Microsoft® Office 2010
Bible

John Walkenbach
Herb Tyson
Michael R. Groh
Faithe Wempen
Lisa A. Bucki

WILEY

Wiley Publishing, Inc.

Microsoft® Office 2010 Bible

Published by
Wiley Publishing, Inc.
10475 Crosspoint Boulevard
Indianapolis, IN 46256
www.wiley.com

Copyright © 2010 by Wiley Publishing, Inc., Indianapolis, Indiana

Published simultaneously in Canada

ISBN: 978-0-470-59185-7

Manufactured in the United States of America

10 9 8 7 6 5 4 3 2

For general information on our other products and services please contact our Customer Care Department within the United States at (877) 762-2974, outside the United States at (317) 572-3993 or fax (317) 572-4002.

Wiley also publishes its books in a variety of electronic formats. Some content that appears in print may not be available in electronic books.

Library of Congress Control Number: 2010930724

About the Authors

John Walkenbach is a bestselling Excel author and has published more than 50 spreadsheet books. He lives amid the saguaros, javelinas, rattlesnakes, bobcats, and gila monsters in Southern Arizona – but the critters are mostly scared away by his clayhammer banjo playing. For more information, Google him.

Herb Tyson is an economist and computer consultant and trainer in the Washington, D.C., area. He earned an interdisciplinary doctorate from Michigan State University in 1977 and an undergraduate degree in Economics and Sociology from Georgetown University in 1973. He is the author of many computer magazine and ezine articles, as well as more than a dozen computing books, including *Teach Yourself Outlook 2000 in 24 Hours*, *Word for Windows Super Book*, *Teach Yourself Web Publishing with Microsoft Word*, *XyWrite Revealed*, *Word for Windows Revealed*, *Your OS/2 Consultant*, and *Navigating the Internet with OS/2 Warp*. Herb is also joint author and technical editor for many other books. He has received the Microsoft MVP (Most Valuable Professional) award each year for more than 15 years in recognition for helping thousands of Microsoft Word users. Widely-recognized for his expertise, Herb's clients have included IBM, Wang, the federal government, and the World Bank, as well as numerous law firms and publishers. Herb is also a singer and songwriter, currently working on his second CD. He and his guitar are no strangers to musical venues in the Washington, D.C., area. He has performed at the Birchmere, the Kennedy Center, Jammin' Java, and coffeehouses, and is a frequent performer at the Mount Vernon Unitarian Church (where he serves as Webmaster). You can visit Herb's website at `www.herbtyson.com`. Questions about this book and Microsoft Office can be pursued at Herb's Word 2010 blog, at `http://word.herbtyson.com/`.

Michael R. Groh is a well-known author, writer, and consultant specializing in Windows database systems. His company, PC Productivity Solutions, provides information-management applications to companies across the country. Over the last 25 years, Mike has worked with a wide variety of programming languages, operating systems, and computer hardware, ranging from programming a DEC PDP-8A using the Focal interpreted language to building distributed applications under Visual Studio .NET and Microsoft SharePoint. Mike was one of the first people outside Microsoft to see Access in action. He was among a select group of journalists and publishers invited to preview the Access 1.0 beta (then called Cirrus) at the 1992 Windows World Conference in Chicago. Since then, Mike has been involved in every Microsoft Access beta program, as an insider and as a journalist and reporter documenting the evolution of this fascinating product. Mike has authored parts of more than 20 different computer books and is a frequent contributor to computer magazines and journals. Mike has written more than 200 articles and editorials over the last 15 years, mostly for Advisor Media (San Diego, CA). He frequently speaks at computer conferences virtually everywhere in the world, and is technical editor and contributor to periodicals and publications produced by Advisor Media. Mike holds a master's degree in Clinical Chemistry from the University of Iowa (Iowa City) and an MBA from Northeastern University (Boston). Mike can be reached at `AccessBible@mikegroh.com`. Please prefix the e-mail subject line with "AccessBible:" to get past the spam blocker on this account.

Faithe Wempen, M.A., is an A+ Certified hardware guru, Microsoft Office Specialist Master Instructor, and software consultant with more than 90 computer books to her credit. She has taught Microsoft Office applications, including PowerPoint, to more than a quarter of a million online students for corporate clients including Hewlett Packard, CNET, Sony, Gateway, and eMachines. When she is not writing, she teaches Microsoft Office classes in the Computer Technology department at Indiana University–Purdue University at Indianapolis (IUPUI), does private computer training and support consulting, and owns and operates Sycamore Knoll Bed and Breakfast in Noblesville, Indiana (www.sycamoreknoll.com).

Lisa A. Bucki is an author, trainer, and consultant and has been writing and teaching about computers and software for more than 15 years. She wrote *Teach Yourself Visually Microsoft Office PowerPoint 2007*, *Microsoft Office Project 2007 Survival Guide*, *Learning Photoshop CS2*, *Dell Guide to Digital Photography: Shooting, Editing, and Printing Pictures*, *Learning Computer Applications: Projects & Exercises* (multiple editions), and *Adobe Photoshop 7 Fast & Easy*. Along with Faithe Wempen, Lisa also co-wrote *Windows 7* (brief and expanded editions) for educational publisher Paradigm Publishing. Lisa has written or contributed to dozens of additional books and multimedia tutorials covering a variety of software and technology topics, including FileMaker Pro 6 for the Mac, iPhoto 2, Fireworks and Flash from Adobe, Microsoft Office applications, and digital photography. She also spearheaded or developed more than 100 computer and trade titles during her association with the former Macmillan Computer Publishing (now a division of Pearson).

About the Technical Editor

Justin Rodino started his instructional career working as a guest lecturer at Purdue University. From Purdue, Justin was a key instructor and courseware developer for Altiris/Symantec where he became more involved with Microsoft technologies. He is an MCT and MVP and heavily involved with the Windows and Office teams at Microsoft. Justin has also helped author and edit many books including the *Microsoft Office 2010 Bible*. As well as authoring material, Justin speaks at many Microsoft events and runs his own consulting company.

Credits

Executive Editor
Carol Long

Senior Project Editor
Adaobi Obi Tulton

Technical Editor
Justin Rodino

Production Editor
Rebecca Anderson

Copy Editor
Cate Caffrey

Editorial Director
Robyn B. Siesky

Editorial Manager
Mary Beth Wakefield

Marketing Manager
Ashley Zurcher

Production Manager
Tim Tate

Vice President and Executive Group Publisher
Richard Swadley

Vice President and Executive Publisher
Barry Pruett

Associate Publisher
Jim Minatel

Project Coordinator, Cover
Lynsey Stanford

Proofreaders
Scott Klemp, Word One New York
Beth Prouty, Word One New York

Indexer
Robert Swanson

Cover Designer
Michael E. Trent

Cover Image
© Joyce Haughey

Acknowledgments

Thanks to Executive Editor Carol Long for sticking with me (Lisa A. Bucki) for my second experience pulling together the contents of this Bible. Carol, it was a pleasure getting the job done for you. I also appreciate the recommendation for this project that I received from my friend Jim Minatel.

Thanks also to Adaobi Obi Tulton, superhero Senior Project Editor. Adaobi, you handled this monster project while also wrangling a three-year-old at home, with the poise of a person rooted firmly in tree pose. Namaste.

The authors who contributed chapters from their individual *Bible* books provided the granite from which this edifice was built. Thanks to these folks for their excellence and expertise:

- John Walkenbach, *Excel 2010 Bible*
- Herb Tyson, *Word 2010 Bible*
- Michael R. Groh, *Access 2010 Bible*
- Faithe Wempen, *PowerPoint 2010 Bible*

I thank Technical Editor Justin Rodino for vetting a huge volume of material under an aggressive schedule. Your MVP experience was invaluable in making this a better book.

Contents at a Glance

Contents at a Glance

Contents

Contents

Contents

Contents

Contents

Contents

Contents

Contents

Contents

Contents

Contents

Contents

Contents

Contents

Chapter 25: Building Animation Effects, Transitions, and Support Materials 741

Contents

Contents

Contents

Contents

Contents

Contents

Contents

Introduction

Welcome to the *Microsoft Office 2010 Bible*. This book provides the information you need to get up and running with the applications in the latest version of the Microsoft Office 2010 suite. Inside, you get coverage of these members of the various versions of the Office Suite:

- Microsoft Word 2010
- Microsoft Excel 2010
- Microsoft PowerPoint 2010
- Microsoft Outlook 2010
- Microsoft Publisher 2010
- Microsoft Access 2010
- Microsoft OneNote 2010

This book brings together chapters from the new versions of the Word, Excel, PowerPoint, and Access *Bibles*. You get the best information from experts in each program so that you can get to work and be productive quickly.

Who Should Read This Book

Office 2010 adds some terrific new features in Word, Excel, PowerPoint, and Access, and fully integrates the Ribbon interface in Outlook, Publisher, and OneNote. As a result, even experienced Office users can use this book to get up to speed with using the new interface quickly. Because this book presents information using the friendly, accessible *Bible* format that combines straightforward steps and concise reference information, beginners with Office can use it to learn Office quickly and expand their skills beyond the basics.

How This Book Is Organized

Microsoft Office 2010 Bible organizes information into several parts. In most cases, a part focuses on a particular application in the suite, so you can jump right to the part for the application you're currently using.

Part I: Common Office Features

The chapters in Part I provide the first introduction to the new user interface in the major Office applications, as well as show how to perform fundamental operations such as working with files.

Part II: Creating Documents with Word

Part II covers using the Microsoft Word 2010 word processing program to create and format text-based documents. In addition to learning how to format words, paragraphs, and pages, you get a shot at working with more sophisticated features such as tables and mail merge, and even the new SmartArt diagrams. You also see how document security settings can help protect information.

Part III: Making the Numbers Work with Excel

The chapters in Part III show you how to use the spreadsheet program Microsoft Excel 2010 to organize and calculate data. After getting a preview of the new features in the program, you learn how to enter, format, and calculate information. You also see how to create powerful charts that tell a story about your data and then summarize that data using data bars, sparklines, and conditional formatting.

Part IV: Persuading and Informing with PowerPoint

In Part IV, you learn how to get the word out with the Microsoft PowerPoint 2010 presentation graphics program. This part explains how to add information, charts, SmartArt diagrams, and graphics to slides. You also see how to animate and automate a slide show and get expert tips about going live with your presentation.

Part V: Organizing Messages, Contacts, and Time with Outlook

The basics for using Microsoft Outlook 2010 appear in Part V. Learn to set up an e-mail account; compose, send, and respond to messages; organize messages and deal with junk mail and security issues; and manage your contacts, appointments, and to-do list.

Part VI: Designing Publications with Publisher

Part VI introduces you to the Microsoft Publisher 2010 page layout and design program. Learn how to not only create great-looking publications with Publisher's flexible tools, but also prep your publications for professional printing.

Part VII: Managing Information with Access and OneNote

If you manage detailed lists — with customer or product data, for example — Microsoft Access 2010 and Part VII's chapters are for you. Get a roadmap here for designing a good database. Learn how to create tables, fields, and forms, and how to select and present data with queries and reports. Also get an overview about using OneNote 2010 to track notes and project details and gather project resources such as links and photos into a notebook-like structure onscreen.

Part VIII: Sharing and Collaboration

Part VIII explains not only how to share information between Office applications, but also how to use Office 2010 applications with SharePoint Workspace 2010 and SkyDrive on a network or the Internet.

What Is on the Website

On the *Office 2010 Bible* website at www.wiley.com/go/office2010bible, you can find three appendixes to provide supplementary information: Appendix A, "Customizing Office"; Appendix B, "Optimizing Your Office Installation"; and Appendix C, "International Support and Accessibility Features."

Conventions and Features

As you work your way through the text, be on the lookout for these icons that bring your attention to important information:

Caution

This information is important and is set off in a separate paragraph with a special icon. Cautions provide information about things to watch out for, whether simply inconvenient or potentially hazardous to your data or systems. ■

Tip

Tips generally are used to provide information that can make your work easier — special shortcuts or methods for doing something more easily than the norm. ■

Note

Notes provide additional, ancillary information that is helpful but somewhat outside of the current presentation of information. ■

Cross-Reference

Cross-references point you to other areas in the book that give more detail about the current topic. ■

The text also uses specific shortcuts for choosing commands:

- **Mouse.** When the text instructs you to choose a command from a menu or the Ribbon (in the new interface), the command is presented like this: "Choose Home ➪ Clipboard ➪ Copy." That means to click the Home tab on the Ribbon, look in the Clipboard group, and click the Copy choice. (Most command sequences include the specific group after the Ribbon tab.) For another example, "Choose File ➪ Save" means to click the File tab and then click Save in the menu that appears. In most command sequences, both parts of a two-level contextual tab on the ribbon will be included. For example, if a command is on the Picture Tools Format tab, it will appear as Picture Tools ⇨ Format in the command sequence.

- **Keyboard.** Any keyboard shortcuts appear like this: Ctrl+C. That means to press the Ctrl key and the C key simultaneously and then release them.

Where to Go from Here

Microsoft has released multiple versions of the Microsoft Office 2010 suite, with different versions including different applications. You can jump right to the parts that offer coverage for the applications offered in the flavor of Office that you own.

Part I

Common Office Features

Welcome to Microsoft Office 2010

Microsoft Office 2010 provides a comprehensive toolkit for tackling day-to-day productivity and communication tasks for business or personal purposes. This chapter introduces the individual Office applications and teaches you skills for getting started using them.

Learning about Office Applications

Microsoft Office 2010 offers a robust set of applications, each tailor-made to provide the best tools for a particular job. For example, if you're creating a letter, you may need to work with commands for formatting text. If you need to total sales figures, you'll need an automated way to sum the numbers.

Office provides applications that enable you to handle each of those aforementioned scenarios and more. Read on to learn which Office applications to use for creating text-based documents, manipulating numbers, presenting your ideas, or even communicating with others.

Note
Microsoft offers several different versions of the Microsoft Office 2010 software suite, some of which are only available via volume licensing. Each version includes a different combination of the individual Office programs. Only Microsoft Word 2010, Microsoft Excel 2010, and Microsoft PowerPoint 2010 are included in all versions. Therefore, depending on the Office version you've purchased, you may not have all of the applications described in this chapter and further throughout the book. Office 2010 also comes in both 32-bit and 64-bit releases. If you have 64-bit computer system and are running a 64-bit operating system, choosing a 64-bit Office release will ensure the best performance possible when using Office. ■

IN THIS CHAPTER

Reviewing the core Microsoft Office business applications

Looking at additional Office applications

Starting and closing an application

Finding a file

Browsing and finding Help

Note

Microsoft also will be offering Office Web apps, Web-browser-based versions of certain core Office apps, helping eliminate the need for the software to be installed locally on your computer, subsequently enabling online file sharing and collaboration. Using Office Web apps will store your files in an online location, in the "cloud," such as on a SharePoint Server or in a Windows Live SkyDrive account. Access to Office Web apps is included free with some Office 2010 versions, and as of this writing, Microsoft also plans to make free ad-supported access available. This book focuses on the locally installed desktop versions of the Office applications, but you can explore Office Web apps and online storage options if you require remote capabilities of either specific office applications or your data. ■

Word

Word processing — typing, editing, formatting letters, reports, fax cover sheets, and so on — is perhaps the most common activity performed on a computer. Whether you need to create a memo at the office or a letter at home, using a word processing program can save you time and help you achieve polished results.

Microsoft Word has long been the leading word processing program. As one of the core applications in the Office suite, Word provides a host of document-creation tools that have been refined to be easy to use, yet have comprehensive feature sets should you wish to extend your document beyond the basics. Using Word to apply a minor bit of text formatting and a graphic can make even a simple document such as the meeting agenda shown in Figure 1-1 have more impact and appeal than just plain text alone.

Word enables you to do more than just make your documents look great. Its features can help you enhance your document text more easily and furthermore create sophisticated elements such as footnotes, endnotes, and more. You'll learn about these powerful Word features, among others, later in this book:

- **Templates.** A *template* is a starter document that supplies the document design, text formatting, and, often, placeholder text or suggested text. Add your own text and your document is finished!

- **Styles.** If you like a particular combination of formatting settings that you've applied to text, you can save the combination as a style that you can easily apply to other text.

- **Tables.** Add a table to organize text in a grid of rows and columns to which you can then apply terrific formatting. In Word 2010, you can add a title and a summary to a table to better describe its contents.

- **Graphics.** You can add all types of pictures to your documents and even create diagrams like the one in Figure 1-2 using the new SmartArt feature. Some SmartArt layouts even enable you to insert pictures as shown in Figure 1-2.

- **Mail Merge.** Create your own, customized "form letter" wherein each copy is automatically customized for a particular recipient (or list entry). Word's Merge feature even enables you to create matching envelopes and labels.

- **Document Security and Review.** Word enables you to protect a document against unwanted changes, as well as to track changes made by other users. Using these features, you can control the document content through a collaboration process.

FIGURE 1-1

Microsoft Word 2010 enables you to create appealing documents.

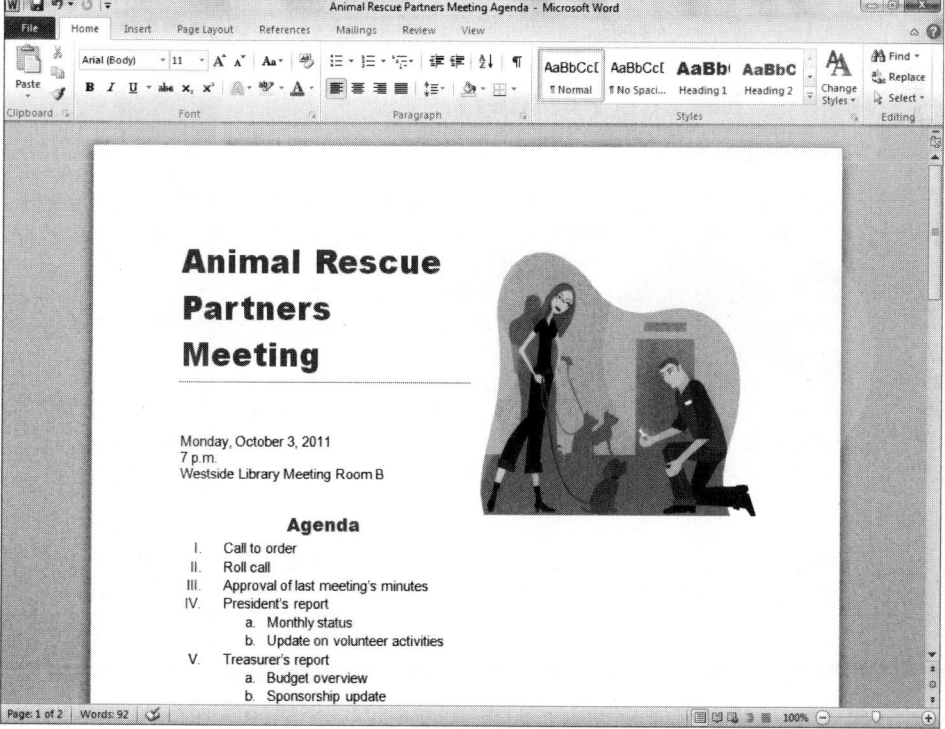

Excel

Spreadsheet programs — which provide formulas and functions that make it easy to calculate numerical data — made a critical technology leap in business computing. Business people no longer need to rely on adding machines, scientific calculators, or accountants to perform detailed sales or financial calculations. Even a beginning salesperson could insert numbers into a spreadsheet, type a few formulas, and have the data automatically calculated. Even better, spreadsheet programs give you the ability to represent data graphically, which communicates the impact of the data more effectively. Microsoft Excel 2010, shown in Figure 1-3, performs the spreadsheet duties in the Microsoft Office suite.

FIGURE 1-2

SmartArt diagrams illustrate information in a document.

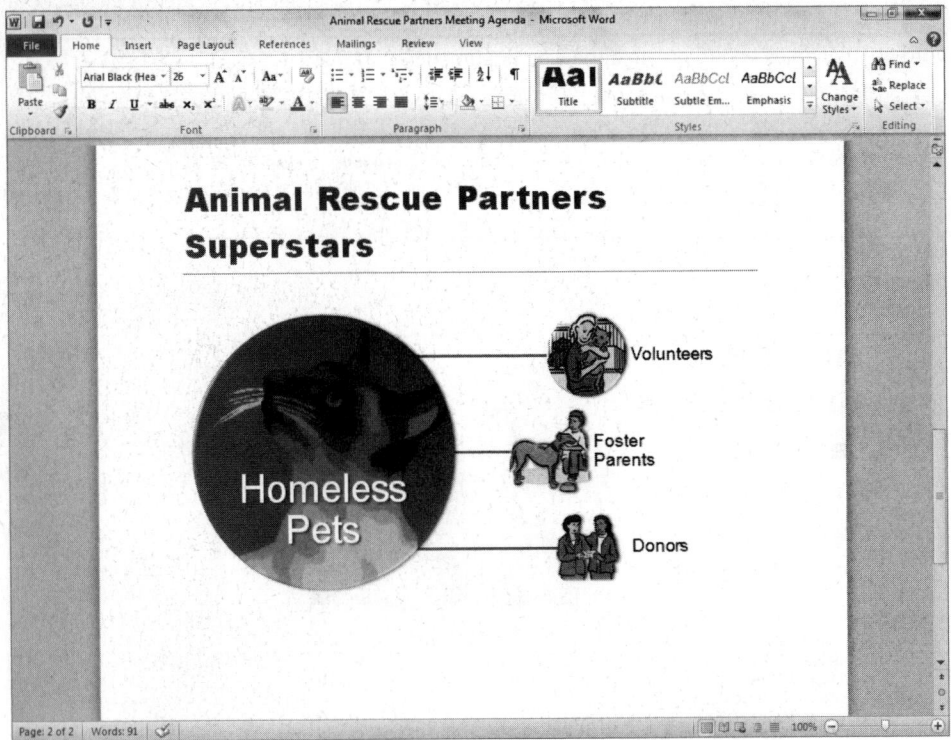

Excel enables you to build a calculation by creating a formula that specifies the values to calculate and which mathematical operators to use to perform the calculation. Excel also offers *functions* — predesigned formulas that perform more complex calculations, such as calculating accrued interest. Many of Excel 2010's functions have been updated for increased accuracy and renamed for consistency with the terminology used in the scientific community. Excel not only provides tools to assist you in building and error-checking spreadsheet formulas, but it also gives you many easy choices for formatting the data to make it more readable and professional. You'll learn these Excel essentials later in the book, as well as more about these key Excel features:

- **Worksheets.** Within each file, you can divide and organize a large volume of data across multiple worksheets or pages of information in the file.

- **Ranges.** You can assign a name to a contiguous area on a worksheet so that you can later select that area by name, or use the name in a formula to save time.

- **Number and Date Value Formatting.** You can apply a number format that defines how Excel should display a cell's contents, indicating details such as how many decimal points should appear and whether a percentage or dollar sign should be included. You can also apply a date format to determine how the date appears.

- **Charts.** Translate your data into a meaningful image by creating a chart in Excel (as shown in Figure 1-4). Excel offers dozens of chart types, layouts, and formats to help you present your results in the clearest way.

FIGURE 1-3

Use the Microsoft Excel 2010 program to organize and calculate numerical data.

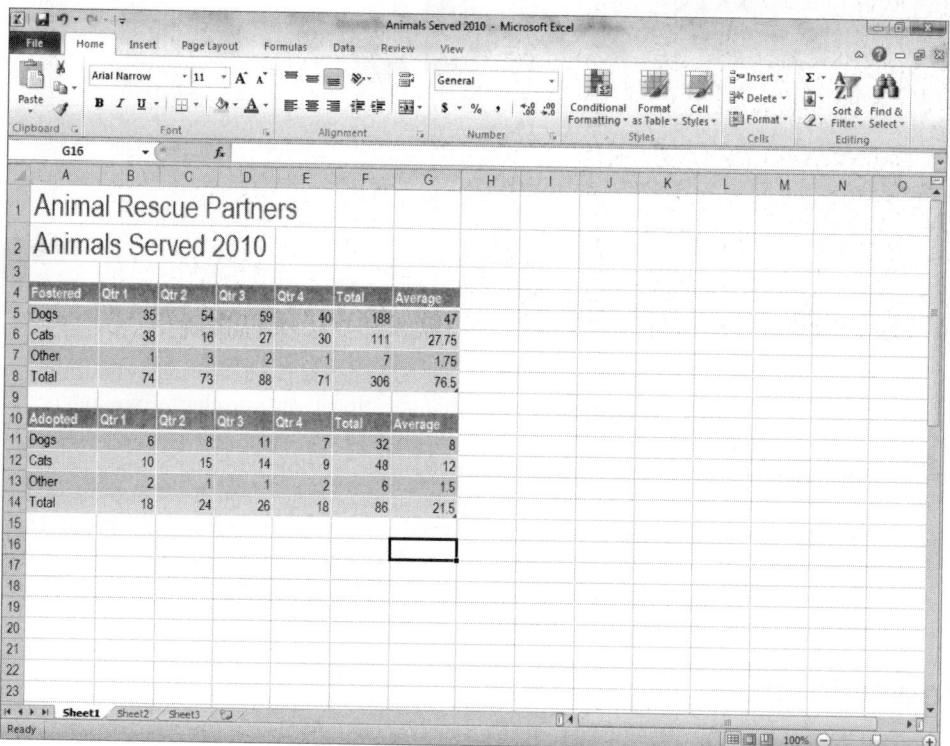

FIGURE 1-4

Excel's data visualization features, such as sparklines and charting, help you make data more compelling and easier to evaluate.

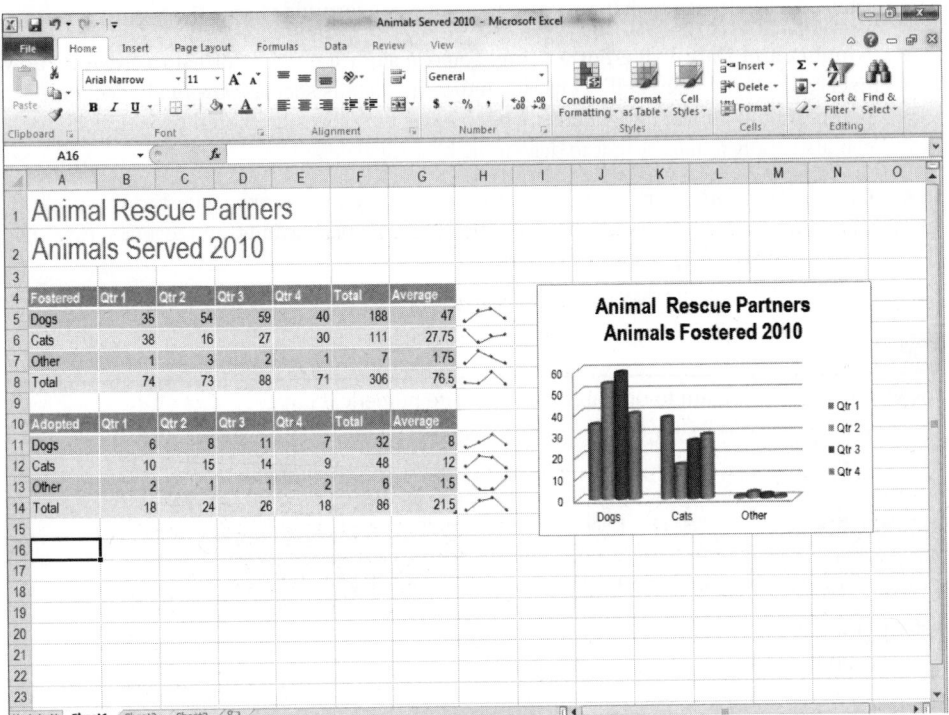

- **Specialized Data Formatting.** Sometimes it's more expedient to use cell formatting to help data have more visual impact rather than creating a separate chart. Excel offers *conditional formatting*, a tool that enables it to apply specialized formatting for selected cells based on the results of the formulas in those cells or the contents of the cells. For example, if you have a spreadsheet calculating grade averages, you can set up the cells to be formatted in one color for a passing average and another for a failing average. The conditional formats include data bars, color scales, icon scales, and more. Excel 2010 offers a new sparklines feature that enables you to create a small chart within a cell. Refer to Figure 1-4 to see an example.

PowerPoint

To achieve positive outcomes in situations such as persuading customers to buy; convincing your company's leadership to invest in developing a new product you've conceived; training members of your team to follow a new operating procedure; or making sure that a group of volunteers understands program requirements — you must deliver your message in a clear, concise, convincing, and often visual way. A presentation graphics program helps you inform your audience in situations like those just described, and more.

The Microsoft PowerPoint 2010 presentation graphics program (see Figure 1-5) enables you to communicate information and ideas via an onscreen slide show or by printing the pages as handouts. Each slide should present a key topic that you want to convey, along with a few supporting points or a graphical reinforcement such as a chart or picture. In this way, PowerPoint helps you to divide information into chunks that audience members can more easily absorb.

FIGURE 1-5

Use PowerPoint to present your message in informative slides.

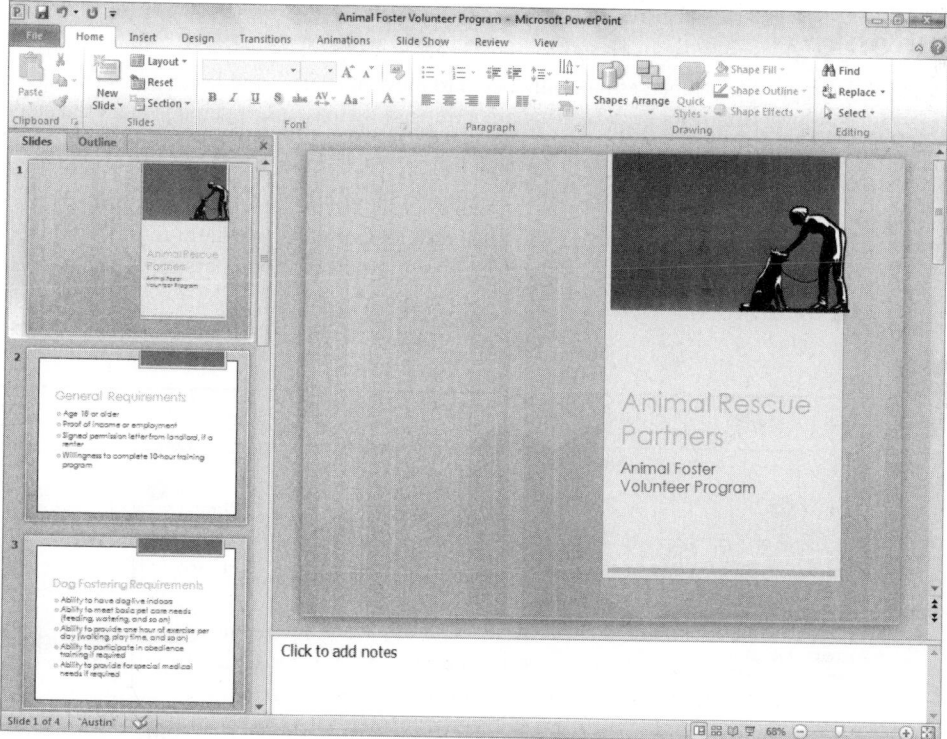

Later in the book, you will learn how to create the basic presentation structure and add information as well as use the following PowerPoint features to help reinforce your message:

- **Layouts, Themes, and Masters.** These PowerPoint features control the content that appears on a slide and how the content is arranged, as well as the appearance of all of the slides. You can quickly redesign a single slide or the entire presentation.

- **Tables and Charts.** Similar to Word and Excel, PowerPoint enables you to arrange information in an attractively formatted grid of rows and columns. PowerPoint works with Excel to deliver charted data, so the Excel charting skills you build make developing charts in PowerPoint even easier.

- **Animations and Transitions.** You can set up the text and other items on slides to make a special entrance, such as appearing to fly onto the screen, when you play them in a slide show. In addition to applying animations on objects, you can apply a transition that animates how the overall slide appears and disappears from the screen, such as dissolving or wiping in and away.

- **Live Presentations.** PowerPoint offers several different ways in which you can customize and control how the presentation looks when played as an onscreen slide show. In this book, you will learn tricks such as hiding slides or jumping between slides onscreen.

Outlook

As technology improves, businesses naturally begin to move at a faster and faster pace. The days of face-to-face conversations for each meeting are a thing of the past, and everyone faces the challenge of tracking more and more contacts and to-dos. The Microsoft Outlook 2010 program in the Microsoft Office suite can handle your e-mail messages (Figure 1-6), appointment scheduling, contact information, and your to-do list, as well as other various communication tasks. This program helps you stay in the loop, keeps you organized, and also keeps you up-to-date with all the action in your work life, including connecting you with social and business networks via the Outlook Social Connector.

FIGURE 1-6

Send and receive e-mail messages in Microsoft Outlook.

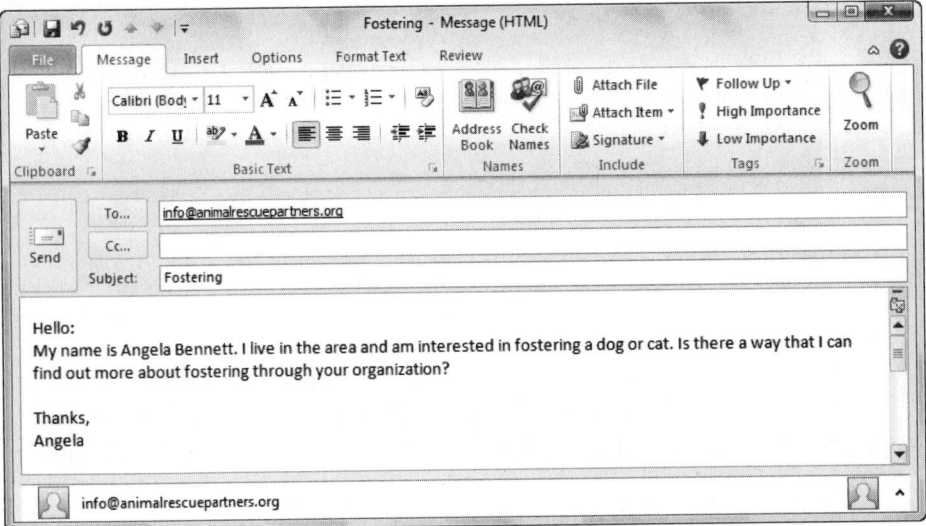

In addition to learning Outlook e-mail, scheduling, contact management, and to-do list basics later in the book, you will learn which Outlook settings and tools help prevent messages with viruses from infecting your computer. Also learn how Outlook can automatically manage annoying yet pervasive junk mail messages.

Taking Advantage of Other Office Applications

You may be a user whose needs extend beyond letter writing and number crunching. If you routinely take on special tasks such as creating printed publications or tracking extensive customer data, you may find yourself working with some of the other applications that are part of certain editions of Microsoft Office 2010. This section gives you a snapshot of those other applications; later chapters of the book revisit these topics.

Publisher

Microsoft Publisher 2010 enables you to create *publications*, which have a greater emphasis on design than a word processing program typically offers. To help the creative process, Publisher includes attractive publication designs and templates with placeholders for text and images as well as other features including decorative rules and backgrounds already in place, as shown in Figure 1-7.

Tip

The distinction between documents and publications often is a very gray area; however, think of a *document* as something printed from a personal printer, either at home or in the office. This usually is something like a report or proposal. On the other hand, a *publication* is something typically printed professionally, like business cards or brochures and flyers. Typically, for example, you wouldn't use Word to prepare a brochure for professional printing, because many professional print shops require more comprehensive page setup and design features such as those found in Publisher. ∎

A later chapter shows you how to handle Publisher's basics of choosing a publication design and then adding the text and graphics. You'll also learn how to add effects such as drop caps and design gallery objects, and even how to prepare a publication for professional printing.

Access

The Microsoft Access 2010 database program can certainly do heavy lifting when it comes to managing detailed mountains of data such as customer detail, stock inventory, and order lists that may have hundreds or thousands of entries. The file that holds such lists is called a database. Each Access database file actually can hold multiple lists of data, each usually stored in a separate table, such as the Current Foster Animals table shown in Figure 1-8.

FIGURE 1-7

Microsoft Publisher provides placeholders and design elements so that you can create eye-catching publications with minimal design effort.

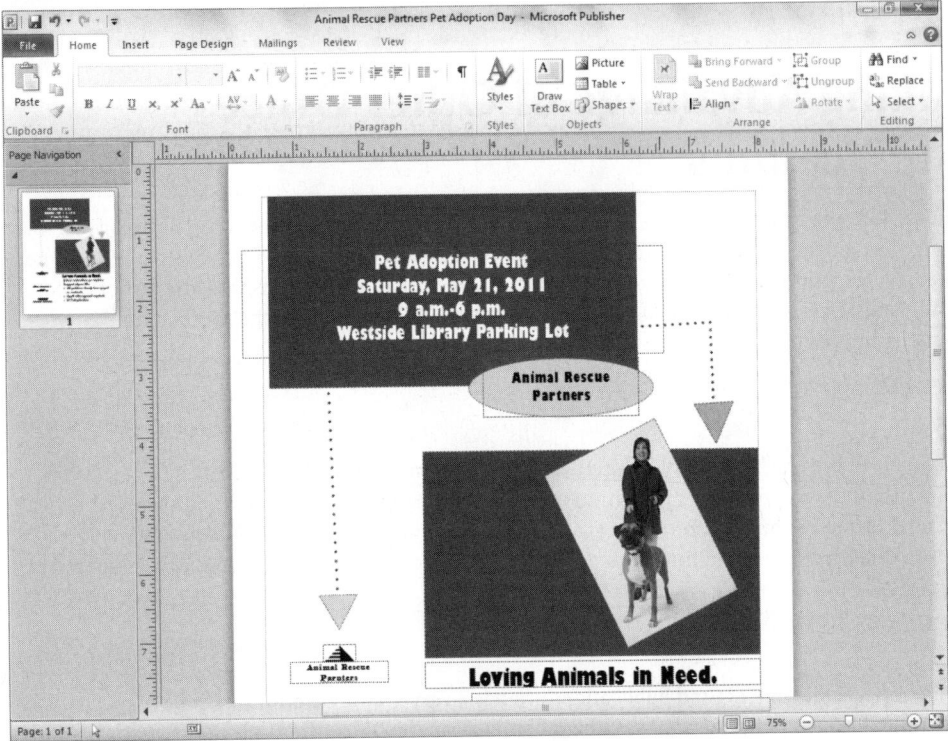

Access enables you to enter and view data using various forms. You also can set up queries to retrieve data that matches certain criteria out of your database tables. These queries can be used to generate reports that consolidate and analyze your data. Later chapters introduce you to these Access skills.

OneNote

It's a risky proposition to track your professional or educational life via notes scribbled on various scraps of paper or notebook pages. As the notes pile up, it becomes harder and harder to find relevant information, making it look as though you can't keep up. If you lose a scrap of paper containing a critical piece of information, you can put a project in jeopardy.

Microsoft Office OneNote 2010, as seen in Figure 1-9, serves as a type of electronic scrapbook for notes, reference materials, and files related to a particular activity or project. This way, when you need to find all the relevant material related to a specific topic or a particular project, you can flip right to the applicable notebook tab. You learn to get yourself together with OneNote in a later chapter.

FIGURE 1-8

A Microsoft Access database organizes lists of information in tables.

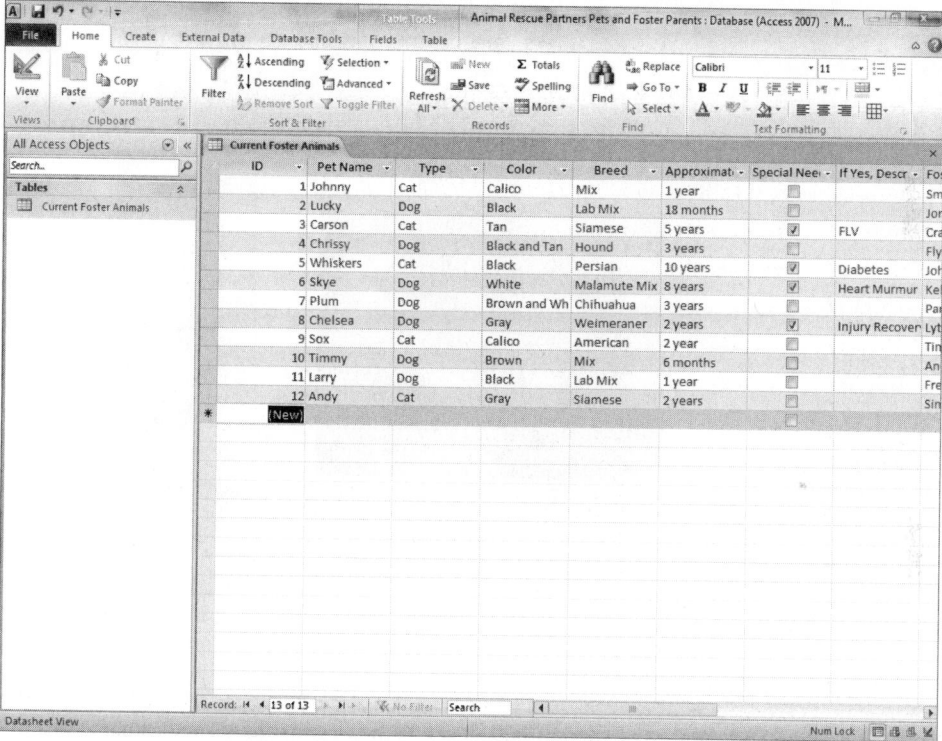

Starting an Application

When you launch any of the Office applications, that program and its respective tool set will be loaded into your computer's RAM (working memory) so that you can begin working. Starting an Office application is similar to starting any other application — first finding it in the Start menu and then clicking on it — however, with Windows Vista and Windows 7, there are new tricks that make starting applications a little bit easier.

FIGURE 1-9

Organize notes, files, pictures, and other material in a OneNote notebook.

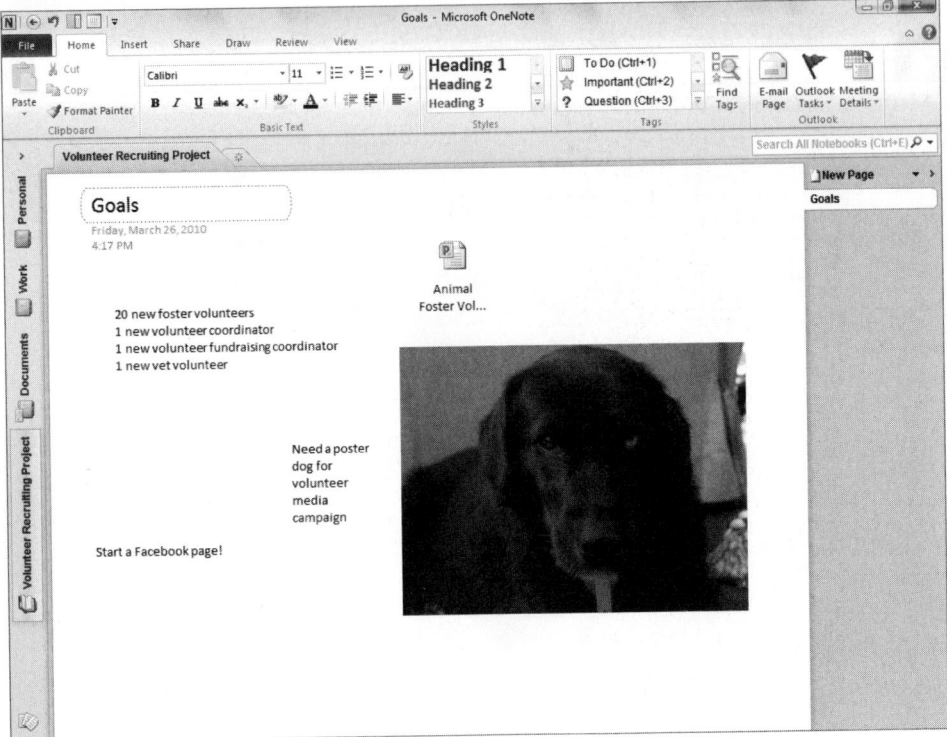

To find the Office programs in the Start menu:

1. **Click the Start button at the left end of the Windows taskbar.** The taskbar appears along the bottom of the Windows desktop. The Start menu opens.

2. **Click All Programs.** A list of available programs appears. In XP, it appears as a sub-menu of the Start menu. In Vista and Windows 7, the list appears in the left column of the Start menu.

3. **Click Microsoft Office.** The available Office programs appear.

4. **Click the desired Office program.** The program window appears onscreen (Figure 1-10).

Note

Some applications automatically open a new, blank file when you start them. Others prompt you to create a new file. Outlook automatically displays personal folder information, whereas OneNote opens the notebook page that you last worked with. ∎

FIGURE 1-10

Use the Start menu to start an Office program

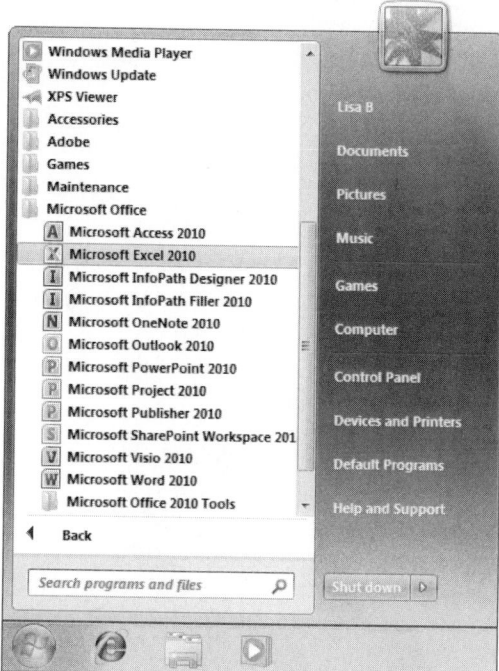

Windows Vista and Windows 7 provide you with a quicker and much simpler way to start any application, including the Office applications. To do this on either operating system:

1. **Click the Start button on the taskbar.** The Start menu opens with the blinking insertion point in the Search Programs and Files textbox at the bottom of the menu.

2. **Type all or part of the name of the application you want to start.** As shown in Figure 1-11, a list of matching applications (and files with the typed information in them) appears.

3. **Click the desired Office program.** The program window appears onscreen.

You also can create a desktop shortcut icon to use to start the program. To do so, simply drag the application name from the Start menu to the desktop. A shortcut icon will appear. You then can double-click that icon to start the program.

FIGURE 1-11

Typing a name in the Search textbox lists matching programs.

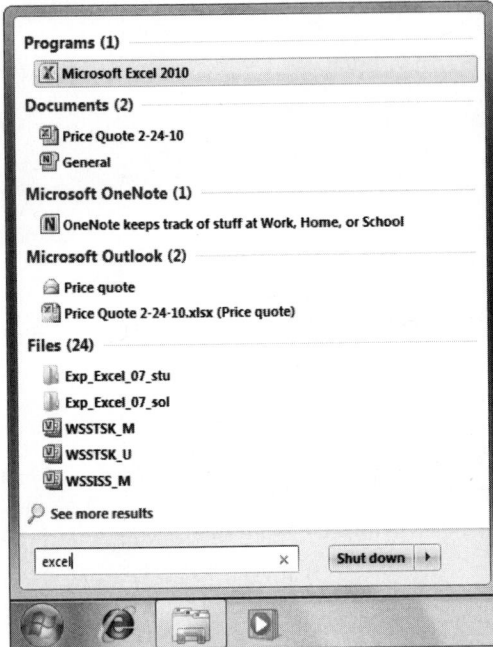

Closing an Application

When you finish your work in an application, shutting the application down removes it from system memory, freeing that memory for other uses. Closing the application also provides the benefit of closing any possibly sensitive open files to prevent unwanted viewing by others.

You can use one of three methods to shut down any program:

- Press the Alt and F4 keys simultaneously (Alt+F4).
- Click the File tab in the upper-left corner of the program window (see Figure 1-12); then click Exit.
- Click the X in the upper-right corner, which denotes you'd like to close the program.

If you see a message box similar to the one in Figure 1-12, it means that you haven't saved all your changes to the file. Click Yes to save your changes. Both the application and file close.

FIGURE 1-12

A prompt appears to remind you to save file changes.

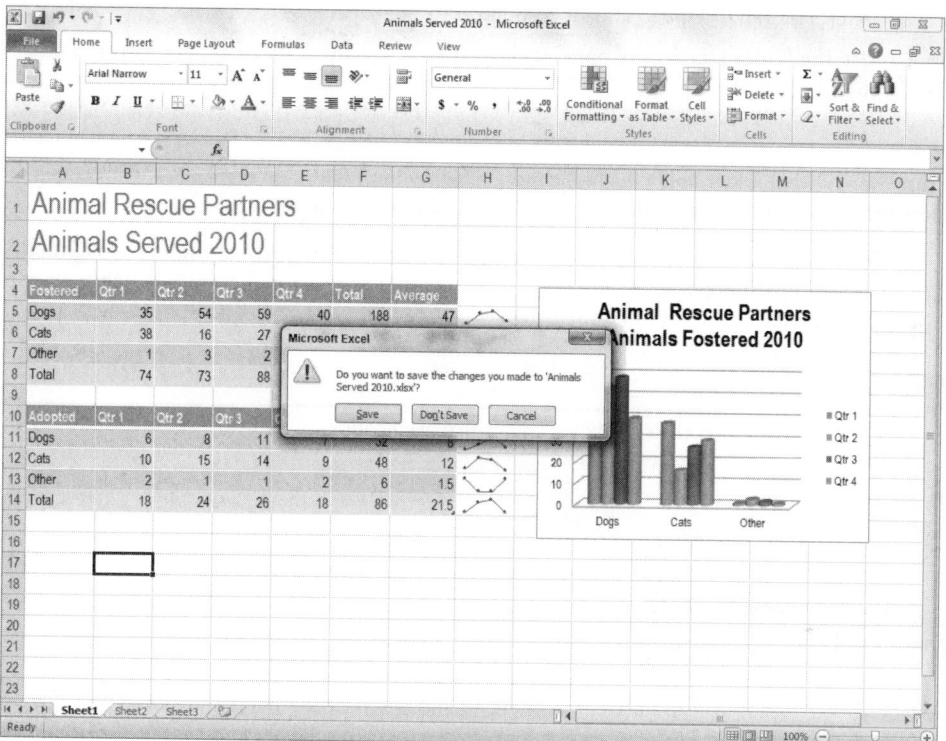

Finding Files

Searching through folders on a computer's hard disk to try to find the file you want to work with sure can waste valuable time you often don't have. If you're using Office with Windows 7 (or with Windows Vista if it has the proper updates installed), you can take advantage of a couple of short-cuts that help you find a file on your system.

As shown previously in Figure 1-12, making an entry in the Search Programs and Files textbox displays not only matching programs but also files with the search text in the filename or file contents. Therefore, you can enter all or part of the filename or topic (provided the metadata exists in the file properties) in the Search Programs and Files textbox on the File menu and then click on the name of the file to open. The application used to create the file opens with the speci-fied file in it.

Alternatively, you can work in the Open dialog box for any Office program to search for a file. Use these steps when you're already working in the application used to create the file:

1. Click File tab ➪ Open. The Open dialog box appears.
2. Use the folder tree in the pane at the left to select the folder that you think holds the file to find.

Tip

If you're not sure even of what folder holds the file, choose a higher-level folder or even a disk icon. Doing so will search more locations, but this means that the search may take more time. ■

3. Type the name of the file to search for in the Search textbox in the upper-right corner of the dialog box. As you type, the Open dialog box lists files with matching names or contents, as shown in Figure 1-13.

FIGURE 1-13

You can search for a file in the Open dialog box for any Office application.

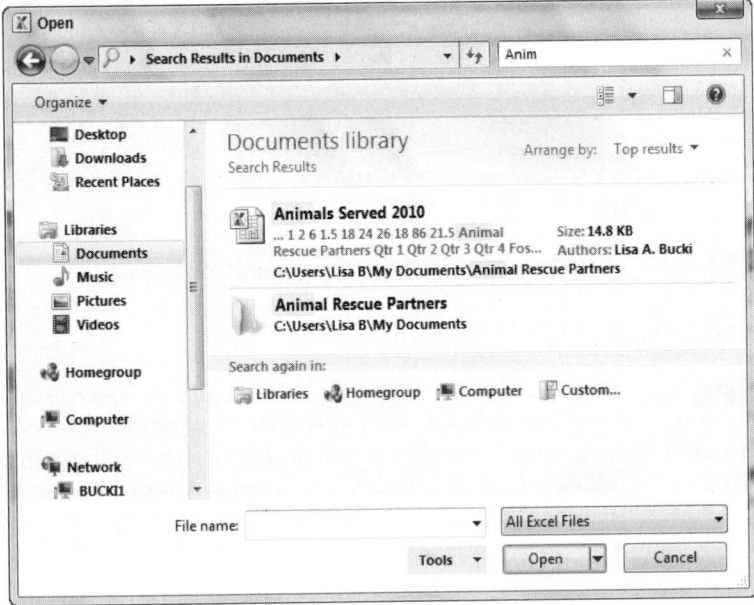

4. Double-click on the name of the file to open. The file appears in the application.

Note

In Windows XP, you will still have search capabilities. Click the Start button and then click Search in the right column of the menu. Then click the Documents link under What Do You Want to Search For? to display the controls where you can then enter information about the file you're looking for. If you've already displayed the Open dialog box in an Office application running under XP, you can right-click on any folder in the Open dialog box and then click Search in the shortcut menu to search for a file. ■

Getting Help

Program features sometimes can seem a little obscure, and because the interface has been heavily redesigned in the Microsoft Office 2010 applications, you may get stuck from time to time when you're trying out a feature that you don't use every day. If you don't have this book handy, it's time to turn to another resource — the Help system for the application that you're using.

Browsing Help Contents

Regardless of whether you have an Internet connection, you can explore and browse the basic Help that is installed with each of the Office applications. With an Internet connection, you can also search Office.com, a repository containing further topics as well as more up-to-date information. To open the application's Help window, click the round Help (question mark) button at the right end of the Ribbon or press F1.

The Help window for the program appears and lists general help categories. Click on a category to view available Help topics in that category (see Figure 1-14). In some cases, you may need to click on a subcategory to display the topic you need. When you see the topic you need, you can click the Print button to print it. To move around to additional topics, use the Back and Forward buttons, as well as clicking on additional links.

When you finish working in the Help window, click the window's Close button to finish.

Searching Office.com

You can search for help about a particular topic or question using the textbox near the top of the Help window. If your system is connected to the Internet, simply type the topic to search for into the textbox and press Enter.

However, if you see Offline displayed near the right end of the Help window status bar, you might need to double-check your connection to ensure you can search online Help. To search online for help:

1. **Click the drop-down arrow for the Search button and click on a choice under Content from Office.com in the menu** (Figure 1-15). The All *Program Name* choice searches all the online Help resources for that application, whereas any of the other choices under Content from Office Online target the Help search to a specific type of information.

2. **Type the search topic into the Search text box.**

3. **Press Enter.** The list of matching Help topics appears.

4. **Click on the desired topic.** The Help for the topic appears in the Help window.

Note

Whether you browse for Help while already connected to the Internet or forced the Help window to search online, in certain cases clicking on a Help topic link will launch your system's Web browser and display the Help and resources there, rather than in the Help window. ■

Tip

If you click the Search button drop-down arrow as noted in the preceding Step 1, you can click the *Program Name* Help choice under Content from This Computer to search only help installed on your system. For simple questions, this method might display the right Help topic a bit quicker. ■

FIGURE 1-14

Browse by clicking on categories, subcategories, and topics.

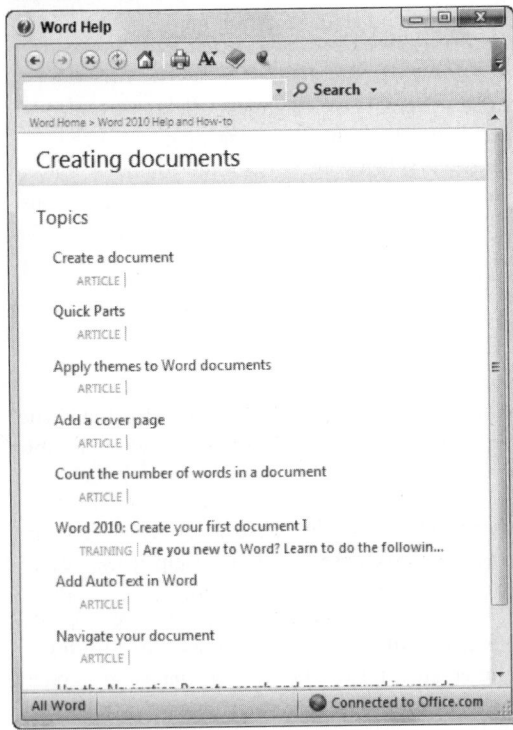

You can request that Office go back online for Help.

Summary

This chapter introduced the programs that are part of the Microsoft Office 2010 system that will be covered in this book. You learned about core features in the Word (word processing), Excel (spreadsheet), PowerPoint (presentation graphics), and Outlook (e-mail scheduling and collaboration) programs. You also learned that you can perform more specialized business functions with Publisher (publication design), Access (database), and OneNote (information management). You moved on to learn how to start and close any application in Microsoft Office, how to find a file that's not quite at your fingertips, and how to use Help, both offline and online, when you need to learn more.

Navigating in Office

Welcome to Office 2010. If you came here from Office 2007, the changes will seem evolutionary. If you arrived from Office 2003 or an even earlier version of Office, the changes are more revolutionary. This chapter provides an overview of what's new since Office 2003 and Office 2007.

If you're completely new to Office and have been using other applications such as OpenOffice, you're likely more accustomed to toolbars and menus than you are to Office 2010's Ribbon, so when contrasting Office 2010's Ribbon with pre-Office 2007's interface, you'll likely immediately grasp just how different the Ribbon is, even if you never touched Office 2003.

The *Ribbon* is a set of contextual tools designed to put what you need where you need it when you need it. When you click one of the major tabs on the Ribbon, the tools you need for specific tasks should be right where you need them. The ideal result is that you don't need to go looking too far for what you need.

In fact, the Ribbon might actually be considered a kind of toolbar. Instead of a list of different toolbars accessed from the View menu, however, the different parts of the Ribbon are organized into *tabs* and *groups*. The result is that more of the tools are exposed to you, making it more likely that you'll discover what you need. At least, that's the theory.

If you've used Office 2003 or earlier versions in the past, Office 2010 will seem strange and different. Imagine that you left Earth in the year 1994 — the last time the Office interface was overhauled — and returned in the year 2010. Over the ensuing 16 years, the interface slowly transitioned from menus and toolbars to the Ribbon.

When considered from that evolutionary perspective, perhaps Office 2010 doesn't look so different. What you, the space traveler, do not realize, however, is that the radical changes occurred not slowly and gradually over more than a decade, but in one giant leap from Office 11 to Office 12, three years before you landed. You're not aware of the "missing link" (Office 2007). Never mind why there was no Office 13.

Discoverability

If pre-2003 versions of Office were driven mostly by functionality and usability, Office 2010's catchwords are *discoverability* and *results*. Studies show that typical Office users use only a fraction of the myriad features contained in Office. Yet the same studies show that users often employ the wrong features. For example, rather than use an indent setting, a user might press the Spacebar five times (gasp!) or the Tab key once (again gasp, but not quite as loud).

Microsoft's challenge, therefore, was to design an interface that made discovering the right features easier, more direct, and more deliberate.

Has it succeeded? Well, you'll have to be the judge.

Let's suppose you want to create a table. Assuming for the moment that you even know that a table is what you want, in Word 2003 and earlier you might choose Table ➪ Draw Table or Table ➪ Insert ➪ Table from the menu. Or perhaps you would click the Table tool on the Standard toolbar, assuming you recognize the icon as representing that functionality.

The point is that you had to navigate through dense menus or toolbars in order to find the needed functionality — perhaps not even knowing what that functionality was called. It's akin to wandering through a hardware store looking for something that will twist a spiraling piece of metal into a piece of wood, without knowing whether such a tool actually exists. You don't even know what the piece of metal is called, so you wander about, and finally discover, to your utter delight, the perfect tool … a hammer. Oops! There's an old saying: when the only tool you have is a hammer, everything looks like a nail.

Like a hammer, the time-proven Spacebar has been used countless times to perform chores for which it was never intended. Yes, a hammer can compel a screw to join two pieces of wood together; and a Spacebar can be used to move text around so it looks like a table. However, just as a hammered screw makes for a shaky wooden table, a word processing table fashioned together with spaces is equally fragile. Add something to the table and it doesn't hold together. Which table? Take your pick.

In Office 2010, there are no dense menus and toolbars. To insert a table — again assuming you even know that a table is what you're looking for — you stare at the Home Ribbon and see nothing that looks remotely like a table.

Thinking that the act of inserting may be what you need, you click Insert, and there you see a grid with the Office Table under it. You click Table, move the mouse, and perhaps you see what's shown in Figure 2-1, as an actual table is previewed inside your document, changing as the mouse moves. Epiphany! Well, maybe just "Yay!"

FIGURE 2-1

Office's Live Preview shows the results of the currently selected Ribbon action.

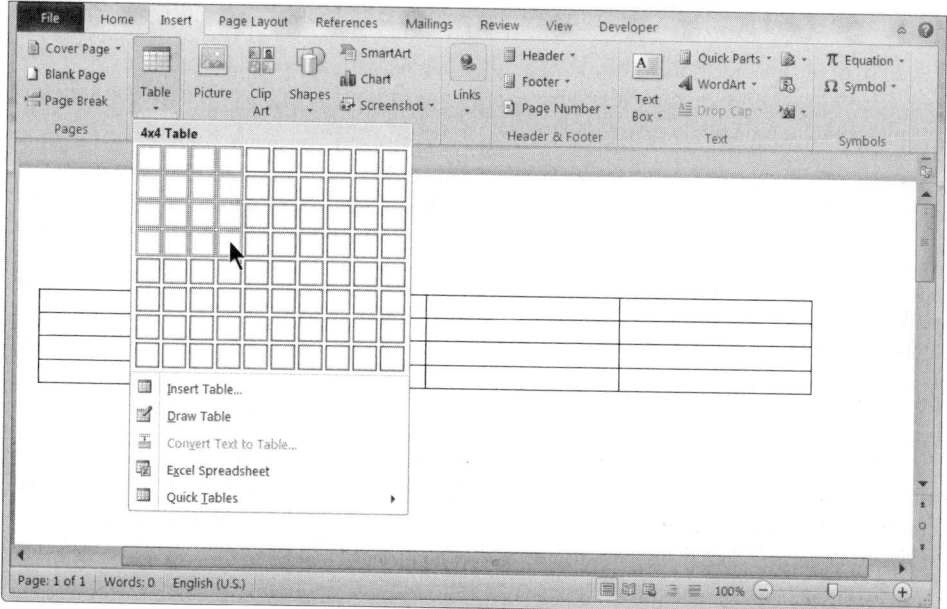

You might be happy to know that pre-Office 2007's proprietary .doc document format was replaced by .docx, which uses XML (eXtensible Markup Language). XML is an open format in the public domain. At its heart are plain-text commands that can be resolved by Office and a variety of other programs. The bottom line for the user is that the mysterious so-called binary format is gone, meaning that Office documents are now harder to corrupt. If they do get corrupted, your work is easier to salvage.

Note

If you're a glutton for punishment or you like taking risks, Office 2010 still supports its legacy formats. You can even tell Office to always save documents in earlier formats. This is a good option when you share your work with users of Office 2003 and earlier. For those same Office 2003 users (as well as Office 2000 and 2002 users), however, Microsoft provides a free compatibility pack that enables them to read Office 2010 documents (although Office 2010–specific enhancements will be lost in the translation). To find the compatibility pack, visit http://office.microsoft.com and search the Downloads tab for *compatibility* or go to www.microsoft.com/downloads to find the download. ■

The "Results-Oriented" User Interface

If you're like most users, when you begin a letter or a report, the first thing you do is check whether you've ever written a letter or report like the one you are about to write. If you have written something similar, then you very likely will open it and use it as a starting point.

If you don't have a document to use as a starting point, then you check whether there's an existing template in Microsoft Office's repertoire. Failing there, you might search online. Indeed, it's not uncommon to come across questions in online communities or newsgroups asking if anyone has a particular type of template, for example, "Does anyone have a template for a resignation letter?"

Knowing that most people don't prefer to begin documents with a clean slate, so to speak, Microsoft designed Office to give users what they want. The goal is to offer them a collection of the results they are probably seeking, to save time and guesswork.

Microsoft has done this in a variety of ways. One of the most prominent is to provide galleries of already formatted options. Coupled with this is something called *Live Preview*, which instantly shows the user the effect of a given option in the current document — not in a preview window!

Rather than focus on a confusing array of tools, Office instead shows a variety of finished document parts or building blocks. It then goes on to provide context-sensitive sets of effects — also tied to Live Preview. These are designed to help you sculpt those document parts into, if not exactly what you want, then something close. The objective at each step is to help you achieve results quickly, rather than combing through myriad menus and toolbars to discover possibilities. If nothing else, the interface eliminates several what-if steps in what necessarily is a process of trial and error.

In addition, with each result, Office's context-sensitive Ribbon changes to show you additional tools that seem most likely to be appropriate for, or relevant to, the document part that is currently selected. For example, if a picture is selected, the Picture Tools ⇨ Format tab is displayed, as shown in Figure 2-2.

FIGURE 2-2

A picture is selected, and the Picture Tools ⇨ Format Ribbon is displayed; the result of the Picture Style gallery selection (Bevel Perspective, in this case) is previewed in the document.

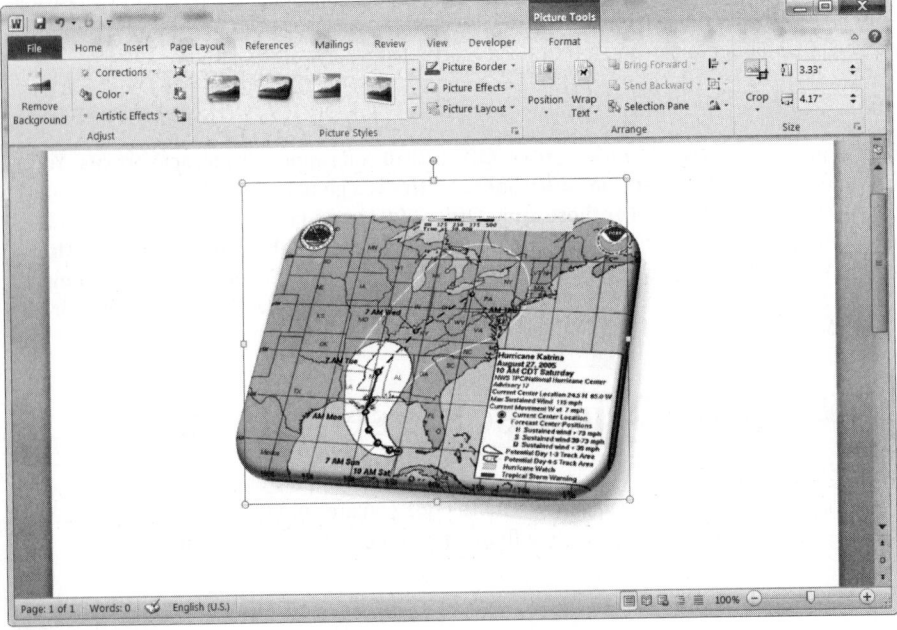

With each action, Office displays a likely set of applicable tools on the Ribbon. The tools provided include several galleries, which contain sets of ready-to-use options — you'll learn more about galleries later. As the mouse pointer moves over different gallery options, such as the picture styles shown here, the image in the actual document shows a live preview of the effect of that choice. As you navigate the Ribbon to additional formatting options and special effects, the Live Preview changes to reflect the currently selected choice, as shown in Figure 2-3.

FIGURE 2-3

Live Preview shows the result of the selected formatting or effect.

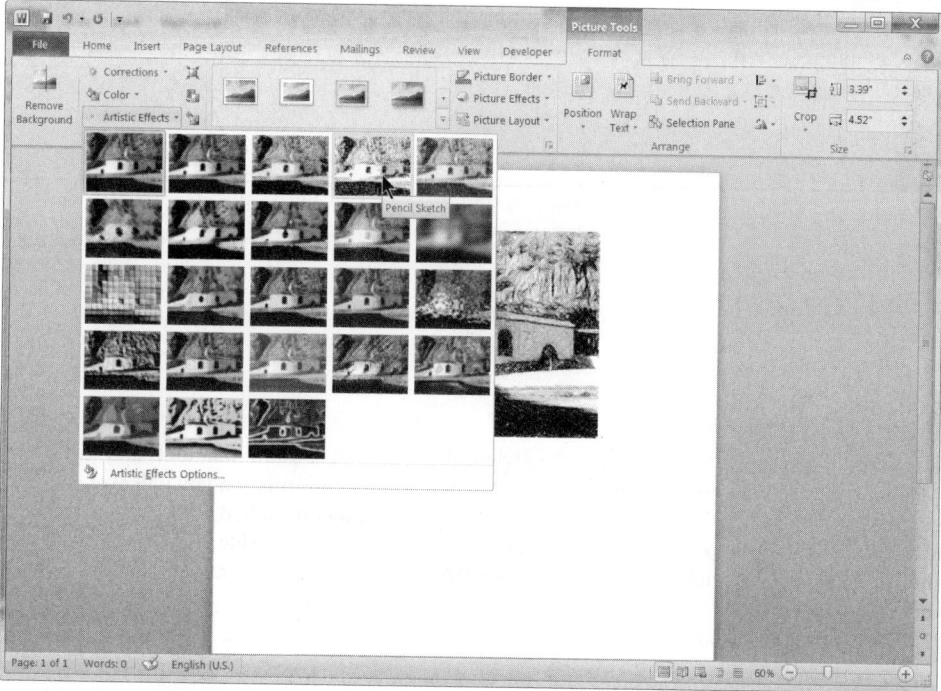

In addition to providing a live preview of many formatting options, Microsoft has also greatly enhanced and expanded the range of different effects and options. The result, optimally, is documents that look more polished and professional than was possible previously.

Ribbons and Things

At the heart of Office 2010's results-oriented interface is the Ribbon. The Ribbon is the area above the document workspace, as shown in Figure 2-4. The Ribbon contains tabs, each with a set of commands on it. Click to select which Ribbon tab is displayed.

Office 2010's Ribbon, shown in home position on a 22-inch monitor with normal resolution

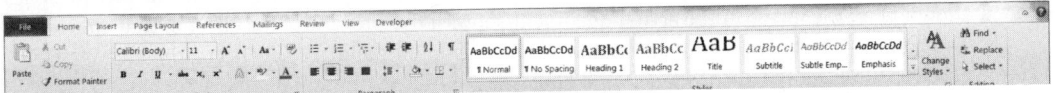

Exactly what you see in any given Ribbon tab is determined by a number of factors, including the size of your monitor, your screen resolution, the size of the current Office window, and whether you're using Windows' display settings to accommodate low vision. Hence, what you see might not always be what is pictured in this book. If you have a very large monitor operating at comparatively high resolution, at most you will see the entirety of the Home tab of the Ribbon, shown in Figure 2-5.

At the highest resolution and largest screen size, Office's Ribbon displays additional gallery options and text labels.

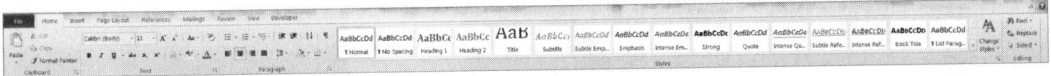

Note

This Home tab of the Ribbon shows 16 styles from the Style Gallery, as well as additional tools and text labels in the Clipboard and Editing groups. This is the maximum amount of information you will ever see in the Home Ribbon. For the picture in Figure 2-5 to be captured, Office was stretched across two 22-inch monitors, and additional detail stopped appearing when Office became 37 inches wide. Therefore, if you're wondering whether you need a 52-inch monitor for Office 2010, you'll be happy to know that a 42-inch model will work just fine. ■

Tip

Ctrl+F1 toggles the Ribbon on and off, as does clicking the arrow button that is the first button to the right of the tabs, next to the round Help button. At times the Ribbon is going to look overly large to you. It will also seem imposing when you're simply reading a document or when you're trying to see a graphic and write about it at the same time. The Ribbon might also be distracting if all you're doing is composing, and are fluent in the keystrokes you need to perform basic formatting. For those times, there is Ctrl+F1. To turn the Ribbon off using the mouse, double-click the current tab; click any tab to turn it back on temporarily. It will automatically hide when you're done using it. Double-click any tab or press Ctrl+F1 to turn it back on full-time. ■

Title Bar

The top bar of the Office window is called the *title bar*, exhibited in Figure 2-6. Double-clicking the title bar toggles Office between maximized and restored states. It's the equivalent of alternately clicking the Maximize and Restore buttons.

FIGURE 2-6

The title bar

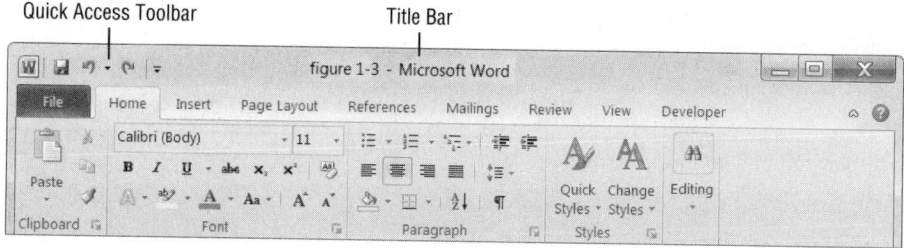

The title bar also contains the Quick Access Toolbar (QAT), the name of the document in the current Office window, and what Windows calls the *application control caption buttons* (the tools for maximizing, minimizing, restoring, and closing application windows). If you've told Office not to Show All Windows in the Taskbar (in Word, File ➪ Options ➪ Advanced ➪ Display section), then these caption buttons control all of Office, rather than just the current document window. In your own case, the title bar might contain other elements as well, such as items placed there by various Office and Windows add-ins.

Tip

Right-click on different areas of the title bar for available options. For example, if you right-click the Quick Access Toolbar, you'll see that it can be customized or placed below the Ribbon; any tool on it can be instantly removed as well. If you right-click the middle area of the title bar, you'll see that the window button options (Move, Size, Minimize, etc.) are available here as well. ■

The Tab Row

Shown below the title bar in Figure 2-6 is the Tab row. In addition to the tabs themselves that you click to control which set of commands is displayed, this line contains the document window control buttons and the Help button (which replaces Help ➪ Microsoft Office Help from 2003 and earlier Office applications). If you've told Office to Show All Windows in the Taskbar (File ➪ Options ➪ Advanced ➪ Display section in Word), the separate document control caption buttons will not be present. The tabs can be accessed via the mouse or hot keys. Unlike in menu-based Windows applications, however, there are no underlined letters showing you the hot keys.

As noted earlier, double-clicking the currently selected tab hides the Ribbon. Double-click any tab to unhide it. Ctrl+F1 toggles the Ribbon on and off as well. Once the Ribbon has been turned off, you can temporarily turn it back on by clicking a tab (or pressing its hot key). Once you've used a tool in that tab, the Ribbon automatically goes back into hiding.

KeyTips

If there are no underlined letters, how do you know which keys to press? Tap the Alt key. As shown in Figure 2-7, when you tap the Alt key, shortcut keys that work in the current context are displayed. "In the current context" might seem like an odd way to phrase it. Why context is relevant will become clear when we talk more about the Ribbon (described in the following section). For now, however, if you're working in an Office document, pressing Alt+H will display the Home tab of the Ribbon, Alt+N the Insert tab, and so on. (Be sure to press Esc to hide all KeyTips before starting again with Alt.)

FIGURE 2-7

Tap the Alt key to display Office's context-sensitive hot keys.

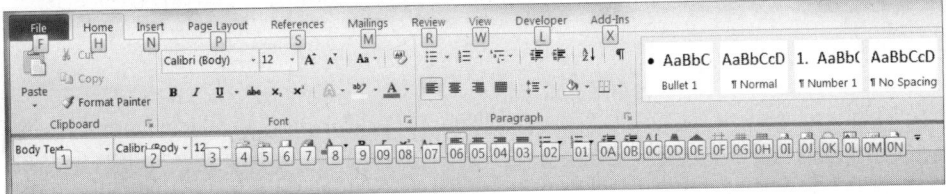

Note that I've added some additional tools to the QAT, shown in its alternate position below the Ribbon in Figure 2-7, and that numbered hot keys are associated with them. In addition to the first nine being accessible via Alt+1 through Alt+9, the last three are accessible via Alt+0L, Alt+0M, and Alt+0N.

Ribbon

The Ribbon is divided into several different tabs that ostensibly correspond to the Office applications' former menus. Unlike with the menus, however, there are no expanded drop-down lists under each main menu item. Instead, each tab exposes a different set of commands. Note that in Figure 2-4, the Home tab is exposed. Contrast that with Figure 2-8, which displays the Insert tab.

FIGURE 2-8

Each of the tabs exposes a different set of commands. The Insert tab is shown here.

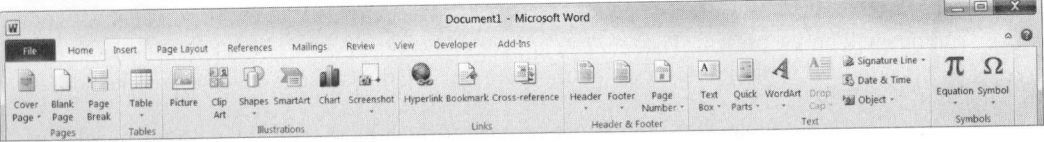

Note that the number of Ribbon tabs you see also varies according to user settings. In Figure 2-8, you can see the Developer and Add-Ins tabs. In your own setup, these tabs might not appear.

Groups, or Chunks

We've already talked about the Ribbon — now it's time to explore a few tricks and some odd nomenclature. At the bottom of the Ribbon shown in Figure 2-7, note the names Clipboard,

Font, and Paragraph. These are known as groups, or chunks. Each contains individual tools or controls.

If you're a veteran Office user — perhaps even if not — you've probably been wondering what to do, for example, if the Ribbon is displaying the Page Layout tab and you really want to access the Home tab's Editing tools (the ones that contain Find, Replace, Go To, and Select).

In pre-2007 incarnations of Office, access to commonly used commands was always available via the menu, and often via the Standard and Formatting toolbars. Indeed, these commands are always available in Office 2010 as well, sort of. When the Page Layout tab is displayed, you can access any of the Home tab items simply by pressing Alt, H (in sequence), or by clicking the Home tab.

What if you want to remain focused on Page Layout?

Any item on the Ribbon — individual tools, groups/chunks, and even Dialog Box Launchers — can be added to the QAT. For example, right-click Bold and choose Add to Quick Access Toolbar. Now Bold will be available all the time, regardless of which tab is displayed. Did I mention that Q stands for Quick? Don't want bold there? Right-click on Bold and choose Remove from the Quick Access Toolbar.

Let's try another navigation trick. Tap Alt+P (Page Layout tab). Now press the arrow keys. If you're unsteady with the mouse, you can use the four arrow keys to navigate. You can also use Tab and Shift+Tab to move forward or backward through all the Ribbon commands. When you get to a command you want to use, press either the Spacebar or the Enter key.

Note

In the previous section, I mentioned that hot keys are context-sensitive. Shouldn't they work the same way all the time? One would think so. Alas, Microsoft does not agree, so while Alt+1 might activate the first QAT command when you tap the Alt key, you cannot count on its always doing the same thing. If you press Alt+H, now the Alt+1 key applies bold formatting. Hence, context is vital. ■

Contextual Tools

In addition to the default set of seven main tabs, additional context-sensitive or contextual tabs appear depending on what kind of document part is selected. For example, if you choose Insert ➪ Header and insert a header from the Header gallery, the Heading & Footer Tools' Design subtab is displayed, as shown in Figure 2-9.

Notice that because this particular header format is enclosed in a table, the Table Tools tab is also exposed. The Table Tools tab has Design and Layout subtabs, each of which is also available in the current view.

Tip

As you are becoming acclimated to Office 2010, whenever a new tab is exposed, you should click it to explore what it has to offer. Think of them as hidden drawers that might contain money! This is an aspect of Office

2010's *discoverability*. If you don't like the design choice in a given gallery, you very likely can change it (and even add new or changed items to the gallery for future use — more on this later). ∎

When a header is selected, the Header & Footer Tools' Design subtab and associated Ribbon are selected.

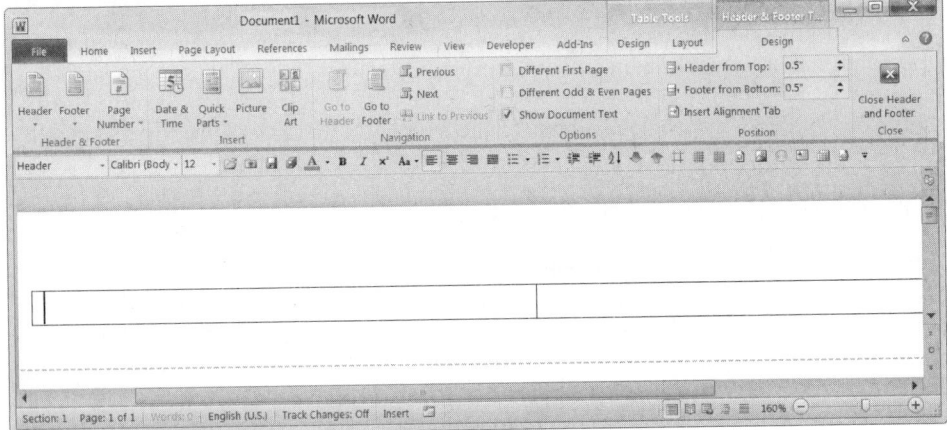

Quick Access Toolbar

If you are a veteran pre-Office 2007 user, you might be asking, "Where have all the toolbars gone?" If you are a longtime veteran, in fact, you might be screaming that question at the top of your lungs, perhaps adding a colorful adjective or two. All of the toolbars have been collapsed into the single and less flexible Quick Access Toolbar, or *QAT* as it is rapidly becoming known. Shown above the Ribbon in Figure 2-10, the QAT can also be placed below the Ribbon.

The Quick Access Toolbar, in its default location above the Ribbon tabs, replaces all of Office's earlier user-customizable toolbars.

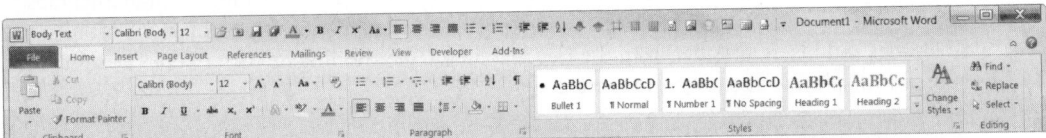

Note

If you have custom templates that rely heavily on carefully crafted custom toolbars and menus, heed caution. The good news is that some of those toolbars might actually still work in Office 2010 if you upgraded from Office 2003. Look for them in the Add-Ins Ribbon. The bad news is that Office 2010 no longer contains customization tools that let you create and modify multiple toolbars. The benefit, though, of Office 2010 is that you can customize the Ribbon. ∎

Live Preview

Live Preview applies the highlighted gallery formatting to the selection in the current document, enabling you to see the results instantly without actually having to apply that formatting, as shown in Figure 2-11. As the mouse pointer moves among the different gallery options, the formatting displayed in the body of the document instantly changes.

FIGURE 2-11

Live Preview, showing the results of the Intense Quote style applied to the current paragraph

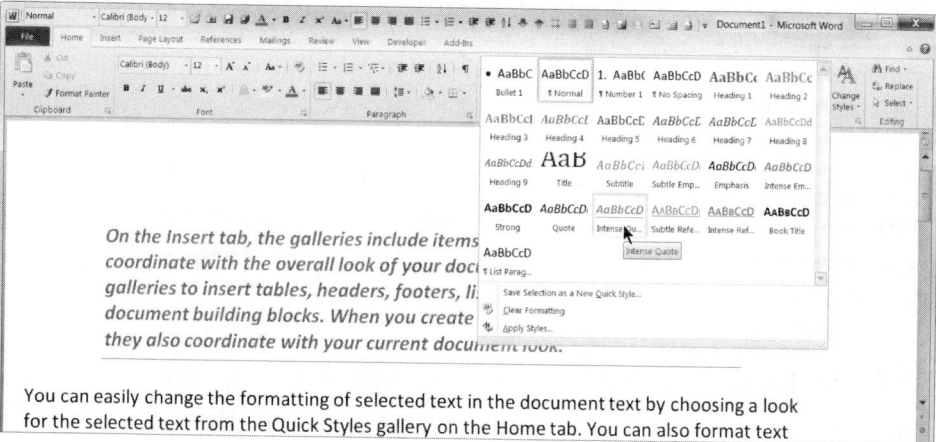

Note that not all galleries and formatting options produce Live Preview results. For example, in the Page Layout tab, none of the Page Setup items produces live previews, nor do the paragraph settings on that Ribbon.

Another time you won't see Live Preview is when working with dialog boxes, such as the Paragraph dialog box. Many of those offer internal Preview panels but do not take advantage of Office 2010's Live Preview capability.

A gotcha in all this newfangled functionality is that sometimes the gallery itself covers up all or part of the live preview. This gets old quickly, and can negate much of Live Preview's functionality, unless you're blessed with lots of screen real estate. Maybe that 52-inch monitor isn't such a bad idea after all.

Fortunately, some galleries and controls have draggable borders that enable you to see more of what you're trying to preview, as shown in Figure 2-12. If a control's border is draggable, this is indicated by three dots. Notice the three dots in the lower-right corner of the Style gallery in Figure 2-11, and in the bottom border of the Fonts drop-down in Figure 2-12. On the lower-right corner, the three dots indicate that the border can be rolled up and to the left. On the bottom, the three dots indicate that the border can be rolled up.

FIGURE 2-12

Some Live Preview controls can be rolled up to reveal document details that otherwise would be covered.

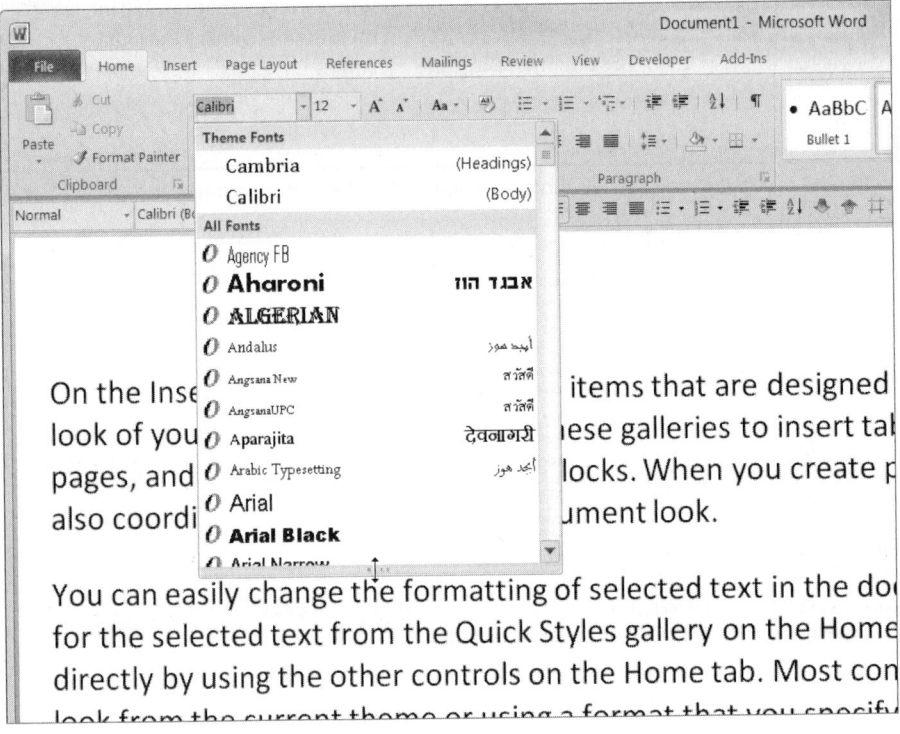

Sometimes, however, it's easiest simply to go ahead and apply the formatting, rather than jump through hoops. If necessary, you can always use the venerable Ctrl+Z (Undo) if you don't like the result.

Caution

When using Live Preview, it's very easy to forget to click on the desired gallery or formatting command when you come to it. Particularly in extensive lists (such as lists of fonts, colors, or styles), it's possible to get exactly the right effect without noticing what it's called. In the case of colors, you usually don't even have a name to use as a guide. Sometimes, the hand really is quicker than the eye. Once you move your mouse away from your selection, the gallery closes. You might have to reinspect that entire list to find exactly what you already found so don't forget to click! ■

Galleries

Up to now, the term gallery has been used as if it were a common everyday Office term. Well, it is — but it has taken on expanded meaning in Ribbon-oriented Office. Simply put, a gallery is a set of formatting results or pre-formatted document parts. Virtually every set of formatting results or document parts in Word 2010 (indeed, in all of Office 2010) might be called a gallery, although Office itself does not use the word gallery to refer to every feature set. Some, such as the lists of bullets, are called libraries instead.

Galleries include document styles, themes, headers, footers, page colors, tables, WordArt, equations, symbols, and more. The Style Gallery is shown in the previous section, in Figure 2-11. Galleries often work hand-in-hand with the Live Preview feature. Imagine that you're paging through a coffee-table volume of paintings, and each time you point to a different painting, your own house and garden are transformed to reflect the style and period of the painting. Point at a different painting, and your house and garden are retransformed, as the selected item is transformed when using Live Preview.

As noted earlier, however, not every gallery results in a Live Preview. As you begin to take advantage of this feature, you will quickly start to miss it when it's not available. Office 2010 has added some new galleries that Office 2007 did not have, such as the Artistic Effects gallery in the Picture Tools Format tab in Word.

The MiniBar or Mini Toolbar

Another feature in Office 2010 is the MiniBar, more formally known as the Mini toolbar. The MiniBar is a set of formatting tools that appears when you first select text. It is not context-sensitive and always contains an identical set of formatting tools. There is no MiniBar for graphics and other non-text objects.

When you first select text, the MiniBar appears as a ghostly apparition. When you move the mouse pointer closer to it, it becomes more solid, as shown in Figure 2-13. If you move the mouse pointer far enough away from it, it fades away completely.

FIGURE 2-13

The MiniBar appears when text is first selected.

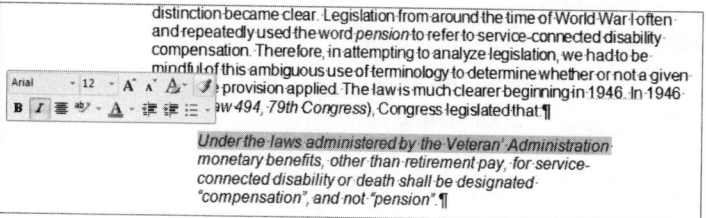

Note

Once the MiniBar disappears, you cannot resurrect it by hovering the mouse over the selection. You can, however, display the MiniBar and the current shortcut menu by right-clicking on the selection. Note also that only the mouse triggers the MiniBar. If you display the pop-up context menu by pressing Shift+F10 or by tapping the Menu button on a Windows keyboard, the MiniBar will not appear. ∎

Some users will love the MiniBar, others will hate it. I recommend that you give it a try. It exists to provide convenient and discoverable access to commands that are otherwise less convenient and less accessible, unless you are an avid keyboarder.

When the Home tab is exposed, the MiniBar might seem superfluous, as all of the MiniBar's components are replicated in that tab. However, consider for a moment how far the mouse has to travel to access those formatting commands. With the MiniBar, the mouse pointer usually has to travel less than an inch or so.

For those with repetitive motion injuries, this can save a lot of wear and tear on the wrist.

If you decide that the MiniBar gets in the way, you can turn it off. Even when it is turned off, however, you can still summon it by right-clicking on the current selection.

Note

Unlike many Ribbon tools, the MiniBar tools do not produce live previews of formatting and other effects. If you need to see a live preview, use the Ribbon instead. ■

Shortcut or Contextual Menus

Although the menu system of Office 2003 and earlier has been almost entirely replaced by Ribbons, Office's shortcut menus, sometimes called contextual or pop-up menus, remain. Shown in Figure 2-14, shortcut menus remain largely unchanged from Office 2003, except for the fact that when text is selected, the MiniBar accompanies the pop-up.

FIGURE 2-14

When you right-click on a selection, a context-sensitive shortcut menu appears, along with the MiniBar.

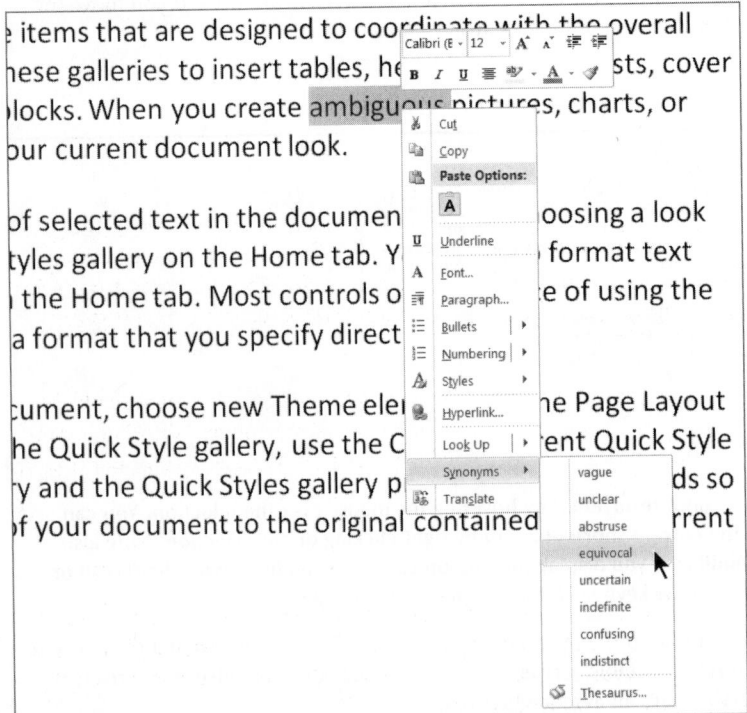

Note

Although shortcut menus remain in Office 2010, the ability to customize them is gone. ■

Enhanced ScreenTips

Another Office 2010 feature is Enhanced ScreenTips. Enhanced ScreenTips are expanded feature descriptions designed to make features more discoverable, as well as to reduce the frequency with which you'll need to press the F1 key for Help.

Shown in Figure 2-15, an Enhanced ScreenTip magically appears when you hover the mouse pointer over a tool. If you hover the mouse pointer over an exposed gallery item (such as a style), however, you will see a Live Preview of the gallery item instead of an Enhanced ScreenTip.

FIGURE 2-15

Enhanced ScreenTips explain the selected feature, reducing the need to press F1.

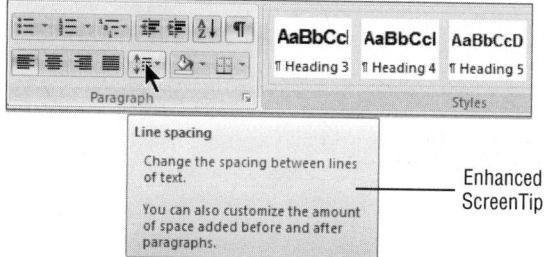

Dialog Boxes and Launchers

Even though Office 2010's philosophy focuses on the results-oriented Ribbon, some features and functions remain tied to traditional dialog boxes. Dialog boxes can be launched in several ways, including by direct keystrokes and what Microsoft calls Dialog Box Launchers. Dialog Box Launchers are the arrows pointing southeast in the lower-right corner of some Ribbon groups, as shown in Figure 2-16.

In many instances, Office's dialog boxes have not been overhauled or greatly enhanced for this release. However, if you look closely, you often will see several changes, some subtle and others not so subtle. Figure 2-17 contrasts the Paragraph dialog boxes from Word 2010 and Word 2007. Sometimes, if you look really closely, new features will leap out at you!

Task Panes

Word 2003 sported a collection of 14 task panes (or more, depending on what features were installed and in use). You activated the task pane by pressing Ctrl+F1, and it included Getting Started, Styles and Formatting, Clipboard, Mail Merge, and others. As noted earlier in this chapter, in Office 2010, Ctrl+F1 toggles the Ribbon on and off.

FIGURE 2-16

Clicking a Dialog Box Launcher displays a dialog box.

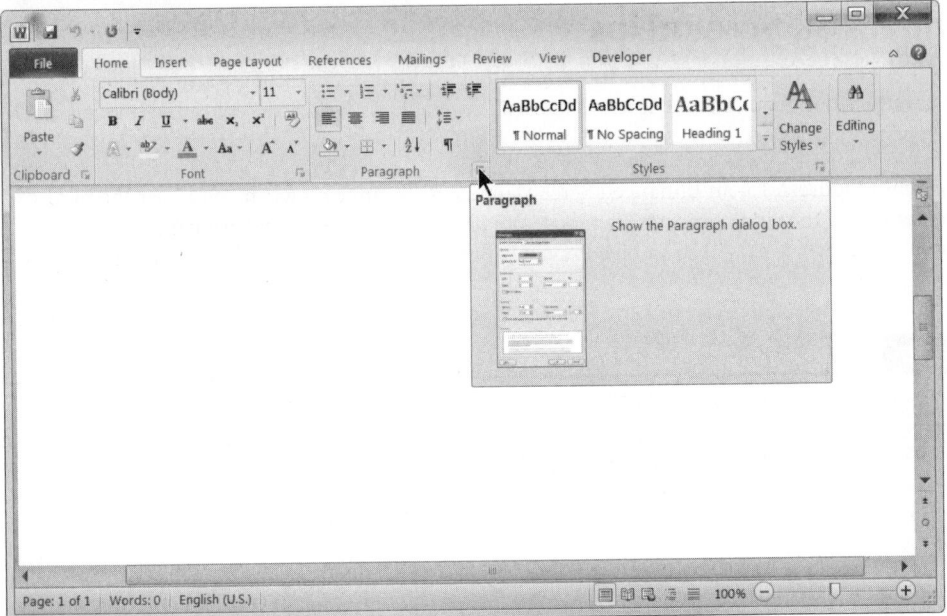

FIGURE 2-17

Can you spot the differences between the Word 2010 and Word 2007 dialog boxes? Without seeing the two versions side-by-side, you might never notice Word 2010's new Text Effects button!

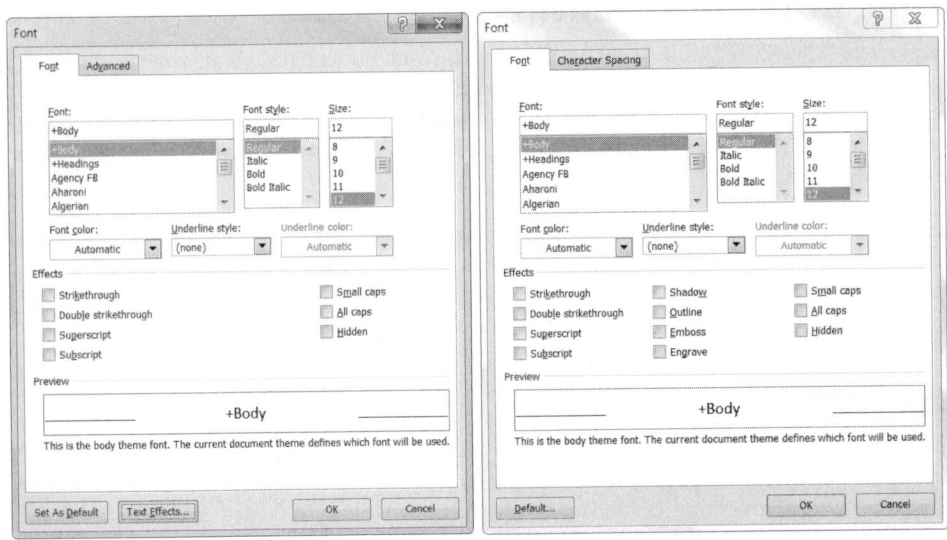

Word 2010 Font Dialog   Word 2007 Font Dialog

If Ctrl+F1 is now used for something else, how do you activate the task panes in Office 2010 applications? The short answer is that task panes, as a cohesive concept, have been mostly abandoned. Office 2010 still has some task panes, but you can't access them using a drop-down menu as you could in Office 2003, and you can't access the entire collection of task panes using a single keystroke. Instead, they will appear as needed (and possibly when you aren't expecting them). Think of them as dialog boxes that enable you to type while they're onscreen.

For example, in the Home tab in Word 2010, click the Styles Dialog Box Launcher. This displays the Styles task pane. Now click the drop-down arrow to the left of the X in the upper-right corner of the task pane, as shown in Figure 2-18. Instead of a list of task panes, you get three options that control only this task pane. Task panes can be docked on the left or right side of the document window, or can be dragged and displayed wherever it's convenient — including completely out of Office's window frame. Just move the mouse pointer over the Styles title bar and drag. To return it, just drag it back, or double-click the floating task pane's title bar.

FIGURE 2-18

Office 2010's task panes are independent of each other and can't be selected from a common pull-down control.

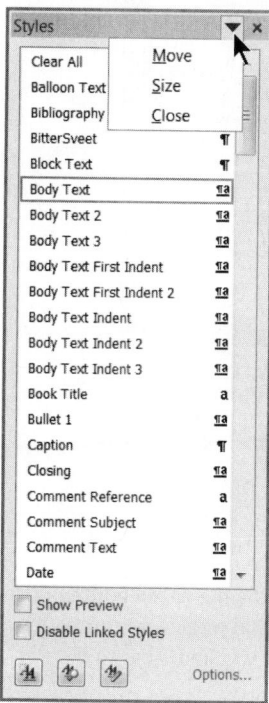

Other Word 2010 features that manifest as independent task panes include the Navigation pane (new in Word 2010), the Mail Merge Wizard, Clip Art, Protect Document, Research, Document Management, the Clipboard, and the Style Inspector. While it might seem a bit odd for Microsoft to have unbundled the task panes, a quick look at Figure 2-19 hints at a decided advantage of the independent approach. While you probably won't need to have them all onscreen at once, it's nice to know that you're not limited to just one task pane at a time.

You can display multiple task panes at the same time, should you feel a compelling need for clutter.

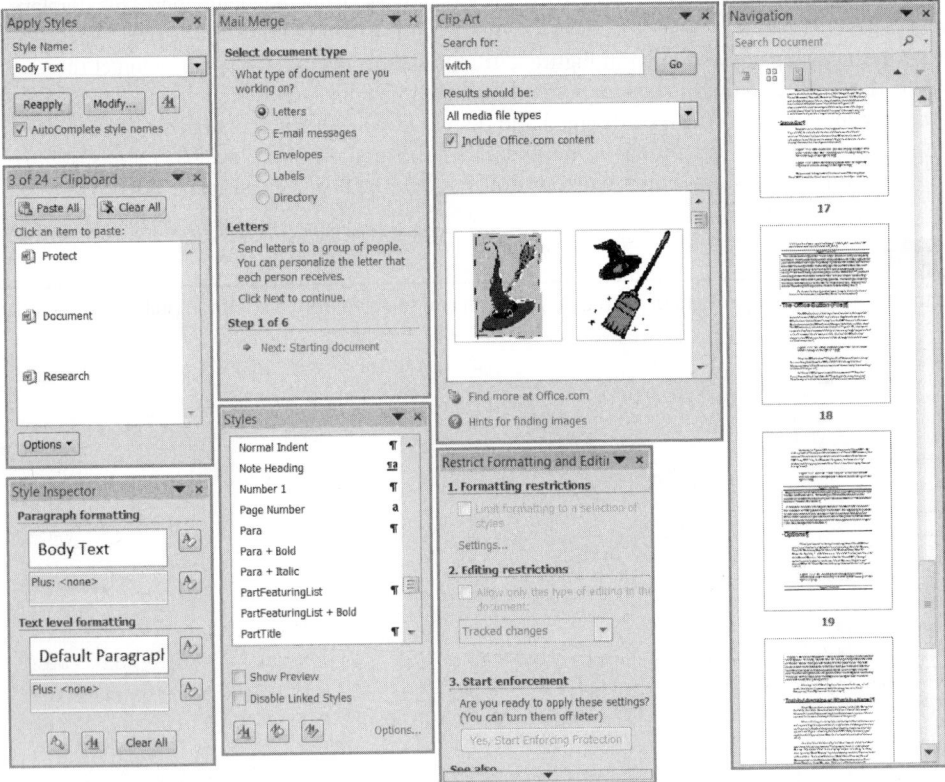

Status Bar

Now we turn to the status bar. Shown in Figure 2-20, the status bar is the bar at the bottom of an Office application window. The status bar provides more than 20 optional pieces of information about the current document, depending on the application. Right-click the status bar to display its customization options.

FIGURE 2-20

Office 2010's status bar adds several new collaboration features.

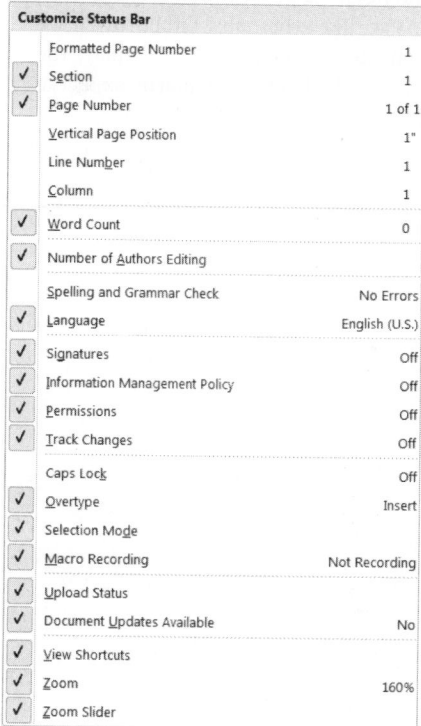

Do you need to keep track of the word count in a Word document? Not only does Word update the Word count continuously, but if you select text, its status bar tells you how many words are selected: *180/5,644* means that 180 words are selected out of a total of 5,644.

Note

The Customize Status Bar menu stays onscreen until you click somewhere else in the application window. That means that you can enable or disable as many options as you want without having to repeatedly right-click the status bar. Notice also that the Customize Status Bar menu displays the current status too, so if you just want to quickly refer to it to find out what language you're using — but don't really want Language on the status bar — you don't have to put it on the status bar and then remove it. Note additionally that the status items aren't just pretty pictures. For example, clicking the Page item takes you to the Go To Page dialog box. Clicking the Macro Recording item opens the Record Macro dialog box. ∎

To dismiss the customization menu, simply click the status bar or anywhere else in the document, press Esc, Enter, or the Spacebar.

Go Backstage with File

Office 2007's Office button has been replaced by a File tab in Office 2010, which displays the Backstage view. Only it's not really a tab because it doesn't act like other tabs. Either way, it will make a lot of users happy. The File button, which has been clicked in Figure 2-21, displays the Backstage view. Here you'll find a number of top-level commands that you ordinarily expect to find in a File menu.

FIGURE 2-21

Office 2010's File tab replaces Office 2007's Office button.

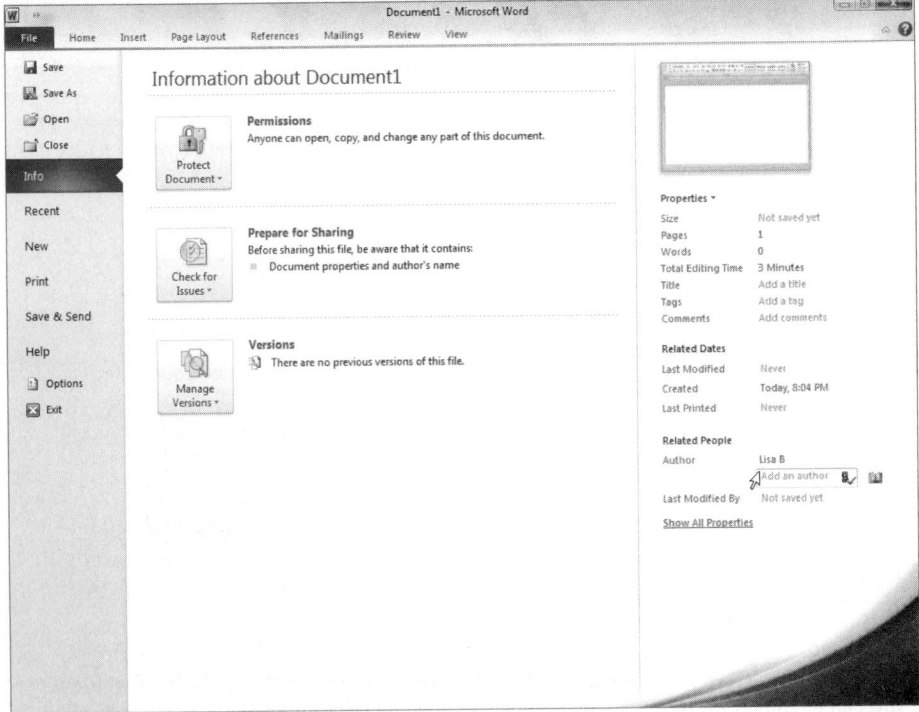

In Office's File tab, some of the commands — Info, Recent, New, Print, Save & Send, and Help — have additional screens and commands.

As shown in Figure 2-22, it pays to explore in Word 2010 and the other Office applications. By clicking each of the expandable commands in Office's File tab or Backstage view, the seasoned Office user will quickly discover several features hiding in each panel — recent files, document templates, printer commands, sharing options, and more. You'll also find legacy features hiding there. Users coming from Word 2007 will be happy to know that you no longer need to download an add-in to gain PDF and XPS capabilities. Those are available in Word 2010 right out-of-the-box.

A cornucopia of sharing options is found in the Backstage Save & Send window.

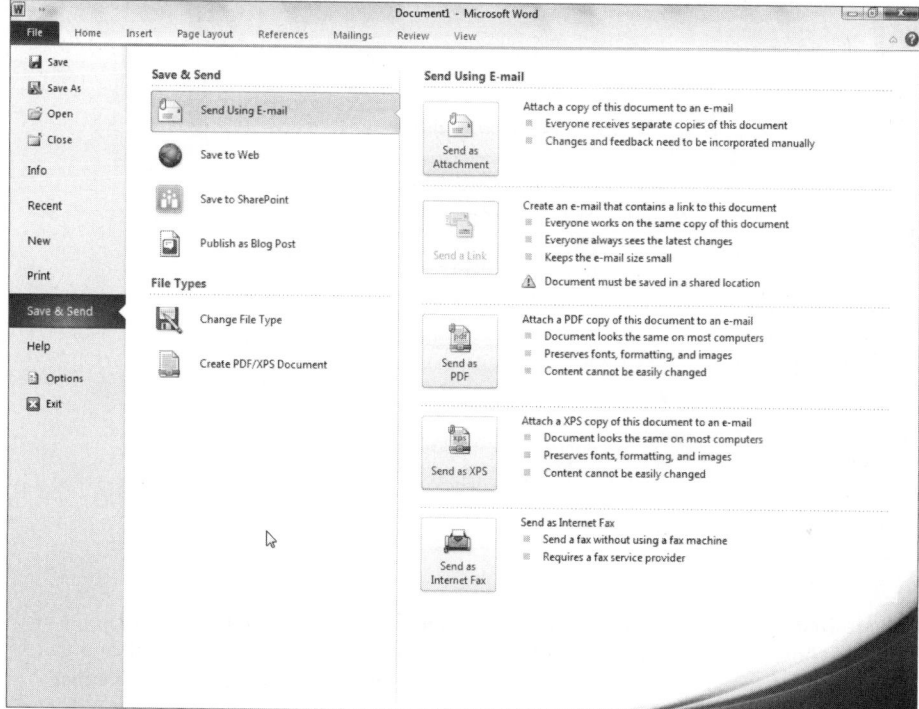

Caution

To exit Backstage view, don't click the X. Instead, press Esc or click a different tab (such as the Home tab). If you click the X in the upper-right corner, Office not only closes Backstage, but closes the program too. ■

Options

When you wanted to change something about Office 2003 or earlier, you had multiple places to look, including Tools ⇨ Options, Tools ⇨ Customize, Help ⇨ About ⇨ Disabled Items, Help ⇨ Check for Updates, File ⇨ Permission, Tools ⇨ Protect, and Tools ⇨ AutoCorrect Options, to name but a few. In Office 2010, "change central" is now one place: Options. To get there, choose File ⇨ Options to display the Options dialog box for the application in use, such as the example shown in Figure 2-23.

FIGURE 2-23

The Options dialog box features Information icons to clarify selected options.

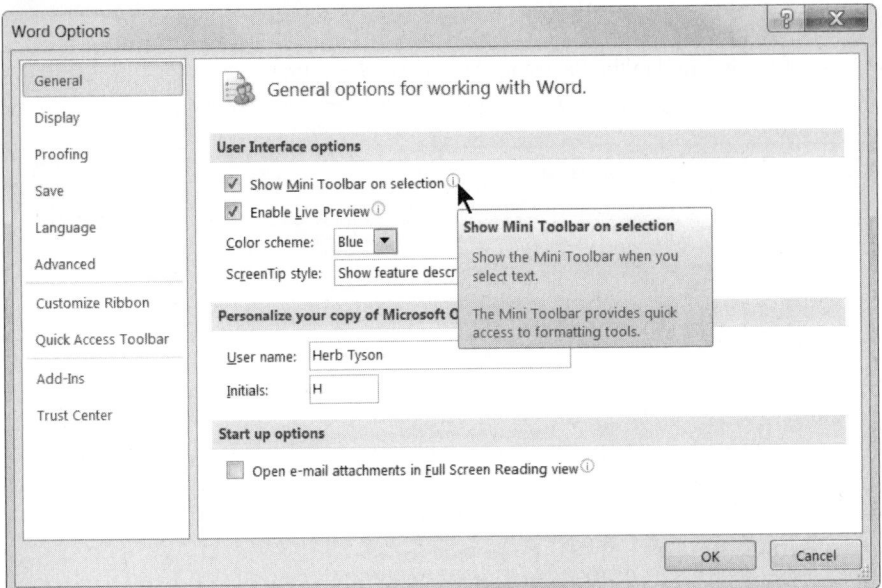

Note

Figure 2-23 is neatly resized so that it's no longer very large, as it initially is. The good news is that you can resize the Options dialog box. The bad news is that Office does not remember that you resized it, and the next time you open it, it's back to full size. In fact, in some dual-monitor configurations, it's possible that Options won't obey Windows' normal rules, and Options will span both monitors each and every time you open it. ■

Although all of Office's options are now in one place in each application, so to speak, that doesn't necessarily make them any easier to find. Navigating Office Options can be daunting.

Truth in Advertising, or What's in a Name?

The Options dialog for each Office application has numerous sections, sometimes called tabs, on the left. Do not be fooled by the labels. Note that one of the tabs is called Advanced. Microsoft's idea of advanced, however, might not be the same as yours. What's optional for someone else might be essential for you.

Microsoft's logic is to try to put at the top of the list the controls and options it thinks you are most likely to want to change. The first set, General, is therefore the group it thinks will matter most to the typical user. If you're reading the *Office 2010 Bible*, however, you might not be a typical user. Keep this in mind as you look at the various tabs.

Another caveat is that the labels aren't even objectively accurate. For example, there is a tab labeled Display in Word. If you don't find the display option you're looking for there, don't give up. Some display options actually reside in General, such as Show Mini Toolbar on Selection, Enable Live Preview, and Open E-mail Attachments in Full Screen Reading View.

Several display options are also sheltered under the Advanced umbrella, including great Word favorites such as the Show Document Content options, the Display options, and Provide Feedback with Animation (under General). If you're keeping track, there's a General tab, and there's a General section within the Advanced tab. Which General are we supposed to salute?

Still other display options are to be found hiding in various other dark corners and recesses. If you can't find something you know must be there, check the index in this book.

Options are covered further in Appendix A, available online at www.wiley.com/go/office-2010bible. I urge you to click on each of the tabs available in the Office application that you're working in to explore the different options that are available. Mostly, this is so you can learn the answer to "Where did they hide it?" Additionally, however, it will enable you to learn about options and features you might not otherwise be aware of.

Advanced . . . versus Not Advanced?

If you're at all like me, you might be wondering, "How did Microsoft decide what's advanced and what's not advanced?" We'll probably never know. More important than understanding the logic, however, is simply becoming familiar with the lay of the land so you know where things are, rather than having to look all over the place every time you want to know how to change a setting.

For example, the Advanced tab for Word, partially shown in Figure 2-24, has 12 major sections (depending on how you count them, of course). Also depending on how you count, the Advanced tab in Word offers more than 150 different settings, including the Layout options.

Remember those nice information icons so prevalent in the General tab? The Advanced tab has only six of them! Out of more than 150 different settings, there are information icons for only six!

Scroll down a bit so you can see both the Save and Preserve Fidelity sections at the same time. Is there any doubt in your mind what Prompt before Saving Normal Template means? Not in mine either.

Now look at Embed Linguistic Data. Do you really know exactly what that means? I didn't (I looked it up, so I know now, but there's no cute information button to tell you). Why, do you suppose, did Microsoft choose to provide cute little information buttons for the options whose meanings, for the most part, are already patently obvious? Clearly, it must not know what Embed Linguistic Data means either!

FIGURE 2-24

Word's Advanced options contain more than 150 settings.

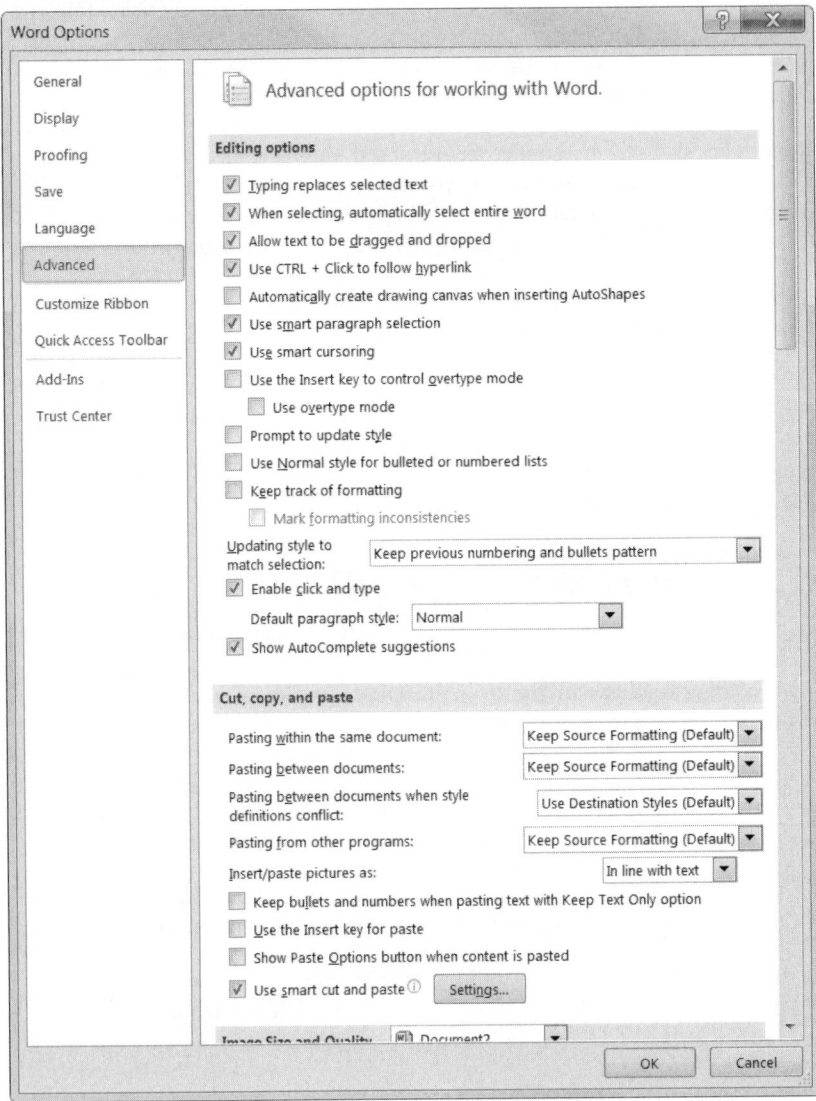

To find out what these advanced options are, simply select the option and press F1. Not much help, right? Okay, then, type **embed linguistic data** into the Search box (including the quotes) and click Search for the really helpful view shown in Figure 2-25.

Tip

In many instances, but not always, you can find help on what you want by typing the exact feature name (e.g., *embed linguistic data*) into the Search box, pressing Enter (which usually returns no results), and then clicking the All of Office.com link. ■

FIGURE 2-25

Office's Help system sometimes does not provide the needed answer.

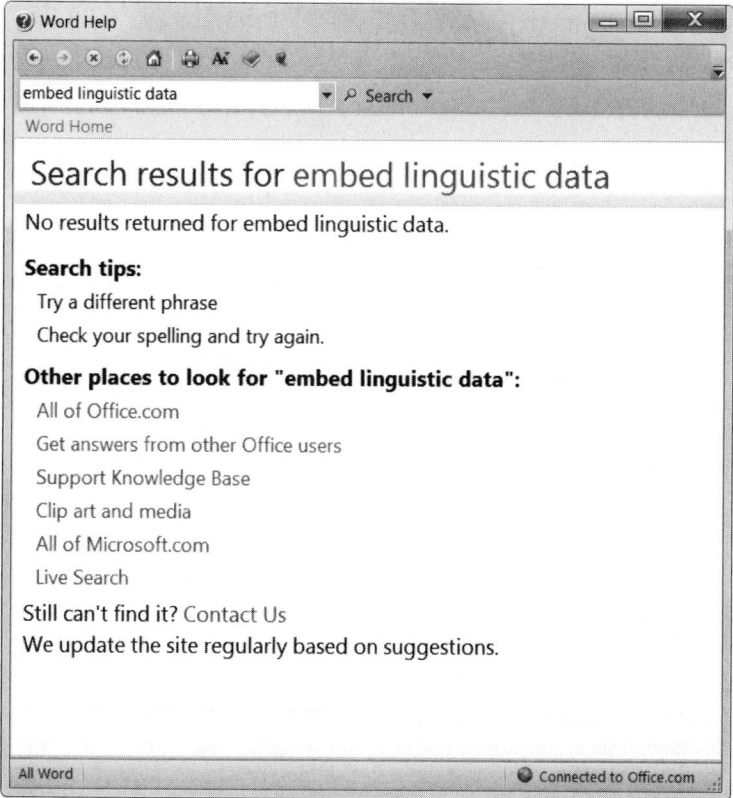

Sometimes you will find useful help much more quickly by following the tip shown above, or simply by searching the Web for information about the feature in question. Note that even when you can find help in Microsoft's Knowledge Base, that help often is couched in technical language or refers you to other locations in Help. Searching other sources online often nets you more useful information because the very existence of such sources likely is the result of someone's frustration in trying to parse the "official" sources.

Working with Dialog Boxes

Many Office commands display a dialog box, which is simply a way of getting more information from you. For example, if you choose Review ➪ Changes ➪ Protect Sheet from Excel's Ribbon, Excel can't carry out the command until you tell it what parts of the sheet you want to protect. Therefore, it displays the Protect Sheet dialog box, shown in Figure 2-26.

FIGURE 2-26

Dialog boxes request additional information about executing a command.

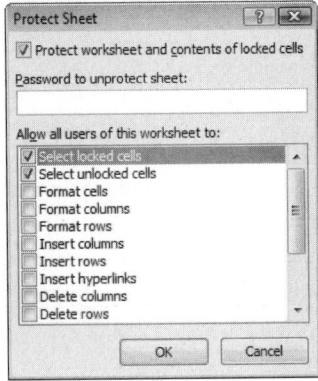

Office dialog boxes vary in how they work. You'll find two types of dialog boxes:

- **Typical Dialog Box.** A modal dialog box takes the focus away from the spreadsheet. When this type of dialog box is displayed, you can't do anything in the worksheet until you dismiss the dialog box. Clicking OK performs the specified actions, and clicking Cancel (or pressing Esc) closes the dialog box without taking any action. Most Office dialog boxes are this type.

- **Stay-on-Top Dialog Box.** A modeless dialog box works in a manner similar to a toolbar. When a modeless dialog box is displayed, you can continue working in the Office application, and the dialog box remains open. Changes made in a modeless dialog box take effect immediately. For example, if you're applying formatting to a chart, changes you make in the Format dialog box appear in the chart as soon as you make them. A modeless dialog box has a Close button but no OK button.

Most people find working with dialog boxes to be quite straightforward and natural. If you've used other programs, you'll feel right at home. You can manipulate the controls either with your mouse or directly from the keyboard.

Navigating Dialog Boxes

Navigating dialog boxes is generally very easy — you simply click the control you want to activate.

Although dialog boxes were designed with mouse users in mind, you can also use the keyboard. Every dialog box control has text associated with it, and this text always has one underlined letter (a hot key or an accelerator key). You can access the control from the keyboard by pressing Alt and then the underlined letter. You also can press Tab to cycle through all the controls on a dialog box. Pressing Shift+Tab cycles through the controls in reverse order.

Tip

When a control is selected, it appears with a dotted outline. You can use the Spacebar to activate a selected control. ■

Using Tabbed Dialog Boxes

Many Office dialog boxes are tabbed dialog boxes: That is, they include notebook-like tabs, each of which is associated with a different panel.

When you click a tab, the dialog box changes to display a new panel containing a new set of controls. Excel's Format Cells dialog box, shown in Figure 2-27, is a good example. It has six tabs, which makes it functionally equivalent to six different dialog boxes.

FIGURE 2-27

Use the dialog box tabs to select different functional areas in the dialog box.

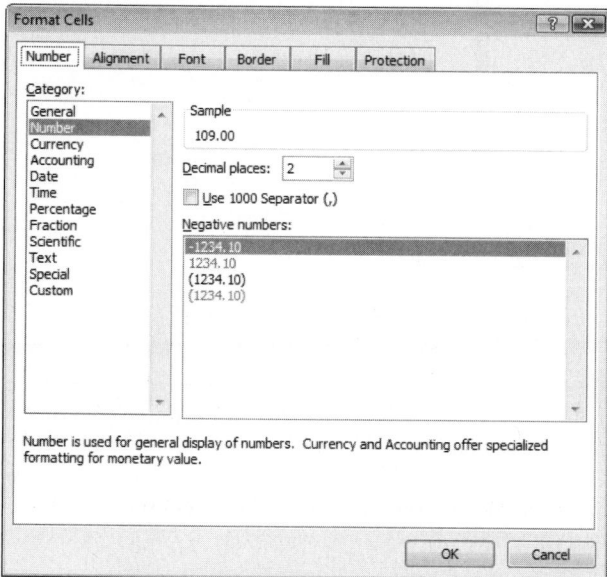

Tabbed dialog boxes are quite convenient because you can make several changes in a single dialog box. After you make all your setting changes, click OK or press Enter.

Tip

To select a tab by using the keyboard, press Ctrl+Page Up or Ctrl+Page Down, or simply press the first letter of the tab that you want to activate. ∎

Office 2007 introduced a new style of modeless tabbed dialog box in which the tabs are on the left, rather than across the top. Office 2010 also uses this style. Figure 2-28 shows the Format Shape dialog box, which is modeless tabbed. To select a tab using the keyboard, press the up- or down-arrow key and then Tab to access the controls.

FIGURE 2-28

A tabbed dialog box with tabs on the left

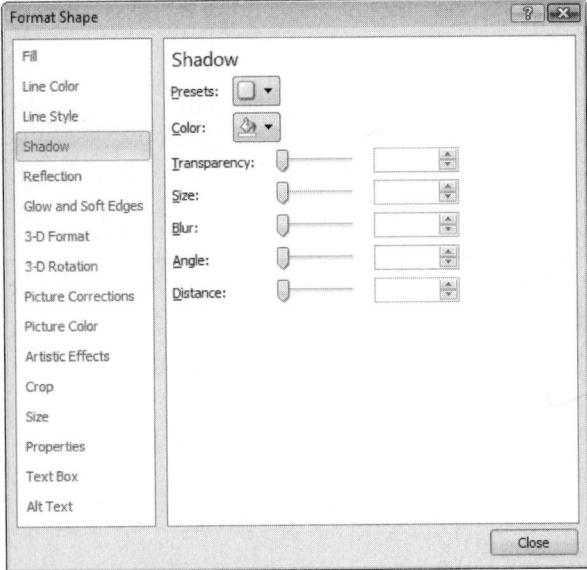

Summary

In this chapter, you've had a look at many of the exciting facets of Office 2010. You've seen the philosophy behind the Ribbon (discoverability). You've also learned several ways in which Office 2010 is similar to earlier versions, and several ways in which it's different. You should now know what people are talking about when they mention Ribbon tabs, the Quick Access Toolbar (QAT), Live Preview, Enhanced ScreenTips, and Galleries.

Mastering Fundamental Operations

Years ago, computer program developers began to standardize commands and functions, even in programs with significantly different purposes. Microsoft's Office suite was a pioneer in meeting the needs of users by standardizing names for menus and commands and by placing familiar tools in all of their applications. This chapter discusses features, commands, and tasks that many of the Microsoft Office 2010 applications have in common.

Working with Files

Computer files are part of a framework for managing data created and stored on a computer. When you create information in a program, such as a letter, you save that information in a file and assign the file a memorable name. When you want to work with the file at a later time, you can identify the file by its name and subsequently open the file in the program. Although the ins and outs of creating and using files can differ among Office programs, after you have learned to work with files in one Office application, you should be able to work with files in any other Office application. The skills you learn next will come in handy when you need to work with files in various Office programs.

Understanding Office 2010 File Formats

Every program saves data in a particular file format that reflects how the program identifies, organizes, and interprets the information contained within the file. You can typically identify which program was used to create a file in one of two ways:

- The file's icon in a Windows folder window or a dialog box, such as the Open dialog box, identifies the program used to create the file. All files created in a particular program use the program's icon. Figure 3-1 shows the file icons for some of the key Office programs. (The size and appearance of the icons vary depend on the view selected in Windows or the dialog box.)

FIGURE 3-1

A file's icon reflects the program used to create the file.

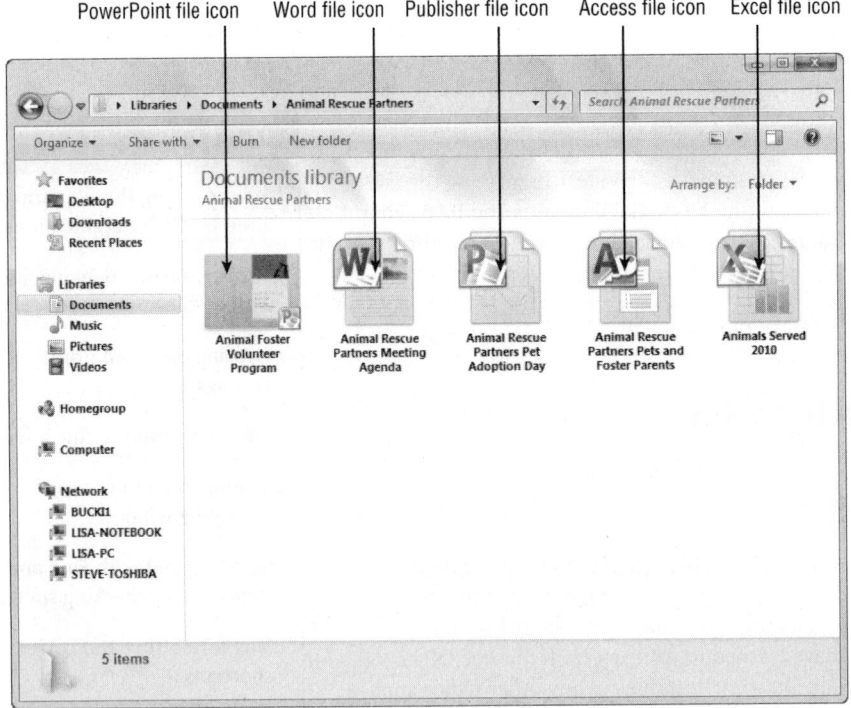

- A three- to five-letter filename extension (such as .docx for Word 2007 files) also identifies the program used to create the file. Although filename extensions often are hidden, you may see the extension when viewing the properties of a file or browsing to find a file in Windows.

The file formats for the 2007 releases of Word, Excel, and PowerPoint dramatically changed to use the Microsoft Office Open XML Formats, and the Office 2010 versions retain the XML formats. The Microsoft Office Open XML format is based on a wider standard called *eXtensible Markup Language* (XML), a method of describing data that was designed to facilitate sharing data between different systems. To signify their XML roots, the filename extensions for Word, Excel, and PowerPoint now include an *x*: .docx for Word documents, .xlsx for Excel workbooks, and .pptx for PowerPoint presentations. The change to XML-based file formats enables the applications to create smaller, more secure files that can be shared more easily.

Note

If an Office 2010 file has been saved in a special macro-enabled format, it will have the .docm **(Word),** .xlsm **(Excel), or** .pptm **(PowerPoint) filename extension and its file icon will include an explanation point on a yellow page.** ∎

Access 2010 also retains the .accdb database file format rather than the older .mdb file format for versions prior to 2007. The Access file format and the database engine that drives it give tighter integration with SharePoint and Outlook 2010. There are also some special variations of the Access file format, including an execute-only database file (.accde) and a runtime version (.accdr). Although Access can read tables from database files created in earlier Access versions for backward compatibility, older Access versions cannot read tables from an Access 2010 database file. Publisher 2010 files continue to use the .pub filename extension.

The Office 2010 Word, Excel, and PowerPoint applications also can save and open files based on the Open Document Format (ODF) v1.1 standard. The specific file format names vary depending on the application — OpenDocument Text (*.odt) for word processing, OpenDocument Spreadsheet (*.ods), and OpenDocument Presentations (*.odp) support of these formats means that Office applications can work with files created using an OpenOffice application, further reducing barriers to collaboration. The primary Office 2010 applications also can save files in the portable XPS (XML Paper Specification) and PDF (Portable Document Format) file types. You can double-click an XPS document in a folder window to open it in XPS Viewer (Windows 7) or Internet Explorer (Windows Vista). Viewing a PDF file requires the free Adobe Reader application that you can download from any number of locations online.

Creating a New, Blank File

When you start some of the Office applications — such as Word, Excel, and PowerPoint — the application automatically opens a new, blank file for you. You can then begin adding and formatting the content you want to preserve for yourself or other readers or viewers.

If you're working with an existing file and need to create another blank file, you can do so at any time, using one of the following two methods:

- Press Ctrl+N. The blank file appears immediately.
- Click the File tab in the upper-left corner of the program window and then click New. The Backstage view appears and presents new file options, like the one for Excel shown in Figure 3-2. Double-click the Blank document type icon, which closes the Backstage view and immediately opens the new document onscreen. Because the Blank document type icon is usually selected by default, you also can simply click the Create button in the lower right, under the document preview.

FIGURE 3-2

You can create a blank file using the New command in Backstage view.

Double-click

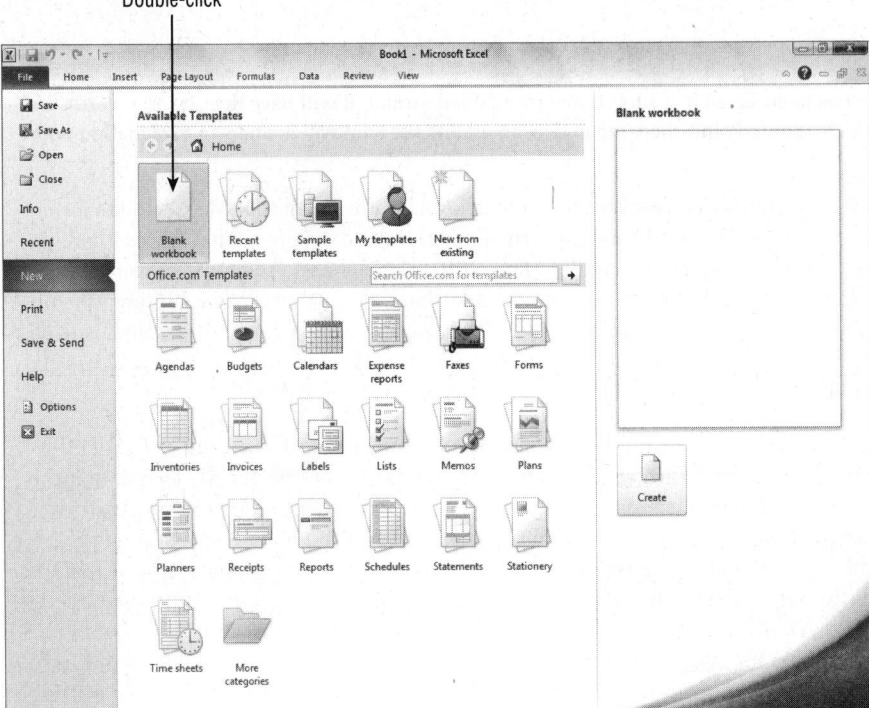

Because of its more complicated file structure, Access requires you to take a few more setup steps when you create a new database file. If you double-click the Blank Database icon after starting Access or choosing the New command, Access prompts you to enter a name for the file. After you click Create (Figure 3-3), you then must set up the first table that will hold the data you'll enter. Chapter 34 covers the process for creating an Access table.

Tip

Outlook doesn't use files, so you'll learn how to work with its messages and information when we cover Outlook. Both the Publisher and OneNote programs have a somewhat unique process for setting up a new file, and you'll learn about each process in the applicable chapters. ■

Creating a File with a Document Template

You can avoid starting from scratch when creating a file by selecting a template. A *template* includes predefined content and attractive formatting, both of which you can adapt for your own uses. For example, Excel includes a Loan Amortization template that includes all the formulas required to calculate payments on a loan; you plug in the loan terms, and it will finalize the results. The worksheet presents you with precise principal and payment information for any payment date in the life of the loan. As shown in Figure 3-4, this template also includes the formatting needed to organize and highlight the information.

FIGURE 3-3

Access prompts you to enter a filename immediately.

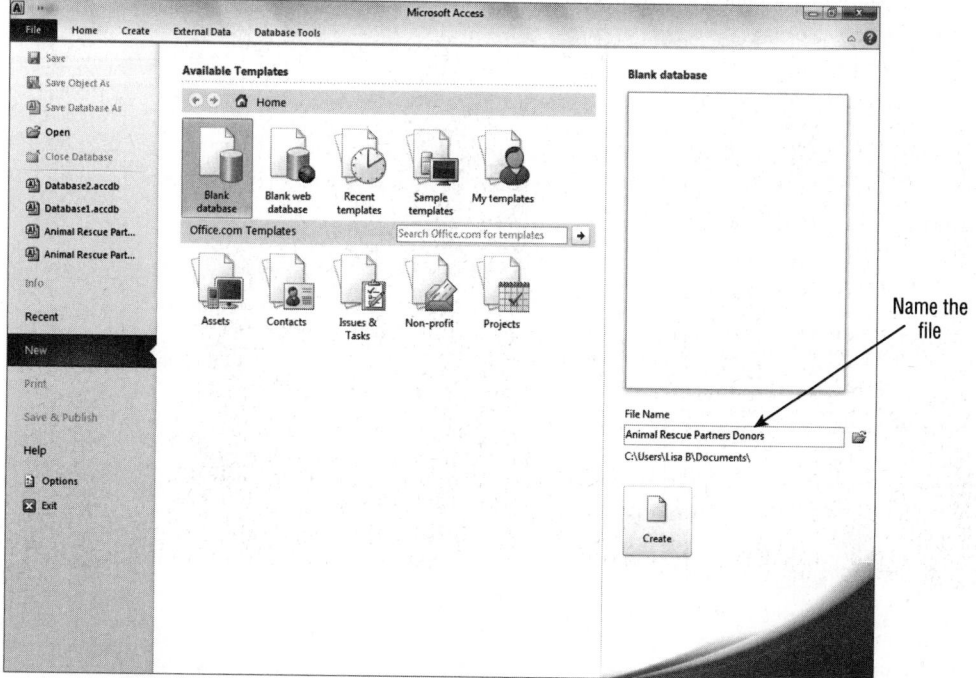

Some templates install on your system's hard disk when you install Office. Microsoft also enables you to browse and download templates stored online at Office.com, giving you the opportunity to take advantage of new templates as Microsoft adds them to the site.

Whether you choose an installed template or download a new template, the process for using a template to create a new file is roughly the same:

1. **Choose File ⇨ New.** The Backstage view appears, showing choices for creating files.

2a. **Click Sample Templates in the Available Templates section in the center of the view.**
    OR

2b. Click on a template category in the Office.com Templates section, and then click on one of the type icons that appears.

3. **Click on a template thumbnail.** As shown in Figure 3-5, a preview of the template appears at the right side of the dialog box.

Templates include starter information and formatting.

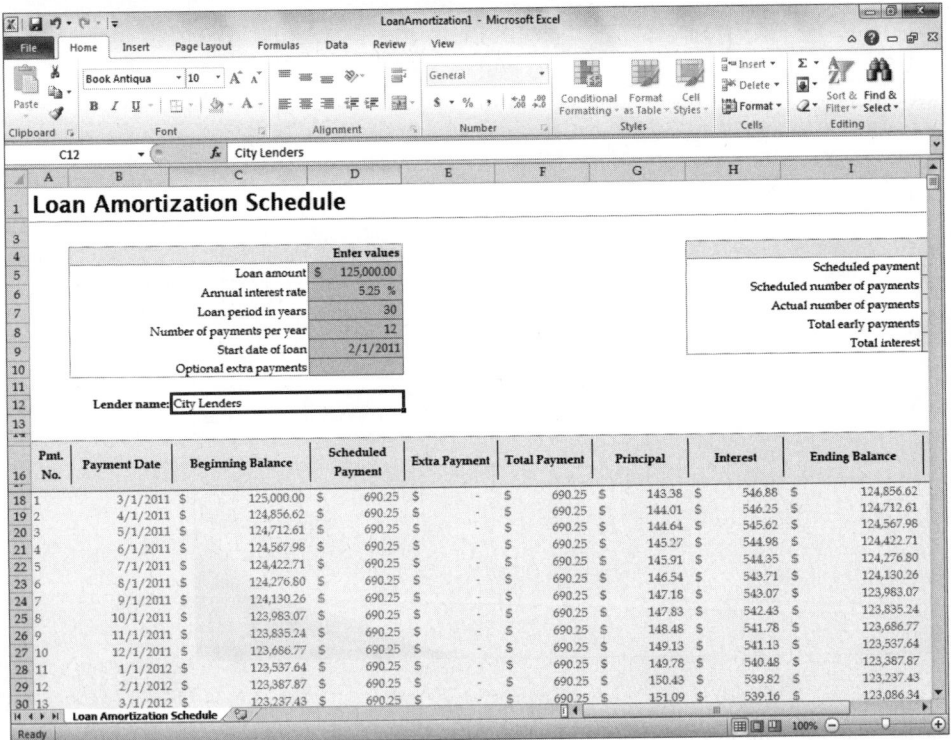

Tip

If you don't see the template you want in one of the available categories, type a keyword or description for the type of template that you need into the Search Office.com for Templates textbox. Then click the Start Searching (right arrow) button beside it to find matching templates. ∎

4. **Click Create (for an installed template) or Download.** If you selected a template installed on your system, the new file appears. An online template may take a few seconds to a few minutes to download, and then the new file will appear.

FIGURE 3-5

The Office application displays a preview of the selected template.

Use this text box to search
for a template online

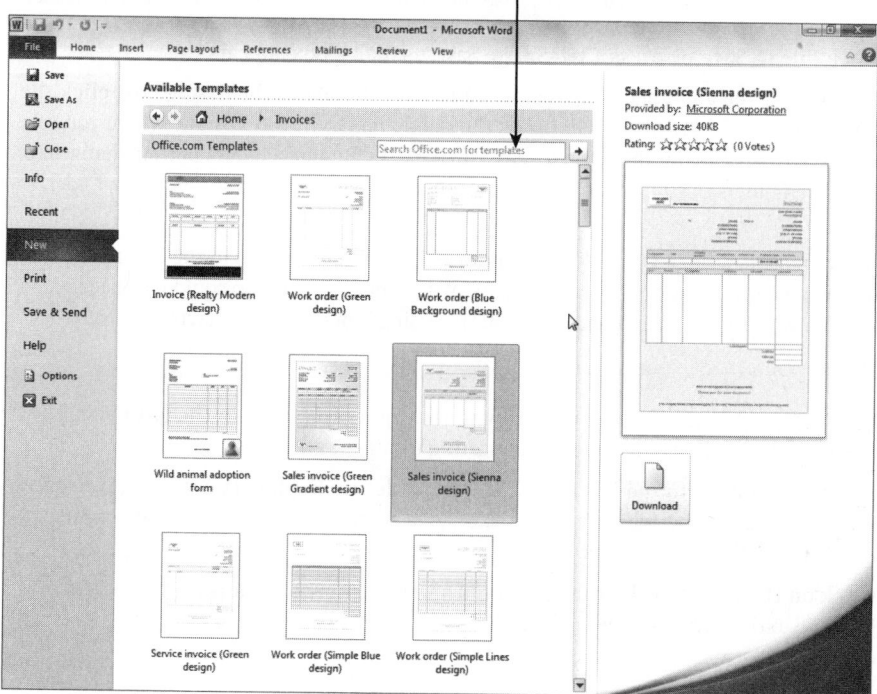

Note

The first time you download a template, the Microsoft Office Genuine Advantage message box may appear to inform you that Microsoft will verify that you have a legitimate copy of Office as a requirement of the download process. To turn off this message for future downloads, click the Do Not Show This Message Again checkbox to check it before clicking Continue. ■

Note

PowerPoint also enables you to create a file by applying a design theme. Although themes don't include any content, they do provide attractive, consistent formatting for all the slides in a presentation. To create a file with a theme, click Themes under Available Templates and Themes in the Backstage view, click on a theme icon to see its preview, and then click Create. ■

Saving and Naming a File

When you create a new file, the application assigns it a temporary name. If you create more than one new file in Excel, for example, the program will assign the temporary filenames sequentially, that is, *Book1*, *Book2*, and so on. To replace the temporary filename and to make sure that your work in a file gets preserved on your computer's hard disk or a network drive, you need to *save* the file. The application you're saving with will automatically apply the file format extension to whatever filename you specify during the Save process.

If you are using Windows Vista or Windows 7, use the following steps to save a newly created file:

1. **Click File ⇨ Save or press Ctrl+S.** The Save As dialog box appears.

2. **If you don't see a navigation pane or list at the left side of the dialog box, click the Browse Folders button.** This expands the dialog box to include a pane where you can choose a disk or folder in which to save the file. The Browse Folders button changes to the Hide Folders button, which you can click at any later time to suppress the folder display.

3a. **If you don't see the list of disks in Windows 7, click the triangle to the left of Computer in the navigation pane.** The list of available disks appears. You also could navigate to a location where you would like to save your file using Libraries in the navigation pane.

   OR

3b. **In Windows Vista, click the up arrow to the right of Folders in the left pane.** The Folders list with the folder tree for navigating to disks and folders expands.

4. **Click the triangle to the left of any disk or folder to display its contents, if needed.** A triangle appears beside only folders that have subfolders within them, so you may not see any triangles beside folder icons.

5. **Click on the desired folder in the tree.** This selects the folder as the save location. Figure 3-6 displays a selected folder.

Note

If you're using Windows XP, select File ⇨ Save to open the Save As dialog box. You can use the Save In drop-down list and the list of folders in the Save As dialog box to navigate to the folder where you want to save the file. Enter a filename in the File Name text box, and then click Save. ∎

6. **Drag over the contents of the File Name text box and type a new name.** Make sure your filename not only describes the file's contents but also includes information such as a date to distinguish it from other similar files.

7. **Click Save.** The program saves the file and displays the new filename in the title bar onscreen.

As you continue working with a file, you should save it periodically to ensure that your latest changes are included in the stored version. That way, in the event of a power surge or problem with your computer, you won't lose much work. Saving every 10 minutes proves good insurance for your file. To save your latest changes, click the Save button on the Quick Access toolbar or press Ctrl+S. If you must, you can click the Microsoft Office button and then click Save, but why choose two steps when you can choose one?

FIGURE 3-6

Choose a save location and enter a filename.

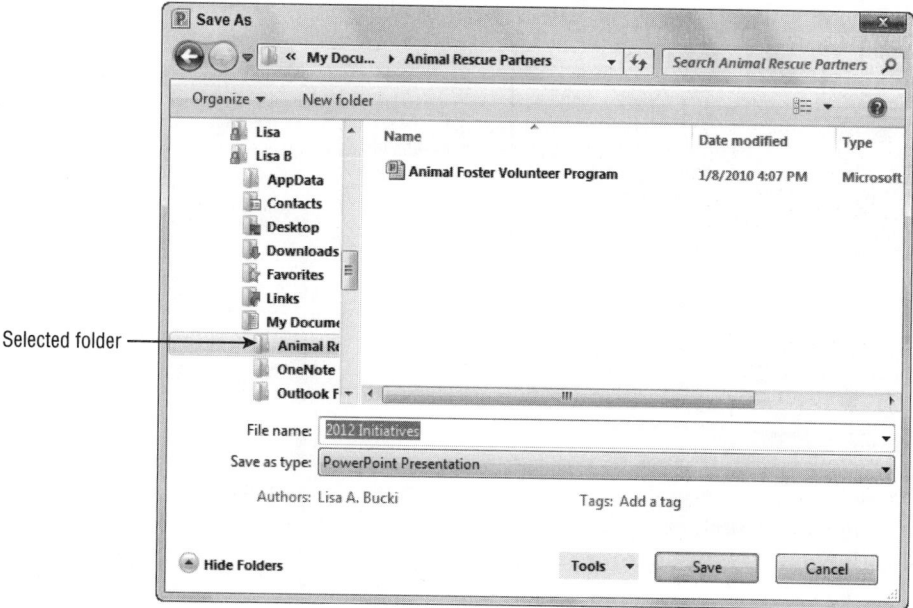

Files created in the 2010 versions of Word, Excel, PowerPoint, and Access cannot be opened with versions of those programs prior to the 2007 versions by default. (You can download and install a compatibility pack to handle the files; information is available by going to the main Office website at http://office.microsoft.com and searching for "office compatibility pack," with or without quotation marks. If the compatibility pack for the 2010 file formats is not available, install and use the one for the 2007 formats.) If a user running an older version of one of these applications needs to open one of your files, you may need to save a copy of the file in a compatible format. Here's how:

1. **Click File ⇨ Save As.** The Save As dialog box appears.

2. **Click the Save As Type drop-down list.** A list of other file formats that you can select for the copy you're creating appears, like the one shown in Figure 3-7.

3. **Click the desired Save As format.**

4. **Specify a save location and filename in the Save As dialog box.** The process works just as described in the previous set of steps about saving a new file.

5. **Click Save.**

FIGURE 3-7

Choose an alternative format for the file copy.

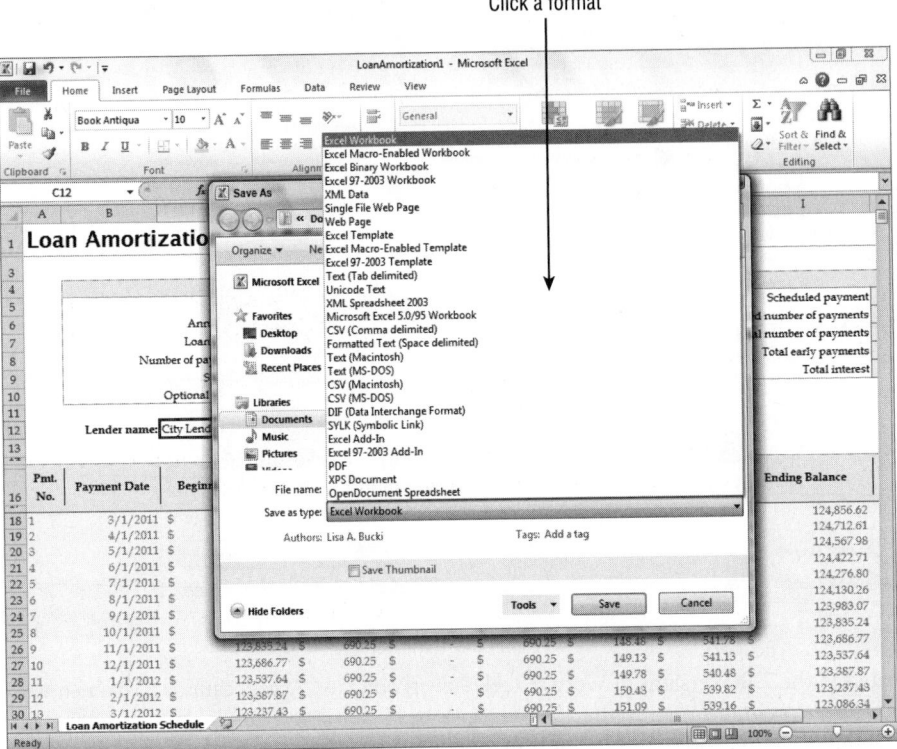

Click a format

Opening a File

Opening a file you've previously saved loads the file back into the program so that you can review, change, or print it. The Open process works a lot like the Save process. You select the folder in which you stored the file and then select the file to open, as follows:

1. **Click File ⇨ Open or press Ctrl+O.** The Open dialog box appears.

2a. **If you don't see the list of disks in Windows 7, click the triangle to the left of Computer in the navigation pane.** The list of available disks appears. You also could navigate to a save location using the Libraries choices in the navigation pane, if desired.

   OR

> **2b.** **In Windows Vista, click the up arrow to the right of Folders in the left pane.** The Folders list with the folder tree for navigating to disks and folders expands.

> **3.** **Click the triangle to the left of any disk or folder to display its contents, if needed.** A triangle appears beside only folders that have subfolders within them, so you may not see any triangles beside folder icons.

> **4.** **Click on the folder that holds the file to open in the tree.** The files stored in the folder appear in the dialog box.

> **5.** **Click on the file to open.**

> **6.** **Click Open.** The file loads in the program.

Note

If you're using Windows XP, select File ⇨ Open to open the Open dialog box. You can use the Look In drop-down list and the list of folders in the dialog box to navigate to the folder that holds the file to open. Click on the file and then click Open. ∎

Tip

In some Office applications, the Open button includes a drop-down list arrow. Click on a file to select it. You can then click the Open button drop-down arrow to see additional options for opening the file, such as the Open and Repair command. ∎

Tip

Double-click on a file's icon in any Windows folder window to open the file within the application in which it was created. ∎

Closing a File

Closing a file that you've finished working on removes the file from the system's working memory. Only a few years ago, closing a file was a necessity because most computers had limited amounts of working memory. Today's powerful computers make that less of an issue, but there are some other equally important reasons to close a file after you finish making changes. For example, you may want to close a file so that it's not visible onscreen for security or privacy reasons. Closing a file also reduces the chance of the file being corrupted by a power fluctuation or a system error; it also gives you a reminder to save your changes to the file if you haven't already done so.

Some Office applications offer a Close (X) button for the file window itself, located below the application Close (X) button near the upper-right corner of the program window. Clicking the file window Close button closes the file. Other Office applications may not include a file window Close button. If that's the case, you can close the current file by clicking the File tab and then clicking Close. The keyboard shortcut Alt+F+C will close the current file as well in some Office applications.

If you haven't saved your most recent changes to the file being closed, a reminder message like the one shown in Figure 3-8 appears.

FIGURE 3-8

Click Save to save the file before closing it.

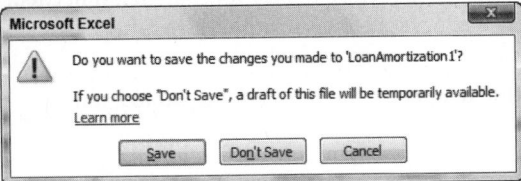

Printing a File

With the crisp, vibrant output produced by today's cheap color printers, who would want a paperless office? Although the Internet and faster computer networks have made electronic transmission a common and accepted means of sharing documents, many circumstances still call for — if not require — that information be shared on paper:

- Legal documents such as contracts that need to be signed, initialed, dated, or otherwise stamped are still largely handled on paper. Standards for digital signatures are still evolving, and most users still print a hard copy of a contract or agreement for official filing.

- When a reader or viewer won't have a computer or connection at hand and will need to take notes, you need to provide a hard copy. For example, participants in seminars typically don't bring along a notebook and prefer to take their notes on a hard copy of a presentation.

- When you want to make a strong impression, hard copy is still preferred. Although e-mail is increasingly accepted as a standard business practice for many communications, sometimes it doesn't measure up. For example, it might be acceptable to e-mail a proposal to a potential new client, but hand-delivering a hard copy and then following up by e-mail shows that you still care enough to make a personal effort to get the business.

- When you need a fresh perspective on a document, you can get it by working from hard copy. Reading through a printed copy of a document can help you catch text and formatting mistakes you previously missed, while also enabling you to make additional notes and engage in proofreading tricks such as reading the document backward.

- When you want to provide a more constant, visible reminder, you need a hard copy. Whether it's putting up a flyer at the grocery store about a found cat or giving a recognition certificate to a valued volunteer, hard copy is still the only useful format.

With all the great documents you can create in Office, you'll be proud to publish and share hard copies. This section explains how to set up and print your files.

Note

This section on printing assumes that a printer is installed on your system or network and that the printer is powered on and has ample paper and ink or toner in it. ■

Performing a Basic Preview and Print

Previewing and printing used to be separate operations in previous versions of Office applications. The Backstage view in Office 2010 enables you to preview the printout and select print settings, so you can adjust the document as needed without having to go back and forth between the preview and a separate setup dialog box. You can preview and print the document using the current settings for the printer with only a few mouse clicks if you want to use the default print settings.

Viewing a preview and printing the document is easy:

1. **Click File ⇨ Print.** The Backstage view shows the preview and printing settings, as shown in Figure 3-9.

FIGURE 3-9

Preview the printout and choose print settings in Backstage view.

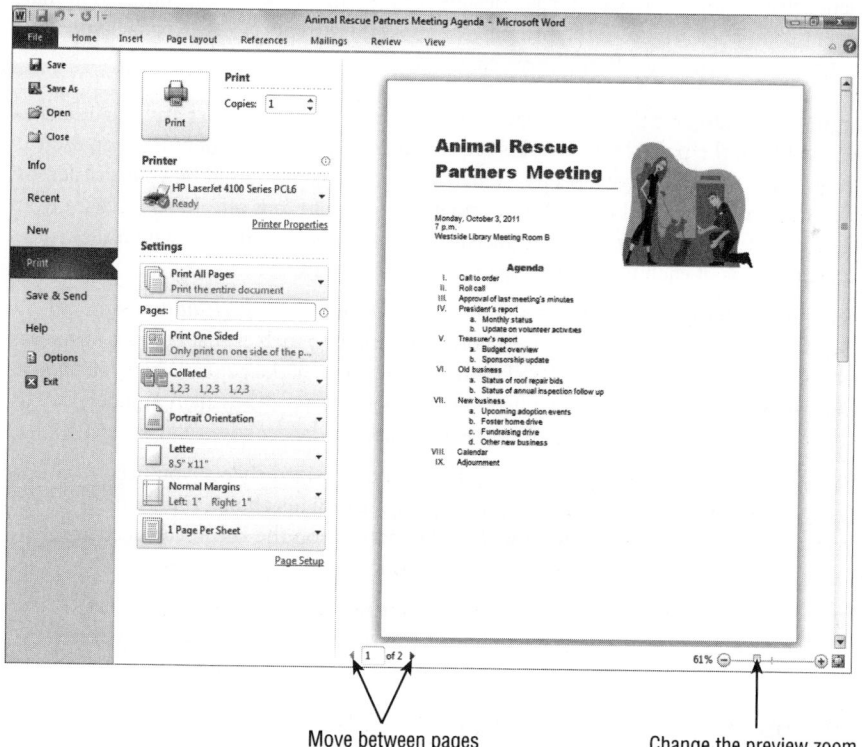

Move between pages   Change the preview zoom

2. **Use the Zoom slider to adjust the preview zoom as desired.** The Zoom slider appears in the lower right of the preview. You also can use the Zoom Out and Zoom In buttons at either end of the slider to adjust the view.

3. **Use the Previous Page and Next Page buttons to move between pages if the document has multiple pages.** These buttons appear at lower left below the preview.

4. **Click Print.** The document prints.

Tip

If you prefer the keyboard to the mouse, you can use this rather long keyboard shortcut for performing a quick print: Alt+F+P+P. ∎

Tip

You can add a Quick Print button to the Quick Access toolbar. Clicking that button then prints the current file directly. To add the button, click the Customize Quick Access Toolbar drop-down arrow at the right end of the Quick Access toolbar; then, click Quick Print. ∎

Understanding Page Design Settings

Some document settings affect the overall page design not only in terms of looks but also in making the document print correctly from the printer. The most important page settings you need to specify when it comes to printing fall into three categories:

- **Margins.** The *margin* is the white space between the edge of the paper and the information printed on the page. Most printers require at least 0.25 inches of margin on each edge of the document. If you specify a smaller margin than required by your printer, you could cause some of the printed information to appear "cut off." In some cases, you need to specify special-purpose margins such as *mirrored margins*, for which the inside (center) margins of each two-page spread are wider to allow for binding the pages.

- **Orientation.** You can choose to present information from a file in *Portrait* (tall) or *Landscape* (wide) format. When you choose a portrait orientation such as that used for a typical letter, the printer prints the text parallel to the shorter edges of the paper. When you choose a landscape orientation such as that often used for worksheets or presentation slides, the printer rotates the information and prints horizontal to the longer edges of the paper.

- **Size.** If you want to print on paper other than standard-sized sheets, you need to choose that paper size for the document's page design or setup. This choice automatically adjusts the document contents to fit within the margins on the specified sheet size.

Because page design settings vary quite a bit between applications, it's not possible to cover each and every choice here. Later chapters detail some of the settings that pertain to particular Office applications. So, here's an idea of where you can find the page settings you need to check or change before sending a file to the printer:

- **On the Page Layout or Design Tab of the Ribbon.** The Ribbon tab can be used to format the page or design and typically includes a Page Layout section with the options for changing crucial page settings. Clicking on a choice here typically displays a menu or gallery, as shown in Figure 3-10, of specific settings; click on the one you want to apply to the document.

The Page Layout or Design tab of the Ribbon offers page design settings.

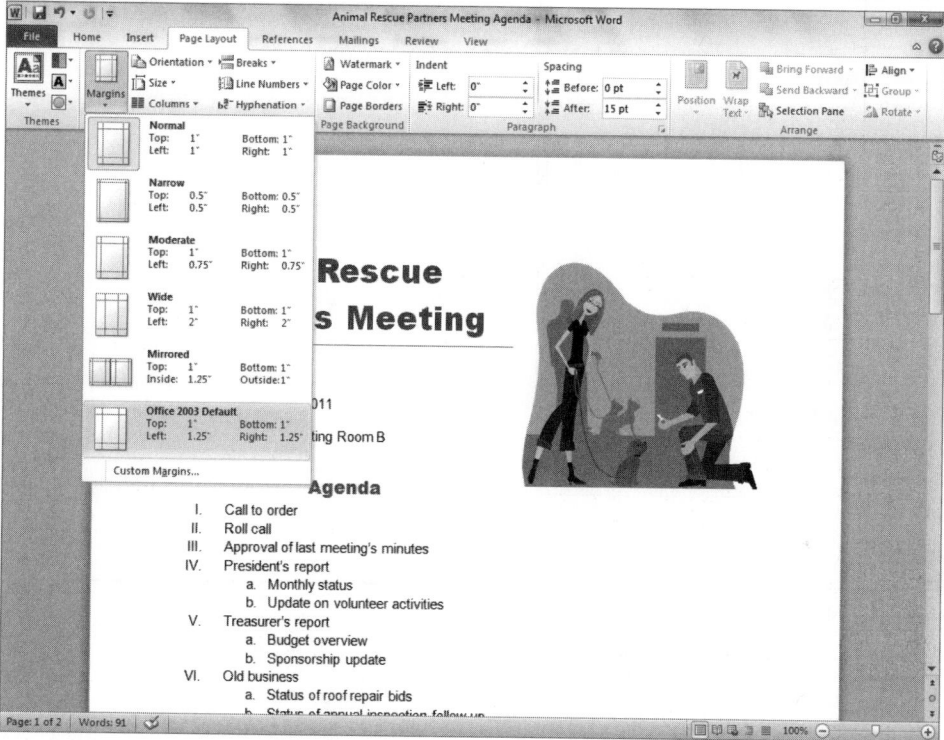

- **In the Backstage View after You Click Print.** As shown in Figure 3-9, the Settings area offers settings for orientation and margin. These settings work just like the corresponding settings found on the Ribbon.

- **In the Page Setup Dialog Box.** The Page Setup dialog box for an application offers general page formatting options such as margin settings, as well as choices specific to the application that you're using. For example, the Page Setup dialog box for Excel includes a Sheet tab, on which you can indicate such details as whether gridlines should print (Figure 3-11). To open the Page Setup dialog box, you can click the Dialog Box Launcher for the Page Setup group on the Page Layout or Design tab of the Ribbon (Figure 3-12). After you make your choices in the dialog box, click OK to apply them to the document.

FIGURE 3-11

Page Setup options vary from application to application.

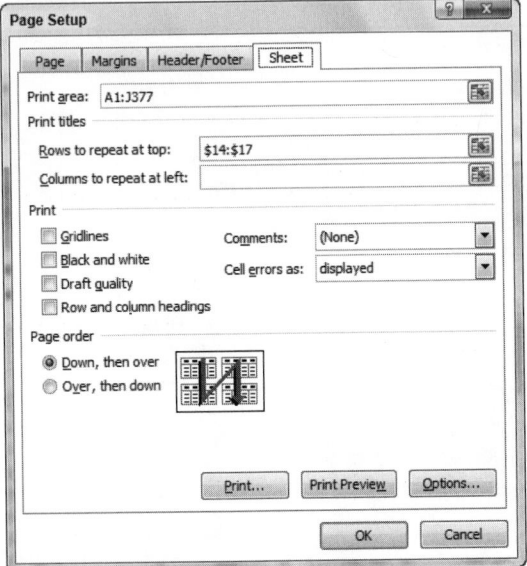

FIGURE 3-12

Click the Dialog Box Launcher for the Page Setup group.

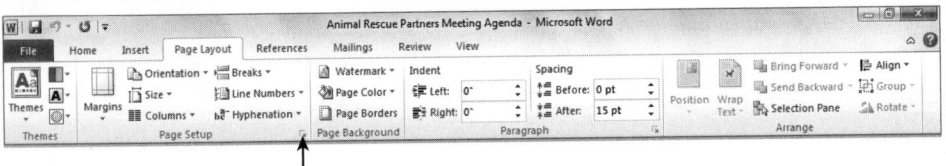

Dialog Box Launcher

Choosing Print Settings and Printing

As opposed to being specific to the design of the pages of the document being printed, additional settings pertain to the nature of the hard copy being produced. These settings include which printer to use, which pages of the file to print, how many copies to print, what print quality to use, and so on. You choose all these types of settings in the Backstage view after clicking Print at the left side of the view.

Although settings such as which pages to print and how many copies to print are the same in most circumstances, other choices vary depending on the application or the selected printer. For example, Excel has additional options for enabling you to print only the current worksheet or the entire workbook file. And choosing an inkjet printer generally enables you to select whether you want to print in just black ink or in full color.

Despite those types of differences, the process for choosing a printer and print settings and finishing the print job is about the same in every application:

1. **Click File ⇨ Print or press Ctrl+P.** The Backstage view appears with its associated print settings.
2. **Select the printer to use from the Printer drop-down list.** The printer becomes the current or active printer (Figure 3-13).

FIGURE 3-13

Choose printout settings in the Backstage view after clicking Print.

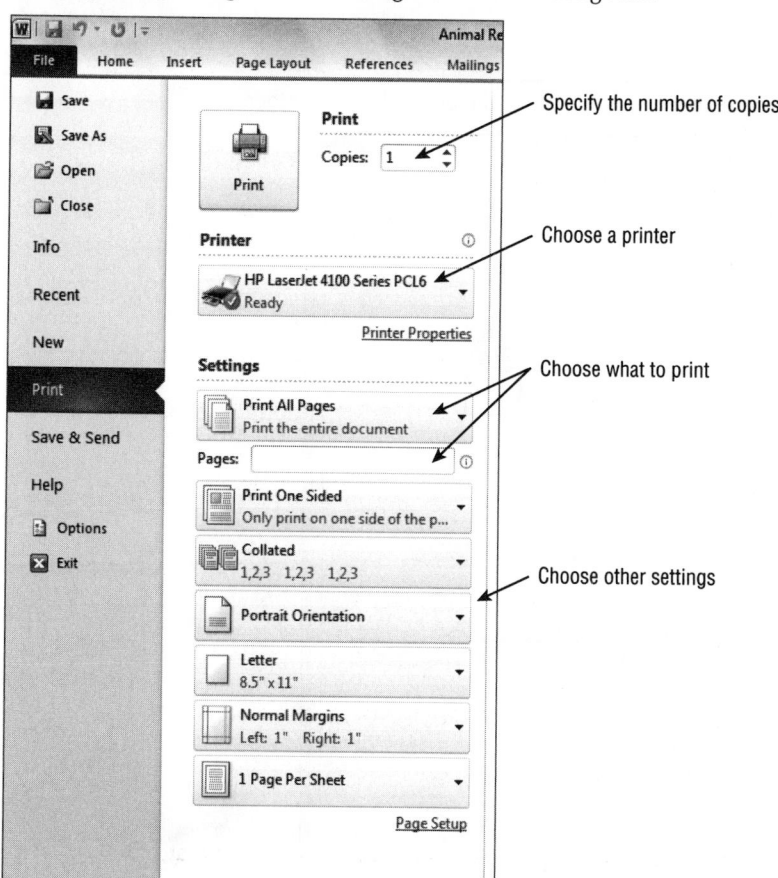

Specify the number of copies

Choose a printer

Choose what to print

Choose other settings

3. **Specify what pages to print in the Pages textbox under settings.** You also can use the drop-down list above the textbox to choose one of the available settings for the current application, such as printing the Document Properties for a Word document.

4. **Specify how many copies to print in the Copies box.** In some cases, you also can choose to collate the printed pages.

5. **Choose other print settings as desired.** For example, you might change zoom settings or print to a file rather than paper.

Note
Clicking the Options button in the lower-left corner of the dialog box opens another dialog box that includes additional print options, such as whether to print hidden text in Word. ∎

6. **Click the Printer Properties link below the selected printer.** The dialog box that appears has additional print settings, as in the example shown in Figure 3-14.

FIGURE 3-14

Properties for the selected printer enable you to fine-tune the print job even further.

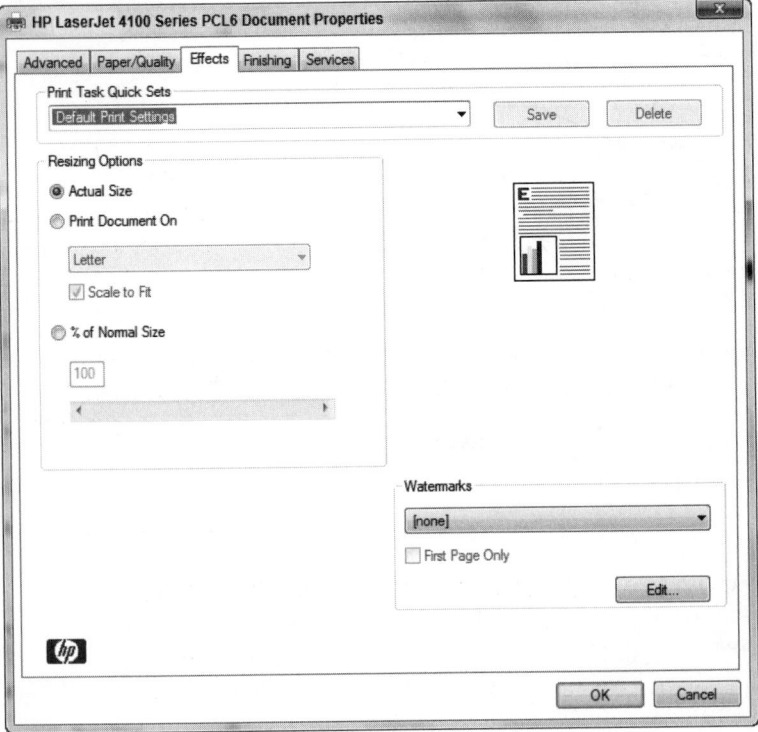

7. **Choose settings in the printer's Properties dialog box as needed, and then click OK.** The Print dialog box reappears.

8. **Click Print.** The application prints the file to the specified printer.

Tip

If you prefer to e-mail a file rather than print it, you can send it from right within some of the Office applications. Select File ⇨ Save & Send ⇨ Send Using E-mail, and then click on the desired sending format to continue the process. ■

Working with Multiple Windows

Every time you open another file in an Office application, the file opens in its own file window. You can have multiple programs and files open to help you multitask — to jump between different jobs you're working on and to look at information stored in a number of different files and applications.

The taskbar is a band or bar that appears by default along the bottom of the Windows desktop. A button for programs that you open appears on the taskbar in Windows 7. In Windows Vista and XP, you may see a separate taskbar button for each open file. The Office applications work with Windows to provide you with multiple options for navigating between open file and application windows, including using the taskbar.

Switching to Another File or Application Window

Switching to another open file makes it the active file in its application. When you use the taskbar to switch between open files, Windows switches to the application for that file, if applicable. You can use one of the following techniques to navigate to another file or application in Office and Windows:

- **View Tab on Ribbon.** To switch to another open file window in an application, click the View tab on the Ribbon, click Switch Windows, and then click on the name of the file to select, as shown in the example in Figure 3-15. The selected file becomes the active file.

FIGURE 3-15

Using the Ribbon to switch between open files.

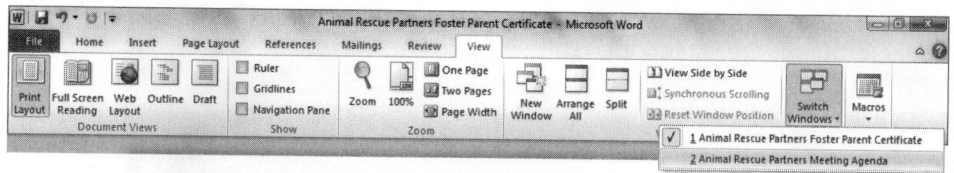

- **Taskbar.** If a single file for the application is open, click the taskbar button for the file to open, which immediately makes the file appear in its application. If the taskbar button represents more than one open file, clicking it displays a menu with the name for each open file in Windows XP or Vista. Windows 7 displays a thumbnail of each open file, instead. Whether you see a menu or a thumbnail, click the file you want to open to select it.

- **Shortcut Key Combination.** If you press and hold the Alt+Tab key combination, a task-switching box with an icon for each open file, as well as for the Windows desktop, appears. Continue holding down the Alt key as you press and release the Tab key until you've highlighted the desired file icon; then, release both keys. The last file you selected opens onscreen in its application.

- **Stack the Windows.** Both Windows 7 and Windows Vista enable you to stack windows on screen, as shown in Figure 3-16, and choose the one you want from the stack. This feature is called Aero Flip 3D in Windows 7. In Windows 7, press the Windows Logo Key+Tab. Press Tab or an arrow key to cycle through the windows, and when the document you want is on top of the stack, click it. In Windows Vista, click the Switch Between Windows button on the Quick Launch toolbar, then click on the window for the file (and application) you want to switch to.

FIGURE 3-16

Windows 7 and Windows Vista provide a visual way to switch between open file and application windows.

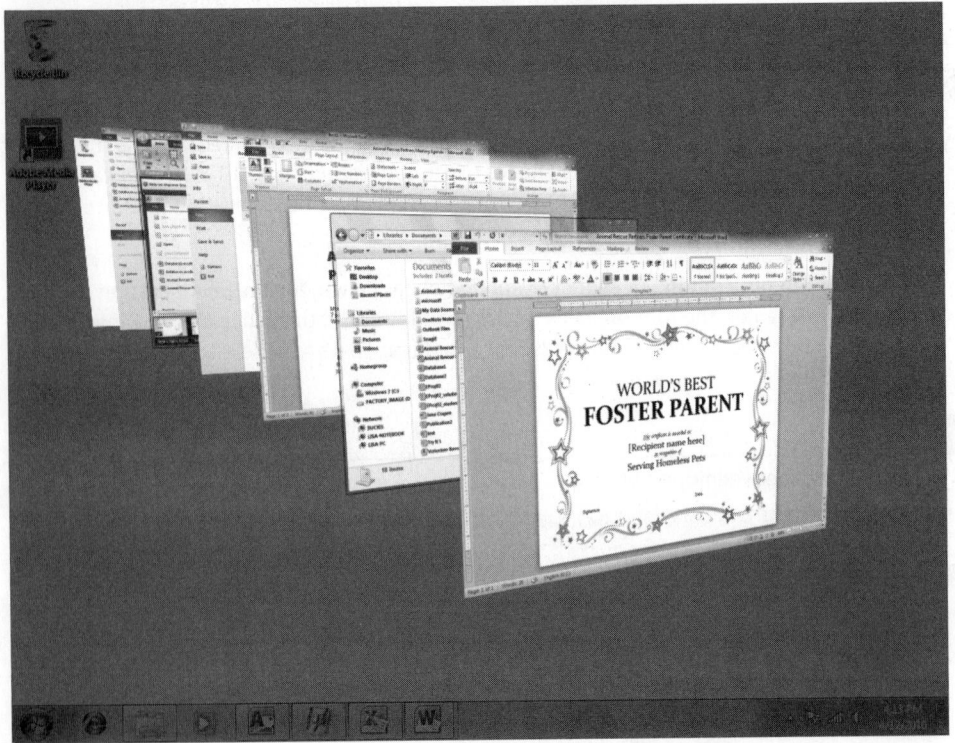

Arranging Windows

Arranging windows sizes all the open files in an application and positions them so that the files fill the available space in the application window without overlapping. (Word and PowerPoint actually size multiple instances of the application window to fill the screen.) This feature enables you to review and compare the information in multiple files more easily, or to perform an action such as moving or copying information from one file to another, as described in the next section.

The View tab of the Ribbon includes an Arrange All button in the Window group. Click that button to arrange the open file windows, as in the example shown in Figure 3-17. Note that some applications also include Cascade, which stacks the open windows so that you can switch to another window by clicking on its title bar.

FIGURE 3-17

Arranging file windows makes file contents more accessible.

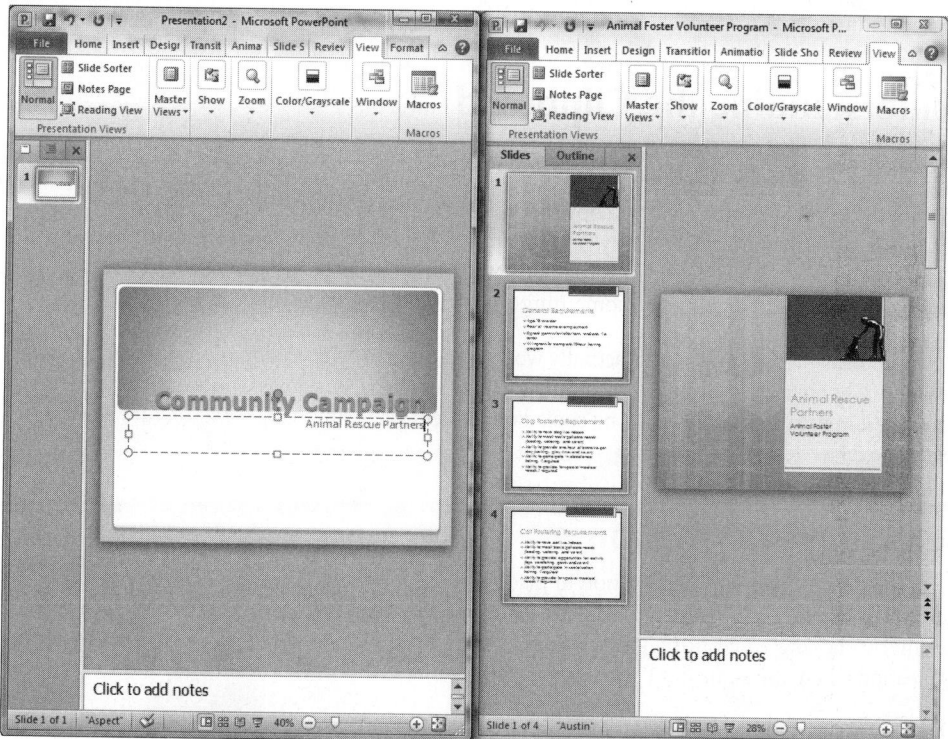

To arrange all the open file and program windows on the Windows desktop, right-click on a blank area of the taskbar (not a taskbar button) and then click Show Windows Side by Side.

Moving and Copying Information

A template can save you time by providing starter content for a document, but that starter content is not your own, unique information. When needed, you can reuse information you've created in one file in a new file by moving or copying that information.

Microsoft has dedicated significant effort over time to ensure that the Office applications can accept information from one to another so that users can build documents that integrate content created from different applications. For example, you can use an Excel worksheet to perform complicated calculations and then reuse that information in Word or PowerPoint.

This section shows you how simple techniques enable you to work quickly and have consistent content by moving or copying information.

Note
See Chapter 41, "Integration with Other Office Applications," to learn more specifics about reusing information between applications. ∎

Understanding the Clipboard

The Windows Clipboard enables users to copy information between virtually any two applications, as long as the applications are relatively compatible in terms of the file formats they use. Windows transfers information you copy or cut from a file to the Clipboard, a temporary holding area in the system's working memory. You can paste the information from the Clipboard into another location in the same file or into another file altogether. The information stays on the Clipboard until you copy or paste something else or shut down the computer.

Many Microsoft Office applications actually work with Office's own version of the Clipboard, called the Office Clipboard, which improves on the capabilities of the Windows Clipboard. Whereas the Windows Clipboard can hold only one copied or cut item, the Office Clipboard (Figure 3-18) can hold up to 24.

Selecting Information

Before you can copy or cut information to place it in the Clipboard, you have to *select,* or highlight, the information. Most users today prefer to use the mouse to select text or other onscreen content by clicking on it or dragging over it. Although selection methods can vary between Office applications, here are some basic techniques to know:

- In Word, drag over text to select it. Word also offers a variety of shortcut techniques, such as double-clicking on a word to select it, or triple-clicking on a paragraph to select the whole paragraph.

- In applications that use text placeholders, such as PowerPoint and Publisher, click on the placeholder to select or activate it, and then drag over the specific text to select.

- In Excel worksheets and Access tables, drag diagonally over cells to select the group of cells. For example, in Figure 3-19, you can see that the range A4:E8 is selected because the heavy black cell selector appears around the selected range and the row and column headings for the selected cells appear highlighted.

FIGURE 3-18

Multiple cut or copied items appear on the Office Clipboard for pasting.

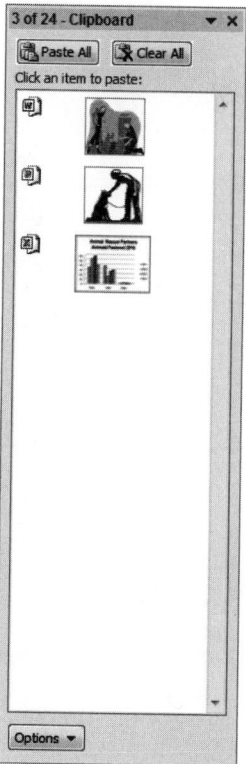

- To select another type of item such as a graphic, simply click on it. Black selection handles and a selection box appear around the object. You can Shift+click additional objects to add them to the selection.

Copying

Copy a selection when you want to reuse information from one location in one or more other locations. Copying a selected item leaves the original intact and places a duplicate on the Clipboard. You can use one of three methods to copy a selection that you've already made:

- Press Ctrl+C.
- Click the Home tab on the Ribbon, and then click the Copy button in the Clipboard group. Figure 3-20 shows the Ribbon buttons for copying, cutting, and pasting.

FIGURE 3-19

Drag diagonally to select worksheet cells.

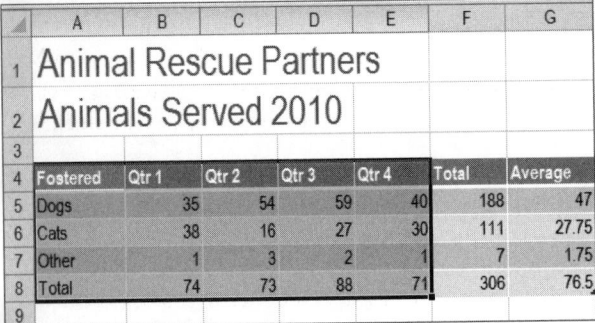

FIGURE 3-20

The Home tab has tools for copying and moving a selection.

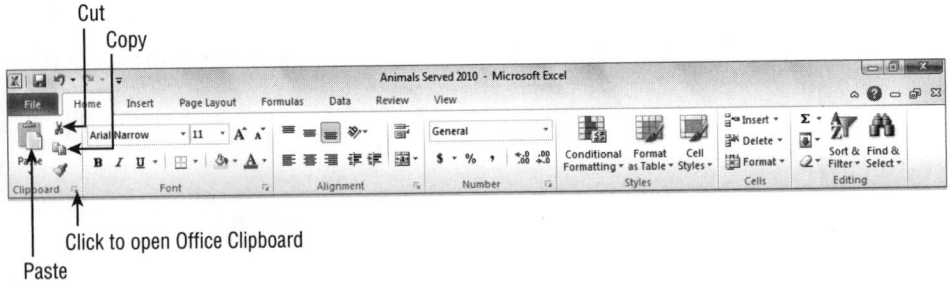

- Right-click on the selection, and choose Copy in the shortcut menu.

Note

After you copy or cut a range of cells in Excel, a flashing marquee appears around the selected range to remind you to paste. Press Esc to clear the marquee if you decide not to paste the information. This also removes the data from the Clipboard. ∎

Cutting

Cutting also places the selection on the Clipboard but removes the selection from its original location rather than make a duplicate. So, when you want to move information from one file to another, you first cut the selection from its original location and then paste it into position in another file.

As with copying, you can use one of three methods to cut:

- Press Ctrl+X.
- Click the Home tab on the Ribbon, and then click the Cut button in the Clipboard group.
- Right-click on the selection, and click Cut in the shortcut menu.

Caution

After you cut information from a text document or placeholder, be sure to take a look at the location from which you cut. In many instances, you might need to delete extra line spaces or add new spaces between words. ■

Pasting

Pasting places an item from the Clipboard into a new location within the same file or in a completely different file or application. For example, Figure 3-21 shows the selection from Figure 3-19 pasted from Excel onto a PowerPoint slide. Pasting finishes the overall activity of either copying or moving information between locations. The method you use to paste in Office depends on whether you need to use the Office Clipboard, which enables you to paste multiple selections or a selection other than the most recent item you cut or copied.

To paste directly:

1. **Click to position the insertion point at the location in which you want to paste the item.** Switch to the file first, if needed. In some cases, you might have to click within a text placeholder first. In Excel, click the upper-left cell in the range to paste to.

2. **Perform the paste.** As when copying or cutting, you can use one of three techniques to issue the Paste command:

   - Press Ctrl+V.
   - Click the Home tab on the Ribbon, and then click the top portion of the Paste button in the Clipboard group.
   - Right-click on the location where you want the selection inserted, and then click on one of the buttons under Paste Options in the shortcut menu.

3. (Optional) **Click the Paste Options button, which appears at the lower-right corner of the pasted selection, and choose one of the formatting or other options that appears.**

Tip

In Excel, you also can press Enter to paste after selecting a destination cell. This method clears the blinking marquee from the copied or cut material, in contrast to the three techniques listed in the previous step. ■

FIGURE 3-21

Pasting to finish copying and moving text enables you to deliver a powerful, consistent message by combining information you've developed in a variety of applications.

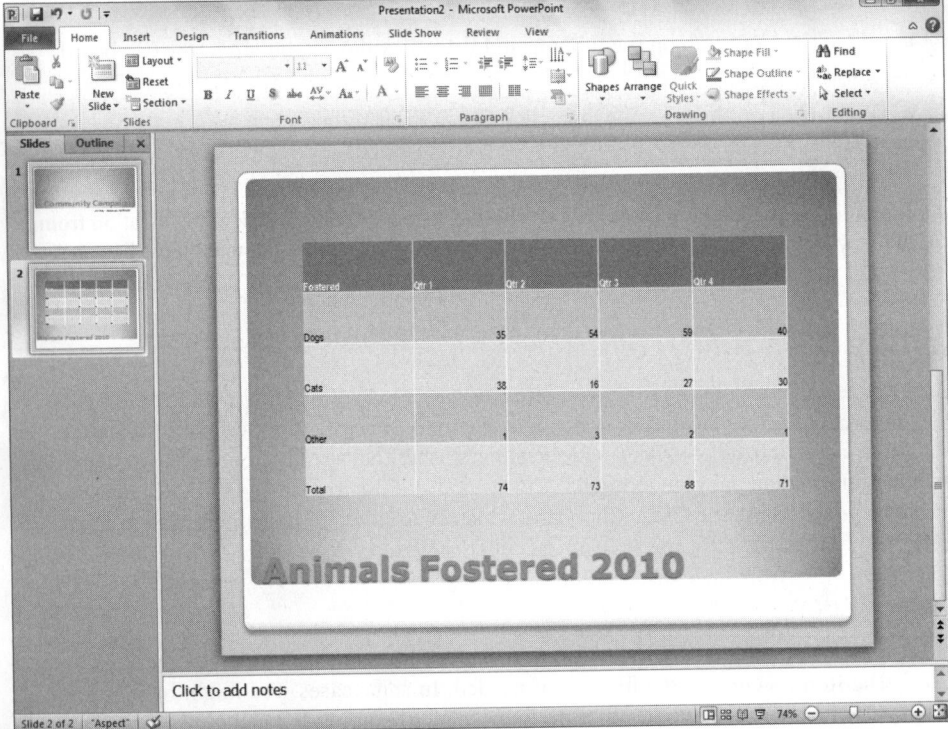

Using the Office Clipboard enables you to take advantage of multiple selections that you've copied or cut. To paste using the Office Clipboard:

1. **Click to position the insertion point at the location in which you want to paste the item.** Again, switch to the destination file first, if needed.

2. **Click the Home tab on the Ribbon.**

3. **Click the Dialog Box Launcher button in the Clipboard group.** The Clipboard task pane opens at the left side of the window.

4. **Click on the item to paste in the task pane.** As shown in Figure 3-22, the pasted item appears in the destination location. You can then resize and format it as needed in the destination.

FIGURE 3-22

Use the Office Clipboard to paste multiple selections.

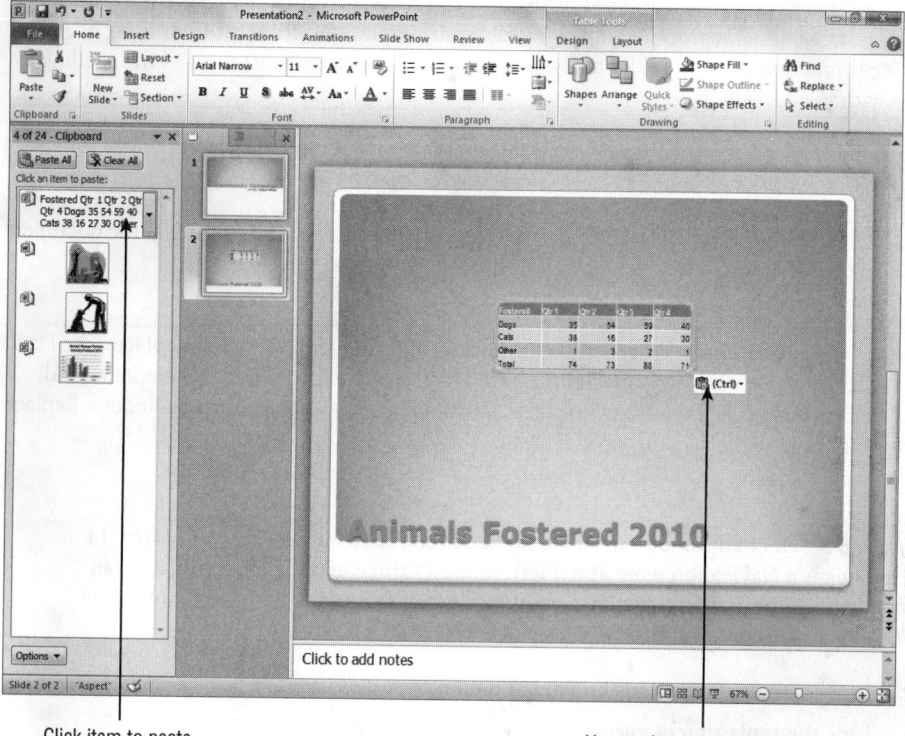

Click item to paste   Use to choose paste options

5. (Optional) **Click the Paste Options button that appears at the lower-right corner of the pasted selection, and choose one of the formatting or other options that appears.**

6. **Select additional paste locations and paste additional selections as needed.**

7. **Click the Close (X) button on the task pane window to close the task pane.**

Tip

If you plan to use the Office Clipboard to paste multiple selections in a document, copy or cut all the selections before opening the Clipboard and pasting. Doing so can save you time moving back and forth between files. ■

Finding and Replacing

Lengthy, complex business files can hold a ton of information, and who wants to spend all day using the Page Down key and scrolling to try to find one bit of information? Luckily, you can use the Find feature to search for a particular word or phrase. For example, if you need to find the section of a construction contract that deals with site remediation, you can find the phrase "site remediation." Even better, you can use the Replace feature to correct words you've misspelled or to change phrases or names. For example, if you've mistakenly spelled *Artur Consulting* as *Arthur Consulting* throughout a proposal for a new client, you can replace all instances of the spelling boo-boo with the correction.

Finding and replacing work in a very similar fashion, so you can use the following steps for either operation:

1. **Press Ctrl+Home.** This step moves the insertion point to the beginning of the document so that the Find or Replace operation starts from the top.

2. **Click the Home tab on the Ribbon.**

3. **Click Find & Replace in the Editing Group, and then click Find or Replace.** The Find and Replace dialog box appears. The Find tab that appears for a find includes a Find What textbox, whereas the Replace tab that appears for a replace also includes a Replace With textbox.

Note
In Excel, click the Find & Select button on the Home tab, and then click either Find or Replace. In Word, clicking Find opens a Navigation pane at the left. In most Office applications, you also can press Ctrl+F to start a find. The Find and Replace dialog box varies in appearance from application to application. ■

4. **Type the entry to find in the Find What textbox.**

5. **Type the replacement entry, if any, in the Replace With textbox.**

6. **Specify additional options, if needed.** The available options vary depending on the application. For example, in Word, you can click the More button and then specify choices such as matching case or matching a prefix or suffix.

7. **Click Find Next.** The application highlights the first matching instance of the search word or phrase, as shown in Figure 3-23.

8. **Click on a button for replacing the found text, if applicable:**
   - **Replace.** Replaces only the highlighted instance of the matching word or phrase.
   - **Replace All.** Replaces all instances of the matching word or phrase.
   - **Find Next.** Skips to the next match without making a replacement.

9. **Repeat Steps 7 and 8 as needed to proceed through the find or replace operation.**

10. **Click OK in the message that tells you that the search has been completed.**

Tip

Some Office applications offer special methods for finding information. For example, Outlook enables you to find messages from a particular sender or having a particular subject. Access enables you to save and reuse a query, which finds information matching one or more criteria. ∎

FIGURE 3-23

The found match is selected (highlighted).

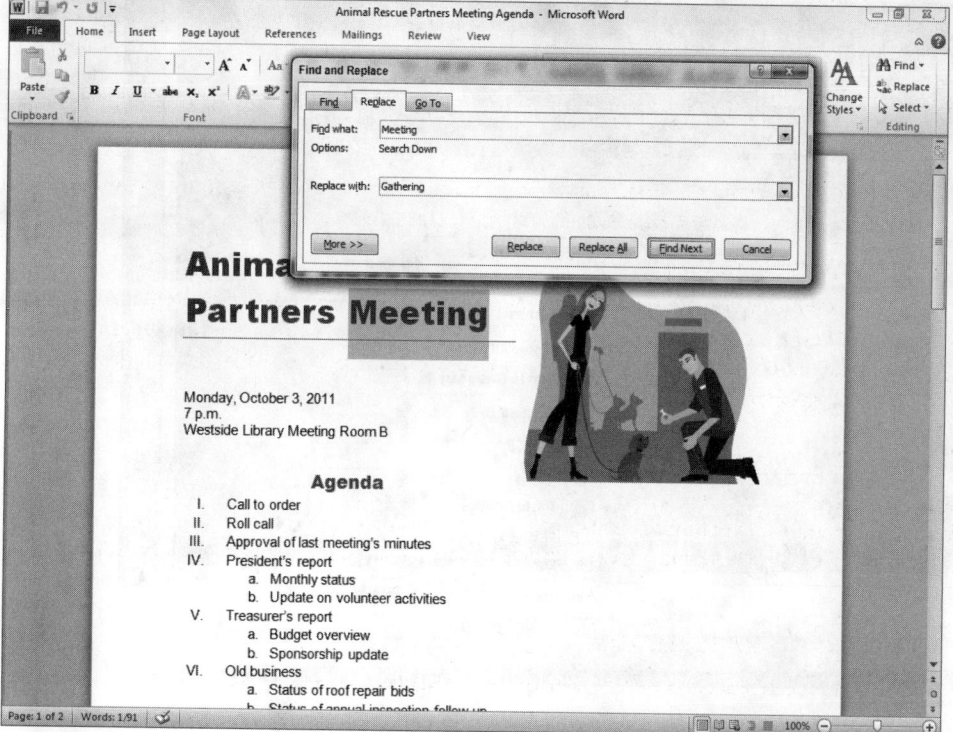

Spell Checking

Typos have no place in professional business documents, whether delivered electronically or in hard-copy form. You always want to put your best foot forward and make sure that your files are attractive, clear and easy to follow, and typo free.

By default, many of the Office applications quietly check your spelling for you as you type. If you see a telltale red squiggle appear underneath a word, that means that the application thinks you've misspelled the word — according to the application's own dictionary, anyway. If you see a wavy red underline underneath a word, right-click on the word. As shown in Figure 3-24, you can then click on a correction in the shortcut menu that appears to replace the typo with the correction, or click Add to Dictionary so that the word is no longer flagged as a misspelling.

FIGURE 3-24

Right-click on any word with a red wavy outline and then click on a correction.

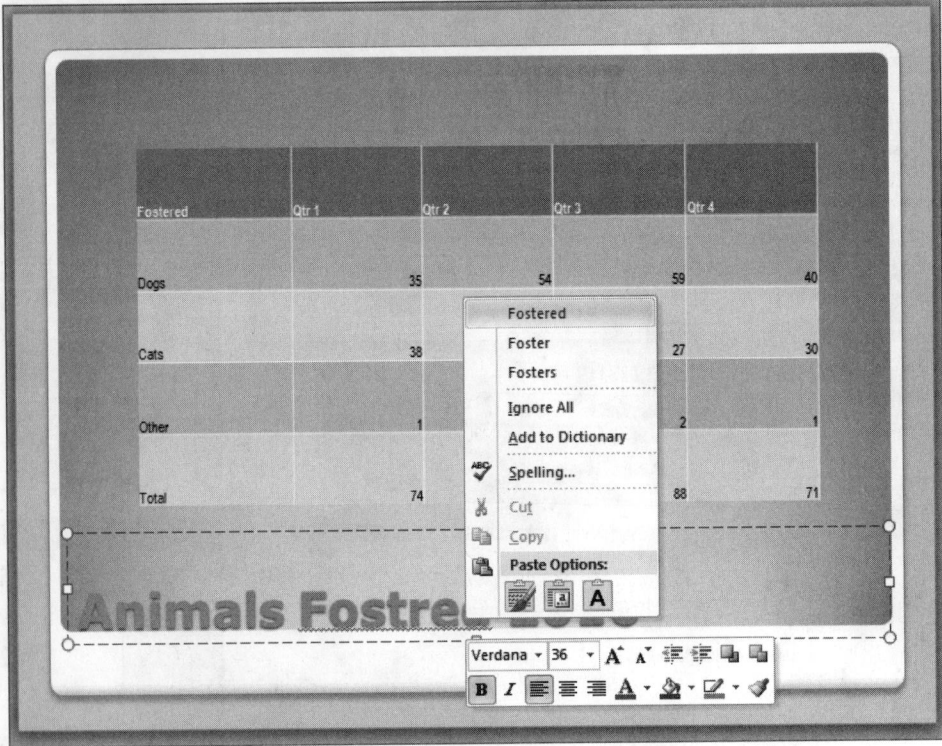

If you've finished creating the document and have moved on to the fine-tuning stage, you should always run a complete spell check to catch any typos that you might have missed earlier. Use these steps to run the check, and use the most common options for dealing with potential misspellings:

1. **Press Ctrl+Home.** This step moves to the beginning of the document so that the spell-checking operation will start from there.

2. **Click the Review tab on the Ribbon.**

3. **Click Spelling & Grammar (Word) or Spelling (other apps) in the Proofing Group.** The Spelling dialog box appears with the first potential misspelling highlighted, as

shown in Figure 3-25. Some applications enable you to start a spelling check simply by pressing F7.

FIGURE 3-25

The spelling check highlights the suspected word and displays it in the Not in Dictionary textbox of the Spelling dialog box.

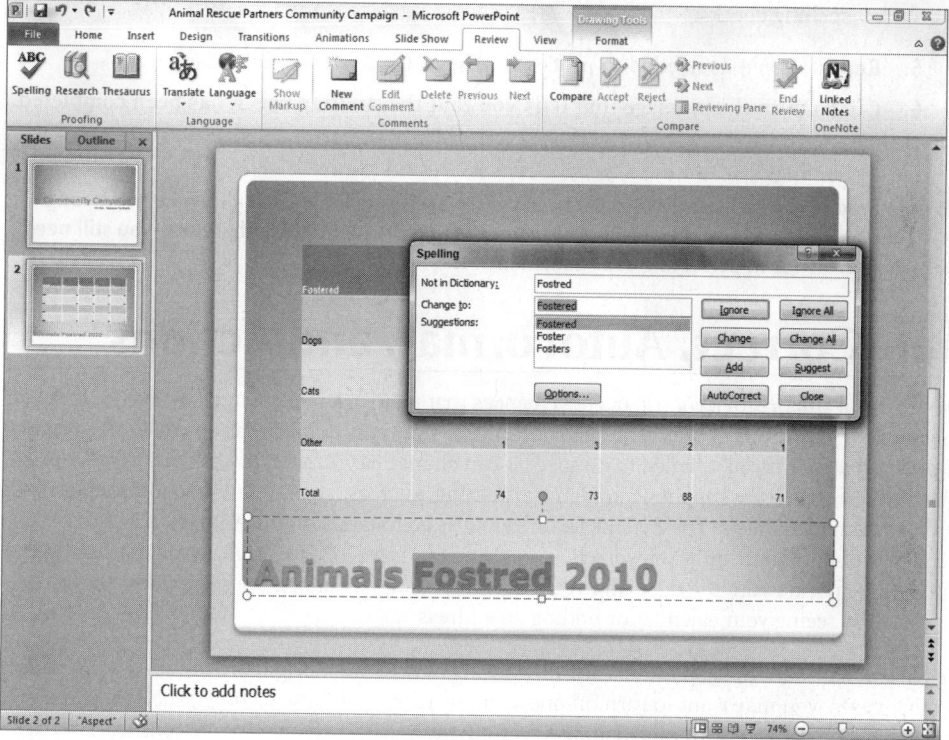

Note

Word can check grammar in addition to spelling every time you run a spell check. A green squiggle may appear under any potential grammar error in the document. Appendix A, which is on this book's website, explains where you can find the settings for controlling how spelling and grammar checking behave in Word. ■

4. Click on a button to tell the spelling check how to proceed:

- **Ignore.** Skips only the currently found instance of the suspected word without replacing it.

- **Ignore All.** Skips all instances of the suspected word without replacing it.

- **Change.** Replaces only the currently found instance of the suspected word with the current selection in the Suggestions list. (Click on another suggestion before clicking on this button, if needed.)

- **Change All.** Replaces all instances of the suspected word with the current selection in the Suggestions list. (Click on another suggestion before clicking on this button, if needed.)

- **Add.** Adds the suspected word to the dictionary so that it will be skipped in future spelling checks.

5. **Repeat Step 4 as needed to proceed through the spelling check.**

6. **Click OK in the message that tells you that the spelling check has been completed.**

Tip

It's critical to proofread your files even after spell checking. No spell checker can pick up on every wrong word choice — such as when you use *then* instead of *than* or *their* instead of *there*. Therefore, you still need to apply your own intelligence in perfecting your documents. ■

AutoCorrect, AutoFormat, and Actions

These three features provide a trio of conveniences that many users have come to take for granted. The AutoCorrect feature makes certain corrections as you type. For example, it capitalizes the first word of a sentence if you've failed to do so, or it can change a typo such as *acessories* to *accessories*. The AutoFormat feature supplies automatic formatting, such as creating true fraction characters or automatic numbered lists. The Actions feature enables commands on the Additional Actions submenu of the shortcut menu when you click on particular types of data such as a date. Click on the button that appears with the data, and you'll see a menu of special operations pertaining to that data, such as seeing your calendar or finding an address.

Most users will want to keep these features working as they were originally installed. However, in other cases, you may want to turn off one or more aspects of these features, such as whether AutoFormat converts web or e-mail addresses to hyperlinks or whether the Actions feature flags dates.

You can access the settings for all three of these features in the AutoCorrect dialog box. To display the dialog box, click the File tab, and then click Options. Click the Proofing category in the list at the left side of the Options dialog box that appears and then click the AutoCorrect Options button. The AutoCorrect dialog box appears.

Change settings on each of the tabs as needed and then click OK to apply your changes. Here's a look at the tabs and the changes you might want to make:

- **AutoCorrect.** Clear the checkbox beside any of the standard corrections that you want the program to stop making. If you want to add your own correction to the list of typos that AutoCorrect fixes, type entries in the Replace and With textboxes (see Figure 3-26), and then click Add.

- **AutoFormat as You Type.** On this tab (Figure 3-27), clear the checkbox beside any of the formatting changes to disable that change.

- **Actions.** As on the other two tabs, clear or check checkboxes as needed to disable or enable Actions features. The Enable Additional Actions in the Right-Click Menu checkbox turns actions on and off altogether.

- **Math AutoCorrect.** Word enables you to type certain keystroke combinations to insert characters not found on the keyboard, many of which are mathematical symbols. The majority of the keystrokes are a backslash (\) followed by two or more additional letters. For example, you can type **\infty** to insert the ∞ (infinity) symbol. Use this tab to learn what symbols you can insert and to add keystroke combinations for other symbols if applicable.

FIGURE 3-26

You can create a new typo correction for AutoCorrect.

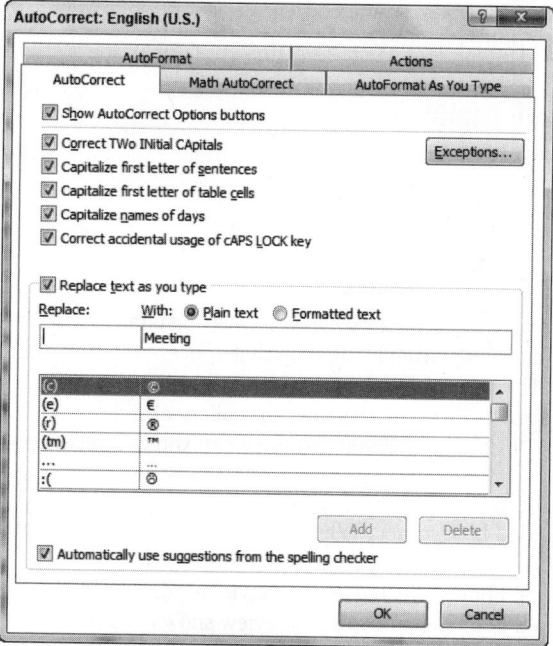

FIGURE 3-27

Choose which AutoFormatting changes the application will make.

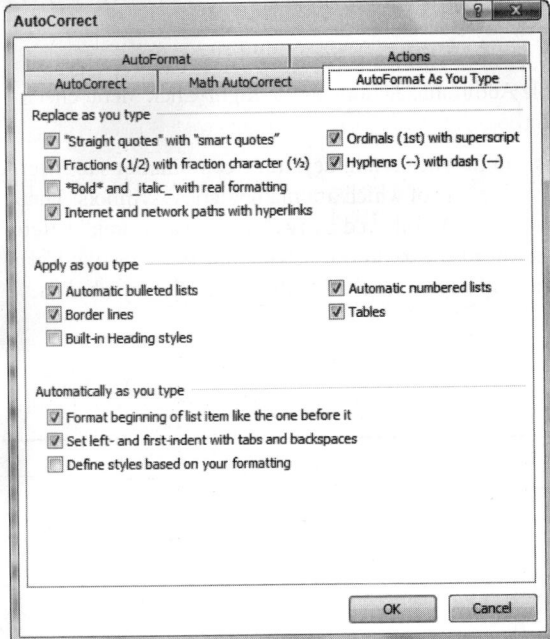

Styles and Live Preview

Word, Excel, PowerPoint, and Publisher, in particular, offer powerful formatting choices loosely known as *styles*, which are typically found on a contextual Design tab that appears when you select an element such as a table onscreen. The styles might be found in a Ribbon group or gallery named *"Styles"* or something similar. For example, Figure 3-28 shows the gallery of styles available in the Table Styles group of the Table Tools Design tab that you can use when you've selected a collection of cells in an Excel worksheet.

Style choices work with an Office feature called *Live Preview*. When you move your mouse pointer over a choice in a gallery like the one shown in Figure 3-28, the selected object temporarily changes to show you how it would look if you applied the highlighted style. In this way, you can quickly "try on" various looks for the selected item. When the Live Preview shows you the look you want, you can click the selected style to apply it to the selected item.

Tip

If you prefer not to use the Live Preview feature, you can turn it off. Click the File tab and click Options, and then clear the Enable Live Preview checkbox in the General options. ■

FIGURE 3-28

Click on a style to apply all its formatting choices to the selected object.

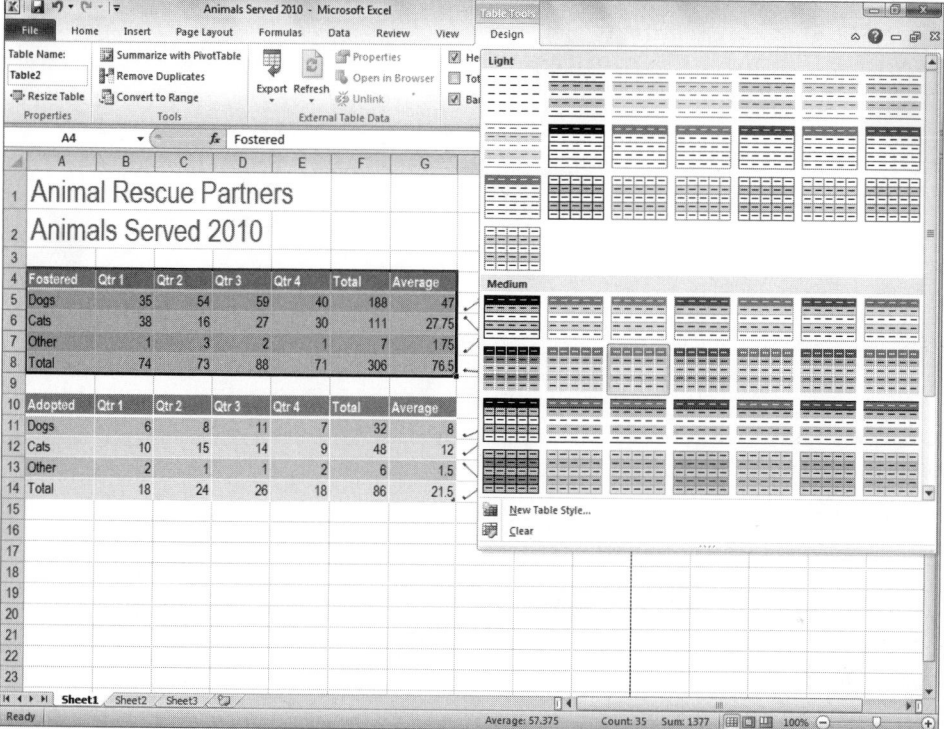

Summary

You now should have a good grounding in tasks common to most of the Office applications. In this chapter, you learned how to create, save, open, and close files. You learned how to check out how a file will look when printed, how to tweak page and printer settings, and how to print. The chapter also showed you how you can work in multiple files and applications, move easily between different files and programs, and how to move or copy information from one file or program to another. Finally, you saw how you can polish a document by replacing text, spell checking, making automatic corrections and formatting changes, and viewing and using the sophisticated styles offered in some Office 2010 applications.

Part II

Creating Documents with Word

Making a Document

Regardless of your background with prior generations of Microsoft Word, this chapter will help you get started quickly. If you're new to Word, this chapter escorts you through the basics, so you're ready to begin your journey toward becoming an expert. If you've been using Word for years, there are many new wrinkles in Word 2010 that I'll point out along the way. This chapter explores navigation nuances, view variations, and saving options. You'll also learn some navigation tricks and take a tour of Word's views.

Creating a Blank File

When you start the Office 2010 Word application using the Start menu, it creates a new, blank document file by default for you. This document file has the placeholder name *Document1* until you save it to assign a more specific name, as described later in the chapter. You can immediately start entering content into this blank document.

If you need another blank document, you can create it at any time by following these steps:

1. **Select File ➪ New.** The New Document dialog box appears.
2. **Click the Blank Document icon if it isn't selected by default.**
3. **Click Create.** The new, blank document appears.

Typing Text

When you create a new, blank document, you can begin typing text to fill the page. As you type, each character appears to the right of the blinking vertical insertion point. You can use the Backspace and Delete keys to delete text, the Spacebar to enter spaces, and all the other keys that you're using for typing.

Word also enables you to start a line of text anywhere on the page using the Click and Type feature. (This feature only works in the Print Layout view, so to learn more about that view, see the section called "Views" later in this chapter.) To take advantage of Click and Type, move the mouse pointer over a blank area of the page. If you don't see formatting symbols below the I-beam mouse pointer, click once. This enables Click and Type and displays its special mouse pointer. Then, you can double-click to position the pointer on the page and type your text. Figure 4-1 shows snippets of text added to a page using Click and Type.

FIGURE 4-1

Double-click and type anywhere on the page.

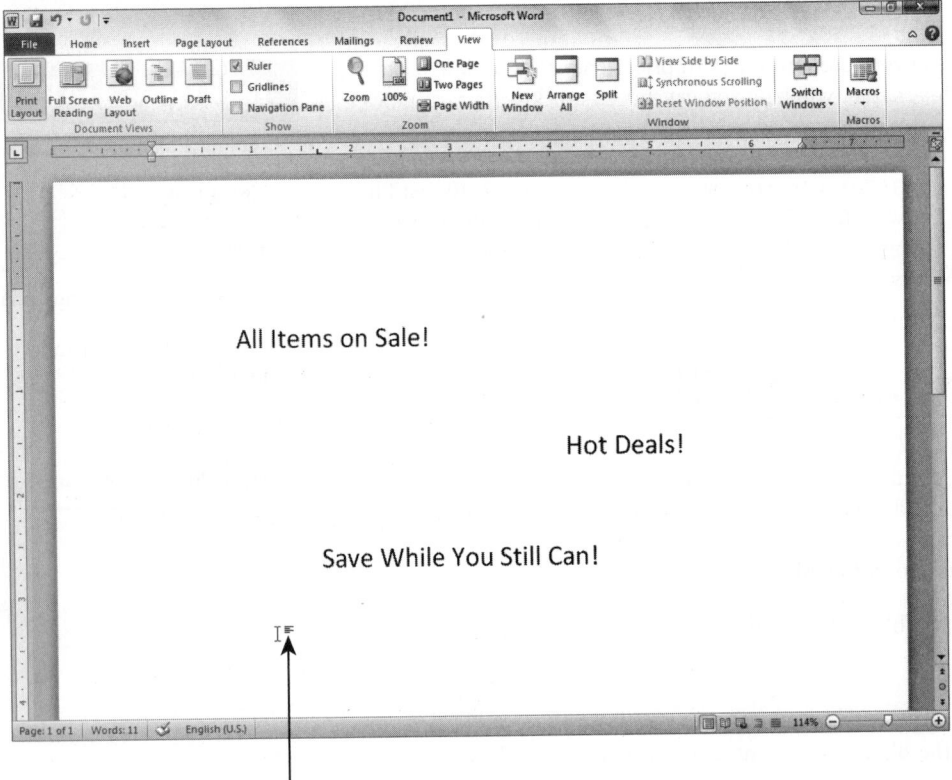

Click and Type mouse pointer

Using Word Wrap

By default, the margins for a blank document in Word 2010 are 1 inch on the left and the right. When you type enough text to fill each line, hitting the right margin boundary, Word automatically moves the insertion point to the next line. This automated feature is called *word wrap*, and it's a heck of a lot more convenient than having to make a manual carriage return at the end of each line.

If you adjust the margins for the document, word wrap always keeps your text within the new margin boundaries. Similarly, if you apply a right indent, divide the document into columns, or create a table and type in a table cell, word wrap automatically creates a new line of text at every right boundary. Just keep typing until you want or need to start a new paragraph (covered shortly). Later chapters cover changing margins and indents and working with tables.

Inserting versus Overtyping

Like its prior versions, Word 2010 offers two modes for entering text: Insert mode and Over-type mode. In Insert mode, the default mode, if you click within existing text and type, Word inserts the added text between the existing characters, moving text to the right of the inser-tion point farther right to accommodate your additions, and rewrapping the line as needed. In contrast, when you switch to Overtype mode, any text you type replaces text to the right of the insertion point.

Overtyping is a fine method of data entry — when it's the mode that you want. Unfortunately, in older Word versions, the Insert key on the keyboard toggled between Insert and Overtype modes by default. Because the Insert key is often found above or right next to the Delete key on the key-board, many a surprised user would accidentally hit the Insert key and then unhappily type right over his text.

In Word 2010, the Insert key's control of Overtype mode is turned off by default. You can use the Word Options dialog box to turn Overtype mode on and off, and also to enable the Insert key's control of Overtype mode. Select File ➪ Word Options, and then click Advanced in the list at the left side of the Word Options dialog box. Use the Use Overtype Mode checkbox (Figure 4-2) to toggle Overtype mode on and off, and the Use the Insert Key to Control Overtype Mode checkbox to toggle the Insert key's control of Overtype mode on and off. Click OK to apply your changes.

Using Default Tabs

Every new, blank document has default tab stops already set up for you. These tabs are set at 1/2-inch (0.5-inch) intervals along the whole width of the document between the margins. To align text to any of these default tab stops, press the Tab key. You can press Tab multiple times if you need to allow more width between the information that you're using the tab stops to align.

Tip
To display the rulers so that you can better work with text alignment features like tabs in a document, click the View Ruler button that appears at the top of the vertical scroll bar at the right side of the Word window. ■

FIGURE 4-2

The Word Options dialog box enables you to turn Overtype mode on and off.

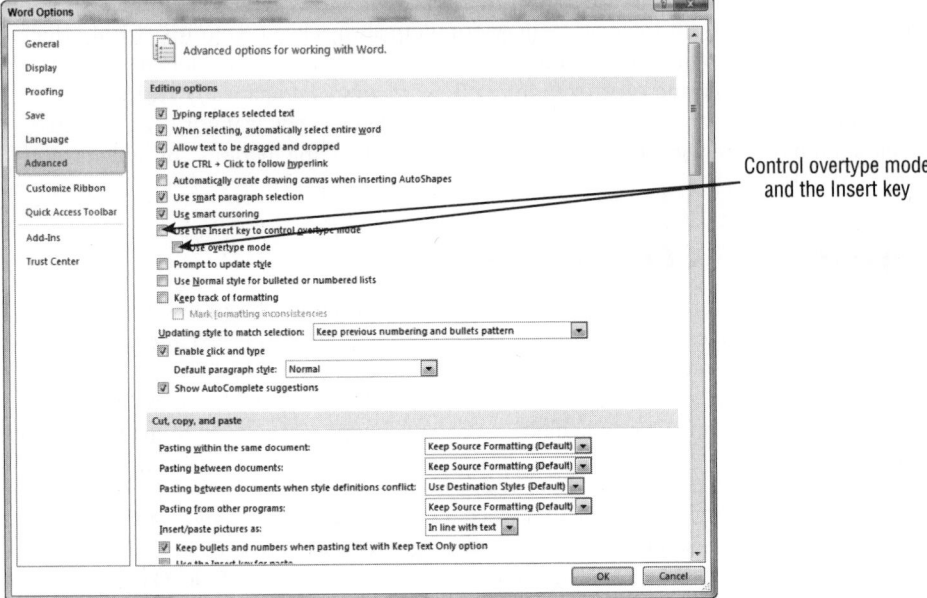

Control overtype mode
and the Insert key

Making a New Paragraph

In legacy versions of Word, when you wanted to create a new paragraph in a blank document, you had to press the Enter key twice. That's because the default body text style didn't provide for any extra spacing after a paragraph mark, which is a hidden symbol inserted when you press Enter.

Starting with Word 2007, pressing Enter by default not only inserts the paragraph mark to create a new paragraph, but also inserts extra spacing between paragraphs to separate them visually and eliminate the need to press Enter twice. As shown in Figure 4-3, when you press Enter after a paragraph, the insertion point moves down to the beginning of a new paragraph, and Word includes spacing above the new paragraph.

Creating a File from a Template

You need not start every document that you create from scratch. You can instead select a *template* that supplies design settings and in many cases starter text on which you can base your own document content. The Office applications offer many templates, both installed on your system and available online. In Word, you can choose from a variety of different templates to get your document started.

FIGURE 4-3

Press Enter to create a new paragraph in Word.

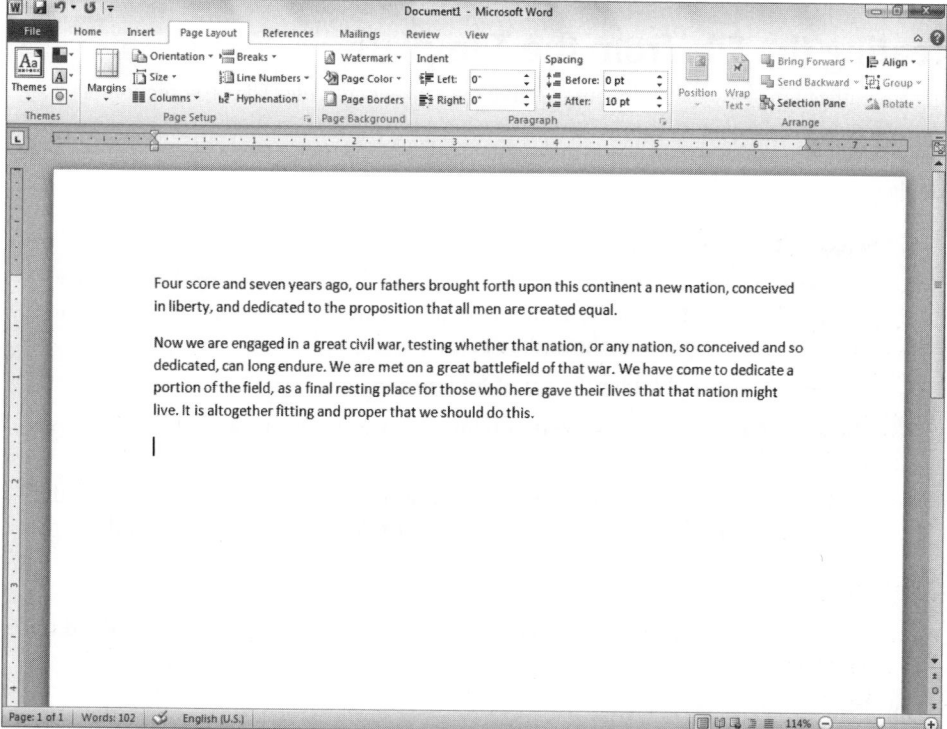

Understanding Templates

Every new document you create in Word 2010 — even a blank document — is based on a template that specifies basic formatting for the document such as margin settings and default text styles. When you create a blank document, Word automatically applies the default global template, `Normal.dotm`.

In other instances, you can select a specific template to use as the basis for a new document. A template can include not only design elements, but also labels and starter text and placeholders for your information. For example, you can select a Fax template that holds predefined labels and positions for recipient name, fax number, and more. Or, you can choose a Resume template that defines a nice layout with placeholders that you select and replace to add your own resume information.

Installing Word 2010 installs a variety of letter, resume, fax, and report templates on your system. Word also enables you to download templates from dozens of different categories from Office.com. There are downloadable templates for brochures, business cards, memos, purchase orders, and more.

Creating the File from the Template

Using a template for a new file starts out just like creating a blank file. The New section of Backstage view enables you to browse for and select a template and, in most cases, to see a preview before you select the template to use. Follow these steps to create a new document based on a template:

1. **Select File ⇨ New.** The New section of Backstage view appears.
2. **Click either Sample Templates in the Templates section or a template category under Office.com Templates.** Thumbnails and names for the available templates in the selected category appear in the middle section of the dialog box.
3. **Click on the desired folder if a set of folders appears.**
4. **Click the thumbnail for the desired template.** A preview for the template appears at the right, as shown in Figure 4-4.
5. **Click the Create button to create the new file from an installed template, or click Download to create the new document from a selected online template.** If you're downloading a template, the Microsoft Office Genuine Advantage dialog box may appear.
6. **If it does, click Continue to validate your software installation and download the template.**

The new document appears onscreen.

Note
Some of the templates available via Office.com were created in earlier Word versions. Those documents will open in Compatibility mode, which is described later in this chapter. ■

Working with Template Content

As shown in Figure 4-5, a template might hold a variety of different sample contents and placeholders.

You can work with these placeholders and other contents as follows to finish your document:

- **Graphics Placeholders.** The box at the top of Figure 4-5 that says *Your Logo Here* is a placeholder for a graphic. Click the placeholder to select it, click the Insert tab on the

Ribbon, and then click the Picture or Clip Art choice in the Illustrations group to select a replacement item. Chapter 9, "Tables and Graphics," provides more information about working with artwork in your Word documents.

- **Labels for Text.** If you were to click to the right of the colon for any of the label items listed immediately below the Project Initiation Checklist in Figure 4-5, the insertion point would appear at a precise position, ready for you to enter the text to go with the label.

- **Gray Field Placeholders.** Template text that appears with square brackets and gray shading is text form fields. Clicking one of these placeholders selects the entire placeholder, and then any text you type replaces the placeholder contents.

- **Other Text.** You can supplement the template's contents by adding your own text anywhere in the document.

- **Styles.** Templates also include predefined styles (formatting) that you can apply to text that you add. See Chapter 7 to learn more about applying styles to text.

FIGURE 4-4

Preview a template before making a new document from it.

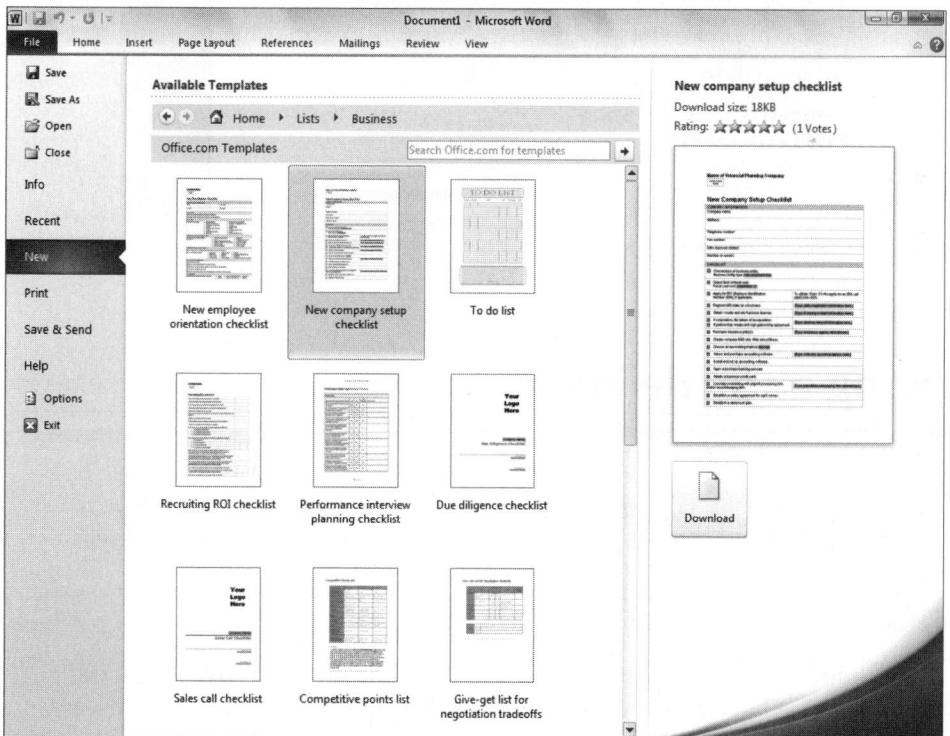

FIGURE 4-5

Replace template placeholders with your own content.

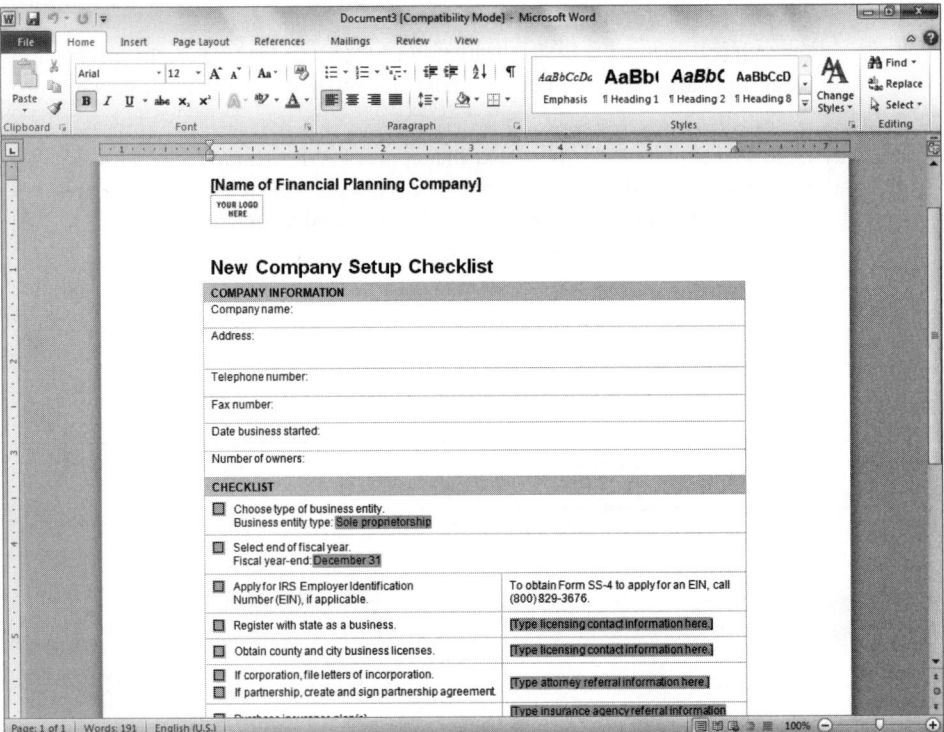

Saving and File Formats

What good are any of these tools if the information never leaves the Word window? At the end of the day, the goal is to create letters, reports, brochures, pamphlets, books, web pages, blogs, and other publications that take on some kind of semi-permanent existence. As long as you see *Document1* in Word's title bar, you run the risk of losing your investment of time and creativity.

Word is like most other Windows programs. When you're ready to commit your work to disk, just choose File ⇨ Save from the menu. Whoops! What menu?

Like most other Windows programs, you can press Ctrl+S to save the current document. If it is new and hasn't been named, you'll see the Save As dialog box shown in Figure 4-6, or something similar. If the document isn't new, Ctrl+S does an immediate save using the existing filename.

FIGURE 4-6

Add frequently used folders to the Favorites area (see the following tip) to make saving and opening files faster.

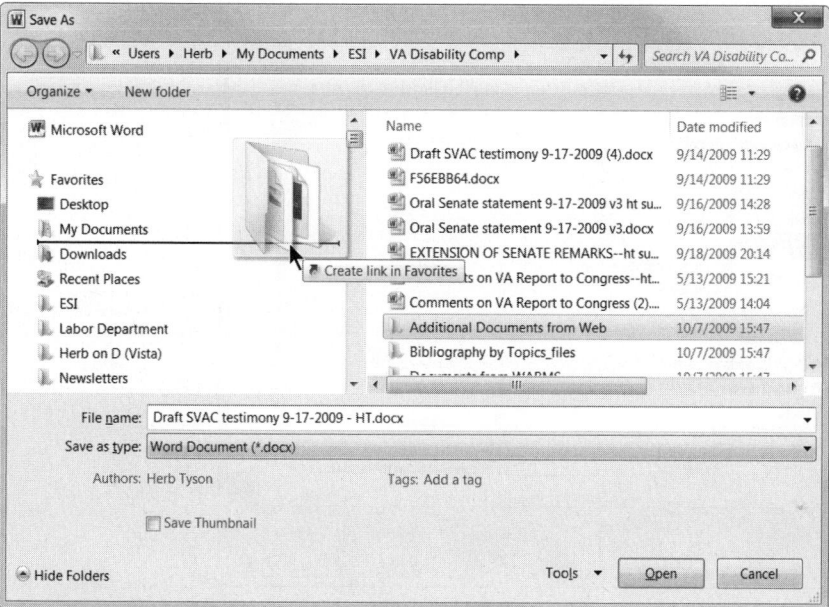

Tip

To add a folder to the Favorites area, select and drag the folder from the list of files and folders and drop it into the Favorites area. For example, in Figure 4-6, the Additional Documents from Web folder is selected. When dragging, make sure that you drop the folder into an existing link. The line and screen tip in Figure 4-6 provide positive confirmation that the folder will land in Favorites — not in an adjacent folder. ∎

Note also the Save as Type field under File Name. The list of formats you will see varies depending on how much of Office was installed. To have the fullest array of save options, you should do two things.

First, in Word or Office setup (in Programs and Features in Windows' Control Panel), navigate to Office 2010's (or Word 2010's) Installation Options section, and set Converters and Filters to Run All from My Computer, as shown in Figure 4-7. Click Continue as needed to complete the installation. Note that you need do this only if the full set of converters isn't already installed.

FIGURE 4-7

To maximize your Save and Open options, install the full set of converters.

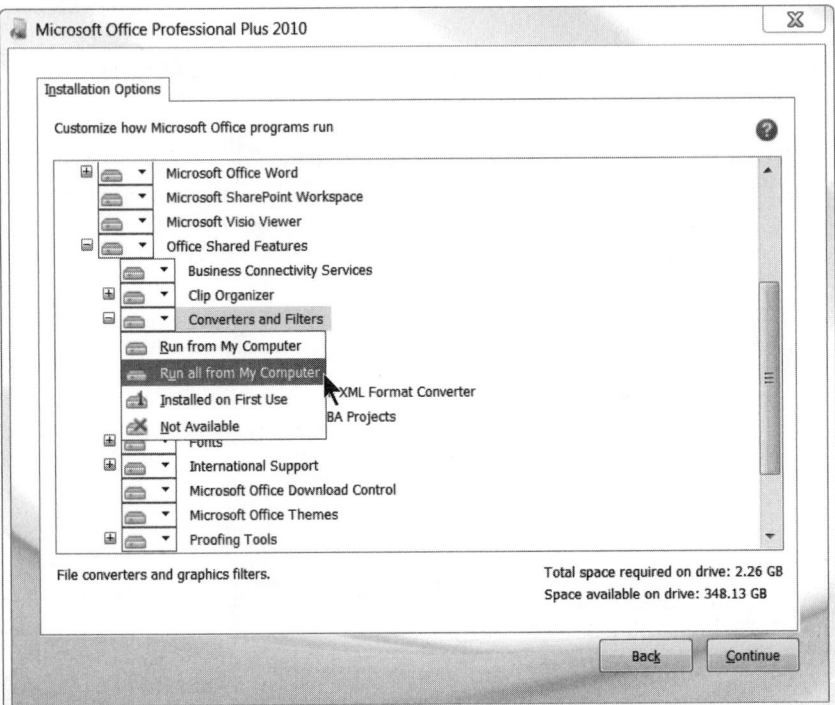

The second thing to do is to go to the Microsoft Office website and download the converter pack. Installed, this pack adds the fullest range of converters to your Office 2010 setup. Note that the location and name of this free add-on varies. At this writing, however, it is located here:

```
www.microsoft.com/downloads/details.aspx?FamilyID=cf196df0-70e5-4595-
8a98-370278f40c57&DisplayLang=en
```

You can also search Microsoft's website for OCONVPCK.EXE.

Convert

You will see the Convert option (in the Info tab when you click File) only if the current file is from an earlier Word format (e.g., Word 97–Word 2003, which causes *[Compatibility Mode]* to appear after the filename in Word's title bar). Clicking the Convert button converts the current file into .docx format.

Caution

Make a copy of the file or save the file under a new name *before* clicking Convert. The Convert option renames the original file — the .doc version will be gone. The first time you convert, Word does alert you to what it's doing, but if you're like most users, you won't read the fine print and you'll click Do Not Ask Me Again about Converting Documents. If you do happen to click that option, in the future there will be no warning; and if you're like me, you will forget it was there the first time.

When you convert, Word converts the document currently displayed to .docx format. At that point, the notation *[Compatibility Mode]* disappears from Word's title bar, but the displayed name still shows .doc instead of .docx. Even so, at this point, you can still recover the original file by closing the file without saving the changes. Until you save, the converted file exists only in the current window.

However, if you now save the file, Word immediately renames it using the new extension (.docx for a plain vanilla Word 2010 document file, or .docm for a Word 2010 document file that contains macros). Once converted, the original .doc file is gone forever! After the fact, you can perform a Save As and resave the file in the original format. However, I'm not going to guarantee that it will be byte-for-byte identical to the original. ■

Save & Send (Formerly Publish)

Word 2010 has replaced Word 2007's Publish set of commands with Share. Shown in Figure 4-8, these options all result in Word content's ending up online. Depending on what else you have installed, you might see different options from those pictured. You can send files using e-mail, save files to the Web, or collaborate with SharePoint.

FIGURE 4-8

Word 2010 has a variety of sharing options for putting Word content online.

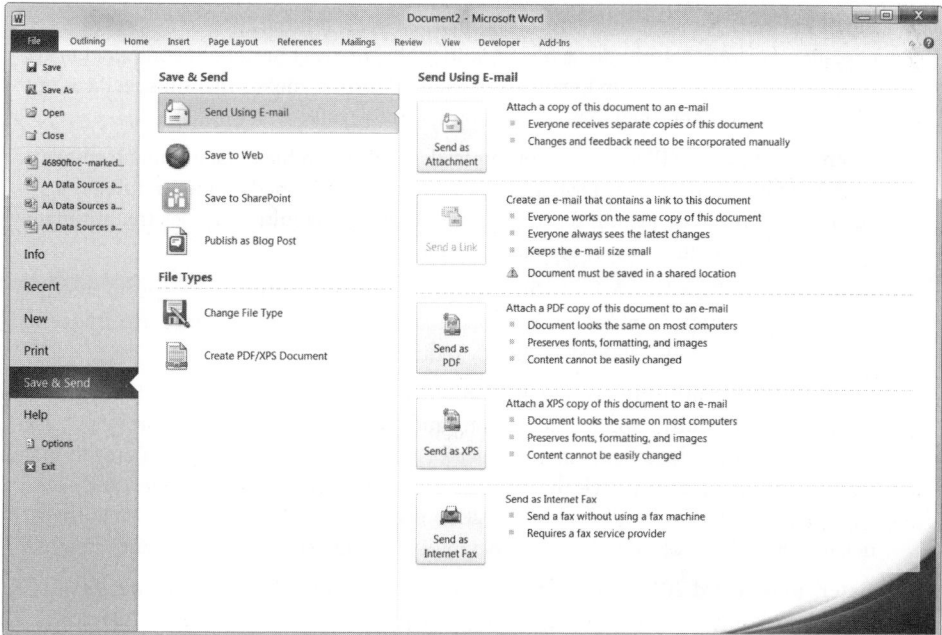

The Publish as Blog Post feature enables you to publish directly from Word to supported blogs. Which blogs are supported? At this time, Windows Live Spaces, Blogger, SharePoint blog, Community Server, TypePad, and WordPress are supported. You might also have success with some services that support common blog APIs.

You also can use Change File Type to save in another file format, or create a document that can be viewed outside of Word with Create PDF/XPS Document.

Compatibility with Previous Versions of Word

Word 2003's file format was basically unchanged since Word 97. Feature enhancements necessitated the modification of Word's binary format over the years, such as when document versioning and floating tables were introduced.

Even so, you can still open most Word 2003 files in Word 97, and the documents will look basically the same. Only if you use newer features will you see a difference, and usually that just means reduced functionality rather than lost data or formatting.

Word 2010, Word 2007, and Word 2003 users will continue to see interoperability. However, Word 2010's and 2007's *native* format is radically different from — and better than — the old format. The new format boasts a number of improvements over the older format:

- **Open Format.** The basic file is in ZIP format, an open standard, which serves as a container for .docx and .docm files. Additionally, many (but not all) components are in XML (eXtensible Markup Language) format. Microsoft makes the full specifications available for free, and they may be used by anyone royalty-free.

- **Compression.** The ZIP format is compressed, resulting in files that are much smaller. Additionally, Word's *binary* format has been mostly abandoned (some components, such as VBA macros, are still written in binary format), resulting in files that ultimately resolve to plain text, and that are much smaller.

- **Robustness.** ZIP and XML are industry-standard formats with precise specifications that offer fewer opportunities to introduce document corruption. Hence, the frequency of corrupted Word files should be greatly reduced.

- **Backward Compatibility.** Although Word 2010 and Word 2007 have a slightly different format, they still fully support the opening and saving of files in legacy formats. A user can opt to save all documents in an earlier format by default. Moreover, Microsoft makes available a Compatibility Pack that enables Word 2000–2003 users to open and save in the new format. In fact, Word 2000–2003 users can make the .docx format their default, providing considerable interoperability among users of the different versions.

- **Extensions.** Word 2010 has four native file formats: .docx (ordinary documents), .docm (macro-enabled documents), .dotx (templates that cannot contain macros), and .dotm (templates that are macro-enabled, such as Normal.dotm).

Calling the x-file format *XML format* actually is a bit of a misnomer. XML is at the heart of Word's x format; however, the files saved by Word are not XML files. You can verify this by trying to open one using Internet Explorer. What you see is decidedly not XML. Some of the components of Word's x files, however, do use XML format.

As indicated, Word 2010 and 2007 or 2000–2003 users will still be able to read and write to each others' files, assuming that the Word 2000–2003 users install the free Office Compatibility Pack. Even so, Word will sometimes warn you that features might be lost when you convert to a different format.

Word itself runs an automatic compatibility check when you attempt to save a document in a format that's different from the current one. You can, without attempting to save, run this check yourself at any time from Word 2010. To see whether features might be lost in the move from one version of Word to another, open the document in Word 2010. Choose File ➪ Info ➪ Check for Issues ➪ Check Compatibility.

For the most part, Word 2010 does a good job of checking compatibility when trying to save a native .docx file in .doc format. For example, if you run the Compatibility Checker on a Word 2010 document containing advanced features, you will be alerted, as shown in Figure 4-9.

FIGURE 4-9

Using the Compatibility Checker to determine whether converting to a different Word version will cause a loss of information or features.

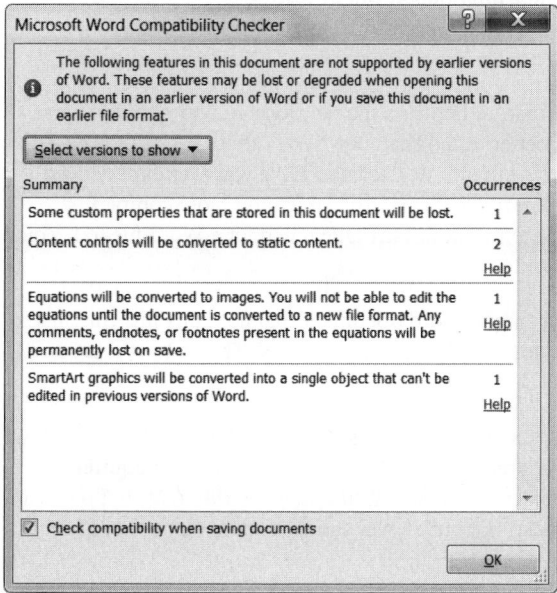

When moving in the other direction — checking a Word 2003 (or earlier) document for compatibility with Word 2010 — the Checker usually will inform you that "No compatibility issues were found." Note, however, that the Compatibility Checker doesn't check when you first open a document formatted for Word 2003 (or earlier). Nor does it check when you convert a file. It's not until you try to save the file that it warns you, as shown in Figure 4-10.

FIGURE 4-10

Word 2010 warns you when saving a document that contains multiple versions saved in Word 2003 or earlier.

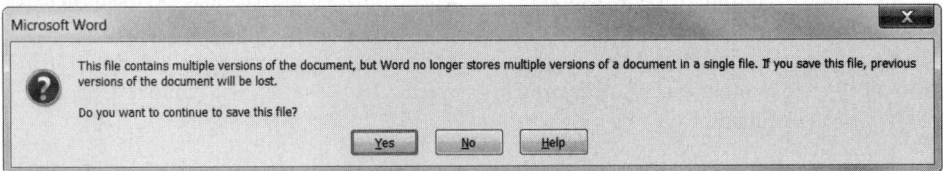

Caution

The Compatibility Checker does not warn you if you open a file that uses Word's Versioning feature. Word 2010 comes with a tool for dealing with multiple document versions that were saved in a single file, but Word will not alert you to the fact that the current file contains versioned changes until or unless you try to save the file in .docx format. Note also that Word 2010 itself cannot fully access or properly save a versioned file, even if you tell Word 2010 to work in Word 2003 format. Hence, if you save such a file in Word 2010 — even if you tell it to save in Word 2003 format — all versioning information will be lost! ■

To .doc or Not to .doc

If you have the option to use Word's old format, rather than the new format, why shouldn't you do that? Isn't old usually more reliable and better tested than new? Well, that's certainly a plausible argument, but consider the fragility of Word's binary .doc format. Have you ever experienced document corruption? With a proprietary binary file format, the larger and more complex the document, the more likely corruption becomes. It doesn't take much for a Word file to become inaccessible to Word's default Open command.

Another issue is document size. Consider a simple Word document that contains just the phrase *Hello, Word*. When saved in Word 97–2003 format, that basic file is 26K. That is to say, to store those 11 characters, it takes Word about 26,000 characters!

The same phrase stored in Word 2010's .docx format requires just 10K. Make no mistake: That's still a lot of storage space for just those 11 characters, but it's a lot less than what's required by Word 2003. The storage savings you get won't always be that dramatically different, but over time you will notice a difference. Smaller files mean not only lower storage requirements but faster communication times as well.

Still another issue is interoperability. When a Word user gives a .doc file to a WordPerfect, OpenOffice, or other word processor user, it's a very sure bet that something is going to get lost in translation, even though WordPerfect claims to be able to work with Word's .doc format. Such documents seldom look identical or print identically, and the larger and more complex they are, the more different they look.

With Word's adoption of an open formatting standard, it is possible for WordPerfect and other programs to more correctly interpret how any given .docx file should be displayed. Just as the same web page looks and prints nearly identically when viewed in different web browsers, a Word .docx file should look and print nearly identically regardless of which program you use to open it (assuming it supports Word's .docx format).

Persistent Save As

If, despite the advantages of using the new format, you wish to use Word's .doc format, you can do so. Choose File ➪ Options ➪ Save choice. As shown in Figure 4-11, set Save Files in this Format to Word 97–2003 Document (*.doc).

FIGURE 4-11

You can tell Word to save in any of a variety of formats by default.

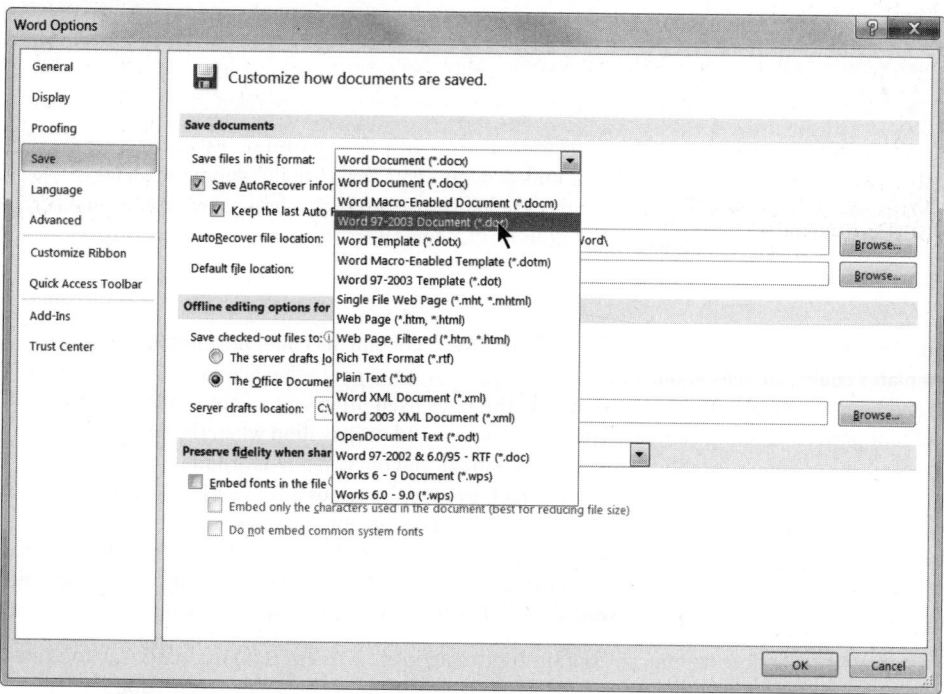

Note that even if you set `.doc` or some other format as your default, you can still override that setting at any time by using Save As and saving to `.docx` or any other supported format. Setting one format as the default does not lock you out of using other formats as needed.

Microsoft Office Compatibility Pack

As noted earlier, Microsoft makes available a free enhancement that enables Word 2003 users to open and save files in the new format. In fact, this enhancement also works with Word 2002.

Instructions for downloading and installing the converters are in flux, as is the location of the Compatibility Pack. Try the following search in Google:

```
site:microsoft.com "office compatibility pack"
```

At this time, the first hit listed is the correct location.

.docx versus .docm

With Word 2010 come four XML-based file formats:

- `.docx`: An ordinary document containing no macros
- `.docm`: A document that either contains macros or is macro-enabled
- `.dotx`: A template that does not contain macros
- `.dotm`: A template that either contains macros or is macro-enabled

It is important for some purposes for users to be able to include macros not just in document templates, but in documents as well. This makes documents that contain automation a lot more portable. Rather than having to send both document and template — or, worse, a template masquerading as a document — you can send a document that has macros enabled.

Note

When Word macro viruses first started appearing, ordinary Word documents could not contain macros — only templates could. Therefore, one of the most popular ways of *packaging* macro viruses was in a `.dot` file that had been renamed with a .doc extension. The virus itself often was an automatic macro (typically AutoExec) that performed some combination of destruction and propagation when the rogue `.dot` file was first opened. A common precaution was to press Shift as you opened any Word file — .doc or `.dot` — to prevent automatic macros from running. In fact, even with various advances in security and anti-virus software, pressing Shift when you open an unfamiliar Word document is still not being overcautious. In recent versions of Word, `.doc` files can legitimately contain macros, so I'm not really sure the situation has improved much. I still reach for the Shift key, do a quick inspection to determine whether any macros are hiding inside, and then proceed. Often, though, Word 2010 will warn you when a document contains macros. ∎

Because Word 2003 documents can contain legitimate macros, there is no outward way to know whether any given `.doc` document file contains macros. If someone sends you a `.doc` file, is opening it safe?

While it's not clear that the new approach — distinct file extensions for documents and templates that are macro-enabled — is going to improve safety a lot, it does provide more information for the user. This is true especially in business environments, where people don't deliberately change file extensions. If you see a file with a .docm or .dotm extension, you know that it contains macros and that it might warrant careful handling.

Moreover, if a document file has been deliberately mis-renamed, Word will refuse to open it. Whether it's a .docx file that's been renamed to .docm or vice versa, you will see the message box shown in Figure 4-12.

FIGURE 4-12

Word 2010 refuses to open a .docx or .docm file that has deliberately been mis-renamed.

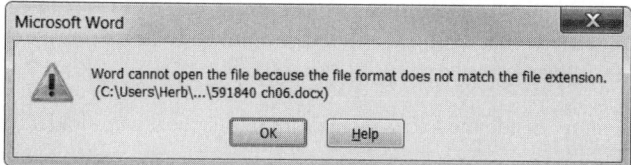

Converting a .docx File into a .docm File

If you want to convert a .docx file so that it can contain macros, you must use Save As and choose Word Macro-Enabled Document (*.docm) as the file type. You can do this at any time — it doesn't have to be when the document is first created. You can also remove any macros from a .docm file by saving it as a Word document (*.docx).

Even so, you can create or record a macro while editing a .docx file, and even tell Word to store it in a .docx file. There will be no error message, and the macro will be available for running in the current session. However, when you first try to save the file, you will be prompted to change the target format or risk losing the VBA project. If you save the file as a .docx anyway and close the file, the macro will not be saved.

Understanding .docx

As indicated earlier, Word's new .docx format doesn't entirely use XML format. Rather, the main body of your document is stored in XML format, but that file isn't stored directly on disk. Instead, it's stored inside a ZIP file, which gets a .docx, .docm, .dotm, or .dotx file extension.

To verify this, create a simple Word 2010 file, and save and close it. Next, rename it to add a .zip extension. Finally, use Windows Explorer to display the contents of that ZIP file, as shown in Figure 4-13.

FIGURE 4-13

When viewed as ZIP files, most .docx files contain three main folders and a Content Types XML document.

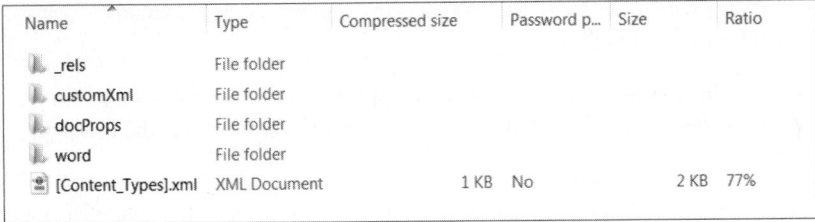

Word .docx files can contain additional folders as well, such as one named customXml. This folder is used if the document contains content control features that are linked to document properties, an external database or forms server, and so on.

The main parts of the Word document are inside the folder named word. A typical word folder for a simple document is shown in Figure 4-14.

FIGURE 4-14

The Word document's main components are stored inside the .docx file in the folder named word.

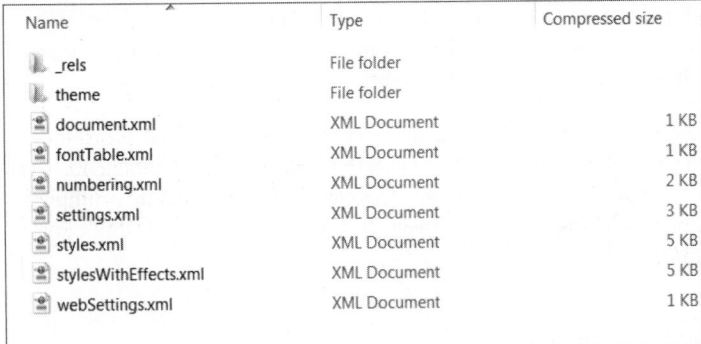

The main text of the document is stored in document.xml. Using an XML Editor, you could actually make changes to the text in document.xml, replace the original file with the changed one, rename the file so that it has a .docx extension instead of .zip, and open the file in Word, and those changes would appear.

What's an XML Editor?

When you double-click an XML file, it just opens Internet Explorer, which doesn't let you edit anything. Luckily, there are specialized XML Editors that you can use. You can also use Expression Web or SharePoint Designer. You can also use anything that edits plain-text files, such as Notepad.

More complex Word files contain additional elements. Shown in Figure 4-15 is an expanded folder view of a .docx file that contains clip art, an embedded Excel chart, several pictures, and some SmartArt, as well as custom XML links to document properties.

FIGURE 4-15

In a .docx file, images are stored in the word\media folder.

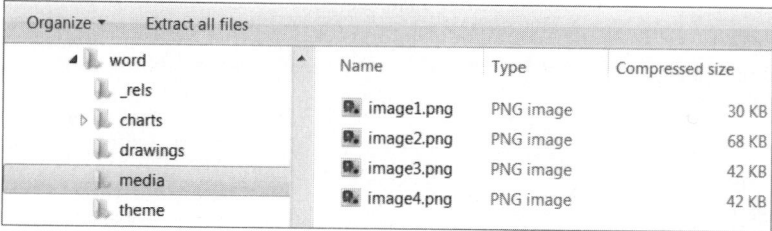

Tip

You can replace the images in a .docx **file without editing the file in Word. Rename the** .docx **file so that it has a** .zip **extension. Extract the images stored in the** word\media **folder so you can see what's what. Give the replacement images the same respective names as the existing ones. Replace the contents of the** word\media **folder with the new images. Finally, replace the** .zip **extension with the original extension. Presto! And you never touched Word! This might not make ergonomic sense for just a few images, but if you have dozens, it could save you a substantial amount of time. ∎**

Navigation Tips and Tricks

Bible readers already know the basics of using the Windows interface, so this book skips the stuff that I think every Windows user already knows about, and instead covers aspects of Word that you might not know about. In our great hurry to get things done, ironically, we often overlook simple tips and tricks that might otherwise make our computing lives easier and less hurried or, at the very least, more entertaining.

Tricks with Clicks

We all know about double-clicking, but not everyone knows the benefits of triple-clicking, Ctrl+clicking, and Alt+clicking.

Triple-Clicking

When you triple-click inside a paragraph, Word selects the entire paragraph. However, where you click makes a difference. If you triple-click in the left margin, rather than in a paragraph, and the mouse pointer's shape is the arrow shown in Figure 4-16, the entire document is selected.

FIGURE 4-16

A right-facing mouse pointer in the left margin indicates a different selection mode.

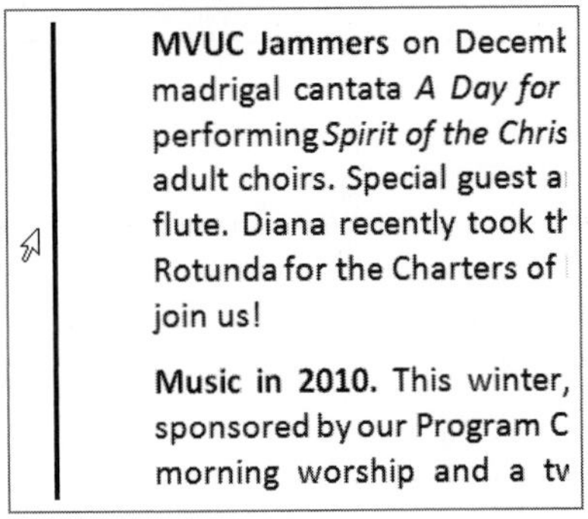

MVUC Jammers on Decemb
madrigal cantata *A Day for*
performing *Spirit of the Chris*
adult choirs. Special guest a
flute. Diana recently took th
Rotunda for the Charters of
join us!

Music in 2010. This winter,
sponsored by our Program C
morning worship and a tv

Is triple-clicking in the left margin faster and easier than pressing Ctrl+A? Not necessarily, but it might be if your hand is already on the mouse. In addition, if you want the MiniBar to appear, the mouse method will summon it, whereas Ctrl+A won't.

Ctrl+Clicking

Want something faster than triple-clicking? If you just happen to have one hand on the mouse and the other on the keyboard, Ctrl+click in the left margin. That also selects the entire document and displays the MiniBar.

If you Ctrl+click in a paragraph, the current sentence is selected. This can be handy when you want to move, delete, or highlight a sentence. As someone who sometimes highlights as they read, you might also find that this can help focus on a particular passage when simply reading rather than editing.

Alt+Clicking

If you Alt+click a word or a selected passage, Word looks up the word or selection using Office's Research pane. Do you ever accidentally invoke the Research pane? Want a good way to turn it off? Well...stop looking, because it doesn't exist.

Note

If you're an advanced Word user, you probably don't want to accept this. You're probably thinking "Herb doesn't know that you can intercept the built-in Research command and replace it with a dummy macro, thereby disabling this behavior." Well, you caught me. Go ahead and try it. I'll wait.

Back already? That's right. You can indeed prevent the Research command on the Review ribbon tab of the Ribbon from doing anything, but that doesn't tame the Alt+click shortcut. It's more persistent than a horsefly. ■

Alt+Dragging

You can use Alt+drag to select a vertical column of text — even if the text is not column-oriented. This can be useful when you are working with monospaced fonts and there is a de facto columnar setup. Once a selection is made, any character- or font-oriented formatting can be applied to it, as shown in Figure 4-17. The selection can also be deleted. Note that if the text is proportionally spaced, anything that affects the size and therefore the ostensible columnar orientation will undo the selection. The effect can be rather bizarre.

FIGURE 4-17

With the Alt key pressed, you can drag to select a vertical swath of text.

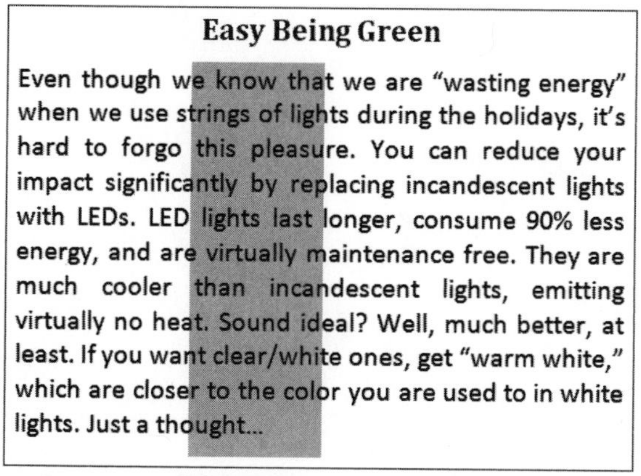

Easy Being Green

Even though we know that we are "wasting energy" when we use strings of lights during the holidays, it's hard to forgo this pleasure. You can reduce your impact significantly by replacing incandescent lights with LEDs. LED lights last longer, consume 90% less energy, and are virtually maintenance free. They are much cooler than incandescent lights, emitting virtually no heat. Sound ideal? Well, much better, at least. If you want clear/white ones, get "warm white," which are closer to the color you are used to in white lights. Just a thought...

Shift+Click

Click where you want a selection to start, and then Shift+click where you want it to end. You can continue Shift+clicking to expand or reduce the selection. This technique can be really useful if you have difficulty dragging to highlight exactly the selection you want.

Multi-Selecting

A few versions of Word ago, it became possible to make multiple noncontiguous selections in a document. While many know this, many more don't. To do it, make your first selection. Then, hold down the Ctrl key to make additional selections. Once you've made as many selections as you want, you can then apply the desired formatting to them, copy all of the selections to the clipboard, paste the contents of the clipboard over all of the selections, and so on.

Seldom Screen

I've already reviewed a few new features that you'll see on the Word screen. Word 2010's repertoire is so vast, however, that you might never notice a few features — some relatively new and some old. In this section, I point out features that are often overlooked (even by longtime users) and that you might find useful.

Split Box

Shown in Figure 4-18, the split box is used to divide the current document into two horizontal views. Move the mouse over the top of the vertical scroll bar so that the pointer changes (refer to Figure 4-18). At that point, you can drag down to divide the window into two panes. Alternatively, you can double-click the split box to divide the window into two equal panes.

FIGURE 4-18

Double-click or drag the split box to display the current document in two panes.

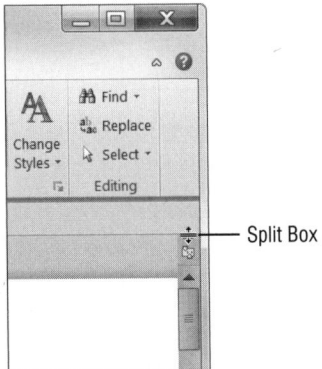

— Split Box

Why would you want to do that? Well, you might not have two monitors, but you need to look at a table or a figure while you write about it. In a single pane this can be challenging, especially if what you type keeps causing the figure to move out of view.

As another example, you might want to have an Outline view of your document in one pane while maintaining a Print Layout view in the other, as shown in Figure 4-19. When viewing a document in two split panes, note that the status bar reflects the status of the currently active pane. Not only can you display different views in multiple panes, but you can display them at different zoom levels as well.

Split panes can be displayed in different views, enabling you see Outline and Print Layout at the same time.

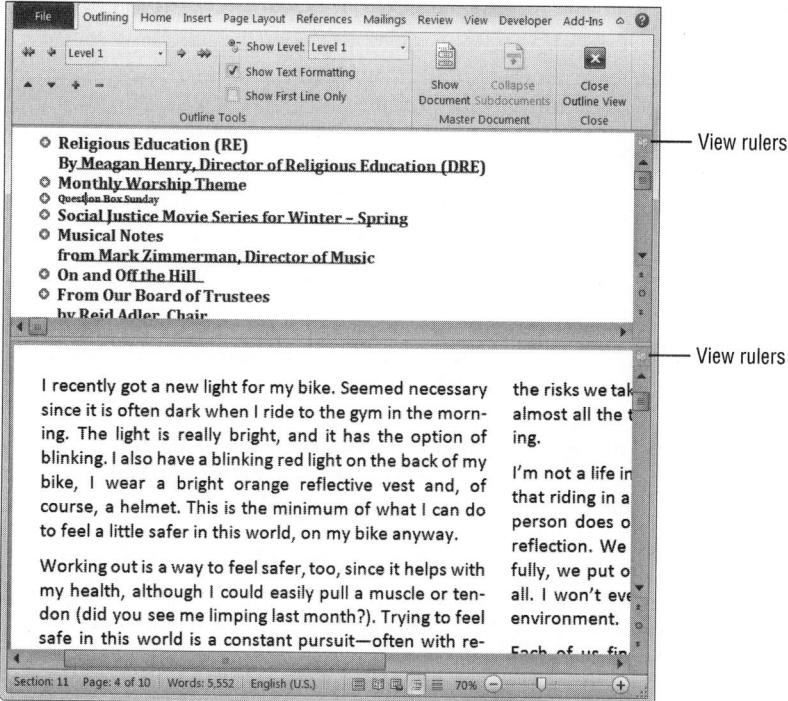

— View rulers

— View rulers

You can remove the split by dragging it up or down, leaving the desired view in place, or double-clicking anywhere on the split line. Alternatively, if the Ribbon's View tab is displayed, click Remove Split in the Window group.

View Rulers

Another sometimes-overlooked tool is the ruler toggle control, also shown in Figure 4-19. This control toggles the horizontal and vertical (if it's on) rulers on and off. It cannot control them separately.

The presence of the ruler toggle on both panes of a split document window might lead you to assume that the upper and lower rulers can be toggled independently. They cannot.

Select Browse Object

While we're visiting over there on that side of the Word screen, let's take a look at another sometimes-overlooked control — Select Browse Object. Shown in Figure 4-20, this control determines what happens when you click the Previous or Next buttons that are immediately above and below the Select Browse Object control. It also determines what happens when you press Ctrl+Page Up or Ctrl+Page Down.

FIGURE 4-20

Select Browse Object determines the actions performed by the Previous and Next buttons.

By default, the browse object is set to Page. Clicking the Previous or Next button performs Page Up or Page Down actions. When the default object type is active, the browse buttons (Up and Down) are black. When a non-default object type is active, the browse buttons change to blue.

For example, click the Select Browse Object button and choose Browse by Table. If you hear an error beep, that means that the current document does not contain any tables between the insertion point and the end of the document. Nonetheless, the browse buttons turn blue, and they now *mean* Previous Table and Next Table.

If you ever click a browse button and don't get the expected default Page Up/Page Down behavior, take a look at the color. If the button is blue, then that's the problem. To reset the browse behavior to the default, click the Select Browse Object button and choose Page.

What makes this a little tricky is that there are ways other than clicking that button to change browse behavior. For example, if you perform a search, the browse buttons now become Find Previous and Find Next. If you perform a Go To and go to the next field, then Previous Field/ Next Field become the browse actions. Hover your mouse pointer over each of the 12 object types to explore the possibilities. If you keep these objects in mind, then this feature can become a tool, rather than just an annoyance.

Note

One browse feature is Browse by Edits. Word remembers the current and previous three places where editing occurred (anything that changes the status of the document from saved to *dirty). Hence, when Browse by Edits is the browse behavior, the Previous and Next buttons cycle the insertion point among those four locations.**

The Shift+F5 keystroke (assigned to the GoBack command) performs the same action as the Previous button when the browse object is set to Browse by Edits. ∎

*When a document contains a savable change — one that will actually change the contents of the file when saved to disk — it is marked by Word as dirty. Some actions make a file dirty, and some don't. If you simply press Page Up or Page Down, or otherwise scroll around in the document, that does not affect the saved/dirty status. If you type a character, perform some formatting, or change a document's properties, however, that will make the file dirty, requiring a save to preserve those changes. Typing a character and immediately deleting it also makes a file dirty.

Keyboard

With Word 2007 and 2010 come some keyboard changes from Word 2003 and earlier. Perhaps surprisingly, as you'll learn, most legacy keystrokes still work, even though Word's menus are gone.

What works differently? One of my favorite keystrokes is Ctrl+Shift+S, which in Word 2003 and earlier moved the focus to the Style control on the Formatting toolbar. Given that there is no Formatting toolbar in Word 2010 and that there is no comparable Style control on the ribbon, Ctrl+Shift+S pretty much has to be at least a little different. If you still have Word 2003, open it, press Ctrl+Shift+S, tap the first letter of a style that's not currently selected, and then use the down-arrow key to go to the style you had in mind. Press Enter to apply the style.

Now try the same thing in Word 2010. Pressing Ctrl+Shift+S activates the Apply Styles task pane, and the keystrokes otherwise seem to work the same way. However, the Apply Styles task pane doesn't go away. It stays there — in your way, more likely than not.

How do you dismiss the Apply Styles task pane? Well, you could click its X, although that defeats the shortcut key non-mouse advantage of Ctrl+Shift+S. Unfortunately, pressing the Esc key simply returns the focus to the document without dismissing Apply Styles. To dismiss it (as well as any other task pane) using the keyboard, press Ctrl+space, C. Note that for this to work, the task pane must have the focus, so you might need to press Ctrl+Shift+S and then Ctrl+space, C to get it to work. Did I mention that not *all* changes are improvements?

Other Built-In Keystrokes

Word boasts a broad array of keystrokes to make writing faster. If you're a fast touch-typist, you might not care to have to reach for the mouse to make a word bold or italic. You might not want to reach for the mouse to create a hyperlink. If you've been using Word for a long time, you very likely have memorized many keystrokes (some of them that apply only to Word, and others not) that make your typing life easier. You'll be happy to know that most of those keystrokes still work in Word 2010.

Rather than provide a list of all of the key assignments in Word, I'm going to show you how to make one yourself. Start by pressing Alt+F8. In the Macro Name field, type **listcommands**, and press Enter. In the List Commands dialog box, choose Current Keyboard Settings, and press Enter.

Presto! You now have a table showing all of Word's current keyboard settings. If you've reassigned any built-in keystrokes to other commands or macros, your own assignments are shown in place of Word's built-in assignments. If you've redundantly assigned any keystrokes, all assignments will be shown. For example, Word assigns Alt+F8 to ToolsMacro. I also assigned Ctrl+Shift+O to it. Therefore, my ListCommands table shows both assignments. The table also shows those assignments and commands you haven't customized.

Tip

If you want a list of Word's default built-in assignments, open Word in safe mode (hold down the control key as Word is starting and then click Yes) and repeat this exercise. ∎

Office 2003 Menu Keystrokes

One of Microsoft's aims was to assign as many legacy menu keystrokes as possible to the equivalent commands in Word 2007 and 2010, so if you're used to pressing Alt+I, B to choose Insert ➪ Break in Word 2003, you'll be glad to know it still works. So does Alt+O, P for Format ➪ Paragraph. Liking this so far, are you? Great!

Now try Alt+H, A for Help ➪ About. It doesn't work. In fact, none of the Help shortcuts work, because that Alt+H shortcut is reserved for the Ribbon's Home tab. Some others don't work either, but at least Microsoft tried.

Some key combinations can't be assigned because the corresponding commands have been eliminated. There are very few in that category. Some other legacy menu assignments haven't been made in Word 2010 because Microsoft is grappling with some conflicts between how the new and old keyboard models work. There are, for example, some problems with Alt+F because that keystroke is used to select the File tab. For now at least, Microsoft has resolved to use a different approach for the Alt+F assignments. Press Alt+I and then press Alt+F to compare the different approaches.

Custom Keystrokes

You can also make your own keyboard assignments. To get a sneak peak, choose File ➪ Options ➪ Customize Ribbon ➪ Customize.

Tip

If you're a keyboard aficionado, to simplify your life, assign Alt+K (it's unassigned by default) to the ToolsCustomizeKeyboard command. Then, whenever you see something you want to assign, press Alt+K and you're off and running. To assign Alt+K, choose File ➪ Options ➪ Customize Ribbon ➪ Customize. Set Categories to All Commands. In Commands, tap the T key to skip to the Ts. Find and select ToolCustomizeKeyboard. Click Press New Keyboard Shortcut Key, and then press Alt+K (or whatever other assignment you might find preferable or more memorable). Make sure that Save Changes In is set to Normal.dotm (assuming you don't want it saved somewhere else). Click Assign, and then click Close, and click Cancel to dismiss the Word Options dialog box. If you've told Word to prompt before saving changes in Normal.dotm, then make sure you say Yes to saving this change (when prompted). ∎

Views

To expand the ways of working with documents, Word offers many different environments you can use, called *views*. For reading and performing text edits on long documents with a minimum of UI (user interface) clutter, you can use Full Screen Reading view. For composing documents and reviewing text and basic text formatting, you can choose a fast-display view called *Draft view*.

For working with documents containing graphics, equations, and other non-text elements, where document design is a strong consideration, there's Print Layout view. If the destination of the document is online (Internet or intranet), Word's Web Layout view removes paper-oriented screen elements, enabling you to view documents as they would appear in a web browser.

For organizing and managing a document, Word's Outline view provides powerful tools that enable you to move whole sections of the document around without having to copy, cut, and paste. An extension of Outline view, Master Document view enables you to split large documents into separate components for easier management and workgroup sharing.

Draft View Is the New Normal View

If you're someone accustomed to working with Word 2003 in Normal view, you might be alarmed to see the view options in Word 2010. Shown in Figure 4-21, they include Print Layout, Full Screen Reading, Web Layout, Outline, and Draft. Where's Normal?

FIGURE 4-21

Word 2003's Normal view is called *Draft view* in Word 2010.

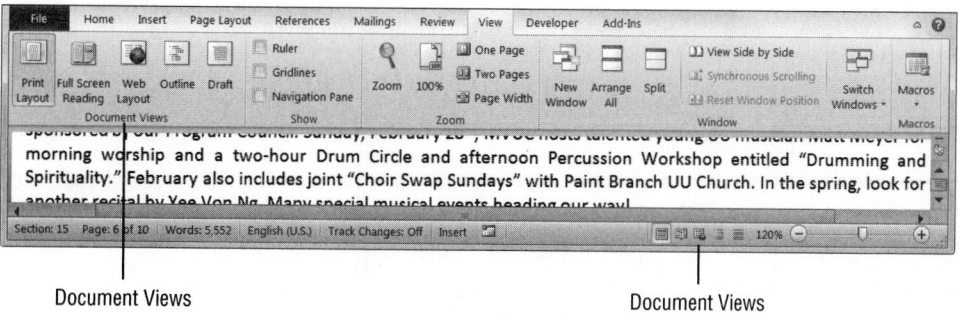

Document Views   Document Views

Normal as a view name is history. What was Normal is now called *Draft*. Internally, though, when you click on Draft either in the View tab of the Ribbon or on the status bar, Word still uses the ViewNormal command. You can confirm this with the following tip.

Tip

You can determine Word's name for most Ribbon or status bar-based commands with a simple keystroke and a click. First, switch to Print Layout view so that the Draft view command will have an effect. Next, press Ctrl+Alt and the plus (+) sign on the number pad. This turns the mouse pointer into the cloverleaf pattern shown in Figure 4-22. Use that pointer to click (just about) any tool. Word responds by displaying the Customize Keyboard dialog. The Commands box displays the actual command's name, as shown in Figure 4-23. When in cloverleaf mode, Word returns to normal when the Customize Keyboard dialog box is closed, or you can hasten the return to normal by pressing the Esc key. ■

FIGURE 4-22

The cloverleaf mouse pointer indicates that the ToolsCustomizeKeyboardShortcut command has been activated.

⌘

FIGURE 4-23

Cloverleaf mode (the result of the ToolsCustomizeKeyboardShortcut command) displays the next Word command or macro you perform in Word; it responds to mouse and keyboard actions.

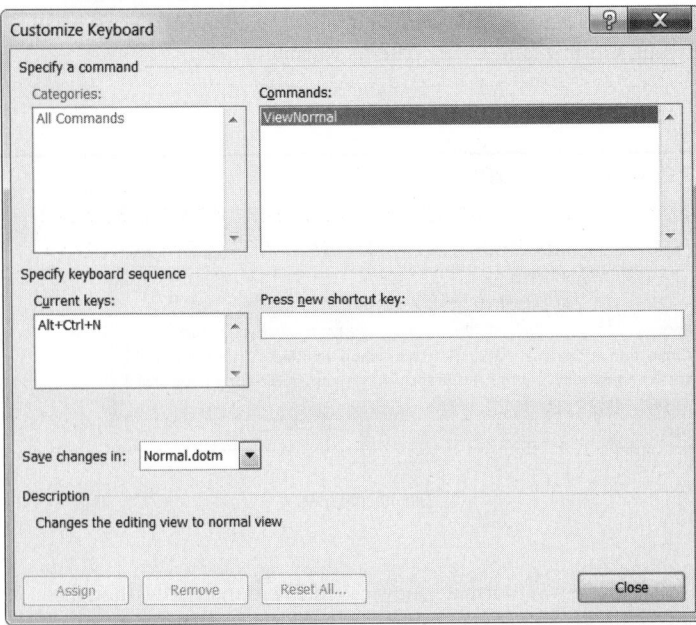

If Word is really running ViewNormal, what happened to Draft view? It's still there. In Word's Options dialog box, choose Advanced. Near the bottom of the Show Document Content options, notice the option to Use Draft Font in Draft and Outline Views. You can also choose the font and point size to use for Draft.

Tip

When you need to distinguish among an uppercase *i* (*I*), a lowercase *L* (*l*), the number one (1), and the vertical line segment (|, usually typed with Shift+\ on most U.S. keyboards), the font that I've found makes the distinction clearest is Comic Sans. It's also a very comfortable and readable font, its non-professional-sounding name notwithstanding. If after applying Comic Sans you're still uncertain as to what's what, try toggling the case. Properly distinguishing among these characters, as well as between 0 (zero) and *O* (capital *o*), can make a world of difference when you are trying to convey part numbers, serial numbers, user names, and passwords. ∎

For editors and writers, Normal view was the workhorse view before Word 2007. It enabled them to focus on just words. When you coupled it with wrapping text to fit the window, you could take off the reading glasses and zoom to any magnification you liked. You didn't have to monkey around with the horizontal scroll bar or bothersome floating pictures to see what was written. It was also faster because its simplicity required less computer memory. You could let the layout editors worry about the placement of pictures and other formatting nuances. If you're used to thinking Normal view, then in Word 2010 think Draft view with the Draft Font view turned off.

If you plan to toggle between Draft and Draft Font views very often, you should know that Word has a built-in ViewDraft command that toggles the Use Draft Font setting on and off. To make it more accessible, you might either assign it to a keyboard shortcut or put it onto the Quick Access Toolbar (QAT) for ready access. In the QAT customization dialog box, it's in the All Commands list.

Caution

If you do use the View ➪ Draft command, be advised that font and point size changes will not be reflected in what you see onscreen. This can be good if the original is a legal contract written in 4-point type. It can be bad, however, if you don't toggle out of Draft mode before sending a .doc file to someone else for review, particularly if you've been careless with the font and point-size formatting. ∎

Print Layout

If Normal view (now Draft view) was the workhorse view for Word 2003, Print Layout is destined to be the workhorse view for Word 2010. That's because one of Word 2010's strongest features, Live Preview, does not work in Draft view. Live Preview works only in Print Layout and Web Layout.

Full Screen Reading

Full Screen Reading view is similar to Word 2003's Reading Layout view. Shown in Figure 4-24, the Word 2010 view uses more of the screen than the comparable Word 2003 view did. By default, Reading mode does not permit editing. Often, this is exactly what you want. But not always. Switch a document into Full Screen Reading view and peruse the different options.

Tip

Full Screen Reading view offers a variety of ways to scroll up and down: Page Down/Page Up, Space/Shift+Space, Enter/Shift+Enter, Right/Left arrow keys, Down/Up arrow keys, the Next/Previous graphic controls at the bottom of the window, and the scroll wheel on your mouse. ■

FIGURE 4-24

Word 2010's Full Screen Reading view features several view options.

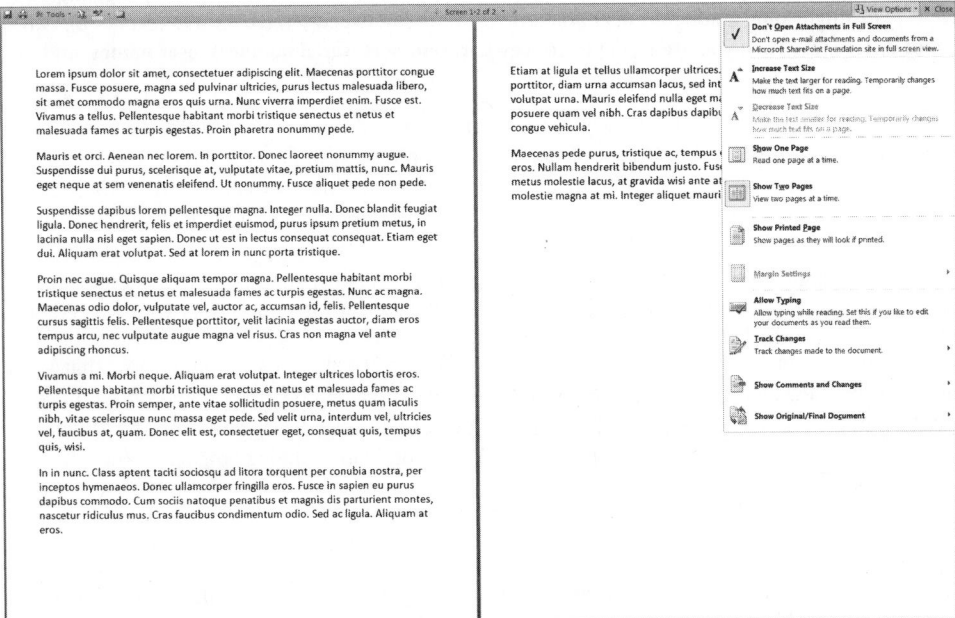

Web Layout

Web Layout is designed for composing and reviewing documents that will be viewed online rather than printed. Hence, information such as page and section numbers is excluded from the status bar. If the document contains hyperlinks, they are displayed underlined by default, as shown in Figure 4-25. Background colors, pictures, and textures are also displayed.

Outline (Master Document Tools)

The final distinct Word view is Outline. Outlining is one of Word's most powerful and least-used tools for writing and organizing your documents. To avail yourself of this tremendous resource, the easiest way is simply to use Word's Heading styles. Heading levels one through nine are available through styles named *Heading 1* through *Heading 9*. You don't need to use all nine levels — most users find that the first three or four are adequate for most structured documents. If your document is organized with the built-in heading levels, then a wonderful world of document organization is at your fingertips.

FIGURE 4-25

Web Layout suppresses paper-oriented information such as page and section numbers, and includes web-oriented features such as underlined hyperlinks and background colors and textures.

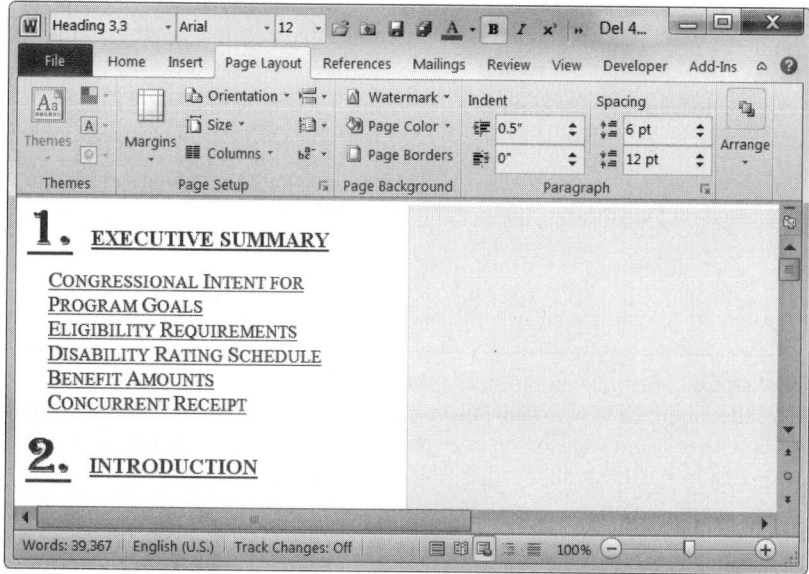

As suggested by the title of this section, Outline view has a split personality, of sorts. As an outline manager, this view can be used on any document with heading styles that are tied to outline levels. (If you don't want to use Word's built-in Heading styles, you can use other styles and assign them to different outline levels.)

Outline view's other personality is the Master Document manager. Compare the two Ribbons shown in Figure 4-26. Both say *Outlining*, yet the lower Ribbon contains additional tools. To display the additional tools, click Show Document.

FIGURE 4-26

Click Show Document to display the Master Document tools.

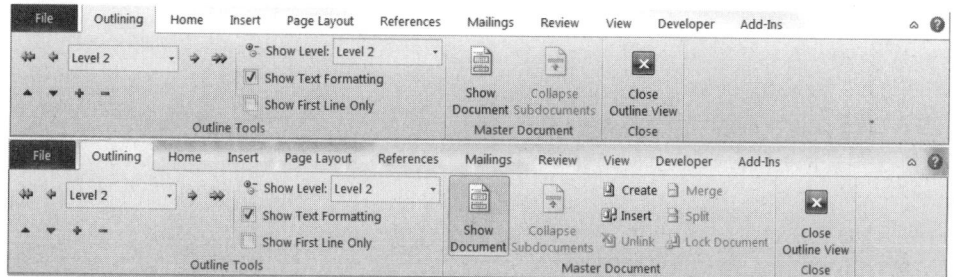

A little warning about the Master Document feature: This is an extremely powerful document control feature for users who are working on parts of the same document. It provides a way to carefully control the checking out and checking in of document parts, as well as to manage problems inherent in working with very large documents.

In previous versions of Word, the Master Document feature was quite unstable, leading to the adage: "There are two kinds of master document users: those whose documents are corrupted, and those whose documents will soon be corrupted." Is this harsh assessment still true, or does the existence of a Word document format based on XML relegate those concerns to history?

The jury is in: the Master Document feature in Word 2010 remains word processing's answer to Conan the Destroyer. Use it only if you enjoy pain and frustration.

Summary

In this chapter, you've seen a variety of ways to start a Word 2010 document as well as several navigation techniques that might be new to you. You've also explored how to modify Word's view to fit your work style and needs, and some of the finer points about saving, converting, and publishing in Word 2010. Finally, putting it all together, you should now have no problem doing the following:

- Creating a blank file or one using a template
- Saving a file
- Converting Word 2003 documents to Word 2010, and vice versa
- Impressing your friends with cool navigation trick and tips
- Viewing your work in different ways for different kinds of writing and editing

Formatting 101: Font/ Character Formatting

O ne of the more difficult conceptual hurdles in understanding Word is the way formatting is conceived. Some people think about formatting as a stream. You turn it on here, and it remains on until you turn it off later.

However, Word's formatting *mindset* is not stream-oriented — it's object-oriented. Rather than turn formatting on in one place and off in another in order to format a block of text, you format objects such as letters, words, paragraphs, tables, pictures, and so on. However, saying the O word (*object*) causes some people's eyes to glaze over.

Another way to think about formatting is in units. Formatting can be applied to any unit you can select. The smallest unit that can be formatted is a single character. Discrete units larger than characters are words, sentences, paragraphs, document sections, and the whole document.

The Big Picture

Word has four levels of formatting: *character, paragraph, section,* and *document.* Things such as bold, italic, points, and superscript are called *character* or *font formatting* and can be applied to as little as a single character. I'll talk about the other levels of formatting in later chapters.

Personally, I don't like the adjective "font" formatting, because most people — including me — think of fonts as things like Times New Roman, Arial, and Tahoma. For me, "character formatting" is a lot clearer and less confusing, but because Word's Home tab on the Ribbon has a group called *Font,* as shown in Figure 5-1, we're kind of stuck with that terminology.

We're all stuck with another term too: *text-level formatting*, which really means the same thing as font and character formatting. It helps, however, to think in terms of *character* formatting, as a character is the smallest thing you can format in Word.

Much, but not all, of the character (or font) formatting is accessible from the Home Ribbon's Font group.

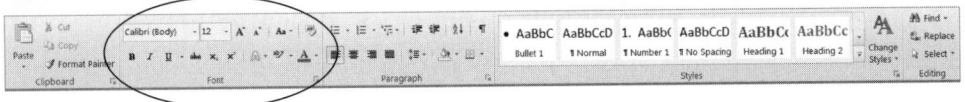

Note

OK. I lied. Technically, the smallest thing you can "format" is a point between two characters, but the word "format" is debatable in this case. To split hairs, you can insert a bookmark at a point so that no characters are enclosed. Is that formatting? I don't think so, but somebody else might. ■

Note also that the Font group on the Home tab does not contain access to all character-level formatting. Language (English, English UK, Spanish, etc.), which can be applied down to a single character, is not shown there. Moreover, the Font group contains case (upper, lower, title, etc.), which isn't formatting at all. This type of capitalization is distinct from small caps and all caps, both of which are considered character formatting.

Styles and Character/Font Formatting

A few Word versions ago, possibly while many users weren't watching, Microsoft added a new type of style to Word. Before that there was just one type of style — the paragraph style — and styles could be applied only to a whole paragraph. It soon became clear, however, that a more flexible, sophisticated style was needed — one that could be applied to characters within a paragraph.

The *character style* was born. Using this new invention, it was suddenly possible to create styles for formatting book titles, article titles, names, phone numbers, Internet links — you name it.

Later in this book (Chapter 7) you'll find an entire chapter dedicated to styles, but to understand character formatting, there's a little you need to know at the outset, so please bear with me for another couple of paragraphs.

Even if you yourself never apply a style using Word's vast array of formatting tools, two styles are always in effect: a paragraph style and a character style. To demonstrate this, display the Styles pane by clicking the Styles Dialog Box Launcher at the bottom-right corner of the Styles group on the Home tab. Then click the middle icon at the bottom of the Styles task pane to display the Style Inspector, shown in Figure 5-2. You can dismiss the Styles pane if it's distracting.

FIGURE 5-2

Use the Style Inspector when you want to fully examine the styles and direct formatting in use (direct formatting is identified by the word *Plus* in the Style Inspector).

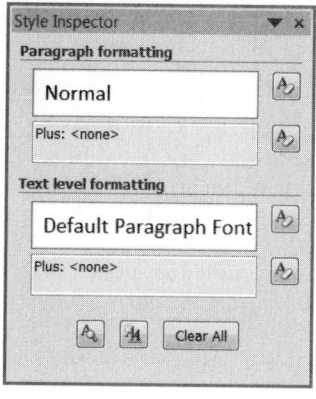
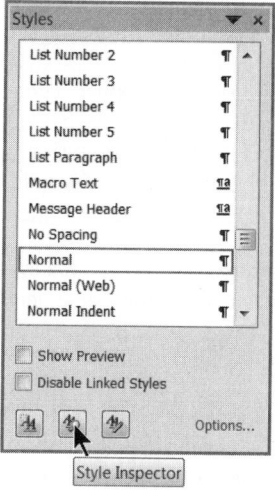

Here the two styles applied are Normal (the default paragraph style) and Default Paragraph Font (the default character style for Normal). The latter is the name of the Normal style's default character style.

Style versus Direct

I just went through that whole rigmarole so that I could explain that you have two ways to apply character formatting. You can use a *style* to apply character formatting, or you can apply character formatting directly. As you're typing along, it's really quite easy to apply bold, italic, or underlining to text. That's called *direct formatting*, and often there's no reason for you to format any other way. After all, the goal is to create a functional document in as short a time as possible.

Given that creating and applying styles involves more thought, preparation, and work than using direct formatting, it would appear that using direct formatting works better for my twin goals of speed and functionality. However, a shortcut is only as good as the time it saves you. If it ends up taking more time, then it wasn't really a shortcut at all.

For example, suppose that each time I need to type a book title I press Ctrl+B (for bold), type the book title, and then press Ctrl+B again to toggle bold off. That doesn't seem too onerous, right? Suppose my editors now tell me that they don't like book titles formatted that way. Instead, they want me to use bold small caps. Now I have to change the book title references so that they match the editors' requirements. If all book titles and only book titles were formatted as bold, I could use Word's Replace feature to simply replace bold with bold and small caps, but what if

I've applied bold to something other than a book title? (The chances are good that I have!) Now I'm left carefully plodding through the document looking for things that look like book titles.

Or worse, suppose I need to correct the formatting error not in just one document file, but in dozens of files? I have a lot of work to do, right? That Ctrl+B shortcut doesn't seem like a very good shortcut anymore, does it?

If, instead, each time I wanted a book title I had applied a character style named *Book Title*, I'd be in much better shape. That way I could simply modify the Book Title style, and all of my book titles would obediently change. Even if the formatting "error" were propagated over dozens of different documents, I could change the definition of the style in the template on which those documents are based, use the Automatically Update Document Styles feature, and I'd be done.

The commandment is this: *If the formatting is something you will need to repeatedly apply to certain categories of text (such as book titles, programming commands, jargon, etc.), create a character style and use it.*

If, conversely, the use is ad hoc and not something for which you'll have a recurring need, then go ahead and use direct formatting. For example, when I'm writing a letter or memo and want to use bold for emphasis, I use direct formatting. When I'm writing a formal report and am formatting the name of a journal and a journal article, I use a style.

Tip

To make using styles less onerous, you can assign keyboard shortcuts to them. From Word Options, select Customize Ribbon in the list at the left and choose Customize. Set Categories to Styles. Choose the style, click Press New Shortcut Key, press the desired key(s) (i.e., the exact combination you want to assign, such as Alt+9, Ctrl+Shift+F7, etc.), and then click Assign ⇨ Close. Don't forget to click Assign! ■

Character Formatting

There are at least six ways of directly applying various kinds of character formatting:

- Using the Font group on the Home tab of the Ribbon
- Using the Font dialog box (Ctrl+D or Ctrl+Shift+F, or click the Font Dialog Box Launcher)
- Using the Mini toolbar (hover the mouse over selected text)
- Using shortcut keys
- Using the Font group or components placed on the Quick Access Toolbar (QAT)
- Using the Language tool on the status bar

In this section I'll describe these methods and try to give you a sense of which ones to use. A lot depends on your working style, but your choice can also depend on what you happen to be doing. On any given day I'll probably use at least five of the six methods.

Formatting Techniques

To apply character formatting, you have three basic options:

- **Stream Method.** Apply formatting before you start typing a word or passage, and then turn it off when you're done. For example, click the Bold tool, type a word, and then click the Bold tool again.
- **Selection Method.** Select the text you want formatted and then apply the formatting.
- **Whole-Word Method.** Click anywhere in a word and then choose the desired formatting.

Note

The whole-word method is settings-dependent. It will work by default, but it will not work if you've turned off When Selecting, Automatically Select Entire Word in the Editing Options section of Word Options ⇨ Advanced. ■

It would be redundant to repeat the basic steps for each and every formatting type. The techniques described here apply to all character formatting described in this chapter.

Repeat Formatting (F4)

A tremendous time-saver in Word is the Repeat Formatting command, invoked by the F4 key. Actually, F4 will repeat typing and many other actions too, but I find it most useful for repeating formatting.

Suppose, for example, that you're scanning a newsletter looking for people's names, which need to be made bold. There's *John Smith*, so you select his name and press Ctrl+B. Thereafter, however, it might be faster to position one hand on the mouse and the other on the F4 key. Click *Jane*; press F4. Click *Doe*; press F4. Or click to select *Jane Doe* as a phrase, and then press F4. The F4 key enables you to temporarily forget about pressing Ctrl+B, right-clicking, or traveling to the top of the Word menu in search of a formatting tool.

Now let's try something else. Click on a word and press Ctrl+B to make it bold. Now press Ctrl+I. Now the text is bold and italic. Click on another word and press F4. It's only italic! That's because F4 repeats only the most recent formatting (or other action).

Note that F4 and Ctrl+Y both do the same thing. Which you use is your choice. Many prefer F4 because it can be pressed with one finger. Others prefer Ctrl+Y because it doesn't involve as much of a stretch as F4.

Tip

If you have multiple or compound character formatting to repeatedly apply to a non-style-formatted series of words or selections, use the Font dialog box instead of individual commands. When you use the Font dialog box, all changes applied when you click OK become a single formatting event to the F4 key, so F4 can now apply multiple types of character formatting all at once. ■

Copy Formatting

Sometimes, the moment for using F4 has passed, yet you're still left needing to reapply compound formatting. I'm assuming that for whatever reason you're not using a character style. Be that as it may, there are two common methods for copying formatting: the Format Painter and the Copy Formatting keystroke. Note that these tools aren't limited to character formatting. They'll work with many other kinds of formatting as well.

Format Painter

To use the Format Painter, click or select the item whose formatting you want to copy. If you want to clone that formatting just once, click the Format Painter in the Clipboard group on the Home tab of the Ribbon, shown in Figure 5-3. If you want to apply that formatting multiple times, double-click the Format Painter.

FIGURE 5-3

Use the Format Painter in the Clipboard group to copy formatting.

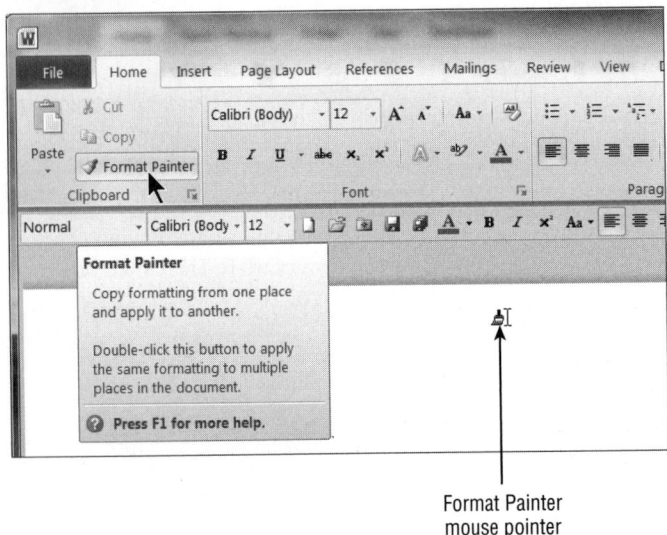

Format Painter
mouse pointer

Note that the mouse pointer turns into a paintbrush.

Honestly! That's what it's supposed to be!

Next, if you're copying formatting to a whole word, click the word you want formatted. Presto! If you're copying to any other group of characters, use the mouse pointer to select the destination text. If you double-clicked the Format Painter, continue this until you're done. Press Esc or click the Format Painter again to exit Format Painting mode.

Keyboard Method

If you don't care for clicking the Format Painter button, that's perfectly OK. You'll need to know about two keystrokes:

- **Ctrl+Shift+C.** Copy Format.
- **Ctrl+Shift+V.** Paste Format.

This works very much like the Format Painter. Click in or select the text whose formatting you want to copy, and press Ctrl+Shift+C. Observe the mouse pointer. It's the Format Painter pointer! Now, move to or select the text onto which you want the formatting copied, and press Ctrl+Shift+V. Note that there is no keyboard equivalent for the multi-copy method (double-clicking on the Format Painter), but you can combine the two methods, initiating the process by double-clicking the Format Painter and then ending it using Ctrl+Shift+V.

Clear Formatting

There are several degrees of clearing formatting. Here I'll talk about two of them:

- Clear direct character formatting (ResetChar)
- Clear all formatting (ClearAllFormatting)

The first is the venerable Ctrl+Spacebar command known and loved by many in every version of Word they can remember. It's also a widely misunderstood command. This command does not remove all character formatting. It removes all *direct* character formatting. So if the selected text's formatting all comes from styles applied to the text — regardless of how bizarre or compound the formatting might be — Ctrl+Spacebar will have no effect whatsoever.

For example, when you apply the Heading 1 style to a section of text, that text becomes bold. Ctrl+Spacebar can't touch that bold formatting since it was applied through the style rather than via Ctrl+B or the Bold tool. If you use direct formatting to italicize a word in an otherwise non-italicized heading, however, now Ctrl+Spacebar can remove it.

The second type of formatting removal is completely new to Word 2007 and 2010. It is accessible via the Clear Formatting tool on the Home tab of the Ribbon, shown in Figure 5-4. This command is quite different from Ctrl+Spacebar.

Using this new command is the functional equivalent of copying a selection to the Clipboard and then using Paste Special ⇨ Unformatted Text to paste it back into the document. It strips out all formatting.

The Font Group

The Font group is shown in Figure 5-5. The Font group is compressed or expanded depending on the width of the current Word window. In its full glory, the Font group can display up to 15 separate tools (not including the Font Dialog Box Launcher, which I'll talk about in a moment).

FIGURE 5-4

The Clear Formatting tool is actually misplaced in the Ribbon. It affects not only character/font formatting, but paragraph and style formatting as well.

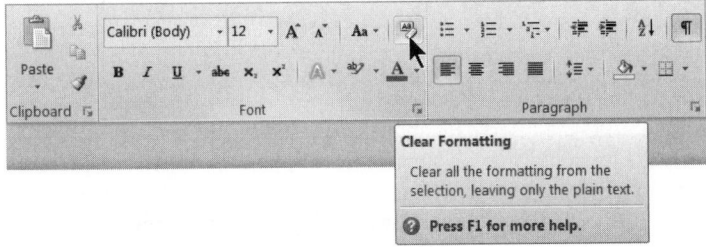

FIGURE 5-5

The Font group is Word's *discoverable* way of applying character formatting.

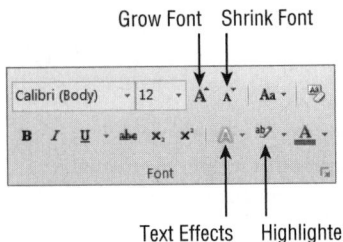

Four of the Font tools feature Live Preview:

- Font (e.g., typeface name, such as Calibri)
- Font/Point Size
- Highlight color
- Text color

As shown in Figure 5-6, Live Preview shows you the results of the selected (but not yet applied) formatting. Two of the Live Preview controls — Font and Font/Point Size — can be rolled up and out of the way, as shown in Figure 5-6. The other two cannot.

As shown in Figure 5-7, there's also a sixteenth control — the Font Dialog Box Launcher. The Font dialog box is nearly identical to its counterpart from Word 2007 — except that Word 2007's Character Spacing tab is now the Advanced tab in Word 2010. If you upgraded directly from Word 2003, you'll also notice that Text Effects have been moved from the Font tab to the Advanced tab and are quite different from the Word 2003 feature. Word 2010's new Text Effects are closely tied to the new implementation of WordArt.

FIGURE 5-6

Dots at the bottom of a Live Preview control indicate that it can be rolled up and out of the way.

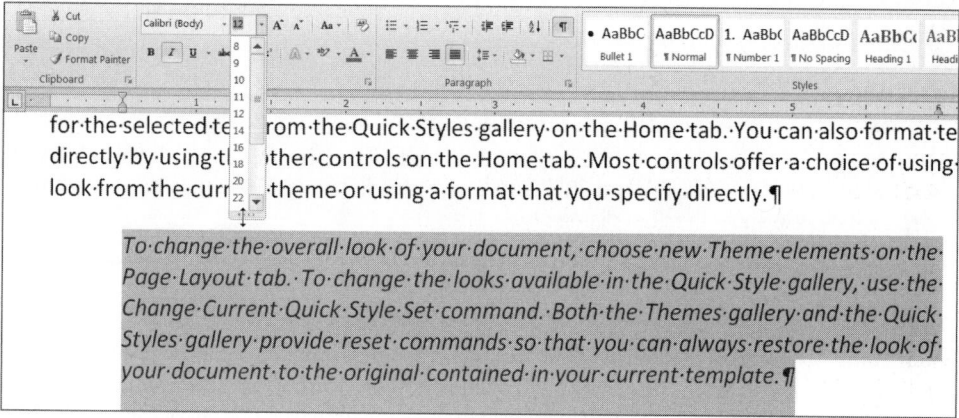

FIGURE 5-7

Use the Font Dialog Box Launcher to display the nearly full-service dialog box.

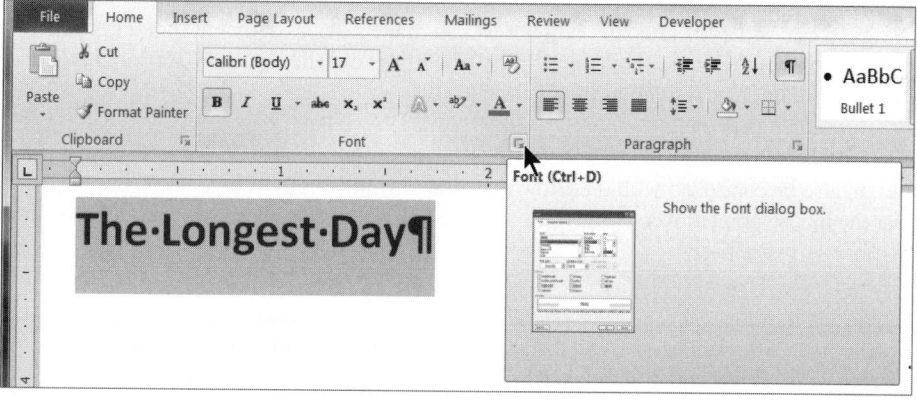

Some of the icons in the Font group might seem a bit obscure and indistinct. Hover the mouse pointer over each of the controls to see what it does. Notice that for many of the controls, if shortcut keys exist, they are indicated in the Enhanced ScreenTip. However, this is not the end of the story. Some tools, for whatever reason, might not show the shortcuts. Jump ahead to "Character-Formatting Shortcut Keys" later in this chapter if you're just dying to know what's assigned to what.

Typeface or Font

Some call it *font*, some call it *typeface*. Some skirt the nomenclature issue by simply saying what typeface or font they want (Times New Roman, Arial, etc.). Whatever you call it, it's key to a document's appearance.

Upgrade Note

In Word 2003, you could move the focus to the Font tool in the toolbar by pressing Ctrl+Shift+F. That precise functionality no longer exists in Word 2007 and later. Instead, that keystroke now does the same thing as Ctrl+D, which is to show the Font dialog box.

Font Size

Font or Point Size controls the height of the font, generally measured in points. A *point* is $1/72$ of an inch, so 12 points would be $12/72$ (or $1/6$) of an inch. For Word, a font set's point size is the vertical distance from the top of the highest ascending character to the bottom of the lowest descending character.

You aren't limited to the range of sizes you see in the Font tab. Word can go as low as 1 point and as high as 1,638 points. Plus, you can set the height in increments of half a point. Hence, a point size of 1,637.5 is perfectly valid.

As with typeface, Word 2007 and later will not let you make a key assignment that takes you directly to the exposed Font Size control. While Ctrl+Shift+P did that in Word 2003 and earlier, Ctrl+Shift+P now simply takes you to the Font dialog box, where *Size* is highlighted.

Grow/Shrink Tools and Keyboard Shortcuts

Text size can also be controlled with the Grow Font and Shrink Font tools (refer to Figure 5-5). If you hover the mouse pointer over these, you'll also learn that they both have shortcuts, Ctrl+Shift+> and Ctrl+Shift+<, respectively.

Note

The ScreenTip actually says Ctrl+> and Ctrl+<, and technically that's right because > and < are a shifted period and comma, respectively. Personally, though, I'd rather have you understand exactly what keys to press than stand on ceremony. ■

If you click the drop-down arrow next to the Font Size tool, you'll notice that the font sizes listed do not consistently increase by twos. Instead, they go from 8 to 12 in increments of one, then from 12 to 28 in increments of two, and then leap to 36, 48, and 72. The Grow and Shrink Font tools follow the listed increments.

If you want a finer degree of control (e.g., when you're trying to make text as large as possible without spilling onto an additional page), you should know about two additional default shortcut keys: Ctrl+[and Ctrl+]. These two commands shrink or enlarge the selected characters by 1 point. The extra granularity often is just what you need to find the largest possible font you can fit inside a given space, such as a page, table, or textbox.

Color

Word has three color settings that can be applied at the character level:

- **Text Color.** The color of the characters themselves
- **Shading.** The color of the background immediately behind the text
- **Highlighting.** The electronic equivalent of those neon-colored felt markers you use to annoy people who ask you to read things you don't want to read

Text Color

Text color is pretty self-explanatory, except when it's not. Most of us know what red, black, and blue are, but what is automatic? Automatic can be black or white, and is based on the shading. If the shading is so dark that black text can't be read without difficulty, Word automatically switches the display color to white.

Shading

We'll talk about design considerations in a later chapter. For now, note a few things about shading that sometimes escape notice. Looking at the Home tab on the Ribbon and the placement of Shading (second from the right under Paragraph), you might be tempted to believe that shading is paragraph-level formatting. Indeed, it sure acts that way. With nothing selected, Shading acts on the entire current paragraph. (You'll learn more about this later.)

However, if you select a single word or character, Shading suddenly acts like a character-formatting attribute. Well, that's what it is. Because people seldom vary the shading within any given paragraph, it is treated as a paragraph attribute by Word's interface. And yet, just like Font, Font/Point Size, Bold, and Italic, shading is a character attribute.

As shown in Figure 5-8, shading also affects the display of text color. In this case, the shading color is maroonish, which you can't tell in the printed version of this book. Keep the character aspect of shading in mind when we look at the Font dialog box, coming up shortly.

FIGURE 5-8

Despite its placement in the Home tab of the Ribbon, shading can be applied to a selection of characters.

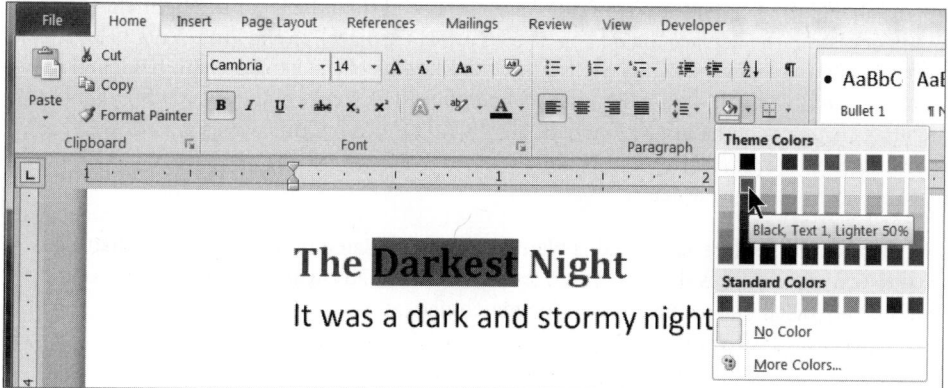

Highlighting

The Text Highlight Color control — more generally known as the *highlighter* — is shown in Figure 5-5. It actually has four modes of operation. Most people are aware of one mode or another, but not all four.

One method is to select text and then click the highlighter. This is the method that most users are aware of. It's pretty effective, but it might not reflect the actual highlighting process.

A second method is to turn the highlighter on by clicking the Text Highlight Color tool, and then to use the mouse to select areas you want highlighted. The highlighter mouse pointer stays active until you click the Text Highlight Color tool again, or until you press the Esc key.

A third method can be used to apply highlighting to all occurrences of a given word or phrase in a document, using the most recently applied highlighting color. Press Ctrl+F to open the Find dialog box. Type the word or phrase of interest, and then choose Reading Highlight ⇨ Highlight All, as shown in Figure 5-9.

FIGURE 5-9

Use Find to apply a *reading highlight* to every occurrence of a word or phrase in your document.

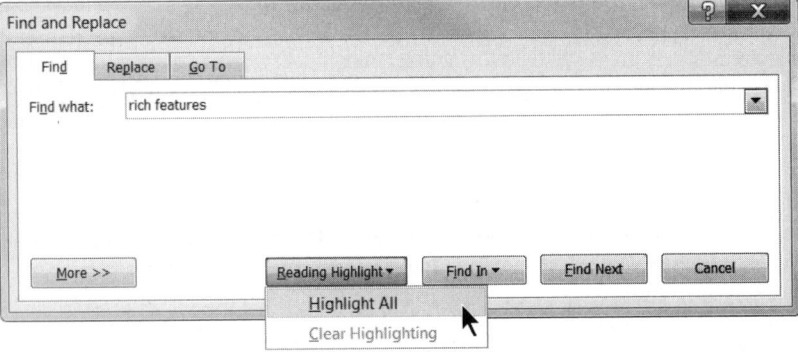

A fourth highlighting method is one I find a bit more useful than the Reading Highlight feature. It works from the Replace dialog box. Press Ctrl+H (Replace). In the Find What field, type the word or phrase you want to highlight. Clear the contents of the Replace With field, and in Replace's lower-left corner, choose Format ⇨ Highlight. Click Replace All to apply highlighting to all occurrences of the Find What text. Highlighting inserted this way is more robust than highlighting inserted via the Reading Highlight feature and will not disappear if you choose to manipulate highlighting manually.

Note that when the Replace With field is blank but has associated formatting, the formatting is applied to text that matches the Find What text. If both formatting and Replace With text are absent, Replace deletes all occurrences of the matching text.

You can also choose not to print highlighting. This gives you the best of both worlds. You can mark up a document for your own benefit, and then — if you wish — print it out without the highlighting. Not only is this good for keeping internal guides private, it also saves money on yellow ink. To prevent the printing (or displaying) of highlighting, choose File ⇨ Options, select Display in the list at the left, and remove the check next to Show Highlighter Marks. If you hover over the information while you're here, the tip informs you that this controls both display and printing. Click OK when you're done.

Tip

If you use the select-and-highlight method, Word undoes the selection after you apply highlighting. This can be really irritating if you use the wrong color, but if you immediately press Ctrl+Z or click Undo, Word not only undoes the highlighting, it also reselects that section of text so you can take another stab at highlighting it. ∎

Change Case

Changing case doesn't really fit in here, but that's precisely why it's included. Case is not formatting. Case is a choice of what capitalization to use — uppercase, lowercase, or some combination thereof. Why does Microsoft put it in the Font group? I don't know for sure, but it's probably because it can affect groups of characters and doesn't really fit anywhere else.

The first thing you need to know is that you cannot use any variation of this command to affect style definitions in your document. For example, you can't apply lowercase to text, turn it into a style, and then use that style to format Internet keywords. It could be useful, but this feature must await some distant version of Word as yet unannounced. (For now, you can include all caps or small caps as elements of a Word style, not that that helps with Internet addresses.)

Language

Note that Language is not included in the Font group of the Home tab. You'll also notice that it's not present in the Font dialog box either, so how do you know it's a character-formatting attribute? Two reasons: First, it can be applied to a single character in a document. Second, it can be included in a character style definition, as shown in Figure 5-10.

You set the language using the Language tool on the status bar. If you don't see it, then right-click the status bar and click to enable Language. Among the Language tool's more useful features is the Do Not Check Spelling or Grammar setting, which you can apply to text. This can be handy for technical jargon and programming keywords that you might not want checked.

Conversely, Detect Language Automatically, the last feature shown in Figure 5-11, can create issues. With that setting turned on, it's possible for text to unintentionally be tagged as some other language, resulting in large sections of text being flagged as misspelled. If the corresponding proofing tools are not installed, the text is not checked at all, even though it's not actually formatted as Do Not Check. This can leave large sections of text unintentionally unchecked. You should turn that setting off unless you actually need it. It is enabled by default!

FIGURE 5-10

Language is included among the attributes associated with a character style.

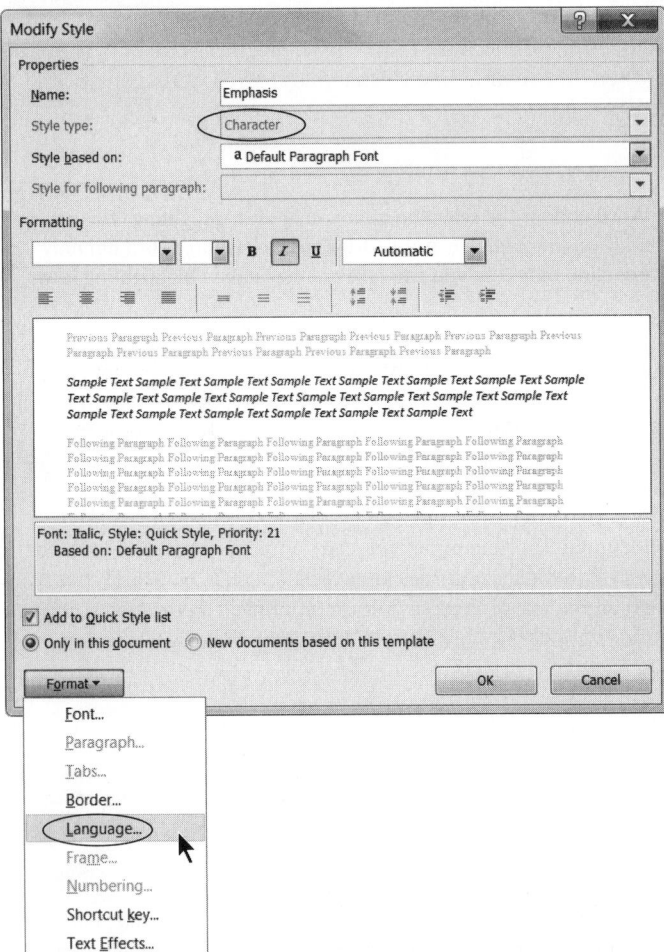

To set the default for all documents based on the current template, choose the desired language as well as the desired settings for the last two options, and then click Default. Confirm the settings by clicking Yes. Note that even though the confirmation box doesn't mention the latter two settings, they are included in the changes made to the underlying template.

The Font Dialog Box

The Font dialog box, shown in Figure 5-12, can be a useful tool when you're applying multiple character format changes at the same time. Note, however, that the Font dialog box and the Font group on the Home tab of the Ribbon do not provide identical capabilities. Not only doesn't the Font dialog provide any Live Preview at all (just the static preview box), it contains different commands and settings.

FIGURE 5-11

The Do Not Check Spelling or Grammar option can be useful for technical writers. Detect Language Automatically can cause problems for chronically bad spellers!

FIGURE 5-12

Only some of the functionality of the Font dialog's two tabs is replicated on the Home tab of the Ribbon.

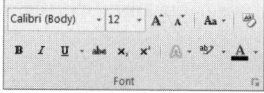

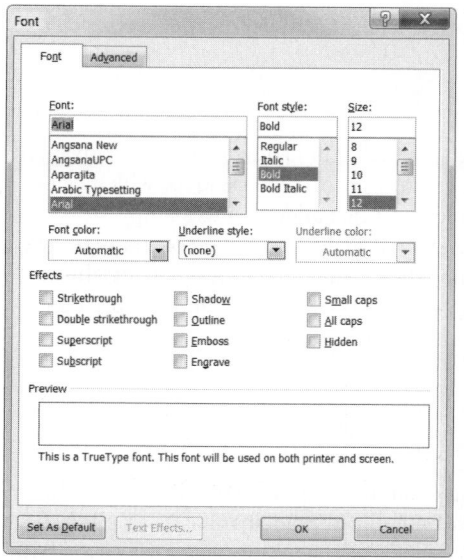

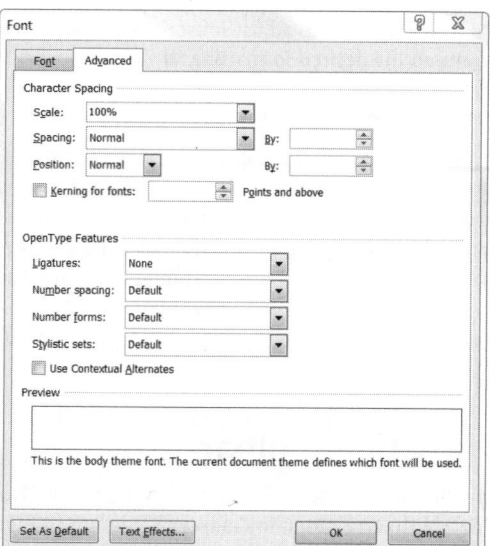

Most font attributes are largely self-explanatory. Experiment with them to see the different effects. Conspicuously missing from the Home tab of the Ribbon are the controls in the Font dialog box's Advanced tab, shown in Figure 5-12. Note the Scale and Spacing controls.

Scale is used to stretch or compress the actual characters. *Spacing* is used to expand or condense only the spacing. Scaling and spacing expansion are demonstrated on the text shown in Figure 5-13. The top sample was scaled up 150 percent. The characters and spaces were all stretched horizontally. The bottom sample was expanded by 2.8 points. An additional 2.8 points of spacing were inserted between each character. Even though both samples are nearly identical in height and width, the top sample actually looks larger.

FIGURE 5-13

Scaling and horizontal spacing can yield texts of identical length and height, but with very different appearances.

Costs and Benefits of Reinvestment

Costs and Benefits of Reinvestment

Position is used to raise or lower the selected characters by a specified number of points. Unlike spacing, which can vary by as little as 0.1 point, position's smallest gradation is 0.5 point. This tool is sometimes used to adjust subscripts and superscripts if the built-in versions don't accomplish the desired effect or you need the subscripts and superscripts to be the same size as the surrounding text.

Tip

If you have a recurring need to adjust subscripts and superscripts, you might consider creating a character style that gives you the desired formatting. ■

OpenType Features

New in Word 2010 are the OpenType features, which are shown in Figure 5-12, in the Advanced tab. Developed largely by Microsoft, OpenType is the successor to TrueType fonts, which helped in making fonts scalable. OpenType adds additional features that allow you to manipulate some of the more intricate aspects of fonts and number spacing. If you have problems aligning numbers in numbered lists, you might care to examine the OpenType features more carefully. I encourage you to consult www.microsoft.com/typography/WhatIsOpenType.mspx and www.microsoft.com/typography/otspec/ or other online sources if you want to know more about these features.

The Mini Toolbar

Yet another tool for applying formatting is the Mini toolbar. Introduced in Word 2007, this feature is fully explained in Chapter 2. Shown in Figure 5-14, the Mini toolbar has a sampling of character-formatting tools from the Home tab of the Ribbon. Unlike the ribbon tools, however, none of the Mini toolbar's tools provide Live Preview.

FIGURE 5-14

The Mini toolbar has a sampling of character-formatting tools from the Home tab of the Ribbon.

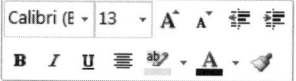

The Mini toolbar's singular but important claim to fame for many users will be its ergonomic utility. When you need something on it, it's right there, close to the text. Many of its tools are easily accessible via direct keystrokes, as you'll see in the next and final section in this chapter.

Character-Formatting Shortcut Keys

Many of the character-formatting commands discussed in this chapter are accessible via built-in keyboard shortcuts. Longtime users of Word undoubtedly have many of them committed to memory. Newcomers, however, might need a quick guide. As you navigate your way through Word 2010, keep your eyes open. Quite often, Word will show you its built-in key assignments. To make sure this happens, do the following:

- In File ⇨ Options ⇨ General, set ScreenTip Style to something other than Don't Show ScreenTips.

- In Word Options ⇨ Advanced ⇨ Display section, enable Show Shortcut Keys in ScreenTips.

Table 5-1 provides a quick reference of keyboard shortcuts related to character formatting. This list might not be exhaustive.

TABLE 5-1

Default Character-Formatting Keyboard Shortcuts

Command	Keystroke
All Caps	Ctrl+Shift+A
Bold	Ctrl+B, Ctrl+Shift+B
Copy formatting	Ctrl+Shift+C
Font dialog box	Ctrl+D, Ctrl+Shift+F
Highlighting	Alt+Ctrl+H

continued

TABLE 5-1 *(continued)*

Command	Keystroke
Hyperlink	Ctrl+K
Italics	Ctrl+I
Paste Formatting	Ctrl+Shift+V
Font/Point size	Ctrl+Shift+P
Font/Point size: decrease by 1 point	Ctrl+[
Font/Point size: decrease to next preset	Ctrl+Shift+<
Font/Point size: increase by 1 point	Ctrl+]
Font/Point size: increase to next preset	Ctrl+Shift+>
Remove non-style character formatting	Ctrl+Spacebar
Small Caps	Ctrl+Shift+K
Subscript	Ctrl+=
Superscript	Ctrl+Shift+=
Symbol font	Ctrl+Shift+Q
Toggle case of selected text	Shift+F3
Underline	Ctrl+U
Words Only Underline Style	Ctrl+W

Summary

For most of us, the most important thing about the documents we create is the choice of words. Character formatting is mostly about formatting words. In this chapter, you've seen the variety of things you can do to words and characters. You should now be able to do the following:

- Apply character formatting to a text selection of any size, from a single character up to a complete document.
- Choose whether to apply formatting directly or to use a character style.
- Decide, from among the variety of formatting tools, which one to use in any given formatting situation.
- Remove unwanted character formatting.
- Save time by using shortcut keystrokes and shortcut techniques.

6

Paragraph Formatting

Everything you type in Word resides in paragraphs. Even if you type nothing at all, in fact, every Word document — even one that you believe is completely empty — contains at least one paragraph. The key to knowing that a paragraph is present is the ubiquitous paragraph mark: ¶. If you don't see them in Word right now, perhaps you have them turned off. Pressing Ctrl+Shift+8 toggles them and the other nonprinting characters on and off.

Also called a *pilcrow* or an *alinea*, in Word the paragraph mark is the repository of paragraph formatting. Delete a paragraph's pilcrow, and you've extinguished its soul. A little dramatic? Perhaps, but Word is filled with drama. Just ask anybody who ever wrestled with numbering in Word 2000.

In this chapter I'll go into detail about paragraph formatting, and along the way I'll try to demystify aspects that seem to leave people scratching their heads. You'll also learn about the interaction between selected Word options and the nuances of paragraph formatting.

IN THIS CHAPTER

Understanding paragraph formatting

Using direct paragraph formatting versus using styles

Indentation and alignment

Applying numbering and bullets

Applying shading and borders

Bonus tips

Styles and Paragraph Formatting

One of Word's challenges is that there often are multiple ways to do the same thing. For any given set of circumstances, however, only one way is the most efficient. The challenge is to see through the clutter and determine which way is best.

"I don't use styles," is something I hear quite frequently, but that can't be true. If you're using Word, you're always using two styles: a paragraph style and a character style. When people say, "I don't use styles," they mean that they use just a single paragraph style, called *Normal*, and a single character style, called *Default Paragraph Font*. More to the point, they mean that they simply ignore the existence of styles.

Any formatting variation such *astylists* might achieve is made through variant or direct formatting. I'm not going to sit here snobbishly and tell you that paying no attention to styles is a sin (although, come to think of it, this is a Bible…). There are times when you have to do something ASAP, and if ignoring styles gets that "The building is on fire!" memo finished sooner than fumbling with unfamiliar tools and concepts, then so be it.

This chapter will tell style-shunners what paragraph formatting is, what it's for, and how to use it. It also will tell style-users the same things, but the latter will have a broader context for it all as well as a strategy, because paragraph formatting is integral to paragraph-style formatting.

When to Use Styles

The same commandment that applies to character-style formatting (see Chapter 5) applies to paragraph-style formatting. If it's a one-time ad hoc need, direct paragraph formatting is entirely appropriate. For example, if it's a centered heading on a one-time announcement you're going to tack to a bulletin board, feel free to simply press Ctrl+E.

On the other hand, if it's formatting that you're going to need again and again, then use a style. For example, if it's one of several headings in a monthly newsletter you're going to be assembling for the next five years, either adopt and adapt built-in heading styles to suit the need, or create your own styles. The more work styles can do for you, the less time you're going to have to spend formatting and reformatting.

What Exactly Is a Paragraph, Anyway?

With apologies to Mrs. Hewitt, my eighth-grade English teacher, a *paragraph* is everything between two different paragraph marks. Shown in Figure 6-1, all of numbered item 1 is a single paragraph. Note, however, that a single sentence separated by two paragraph marks is also a complete paragraph — to Word — as is a paragraph mark that contains no associated text at all.

Many new Word users often are distracted by the display of nonprinting characters (such as paragraph marks, manual line breaks, spaces, and tabs). As shown in Figure 6-1, however, displaying them can give you essential clues about what's going on in a document.

Sometimes it's useful to use a manual line break within a paragraph while still keeping it as a single paragraph. This most often is done within numbered or bulleted paragraphs. That way, any paragraph formatting you do to any part of the paragraph is done to the entire paragraph (such as the main indentation and numbering), despite its disjointed appearance. If the paragraphs are numbered or bulleted, a manual line break prevents a new number or bullet from being assigned to the disjointed portion.

FIGURE 6-1

A paragraph is everything between two paragraph marks.

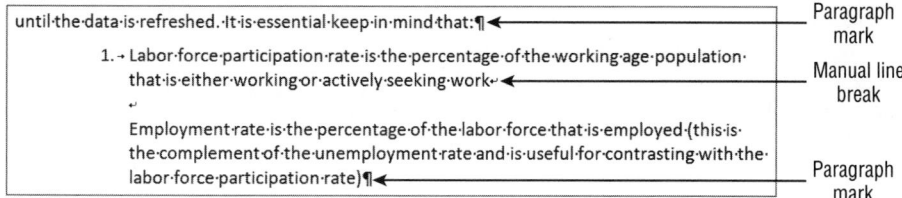

If you're in the habit of working with nonprinting characters turned off, you might find that it's useful to occasionally turn them on when trying to diagnose the behavior of text. You can toggle them by pressing Ctrl+Shift+8. If any marks don't toggle, then check File ⇨ Options ⇨ Display to see whether any are set to be displayed all the time.

Another useful diagnostic aid in analyzing paragraph formatting is the Reveal Formatting pane, shown in Figure 6-2. You display it by pressing Shift+F1. It shows all the formatting that's common to the selected text or that's applied at the insertion point. It has three segments: Font (character formatting), Paragraph, and Section. (Thanks to Word's thesaurus, I just neatly sidestepped having to refer to the bottom segment as the *section section*.) It also displays the selected text, if any, using the current common formatting, as best it can. If nothing is selected, it displays the words *Sample Text* using common current formatting.

Why do I say that it displays the common formatting? That's because the selected text might not be formatted homogeneously. In this case, although you can't see it, the sentence in the text was, "It was a **dark** and *stormy* night." Because some formatting (bold and italic in this case) might not be common to the entire selection, you can't use Reveal Formatting to determine whether a given selection contains any formatting of a particular type.

Notice that the Reveal Formatting pane does not tell you what style is applied. We will look at other tools later on that help us with styles. In this chapter, we focus only on the paragraph segment.

Tip

The Reveal Formatting pane is not accessible from the Ribbon interface. If you want to be able to access it from the QAT, you can add it. To do so, right-click the QAT and choose Customize Quick Access Toolbar. Set Choose Commands From to Commands Not in the Ribbon. Click in the list and tap the S key to accelerate to that part of the alphabet, and then tap the up-arrow key five times to select Reveal Formatting. Click Add ⇨ OK, and you're done. ∎

FIGURE 6-2

Press Shift+F1 to toggle the Reveal Formatting pane. It shows all the formatting in effect for the selection.

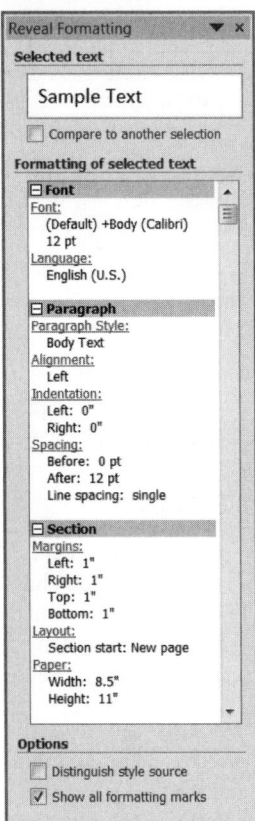

Paragraph-Formatting Attributes

Paragraph formatting, like character formatting, can be applied with a wide variety of tools that apply certain paragraph attributes. Many of those attribute controls, but not all, can be found in the Paragraph group in the Home tab of the Ribbon, shown in Figure 6-3. Indents and spacing, both of which are paragraph attributes, are located on the Paragraph group of the Page Layout tab of the Ribbon, also shown in Figure 6-3. Several attributes missing from the Ribbon are on the horizontal rulers: left and right indent, hanging and paragraph indent, and tab settings.

Many paragraph attributes — but again, not all — are also found in the Paragraph dialog box, shown in Figure 6-4. You can display the Paragraph dialog box by clicking the Dialog Box

Launcher in the lower-right corner of the Ribbon's Paragraph groups, by double-clicking any of the indent controls on the horizontal ruler, or by pressing the legacy keystrokes Alt+O followed immediately by Alt+P.

FIGURE 6-3

The Paragraph sections in the Home and Page Layout tabs of the Ribbon contain several paragraph-formatting controls.

 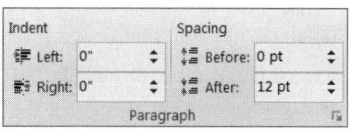

Paragraph group from
Home Ribbon tab

Paragraph group from
Page Layout Ribbon tab

FIGURE 6-4

The Paragraph dialog box contains controls for most, but not all, of Word's paragraph attributes.

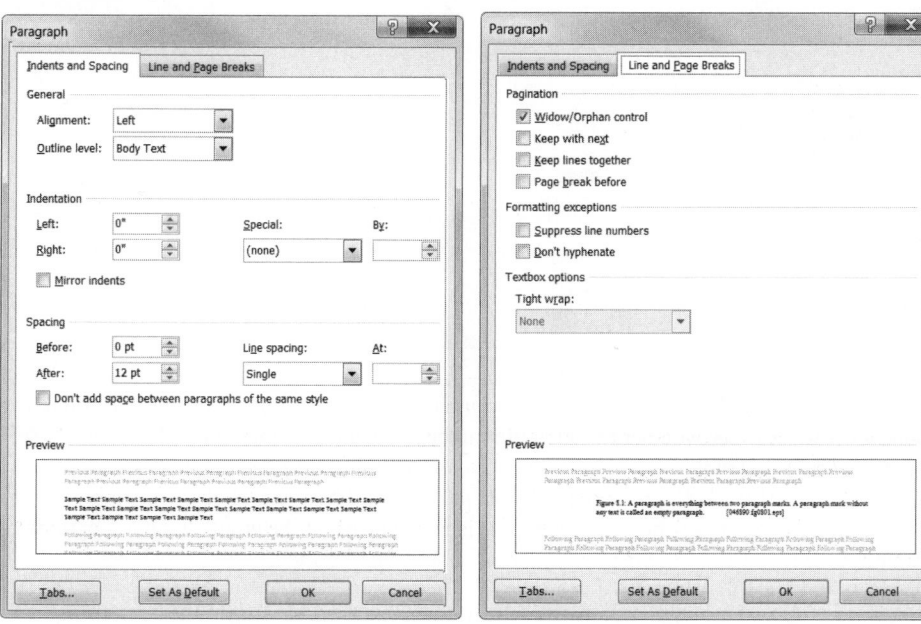

Missing from the dialog box, of course, are tab settings, which you can access by clicking Tabs in the Indents and Spacing section of the dialog box. Also missing are borders and shading, which you can access by clicking Borders and Shading from the bottom of the Border tool's list of settings (in the Home tab of the Ribbon), shown in Figure 6-5.

FIGURE 6-5

The Borders and Shading dialog box can be accessed from the bottom of the Borders control in the Paragraph group of the Home tab.

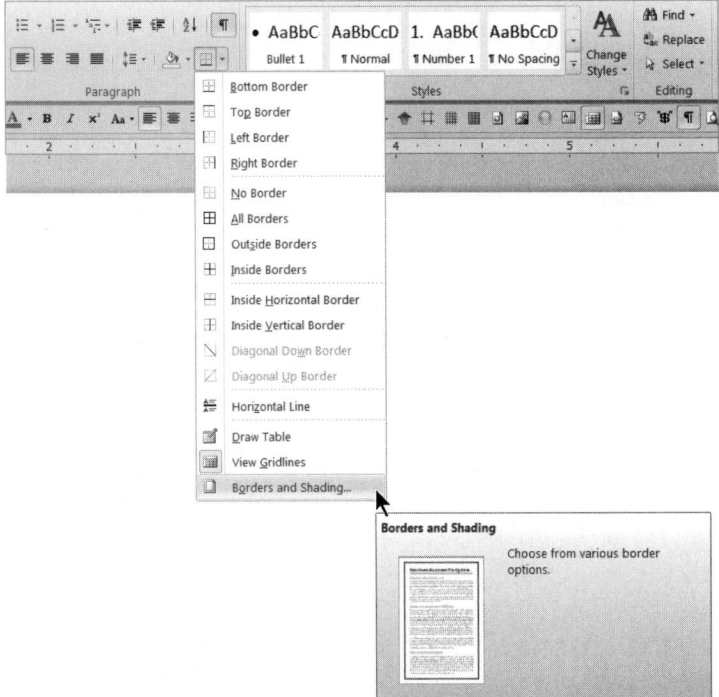

You might be wondering from all this how to determine whether a setting is a paragraph-formatting attribute. One way is to see whether the attribute can be applied to a paragraph without the whole paragraph's being selected. For example, if you click anywhere inside a paragraph and click the Center button in the Paragraph group of the Home tab of the Ribbon, the whole paragraph is centered. The same "anywhere-in-the-paragraph" rule is true for each of the other alignment options. The same applies to borders, shading, indentation, bullets, numbering, and line spacing.

Note, however, that two "paragraph-formatting" attributes behave according to the "if nothing is selected, format the whole paragraph" rule, but behave differently if part (but not all) of a paragraph is selected. These two are Shading and Borders. While they generally are considered paragraph formatting, they also can be character formatting.

Paragraph-Formatting Techniques

Two techniques can be used for all paragraph-formatting attributes. As noted, you can simply place the insertion point in the paragraph you want and then choose the attribute (using the Ribbon, a dialog box, a keystroke, the shortcut menu, or the Mini toolbar).

The other technique is to select a range of paragraphs (up to and including the entire document). Note that even though shading and border formatting can apply to a selection of characters/ words, if the selection includes or spans a paragraph mark, the formatting is applied to the entirety of all the paragraphs in the selection, even those that aren't fully selected.

Structural Formatting

Paragraph formatting can be thought of as encompassing two concepts:

- **Structural Formatting.** Attributes that affect the overall structure of the text, such as alignment, indentation, tabs, and so on
- **Decorative Formatting.** Attributes that affect the interior appearance of the text, such as shading, borders, numbering, and bullets

This section deals with structural formatting. Decorative formatting is addressed in the section that follows.

Indentation

Indentation typically is used for automatically indenting the first line of paragraphs, block-indenting quotes, and setting up hanging indentation for bulleted or numbered text. Preset indentation can be set via the Decrease Indent and Increase Indent controls in the Paragraph group of the Home tab on the Ribbon.

Tip

You can also perform Decrease Indent and Increase Indent using the Backspace and Tab keys, respectively. To do this, first choose File ⇨ Options ⇨ Proofing ⇨ AutoCorrect Options. Click the AutoFormat As You Type tab, and then in the bottom set of options, click Set Left- and First-Indent with Tabs and Backspaces to select it. Then click OK twice. This feature is enabled by default in Word, but many people turn it off because the feature sometimes appears to be *broken* (i.e., doesn't work the way the user expects it to). Also note that it does not perform identically to the Ribbon Decrease Indent and Increase Indent controls.

When this setting is enabled, the Tab and Backspace (also Shift+Tab, if you prefer symmetry) work as adver-tised, but only when the paragraph is not empty, and only if the insertion point is as far left as it can go (in any line in the paragraph). If the insertion point is anywhere else, the keys have their normal effects. Note that the first press of the Tab key (if the insertion point is at the beginning of the paragraph) indents only the first line of the paragraph. Subsequent presses indent the entire paragraph.

Special rules apply for the Backspace key. Backspace decreases the indent only when an indentation is actually set. If there is a negative indent and a first-line or hanging indent, the first Backspace press removes the hanging or first-line indent. If there is a negative indent and no hanging/first-line indent, Backspace resets the indent to zero.

This is all potentially confusing enough that you might want to turn the setting off. In any case, if you turn it on, watch the ruler and the text when you press Tab or Backspace. One last thing: To insert an actual tab at the beginning of a paragraph when this setting is enabled, press Ctrl+Tab. This is also how you insert a tab into a table. ■

You can set more precise indentation using the Indent Left and Right settings controls in the Paragraph group of the Page Layout tab of the Ribbon. A first-line or hanging indent typically is set with the mouse drag controls on the horizontal ruler, as shown in Figure 6-6.

FIGURE 6-6

The ruler provides GUI controls for indentation.

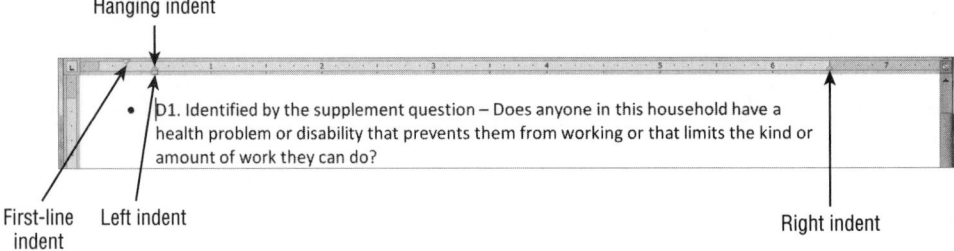

Hanging indent

D1. Identified by the supplement question – Does anyone in this household have a health problem or disability that prevents them from working or that limits the kind or amount of work they can do?

First-line   Left indent
indent

Right indent

Tip

If you have trouble grabbing the ruler's tiny indent controls, you can use the tab/indent selection control at the left end of the horizontal ruler. Click the (usually) L-shaped control to cycle through the different tabs and indents and stop at the indent control that's giving you problems. With that control selected, you can now set a first-line or hanging indent by clicking the desired position on the ruler. ■

If you press the Alt key while manipulating the ruler's indent controls, Word displays the measurement, allowing for more informed positioning. Depending on your screen's resolution, however, you might sometimes need to use the Paragraph dialog box's Special settings, shown in Figure 6-7. Here the settings are identical to those shown in Figure 6-6.

Mirror Indents

Word 2007 and Word 2010 aren't all just a flashy new interface. Keen observers who've used Word 2003 or earlier versions no doubt notice the Mirror Indents addition to the Paragraph dialog box. When this is enabled, Left and Right become Inside and Outside, as shown in Figure 6-8. This enables your indent settings to accommodate book-style printing. Note that this is different from Mirror Margins, which is a Page Setup setting discussed in Chapter 8, "Page Setup and Sections."

FIGURE 6-7

The Paragraph dialog box is ideally suited to users who need more precision for their settings.

Alignment

Horizontal alignment determines how any given paragraph is oriented. The four options are Left, Right, Centered, and Justified. You can set these using the respective controls in the Paragraph group on the Home tab of the Ribbon. They can also be made with the four Alignment options in the Paragraph dialog box. And finally, they can be set with Ctrl+L, Ctrl+R, Ctrl+E, and Ctrl+J.

Note

How Ctrl+E ever came to mean *center* is a mystery to me, but it seems to mean *center* in a wide variety of Windows programs. Maybe it's because it contains two *Es*. In any case, Ctrl+C is reserved for Copy to Clipboard, so the purely intuitive choice for Center was already taken. ■

FIGURE 6-8

Mirror Indents was introduced in Word 2007.

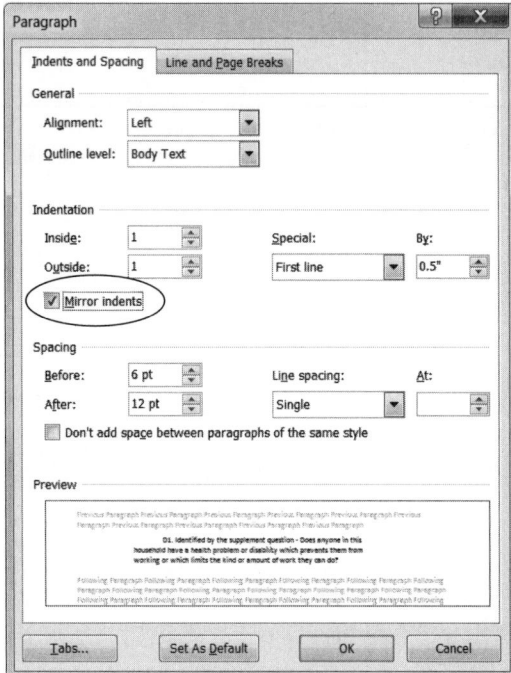

Tabs

Tab is largely passé for many modern computer users. That's because better control can be effected with tables. Ever wonder why we call them *tabs* and *tables*? We call them *tabs* because that's short for "tabulation." And we call them *tables* for the same reason. If you want the exact etymology, try the Oxford English Dictionary (OED).

By default, a new document doesn't have any explicit tabs set. However, when no explicit tabs are set, Word uses default preset tabs every 0.5 inch. When you set a tab, all the built-in preset tabs to the left of the one you set are removed, leaving the manually inserted tab and all remaining preset tabs to the right.

You can set tabs using the horizontal ruler line or the Tabs dialog box. Using the ruler line, you first determine the type of tab by clicking the Tab control at the left end of the ruler. As indicated earlier, this control cycles not only among Word's built-in five tabs, but also among first-line and hanging indent controls as well. The five built-in Tab types are shown in Figure 6-9. When the desired tab type is displayed, click the lower portion of the ruler (below the eighth-inch marks) to set the desired tab(s). You can drag them for better placement; holding the Alt key while dragging shows you the exact location.

FIGURE 6-9

Tabs can be set visually by means of the ruler line.

L	Left tab sets the starting position of text
⊥	Center tab centers text at the set position
⌐	Right tab sets the ending position
⊥	Decimal tab aligns all numbers at the decimal point, regardless of length
I	Bar tab causes a vertical bar to be inserted at the location of the tab

To remove a tab using the ruler, simply drag it down and away from the ruler until the mouse pointer is no longer in the ruler area.

If you prefer the steadiness and precision of typing in the settings you want, use the Tabs dialog box, shown in Figure 6-10. Activate the Tabs dialog box by choosing Tabs from the Paragraph dialog box, or by double-clicking any existing tab in the ruler line.

FIGURE 6-10

Use the Tabs dialog box to set and clear tabs, set the default tab stop interval, and set a tab leader.

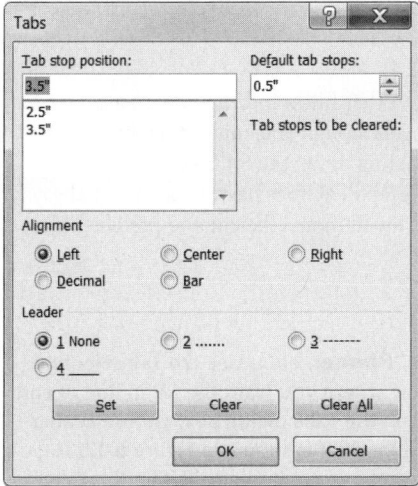

Notice that the Tab dialog box also lets you set tab leaders — dashed or solid lines typically used to help the reader visually line up text and numbers. Tab leaders often are used in tables of contents and indexes, such as the one shown in Figure 6-11.

FIGURE 6-11

Tab leaders are a visual aid that help the reader correctly align associated text.

I. Introduction I-1
ORGANIZATION OF REPORT I-2
II. Current Population Survey and Survey of Income and Program Participation II-1
CURRENT POPULATION SURVEY DATA II-1
Measures of Disability II-2
SURVEY OF INCOME AND PROGRAM PARTICIPATION II-6
Measures of Disability II-6
COMPARING CPS AND SIPP DISABILITY TRENDS II-7
III. Demographics of the Population with Disabilities III-1
CPS DISABILITY TRENDS III-1
AGE AND SEX III-2

Tabs versus Tables

If you can use tabs and you can use tables, when should you use which? Years of using Word has convinced me that *pseudo-tables*, as I like to call tables that are created using tabs, are a lot more fragile than actual tables. They're also a lot less flexible.

Even so, there are times when tabs give you precisely what you want, and in a way that a table either can't or can't without your jumping through hoops. If you want lines connecting two tabbed items, while there are other ways to accomplish the same effect, it's almost always faster and easier to use tab leaders.

If you need to create an underscored area for a signature or other fill-in information on a paper form, the solid tab leader line is definitely the way to go, even though you could draw lines where you want them instead, using Insert ➪ Shapes ➪ Line (holding down the Shift key as you draw to keep the line perfectly horizontal, of course). However, graphical lines have a way of not always staying where you put them, so you'll usually find that it's much more efficient and predictable to just use a leader line.

Tip

To create a signature or other fill-in area, type the prompt (Name:, Phone:, etc.). Use the Tab selection tool to choose a right tab, and then click on the horizontal ruler line where you want the fill-in line to end, to insert a right-aligned tab. Double-click the tab you just created. In the Tabs dialog box, choose Leader Option 4 (solid underscore), and click OK. This creates something like what is shown in Figure 6-12. (If you accidentally insert a new tab when you try to double-click, make sure you zap it while visiting the Tabs dialog box.) ■

FIGURE 6-12

Tab leader lines are ideal for creating underscored fill-in areas for paper forms.

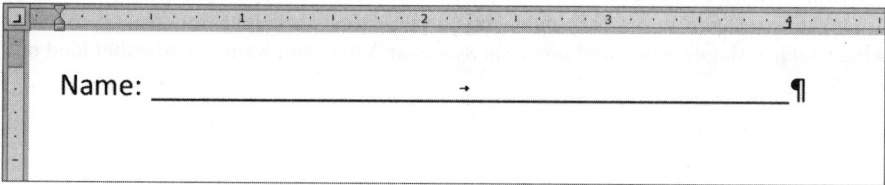

Incidentally, using a table, you can create a fill-in area that looks identical to that one. Create a table with one row. Size it so that *Name:* is a narrower column and the second column ends where you want the fill-in area to end. Next, use the Borders tool to turn off all borders in the table. Finally, use the Bottom Border tool to turn on just the bottom border in the second column's cell. For me, however, this is a lot more work just to prove a point.

Another situation in which tabs give you what you want is with simple document headers. The default header for Word 2010 documents contains a center tab and a right-align tab. This enables you to easily create a header with text to the left, centered text, and right-aligned text, simply by separating those three components with tabs. Tabs also can be useful inside actual tables for aligning numbers at the decimal point. (As noted earlier, to insert a tab inside a table, press Ctrl+Tab.)

However, for more complex presentations of information, particularly when you might need organizational control (copying and moving rows and columns), it's much better and much more natural to use a table.

Paragraph Decoration

A second kind of paragraph formatting is something that might be termed paragraph decoration. This includes shading, boxes, bullets, and other semi-graphical elements that help the writer call attention to particular paragraphs, or that help the reader understand the text better.

Numbering/Bullets

Numbering in Word has always been a bit of a sore point. That's because, historically, it has proven to be both confusing and fraught with odd quirks. Let's pretend for the moment that numbering and bullets work perfectly and never give the user grief. To test this, let's assume we're using the Word 2007/2010 .docx format, rather than Word 2003's (or earlier) legacy .doc format.

You can apply numbering or bullets simply by clicking the Numbering or Bullets button on the Paragraph tab of the Ribbon's Home tab. You can click the Numbering or Bullets button and just start typing. When you're done with your list, simply press Enter twice.

Note

If Automatic bulleted lists or Automatic numbered lists are enabled, then you don't even need to click the Numbering or Bullets tool. To begin a numbered list, simply type 1. and press the Spacebar, and Word automatically replaces what you typed with automatic number formatting. Other variations work, too, such as 1<tab>. To begin a bulleted list, simply type * and press the Spacebar. When you want to end either kind of list, press Enter twice. ■

You can also apply numbering or bullets to an existing list. Just select the list and click either tool. If the list has levels (e.g., created by a Tab press before certain subitems), then the Numbering tool uses different and appropriate numbering schemes for each level.

Note that Bullets and Numbering both offer Live Preview of the resulting list. Multilevel List, however, does not.

Line Numbering

Line numbering, which is different from numbered lists, often is used in legal documents such as affidavits. The numbering allows for ready reference to testimony by page and line number. Line numbering itself, however, is not a paragraph-formatting attribute. It is a section-formatting attribute. Line numbering is turned on with the Line Numbers menu in the Page Setup group of the Page Layout tab of the Ribbon, or the Line Numbers option in the Layout tab of the Page Setup dialog box, shown in Figure 6-13.

FIGURE 6-13

Line numbering is a section-formatting attribute, but it can be turned off in any given paragraph.

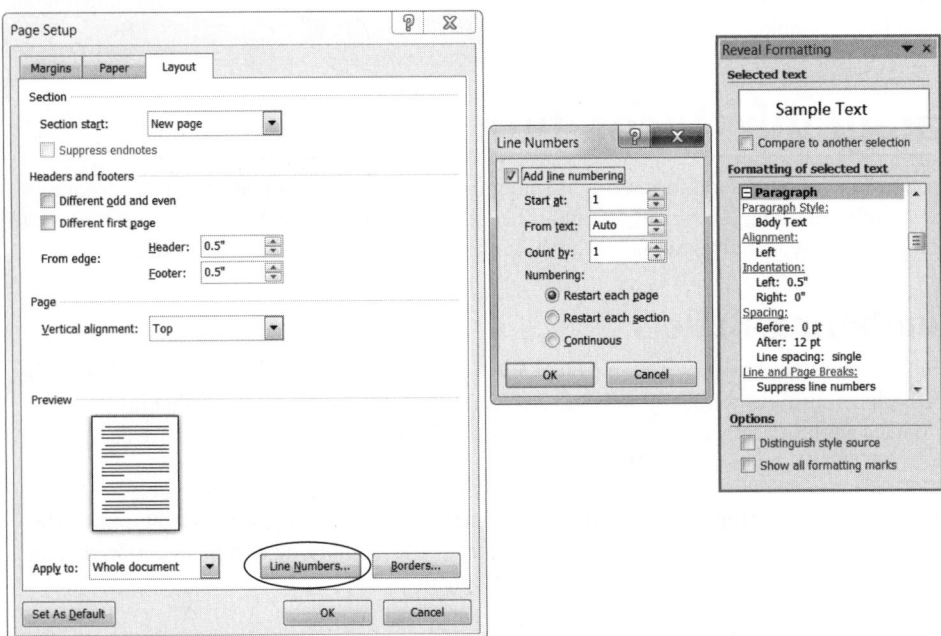

So why am I talking about line numbering here if it's not a paragraph-formatting attribute? I'm talking about it here because although line numbering isn't a paragraph attribute, suppressing line numbering *is* a paragraph attribute. Figure 6-14 shows examples of line numbering suppressed for the heading paragraphs but not the body text paragraphs. (Note that line numbers do not display in Draft or Outline views.)

FIGURE 6-14

While line numbering is a section-formatting attribute, the ability to suppress it is a paragraph attribute.

```
 8    Researchers comparing this work with other studies should look to these basic tables to
 9    determine whether the different studies are using the same data. Our data extracts were made
10    in early March 2009, and reflect the data and all included corrections as of that time.

      Measures of Disability

11    For several decades, many researchers have focused on the CPS as a largely-consistent source
12    of data for labor statistics and the incidence of disability in the U.S. During this time, many have
13    relied upon a question asking if individuals have a disability that prevents or limits their ability
14    to work. At least since 1994, there have been seven other related questions that have been
15    used to form a more complete indicator of disability, including distinguishing severe from
16    moderate disabilities. In the discussion below, we refer to these as "established indicators."
17    Beginning in mid-2008, "new indicators" have been available that may provide a more reliable
18    research tool for future research.

      Established Indicators

19    The CPS contains seven survey elements that Census and researchers use in some form as a
20    basis for classifying survey respondents as having or not having disabilities. Until recently, these
21    seven items have been a key way that Census and researchers have attempted to identify
22    Americans with disabilities in investigating trends and the relationship between disability and
23    other factors.
```

To suppress line numbering in any given paragraph, put the insertion point in that paragraph, display the Paragraph dialog box (double-click any of the indent controls on the horizontal ruler), and enable Suppress Line Numbers in the Line and Page Breaks tab, as shown in Figure 6-15.

Additional Paragraph Controls

Figure 6-15 shows additional paragraph-level formatting controls:

- **Widow/Orphan Control.** Prevents a solitary paragraph line from being *stranded* on a page all by itself (widows precede the main portion of the paragraph, while orphans follow it).

- **Keep with Next.** Forces a paragraph to appear with the paragraph that follows. This is used to keep headings together with at least the first few lines of the first paragraph under that heading. It is also used to keep captions and pictures, figures, tables, and so on, on the same page.

- **Keep Lines Together.** Prevents a paragraph from breaking across two pages.

- **Page Break Before.** Forces an automatic page break before the paragraph. This often is used to force each chapter to begin on a new page.

- **Don't Hyphenate.** Instructs Word not to perform hyphenation in a given paragraph. This often is done by those trying to reproduce a quote and maintain its integrity with respect to the words and position of the original being quoted.

FIGURE 6-15

Line numbers can be suppressed on a paragraph-by-paragraph basis.

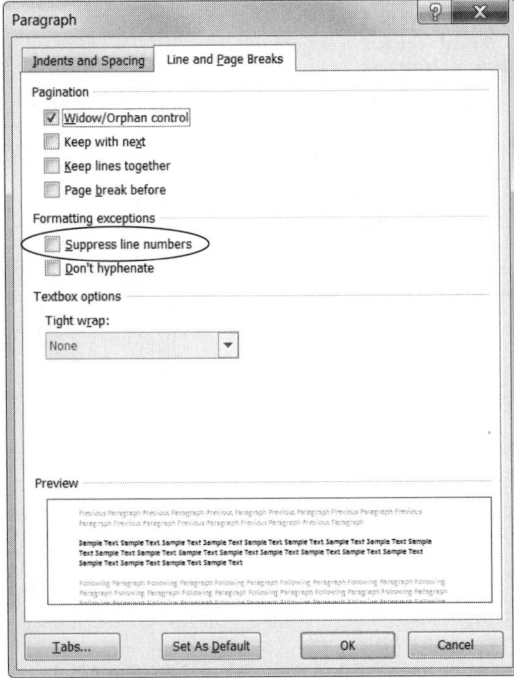

Shading

Paragraph shading, as well as shading of individual words, can be performed graphically with Live Preview via the Shading choice in the Paragraph group of the Home tab of the Ribbon, shown in Figure 6-16.

Additional shading options can be viewed in the Shading tab in the Borders and Shading dialog box. In addition to color shading, you can also choose to apply *patterns*. Patterns often are more useful when you're preparing documents for grayscale printing in which shading variations might be too subtle. To display the Borders and Shading dialog box, click the drop-down arrow next to the Border button in the Paragraph group of the Home tab of the Ribbon, and select Borders and Shading (at the bottom of the list).

FIGURE 6-16

When nothing is selected, shading is applied to the whole paragraph. Unlike many other paragraph formatting attributes, shading can be a character-formatting attribute as well.

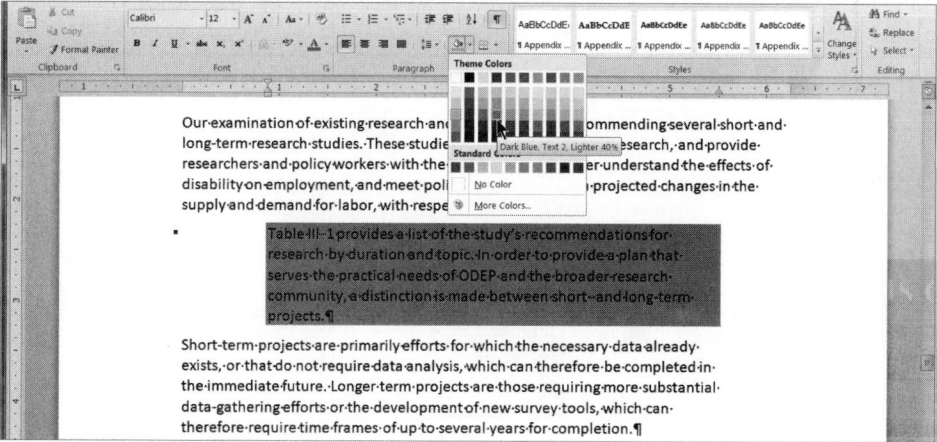

Caution

Note that the Border button changes to the last border option you picked using the drop-down arrow. Therefore, if the last option you picked was Borders and Shading, that's what the main Border button becomes (for now, anyway). ■

What's That Dot?

In Figure 6-16, notice the square dot to the left of the shaded paragraph. That dot has nothing to do with the shading or with the fact that that paragraph is selected. The square dot appears to the left of a paragraph when any of the following attributes are assigned to that paragraph:

- Keep with next
- Keep lines together
- Page break before
- Suppress line numbers

These options can all be found in the Line and Page Breaks tab of the Paragraph dialog box, shown in Figure 6-15.

Borders and Boxes

Some call them *borders*, some call them *boxes*. I call them ... *borders and boxes*. Unlike Shading, Borders do not provide Live Preview. You can choose from the Border control's drop-down options, or you can instead select the Borders and Shading option at the end of the drop-down list to display the dialog box shown in Figure 6-17.

FIGURE 6-17

The Borders and Shading dialog box provides complete control over a paragraph's border.

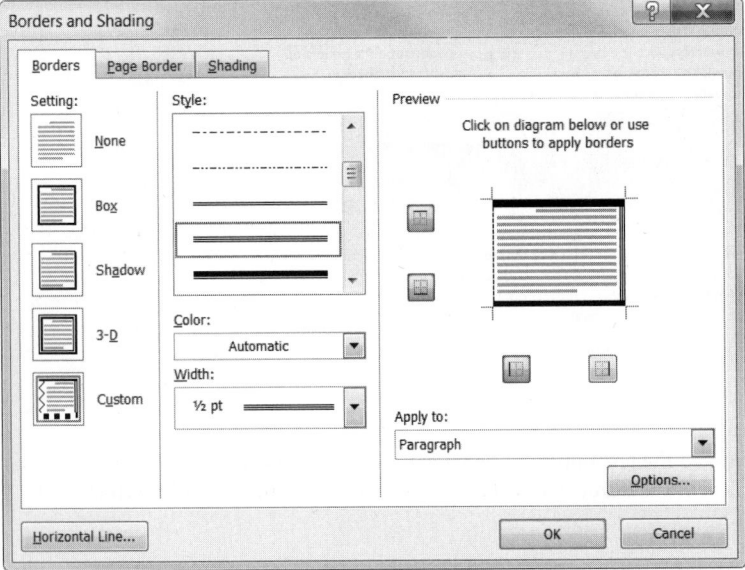

Because the drop-down doesn't provide Live Preview, I often find working in the dialog box to involve a bit less trial-and-error. The basic technique is to choose a box/border design (Box, Shadow, or 3-D), and then customize as you see fit. You can click the boxes or the borders in the Preview area to turn individual sides on or off. By alternately clicking Style, Color, or Width and the line segments you want to format, you can even create a box with four completely different sides. (Did I fail to mention that this chapter is about formatting, not tacky design?)

Additionally, you can adjust the distance between the border and paragraph text by clicking Options in the lower-right corner of the dialog box. You can individually adjust the distance for any of the four sides.

Random Bonus Tip #1 — Sort Paragraphs That Aren't in a Table

You've seen Sort in the Paragraph group and in the Table Layout tab of the Ribbon, but you might not know that it works on any list — even one that's not in a table. Select the items you want sorted, and click the Sort tool in the Home Ribbon's Paragraph group. Or, if you're a keyboard junkie, try using the same menu keystrokes you used in earlier versions of Word (Alt+A, Alt+S).

Random Bonus Tip #2 — Move Paragraphs Easily

If you ever have two paragraphs that you need to quickly swap, don't reach for the mouse. Instead, put the insertion point into either paragraph and use Shift+Alt+Up or Shift+Alt+Down to drag the current paragraph up or down so that it changes places with the other paragraph. These are outlining keystrokes, but they work great for this sort of thing as well. You can also quickly move rows around in tables.

Summary

In this chapter we've explored the ins and outs of direct paragraph formatting. You should have also learned that anything you can do to a paragraph, you can enshrine in a style. You should now be able to do the following:

- Decide when to use direct formatting, and when to use a style.
- Distinguish between paragraph-formatting attributes and other kinds of attributes.
- Properly indent and align any paragraph, as well as determine how to find and use the appropriate tools.
- Apply and remove bullets and numbering.
- Use shading and boxes to highlight paragraphs.
- Explain at the next cocktail party what those strange square dots are at the left side of certain paragraphs.
- Decide when to use tabs versus when to use a table.

Styles

Styles are the seat of power in Word — any version, not just Word 2010. Word 2007 introduced additional tools that make using styles for formatting more powerful and more flexible. The dizzying array of options might leave you scratching your head in wonder and amazement, but perhaps in confusion as well. In fact, much of how Word 2010 goes about its business might seem shrouded in mystery, since there are so many unfamiliar elements, particularly if you leapfrogged past Word 2007.

This chapter sorts things out — solving the mysteries, reducing the confusion, and giving you a handle on which tools to use for what. It looks at concepts and tools, such as Quick Styles and Quick Style Sets, the Style Inspector, the Apply Styles task pane, and the Styles task pane. It ties these features together and shows how they relate to legacy Word 2003 tools, such as the Modify Styles dialog box and the Organizer.

> **IN THIS CHAPTER**
>
> **Understanding the ins and outs of the Styles group on the Ribbon**
>
> **Using, creating, and modifying styles**
>
> **Using, creating, and modifying Quick Style Sets**
>
> **Managing styles**
>
> **Inspecting styles**

Styles Group

The most visible Ribbon control for applying and changing styles is the Styles group in the Home tab of the Ribbon. Seemingly simple, the Styles group is the tip of a rather large iceberg.

On its face are four controls, shown in Figure 7-1: the Quick Style Gallery, Style Sets, Expand gallery, and the Dialog Box Launcher, which displays the Styles task pane.

Note

The word *quick* very likely will confuse many users. You might also notice that the term *Quick Style* also applies to the gallery used for SmartArt. These are not related. One way to deal with the disconnect is to think of them as different kinds of styles — one you apply to text elements, the other you apply to certain kinds of graphic elements. We will look at SmartArt styles in Chapter 9, "Tables and Graphics." ■

FIGURE 7-1

The Styles group is the command and control center for styles.

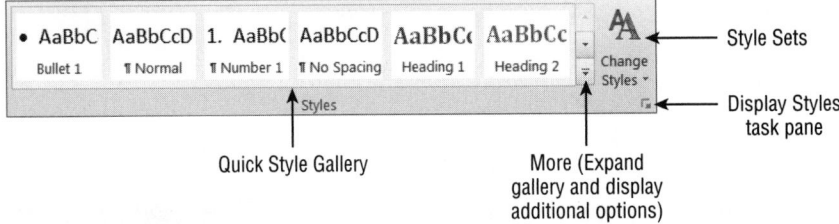

In a normal screen configuration and resolution, the Quick Style Gallery shows only three to eight styles. In a very high-resolution setup with a sufficiently wide monitor, it can show up to 17 styles. Clicking the More button shows more of the styles in the Quick Style Gallery, as shown in Figure 7-2. If there are still more styles in the gallery, you can access them using the vertical scroll bar or by dragging the right corner control to expand or shrink the size of the gallery.

FIGURE 7-2

The Style Gallery can be scrolled and made larger or smaller.

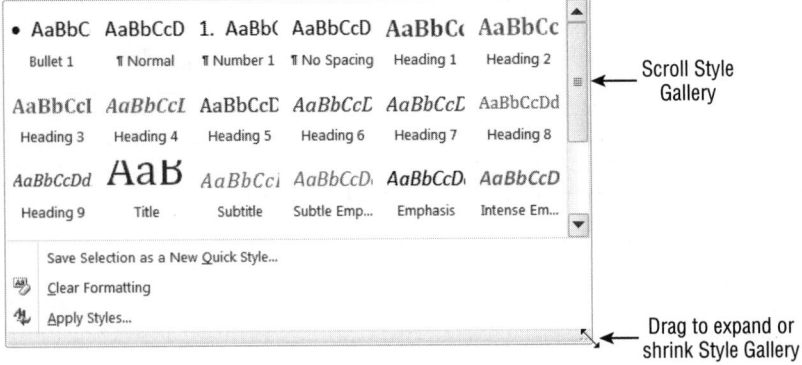

The Styles group also provides access to Style Sets. If you click Change Styles, you see additional choices, as shown in Figure 7-3. The options shown — Clean, Default (Black and White), Distinctive, and so on, are carefully constructed sets of styles that are coordinated to help you quickly change the look of your document. (You'll see where those Style Sets come from later in this chapter.)

FIGURE 7-3

Style Sets offer additional coordinated styles to help you achieve a different *look* for your documents.

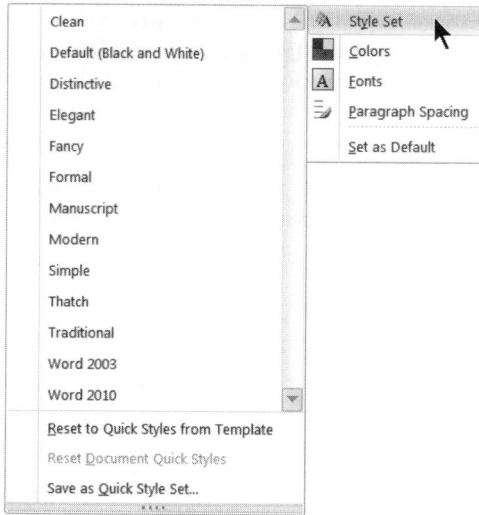

Notice also the Colors and Fonts controls. These tools work with themes, which aren't the same thing as styles. Like Style Sets, themes can be used to dramatically change the appearance of your document. Unlike Style Sets, however, they are tied to the use of theme elements in your document. One way to think about themes is as design elements that affect the aesthetic appearance of a document. Styles, on the other hand, are geared more to the formatting of text and paragraphs.

Note

Themes were a feature new to Word 2007 and do not work with compatibility mode documents. In the Change Styles list, Style Set is available, but Colors and Fonts are not. These features are available not only when you're working with *.docx documents, but also when you're working with Web-oriented documents (*.mht, *.htm, *.html, etc.). Themes are explored in Chapter 8, "Page Setup and Sections." ■

The effect of different Style Sets — indeed, seeing any effect at all — depends on your having used styles in your document. If you simply use the style Normal, then at most applying a new Style Set will change the font. For maximum benefit from Word's style features, you need to lay the proper foundation, which means using styles to differentiate different kinds of text (headings, body, captions, etc.).

Using Styles

When you first start typing in any Word document, you're automatically using the default style. Ordinarily, that would be Normal.

Note

The style named *Normal* is wholly independent of the Word template named Normal.dotm. Normal.dotm contains many different styles, and one of them happens to be named *Normal*. In fact, every Word template contains a style named *Normal*. This is nothing more than an unfortunate, confusing, and creativity-challenged choice of names. They could have named Word's default style *Base* or *Body*, and I really wish they had. It would make notes like this one unnecessary. Fortunately, *Normal view* was renamed *Draft view* as of Word 2007, so at least we no longer have to deal with that added bit of confusion. ■

As you type different parts of any document, you should consider applying an appropriate style. For example, if you type a heading, consider applying a heading style to it, such as Heading 1, 2, or 3. To do this, click the heading style in the Quick Styles Gallery, as shown in Figure 7-4. If Heading 1 isn't showing, click the More button to the right of the Styles, also shown in Figure 7-4.

FIGURE 7-4

Click a style in the Quick Style Gallery to apply it to the current paragraph or selection.

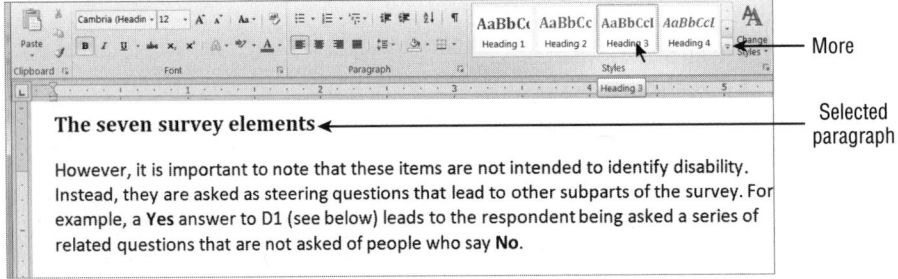

Apply Styles Task Pane

If you're accustomed to Word 2003 or earlier, you can also apply a style in a way that's similar. In Word 2003 you could either click in the Style drop-down tool or press Ctrl+Shift+S. There is no default Style drop-down in Word 2010, but Ctrl+Shift+S activates the Apply Styles task pane, shown in Figure 7-5. Once the Apply Styles task pane is visible, it can be used much like Word 2003's Style tool.

FIGURE 7-5

Press Ctrl+Shift+S to activate the Apply Styles task pane, which is Word 2010's substitute for pre-Ribbon Word's Style tool in the Formatting toolbar.

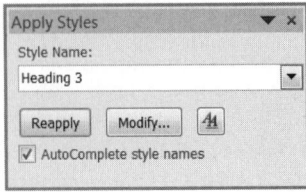

Tip

In the preceding paragraph, I said that there is no *default* Style drop-down tool. However, there is one that you can add to the Quick Access Toolbar (QAT) — it is the "classic" Style drop-down tool that appeared in the Formatting toolbar in Word 2003 and earlier. You can use it for setting the style using the mouse. More importantly, it displays the style assigned to the insertion point all the time, unlike the Quick Style Gallery.

To add this tool to your QAT, right-click the QAT and choose Customize Quick Access Toolbar. Make sure that For All Documents (Default) is selected in the Customize Quick Access Toolbar drop-down list. Open the Choose Commands From drop-down list, and click Commands Not in the Ribbon. Click in the list of commands and tap the T key. This displays the first command starting with *T* but also exposes all the commands beginning with *Style*. Click on the command named just *Style*. When you hover the mouse over it, the ScreenTip says Style (StyleGalleryClassic). With Style selected, click Add to add it to the QAT. Click OK, and you're done. ∎

Creating and Modifying Styles

Often, when you use a built-in heading style, it does not suit your needs. The font or point size might be wrong, or the spacing might be off. No problem — you can change it. Or, if you still need the existing style but want a slightly different version for another purpose, create a new style.

Caution

When experimenting with styles, do not experiment on the only copy of a document or template that you have. Make a copy of the document and/or template in question and work with the copy. That way, you have a fallback position when and if you either change your mind or make a colossal formatting mistake. ∎

To change an existing style, right-click the style in the Quick Style Gallery and choose Modify. This displays the Modify Style dialog box shown in Figure 7-6. Make the desired change to the style. If the formatting you need to change isn't shown, click Format in the lower-left corner, and choose from the seven different categories of formatting.

Caution

Keep Automatically Update turned off unless you absolutely need it (e.g., if your company's policy requires that it be used). The Automatically Update setting can bring much joy or much sorrow. If it is enabled, when you make changes to Heading 3, for example, those changes are automatically incorporated into the style's definition. All other text in the document formatted with that style will automatically change to reflect the changes in the style's definition. If you're using styles correctly, this can bring great joy.

If, on the other hand, you've misused Body Text throughout the document, applying direct formatting in various locations to make it *look right*, then you could be in for an unpleasant shock. Suppose a modified Body Text style is sometimes used on a heading, other times used for a caption, and yet other times used for other purposes. Each time you modify the Body Text style in one place, all other instances in your document will also change, undoing your careful direct formatting. This can happen without your realizing it because the updated instances may be miles away in another part of the document. By the time you see what's happening, it might be too late for a Ctrl+Z miracle. On the bright side, the Automatically Update option does not exist for the Normal style. This option was the cause of much grief in Word 2003 and earlier. Its post–Word 2003 removal from the Normal style has prevented a great many mishaps! ■

While there is a special New Style dialog box you can use (available from the bottom of the Styles task pane and the Manage Styles dialog box, e.g.), you aren't limited to that method. In Figure 7-6, where it says "Heading 3," you can type a new style name. When you click OK, the style is created!

FIGURE 7-6

Use the Modify Style dialog box to make changes to a style.

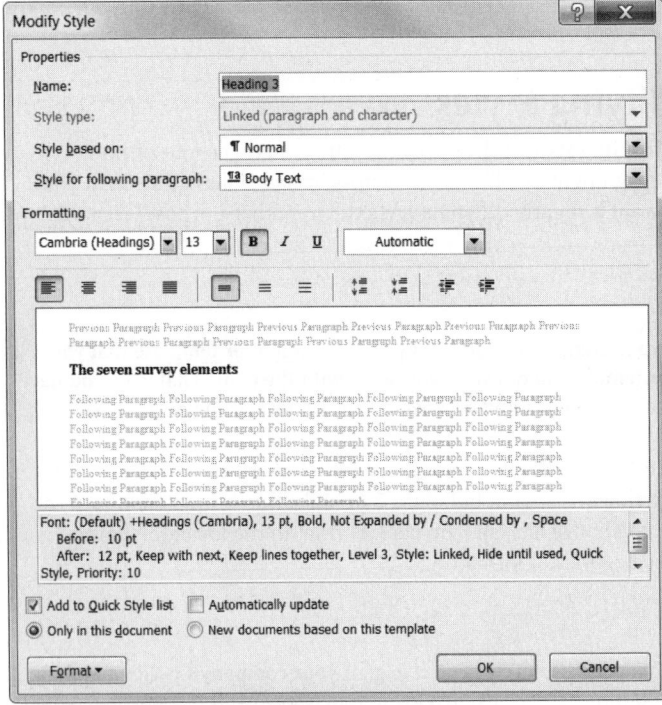

Style-by-Example

Another way to modify a style assumes that Automatically Update is *not* enabled, and that Prompt to Update Style *is* enabled. Choose File ➪ Options ➪ Advanced, and in the Editing options section, click to enable Prompt to Update Style. Assuming that Automatically Update is not enabled for a given style, you can now perform what's sometimes called *style-by-example*. We also need to assume that you're not using the Normal style, as it plays by different rules (Automatically Update doesn't work for Normal).

Use whatever formatting controls you like — Ribbon, keyboard shortcuts, dialog boxes, and so on — to tweak text so that it looks the way you want. When you've got it looking just so, you can either create a new style or modify the current one. Note that you should modify a given style only if you want all other text formatted with that style to be formatted the same way.

To create a new style, type the new style name in the Style Name box in the Apply Styles task pane, and then press Enter to apply it.

To modify the existing style, click Reapply on the Apply Styles task pane. Or reapply the current style using some other method, such as the Quick Style Gallery or a keyboard shortcut. Word now prompts you with the dialog box shown in Figure 7-7. Note that you will never see this dialog box if the current style is Normal. Normal is designed to resist easy changes that might have major unintended consequences.

The Advanced Word option Prompt to Update Style tells Word to prompt you when you attempt to reapply a style (other than Normal) to text that contains formatting that differs from the current style's settings.

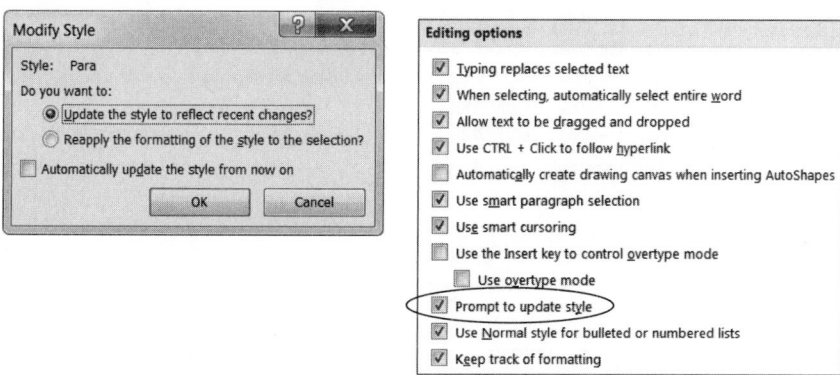

Choose the Update option to redefine the current style according to the formatting in the current selection (that's what "recent changes" really means — it doesn't mean "changes made in the last week or two"). The Reapply option will undo your direct formatting and reapply the original style. Note that Automatically Update the Style from Now On enables the Automatically Update checkbox in the Modify Style dialog box. Think long and hard before you ever check that checkbox!

Quick Style Sets

Quick Style Sets are a potentially confusing weapon in Word's formatting arsenal. Quick Style Sets get their information from a set of .dotx (not macro-enabled) templates. In the Styles group of the Home tab of the Ribbon, choose Change Styles ➪ Style Set and look at the names: Clean, Default (Black and White), Distinctive, Elegant, and so on.

These sets correspond to .dotx files stored in C:\Program Files\Microsoft Office\ OFFICE14\1033\QuickStyles, as shown in Figure 7-8. (The path may vary depending on what Windows and Office builds — 64-bit versus 32-bit — and versions you have installed.)

Note

These `.dotx` files contain no text or other formatting, but only style information for 135 built-in styles that Microsoft's designers chose to include. (No, this is not the entire list; a few notable missing styles are footnote, endnote, header, and footer, which come from the underlying document template, rather than from the Quick Style Set.) To see a list of these styles, copy one of the `.dotx` files to another file and give it an extension of `.zip`. Using the technique described in Chapter 4, drill down to the Word folder and take a look at `styles.xml`. ■

FIGURE 7-8

The Quick Style Sets are stored as .dotx files and can be changed or customized by the user.

Name	Type	Size
Classic.dotx	Microsoft Word Template	9 KB
Clean.dotx	Microsoft Word Template	20 KB
Default.dotx	Microsoft Word Template	9 KB
DefaultBlackAndWhite.dotx	Microsoft Word Template	9 KB
Distinctive.dotx	Microsoft Word Template	9 KB
Elegant.dotx	Microsoft Word Template	9 KB
Fancy.dotx	Microsoft Word Template	9 KB
Formal.dotx	Microsoft Word Template	9 KB
Manuscript.dotx	Microsoft Word Template	9 KB
Modern.dotx	Microsoft Word Template	9 KB
Simple.dotx	Microsoft Word Template	9 KB
Thatch.dotx	Microsoft Word Template	20 KB
Traditional.dotx	Microsoft Word Template	9 KB

When you apply a new Quick Style Set by choosing Change Styles ➪ Style Set in the Styles group and clicking one of the displayed sets, Word replaces the style definitions in the current document with those contained in the corresponding `.dotx` file. It effectively overlays a new document template over what you're already using (even though the name of the underlying document template does not change). All *style-formatted* text that uses any of the styles in the replaced Quick Style Set is affected.

I emphasize *style-formatted* because if paragraphs have direct formatting applied, that formatting will not be overridden. Only the attributes of the selected text that are applied through a style are changed. For example, if you manually change the alignment of a series of paragraphs from centered to left-aligned, any alignment formatting in a Quick Style Set you apply will be ignored.

Modifying and Creating Quick Style Sets

Quick Style Sets are not carved into stone. You can modify the ones that Microsoft provides, and you can create your own.

You should modify the ones that Microsoft provides, by the way, only when a built-in Quick Style Set's original form is something you wouldn't be caught dead using. While you can recover the original, it's easier to simply use a different name, such as *Classic Bert*, so you recognize the variation as your own (assuming your name is Bert).

To easily modify a set that Microsoft provides, open a document that is affected by a Quick Style Set, and apply the Style Set you want to use, using Change Styles ⇨ Style Set in the Styles group of the Home tab. Next, modify any styles you want changed. Finally, choose Change Styles ⇨ Style Set ⇨ Save as Quick Style Set, as shown in Figure 7-9.

FIGURE 7-9

You can modify the built-in Quick Style Sets or add your own.

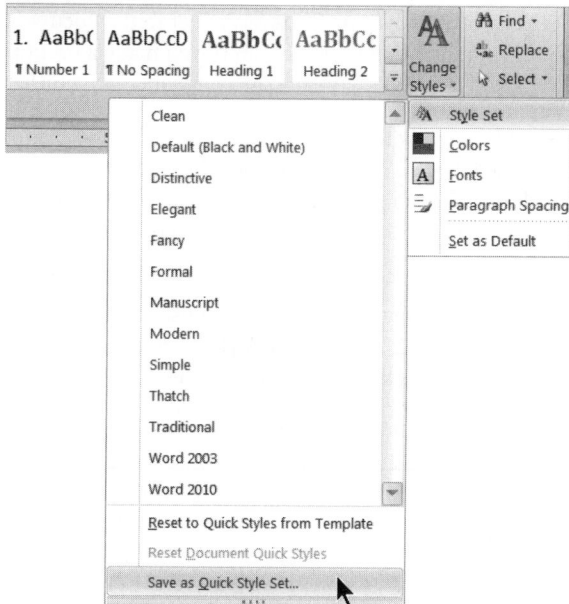

In the Save Quick Style Set dialog, specify the name of the built-in set you want to modify or override. Suppose, for example, that you want a custom version of the Elegant Quick Style Set. In the File Name field, type **Elegant** (you don't need to type the .dotx extension). Note that this will not actually modify or overwrite the original file. Then click Save. Or, to create your own Quick Style Set, type a new name (such as **My Elegant**) and choose Save.

If creating your own Style Set named *Elegant* doesn't overwrite Word's version, then how does Word know to use yours instead of its own? As indicated earlier in this chapter, Word keeps its own Quick Style Sets in one of the Microsoft Office Program Files folders. It saves your Quick Style Sets, however, to the C:\Users*username*\AppData\Roaming\Microsoft\ QuickStyles folder (in Windows 7). When you display the Quick Style Sets list by choosing Change Styles ⇨ Style Set from the Styles group, Word builds the list from a combination of the user folder and its *own* folder, giving priority to any user-created Quick Style Set names that are the same as any Quick Style Set names that ship with Word.

To revert to a Quick Style Set that comes with Word, simply delete or rename your own. In general, however, you increase your options by not giving your Quick Style Sets the same names as those that come with Word.

Tip

Do you have customized styles in your `Normal.dotm` **file? (If you don't know, then this tip does not apply to you.) If you do, before working with Quick Style Sets, protect your original** `Normal.dotm` **Quick Style Set by saving it as a unique Quick Style Set. To do this, press Ctrl+N to create a new document window based on** `Normal.dotm`**. In the Styles group of the Home tab, choose Change Styles ⇨ Style Set ⇨ Save as Quick Style Set. In File Name, choose a name that's unambiguous, such as** My normal dotm quick styles. ■

Changing Your Mind

If you've been experimenting with Quick Style Sets but now want to revert either to the document's own styles or to those of the underlying template, you probably can (if you made a backup copy of the document and/or template, as suggested earlier, then there's no "probably" about it).

Using the built-in Reset method, for you to be able to revert to the document's own original styles, the document must not have been saved and closed. Even when the document has been saved, you often can revert to the document's original styles as of when the document was opened by pressing Ctrl+Z repeatedly until it stops doing anything. However, if you have done a lot of editing, you sometimes cannot Undo all the way back to the beginning of the editing session.

Assuming that you have not yet saved the document, to revert to the document styles that were in effect at the beginning of the current editing session, choose Change Styles ⇨ Style Set in the Styles group of the Home tab. Click Reset Document Quick Styles, highlighted in Figure 7-10.

FIGURE 7-10

As long as the current document hasn't been saved and closed since the last Quick Style Set change, you can revert to the document's original set of Quick Styles.

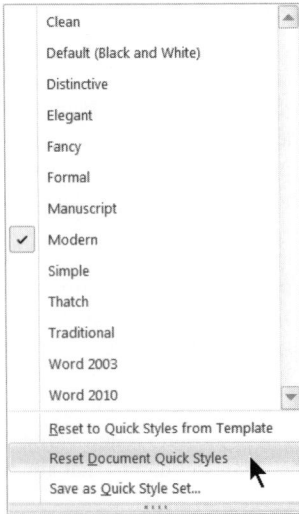

To be able to revert to the styles of the underlying template, you must not have saved Quick Style Set changes to the underlying template. Otherwise, reverting won't do anything other than reapply styles that are already in effect. Unlike in the document itself, where a mere Save doesn't prevent you from being able to go back to square one, saving to the underlying template does commit the style changes. If you did that, see the tip at the end of the preceding section.

Assuming that you haven't saved a Quick Style Set to your current document template, you can revert to its styles. Choose Change Styles ⇨ Style Set ⇨ Reset to Quick Styles from Template (refer to Figure 7-10) in the Styles group of the Home tab.

Styles Task Pane

Conceptually, the Styles task pane is the replacement for Word 2003's Styles and Formatting task pane. Shown in Figure 7-11, the Styles task pane provides some of the same functionality, but not all. It also offers some functionality that Word 2003's earlier task pane didn't have. Remember that you open this pane by clicking the Dialog Box Launcher in the Styles group of the Home tab.

FIGURE 7-11

Right-click a style in the Styles task pane for style-specific options.

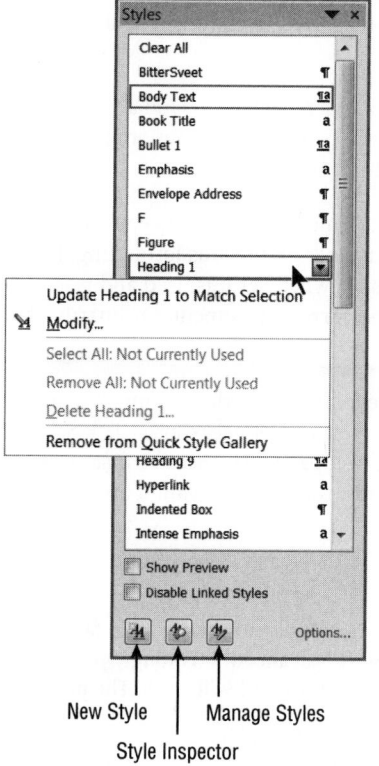
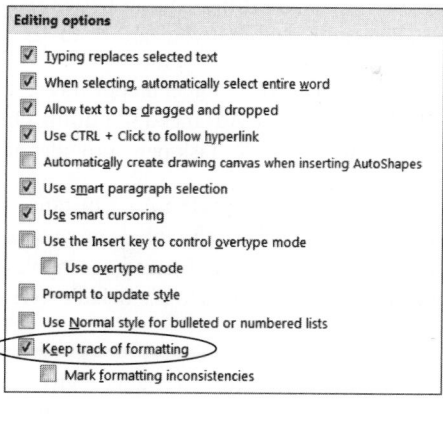

In Figure 7-11, notice that the styles have three kinds of icons next to them: ¶, **a**, or ¶**a**.

The ¶ means that it's a paragraph style only. You cannot apply it to only part of a paragraph, and you can apply it by placing the insertion point anywhere in the target paragraph.

The **a** icon means that it's a character/text style. It is applied only to selected text. You can apply it to a single word (assuming that When Selecting, Automatically Select Entire Word is enabled in the Editing Options section of Word Options — accessed using File ➪ Options). You can also apply it to a single character or an entire document.

The ¶**a** icon means that the style can be used as either a character style or a paragraph style. If nothing is selected or if parts of two or more paragraphs are selected, the style is applied to the entire paragraph(s) touched by the selection. If only part of a single paragraph is selected, the style is applied only to selected text.

Does this mean that Heading styles, which use ¶**a**, can be applied to something less than a full paragraph? You betcha! This can be exceedingly useful when you want to include headings at the beginning of paragraphs, particularly when you want to save vertical space in the document. This is not a new feature, by the way; you could do it as far back as Word 2000.

The options you get when you right-click or use the drop-down arrow in the Styles task pane vary according to Word's Options settings as well as whether the selected style is built in or user-created. In Figure 7-11 the built-in Heading 1 style excludes the Delete option. You cannot delete a built-in style. You can hide it, but you can't deep-six it.

The Update option at the top of the menu appears even if the option Prompt to Update Styles is not enabled (File ➪ Options ➪ Advanced ➪ Editing Options). If you have that option turned off but need the capability, the Styles task pane provides ad hoc access to it.

Two extremely useful options are Select All # Instance(s) and Remove All # Instance(s). The Remove All option is extremely useful for cleaning up a document's extraneous formatting. It does not delete the text in question. Instead, it removes the style wherever it is used and resets the formatting of those occurrences to the default style for the current document. Ordinarily, that would be Normal.

The Select option is equally useful. To change a given style to a different style, you might consider using Find and Replace. Indeed, that is an option. However, it's not necessary. Click Select All # Instances, and then click the desired style in the Styles task pane. Or, once the instances are selected, use manual/direct formatting to sculpt the text just the way you want it, and then choose New Style at the bottom of the Styles task pane.

Note

In Figure 7-11, why would Select All and Remove All say "Not Currently Used" when the style is, in fact, in use? This is an artifact of a Word Options setting. Choose File ➪ Options ➪ Advanced ➪ Editing Options section and click to disable Keep Track of Formatting. Now Select All and Remove All will work. The problem stems from the way in which Word keeps track of formatting, which it does by making tiny incremental changes to the underlying style. The result is that when Keep Track of Formatting is used, Word disallows the Select All and Remove All features. ■

Remove from Quick Style Gallery does not remove the style from the document. Instead, it removes the style from the Quick Style Gallery listing of styles. If the style is not currently in the Quick Style Gallery, the command in the pop-up will be Add to Quick Gallery instead.

Manage Styles

Another option available from the Styles task pane is the Style Manager button, which opens the Manage Styles dialog box shown in Figure 7-12. Use this dialog box to create, modify, and (if they are user-created) delete styles.

FIGURE 7-12

Manage Styles gives you complete control over styles.

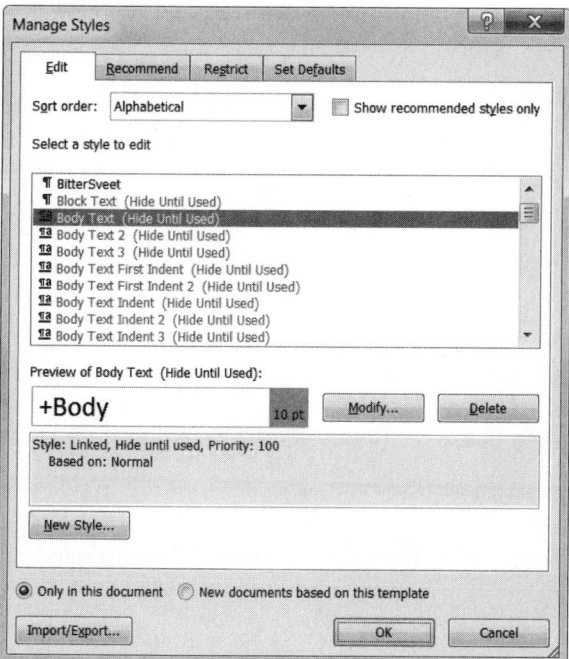

Use the manager also as a launch pad for the Organizer, via the Import/Export button, which enables you to copy styles between different templates and documents, as well as to rename and delete styles. (Again, only user-created styles can be deleted.)

Recommended Styles

The Recommend tab, shown in Figure 7-13, controls which styles show up on the list of recommended styles. The "recommended" option shows up in each of the style-related task panes, and applies to the styles that are displayed in the Quick Style Gallery. For any style you can choose to Show, Hide Until Used, or Hide. It's a great way to focus the options when you want to exercise strong control over document formatting.

FIGURE 7-13

Use the Recommend tab to control what styles show up when you restrict style controls to displaying "recommended" styles.

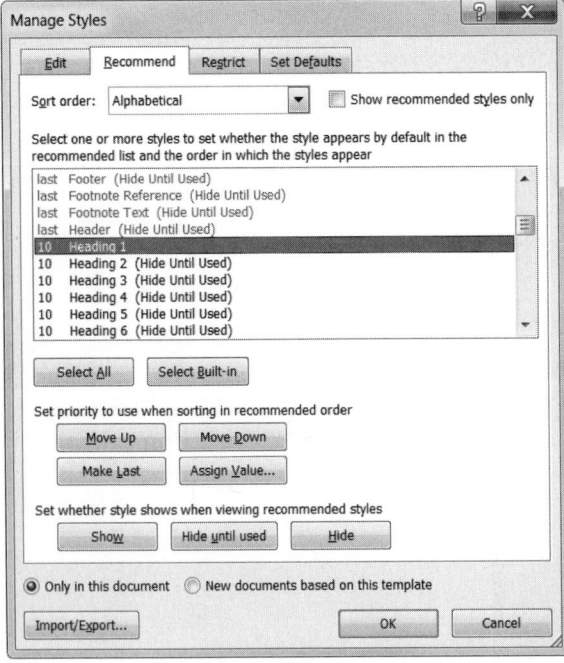

In the recommended list of styles, you can apply your changes one at a time or by using standard Windows selection techniques to select multiple styles. Note the Select All and Select Built-in buttons, too, which enable you to quickly distinguish between Word's standard styles and user-created styles.

Use the Move Up/Move Down/Make Last/Assign Value tools to determine the recommended order. You can even alphabetize them, if that makes more sense to you.

Restricted Styles

You've heard of the style police? Well, grab your badge! For even stronger style enforcement, the Restrict tab lets you restrict which styles can be used. This is a good tool for designing templates and forms in which you want extremely tight control over the formatting of content. It's also useful in setting up training classes for Word, when you might want to tame the options a bit to avoid overwhelming the novice user.

Additionally, if you want to enforce the use of only styles — and not direct formatting — the restricted styles capability provides a way to do it. Use Limit Formatting to Permitted Styles, shown at the bottom of Figure 7-14, to accomplish this feat. This can be useful when you're setting up forms and templates for specific tasks for which the resulting document formatting must adhere to strict requirements.

FIGURE 7-14

The Restrict tab enables you to make direct formatting off-limits.

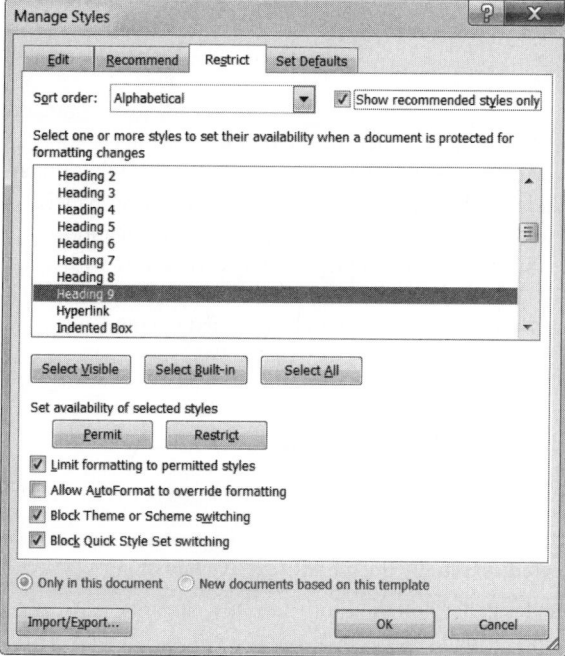

By restricting formatting only to certain styles, you effectively prevent the use of direct formatting tools. As shown in Figure 7-15, when formatting is restricted to Normal and Heading 1 through Heading 5, most of the Font and Paragraph group controls on the Home tab of the Ribbon are dimmed as unavailable.

Note that not only can you limit formatting only to permitted styles; you can also block Theme and Quick Style switching. If you want to tame *artistic* tendencies of users whose mission statement doesn't include using up all the colored ink or toner, this provides an avenue of attack. Did I mention that this stuff is better than a whip?

FIGURE 7-15

In this scenario, formatting is limited to Normal and Headings 1 through 5, which puts the Font and Paragraph direct formatting controls off-limits.

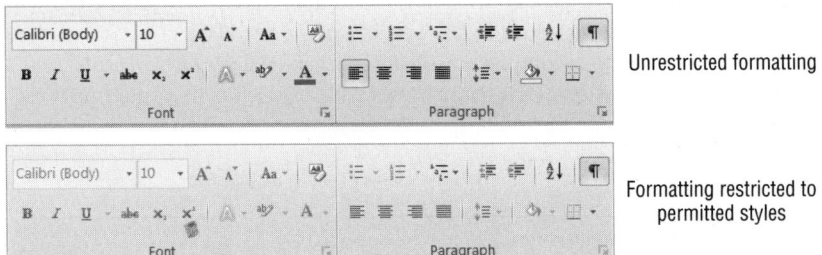

Unrestricted formatting

Formatting restricted to permitted styles

Style Inspector

The Style Inspector enables you to quickly determine whether the current formatting is applied wholly through a style, or whether direct formatting is in effect. In Figure 7-16, notice that under the paragraph and text (character) styles there is a box with the word *Plus*. In the lower panel it says "Plus: <none>," which indicates that no direct text/character formatting has been applied. In the upper panel, however, it shows that left alignment has been applied directly, along with a left indent of 0.38 inch and a line spacing of 1.5 lines. In the current mystery, it appears that someone mistakenly applied the Heading 3 style to regular body text and then tried to compensate using direct formatting.

FIGURE 7-16

The Style Inspector can help you diagnose formatting ailments.

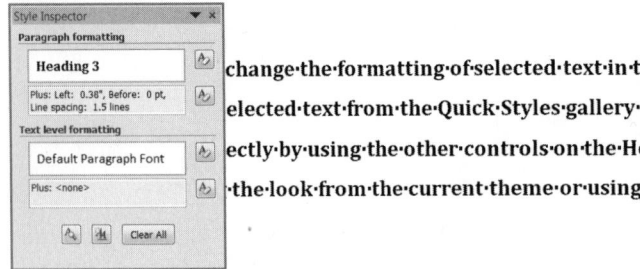

change·the·formatting·of·selected·text·in·the·document·text·by·choosing·

elected·text·from·the·Quick·Styles·gallery·on·the·Home·tab.·You·can·also·

ectly·by·using·the·other·controls·on·the·Home·tab.·Most·controls·offer·a·

·the·look·from·the·current·theme·or·using·a·format·that·you·specify·

Summary

In this chapter we've explored a variety of features. You now know how to apply Quick Styles; how to choose and modify Quick Style Sets (as well as create your own); and how to create, modify, and delete user-created styles. In addition, when a style can't be deleted, you now know why. You should also be able to do the following:

- Use the Manage Styles dialog box to hide and restrict styles and direct formatting.
- Use Apply Styles to apply, create, and modify styles.
- Use the Styles pane to quickly select all occurrences of any given style.
- Use the Style Inspector to solve formatting mysteries.

Page Setup and Sections

This chapter examines some concepts that might be a bit challenging if you're new to Word, or perhaps even if you're not new to Word. Grasping these concepts, however, opens up the marvelous and potential-filled world of section formatting, which enables you to do wonderfully creative things with your documents.

Page Setup Basics

To fully grasp what this part of the chapter is about, you're going to have to make sure that you can see section breaks and other nonprinting formatting characters. Although some users think these characters are an eyesore and distract from the basic business of putting words into the computer, they should instead be viewed as flashlights that illuminate otherwise dark corners that are home to the secret and mysterious powers of Microsoft Word.

It's time to turn on those flashlights, assuming they're not already on. In Figure 8-1, the upper paragraph has nonprinting formatting marks turned on, whereas the lower paragraph has them turned off. You press Ctrl+Shift+8 to toggle them on and off, or click the Show/Hide (¶) button in the Paragraph section of the Home Ribbon tab. To truly understand what's happening in this chapter, as well as what's happening in your documents, you should toggle those nonprinting formatting characters on — at least for now. From here on out in this chapter, it's assumed that you can actually see what's being talked about. Otherwise you'll miss out on all the fun, and you'll remain in the dark.

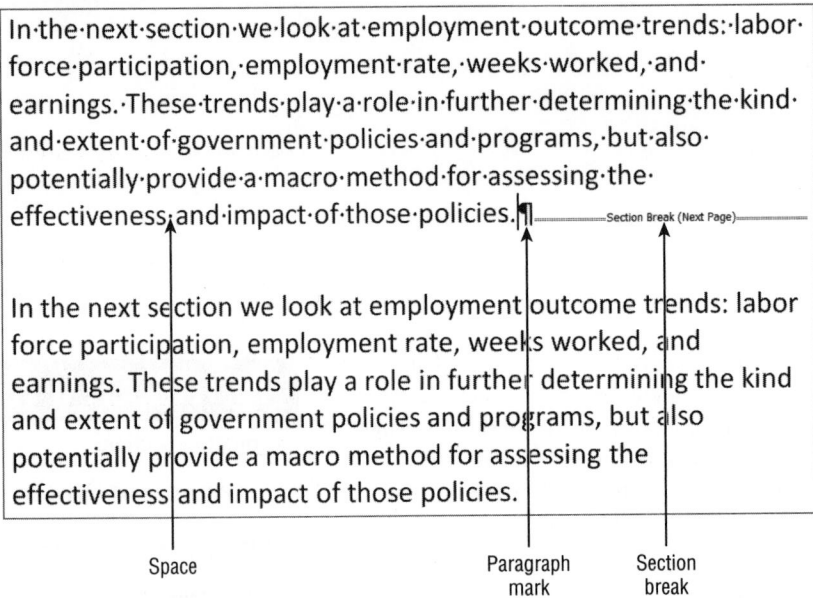

FIGURE 8-1

These two paragraphs are identical, but in the upper one, Ctrl+Shift+8 has been pressed to toggle nonprinting formatting marks on.

In·the·next·section·we·look·at·employment·outcome·trends:·labor·
force·participation,·employment·rate,·weeks·worked,·and·
earnings.·These·trends·play·a·role·in·further·determining·the·kind·
and·extent·of·government·policies·and·programs,·but·also·
potentially·provide·a·macro·method·for·assessing·the·
effectiveness,·and·impact·of·those·policies.¶————Section Break (Next Page)————

In the next section we look at employment outcome trends: labor
force participation, employment rate, weeks worked, and
earnings. These trends play a role in further determining the kind
and extent of government policies and programs, but also
potentially provide a macro method for assessing the
effectiveness and impact of those policies.

Space   Paragraph Section
          mark break

Page setup is an interesting concept in Word. It's interesting because the phrase really isn't about "setting up" a page. It's really about setting up section formatting. We've talked earlier about distinct units of formatting — letters, words, sentences, and paragraphs. For Microsoft Word, section formatting is large-scale formatting that usually affects the entire document. The scale of section formatting is so encompassing, in fact, that it can't be contained in styles. To contain section formatting, you need a whole document or a whole document template.

Section Formatting

Word uses section breaks to separate distinctly formatted parts of a document. Most documents, in fact, have just a single section. Only when you need to apply different section formatting within the same document do you need to create a document that contains more than one section. Different sections are necessary for variations in the following kinds of formatting:

- **Headers and Footers.** Includes changes in page numbering style (except for Different First Page settings).

- **Footnotes.** Can be set to be numbered continuously or set to restart numbering on every new page or section.

- **Changes in Line Numbering Style.** Except for suppression on a paragraph-by-paragraph basis.
- **Margins.** Indentation can vary within a section, but not margins.
- **Orientation.** Landscape versus portrait (actually done through paper size).
- **Paper Size.** 8.5 × 11 (letter), 8.5 × 14 (legal), 7.25 × 10.5 (executive), A4 (210.03 × 297.03 mm), and so on.
- **Paper Source.** Upper tray, envelope feed, manual feed, and so on.
- **Columns.** Snaking newspaper-style columns, the number of which cannot vary within a document section.

Section Breaks

Word uses four kinds of section breaks. What kind of break you use depends on why you're breaking:

- **Next Page.** Causes the new section to begin on the next page.
- **Continuous.** Enables the current and next section to coexist on the same page. Not all kinds of formatting can coexist on the same page, so even if you choose Continuous, Word will sometimes force the differently formatted content onto a new page. Section formatting that can be different on different parts of the same page includes the number of columns, left and right margins, and line numbering.
- **Even Page.** Causes the new section to begin on the next even page. If the following page would have been odd, then that page will be blank (unless it has header/footer content, which can include watermarks).
- **Odd Page.** Causes the new section to begin on the next odd page. If the following page would have been even, then that page will be blank, except as noted for the Even Page break.

If you set up a letter in which the first page is to be printed on letterhead, but subsequent pages are to be printed on regular stock (using different paper feed methods), the first page must be in a separate document *section*. If you set up a letter for which the first or last page is an envelope, the envelope must be in a separate *section* — for multiple reasons, because envelopes typically use a different printer paper source, different orientation (landscape), and different margin settings.

Inserting Section Breaks

To insert a section break, in the Page Setup group of the Page Layout tab on the Ribbon, as shown in Figure 8-2, click Breaks. Word displays a variety of different kinds of breaks, including the four types of section breaks. Click the desired section break.

Tip

If you're inserting multiple breaks of the same kind to section off part of a document to be formatted, after inserting the first section break you can use F4 (Repeat) to insert subsequent breaks. Keep in mind that if you do something else after inserting a break, F4 will repeat that other action rather than insert another break. ∎

FIGURE 8-2

The icons next to the four section break types provide a graphic hint of what the different breaks do.

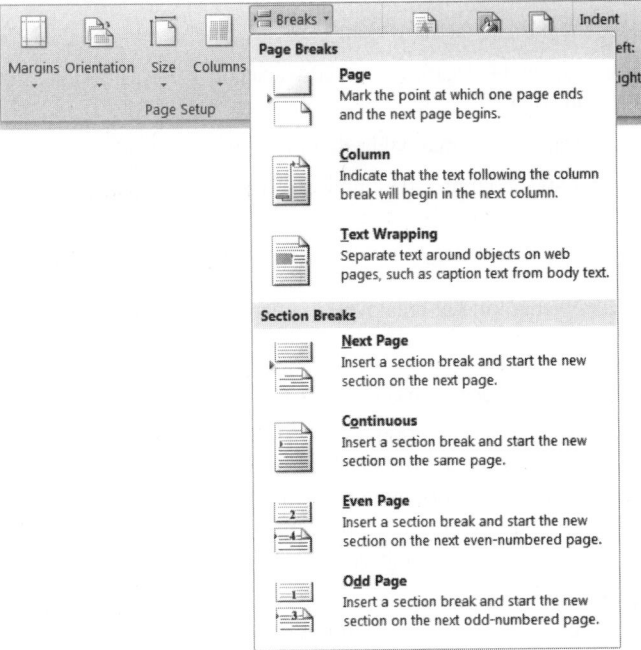

Automatic Section Breaks

Because some kinds of formatting require a section break in order to vary within a document, Word automatically inserts one or more section breaks when you apply "qualifying" formatting to selected text. Sometimes it gets those breaks right, sometimes not. You'll have to be vigilant if you're going to rely on this feature.

For example, suppose you want an interior set of paragraphs to be formatted in three columns, while the adjacent areas are formatted as a single column. Select the paragraphs you want to differentiate, and in the Page Setup group of the Page Layout tab on the Ribbon, choose Columns ⇨ Three Columns. Word automatically inserts Continuous section breaks before and after the selected text to cordon it off for the distinct formatting. If you're lucky, that's what it does, that is.

Sometimes, but not always, Word will insert the wrong kind of section break before and/or after the selected text. It's never quite clear why, but when that happens the best recourse is to press Ctrl+Z to undo the attempt, bracket the target text with the desired type of section breaks, and then apply the formatting to the section you want formatted differently.

Styles, Section Formatting, and Paragraph Formatting

Styles can contain font/character-formatting attributes and paragraph-formatting attributes. However, they cannot contain section-formatting attributes. Therefore, for example, you cannot create a style that would enable you to format a given selection with three columns and 1.5-inch left and right margins. Stand by for a few minutes, however, and you'll see how you can indeed effectively create a style for section formatting, although it's not really a style.

Recall that in Chapter 6, "Paragraph Formatting," you learned that the paragraph mark is the repository of paragraph formatting. Similarly, the section break is the repository of section formatting. If you delete a section break, the current section adopts the formatting of the section that follows, that is, the section whose section break is still intact.

Where is the section break in a document that has only one section? In fact, most documents have only a single section, so this is a serious and valid question. There is an implied section break at the end of the document, so if you insert a section break into a single-section document, the formatting for section 1 resides in that section break, and the formatting for section 2 effectively resides in the permanent paragraph mark at the end of the document.

Permanent? Yes, permanent. If you don't believe it, with paragraph marks displayed, delete everything in a document. Now delete that last paragraph mark. You can't do it! (You can hide it by clicking the Show/Hide button in the Paragraph group in the Home ribbon, but that's cheating, because it's not really gone.)

Saving Section Formatting for Reuse

If section formatting can't reside in a style, then how can you save it for later use? Suppose you often use a very precise set of section formatting attributes — margins and columns, for example — and want to save them for use in other documents. There is a way, but it doesn't involve using what's traditionally called a style. Instead, use a Quick Part or a Building Block.

To do this, insert section breaks — Continuous or Next Page, as needed — to bracket the area to be formatted. Format the first section break in as vanilla or typical a way as possible. This first section break will be used to shield existing text from the new formatting when the Building Block or Quick Part is inserted into an existing document. If it's inserted at the beginning of a document, the vestigial section break can then be deleted.

Format the area between the first section break and the second as needed (see the next section, "Page Setup Choices," to learn about a handy all-in-one-place location to set section formatting, or display the Page Layout tab).

Finally, select both section breaks and the interior matter (it doesn't have to contain text because section formatting resides in the section break), and choose Insert ➪ Text ➪ Quick Parts ➪ Save Selection to Quick Part Gallery. In the Create New Building Block dialog box, in the Name box, type a descriptive name for the item as well as a longer description. If you'll need this item frequently, save it to the Quick Parts Gallery. (Otherwise, you might as well save it as AutoText.) Use the Category drop-down setting to choose Create New Category. In the Create New Category dialog box, as shown on the right in Figure 8-3, type a category name that you can later recall to access all your custom section formatting. Click OK, twice.

FIGURE 8-3

Use Quick Parts or Building Blocks to create reusable section *styles*.

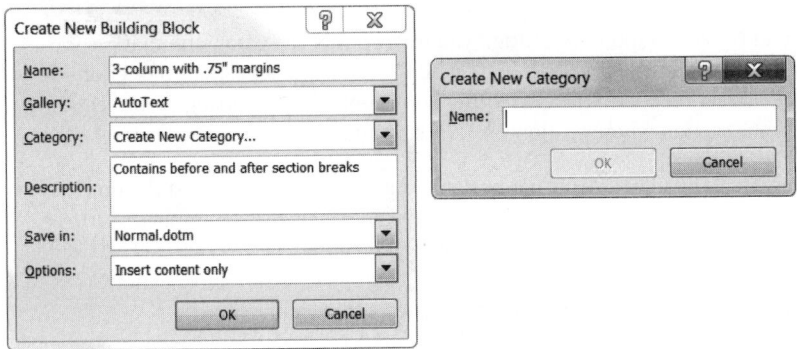

Now, whenever you want this particular kind of formatting, it's there waiting for you. Choose Insert ⇨ Text ⇨ Quick Parts, and if it's in the Quick Parts Gallery, click it to insert it. If it's in AutoText or elsewhere, choose the Building Blocks Organizer. Click the Category heading to sort by category, select the item, and then click Insert. Or, if it's a simple name, type it and press F3. Or press Enter when the AutoComplete tip appears, assuming AutoComplete tips are turned on: File ⇨ Options ⇨ Advanced ⇨ Editing Options (last one in the list).

Page Setup Choices

For access to section formatting, click the Page Layout tab on the Ribbon. The Page Setup group provides access to several section formatting attributes, as well as to the Page Setup dialog box, as shown in Figure 8-4. (Click the group's Dialog Box Launcher to display it.) The Page Setup group also contains Hyphenation, which is not a section-formatting attribute. As discussed in Chapter 6, hyphenation is a paragraph-formatting attribute. (The Margins and Paper tabs of the Page Setup dialog box are shown in later figures.)

Tip

If the Page Layout tab isn't selected, you can also activate the Page Setup dialog box by double-clicking the vertical ruler, if it's displayed, or even by double-clicking the left edge of the Word window in the document area (i.e., anywhere below the horizontal ruler and above the horizontal scroll bar). ■

If you click the Line Numbers drop-down arrow, note that the fifth option — Suppress for Current Paragraph, shown in Figure 8-5 — actually is inaccurate. The feature should say

Suppress for *Selected* Paragraphs. If you choose this option, line numbers for the current paragraph (even if no text is selected) or for the entire selection are suppressed.

The Page Setup group of the Page Layout tab on the Ribbon provides access to section formatting and the Page Setup dialog box.

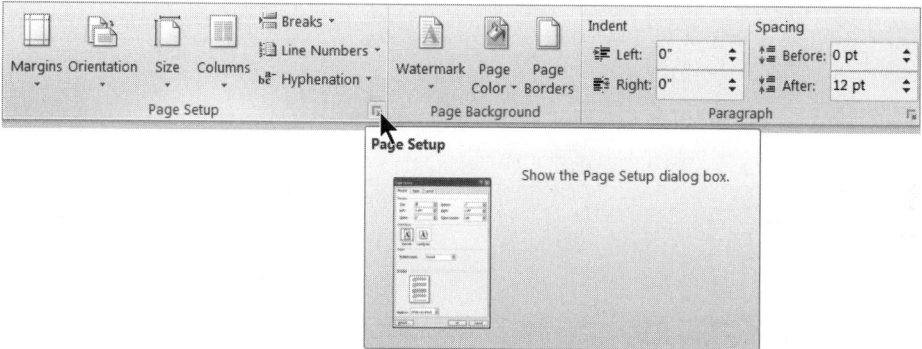

Suppress for Current Paragraph suppresses line numbering for the current paragraph or all paragraphs in the current selection.

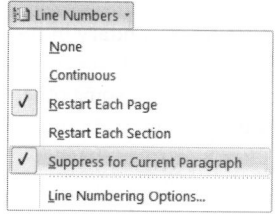

Margins

Using the Margins drop-down in the Page Setup group of the Page Layout tab, shown in Figure 8-6, you can apply a variety of different preset margin settings. If the document contains multiple sections, each of the presets will be applied only to the current document section if nothing is selected, or only to the selected sections if multiple sections are included in the selection.

If you want more precise control, choose Custom Margins, which opens the Page Setup dialog box to the Margins tab, shown in Figure 8-7. From here you can control all margins as needed and apply the change where you want. If text is selected, then Selected Sections and Selected Text replace This Section and This Point Forward, respectively, in the Apply To drop-down list.

FIGURE 8-6

The Margins drop-down offers a selection of preset margins, including the Office 2003 Default, just in case you want to reminisce.

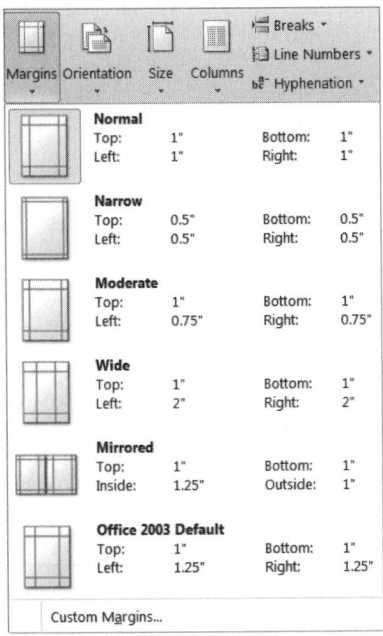

You can also adjust the top and bottom margins by dragging the gray-and-white boundary in the vertical ruler to the left of the document window (depending on your Color Scheme choice in the General settings in the Word Options dialog box, you might see shades of blue or some other color rather than gray). To increase the top margin, drag the top border down. To increase the bottom margin, draw the bottom border up. In either case, press the Alt key to display the margin setting as you're dragging.

Orientation

Orientation refers to whether the page is laid out horizontally (Landscape) or vertically (Portrait — the default orientation). You might sometimes need to rotate a page to Landscape in order to fit a particular picture, chart, table, or other object. It should be emphasized, however, that making a single page Landscape carries with it many consequences that might be considerably worse and harder to deal with than trying to find a way to rotate the object itself.

Consider page numbers and other header and footer content. If the whole page is changed to Landscape, then the header and footer now rotate as well. To have the headers and footers located in the correct positions relative to Portrait-oriented pages takes a bit of strategizing. The usual approach is to set up different headers and footers for the solitary Landscape page. To get the orientation correct, you might consider putting the header and footer material into either a textbox or a single-cell borderless table in which the text has been rotated 90 degrees.

Using the Margins tab of the Page Setup dialog box, you can control how/where the new formatting is applied.

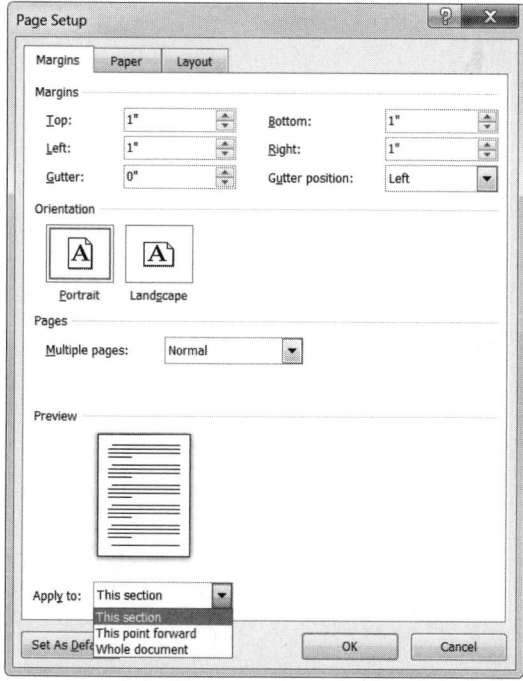

Alternatively, you can keep the orientation as Portrait and rotate the table, chart, or picture instead. For pictures and charts, rotation isn't challenging. With Wrapping (Picture Tools Format tab of the Ribbon, in the Arrange group) set to anything other than In Line with Text, simply rotate the picture or chart 90 degrees using the rotation handle.

Tables are a bit more challenging, but you have several options. If you're just now creating the table, select the entire table and in the Table Tools Layout tab, Alignment group, click Text Direction to rotate the text so that it can be read if you tilt your head to the right or left. Keep in mind that columns and rows are reversed. It's not necessarily easy to work this way, but it can be done, as shown in Figure 8-8.

FIGURE 8-8

With all text in a table rotated 90 degrees, it's possible to create a sideways table, rather than have to change orientation within a document.

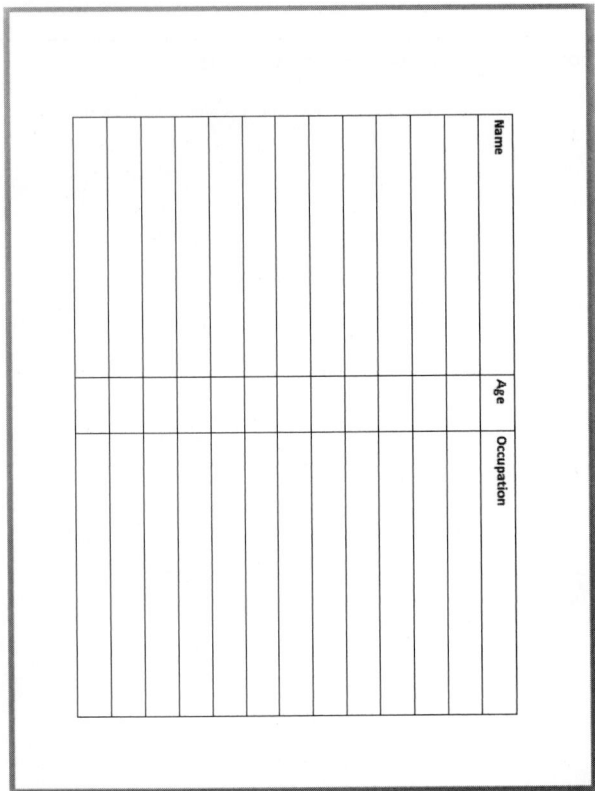

Another option would be to copy the table to the clipboard, choose Home ➪ Clipboard ➪ Paste ➪ Paste Special, and paste the table into the document as a picture. Because it's now a picture, you can choose any floating wrapping style and then rotate the table as needed so that it fits comfortably, but sideways, in a Portrait-oriented Word document page. As above, headers and footers will display in Portrait mode because you haven't changed the paper orientation.

The downside is that sometimes the graphics resolution of this technique isn't perfect. You'll have to decide if it's acceptable and legible. Plus, to make changes in the table, you need to maintain a copy of the actual table and remake the *conversion* as needed.

Another negative is that once you've done this to a table, you won't be able to edit it anymore. If you decide to go this route, you might consider saving the non-graphic version of the table as a Building Block in the current template. This way it will still be accessible if you need to modify it.

A variation on this approach, if the table fits into a window from which you can copy it, is to use screen-capture software to take a picture of the table. This approach often yields more predictable and better-quality graphics, but it has the same drawbacks as the previous approach, and you must have a sufficiently large monitor and amenable screen-capture software (such as the Snipping Tool built into Windows 7 or SnagIt, from www.TechSmith.com, which is highly flexible).

Size

Size refers to paper size. Several preset standard sizes are available from the Size drop-down in the Page Setup group of the Page Layout tab on the Ribbon, as shown in Figure 8-9. Clicking More Paper Sizes displays the Paper tab in the Page Setup dialog box. Although it says "More Paper Sizes," that's not actually what you get. The *more* refers to the Custom Size setting at the bottom of the Paper Size list, which enables you to set any size up to 22 inches. This assumes that your printer supports something that large.

FIGURE 8-9

Click More Paper Sizes to display the Paper tab in the Page Setup dialog box.

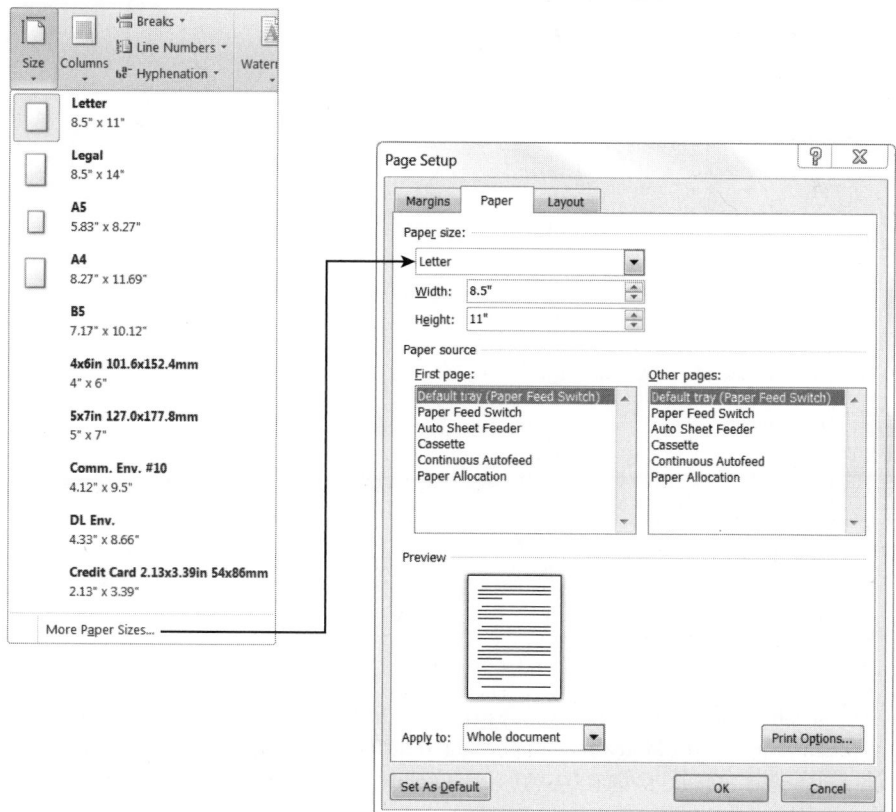

Columns

Use the Columns tool in the Page Setup group on the Page Layout tab of the Ribbon to set the number of columns either in the current section or in all sections in the current selection if text is selected.

Page Layout Settings

We've already looked at the Margins and Paper tabs in the Page Setup dialog box. The Layout tab, visible in Figure 8-10, houses additional settings, some of which often go unnoticed. Headers and Footers settings are also set in the Layout tab; see "Header and Footer Navigation and Design" later in this chapter for a full discussion.

FIGURE 8-10

The Different Odd and Even and Different First Page header/footer settings enable you to set different headers and footers without using another section break.

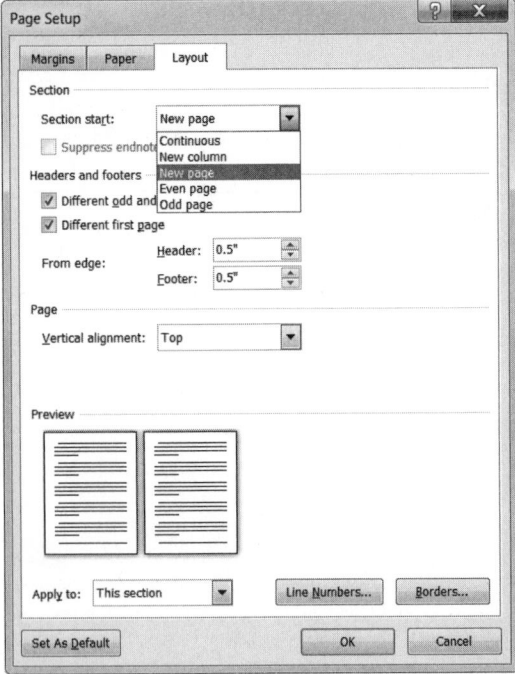

If the Page Layout tab is selected, the quickest way to display the Layout tab of the Page Setup dialog box is to click Line Numbers ⇨ More Line Numbering in the Page Setup group, even if you're not interested in line numbering. If the Page Layout tab isn't showing, you can double-click on the vertical ruler or between the horizontal ruler and the bottom of the ribbon area to display the Page Setup dialog box, and then click the Layout tab.

Fixing or Changing a Section Break

The Section Start setting shown in Figure 8-10 is a bit cryptic and confusing to many users, but it can be extremely useful. Have you ever ended up with the wrong kind of section break? For example, suppose you want a Continuous section break, but you have a New Page, Odd, or Even section break instead. This can happen either because you inserted the wrong kind of break or because Word inserted the wrong kind of break automatically.

The ordinary impulse is to delete the wrong one and insert the kind you want. Sometimes, however, despite your best efforts, you still end up with the wrong kind of break.

To cure this, put the insertion point into the section that is preceded by the wrong kind of break. Activate the Page Setup dialog box using any of the techniques described earlier. Click the Layout tab to display the dialog box view shown in Figure 8-10. Set Section Start to the kind of section break you want, and click OK.

Vertical Page Alignment

Another often-unnoticed feature in Word is the Vertical Alignment setting on the Layout tab of the Page Setup dialog box. By default, Word sets the vertical alignment to Top, and most users never discover the additional options shown in Figure 8-11. Because it is a section formatting attribute, you can set vertical alignment for the whole document or just for selected sections.

FIGURE 8-11

Word provides four different types of vertical page alignment.

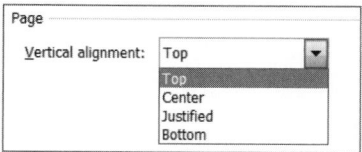

Vertical alignment can be extremely useful for particular parts of a publication — such as the title page for a format report, booklet, or book — as well as for short letters, brochures, newsletters, and flyers. For title pages, setting the vertical alignment to Centered is almost always more efficient than trying to insert the right number of empty paragraphs above the top line, or trying to set the Spacing Before to just the right amount (in the Paragraph group of the Page Layout tab of the Ribbon). For one-page notices, vertical alignment is also often just what the doctor ordered.

For some newsletters and other page-oriented publications, setting the alignment to Justified serves a couple of purposes. Not only does it make the most use of the whole sheet of paper, but it adjusts line spacing to do it. Hence the appearance is smoother than it might be otherwise.

This setting also lets you optimize the point size if you want to make the font as large as possible without spilling onto another page.

Page Borders

The last Page Setup setting we'll look at is page borders. A *page border* is a line, a set of lines, or decorative artwork that appears around the perimeter of the page. You see them a lot on title pages as well as on flyers and brochures.

To insert a page border, in the Page Layout tab of the Ribbon, choose Page Borders in the Page Background group, which displays the dialog box shown in Figure 8-12. The dialog box offers the same options you saw earlier in Chapter 6, "Paragraph Formatting," under "Borders and Boxes." In addition, however, you have more than 150 Art options you can use to create decorative borders, although some of these might look pretty cheesy compared to the professional graphics you can create with SmartArt.

FIGURE 8-12

For page borders, you can insert a variety of different lines, or choose from more than 150 built-in Art items.

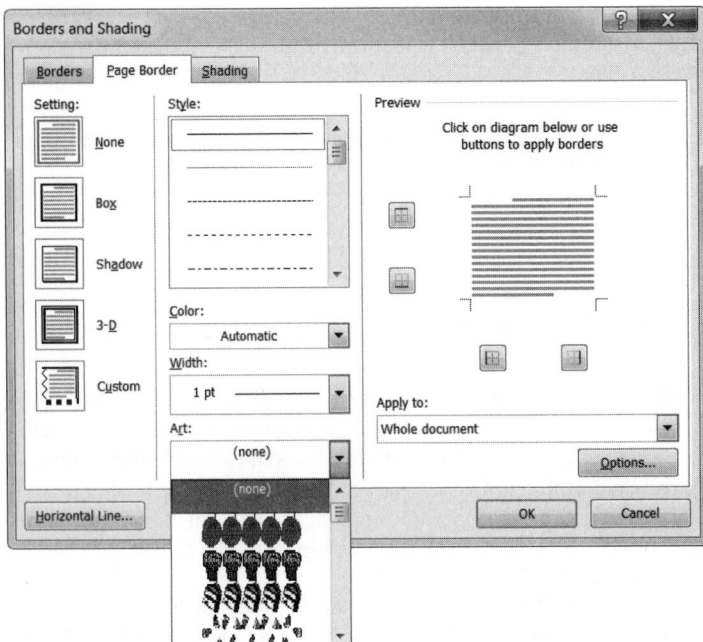

For placing a border around a title page, you can set Apply to This Section — First Page Only. Other options here are Whole Document, This Section, and This Section — All Except First Page.

To control the placement of the page border with respect to the edge of the text or paper, click Options to open the Border and Shading Options dialog box, shown in Figure 8-13. Note that when you're setting page borders, paragraph-related options are grayed out. Using the Measure From box, you can set the distance of the page border either from the text or from the edge of the paper.

Use Border and Shading Options if your page border crowds the text too much.

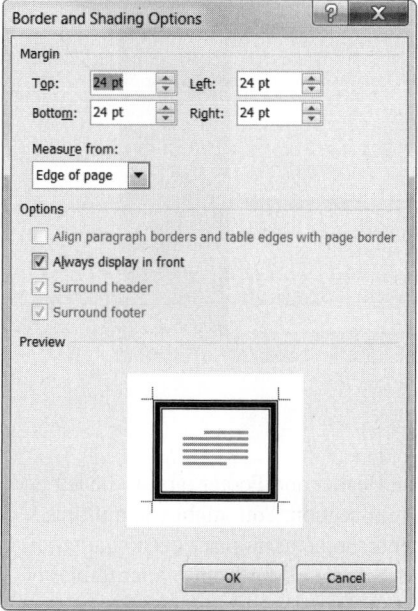

The Header and Footer Layer

When you're working in Print Layout view, any text in the header and footer layer usually shows up as grayish text at the top, bottom, or side of your document. To access those areas, double-click where you want to edit — even if you don't see any text there. This brings the header and footer areas to the surface, as shown in Figure 8-14.

Headers and footers also display in the Print Preview in Backstage view. There, however, because the view is supposed to represent what you'll see when the document is printed, the header and footer areas aren't gray and isolated. The same is true in Full Screen Reading view. Note that in the Print Preview and Full Screen Reading view, you cannot perform normal editing — neither to normal text nor to text in headers and footers. In Full Screen Reading view, however, you can insert comments. This chapter assumes that you are working in Print Layout view, so that all kinds of editing are possible. If you don't see what's shown in the screen shots, then check your view setting.

FIGURE 8-14

Header and Footer tabs clarify what and where headers and footers are. With headers and footers open for editing, the document body text turns gray.

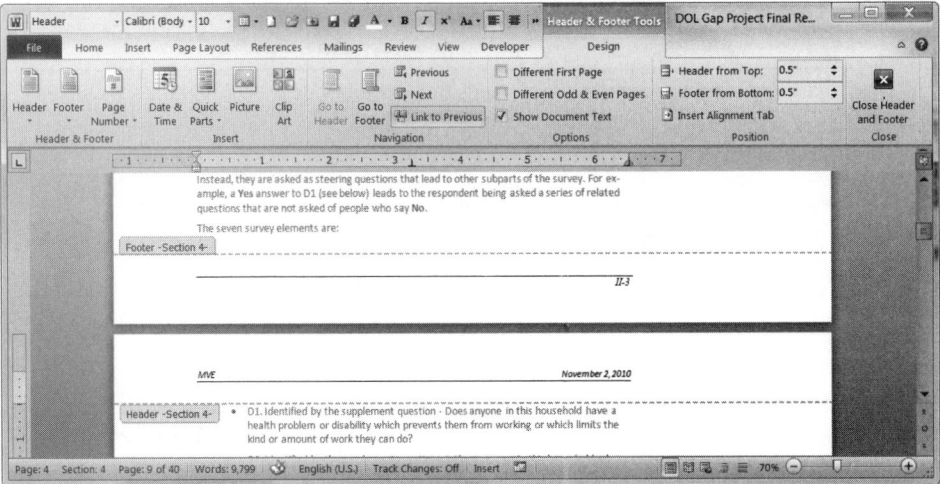

Document Sections

Figure 8-14 indicates the document section number in the Header and Footer tabs at the left end of each area. Word documents can be single-section or multi-section. You might use multiple sections for a variety of reasons, particularly in long documents. Some users place each chapter of a document in a separate section, with additional sections being used for front matter (tables of contents, tables of figures, foreword, etc.) and back matter (index, glossary, etc.).

Section formatting enables you to use different kinds of numbering for different sections. It also allows different header and footer text in different sections. For example, the header or footer might include the name of each chapter, or the word *Index* or *Glossary*.

Header and Footer Navigation and Design

Word provides several different tools that enable you to control the way headers and footers are displayed and formatted. In this section you'll learn what those are and where to find them in Word 2010.

Editing the Header and Footer Areas

The main set of controls is contained in the Header & Footer Tools Design tab of the Ribbon, shown in Figure 8-15. To display the tab, double-click the header or footer area in a document. Or, from the Insert tab, choose Header ➪ Edit Header (or Footer ➪ Edit Footer) in the Header & Footer group. Once the header/footer layer is open for editing, either the header or footer can be edited, as can items inserted into the side area (e.g., page numbers in the side margins), as well as watermarks.

FIGURE 8-15

The Header & Footer Tools Design tab on the Ribbon provides complete control over headers and footers.

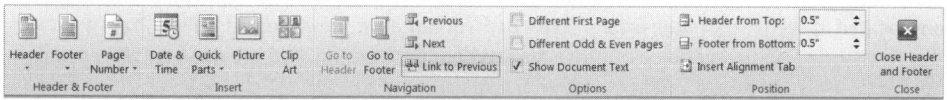

Notice the Go to Header and Go to Footer commands in the Navigation group of the tab. You can use those commands to quickly switch back and forth between the header and footer areas, but, as suggested by Figure 8-14, both areas are equally accessible. You do not need to click Go to Header or Go to Footer — you can simply click where you want to edit.

Note

Although header and footer material can reside in the side margins, you cannot open the header or footer area for editing by double-clicking in the side margins. The double-click method for opening headers and footers works only in the top and bottom margin areas. ∎

Header and Footer Styles

By default, Word's headers and footers use built-in paragraph styles named *Header* and *Footer*. Each is formatted with a center tab and a right-aligned tab to facilitate placement of text and other items. This enables you to have three distinct components, one each at the left, center, and right within the header or footer, without having to resort to using a table, textbox, or other device (although tables and textboxes are perfectly acceptable in headers and footers).

For example, to create a header with a left-adjusted document name, a centered date, and a right-adjusted author's name, you would enter the document name, press Tab, enter the date, press Tab, and finally type the author's name, as shown in Figure 8-16.

FIGURE 8-16

The default header style makes three-part headers easy.

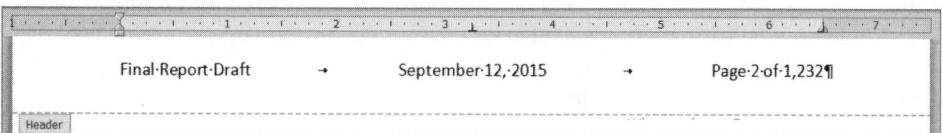

Section Surfing

When editing the header/footer layer of a document, you can use the mouse or keyboard keys to navigate as needed. As long as you don't double-click in the text area of the document, the header and footer area remains open for business.

In a long document that contains many sections, however, scrolling can be tedious and imprecise. For greater control and precision, you can use the Previous Section and Next Section tools in the Navigation group of the Header & Footer Tools Design tab.

Note
When the header and footer areas are open for editing, the Browse Object's Next Section and Previous Section buttons located at the base of the vertical scroll bar will not have the expected effects. Yes, they move you to the next and previous sections, but they also switch the focus back to the main text layer. ■

Link to Previous

Different document sections can contain different headers and footers. When Link to Previous is selected for any given header or footer, that header or footer is the same as that for the previous section. By default, when you add a new document section, its headers and footers inherit the header and footer settings of the previous section.

To unlink the currently selected header or footer from the header or footer in the previous section (which will allow the current section to maintain a distinct header or footer), click Link to Previous in the Navigation group of the Header & Footer Tools Design tab to toggle it off. Observe the difference between the upper and lower Link to Previous buttons shown in Figure 8-17.

FIGURE 8-17

Link to Previous is a toggle that can be turned on or off independently for the header and footer in each document section.

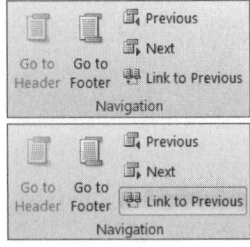

Note that headers and footers in any section have independent Link to Previous settings. While Link to Previous initially is turned on for all new sections that are created, when you turn it off for any given header, the corresponding footer remains linked to the previous footer. This gives you additional control over how document information is presented.

Different First Page

Most formal reports and, indeed, many other formal documents do not use page numbers on the first page. To keep users from having to make such documents multi-section documents, Word lets you set an exception for the first page of each document section. To enable this option for any given document section, display a header or footer in that section and click the Different First Page option in the Options group of the Header & Footer Tools Design tab (refer to Figure 8-15).

In a way, this is like a "link to previous" option that you can apply to different document sections. Unlike with Link to Previous, however, there is no telltale toggle tool to tell you the setting for the current section. Instead, there's a checkbox that indicates whether the option is turned on or off. As you navigate across different header and footer areas in a multi-section document, the checkmark appears or disappears to indicate the setting for the current section. Also unlike with the Link to Previous option, Different First Page cannot be different for the header and the footer. You cannot suppress just one. To accomplish that you would need distinct document sections (separated by a section break).

Different Odd & Even Pages

You can, without using section breaks, instruct Word to maintain different headers and footers on odd and even pages. This feature is often used in book/booklet printing, where the header/footer always appears closest to the outside edge of the paper — on the left for left-hand pages, and on the right for right-hand pages. The Different Odd & Even Pages checkbox, also in the Options group of the Header & Footer Tools Design tab, works in the same way as the Different First Page option and is set per section, not individually for each header and footer.

Show Document Text

Sometimes having document text showing is useful and helps provide a frame of reference for headers and footers. At other times, however, it can be distracting and can make it harder to identify header and footer text, particularly if you're actually using gray fonts in the header or footer area. Displayed text also can make it difficult to access graphics that are stored in the header or footer layer.

By default, Show Document Text is enabled. To hide document text, click to remove the check mark next to Show Document Text in the Options group of the Header & Footer Tools Design tab.

Distance from Edge of Paper

Headers and footers are printed in the margin area. The *margin* is the area between the edge of the paper and the edge of the text layer in the body of the document. If the header or footer is too tall for a given page, Word reduces the height of the text layer on the fly so that the header or footer can be printed. That is, it will be printed if the distance between the top of the header or the bottom of the footer and the respective edge of the paper is as large as the nonprintable areas of the paper.

Printers have a *nonprintable area* around the perimeter of the paper. This is an area in which it is mechanically impossible for a given printer to print. Windows' printer drivers do a good job of calculating the margin so that the printer does not try to print in the nonprintable region. When the margin is too small, Word will warn you.

Word does not warn you, however, if the header or footer extends too far into the margin. When this happens, all or part of the header or footer is cut off. Everything might look fine in the Print Preview in Backstage view and there is no warning, but part of the footer or header will be printed in the "twilight zone."

You can rein the document in using the Header from Top and Footer from Bottom settings in the Header & Footer Tools Design tab's Position group. If you find that the header or footer is being cut off, determine how much is being cut off and make that much additional allowance. For example, if 0.25 inch of text is being cut off of the footer, then increase Footer from Bottom by that amount.

Adding Header and Footer Material

You can put a variety of things into headers and footers, ranging from filenames and various other document properties (author, title, date last printed/modified, etc.) to page numbers and even watermarks. Inserting most text and graphics that will actually be printed in the top or bottom margin is straightforward. There are some special cases, however, such as page numbers, side margin matter, and background images and watermarks that require special attention.

Page Numbers

A common use for headers and footers is to display page numbers. To include page numbers in Word 2010, several methods are available — some new as of Word 2007, and some legacy. This section focuses mostly on the new ways because they provide extraordinary ease, flexibility, and variety not found in pre-Ribbon Word (2003 and earlier). When the legacy ways are best, however, that's where we'll turn.

Insert Page Numbers

Inserting page numbers in Word has never been easier. First, decide where you want the page numbers to appear (top, bottom, or side margin). Then click anywhere on the first page in the document section where you want the number to appear. As noted earlier, documents can contain multiple sections, and each section can have independent headers and footers, which means they also can be numbered independently.

In the Insert tab's Header & Footer group, use the Page Number drop-down, as shown in Figure 8-18, and choose Top of Page, for example.

Select the option that corresponds to where you want the page number to appear:

- Top of Page
- Bottom of Page

- Page Margins (see "Where Do Page Margin Numbers Really Go?" a little later in this section)
- Current Position (use this option when the insertion point is already exactly where you want the page number to appear)

FIGURE 8-18

Word 2010 has extensive galleries with a variety of page number formats from which to choose.

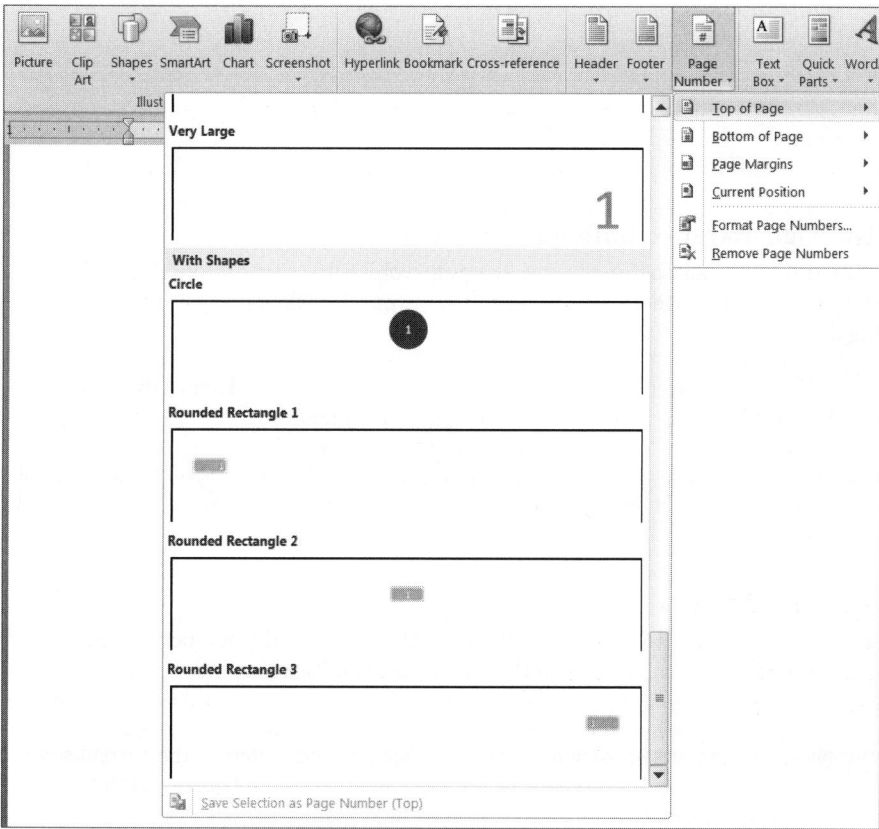

The bottom of the page is the most common choice for word processing documents, but there are times when the top or side works better for a particular document. Select the desired destination. Word displays several preset page number options.

When you find a Page Number Gallery item that suits your fancy, click it to insert the page number into the header or footer (according to which option you chose to get here). Note that you can also right-click the gallery item to see additional options, which are shown in Figure 8-19.

FIGURE 8-19

Right-click a Page Number Gallery item for additional options.

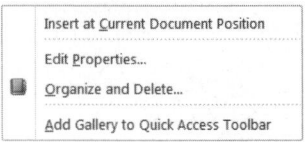

To see the true nature of a Page Number Gallery item, right-click it and choose Edit Properties.

Where Do Page Margin Numbers Really Go?

When you insert the page number in the page margin, Word 2010 inserts it into the header as a floating textbox to which a page field code was added. If you try to double-click that page number, nothing happens!

You can, however, use the Select Objects tool (in the Editing group in the Home tab of the Ribbon, choose Select ⇨ Select Objects), which can grasp any graphic.

Another way to bring the number into reach is to edit the header. In the Header & Footer group of the Insert tab, choose Header ⇨ Edit Header. You can now click the side page number and edit to your heart's content.

Deleting Page Numbers

To delete page numbers, move to the document section that contains the numbering you want to remove. In the Header & Footer group of the Insert tab, click Page Number ⇨ Remove Page Numbers.

Remove Page Numbers removes all page numbers from headers and footers in the current section — including those in the side margins. It does not remove page numbers from other document sections.

Formatting Page Numbers

You can choose the page numbering format before or after you insert a page number. On the Insert tab of the Ribbon, choose Page Number ⇨ Format Page Numbers, to display the Page Number Format dialog box, shown in Figure 8-20. Options are explained in Table 8-1.

FIGURE 8-20

Word provides flexible page numbering options.

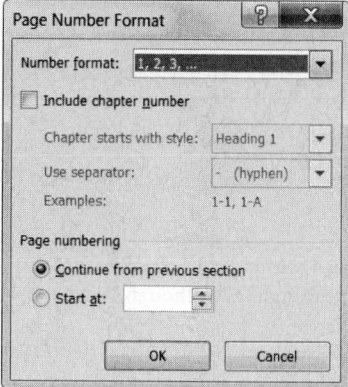

TABLE 8-1

Page Number Options

Option	Purpose
Number format	Specifies numbering scheme: 1, 2, 3; A, B, C; a, b, c; I, II, III; or i, ii, iii. Provides an additional option to bracket Arabic numbers with dashes (to bracket others, edit the header or footer directly, as shown later in this chapter).
Include chapter number	Applies a chapter numbering scheme such as I-1, II-5, III-43, where I, II, and III are chapter numbers and chapters are formatted in a Heading 1 through Heading 9 style, with numbering included in the style definition.
Chapter starts with style	Available only if "Include chapter number" is enabled. For this option to work, chapter numbers must be formatted in a Heading 1 through Heading 9 style, and numbering must be included in the style.
Use separator	Specifies the separator to use between chapter and page numbers.
Continue from previous section	Indicates whether the current section's numbering is connected with that of the previous section. Use this option when distinct sections are being used for a reason other than to create distinct numbering, such as when switching sections to accommodate changes from Portrait to Landscape and back again.
Start at	Use this to specify a starting number other than 1.

Additional options that affect page numbers, such as whether headers or footers are displayed on the first page of a document or document section, were discussed earlier in this chapter, under "Different First Page."

Themes

Before you leave the overall topic of formatting Word documents, you should consider one last formatting *quick change* you can make in a document — changing its *theme*.

Note

Note also that the Themes feature set does not work in Compatibility Mode. There is no mechanism for storing Word 2010 theme information in the standard Word 97–2003 document format, even though Word 2003 has its own different brand of theme formatting. ■

What Are Themes?

Themes are coordinated sets of colors, fonts, table formats, and other graphic elements used to change the overall look of a document while leaving its content unchanged. Word 2010 comes with more than three dozen built-in themes.

The use of themes hinges on using certain Word 2010 formatting features in a particular way. Unless a given document has been designed to use theme elements, you might quickly conclude that themes are broken. They are not.

Another important thing to know about themes is that they are not part of style formatting. There is no way to associate or assign a theme with a particular style. Themes are applied to the entire document, wholly apart from styles.

Each overall theme encompasses three different elements:

- **Theme Colors.** Controls the colors used in tables, graphic objects, and some other document elements like headers and footers.
- **Theme Fonts.** Controls the heading and body fonts used in the document.
- **Theme Effects.** Controls whether certain document elements use effects like glows or shadows.

Using Built-In Themes

The themes appear in a gallery, and when Live Preview is enabled, you can try on themes for the document before applying the one you want. To change the theme, click the Page Layout tab on the Ribbon, and then click the Themes button in the Themes group. Move the mouse pointer over various themes to preview the look each applies (Figure 8-21), and then click the theme to apply.

FIGURE 8-21

Choosing a theme updates the colors and fonts in the document.

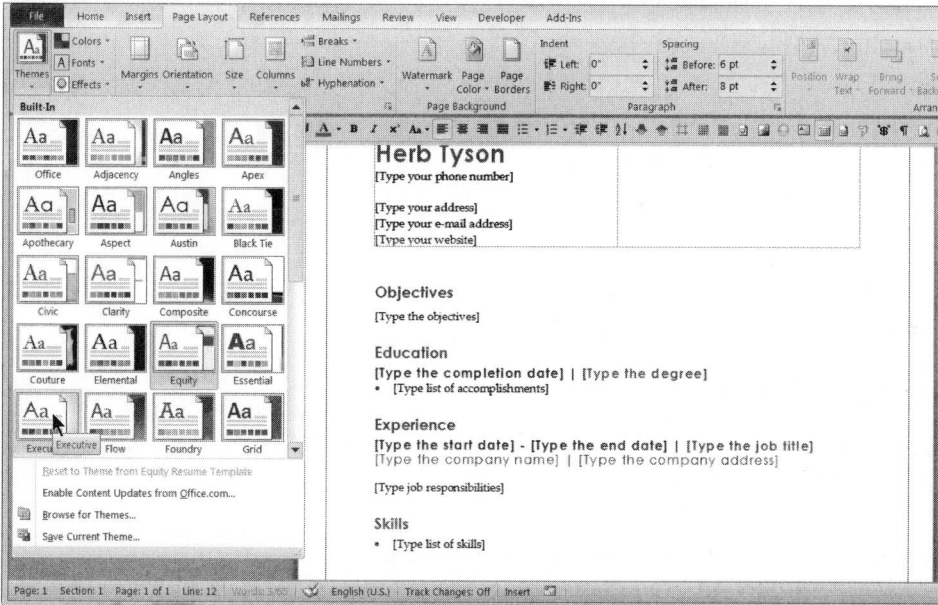

Notice that there are three additional buttons in the Themes group. These are the Theme Colors, Theme Fonts, and Theme Effects buttons, respectively, and you can use them to change overall factors of the document's appearance without changing the whole theme. You can save any combination of Theme Colors, Theme Fonts, and Theme Effects settings as a new overall document theme; to start the process, click the Themes button and then click the Save Current Theme choice at the bottom of the gallery that appears.

Summary

In this chapter, you've learned about the difference between section and paragraph formatting, and exactly what section formatting is. You now know how to create new document sections, as well as why you might want to. You've also learned what headers and footers are, what they're used for, how to use them, and how to navigate them. You finished by seeing how applying a new theme can polish the look of your document. You should now be able to do the following:

- Convert a next page section break into a continuous section break, and vice versa.
- Vertically align a section of a document.
- Change the paper size and paper feed for the envelope section of a document.

- Place decorative or line borders around specific pages.
- Create page numbers in your documents.
- Edit headers and footers.
- Apply a new theme.

Tables and Graphics

T ables are one of Word's most powerful and useful tools. They're extremely flexible and easy to create and manipulate, both directly and via the Ribbon. Thanks to a gaggle of galleries, it's easy to create professional-looking tables quickly and with minimal effort. Live Preview comes to life when it comes to working with tables.

This chapter won't help you decide whether to include pictures. It won't tell you what pictures to use. It will, however, show you where to find pictures if you don't have any, how to insert pictures and other graphics, how to work with pictures once they're in your document, and how to negotiate the precarious relationship between pictures and text.

So, pull up a chair!

Quick Start

The quickest way to create a table in Word is to use one that already exists. It might not be exactly what you want, but it often will be closer to what you want than if you create one from scratch. It helps if you can see a picture, of course, and Word 2010 includes many images of tables. From the Insert tab on the Ribbon, choose Table ⇨ Quick Tables for a view similar to what is shown in Figure 9-1.

Scroll through the gallery to see if there's something you like — something that compares favorably with the table in your mind's eye. If there is, click on it. If it has too many rows, you can delete the ones you don't need. If it has too few columns, you can add a few more. If the proportions and other attributes aren't quite right, you can use Word's table tools to make them right. The point is that you hit the ground running.

IN THIS CHAPTER

Creating a table quickly

Creating tables from scratch

Using table styles

Handling tables, rows, columns, and cells

Understanding table layout and design

Inserting pictures from files

Finding pictures on the Internet

Working with graphics

Using clip art

Using Word 2010's SmartArt tools

FIGURE 9-1

The Quick Tables Gallery offers several pre-formatted tables.

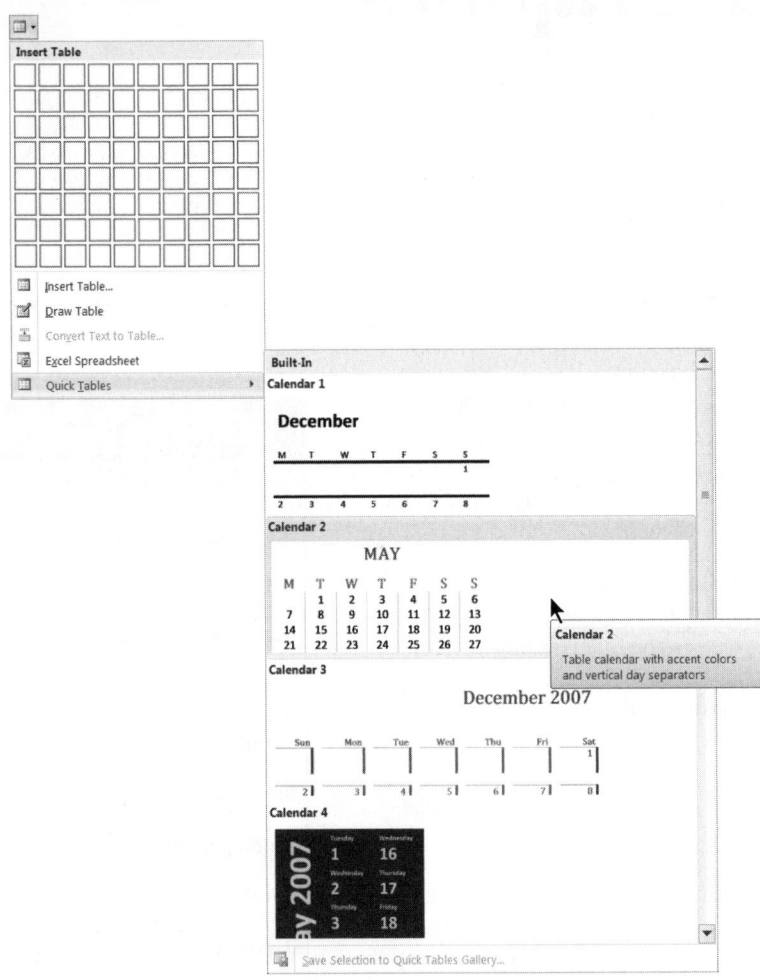

Table Basics

One way to think about a table is as a container for information. The container consists of horizontal rows and vertical columns. If someone speaks of a five-by-four (5 × 4) table, by convention and agreement this refers to a table that is five columns wide and four rows high.

If the terminology is foreign to you, think of rows as you would rows of seats in a theater. Think of columns as vertical columns on a building. Rows go across, and columns go up and down.

Inserting Tables from Scratch

There are three basic methods for creating a table from scratch. One is to use the Table tool to select the numbers of rows and columns you want. On the Insert tab of the Ribbon, click Table in the Tables group. After you release the mouse button, drag the mouse down through the table grid. As you move the mouse, the selected table dimensions change, and Word shows a Live Preview in the document window, as shown in Figure 9-2. Click the mouse when you see what you want.

FIGURE 9-2

When a 5 × 4 table is selected in the Table tool grid, a 5 × 4 Live Preview appears in the document window.

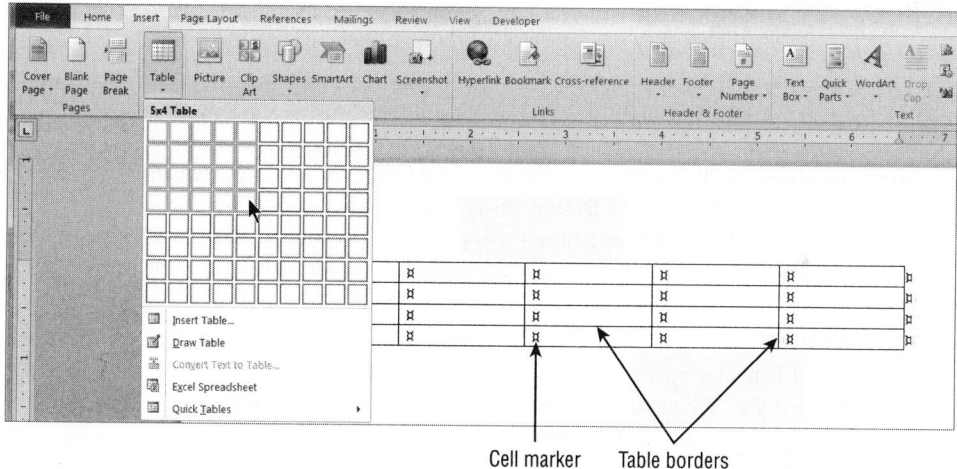

Cell marker   Table borders

A second method for creating a table from scratch is by using the Insert Table dialog box. To get its attention, choose Table ⇨ Insert Table in the Tables group of the Insert tab of the Ribbon. As shown in Figure 9-3, you choose the number of columns and rows, select an AutoFit behavior, and click OK. If you'd like Word to remember to default to the dimensions you choose, then click the Remember Dimensions for New Tables option.

Tip

When nonprinting formatting marks are displayed (Ctrl+Shift+8), cell markers display in each cell, showing where the cells are, as indicated in Figure 9-2. Toggling the cell markers reveals the location for table cells in a table without borders when no gridlines are displayed. Cell markers, incidentally, display whenever paragraph marks do. ∎

FIGURE 9-3

If your hands aren't steady, use the old-fashioned dialog box to choose the number of columns and rows using spin controls.

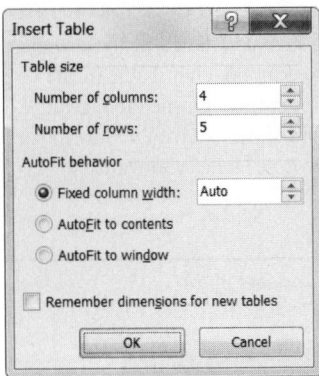

The third method for inserting a table from scratch is to draw it using the Draw Table tool. To begin, choose Insert ⇨ Tables ⇨ Table ⇨ Draw Table. Drag a rectangle to inscribe the outer boundary of your table shell, and then use the Draw Table tool (or pen) to carve out the desired cells. Use the tools in the Table Tools Design tab's Draw Borders group to set line style, weight, and color for the table borders. Use the Eraser tool to remove unwanted table parts. See "Borders and Table Drawing" and "The Table Eraser" later in this chapter for additional information.

AutoFit Behavior

Notice the AutoFit Behavior options shown in Figure 9-3. These same AutoFit options are also available from the right-click menu, as shown in Figure 9-4. Keep this in mind if you need to change the formatting once a table is fully populated.

The Fixed Column Width option is straightforward enough. When you choose this option, the column widths remain fixed unless you explicitly change them by dragging or by using some other method. Note that *fixed* is not the same as *equal*. The column widths might be equal also, but that's a different concept.

The middle option — AutoFit to Contents — is a formatting attribute that causes a table to automatically resize as you add or remove material. It's not a temporary setting, so don't freak out when the table acts as if it were made out of elastic when you add or remove text in existing cells.

The third option — AutoFit to Window — is misnamed. It should be "AutoFit to left and right margins." This option means that the table will remain as wide as the document text itself, regardless of how much text you stuff into the cells. If you add text disproportionately to any given column, that column will automatically resize, making the other columns correspondingly narrower. But the table itself will maintain the width of the document text.

FIGURE 9-4

When the insertion point is inside a table, table-related options are displayed on the right-click menu.

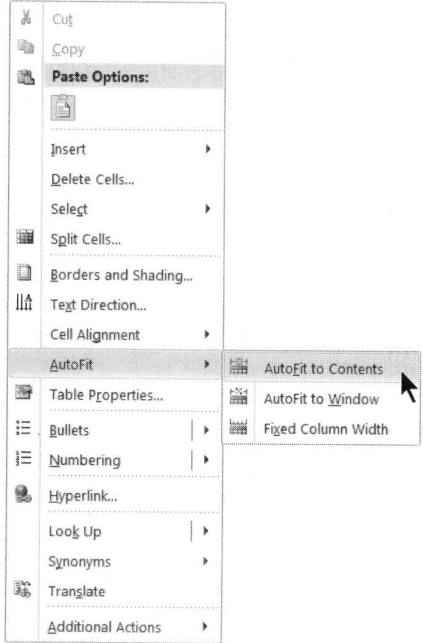

Inserting Tables Based on Existing Data

As suggested elsewhere in this book, there is a correspondence between the word *tab* and the word *table*. Although the proportion of the word processing population that was raised on type-writers is rapidly dwindling, many of us still survive in the wild. Those who took typing classes learned how to fashion tables using the tab stops and the Tab key. Tab stops are metal hardware on a typewriter that literally stop the carriage when you press the Tab key.

Microsoft knows that *tab* and *table* both have the same root. As a result, Word can readily convert your tab-delineated tables into real tables. The easiest way begins with selecting the "table" (although it might look like a table, Word doesn't agree). In the Tables group on the Insert tab of the Ribbon, click Table ⇨ Insert Table. Word instantly determines how many rows and columns there are and encloses your data in a table. As shown in Figure 9-5, the results are basic, but functional. For example, although you often end up with the expected number of rows and columns, one or both might be too wide.

You can fix the width problem easily. Right-click anywhere in the table and choose AutoFit ⇨ AutoFit to Contents (refer to Figure 9-4).

FIGURE 9-5

Word easily converts a tabbed "table" into an actual Word table.

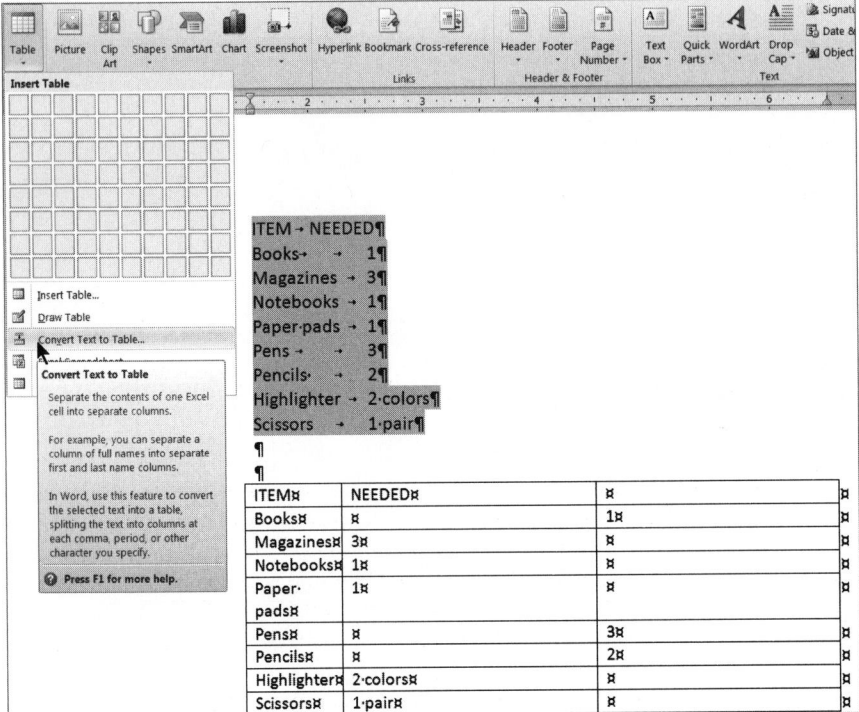

Note

There are other methods for converting text to tables, but they all take more effort. For example, you can create a table shell (an empty table) that fits the dimensions of the data you have, select it, and then drag your tabbed data into it. ■

Convert Text to Table Dialog Box

Alternatively, you can use the Convert Text to Table dialog box as an intermediary. Select the data to be converted, and choose Table ➪ Convert Text to Table in the Tables group of the Insert tab. This displays the Convert Text to Table dialog box, shown in Figure 9-6.

This method doesn't produce instant results, but it does let you set the AutoFit behavior ahead of time, as well as choose a different column delimiter if the one Word guesses (usually tabs) is incorrect.

It's also a useful diagnostic tool when the quick method illustrated earlier yields unexpected results, such as more or fewer columns than you expected. When you get the wrong table dimensions, press Ctrl+Z, investigate the data, make any corrections, and try again.

FIGURE 9-6

The Convert Text to Table dialog box guesses how many rows and columns to create.

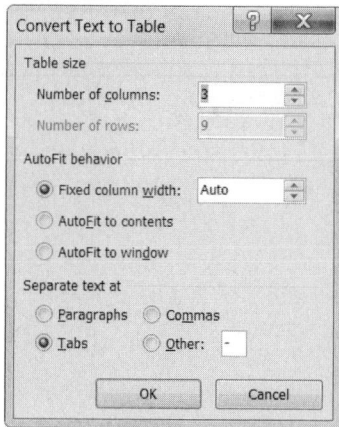

You can get the wrong number of columns if there are too many tabs (sometimes obscured as a result of formatting issues) or if some rows use spaces instead of tabs to achieve the table *look*. Figure 9-5 demonstrates the utility of displaying nonprinting formatting characters, such as tabs. In this case, the user relied on built-in tab stops rather than setting a custom tab in the tabbed table. As a result, alignment required two tabs for some of the shorter items (*Books*, *Pens*, and *Pencils*), and only one tab for each of the others. The result confuses Word, which assumes that there are three columns, rather than two. When this happens, dismiss the dialog box, find and remove the extra tabs, and try again. Don't worry about setting a properly aligned tab, because you're converting the tabbed data into a table anyway; the table will handle the alignment for you.

Convert Table to Text Dialog Box

What goes around comes around. Sometimes it's necessary or useful to convert an existing table to text. You might want to do this if the data needs to be provided to someone else in a different form. Some statistical programs will accept CSV (comma-separated values) data, but not Word tables. Or you might simply find it easier to manipulate the data in text form and then transform it back into a table. Whatever the reason, it's easy.

First, save your document (because it's easy to make mistakes too). Next, select the table you want to convert. On the Table Tools Layout tab of the Ribbon, click Convert to Text in the Data group at the right. In the Convert Table to Text dialog box, choose the desired horizontal delimiter and then click OK. Note that if the table contains nested tables, then the Convert Nested Tables option will be available.

Handling Tables

Word tables feature several kinds of handles and mouse pointers that enable you to manipulate and select cells, rows, columns, and entire tables. The table handle, shown in Figure 9-7, is displayed only when part of the table is selected, and only when all formatting marks are displayed (File ⇨ Options ⇨ Display ⇨ Show All Formatting Marks). Row- and column-sizing handles, on the other hand, are not affected by the display setting.

Handles enable you to resize rows and columns by dragging, as well as to select and move whole tables.

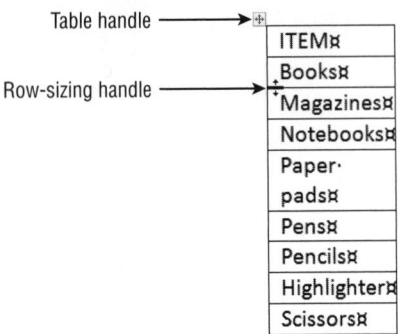

Use the row-sizing handle to drag the row to make it larger or smaller. Press the Alt key while dragging to display the measurements on the vertical ruler (even if the vertical ruler currently is not displayed).

You can resize columns in a similar way by dragging the column-sizing handles (they look like the row handles flipped 90°). Again, pressing the Alt key while dragging displays the measurements, this time on the horizontal ruler, enabling you to drag with a little more precision. You can modify the results by pressing the Ctrl (control) or Shift keys while dragging. Experiment to see which method yields the desired results. Remember: Ctrl+Z is your friend.

The entire table can be resized proportionally with the resize handle that appears at the lower-right corner. Hover the mouse pointer over that corner until you see a diagonal arrow, and drag to expand or shrink the table.

Selecting Tables, Rows, and Columns

Click the table handle to select the entire table. You can also select an entire table by right-clicking anywhere in it and choosing Select Table. If you're Ribbon-oriented, you can always select the table by clicking anywhere in it to reveal the Table Tools tabs, shown in Figure 9-8, and then clicking Select ⇨ Select Table in the Table group of the Table Tools Layout tab.

There is also a keyboard method for selecting tables but it's a nuisance to remember and to use. With the insertion point anywhere in the table, and Num Lock engaged, press Alt+Shift+5 on the numeric keypad. If Num Lock isn't engaged, press Shift+5 on the numeric keypad instead. Unless it's Thursday, of course, in which case…

FIGURE 9-8

Use the Table Tools Layout tab to access various table selection and manipulation tools.

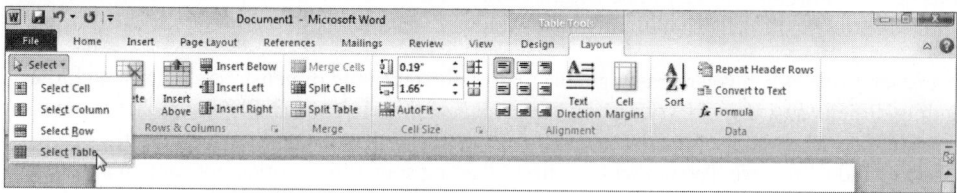

If you're using the keyboard, selecting the cell marker selects the cell. Hold down the Shift key and use the arrow keys to expand the selection to other cells. If you're using the direct mouse method, move the mouse pointer so that it is the small diagonal black arrow indicated in Figure 9-9. You can drag to expand the selection to include additional cells. Or hold the Ctrl key and use the select cell pointer to select additional discrete cells.

FIGURE 9-9

Word's mouse pointer changes shape to indicate what action a click will perform.

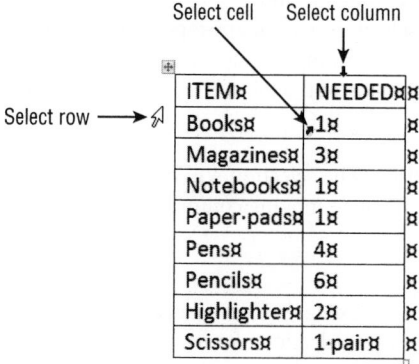

To select a row without using the Ribbon, move the mouse pointer to the left of the row so that it assumes the Select Row shape, and click. Drag to expand the selection to include contiguous rows, or Ctrl+click using the select row pointer to select additional noncontiguous rows.

To select a column without using the Ribbon, move the mouse pointer so that it takes on the Select Column shape, and click. Again, drag to expand the selection to include additional contiguous columns, or Shift+click using the Select Column Pointer to select additional discrete/noncontiguous columns.

Copying Table Matter

When copying all or part of a table from one table to another, you need to consider the dimensions of the source and the target. Sometimes when you paste into the new table, the whole table is pasted into a single cell! That's hardly ever what you want!

As a general rule, when you're pasting table matter, the receiving dimensions should match the sending dimensions. If you're trying to paste a 4 × 5 set of cells into a table whose dimensions are 6 × 8, copy the 4 × 5 source to the Clipboard, select the desired 4 × 5 location in the receiving table, and then paste. Pasting without first selecting sometimes works, but sometimes doesn't. The situation can get even weirder when you're pasting between Word and Excel, so have that Ctrl+Z (undo) command standing by.

To control what happens with respect to formatting, see the File ➪ Options ➪ Advanced ➪ Cut, Copy, and Paste section. Use the top four pasting options to specify what happens when you paste under a variety of circumstances. If necessary, temporarily enable the desired behavior, perform the paste, and then go back to reset the defaults.

Moving and Copying Columns

To move one or more adjacent columns, select them and then drag to the desired column. Release the mouse button anywhere in the destination column. The selected column(s) will move to the position of the destination column, which will scoot to the right. To move one or more selected columns to the right of the rightmost column, drop the selection at what appears to be outside the right edge of the table. As shown in Figure 9-9, there are cell markers to the right of the table's right boundary. When moving columns to the right side of the table, drop them on those exterior markers.

To copy one or more columns, hold the Ctrl key as you drop. The selection will be inserted at the drop point, using the same location rules that apply when you're moving columns.

Moving and Copying Rows

Rows can be moved and copied in the same way as columns, except with respect to the last row. The last row does not have exterior cell markers. If you drop a selection of one or more rows onto the last row of a table, the selection will be placed above the last row. If you drop it after the last row, the selection will be appended to the table, but the formatting will often change.

Instead, when you want to move rows after the last current row, drop them on the last row. Then put the insertion point anywhere in the last row and press Ctrl+Shift+up-arrow to move the last row up to where you want it.

Tip

Anytime you want to move table rows around, Ctrl+Alt+up-arrow and Ctrl+Alt+down-arrow can be used to push the current row up or down in the table. If you're moving a single row, you don't need to select anything. If you're moving multiple contiguous rows, select them first. ■

Table Properties

If you prefer to manipulate tables non-graphically, click Properties in the Table Tools Layout tab, or right-click a table and choose Table Properties to display the dialog box shown in Figure 9-10. Use the Table tab to control overall layout and behavior; use the other tabs to control row, column, and cell characteristics.

FIGURE 9-10

Use Table Properties to control overall alignment, indentation, and positioning of tables.

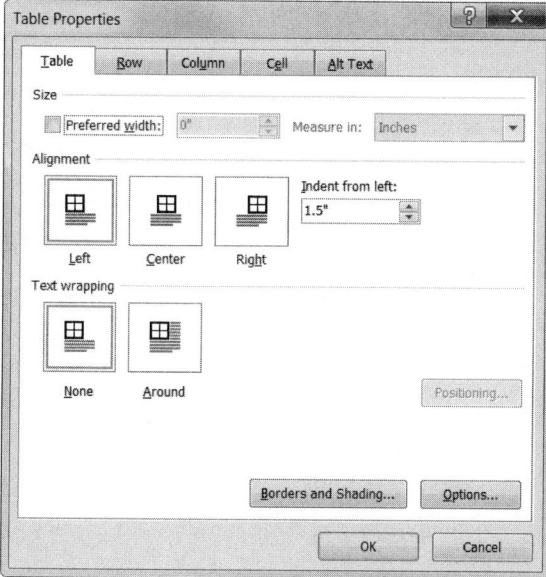

Preferred Width

Preferred width sets a target width for the table. The preferred width can't be absolute, however, because tables contain text and data and are further constrained by paper and margin settings. Note that the preferred width is overridden by AutoFit settings.

Alignment

The Table Alignment setting in the Table Properties dialog box affects the entire table with respect to the current left and right margins. If the table extends from the left margin to the right margin, which is the default for tables inserted in Word, then the alignment controls seemingly will have no effect. This makes it easy not to notice if they're changed. If you later narrow the table, its placement on the page might suddenly seem askew. That's the time to visit the Table Properties dialog box to see what's going on.

Table alignment is a sore spot for some users because table alignment and text alignment within cells are different things. Whereas table alignment can be set via the alignment tools on the Ribbon, if the entire table is not selected, then the Home tab's paragraph alignment tools affect only the selected portion of the table.

The Cell Alignment option, shown in Figure 9-11, affects only selected cells. The Alignment group tools in the Table Tools Layout tab also affect only selected cells.

FIGURE 9-11

Cell Alignment affects only the text inside cells, even if the entire table is selected.

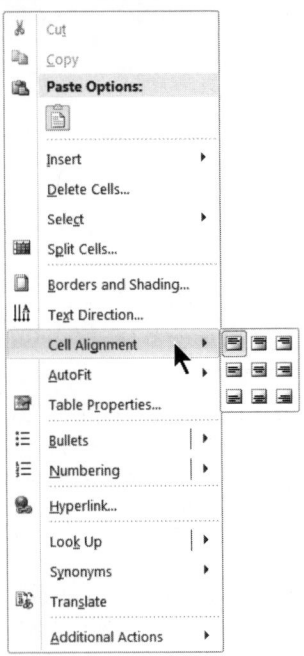

The bottom line is that if you're having trouble centering your table, center it using the Alignment control in the Table tab of the Table Properties dialog box.

The Indent from Left setting beside the Alignment settings in the Table Properties dialog box controls how far the table is from the left margin. There is no Ribbon control for this setting, and it cannot be set with the ruler line.

Note that Indent from Left is available only when Text Wrapping is set to None (see Figure 9-10) and Alignment is set to Left. When Around is enabled under Text Wrapping, use Positioning to set the distance from the left, as shown in the section that follows.

Text Wrapping

Tables can be inserted in line with other text, or they can be moved/dragged so that text outside the table wraps around them, as shown in Figure 9-12. You can achieve wrapping by selecting the appropriate option in the Table Properties dialog box, or you can force it by dragging a table to the desired location using its handle. This automatically changes the Text Wrapping setting from None to Around.

FIGURE 9-12

Tables can be positioned for text wrapping, like graphics.

Major revisions were made to the CPS in 1994, making some comparisons with previous years tenuous. Our use of CPS data for this study includes data from 1994 through 2008. Table II-1 provides a summary of the data we are using, using unweighted observations. For purposes of this study, we use the March Supplement weights provided in the CPS data. These weights are based upon the estimated US population as of March in each year, so that the percentages and other statistics used in this study are a statistically accurate reflection of the estimated proportions, groups, and subgroups as they occur in the population.

CPS Year	16-17	18-20
1994	4,224	5,506
1995	4,269	5,550

When Text Wrapping is set to Around, the Position button becomes active. Click it to open the Table Positioning dialog box. The dialog box settings work much like the positioning settings for graphics. Most of the settings here need no further explanation.

The Move with Text option controls whether the table's vertical position is governed by the paragraph to which it is anchored. If Move with Text is enabled, the vertical position can be relative to only the paragraph. Use this setting if the paragraph's content and the table's content are intertwined so that the table would not make sense except in that paragraph. This often is the setting you want for research reports.

Turn off Move with Text if the location of the table is not logically tied to a particular paragraph. This setting might be more in keeping with the design of a brochure or a newsletter in which the table's contents are relevant to the entire document and should appear in a particular location for aesthetic reasons.

Table Layout and Design

Word 2010's Table Tools Layout and Table Tools Design tabs provide you with most of what you need to create tables that are both aesthetically appealing and functional. Naturally, Word can't do all of the work. It's up to you to decide on presentation. When you get stuck for ideas, however, sometimes the Ribbon provides just the touch of inspiration, or just the right suggestion or hint to speed you along your way.

In many ways, although the Table Tools Design tab appears first in the Ribbon, Table Tools Layout logically comes first. Layout determines whether or not your presentation is logical, whether it is meaningful to the reader, and ultimately whether it helps prove whatever point you're trying to make. After all that, design is icing on the cake.

So far we've looked at several basic tools that help you achieve the right structure for your tables. In this section we're going to look at how to mold tables into shape and then polish them for presentation.

Note
Many of the Ribbon techniques described in this section are also available in the right-click shortcut menu. If you prefer the shortcut menu to the Ribbon, press Ctrl+F1 to dismiss the Ribbon and go for it! ■

Modifying Table Layout

Once you have your basic table, what do you do with it? We all know that situations, ideas, and data change. Let's look at how to cope with change.

Note that all references to the Layout tab in this section actually refer to the Table Tools Layout tab on the Ribbon. We can save ink and trees by saying that up front rather than each and every time the need arises. Note that none of the layout tools provide Live Preview. Live Preview must wait for the Table Tools Design tab discussion.

Deleting Tables and Table Parts

Sometimes you need to trim your tables by deleting rows or columns. Sometimes you have to delete the entire table. Sometimes this simple act can prove more daunting and challenging than you expect. If you select a table and tap the Delete key, the data inside the table is deleted, but the table shell itself is still there! "Good trick! Now make it go away!" you exclaim. The same thing sometimes happens when you try to delete a cell, a row, or a column.

Tip
When the Delete key doesn't do what you want, try the Backspace key instead. ■

Rather than say this a half dozen times, let's just say it once. If you want to remove the contents of a cell, row, column, or table, select what you want to remove and tap the Delete key. In the sections that follow we'll be looking at table structure, not contents.

Deleting Tables

As you've seen, you can't just select a table and tap the Delete key. That would be too logical and easy. Instead, select the table and tap the Backspace key. Goodbye, table. Why? Who knows? It works.

Alternatively, click anywhere in the table (no need to select anything) and in the Table Tools Layout tab's Rows & Columns group, choose Delete ➪ Delete Table, as shown in Figure 9-13. Again, the table is gone. If you absolutely, positively need to know how to do it using the Delete key, insert a paragraph above or below the table (but outside the table) and include it in the selection. Now when you press Delete the table disappears.

FIGURE 9-13

Delete the current cell, column, row, or table using the Layout tab's Delete tool.

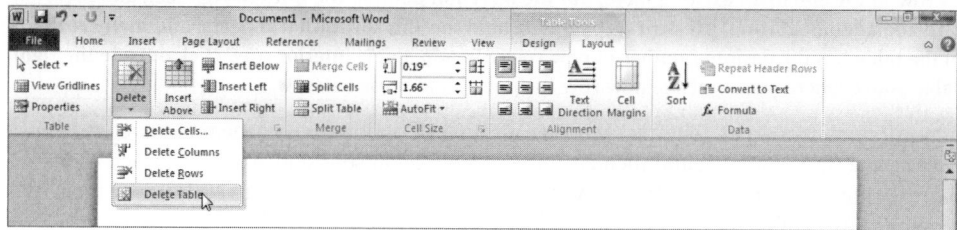

You can also delete the table by cutting it to the Clipboard. Select the table and click the Cut tool on the Home tab, or press Ctrl+X (or Shift+Delete). Of course, this clutters the Clipboard, which you might not want cluttered.

Deleting Rows, Columns, and Cells

To delete the current row or column, you have the same options: Select the offending rows or columns and press Backspace, or choose Delete ➪ Delete Columns, Delete ➪ Rows, or Delete ➪ Cells from the Table Tools Layout tab's Delete menu in the Rows & Columns group (refer to Figure 9-13).

When deleting cells, Word needs a little more information. You are prompted as shown in Figure 9-14. Make your selection and click OK. Now you know how those rag-eared tables you sometimes see lost their corner cells!

FIGURE 9-14

Word prompts to find out how to handle the rest of the column or row when you delete a single cell.

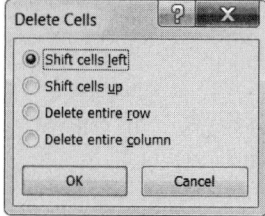

Inserting Rows, Columns, and Cells

To insert a row or column into a table, click in the row or column adjacent to where you want to insert, and then click Insert Above, Insert Below, Insert Left, or Insert Right in the

Rows & Columns group of the Table Tools Layout tab, depending on where you want the new row or column to appear. If you miss, you can always drag the new row or column where you want it.

Tip

To add a new row to the end of an existing table, put the insertion point in the bottom-right cell and press the Tab key. To add additional rows, press F4 (repeat). Or hold the Tab key until it repeats, and then continue holding until the table has the desired number of new rows. To add a new interior row, click outside the right side of the table above where you want the new row to appear, and press Enter. ∎

To insert multiple rows or columns, you have a couple of options. Select the number of rows or columns you want to insert, and then click the appropriate insert tool. Word will insert as many rows or columns as you have selected. Alternatively, insert a single row or column, and then press the F4 (repeat) key for each additional row or column you need.

To insert cells, select the cell(s) adjacent to where you want the new one(s) to appear, and click the Dialog Box Launcher in the bottom-right corner of the Rows & Columns group of the Table Tools Layout tab. You'll see a dialog box containing the identical options shown in Figure 9-14. Choose your desired action and click OK.

Controlling How Tables Break

Sometimes you don't particularly care how tables break across pages, but sometimes you do. When you have an opinion, select the row or rows in question, and click Properties in the Table group of the Table Tools Layout tab (or right-click the selection and choose Table Properties from the shortcut menu). In the Row tab under Options, Allow Row to Break across Pages is enabled by default. Clear this option if you absolutely, positively don't want the selected row(s) to break, and then click OK.

To force a table to break at a particular point, move the insertion point to anywhere in the row where you want the break to occur, and then press Ctrl+Enter. Note that this doesn't simply force the table to break at that point; it actually breaks the table into two tables. If the Repeat as header row at the top of each page checkbox is enabled on the Row tab of the Table Properties dialog box, it won't be inherited by the *new* table. You'll need to copy the heading row to the new table and reinstate the setting, if needed.

Merge

Sometimes you need to merge columns, rows, or cells. Merging cells is easy. Select the cells you want to merge, and click Merge Cells in the Merge group of the Table Tools Layout tab (refer to Figure 9-13).

Tip

You want it even easier? Use the table eraser in the Table Tools Design tab. Click the Eraser tool in the Draw Borders group, and then click on the table line segment. Click the Eraser tool again, or press the Esc key to turn it off. Jump ahead to "The Table Eraser" later in this chapter for more exciting details. ∎

Word can't really merge rows or columns. Suppose, for example, that your table has three columns, and you need to merge each of the cells in two adjoining rows. What you want to end up with is one new row with three new combined cells. If you select both rows and click Merge Cells, however, Word treats that as a request to merge all the cells in the selection, and you end up with one big cell. This is illustrated in Figure 9-15. There is no way around this. If you want the middle result, you must merge each set of cells separately (in other words, merge A and F, and then merge B and G). To effect a merge of the columns while retaining the rows, you would need to merge A and B, and then F and G.

FIGURE 9-15

Word cannot merge into multiple cells.

What you have...

Bob	Ted
Carol	Alice

What you want...

Bob	Ted
Carol	Alice

What you get...

Bob
Ted
Carol
Alice

Splitting Cells, Rows, and Columns

At first it seemed that one cell, row, or column was fine, but later you decide that the logic of the presentation calls for two (or more) where there once was one. In any divorce, amicable or not, one has to divvy up the jointly held property. Like a few of the shadier attorneys, Word seems to think that everything should go to one party, while the other gets nothing.

If we reverse the situation illustrated in Figure 9-15, to make a long story short, we end up with all of the data in the upper row, as shown in Figure 9-16.

FIGURE 9-16

When you split cells, Word's distribution logic probably won't agree with yours.

Bob	Carol
Ted	Alice

When you split cells using Word's default divorce attorney, you're going to have to manually redistribute the goodies after the split. You get to be the judge!

A better way to manage and control split-ups is to use the Draw Table tool, described later in this chapter. In the Draw Borders group of the Table Tools Design tab, click the Draw Table tool to set it in motion. Use the tool to draw a line in a cell between the items you want to separate. The items above the new line go north, and the ones below the line head south.

Horizontal splits are often harder to control. The trick is to make sure that items are horizontally displayed and separated either by at least two spaces or by a tab (press Ctrl+Tab to insert a tab inside a table). It can still be tedious, but it's a bit more direct than using the dialog box, and you have a bit more control and precision.

With luck you'll only have four cells to contend with, rather than 400. If you have 400, it might be time to record a macro.

Cell Size

When you're using a table to lay out a form, cell measurements sometimes have to be precise, especially when you're trying to align a Word document with preprinted forms. When cell height and width need to be controlled precisely, click the corresponding boxes in the Cell Size group on the Table Tools Layout tab, shown in Figure 9-17. Note that cell height cannot vary for any cell within any given row.

FIGURE 9-17

Use the Cell Size group to specify the precise height and width of rows and columns.

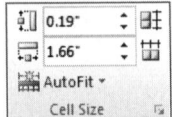

When you need rows to have a uniform height, click the Distribute Rows button. If rows are of different heights — as sometimes happens when you're converting part of an Excel spreadsheet into a Word table — this command determines the optimal height and equalizes the height of all selected rows or of all rows in the table if no rows are selected.

Similarly, click Distribute Columns to set selected or all columns to the same width. If different rows have different widths, this command will not equalize the whole table. It works only when all the rows have the same width. If any differ (e.g., if row 2 is 4 inches and all the other rows are 3.5 inches, giving the table a ragged left and/or right edge), it won't equalize them all. To remedy this, drag the right border(s) of shorter or longer rows so that they all align on the left and right.

Alignment

Alignment offers nine options, as shown in Figure 9-18. To set or change cell alignment, click in or select the cells you want to change, and then click the desired tool. As noted elsewhere, many users confuse cell alignment with table alignment. With the whole table selected, this tool will at most set the individual alignment of each cell and won't have any effect on table alignment. Instead, select the whole table and use the Paragraph Alignment tool in the Home tab, or use the Alignment setting in the Table Properties dialog box.

FIGURE 9-18

Word offers nine options for cell alignment.

Text Direction

To control text direction in table cells, click the Text Direction tool in the Alignment group of the Table Tools Layout tab. This option often enables you to simulate rotating a wide table so it fits on a page using Portrait orientation.

Cell Margins and Cell Spacing

Word provides several different kinds of controls for cell margins. *Cell margin* is the distance between the cell contents and the cell walls. Proper margins can keep cells from becoming too crowded. Additional spacing sometimes helps achieve a precise look. It can also prevent data from printing over the borders when you're using a table to format data for printing on pre-printed forms. To set cell margins and cell spacing, click Cell Margins in the Alignment group of the Table Tools Layout tab, shown in Figure 9-18. This displays the Table Options dialog box shown in Figure 9-19.

FIGURE 9-19

If your table is too crowded, increase the default cell margins.

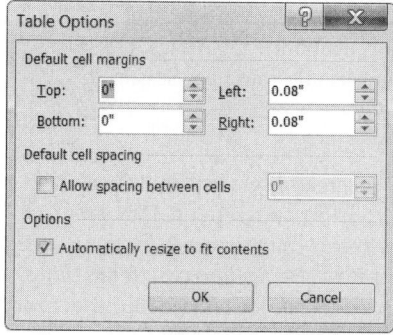

Despite the text in the dialog box, it does not set the default cell margins or spacing for tables. It sets those only for the currently selected table.

Cell spacing can be used to create the rather cool effect shown in Figure 9-20. This gives the table the appearance of having a distinct box inside each table cell.

FIGURE 9-20

Cell spacing can give tables a more dramatic appearance.

CPS Year	16-17	18-20	21-24	25-29	30-39	40-49	50-59	60-64	Total Working Age
1994	4,224	5,506	8,063	11,030	25,016	20,848	13,747	5,832	94,266
1995	4,269	5,550	7,821	10,572	24,743	21,197	14,124	5,701	93,977
1996	3,859	5,029	6,486	9,017	21,265	19,087	12,242	4,917	81,902
1997	4,032	5,161	6,414	9,278	21,094	19,266	12,963	5,048	83,256
1998	3,980	5,122	6,250	8,990	20,723	19,545	13,642	5,044	83,296
1999	3,955	5,189	6,397	8,697	20,538	20,098	14,020	5,024	83,918
2000	3,963	5,395	6,609	8,828	20,358	20,255	14,696	5,168	85,272
2001	3,851	5,124	6,443	8,203	19,240	19,902	14,564	5,044	82,371
2002	7,677	8,799	9,800	12,814	33,507	35,006	22,305	7,067	136,975
2003	7,583	8,803	9,938	12,707	32,293	35,212	22,967	7,540	137,043
2004	7,608	8,635	9,939	12,373	30,770	34,694	23,792	7,608	135,419
2005	7,353	8,346	9,873	12,512	30,110	33,540	23,920	7,656	133,310
2006	7,626	8,414	9,897	12,614	29,253	32,950	24,481	7,730	132,965
2007	7,425	8,316	9,460	12,688	28,676	32,230	24,925	8,131	131,851
2008	7,408	8,344	9,609	12,731	28,275	31,697	25,268	8,728	132,060

Tables That Span Multiple Pages

When a table spans multiple pages, Word can automatically repeat one or more heading rows to make the table more manageable. When the need arises, select the target table's heading rows (you can have multiple heading rows), and click Repeat Header Rows in the Data group of the Table Tools Layout tab. The selected heading rows are then repeated where necessary. The setting can be toggled on or off for each individual table. Because the number of heading rows can vary, this setting cannot be made the default for all tables, nor incorporated into a style definition.

This setting has no observable effect on tables that display or print on a single page. It also has no effect on pages displayed in Web view, because web pages are seamless and pageless in concept.

Sorting Tables

Word provides a flexible and fast way to sort data in tables. It can also sort lists that aren't in tables. To sort a table, click anywhere in the table and click the Sort button in the Data group of the Table Tools Layout tab. Word displays the Sort dialog box, shown in Figure 9-21. If the table has headings at the top of each column, enabling the Header Row setting does two things. First, it provides labels in the Sort By and Then By drop-down lists. Second, it excludes the header row from the sort. Unlike the previous feature, this one allows only a single header row.

FIGURE 9-21

The Sort command lets you sort by up to three fields.

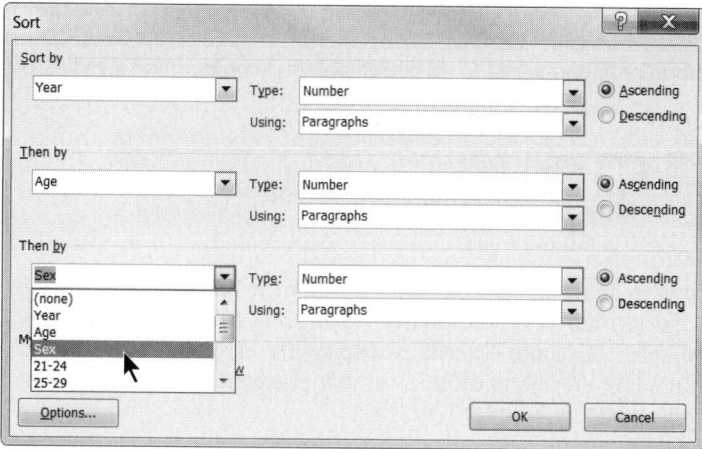

To sort, set Sort By to the first field. Setting Type to Text, Number, or Date affects the way data is sorted. For Year and Age, shown here, sorting by number ensures that the correct sorting order will be used. Choose the desired order, Ascending or Descending. If you have additional sort fields, use Then By to include up to two of them. Click Options to determine additional settings, including how fields are separated (for non-table sorts), whether to make the sort case-sensitive, and the sorting language. Click OK to close Sort Options, and then click OK to do the sort.

Table Math

Word can perform some calculations using the Formula choice in the Data group of the Table Tools Layout tab shown earlier in Figure 9-8. However, this feature is limited and subject to hard-to-spot errors. If you use Word for math, double-check all calculations using a calculator or Excel. But if you have Excel and you need math in tables, then use Excel, period. You can then link the results to Word. See Chapter 41 for additional information on using Excel with Word.

Modifying Table Design

Word 2010 provides several powerful tools to help you quickly enhance the look and feel of your tables. One of these tools, Table Styles, features Live Preview. In this section, we'll look only at the features contained in the Table Tools Design tab of the Ribbon, shown in Figure 9-22.

Table Styles

Word 2010 has several preset table styles that you can apply to any table. They provide a wide variety of different kinds of formatting that can be previewed live in your table. You can use these styles to ensure a consistent, professional look. You can also modify them and save the modified versions for later use.

FIGURE 9-22

The Table Tools Design tab on the Ribbon provides access to six preset table style options and a gallery of table styles.

To use a table style, click anywhere in the target table, and then click the Table Tools Design tab on the Ribbon. In the Table Styles group, hover the mouse over different styles and observe the changes to your table. As you move the mouse, ScreenTips displays the name of the selected table style (such as *Table Colorful 2*). A Live Preview of the selected style also appears on the table, as shown in Figure 9-23.

FIGURE 9-23

As you move the mouse over different table styles, the currently selected table displays a Live Preview of the formatting.

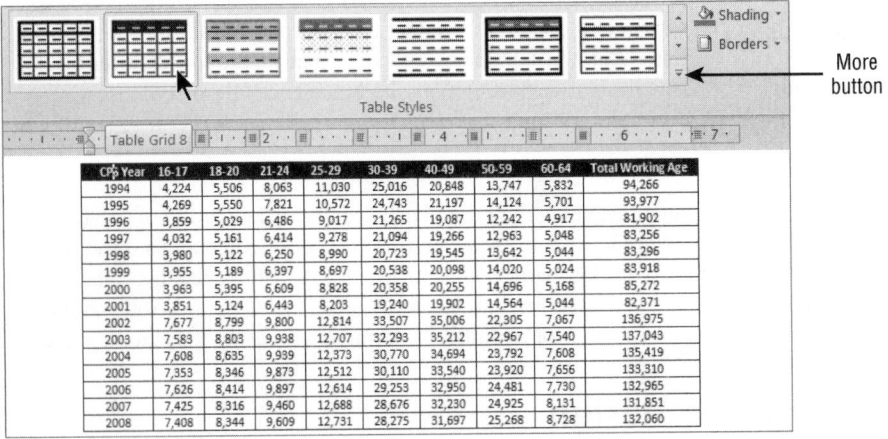

More button

CPI Year	16-17	18-20	21-24	25-29	30-39	40-49	50-59	60-64	Total Working Age
1994	4,224	5,506	8,063	11,030	25,016	20,848	13,747	5,832	94,266
1995	4,269	5,550	7,821	10,572	24,743	21,197	14,124	5,701	93,977
1996	3,859	5,029	6,486	9,017	21,265	19,087	12,242	4,917	81,902
1997	4,032	5,161	6,414	9,278	21,094	19,266	12,963	5,048	83,256
1998	3,980	5,122	6,250	8,990	20,723	19,545	13,642	5,044	83,296
1999	3,955	5,189	6,397	8,697	20,538	20,098	14,020	5,024	83,918
2000	3,963	5,395	6,609	8,828	20,358	20,255	14,696	5,168	85,272
2001	3,851	5,124	6,443	8,203	19,240	19,902	14,564	5,044	82,371
2002	7,677	8,799	9,800	12,814	33,507	35,006	22,305	7,067	136,975
2003	7,583	8,803	9,938	12,707	32,293	35,212	22,967	7,540	137,043
2004	7,608	8,635	9,939	12,373	30,770	34,694	23,792	7,608	135,419
2005	7,353	8,346	9,873	12,512	30,110	33,540	23,920	7,656	133,310
2006	7,626	8,414	9,897	12,614	29,253	32,950	24,481	7,730	132,965
2007	7,425	8,316	9,460	12,688	28,676	32,230	24,925	8,131	131,851
2008	7,408	8,344	9,609	12,731	28,275	31,697	25,268	8,728	132,060

If you see a style you like, click it to apply it to your table. If it's not perfect, you can modify it. If you don't see a style you like, click the More button to the right of the table styles that are showing. Word will display the full Table Style Gallery, showing custom, plain, and built-in table styles, as shown in Figure 9-24.

FIGURE 9-24

The Table Style Gallery enables you to test-drive dozens of built-in table styles.

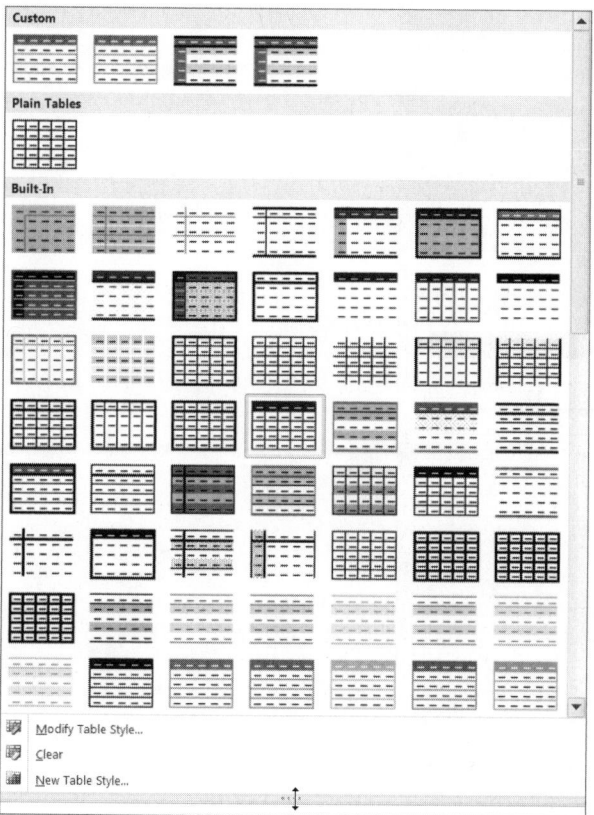

To modify the currently displayed table style, click Modify Table Style just below the Table Style Gallery, which will display the Modify Style dialog box, shown in Figure 9-25. You can use the Modify Style dialog box to apply style formatting, as described in Chapter 7.

For additional options, right-click a table style in the gallery to call up the menu shown in Figure 9-26. Note the Set as Default option, which enables you to set the selected table style as the default for all tables in the current document or as the default for all future tables in documents based on the current template. This enables you to easily achieve a consistent look for tables you add to your documents.

FIGURE 9-25

If you type a new name, the style will be saved as a custom style in the Table Styles Gallery.

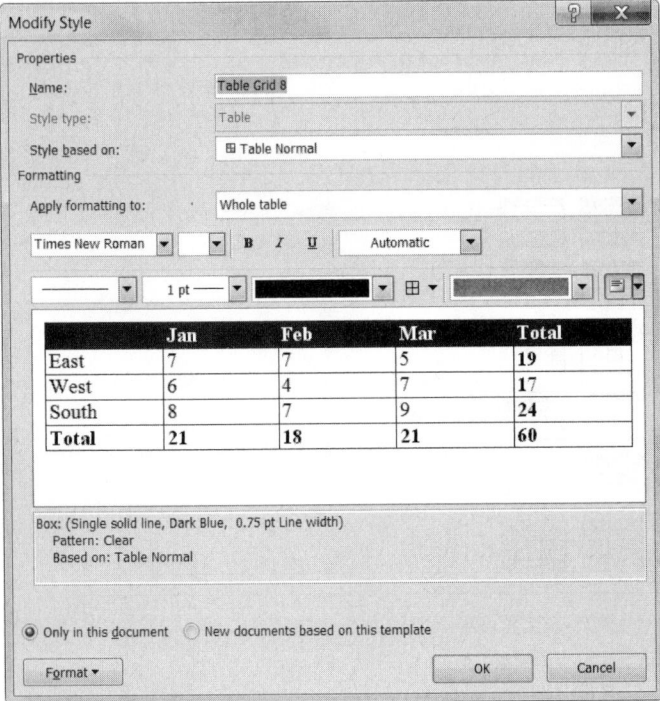

FIGURE 9-26

For additional options, right-click any table style in the gallery.

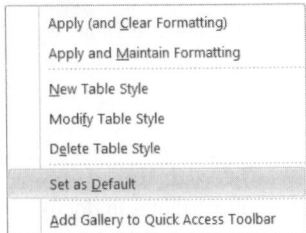

Note

Making this your default table style does not apply the style to existing tables. You would need to do that using the method described earlier (albeit one table at a time). Note also that the Modify Style dialog box for table styles lacks the Automatically Update option. That denies you the potential utility or the disastrous consequences (take your pick) to which that button might lead given the preponderance of documents based on the `Normal.dotm` templates. ∎

Table Style Options

The Table Style Options group on the Table Tools Design tab provides access to six options, shown earlier in Figure 9-22, that it can automatically apply to your table. For these to work, the table must have been formatted with one of the Built-In table styles instead of the style under Plain tables shown in Figure 9-24. Click to apply those features to your tables, or remove checks to turn the corresponding features off. The table style options provided are as follows:

- **Header Row.** Applies special formatting to the entire top row in your table.
- **First Column.** Applies special formatting to the entire first column.
- **Total Row.** Applies special formatting to the last row, except for the first cell.
- **Last Column.** Applies special formatting to the last column, except for the top cell.
- **Banded Rows.** Alternates shading in rows to create a horizontal striping effect. This helps the reader focus on specific rows.
- **Banded Columns.** Alternates shading in columns to create vertical stripes, focusing the reader on columnar comparisons.

Each of the style options works together with the table styles. Each table style might have any of these attributes enabled. Use the checkboxes to add or remove attributes.

Shading

Shading refers to the background color for tables, which can be applied individually to cells, rows, or columns, or to a complete table. Shading sometimes is used to draw attention to one or more elements of a table.

Shading is a Live Preview attribute. Similar to the method shown in Chapters 5 and 6, you apply shading to a table by selecting the part of the table you want shaded and then using the Shading tool, as shown in Figure 9-27. You also can use the Shading tool on the Home tab of the Ribbon to shade a table.

FIGURE 9-27

If you apply one of the theme colors to shade a table, the table shading will change when different themes are applied.

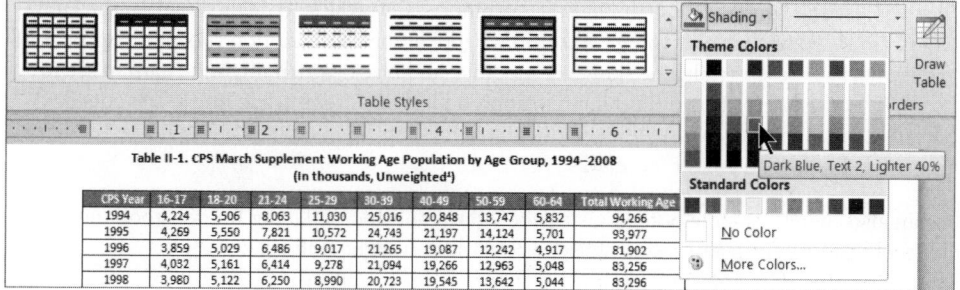

Borders and Table Drawing

Borders are lines that separate a table into cells, rows, and columns. You've seen in other chapters that borders are not unique to tables and can be applied to characters and paragraphs as well. They also can be applied to other Word document elements, such as textboxes, frames, and graphics. Any of the border tools can be used to control borders in tables. None of the border tools offers Live Preview, although the Borders and Shading dialog box does provide a generic preview.

You have two strategies for working with borders. You can use the holistic approach by launching the Borders and Shading dialog box. For a detailed description of how to apply borders using the Borders and Shading dialog box, see the "Borders and Boxes" section in Chapter 6.

The second strategy uses an ad hoc approach, by using the Borders, Line Style, Line Weight, Pen Color, Draw Table, and Eraser tools in the Table Tools Design tab, shown in Figure 9-28. Much, if not all, of what you can do using the Borders and Shading dialog box you can also do using the Borders tool, in combination with the Draw Borders group choices in the Table Tools Design tab. Use whichever method works better for you, and it doesn't have to be the same method or set of tools each time.

FIGURE 9-28

Use the Borders tool and its friends to perform ad hoc editing on table borders.

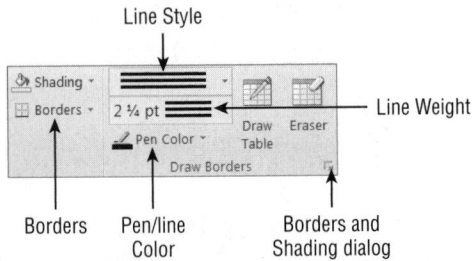

You should experiment with the Borders tool and its friends to get a feel for how they work. Even if you generally prefer the dialog box approach, the individual tools are great when you want to touch up or polish the look of a table. Keep in mind that you can use Ctrl+Z to remove the last effect applied, and F4 to reapply the most recent effect to a new selection.

When you use the Borders tool, it applies the current style, weight, and color shown in the Draw Borders group. For example, if you use the Borders tool in the configuration shown in Figure 9-28, the line style will be the triple line shown, 2¼ points, and black (which might be hard to see in a book with grayscale pictures). Therefore, to apply a black, 2¼ point triple line to the outside perimeter of the currently selected table cells, rows, columns, or complete table, choose Borders ➪ Outside Borders, as shown in Figure 9-29.

You can also change existing borders using the Draw Table tool. Like the Borders tool, the Draw Table tool takes its cue from the currently selected style, weight, and color.

FIGURE 9-29

Use the Borders tool to apply borders by name, remove borders (No Border), draw a horizontal line, display gridlines, and launch the Borders and Shading dialog box.

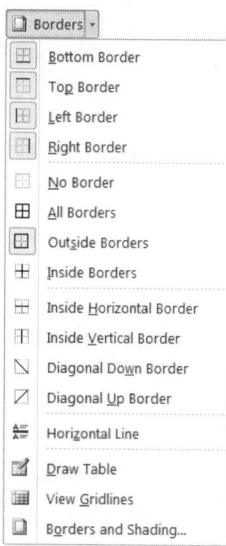

To change a particular border to blue without changing the other border attributes, for example, use the style and weight controls to reset those controls so that they match the current border settings. Use the Pen Color control to choose the shade of blue that you want. Finally, click Draw Table to turn the tool on (the button will look pushed in), and then click each of the borders you want to be blue. Note that the Draw Table tool affects only one border at a time.

To turn the Draw Table tool off, either click it again (it's a toggle) or press the Esc key.

Note

Using either the Draw Table tool or the Borders tool, it's possible to place *ugly* diagonal lines in table cells. Unfortunately, the effect is purely visual, not functional. You cannot place data above and below those lines. Some folks use these lines to indicate that the cells contain no data. Some might well imagine that emptiness or subtle shading conveys the same information, and somewhat more elegantly and eloquently. It's all a matter of style and aesthetics. If you want ugly diagonal lines and X marks in your tables (yes, the diagonals can go both ways at the same time), it's entirely up to you. It's your table. ∎

Drawing Tables from Scratch

You can also use the Draw Table tool to draw tables from scratch. In the Tables group of the Insert tab of the Ribbon, choose Table ➪ Draw Table. Use the table pen to drag to form an overall outline of the table. Then use the pen to add rows or columns, as shown in Figure 9-30. If necessary, you can use the Table Tools Layout tab tools later to touch up any cell, row, or column dimensions that need to be adjusted.

FIGURE 9-30

Use the Draw Table tool to create tables from scratch, as well as to expand, extend, and modify existing tables.

The Table Eraser

The Eraser tool in the Draw Borders group of the Table Tools Design tab is a powerful tool, and perhaps misunderstood. The Eraser actually erases parts of tables. It doesn't merely remove border lines. It actually deletes the table structure it touches.

No, it won't leave a hole in the middle of the table where non-table text can leak through (although that would be really cool). What it can do, however, is turn interior cells into a larger interior cell. Or, if you've ever wanted to knock a table's block off, now's your chance. You can use the table eraser to remove corner cells from tables. In some presentations the top-left corner cell serves no purpose, so why tolerate its presence? Erase it!

To dismiss the Eraser, either click the Eraser tool again to toggle it off, or press the Esc key. The Eraser also goes away if you click outside a table, that is, in regular text.

Inserting Pictures from Files

Is a picture really worth a thousand words? It's up to you. Pictures that are merely decorative might simply clutter up a document and make it more time-consuming to send to somebody and more expensive to print. But used carefully, pictures enable you to show the reader what you mean. Yes, used the right way, pictures can save many paragraphs of explanation, so perhaps a picture is worth a thousand words — maybe more. If not, there wouldn't be so many pictures in this book, helping to illustrate ideas.

You can insert pictures in Word in several ways, using pictures from a variety of different graphics formats. We'll look at formats shortly.

If you have pictures on removable media — such as SD (secure digital), CF (compact flash), CD, DVD, or USB drive — it's usually best if those pictures have been copied to your hard drive before you proceed. While you can insert directly from such sources, or from a local area network (LAN) or over the Internet, you have more options available to you if the files are on your own computer in a location that is always accessible.

You might also have pictures available from a webcam, another camera, or a scanner connected to your computer. Assuming that the formats are supported, those also can be inserted into Word — but usually not directly. You'll usually copy them to your hard drive first.

While it's not necessary, computing life is usually easier when pictures, sounds, and other files are where Word and other programs expect them to be. In the case of pictures, the expected location is your Pictures Library (or My Pictures, if you're not using Windows 7). You'll see why in this chapter. I'm going to assume that you've either copied the picture(s) you want to use to one of the folders in the Pictures Library or that you otherwise know where to find them.

I'm also going to assume that you're working with Word 2010 .docx files, and not Word 97–2003 Compatibility Mode files. This matters because things are a bit different in Compatibility Mode. In Compatibility Mode, linking of picture files is accomplished with the INCLUDEPICTURE field. In Word 2010 mode, linking is accomplished with XML relationships.

To insert a picture at the current insertion point, choose Picture in the Illustrations group of the Insert tab, which displays the Insert Picture dialog box. Assuming that the picture is listed there, select it, but don't double-click it yet. As shown in Figure 9-31, click the drop-down arrow next to Insert to view the Insert options.

FIGURE 9-31

When you insert a picture, Word's default search location is the Pictures Library.

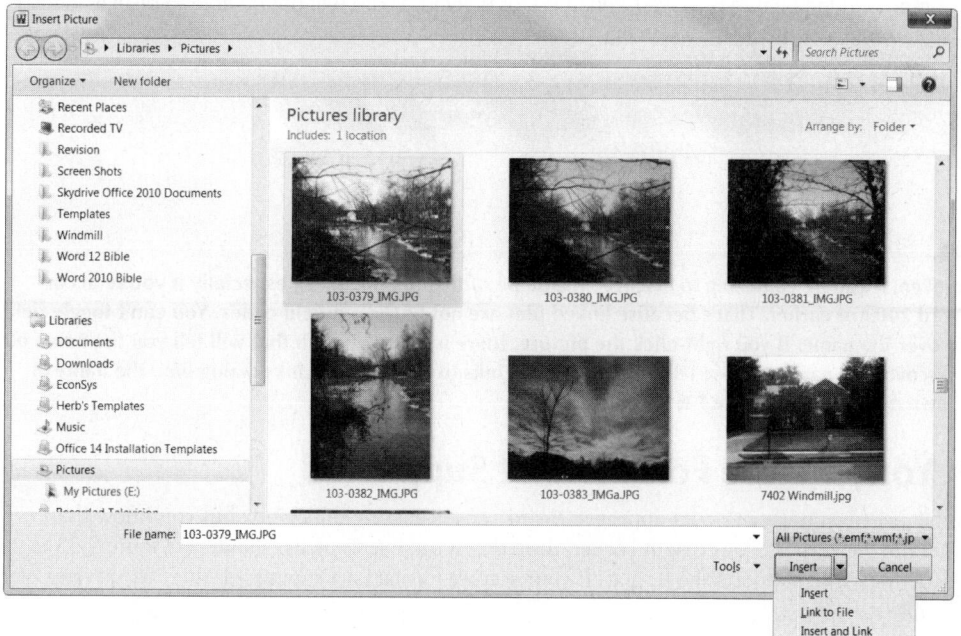

When you're inserting a picture this way, Word offers three options:

- **Insert.** The picture is embedded in the current document. If the original is ever deleted or moved, it will still exist in your document. If the original is ever updated, however, your document will not reflect the update. The document file will be larger because the original image is stored in the .docx file. If neither file size nor updates are important, this is the best option.

- **Link to File.** A link to the picture is inserted, and the picture is displayed in the document. The document file will be smaller — often dramatically smaller — because the image is external to the Word document. If the original file is moved or deleted, it will no longer be available for viewing in the document, and you will see the upsetting and confusing message shown in Figure 9-32 (see the following Caution for more information). On the other hand, if the image is modified or updated, the update will be available and displayed in Word. If file size is an issue but the availability of the image file is not, then this is the best option.

- **Insert and Link.** The image is both embedded in the document and linked to the original file. If the original file is updated, the picture in the document will be updated to reflect changes in the original. Because the file is embedded, the document will be larger than it would be if only linked. However, the document will not be larger than it would be if only inserted. If file size is not an issue but updates are, this is the best option.

FIGURE 9-32

If a linked, non-embedded picture is moved, renamed, or deleted, Word will not be able to display it.

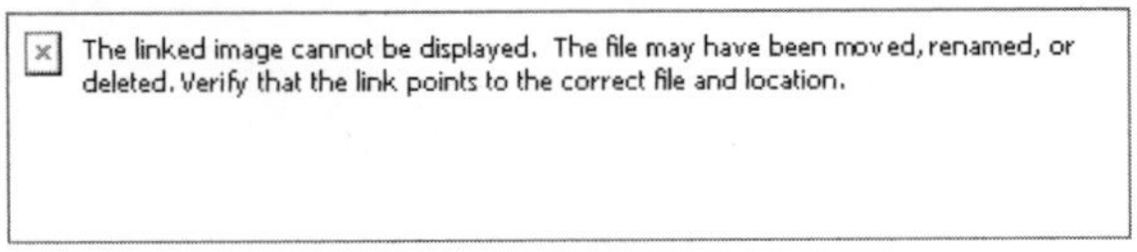

> ☒ The linked image cannot be displayed. The file may have been moved, renamed, or deleted. Verify that the link points to the correct file and location.

Caution

If a link is broken, it can be confusing to discover the name of the missing file(s), especially if you're accustomed to Word 2003 or earlier. That's because linked files are not linked via field codes. You can't toggle field codes to discover the name. If you right-click the picture, there is no menu item that will tell you the name of the file. To discover the name, choose File ⇨ Info ⇨ Edit Links to Files. In the Links dialog box, the name of the file is shown next to "Source File." ∎

If Your Picture Format Isn't Supported

If the picture you want doesn't appear in Word's Insert Picture dialog box but you know that it's really there, in the lower-right corner, drop down the File Type list shown in Figure 9-33 to verify that Word supports the format. If your picture format isn't supported, there are several possible reasons.

FIGURE 9-33

Word supports many popular graphics formats, but some formats do not come with Word 2010.

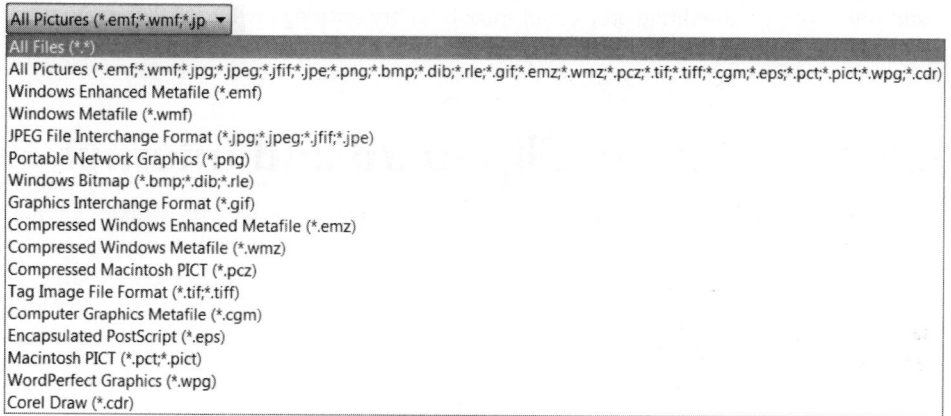

The most popular picture format, used by most digital cameras, is JPEG or JPG, which stands for *Joint Photographic Experts Group*. Word 2010 comes with a converter that supports .jpg files. Other Word 2010–supported popular formats include .gif, which is heavily used on the Internet (because of support for transparent backgrounds, which makes such images better suited for web page design), .png, .wmf, and .bmp. Note that the latter three formats are natively supported by Word and do not require special converters.

Which formats are supported by your installation of Word depends on several things. Several graphics converters are installed as part of Office 2010's Shared Features. Other converters installed by other programs might also be available. If you had Office 2000 or Office XP installed on your computer and upgraded to Office 2010, additional converters possibly were installed as well.

If your file uses any of the formats that come with Office 2010 but they don't show up in the Pictures Library, it's probable that you didn't install any of the converters. To add the missing converters, from the Windows Control Panel search for Programs and Features, and locate Microsoft Office 2010. The precise name depends on which flavor of Office 2010 you have.

Click Change ⇨ Add or Remove Features ⇨ Continue. Expand Office Shared Features ⇨ Converters and Filters ⇨ Graphics Filters. Drop down the arrow by Graphics Filters and choose Run All from My Computer. While you're here, you might want to install all the text filters as well. You never know when they might come in handy. Click Continue and follow any instructions (which might or might not include inserting the original Office 2010 install disc). When you're done, go back and check whether your picture format is now supported.

If your file format isn't supported natively by Word 2010, try searching for a *converter pack* on Microsoft's support site for Office and see what you can find. Choose File ⇨ Help ⇨ Check for

Updates. Once there, type **converter pack** in the Search box, and click Go. As of this writing, several are listed, although it's not clear that they add any graphics-conversion capabilities to Word 2010. A specific Internet search for the format you need might be more productive. If that fails and you have a photo-editing program of some kind, try opening the file using that program, then save the file in a format that Word can handle, such as JPEG.

Pictures from the Clipboard and Internet

You can also insert pictures from the Clipboard and from your Internet browser (usually, but not always). To use the Clipboard, display the picture in any Windows program that supports graphics, and use that program's controls to select and copy the picture to the Clipboard. If all else fails, try right-clicking the picture and choosing Copy or Copy Picture. Then, in Word, move to where you want the picture, and press Ctrl+V (or click Paste in the Clipboard group of the Home tab of the Ribbon).

Sometimes the copy-and-paste method works from Internet Explorer, Firefox, Google Chrome, and other popular browsers — other times not. When the Clipboard method fails or when you want a copy of the file itself (not simply the embedded version in a Word document), you can try several things.

In Firefox, right-click the picture and choose Save Image As. In Save Image, navigate to where you want to store the file, accept the name shown or type a new one (no need to type an extension — Firefox automatically supplies it), and click Save. In Internet Explorer, right-click the picture and choose Save Picture As. Again, navigate to the desired location, pick a filename, and click Save.

Tip

If you're harvesting several files from an Internet browser, open a copy of Windows Explorer and navigate to where you want to store the pictures. Using the left mouse button, drag the pictures from your browser and drop them into Windows Explorer. Click Yes to confirm the copying of each file, and then continue. Before doing this, however, please make sure that you have a right to do this. Many pictures on the Internet are copyright protected. ∎

There are a number of ways to find pictures on the Internet, from surfing to explicitly searching. Google itself has an Image Search feature. From Google's home page, click Images. In the Image Search page, type the search text (enclose in quotes to search for a whole name), and click Search Images. Another common technique is to include the word "gallery" in the search, although these days you'd probably find a lot of Office 2010 gallery hits!

Manipulation 101

Now that you've got those pictures, what are you going to do with them? Word 2010 provides many cool tools that really expand your presentation options. What you can do with pictures depends on how they *live* in the Word document. We'll look at the various wrapping options and their implications and then move on to working with pictures, knowing that there are some constraints. Keep in mind also that this discussion is about working with Word 2010 format documents. If we were to deal with Word 97–2003 format, this book might need another 900 pages because the methods are so different.

Wrapping

Wrapping is the term used to classify the various ways in which pictures (as well as other graphics) are used in a Word document. It helps to understand that a Word document has several different layers. Where you normally compose text is called the *text layer*. There are also *drawing layers* that are both in front of and behind the text layer. A graphic inserted in front of the text layer will cover up text, unless the graphic is semi-transparent, in which case it will modify the view of the text. Graphics inserted behind the text layer act as a backdrop, or *background*, for the text.

Additionally, there is the header and footer layer. This is where headers and footers reside. This area is behind the text area. If you place a graphic into a header or footer, the graphic will appear behind the text. Dim graphics placed in the header and footer layer often serve as watermarks. Sometimes the word *CONFIDENTIAL* will be used in the header and footer layer, branding each page of the document as a caution to readers.

Setting Wrapping and Wrapping Defaults

Wrapping determines how graphics interact with each other and with text. To set the wrapping behavior of a graphic, click the graphic and then click the Wrap Text tool in the Arrange group of the Picture Tools Format tab, or in the Page Layout tab. Choose the desired wrapping from the menu that appears.

You can also set the default wrapping. If you're a long-time Word user, you likely already have a default wrapping style that suits your generic needs. If not, then in time you likely will find that you frequently change the wrapping from the default to something else. If that happens a lot, you can save yourself a step by setting the wrapping default to your usual setting.

To set the default wrapping style for most graphic objects you insert, paste, or create, choose File ⇨ Options ⇨ Advanced. In the Cut, Copy, and Paste section, use Insert/Paste Pictures As to set wrapping to any of the options shown in Figure 9-34. This setting determines the default for most, but not all, graphics inserted into Word.

Notable exceptions are shapes and textboxes. Shapes and textboxes can be set to any wrapping style after the fact, but they are always inserted as In Front of Text. Another exception, of sorts, stems from the fact that if you copy a picture from one part of a document and paste it elsewhere, it will inherit the wrapping style of the original picture and won't use your default.

Knowing how you plan to use a picture and what you need to do to it should determine the wrapping setting. Wrapping effects and typical uses are shown in Table 9-1. Wrapping comes in two basic flavors: In line with text (in the text layer) and floating (in the graphics layer, which includes the other six wrapping formats shown in Table 9-1). *Floating* means that the picture can be dragged anywhere in the document and isn't constrained in the way that pictures in the text layer of the document are.

FIGURE 9-34

Wrapping behavior determines what you can do with a picture in Word.

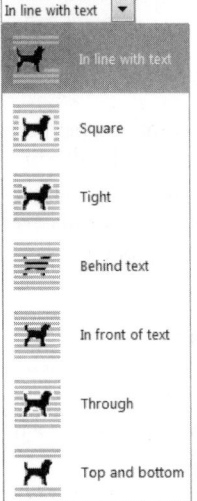

TABLE 9-1

Wrapping Styles

Wrapping Setting	Effect/Application
In line with text	Inserted into text layer. Graphic can be dragged, but only from one paragraph marker to another. Typically used in simple presentations and formal reports.
Square	Creates a square *hole* in the text where the graphic is. Text wraps around the graphic, leaving a gap between the text and the graphic. The graphic can be dragged anywhere in the document. Typically used in newsletters and flyers with a fair amount of white space.
Tight	Effectively creates a *hole* in the text where the graphic is, of the same shape as the overall outline of the graphic, so that text flows around the graphic. Wrapping points can be changed to reshape the hole that the text flows around. The graphic can be dragged anywhere in the document. Typically used in denser publications in which paper space is at a premium and where irregular shapes are acceptable and even desirable.
Behind text	Inserted into the bottom or back drawing layer of a document. The graphic can be dragged anywhere in the document. Typically used for watermarks and page background pictures. Text flows in front of the graphic. Also used in the assembling of pictures from different vector elements.

Wrapping Setting	Effect/Application
In front of text	Inserted into the top drawing layer of a document. The graphic can be dragged anywhere in the document. Text flows behind the graphic. Typically used only on top of other pictures or in the assembling of vector drawings, or when you deliberately need to cover or veil text in some way to create a special effect.
Through	Text flows around the graphic's wrapping points, which can be adjusted. Text is supposed to flow into any open areas of the graphic, but evidence that this actually works is in short supply. For all practical purposes, this appears to have the same effects and behavior as Tight wrapping.
Top and bottom	Effectively creates a rectangular hole the same width as the margin. Text flows above and below, but not beside, the graphic. The picture can be dragged anywhere in the document. Typically used when the graphic is the focal point of the text.

For Tight and Through wrapping, you can change the wrap points. To edit the wrap points, click the picture (you might need to click twice), and then choose Wrap Text ⇨ Edit Wrap Points from the Arrange group in the Picture Tools Format tab, or from the Arrange group in the Page Layout tab, as shown in Figure 9-35. If too much white space is showing, you can reduce it by moving the wrap points closer to the object. If you want to create a special effect in the form of a starburst or other pattern, you can drag the wrap points outward and inward.

FIGURE 9-35

Use Edit Wrap Points to change the way text flows around a picture.

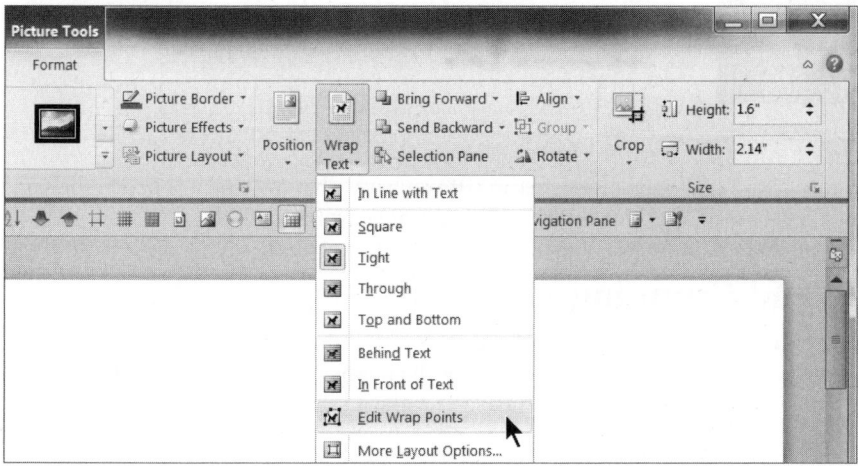

Dragging and Nudging

You can move any graphic by dragging it, and some graphics can be dropped anywhere in the document. Graphics inserted as In Line with Text, however, can be dropped only at a paragraph mark. All other graphics can be dragged and dropped anywhere. The techniques described in this section apply only to floating graphics (i.e., not In Line with Text). As described earlier, what happens when you drag a graphic is determined by the wrapping that is applied.

To drag a graphic, click to select it, and then drag it where you want it to go. You can also nudge a selected floating graphic. Select it, and then use the arrow keys to nudge it in any of the four directions.

To drag in discrete steps using Word's built-in invisible drawing grid, hold the Alt key as you drag. If you make Word's gridlines visible (View ➪ Show ➪ Gridlines), however, the effect of the Alt key is reversed. Now holding Alt while dragging makes Word ignore the grid, as shown in Figure 9-36. With the grid displayed, arrow key nudging also changes. Now the arrow keys move the picture in grid steps. Press the Ctrl key to nudge in smaller gradations. Each grid mark is an eighth of an inch.

FIGURE 9-36

Enable Gridlines in the View tab for help in planning graphic placement.

At sunset, the old restored windmill is visible through the trees. At the left, the edge of the greenhouse projects into the background. In mid-January, a tangle of trees and vines lend their silhouettes to the artistry of Mother Nature's paintbrush.

Note that gridlines is a Word-wide display setting. If you have other documents open in the same Word session, they too will be gridded. Why am I suddenly craving waffles?

Resizing and Cropping

Resizing changes the physical dimensions of the picture as it is displayed in your document. Resizing in Word will not make the associated file (or the image stored in the .docx file) any larger or smaller. If you make it smaller and then later make it larger, you still retain the original file resolution.

Cropping refers to blocking out certain portions of a picture by changing its exterior borders. You can crop out distracting or unnecessary details. Again, cropping in Word does not affect the actual picture itself, only the way it is displayed in Word. The fact that Word doesn't change the actual image is a big plus, because you preserve your options if you later change your mind.

Caution

Resizing and cropping in Microsoft Office Picture Manager and other graphics programs does change the picture itself. Keep this distinction in mind. Once you've saved a cropped or resized picture in Picture Manager, you can't get the original back (unless you saved a backup copy, of course). ■

Resizing

You can resize a picture by typing the measurements or by dragging. To resize by dragging, click on the picture and then move the mouse pointer so that it's over one of the eight sizing handles. The mouse pointer changes into a double arrow, as shown in Figure 9-37. Drag until the picture is the desired size and then release the mouse button. Note that dragging the corner handles maintains the aspect ratio of the picture, whereas dragging the side handles can be used to stretch or compress the picture.

FIGURE 9-37

Resize a picture or other graphic by dragging any of the eight sizing handles.

Hold down the Ctrl and/or Alt keys while dragging to modify the way resizing occurs:

- To resize symmetrically, causing the picture to increase or decrease by the same amount in opposite directions, hold down the Ctrl key while dragging.

- To drag in discrete steps, hold down the Alt key while dragging; if gridlines are displayed, the Alt key's behavior is reversed, as indicated earlier.

You can combine these options. For example, holding down the Alt and Ctrl keys at the same time forces Word to resize in discrete steps while resizing symmetrically.

Note

Use the solitary green handle above the center of the picture to rotate the picture. ■

To specify the size of the picture exactly, click in the Height and/or Width box in the Size group in the Picture Tools Format tab and specify the desired dimension. By default, these settings maintain the aspect ratio automatically. To distort the picture, click the Dialog Box Launcher in the Size group of the Picture Tools Format tab. Remove the check next to Lock Aspect Ratio, as shown in Figure 9-38.

FIGURE 9-38

Lock Aspect Ratio is enabled by default; to distort a picture's dimensions, turn it off.

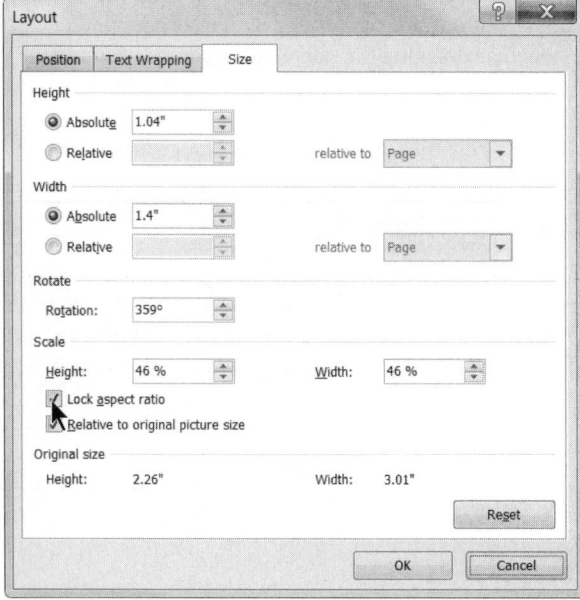

Tip

If a picture is not in line with text, you can resize and rotate using the arrow keys. Alt+left-arrow/right-arrow rotates the picture. Shift+up-arrow/down-arrow/left-arrow/right-arrow resizes the picture symmetrically. If you add the Ctrl key at the same time, the rotation or resizing is done in finer gradations. ■

Cropping

To crop a picture, click the Crop button in the Size group in the Picture Tools Format tab. The selected picture sprouts cropping handles, as does the mouse pointer. Move the pointer over any of the eight cropping handles and drag to remove the part of the picture you want to hide, as in the example in Figure 9-39. Note that the Alt key crops in discrete steps. You can also crop using the Size dialog box, as shown in Figure 9-39.

Crop to hide part of a picture to focus the reader's attention.

Picture Styles

Word 2010 provides a variety of tools for controlling the presentation of graphics. To the extent possible, use the Ribbon to apply the basic effects; then use additional tools to refine the effect for more precision, if needed. The Picture Styles Gallery provides a variety of different presentation styles. Click a picture to activate the Picture Tools Format tab. In the Picture Styles group, shown in Figure 9-40, click the More tool to expose more of the gallery.

Click the More button to expose more picture styles.

As suggested by Figure 9-41, when you move the mouse, each style is applied to the selected picture (or pictures). Note that the speed of Live Preview is heavily affected by the size of the graphic file. If the picture is 2 MB, Live Preview is going to be a lot slower than if the file were only 50 KB.

FIGURE 9-41

Effects of each style are previewed as you move the mouse.

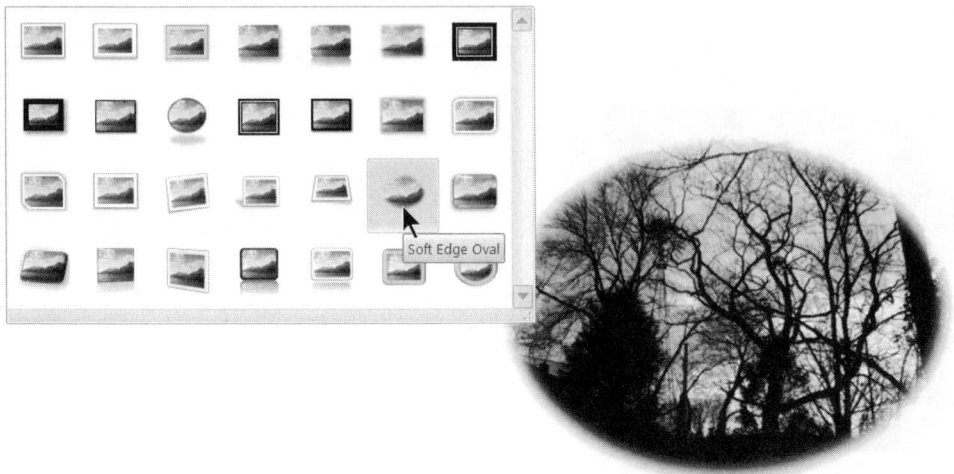

Picture Effects

Additional effects can be applied and refined with the Picture Effects tool, also contained in the Picture Styles group of the Picture Tools Format tab. There are literally millions of different permutations of effects you can apply, a small sampling of which are shown in Figure 9-42. Take a few years off to explore the different combinations.

Adjust

Word also features seven tools for adjusting picture attributes, shown in Figure 9-43. Use the tools to accomplish a number of common tasks:

- **Remove Background.** Lets you automatically/selectively remove portions of a picture based on color patterns. For example, this feature can remove everything from a picture except for a single object, such as a flower or a car. This set of tools requires considerable practice to get the desired results, so I encourage you to practice with the tools provided in the Background Removal tab until you get the hang of them.

- **Corrections.** Sharpen, soften, and adjust the brightness of images for better printing or onscreen presentation (Live Preview).

- **Color.** Applies different color masks to achieve antiquing, sepia tone, grayscale, and a variety of other color effects (Live Preview).

- **Artistic Effects.** Provides 23 special effects, such as pencil sketch, blurring, charcoal sketch, paint strokes, and others (Live Preview).

- **Compress Pictures.** Reduces the size of the picture stored in the file to the minimum needed for a given application.

- **Change Picture.** Replaces the picture with a different one. Picture Styles and Effects applied carry over to the replacement picture, as do changes applied with other tools in the Adjust group. Cropping and resizing, however, do not.

- **Reset Picture.** Removes formatting applied with Picture Styles, Picture Effects, and other Adjust tools (except for Change and Compress).

FIGURE 9-42

Applying picture effects to different Picture Styles Gallery effects produces myriad combinations.

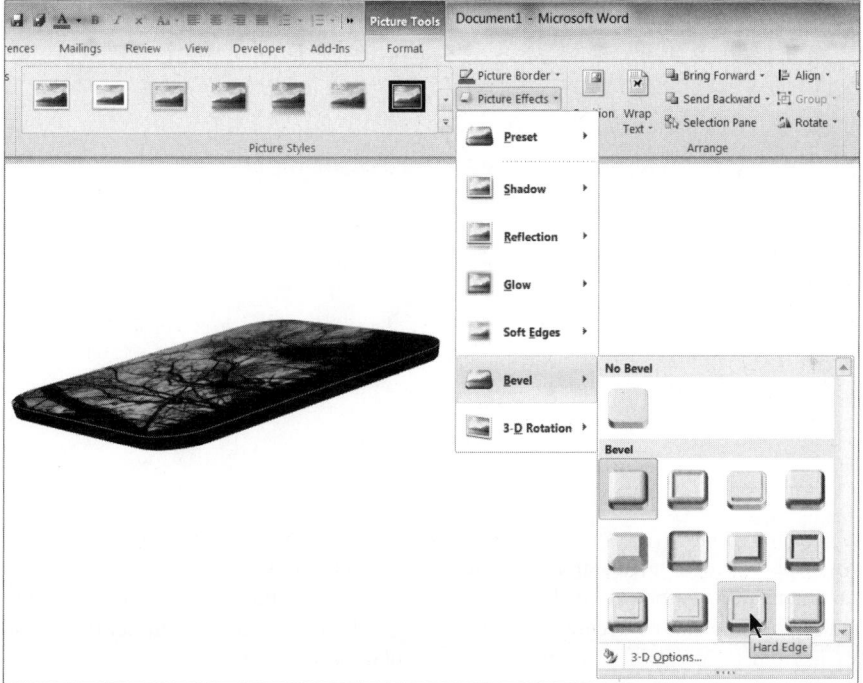

FIGURE 9-43

Word 2010 has seven tools for *adjusting* pictures.

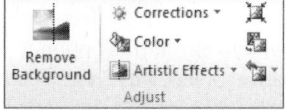

Arranging Pictures on the Page

Word has additional tools for quickly controlling the position of pictures, both two-dimensionally on the document page and with respect to other objects in the graphical layer. In the Arrange group of the Picture Tools Format tab (see Figure 9-44), click Position. The In Line with Text option here is identical to the one listed under Wrap Text. The other options, however, aren't duplicated elsewhere.

FIGURE 9-44

Position gives you a Live Preview of nine fixed positions.

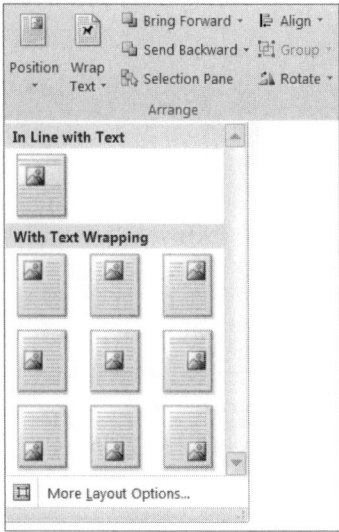

Some pictures need to be in a particular location in order to make sense. In newsletters, brochures, and many other publications, however, some pictures are intended as general illustrations. Position on the page can be decided on the basis of aesthetics and balance rather than logic and the relationship between a given picture and a particular passage in the text.

More Layout Options invokes the Layout dialog box, shown in Figure 9-45. This replaces the Advanced Layout dialog box from Word 2007 and earlier, which had only two tabs.

Additional options of interest include the following:

- **Move Object with Text.** Associates a picture with a particular paragraph so that the paragraph and the picture will always appear on the same page. This setting affects only the vertical position on the page. Although Word will allow you to check this option and Lock Anchor at the same time, once you click OK, the Move Object with Text option is cleared.

- **Lock Anchor.** This setting locks the picture's current position on the page. If you have trouble dragging a picture, verify that it is set to one of the floating wrapping options (anything but In Line with Text) and that Lock Anchor is turned off. Pictures that have been positioned with any of the nine Position presets shown in Figure 9-16 will also resist dragging.

- **Allow Overlap.** Use this setting to allow graphical objects to cover each other up. One use for this is to create a stack of photographs or other objects. This feature is also needed for layered drawings.

- **Layout in Table Cell.** This setting enables you to use tables for positioning graphics on the page.

FIGURE 9-45

Layout enables you to precisely control and set the position of graphics on the page.

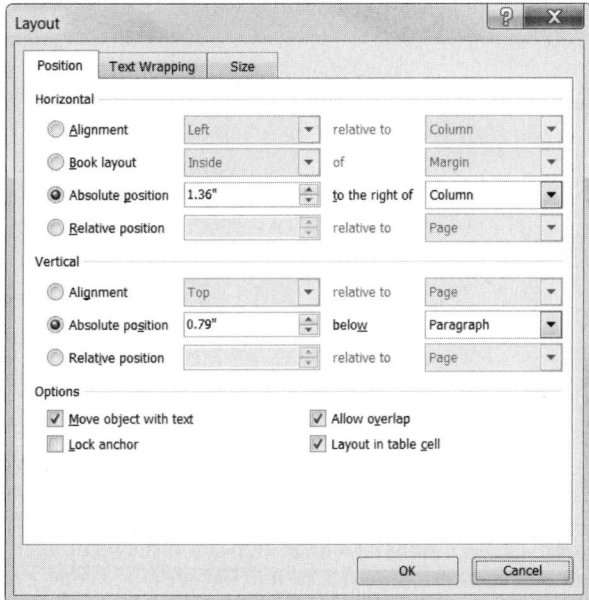

Inserting Clip Art

Clip art provides another source of decoration for your documents and is frequently used in newsletters and flyers. Part of Office's Shared Features set, depending on what Office program you have and how much of the Shared Features you have installed, Clip Art has hundreds or even thousands of little pieces of royalty-free art that you can use anywhere.

To insert clip art at the insertion point, click Insert ⇨ Illustrations ⇨ Clip Art. To accept the defaults, type a search term (e.g., **cars**) and click Go, as shown in Figure 9-46. When clip art appears, scroll through the list. When you find something you want to use, click it to insert it into your document.

FIGURE 9-46

The Clip Art pane uses local clip art as well as clip art from Office.com.

To control where the Clip Art pane searches, use the Results should be drop-down shown in Figure 9-47. To search only your local collection, remove the check next to Include Office.com Content. You can further control the scope of the search by limiting the search to only a particular kind of media. By default, Word searches for all media types — including videos and audio. Note also that we talked earlier about where to find photographs on the Web. Now you know another source. With Results should be set only to Photographs and with Include Office.com Content enabled, you can quickly see a list of photographs available for download from Microsoft.

Note

As shown in the section, "If Your Picture Format Isn't Supported," earlier in this chapter, if you lack local clip art, check Office 2010's Setup settings and verify that clip art was actually fully installed. Check the Clip Organizer choice, and choose Run All from My Computer. Or, you can selectively install individual components. ∎

FIGURE 9-47

Use the Results Should Be drop-down list to control the scope of a search for clip art.

SmartArt

Thanks to SmartArt there's a cornucopia of professional graphics available for use in Word 2010. If this book had color screen shots you would be dazzled by the kinds of sparkling, shiny, bubbly diagrams you can now make with Word. Best of all, although SmartArt is seemingly bottomless in its variety, the techniques are intuitive and simple to use.

SmartArt, introduced in Word 2007, replaced the Insert Diagram and Insert Organization Chart features of Word 2003 (and earlier). The legacy six-item Diagram Gallery (still available in Compatibility Mode) has been completely revamped and replaced with SmartArt. Moreover, the plain two-dimensional (2-D) formatting has been replaced by 3-D formatting that's so slick it looks like something you'd find in the pages of a major magazine. Let's just hope that Word users have some excellent data and content to go with all this slickness.

Inserting SmartArt

To insert SmartArt, in the Illustrations group of the Insert tab, click SmartArt. As shown in Figure 9-48, there are eight categories, plus All, which enables you to peruse the entire gallery. Clicking a thumbnail preview in the middle panel displays a larger preview on the right. A description lists the intended use of the selected item. When you find something that looks appropriate, either double-click it or click it and then choose OK. Note that SmartArt is inserted like other graphics, such as pictures, and will use your default wrapping style. See "Wrapping" earlier in this chapter.

Word inserts the shape into your document with the text entry area ready to accept information, as shown in Figure 9-49. To enter text for the SmartArt diagram, click in the Type Your Text

Here box (the text pane) and start typing. As you type on the left, text is displayed in the corresponding SmartArt component on the right.

FIGURE 9-48

Word 2010 has more than 160 different SmartArt gallery items divided into eight different categories.

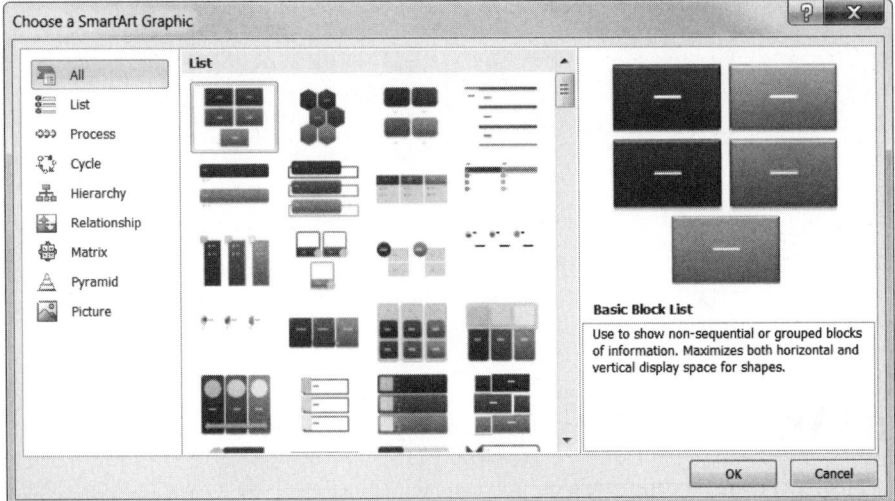

FIGURE 9-49

A new SmartArt object.

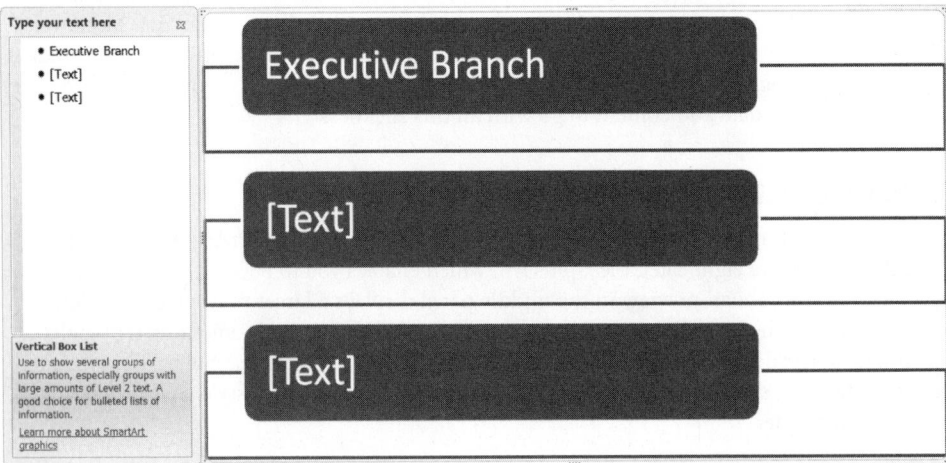

There are a variety of different ways to enter and format text. The following is not intended to be exhaustive; it's simply a list of things that work. Note that some actions can also be performed via the Create Graphic group in the SmartArt Tools Design tab, shown at the left in Figure 9-50.

The SmartArt Tools Design tab provides direct access to many useful tools.

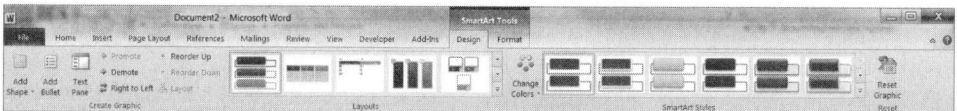

- To move to the next item, press the down arrow. Use the other arrow keys to navigate in the text entry box as well.

- To add a new item to the list, press Enter, either at the end of the list of items or above an existing item.

- To demote the current item, press the Tab key.

- To promote the current item, press Shift+Tab.

- To delete an item, select it and press the Backspace key.

- To change the font for an item, select the text you want to change, mouse over the selection, and use the Mini toolbar.

- The text pane can be moved and resized if it's in the way: Drag it to a more convenient location or drag any of the four sides to resize the text area.

- To dismiss the text pane, click the X. To redisplay the text pane, click either of the arrows at the left end of the diagram (see Figure 9-51).

Click the arrows at the left end of the diagram to toggle the text pane.

You can also enter text directly without using the text pane. Click in the SmartArt item and type. Right-click the item to see a list of options, as shown in Figure 9-52. To add a shape above the selected item, right-click and choose Add Shape ⇨ Add Shape Before.

Note that basic paragraph and character formatting can be applied to SmartArt shapes. Indents, bullets, and numbering cannot be; nor can styles. You can assign a style to the overall diagram; however, effects are limited unless the SmartArt item is In Line with Text.

FIGURE 9-52

When working directly with the SmartArt item, right-click to see actions and formatting options.

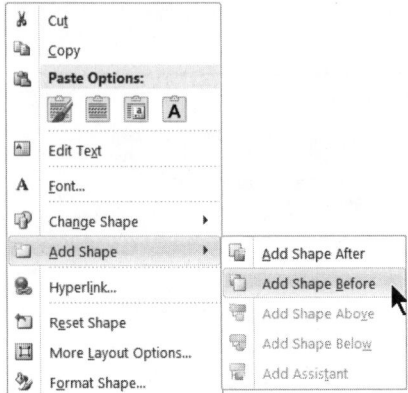

To change the font used in all the text in a SmartArt object, display the text pane, click in it, press Ctrl+A to select the contents of the text area, and then right-click and set the desired font.

You're not limited to the shapes you start out with, nor must each item be the same shape. To change the shape of any given item, select the item, right-click it, choose Change Shape, and select an alternative. Keep in mind, however, that not every shape works for every type of diagram.

Tip

If you have a list — hierarchical or not — that you would like to convert into a SmartArt object, select the list and copy it to the Clipboard before choosing the SmartArt tool. Once your SmartArt object appears, click in the text pane. Press Ctrl+A to select the placeholder list, and then press Ctrl+V to paste the list over the placeholder. ■

Changing Layout

You can change layout at any time. Select the SmartArt graphic and use the Layouts gallery on the SmartArt Tools Design tab, shown in Figure 9-53, to choose a different layout. Note that the gallery provides a Live Preview. You aren't limited to applying the same class (List, Hierarchy, Process, Cycle, etc.). SmartArt will adapt the different designs using the relationship levels currently applied.

SmartArt Styles

SmartArt Styles apply a variety of preset formatting to your SmartArt diagrams — again, using Live Preview. As suggested by Figure 9-54, a great deal of care, thought, and artistry has gone into the design of SmartArt Quick Styles.

FIGURE 9-53

SmartArt will apply any layout to any hierarchical list.

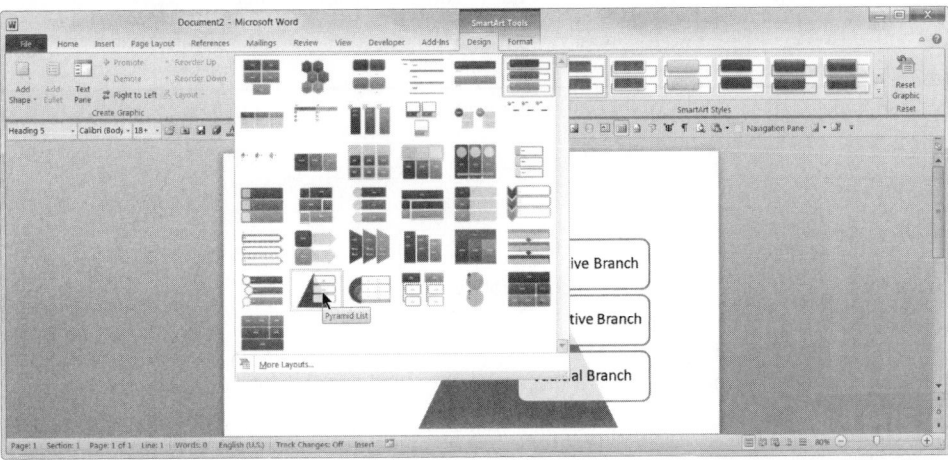

FIGURE 9-54

The Quick Style Gallery puts a basic spin on your graphics; you can refine these further using the SmartArt Tools Format Ribbon.

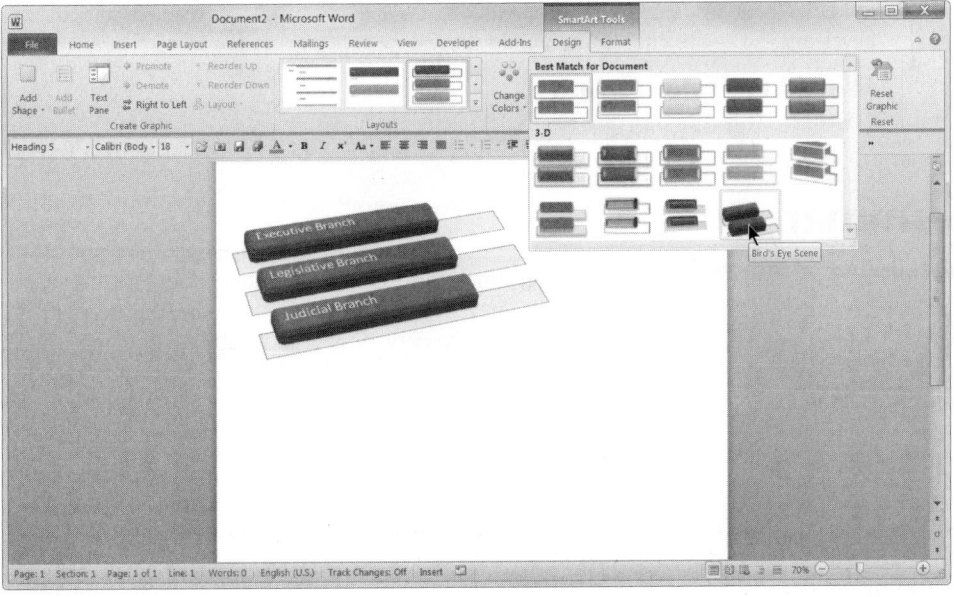

SmartArt Formatting

SmartArt provides several additional tools for further sculpting your diagrams. Shown in Figure 9-55, use the SmartArt Tools Format tab to add the finishing touches.

FIGURE 9-55

Formatting tools include Shapes, Shape Styles, and WordArt Styles.

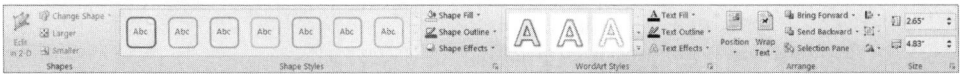

Use the SmartArt Tools Format tab choices as follows:

Shapes Group

- **Edit in 2-D.** When you click a shape, a 2-D version appears for more direct editing.
- **Change Shape.** Change the selected shape into any of dozens of Word's shapes.
- **Larger or Smaller.** Expand or shrink the selected shape.

Shape Styles Group

- **Shape Style Gallery.** Choose from three dozen different patterns of outlines and fills.
- **Shape Fill.** Choose your own custom fill for the selected shape.
- **Shape Outline.** Choose a custom outline for the selected shape.
- **Shape Effects.** Choose from a variety of effects — shadow, reflection, glow, soft edges, bevel, and 3-D — to change individual shapes.

WordArt Styles Group

Choose from several different filled-block lettering styles.

Summary

In this chapter, you've learned just about everything there is to know about tables and graphics. You know a quick way to insert a whole table, and several ways to create a table from scratch. You also know how to modify and format tables using a variety of tools and techniques. You learned how to insert graphics, Clip Art, and SmartArt, and how to work with the formatting for those objects. You should now be able to do the following:

- Copy material from one table into another, even if the dimensions don't match. Use the table Eraser to remove unwanted parts of tables.
- Use table styles to add zest and color to your tables.

- Create tables from existing non-tabular data.
- Use the Ribbon tools to modify table layout and design.
- Determine whether Word supports the graphic format of your pictures.
- Achieve any wrapping effect when working with text and graphics.
- Present a hierarchical text list into SmartArt.

Data Documents and Mail Merge

L et's face it. The term *mail merge* is entirely too narrow to fully reflect the range of what can be done using Word's Mail Merge features.

Setting up a mail merge or data document involves several steps, some of which must be done before others can happen:

1. **Set the document type.** Letter, e-mail, envelope, labels, or directory.

2. **Associate a data source with the document.** New, Outlook contact, or some other source.

3. **Design your data document by combining ordinary document features with Word merge fields.**

4. **Preview the finished document by testing to see how it looks with different data records.**

5. **Finish the process by merging the data document with the data source, creating a printed result, a saved document, or an e-mailed document.**

Understanding Data Sources

When you perform a mail merge, Word inserts an individual set of information (such as a recipient's name and mailing address) into a copy of a document to customize or personalize the document. The sets of information come from a *data source* — a file that organizes information into fields and records of information. For example, for a mailing address, the person's first name, last name, street number, city, state, and ZIP code represent the different *fields*; all the field entries for a single recipient comprise a single *record*.

In most cases, the data source that you use for a merge will be a file created in another application, most typically in Excel or Access. You also can use the contact information from Outlook. You can even use information from a Word file or other Word processing file. The key with data sources is that the information in the data source file must be properly divided into fields and records. In Excel, you can enter the field names in row 1 and each record below the field names. In Access, the table will already define the field names and records. In a word processing file, you can enter the field names on the first line, and press Enter to start each new record; you include a delimiter such as a comma or a tab between each field name and field entry so that Word can correctly separate the information to perform the merge.

Chances are, your data source may be a file that's already been created for another purpose. If you use an existing source, your file format options include the following:

- Outlook contacts
- Office Database Connections (*.odc)
- Access Databases (pre-version 12: *.mdb, *.mde)
- Access 12 and later Databases (*.accdb, *.accde)
- Microsoft Office Address Lists (*.mdb)
- Microsoft Office List Shortcuts (*.ols)
- Access Projects (*.ade, *.adp)
- Microsoft Data links (*.udl)
- ODBC File DSNs (*.dsn)
- Excel Files (*.xlsx, *.xlsm, *.xlsb, *.xls)
- Web Pages (*.htm, *.html, *.asp, *.mht, *.mhtml)
- Rich Text Format (*.rtf)
- Word Documents (*.docx, *.doc, *.docm, *.dot)
- Text Files (*.txt, *.prn, *.csv, *.tab, *.asc)
- Microsoft Works Databases (*.wdb)
- Outlook Personal Address Books (*.pab)
- Lotus 1-2-3 Files (*.wk?, *.wj?)
- Paradox Files (*.db)
- dBASE Files (*.dbf)
- Database Queries (*.dqy, *.rqy)

If your data isn't already entered in another type of file, many users create a data source file first, but Word can accommodate creating a data source on-the-fly during the merge process described in this chapter.

Choosing the Type of Data Document

To choose the type of data document, in the Start Mail Merge group of the Mailings tab, click Start Mail Merge, as shown in Figure 10-1. Some of the options are obvious, others are not. There are basically two kinds of data documents you can design. For one kind, each *data record* (a set of data items or fields describing a person, company, product, etc.) will result in a single document, such as a form letter, a mass e-mail, a product specification sheet, or an invoice. For the other kind, a single document is produced in which multiple records can appear on any given page. This approach is needed for creating directories, catalogs, and sheets of labels.

FIGURE 10-1

Letters, e-mail messages, and envelopes use one record per output document, whereas labels and directories use multiple records for each output document.

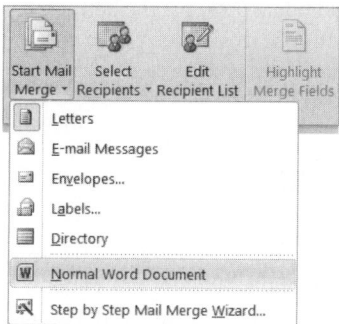

Contrast, for example, using an envelope (with a different address on each envelope) with using a sheet of labels (with a different address on each label). If you have only one address and want to print only one envelope or label, you don't need a data document. When you plan to crank out stacks of envelopes, each with a different address, or sheets of labels for which no two contain the same information, you need the approach described in this chapter.

As shown in Figure 10-1, Word offers five flavors of the two basic types of data documents:

- **Letters.** Use this option for composing and designing mass mailings for which only the recipient information varies from page to page. Use this approach too when you're preparing sheets containing product or other item specifications with one piece of paper per product or item. You might use this approach, for example, not only when sending out a form letter or invoices, but also when producing a job manual wherein each page describes a different job title, and job information is stored in a database.

- **E-mail Messages.** This is identical in concept to the form letter, except that it is geared to paperless online distribution. Contrast this with using multiple e-mail addresses in the To, Cc, or Bcc fields. Using e-mail *merge*, each recipient can receive a personalized e-mail. Using multiple addresses, each recipient receives the identical e-mail.

- **Envelopes.** This is also identical in concept to the form letter, except that the resulting document will be envelopes. As a result, when you choose this option, Word begins by displaying the Envelope Options dialog box.

- **Labels.** Use this option to print to one or more sheets of labels. This combines Word's capability to print to any of hundreds of different label formats with the capability to associate a database with a document, printing many addresses (data records) on the same page, rather than the same address on each label.

- **Directory.** This is similar in concept to labels, in that you print from multiple data records on a single page. Use the directory approach when printing a catalog or any other document that requires printing multiple records per page.

To choose the kind of document, choose Start Mail Merge in the Start Mail Merge group of the Mailings tab, and click the kind of document you want to create.

If you want step-by-step guidance through the process, note an additional option at the bottom of the Start Mail Merge list — the Step by Step Mail Merge Wizard. Use this option if you're unfamiliar with the mail merge process. The Mail Merge Wizard process is described later in this chapter.

Restoring a Word Document to Normal

Sometimes, either by accident, temporary need, or whatever, a Word document becomes associated with a data file, and you want to restore a document to normal non–mail-merge status. To restore a Word document to normal, in the Start Mail Merge group of the Mailings tab, choose Start Mail Merge ⇨ Normal Word Document. Note that when you restore a document to Normal status, several tools on the Mailings tab that were formerly available are now grayed out as unavailable. If you later decide that you need to again make the document into a data document, you will need to reestablish the data connection.

Tip
If there's a chance that you'll later need to restore a data connection and if document storage space isn't a concern, rather than break the data connection for a document, save a copy of the document, giving it a name that lets you know that it has a data connection. Although establishing a data connection isn't all that difficult or time-consuming, you can usually save some time and guesswork by not having to reinvent that particular wheel. ■

Attaching a Data Source

After you establish the type of data document for the merge, you need to attach a data source to it. In the Start Mail Merge group of the Mailings tab, choose Select Recipients, as shown in Figure 10-2.

Note that once you've attached a data source to the document, Edit Recipient List and a number of other tools on the Mailings tab are no longer grayed out. If you plan to use the entire database, you can skip the following section.

FIGURE 10-2

A document isn't really a data document until you attach a data source to it using one of the Select Recipients options.

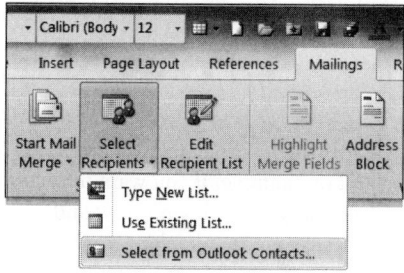

Selecting Recipients

If you don't plan to use the entire database, you can use the Mail Merge Recipients dialog box, shown in Figure 10-3, to select just the recipients you want to use. Use the check boxes shown to include or exclude records. To quickly deselect all records, clear or select the check box at the top of the list, just to the right of Data Source.

FIGURE 10-3

Select just the target recipients using the Mail Merge Recipients dialog box.

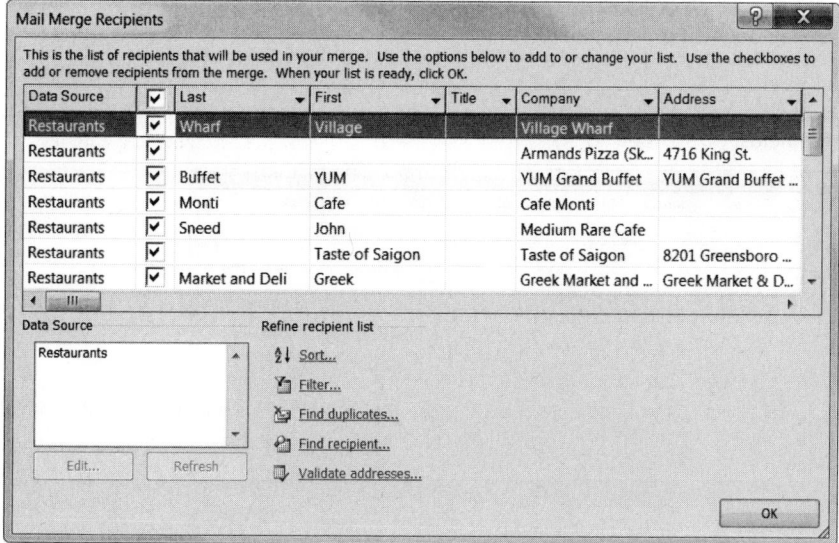

Editing Data

Depending on your data source, you sometimes can edit it by clicking the database in the Data Source box and then clicking Edit. When your data source is Outlook contacts, note that Edit is not an option. To change your Outlook data, you must use Outlook. Once you've made your change in Outlook, you can then refresh the records you see in the Mail Merge Recipients list by highlighting the data source and clicking Refresh.

Sorting Records

When editing non-Outlook data, you can sort using Word controls. Click the arrow next to a field to drop down a list of sort options, shown in Figure 10-4. For example, if you want to filter out records for which the company name is blank, click the Company drop-down arrow and choose Blanks. To select only records for which the e-mail address is not blank, click Nonblanks. To restore the list to show all records, choose the All option.

FIGURE 10-4

Quickly select records for which the current field is blank or nonblank by choosing Blanks or Nonblanks.

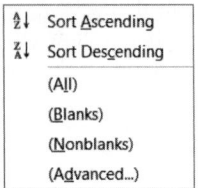

To sort by multiple fields at the same time, in the Mail Merge Recipients dialog box, choose Sort under Refine Recipient List. This displays the Filter and Sort dialog box, shown in Figure 10-5.

FIGURE 10-5

You can sort by up to three fields.

Use this dialog box to sort by multiple criteria. For example, if letters are being hand-delivered within a company, it might be useful to sort by floor and then by room number, assuming those are separate fields. (Often, sorting just by room number accomplishes both at the same time.)

Filtering Records

Word also enables you to filter records to either include or exclude records with data fields matching specific criteria. To filter records, click Filter under Refine Recipient List. Here, you again get the Filter and Sort dialog box, but the Filter Records tab this time, as shown in Figure 10-6. Use the options shown to filter by specific values. As shown here, you can use it to include specific ZIP codes. Although the dialog box initially shows just six filter fields, you are not limited to that many. It's not clear what the upper limit is, but you can specify 94, I'm told. I stopped testing at 45.

FIGURE 10-6

You can specify multiple filter criteria.

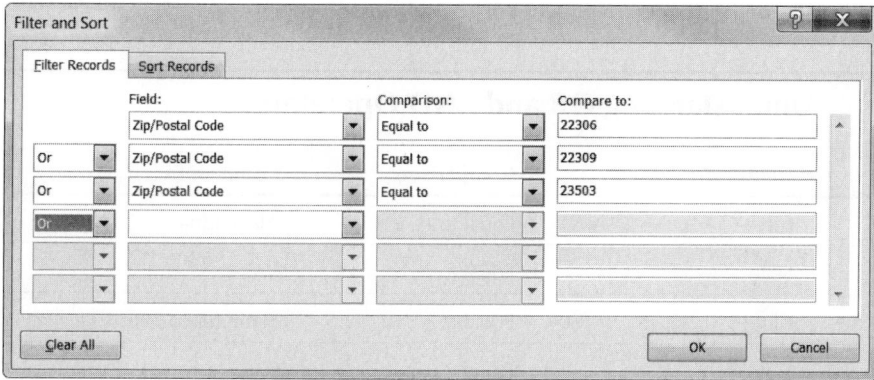

Although the dialog box shown in Figure 10-6 shows just the Equal To comparison, you can make a total of 10 comparisons (see Figure 10-7).

FIGURE 10-7

Include records based on 10 comparison operators.

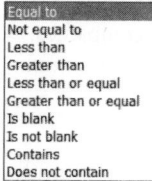

Tip

When filtering by ZIP code, if your database contains nine-digit ZIP codes, use the Contains filter rather than the Equal To filter. Using Equal To, you would need to specify all nine digits in the filter. ■

Understanding AND and OR

When setting up filters, you can make two kinds of comparisons: AND and OR. If all we had were one or the other, there would be no problem; but we have both, and we don't have parentheses to help clarify the comparisons.

It helps to understand that AND and OR apply to each pair of rules. You also need to understand that the AND rule is harder to satisfy, in that it requires that two conditions be met. Depending on what comes before or follows, each AND/OR effectively divides the list of filters into sets of filters that are being evaluated. However, by being careful with filters, you can avoid combinations that are impossibly difficult to understand.

Suppose the filters contain the comparisons shown in Table 10-1. The first AND applies to the Alexandria and VA filters. The second AND applies to the Hampton and VA filters. This set of filters requires that records must be in Alexandria, VA, OR in Hampton, VA.

TABLE 10-1

Understanding OR and AND Operators

Operator	Field	Comparison	Compare to
	City	Equal to	Alexandria
AND	State	Equal to	VA
OR	City	Equal to	Hampton
AND	State	Equal to	VA

Finally, understand that it's perfectly possible to set up filters that make no logical sense. Hence, Table 10-1 could have been set up with all of the Operators set to AND. There would be no matching records, of course. It's up to you to examine the collection of resulting data records to make sure that your logic is being applied as you think it should be.

Duplicates

Databases often contain duplicate records. When mailing or e-mailing, especially, you want to avoid sending the same person duplicate messages. When sending invoices to large companies, this can cause problems, especially if they are received and processed by different people, resulting in double payment and further paperwork downstream.

To find duplicates, click the Find Duplicates link in the lower section of the Mail Merge Recipients dialog box. Word now displays the Find Duplicates dialog box, shown in Figure 10-8.

If you identify duplicates, remove the checks next to them to exclude them from the data merge. Look carefully, however, because Word's criteria for what constitutes a duplicate might be different from your own.

Beware of Word's ability to find duplicates. Some "duplicates" aren't duplicates at all!

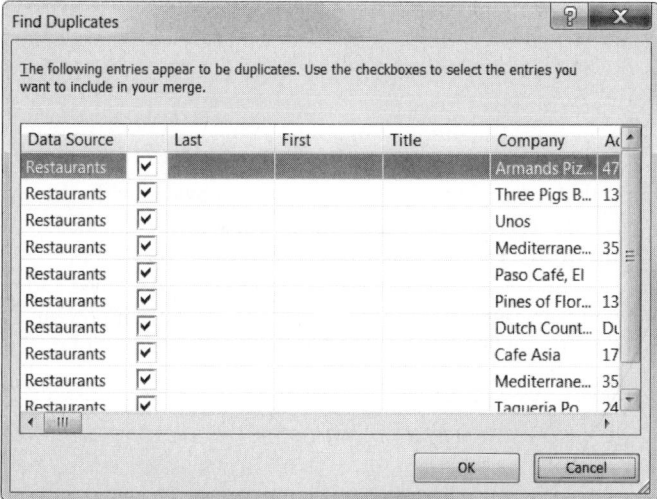

Caution

Caveat duplicates! In Figure 10-8, Word identifies nine entries as duplicates, which clearly aren't. Word uses First and Last Name to identify duplicates. If your database contains only company names and no First and Last Name fields (which isn't unexpected when all you have is the name of the establishment), you cannot use this feature to reliably identify duplicates. ∎

Find Recipient

If your database is especially large, using Find Recipient can be faster than pawing through the listings manually. Click the Find Recipient link in the lower portion of the Mail Merge Recipients dialog box to display the Find Entry dialog box shown in Figure 10-9. Alternatively, click the Find Recipient tool in the Preview Results group of the Mailings tab of the Ribbon.

Type the search text in the Find field, choose All Fields or a specific field, and then click Find Next. Note that the search is not case-sensitive. If there are matches, Word highlights the first match in the Mail Merge Recipients dialog, and the Find Entry dialog box stays onscreen. Click Find Next to move to successive matches in the database.

Return to this tool later, after your data document has been constructed, to preview specific data records. It's better to iron out problems before committing your merge to paper or e-mail.

FIGURE 10-9

Use Find Entry to search for text in any or all data fields.

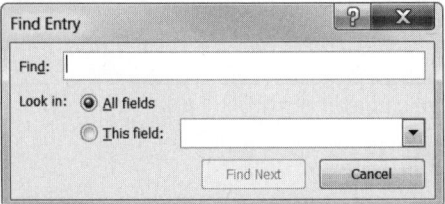

Validate Addresses

The Validate Addresses link works with third-party software, such as that provided with stamps.com and other electronic postage services. If you don't have such software installed, you'll see the message shown in Figure 10-10. These services vary, but basically they check against a huge database of valid street addresses to determine whether the selected address and ZIP code combination really exists. This can save considerably on costs because it can prevent you from mailing to addresses that might actually be somewhere in the middle of a lake (if the street were extended to where an address logically would fall).

FIGURE 10-10

If you don't have address validation software installed, Word invalidates your attempt to run the Validate address command.

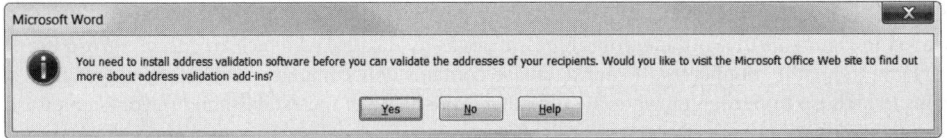

Assembling a Data Document

Regardless of which data document type you choose (letter, e-mail, envelopes, labels, or directory), the process is similar. There are some additional considerations for multi-record-per-page documents, however, so we will look at those separately after discussing the common elements.

When designing a letter or e-mail you plan to send to multiple recipients using the Merge feature, it's often a good idea to draft the document as you want it to appear, using placeholders for information pertaining to the intended recipient, as shown in the following example:

Dear [name]:

We are writing to inform you that the warranty for [product] which you purchased on [purchasedate] will expire on [expirationdate].

If you would like to extend your warranty, you must take advantage of our extended warranty coverage plans before [expirationdate]. Costs for extending the warranty are:

1 Year: [oneyearwarranty]

2 Years: [twoyearwarranty]

3 Years: [threeyearwarranty]

Please use the enclosed card and envelope to extend your warranty before it's too late!

Yours truly,

[salesagent]

When you're done, edit your document and substitute merge fields for the placeholders.

Merge Fields

After setting the data document type (using Start Mail Merge), associating a database with it (using Select Recipients), narrowing the list of recipients or records just to those records you plan to use, and drafting the data document, the next step is to insert merge fields into your document where you want the corresponding data fields to appear.

Note

Merge fields are special Word fields that correspond to the data fields in your database. For example, if you have a data field called *Company,* then you would insert the company name into your data document by using a MergeField field code with the name *Company* in it: { MERGEFIELD Company }. In your data document, that field displays either as «Company» or as the name of the company associated with the current record in the data set. Use the Mailings tab's Preview Results button in the Preview Results group to toggle between the merge field name and actual data. ∎

To insert a merge field, position the insertion point where you want the field to appear (or select the placeholder if you're replacing a placeholder with a merge field). In the Write & Insert Fields group of the Mailings tab, choose Insert Merge Field, as shown in Figure 10-11. Click the field you want to insert. Using a combination of text and merge fields that you insert, complete the assembly and wording of your document. Note that in addition to individual merge fields that you can insert using the Insert Merge Field tool, you can use special sets of merge fields to save time: Address Block and Greeting Line.

Merge fields are data tokens that you use where you want actual data fields to appear in the data document.

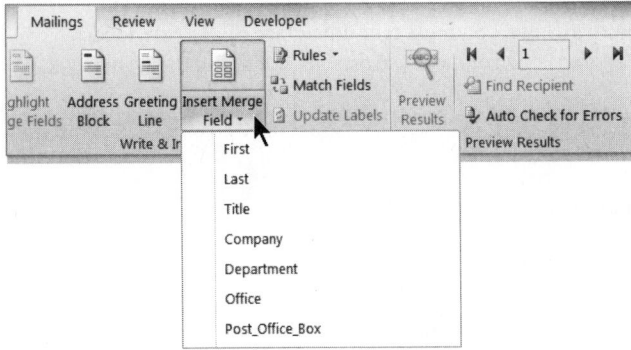

Address Block

The Address Block contains several elements that you can select from the Insert Address Block dialog box. To determine the contents of the address block, click Address Block in the Write & Insert Fields group of the Mailings tab, as shown in Figure 10-12.

Use the Address Block tool to launch the Insert Address Block dialog box.

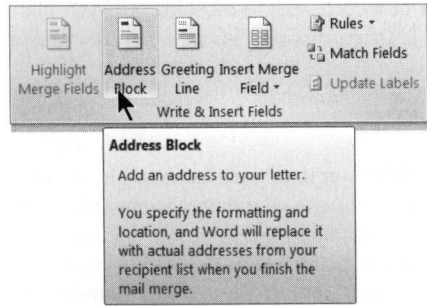

When you click Address Block, the Insert Address Block dialog box, shown in Figure 10-13, appears. Notice that it contains three sections for selecting, previewing, and correcting your Address Block information (if there are problems). Make your selections as indicated, and then click OK.

- **Specify Address Elements.** Use this section to tell Word how to define the Address Block. You can include the recipient's name (in a variety of formats), the company name, and the postal address, as well as the country or region. If desired, you can suppress the country or region, always include it, or include it only if it's different from the country selected. You can also tell Word to format the address according to the destination country or region.

FIGURE 10-13

Use the Insert Address Block dialog box to choose the Address Block elements for the current data document.

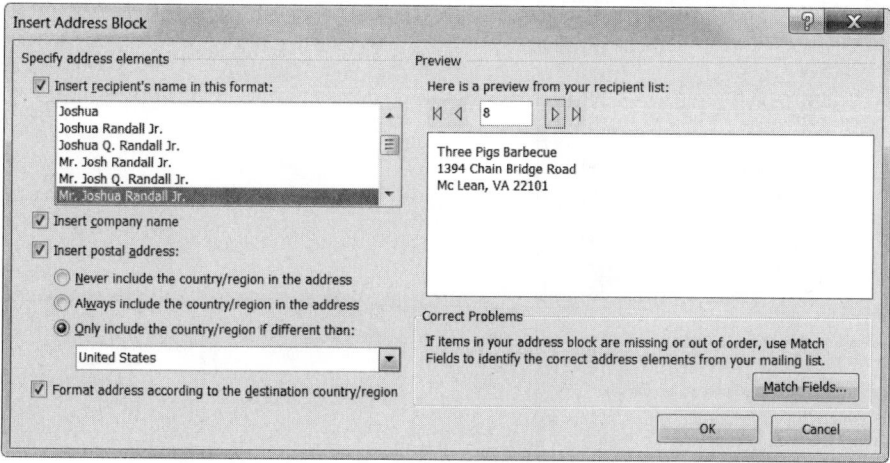

- **Preview.** Use the First, Previous, Next, and Last buttons to preview different addresses as they will appear with the selected options. It's a good idea to preview a good sampling in case some parts of the address are treated differently from how you expect, or if there are problems with missing data that will leave *holes* in the Address Block. (Click Preview Results if you see merge field names instead of data.)

- **Correct Problems.** If the preview isn't what you expect, click Match Fields to change the different data elements with which each of the fields listed is associated, as shown in Figure 10-14.

If you plan to reuse the Address Block data either for the same database or for other databases that contain the same field names, click to enable the Remember This Matching ... setting.

Greeting Line

The Greeting Line merge field, like the Address Block field, is a collection of different data elements and plain text designed to save you entry time when composing data documents. Click Greeting Line in the Write & Insert Fields group of the Mailings tab. This displays the Insert Greeting Line dialog box shown in Figure 10-15. Proper operation of a number of aspects of the Greeting Line merge field depends on your having several potentially obscure data elements available and filled out, such as nickname, spouse's nickname, and the color of their children's socks. Unless you or someone with whom you work is obsessively compulsive about data entry, you're not likely to find some aspects of this terribly useful.

FIGURE 10-14

Use the Match Fields dialog box to associate each of 11 items with data fields from your database for the Address Block.

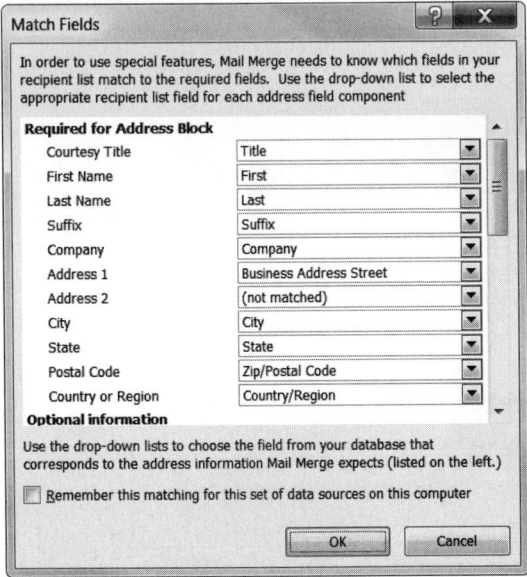

FIGURE 10-15

Set and preview Greeting Line components.

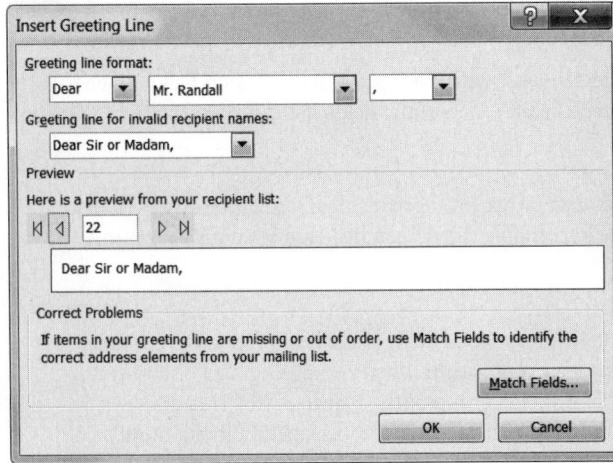

Use the Preview buttons to test your selected Greeting Line options against your actual data. If something doesn't look quite right, click Match Fields and use the controls shown in Figure 10-16 to associate the Greeting Line components with the correct merge data fields.

Use the Match Fields dialog box to associate Greeting Line merge field components with data elements from your database.

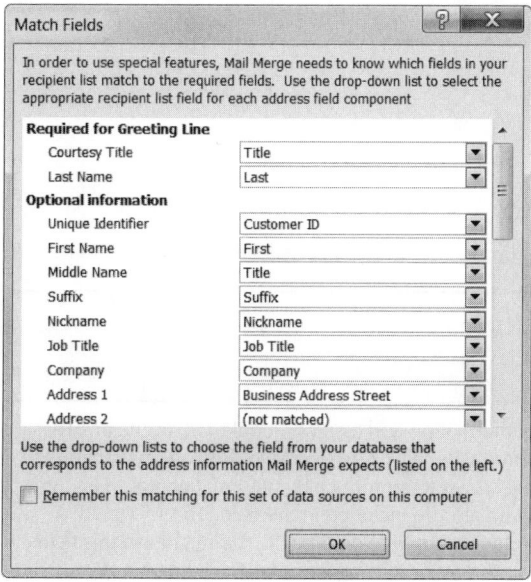

Rules

In assembling a data document, you sometimes need to control or modify how data and records are processed. Word provides nine commands to help you do that, as shown in Figure 10-17. The entries in the Rules drop-down list of the Write & Insert Fields group show how those Rule keywords are displayed in the data document.

These rules are tied to specific Word field codes, and are explained in Table 10-2. Note that many of these are supported by dialog boxes that guide you through proper syntax, making them easy to use and understand.

FIGURE 10-17

Use the Rules drop-down list of Word fields to control how data is merged with the data document.

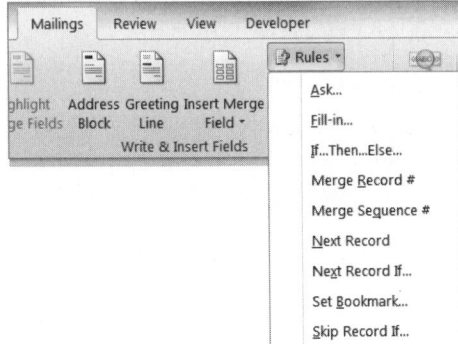

TABLE 10-2

Merge Rules

Field	Usage/Purpose
ASK	This field prompts you to provide information and assigns a bookmark to the answer you provide; the information is stored internally. A reference to the bookmark can then be used in the mail merge document to reproduce the information you type. A default response to the prompt can also be included in the field. The ASK field displays as an empty bookmark in the mail merge document. You might use this field in conjunction with an IF field to prompt for missing information during a merge.
FILLIN	This field prompts you to enter text and then uses your response in place of the field in the mail merge document. This is similar to the ASK field, except that the information can be used only in one place.
IF	This is used in mail merge documents to control the flow and to create a conditional statement that controls whether specific mail merge fields are printed or included in the merged document.
MERGESEQ	This field provides a counter of mail merge documents that actually result from a merge. If you merge the entire database and do not change the base sorting and if no records are skipped, then MERGESEQ and MERGEREC will be identical.
MERGEREC	When doing a mail merge, the MERGEREC field serves as a counter of records in the data file and doesn't count the number of documents actually printed. This field is incremented by the presence of NEXT and NEXTIF fields. If you skip records using SKIPIF, MERGEREC is incremented nonetheless.

Field	Usage/Purpose
NEXT	The NEXT field is used to include more than one record in a given document. Ordinarily, when doing a mail merge, one document is printed for each record. With the NEXT field, however, you can include multiple records in a single document. This can be useful when you need to refer to several addresses from a data file. When doing a label merge, the NEXT field is provided automatically, and appears as « Next Record ».
NEXTIF	The NEXTIF statement works like the NEXT field except that it advances to the next record only if an expression being evaluated is true. A typical use is to skip a given record if a particular key field is blank. For example, in an e-mail merge, if you haven't otherwise excluded records with blank e-mail addresses, you can use NEXTIF to do it.
SET	The SET field is used to change the text referred to by a bookmark. SET often is used in conjunction with IF to conditionally change how particular text is defined based on external factors, such as the current date, or internal factors, such as the value(s) of particular fields.
SKIPIF	The SKIPIF field is used to cancel processing of the current database record during a mail merge. For example, you might use it to screen out a particular ZIP code.

Match Fields

The Match Fields button in the Write & Insert Fields group displays the Match Fields dialog box shown in Figure 10-18. If the dialog box and fields look familiar, it's no accident. The "special features" notation referred to at the top of the Match Fields dialog box refers to the Address Block and Greeting Line. If you've already visited the Match Fields dialog boxes in those respective dialogs, you can forego the pleasure of another visit. In addition, if you aren't using Address Block and Greeting Line fields, you can safely ignore this tool.

Preview Results

At any time as you go along, if you want to see what actual data will look like in your document, click the Preview Results button in the Preview Results group of the Mailings tab of the Ribbon to toggle between a data token (merge field name) and actual data, as shown in Figure 10-19. Note that because the merge fields actually are field codes, they can also be displayed in a third way, also shown in Figure 10-19.

In the Preview Results section of the Mailings toolbar, shown in Figure 10-20, you can use the First, Previous, Next, Last, and Go To Record tools to display any data record.

Find Recipient

To search for a specific data record or for records whose data you want to preview, click the Find Recipient tool in the Preview Results group. This displays the Find Entry dialog box shown earlier in Figure 10-9. Refer to the discussion earlier in this chapter.

FIGURE 10-18

When launched from the Mailings tab, the Match Fields dialog box is a marriage of the Match Fields dialogs available from within the Insert Address Block and Insert Greeting Line dialog boxes.

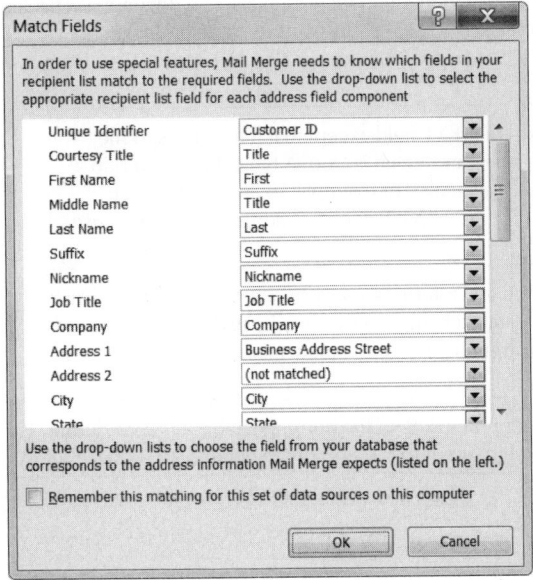

FIGURE 10-19

Data merge fields can be displayed in three different ways in your document.

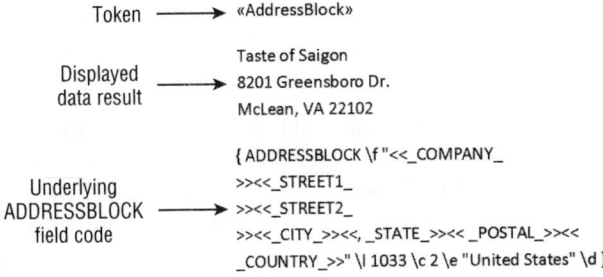

Use the Preview Results tools to ensure that the merge will produce the results you want.

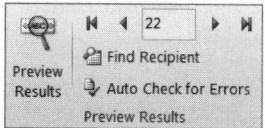

Update Labels

When the data document type is Labels, there are two ways to proceed. The easy way is to carefully edit just the first label cell by inserting whatever merge fields you need. When you're finished, click Update Labels. Word copies all text, merge fields, and formatting from the first cell into each of the other cells, after the Next Record control. The result is that each sheet of labels will contain data from the same number of label cells. A sheet containing nine labels will use data from nine database records.

The hard way to do labels is to ignore the existence of the Update Labels tool and to carefully edit each of the table cells, inserting the merge fields you want to use. Note that Word automatically provides the Next Record field in each of the table cells, as shown in Figure 10-21. If you manually populate the cells, additional merge fields should be inserted after the Next Record control. If you insert merge fields before the Next Record control, data from the same record used for the first cell will be used.

When you insert a merge field into the first label cell, Word automatically puts the Next Record field into each of the other cells.

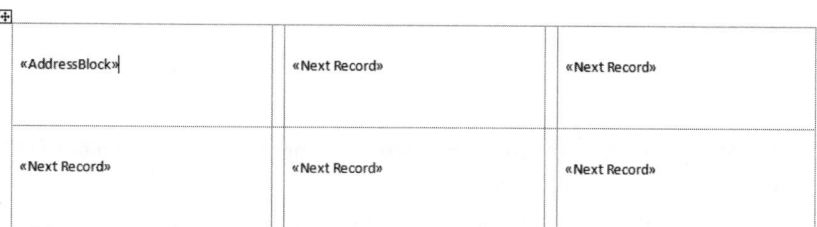

Why would you choose to do it the hard way? You might do it that way if you need to do something else in each data field that can't be accomplished by Word automatically copying the first table cell to each of the other label cells.

Highlight Merge Fields

Use the Highlight Merge Fields tool to highlight all of the merge fields in your data. This can be useful if you're working on a complex document and need to recheck the logic and placement of merge fields. This is especially true if you've turned on Preview Results and are looking at actual data results, rather than the merge fields themselves.

If, for example, you expect a given merge field result to appear in two places in the document, this tool enables you to find those locations more easily so you can verify that the correct text appears. If you're using conditional rules, such as Skip Record If, Next Record If, and If, this also helps you focus on the results so you can verify that the rules are working as expected.

Auto Check for Errors

To avoid wasting paper and other resources, when you think you're done, click Auto Check for Errors in the Preview Results group to display the options shown in Figure 10-22.

FIGURE 10-22

Rather than waste paper or send out errant e-mails, use the error checking tool to avoid logical errors or other unwanted surprises.

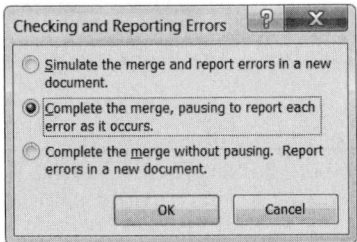

The options are as follows:

- **Simulate the Merge and Report Errors in a New Document.** Use this option to examine any and all errors in a new document.

- **Complete the Merge, Pausing to Report Each Error as It Occurs.** Use this option once you've determined that there are errors, so you can observe the error in action.

- **Complete the Merge without Pausing. Report Errors in a New Document.** Use this option to go ahead and complete the merge without stopping at each error, sending the error report to a new document.

Finishing the Merge

Once the data document is ready and has been thoroughly debugged and certified as error-free, it's time to go through the final motions. The Finish & Merge button in the Finish group of the Mailings tab provides three options, shown in Figure 10-23, regardless of the type of data document chosen. Think twice before accidentally clicking Send E-mail Messages if the document is a set of labels or a directory!

Word offers three options for completing the merge.

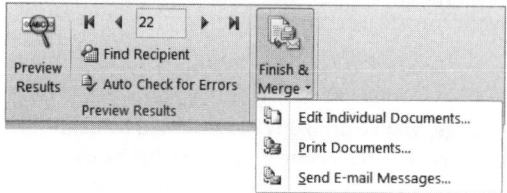

Edit Individual Documents

Use the Edit Individual Documents option if you want to save your merged results for future use. For example, suppose you have a set of labels that seldom changes and that you need to print out every week. Rather than go through the mail merge exercise each week, save a copy of the labels and then print them each time you need them. That way, you don't need to go through the whole mail merge routine unless the underlying database changes.

You might also choose this option if you don't trust other ways of proofing the results. Instead of printing from the Mailings tab controls, send the results to a new document where you can examine each of them, and then print when you're ready.

When you choose this option, Word displays the Merge to New Document dialog box, shown in Figure 10-24. If you want Word to create a limited number of output documents, either choose Current Record or indicate a From/To range. Click OK to create the new document with the merged data.

Select the desired records to merge, and click OK.

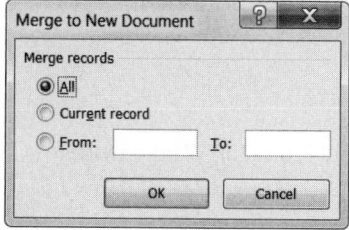

Note

If you choose this option for an e-mail merge, the resulting document(s) will not be useful except for proofing the e-mails. To actually send the e-mails, you have to choose the Send E-mail Messages option. ■

Print Documents

Choose the Print Documents option when you're certain that the merge will give you the results you want and your boss is at the door asking, "Where are those letters?" When you click Print Documents, Word displays the dialog box shown earlier in Figure 10-24, this time sporting a Merge to Printer title bar. The same options prevail. Choose wisely and click OK to immediately launch yet another dialog box, the Print dialog box. Make any additional choices and decisions, including which printer to use, cross your fingers, and click OK.

Tip

If you don't trust all of the previews and error checks at this stage, you've probably been burned by mail merge in the past. If you still want to be sure before wasting a tree, use the Name drop-down list to see whether you have an option that produces electronic images of printed pages, rather than actual printed pages. Using Office 2010 and Windows 7, you have both XPS and PDF options to create digital documents in lieu of actual printouts. Then you can review what amounts to your best possible Print Preview. ■

Send E-mail Messages

Choose the Send E-mail Messages option if you're working on an e-mail merge. When you click Send E-mail Messages, Word displays the Merge to E-mail dialog box, shown in Figure 10-25.

FIGURE 10-25

Make sure you fill out the Subject line field!

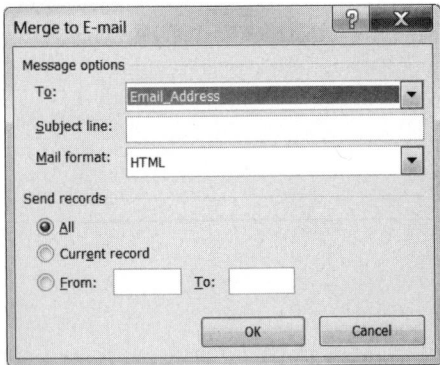

In addition to the Send Records options (All, Current Record, and From/To), Word provides three additional options:

- **To.** If the proposed e-mail address data field is not correct, used the drop-down arrow to replace it with the correct address field.

- **Subject Line.** This is very important. Not including a Subject line will often flag the e-mail as spam by various systems. Be sure to include the subject for an added level of completeness.

- **Mail Format.** Many e-mail recipients wisely have their e-mail options set up to read all e-mail as plain text (this gives them a shot at preventing any automatic naughtiness from being executed when e-mail is opened). The options provided are Attachment, Plain Text, and HTML, the latter being the default. Although Attachment seems like a good compromise for formatted e-mail, this option provides no way for you to include any message text for the body of the e-mail. When and if you use this option, make sure the Subject line isn't blank.

Mail Merge Task Pane/Wizard

YAHOO stands for *you always have other options*. YAHOO applies here as well. Your other option is to use the Mail Merge Wizard, rather than the individual tools in the Mailings tab. If you need a little more hand-holding when doing a mail merge, Word has the hand ready and waiting, in the form of the Mail Merge Wizard. To travel down this particular road, start a new blank document (or open a document you want to use as the basis for a data document). On the Mailings tab, click the Start Mail Merge button in the Start Mail Merge group, and choose the Step by Step Mail Merge Wizard. This opens the Mail Merge task pane, shown in Figure 10-26.

FIGURE 10-26

Choosing the Mail Merge Wizard opens the Mail Merge task pane.

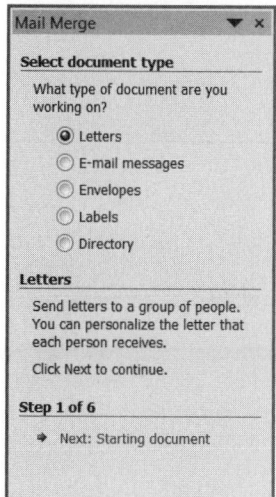

Step 1: Document Type

In Step 1, shown in Figure 10-26, choose the type of data document you want to create. Later, if you need to restore this to a normal document, in the Mailings tab, choose Start Mail Merge ➪ Normal Word Document. Click Next: Starting Document.

Step 2: Starting Document

In Starting Document, Word provides three options. Note that when you choose any of these options, Word explains the option in the lower part of the task pane. The options are as follows:

- **Use the Current Document.** Start from the current document and use the Mail Merge Wizard to add recipient information (merge fields).

- **Start from a Template.** Start from a template, which you can customize as needed by adding merge fields and/or other contents. If you choose this option, click "Select Template" to be shown a list of all of the available templates (at least the ones that Word knows about). Note that despite the option's wording, it does *not* present you with a list of "ready-to-use mail merge" templates.

- **Start from Existing Document.** Open an existing mail merge or other document, and change it to fit the current need by changing the contents or recipients. Recent mail merge documents, if any, will be listed. If the one you want isn't listed, click Open to navigate to the one you want, select it, and then click Open again.

After homing in on the starting document, choose Next: Select Recipients at the bottom of the task pane.

Step 3: Select Recipients

In Step 3, select from Use an Existing List, Select from Outlook Contacts, and Type a New List. These options are shown in Figure 10-27.

FIGURE 10-27

Select the desired recipients option and then click Next: Write Your Letter.

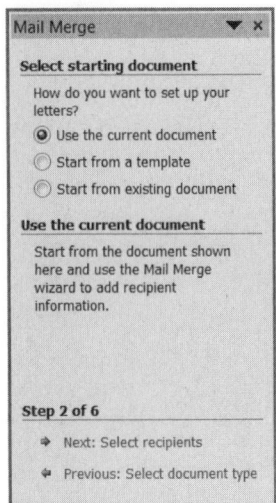
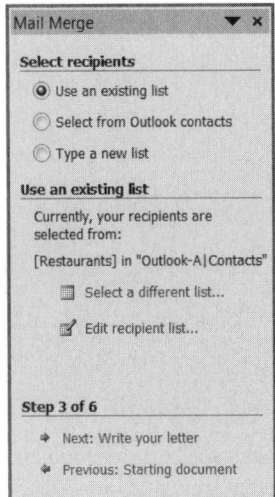

If you click Type a New List and then click Create, Word displays the New Address List dialog box. Type your data into the fields shown, tabbing or clicking to get to the next entry field. To accept the current entry and enter a new record, click New Entry. To remove an entry, click Delete Entry.

The New Address List dialog box can be used for addresses, but doesn't need to be. If the list of data elements or fields doesn't meet your needs, click Customize Columns, which displays the Customize Address List dialog box. To add a field, select the field above where you want to add the new field, and click Add. Type the field name in the space provided, and click OK. To delete a field, select the field and click Delete. To rename a field, select it, click Rename, type a new name in the To field, and click OK. (To add a field at the beginning, select the first field and click Add, as before. The added field will be second on the list, not first. Select the added field, and then click Move Up.) To rearrange the fields, click a field you want to move, and then click Move Up or Move Down, as needed. When you're done customizing the fields, click OK to return to the New Address List dialog box.

When you're finished entering data, click OK. Word now prompts you to save the file as a Microsoft Office Address Lists file (Access Database). Note that this is the only Save as Type option. Type a name and click Save.

Step 4: Write Your Letter

In Step 4, you are greeted with four options:

- **Address Block.** This leads to the dialog box shown in Figure 10-13. See the discussion under "Address Block" for additional details.

- **Greeting Line.** The Greeting Line option displays the dialog box shown in Figure 10-15. See the "Greeting Line" section for more information.

- **Electronic Postage.** As indicated previously, the functioning of this option requires the installation of third-party software that enables you to apply postage to items you send.

- **More Items.** This option displays the dialog box shown in Figure 10-28. It is a shame that this thoroughly confusing dialog box appears as part of the Mail Merge Wizard. If you choose Address Fields, the dialog box shows you a list of all of the fields in its vocabulary, many or most of which are probably irrelevant to the attached database. Choose Database Fields instead to see a list of what's actually available for use in this merge.

Tip

In theory, you move the insertion point to where you want a merge field to appear, click More items, select the field, and click Insert. Dismiss the dialog box and repeat this series of actions for each merge field. In practice, however, if you know which fields you want to insert, go ahead and insert them all at once, and then cut-and-paste them where you want them to go. ■

Use a combination of text and merge fields to write the data document, inserting merge fields where you want database fields to appear. When you're done, click Step 5: Preview Your Letters.

FIGURE 10-28

Ignore the Address Fields option. The associated database fields are listed when you choose Database Fields.

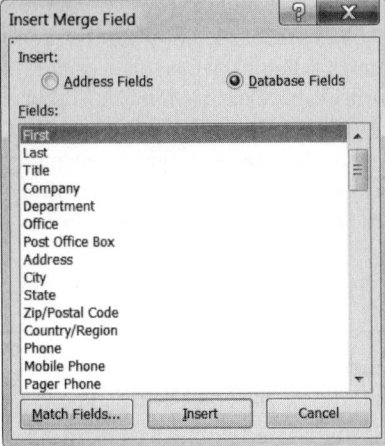

Step 5: Preview Your Letters

In Step 5, shown in Figure 10-29, use the controls shown to move from record to record in your database. Note that the << and >> tools correspond to the Previous and Next buttons in the Mailings tab of the Ribbon. There's no reason you can't use the far more flexible and useful tools in the Ribbon.

Notice that the Find a Recipient and Edit Recipient List options perform identical actions, respectively, as the Find Recipient and Edit Recipient List Ribbon tools discussed earlier in this chapter. About the only useful tool in this set is the Exclude This Recipient option, which is the equivalent of choosing Edit Recipient List from the Mailings tab and removing the check next to the currently selected record.

Step 6: Complete the Merge

The contents of the Step 6 panel vary depending on the document type. As shown in Figure 10-29, when the document type is a letter, the options are to send the merged results to the printer or to send them to "individual letters." Actually, that's not at all what the option does. Instead, it sends all of the merged letter results to a single new document, in which the individual letters are separated by section breaks.

FIGURE 10-29

Use Steps 5 and 6 to preview the data document and complete the merge.

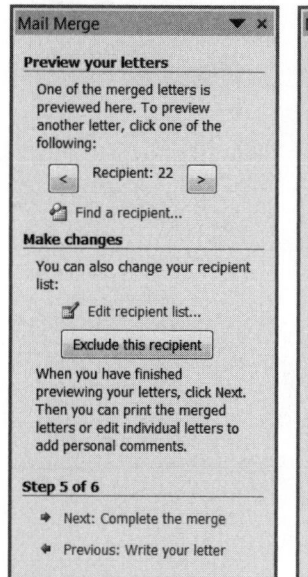 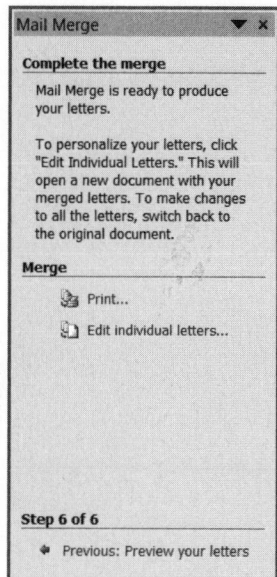

Summary

In this chapter, you've learned how to use each of the Mail Merge tools in the Mailings Ribbon to begin a mail merge, attach a database to a data document, insert merge fields, and complete a data merge. You've also seen that this feature isn't just for mail merge, but has many other uses as well. You should now be able to do the following:

- Attach a data source to a Word document and select just the records you want.

- Within limits, use Word tools to discover duplicate data records.

- Insert composite merge fields, such as the Address Block and Greeting Line, as well as control how those fields are constituted.

- Use the Mail Merge Wizard.

Security, Tracking, and Comments

N ot too terribly long ago, about the only way you could protect a Word document was to password-protect it using a password technology that was decidedly easy to crack. Password-cracking solutions abounded and were available free or practically free. Word has come a long way since then and now offers a variety of different kinds of protection that are a lot better than what was available for Word 97 and earlier, although nothing is 100 percent secure.

Not only does improved technology make protection stronger, but the variety of types of protection has expanded as well. This chapter looks at the types of document protection available to Word users and describes how to use them.

Protection Types

One of the unfortunate things about a piece of software as complicated as Word 2010 is that privacy settings aren't all centrally located. This can make discovering the full range of what's available a bit difficult. Word 2010 is a bit improved over Word 2007 on this score, but it still helps to have a guide. To save you the trouble of searching desperately to find what you can control, here's the definitive list of the different types of protection (and pseudo-protection) Word 2010 offers, and where to find them:

- **Permission.** Restricts a document so that it can be opened and/or changed only by specific individuals. Select File ➪ Info ➪ Protect Document ➪ Restrict Permission by People.

- **Digital Signature.** Signs a document with a digital signature to provide assurance that you are the source of the document. Select File ➪ Info ➪ Protect Document ➪ Add a Digital Signature.

- **Inspect Document.** Inspects the document to see if it contains private or sensitive information or data. Select File ⇨ Info ⇨ Check for Issues ⇨ Inspect Document.

- **Mark as Final.** Marks a document as *final* to let recipients know that the document is considered the final revision. This setting makes the document read-only and makes it unavailable for additional typing, editing, proofing, or tracking changes. Note that this setting is advisory only — you can still click the big Edit Anyway button and remove the Mark as Final setting. Recipients with earlier versions of Word who have installed the Office 2010 Compatibility Pack won't even see the file as read-only. Hence, this kind of gentle protection would have to be combined with something more substantial to be meaningful.

- **Style Formatting Restrictions.** Limits formatting to a selection of styles, as well as blocks Theme, Scheme, or Quick Style Set switching. Protection here is by password and is therefore less secure and robust than when using permissions. Select File ⇨ Info ⇨ Protect Document ⇨ Restrict Editing ⇨ Limit Formatting to a Selection of Styles.

- **Editing Restrictions — Read Only.** Offers password protection, which is not very secure, along with exceptions of specific areas of the document. Exceptions can be made wholesale, or you can limit them to individuals with specific Windows Live ID–associated e-mail addresses. Select File ⇨ Info ⇨ Protect Document ⇨ Restrict Editing ⇨ Allow Only This Type of Editing in the Document ⇨ Read only.

- **Editing Restrictions — Tracked Changes.** Allows only tracked changes to be made. Select File ⇨ Info ⇨ Protect Document ⇨ Restrict Editing ⇨ Allow Only This Type of Editing in the Document ⇨ Tracked Changes.

- **Editing Restrictions — Fill-In Forms.** Allows filling in of form fields and content controls. Select File ⇨ Info ⇨ Protect Document ⇨ Restrict Editing ⇨ Allow Only This Type of Editing in the Document ⇨ Filling in Forms.

- **Editing Restrictions — Comments.** Allows only comments. Exceptions can be made for selected areas of the document, for everyone, or for specific individuals (using Windows Live ID–associated e-mail addresses). Select File ⇨ Info ⇨ Protect Document ⇨ Restrict Editing ⇨ Allow Only This Type of Editing in the Document ⇨ Comments.

- **Password to Open/Modify.** Lets you specify a password to open and/or modify the document. This protection is not the same as the Editing Restrictions' No Changes setting. You must choose one or the other. Select File ⇨ Save As ⇨ Tools ⇨ General Options.

The rest of this section looks at each of these, showing how you enable protection and assessing the degree of protection provided.

Restricting Permission (Information Rights Management)

A relatively new and strong way to protect your documents uses an Information Rights Management server to authenticate users who create or receive documents or e-mail that have restricted permissions. To begin the process — assuming you're using an enterprise-enabled version of Office — choose File ➪ Protect Document ➪ Restrict Permission by People ➪ Manage Credentials ➪ Add. As noted in Figure 11-1, some enterprises have their own rights management servers. If you don't have access to one, you can use Microsoft's free trial Information Rights Management service.

FIGURE 11-1

If you don't already have access to an Information Rights Management service, you can sign up to use a free trial service.

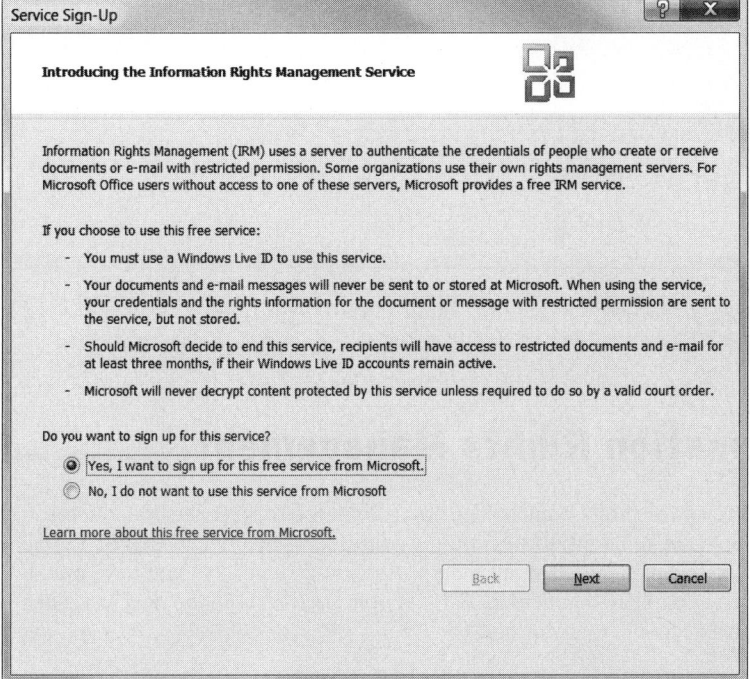

To use this service, you and all users with whom you share rights-managed documents or e-mail must have Windows Live ID–registered e-mail addresses. The biggest risk is that Microsoft might at some point end the free trial service. You'll then have three months in which to move to a different rights management server, subscribe to whatever service Microsoft offers (assuming it replaces the free trial service with a for-pay service), or remove rights management protection from your documents so you don't lose access to them.

To restrict permission by using Information Rights Management, choose File ➪ Info ➪ Protect Document ➪ Restrict Permission by People ➪ Restricted Access. If you do not have Rights Management software installed on your computer, the dialog box shown in Figure 11-1 appears. If you choose to proceed, a five-step wizard walks you through the process of setting up rights management and associating your Windows Live account.

If you are not logged on to the rights management server account you want to use, or if you need to specify, add, or remove a user account, choose File ⇨ Info ⇨ Protect Document ⇨ Restrict Permission by People ⇨ Manage Credentials, which displays the Select User dialog box, shown in Figure 11-2. If you need to add a Windows Live or other account, click Add. To remove an account, select the one you want to remove and click Remove. Select the account you want to use (if desired, enable Always Use this Account), and then click OK.

FIGURE 11-2

Most rights management users have only one rights management account.

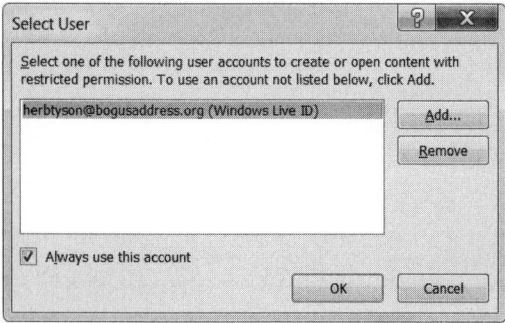

Setting Up Information Rights Management

In the Service Sign-Up dialog box, choose Yes, I Want to Sign up for This Free Trial Service from Microsoft and click Next. In the Welcome to the Windows RM Account Certification Wizard, choose Yes, I Have a Windows Live ID. (They are so prevalent at this point that this section assumes that you have one. If you don't, choose the No option and follow that detour, and then join back up with the next step once you've set up your Windows Live account). Click Next.

In Specify Your E-mail Address, type the address associated with the Windows Live account you want to use for rights management, and then click Next. In Select Certificate Type, read the descriptions of Standard and Temporary, make your choice, and then click Next ⇨ Finish.

If credentials are already associated, and/or when you click OK in the dialog box shown in Figure 11-2, Word displays the Permission dialog box shown in Figure 11-3. Type the e-mail addresses of people with permission to read and change the document in the boxes provided. E-mail addresses should be separated with semicolons. The system automatically checks e-mail addresses you enter, but if it doesn't happen quickly enough for you, click the Check Names tools to the right of the address boxes. A colored icon next to the name means that the person has a Windows Live ID and is currently online. A gray icon means either that they're not online or that the address isn't a valid Windows Live ID.

FIGURE 11-3

You can use rights management to limit who can read and change a document.

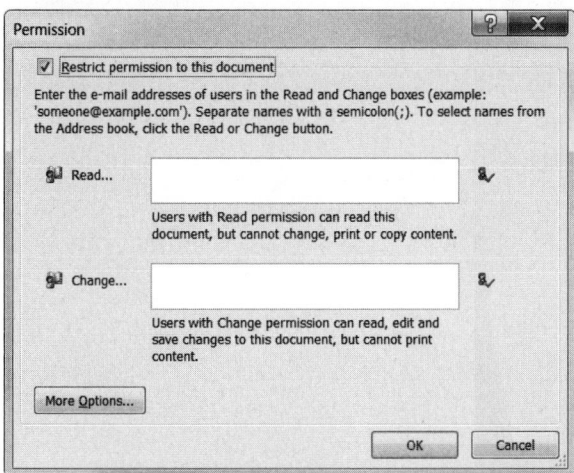

To see more options, click More Options, not surprisingly, which displays the different Permission dialog box shown in Figure 11-4. Note that you can set an expiration date for permissions you grant. In addition, recipients of the document will not be able to print, copy, or access document content programmatically (e.g., use a program to extract XML data) unless the corresponding options are checked. For additional protection, if you don't want to receive requests for additional permission, remove the check next to Users Can Request Additional Permissions From. Once you've selected permissions, click Set Defaults to make the selected permissions the default for future documents upon which you restrict permissions.

Click Require a Connection to Verify a User's Permission to require that individuals to whom you are granting permissions be connected to the rights management server, either over the Internet or over the respective intranet. Note that if you have not installed the Windows RMS client for Rights Management Services, this option will be grayed out as unavailable.

When you click OK in either of the dialog boxes shown in Figure 11-3 or Figure 11-4, Word adds the Permission Is Currently Restricted bar at the top of the document window, as shown in Figure 11-5.

Removing Access Restrictions

When and if there is no longer a need to restrict access to a document, choose File ➪ Info ➪ Protect Document ➪ Restrict Permission by People ➪ Unrestricted Access. Click Yes to the prompt that asks if you're sure you want to remove permission. Note that you're not removing *permission*. Rather, you're removing permission *restrictions*.

FIGURE 11-4

You can set an expiration date as well as restrict permission to copy or print a document.

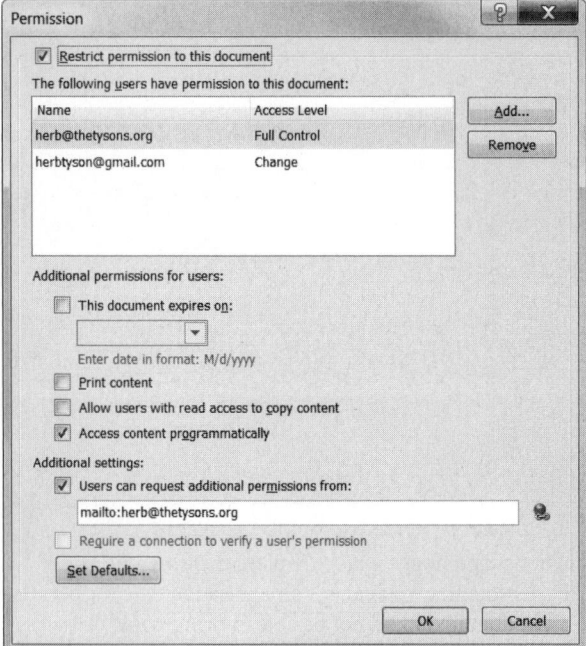

FIGURE 11-5

The Permission Is Currently Restricted message bar appears when you limit access to the document.

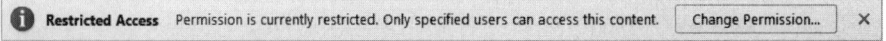

Digital Signatures

A digital signature is an electronic certificate that provides a way for recipients to verify that a document or e-mail actually came from the sender. Can these certificates really provide such verification? That's an article of faith, perhaps — an appropriate enough concept for a Bible, one supposes. Use and trust digital signatures according to your own personal beliefs. You assume any and all risks.

Note

Personally, I don't trust digital signatures. When I receive e-mail containing a digital signature, warning bells immediately go off because nobody with whom I exchange e-mail uses digital signatures. Hence, the only e-mails I ever get that have digital signatures have been part of some scam to try to convince me to share various account numbers. The bottom line? If you receive something important and the validity of the signature is an issue, call the sender to verify the contents. ■

How to Digitally Sign a Word Document

To digitally sign a Word document, choose File ⇨ Info ⇨ Protect Document ⇨ Add a Digital Signature. If this is the first time you've used this feature or if you didn't previously choose Don't Show This Message Again, Word displays the dialog box shown in Figure 11-6. If you already have a digital signing certificate, click Yes. Otherwise, you can dismiss the dialog box (if you've changed your mind) or click Signature Services from the Office Marketplace.

FIGURE 11-6

If you don't already have a digital signing certificate, click Signature Services from the Office Marketplace to learn about for-fee and for-free services.

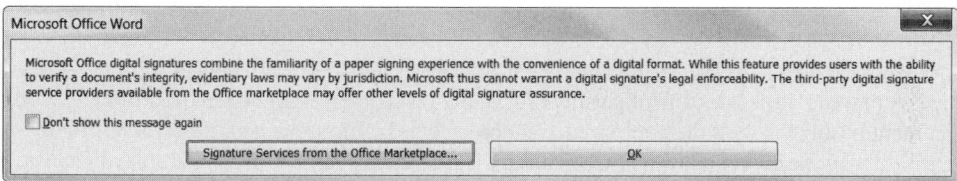

If you choose the Signature Services option, Word takes you to a Digital Signing site on the Microsoft Office website. There, you can use a commercial service to buy a digital certificate. As this is being written, at least one certificate authority is offering a free digital signature to private individuals (non-business).

If you choose OK and the document has not been saved, you are prompted to save the file as a Word document. Word then displays the Sign dialog box, shown in Figure 11-7. You do not need to provide a purpose for signing the document, but you can if you want. To see exactly what you are signing and what information is provided along with the signature, click the link at the top of the dialog box: See Additional Information about What You Are Signing. If the Signing As identity/certificate isn't the one you want to use, click Change. If everything is as you want it, click Sign, and the Signature Confirmation message appears, as shown in Figure 11-8.

FIGURE 11-7

If you're not sure about the signing identity, click Change to see additional signing certificates as well as information about this one.

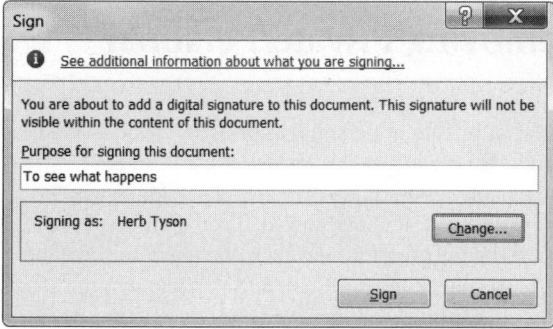

FIGURE 11-8

Don't sign a document until you're finished making changes to it.

Removing a Signature

Once you've signed a document, the document is locked against further changes until the signature is removed. Unlike document permissions, a digital signature can be removed from a Word document by anyone with the appropriate version of Word. Once removed, however, it can be signed only by the owner of a signing certificate. Hence, if you remove my signature, you can edit the file I sent you and make any changes you want to. However, you will not be able to restore my signature.

Caution

Let's be honest here. You can use a free service to obtain a certificate with my name on it and affix that signature to a document and claim that I signed it. However, if it comes from the same CA (Certificate Authority) I used, it can't be associated with my e-mail address, which proves it's not really my signature; and if it doesn't come from the same CA, I can use that as proof that it's not really my signature. Presumably, there are ways to determine whether a signature is valid, but there are ways to make a forged signature look valid, and not everyone is sufficiently skeptical. Forewarned is forearmed. ■

To remove a signature from a document, choose File ➪ Info ➪ View Signatures (unless the Signatures pane is already showing). Right-click the signature and choose Remove Signature. In the Remove Signature prompt dialog box, click Yes.

Don't let the words "permanently" and "cannot be undone" throw you. This simply means that you can't remove someone's signature, change that $1,000 fee to $100,000, and then reaffix their signature. Once you remove someone's signature, only they can put it back.

Document Inspector (Removing Private/Personal Information)

You can use the Document Inspector to see what private or personal information resides in a file and remove it. The Document Inspector checks for the kinds of information and content shown in Figure 11-9. To display the Document Inspector, choose File ➪ Info ➪ Check for Issues ➪ Inspect Document. By default, all six areas are checked. Remove checks if you don't want those kinds of information removed. For example, if the purpose for sending a document to someone is to convey the XML data it contains, remove the check next to Custom XML Data. On the other hand, if the document might contain colorful comments about someone's draft, you probably do want to inspect it for those. When the right checks are checked and the wrong checks are unchecked, click Inspect.

Use the Document Inspector to remove private/proprietary information before passing a document along to someone else.

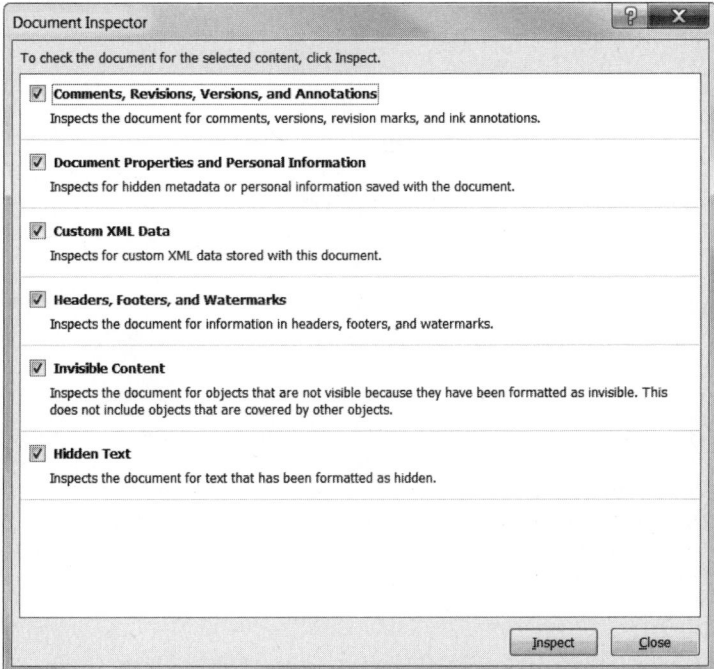

The Document Inspector inspects the current document for each of the types of material or data indicated. If it finds any, the Document Inspector dialog box is redisplayed, with Remove All buttons next to each type of content that was found, as shown in Figure 11-10.

Caution

Make a backup copy of the document before using Remove All. Once you remove the content using the Document Inspector, you can't get it back using Undo. Particularly for comments and data, if they are content you need to preserve, make a backup copy of the document. ■

There is no facility in the Document Inspector for further inspecting to see exactly what it found. You have two options: Click Remove All to do exactly that, or click Close and conduct a closer personal inspection. You can remove the content yourself manually or you can return to the Document Inspector and use Remove All once you're satisfied that you really want it removed.

FIGURE 11-10

A red exclamation mark means that the Document Inspector found potentially sensitive content, and the check mark indicates that the specified type of content was not found.

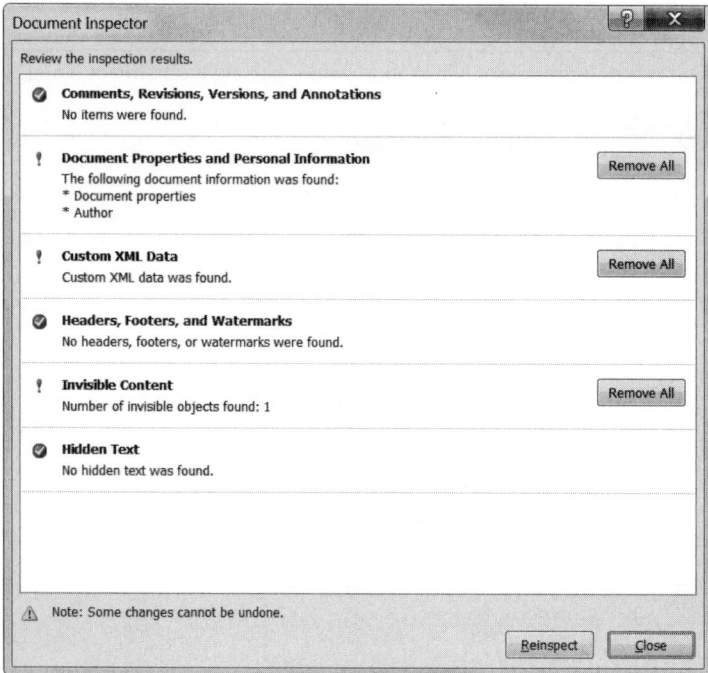

What Is Invisible Content?

A new feature in Word 2010 — one that both Excel and PowerPoint 2007 had — is the ability to format graphical objects as invisible, as long as they do not have wrapping set to In Line with Text. To see how this works, open any .docx document that contains floating graphics. In the Editing group of the Home tab on the Ribbon, choose Select ➪ Selection Pane.

Each *qualified* object will have an eye icon (or, an *eye-con*) next to it. Clicking the icon makes the associated object invisible. You can use this to hide shapes, text boxes, SmartArt, and charts. You cannot unbundle parts of a chart or SmartArt object — it's all or nothing.

When you click Remove All in the Document Inspector, it actually does remove the hidden objects. It doesn't just make them visible. So, exercise caution if you really do need those objects — it's a good idea to create a for-distribution copy of the document.

Formatting and Editing Restrictions

Rights management represents one general area of document protection, and it is certainly more formidable and secure than most of what you can do using formatting and editing restrictions.

However, if you choose not to install and use rights management software, the Restrict Formatting and Editing settings can provide a measure of protection.

Limit Formatting to a Selection of Styles

To limit formatting to certain styles, in the Review or Developer tabs of the Ribbon, choose Restrict Editing in the Protect Group of the Review tab on the Ribbon, which displays the Restrict Formatting and Editing pane shown in Figure 11-11, and then click to place a check next to Limit Formatting to a Selection of Styles. To choose which styles, click Settings. The Formatting Restrictions dialog box now appears, also shown in Figure 11-11.

FIGURE 11-11

With Limit Formatting to a Selection of Styles checked, click Settings to choose those limits.

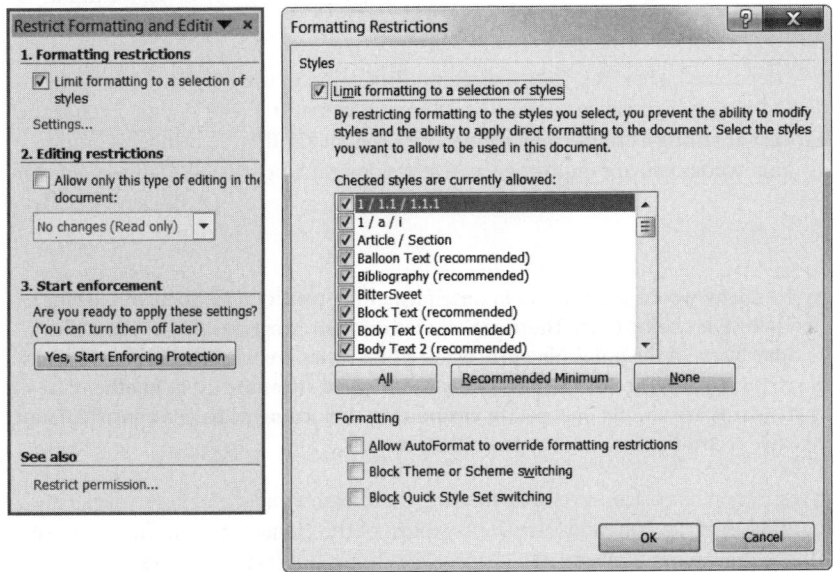

The Formatting Restrictions dialog box provides the following options:

- **Checked Styles.** Place a check next to each style you want to allow. Remove checks for styles you want to disallow. Note that the styles listed might be limited based on settings in the Manage Styles dialog box, discussed in Chapter 7. See Chapter 7 if you need to liberate additional styles from captivity before they will display here. Note that Normal is not included in the list. As much as you might like to, you can't deny access to the Normal style.

- **Recommended Minimum.** If the list is too inclusive, click Recommended Minimum, and then add or remove checks as needed.

- **None.** If the style list is way too inclusive, then choose None, and place a check next to just those you want to allow.

- **All.** If the style list is way too restrictive, then click All and remove the check next to those you want to disallow.

- **Allow AutoFormat to Override Formatting Restrictions.** If AutoFormat's rules and practices are sufficiently rigorous for your purposes, click to allow this option.

- **Block Theme or Scheme Switching.** Choose this option to limit formatting to the currently applied theme or scheme.

- **Block Quick Style Set Switching.** Choose this option to use style definitions from the current document and template only.

When you're ready to proceed, click OK in the Formatting Restrictions dialog box. Word next displays a message box informing you that the document may include styles that are not allowed. Click Yes if you want disallowed styles or formatting removed. Note that if any styles are removed, text will be reformatted using Normal (even if the default paragraph style, set in File ➪ Options ➪ Advanced ➪ Editing Options, is set to something else).

When you're ready to proceed, click Yes, Start Enforcing Protection in the Restrict Formatting and Editing pane. Optionally, you can password-protect your formatting restrictions. Even if the level of protection isn't as strong as rights management, it's still better than nothing, assuming the hapless users upon whom you are imposing the restrictions can't be trusted. (Sniff.) Click OK when you're done.

Note

Other than being an ornery cuss, why would you want to impose formatting restrictions? Some publishing processes depend on only certain styles being used. There are macros or other programs that process files so that they can be fed into other parts of the publishing process. If other styles are used, the process breaks down and requires manual intervention. Hence, it's better if only the allowed styles are used. In other cases, enterprise-wide formatting standards are strictly imposed to ensure that all documents have a consistent and professional look. Enforcing style restrictions is one way to do that. ■

With formatting restrictions in place, several formatting tools, commands, and keystrokes are grayed out as unavailable in the Font and Paragraph groups of the Home tab. The Change Case "formatting" tool isn't grayed out, however. That's because case is not formatting; it's simply a choice of which characters to use.

No Changes (Read-Only)

You can protect all or part of a document against changes. You can make different exceptions for different users. Suppose, for example, that you have a document that has been written by a group of people. You want each individual to be able to edit his or her own section, but not that of others. At the same time, you don't want to have to manage different documents.

The solution is to create a document with a specific area for each individual. You make the entire document read-only, but you make an exception for each individual's section so that the individual responsible can make changes as needed.

To set a document as read-only, click Restrict Editing in the Protect Group of the Review tab on the Ribbon to display the Restrict Formatting and Editing pane. In the Editing restrictions section, click the check box to Allow Only This Type of Editing in the Document, and use the drop-down arrow to set it to No Changes (Read Only).

To make an exception, select the part of the document to which you want to allow changes by someone (or everyone). This selection can be any part of the document — a single letter, word, sentence, line, paragraph, and so on. If you want the exception to apply to everyone, click the check box next to Everyone. Or, if other groups are listed, you can place a check next to any of them.

To make an exception for individuals, if they are listed, click to place a check by their names. If the individuals aren't listed (or if no individuals are listed at all), click More Users. In Add Users, type the user IDs or e-mail addresses for the individuals you want to exempt from the read-only proscription, as shown in Figure 11-12. When you click OK, Word attempts to verify the names/addresses you added. If they are verified, they are added to the list of individuals.

FIGURE 11-12

You can combine network and Internet e-mail addresses.

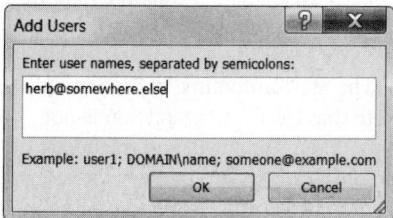

Back in the Restrict Formatting and Editing pane, you need to place a check by the name(s) and e-mail address(es) you added, and then click Yes, Start Enforcing Protection. Add and confirm a password if desired, as shown in Figure 11-13, noting that the document is not encrypted and is susceptible to hacking by malicious users. If you enabled User Authentication, the top part of the dialog box becomes unavailable, and Word will use Information Rights Management to control the permissions. The document is encrypted, and users are authenticated using Windows Live.

Comments

This protection option is identical to the No Changes (Read Only) type of protection except that all users can insert comments wherever they want to. Refer to the preceding discussion, adding to it that comments are enabled everywhere.

FIGURE 11-13

Choose the degree of protection desired.

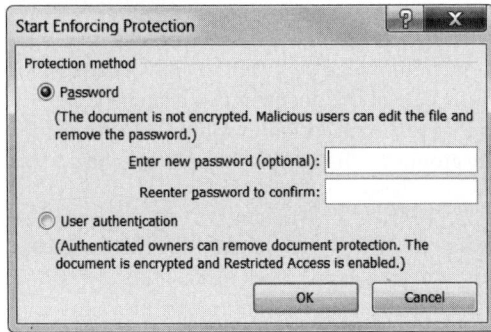

Tracked Changes

Another option is to allow editing, but only tracked changes. That way, you can see who changed what, and when. This is an important feature in controlling the editing/revision process. To protect a document for tracked changes, click Restrict Editing in the Protect group of the Review tab on the Ribbon. In the Restrict Formatting and Editing pane, click to enable Editing Restrictions, and set the drop-down type to Tracked Change.

To turn protection on, click Yes, Start Enforcing Protection. The Start Enforcing Protection dialog box appears, where you can set and confirm a password. Note that User Authentication is not available for this kind of protection. When you click OK, protection is enabled, and the document switches into Track Changes mode. To turn protection off — which is necessary for accepting/rejecting tracked changes — click Stop Protection. If the Restrict Formatting and Editing pane has long since disappeared and the time comes to turn protection off, you can toggle it back on using the Protect Document tool in the Review tab.

Filling in Forms

To protect a fill-in form that you've created in Word, click Restrict Editing in the Protect group of the Review tab of the Ribbon. In the Restrict Formatting and Editing pane, click to enable Allow Only This Type of Editing in the Document, open the drop-down list, and click Filling in Forms. Click Yes, Start Enforcing Protection.

Password to Open/Modify

A final kind of protection is well hidden in Word 2010. It was a bit less hidden in Word 2003 and earlier, although still not overly conspicuous. This legacy feature offers the same weak protection already noted, in that passwords aren't impossibly difficult to hack and crack. The bottom line:

Use this kind of protection at your own risk. It is essentially worthless and offers minimal, if any, protection. Worse, it offers the illusion of protection, and thinking a document is well protected when it's not is perhaps worse than no protection at all, because you are unlikely to be as careful with the document as you would be if you knew it were completely unprotected.

Applying Passwords to Open and/or Modify a Word Document

You can set two different passwords — one that enables a user to open the document, and another that enables the user to make changes. To enable this kind of password protection, choose File ➪ Save As. In the lower-right corner of the Save As dialog box, choose Tools ➪ General Options, to display the General Options dialog box shown in Figure 11-14. Type a password in Password to Open, and/or in Password to Modify. Both are optional.

FIGURE 11-14

File encryption options are not available when applying Open and Modify passwords to a Word document.

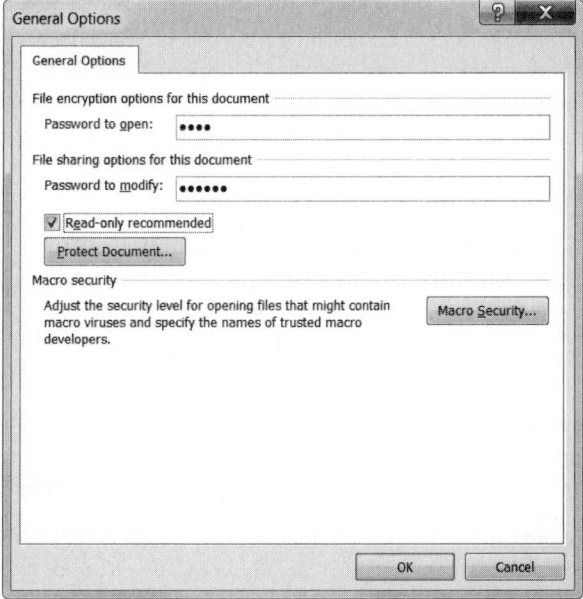

The Read-Only Recommended option applies only if there is no password for modifying the document. If this option is enabled, the user is provided a read-only recommendation when the file is opened, and an easy way to select read-only.

When you click OK, you are prompted to confirm any passwords and are returned to the Save As dialog box. Click Save to save the document with the password settings.

Note

If you click the Protect Document button and the Restrict Formatting and Editing pane is not already show-ing, it is displayed behind the Save As dialog box, and the General Options dialog box goes away. If the Restrict Formatting and Editing pane is not already showing, clicking the Protect Document button simply causes the General Options dialog box to close, leaving users scratching their heads. ■

When you try to open the file, you are prompted for the relevant passwords. If you know the password to open but not the password to modify, you can click Read Only to open the docu-ment in "read-only" mode. Why the quotes? Because it's only the file itself that is read-only. The document can be edited, unlike when using other kinds of protection discussed earlier. If you save the file under a new name, the new file will inherit the password settings, but if you copy the file to the Clipboard and then paste it and save it under a new name, the protection is history.

Comments and Tracked Changes

Comments and tracked changes are two ways Word provides for reviewing others' Word docu-ments. *Comments* themselves are pretty easy to explain. They are notes, questions, suggestions, and other kibitzing that a reader engages in when reading a Word document. Comments are not integrated into the text as edits. They might suggest edits, and it's not unusual to copy the text of a suggestion from inside a comment and paste it into the text, but comments themselves aren't part of the flow.

Tracked changes, however, are part of the flow. *Tracked changes* are insertions and deletions made to a Word document. You can see what was inserted or deleted, by whom, and when. That way, if you have multiple edits, you can see which edit was made first. This can help in deciding how to integrate competing edits, as can "by whom" — especially if one "whom" is higher up the food chain than the other.

With comments and tracked changes, as with many Word features, there is the proverbial chicken-and-egg problem. Do you need to learn how to insert tracked changes and comments first, or how to view them first? If starting with viewing seems odd, a little explanation is in order.

If you're already familiar with comments and tracked changes, it doesn't really matter. You'll be reading these sections for nuance — looking for things you didn't already know. If you aren't familiar with tracking and comments, however, chances are good that your first exposure will come not from wanting to know how to insert them, but from encountering them and wondering how to deal with them. Is this the chicken or the egg? That depends on which comes first....

Comments

Comments are much like footnotes. In fact, it's not at all unusual to convert comments into footnotes or endnotes. The point is that they are references in the text, but aren't part of the text themselves. Instead, they are like meta text. They comment about the text itself. It would inter-rupt the flow if comments displayed inline with the text.

Viewing Comments

There are multiple ways to display comments and tracked changes: inline, in a Reviewing pane, and as balloons. Comments themselves aren't actually displayed inline, although indicators that a comment is present are. When comments are displayed inline, they are indicated by initials and brackets in the text, as shown in Figure 11-15. When they are displayed in balloons, only the brackets show inline with the text.

FIGURE 11-15

The text of a comment is not displayed inline with text in the document.

> You can easily change the formatting of selected text in the document text by choosing a look for the selected text from the Quick Styles[H1] gallery on the Home tab. You can also format text directly by using the other controls on the Home tab. Most controls offer a choice of using the look from the current theme or using a format that you specify directly.

Comment text itself displays in one of three ways:

- **ScreenTip.** Shown in Figure 11-16. Comments display as ScreenTips regardless of whether display is set to inline or balloon. Hover the mouse over the bracketed area to display the ScreenTip.
- **Reviewing Pane.** Shown in Figure 11-17. Editing of Comments takes place in the Reviewing pane when display is set to inline.
- **Balloon.** Shown in Figure 11-18. Editing of comments takes place in the margin when display is set to balloon.

FIGURE 11-16

Hover the mouse over a comment (inside the brackets) to display the text of the comment as a ScreenTip.

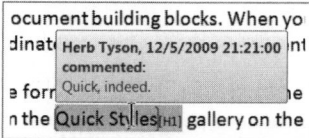

FIGURE 11-17

When the reviewer's initials are inline, right-click them and choose Edit Comment to display the Reviewing pane.

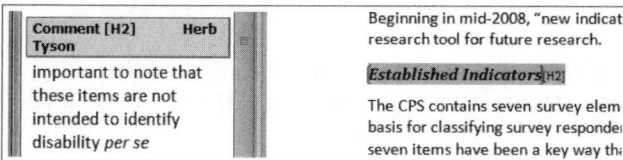

FIGURE 11-18

Balloons are displayed and edited in the margin.

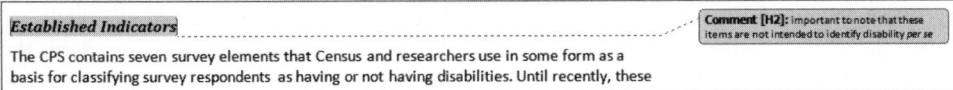

To set comments to display as balloons, in the Tracking group of the Review tab on the Ribbon, choose Show Markup ➪ Balloons ➪ Show Revisions in Balloons, as shown in Figure 11-19. Alternatively, choose Show Only Comments and Formatting in Balloons. To set comments to display inline (which isn't really correct, because comments themselves do not display inline), choose Show All Revisions Inline.

FIGURE 11-19

Two of the three Balloons options put comments in balloons.

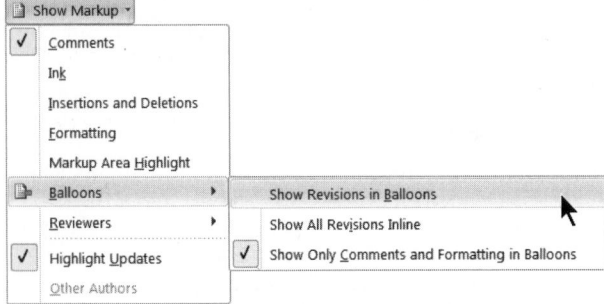

Inserting, Editing, and Deleting Comments

To insert a new comment, click New Comment in the Comments group of the Review tab on the Ribbon. If display is set to inline, type the comment in the Reviewing pane. If display is set to balloons, you'll type your comment inside a balloon in the margin of your document. When you're done, you can click in the text to return to normal editing. If you entered the text in the Reviewing pane, you can also click the X or press Alt+Shift+C to close the Reviewing pane.

To edit a comment, right-click the comment (brackets or initials) and choose Edit Comment. As mentioned, where editing takes place depends on whether display is set to inline or balloons.

To delete a comment, right-click the comment in the text (brackets or initials), and choose Delete Comment. Or, if your wrist needs more exercise, click the comment until Delete becomes available in the Comments group of the Review tab, and then click Delete.

Tracked Changes

Unlike comments, tracked changes can be displayed inline. You also have a variety of options regarding which aspects of tracked changes to display.

Track Changes Options

To see the main set of tracking options, choose Track Changes ➪ Change Tracking Options in the Tracking group of the Review tab on the Ribbon. This displays the considerable Track Changes Options dialog box shown in Figure 11-20. Options are in five groups:

- **Markup.** These control the formatting and colors to use when displaying insertions, deletions, and comments, as well as how to display lines indicating where changes have been made. The default formatting is to use underlining for insertions and strikethrough for deletions. If Color is set to By Author, Word automatically chooses different colors for different authors. Note, however, that while your comments might display as green on your computer, they might display as magenta on somebody else's. Therefore, if you're describing a change in a phone conversation, don't assume the other party is seeing exactly what you're seeing.

- **Moves.** These control the formatting and colors to use when displaying text that was moved from one location to another in the document. If you don't want to track moves, remove the check next to Track Moves.

- **Table Cell Highlighting.** These options control the display of table edits — inserted, deleted, merged, and split cells.

- **Formatting.** These control how formatting changes are represented. If you don't want to track formatting changes, remove the check next to Track Formatting. Note that this doesn't affect the display of tracked formatting. It controls whether formatting is tracked at all. When you turn this off, existing tracked formatting changes remain in the document, but subsequent formatting changes are not tracked at all. To hide tracked formatting changes, choose Show Markup and remove the check next to Formatting.

- **Balloons.** The balloon settings here correspond to the Balloons settings in the Review tab on the Ribbon. When set to Never, all of the additional settings in the Balloons section of the Track Changes Options dialog box are grayed as unavailable. When set to Always or Only for comments/formatting, you can set the width of balloons, which margin they appear in, and whether there are lines connecting tracked change balloons with the location of the changes in the text. Use the Paper orientation setting to rotate pages as needed (to Landscape) if you want to fit the full text width in addition to showing tracked changes in balloons.

Turn on Tracked Changes

To enable tracked changes, click the Track Changes button in the Tracking group of the Review tab. Notice that the upper and lower portions of that button are separate. Use the upper portion to toggle tracked changes, and use the lower portion to choose Track Changes, Change Tracking Options, or Change User Name.

FIGURE 11-20

Use Track Changes Options to change how/if changes are tracked and displayed.

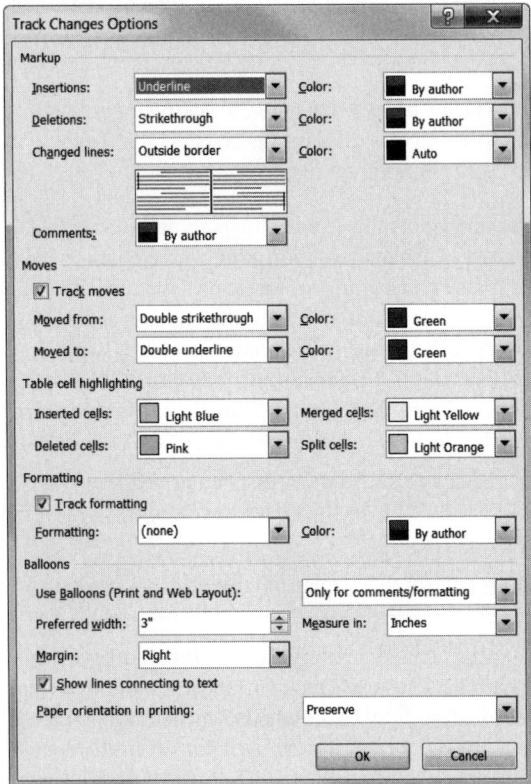

Alternatively, if Track Changes is displayed in the status bar, you can click it to toggle tracking on and off. If Track Changes is not displayed, right-click the Status bar and click to place a check next to Track Changes. Once there, click Track Changes to turn tracking on or off. Track Changes can also be toggled using Ctrl+Shift+E.

Show Markup

If your comments don't display, it's possible that they are turned off. In the Review tab, click the drop-down arrow next to Show Markup in the Tracking group to display the options shown in Figure 11-21.

FIGURE 11-21

Click Show Markup in the Tracking group of the Review tab to control the kinds of markup that Word displays.

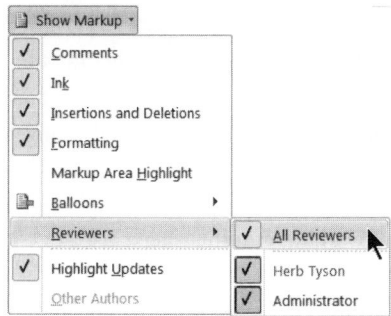

Show Markup options affect only the display of markup. They do not affect whether changes are tracked. The display options are as follows:

- **Comments.** Choose to display or not display comments.

- **Ink.** When using a table or other system that supports pen annotations, use this option to choose whether to display the original ink markup (in addition to the text conversion thereof).

- **Insertions and Deletions.** Use this setting to control the display of textual edits (insertions and deletions). Some users prefer to deal separately with textual and formatting edits. With this option enabled and Formatting display turned off, you can selectively focus.

- **Formatting.** Use this setting to hide or show formatting changes.

- **Markup Area Highlight.** Use this setting to turn shading of the markup area (i.e., where balloons display) on or off.

- **Balloons.** Use to control the use of "balloons" for revisions and comments.

- **Reviewers.** Use this setting to selectively show or hide specific reviewers' edits and comments.

- **Highlight Updates.** When co-authoring a document on a SharePoint server, this option highlights updates by the other author(s).

- **Other Authors.** When co-authoring, this option lists other authors currently working on the same document.

Display for Review

Use the Display for Review drop-down list in the Tracking group of the Review tab to determine exactly what displays when a document contains tracked changes. The Display for Review drop-down list offers four choices (shown in Figure 11-22):

- **Final: Show Markup.** Inserts are shown in context with deletions shown either in balloons or in the Reviewing pane.

- **Final.** All markup is hidden, and you see the document as it would appear if all changes were accepted.

- **Original: Show Markup.** Inserts are shown in balloons or in the Reviewing pane, and deletions are shown in context with strikethrough (or whatever formatting is used to indicate deletion).

- **Original.** All markup is hidden, and you see the document as it appeared before any markup occurred. This is how the document would appear if all changes were rejected.

FIGURE 11-22

Word can display the document from four different points of view.

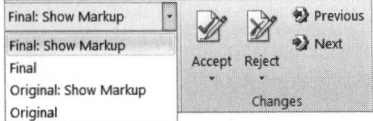

Tip

It's often hard to gauge the effects of changes. It can be helpful to switch between Final and Original so you can properly assess the full impact of changes, especially when comparing paragraphs that have undergone substantial editing. ■

Reviewing Pane

The Reviewing pane is potentially much more substantial than what's shown in Figure 11-17. The Reviewing pane can be displayed vertically, as shown there, or horizontally as shown in Figure 11-23. In the latter, you see a cross-section of the different elements contained in the Reviewing pane.

To toggle the Reviewing pane, click Reviewing Pane in the Tracking group of the Review tab on the Ribbon. To choose between vertical and horizontal display, click the drop-down arrow next to Reviewing Pane, and choose Reviewing Pane Vertical or Horizontal.

The Reviewing pane is independent of balloons. If you prefer to edit some comments in the balloons and others in the Reviewing pane, the choice is yours. However, choosing one or the other will give you more screen real estate to work with.

FIGURE 11-23

The Reviewing pane shows comments and tracked changes, as well as changes in headers, footers, text boxes, footnotes, and endnotes.

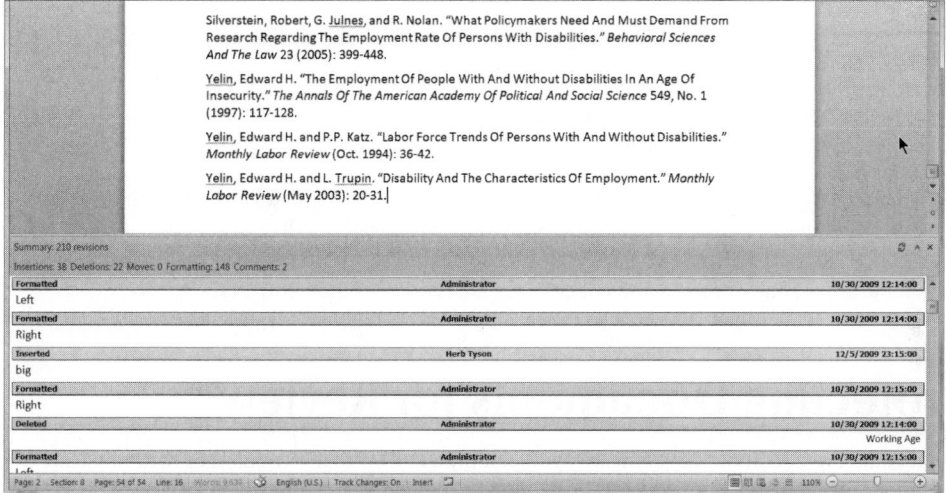

Reviewing Comments and Changes

Use the Changes group in the Review tab of the Ribbon, shown in Figure 11-24, to review changes to determine whether you want to accept or reject them. Use Next or Previous to navigate to the nearest comment or change. Use Accept and Reject to integrate or remove changes. You can also right-click a change and choose Accept or Reject.

FIGURE 11-24

Accept All Changes Shown is available only when some changes are hidden.

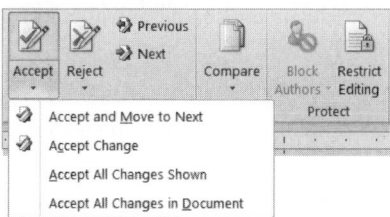

Accepting and Rejecting Comments

You cannot accept or reject a comment per se. Accepting a comment leaves it alone. Rejecting a comment deletes it.

Accepting and Rejecting Changes

When you accept a change, it is converted from a tracked change into regular text. When you accept a deletion, it is removed entirely from the document.

When you reject an insertion, it is deleted. When you reject a deletion, the original text is restored.

When you accept formatting changes, they are applied to the final version of the text. When you reject formatting changes, the formatting is removed.

Note that the Accept and Reject buttons in the Changes group of the Review tab both have upper and lower sections. The lower section of the Accept button features the options shown in Figure 11-24. Reject has similar options. Note that the third option, Accept All Changes Shown, is available only if one or more kinds of changes are hidden in the Show Markup tool.

Protecting Documents for Review

When you send a document to someone, you can protect it so that any changes they make are marked as changes. You can protect it for Tracked Changes or for Comments, but not both at the same time. See the "Comments" and "Tracked Changes" sections earlier in this chapter in the material on document protection.

Summary

In this chapter, you've learned about the many different and potentially confusing kinds of document protection and security available in Word. You should now have a good idea about which forms of protection and security are useful, and which ones give only a false sense of security. You've also learned about tracking changes and commenting on Word documents. You should now be able to do the following:

- Enable Track Changes in a document, and protect that document so that only that kind of editing can be performed.
- Use Information Rights Management to set strong protection for Word documents.
- Use Word's legacy password protection, while understanding that it's feeble protection at best.
- Set options that let you display a variety of different elements when tracking changes in a document.

Part III

Making the Numbers Work with Excel

Using Excel Worksheets and Workbooks

This chapter serves as an introductory overview of Excel 2010. If you're already familiar with a previous version of Excel, reading this chapter is still a good idea. You'll find that Excel 2010 is very similar to Excel 2007. However, both Excel 2007 and Excel 2010 are different from every previous version — very different.

What Is Excel Good For?

Excel, as you probably know, is the world's most widely used spreadsheet program and is part of the Microsoft Office suite. Other spreadsheet programs are available, but Excel is by far the most popular and has become the world standard.

Much of the appeal of Excel is due to the fact that it's so versatile. Excel's forte, of course, is performing numerical calculations, but Excel is also very useful for non-numeric applications. Here are just a few of the uses for Excel:

- **Number Crunching.** Create budgets, analyze survey results, and perform just about any type of financial analysis you can think of.

- **Creating Charts.** Create a wide variety of highly customizable charts.

- **Organizing Lists.** Use the row-and-column layout to store lists efficiently.

- **Accessing Other Data.** Import data from a wide variety of sources.

- **Creating Graphical Dashboards.** Summarize a large amount of business information in a concise format.

- **Creating Graphics and Diagrams.** Use Shapes and SmartArt to create professional-looking diagrams.

- **Automating Complex Tasks.** Perform a tedious task with a single mouse click with Excel's macro capabilities.

What's New in Excel 2010?

When a new version of Microsoft Office is released, sometimes Excel gets lots of new features. And sometimes it gets very few new features. In the case of Office 2010, there weren't very many radical changes; however, Excel did get a makeover. Here's a quick summary of what's new in Excel 2010 compared to its predecessor, Excel 2007:

- **64-bit Version.** If your hardware (and Windows version) supports it, you can install the 64-bit version, which enables you to take full advantage of the speed of a 64-bit computer and operating system, if your computer has both.

Note
Most people do not require the 64-bit version, and using it might cause some add-ins to not function; however, the functionality has been added to support this architecture, which is creating more of a stronghold in today's marketplace. ■

- **Sparkline Charts.** Create small in-cell charts to summarize a range of data graphically. See Chapter 19.

- **Slicers.** This is a new feature in Excel that allows you to filter and display data in pivot tables, by clicking buttons

- **New Pivot Table Formatting Options.** You have more control over the appearance of pivot table reports.

- **Draft Mode for Charts.** If you use many heavily formatted charts, you can choose to display them in draft mode for improved performance.

- **Conditional Formatting Enhancements.** Data bar conditional formatting can display in a solid color, and the bars provide a more accurate display. See Chapter 19.

- **Function Enhancements.** Some Excel worksheet financial and statistical functions have been improved in terms of numerical accuracy.

- **Image Editing Enhancements.** You have much more control over graphic images inserted into a workbook, including the ability to remove nonessential parts from the background of an image.

- **Screen Capture Tool.** You can easily capture a window from a different program and then insert the image on a worksheet with a single click.

- **Paste Preview.** When you copy a range of cells, the Paste command displays various options with a live preview so you can see how the paste operation will look.

- **Equation Editor.** Creates and displays (non-calculating) mathematical equations and embeds them on a worksheet.

- **Faster.** Microsoft made some improvements to the calculation engine, and files load a bit faster.

- **New Security Features.** Workbooks downloaded from the Internet or from e-mail attachments are opened in Protected View mode. Workbooks can be designated as *trusted* and don't need to reside in special trusted folders.

- **Solver.** Excel 2010 includes a new version of the Solver add-in, which is useful for solving some complex problems.

- **Enhancements to VBA.** Operations that used to require old XLM macros can now be performed directly using VBA macro commands. In addition, macro recording now works for operations such as chart shape formatting.

Note

This book includes coverage of some of the new features, but not all. For a comprehensive look at what Excel now offers, look for the *Excel 2010 Bible* by John Walkenbach (2010, Wiley, New York). ∎

Understanding Workbooks and Worksheets

The work you do in Excel is performed in a *workbook* file, which appears in its own window. You can have as many workbooks open as you need. By default, Excel 2010 workbooks use an .xlsx file extension.

Each workbook comprises one or more *worksheets*, and each worksheet is made up of individual *cells*. Each cell contains a value, a formula, or text. A worksheet also has an invisible draw layer, which holds charts, images, or diagrams. Each worksheet in a workbook is accessible by clicking the tab at the bottom of the workbook window. In addition, workbooks can store chart sheets. A chart sheet displays a single chart and is also accessible by clicking a tab.

Newcomers to Excel are often intimidated by all the different elements that appear within Excel's window. After you become familiar with the various parts, it all starts to make sense.

Figure 12-1 shows the default layout of Excel when opening a new workbook. As you look at the figure, refer to Table 12-1 for a brief explanation of the items shown in the figure.

Part III: Making the Numbers Work with Excel

FIGURE 12-1

The Excel screen has many useful elements that you will use often.

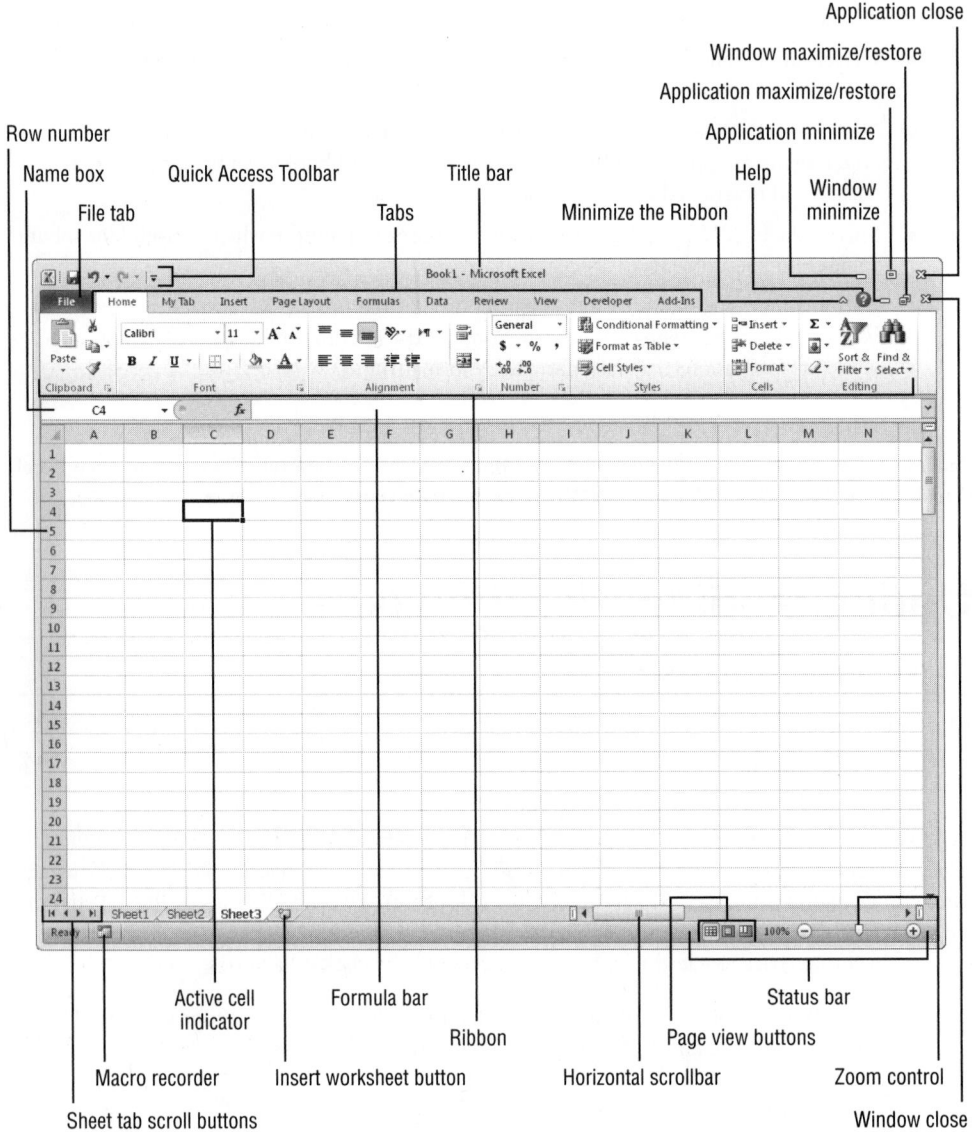

TABLE 12-1

Parts of the Excel Screen That You Need to Know

Name	Description
Active cell indicator	The dark outline seen in cell A1 indicates the currently active cell (one of the 17,179,869,184 cells on each worksheet).
Application Close button	The X button in the upper-right corner. Clicking this button closes Excel.
Application Minimize button	Clicking this button to the left of the Close button minimizes the Excel window.
Column letters	Letters across the top of the worksheet ranging from A to XFD — one for each of the 16,384 columns in the worksheet. You can click a column heading to select an entire column of cells or drag a column border to change its width.
File tab	Click this button to open Backstage view, which contains many options for working with your document such as printing and setting Excel options.
Formula bar	When you enter information or formulas into a cell, it appears in this line.
Help button	Clicking this button displays the Excel Help system window.
Horizontal scrollbar	Use this tool to scroll the sheet horizontally.
Macro recorder indicator	Click to start recording a VBA macro. The icon changes while your actions are being recorded. Click again to stop recording.
Minimize Ribbon button	Clicking this small button with the up arrow just to the left of the Help button hides the Ribbon, giving you a bit more space onscreen. When you click a tab, the Ribbon reappears.
Name box	Located to the left of the formula bar, this box displays the active cell address or the name of the selected cell, range, or object.
Page View buttons	Change the way the worksheet is displayed by clicking one of these buttons.
Quick Access Toolbar	This customizable toolbar above the File tab holds commonly used commands. The Quick Access Toolbar is always visible, regardless of which tab is selected.
Ribbon	This is the main location for Excel's commands. Clicking an item in the tab list changes the Ribbon that displays.
Row numbers	Numbers along the left side ranging from 1 to 1,048,576 — one for each row in the worksheet. You can click a row number to select an entire row of cells.

continued

TABLE 12-1 *(continued)*

Name	Description
Sheet tabs	Each of these notebook-like tabs represents a different sheet in the workbook. A workbook can have any number of sheets, and each sheet has its name displayed in a Sheet tab.
Insert Worksheet button	By default, each new workbook that you create contains three sheets. Add a new sheet by clicking the Insert Worksheet button (which is displayed to the right of the last sheet tab).
Sheet tab scroll buttons	Use these buttons to scroll the sheet tabs to display tabs that aren't visible.
Status bar	This bar displays various messages as well as the status of the Num Lock, Caps Lock, and Scroll Lock keys on your keyboard. It also shows summary information about the range of cells that is selected. Right-click the status bar to change the information that's displayed.
Tabs	Click these tabs to display a different Ribbon, similar to a menu.
Title bar	This displays the name of the program and the name of the current workbook, and also holds some control buttons that you can use to modify the window.
Vertical scrollbar	Use this to scroll the sheet vertically.
Window Close button	Clicking this button closes the active workbook window.
Window Maximize/ Restore button	Clicking this button increases the workbook window's size to fill Excel's complete workspace. If the window is already maximized, clicking this button "unmaximizes" Excel's window so that it no longer fills the entire screen.
Window Minimize button	Clicking this button minimizes the workbook window, and it displays as an icon.
Zoom control	Use this slider to zoom your worksheet in and out.

Moving around a Worksheet

This section describes various ways to navigate through the cells in a worksheet. Every worksheet consists of rows (numbered 1 through 1,048,576) and columns (labeled A through XFD). After column Z comes column AA, which is followed by AB, AC, and so on. After column AZ comes BA, BB, and so on. After column ZZ is AAA, AAB, and so on.

The intersection of a row and a column is a single cell. At any given time, one cell is the *active cell*. You can identify the active cell by its darker border, as shown in Figure 12-2. Its *address* (its column letter and row number) appears in the Name box. Depending on the technique that you use to navigate through a workbook, you may or may not change the active cell when you navigate.

Notice that the row and column headings of the active cell appear in different colors to make it easier to identify the row and column of the active cell.

FIGURE 12-2

The active cell is the cell with the dark border—in this case, cell C8.

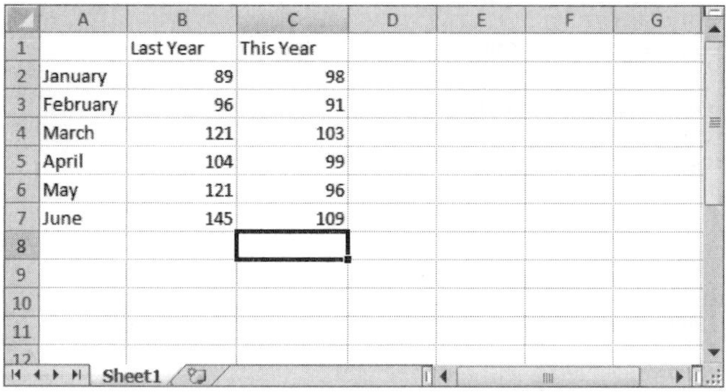

	A	B	C	D	E	F	G
1		Last Year	This Year				
2	January	89	98				
3	February	96	91				
4	March	121	103				
5	April	104	99				
6	May	121	96				
7	June	145	109				
8							
9							
10							
11							
12							

Sheet1

Navigating with Your Keyboard

Not surprisingly, you can use the standard navigational keys on your keyboard to move around a worksheet. These keys work just as you'd expect: The down arrow moves the active cell down one row, the right arrow moves it one column to the right, and so on. Page Up and Page Down move the active cell up or down one full window. (The actual number of rows moved depends on the number of rows displayed in the window.)

Tip

You can use the keyboard to scroll through the worksheet without changing the active cell by turning on Scroll Lock, which is useful if you need to view another area of your worksheet and then quickly return to your original location. Just press the Scroll Lock key and use the navigation keys to scroll through the worksheet. When you want to return to the original position (the active cell), press Ctrl+Backspace. Then, press Scroll Lock again to turn it off. When Scroll Lock is turned on, Excel displays *Scroll Lock* in the status bar at the bottom of the window, just below the worksheet tabs. ■

The Num Lock key on your keyboard controls how the keys on the numeric keypad (should you have one) behave. When Num Lock is on, the keys on your numeric keypad generate numbers. Many keyboards have a separate set of navigation (arrow) keys located to the left of the numeric keypad. The state of the Num Lock key doesn't affect these keys.

Table 12-2 summarizes all the worksheet movement keys available in Excel.

TABLE 12-2

Excel Worksheet Movement Keys

Key	Action
Up arrow (↑)	Moves the active cell up one row.
Down arrow (↓)	Moves the active cell down one row.
Left arrow (←) or Shift+Tab	Moves the active cell one column to the left.
Right arrow (→) or Tab	Moves the active cell one column to the right.
Page Up	Moves the active cell up one screen.
Page Down	Moves the active cell down one screen.
Alt+Page Down	Moves the active cell right one screen.
Alt+Page Up	Moves the active cell left one screen.
Ctrl+Backspace	Scrolls the screen so that the active cell is visible.
↑[a]	Scrolls the screen up one row (active cell does not change).
↓[a]	Scrolls the screen down one row (active cell does not change).
←[a]	Scrolls the screen left one column (active cell does not change).
→[a]	Scrolls the screen right one column (active cell does not change).

[a] With Scroll Lock on.

Navigating with Your Mouse

To change the active cell by using the mouse, click another cell; it becomes the active cell. If the cell that you want to activate isn't visible in the workbook window, you can use the scroll bars to scroll the window in any direction. To scroll one cell, click either of the arrows on the scroll bar. To scroll by a complete screen, click either side of the scroll bar's scroll box. You also can drag the scroll box for faster scrolling.

Tip

If your mouse has a wheel, you can use the mouse wheel to scroll vertically. Also, if you click the wheel and move the mouse in any direction, the worksheet scrolls automatically in that direction. The more you move the mouse, the faster the scrolling. ■

Press Ctrl while you use the mouse wheel to zoom the worksheet. If you prefer to use the mouse wheel to zoom the worksheet without pressing Ctrl, choose File ➪ Options and select the Advanced section. Place a check mark next to the Zoom on Roll with Intellimouse checkbox.

Using the scroll bars or scrolling with your mouse doesn't change the active cell. It simply scrolls the worksheet. To change the active cell, you must click on a new cell after scrolling.

Introducing Excel's Ribbon Tabs

Excel offers the same command and user interface features as the other Office 2010 applications, including the Ribbon, shortcut menus, dialog boxes, and more. Chapter 2 provides more details about how to choose commands and settings. The tabs on the Ribbon vary depending on which application you're using, so this section provides a brief introduction to the tabs offered by Excel.

Ribbon Tabs

The commands available in the Ribbon vary, depending on which tab is selected. Excel's Ribbon is arranged into groups of related commands. Here's a quick overview of Excel's tabs.

- **Home.** You'll probably spend most of your time with the Home tab selected. This tab contains the basic Clipboard commands, formatting commands, style commands, commands to insert and delete rows or columns, plus an assortment of worksheet editing commands.

- **Insert.** Select this tab when you need to insert something in a worksheet — a table, a diagram, a chart, a symbol, and the like.

- **Page Layout.** This tab contains commands that affect the overall appearance of your worksheet, including some settings that deal with printing.

- **Formulas.** Use this tab to insert a formula, name a cell or a range, access the formula auditing tools, or control how Excel performs calculations.

- **Data.** Excel's data-related commands are on this tab.

- **Review.** This tab contains tools to check spelling, translate words, add comments, or protect sheets.

- **View.** The View tab contains commands that control various aspects of how a sheet is viewed. Some commands on this tab are also available in the status bar.

- **Developer.** This tab isn't visible by default. It contains commands that are useful for programmers. To display the Developer tab, choose File ⇨ Options and then select Customize Ribbon. In the Customize the Ribbon section on the right, place a check mark next to Developer and then click OK.

- **Add-Ins.** This tab is visible only if you loaded an older workbook or add-in that customizes the menu or toolbars. Because menus and toolbars are no longer available in Excel 2010, these user interface customizations appear on the Add-Ins tab.

The appearance of the commands on the Ribbon varies, depending on the width of Excel window. When the window is too narrow to display everything, the commands adapt; some of them might seem to be missing, but the commands are still available. Figure 12-3 shows the Home tab of the Ribbon with all controls fully visible. When you make the Excel window narrower, some groups may display a single icon. However, if you click the icon, all the group commands are available to you.

FIGURE 12-3

The Home tab of the Ribbon

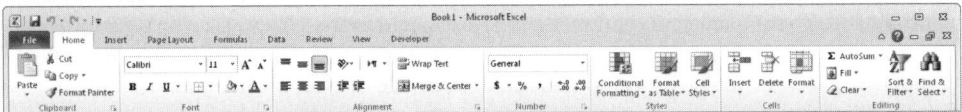

Contextual Tabs

In addition to the standard tabs, Excel 2010 also includes *contextual tabs* like the other Office applications. Whenever an object (such as a chart, a table, or a SmartArt diagram) is selected, specific tools for working with that object are made available in the Ribbon.

Figure 12-4 shows the contextual tab that appears when a chart is selected. In this case, it has three contextual tabs: Design, Layout, and Format. These tabs offer the commands for working with charts in Excel, so you are likely to use them often. Notice that the contextual tabs contain a description (Chart Tools) in Excel's title bar. When contextual tabs appear, you can, of course, continue to use all the other tabs.

FIGURE 12-4

When you select an object, contextual tabs contain tools for working with that object.

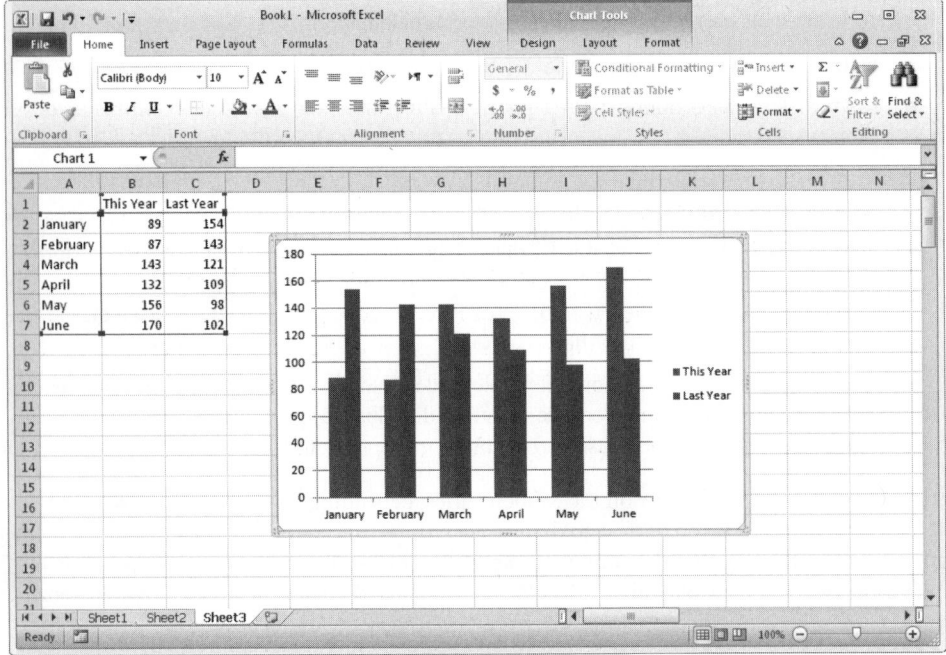

Creating Your First Excel Worksheet

This section presents an introductory hands-on session with Excel. If you haven't used Excel, you may want to follow along on your computer to get a feel for how this software works.

In this example, you create a simple monthly sales projection table along with a chart.

Getting Started on Your Worksheet

Start Excel (Start ⇨ All Programs ⇨ Microsoft Office ⇨ Microsoft Excel 2010) and make sure that you have an empty workbook displayed. To create a new, blank workbook if one is not open, press Ctrl+N (the shortcut key for File ⇨ New ⇨ Blank Workbook ⇨ Create).

This example sales projection workbook will consist of two columns of information. Column A will contain the month names, and column B will store the projected sales numbers. Start by entering some descriptive titles into the worksheet. Here's how to begin:

1. **If needed, move the cell pointer to cell A1 (the upper-left cell in the worksheet) by using the navigation (arrow) keys.** The Name box displays the cell's address.

2. **Type** Month **into cell A1 and press Enter.** Depending on your setup, Excel either moves the cell pointer to a different cell, or the pointer remains in cell A1.

3. **Move the cell pointer to B1.**

4. **Type** Projected Sales, **and again press Enter.**

    The text extends beyond the cell width, but don't worry about that for now.

Filling in the Month Names

In this step, you enter the month names in column A.

1. **Move the cell pointer to A2 and type** Jan **(an abbreviation for January).** At this point, you can enter the other month name abbreviations manually; alternatively, you can let Excel do some of the work by taking advantage of the Auto Fill feature.

2. **Make sure that cell A2 is selected.** Notice that the active cell is displayed with a heavy outline. At the bottom-right corner of the outline, you'll see a small square known as the *fill handle*. Move your mouse pointer over the fill handle, click, and drag down until you've highlighted from A2 down to A13.

3. **Release the mouse button, and Excel automatically fills in the month names.**

Your worksheet should resemble the one shown in Figure 12-5.

Entering the Sales Data

Next, you provide the sales projection numbers in column B. Assume that January's sales are projected to be $50,000, and that sales will increase by 3.5 percent in each subsequent month.

FIGURE 12-5

Your worksheet, after entering the column headings and month names

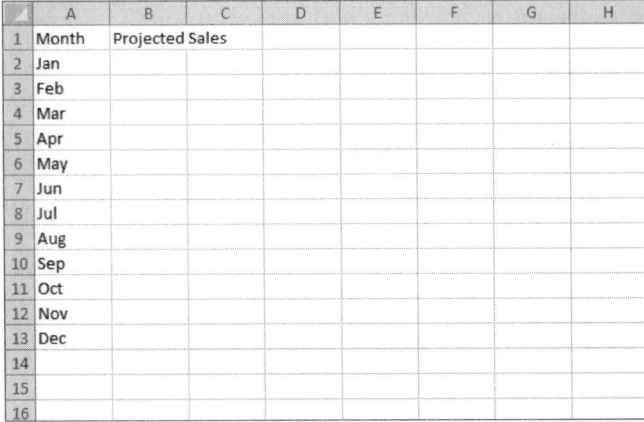

1. **Move the cell pointer to B2 and type** 50000, **the projected sales for January.** You could type a dollar sign and comma to make the number more legible, but you do the number formatting a bit later.

2. **To enter a formula to calculate the projected sales for February, move to cell B3 and enter the following:** =B2*103.5%. When you press Enter, the cell displays **51750**. The formula returns the contents of cell B2, multiplied by 103.5%. In other words, February sales are projected to be 3.5% greater than January sales.

3. **The projected sales for subsequent months use a similar formula.** But rather than retype the formula for each cell in column B, once again take advantage of the Auto Fill feature. Make sure that cell B3 is selected. Click the cell's fill handle, drag down to cell B13, and release the mouse button.

At this point, your worksheet should resemble the one shown in Figure 12-6. Keep in mind that except for cell B2, the values in column B are calculated with *formulas*. To demonstrate, try changing the projected sales value for the initial month, January (in cell B2). You'll find that the formulas recalculate and return different values. These formulas all depend on the initial value in cell B2.

Formatting the Numbers

The values in the worksheet are difficult to read because they aren't formatted. In this step, you apply a number format to make the numbers easier to read and more consistent in appearance:

1. **Select the numbers by dragging from cell B2 down to cell B13.**

Tip

Don't drag the fill handle this time, though, because you're selecting cells, not filling a range. ∎

2. **Choose Home ➪ Number, click the drop-down Number Format control (it initially displays General), and select Currency from the list.** The numbers now display with a currency symbol and two decimal places. Much better!

FIGURE 12-6

Your worksheet, after creating the formulas

	A	B	C	D	E	F
1	Month	Projected Sales				
2	Jan	50000				
3	Feb	51750				
4	Mar	53561.25				
5	Apr	55435.89				
6	May	57376.15				
7	Jun	59384.32				
8	Jul	61462.77				
9	Aug	63613.96				
10	Sep	65840.45				
11	Oct	68144.87				
12	Nov	70529.94				
13	Dec	72998.49				
14						
15						

Making Your Worksheet Look a Bit Fancier

At this point, you have a functional worksheet, but it could use some help in the appearance department. Converting this range to an "official" (and attractive) Excel table is a snap:

1. **Move to any cell within the range you've just entered.**

2. **Choose Insert ➪ Tables ➪ Table.** Excel displays its Create Table dialog box to make sure that it guessed the range properly.

3. **Click OK to close the Create Table dialog box.** Excel applies its default table formatting and also displays its Table Tools Design contextual tab.

4. **Click outside the table so you can see it.** Your worksheet should look like Figure 12-7.

5. **If you don't like the default table style, just select another one from the Table Tools ➪ Design ➪ Table Styles group.** Notice that you can get a preview of different table styles by moving your mouse over the Ribbon. When you find one you like, click it, and style will be applied to your table.

FIGURE 12-7

Your worksheet, after converting the range to a table

	A	B	C	D	E	F
1	Month	Projected Sales				
2	Jan	$50,000.00				
3	Feb	$51,750.00				
4	Mar	$53,561.25				
5	Apr	$55,435.89				
6	May	$57,376.15				
7	Jun	$59,384.32				
8	Jul	$61,462.77				
9	Aug	$63,613.96				
10	Sep	$65,840.45				
11	Oct	$68,144.87				
12	Nov	$70,529.94				
13	Dec	$72,998.49				
14						
15						
16						

Summing the Values

The worksheet displays the monthly projected sales, but what about the total projected sales for the year? Because this range is a table, it's simple:

1. **Choose any cell in the table.**

2. **Choose Table Tools ⇨ Design ⇨ Table Style Options ⇨ Total Row.** Excel automatically adds a new row to the bottom of your table, including a formula that calculated the total of the Projected Sales column.

3. **If you'd prefer to see a different summary formula (for example, average), click cell B14 and choose a different summary formula from the drop-down list.**

Creating a Chart

How about a chart that shows the projected sales for each month?

1. **Activate any cell in the table.**

2. **Choose Insert ⇨ Charts ⇨ Column, and then select one of the 2D (two-dimensional) column chart types.** Excel inserts the chart in the center of your screen.

Tip

To move the chart to another location, move the mouse pointer over its border and drag it. To change the appearance and style of the chart, use the commands on the three Chart Tools contextual tabs. ■

Figure 12-8 shows the worksheet with a column chart. Your chart may look different, depending on the chart layout or style you selected.

FIGURE 12-8

The table and chart

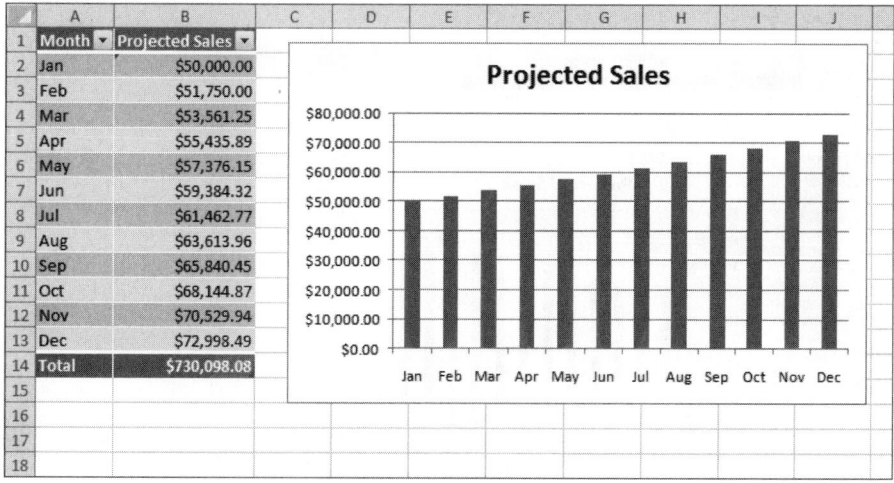

Printing Your Worksheet

Printing your worksheet is very easy (assuming that you have a printer attached and that it works properly):

1. **Make sure that the chart isn't selected.** If a chart is selected, it will print on a page by itself. To deselect the chart, just press Esc or click any cell.

2. **To make use of Excel's page layout view, click the Page Layout View button on the right side of the status bar.** (The Page Layout View button is the middle button in the cluster of three located just to the left of the zoom control in the bottom-right corner of the screen.) Excel then displays the worksheet page by page so that you can easily see how your printed output will look. Figure 12-9 shows the worksheet zoomed out to show a complete page. In Page Layout view, you can tell immediately whether the chart is too wide to fit on one page. If the chart is too wide, drag a corner to resize it. Alternatively, you can move the chart below the table of numbers or modify the page margins.

3. **When you're ready to print, choose File ➪ Print.**

At this point, you can change certain print settings. For example, you can choose to print in landscape rather than portrait orientation. Make the change, and you see the result in the preview area. When you're satisfied, click the Print button in the upper-left corner. The page is printed, and you're returned to your workbook.

FIGURE 12-9

Viewing the worksheet in Page Layout mode

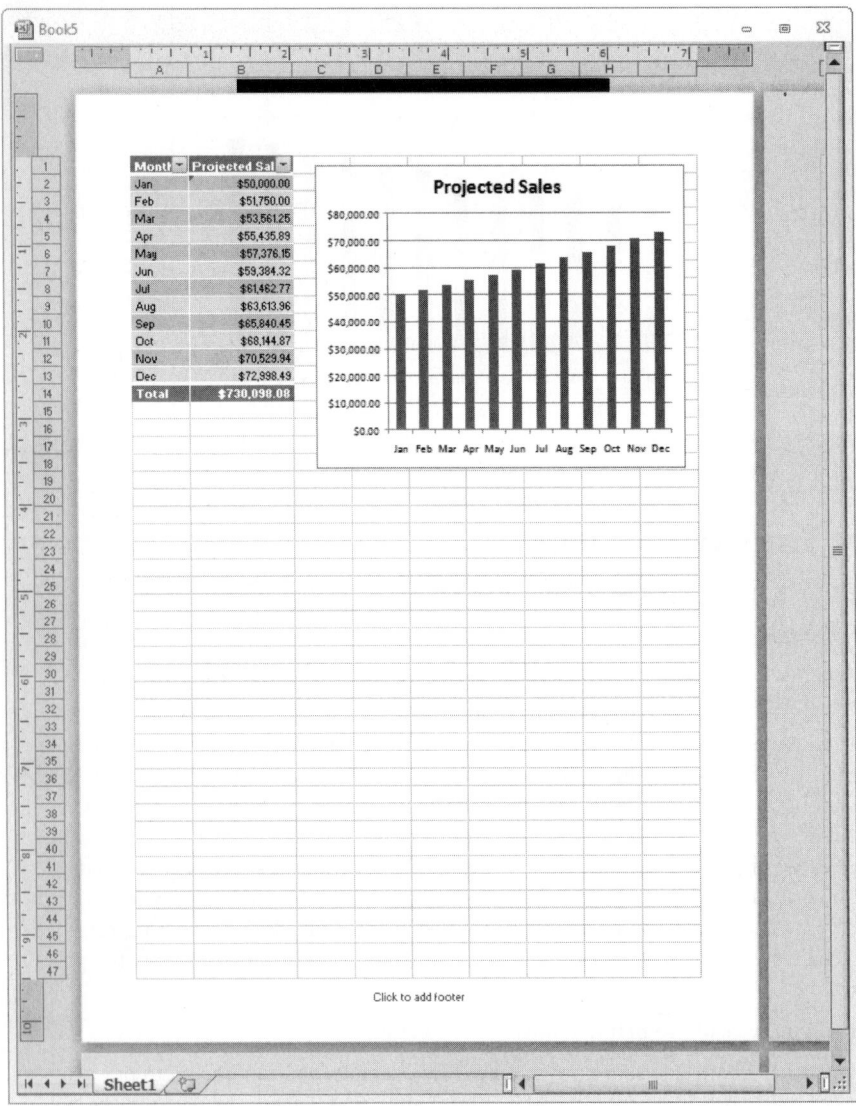

Saving Your Workbook

Until now, everything that you've done has occurred in your computer's memory. If the power should fail, all may be lost — unless Excel's AutoRecover feature happened to kick in. It's time to save your work to a file on your hard drive.

1. **Click the Save button on the Quick Access Toolbar.** (This button looks like an old-fashioned floppy disk, popular in the previous century.) Because the workbook hasn't been saved yet and still has its default name, Excel responds with the Save As dialog box.

2. **In the box labeled File Name, enter a name (such as *Monthly Sales Projection*), and then click Save or press Enter.** Excel saves the workbook as a file. The workbook remains open so that you can work with it some more.

Note

By default, Excel saves a backup copy of your work automatically every 10 minutes. To adjust the AutoRecover setting (or turn it off), choose File ➪ Options, and click the Save choice in the Excel Options dialog box. However, you should never rely on Excel's AutoRecover feature. Saving your work frequently is a good idea. ∎

If you've followed along, you may have realized that creating this workbook was not at all difficult. But, of course, you've barely scratched the surface. The remainder of this book covers these tasks (and many, many more) in much greater detail.

Summary

This chapter touched on the new features of the Excel 2010 spreadsheet program. You learned the difference between a workbook and a worksheet, as well as how to navigate around Excel. You finished up by creating your first spreadsheet, including adding labels and values, building a simple sum formula, treating your information as a table, and even charting and printing. Well done!

Entering and Editing Worksheet Data

This chapter describes what you need to know about entering, using, and modifying data in your Excel worksheets. As you will see, Excel doesn't treat all data equally. Therefore, you need to learn about the various types of data that you can use in an Excel worksheet.

Exploring the Types of Data You Can Use

An Excel workbook can hold any number of worksheets, and each worksheet is made up of more than 17 billion cells. A cell can hold any of three basic types of data:

- A numerical value

- Text

- A formula

A worksheet can also hold charts, diagrams, pictures, buttons, and other objects. These objects aren't contained in cells. Rather, they reside on the worksheet's *draw layer*, which is an invisible layer on top of each worksheet.

About Numeric Values

Numeric values represent a quantity of some type: sales amounts, number of employees, atomic weights, test scores, and so on. Values also can be dates (such as Feb-26-2011) or times (such as 3:24 a.m.).

Cross-Reference

Excel can display values in many different formats. Later in this chapter, you see how different format options can affect the display of numerical values (see "Applying Number Formatting"). ∎

Excel's Numeric Limitations

You may be curious about the types of numeric values that Excel can handle. In other words, how large can numbers be? And how accurate are large numbers?

Excel's numbers are precise up to 15 digits. For example, if you enter a large value, such as **123,456,789,123,456,789** (18 digits), Excel actually stores it with only 15 digits of precision. This 18-digit number displays as *123,456,789,123,456,000*. This precision may seem quite limiting, but in practice, it rarely causes any problems.

One situation in which the 15-digit accuracy can cause a problem is when entering credit card numbers. Most credit card numbers are 16 digits, but Excel can handle only 15 digits, so it substitutes a zero for the last credit card digit. Even worse, you may not even realize that Excel made the card number invalid. The solution? Enter credit card numbers as text. The easiest way is to pre-format the cell as Text (choose Home ➪ Number and choose Text from the drop-down Number Format list). Or you can precede the credit card number with an apostrophe. Either method prevents Excel from interpreting the entry as a number.

Here are some of Excel's other numeric limitations:

Largest positive number: 9.9E+307

Smallest negative number: –9.9E+307

Smallest positive number: 1E–307

Largest negative number: –1E–307

These numbers are expressed in scientific notation. For example, the largest positive number *9.9E+307* is "9.9 times 10 to the 307th power" — in other words, 99 followed by 306 zeros. Keep in mind, though, that this number has only 15 digits of accuracy.

About Text Entries

Most worksheets also include text in their cells. You can insert text to serve as labels for values, headings for columns, or instructions about the worksheet. Text is often used to clarify what the values in a worksheet mean.

Text that begins with a number is still considered text. For example, if you type **12 Employees** into a cell, Excel considers the entry to be text rather than a value. Consequently, you can't use this cell for numeric calculations. If you need to both use the number 12 in calculations and indicate that the number 12 refers to employees, enter **12** into a cell and then type **Employees** into the cell to the right.

About Formulas

Formulas are what make a spreadsheet a spreadsheet. Excel enables you to enter powerful formulas that use the values (or even text) in cells to calculate a result. When you enter a formula into a cell, the formula's result appears in the cell. If you change any of the values used by a formula, the formula recalculates and shows the new result.

Formulas can be simple mathematical expressions, or they can use some of the powerful functions that are built into Excel. Figure 13-1 shows an Excel worksheet set up to calculate a monthly loan payment. The worksheet contains values, text, and formulas. The cells in column A contain text. Column B contains four values and two formulas. The formulas are in cells B6 and B10. Column D, for reference, shows the actual contents of the cells in column B.

FIGURE 13-1

You can use values, text, and formulas to create useful Excel worksheets.

	A	B	C	D	E
1	**Loan Payment Calculator**				
2					
3				Column B Contents	
4	Purchase Amount:	$475,000		475000	
5	Down Payment Pct:	20%		0.2	
6	Loan Amount:	$380,000		=B4*(1-B5)	
7	Term (months):	360		360	
8	Interest Rate (APR):	6.25%		0.0625	
9					
10	Monthly Payment:	$2,339.73		=PMT(B8/12,B7,-B6)	
11					
12					

Cross-Reference

You can find out much more about formulas in Chapter 15. ■

Entering Text and Values into Your Worksheets

To enter a numeric value into a cell, move the cell pointer to the appropriate cell, type the value, and then press Enter or one of the navigation keys. The value is displayed in the cell and also appears in the Formula bar when the cell is selected. You can include decimal points and currency symbols when entering values, along with plus signs, minus signs, and commas (to separate thousands).

Note

If you precede a value with a minus sign or enclose it in parentheses, Excel considers it to be a negative number. ■

Entering text into a cell is just as easy as entering a value: Activate the cell, type the text, and then press Enter or a navigation key. A cell can contain a maximum of about 32,000 characters — more than enough to hold a typical chapter in this book. Even though a cell can hold a large number of characters, you'll find that it's not possible to actually display all these characters.

Tip

If you type an exceptionally long text entry into a cell, the Formula bar may not show all the text. To display more of the text in the Formula bar, click the bottom of the Formula bar and drag down to increase the height (see Figure 13-2). Also useful is the Ctrl+Shift+U keyboard shortcut. Pressing this key combination toggles the height of the formula bar to show either one more row or the previous size. ■

FIGURE 13-2

The Formula bar, expanded in height to show more information in the cell.

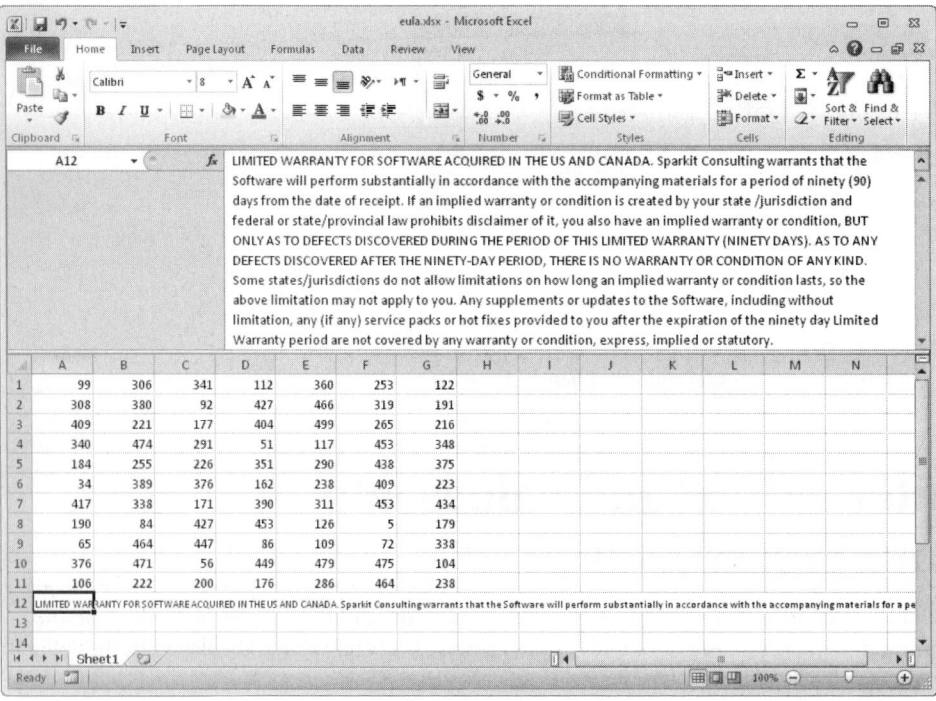

What happens when you enter text that's longer than the current width of its column? If the cells to the immediate right are blank, Excel displays the text in its entirety, appearing to spill the entry into adjacent cells. If an adjacent cell isn't blank, Excel displays as much of the text as possible. (The full text is contained in the cell; it's just not displayed.) If you need to display a long text string in a cell that's adjacent to a non-blank cell, you can take one of several actions:

- Edit your text to make it shorter.
- Increase the width of the column.
- Use a smaller font.
- Wrap the text within the cell so that it occupies more than one line. Choose Home ⇨ Alignment ⇨ Wrap Text to toggle wrapping on and off for the selected cell or range.

Entering Dates and Times into Your Worksheets

Excel treats dates and times as special types of numeric values. Typically, these values are formatted so that they appear as dates or times because we humans find it far easier to understand these values when they appear in the correct format. If you work with dates and times, you need to understand Excel's Date and Time system.

Entering Date Values

Excel handles dates by using a serial number system. The earliest date that Excel understands is January 1, 1900. This date has a serial number of 1. January 2, 1900, has a serial number of 2, and so on. This system makes it easy to deal with dates in formulas. For example, you can enter a formula to calculate the number of days between two dates.

Most of the time, you don't have to be concerned with Excel's serial number date system. You can simply enter a date in a familiar date format, and Excel takes care of the details behind the scenes. For example, if you need to enter *June 1, 2007*, you can simply enter the date by typing **June 1, 2007** (or use any of several different date formats). Excel interprets your entry and stores the value 39234, which is the serial number for that date.

Note

The date examples in this book use the U.S. English system. Depending on your Windows regional settings, entering a date in a format (such as "June 1, 2011") may be interpreted as text rather than a date. In such a case, you need to enter the date in a format that corresponds to your regional date settings — for example, 1 June 2011. ■

Cross-Reference

For more information about working with dates, see Chapter 16. ■

Entering Time Values

When you work with times, you simply extend Excel's date serial number system to include decimals. In other words, Excel works with times by using fractional days. For example, the date serial number for June 1, 2011, is 40695. Noon on June 1, 2011 (halfway through the day), is represented internally as 40695.5 because the time fraction is added to the date serial number to get the full date/time serial number.

Again, you normally don't have to be concerned with these serial numbers (or fractional serial numbers, for times). Just enter the time into a cell in a recognized format.

Cross-Reference
See Chapter 16 for more information about working with time values. ■

Modifying Cell Contents

After you enter a value or text into a cell, you can modify it in several ways:

- Erase the cell's contents.
- Replace the cell's contents with something else.
- Edit the cell's contents.

Note
You can also modify a cell by changing its formatting. However, formatting a cell affects only a cell's appearance. Formatting does not affect its contents. Later sections in this chapter cover formatting. ■

Erasing the Contents of a Cell

To erase the contents of a cell, just click on the cell and press Delete. To erase more than one cell, select all the cells that you want to erase and then press Delete. Pressing Delete removes the cell's contents but doesn't remove any formatting (such as bold, italic, or a different number format) that you may have applied to the cell.

For more control over what gets deleted, you can choose Home ➪ Editing ➪ Clear. This command's drop-down list has five choices:

- **Clear All.** Clears everything from the cell — its contents, its formatting, and its cell comment (if it has one).
- **Clear Formats.** Clears only the formatting and leaves the value, text, or formula.
- **Clear Contents.** Clears only the cell's contents and leaves the formatting (similar to using the Delete key).
- **Clear Comments.** Clears the comment(s) (if any) attached to the cell.
- **Clear Hyperlinks.** Removes hyperlinks contained in the selected cells. The text remains, but the cell no longer functions as a clickable hyperlink.

Note

Clearing formats doesn't clear the background colors in a range that has been designated as a table unless you replace the table style background colors manually. ∎

Replacing the Contents of a Cell

To replace the contents of a cell with something else, just activate the cell and type your new entry, which replaces the previous contents. Any formatting applied to the cell remains in place and is applied to the new content.

Tip

You can also replace cell contents by dragging and dropping or by pasting data from the Clipboard. In both cases, the cell formatting will be replaced by the format of the new data. To avoid pasting formatting, choose Home ⇨ Clipboard ⇨ Paste ⇨ Values, or Home ⇨ Clipboard ⇨ Paste ⇨ Formulas. ∎

Editing the Contents of a Cell

If the cell contains only a few characters, replacing its contents by typing new data usually is easiest. However, if the cell contains lengthy text or a complex formula and you need to make only a slight modification, you probably want to edit the cell rather than re-enter information.

When you want to edit the contents of a cell, you can use one of the following ways to enter Edit mode:

- Double-click the cell to edit the cell contents directly in the cell.
- Select the cell and press F2 to edit the cell contents directly in the cell.
- Select the cell that you want to edit, and then click inside the Formula bar to edit the cell contents in the Formula bar.

You can use whichever method you prefer. Some people find editing directly in the cell easier; others prefer to use the Formula bar to edit a cell.

Note

After you click Advanced in the list at the left side of the Excel Options dialog box, the options that appear at the right contain a section called Editing Options. These settings affect how editing works. (To access this dialog box, choose File ⇨ Options.) If the Allow Editing Directly In Cells option isn't enabled, you can't edit a cell by double-clicking. In addition, pressing F2 allows you to edit the cell in the Formula bar (not directly in the cell). ∎

All of these methods cause Excel to go into *Edit mode*. (The word *Edit* appears at the left side of the status bar at the bottom of the screen, replacing the word *Ready*.) When Excel is in Edit mode, the Formula bar displays two new icons: the X and the CheckMark (see Figure 13-3). These icons are also called the Cancel and Enter buttons, respectively. Clicking the X icon cancels editing without changing the cell's contents. (Pressing Esc has the same effect.) Clicking the CheckMark icon completes the editing and enters the modified contents into the cell; pressing Enter has the same effect.

FIGURE 13-3

While editing a cell, the Formula bar displays two new icons.

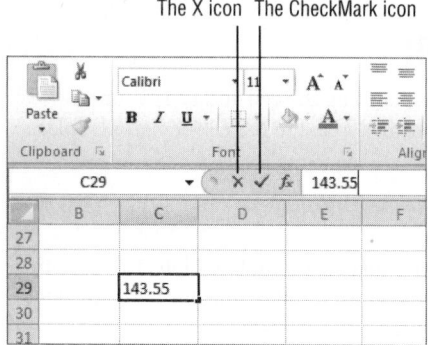

The X icon   The CheckMark icon

When you begin editing a cell, the insertion point appears as a vertical bar, and you can perform the following tasks:

- Add new characters at the location of the insertion point. You can move the insertion point by:
  - Using the navigation keys to move within the cell.
  - Pressing Home to move the insertion point to the beginning of the cell.
  - Pressing End to move the insertion point to the end of the cell.
- Select multiple characters. Press Shift while you use the navigation keys.
- Select characters while you're editing a cell. Use the mouse. Simply click and drag the mouse pointer over the characters that you want to select.

Learning Some Handy Data-Entry Techniques

You can simplify the process of entering information into your Excel worksheets and make your work go quite a bit faster by using several useful tricks, described in the following sections.

Automatically Moving the Cell Pointer after Entering Data

By default, Excel automatically moves the cell pointer to the next cell down when you press the Enter key after entering data into a cell. To change this setting, choose File ➪ Options and click Advanced at the left (see Figure 13-4). The checkbox that controls this behavior is labeled After Pressing Enter, Move Selection. If you enable this option, you can choose the direction in which the cell pointer moves (down, up, left, or right). Your choice is completely a matter of personal preference. I prefer to keep this option turned off. When entering data, I use the navigation keys rather than the Enter key (see the next section).

FIGURE 13-4

You can use the Advanced tab in Excel Options to select several helpful input option settings.

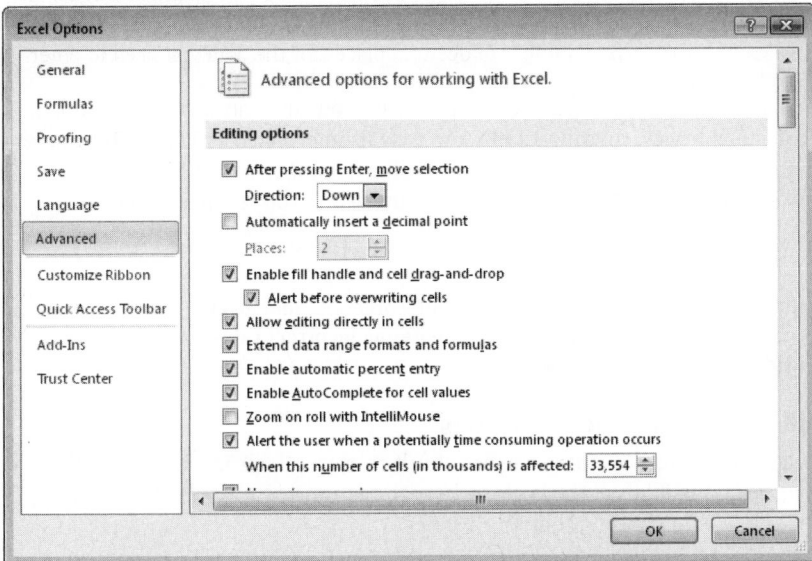

Using Navigation Keys instead of Pressing Enter

Instead of pressing the Enter key when you're finished making a cell entry, you also can use any of the navigation keys to complete the entry. Not surprisingly, these navigation keys send you in the direction that you indicate. For example, if you're entering data in a row, press the right-arrow (→) key rather than Enter. The other arrow keys work as expected, and you can even use Page Up and Page Down.

Selecting a Range of Input Cells before Entering Data

Here's a tip that most Excel users don't know about: When a range of cells is selected, Excel automatically moves the cell pointer to the next cell in the range when you press Enter. If the selection consists of multiple rows, Excel moves down the column; when it reaches the end of the selection in the column, it moves to the first selected cell in the next column.

To skip a cell, just press Enter without entering anything. To go backward, press Shift+Enter. If you prefer to enter the data by rows rather than by columns, press Tab rather than Enter. Excel continues to cycle through the selected range until you select a cell outside of the range.

Using Ctrl+Enter to Place Information into Multiple Cells Simultaneously

If you need to enter the same data into multiple cells, Excel offers a handy shortcut. Select all the cells that you want to contain the data; enter the value, text, or formula; and then press Ctrl+Enter. The same information is inserted into each cell in the selection.

Entering Decimal Points Automatically

If you need to enter lots of numbers with a fixed number of decimal places, Excel has a useful tool that works like some adding machines. Access the Excel Options dialog box (File ⇨ Options) and click the Advanced tab. Select the checkbox Automatically Insert a Decimal Point, and make sure that the Places box is set for the correct number of decimal places for the data you need to enter.

When this option is set, Excel supplies the decimal points for you automatically. For example, if you specify two decimal places, entering **12345** into a cell is interpreted as 123.45. To restore things to normal, just clear the Automatically Insert a Decimal Point checkbox in the Excel Options dialog box. Changing this setting doesn't affect any values you've already entered.

Caution

The fixed decimal places option is a global setting and applies to all workbooks (not just the active workbook). If you forget that this option is turned on, you can easily end up entering incorrect values or cause some major confusion if you are using a shared computer. ■

Using Auto Fill to Enter a Series of Values

The Excel Auto Fill feature makes inserting a series of values or text items in a range of cells easy. It uses the fill handle (the small box at the lower right of the active cell). You can drag the fill handle to copy the cell or automatically complete a series.

Figure 13-5 shows an example. I entered **1** into cell A1 and **3** into cell A2. Then I selected both cells and dragged down the fill handle to create a linear series of odd numbers. The figure also shows that the Auto Fill Options button that, when clicked, displays some additional Auto Fill options.

FIGURE 13-5

This series was created by using Auto Fill.

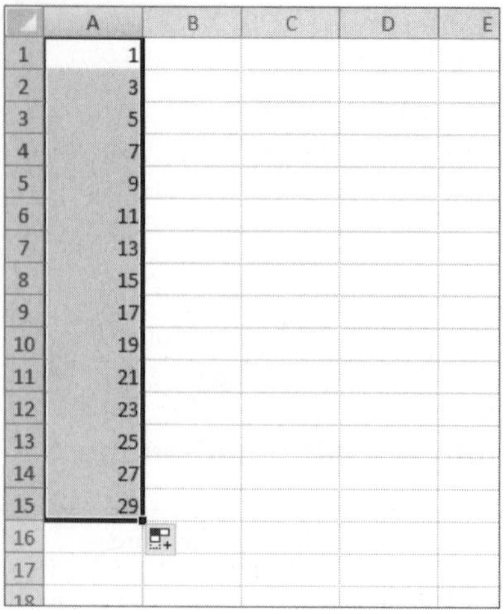

Tip

If you drag the fill handle while you press and hold the right mouse button, Excel display a shortcut menu with additional fill options. ■

Using AutoComplete to Automate Data Entry

The Excel AutoComplete feature makes entering the same text into multiple cells easy. With AutoComplete, you type the first few letters of a text entry into a cell, and Excel automatically completes the entry based on other entries that you already made in the column. Besides reducing typing, this feature also ensures that your entries are spelled correctly and are consistent.

Here's how it works. Suppose that you're entering product information in a column. One of your products is named *Widgets*. The first time that you enter **Widgets** into a cell, Excel remembers it. Later, when you start typing **Widgets** in that same column, Excel recognizes it by the first few letters and finishes typing it for you. Just press Enter, and you're done. To override the suggestion, just keep typing.

AutoComplete also changes the case of letters for you automatically. If you start entering **widget** (with a lowercase *w*) in the second entry, Excel makes the *w* uppercase to be consistent with the previous entry in the column.

Tip

You also can access a mouse-oriented version of AutoComplete by right-clicking on the cell and choosing Pick From Drop-Down List from the shortcut menu. Excel then displays a drop-down box that has all the entries in the current column, and you just click the one that you want. ■

Keep in mind that AutoComplete works only within a contiguous column of cells. If you have a blank row, for example, AutoComplete identifies only the cell contents below the blank row.

If you find the AutoComplete feature distracting, you can turn it off by clicking Advanced in the list at the left side of the Excel Options dialog box. Remove the check mark from Enable AutoComplete for cell values.

Forcing Text to Appear on a New Line within a Cell

If you have lengthy text in a cell, you can force Excel to display it in multiple lines within the cell: Press Alt+Enter to start a new line in a cell.

Note

When you add a line break, Excel automatically changes the cell's format to Wrap Text. But unlike normal text wrap, your manual line break forces Excel to break the text at a specific place within the text, which gives you more precise control over the appearance of the text than if you rely on automatic text wrapping. ■

Tip

To remove a manual line break, edit the cell and press Delete when the insertion point is located at the end of the line that contains the manual line break. You won't see any symbol to indicate the position of the manual line break, but the text that follows it will move up when the line break is deleted. ■

Using AutoCorrect for Shorthand Data Entry

You can use the AutoCorrect feature to create shortcuts for commonly used words or phrases. For example, if you work for a company named *Consolidated Data Processing Corporation*, you can create an AutoCorrect entry for an abbreviation, such as *cdp*. Then, whenever you type **cdp**, Excel automatically changes it to **Consolidated Data Processing Corporation**.

Excel includes quite a few built-in AutoCorrect terms (mostly common misspellings); furthermore, you can add your own. To set up your custom AutoCorrect entries, access the Excel Options dialog box (File ⇨ Options) and click the Proofing tab. Then click the AutoCorrect Options button to display the AutoCorrect dialog box. In the dialog box, click the AutoCorrect tab, check the option labeled Replace Text As You Type, and then enter your custom entries. (Figure 13-6 shows an example.) You can set up as many custom entries as you like. Just be careful not to use an abbreviation that might appear normally in your text.

FIGURE 13-6

AutoCorrect allows you to create shorthand abbreviations for text you enter often.

Tip

Excel shares your AutoCorrect list with other Office applications. For example, any AutoCorrect entries you created in Word also work in Excel. ∎

Entering Numbers with Fractions

To enter a fractional value into a cell, leave a space between the whole number and the fraction. For example, to enter 6 7/8, enter **6 7/8** and then press Enter. When you select the cell, 6.875 appears in the Formula bar, and the cell entry appears as a fraction. If you have a fraction only (e.g., $1/8$), you must enter a zero first, like this — **0 1/8** — or Excel will likely assume that you're entering a date. When you select the cell and look at the Formula bar, you see 0.125. In the cell, you see $1/8$.

Simplifying Data Entry by Using a Form

Many people use Excel to manage lists in which the information is arranged in rows. Excel offers a simple way to work with this type of data through the use of a data entry form that Excel can create automatically. This data form works with either a normal range of data or with a range that has been designated as a table (choose Insert ➪ Tables ➪ Table). Figure 13-7 shows an example.

FIGURE 13-7

Excel's built-in data form can simplify many data-entry tasks.

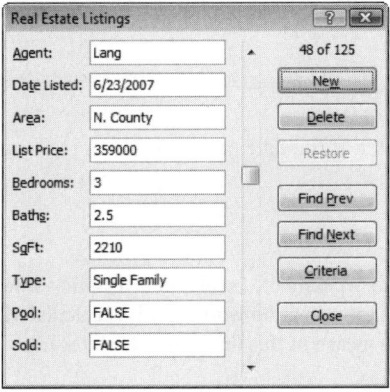

Unfortunately, the command to access the data form is not on the Ribbon. To use the data form, you must add it to your Quick Access Toolbar or add it to the Ribbon. The instructions that follow describe how to add this command to your Quick Access Toolbar:

1. **Right-click the Quick Access Toolbar, and choose Customize Quick Access Toolbar.** The Quick Access Toolbar choices in the Excel Options dialog box appear.

2. **In the Choose Commands From drop-down list, choose Commands Not in the Ribbon.**

3. **In the list box on the left, select Form.**

4. **Click the Add button to add the selected command to your Quick Access Toolbar.**

5. **Click OK to close the Excel Options dialog box.**

After performing these steps, a new icon appears on your Quick Access Toolbar.

To use a data entry form, follow these steps:

1. **Arrange your data so that Excel can recognize it as a table by entering headings for the columns in the first row of your data entry range.**

2. **Select any cell in the table, and click the Form button on your Quick Access Toolbar.** Excel displays a dialog box customized to your data (refer to Figure 13-7).

3. **Fill in the information.** Press Tab to move between the textboxes. If a cell contains a formula, the formula result appears as text (not as an edit box). In other words, you can't modify formulas using the data entry form.

4. **When you complete the data form, click the New button.** Excel enters the data into a row in the worksheet and clears the dialog box for the next row of data.

Entering the Current Date or Time into a Cell

If you need to date-stamp or time-stamp your worksheet, Excel provides two shortcut keys that do this task for you:

- **Current Date.** Ctrl+; (semicolon)
- **Current Time.** Ctrl+Shift+; (semicolon)

The date and time are from the system time in your computer. If the date or time is not correct in Excel, use the Windows Control Panel to make the adjustment.

Note

When you use either of these shortcuts to enter a date or time into your worksheet, Excel enters a static value into the worksheet. In other words, the date or time entered doesn't change when the worksheet is recalculated. In most cases, this setup is probably what you want, but you should be aware of this limitation. If you want the date or time display to update, use one of these formulas:

```
=TODAY()
```

or

```
=NOW()  ■
```

Applying Number Formatting

Number formatting refers to the process of changing the appearance of values contained in cells. Excel provides a wide variety of number formatting options. In the following sections, you see how to use many of Excel's formatting options to quickly improve the appearance of your worksheets.

Note

The formatting that you apply works with the selected cell or cells. Therefore, you need to select the cell (or range of cells) before applying the formatting. Also remember that changing the number format does not affect the underlying value. Number formatting affects only the *appearance*. ■

Values that you enter into cells normally are unformatted. In other words, they simply consist of a string of numerals. Typically, you want to format the numbers so that they're easier to read or are more consistent in terms of the number of decimal places shown.

Figure 13-8 shows a worksheet that has two columns of values and a third column to help explain the format. The first column consists of unformatted values. The cells in the second column are formatted to make the values easier to read. The third column describes the type of formatting that was applied.

FIGURE 13-8

Use numeric formatting to make it easier to understand what the values in the worksheet represent.

	A	B	C	D
1				
2	Unformatted	Formatted	Type	
3	1200	$1,200.00	Currency	
4	0.231	23.1%	Percentage	
5	2/3/2010	2/3/2008	Short Date	
6	2/3/2010	Sunday, February 03, 2008	Long Date	
7	123439832	123,439,832.00	Accounting	
8	5559832	555-9832	Phone Number	
9	434988723	434-98-8723	Social Security Number	
10	0.552	1:14:53 PM	Time	
11	0.25	1/4	Fraction	
12	12332354090	1.23E+10	Scientific	
13				

Tip

If you move the cell pointer to a cell that has a formatted value, the Formula bar displays the value in its unformatted state because the formatting affects only how the value appears in the cell — not the actual value contained in the cell. ■

Using Automatic Number Formatting

Excel is smart enough to perform some formatting for you automatically. For example, if you enter **12.2%** into a cell, Excel knows that you want to use a percentage format and applies it for you automatically. If you type commas to separate thousands (such as **123,456**), Excel applies comma formatting for you. And if you precede your value with a dollar sign, the cell is formatted for currency (assuming that the dollar sign is your system currency symbol).

Tip

A handy default feature in Excel makes entering percentage values into cells easier. If a cell is formatted to display as a percent, you can simply enter a normal value (e.g., 12.5 for 12.5%). To enter values less than 1%, precede the value with a zero and a period (e.g., 0.52 for 0.52%). If this automatic percent-entry feature isn't working (or if you prefer to enter the actual value for percentages), access the Excel Options dialog box and click Advanced in the list at the left. In the Editing Options section, locate the Enable Automatic Percent Entry checkbox and remove the check mark. ■

Formatting Numbers by Using the Ribbon

The Home ➪ Number group in the Ribbon contains controls that let you quickly apply common number formats (see Figure 13-9).

FIGURE 13-9

You can find number formatting commands in the Number group of the Home tab.

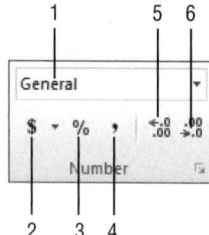

Figure 13-9 identifies the tools in the Number group by number. Following is a description of each of those tools:

1. The Number Format drop-down list contains 11 common number formats.

2. The Accounting Number Format button applies a dollar sign, thousands separator (comma), and two decimal places. Use its drop-down list to select a currency format.

3. The Percent Style formats the cell value with a percent sign. Enter values as decimals to create percentages, such as .75 for 75%.

4. The Comma Style button adds a thousands separator (comma) and two decimal places.

5. Click the Increase Decimal button to add decimal places.

6. Click the Decrease Decimal button to remove decimal places.

When you select one of these controls, the active cell takes on the specified number format. You also can select a range of cells (or even an entire row or column) before clicking these buttons. If you select more than one cell, Excel applies the number format to all the selected cells.

Using Shortcut Keys to Format Numbers

Another way to apply number formatting is to use shortcut keys. Table 13-1 summarizes the shortcut-key combinations that you can use to apply common number formatting to the selected cells or range.

TABLE 13-1

Number-Formatting Keyboard Shortcuts

Key Combination	Formatting Applied
Ctrl+Shift+~	General number format (i.e., unformatted values)
Ctrl+Shift+$	Currency format with two decimal places (negative numbers appear in parentheses)
Ctrl+Shift+%	Percentage format, with no decimal places
Ctrl+Shift+^	Scientific notation number format, with two decimal places
Ctrl+Shift+#	Date format with the day, month, and year
Ctrl+Shift+@	Time format with the hour, minute, and a.m. or p.m.
Ctrl+Shift+!	Two decimal places, thousands separator, and a hyphen for negative values

Formatting Numbers Using the Format Cells Dialog Box

In most cases, the number formats that are accessible from the Number group on the Home tab are just fine. Sometimes, however, you might want more control over how your values appear. Excel offers a great deal of control over number formats through the use of the Format Cells dialog box, shown in Figure 13-10. For formatting numbers, you need to use the Number tab.

You can bring up the Format Cells dialog box in several ways. Start by selecting the cell or cells that you want to format, and then do one of the following:

- Choose Home ⇨ Number and click the small Dialog Box Launcher icon (arrow in the lower-right corner of the Number group).
- Choose Home ⇨ Number, click the Number Format drop-down list, and choose More Number Formats from the drop-down list.
- Right-click on the cell, and choose Format Cells from the shortcut menu.
- Press Ctrl+1 (the number one).

The Number tab of the Format Cells dialog box displays 12 categories of number formats from which to choose. When you select a category from the list box, the right side of the tab changes to display the appropriate options.

The Number category on the Number tab has three options that you can control: the number of decimal places displayed, whether to use a thousands separator, and how you want negative numbers displayed. Notice that the Negative Numbers list box has four choices (two of which display negative values in red), and the choices change depending on the number of decimal places and whether you choose to separate thousands.

FIGURE 13-10

When you need more control over number formats, use the Number tab of the Format Cells dialog box.

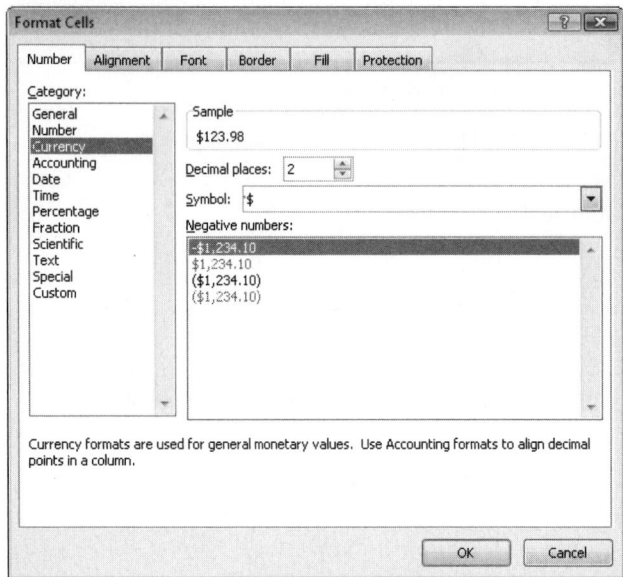

The top of the tab displays a sample of how the active cell will appear with the selected number format (visible only if a cell with a value is selected). After you make your choices, click OK to apply the number format to all the selected cells.

When Numbers Appear to Add Incorrectly

Applying a number format to a cell doesn't change the value — only how the value appears in the worksheet. For example, if a cell contains 0.874543, you may format it to appear as 87%. But if that cell is used in a formula, the formula uses the full value (0.874543), not the displayed value (87%).

In some situations, formatting may cause Excel to display calculation results that appear incorrect, such as when totaling numbers with decimal places. For example, if values are formatted to display two decimal places, you may not see the actual numbers used in the calculations. But because Excel uses the full precision of the values in its formula, the sum of the two values may appear to be incorrect.

Several solutions to this problem are available. You can format the cells to display more decimal places. You can use the ROUND function on individual numbers and specify the number of decimal places Excel should round to. Alternatively, you can instruct Excel to change the worksheet values to match their displayed format. To do so, access the Excel Options dialog box and click the Advanced tab. In the When Calculating This Workbook section, check the Set Precision as Displayed checkbox.

Caution

Selecting the Set Precision as Displayed option changes the numbers in your worksheets to permanently match their appearance onscreen. This setting applies to all sheets in the active workbook. Most of the time, this option is *not* what you want. Make sure that you understand the consequences of using the Set Precision as Displayed option. ■

The following are the number-format categories, along with some general comments:

- **General.** The default format; it displays numbers as integers, as decimals, or in scientific notation if the value is too wide to fit in the cell.

- **Number.** Enables you to specify the number of decimal places, whether to use a thousands separator (or 1000 separator, usually a comma in the U.S.) to separate thousands, and how to display negative numbers (with a minus sign, in red, in parentheses, or in red and in parentheses).

- **Currency.** Enables you to specify the number of decimal places, whether to use a currency symbol, and how to display negative numbers (with a minus sign, in red, in parentheses, or in red and in parentheses). This format always uses a thousands separator.

- **Accounting.** Differs from the Currency format in that the currency symbols always align vertically.

- **Date.** Enables you to choose from several different date formats.

- **Time.** Enables you to choose from several different time formats.

- **Percentage.** Enables you to choose the number of decimal places and always displays a percent sign.

- **Fraction.** Enables you to choose from among nine fraction formats.

- **Scientific.** Displays numbers in exponential notation (with an E), for example, $2.00E+05 = 200,000$; $2.05E+05 = 205,000$. You can choose the number of decimal places to display to the left of E.

- **Text.** When applied to a value, causes Excel to treat the value as text (even if it looks like a number). This feature is useful for such items as part numbers.

- **Special.** Contains additional number formats. As an example, in the U.S. version of Excel, the additional number formats are Zip Code, Zip Code +4, Phone Number, and Social Security Number.

- **Custom.** Enables you to define custom number formats that aren't included in any other category.

Tip

If a cell displays a series of hash marks (such as ########), it usually means that the column isn't wide enough to display the value in the number format that you selected. Either make the column wider or change the number format. If that doesn't fix the problem, try applying a different number format, as the applied format may not match the data. ■

Summary

This chapter showed you the techniques you need to know to enter the contents for any worksheet in Excel. You learned how Excel treats different types of information — text, numbers, and formulas. You saw how to enter each type of information into a cell, as well as how to edit or replace a cell entry. The chapter shared handy data-entry shortcuts such as Auto Fill and finished by explaining what number formats are and how to apply them. Continue in the book to learn how to work with groups of cells called *ranges*.

14

Essential Worksheet and Cell Range Operations

T his chapter covers some basic information regarding workbooks, worksheets, and windows. You will discover tips and techniques to help take control of your worksheets. The result? You'll be a more efficient Excel user.

Learning the Fundamentals of Excel Worksheets

In Excel, each file is called a *workbook*, and each workbook can contain one or more *worksheets*. You may find it helpful to think of an Excel workbook as a paper notebook and worksheets as pages in the notebook. As with a notebook, you can view a particular sheet, add new sheets, remove sheets, and copy sheets.

The following sections describe the operations you can perform with worksheets.

Working with Excel Windows

Each Excel workbook file is displayed in a *window*. A workbook can hold any number of sheets, and these sheets can be either worksheets (sheets consisting of rows and columns) or *chart sheets* (sheets that hold a single chart). A worksheet is what people usually think of when they think of a *spreadsheet*. You can open as many Excel workbooks as necessary at the same time.

Figure 14-1 shows Excel with four workbooks open, each in a separate window. One of the windows is minimized and appears near the lower-left

IN THIS CHAPTER

Understanding Excel worksheet essentials

Controlling your views

Manipulating the rows and columns

Understanding Excel cells and ranges

Selecting cells and ranges

Copying or moving ranges

Using names to work with ranges

Adding comments to cells

corner of the screen. (When a workbook is minimized, only its title bar is visible.) Worksheet windows can overlap, and the title bar of one window is a different color. That's the window that contains the active workbook.

FIGURE 14-1

You can open several Excel workbooks at the same time.

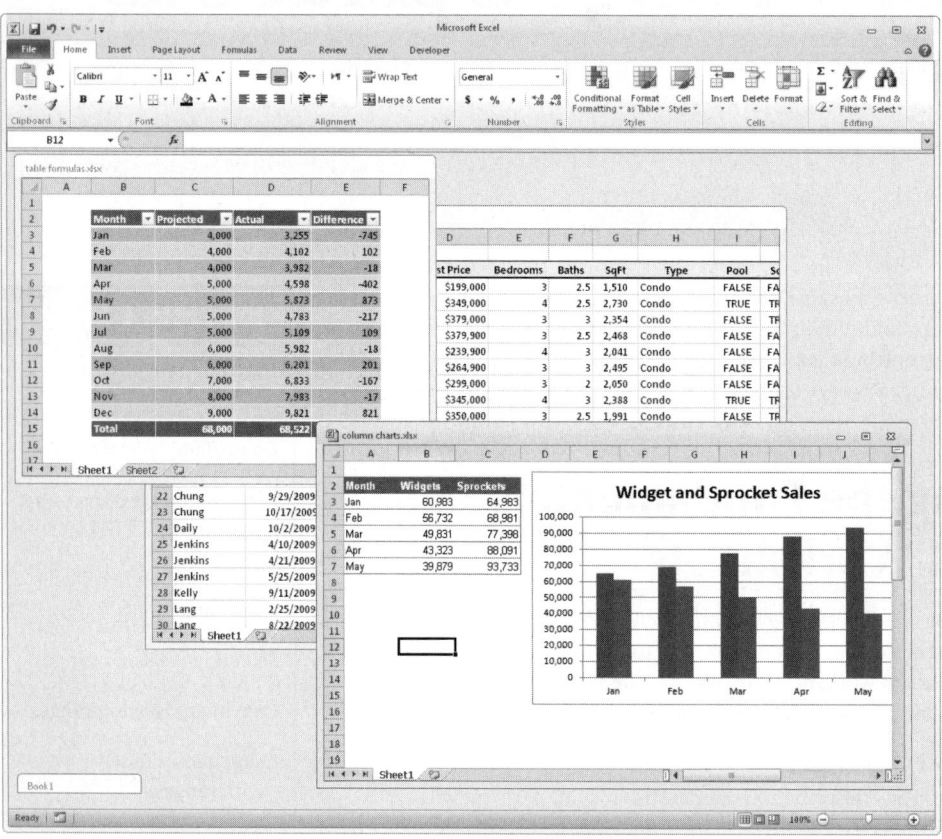

The workbook windows that Excel uses work much like the windows in any other Windows program. Each window has three buttons at the right side of its title bar. From left to right, they are Minimize, Maximize (or Restore), and Close. When a workbook window is maximized, the three buttons appear directly below the Excel title bar.

Workbook windows can be in one of the following states:

- **Maximized.** Fills the entire Excel workspace. A maximized window doesn't have a title bar, and the workbook's name appears in the title bar for Excel. To maximize a window, click its Maximize button.

- **Minimized.** Appears as a small window with only a title bar. To minimize a window, click its Minimize button.

- **Restored.** A non-maximized size. To restore a maximized or minimized window, click its Restore button.

If you work with more than one workbook simultaneously (which is quite common), you need to know how to move, resize, and switch among the workbook windows.

Moving and Resizing Windows

To move a window, make sure that it's not maximized. Then drag its title bar with your mouse.

To resize a window, drag any of its borders until it's the size that you want it to be. When you position the mouse pointer on a window's border, the mouse pointer changes to a double-sided arrow, which lets you know that you can now drag to resize the window. To resize a window horizontally and vertically at the same time, drag any of its corners.

Note

You can't move or resize a workbook window if it's maximized. You can move a minimized window, but doing so has no effect on its position when it is subsequently restored. ■

If you want all of your workbook windows to be visible (i.e., not obscured by another window), you can move and resize the windows manually, or you can let Excel do it for you. Choosing View ➪ Window ➪ Arrange All displays the Arrange Windows dialog box, shown in Figure 14-2. This dialog box has four window-arrangement options. Just select the one that you want and click OK. Windows that are minimized aren't affected by this command.

FIGURE 14-2

Use the Arrange Windows dialog box to quickly arrange all open non-minimized workbook windows.

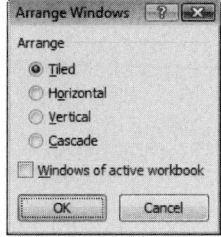

Switching among Windows

At any given time, only one workbook window can be the active window. The active window accepts your input and is the window upon which your commands work. The active window's title bar is a different color, and the window appears on top of all of the other windows. To work in a different window, you need to make *that* window active. You can make a different window the active workbook in several ways:

- Click on another window, if it's visible. The window you click on moves to the top and becomes the active window. This method isn't possible if the current window is maximized.

- Press Ctrl+Tab (or Ctrl+F6) to cycle through all open windows until the window that you want to work with appears on top as the active window. Pressing Shift+Ctrl+Tab (or Shift+Ctrl+F6) cycles through the windows in the opposite direction.

- Choose View ➪ Window ➪ Switch Windows, and select the window that you want from the drop-down list (the active window has a check mark next to it). This menu can display as many as nine windows. If you have more than nine workbook windows open, choose More Windows (which appears below the nine window names).

- Click on the icon for the window in the Windows taskbar. This technique is available only if the Show All Windows in the Taskbar option is turned on. You can control this setting from the Advanced tab of the Excel Options dialog box (in the Display section).

Tip

Most people prefer to do most of their work with maximized workbook windows, which enables you to see more cells and eliminates the distraction of other workbook windows getting in the way. At times, however, viewing multiple windows is preferred. For example, displaying two windows is more efficient if you need to compare information in two workbooks or if you need to copy data from one workbook to another. ■

When you maximize one window, all of the other windows are maximized, too (even though you don't see them). Therefore, if the active window is maximized and you activate a different window, the new active window is also maximized.

Tip

You also can display a single workbook in more than one window. For example, if you have a workbook with two worksheets, you may want to display each worksheet in a separate window to compare the two sheets. All of the window-manipulation procedures described previously still apply. Choose View ➪ Window ➪ New Window to open an additional window in the active workbook. ■

Closing Windows

If you have multiple windows open, you may want to close those windows that you no longer need. Excel offers several ways to close the active window:

- Choose File ➪ Close.

- Click the Close button (the X icon) on the workbook window's title bar. If the workbook window is maximized, its title bar is not visible, so its Close button appears directly below the Excel Close button.

- Press Ctrl+W.

When you close a workbook window, Excel checks whether you made any changes since the last time you saved the file. If you have made unsaved changes, Excel prompts you to save the file before it closes the window. If not, the window closes without a prompt from Excel.

Activating a Worksheet

At any given time, one workbook is the active workbook, and one sheet is the active sheet in the active workbook. To activate a different sheet, just click its sheet tab, located at the bottom of the workbook window. You also can use the following shortcut keys to activate a different sheet:

- **Ctrl+Page Up**. Activates the previous sheet, if one exists.
- **Ctrl+Page Down**. Activates the next sheet, if one exists.

If your workbook has many sheets, all of its tabs may not be visible. Use the tab scrolling controls (see Figure 14-3) to scroll the sheet tabs. The sheet tabs share space with the worksheet's horizontal scroll bar. You also can drag the tab split control to display more or fewer tabs. Dragging the tab split control simultaneously changes the number of tabs and the size of the horizontal scroll bar.

FIGURE 14-3

Use the tab controls to activate a different worksheet or to see additional worksheet tabs.

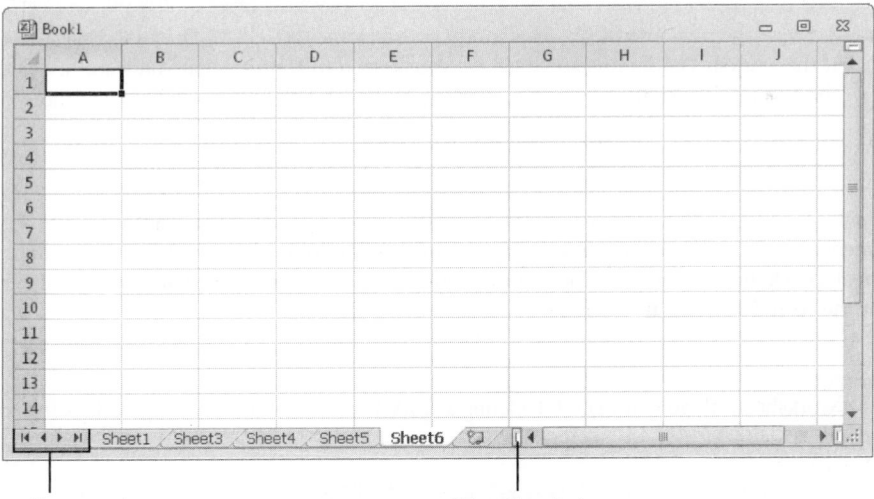

Tab scrolling controls Tab split control

Tip

When you right-click on any of the tab scrolling controls, Excel displays a list of all of the sheets in the workbook. You can quickly activate a sheet by selecting it from the list. ■

Adding a New Worksheet to Your Workbook

Worksheets can be an excellent organizational tool. Instead of placing everything on a single worksheet, you can use additional worksheets in a workbook to separate various workbook elements logically. For example, if you have several products whose sales you track individually, you may want to assign each product to its own worksheet and then use another worksheet to consolidate your results.

The following are three ways to add a new worksheet to a workbook:

- Click the Insert Worksheet control, which is located to the right of the last sheet tab. This method inserts the new sheet *after* the last sheet in the workbook.

- Press Shift+F11. This method inserts the new sheet *before* the active sheet.

- Right-click a sheet tab, choose Insert from the shortcut menu, and click the General tab of the Insert dialog box that appears. Then select the Worksheet icon and click OK. This method inserts the new sheet *before* the active sheet.

Deleting a Worksheet You No Longer Need

If you no longer need a worksheet or if you want to get rid of an empty worksheet in a workbook, you can delete it in either of two ways:

- Right-click on its sheet tab and choose Delete from the shortcut menu.

- Activate the unwanted worksheet, and choose Home ➪ Cells ➪ Delete ➪ Delete Sheet. If the worksheet contains any data, Excel asks you to confirm that you want to delete the sheet. If you've never used the worksheet, Excel deletes it immediately without asking for confirmation.

Tip

You can delete multiple sheets with a single command by selecting the sheets that you want to delete. To select multiple sheets, press Ctrl while you click the sheet tabs that you want to delete. To select a group of contiguous sheets, click the first sheet tab, press Shift, and then click the last sheet tab. Then use either method to delete the selected sheets. ∎

Caution

When you delete a worksheet, it's gone for good. Deleting a worksheet is one of the few operations in Excel that can't be undone. ∎

Changing the Default Number of Sheets in Your Workbooks

By default, Excel automatically creates three worksheets in each new workbook. You can change this default behavior. For example, I prefer to start each new workbook with a single worksheet. After all, you can easily add new sheets if and when they're needed. To change the default number of worksheets:

1. Choose File ➪ Options to display the Excel Options window.

2. Click General in the list at the left.

3. Under the section When Creating New Workbooks, change the value for the Include This Many Sheets setting and then click OK.

This change affects all new workbooks but has no effect on existing workbooks.

Changing the Name of a Worksheet

The default names that Excel uses for worksheets — *Sheet1, Sheet2*, and so on — aren't very descriptive. If you don't change the worksheet names, remembering where to find things in multiple-sheet workbooks can be a bit difficult. That's why providing more meaningful names for your worksheets is often a good idea.

To change a sheet's name, double-click on the sheet tab. Excel highlights the name on the sheet tab so that you can edit the name or replace it with a new name.

Sheet names can be up to 31 characters, and spaces are allowed.

Caution

The following characters *CANNOT* be used in sheet names:

: colon

/ slash

\ backslash

[ ] square brackets

? question mark

* asterisk ■

Keep in mind that a longer worksheet name results in a wider tab, which takes up more space onscreen. Therefore, if you use lengthy sheet names, you won't be able to see very many sheet tabs without scrolling the tab list.

Changing a Sheet Tab Color

Excel allows you to change the color of your worksheet tabs. For example, you may prefer to color-code the sheet tabs to make identifying the worksheet's contents easier.

To change the color of a sheet tab, right-click on the tab and choose Tab Color from the shortcut menu. Then select the color from the color submenu (gallery) that appears.

Rearranging Your Worksheets

You may want to rearrange the order of worksheets in a workbook. If you have a separate worksheet for each sales region, for example, arranging the worksheets in alphabetical order may be helpful. You may want to move a worksheet from one workbook to another. (To move a worksheet to a different workbook, both workbooks must be open.) You can also create copies of worksheets.

You can move or copy a worksheet in the following ways:

- Right-click on the sheet tab and choose Move or Copy to display the Move or Copy dialog box (see Figure 14-4). Use this dialog box to specify the operation and the location for the sheet.

- To move a worksheet, move the mouse pointer over the worksheet tab, press and hold the left mouse button, and drag it to its desired location (either in the same workbook or in a different workbook). When you drag, the mouse pointer changes to a small sheet, and a small arrow guides you.

- To copy a worksheet, click on the worksheet tab and press Ctrl while dragging the tab to its desired location (either in the same workbook or in a different workbook). When you drag, the mouse pointer changes to a small sheet with a plus sign on it.

FIGURE 14-4

Use the Move or Copy dialog box to move or copy worksheets in the same or another workbook.

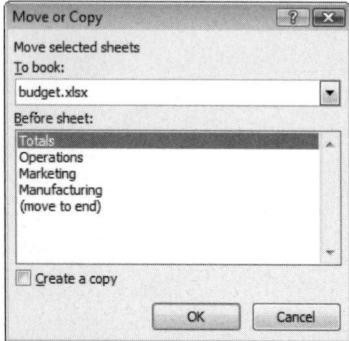

Tip

You can move or copy multiple sheets simultaneously. First, select the sheets by clicking their sheet tabs while holding down the Ctrl key (or the Shift key for sequential sheets). Then you can move or copy the set of sheets by using the preceding methods. ■

If you move or copy a worksheet to a workbook that already has a sheet with the same name, Excel changes the name to make it unique. For example, *Sheet1* becomes *Sheet1 (2)*. You probably want to rename the copied sheet to give it a more meaningful name. See "Changing the Name of a Worksheet," earlier in this chapter.

Note

When you move or copy a worksheet to a different workbook, any defined names and custom formats also get copied to the new workbook. ∎

Hiding and Unhiding a Worksheet

In some situations, you may want to hide one or more worksheets. Hiding a sheet may be useful if you don't want others to see it or if you just want to get it out of the way. When a sheet is hidden, its sheet tab is also hidden. You can't hide all the sheets in a workbook; at least one sheet must remain visible.

To hide a worksheet, right-click on its sheet tab and choose Hide. The active worksheet (or selected worksheets) will be hidden from view.

To unhide a hidden worksheet, right-click on any sheet tab and choose Unhide. Excel opens its Unhide dialog box that lists all hidden sheets. Choose the sheet that you want to redisplay and click OK. When you unhide a sheet, it appears in its previous position among the sheet tabs.

Note

You can only unhide one sheet at a time; therefore, if you wish to unhide multiple hidden sheets, you must repeat these steps for each sheet. ∎

Preventing Sheet Actions

To prevent others from unhiding hidden sheets, inserting new sheets, renaming sheets, copying sheets, or deleting sheets, protect the workbook's structure as follows:

1. Choose Review ➪ Changes ➪ Protect Workbook.

2. In the Protect Workbook dialog box, click the Structure option.

3. (Optional) Provide a password.

After performing these steps, several commands will no longer be available when you right-click on a sheet tab: Insert, Delete Sheet, Rename Sheet, Move or Copy Sheet, Tab Color, Hide Sheet, and Unhide Sheet.

Caution

There are tools on the Internet that will assist in cracking Excel's password protection mechanisms, so don't assume that any workbook is 100% secure. ∎

Controlling the Worksheet View

As you add more information to a worksheet, you may find that navigating and locating what you want gets more difficult. Excel includes a few options that enable you to view your sheet, and sometimes multiple sheets, more efficiently. This section discusses a few additional worksheet options at your disposal.

Zooming in or out for a Better View

Normally, everything you see onscreen is displayed at 100%. You can change the zoom percentage from 10% (very tiny) to 400% (huge). Using a small zoom percentage can help you to get a bird's-eye view of your worksheet to see how it's laid out. Zooming in is useful if your eyesight isn't quite what it used to be and you have trouble deciphering tiny type. Zooming doesn't change the font size, nor does it have any effect on printed output.

Tip

Excel contains separate options for changing the size of your printed output. (Use the controls in the Page Layout ⇨ Scale to Fit group.) ∎

Figure 14-5 shows a window zoomed to 10% and a window zoomed to 400%.

You can easily change the zoom factor of the active worksheet by using the Zoom slider located on the right side of the status bar. Drag the slider, and your screen transforms instantly.

Another way to zoom is to choose View ⇨ Zoom ⇨ Zoom, which displays a dialog box. Choosing View ⇨ Zoom ⇨ Zoom to Selection zooms the worksheet to display only the selected cells (useful if you want a particular range of cells to fill the workbook window).

Tip

Zooming only affects the active worksheet, so you can use different zoom factors for different worksheets. Also, if you have a worksheet displayed in two different windows, you can set a different zoom factor for each of the windows. ∎

Cross-Reference

If your worksheet uses named ranges (see "Using Names to Work with Ranges" later in the chapter), zooming your worksheet to 39% or less displays the name of the range overlaid on the cells. Viewing named ranges in this manner is useful for getting an overview of how a worksheet is laid out. ∎

Viewing a Worksheet in Multiple Windows

Sometimes, you may want to view two different parts of a worksheet simultaneously — perhaps to make referencing a distant cell in a formula easier. Or you may want to examine more than one sheet in the same workbook simultaneously. You can accomplish either of these actions by opening a new view to the workbook, using one or more additional windows.

FIGURE 14-5

You can zoom in or out for a different view of your worksheets.

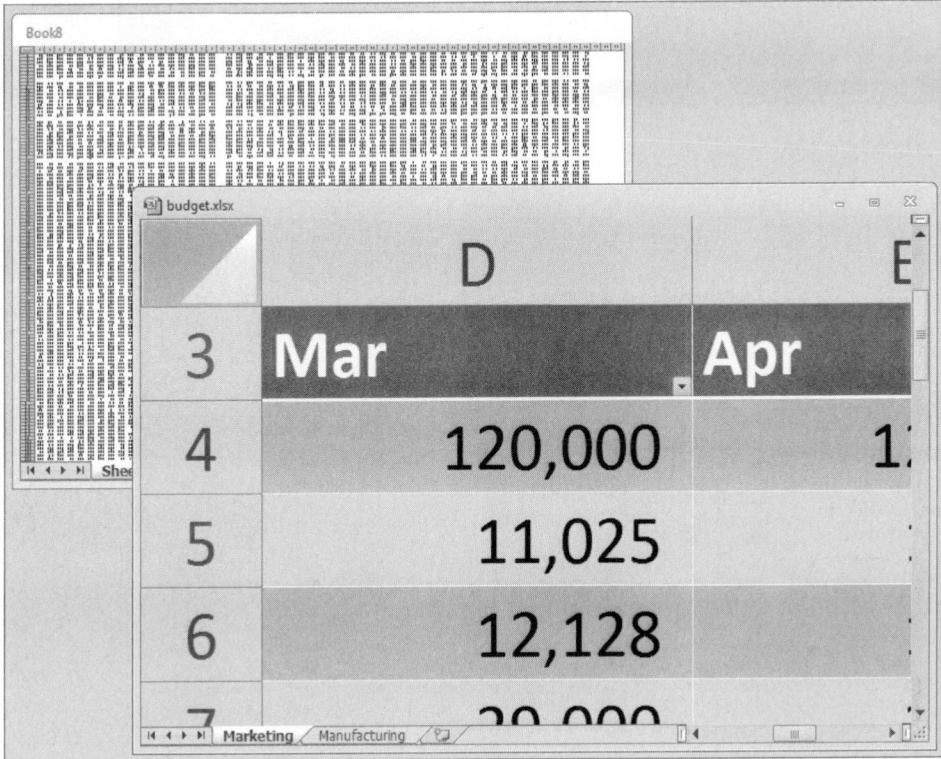

To create and display a new view of the active workbook, choose View ➪ Window ➪ New Window.

Excel displays a new window for the active workbook, similar to the one shown in Figure 14-6. In this case, each window shows a different worksheet in the workbook. Notice the text in the windows' title bars: *climate data.xlsx:1* and *climate data.xlsx:2*. To help you keep track of the windows, Excel appends a colon and a number to each window.

Tip

If the workbook is maximized when you create a new window, you may not even notice that Excel created the new window. If you look at the Excel title bar, though, you'll see that the workbook title now has *:2* appended to the name. Choose View ➪ Window ➪ Arrange All and choose one of the Arrange options in the Arrange Windows dialog box to display the open windows. If you select the Windows of Active Workbook checkbox, only the windows of the active workbook are arranged. ∎

FIGURE 14-6

Use multiple windows to view different sections of a workbook at the same time.

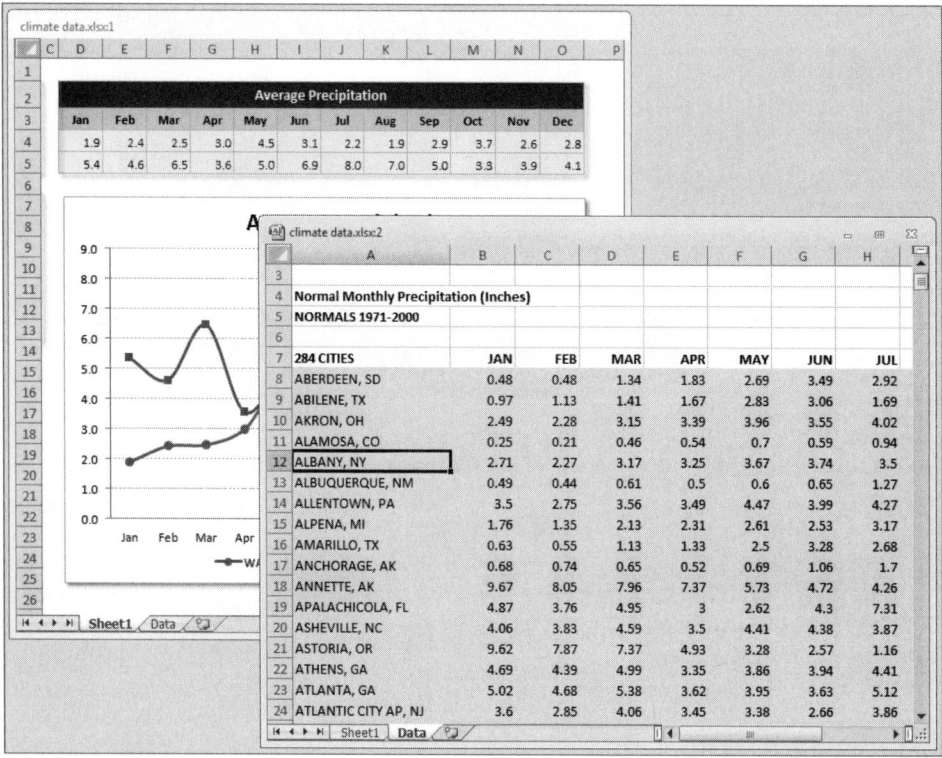

A single workbook can have as many views (i.e., separate windows) as you want. Each window is independent. In other words, scrolling to a new location in one window doesn't cause scrolling in the other window(s). However, if you make changes to the worksheet shown in a particular window, those changes are also made in all views of that worksheet.

You can close these additional windows when you no longer need them. For example, clicking the Close button on the active window's title bar closes the active window but doesn't close the other windows for the workbook.

Tip

Multiple windows make copying or moving information from one worksheet to another easier. You can use Excel's drag-and-drop procedures to copy or move ranges. ■

Comparing Sheets Side-by-Side

In some situations, you may want to compare two worksheets that are in different windows. The View Side by Side feature makes this task a bit easier.

First, make sure that the two sheets are displayed in separate windows. (The sheets can be in the same workbook or in different workbooks.) If you want to compare two sheets in the same workbook, choose View ➪ Window ➪ New Window to create a new window for the active workbook. Activate the first window; then choose View ➪ Window ➪ View Side by Side. If more than two windows are open, you see a dialog box that lets you select the window for the comparison. The two windows appear next to each other.

When using the View Side by Side feature, scrolling in one of the windows also scrolls the other window. If you don't want this simultaneous scrolling, choose View ➪ Window ➪ Synchronous Scrolling (which is a toggle). If you have rearranged or moved the windows, choose View ➪ Window ➪ Reset Window Position to restore the windows to the initial side-by-side arrangement. To turn off the side-by-side viewing, choose View ➪ Window ➪ View Side by Side again.

Keep in mind that this feature is for manual comparison only. Unfortunately, Excel doesn't provide a way to actually point out the differences between two sheets.

Splitting the Worksheet Window into Panes

If you prefer not to clutter your screen with additional windows, Excel provides another option for viewing multiple parts of the same worksheet. Choosing View ➪ Window ➪ Split splits the active worksheet into two or four separate panes. The split occurs at the location of the cell pointer. If the cell pointer is in row 1 or column A (but not cell A1), this command results in a two-pane split. Otherwise, it gives you four panes. You can use the mouse to drag the individual panes to resize them.

Figure 14-7 shows a worksheet split into two panes. Notice that row numbers aren't continuous. The top pane shows rows 8 through 21, and the bottom pane shows rows 1020 through 1029. In other words, splitting panes enables you to display widely separated areas of a worksheet in a single window. To remove the split panes, choose View ➪ Window ➪ Split again.

Keeping the Titles in View by Freezing Panes

If you set up a worksheet with row or column headings, these headings will not be visible when you scroll down or to the right (unless you are in a table, which you'll learn about later). Excel provides a handy solution to this problem: freezing panes. Freezing panes keeps the headings visible while you're scrolling through the worksheet.

To freeze panes, start by moving the cell pointer to the cell below the row that you want to remain visible while you scroll vertically, and to the right of the column that you want to remain visible while you scroll horizontally. Then, choose View ➪ Window ➪ Freeze Panes, and select the Freeze Panes option from the drop-down list. Excel inserts dark lines to indicate the frozen rows and columns. The frozen row and column remain visible while you scroll throughout the worksheet. To remove the frozen panes, choose View ➪ Window ➪ Freeze Panes, and select the Unfreeze Panes option from the drop-down list.

FIGURE 14-7

You can split the worksheet window into two or four panes to view different areas of the worksheet at the same time.

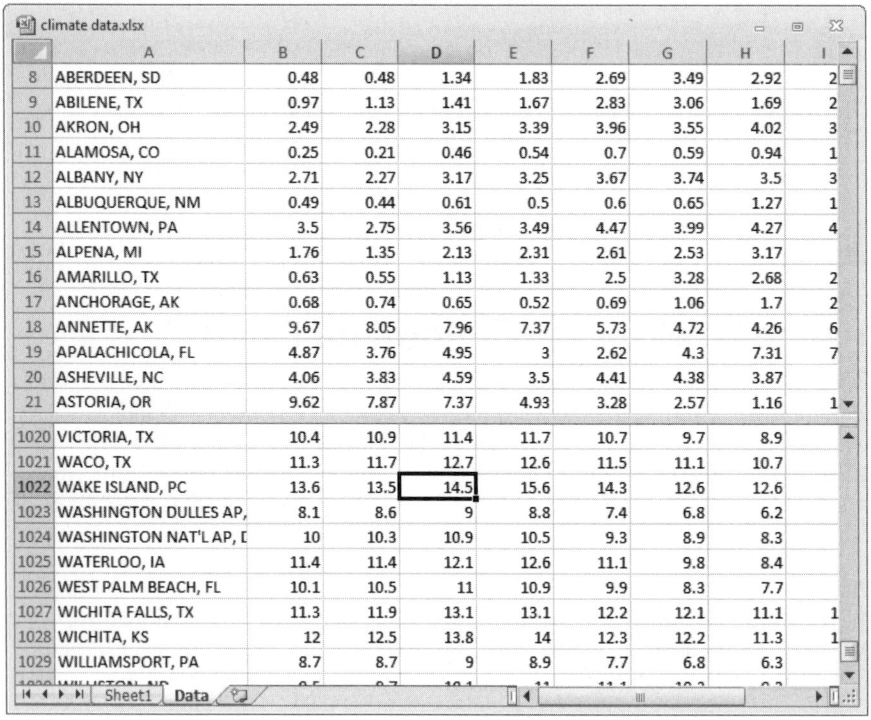

climate data.xlsx								
	A	B	C	D	E	F	G	H	I
8	ABERDEEN, SD	0.48	0.48	1.34	1.83	2.69	3.49	2.92	2
9	ABILENE, TX	0.97	1.13	1.41	1.67	2.83	3.06	1.69	2
10	AKRON, OH	2.49	2.28	3.15	3.39	3.96	3.55	4.02	3
11	ALAMOSA, CO	0.25	0.21	0.46	0.54	0.7	0.59	0.94	1
12	ALBANY, NY	2.71	2.27	3.17	3.25	3.67	3.74	3.5	3
13	ALBUQUERQUE, NM	0.49	0.44	0.61	0.5	0.6	0.65	1.27	1
14	ALLENTOWN, PA	3.5	2.75	3.56	3.49	4.47	3.99	4.27	4
15	ALPENA, MI	1.76	1.35	2.13	2.31	2.61	2.53	3.17	
16	AMARILLO, TX	0.63	0.55	1.13	1.33	2.5	3.28	2.68	2
17	ANCHORAGE, AK	0.68	0.74	0.65	0.52	0.69	1.06	1.7	2
18	ANNETTE, AK	9.67	8.05	7.96	7.37	5.73	4.72	4.26	6
19	APALACHICOLA, FL	4.87	3.76	4.95	3	2.62	4.3	7.31	7
20	ASHEVILLE, NC	4.06	3.83	4.59	3.5	4.41	4.38	3.87	
21	ASTORIA, OR	9.62	7.87	7.37	4.93	3.28	2.57	1.16	1
1020	VICTORIA, TX	10.4	10.9	11.4	11.7	10.7	9.7	8.9	
1021	WACO, TX	11.3	11.7	12.7	12.6	11.5	11.1	10.7	
1022	WAKE ISLAND, PC	13.6	13.5	14.5	15.6	14.3	12.6	12.6	
1023	WASHINGTON DULLES AP,	8.1	8.6	9	8.8	7.4	6.8	6.2	
1024	WASHINGTON NAT'L AP, [	10	10.3	10.9	10.5	9.3	8.9	8.3	
1025	WATERLOO, IA	11.4	11.4	12.1	12.6	11.1	9.8	8.4	
1026	WEST PALM BEACH, FL	10.1	10.5	11	10.9	9.9	8.3	7.7	
1027	WICHITA FALLS, TX	11.3	11.9	13.1	13.1	12.2	12.1	11.1	1
1028	WICHITA, KS	12	12.5	13.8	14	12.3	12.2	11.3	1
1029	WILLIAMSPORT, PA	8.7	8.7	9	8.9	7.7	6.8	6.3	

Sheet1 | Data

Figure 14-8 shows a worksheet with frozen panes. In this case, rows 1 through 4 and column A are frozen in place. This technique allows you to scroll down and to the right to locate some information while keeping the column titles and the column A entries visible.

The vast majority of the time, you'll want to freeze either the first row or the first column. The View ➪ Window ➪ Freeze Panes drop-down list has two additional options: Freeze Top Row and Freeze First Column. Using these commands eliminates the need to position the cell pointer before freezing panes.

FIGURE 14-8

Freeze certain columns and rows to make them remain visible while you scroll the worksheet.

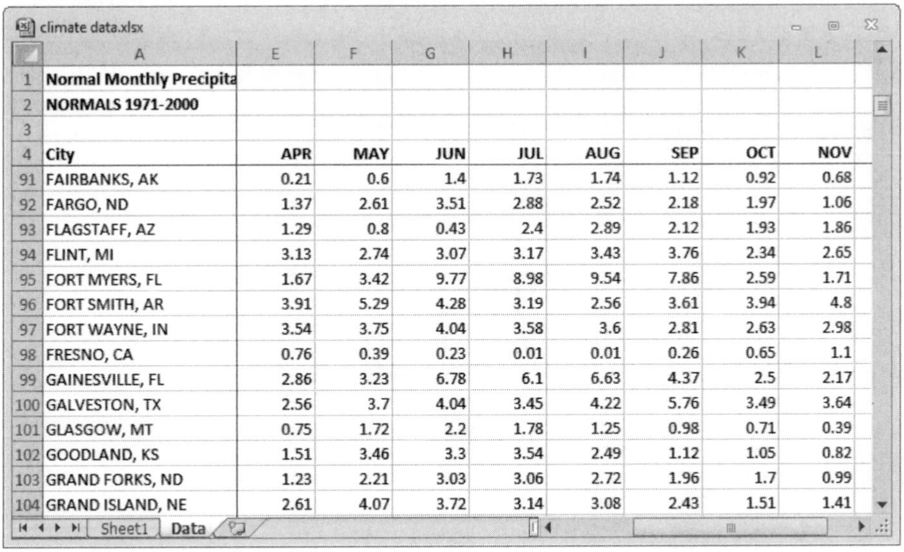

	A	E	F	G	H	I	J	K	L
1	Normal Monthly Precipita								
2	NORMALS 1971-2000								
3									
4	City	APR	MAY	JUN	JUL	AUG	SEP	OCT	NOV
91	FAIRBANKS, AK	0.21	0.6	1.4	1.73	1.74	1.12	0.92	0.68
92	FARGO, ND	1.37	2.61	3.51	2.88	2.52	2.18	1.97	1.06
93	FLAGSTAFF, AZ	1.29	0.8	0.43	2.4	2.89	2.12	1.93	1.86
94	FLINT, MI	3.13	2.74	3.07	3.17	3.43	3.76	2.34	2.65
95	FORT MYERS, FL	1.67	3.42	9.77	8.98	9.54	7.86	2.59	1.71
96	FORT SMITH, AR	3.91	5.29	4.28	3.19	2.56	3.61	3.94	4.8
97	FORT WAYNE, IN	3.54	3.75	4.04	3.58	3.6	2.81	2.63	2.98
98	FRESNO, CA	0.76	0.39	0.23	0.01	0.01	0.26	0.65	1.1
99	GAINESVILLE, FL	2.86	3.23	6.78	6.1	6.63	4.37	2.5	2.17
100	GALVESTON, TX	2.56	3.7	4.04	3.45	4.22	5.76	3.49	3.64
101	GLASGOW, MT	0.75	1.72	2.2	1.78	1.25	0.98	0.71	0.39
102	GOODLAND, KS	1.51	3.46	3.3	3.54	2.49	1.12	1.05	0.82
103	GRAND FORKS, ND	1.23	2.21	3.03	3.06	2.72	1.96	1.7	0.99
104	GRAND ISLAND, NE	2.61	4.07	3.72	3.14	3.08	2.43	1.51	1.41

Tip

If you designated a range to be a table (by choosing Insert ⇨ Tables ⇨ Table), you may not even need to freeze panes. When you scroll down, Excel displays the table column headings in place of the column letters. Figure 14-9 shows an example. The table headings replace the column letters only when a cell within the table is selected. ■

Monitoring Cells with a Watch Window

In some situations, you may want to monitor the value in a particular cell as you work. As you scroll through the worksheet, that cell may disappear from view. A feature known as *Watch Window* can help. A Watch Window displays the value of any number of cells in a handy window that's always visible.

To display the Watch Window, choose Formulas ⇨ Formula Auditing ⇨ Watch Window. The Watch Window appears in the task pane, but you can also drag it and make it float over the worksheet.

To add a cell to watch, click Add Watch and specify the cell that you want to watch. The Watch Window displays the value in that cell. You can add any number of cells to the Watch Window, and you can move the window to any convenient location. Figure 14-10 shows the Watch Window monitoring four cells.

FIGURE 14-9

When using a table, scrolling down displays the table headings where the column letters normally appear.

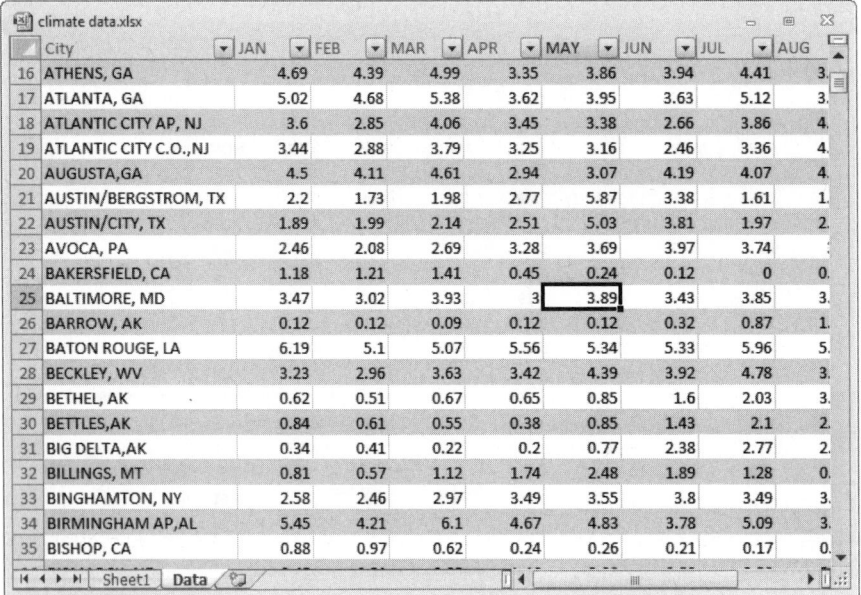

	City	JAN	FEB	MAR	APR	MAY	JUN	JUL	AUG
16	ATHENS, GA	4.69	4.39	4.99	3.35	3.86	3.94	4.41	3.
17	ATLANTA, GA	5.02	4.68	5.38	3.62	3.95	3.63	5.12	3.
18	ATLANTIC CITY AP, NJ	3.6	2.85	4.06	3.45	3.38	2.66	3.86	4.
19	ATLANTIC CITY C.O.,NJ	3.44	2.88	3.79	3.25	3.16	2.46	3.36	4.
20	AUGUSTA,GA	4.5	4.11	4.61	2.94	3.07	4.19	4.07	4.
21	AUSTIN/BERGSTROM, TX	2.2	1.73	1.98	2.77	5.87	3.38	1.61	1.
22	AUSTIN/CITY, TX	1.89	1.99	2.14	2.51	5.03	3.81	1.97	2.
23	AVOCA, PA	2.46	2.08	2.69	3.28	3.69	3.97	3.74	
24	BAKERSFIELD, CA	1.18	1.21	1.41	0.45	0.24	0.12	0	0.
25	BALTIMORE, MD	3.47	3.02	3.93	3	3.89	3.43	3.85	3.
26	BARROW, AK	0.12	0.12	0.09	0.12	0.12	0.32	0.87	1.
27	BATON ROUGE, LA	6.19	5.1	5.07	5.56	5.34	5.33	5.96	5.
28	BECKLEY, WV	3.23	2.96	3.63	3.42	4.39	3.92	4.78	3.
29	BETHEL, AK	0.62	0.51	0.67	0.65	0.85	1.6	2.03	3.
30	BETTLES,AK	0.84	0.61	0.55	0.38	0.85	1.43	2.1	2.
31	BIG DELTA,AK	0.34	0.41	0.22	0.2	0.77	2.38	2.77	2.
32	BILLINGS, MT	0.81	0.57	1.12	1.74	2.48	1.89	1.28	0.
33	BINGHAMTON, NY	2.58	2.46	2.97	3.49	3.55	3.8	3.49	3.
34	BIRMINGHAM AP,AL	5.45	4.21	6.1	4.67	4.83	3.78	5.09	3.
35	BISHOP, CA	0.88	0.97	0.62	0.24	0.26	0.21	0.17	0.

Sheet1 | **Data**

FIGURE 14-10

Use the Watch Window to monitor the value in one or more cells.

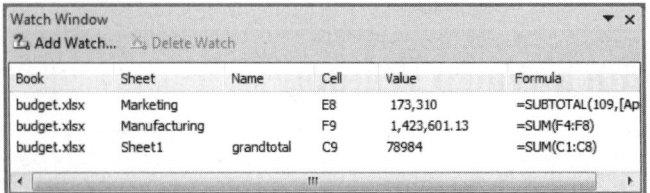

Watch Window
Add Watch...   Delete Watch

Book	Sheet	Name	Cell	Value	Formula
budget.xlsx	Marketing		E8	173,310	=SUBTOTAL(109,[Ap
budget.xlsx	Manufacturing		F9	1,423,601.13	=SUM(F4:F8)
budget.xlsx	Sheet1	grandtotal	C9	78984	=SUM(C1:C8)

Tip

Double-click on a cell in the Watch Window to immediately select that cell. ■

Working with Rows and Columns

This section discusses worksheet operations that involve complete rows and columns (rather than individual cells). Every worksheet has exactly 1,048,576 rows and 16,384 columns, and these values can't be changed.

Note

If you open a workbook that was created in a version of Excel prior to Excel 2007, the workbook is opened in Compatibility Mode. These workbooks have 65,536 rows and 256 columns. To increase the number of rows and columns, save the workbook as an Excel 2010 .xlsx file and then reopen it. ∎

Inserting Rows and Columns

Although the number of rows and columns in a worksheet is fixed, you can still insert and delete rows and columns if you need to make room for additional information. These operations don't change the total number of available rows or columns, rather, inserting a new row moves down the other rows to accommodate the new row. The last row is simply removed from the worksheet if it's empty. Inserting a new column shifts the columns to the right, and the last column is removed if it is empty.

Note

If the last row isn't empty, you can't insert a new row. Similarly, if the last column contains information, Excel doesn't let you insert a new column. Attempting to add a row or column in such cases displays a warning dialog box. Click OK and then remove the contents of the non-blank cells to continue. ∎

To insert a new row or rows, you can:

- Select an entire row or multiple rows by clicking the row numbers in the worksheet border. Right-click and choose Insert from the shortcut menu.

- Move the cell pointer to the row that you want to insert and then choose Home ➪ Cells ➪ Insert ➪ Insert Sheet Rows. If you select multiple cells in the column, Excel inserts additional rows that correspond to the number of cells selected in the column and moves the rows below the insertion down.

The procedures for inserting a new column or columns is similar, but you choose Home ➪ Cells ➪ Insert ➪ Insert Sheet Columns.

You also can insert cells, rather than just rows or columns. Select the range into which you want to add new cells and then choose Home ➪ Cells ➪ Insert ➪ Insert Cells (or right-click on the selection and choose Insert). To insert cells, the existing cells must be shifted to the right or shifted down. Therefore, Excel displays the Insert dialog box shown in Figure 14-11 so that you can specify the direction in which you want to shift the cells.

FIGURE 14-11

You can insert partial rows or columns by using the Insert dialog box.

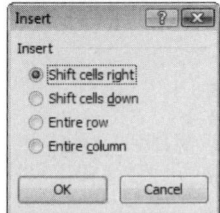

Deleting Rows and Columns

You may also want to delete rows or columns in a worksheet. For example, your sheet may contain old data that is no longer needed.

To delete a row or rows, use either of these methods:

- Select an entire row or multiple rows by clicking on the row numbers in the worksheet border. Right-click and choose Delete from the shortcut menu.
- Move the cell pointer to the row that you want to delete, and then choose Home ➪ Cells ➪ Delete Sheet Rows. If you select multiple cells in the column, Excel deletes all rows in the selection.

Deleting columns works in a similar way. If you discover that you accidentally deleted a row or column, select Undo from the Quick Access Toolbar (or press Ctrl+Z) to undo the action.

Hiding Rows and Columns

In some cases, you may want to hide particular rows or columns. Hiding rows and columns may be useful if you don't want users to see particular information, or if you need to print a report that summarizes the information in the worksheet without showing all the details.

To hide rows or columns in your worksheet, select the row or rows that you want to hide by clicking in the row or column header. Then right-click and choose Hide from the shortcut menu. Or, you can use the commands on the Home ➪ Cells ➪ Format ➪ Hide & Unhide drop-down list.

A hidden row is actually a row with its height set to zero. Similarly, a hidden column has a column width of zero. When you use the navigation keys to move the cell pointer, cells in hidden rows or columns are skipped. In other words, you can't use the navigation keys to move to a cell in a hidden row or column.

Unhiding a hidden row or column can be a bit tricky because selecting a row or column that's hidden is difficult. The solution is to select the columns or rows that are adjacent to the hidden column or row. (Select at least one column or row on either side.) Then right-click and choose Unhide. For example, if column G is hidden, select columns F and H.

Another method is to choose Home ➪ Editing ➪ Find & Select ➪ Go To (or press F5) to select a cell in a hidden row or column. For example, if column A is hidden, you can press F5 and specify cell A1 (or any other cell in column A) to move the cell pointer to the hidden column. Then you can choose Home ➪ Cells ➪ Format ➪ Hide & Unhide ➪ Unhide Columns.

Changing Column Widths and Row Heights

Often, you'll want to change the width of a column or the height of a row. For example, you can make columns narrower to accommodate more information on a printed page. Or you may want to increase row height to create a "double-spaced" effect.

Excel provides several different ways to change the widths of columns and the height of rows.

Changing Column Widths

Column width is measured in terms of the number of characters of a *fixed pitch font* that will fit into the cell's width. By default, each column's width is 8.43 units, which equates to 64 pixels (px).

Tip

If hash marks (#) fill a cell that contains a numerical value, the column isn't wide enough to accommodate the information in the cell. Widen the column to solve the problem. ■

Before you change the column width, you can select multiple columns so that the width will be the same for all selected columns. To select multiple columns, either click-and-drag in the column border or press Ctrl while you select individual columns. To select all columns, click the button where the row and column headers intersect. You can change column widths by using any of the following techniques:

- Drag the right column border with the mouse until the column is the desired width.
- Choose Home ➪ Cells ➪ Format ➪ Column Width, and enter a value in the Column Width dialog box.
- Choose Home ➪ Cells ➪ Format ➪ AutoFit Column Width to adjust the width of the selected column so that the widest entry in the column fits. Rather than selecting an entire column, you can just select cells in the column, and the column is adjusted based on the widest entry in your selection.
- Double-click on the right border of a column header to set the column width automatically to the widest entry in the column.

Tip

To change the default width of all columns, choose Home ➪ Cells ➪ Format ➪ Default Width. This command displays a dialog box into which you enter the new default column width. All columns that haven't been previously adjusted take on the new column width. ■

Caution

After you manually adjust a column's width, Excel will no longer automatically adjust the column to accommodate longer numerical entries. You need to change the column width manually. ■

Changing Row Heights

Row height is measured in points (a standard unit of measurement in the printing trade — 72 pt is equal to 1 inch). The default row height using the default font is 15 pt, or 20 px.

The default row height can vary, depending on the font defined in the Normal style. In addition, Excel automatically adjusts row heights to accommodate the tallest font in the row. So, if you change the font size of a cell to 20 pt, for example, Excel makes the row taller so that the entire text is visible.

You can set the row height manually, however, by using any of the following techniques. As with columns, you can select multiple rows.

- Drag the lower row border with the mouse until the row is the desired height.
- Choose Home ➪ Cells ➪ Format ➪ Row Height, and enter a value (in points) in the Row Height dialog box.
- Double-click on the bottom border of a row to set the row height automatically to the tallest entry in the row. You also can choose Home ➪ Cells ➪ Format ➪ AutoFit Row Height for this task.

Changing the row height is useful for spacing out rows and is almost always preferable to inserting empty rows between lines of data.

Understanding Cells and Ranges

Most of the work you do in Excel involves cells and ranges. Understanding how best to manipulate cells and ranges will save you time and effort. The remainder of this chapter discusses a variety of techniques that you can use to help increase your efficiency.

A *cell* is a single element in a worksheet that can hold a value, some text, or a formula. A cell is identified by its address, which consists of its column letter and row number. For example, cell D12 is the cell in the fourth column and the twelfth row.

A group of cells is called a *range*. You designate a range address by specifying its upper-left cell address and its lower-right cell address, separated by a colon.

Some examples of range addresses are shown in Table 14-1.

TABLE 14-1

Range Addresses

C24	A range that consists of a single cell (column C, row 24)
A1:B1	Two cells that occupy one row and two columns (row 1, columns A and B)
A1:A100	100 cells in column A
A1:D4	16 cells (four rows by four columns, rows 1 to 4, columns A to D)
C1:C1048576	An entire column of cells. This range also can be expressed as C:C.
A6:XFD6	An entire row of cells. This range also can be expressed as 6:6.
A1:XFD1048576	All cells in a worksheet. This range also can be expressed as either A:XFD or 1:1048576.

Selecting Ranges

To perform an operation on a range of cells in a worksheet, you must first select the range. For example, if you want to make the text bold for a range of cells, you must select the range and then choose Home ➪ Font ➪ Bold (or press Ctrl+B).

When you select a range, the cells appear highlighted. The exception is the active cell, which remains its normal color. Figure 14-12 shows an example of a selected range (B5:C8) in a worksheet. Cell B5, the active cell, is selected but not highlighted.

FIGURE 14-12

When you select a range, it appears highlighted, but the active cell within the range is not highlighted.

	A	B	C	D	E
1	Product	Sold By	Month		
2	Widget	Gomez	January		
3	Widget	Gomez	March		
4	Sprocket	Gomez	January		
5	Widget	Gomez	March		
6	Sprocket	Gomez	February		
7	Sprocket	Gomez	January		
8	Sprocket	Gomez	March		
9	Widget	Gomez	March		
10	Widget	Gomez	January		
11	Sprocket	Gomez	March		
12	Sprocket	Jones	March		
13	Sprocket	Jones	February		

You can select a range in several ways:

- Press and hold the left mouse button and drag, highlighting the range. Then release the mouse button. If you drag to the end of the screen, the worksheet will scroll.

- Press the Shift key while you use the arrow keys to select a range.

- Press F8 and then move the cell pointer with the arrow keys to highlight the range. Press F8 again to return the arrow keys to normal movement.

- Type the cell or range address into the Name box and press Enter. Excel selects the cell or range that you specified.

- Choose Home ➪ Editing ➪ Find & Select ➪ Go To (or press F5) and enter a range's address manually into the Go To dialog box. When you click OK, Excel selects the cells in the range that you specified.

Tip

While you're selecting a range, Excel displays the number of rows and columns in your selection in the Name box (located on the left side of the Formula bar). As soon as you finish the selection, the Name box reverts to showing the address of the active cell. ■

Selecting Complete Rows and Columns

Often, you'll need to select an entire row or column. For example, you may want to apply the same numerical format or the same alignment options to an entire row or column. You can select entire rows and columns in much the same manner as you select ranges:

- Click on the row or column border to select a single row or column.

- To select multiple adjacent rows or columns, click on a row or column border and drag to highlight additional rows or columns.

- To select multiple (nonadjacent) rows or columns, press Ctrl while you click on the row or column borders that you want.

- Press Ctrl+Spacebar to select a column. The column of the active cell (or columns of the selected cells) is highlighted.

- Press Shift+Spacebar to select a row. The row of the active cell (or rows of the selected cells) is highlighted.

Tip

Press Ctrl+A to select all cells in the worksheet, which is the same as selecting all rows and all columns. If the active cell is within a table, you may need to press Ctrl+A two or even three times to select all cells in the worksheet, as it will select table data first, select the header rows second, and select all the cells in the worksheet last. You can also click the area at the intersection of the row and column borders to select all cells. ■

Selecting Noncontiguous Ranges

Most of the time, the ranges that you select are *contiguous* — a single rectangle of cells. Excel also enables you to work with noncontiguous ranges, which consist of two or more ranges (or single cells) that aren't next to each other. Selecting noncontiguous ranges is also known as a *multiple selection*. If you want to apply the same formatting to cells in different areas of your worksheet, one approach is to make a multiple selection. When the appropriate cells or ranges are selected, the formatting that you select is applied to them all. Figure 14-13 shows a noncontiguous range selected in a worksheet. Three ranges are selected: A2:C3, A5:C5, and A9:C10.

You can select a noncontiguous range in several ways:

- Select the first range (or cell). Then press and hold Ctrl as you drag the mouse to highlight additional cells or ranges.

- From the keyboard, select a range as described previously (using F8 or the Shift key). Then press Shift+F8 to select another range without canceling the previous range selections.

- Enter the range (or cell) address in the Name box and press Enter. Separate each range address with a comma.

- Choose Home ➪ Editing ➪ Find & Select ➪ Go To (or press F5) to display the Go To dialog box. Enter the range (or cell) address in the Reference box, and separate each range address with a comma. Click OK, and Excel selects the ranges.

FIGURE 14-13

Excel enables you to select noncontiguous ranges.

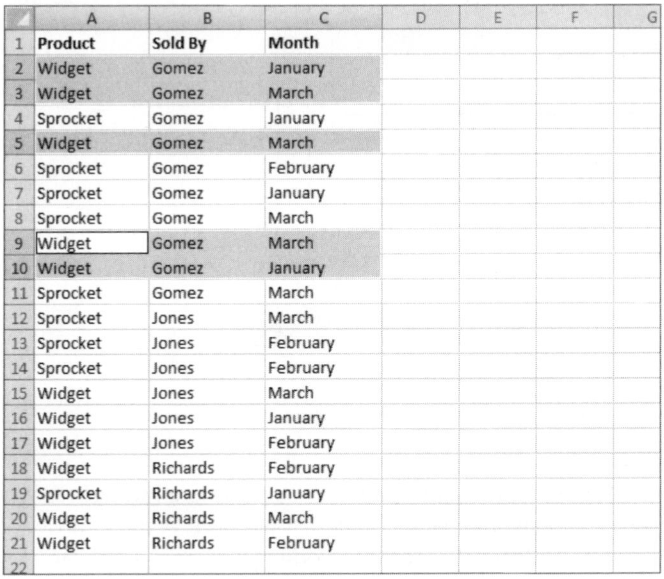

	A	B	C	D	E	F	G
1	Product	Sold By	Month				
2	Widget	Gomez	January				
3	Widget	Gomez	March				
4	Sprocket	Gomez	January				
5	Widget	Gomez	March				
6	Sprocket	Gomez	February				
7	Sprocket	Gomez	January				
8	Sprocket	Gomez	March				
9	Widget	Gomez	March				
10	Widget	Gomez	January				
11	Sprocket	Gomez	March				
12	Sprocket	Jones	March				
13	Sprocket	Jones	February				
14	Sprocket	Jones	February				
15	Widget	Jones	March				
16	Widget	Jones	January				
17	Widget	Jones	February				
18	Widget	Richards	February				
19	Sprocket	Richards	January				
20	Widget	Richards	March				
21	Widget	Richards	February				
22							

Note

Noncontiguous ranges differ from contiguous ranges in several important ways. One obvious difference is that you can't use drag-and-drop methods (described later) to move or copy noncontiguous ranges. ■

Selecting Multisheet Ranges

In addition to two-dimensional (2-D) ranges on a single worksheet, ranges can extend across multiple worksheets to be 3-D ranges.

Suppose that you have a workbook set up to track budgets. A common approach is to use a separate worksheet for each department, making it easy to organize the data. You can click a sheet tab to view the information for a particular department.

Say you have a workbook with four sheets: Totals, Operations, Marketing, and Manufacturing. The sheets are laid out identically. The only difference is the values. The Totals sheet contains formulas that compute the sum of the corresponding items in the three departmental worksheets.

Assume that you want to apply formatting to the sheets — for example, make the column headings bold with background shading. One (albeit not-so-efficient) approach is to format the cells in each worksheet separately. A better technique is to select a multisheet range and format the cells in all the sheets simultaneously. The following is a step-by-step example of multisheet formatting, using the workbook shown in Figure 14-14.

FIGURE 14-14

In Group mode, you can work with a 3-D range of cells that extend across multiple worksheets.

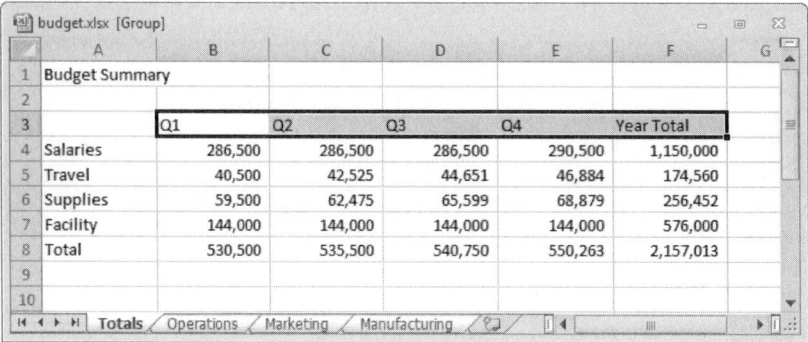

1. Activate the Totals worksheet by clicking its tab.

2. Select the range B3:F3.

3. **Press Shift and click the Manufacturing sheet tab.** This step selects all worksheets between the active worksheet (Totals) and the sheet tab that you click — in essence, a 3-D range of cells (see Figure 14-14). Notice that the workbook window's title bar displays [Group] to remind you that you've selected a group of sheets and that you're in Group mode.

4. **Choose Home ⇨ Font ⇨ Bold, and then choose Home ⇨ Font ⇨ Fill Color to apply a colored background.** Excel applies the formatting to the selected range across the selected sheets.

5. **Click one of the other sheet tabs.** This step selects the sheet and also cancels Group mode; [Group] is no longer displayed in the title bar.

When a workbook is in Group mode, any changes that you make to cells in one worksheet also apply to all the other grouped worksheets. You can use this to your advantage when you want to set up a group of identical worksheets because any labels, data, formatting, or formulas you enter are automatically added to the same cells in all the grouped worksheets.

Note

When Excel is in Group mode, some commands are disabled and can't be used. In the preceding example, for example, you can't convert all these ranges to tables by choosing Insert ⇨ Tables ⇨ Table. ∎

In general, selecting a multisheet range is a simple two-step process: select the range in one sheet, and then select the worksheets to include in the range. To select a group of contiguous worksheets, you can press Shift and click the sheet tab of the last worksheet that you want to include in the selection. To select individual worksheets, press Ctrl and click the sheet tab of each worksheet that you want to select. If all the worksheets in a workbook aren't laid out the same, you can skip the sheets that you don't want to format. When you make the selection, the sheet tabs of the selected sheets appear with a white background, and Excel displays [Group] in the title bar.

Tip

To select all sheets in a workbook, right-click on any sheet tab, and choose Select All Sheets from the shortcut menu. ■

Selecting Special Types of Cells

As you use Excel, you may need to locate specific types of cells in your worksheets. For example, wouldn't it be handy to be able to locate every cell that contains a formula — or perhaps all the cells whose value depends on the current cell? Excel provides an easy way to locate these and many other special types of cells. Simply choose Home ➪ Editing ➪ Find & Select ➪ Go To Special to display the Go to Special dialog box, shown in Figure 14-15.

Use the Go to Special dialog box to select specific types of cells.

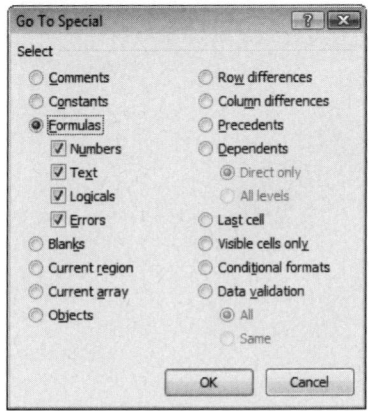

After you make your choice in the dialog box, Excel selects the qualifying subset of cells in the current selection. Often, this subset of cells is a multiple selection. If no cells qualify, Excel lets you know with the message "No cells were found."

Tip

If you bring up the Go to Special dialog box with only one cell selected, Excel bases its selection on the current worksheet. Otherwise, the selection is based on the selected range. ■

Tip

When you select an option in the Go to Special dialog box, be sure to note which suboptions become available. For example, when you select Constants, the suboptions under Formulas become available to help you further refine the results. Likewise, the suboptions under Dependents also apply to Precedents, and those under Data Validation also apply to Conditional Formats. ■

Selecting Cells by Searching

Another way to select cells is to use Home ➪ Editing ➪ Find & Select ➪ Find (or press Ctrl+F), which allows you to select cells by their contents. Click the Options button to display additional choices for refining the search.

Enter the text that you're looking for; then click Find All. The dialog box expands to display all the cells that match your search criteria. For example, Figure 14-16 shows the dialog box after Excel has located all cells that contain the text *March*. You can click on an item in the list, and the screen will scroll so that you can view the cell in context. To select all the cells in the list, first select any single item in the list. Then press Ctrl+A to select them all. Note that the Find and Replace dialog box allows you to return to the worksheet without dismissing the dialog box.

FIGURE 14-16

The Find and Replace dialog box, with its results listed.

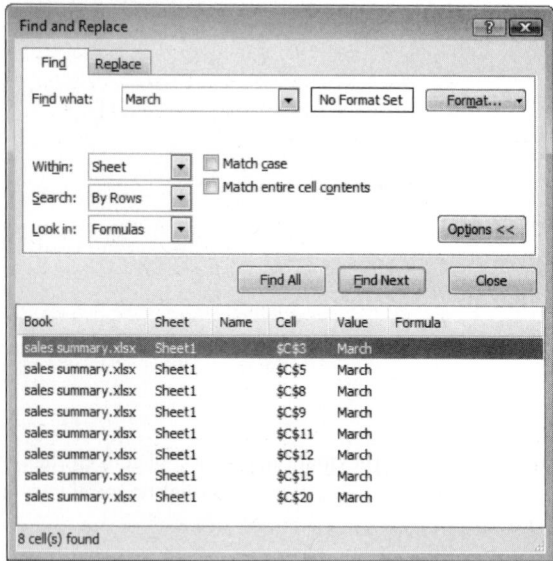

Tip

You can use the ? (matches a single character) or * (matches multiple characters) wildcards to search. To search for a question mark or an asterisk, precede the character with a tilde character (~). ■

Copying or Moving Ranges

As you create a worksheet, you may find it necessary to copy or move information from one location to another. Excel makes copying or moving ranges of cells easy. Here are some common things you might do:

- Copy a cell to another cell.
- Copy a cell to a range of cells. The source cell is copied to every cell in the destination range.
- Copy a range to another range. Both ranges must be the same size.
- Move a range of cells to another location.

The primary difference between copying and moving a range is the effect of the operation on the source range. When you copy a range, the source range is unaffected. When you move a range, the contents are removed from the source range.

Note

Copying a cell normally copies the cell's contents, any formatting that is applied to the original cell (including conditional formatting and data validation), and the cell comment (if it has one). When you copy a cell that contains a formula, the cell references in the copied formulas are changed automatically to be relative to their new destination (unless you have formatted the cell references to be absolute). ∎

Copying or moving consists of two steps (although shortcut methods do exist):

1. Select the cell or range to copy (the source range) and copy it to the Clipboard. To move the range instead of copying it, cut the range rather than copying it.

2. Move the cell pointer to the range that will hold the copy (the destination range) and paste the Clipboard contents.

Caution

When you paste information, Excel overwrites any cells that get in the way without warning you. If you find that pasting overwrote some essential cells, choose Undo from the Quick Access Toolbar (or press Ctrl+Z). ∎

Note

When you copy a cell or range, Excel surrounds the copied area with an animated border (sometimes referred to as *marching ants*). As long as that border remains animated, the copied information is available for pasting. If you press Esc to cancel the animated border, Excel removes the information from the Clipboard. ∎

Because copying (or moving) is used so often, Excel provides many different methods. I discuss each method in the following sections. Copying and moving are similar operations, so I point out only important differences between the two.

Copying by Using Ribbon Commands

Choosing Home ⇨ Clipboard ⇨ Copy transfers a copy of the selected cell or range to the Windows Clipboard and the Office Clipboard. After performing the copy part of this operation, select the cell that will hold the copy and choose Home ⇨ Clipboard ⇨ Paste.

Rather than choosing Home ⇨ Clipboard ⇨ Paste, you can just activate the destination cell and press Enter. If you use this technique, Excel removes the copied information from the Clipboard so that it can't be pasted again. If you're copying a range, you don't need to select an entire same-sized range before you click the Paste button. You need only activate the upper-left cell in the destination range.

Note

If you click the Copy button more than once before you click the Paste button, Excel may automatically display the Office Clipboard task pane. To prevent this pane from appearing, click the Options button at the bottom and then click Show Office Clipboard Automatically. You can display the Office Clipboard when needed by clicking the Dialog Box Launcher icon in the bottom-right corner of the Home ⇨ Clipboard group. Chapter 3 explains how to use the Clipboard. ∎

New Feature

The Home ⇨ Clipboard ⇨ Paste control contains a drop-down arrow that, when clicked, gives you additional Paste Option icons. The Paste Preview icons are new to Excel 2010. These icons are explained later in this chapter (see "Pasting in Special Ways"). The difference is that you can preview how the pasted information will appear.

Copying by Using Shortcut Menu Commands

If you prefer, you can use the following shortcut menu commands for copying and pasting:

- Right-click on the range, and choose Copy (or Cut) from the shortcut menu to copy the selected cells to the Clipboard.
- Right-click and choose Paste from the shortcut menu that appears to paste the Clipboard contents to the selected cell or range.

For more control over how the pasted information appears, use one of the buttons under Paste Options in the shortcut menu (see Figure 14-17).

The copy and paste operations also have shortcut keys associated with them:

- Ctrl+C copies the selected cells to both the Windows and Office Clipboards.
- Ctrl+X cuts the selected cells to both the Windows and Office Clipboards.
- Ctrl+V pastes the Windows Clipboard contents to the selected cell or range.

FIGURE 14-17

The Paste Icons on the shortcut menu provide more control over how the pasted information appears.

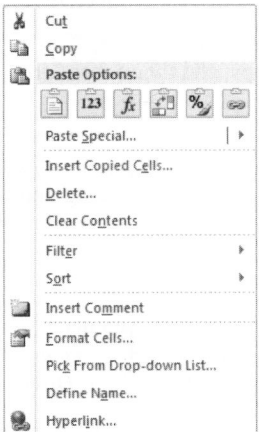

Tip

Most other Windows applications also use these shortcut keys. ∎

Using Paste Options Buttons When Inserting and Pasting

Some cell and range operations — specifically inserting, pasting, and filling cells by dragging — result in the display of an Options button. Clicking the Options button displays choices for completing the insert or paste, such as whether to keep the original formatting from the copied material. For example, if you copy a range and then paste it to a different location, a Paste Options button appears at the lower-right of the pasted range. Click the Paste Options button (or press Ctrl), and you see choices that enable you to specify how the data should be pasted, such as values only or formatting only.

Some users find these Options buttons helpful, and others think that they're annoying. (Count me in the latter group.) To turn off these Options buttons, choose File ➪ Options and click Advanced in the list at the left. Remove the check marks from the two options under Cut, Copy, and Paste labeled Show Paste Options Buttons When Content is Pasted and Show Insert Options Buttons, and then click OK.

Copying or Moving by Using Drag-and-Drop

Excel also enables you to copy or move a cell or range by dragging. Be aware, however, that dragging and dropping does not place any information on either the Windows Clipboard or the Office Clipboard.

Caution

The drag-and-drop method of moving does offer one advantage over the cut-and-paste method — Excel warns you if a drag-and-drop move operation will overwrite existing cell contents. However, you do *not* get a warning if a drag-and-drop copy operation will overwrite existing cell contents. ■

To *copy* using drag-and-drop, select the cell or range that you want to copy, and then press Ctrl and move the mouse to one of the selection's borders (the mouse arrow pointer is augmented with a small plus sign). Then, simply drag the selection to its new location while you continue to press the Ctrl key. The original selection remains behind, and Excel makes a new copy when you release the mouse button. To *move* a range using drag-and-drop, don't press Ctrl while dragging the border.

Tip

If the mouse pointer doesn't turn into an arrow when you point to the border of a cell or range, you need to make a change to your settings. Access the Excel Options (File ⇨ Options) dialog box, click Advanced in the list at the left, and place a check mark on the option labeled Enable Fill Handle and Cell Drag-and-Drop under Editing Options. Click OK to apply the change. ■

Copying to Adjacent Cells

Often, you need to copy a cell to an adjacent cell or range. This type of copying is quite common when working with formulas. For example, if you're working on a budget, you might create a formula to add the values in column B. You can use the same formula to add the values in the other columns. Rather than re-enter the formula, you can copy it to the adjacent cells.

Excel provides additional options for copying to adjacent cells. To use these commands, activate the cell that you're copying *and* extend the cell selection to include the cells that you're copying to. Then issue the appropriate command from the following list for one-step copying:

- Home ⇨ Editing ⇨ Fill ⇨ Down (or Ctrl+D) copies the cell to the selected range below.
- Home ⇨ Editing ⇨ Fill ⇨ Right (or Ctrl+R) copies the cell to the selected range to the right.
- Home ⇨ Editing ⇨ Fill ⇨ Up copies the cell to the selected range above.
- Home ⇨ Editing ⇨ Fill ⇨ Left copies the cell to the selected range to the left.

None of these commands places information on either the Windows Clipboard or the Office Clipboard.

Tip

You also can use Auto Fill to copy to adjacent cells by dragging the selection's fill handle (the small square in the bottom-right corner of the selected cell or range). Excel copies the original selection to the cells that you highlight while dragging. For more control over the Auto Fill operation, drag the fill handle with the right mouse button, and if you click the Auto Fill Options button, you'll get a shortcut menu with additional options after completing the Auto Fill. ■

Copying a Range to Other Sheets

You can use the copy procedures described previously to copy a cell or range to another worksheet, even if the worksheet is in a different workbook. You must, of course, activate the other worksheet before you select the location to which you want to copy.

Excel offers a quicker way to copy a cell or range and paste it to other worksheets in the same workbook.

1. **Select the range to copy.**

2. **Press Ctrl and click the sheet tabs for the worksheets to which you want to copy the information.** Excel displays [Group] in the workbook's title bar.

3. **Choose Home ⇨ Editing ⇨ Fill ⇨ Across Worksheets.** A dialog box appears to ask you what you want to copy (All, Contents, or Formats).

4. **Make your choice and then click OK.** Excel copies the selected range to the selected worksheets; the new copy occupies the same cells in the selected worksheets as the original occupies in the initial worksheet.

Caution

Be careful with the Home ⇨ Editing ⇨ Fill ⇨ Across Worksheets command because Excel doesn't warn you if the destination cells contain information. You can quickly overwrite lots of cells with this command and not realize it! Make sure you check your work, and use Undo if the result isn't what you expected. ■

Using the Office Clipboard to Paste

Whenever you cut or copy information in an Office program, such as Excel, you can place the data on both the Windows Clipboard and the Office Clipboard. When you copy information to the Office Clipboard, you append the information to the Office Clipboard instead of replacing what is already there. With multiple items stored on the Office Clipboard, you can then paste the items either individually or as a group.

To use the Office Clipboard, you first need to open it. Use the dialog launcher on the bottom right of the Home ⇨ Clipboard group to toggle the Clipboard task pane on and off.

Tip

To make the Clipboard task pane open automatically, click the Options button near the bottom of the task pane, and choose the Show Office Clipboard Automatically option. ■

After you open the Clipboard task pane, select the first cell or range that you want to copy to the Office Clipboard, and copy it by using any of the preceding techniques. Repeat this process, selecting the next cell or range that you want to copy. As soon as you copy the information, the Office Clipboard task pane shows you the number of items that you've copied and a brief description (it will hold up to 24 items). Figure 14-18 shows the Office Clipboard with four copied items.

FIGURE 14-18

Use the Clipboard task pane to copy-and-paste multiple items.

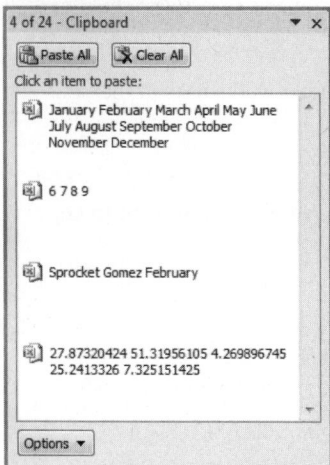

When you're ready to paste information, select the cell into which you want to paste information. To paste an individual item, click on it in the Clipboard task pane. To paste all the items that you've copied, click the Paste All button (which is at the top of the Clipboard task pane). The items are pasted, one after the other. The Paste All button is probably more useful in Word, for situations in which you copy text from various sources and then paste it all at once.

You can clear the contents of the Office Clipboard by clicking the Clear All button.

The following items about the Office Clipboard and its functioning are worth noting:

- Excel pastes the contents of the Windows Clipboard (the last item you copied to the Office Clipboard) when you paste by choosing Home ➪ Clipboard ➪ Paste, by pressing Ctrl+V, or by right-clicking and choosing Paste from the shortcut menu.

- The last item that you cut or copied appears on both the Office Clipboard and the Windows Clipboard.

- Pasting from the Office Clipboard also places that item on the Windows Clipboard. If you choose Paste All from the Office Clipboard toolbar, you paste all items stored on the Office Clipboard onto the Windows Clipboard as a single item.

- Clearing the Office Clipboard also clears the Windows Clipboard.

Caution
The Office Clipboard has a serious problem that makes it virtually worthless for Excel users: if you copy a range that contains formulas, the formulas are not transferred when you paste to a different range. Only the values are pasted. Furthermore, Excel doesn't even warn you about this fact. ∎

Pasting in Special Ways

You may not always want to copy everything from the source range to the destination range. For example, you may want to copy only the formula results rather than the formulas themselves. Or you may want to copy the number formats from one range to another without overwriting any existing data or formulas.

To control what is copied into the destination range, choose Home ⇨ Clipboard ⇨ Paste, and use the drop-down menu shown in Figure 14-19. When you hover your mouse pointer over an icon, you'll see a preview of the pasted information in the destination range. Click on the icon to use the selected Paste option.

FIGURE 14-19

Excel offers several pasting options, with preview. Here, the information is copied from D4:E7 and is being pasted beginning at cell D10.

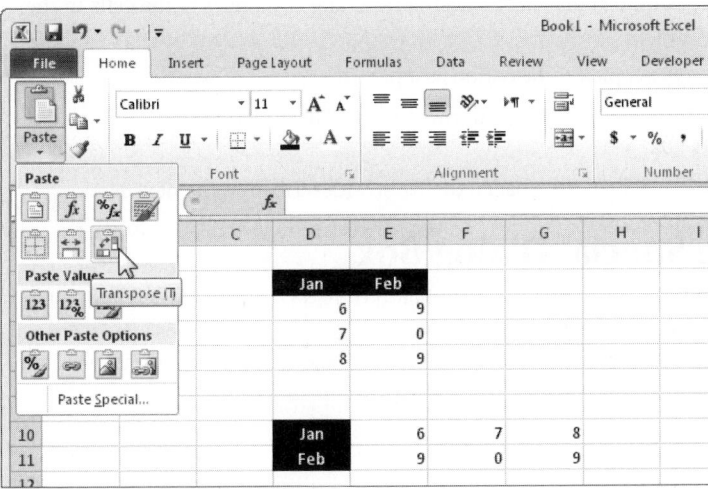

The Paste options are as follows:

- **Paste (P).** Pastes the cell's contents, formats, and data validation from the Windows Clipboard.

- **Formulas (F).** Pastes formulas, but not formatting.

- **Formulas & Number Formatting (O).** Pastes formulas and number formatting only.

- **Keep Source Formatting (K).** Pastes formulas and all formatting.

- **No Borders (B).** Pastes everything except borders that appear in the source range.

- **Keep Source Column Width (W).** Pastes formulas, and also duplicates the column width of the copied cells.

- **Transpose (T).** Changes the orientation of the copied range. Rows become columns, and columns become rows. Any formulas in the copied range are adjusted so that they work properly when transposed.

- **Merge Conditional Formatting (G).** This icon is displayed only when the copied cells contain conditional formatting. When clicked, it merges the copied conditional formatting with any conditional formatting in the destination range.

- **Values (V).** Pastes the results of formulas. The destination for the copy can be a new range or the original range. In the latter case, Excel replaces the original formulas with their current values.

- **Values & Number Formatting (A).** Pastes the results of formulas, plus the number formatting.

- **Values & Source Formatting (E).** Pastes the results of formulas, plus all formatting.

- **Formatting (R).** Pastes only the formatting of the source range.

- **Paste Link (N).** Creates formulas in the destination range that refer to the cells in the copied range.

- **Picture (U).** Pastes the copied information as a picture.

- **Linked Picture (I).** Pastes the copied information as a "live" picture that is updated if the source range is changed.

- **Paste Special.** Displays the Paste Special dialog box (described in the next section).

Using the Paste Special Dialog Box

For yet another pasting method, choose Home ⇨ Clipboard ⇨ Paste ⇨ Paste Special to display the Paste Special dialog box (see Figure 14-20). You can also right-click and choose Paste Special from the shortcut menu to display this dialog box. This dialog box has several options, which I explain in the following list.

Note
Excel actually has several different Paste Special dialog boxes, each with different options. The one displayed depends on what's copied. This section describes the Paste Special dialog box that appears when a range or cell has been copied. ∎

Tip
For the Paste Special command to be available, you need to copy a cell or range. (Choosing Home ⇨ Clipboard ⇨ Cut doesn't work.) ∎

- **All.** Pastes the cell's contents, formats, and data validation from the Windows Clipboard.

- **Formulas.** Pastes values and formulas, with no formatting.

- **Values.** Pastes values and the results of formulas (no formatting). The destination for the copy can be a new range or the original range. In the latter case, Excel replaces the original formulas with their current values.

- **Formats.** Copies only the formatting.

- **Comments.** Copies only the cell comments from a cell or range. This option doesn't copy cell contents or formatting.

- **Validation.** Copies the validation criteria so the same data validation will apply. Data validation is applied by choosing Data ➪ Data Tools ➪ Data Validation.

- **All Using Source Theme.** Pastes everything, but uses the formatting from the document theme of the source. This option is relevant only if you're pasting information from a different workbook and the workbook uses a different document theme from that of the active workbook.

- **All Except Borders.** Pastes everything except borders that appear in the source range.

- **Column Widths.** Pastes only column width information.

- **Formulas and Number Formats.** Pastes all values, formulas, and number formats (but no other formatting).

- **Values and Number Formats.** Pastes all values and numeric formats, but not the formulas themselves.

- **All Merging Conditional Formats.** Merges the copied conditional formatting with any conditional formatting in the destination range. This option is enabled only when you are copying a range that contains conditional formatting.

In addition, the Paste Special dialog box enables you to perform other operations, described in the following sections.

FIGURE 14-20

The Paste Special dialog box

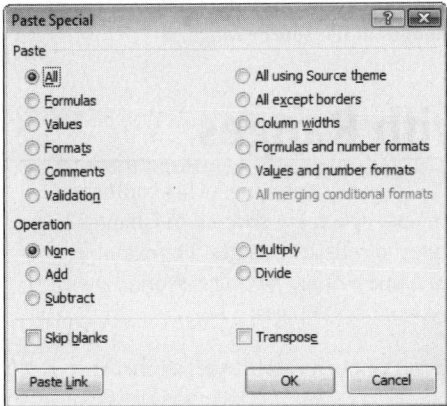

Performing Mathematical Operations without Formulas

The options listed in the Operation section of the Paste Special dialog box let you perform an arithmetic operation on values and formulas in the destination range. For example, you can copy a range to another range and select the Multiply operation. Excel multiplies the corresponding values in the source range and the destination range and replaces the destination range with the new values.

This feature also works with a single copied cell, pasted to a multicell range. Assume that you have a range of values and you want to increase each value by five percent. Enter **105%** into any blank cell, and copy that cell to the Clipboard. Then select the range of values, and bring up the Paste Special dialog box. Select the Multiply option, and each value in the range is multiplied by 105 percent.

Caution

If the destination range contains formulas, the formulas are also modified. In many cases, this is *not* what you want. ■

Skipping Blanks when Pasting

The Skip Blanks option in the Paste Special dialog box prevents Excel from overwriting cell contents in your paste area with blank cells from the copied range. This option is useful if you're copying a range to another area but don't want the blank cells in the copied range to overwrite existing data.

Transposing a Range

The Transpose option in the Paste Special dialog box changes the orientation of the copied range. Rows become columns, and columns become rows. Refer to Figure 14-19 to see an example. Any formulas in the copied range are adjusted so that they work properly when transposed. Note that you can use this checkbox with the other options in the Paste Special dialog box.

Tip

If you click the Paste Link button in the Paste Special dialog box, you create formulas that link to the source range. As a result, the destination range automatically reflects changes in the source range. ■

Using Names to Work with Ranges

Dealing with cryptic cell and range addresses can sometimes be confusing. (This confusion becomes even more apparent when you deal with formulas, which are covered in Chapter 15.) Fortunately, Excel allows you to assign descriptive names to cells and ranges. For example, you can give a cell a name such as *Interest_Rate*, or you can name a range *JulySales*. Working with these names (rather than cell or range addresses) has several advantages:

- A meaningful range name (such as *Total_Income*) is much easier to remember than a cell address (such as AC21).
- Entering a name is less error-prone than entering a cell or range address.

- You can quickly move to areas of your worksheet either by using the Name box, located at the left side of the Formula bar (click on the arrow to drop down a list of defined names) or by choosing Home ➪ Editing ➪ Find & Select ➪ Go To (or F5) and specifying the range name.

- Creating formulas is easier. You can paste a cell or range name into a formula by using Formula AutoComplete.

- Names make your formulas more understandable and easier to use. A formula such as =Income-Taxes is more intuitive than =D20-D40.

Creating Range Names in Your Workbooks

Excel provides several different methods that you can use to create range names. Before you begin, however, you should be aware of some important rules about what is acceptable:

1. **Names can't contain any spaces.** You may want to use an underscore character to simulate a space (such as Annual_Total).

2. **You can use any combination of letters and numbers, but the name must begin with a letter.** A name can't begin with a number (such as 3rdQuarter) or look like a cell reference (such as QTR3). If these are desirable names, though, you can precede the name with an underscore, for example, _3rd Quarter and _QTR3.

3. **Symbols (except for underscores and periods) aren't allowed.**

4. **Names are limited to 255 characters,** but it's a good practice to keep names as short as possible yet still meaningful and understandable.

Caution
Excel also uses a few names internally for its own use. Although you can create names that override Excel's internal names, you should avoid doing so. To be on the safe side, avoid using the following for names: Print_Area, Print_Titles, Consolidate_Area, and Sheet_Title.

To delete a range name or rename a range, see "Managing Names," later in this chapter. ■

Using the New Name Dialog Box
To create a range name, start by selecting the cell or range that you want to name. Then, choose Formulas ➪ Defined Names ➪ Define Name. Excel displays the New Name dialog box, shown in Figure 14-21. Note that this is a resizable dialog box. Drag a border to change the dimensions.

Type a name in the Name text field (or use the name that Excel proposes, if any). The selected cell or range address appears in the Refers To text field. Use the Scope drop-down list to indicate the scope for the name. The scope indicates where the name will be valid, and it's either the entire workbook or a particular sheet. If you like, you can add a comment that describes the named range or cell. Click OK to add the name to your workbook and close the dialog box.

FIGURE 14-21

Create names for cells or ranges by using the New Name dialog box.

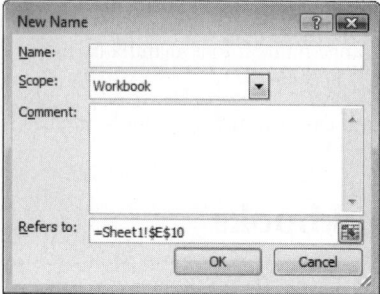

Using the Name Box

A faster way to create a name is to use the Name box (to the left of the Formula bar). Select the cell or range to name, click the Name box, and type the name. Press Enter to create the name. (You must press Enter to actually record the name; if you type a name and then click in the worksheet, Excel doesn't create the name.)

The Name box is a drop-down list and shows all names in the workbook. To choose a named cell or range, click the Name box and choose the name. The name appears in the Name box, and Excel selects the named cell or range in the worksheet.

Using the Create Names from Selection Dialog Box

You may have a worksheet that contains text that you want to use for names for adjacent cells or ranges. For example, you may want to use the text in column A to create names for the corresponding values in column B. Excel makes this task easy to do.

To create names by using adjacent text, start by selecting the name text and the cells that you want to name. (These items can be individual cells or ranges of cells.) The names must be adjacent to the cells that you're naming. (A multiple selection is allowed.) Then, choose Formulas ⇨ Defined Names ⇨ Create from Selection. Excel displays the Create Names from Selection dialog box, shown in Figure 14-22. The check marks in this dialog box are based on Excel's analysis of the selected range. For example, if Excel finds text in the first row of the selection, it proposes that you create names based on the top row. If Excel didn't guess correctly, you can change the checkboxes. Click OK, and Excel creates the names. Using the data in Figure 14-22, Excel creates six names: January for cell B1, February for cell B2, and so on.

Note

If the text contained in a cell would result in an invalid name, Excel modifies the name to make it valid. For example, if a cell contains the text *Net Income* (which is invalid for a name because it contains a space), Excel converts the space to an underscore character. If Excel encounters a value or a numeric formula where text should be, however, it doesn't convert it to a valid name. It simply doesn't create a name — and does not inform you of that fact. ∎

Caution

If the upper-left cell of the selection contains text and you choose the Top Row and Left Column options, Excel uses that text for the name of the entire data, excluding the top row and left column. So, after Excel creates the names, take a minute to make sure that they refer to the correct ranges. If Excel creates a name that is incorrect, you can delete or modify it by using the Name Manager (described next). ∎

FIGURE 14-22

Use the Create Names from Selection dialog box to name cells using labels that appear in the worksheet.

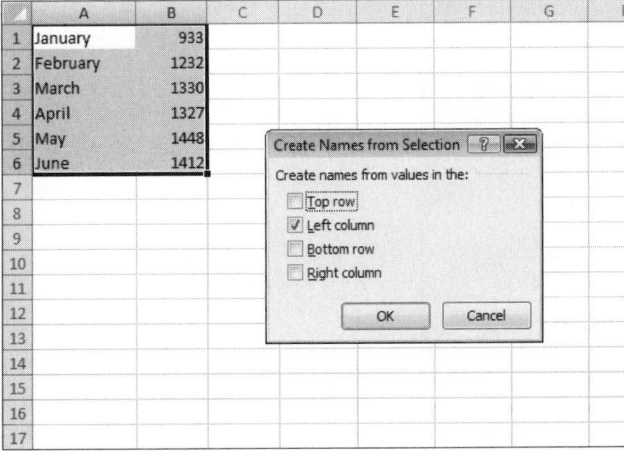

Managing Names

A workbook can have any number of names. If you have many names, you should know about the Name Manager, shown in Figure 14-23.

The Name Manager appears when you choose Formulas ➪ Defined Names ➪ Name Manager (or press Ctrl+F3). The Name Manager has the following features:

- Displays information about each name in the workbook. You can resize the Name Manager dialog box and widen the columns to show more information. You can also click on a column heading to sort the information by the column.

- Allows you to filter the displayed names. Clicking the Filter button lets you show only those names that meet a certain criterion. For example, you can view only the worksheet level names.

- Provides quick access to the New Name dialog box. Click the New button to create a new name without closing the Name Manager.

- Lets you edit names. To edit a name, select it in the list and then click the Edit button. You can change the name itself, modify the Refers To range, or edit the comment.

- Lets you quickly delete unneeded names. To delete a name, select it in the list and click Delete.

FIGURE 14-23

Use the Name Manager to work with range names.

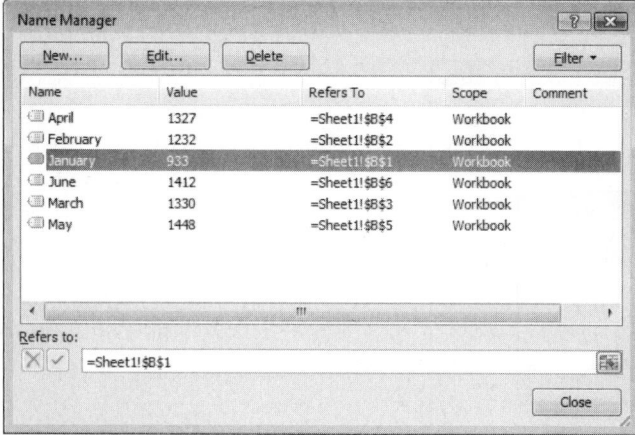

Caution

Be extra careful when deleting names. If the name is used in a formula, deleting the name causes the formula to become invalid. (#NAME? is displayed.) However, deleting a name can be undone, so if you find that formulas return #NAME? after you delete a name, choose Undo from the Quick Access toolbar (or press Ctrl+Z) to get the name back. ■

If you delete the rows or columns that contain named cells or ranges, the names contain an invalid reference. For example, if cell A1 on Sheet1 is named *Interest* and you delete row 1 or column A, the name *Interest* then refers to =Sheet1!#REF! (i.e., to an erroneous reference). If you use *Interest* in a formula, the formula displays #REF.

Tip

The Name Manager is useful, but it has a shortcoming: it doesn't let you display the list of names in a worksheet range so you can view or print them. Such a feat is possible, but you need to look beyond the Name Manager.

To create a list of names in a worksheet, first move the cell pointer to an empty area of your worksheet — the list is created at the active cell position and overwrites any information at that location. Press F3 to display the Paste Name dialog box, which lists all the defined names. Then click the Paste List button. Excel creates a list of all names in the workbook and their corresponding addresses. ■

Adding Comments to Cells

Documentation that explains certain elements in the worksheet can often be helpful. One way to document your work is to add comments to cells. This feature is useful when you need to describe a particular value or explain how a formula works.

To add a comment to a cell, select the cell and use any of these actions:

- Choose Review ➪ Comments ➪ New Comment.
- Right-click the cell and choose Insert Comment from the shortcut menu.
- Press Shift+F2.

Excel inserts a comment that points to the active cell. Initially, the comment consists of your name, as specified in the Excel Options dialog box. Enter the text for the cell comment, and then click anywhere in the worksheet to hide the comment. You can change the size of the comment by dragging any of its borders. Figure 14-24 shows a cell with a comment.

You can add comments to cells to help clarify important items in your worksheets.

	A	B	C	D	E	F	G
1	January	933					
2	February	1232					
3	March	1330		John:			
4	April	1327					
5	May	643		What happened in May?			
6	June	1412					
7							
8							
9							
10							

Cells that have a comment display a small red triangle in the upper-right corner. When you move the mouse pointer over a cell that contains a comment, the comment becomes visible.

You can force a comment to be displayed even when its cell is not activated. Right-click on the cell and choose Show/Hide Comments. Although this command refers to "comments" (plural), it affects only the comment in the active cell. To return to normal (make the comment appear only when its cell is activated), right-click on the cell and choose Hide Comment.

Tip

You can control how comments are displayed. Display the Advanced settings in the Excel Options dialog box (File ➪ Options). In the Display section, select the No Comments or Indicators option from the For Cells with Comments, Show list. ■

Formatting Comments

If you don't like the default look of cell comments, you can make some changes. Right-click on the cell and choose Edit Comment. Select the text in the comment and use the commands of the Font and the Alignment groups (on the Home tab) to make changes to the comment's appearance.

For even more formatting options, right-click on the open comment, and choose Format Comment from the shortcut menu. Excel responds by displaying the Format Comment dialog box, which allows you to change many aspects of its appearance, including color, border, and margins.

Tip

You can also display an image inside a comment. Right-click on the cell, and choose Edit Comment. Then right-click the comment's border and choose Format Comment. Select the Colors and Lines tab in the Format Comment dialog box. Click the Color drop-down list and select Fill Effects. In the Fill Effects dialog box, click the Picture tab and then click the Select Picture button to specify a graphics file. Figure 14-25 shows a comment that contains a picture. ∎

FIGURE 14-25

This comment contains a graphics image.

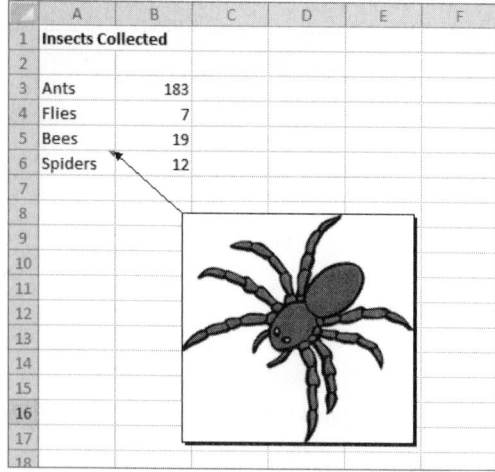

Working Further with Comments

Comments are there to present information, and you need to know how to read and display comments. Here are additional key actions you'll perform with comments:

- **Reading Comments.** To read all comments in a workbook, choose Review ⇨ Comments ⇨ Next. Keep clicking Next to cycle through all the comments in a workbook. Choose Review ⇨ Comments ⇨ Previous to view the comments in reverse order.

- **Hiding and Showing Comments.** If you want all cell comments to be visible (regardless of the location of the cell pointer), choose Review ➪ Comments ➪ Show All Comments. This command is a toggle; select it again to hide all cell comments. To toggle the display of an individual comment, select its cell and then choose Review ➪ Comments ➪ Show/Hide Comment.

- **Editing Comments.** To edit a comment, activate the cell, right-click, and then choose Edit Comment from the shortcut menu. Or, select the cell and press Shift+F2. After you make your changes, click any cell.

- **Deleting Comments.** To delete a cell comment, activate the cell that contains the comment, and then choose Review ➪ Comments ➪ Delete. Or, right-click and then choose "Delete Comment" from the shortcut menu.

- **Printing Comments.** Comments do not print by default. Click the Dialog Box Launcher in the Page Layout ➪ Page Setup group. In the Page Setup dialog box, click the Sheet tab. Make your choice from the Comments drop-down list — At End of Sheet or As Displayed on Sheet. Click OK to close the Page Setup dialog box. Or, click the Print button to print the worksheet.

Summary

This chapter taught essential skills dealing with worksheets, cells, and ranges. Among the wide variety of skills covered, you learned to create, copy, move, rename, and change the view of worksheets. You also learned to work with rows and columns within sheets, performing actions including resizing, inserting, and deleting rows and columns. The chapter moved on to teach you about cells and ranges, covering how to make various kinds of selections, to naming ranges and adding comments to cells. The next chapter moves on to covering formulas and functions to perform calculations.

Introducing Formulas and Functions

Formulas are what make a spreadsheet program so useful. If it weren't for formulas, a spreadsheet would simply be a glorified word processing document that has great support for tabular information. You use formulas in your Excel worksheets to calculate results from the data stored in the worksheet. When data changes, the formulas calculate updated results with no extra effort on your part. This chapter introduces formulas and functions and helps you get up to speed with these important elements.

Understanding Formula Basics

A formula consists of special code entered into a cell. It performs a calculation of some type and returns a result, which is displayed in the cell. Formulas use a variety of operators and worksheet functions to work with values and text. The values and text used in formulas can be located in other cells, which makes changing data easy and gives worksheets their dynamic nature. For example, you can see multiple scenarios quickly by changing the data in a worksheet and letting your formulas do the work.

A formula can consist of any of these elements:

- Mathematical operators, such as + (for addition) and * (for multiplication)
- Cell references (including named cells and ranges)
- Values or text
- Worksheet functions (such as SUM or AVERAGE)

IN THIS CHAPTER

Understanding formula basics

Entering formulas and functions into your worksheets

Understanding how to use references in formulas

Correcting common formula errors

Tips for working with formulas

Note

When you're working with a table, a feature introduced in Excel 2007 enables you to create formulas that use column names from the table, which can make your formulas much easier to read. I discuss table formulas later in this chapter. (See "Using Formulas in Tables.") ∎

After you enter a formula, the cell displays the calculated result of the formula. The formula itself appears in the Formula bar when you select the cell, however.

Table 15-1 shows a few examples of formulas.

TABLE 15-1

Sample Formulas

Formula	Description
=150*.05	Multiplies 150 times 0.05. This formula uses only values, and it always returns the same result. Alternatively, you could enter the value **7.5** into the cell.
=A1+A2	Adds the values in cells A1 and A2.
=Income-Expenses	Subtracts the value in the cell named *Expenses* from the value in the cell named *Income*.
=SUM(A1:A12)	Adds the values in the range A1:A12.
=A1=C12	Compares cell A1 with cell C12. If the cells are identical, the formula returns TRUE; otherwise, it returns FALSE.

Tip

Formulas always begin with an equal sign so that Excel can distinguish them from text. ∎

Using Operators in Formulas

Excel lets you use a variety of operators in your formulas. Operators are symbols that indicate what mathematical operation you want the formula to perform. Table 15-2 lists the operators that Excel recognizes. In addition to these, Excel has many built-in functions that enable you to perform additional calculations.

TABLE 15-2

Operators Used in Formulas

Operator	Name
+	Addition
−	Subtraction

Operator	Name
*	Multiplication
/	Division
^	Exponentiation
&	Concatenation
=	Logical comparison (equal to)
>	Logical comparison (greater than)
<	Logical comparison (less than)
>=	Logical comparison (greater than or equal to)
<=	Logical comparison (less than or equal to)
<>	Logical comparison (not equal to)

You can, of course, use as many operators as you need to perform the desired calculation.

Table 15-3 shows some examples of formulas that use various operators.

TABLE 15-3

Formulas with Operators

Formula	What It Does
="Part-"&"23A"	Joins (concatenates) the two text strings to produce Part-23A.
=A1&A2	Concatenates the contents of cell A1 with cell A2. Concatenation works with values as well as text. If cell A1 contains 123 and cell A2 contains 456, this formula would return the text 123456.
=6^3	Raises 6 to the third power (216).
=216^(1/3)	Raises 216 to the 1/3 power. This is mathematically equivalent to calculating the cube root of 216, which is 6.
=A1<A2	Returns TRUE if the value in cell A1 is less than the value in cell A2. Otherwise, it returns FALSE. Logical-comparison operators also work with text. If A1 contains Bill and A2 contains Julia, the formula would return TRUE because *Bill* comes before *Julia* in alphabetical order.
=A1<=A2	Returns TRUE if the value in cell A1 is less than or equal to the value in cell A2. Otherwise, it returns FALSE.
=A1<>A2	Returns TRUE if the value in cell A1 is not equal to the value in cell A2. Otherwise, it returns FALSE.

Understanding Operator Precedence in Formulas

When Excel calculates the value of a formula, it uses certain rules to determine the order in which the various parts of the formula are calculated. You need to understand these rules if you want your formulas to produce the desired results.

Table 15-4 lists the Excel operator precedence. This table shows that exponentiation has the highest precedence (performed first), and logical comparisons have the lowest precedence (performed last).

TABLE 15-4

Operator Precedence in Excel Formulas

Symbol	Operator	Precedence
^	Exponentiation	1
*	Multiplication	2
/	Division	2
+	Addition	3
−	Subtraction	3
&	Concatenation	4
=	Equal to	5
<	Less than	5
>	Greater than	5

You can use parentheses to override Excel's built-in order of precedence. Expressions within parentheses are always evaluated first. For example, the following formula uses parentheses to control the order in which the calculations occur. In this case, cell B3 is subtracted from cell B2, and then the result is multiplied by cell B4:

    =(B2-B3)*B4

Excel computes a different answer if you enter the formula without the parentheses:

    =B2-B3*B4

Because multiplication has a higher precedence, first cell B3 is multiplied by cell B4. Then this result is subtracted from cell B2.

It's a good idea to use parentheses even when they aren't strictly necessary. Doing so helps to clarify what the formula is intended to do. For example, the following formula makes it perfectly clear that cell B3 should be multiplied by cell B4, and the result subtracted from cell B2. Without the parentheses, you would need to remember Excel's order of precedence.

```
=B2-(B3*B4)
```

You can also nest parentheses within formulas — that is, put them inside other parentheses. If you do so, Excel evaluates the most deeply nested expressions first — and then works its way out. Here's an example of a formula that uses nested parentheses:

```
=((B2*C2)+(B3*C3)+(B4*C4))*B6
```

This formula has four sets of parentheses — three sets are nested inside the fourth set. Excel evaluates each nested set of parentheses and then sums the three results. This result is then multiplied by the value in cell B6.

Although the preceding formula uses four sets of parentheses, only the outer set is really necessary. If you understand operator precedence, it should be clear that you can rewrite this formula as:

```
=(B2*C2+B3*C3+B4*C4)*B6
```

But most would agree that using the extra parentheses makes the calculation much clearer.

Every left parenthesis, of course, must have a matching right parenthesis. If you have many levels of nested parentheses, keeping them straight can sometimes be difficult. If the parentheses don't match, Excel displays a message explaining the problem — and won't let you enter the formula.

Caution

In some cases, if your formula contains mismatched parentheses, Excel may propose a correction to your formula. Figure 15-1 shows an example of the Formula AutoCorrect feature. You may be tempted simply to accept the proposed correction, but be careful — in many cases, the proposed formula, although syntactically correct, isn't the formula you intend, and it will produce an incorrect result. ∎

FIGURE 15-1

The Excel Formula AutoCorrect feature sometimes suggests a syntactically correct formula, but not the formula you had in mind.

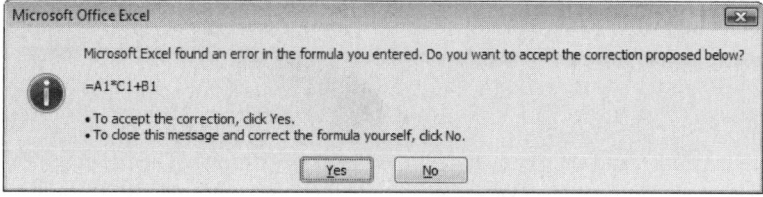

Tip

Excel lends a hand in helping you match parentheses. When the insertion point moves over a parenthesis while you're editing a cell, Excel momentarily makes the parenthesis character bold and displays it in a different color — and does the same with its matching parenthesis. ∎

Using Functions in Your Formulas

Many formulas you create use worksheet functions. These functions enable you to greatly enhance the power of your formulas and perform calculations that are difficult (or even impossible) if you use only the operators discussed previously. For example, you can use the TAN function to calculate the tangent of an angle. You can't do this complicated calculation by using the mathematical operators alone.

Examples of Formulas That Use Functions

A worksheet function can simplify a formula significantly.

Here's an example. To calculate the average of the values in 10 cells (A1:A10) without using a function, you'd have to construct a formula like this:

    =(A1+A2+A3+A4+A5+A6+A7+A8+A9+A10)/10

Not very pretty, is it? Even worse, you would need to edit this formula manually if you added another cell to the range. Fortunately, you can replace this formula with a much simpler one that uses one of Excel's built-in worksheet functions, AVERAGE:

    =AVERAGE(A1:A10)

The following formula demonstrates how using a function can enable you to perform calculations that are not otherwise possible. Say you need to determine the largest value in a range. A formula can't tell you the answer without using a function. Here's a formula that uses the MAX function to return the largest value in the range A1:D100:

    =MAX(A1:D100)

Functions also can sometimes eliminate manual editing. Assume that you have a worksheet that contains 1,000 names in cells A1:A1000, and the names appear in all-capital letters. Your boss sees the listing and informs you that the names will be mail-merged with a form letter. All-uppercase letters is not acceptable; for example, JOHN F. SMITH must now appear as John F. Smith. You could spend the next several hours re-entering the list — ugh — or you could use a formula, such as the following, which uses the PROPER function to convert the capitalized text in cell A1 to the "proper case," upper and lowercase:

    =PROPER(A1)

Enter this formula once in cell B1, and then copy it down to the next 999 rows. Then select B1:B1000 and choose Home ➪ Clipboard ➪ Copy to copy the range. Next, with B1:B1000 still selected, choose Home ➪ Clipboard ➪ Paste Values (V) to convert the formulas to values. Delete the original column, and you've just accomplished several hours of work in less than a minute.

One last example should convince you of the power of functions. Suppose you have a worksheet that calculates sales commissions. If the salesperson sold more than $100,000 of product, the commission rate is 7.5 percent; otherwise, the commission rate is 5.0 percent. Without using a function, you would have to create two different formulas and make sure that you use the correct formula for each sales amount. A better solution is to write a formula that uses the IF function to ensure that you calculate the correct commission, regardless of sales amount:

```
=IF(A1<100000,A1*5%,A1*7.5%)
```

This formula performs some simple decision-making. The formula checks the value of cell A1. If this value is less than 100,000, the formula returns cell A1 multiplied by 5 percent. Otherwise, it returns what's in cell A1 multiplied by 7.5 percent. This example uses three arguments, separated by commas. This is discussed further in the upcoming section, "Function Arguments."

New Functions in Excel 2010

Excel 2010 contains more than 50 new worksheet functions.

Before you get too excited, understand that nearly all of the new functions are simply improved versions of existing statistical functions. For example, you'll find five new functions that deal with the Chi Square distribution: CHISQ.DIST, CHISQ.DIST.RT, CHISQ.INV, CHISQ.INV.RT, and CHISQ.TEST. These are very specialized functions, and the average Excel user will have no need for them.

Excel 2010 offers only three new functions that might appeal to a more general audience:

- AGGREGATE. A function that calculates sums, averages, and so on, with the ability to ignore errors and/or hidden rows
- NETWORKDAYS.INTL. An international version of the NETWORKDAYS function, which returns the number of workdays between two dates
- WORKDAY.INTL. An international version of the WORKDAY function, which returns a date before or after a specified number of workdays

Keep in mind that if you use any of these new functions, you can't share your workbook with someone who uses an earlier version of Excel.

Function Arguments

In the preceding examples, you may have noticed that all the functions used parentheses. The information inside the parentheses is the list of *arguments*.

Functions vary in how they use arguments. Depending on the function, it may use

- No arguments
- One argument
- A fixed number of arguments
- An indeterminate number of arguments
- Optional arguments

An example of a function that doesn't use an argument is the NOW function, which returns the current date and time. Even if a function doesn't use an argument, you must still provide a set of empty parentheses, like this:

=NOW()

If a function uses more than one argument, you must separate each argument with a comma. The examples at the beginning of the chapter used cell references for arguments. Excel is quite flexible when it comes to function arguments. An argument can consist of a cell reference, literal values, literal text strings, expressions, and even other functions. Here are some examples of functions that use various types of arguments:

- **Cell Reference.** =SUM(A1:A24)
- **Literal Value.** =SQRT(121)
- **Literal Text String.** =PROPER("john smith")
- **Expression.** =SQRT(183+12)
- **Other Functions.** =SQRT(SUM(A1:A24))

Note

A comma is the list-separator character for the U.S. version of Excel. Some other versions may use a semicolon. The list separator is a Windows setting, which can be adjusted in the Windows Control Panel (the Region and Language Options dialog box, Additional Settings button in Windows 7). ■

More about Functions

All told, Excel includes more than 400 functions. And if that's not enough, you can purchase additional specialized functions from third-party suppliers — and even create your own custom functions (by using VBA) if you're so inclined.

Some users feel a bit overwhelmed by the sheer number of functions, but you'll probably find that you use only a dozen or so on a regular basis. And as you'll see, the Excel Insert Function dialog box (described later in this chapter) makes it easy to locate and insert a function, even if it's not one that you use frequently.

Cross-Reference

You'll find many examples of Excel's built-in functions in Chapters 16 and 17. ■

Entering Formulas into Your Worksheets

As mentioned earlier, a formula must begin with an equal sign to inform Excel that the cell contains a formula rather than text. Excel provides two ways to enter a formula into a cell: manually or by pointing to cell references. The following sections discuss each way in detail.

Excel provides additional assistance when you create formulas by displaying a drop-down list that contains function names and range names. The items displayed in the list are determined by what you've already typed. For example, if you're entering a formula and then type the letter *L*, you'll see the drop-down list shown in Figure 15-2. If you type an additional letter, the list is shortened to show only the matching functions. To have Excel autocomplete an entry in that list, use the navigation keys to highlight the entry, and then press Tab. Notice that highlighting a function in the list also displays a brief description of the function. See the sidebar "Using Formula AutoComplete" for an example of how this feature works.

FIGURE 15-2

Excel displays a drop-down list when you enter a formula.

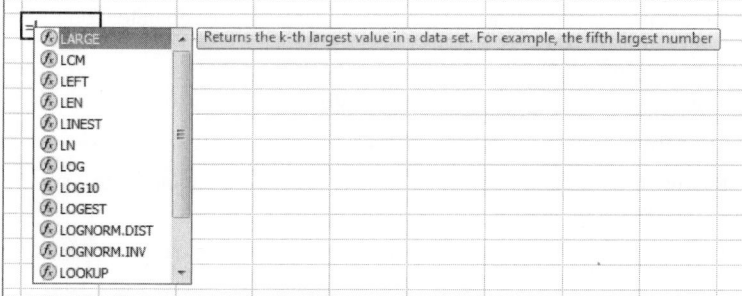

Using Formula AutoComplete

The Formula AutoComplete feature (introduced in Excel 2007) makes entering formulas easier than ever. Here's a quick walk-through that demonstrates how it works. The goal is to create a formula that uses the AGGREGATE function to calculate the average value in a range that I named *TestScores*. The AVERAGE function will not work in this situation because the range contains an error value.

1. Select the cell that will hold the formula, and type an equal sign (=) to signal the start of a formula.

2. Type the letter **A.** You get a list of functions and names that begin with *A*. This feature is not case-sensitive, so you can use either uppercase or lowercase characters.

3. Scroll through the list, or type another letter to narrow down the choices.

4. When AGGREGATE is highlighted, press Tab to select it. Excel adds the opening parenthesis and displays another list that contains options for the first argument for AGGREGATE.

5. Select 1 - AVERAGE and then press Tab. Excel inserts 1, which is the code for calculating the average.

6. Type a comma to separate the next argument.

continued

continued

7. When Excel displays a list of items for the `AGGREGATE` function's second argument, select 2 - Ignore Error Values, and then press Tab.

8. Type a comma to separate the third argument (the range of test scores).

9. Type a **T** to get a list of functions and names that begin with *T*. You're looking for *TestScores*, so narrow it down a bit by typing the second character (**e**).

10. Highlight TestScores and then press Tab.

11. Type a closing parenthesis and then press Enter.

The completed formula is

`=AGGREGATE(1,2,TestScores)`

Formula AutoComplete includes the following items (and each type is identified by a separate icon):

- Excel built-in functions
- User-defined functions (functions defined by the user through VBA or other methods)
- Defined names (named using the Formulas ➪ Defined Names ➪ Define Name command)
- Enumerated arguments that use a value to represent an option (only a few functions use such arguments, and `AGGREGATE` is one of them)
- Table structure references (used to identify portions of a table)

Entering Formulas Manually

Entering a formula manually involves, well, entering a formula manually. In a selected cell, you simply type an equal sign (=) followed by the formula. As you type, the characters appear in the cell and in the Formula bar. You can, of course, use all the normal editing keys when entering a formula.

Entering Formulas by Pointing

Even though you can enter formulas by typing in the entire formula, Excel provides another method of entering formulas that is generally easier, faster, and less error-prone. This method still involves some manual typing, but you can simply point to the cell references instead of typing their values manually. For example, to enter the formula =A1+A2 into cell A3, follow these steps:

1. **Move the cell pointer to cell A3.**

2. **Type an equal sign (=) to begin the formula.** Notice that Excel displays *Enter* in the status bar (bottom left of your screen).

3. **Press the up arrow twice.** As you press this key, Excel displays a faint moving border around cell A1, and the cell reference appears in cell A3 and in the Formula bar. In addition, Excel displays *Point* in the status bar.

4. **Type a plus sign (+).** A solid-color border replaces the faint border, and *Enter* reappears in the status bar.

5. **Press the up arrow again.** The moving border encompasses cell A2, and adds that cell address to the formula.

6. **Press Enter to end the formula.**

Tip

You can also point to the data cells (select them) by using your mouse. ∎

Pasting Range Names into Formulas

If your formula uses named cells or ranges, you can either type the name in place of the address or choose the name from a list and have Excel insert the name for you automatically. Two ways to insert a name into a formula are available:

- Select the name from the drop-down list. To use this method, you must know at least the first character of the name. When you're entering the formula, type the first character and then select the name from the drop-down list.

- Press F3. This action displays the Paste Name dialog box. Select the name from the list, and then click OK (or just double-click on the name). Excel will enter the name into your formula. If no names are defined, pressing F3 has no effect.

Figure 15-3 shows an example. The worksheet contains two defined names: *Expenses* and *Sales*. The Paste Name dialog box is being used to insert a name (Sales) into the formula being entered in cell B10.

FIGURE 15-3

Use the Paste Name dialog box to quickly enter a defined name into a formula.

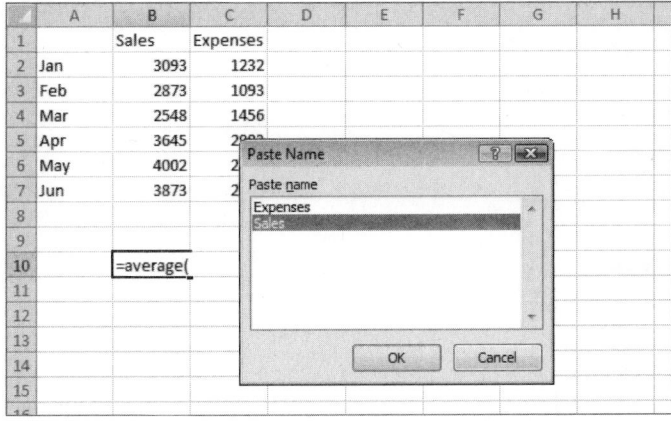

Cross-Reference

See Chapter 14 for information about defining names. ∎

Inserting Functions into Formulas

The easiest way to enter a function into a formula is to use Formula AutoComplete (the drop-down list that Excel displays while you type a formula). To use this method, however, you must know at least the first character of the function's name.

Another way to insert a function is to use the Function Library group on the Formulas tab (see Figure 15-4). This method is especially useful if you can't remember which function you need. When entering a formula, click the function category (Financial, Logical, Text, etc.) to get a list of the functions in that category. Click on the function that you want, and Excel displays its Function Arguments dialog box. This is where you can enter the function's arguments. In addition, you can click the Help on This Function link to learn more about the selected function.

FIGURE 15-4

You can insert a function by selecting it from one of the function categories.

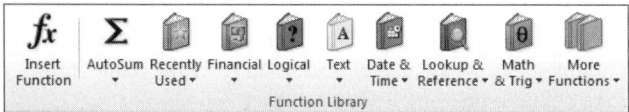

Yet another way to insert a function into a formula is to use the Insert Function dialog box (see Figure 15-5). You can access this dialog box in several ways, listed on the next page.

FIGURE 15-5

The Insert Function dialog box

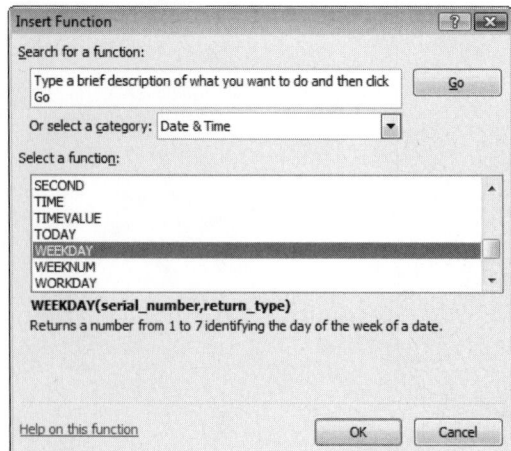

- Choose Formulas ⇨ Function Library ⇨ Insert Function.
- Use the Insert Function command, which appears at the bottom of each drop-down list in the Formulas ⇨ Function Library group.
- Click the Insert Function icon, which is directly to the left of the Formula bar. This button displays *fx*.
- Press Shift+F3.

The Insert Function dialog box shows a drop-down list of function categories. Select a category, and the functions in that category are displayed in the list box. To access a function that you recently used, select Most Recently Used from the drop-down list.

If you're not sure which function you need, you can search for the appropriate function by using the Search for a Function field at the top of the dialog box.

1. **Enter your search terms and click Go.** You get a list of relevant functions. When you select a function from the Select a Function list, Excel displays the function (and its argument names) in the dialog box along with a brief description of what the function does.

2. **When you locate the function you want to use, highlight it and click OK.** Excel then displays its Function Arguments dialog box, as shown in Figure 15-6.

3. **Specify the arguments for the function.** The Function Arguments dialog box will vary, depending on the function you're inserting, and it will show one textbox for each of the function's arguments. To use a cell or range reference as an argument, you can enter the address manually or click inside the argument box and then select (i.e., point to) the cell or range in the sheet.

4. **After you specify all the function arguments, click OK.**

FIGURE 15-6

The Function Arguments dialog box

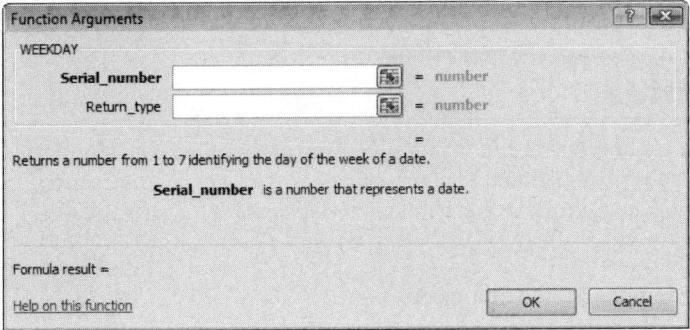

Tip

Yet another way to insert a function while you're entering a formula is to use the Function List to the left of the Formula bar. When you're entering or editing a formula, the space typically occupied by the Name box displays a list of the functions you've used most recently. After you select a function from this list, Excel displays the Function Arguments dialog box. ∎

Function Entry Tips

Here are some additional tips to keep in mind when you use the Insert Function dialog box to enter functions:

- You can use the Insert Function dialog box to insert a function into an existing formula. Just edit the formula and move the insertion point to the location at which you want to insert the function. Then open the Insert Function dialog box (using any of the methods described earlier) and select the function.

- You can also use the Function Arguments dialog box to modify the arguments for a function in an existing formula. Click the function in the Formula bar, and then click the Insert Function button (the *fx* button, to the left of the Formula bar).

- If you change your mind about entering a function, click the Cancel button.

- How many boxes you see in the Function Arguments dialog box depends on the number of arguments used in the function you selected. If a function uses no arguments, you won't see any boxes. If the function uses a variable number of arguments (such as the AVERAGE function), Excel adds a new box every time you enter an optional argument.

- As you provide arguments in the Function Arguments dialog box, the value of each argument is displayed to the right of each box.

- A few functions, such as INDEX, have more than one form. If you choose such a function, Excel displays another dialog box that lets you choose which form you want to use.

- As you become familiar with the functions, you can bypass the Insert Function dialog box and type the function name directly. Excel prompts you with argument names as you enter the function.

Editing Formulas

After you enter a formula, you can (of course) edit that formula. You may need to edit a formula if you make some changes to your worksheet and then have to adjust the formula to accommodate the changes. Or the formula may return an error value, in which case you have to edit the formula to correct the error.

The following are some of the ways to get into Edit mode:

- Double-click on the cell, which enables you to edit the cell contents directly in the cell.

- Press F2, which enables you to edit the cell contents directly in the cell.

- Select the cell that you want to edit, and then click in the Formula bar. This enables you to edit the cell contents in the Formula bar.

- If the cell contains a formula that returns an error, Excel will display a small triangle in the upper-left corner of the cell. Activate the cell, and you'll see an Error Checking button. Click the button, and you can choose one of the options for correcting the error. (The options will vary according to the type of error in the cell.)

Tip

You can control whether Excel displays these formula-error-checking indicators in the Formulas section of the Excel Options dialog box. To display this dialog box, choose File ➪ Options, and then click Formulas. If you remove the check mark from Enable Background Error Checking, Excel no longer displays the indicators. ∎

While you're editing a formula, you can select multiple characters either by dragging the mouse pointer over them or by pressing Shift while you use the navigation keys.

Tip

If you have a formula that you can't seem to edit correctly, you can convert the formula to text and tackle it again later. To convert a formula to text, just remove the initial equal sign (=). When you're ready to try again, type the initial equal sign to convert the cell contents back to a formula. ∎

Using Cell References in Formulas

Most formulas you create include references to cells or ranges. These references enable your formulas to work dynamically with the data contained in those cells or ranges. For example, if your formula refers to cell A1 and you change the value contained in A1, the formula result changes to reflect the new value. If you didn't use references in your formulas, you would need to edit the formulas themselves in order to change the values used in the formulas.

Using Relative, Absolute, and Mixed References

When you use a cell (or range) reference in a formula, you can use three types of references:

- **Relative.** The row and column references can change when you copy the formula to another cell because the references are actually offsets from the current row and column. By default, Excel creates relative cell references in formulas.

- **Absolute.** The row and column references do not change when you copy the formula because the reference is to an actual cell address. An absolute reference uses two dollar signs in its address: one for the column letter and one for the row number (e.g., $A$5).

- **Mixed.** Either the row or column reference is relative, and the other is absolute. Only one of the address parts is absolute (e.g., $A4 or A$4).

The type of cell reference is important only if you plan to copy the formula to other cells (cutting-and-pasting has a differing effect, as described further on in this section). The following examples illustrate this point.

Figure 15-7 shows a simple worksheet. The formula in cell D2, which multiplies the quantity by the price, is

```
=B2*C2
```

FIGURE 15-7

Copying a formula that contains relative references

	A	B	C	D	E
	D3			fx	=B3*C3
1	Item	Quantity	Price	Total	
2	Chair	4	$ 125.00	$ 500.00	
3	Desk	4	$ 695.00	$2,780.00	
4	Lamp	3	$ 39.95	$ 119.85	
5					

This formula uses relative cell references. Therefore, when the formula is copied to the cells below it, the references adjust in a relative manner. For example, the formula in cell D3 is

```
=B3*C3
```

But what if the cell references in D2 contained absolute references, like this?

```
=$B$2*$C$2
```

In this case, copying the formula to the cells below would produce incorrect results. The formula in cell D3 would be exactly the same as the formula in cell D2.

Now I'll extend the example to calculate sales tax based on a sales tax rate stored in cell B7 (see Figure 15-8). In this situation, the formula in cell E2 is

```
=(B2*C2)*$B$7
```

FIGURE 15-8

Formula references to the sales tax cell should be absolute.

	A	B	C	D	E
	E3			fx	=(B3*C3)*$B$7
1	Item	Quantity	Price	Total	Sales Tax
2	Chair	4	$ 125.00	$ 500.00	$ 37.50
3	Desk	4	$ 695.00	$2,780.00	$ 208.50
4	Lamp	3	$ 39.95	$ 119.85	$ 8.99
5					
6					
7	Sales Tax:	7.50%			
8					

The quantity is multiplied by the price, and the result is multiplied by the sales tax rate stored in cell B7. Notice that the reference to B7 is an absolute reference. When the formula in E2 is copied to the cells below it, cell E3 will contain this formula:

```
=(B3*C3)*$B$7
```

Here, the references to cells B2 and C2 were adjusted, but the reference to cell B7 was not — which is exactly what I want because the cell that contains the sales tax never changes.

Figure 15-9 demonstrates the use of mixed references. The formulas in the C3:F7 range calculate the area for various lengths and widths. The formula in cell C3 is

```
=$B3*C$2
```

FIGURE 15-9

Using mixed cell references

	A	B	C	D	E	F	G
1				Width			
2			1.0	1.5	2.0	2.5	
3		1.0	1.0	1.5	2.0	2.5	
4	Length	1.5	1.5	2.3	3.0	3.8	
5		2.0	2.0	3.0	4.0	5.0	
6		2.5	2.5	3.8	5.0	6.3	
7		3.0	3.0	4.5	6.0	7.5	
8							
9							

Notice that both cell references are mixed. The reference to cell B3 uses an absolute reference for the column ($B), and the reference to cell C2 uses an absolute reference for the row ($2). As a result, this formula can be copied down and across, and the calculations will be correct. For example, the formula in cell F7 is

```
=$B7*F$2
```

If C3 used either absolute or relative references, copying the formula would produce incorrect results.

Note

When you cut and paste a formula (move it to another location), the cell references in the formula aren't adjusted. Again, this is usually what you want to happen. When you move a formula, you generally want it to continue to refer to the original cells. ∎

Changing the Types of Your References

You can enter non-relative references (i.e., absolute or mixed) manually by inserting dollar signs in the appropriate positions of the cell address. Or you can use a handy shortcut: the F4 key. When you've entered a cell reference (by typing it or by pointing), you can press F4 repeatedly to have Excel cycle through all four reference types.

For example, if you enter **=A1** to start a formula, pressing F4 converts the cell reference to =$A$1. Pressing F4 again converts it to =A$1. Pressing it again displays =$A1. Pressing it one more time returns to the original =A1. Keep pressing F4 until Excel displays the type of reference that you want.

Note

When you name a cell or range, Excel (by default) uses an absolute reference for the name. For example, if you give the name *SalesForecast* to B1:B12, the Refers To box in the New Name dialog box lists the reference as $B$1:$B$12. This is almost always what you want. If you copy a cell that has a named reference in its formula, the copied formula contains a reference to the original name. ■

Referencing Cells outside the Worksheet

Formulas can also refer to cells in other worksheets — and the worksheets don't even have to be in the same workbook. Excel uses a special type of notation to handle these types of references.

Referencing Cells in Other Worksheets

To use a reference to a cell in another worksheet in the same workbook, use this format:

```
SheetName!CellAddress
```

In other words, precede the cell address with the worksheet name, followed by an exclamation point. Here's an example of a formula that uses a cell on the Sheet2 worksheet:

```
=A1*Sheet2!A1
```

This formula multiplies the value in cell A1 on the current worksheet by the value in cell A1 on Sheet2.

Tip

If the worksheet name in the reference includes one or more spaces, you must enclose it in single quotation marks. (Excel does that automatically if you use the point-and-click method.) For example, here's a formula that refers to a cell on a sheet named *All Depts*:

```
=A1*'All Depts'!A1
```
■

Referencing Cells in Other Workbooks

To refer to a cell in a different workbook, use this format:

```
=[WorkbookName]SheetName!CellAddress
```

In this case, the workbook name (in square brackets), the worksheet name, and an exclamation point precede the cell address. The following is an example of a formula that uses a cell reference in the Sheet1 worksheet in a workbook named *Budget*:

```
=[Budget.xlsx]Sheet1!A1
```

If the workbook name in the reference includes one or more spaces, you must enclose it (and the sheet name) in single quotation marks. For example, here's a formula that refers to a cell on Sheet1 in a workbook named *Budget For 2011*:

```
=A1*'[Budget For 2011.xlsx]Sheet1'!A1
```

When a formula refers to cells in a different workbook, the other workbook doesn't have to be open. If the other workbook is open, you can simply enter the file name. If the workbook is closed, however, you must add the complete path to the reference so that Excel can find it. Here's an example:

```
=A1*'C:\My Documents\[Budget For 2011.xlsx]Sheet1'!A1
```

A linked file can also reside on another system that's accessible on your corporate network. The following formula refers to a cell in a workbook in the files directory of a computer named *DataServer*:

```
='\\DataServer\files\[budget.xlsx]Sheet1'!$D$7
```

Tip

To create formulas that refer to cells not in the current worksheet, point to the cells rather than entering their references manually. Excel takes care of the details regarding the workbook and worksheet references. The workbook you're referencing in your formula must be open if you're going to use the pointing method. ■

Note

If you point to a different worksheet or workbook when creating a formula, you'll notice that Excel always inserts absolute cell references. Therefore, if you plan to copy the formula to other cells, make sure that you change the cell references to relative before you copy. ■

Using Formulas in Tables

A table is a specially designated range of cells, set up with column headers. In this section, you'll learn how to work with formulas inside tables.

Summarizing Data in a Table

Figure 15-10 shows a simple table with three columns. To create a table, enter the data including a header row with the column names. Click within the table range, and then convert the range to a table by choosing Insert ➪ Tables ➪ Table. Note that the table is named *Table1* by default (provided it is the first table you create in the workbook).

FIGURE 15-10

A simple table with three columns of information

	A	B	C	D	E	F
1						
2		Month	Projected	Actual		
3		Jan	4,000	3,255		
4		Feb	4,000	4,102		
5		Mar	4,000	3,982		
6		Apr	5,000	4,598		
7		May	5,000	5,873		
8		Jun	5,000	4,783		
9		Jul	5,000	5,109		
10		Aug	6,000	5,982		
11		Sep	6,000	6,201		
12		Oct	7,000	6,833		
13		Nov	8,000	7,983		
14		Dec	9,000	9,821		
15						

If you'd like to calculate the total projected and total actual sales, you don't even need to write a formula. Simply click a button to add a row of summary formulas to the table:

1. **Activate any cell in the table.**

2. **Place a check mark next to Table Tools ➪ Design ➪ Table Style Options ➪ Total Row.**

3. **Activate a cell in the Total Row and use the drop-down list to select the type of summary formula to use (see Figure 15-11).** For example, to calculate the sum of the `Actual` column, select SUM from the drop-down list in cell D15. Excel creates this formula:

   ```
   =SUBTOTAL(109,[Actual])
   ```

For the SUBTOTAL function, 109 is an enumerated argument that represents SUM. The second argument for the SUBTOTAL function is the column name, in square brackets. Using the column name within brackets creates "structured" references within a table. (This is discussed further in the upcoming section, "Referencing Data in a Table.")

Note

You can toggle the Total Row display via Table Tools ➪ Design ➪ Table Style Options ➪ Total Row. If you turn it off, the summary options you selected will be displayed again when you turn it back on. ∎

Using Formulas within a Table

In many cases, you'll want to use formulas within a table to perform calculations that use other columns. For example, in the table shown in Figure 15-11, you may want a column that shows the difference between the Actual and Projected amounts. To add this formula:

1. **Activate cell E2 and type** Difference **for the column header.** Excel automatically expands the table for you to include the new column.

2. **Move to cell E3 and type an equal sign to signify the beginning of a formula.**

3. **Press the left arrow key.** Excel displays [@Actual], which is the column heading, in the Formula bar.

4. **Type a minus sign (hyphen) and then press the left arrow key twice.** Excel displays [@Projected] in your formula.

5. **Press Enter to end the formula.** Excel copies the formula to all rows in the table.

FIGURE 15-11

A drop-down list enables you to select a summary formula for a table column.

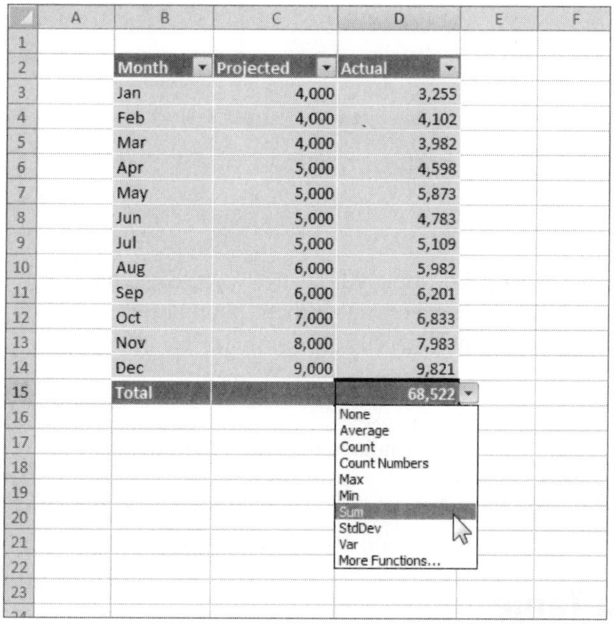

	A	B	C	D	E	F
1						
2		Month	Projected	Actual		
3		Jan	4,000	3,255		
4		Feb	4,000	4,102		
5		Mar	4,000	3,982		
6		Apr	5,000	4,598		
7		May	5,000	5,873		
8		Jun	5,000	4,783		
9		Jul	5,000	5,109		
10		Aug	6,000	5,982		
11		Sep	6,000	6,201		
12		Oct	7,000	6,833		
13		Nov	8,000	7,983		
14		Dec	9,000	9,821		
15		Total		68,522		

None
Average
Count
Count Numbers
Max
Min
Sum
StdDev
Var
More Functions...

Figure 15-12 shows the table with the new column.

Examine the table, and you find this formula for all cells in the Difference column:

=[@Actual]-[@Projected]

Although the formula was entered into the first row of the table, it's not necessary to enter it in that row. Any time a formula is entered into an empty table column, it will automatically fill all the cells in that column. And if you need to edit the formula, Excel will automatically copy the edited formula to the other cells in the column.

Note

The "at" (@) symbol that precedes the column header represents "this row." ∎

FIGURE 15-12

The Difference column contains a formula.

	A	B	C	D	E	F
1						
2		Month	Projected	Actual	Difference	
3		Jan	4,000	3,255	-745	
4		Feb	4,000	4,102	102	
5		Mar	4,000	3,982	-18	
6		Apr	5,000	4,598	-402	
7		May	5,000	5,873	873	
8		Jun	5,000	4,783	-217	
9		Jul	5,000	5,109	109	
10		Aug	6,000	5,982	-18	
11		Sep	6,000	6,201	201	
12		Oct	7,000	6,833	-167	
13		Nov	8,000	7,983	-17	
14		Dec	9,000	9,821	821	
15		Total	68,000	68,522		
16						
17						

These steps use the pointing technique to create the formula. Alternatively, you could have entered the formula manually using standard cell references rather than column headers. For example, you could have entered the following formula in cell E3:

```
=D3-C3
```

If you type the cell references, Excel will still copy the formula to the other cells automatically.

One thing should be clear, however, about formulas that use the column headers instead of cell references: they are much easier to understand.

Referencing Data in a Table

Excel offers some other ways to refer to data that's contained in a table, by using the table name and column headers.

Note

Remember that you don't need to create names for tables and columns. The table itself has a range name, which is provided when you create the table (e.g., *Table1*), and you can refer to data within the table by using the column headers — which are *not* range names. ∎

You can, of course, use standard cell references to refer to data in a table, but using the table name and column headers has a distinct advantage: The names adjust automatically if the table size changes by adding or deleting rows. In addition, formulas that use table names and column headers will adjust automatically if you change the name of the table or give a new name to a column.

Refer to the table (Table1) shown in Figure 15-11. To calculate the sum of all the data in the table, use this formula:

    =SUM(Table1)

This formula will always return the sum of all the data (excluding calculated Total Row values, if any), even if rows or columns are added or deleted. And if you change the name of Table1, Excel will adjust formulas that refer to that table automatically. For example, if you renamed Table1 to *AnnualData* (by using the Name Manager or by using Table Tools ➪ Design ➪ Properties ➪ Table Name), the preceding formula would change to:

    =SUM(AnnualData)

Most of the time, you want to refer to a specific column in the table. The following formula returns the sum of the data in the Actual column:

    =SUM(Table1[Actual])

Notice that the column name is enclosed in square brackets. Again, the formula adjusts automatically if you change the text in the column heading.

Even better, Excel provides some helpful assistance when you create a formula that refers to data within a table. Figure 15-13 shows the Formula AutoComplete feature helping to create a formula by showing a list of the elements in the table. Notice that, in addition to the column headers in the table, Excel lists other table elements that you can reference: #All, #Data, #Headers, #Totals, and @ - This Row.

FIGURE 15-13

The Formula AutoComplete feature is useful when creating a formula that refers to data in a table.

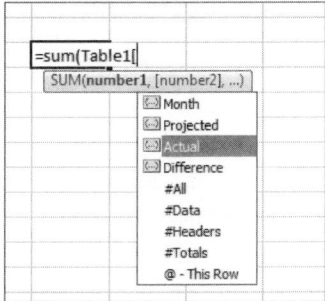

Correcting Common Formula Errors

Sometimes, when you enter a formula, Excel displays a value that begins with a hash mark (#). This is a signal that the formula is returning an error value. You must correct the formula (or correct a cell that the formula references) to get rid of the error display.

Tip

If the entire cell is filled with hash-mark characters, the column isn't wide enough to display the value. You can either widen the column or change the number format of the cell. ■

In some cases, Excel won't even let you enter an erroneous formula. For example, the following formula is missing the closing parenthesis:

```
=A1*(B1+C2
```

If you attempt to enter this formula, Excel informs you that you have unmatched parentheses, and it proposes a correction. Often, the proposed correction is accurate, but check it carefully just in case it's not quite right.

Table 15-5 lists the types of error values that may appear in a cell that has a formula. Formulas may return an error value if a cell to which they refer has an error value. This is known as the *ripple effect* — a single error value can make its way into lots of other cells that contain formulas that depend on that one cell.

TABLE 15-5

Excel Error Values

Error Value	Explanation
#DIV/0!	The formula is trying to divide by zero. This also occurs when the formula attempts to divide by what's in a cell that is empty (i.e., by nothing).
#NAME?	The formula uses a name that Excel doesn't recognize. This can happen if you delete a name that's used in the formula or if you have unmatched quotes when using text.
#N/A	The formula is referring (directly or indirectly) to a cell that uses the NA function to signal that data is not available. Some functions (e.g., VLOOKUP) can also return #N/A.
#NULL!	The formula uses an intersection of two ranges that don't intersect. (This concept is described later in the chapter.)
#NUM!	A problem with a value exists; for example, you specified a negative number where a positive number is expected.
#REF!	The formula refers to a cell that isn't valid. This can happen if the cell has been deleted from the worksheet.
#VALUE!	The formula includes an argument or operand of the wrong type. An *operand* is a value or cell reference that a formula uses to calculate a result.

Handling Circular References

When you're entering formulas, you may occasionally see a Circular Reference Warning message, as shown in Figure 15-14, indicating that the formula you just entered will result in a circular reference. A circular reference occurs when a formula refers to its own value — either directly or indirectly. For example, you create a circular reference if you enter **=A1+A2+A3** into cell A3 because the formula in cell A3 refers to cell A3. Every time the formula in A3 is calculated, it must be calculated again because A3 has changed. The calculation could go on forever.

FIGURE 15-14

If you see this warning, you know that the formula you entered will result in a circular reference.

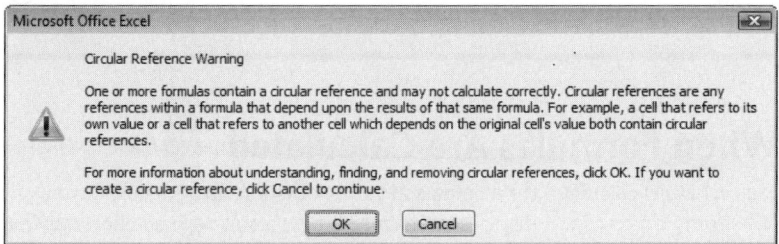

When you get the circular reference message after entering a formula, Excel gives you two options:

- Click OK, and Excel displays a Help screen that tells you more about circular references.
- Click Cancel to enter the formula as is.

Regardless of which option you choose, Excel displays a message in the left side of the status bar to remind you that a circular reference exists.

Caution

Excel won't tell you about a circular reference if the Enable Iterative Calculation setting is in effect. You can check this setting in the Formulas section of the Excel Options dialog box. If Enable Iterative Calculation is turned on, Excel performs the circular calculation exactly the number of times specified in the Maximum Iterations field (or until the value changes by less than 0.001 or whatever value is in the Maximum Change field). In a few situations, you may use a circular reference intentionally. In these cases, the Enable Iterative Calculation setting must be on. However, it's best to keep this setting turned off so that you're warned of circular references. Usually a circular reference indicates an error that you must correct. ■

Usually, a circular reference is quite obvious and easy to identify and correct. But when a circular reference is indirect (as when a formula refers to another formula that refers to yet another formula that refers back to the original formula), it may require a bit of detective work to get to the root of the problem.

Intentional Circular References

You can sometimes use a circular reference to your advantage. For example, suppose your company has a policy of contributing 5 percent of its net profit to charity. The contribution itself, however, is considered an expense — and is therefore subtracted from the net profit figure. This produces a circular reference.

The Contributions cell contains the following formula:

```
=5%*Net_Profit
```

The Net Profit cell contains the following formula:

```
=Gross_Income-Expenses-Contributions
```

These formulas produce a resolvable circular reference. If the Enable Iterative Calculation setting is on, Excel keeps calculating until the Contributions value is, indeed, 5 percent of Net Profit. In other words, the result becomes increasingly accurate until it converges on the final solution.

Specifying When Formulas Are Calculated

You've probably noticed that Excel calculates the formulas in your worksheet immediately. If you change any cells that the formula uses, Excel displays the formula's new result with no effort on your part. All this happens when Excel's Calculation mode is set to Automatic. In Automatic Calculation mode (which is the default mode), Excel follows these rules when it calculates your worksheet:

- When you make a change — enter or edit data or formulas, for example — Excel immediately calculates those formulas that depend on new or edited data.

- If Excel is in the middle of a lengthy calculation, it temporarily suspends the calculation when you need to perform other worksheet tasks; it resumes calculating when you're finished with your other worksheet tasks.

- Formulas are evaluated in a natural sequence. In other words, if a formula in cell D12 depends on the result of a formula in cell D11, Excel calculates cell D11 before calculating D12.

Sometimes, however, you may want to control when Excel calculates formulas. For example, if you create a worksheet with thousands of complex formulas, you'll find that processing can slow to a snail's pace while Excel does its thing. In such a case, set Excel's calculation mode to Manual — which you can do by choosing Formulas ➪ Calculation ➪ Calculation Options ➪ Manual (see Figure 15-15).

Tip

If your worksheet uses any tables with extensive amounts of data, you may want to select the Automatic Except for Data Tables option. Large data tables calculate notoriously slowly. ∎

Note

A *data table* is not the same as a table created by choosing Insert ➪ Tables ➪ Table. ∎

FIGURE 15-15

You can control when Excel calculates formulas.

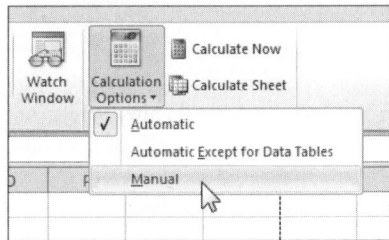

When you're working in Manual Calculation mode, Excel displays *Calculate* in the status bar when you have any uncalculated formulas. You can use the following shortcut keys to recalculate the formulas:

- **F9.** Calculates the formulas in all open workbooks.
- **Shift+F9.** Calculates only the formulas in the active worksheet. Other worksheets in the same workbook aren't calculated.
- **Ctrl+Alt+F9.** Forces a complete recalculation of all formulas.

Note
Excel's Calculation mode isn't specific to a particular worksheet. When you change the Calculation mode, it affects all open workbooks, not just the active workbook. ■

Tips for Working with Formulas

In this section, you'll find a few additional tips and pointers relevant to formulas.

Don't Hard-Code Values

When you create a formula, think twice before you use any specific value in the formula. For example, if your formula calculates sales tax (which is 6.5%), you may be tempted to enter a formula, such as the following:

```
=A1*.065
```

A better approach is to insert the sales tax rate in a cell — and use the cell reference. Or you can define the tax rate as a named constant, using the technique presented earlier in this chapter. Doing so makes modifying and maintaining your worksheet easier. For example, if the sales tax rate changed to 6.75 percent, you would have to modify every formula that used the old value. If you store the tax rate in a cell, however, you simply change that one cell — and Excel updates all the formulas.

Using the Formula Bar as a Calculator

If you need to perform a quick calculation, you can use the Formula bar as a calculator. For example, enter the following formula — but don't press Enter:

```
=(145*1.05)/12
```

If you press Enter, Excel enters the formula into the cell. But because this formula always returns the same result, you may prefer to store the formula's result rather than the formula itself. To do so, press F9 and watch the result appear in the Formula bar. Press Enter to store the result in the active cell. (This technique also works if the formula uses cell references or worksheet functions.)

Making an Exact Copy of a Formula

When you copy a formula, Excel adjusts its cell references when you paste the formula to a different location. Sometimes, you may want to make an exact copy of the formula. One way to do this is to convert the cell references to absolute values, but this isn't always desirable. A better approach is to select the formula in Edit mode and then copy it to the Clipboard as text. You can do this in several ways. Here's a step-by-step example of how to make an exact copy of the formula in A1 and copy it to A2:

1. **Double-click A1 (or press F2) to get into Edit mode.**
2. **Drag the mouse to select the entire formula.** You can drag from left to right or from right to left. To select the entire formula with the keyboard, press Shift+Home.
3. **Choose Home ⇨ Clipboard ⇨ Copy (or press Ctrl+C).** This copies the selected text (which will become the copied formula) to the Clipboard.
4. **Press Esc to leave Edit mode.**
5. **Select cell A2.**
6. **Home ⇨ Clipboard ⇨ Paste (or press Ctrl+V) to paste the text into cell A2.**

You also can use this technique to copy just part of a formula, if you want to use that part in another formula. Just select the part of the formula that you want to copy by dragging the mouse, and then use any of the available techniques to copy the selection to the Clipboard. You can then paste the text to another cell.

Formulas (or parts of formulas) copied in this manner won't have their cell references adjusted when they are pasted to a new cell. That's because the formulas are being copied as text, not as actual formulas.

Tip
You can also convert a formula to text by adding an apostrophe (') in front of the equal sign. Then, copy the formula as usual and paste it to its new location. Remove the apostrophe from the pasted formula, and it will be identical to the original formula. And don't forget to remove the apostrophe from the original formula as well. ∎

Converting Formulas to Values

If you have a range of formulas that will always produce the same result (so-called *dead formulas*), you may want to convert them to values. For example, if you use the RANDBETWEEN function to create a set of random numbers (in cells A1:A20) and you don't want Excel to recalculate those random numbers each time you press Enter, you can convert the formulas to values. Just follow these steps:

1. Select A1:A20.
2. Choose Home ⇨ Clipboard ⇨ Copy (or press Ctrl+C).
3. Choose Home ⇨ Clipboard ⇨ Paste Values (V).
4. Press Esc to cancel Copy mode.

Summary

This chapter taught you the key details about entering formulas to perform calculations in cells. You learned about formula operators and the correct precedence in formulas, as well as how built-in functions help you perform sophisticated calculations. You also saw a host of techniques and shortcuts that will make your formula building faster and easier than ever.

Working with Dates and Times

M any worksheets contain dates and times in cells. For example, you might track information by date or create a schedule based on time. Beginners often find that working with dates and times in Excel can be frustrating. To work with dates and times, you need a good understanding of how Excel handles time-based information. This chapter provides the information you need to create powerful formulas that manipulate dates and times.

Note

The dates in this chapter correspond to the U.S. English language date format: month/day/year. For example, the date *3/1/1952* refers to March 1, 1952, not January 3, 1952. I realize that this setup may seem illogical, but that's the way Americans have been trained. I trust that the non-American readers of this book can make the adjustment. ■

How Excel Handles Dates and Times

This section presents a quick overview of how Excel deals with dates and times. It includes coverage of the Excel program's date and time serial number system, and it offers tips for entering and formatting dates and times.

Understanding Date Serial Numbers

To Excel, a *date* is simply a number. More precisely, a date is a *serial number* that represents the number of days since the fictitious date of January 0, 1900. A serial number of 1 corresponds to January 1, 1900; a serial number

> **IN THIS CHAPTER**
>
> **Using dates and times in Excel**
>
> **Reviewing Excel date-related functions**
>
> **Exploring Excel time-related functions**

of 2 corresponds to January 2, 1900, and so on. This system makes it possible to deal with dates in formulas. For example, you can create a formula to calculate the number of days between two dates (just subtract one from the other).

Excel support dates from January 1, 1900, through December 31, 9999 (serial number = 2,958,465).

You may wonder about January 0, 1900. This *nondate* (which corresponds to date serial number 0) is actually used to represent times that aren't associated with a particular day. This concept becomes clear later in this chapter (see "Entering Times").

To view a date serial number as a date, you must format the cell as a date. Choose Home ➪ Number ➪ Number Format. This drop-down control provides you with two date formats. To select from additional date formats, see "Formatting Dates and Times," later in this chapter.

Choose Your Date System: 1900 or 1904

Excel supports two date systems: the 1900 date system and the 1904 date system. Which system you use in a workbook determines what date serves as the basis for dates. The 1900 date system uses January 1, 1900, as the day assigned to date serial number 1. The 1904 date system uses January 1, 1904, as the base date. By default, Excel for Windows uses the 1900 date system, and Excel for Macintosh uses the 1904 date system. Excel for Windows supports the 1904 date system for compatibility with Macintosh files. You can choose the date system for the active workbook in the Advanced section of the Excel Options dialog box. (It's in the When Calculating This Workbook subsection.) You can't change the date system if you use Excel for Macintosh.

Generally, you should use the default 1900 date system. And you should exercise caution if you use two different date systems in workbooks that are linked. For example, assume that Book1 uses the 1904 date system and contains the date 1/15/1999 in cell A1. Assume that Book2 uses the 1900 date system and contains a link to cell A1 in Book1. Book2 displays the date as *1/14/1995*. Both workbooks use the same date serial number (34713), but they're interpreted differently.

One advantage to using the 1904 date system is that it enables you to display negative time values. With the 1900 date system, a calculation that results in a negative time (e.g., 4:00 PM – 5:30 PM) cannot be displayed. When using the 1904 date system, the negative time displays as *–1:30* (i.e., a difference of 1 hour and 30 minutes).

Entering Dates

You can enter a date directly as a serial number (if you know the serial number) and then format it as a date. More often, you enter a date by using any of several recognized date formats. Excel automatically converts your entry into the corresponding date serial number (which it uses for calculations), and it also applies the default date format to the cell so that it displays as an actual date rather than as a cryptic serial number.

For example, if you need to enter June 18, 2010, into a cell, you can enter the date by typing **June 18, 2010** (or any of several different date formats). Excel interprets your entry and stores the value 40347, the date serial number for that date (provided you're using the 1900 date system, which I'll assume from here on in my descriptions). It also applies the default date format, so the cell contents may not appear exactly as you typed them.

Note

Depending on your regional settings, entering a date in a format such as June 18, 2010, may be interpreted as a text string. In such a case, you need to enter the date in a format that corresponds to your regional settings, such as 18 June 2010. ∎

When you activate a cell that contains a date, the Formula bar shows the cell contents formatted by using the default date format — which corresponds to your system's *short date format*. The Formula bar doesn't display the date's serial number. If you need to find out the serial number for a particular date, format the cell with a nondate number format.

Tip

To change the default date format, you need to change a system-wide setting. From the Windows Control Panel, select Clock, Language, and Region (Windows 7 and Vista) or Regional and Language Options (Windows XP). The exact procedure varies, depending on the version of Windows you use. Look for the drop-down list that enables you to change the Short Date Format. The setting you choose determines the default date format that Excel uses to display dates in the Formula bar. ∎

Table 16-1 shows a sampling of the date formats that Excel recognizes (using the U.S. settings). Results will vary if you use a different regional setting.

TABLE 16-1

Date Entry Formats Recognized by Excel

Entry	Excel Interpretation (U.S. Settings)
6-18-10	June 18, 2010
6-18-2010	June 18, 2010
6/18/10	June 18, 2010
6/18/2010	June 18, 2010
6-18-10	June 18, 2010
June 18, 2010	June 18, 2010
Jun 18	June 18 of the current year
June 18	June 18 of the current year

continued

TABLE 16-1 *(continued)*

Entry	Excel Interpretation (U.S. Settings)
6/18	June 18 of the current year
6-18	June 18 of the current year
18-Jun-2010	June 18, 2010
2010/6/18	June 18, 2010

As you can see in Table 16-1, Excel is rather flexible when it comes to recognizing dates entered into a cell. It's not perfect, however. For example, Excel does *not* recognize any of the following entries as dates:

- June 18 2010
- Jun-18 2010
- Jun-18/2010

Rather, it interprets these entries as text. If you plan to use dates in formulas, make sure that Excel can recognize the date you enter as a date; otherwise, the formulas that refer to these dates will produce incorrect results.

If you attempt to enter a date that lies outside of the supported date range, Excel interprets it as text. If you attempt to format a serial number that lies outside of the supported range as a date, the value displays as a series of hash marks (#########).

Searching for Dates

If your worksheet uses many dates, you may need to search for a particular date by using the Find and Replace dialog box (Home ➪ Editing ➪ Find & Select ➪ Find; or Ctrl+F). Excel is rather picky when it comes to finding dates. You must enter the date as it appears in the Formula bar. For example, if a cell contains a date formatted to display as *June 19, 2010*, the date appears in the Formula bar using your system's short date format (e.g., 6/19/2010). Therefore, if you search for the date as it appears in the cell, Excel won't find it. But it will find the cell if you search for the date in the format that appears in the Formula bar.

Understanding Time Serial Numbers

When you need to work with time values, you extend the Excel date serial number system to include decimals. In other words, Excel works with times by using fractional days. For example, the date serial number for June 1, 2010, is 40330. Noon (halfway through the day) is represented internally as 40330.5.

The serial number equivalent of 1 minute is approximately 0.00069444. The formula that follows calculates this number by multiplying 24 hours by 60 minutes, and dividing the result into 1. The denominator consists of the number of minutes in a day (1,440).

```
=1/(24*60)
```

Similarly, the serial number equivalent of 1 second is approximately 0.00001157, obtained by the following formula:

1/(24 hours × 60 minutes × 60 seconds)

In this case, the denominator represents the number of seconds in a day (86,400).

```
=1/(24*60*60)
```

In Excel, the smallest unit of time is one one-thousandth of a second. The time serial number shown here represents 23:59:59.999 (one one-thousandth of a second or .001 second before midnight):

```
0.99999999
```

Table 16-2 shows various times of day along with each associated time serial number.

TABLE 16-2

Times of Day and Their Corresponding Serial Numbers

Time of Day	Time Serial Number
12:00:00 AM (midnight)	0.00000000
1:30:00 AM	0.06250000
7:30:00 AM	0.31250000
10:30:00 AM	0.43750000
12:00:00 PM (noon)	0.50000000
1:30:00 PM	0.56250000
4:30:00 PM	0.68750000
6:00:00 PM	0.75000000
9:00:00 PM	0.87500000
10:30:00 PM	0.93750000

Entering Times

As with entering dates, you normally don't have to worry about the actual time serial numbers. Just enter the time into a cell using a recognized format. Table 16-3 shows some examples of time formats that Excel recognizes.

TABLE 16-3

Time Entry Formats Recognized by Excel

Entry	Excel Interpretation
11:30:00 am	11:30 AM
11:30:00 AM	11:30 AM
11:30 pm	11:30 PM
11:30	11:30 AM
13:30	1:30 PM

Because the preceding samples don't have a specific day associated with them, Excel (by default) uses a date serial number of 0, which corresponds to the nonday January 0, 1900. Often, you'll want to combine a date and time. Do so by using a recognized date-entry format, followed by a space, and then a recognized time-entry format. For example, if you enter **6/18/2010 11:30** in a cell, Excel interprets it as 11:30 a.m. on June 18, 2010. Its date/time serial number is 40347.479166667.

When you enter a time that exceeds 24 hours, the associated date for the time increments accordingly. For example, if you enter **25:00:00** into a cell, it's interpreted as 1:00 a.m. on January 1, 1900. The day part of the entry increments because the time exceeds 24 hours. Keep in mind that a time value without a date uses January 0, 1900, as the date.

Similarly, if you enter a date *and* a time (and the time exceeds 24 hours), the date that you entered is adjusted. If you enter **9/18/2010 25:00:00**, for example, it's interpreted as 9/19/2010 1:00:00 a.m.

If you enter a time only (without an associated date) into an unformatted cell, the maximum time that you can enter into a cell is **9999:59:59** (just less than 10,000 hours). Excel adds the appropriate number of days. In this case, **9999:59:59** is interpreted as 3:59:59 p.m. on 02/19/1901. If you enter a time that exceeds 10,000 hours, the entry is interpreted as a text string rather than a time.

Formatting Dates and Times

You have a great deal of flexibility in formatting cells that contain dates and times. For example, you can format the cell to display the date part only, the time part only, or both the date and time parts.

You format dates and times by selecting the cells and then using the Number tab of the Format Cells dialog box, as shown in Figure 16-1. To display this dialog box, click the Dialog Box Launcher icon in the Number group of the Home tab. Or, click Number Format and choose More Number Formats from the list that appears.

Use the Number tab in the Format Cells dialog box to change the appearance of dates and times.

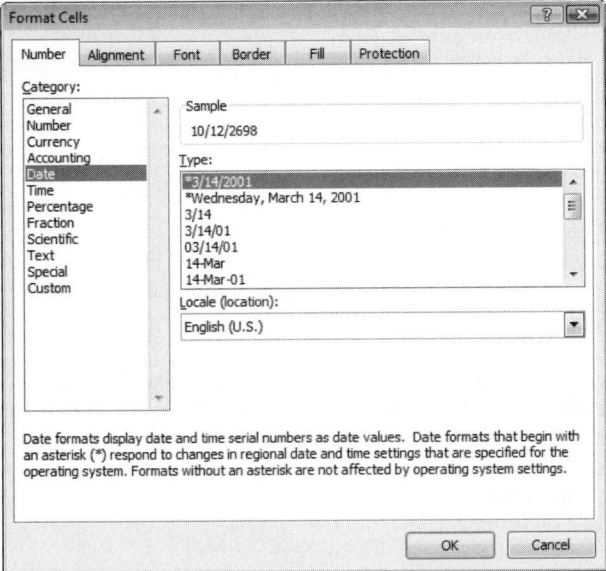

The Date category shows built-in date formats, and the Time category shows built-in time formats. Some formats include both date and time displays. Just select the desired format from the Type list and then click OK.

Tip

When you create a formula that refers to a cell containing a date or a time, Excel sometimes automatically formats the formula cell as a date or a time. Often, this automation can be helpful; other times, it can be an annoyance. To return the number formatting to the default General format, choose Home ⇨ Number ⇨ Number Format and choose General from the drop-down list. Or, press Ctrl+Shift+~. ∎

If none of the built-in formats meets your needs, you can create a custom number format. Select the Custom category and then type the custom format codes into the Type box.

Problems with Dates

Excel has some problems when it comes to dates. Many of these problems stem from the fact that Excel was designed many years ago. Excel designers basically emulated the Lotus 1-2-3 program's limited date and time features, which contain a bug that was duplicated intentionally in Excel. (You can read why in a bit.) If Excel were being designed from scratch today, I'm sure it would be much more versatile in dealing with dates. Unfortunately, users are currently stuck with a product that leaves much to be desired in the area of dates.

Excel's Leap Year Bug

A *leap year*, which occurs every four years, contains an additional day (February 29). Specifically, years that are evenly divisible by 100 are not leap years, unless they are also evenly divisible by 400. Although the year 1900 was not a leap year, Excel treats it as such. In other words, when you type **2/29/1900** into a cell, Excel interprets it as a valid date and assigns a serial number of 60.

If you type **2/29/1901**, however, Excel correctly interprets it as a mistake and doesn't convert it to a date. Rather, it simply makes the cell entry a text string.

How can a product used daily by millions of people contain such an obvious bug? The answer is historical. The original version of Lotus 1-2-3 contained a bug that caused it to treat 1900 as a leap year. When Excel was released some time later, the designers knew of this bug and chose to reproduce it in Excel to maintain compatibility with Lotus worksheet files.

Why does this bug still exist in later versions of Excel? Microsoft asserts that the disadvantages of correcting this bug outweigh the advantages. If the bug were eliminated, it would mess up millions of existing workbooks. In addition, correcting this problem would possibly affect compatibility between Excel and other programs that use dates. As it stands, this bug rarely causes problems because most users don't use dates prior to March 1, 1900.

Pre-1900 Dates

The world, of course, didn't begin on January 1, 1900. People who use Excel to work with historical information often need to work with dates before January 1, 1900. Unfortunately, the only way to work with pre-1900 dates is to enter the date into a cell as text. For example, you can enter **July 4, 1776**, into a cell, and Excel won't complain.

Tip

If you plan to sort information by old dates, you should enter your text dates with a four-digit year, followed by a two-digit month, and then a two-digit day: for example, 1776-07-04. This format will enable accurate sorting. ■

Using dates as text works in some situations, but the main problem is that you can't perform any manipulation on a date that's entered as text. For example, you can't change its numerical formatting, you can't determine which day of the week this date occurred on, and you can't calculate the date that occurs 7 days later.

Inconsistent Date Entries

You need to exercise caution when entering dates by using two digits for the year. When you do so, Excel has some rules that kick in to determine which century to use. And those rules vary, depending on the version of Excel that you use.

Two-digit years between 00 and 29 are interpreted as twenty-first century dates, and two-digit years between 30 and 99 are interpreted as twentieth century dates. For example, if you enter **12/15/28**, Excel interprets your entry as December 15, 2028. But if you enter **12/15/30**, Excel sees it as December 15, 1930, because Windows uses a default boundary year of 2029. You can keep the default as is or change it via the Windows Control Panel. From the Region and Language Options dialog box, click the Additional Settings button to display the Customize Format dialog box. Select the Date tab and then specify a different year.

Figure 16-2 shows this dialog box in Windows 7. This procedure may vary with different versions of Windows.

FIGURE 16-2

Use the Windows Control Panel to specify how Excel interprets two-digit years.

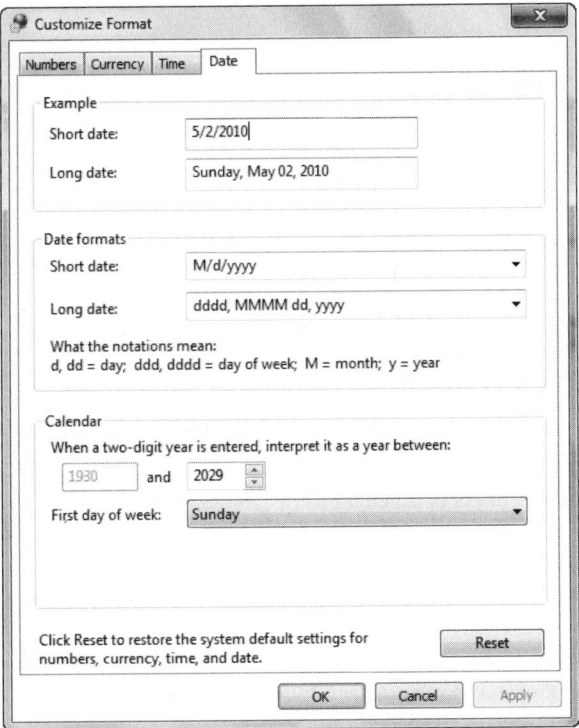

Tip

The best way to avoid any surprises is to simply enter *all* years using all four digits for the year. ∎

Date-Related Worksheet Functions

Excel has quite a few functions that work with dates. These functions are accessible by choosing Formulas ➪ Function Library ➪ Date & Time.

Table 16-4 summarizes the date-related functions available in Excel.

TABLE 16-4

Date-Related Functions

Function	Description
DATE	Returns the serial number of a particular date.
DATEVALUE	Converts a date in the form of text to a serial number.
DAY	Converts a serial number to a day of the month.
DAYS360	Calculates the number of days between two dates based on a 360-day year.
EDATE[a]	Returns the serial number of the date that represents the indicated number of months before or after the start date.
EOMONTH[a]	Returns the serial number of the last day of the month before or after a specified number of months.
MONTH	Converts a serial number to a month.
NETWORKDAYS[a]	Returns the number of whole workdays between two dates.
NETWORKDAYS.INTL [b]	An international version of the NETWORKDAYS function, which allows non-standard weekend days.
NOW	Returns the serial number of the current date and time.
TODAY	Returns the serial number of today's date.
WEEKDAY	Converts a serial number to a day of the week.
WEEKNUM[a]	Returns the week number in the year.
WORKDAY*	Returns the serial number of the date before or after a specified number of workdays.

Function	Description
WORKDAY .INTL [b]	An international version of the WORKDAY function, which allows non-standard weekend days.
YEAR	Converts a serial number to a year.
YEARFRAC [a]	Returns the year fraction representing the number of whole days between start_date and end_date.

[a]In versions prior to Excel 2007, these functions are available only when the Analysis ToolPak add-in is installed.
[b]Indicates a function new to Excel 2010.

Note

Excel 2010 includes two new worksheet functions related to dates: NETWORKDAYS.INTL and WORKDAY.INTL. These functions include an additional argument in which you can specify non-standard weekend days. If you consider Saturday and Sunday to be non-working weekend days, the older versions of these functions will work fine, otherwise, use the new functions to have the option of including weekend days. ■

Displaying the Current Date

The following formula uses the TODAY function to display the current date in a cell:

```
=TODAY()
```

You can also display the date combined with text. The formula that follows, for example, displays text, such as *Today is Friday, April 9, 2010*:

```
="Today is "&TEXT(TODAY(),"dddd, mmmm d, yyyy")
```

It's important to understand that the TODAY function is not a date stamp. The function is updated whenever the worksheet is calculated. For example, if you enter either of the preceding formulas into a worksheet, the formulas display the current date. And when you open the workbook tomorrow, they will display the current date (*not* the date when you entered the formula).

Tip

To enter a date stamp into a cell, press Ctrl+; (semicolon). This action enters the date directly into the cell and does not use a formula. Therefore, the date will not change. ■

Displaying Any Date

You can easily enter a date into a cell by simply typing it while using any of the date formats that Excel recognizes. You can also create a date by using the DATE function, which takes three arguments: the year, the month, and the day. The following formula, for example, returns a date comprising the year in cell A1, the month in cell B1, and the day in cell C1:

```
=DATE(A1,B1,C1)
```

Note

The DATE function accepts invalid arguments and adjusts the result accordingly. For example, the following formula uses 13 as the month argument and returns January 1, 2010. The month argument is automatically translated as month 1 of the following year.

    =DATE(2009,13,1) ∎

Often, you'll use the DATE function with other functions as arguments. For example, the formula that follows uses the YEAR and TODAY functions to return the date for the U.S. Independence Day (July 4) of the current year:

    =DATE(YEAR(TODAY()),7,4)

The DATEVALUE function converts a text string that looks like a date into a date serial number. The following formula returns 40412, which is the date serial number for August 22, 2010:

    =DATEVALUE("8/22/2010")

To view the result of this formula as a date, you need to apply a date number format to the cell.

Caution

Be careful when using the DATEVALUE function. A text string that looks like a date in your country may not look like a date in another country. The preceding example works fine if your system is set for U.S. date formats, but it returns an error for other regional date formats because Excel is looking for the eighth day of the 22nd month! Doing so will return #VALUE! ∎

Generating a Series of Dates

Often, you want to insert a series of dates into a worksheet. For example, in tracking weekly sales, you may want to enter a series of dates, each separated by 7 days. These dates will serve to identify the sales figures.

In some cases you can use the Excel Auto Fill feature to insert a series of dates. Enter the first date, and drag the cell's fill handle while holding the right mouse button. Release the mouse button and select an option from the shortcut menu (see Figure 16-3) — Fill Days, Fill Weekdays, Fill Months, or Fill Years.

For more flexibility, enter the first two dates in the series, and choose Fill Series from the shortcut menu. For example, to enter a series of dates separated by 7 days, enter the first two dates of the series, and select both cells. Drag the cell's fill handle while holding the right mouse button. In the shortcut menu, choose Fill Series. Excel completes the series by entering additional dates, separated by seven days.

The advantage of using formulas (instead of Auto Fill) to create a series of dates is that when you change the first date, the others update automatically. You need to enter the starting date into a cell and then use formulas (copied down the column) to generate the additional dates.

The following examples assume that you enter the first date of the series into cell A1 and the formula into cell A2. You can then copy this formula down the column as many times as needed.

FIGURE 16-3

Using Auto Fill to create a series of dates

To generate a series of dates separated by 7 days, use this formula:

```
=A1+7
```

To generate a series of dates separated by 1 month, you need to use a more complicated formula because months don't all have the same number of days. This formula creates a series of dates, separated by 1 month:

```
=DATE(YEAR(A1),MONTH(A1)+1,DAY(A1))
```

To generate a series of dates separated by 1 year, use this formula:

```
=DATE(YEAR(A1)+1,MONTH(A1),DAY(A1))
```

To generate a series of weekdays only (no Saturdays or Sundays), use the formula that follows. This formula assumes that the date in cell A1 is not a weekend day.

```
=IF(WEEKDAY(A1)=6,A1+3,A1+1)
```

Converting a Nondate String to a Date

You may import data that contains dates coded as text strings. For example, the following text represents August 21, 2010 (a four-digit year followed by a two-digit month, followed by a two-digit day):

```
20100821
```

To convert this string to an actual date, you can use a formula, such as the following. (It assumes that the coded data is in cell A1.)

```
=DATE(LEFT(A1,4),MID(A1,5,2),RIGHT(A1,2))
```

This formula uses text functions (LEFT, MID, and RIGHT) to extract the digits, and then it uses these extracted digits as arguments for the DATE function.

Calculating the Number of Days Between Two Dates

A common type of date calculation determines the number of days between two dates. For example, say you have a financial worksheet that calculates interest earned on a deposit account. The interest earned depends on the number of days the account is open. If your sheet contains the open date and the close date for the account, you can calculate the number of days the account was open.

Because dates are stored as consecutive serial numbers, you can use simple subtraction to calculate the number of days between two dates. For example, if cells A1 and B1 both contain a date, the following formula returns the number of days between these dates:

```
=A1-B1
```

If cell B1 contains a more recent date than the date in cell A1, the result will be negative.

Note

If this formula does not display the correct value, make sure that cells A1 and B1 both contain actual dates — not text that *looks* like a date. ■

Sometimes, calculating the difference between two days is more difficult. To demonstrate, consider the common fence-post analogy. If somebody asks you how many units make up a fence, you can respond with either of two answers: the number of fence posts or the number of gaps between the fence posts. The number of fence posts is always one more than the number of gaps between the posts.

To bring this analogy into the realm of dates, suppose that you start a sales promotion on February 1 and end the promotion on February 9. How many days was the promotion in effect? Subtracting February 1 from February 9 produces an answer of 8 days. Actually, though, the promotion lasted 9 days. In this case, the correct answer involves counting the fence posts, not the gaps. The formula to calculate the length of the promotion (assuming that you have appropriately named cells) appears like this:

```
=EndDay-StartDay+1
```

Calculating the Number of Workdays between Two Dates

When calculating the difference between two dates, you may want to exclude weekends and holidays. For example, you may need to know how many business days fall in the month of November. This calculation should exclude Saturdays, Sundays, and holidays. The NETWORKDAYS function can help out.

Note

In versions prior to Excel 2007, the NETWORKDAYS function was available only when the Analysis ToolPak add-in was installed. This function is now part of Excel and doesn't require an add-in. ■

The NETWORKDAYS function calculates the difference between two dates, excluding weekend days (Saturdays and Sundays). As an option, you can specify a range of cells that contain the dates of holidays, which are also excluded. Excel has no way of determining which days are holidays, so you must provide this information in a range.

Figure 16-4 shows a worksheet that calculates the workdays between two dates. The range A2:A11 contains a list of holiday dates. The two formulas in column C calculate the workdays between the dates in column A and column B. For example, the formula in cell C15 is

```
=NETWORKDAYS(A15,B15,A2:A11)
```

FIGURE 16-4

Using the NETWORKDAYS function to calculate the number of working days between two dates

	A	B	C	D
1	Date	Holiday		
2	1/1/10	New Year's Day		
3	1/18/10	Martin Luther King Jr. Day		
4	2/15/10	Presidents' Day		
5	5/31/10	Memorial Day		
6	7/4/10	Independence Day		
7	9/6/10	Labor Day		
8	10/11/10	Columbus Day		
9	11/11/10	Veterans Day		
10	11/25/10	Thanksgiving Day		
11	12/25/10	Christmas Day		
12				
13				
14	First Day	Last Day	Working Days	
15	Friday 1/1/2010	Thursday 1/7/2010	4	
16	Friday 1/1/2010	Friday 12/31/2010	253	
17				

This formula returns 4, which means that the 7-day period beginning with January 1 contains four workdays. In other words, the calculation excludes one holiday, one Saturday, and one Sunday. The formula in cell C16 calculates the total number of workdays in the year.

Note

Excel 2010 includes an updated version of the NETWORKDAYS function, named NETWORKDAYS.INTL. This new version is useful if you consider weekend days to be days other than Saturday and Sunday. ■

Offsetting a Date Using only Workdays

The WORKDAY function is the opposite of the NETWORKDAYS function. For example, if you start a project on January 4 and the project requires 10 working days to complete, the WORKDAY function can calculate the date you will finish the project.

Note

In versions prior to Excel 2007, the WORKDAY function was available only when the Analysis ToolPak add-in was installed. The function is now part of Excel and doesn't require an add-in. ■

The following formula uses the WORKDAY function to determine the date that is 10 working days from January 4, 2010. A working day consists of a weekday (Monday through Friday).

```
=WORKDAY("1/4/2010",10)
```

The formula returns a date serial number, which must be formatted as a date. The result is January 18, 2010 (four weekend dates fall between January 4 and January 18).

Caution

The preceding formula may return a different result, depending on your regional date setting. (The hard-coded date may be interpreted as April 1, 2010.) A better formula is

```
=WORKDAY(DATE(2010,1,4),10) ■
```

The second argument for the WORKDAY function can be negative. And, as with the NETWORKDAYS function, the WORKDAY function accepts an optional third argument (a reference to a range that contains a list of holiday dates).

Note

Excel 2010 includes an updated version of the WORKDAY function, named WORKDAY.INTL. This new version is useful if you consider weekend days to be days other than Saturday and Sunday. ■

Calculating the Number of Years between Two Dates

The following formula calculates the number of years between two dates. This formula assumes that cells A1 and B1 both contain dates:

```
=YEAR(A1)-YEAR(B1)
```

This formula uses the YEAR function to extract the year from each date and then subtracts one year from the other. If cell B1 contains a more recent date than the date in cell A1, the result is negative.

Note that this function doesn't calculate full years. For example, if cell A1 contains *12/31/2010* and cell B1 contains *01/01/2011*, the formula returns a difference of 1 year even though the dates differ by only 1 day. See the next section for another way to calculate the number of full years.

Calculating a Person's Age

A person's age indicates the number of full years that the person has been alive. The formula in the previous section (for calculating the number of years between two dates) won't calculate this value correctly. You can use two other formulas, however, to calculate a person's age.

The following formula returns the age of the person whose date of birth you enter into cell A1. This formula uses the YEARFRAC function. (The third argument is for the basis, which basically means to count in increments of one day.)

```
=INT(YEARFRAC(TODAY(),A1,1))
```

Note
In versions prior to Excel 2007, the YEARFRAC function was available only when the Analysis ToolPak add-in was installed. The function is now part of Excel, and does not require an add-in. ■

The following formula uses the DATEDIF function to calculate an age. (See the sidebar, "Where's the DATEDIF Function?")

```
=DATEDIF(A1,TODAY(),"Y")
```

Where's the DATEDIF Function?

One of Excel's mysteries is the DATEDIF function. You may notice that this function does not appear in the drop-down function list for the Date & Time category; nor does it appear in the Insert Function dialog box. Therefore, when you use this function, you must always enter it manually.

The DATEDIF function has its origins in Lotus 1-2-3, and apparently Excel provides it for compatibility purposes. For some reason, Microsoft wants to keep this function a secret. The function has been available since Excel 5, but Excel 2000 is the only version that ever documented it in its Help system.

DATEDIF is a handy function that calculates the number of days, months, or years between two dates. The function takes three arguments: start_date, end_date, and a code that represents the time unit of interest. Here's an example of a formula that uses the DATEDIF function (it assumes that cells A1 and A2 contain dates). The formula returns the number of complete years between those two dates.

```
=DATEDIF(A1,A2,"y")
```

continued

continued

The following table displays valid codes for the third argument. (You must enclose the codes in quotation marks.)

Unit Code	Returns
"y"	The number of complete years in the period
"m"	The number of complete months in the period
"d"	The number of days in the period
"md"	The difference between the days in start_date and end_date. The months and years of the dates are ignored.
"ym"	The difference between the months in start_date and end_date. The days and years of the dates are ignored.
"yd"	The difference between the days of start_date and end_date. The years of the dates are ignored.

The start_date argument must be earlier than the end_date argument or else the function returns an error.

Determining the Day of the Year

January 1 is the first day of the year, and December 31 is the last day. But what about all of the days in between? The following formula returns the day of the year for a date stored in cell A1:

```
=A1-DATE(YEAR(A1),1,0)
```

Here's a similar formula that returns the day of the year for the current date:

```
=TODAY()-DATE(YEAR(TODAY()),1,0)
```

The following formula returns the number of days remaining in the year after a particular date (assumed to be in cell A1):

```
=DATE(YEAR(A1),12,31)-A1
```

Here's the formula modified to use the current date:

```
=DATE(YEAR(TODAY()),12,31)-TODAY()
```

When you enter either formula, Excel may apply date formatting to the cell. You may need to apply a nondate number format to view the result as a number.

To convert a particular day of the year (e.g., the 90th day of the year) to an actual date in a specified year, use the following formula, which assumes that the year is stored in cell A1 and that the day of the year is stored in cell B1:

```
=DATE(A1,1,B1)
```

Determining the Day of the Week

The WEEKDAY function accepts a date argument and returns an integer between 1 and 7 that corresponds to the day of the week. The following formula, for example, returns 7 because the first day of the year 2011 falls on a Saturday:

```
=WEEKDAY(DATE(2011,1,1))
```

The WEEKDAY function uses an optional second argument that specifies the day-numbering system for the result. If you specify 2 as the second argument, the function returns 1 for Monday, 2 for Tuesday, and so on. If you specify 3 as the second argument, the function returns 0 for Monday, 1 for Tuesday, and so on.

Tip

You can also determine the day of the week for a cell that contains a date by applying a custom number format. A cell that uses the following custom number format displays the day of the week, spelled out:

dddd ∎

Determining the Date of the Most Recent Sunday

You can use the following formula to return the date for the previous Sunday (or any other day of the week). If the current day is a Sunday, the formula returns the current date:

```
=TODAY()-MOD(TODAY()-1,7)
```

To modify this formula to find the date of a day other than Sunday, change the 1 to a different number between 2 (for Monday) and 7 (for Saturday).

Determining the First Day of the Week after a Date

This next formula returns the specified day of the week that occurs after a particular date. For example, use this formula to determine the date of the first Monday after June 1, 2010. The formula assumes that cell A1 contains a date and cell A2 contains a number between 1 and 7 (1 for Sunday, 2 for Monday, etc.).

```
=A1+A2-WEEKDAY(A1)+(A2<WEEKDAY(A1))*7
```

If cell A1 contains June 1, 2010 (a Tuesday), and cell A2 contains 7 (for Saturday), the formula returns June 5, 2010. This is the first Saturday after June 1, 2010.

Determining the *N*th Occurrence of a Day of the Week in a Month

You may need a formula to determine the date for a particular occurrence of a weekday. For example, suppose that your company's payday falls on the second Friday of each month and you need to determine the paydays for each month of the year. The following formula makes this type of calculation:

```
=DATE(A1,A2,1)+A3-WEEKDAY(DATE(A1,A2,1))+
(A4-(A3>=WEEKDAY(DATE(A1,A2,1))))*7
```

The formula in this section assumes that

- Cell A1 contains a year.
- Cell A2 contains a month.
- Cell A3 contains a day number (1 for Sunday, 2 for Monday, etc.).
- Cell A4 contains the occurrence number (e.g., 2 to select the second occurrence of the weekday specified in cell A3).

If you use this formula to determine the date of the second Friday in November 2010, it returns November 12, 2010.

Note
If the value in cell A4 exceeds the number of the specified day in the month, the formula returns a date from a subsequent month. For example, if you attempt to determine the date of the fifth Friday in November 2010 (there is no such date), the formula returns the first Friday in December. ■

Calculating Dates of Holidays

Determining the date for a particular holiday can be tricky. Some, such as New Year's Day and U.S. Independence Day, are no-brainers because they always occur on the same date. For these kinds of holidays, you can simply use the DATE function. To enter New Year's Day (which always falls on January 1) for a specific year in cell A1, you can enter this function:

```
=DATE(A1,1,1)
```

Other holidays are defined in terms of a particular occurrence of a particular weekday in a particular month. For example, Labor Day falls on the first Monday in September.

Figure 16-5 shows a workbook with formulas that calculate the date for 11 U.S. holidays. The formulas, which reference the year in cell A1, are listed in the sections that follow.

New Year's Day

This holiday always falls on January 1:

```
=DATE(A1,1,1)
```

Martin Luther King, Jr. Day

This holiday occurs on the third Monday in January. This formula calculates Martin Luther King, Jr. Day for the year in cell A1:

```
=DATE(A1,1,1)+IF(2<WEEKDAY(DATE(A1,1,1)),7-WEEKDAY
(DATE(A1,1,1))+2,2-WEEKDAY(DATE(A1,1,1)))+((3-1)*7)
```

FIGURE 16-5

Using formulas to determine the date for various holidays

	A	B	C	D	E	F
1	2010	<-- Enter the year				
2						
3			Holiday Calculations			
4						
5		Holiday	Description	Date	Weekday	
6		New Year's Day	1st Day in January	January 1, 2010	Friday	
7		Martin Luther King Jr. Day	3rd Monday in January	January 18, 2010	Monday	
8		Presidents' Day	3rd Monday in February	February 15, 2010	Monday	
9		Easter	Complicated	April 4, 2010	Sunday	
10		Memorial Day	Last Monday in May	May 31, 2010	Monday	
11		Independence Day	4th Day of July	July 4, 2010	Sunday	
12		Labor Day	1st Monday in September	September 6, 2010	Monday	
13		Columbus Day	2nd Monday in October	October 11, 2010	Monday	
14		Veterans Day	11th Day of November	November 11, 2010	Thursday	
15		Thanksgiving Day	4th Thursday in November	November 25, 2010	Thursday	
16		Christmas Day	25th Day of December	December 25, 2010	Saturday	
17						

Presidents' Day

Presidents' Day occurs on the third Monday in February. This formula calculates Presidents' Day for the year in cell A1:

```
=DATE(A1,2,1)+IF(2<WEEKDAY(DATE(A1,2,1)),7-WEEKDAY
(DATE(A1,2,1))+2,2-WEEKDAY(DATE(A1,2,1)))+((3-1)*7)
```

Easter

Calculating the date for Easter is difficult because of the complicated manner in which Easter is determined. Easter Day is the first Sunday after the next full moon that occurs after the vernal equinox. I found these formulas to calculate Easter on the Web. I have no idea how they work. And they don't work if your workbook uses the 1904 date system. (Read about the difference between the 1900 and the 1904 date system earlier in this chapter.)

```
=DOLLAR(("4/"&A1)/7+MOD(19*MOD(A1,19)-7,30)*14%,)*7-6
```

This one is slightly shorter, but equally obtuse:

```
=FLOOR("5/"&DAY(MINUTE(A1/38)/2+56)&"/"&A1,7)-34
```

Memorial Day

The last Monday in May is Memorial Day. This formula calculates Memorial Day for the year in cell A1:

```
=DATE(A1,6,1)+IF(2<WEEKDAY(DATE(A1,6,1)),7-WEEKDAY
(DATE(A1,6,1))+2,2-WEEKDAY(DATE(A1,6,1)))+((1-1)*7)-7
```

Notice that this formula actually calculates the first Monday in June and then subtracts 7 from the result to return the last Monday in May.

Independence Day

This holiday always falls on July 4:

```
=DATE(A1,7,4)
```

Labor Day

Labor Day occurs on the first Monday in September. This formula calculates Labor Day for the year in cell A1:

```
=DATE(A1,9,1)+IF(2<WEEKDAY(DATE(A1,9,1)),7-WEEKDAY
(DATE(A1,9,1))+2,2-WEEKDAY(DATE(A1,9,1)))+((1-1)*7)
```

Columbus Day

This holiday occurs on the second Monday in October. This formula calculates Columbus Day for the year in cell A1:

```
=DATE(A1,10,1)+IF(2<WEEKDAY(DATE(A1,10,1)),7-WEEKDAY
(DATE(A1,10,1))+2,2-WEEKDAY(DATE(A1,10,1)))+((2-1)*7)
```

Veterans Day

This holiday always falls on November 11:

```
=DATE(A1,11,11)
```

Thanksgiving Day

Thanksgiving Day is celebrated on the fourth Thursday in November. This formula calculates Thanksgiving Day for the year in cell A1:

```
=DATE(A1,11,1)+IF(5<WEEKDAY(DATE(A1,11,1)),7-WEEKDAY
(DATE(A1,11,1))+5,5-WEEKDAY(DATE(A1,11,1)))+((4-1)*7)
```

Christmas Day

This holiday always falls on December 25:

```
=DATE(A1,12,25)
```

Determining the Last Day of a Month

To determine the date that corresponds to the last day of a month, you can use the DATE function. However, you need to increment the month by 1 and use a day value of 0. In other words, the "0th" day of the next month is the last day of the current month.

The following formula assumes that a date is stored in cell A1. The formula returns the date that corresponds to the last day of the month.

```
=DATE(YEAR(A1),MONTH(A1)+1,0)
```

You can use a variation of this formula to determine how many days are in a specified month. The formula that follows returns an integer that corresponds to the number of days in the month for the date in cell A1:

```
=DAY(DATE(YEAR(A1),MONTH(A1)+1,0))
```

Determining whether a Year Is a Leap Year

To determine whether a particular year is a leap year, you can write a formula that determines whether the 29th day of February occurs in February or March. You can take advantage of the fact that the Excel DATE function adjusts the result when you supply an invalid argument — for example, a day of 29 when February contains only 28 days.

The following formula returns TRUE if the year of the date in cell A1 is a leap year. Otherwise, it returns FALSE.

```
=IF(MONTH(DATE(YEAR(A1),2,29))=2,TRUE,FALSE)
```

Caution

This function returns the wrong result (TRUE) if the year is 1900. See "Excel's Leap Year Bug," earlier in this chapter. ∎

Determining a Date's Quarter

For financial reports, you may find it useful to present information in terms of quarters. The following formula returns an integer between 1 and 4 that corresponds to the calendar quarter for the date in cell A1:

```
=ROUNDUP(MONTH(A1)/3,0)
```

This formula divides the month number by 3 and then rounds up the result.

Time-Related Functions

Excel also includes several functions that enable you to work with time values in your formulas. This section contains examples that demonstrate the use of these functions.

Table 16-5 summarizes the time-related functions available in Excel. These functions work with date serial numbers. When you use the Insert Function dialog box, these functions appear in the Date & Time function category.

TABLE 16-5

Time-Related Functions

Function	Description
HOUR	Returns the hour part of a serial number.
MINUTE	Returns the minute part of a serial number.
NOW	Returns the serial number of the current date and time.
SECOND	Returns the second part of a serial number.
TIME	Returns the serial number of a specified time.
TIMEVALUE	Converts a time in the form of text to a serial number.

Displaying the Current Time

This formula displays the current time as a time serial number (or as a serial number without an associated date):

```
=NOW()-TODAY()
```

You need to format the cell with a time format to view the result as a recognizable time. The quickest way is to choose Home ➪ Number ➪ Number Format and select Time from the drop-down list.

Note
This formula is updated only when the worksheet is calculated. ∎

Tip
To enter a time stamp (that doesn't change) into a cell, press Ctrl+Shift+: (colon). ∎

Displaying any Time

One way to enter a time value into a cell is to just type it, making sure that you include at least one colon (:). You can also create a time by using the TIME function. For example, the following formula returns a time comprised of the hour in cell A1, the minute in cell B1, and the second in cell C1:

```
=TIME(A1,B1,C1)
```

Similar to the DATE function, the TIME function accepts invalid arguments and adjusts the result accordingly. For example, the following formula uses 80 as the minute argument and returns 10:20:15 AM. The 80 minutes are simply added to the hour, with 20 minutes remaining.

```
=TIME(9,80,15)
```

Caution
If you enter a value greater than 24 as the first argument for the TIME function, the result may not be what you expect. Logically, a formula such as the one that follows should produce a date/time serial number of 1.041667 (i.e., 1 day and 1 hour).

```
=TIME(25,0,0)
```

In fact, this formula is equivalent to the following:

```
=TIME(1,0,0)
```
∎

You can also use the DATE function along with the TIME function in a single cell. The formula that follows generates a date and time with a serial number of 39420.7708333333 — which represents 6:30 p.m. on December 4, 2010:

```
=DATE(2010,12,4)+TIME(18,30,0)
```

The TIMEVALUE function converts a text string that looks like a time into a time serial number. This formula returns 0.2395833333, the time serial number for 5:45 a.m.:

```
=TIMEVALUE("5:45 am")
```

To view the result of this formula as a time, you need to apply number formatting to the cell. The TIMEVALUE function doesn't recognize all common time formats. For example, the following formula returns an error because Excel doesn't like the periods in "a.m."

```
=TIMEVALUE("5:45 a.m.")
```

Calculating the Difference between Two Times

Because times are represented as serial numbers, you can subtract the earlier time from the later time to get the difference. For example, if cell A2 contains 5:30:00 and cell B2 contains 14:00:00, the following formula returns 08:30:00 (a difference of 8 hours and 30 minutes):

```
=B2-A2
```

If the subtraction results in a negative value, however, it becomes an invalid time; Excel displays a series of hash marks (#######) because a time without a date has a date serial number of 0. A negative time results in a negative serial number, which cannot be displayed — although you can still use the calculated value in other formulas.

If the direction of the time difference doesn't matter, you can use the ABS function to return the absolute value of the difference:

```
=ABS(B2-A2)
```

This "negative time" problem often occurs when calculating an elapsed time — for example, calculating the number of hours worked given a start time and an end time. This presents no problem if the two times fall in the same day. But if the work shift spans midnight, the result is an invalid negative time. For example, you may start work at 10:00 p.m. and end work at 6:00 a.m. the next day. Figure 16-6 shows a worksheet that calculates the hours worked. As you can see, the shift that spans midnight presents a problem (cell C3).

FIGURE 16-6

Calculating the number of hours worked returns an error if the shift spans midnight.

	A	B	C	D	E
1	Start Shift	End Shift	Hours Worked		
2	8:00 AM	5:30 PM	9:30		
3	10:00 PM	6:00 AM	##############		
4	9:00 AM	4:30 PM	7:30		
5	11:30 AM	7:45 PM	8:15		
6	6:15 AM	1:45 PM	7:30		
7					
8					

Using the ABS function (to calculate the absolute value) isn't an option in this case because it returns the wrong result (16 hours). The following formula, however, *does* work by essentially calculating the hours as if they occurred on the same day:

```
=IF(B2<A2,B2+1,B2)-A2
```

Tip

Negative times *are* permitted if the workbook uses the 1904 date system. To switch to the 1904 date system, use the Advanced section of the Excel Options dialog box. Select the Use 1904 Date System option. But beware! When changing the workbook's date system, if the workbook uses dates, the dates will be off by 4 years. For more information about the 1904 date system, see the sidebar, "Choose Your Date System: 1900 or 1904," earlier in this chapter. ∎

Summing Times that Exceed 24 Hours

Many people are surprised to discover that when you sum a series of times that exceed 24 hours, Excel doesn't display the correct total. Figure 16-7 shows an example. The range B2:B8 contains times that represent the hours and minutes worked each day. The formula in cell B9 is

```
=SUM(B2:B8)
```

As you can see, the formula returns a seemingly incorrect total (17 hours, 45 minutes). The total should read 41 hours, 45 minutes. The problem is that the formula is displaying the total as a date/time serial number of 1.7395833, but the cell formatting is not displaying the *date* part of the date/time. The answer is incorrect because cell B9 has the wrong number format.

To view a time that exceeds 24 hours, you need to apply a custom number format for the cell so that square brackets surround the *hour* part of the format string. Applying the number format here to cell B9 displays the sum correctly:

```
[h]:mm
```

FIGURE 16-7

Incorrect cell formatting makes the total appear incorrectly.

	A	B	C	D
1	Day	Hours Worked		
2	Sunday	0		
3	Monday	8:30		
4	Tuesday	8:00		
5	Wednesday	9:00		
6	Thursday	9:30		
7	Friday	4:15		
8	Saturday	2:30		
9	Total Hours	17:45		
10				
11				
12				
13				

Figure 16-8 shows another example of a worksheet that manipulates times. This worksheet keeps track of hours worked during a week (regular hours and overtime hours).

FIGURE 16-8

An employee timesheet workbook

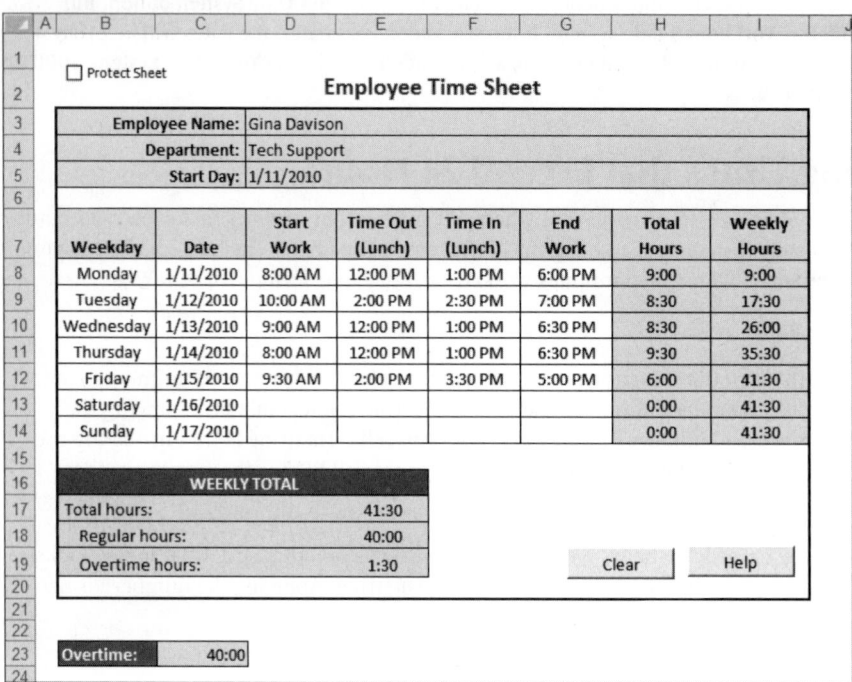

The week's starting date appears in cell D5, and the formulas in column B fill in the dates for the days of the week. Times appear in the range D8:G14, and formulas in column H calculate the number of hours worked each day. For example, the formula in cell H8 is

```
=IF(E8<D8,E8+1-D8,E8-D8)+IF(G8<F8,G8+1-G8,G8-F8)
```

The first part of this formula subtracts the time in column D from the time in column E to get the total hours worked before lunch. The second part subtracts the time in column F from the time in column G to get the total hours worked after lunch. Next, the IF function is used to accommodate overnight shift cases that span midnight — for example, an employee may start work at 10:00 p.m. and begin lunch at 2:00 a.m. Without the IF function, the formula returns a negative result.

The following formula in cell H17 calculates the weekly total by summing the daily totals in column H:

```
=SUM(H8:H14)
```

This worksheet assumes that hours in excess of 40 hours in a week are considered overtime hours. The worksheet contains a cell named *Overtime*, in cell C23. This cell contains a formula that returns 40:00. If your standard workweek consists of something other than 40 hours, you can change this cell.

The following formula (in cell H18) calculates regular (non-overtime) hours. This formula returns the smaller of two values: the total hours or the overtime hours.

```
=MIN(E17,Overtime)
```

The final formula, in cell H19, simply subtracts the regular hours from the total hours to yield the overtime hours.

```
=E17-E18
```

The times in I8:I14 may display time values that exceed 24 hours, so these cells use a custom number format:

```
[h]:mm
```

Converting from Military Time

Military time is expressed as a four-digit number from 0000 to 2359. For example, 1:00 a.m. is expressed as 0100 hours, and 3:30 p.m. is expressed as 1530 hours. The following formula converts such a number (assumed to be in cell A1) to a standard time:

```
=TIMEVALUE(LEFT(A1,2)&":"&RIGHT(A1,2))
```

The formula returns an incorrect result if the contents of cell A1 do not contain four digits. The following formula corrects the problem, and it returns a valid time for any military time value from 0 to 2359:

```
=TIMEVALUE(LEFT(TEXT(A1,"0000"),2)&":"&RIGHT(A1,2))
```

Following is a simpler formula that uses the TEXT function to return a formatted string, and then uses the TIMEVALUE function to express the result in terms of a time:

```
=TIMEVALUE(TEXT(A1,"00\:00"))
```

Converting Decimal Hours, Minutes, or Seconds to a Time

To convert decimal hours to a time, divide the decimal hours by 24. For example, if cell A1 contains 9.25 (representing hours), this formula returns 09:15:00 (9 hours, 15 minutes):

```
=A1/24
```

To convert decimal minutes to a time, divide the decimal hours by 1,440 (the number of minutes in a day). For example, if cell A1 contains 500 (representing minutes), the following formula returns 08:20:00 (8 hours, 20 minutes):

```
=A1/1440
```

To convert decimal seconds to a time, divide the decimal hours by 86,400 (the number of seconds in a day). For example, if cell A1 contains 65,000 (representing seconds), the following formula returns 18:03:20 (18 hours, 3 minutes, and 20 seconds):

```
=A1/86400
```

Adding Hours, Minutes, or Seconds to a Time

You can use the TIME function to add any number of hours, minutes, or seconds to a time. For example, assume that cell A1 contains a time. The following formula adds 2 hours and 30 minutes to that time and displays the result:

```
=A1+TIME(2,30,0)
```

You can use the TIME function to fill a range of cells with incremental times. Figure 16-9 shows a worksheet with a series of times in 10-minute increments. Cell A1 contains a time that was entered directly. Cell A2 contains the following formula, which is copied down the column:

```
=A1+TIME(0,10,0)
```

Rounding Time Values

You may need to create a formula that rounds a time to a particular value. For example, you may need to enter your company's time records rounded to the nearest 15 minutes. This section presents examples of various ways to round a time value.

The following formula rounds the time in cell A1 to the nearest minute:

```
=ROUND(A1*1440,0)/1440
```

FIGURE 16-9

Using a formula to create a series of incremental times

	A	B	C	D
1	8:00 AM			
2	8:10 AM			
3	8:20 AM			
4	8:30 AM			
5	8:40 AM			
6	8:50 AM			
7	9:00 AM			
8	9:10 AM			
9	9:20 AM			
10	9:30 AM			
11	9:40 AM			
12	9:50 AM			
13				
14				

The formula works by multiplying the time by 1,440 (to get total minutes). This value is passed to the ROUND function, and the result is divided by 1,440. For example, if cell A1 contains 11:52:34, the formula returns 11:53:00.

The following formula resembles this example, except that it rounds the time in cell A1 to the nearest hour:

```
=ROUND(A1*24,0)/24
```

If cell A1 contains 5:21:31, the formula returns 5:00:00.

The following formula rounds the time in cell A1 to the nearest 15 minutes (a quarter of an hour):

```
=ROUND(A1*24/0.25,0)*(0.25/24)
```

In this formula, 0.25 represents the fractional hour. To round a time to the nearest 30 minutes, change 0.25 to 0.5, as in the following formula:

```
=ROUND(A1*24/0.5,0)*(0.5/24)
```

Working with Non-Time-of-Day Values

Sometimes, you may want to work with time values that don't represent an actual time of day. For example, you may want to create a list of the finish times for a race or record the amount of time you spend in meetings each day. Such times don't represent a time of day. Rather, a value represents the time for an event (in hours, minutes, and seconds). The time to complete a test, for example, may be 35 minutes and 45 seconds. You can enter that value into a cell as **00:35:45**.

Excel interprets such an entry as 12:35:45 a.m., which works fine. (Just make sure that you format the cell so that it appears as you like.) When you enter such times that do not have an hour component, you must include at least one zero for the hour. If you omit a leading zero for a missing hour, Excel interprets your entry as 35 hours and 45 minutes.

Figure 16-10 shows an example of a worksheet set up to keep track of a person's jogging activity. Column A contains simple dates. Column B contains the distance in miles. Column C contains the time it took to run the distance. Column D contains formulas to calculate the speed in miles per hour. For example, the formula in cell D2 is

```
=B2/(C2*24)
```

Column E contains formulas to calculate the pace, in minutes per mile. For example, the formula in cell E2 is

```
=(C2*60*24)/B2
```

FIGURE 16-10

This worksheet uses times not associated with a time of day.

	A	B	C	D	E	F	G	H
1	Date	Distance	Time	Speed (mph)	Pace (min/mile)	YTD Distance	Cumulative Time	
2	1/1/2010	1.50	00:18:45	4.80	12.50	1.50	00:18:45	
3	1/2/2010	1.50	00:17:40	5.09	11.78	3.00	00:36:25	
4	1/3/2010	2.00	00:21:30	5.58	10.75	5.00	00:57:55	
5	1/4/2010	1.50	00:15:20	5.87	10.22	6.50	01:13:15	
6	1/5/2010	2.40	00:25:05	5.74	10.45	8.90	01:38:20	
7	1/6/2010	3.00	00:31:06	5.79	10.37	11.90	02:09:26	
8	1/7/2010	3.80	00:41:06	5.55	10.82	15.70	02:50:32	
9	1/8/2010	5.00	01:09:00	4.35	13.80	20.70	03:59:32	
10	1/9/2010	4.00	00:45:10	5.31	11.29	24.70	04:44:42	
11	1/10/2010	3.00	00:29:06	6.19	9.70	27.70	05:13:48	
12	1/11/2010	5.50	01:08:30	4.82	12.45	33.20	06:22:18	
13								
14								

Columns F and G contain formulas that calculate the year-to-date distance (using column B) and the cumulative time (using column C). The cells in column G are formatted using the following number format (which permits time displays that exceed 24 hours):

```
[hh]:mm:ss
```

Summary

In this chapter, you learned how Excel treats dates and times as serial numbers. You can use dates and times in formulas, so long as you understand how the serial numbers work. This chapter also introduced you to some Excel functions that work with dates and times, and showed you specific, handy examples of formulas you can build to tackle certain date and time calculation tasks.

Creating Formulas That Count and Sum

Many of the most common spreadsheet questions involve counting and summing values and other worksheet elements. It seems that people are always looking for formulas to count or to sum various items in a worksheet. This chapter attempts to answer the vast majority of such questions. It contains many examples that you can easily adapt to your own situation.

Counting and Summing Worksheet Cells

Generally, a *counting formula* returns the number of cells in a specified range that meet certain criteria. A *summing formula* returns the sum of the values of the cells in a range that meet certain criteria. The range you want counted or summed may or may not consist of a worksheet database.

Table 17-1 lists the Excel worksheet functions that come into play when creating counting and summing formulas. Not all these functions are covered in this chapter.

Note

If your data is in the form of a table, you can use filtering to accomplish many counting and summing operations. Just set the filter criteria, and the table displays only the rows that match your criteria (the non-qualifying rows in the table are hidden). Then you can select formulas to display counts or sums in the table's total row. ■

TABLE 17-1

Excel Counting and Summing Functions

Function	Description
COUNT	Returns the number of cells that contain a numeric value.
COUNTA	Returns the number of non-blank cells.
COUNTBLANK	Returns the number of blank cells.
COUNTIF	Returns the number of cells that meet a specified criterion.
COUNTIFS[a]	Returns the number of cells that meet multiple criteria.
DCOUNT	Counts the number of records that meet specified criteria; used with a worksheet database.
DCOUNTA	Counts the number of non-blank records that meet specified criteria; used with a worksheet database.
DEVSQ	Returns the sum of squares of deviations of data points from the sample mean; used primarily in statistical formulas.
DSUM	Returns the sum of a column of values that meet specified criteria; used with a worksheet database.
FREQUENCY	Calculates how often values occur within a range of values and returns a vertical array of numbers. Used only in a multicell array formula.
SUBTOTAL	When used with a first argument of 2, 3, 102, or 103, returns a *count* of cells that comprise a subtotal; when used with a first argument of 9 or 109, returns *the sum* of cells that comprise a subtotal.
SUM	Returns the sum of its arguments.
SUMIF	Returns the sum of cells that meet a specified criterion.
SUMIFS[a]	Returns the sum of cells that meet multiple criteria.
SUMPRODUCT	Multiplies corresponding cells in two or more ranges and returns the sum of those products.
SUMSQ	Returns the sum of the squares of its arguments; used primarily in statistical formulas.
SUMX2PY2	Returns the sum of the sum of squares of corresponding values in two ranges; used primarily in statistical formulas.
SUMXMY2	Returns the sum of squares of the differences of corresponding values in two ranges; used primarily in statistical formulas.
SUMX2MY2	Returns the sum of the differences of squares of corresponding values in two ranges; used primarily in statistical formulas.

[a]These functions were introduced in Excel 2007.

Getting a Quick Count or Sum

The Excel status bar can display useful information about the currently selected cells — no formulas required. Normally, the status bar displays the sum and count of the values in the selected range. You can, however, right-click to bring up a menu with other options. You can choose any or all the following: Average, Count, Numerical Count, Minimum, Maximum, and Sum.

Basic Counting Formulas

The basic counting formulas presented in this section are all straightforward and relatively simple. They demonstrate the capability of the Excel counting functions to count the number of cells in a range that meet specific criteria. Figure 17-1 shows a worksheet that uses formulas (in column E) to summarize the contents of range A1:B10 — a 20-cell range named *Data*. This range contains a variety of information, including values, text, logical values, errors, and empty cells.

FIGURE 17-1

Formulas in column E display various counts of the data in A1:B10.

	A	B	C	D	E	F
1	Jan	Feb		Total cells:	20	
2	525	718		Blank cells:	6	
3				Nonblank cells:	14	
4	3			Numeric values:	7	
5	552	911		Non-text cells:	17	
6	250	98		Text cells:	3	
7				Logical values:	2	
8	TRUE	FALSE		Error values:	2	
9		#DIV/0!		#N/A errors:	0	
10	Total	#NAME?		#NULL! errors:	0	
11				#DIV/0! errors:	1	
12				#VALUE! errors:	0	
13				#REF! errors:	0	
14				#NAME? errors:	1	
15				#NUM! errors:	0	
16						

About This Chapter's Examples

Most of the examples in this chapter use named ranges for function arguments. When you adapt these formulas for your own use, you'll need to substitute either the actual range address or a range name defined in your workbook.

continued

continued

Also, some examples consist of array formulas. An *array formula* is a special type of formula that enables you to perform calculations that would not otherwise be possible. You can spot an array formula because it's enclosed in curly brackets when it's displayed in the Formula bar. In addition, this syntax is used for the array formula examples presented in this book. For example:

```
{=Data*2}
```

When you enter an array formula, press **Ctrl+Shift+Enter** (not just Enter) but *don't* type the curly brackets (Excel inserts the brackets for you). If you need to edit an array formula, don't forget to use **Ctrl+Shift+Enter** when you finish editing (otherwise, the array formula will revert to a normal formula, and it will return an incorrect result).

Counting the Total Number of Cells

To get a count of the total number of cells in a range (empty and non-empty cells), use the following formula. This formula returns the number of cells in a range named *Data*. It simply multiplies the number of rows (returned by the ROWS function) by the number of columns (returned by the COLUMNS function).

```
=ROWS(Data)*COLUMNS(Data)
```

This formula will not work if the Data range consists of noncontiguous cells. In other words, Data must be a rectangular range of cells.

Counting Blank Cells

The following formula returns the number of blank (empty) cells in a range named *Data*:

```
=COUNTBLANK(Data)
```

The COUNTBLANK function also counts cells containing a formula that returns an empty string. For example, the formula that follows returns an empty string if the value in cell A1 is greater than 5. If the cell meets this condition, the COUNTBLANK function counts that cell.

```
=IF(A1>5,"",A1)
```

You can use the COUNTBLANK function with an argument that consists of entire rows or columns. For example, this next formula returns the number of blank cells in column A:

```
=COUNTBLANK(A:A)
```

The following formula returns the number of empty cells on the entire worksheet named *Sheet1*. You must enter this formula on a sheet other than Sheet1, or it will create a circular reference.

```
=COUNTBLANK(Sheet1!1:1048576)
```

Counting Non-Blank Cells

To count non-blank cells, use the COUNTA function. The following formula uses the COUNTA function to return the number of non-blank cells in a range named *Data*:

    =COUNTA(Data)

The COUNTA function counts cells that contain values, text, or logical values (TRUE or FALSE).

Note
If a cell contains a formula that returns an empty string, that cell is included in the count returned by COUNTA, even though the cell appears to be blank. ■

Counting Numeric Cells

To count only the numeric cells in a range, use the following formula (which assumes the range is named *Data*):

    =COUNT(Data)

Cells that contain a date or a time are considered to be numeric cells. Cells that contain a logical value (TRUE or FALSE) aren't considered to be numeric cells.

Counting Text Cells

To count the number of text cells in a range, you need to use an *array formula*. The array formula that follows returns the number of text cells in a range named *Data*:

    {=SUM(IF(ISTEXT(Data),1))}

Counting Non-text Cells

The following array formula uses the Excel ISNONTEXT function, which returns TRUE if its argument refers to any nontext cell (including a blank cell). This formula returns the count of the number of cells not containing text (including blank cells):

    {=SUM(IF(ISNONTEXT(Data),1))}

Counting Logical Values

The following array formula returns the number of logical values (TRUE or FALSE) in a range named *Data*:

    {=SUM(IF(ISLOGICAL(Data),1))}

Counting Error Values in a Range

Excel has three functions that help you determine whether a cell contains an error value:

- ISERROR: Returns TRUE if the cell contains any error value (#N/A, #VALUE!, #REF!, #DIV/0!, #NUM!, #NAME?, or #NULL!).
- ISERR: Returns TRUE if the cell contains any error value except #N/A.
- ISNA: Returns TRUE if the cell contains the #N/A error value.

You can use these functions in an array formula to count the number of error values in a range. The following array formula, for example, returns the total number of error values in a range named *Data*:

```
{=SUM(IF(ISERROR(data),1))}
```

Depending on your needs, you can use the ISERR or ISNA function in place of ISERROR.

If you would like to count specific types of errors, you can use the COUNTIF function. The following formula, for example, returns the number of #DIV/0! error values in the range named *Data*:

```
=COUNTIF(Data,"#DIV/0!")
```

Advanced Counting Formulas

Most of the basic examples presented earlier in this chapter use functions or formulas that perform conditional counting. The advanced counting formulas represented here contain more complex examples for counting worksheet cells, based on various types of criteria.

Counting Cells by Using the COUNTIF Function

The COUNTIF function, which is useful for single-criterion counting formulas, takes two arguments:

- **Range:** The range that contains the values that determine whether to include a particular cell in the count
- **Criteria:** The logical criteria that determine whether to include a particular cell in the count

Table 17-2 lists several examples of formulas that use the COUNTIF function. These formulas all work with a range named *Data*. As you can see, the criteria argument proves quite flexible. You can use constants, expressions, functions, cell references, and even wildcard characters (* and ?).

TABLE 17-2

Examples of Formulas Using the COUNTIF Function

Formula	Description
=COUNTIF(Data,12)	Returns the number of cells containing the value 12.
=COUNTIF(Data,"<0")	Returns the number of cells containing a negative value.
=COUNTIF(Data,"<>0")	Returns the number of cells not equal to 0.
=COUNTIF(Data,">5")	Returns the number of cells greater than 5.
=COUNTIF(Data,A1)	Returns the number of cells equal to the contents of cell A1.
=COUNTIF(Data,">"&A1)	Returns the number of cells greater than the value in cell A1.
=COUNTIF(Data,"*")	Returns the number of cells containing text.
=COUNTIF(Data,"???")	Returns the number of text cells containing exactly three characters.
=COUNTIF(Data,"budget")	Returns the number of cells containing the single word *budget* (not case sensitive)
=COUNTIF(Data,"*budget*")	Returns the number of cells containing the text *budget* anywhere within the text.
=COUNTIF(Data,"A*")	Returns the number of cells containing text that begins with the letter *A* (not case-sensitive).
=COUNTIF(Data,TODAY())	Returns the number of cells containing the current date.
=COUNTIF(Data,">"&AVERAGE(Data))	Returns the number of cells with a value greater than the average.
=COUNTIF(Data,">"&AVERAGE(Data)+ STDEV(Data)*3)	Returns the number of values exceeding three standard deviations above the mean.
=COUNTIF(Data,3)+COUNTIF(Data,-3)	Returns the number of cells containing the value 3 or –3.
=COUNTIF(Data,TRUE)	Returns the number of cells containing logical TRUE.
=COUNTIF(Data,TRUE)+COUNTIF (Data,FALSE)	Returns the number of cells containing a logical value (TRUE or FALSE).
=COUNTIF(Data,"#N/A")	Returns the number of cells containing the #N/A error value.

Counting Cells Based on Multiple Criteria

In many cases, your counting formula will need to count cells only if two or more criteria are met. These criteria can be based on the cells that are being counted or based on a range of corresponding cells.

Figure 17-2 shows a simple worksheet that I use for the examples in this section. This sheet shows sales data categorized by Month, SalesRep, and Type. The worksheet contains named ranges that correspond to the labels in row 1.

FIGURE 17-2

This worksheet demonstrates various counting techniques that use multiple criteria.

	A	B	C	D
1	Month	SalesRep	Type	Amount
2	January	Albert	New	85
3	January	Albert	New	675
4	January	Brooks	New	130
5	January	Cook	New	1350
6	January	Cook	Existing	685
7	January	Brooks	New	1350
8	January	Cook	New	475
9	January	Brooks	New	1205
10	February	Brooks	Existing	450
11	February	Albert	New	495
12	February	Cook	New	210
13	February	Cook	Existing	1050
14	February	Albert	New	140
15	February	Brooks	New	900
16	February	Brooks	New	900
17	February	Cook	New	95
18	February	Cook	New	780
19	March	Brooks	New	900
20	March	Albert	Existing	875
21	March	Brooks	New	50
22	March	Brooks	New	875
23	March	Cook	Existing	225
24	March	Cook	New	175
25	March	Brooks	Existing	400
26	March	Albert	New	840
27	March	Cook	New	132

Note

Several of the examples in this section use the COUNTIFS function, which was introduced in Excel 2007. There are alternative versions of the formulas, which should be used if you plan to share your workbook with others who use an earlier version of Excel. ∎

Using And Criteria

An And criterion counts cells if all specified conditions are met. A common example is a formula that counts the number of values that fall within a numerical range. For example, you may want to count cells that contain a value greater than 100 *and* less than or equal to 200. For this example, the COUNTIFS function will do the job:

```
=COUNTIFS(Amount,">100",Amount,"<=200")
```

Note

If the data is contained in a table, you can use table referencing in your formulas. For example, if the table is named *Table 1*, you can rewrite the preceding formula as:

```
=COUNTIFS(Table1[Amount],">100",Table1[Amount],"<=200")
```

This method of writing formulas does not require named ranges. ■

The COUNTIFS function accepts any number of paired arguments. The first member of the pair is the range to be counted (in this case, the range named *Amount*); the second member of the pair is the criterion. The preceding example contains two sets of paired arguments and returns the number of cells in which *Amount* is greater than 100 and less than or equal to 200.

Prior to Excel 2007, you would need to use a formula like this:

```
=COUNTIF(Amount,">100")-COUNTIF(Amount,">200")
```

The formula counts the number of values that are greater than 100 and then subtracts the number of values that are greater than or equal to 200. The result is the number of cells that contain a value greater than 100 and less than or equal to 200. This formula can be confusing because the formula refers to a condition — ">200" — even though the goal is to count values that are less than or equal to 200. Yet another alternative technique is to use an array formula, like the one that follows. You may find it easier to create this type of formula:

```
{=SUM((Amount>100)*(Amount<=200))}
```

Note

When you enter an array formula, remember to use Ctrl+Shift+Enter but don't type the brackets. Excel includes the brackets for you. ■

Sometimes, the counting criteria will be based on cells other than the cells being counted. You may, for example, want to count the number of sales that meet the following criteria:

- Month is January, *and*
- SalesRep is Brooks, *and*
- Amount is greater than 1000

The following formula (for Excel 2007 and Excel 2010) returns the number of items that meet all three criteria. Note that the COUNTIFS function uses three sets of pairs of arguments:

```
=COUNTIFS(Month,"January",SalesRep,"Brooks",Amount,">1000")
```

An alternative formula, which works with all versions of Excel, uses the SUMPRODUCT function. The following formula returns the same result as the previous formula:

```
=SUMPRODUCT((Month="January")*(SalesRep="Brooks")*(Amount>1000))
```

Yet another way to perform this count is to use an array formula:

```
{=SUM((Month="January")*(SalesRep="Brooks")*(Amount>1000))}
```

Using Or Criteria

To count cells by using an Or criterion, you can sometimes use multiple COUNTIF functions. The following formula, for example, counts the number of sales made in January or February:

```
=COUNTIF(Month,"January")+COUNTIF(Month,"February")
```

You can also use the COUNTIF function in an array formula. The following array formula, for example, returns the same result as the previous formula:

```
{=SUM(COUNTIF(Month,{"January","February"}))}
```

But if you base your Or criteria on cells other than the cells being counted, the COUNTIF function won't work. (Refer to Figure 17-2.) Suppose that you want to count the number of sales that meet the following criteria:

- Month is January, *or*
- SalesRep is Brooks, *or*
- Amount is greater than 1000

If you attempt to create a formula that uses COUNTIF, some double counting will occur. The solution is to use an array formula like this:

```
{=SUM(IF((Month="January")+(SalesRep="Brooks")+(Amount>1000),1))}
```

Combining And and Or Criteria

In some cases, you may need to combine And and Or criteria when counting. For example, perhaps you want to count sales that meet the following criteria:

- Month is January, *and*
- SalesRep is Brooks, *or* SalesRep is Cook

This array formula returns the number of sales that meet the criteria:

```
{=SUM((Month="January")*IF((SalesRep="Brooks")+
(SalesRep="Cook"),1))}
```

Counting the Most Frequently Occurring Entry

The MODE function returns the most frequently occurring value in a range. Figure 17-3 shows a worksheet with values in the range A1:A10 (named *Data*). The formula that follows returns 10 because that value appears most frequently in the Data range:

    =MODE(Data)

The MODE function returns the most frequently occurring value in a range.

	A	B	C	D	E	F
1	1			10	<- Mode	
2	4			5	<- Frequency of the mode	
3	4					
4	10					
5	10					
6	10					
7	10					
8	10					
9	12					
10	12					
11						

To count the number of times the most frequently occurring value appears in the range (in other words, the frequency of the mode), use the following formula:

    =COUNTIF(Data,MODE(Data))

This formula returns 5 because the modal value (10) appears five times in the Data range.

The MODE function will only work with numeric values. It simply ignores cells that contain text. To find the most frequently occurring text entry in a range, you need to use an array formula.

To count the number of times the most frequently occurring item (text or values) appears in a range named *Data*, use the following array formula:

    {=MAX(COUNTIF(Data,Data))}

This next array formula operates like the MODE function except that it works with both text and values:

    {=INDEX(Data,MATCH(MAX(COUNTIF(Data,Data)),COUNTIF(Data,Data),0))}

Counting the Occurrences of Specific Text

The examples in this section demonstrate various ways to count the occurrences of a character or text string in a range of cells. Figure 17-4 shows a worksheet used for these examples. Various text strings appear in the range A1:A10 (named *Data*); cell B1 is named *Text*.

FIGURE 17-4

This worksheet demonstrates various ways to count character strings in a range.

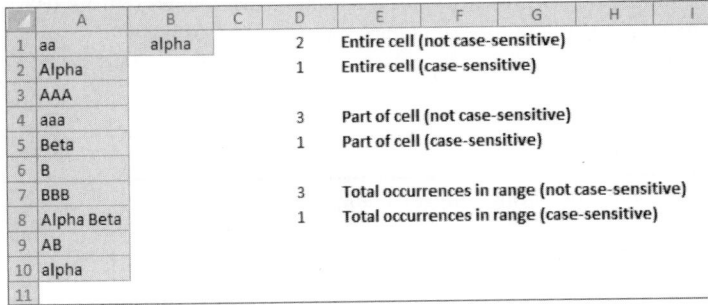

Entire Cell Contents

To count the number of cells containing the contents of the Text cell (and nothing else), you can use the COUNTIF function as the following formula demonstrates:

    =COUNTIF(Data,Text)

For example, if the Text cell contains the string *Alpha*, the formula returns 2 because two cells in the Data range contain this text. This formula is not case-sensitive, so it counts both *Alpha* (cell A2) and *alpha* (cell A10). Note, however, that it does not count the cell that contains *Alpha Beta* (cell A8).

The following array formula is similar to the preceding formula, but this one is case-sensitive:

    {=SUM(IF(EXACT(Data,Text),1))}

Partial Cell Contents

To count the number of cells that contain a string that includes the contents of the Text cell, use this formula:

    =COUNTIF(Data,"*"&Text&"*")

For example, if the Text cell contains the text *Alpha*, the formula returns 3 because three cells in the Data range contain the text *alpha* (cells A2, A8, and A10). Note that the comparison is not case-sensitive.

If you need a case-sensitive count, you can use the following array formula:

    {=SUM(IF(LEN(Data)-LEN(SUBSTITUTE(Data,Text,""))>0,1))}

If the Text cells contain the text *Alpha*, the preceding formula returns 2 because the string appears in two cells (A2 and A8).

Total Occurrences in a Range

To count the total number of occurrences of a string within a range of cells, use the following array formula:

```
{=(SUM(LEN(Data))-SUM(LEN(SUBSTITUTE(Data,Text,""))))/
LEN(Text)}
```

If the Text cell contains the character *B*, the formula returns 7 because the range contains seven instances of the string. This formula is case-sensitive.

The following array formula is a modified version that is not case-sensitive:

```
{=(SUM(LEN(Data))-SUM(LEN(SUBSTITUTE(UPPER(Data),
UPPER(Text),""))))/LEN(Text)}
```

Counting the Number of Unique Values

The following array formula returns the number of unique values in a range named *Data*:

```
{=SUM(1/COUNTIF(Data,Data))}
```

Note
The preceding formula is one of those "classic" Excel formulas that gets passed around the Internet. I don't know who originated it. ■

Useful as it is, this formula does have a serious limitation: If the range contains any blank cells, it returns an error. The following array formula solves this problem:

```
{=SUM(IF(COUNTIF(Data,Data)=0,"",1/COUNTIF(Data,Data)))}
```

Creating a Frequency Distribution

A *frequency distribution* basically comprises a summary table that shows the frequency of each value in a range. For example, an instructor may create a frequency distribution of test scores. The table would show the count of A's, B's, C's, and so on. Excel provides several ways to create frequency distributions. You can

- Use the FREQUENCY function.
- Create your own formulas.
- Use the Analysis ToolPak add-in.
- Use a pivot table.

The FREQUENCY Function

Using the FREQUENCY function to create a frequency distribution can be a bit tricky. This function always returns an array, so you must use it in an array formula that's entered into a multicell range.

Figure 17-5 shows some data in the range A1:E25 (named *Data*). These values range from 1 to 500. The range G2:G11 contains the bins used for the frequency distribution. Each cell in this bin range contains the upper limit for the bin. In this case, the bins consist of <=50, 51–100, 101–150, and so on.

FIGURE 17-5

Creating a frequency distribution for the data in A1:E25.

	A	B	C	D	E	F	G	H
1	55	316	223	185	124		Bins	
2	124	93	163	213	314		50	
3	211	41	231	241	212		100	
4	118	113	400	205	254		150	
5	262	1	201	12	101		200	
6	167	479	205	337	118		250	
7	489	15	89	362	148		300	
8	179	248	125	197	177		350	
9	456	153	269	49	127		400	
10	289	500	198	317	300		450	
11	126	114	303	314	270		500	
12	151	279	347	314	170			
13	250	175	93	209	61			
14	166	113	356	124	242			
15	152	384	157	233	99			
16	277	195	436	6	240			
17	147	80	173	211	244			
18	386	93	330	400	141			
19	332	173	129	323	188			
20	338	263	444	84	220			
21	221	402	498	98	2			
22	201	400	3	190	105			
23	35	225	12	265	329			
24	43	302	125	301	444			
25	56	9	135	500	398			

To create the frequency distribution, select a range of cells that corresponds to the number of cells in the bin range (in this example, select H2:H11 because the bins are in G2:G11). Then enter the following array formula into the selected range (press **Ctrl+Shift+Enter**):

```
{=FREQUENCY(Data,G2:G11)}
```

The array formula returns the count of values in the Data range that fall into each bin. To create a frequency distribution that consists of percentages, use the following array formula:

```
{=FREQUENCY(Data,G2:G11)/COUNT(Data)}
```

Figure 17-6 shows two frequency distributions — one in terms of counts and one in terms of percentages. The figure also shows a chart (histogram) created from the frequency distribution.

FIGURE 17-6

Frequency distributions created by using the FREQUENCY function.

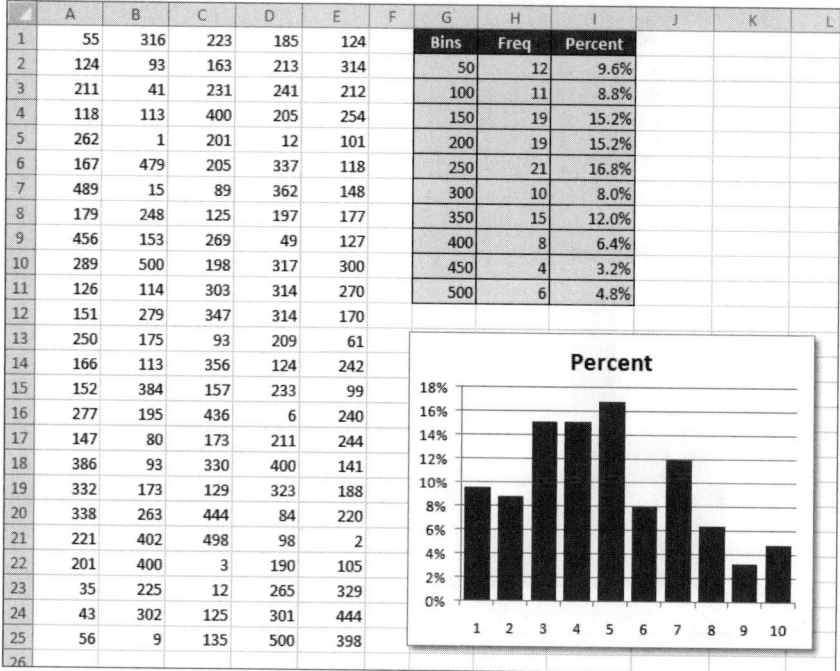

	A	B	C	D	E	F	G	H	I	J	K	L
1	55	316	223	185	124		**Bins**	**Freq**	**Percent**			
2	124	93	163	213	314		50	12	9.6%			
3	211	41	231	241	212		100	11	8.8%			
4	118	113	400	205	254		150	19	15.2%			
5	262	1	201	12	101		200	19	15.2%			
6	167	479	205	337	118		250	21	16.8%			
7	489	15	89	362	148		300	10	8.0%			
8	179	248	125	197	177		350	15	12.0%			
9	456	153	269	49	127		400	8	6.4%			
10	289	500	198	317	300		450	4	3.2%			
11	126	114	303	314	270		500	6	4.8%			
12	151	279	347	314	170							
13	250	175	93	209	61							
14	166	113	356	124	242				Percent			
15	152	384	157	233	99							
16	277	195	436	6	240							
17	147	80	173	211	244							
18	386	93	330	400	141							
19	332	173	129	323	188							
20	338	263	444	84	220							
21	221	402	498	98	2							
22	201	400	3	190	105							
23	35	225	12	265	329							
24	43	302	125	301	444							
25	56	9	135	500	398							
26												

Using Formulas to Create a Frequency Distribution

Figure 17-7 shows a worksheet that contains test scores for 50 students in column B (the range is named *Grades*). Formulas in columns G and H calculate a frequency distribution for letter grades. The minimum and maximum values for each letter grade appear in columns D and E. For example, a test score between 80 and 89 (inclusive) earns a B. In addition, a chart displays the distribution of the test scores.

The formula in cell G2 that follows counts the number of scores that qualify for an A:

```
=COUNTIFS(Grades,">="&D2,Grades,"<="&E2)
```

You may recognize this formula from a previous section in this chapter (see "Counting Cells Based on Multiple Criteria"). This formula was copied to the four cells below G2.

Note

The preceding formula uses the COUNTIFS function, which first appeared in Excel 2007. For compatibility with previous Excel versions, use this array formula:

```
{=SUM((Grades>=D2)*(Grades<=E2))}
```  ■

FIGURE 17-7

Creating a frequency distribution of test scores.

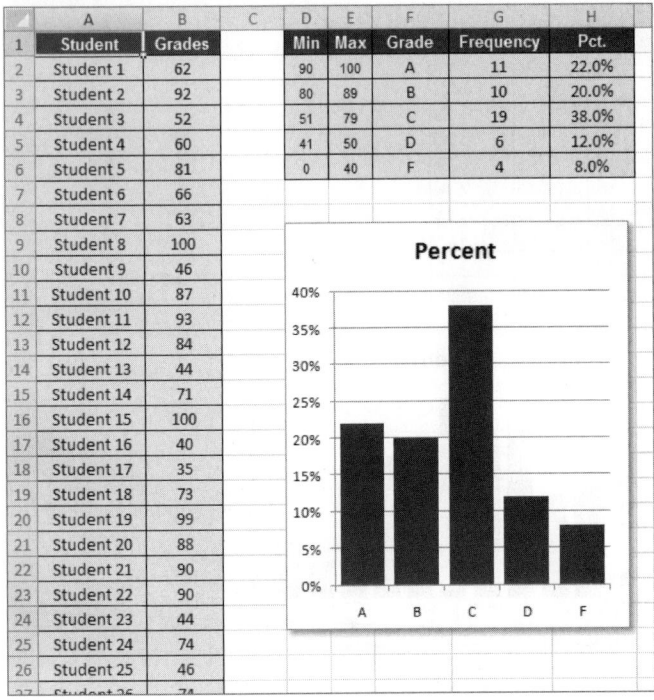

	A	B	C	D	E	F	G	H
1	**Student**	**Grades**		**Min**	**Max**	**Grade**	**Frequency**	**Pct.**
2	Student 1	62		90	100	A	11	22.0%
3	Student 2	92		80	89	B	10	20.0%
4	Student 3	52		51	79	C	19	38.0%
5	Student 4	60		41	50	D	6	12.0%
6	Student 5	81		0	40	F	4	8.0%
7	Student 6	66						
8	Student 7	63						
9	Student 8	100						
10	Student 9	46						
11	Student 10	87						
12	Student 11	93						
13	Student 12	84						
14	Student 13	44						
15	Student 14	71						
16	Student 15	100						
17	Student 16	40						
18	Student 17	35						
19	Student 18	73						
20	Student 19	99						
21	Student 20	88						
22	Student 21	90						
23	Student 22	90						
24	Student 23	44						
25	Student 24	74						
26	Student 25	46						

The formulas in column H calculate the percentage of scores for each letter grade. The formula in H2, which was copied to the four cells below H2, is

```
=G2/SUM($G$2:$G$6)
```

Using the Analysis ToolPak to Create a Frequency Distribution

The Analysis ToolPak add-in, distributed with Excel, provides another way to calculate a frequency distribution.

1. **Enter your bin values in a range.**
2. **Choose Data ⇨ Analysis ⇨ Analysis to display the Data Analysis dialog box.** If this command is not available, see the sidebar, "Is the Analysis ToolPak Installed?".
3. **In the Data Analysis dialog box, select Histogram and then click OK.** You should see the Histogram dialog box shown in Figure 17-8.
4. **Specify the ranges for your data (Input Range), bins (Bin Range), and results (Output Range), and then select any options.** Click OK. Figure 17-9 shows a frequency distribution (and chart) created with the Histogram option.

FIGURE 17-8

The Analysis ToolPak's Histogram dialog box.

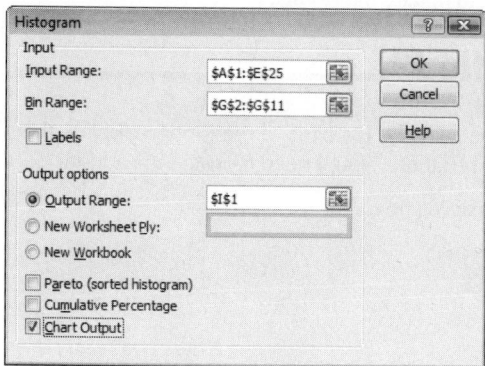

FIGURE 17-9

A frequency distribution and chart generated by the Analysis ToolPak's Histogram option.

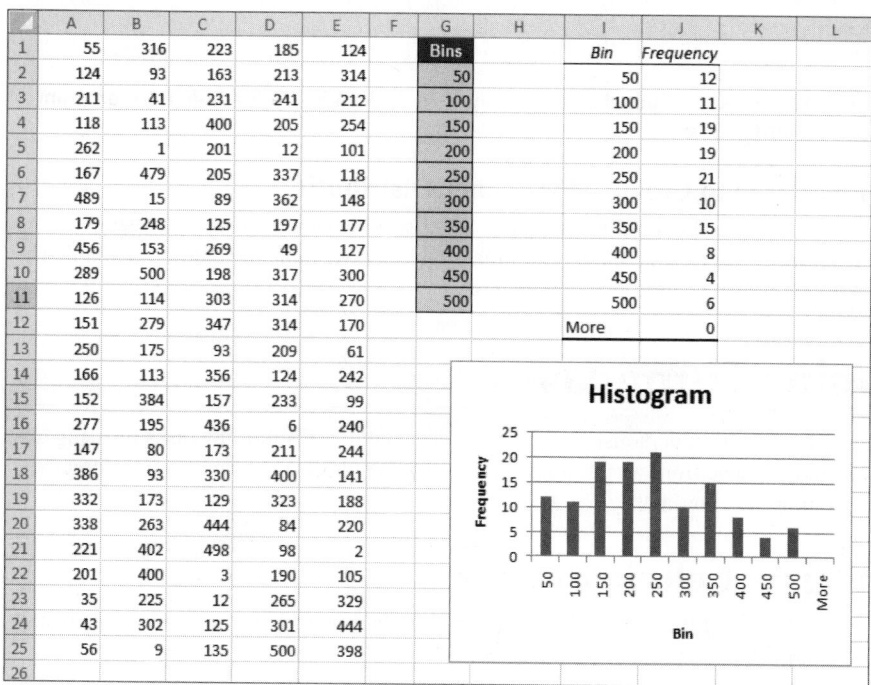

	A	B	C	D	E	F	G	H	I	J	K	L
1	55	316	223	185	124		**Bins**		Bin	Frequency		
2	124	93	163	213	314		50		50	12		
3	211	41	231	241	212		100		100	11		
4	118	113	400	205	254		150		150	19		
5	262	1	201	12	101		200		200	19		
6	167	479	205	337	118		250		250	21		
7	489	15	89	362	148		300		300	10		
8	179	248	125	197	177		350		350	15		
9	456	153	269	49	127		400		400	8		
10	289	500	198	317	300		450		450	4		
11	126	114	303	314	270		500		500	6		
12	151	279	347	314	170				More	0		
13	250	175	93	209	61							
14	166	113	356	124	242							
15	152	384	157	233	99							
16	277	195	436	6	240							
17	147	80	173	211	244							
18	386	93	330	400	141							
19	332	173	129	323	188							
20	338	263	444	84	220							
21	221	402	498	98	2							
22	201	400	3	190	105							
23	35	225	12	265	329							
24	43	302	125	301	444							
25	56	9	135	500	398							
26												

Caution

Note that the frequency distribution consists of values, not formulas. Therefore, if you make any changes to your input data, you need to rerun the Histogram procedure to update the results. ■

Is the Analysis ToolPak Installed?

To make sure that the Analysis ToolPak add-in is installed, click the Data tab. If the Ribbon displays the Data Analysis command in the Analysis group, you're all set. If not, you'll need to install the add-in:

1. Choose File ➪ Options to display the Excel Options dialog box.
2. Click Add-Ins in the list on the left.
3. Select Excel Add-Ins from the Manage drop-down list.
4. Click Go to display the Add-Ins dialog box.
5. Place a check mark next to Analysis ToolPak.
6. Click OK.

If you've enabled the Developer tab, you can display the Add-Ins dialog box by choosing Developer ➪ Add-Ins ➪ Add-Ins.

Note

In the Add-Ins dialog box, you see an additional add-in, Analysis ToolPak - VBA. This add-in is for programmers, and you don't need to install it. ■

Using a PivotTable to Create a Frequency Distribution

If your data is in the form of a table, you may prefer to use a PivotTable to create a histogram. Figure 17-10 shows the student grade data summarized in a PivotTable in columns D and E. The data bars were added using conditional formatting.

Summing Formulas

The examples in this section demonstrate how to perform common summing tasks by using formulas. The formulas range from very simple to relatively complex array formulas that compute sums by using multiple criteria.

Summing All Cells in a Range

It doesn't get much simpler than this. The following formula returns the sum of all values in a range named *Data*:

```
=SUM(Data)
```

FIGURE 17-10

Using data bars within a PivotTable to display a histogram.

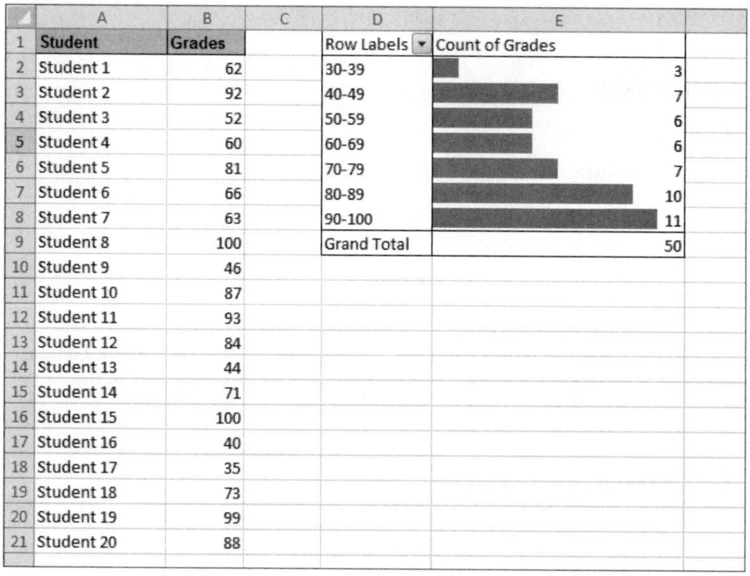

	A	B	C	D	E
1	**Student**	**Grades**		Row Labels ▼	Count of Grades
2	Student 1	62		30-39	3
3	Student 2	92		40-49	7
4	Student 3	52		50-59	6
5	Student 4	60		60-69	6
6	Student 5	81		70-79	7
7	Student 6	66		80-89	10
8	Student 7	63		90-100	11
9	Student 8	100		Grand Total	50
10	Student 9	46			
11	Student 10	87			
12	Student 11	93			
13	Student 12	84			
14	Student 13	44			
15	Student 14	71			
16	Student 15	100			
17	Student 16	40			
18	Student 17	35			
19	Student 18	73			
20	Student 19	99			
21	Student 20	88			

The SUM function can take up to 255 arguments. The following formula, for example, returns the sum of the values in five noncontiguous ranges:

```
=SUM(A1:A9,C1:C9,E1:E9,G1:G9,I1:I9)
```

You can use complete rows or columns as an argument for the SUM function. The formula that follows, for example, returns the sum of all values in column A. If this formula appears in a cell in column A, it generates a circular reference error:

```
=SUM(A:A)
```

The following formula returns the sum of all values on Sheet1 by using a range reference that consists of all rows. To avoid a circular reference error, this formula must appear on a sheet other than Sheet1:

```
=SUM(Sheet1!1:1048576)
```

The SUM function is very versatile. The arguments can be numerical values, cells, ranges, text representations of numbers (which are interpreted as values), logical values, and even embedded functions. For example, consider the following formula:

```
=SUM(B1,5,"6",,SQRT(4),A1:A5,TRUE)
```

This odd formula, which is perfectly valid, contains all the following types of arguments, listed here in the order of their presentation:

- A single cell reference: B1
- A literal value: 5
- A string that looks like a value: "6"
- A missing argument: , ,
- An expression that uses another function: SQRT(4)
- A range reference: A1:A5
- A logical value: TRUE

Caution

The SUM **function is versatile, but it's also inconsistent when you use logical values (TRUE or FALSE). Logical values stored in cells are always treated as 0. However, logical TRUE, when used as an argument in the** SUM **function, is treated as 1.** ∎

Computing a Cumulative Sum

You may want to display a cumulative sum of values in a range — sometimes known as a *running total*. Figure 17-11 illustrates a cumulative sum. Column B shows the monthly amounts, and column C displays the cumulative (year-to-date) totals.

FIGURE 17-11

Simple formulas in column C display a cumulative sum of the values in column B.

	A	B	C	D
1	Month	Amount	Year-to-Date	
2	January	850	850	
3	February	900	1,750	
4	March	750	2,500	
5	April	1,100	3,600	
6	May	600	4,200	
7	June	500	4,700	
8	July	1,200	5,900	
9	August		5,900	
10	September		5,900	
11	October		5,900	
12	November		5,900	
13	December		5,900	
14	TOTAL	5,900		
15				
16				

The formula in cell C2 is

=SUM(B$2:B2)

Notice that this formula uses a *mixed reference* — that is, the first cell in the range reference always refers to the same row (in this case, row 2). When this formula is copied down the column, the range argument adjusts such that the sum always starts with row 2 and ends with the current row. For example, after copying this formula down column C, the formula in cell C8 is

```
=SUM(B$2:B8)
```

You can use an IF function to hide the cumulative sums for rows in which data hasn't been entered. The following formula, entered in cell C2 and copied down the column, is

```
=IF(B2<>"",SUM(B$2:B2),"")
```

Figure 17-12 shows this formula at work.

FIGURE 17-12

Using an IF function to hide cumulative sums for missing data.

	A	B	C	D
1	Month	Amount	Year-to-Date	
2	January	850	850	
3	February	900	1,750	
4	March	750	2,500	
5	April	1,100	3,600	
6	May	600	4,200	
7	June	500	4,700	
8	July	1,200	5,900	
9	August			
10	September			
11	October			
12	November			
13	December			
14	TOTAL	5,900		
15				
16				

Summing the "Top *n*" Values

In some situations, you may need to sum the *n* largest values in a range — for example, the top 10 values. If your data resides in a table, you can use autofiltering to hide all but the top *n* rows and then display the sum of the visible data in the table's total row.

Another approach is to sort the range in descending order and then use the SUM function with an argument consisting of the first *n* values in the sorted range.

A better solution — which doesn't require a table or sorting — uses an array formula like this one:

```
{=SUM(LARGE(Data,{1,2,3,4,5,6,7,8,9,10}))}
```

This formula sums the 10 largest values in a range named *Data*. To sum the 10 smallest values, use the SMALL function instead of the LARGE function:

```
{=SUM(SMALL(Data,{1,2,3,4,5,6,7,8,9,10}))}
```

These formulas use an array constant comprised of the arguments for the LARGE or SMALL function. If the value of *n* for your top-*n* calculation is large, you may prefer to use the following variation. This formula returns the sum of the top 30 values in the Data range. You can, of course, substitute a different value for 30.

```
{=SUM(LARGE(Data,ROW(INDIRECT("1:30"))))}
```

Conditional Sums Using a Single Criterion

Often, you need to calculate a *conditional sum*. With a *conditional sum*, values in a range that meet one or more conditions are included in the sum. This section presents examples of conditional summing by using a single criterion.

The SUMIF function is very useful for single-criterion sum formulas. The SUMIF function takes three arguments:

- **Range:** The range containing the values that determine whether to include a particular cell in the sum.

- **Criteria:** An expression that determines whether to include a particular cell in the sum.

- **Sum_range:** Optional. The range that contains the cells you want to sum. If you omit this argument, the function uses the range specified in the first argument.

The examples that follow demonstrate the use of the SUMIF function. These formulas are based on the worksheet shown in Figure 17-13, set up to track invoices. Column F contains a formula that subtracts the date in column E from the date in column D. A negative number in column F indicates a past-due payment. The worksheet uses named ranges that correspond to the labels in row 1.

FIGURE 17-13

A negative value in column F indicates a past-due payment.

	A	B	C	D	E	F	G
1	InvoiceNum	Office	Amount	DateDue	Today	Difference	
2	AG-0145	Oregon	$5,000.00	4/1/2010	5/5/2010	-34	
3	AG-0189	California	$450.00	4/19/2010	5/5/2010	-16	
4	AG-0220	Washington	$3,211.56	4/28/2010	5/5/2010	-7	
5	AG-0310	Oregon	$250.00	4/30/2010	5/5/2010	-5	
6	AG-0355	Washington	$125.50	5/4/2010	5/5/2010	-1	
7	AG-0409	Washington	$3,000.00	5/10/2010	5/5/2010	5	
8	AG-0581	Oregon	$2,100.00	5/24/2010	5/5/2010	19	
9	AG-0600	Oregon	$335.39	5/24/2010	5/5/2010	19	
10	AG-0602	Washington	$65.00	5/28/2010	5/5/2010	23	
11	AG-0633	California	$250.00	5/31/2010	5/5/2010	26	
12	TOTAL		$14,787.45			29	
13							

Let a Wizard Create Your Formula

Excel ships with the Conditional Sum Wizard add-in. After you install this add-in, you can invoke the wizard by choosing Formulas ➪ Solutions ➪ Conditional Sum.

You can specify various conditions for your summing, and the add-in creates the formula for you (always an array formula). The Conditional Sum Wizard add-in, although a handy tool, is not all that versatile. For example, you can combine multiple criteria by using an And condition but not an Or condition.

To install the Conditional Sum Wizard add-in:

1. Choose File ➪ Options to display the Excel Options dialog box.
2. Click the Add-Ins tab on the left.
3. Select Excel Add-Ins from the Manage drop-down list.
4. Click Go to display the Add-Ins dialog box.
5. Place a check mark next to Conditional Sum Wizard.
6. Click OK.

If you've enabled the Developer tab, you can display the Add-Ins dialog box by choosing Developer ➪ Add-Ins ➪ Add-Ins.

Summing Only Negative Values

The following formula returns the sum of the negative values in column F. In other words, it returns the total number of past-due days for all invoices. For this worksheet, the formula returns –63.

```
=SUMIF(Difference,"<0")
```

Because you omit the third argument, the second argument ("<0") applies to the values in the Difference range.

You don't need to hard-code the arguments for the SUMIF function into your formula. For example, you can create a formula, such as the following, which gets the criteria argument from the contents of cell G2:

```
=SUMIF(Difference,G2)
```

This formula returns a new result if you change the criteria in cell G2.

Summing Values Based on a Different Range

The following formula returns the sum of the past-due invoice amounts (in column C):

```
=SUMIF(Difference,"<0",Amount)
```

This formula uses the values in the Difference range to determine whether the corresponding values in the Amount range contribute to the sum.

Summing Values Based on a Text Comparison

The following formula returns the total invoice amounts for the Oregon office:

```
=SUMIF(Office,"=Oregon",Amount)
```

Using the equal sign in the argument is optional. The following formula has the same result:

```
=SUMIF(Office,"Oregon",Amount)
```

To sum the invoice amounts for all offices *except* Oregon, use this formula:

```
=SUMIF(Office,"<>Oregon",Amount)
```

Summing Values Based on a Date Comparison

The following formula returns the total invoice amounts that have a due date after May 1, 2010:

```
=SUMIF(DateDue,">="&DATE(2010,5,1),Amount)
```

Notice that the second argument for the SUMIF function is an expression. The expression uses the DATE function, which returns a date. Also, the comparison operator, enclosed in quotes, is concatenated (using the & operator) with the result of the DATE function.

The formula that follows returns the total invoice amounts that have a future due date (including today):

```
=SUMIF(DateDue,">="&TODAY(),Amount)
```

Conditional Sums Using Multiple Criteria

The examples in the preceding section all used a single comparison criterion. The examples in this section involve summing cells based on multiple criteria.

Figure 17-14 shows the sample worksheet again, for your reference. The worksheet also shows the result of several formulas that demonstrate summing by using multiple criteria.

Using And Criteria

Suppose that you want to get a sum of the invoice amounts that are past due *and* associated with the Oregon office. In other words, the value in the Amount range will be summed only if both of the following criteria are met:

- The corresponding value in the Difference range is negative.
- The corresponding text in the Office range is *Oregon*.

If the worksheet won't be used by anyone running a version prior to Excel 2007, the following formula does the job:

```
=SUMIFS(Amount,Difference,"<0",Office,"Oregon")
```

This worksheet demonstrates summing based on multiple criteria.

	A	B	C	D	E	F
1	InvoiceNum	Office	Amount	DateDue	Today	Difference
2	AG-0145	Oregon	$5,000.00	4/1/2010	5/5/2010	-34
3	AG-0189	California	$450.00	4/19/2010	5/5/2010	-16
4	AG-0220	Washington	$3,211.56	4/28/2010	5/5/2010	-7
5	AG-0310	Oregon	$250.00	4/30/2010	5/5/2010	-5
6	AG-0355	Washington	$125.50	5/4/2010	5/5/2010	-1
7	AG-0409	Washington	$3,000.00	5/10/2010	5/5/2010	5
8	AG-0581	Oregon	$2,100.00	5/24/2010	5/5/2010	19
9	AG-0600	Oregon	$335.39	5/24/2010	5/5/2010	19
10	AG-0602	Washington	$65.00	5/28/2010	5/5/2010	23
11	AG-0633	California	$250.00	5/31/2010	5/5/2010	26
12	TOTAL		$14,787.45			29
13						
14						
15		-63	Total past due days			
16		-63	Total past due days (array formula)			
17						
18		$9,037.06	Total amount past due			
19		$9,037.06	Total amount past due (array formula)			
20						
21		$7,685.39	Total for Oregon only			
22						
23		$7,102.06	Total for all except Oregon			
24						
25		$14,787.45	Total amount with due date beyond May 1			
26						
27		$5,250.00	Total past due amount for Oregon (Excel 2007 or later only)			
28		$5,250.00	Total past due amount for Oregon (array formula)			
29						
30		$5,000.00	Total past due amounts OR amounts for Oregon (array formula)			
31						
32		$5,700.00	Total past due amounts for Oregon and California (array formula)			
33						

The array formula that follows returns the same result and will work in all versions of Excel:

```
{=SUM((Difference<0)*(Office="Oregon")*Amount)}
```

Using Or Criteria

Suppose that you want to get a sum of past-due invoice amounts *or* ones associated with the Oregon office. In other words, the value in the Amount range will be summed if either of the following criteria is met:

- The corresponding value in the Difference range is negative.
- The corresponding text in the Office range is *Oregon*.

This example requires an array formula:

```
{=SUM(IF((Office="Oregon")+(Difference<0),1,0)*Amount)}
```

A plus sign (+) joins the conditions; you can include more than two conditions.

Using And and Or Criteria

As you may expect, things get a bit tricky when your criteria consist of both And and Or operations. For example, you may want to sum the values in the Amount range when both of the following conditions are met:

- The corresponding value in the Difference range is negative.
- The corresponding text in the Office range is *Oregon* or *California*.

Notice that the second condition actually consists of two conditions joined with *Or*. The following array formula does the trick:

```
{=SUM((Difference<0)*IF((Office="Oregon")+
(Office="California"),1)*Amount)}
```

Summary

This chapter provided valuable tips and tricks that will assist in creating formulas that handle particular counting and summing operations in a worksheet. Applying any of the previous examples covered here will save you significant time while making our worksheets into more powerful business tools.

18

Getting Started Making Charts

IN THIS CHAPTER

Exploring charting in Excel

Understanding how Excel handles charts

Using embedded charts versus chart sheets

Reviewing the parts of a chart

Seeing some chart examples

When most people think of Excel, they think of crunching rows and columns of numbers. But as you probably know already, Excel is no slouch when it comes to presenting data visually in the form of a chart. In fact, Excel is probably the most commonly used software for creating charts.

This chapter presents an introductory overview of the Excel program's charting ability.

Note

One of the new features in Excel 2010 is sparklines. A *sparkline* is a mini-chart that's displayed in a single cell. Because this feature is significantly different from standard charts, I devote a significant portion of Chapter 19 to sparklines. ■

What Is a Chart?

A *chart* is a visual representation of numerical values. Charts (also known as *graphs*) have been an integral part of spreadsheets since the early days of Lotus 1-2-3. Charts generated by early spreadsheet products were quite rudimentary, but they have improved significantly over the years. Excel provides you with the tools to create a wide variety of highly customizable charts.

Displaying data in a well-conceived chart can make your numbers more understandable. Because a chart presents a picture, charts are particularly useful for summarizing a series of numbers and their interrelationships. Making a chart can often help you spot trends and patterns that may otherwise go unnoticed. If you're unfamiliar with the elements of a chart, see the sidebar later in this chapter, "Parts of a Chart."

Figure 18-1 shows a worksheet that contains a simple column chart that depicts a company's sales volume by month. Viewing the chart makes it very apparent that sales were down in the summer months (June through August), but they increased steadily during the final four months of the year. You could, of course, arrive at this same conclusion simply by studying the numbers. But viewing the chart makes the point much more quickly.

FIGURE 18-1

A simple column chart depicts the monthly sales volume.

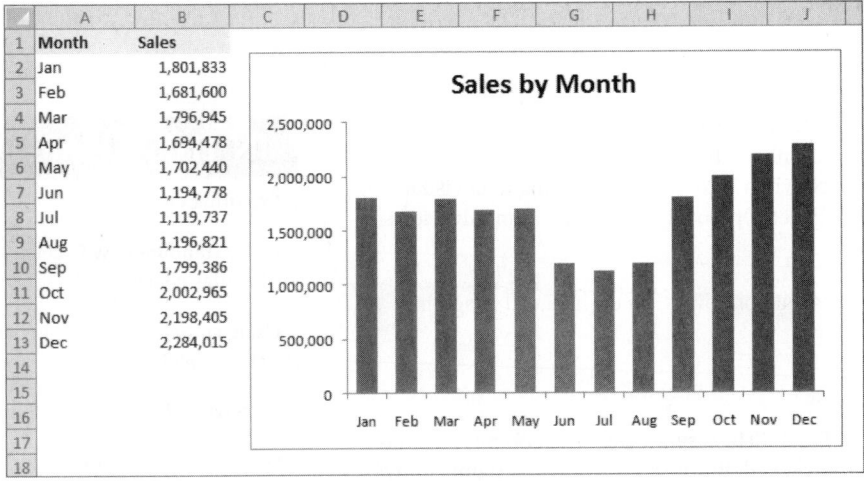

A column chart is just one of many different types of charts that you can create with Excel. I discuss all chart types later in this chapter so that you can make the right choice for your data.

Understanding How Excel Handles Charts

Before you can create a chart, you must have some numbers — sometimes known as data. The data, of course, is stored in the cells in a worksheet. Normally, the data that a chart uses resides in a single worksheet, but that's not a strict requirement. A chart can use data that's stored in a different worksheet or even in a different workbook.

A chart is essentially an object that Excel creates upon request. This object consists of one or more data series, displayed graphically. The appearance of the data series depends on the selected chart type. For example, if you create a line chart that uses two data series, the chart contains two lines, each representing one data series. The data for each series is stored in a separate row or column. Each point on the line is determined by the value in a single cell and is represented by a marker. You can distinguish each of the lines by its thickness, line style, color, or data markers (squares, circles, etc.).

Figure 18-2 shows a line chart that plots two data series across a 12-month period. Different data markers are used (squares versus circles) to identify the two series, as shown in the legend at the bottom of the chart. The chart clearly shows that the sales in the Eastern Region are declining steadily, while Western Region sales are relatively constant.

FIGURE 18-2

This line chart displays two data series.

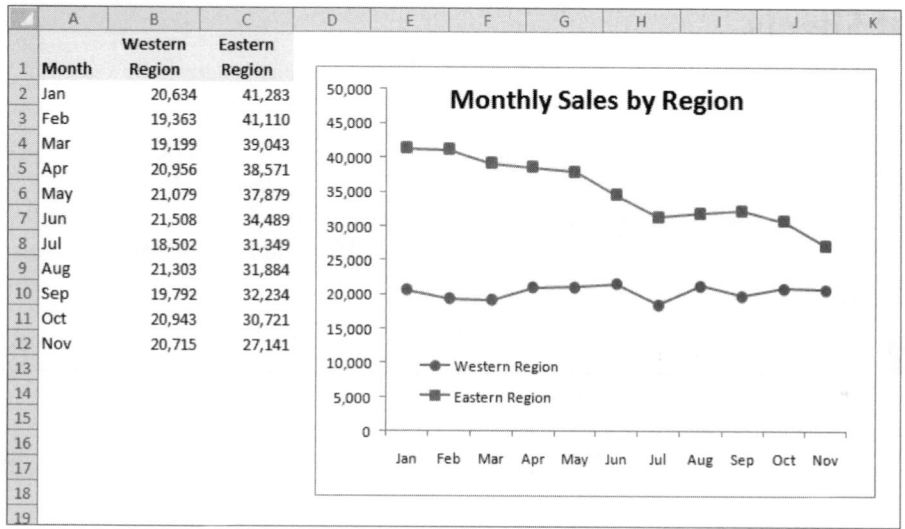

A key point to keep in mind is that charts are *dynamic*. In other words, a chart series is linked to the data in your worksheet. If the data changes, the chart is automatically updated to reflect the changes.

After you create a chart, you can always change its type, change the formatting, add new data series to it, or change an existing data series so that it uses data in a different range.

A chart is either embedded in a worksheet or displayed on a separate chart sheet. It's very easy to move an embedded chart to a chart sheet (and vice versa).

Embedded Charts

An *embedded chart* basically floats on top of a worksheet, on the worksheet's drawing layer. The charts shown previously in this chapter are both embedded charts.

As with other drawing objects (such as Shapes or SmartArt), you can move an embedded chart, resize it, change its proportions, adjust its borders, and perform other operations. Using embedded charts enables you to print the chart next to the data that it uses.

To make any changes to the actual chart in an embedded chart object, you must click on it to activate the chart. When a chart is activated, Excel displays the Chart Tools context tab. The Ribbon provides many tools for working with charts.

With one exception, every chart starts out as an embedded chart. The exception is when you create a default chart by selecting the data and pressing F11. In that case, a column chart using default settings is immediately created on a chart sheet.

Chart Sheets

When a chart is on a chart sheet, you view it by clicking on its sheet tab. Chart sheets and worksheets can be interspersed in a workbook.

To move an embedded chart to a chart sheet, click on the chart to select it, and then choose Chart Tools ➪ Design ➪ Location ➪ Move Chart. Excel displays the Move Chart dialog box, shown in Figure 18-3. Select the New Sheet option and provide a name for the chart sheet (or accept Excel's default name). Click OK, and the chart is moved, and the new chart sheet is activated.

FIGURE 18-3

The Move Chart dialog box lets you move a chart to a chart sheet.

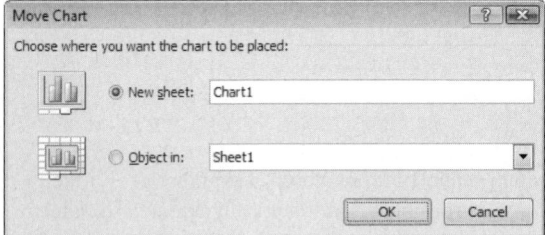

Tip
This operation also works in the opposite direction: You can select a chart on a chart sheet and relocate it to a worksheet as an embedded chart. In the Move Chart dialog box, choose Object In, and then select the worksheet from the drop-down list. ∎

When you place a chart on a chart sheet, the chart occupies the entire sheet. If you plan to print a chart on a page by itself, using a chart sheet is often your better choice. If you have many charts, you may want to put each one on a separate chart sheet to avoid cluttering your worksheet. This technique also makes locating a particular chart easier because you can change the names of the chart sheets' tabs to provide a description of the chart that it contains.

The Excel Ribbon changes when a chart sheet is active, similar to the way it changes when you select an embedded chart.

Excel displays a chart in a chart sheet in WYSIWYG (What You See Is What You Get) mode: The printed chart looks just like the image on the chart sheet. If the chart doesn't fit in the window, you can use the scroll bars to scroll it or adjust the zoom factor. You also can change its orientation (tall or wide) by choosing Page Layout ⇨ Page Setup ⇨ Orientation.

Parts of a Chart

Refer to the accompanying chart as you read the following description of the chart's elements.

The particular chart is a combination chart that displays two data series: Calls and Sales. Calls are plotted as vertical columns, and the Sales are plotted as a line with square markers. Each column (or marker on the line) represents a single *data point* (the value in a cell). The chart data is stored in the range A1:C7.

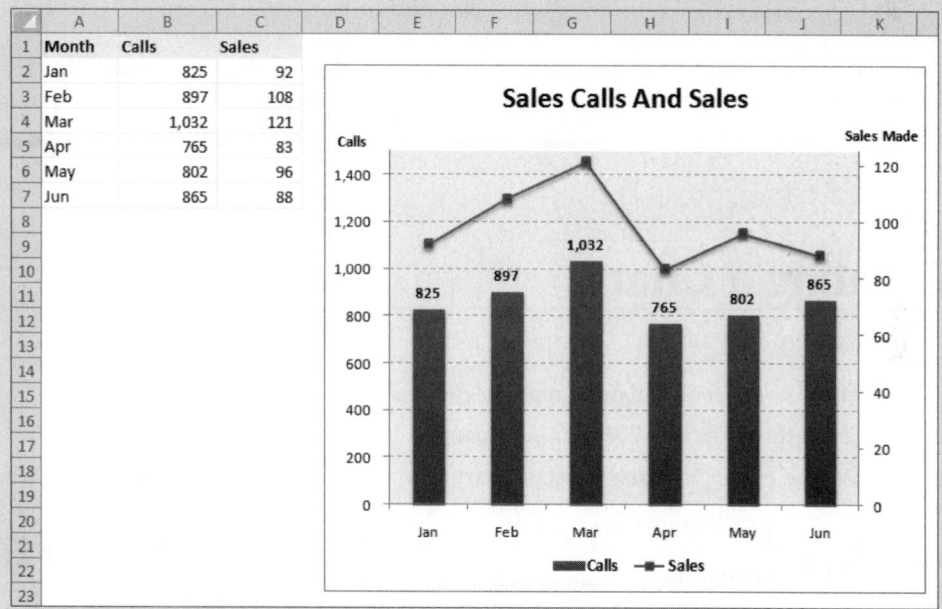

It has a horizontal axis, known as the category axis. This axis represents the category for each data point (January, February, etc.).

It has two vertical axes, known as value axes, and each one has a different scale. The axis on the left is for the columns (Calls), and the axis on the right is for the line (Sales).

The value axes also display scale values. The axis on the left displays scale values from 0 to 1,400, in major unit increments of 200. The value axis on the right uses a different scale: 0 to 120, in increments of 20.

continued

continued

A chart with two value axes is appropriate because the two data series vary dramatically in scale. If the Sales data was plotted using the left axis, the line would barely be visible.

Most charts provide some method of identifying the data series or data points. A legend, for example, is often used to identify the various series in a chart. In this example, the legend appears on the bottom of the chart. Some charts also display data labels to identify specific data points. This chart displays data labels for the Calls series, but not for the Sales series. In addition, most charts (including the example chart) contain a chart title and additional labels to identify the axes or categories.

It also contains horizontal grid lines (which correspond to the left value axis). Grid lines are basically extensions of the value axis scale, which makes it easier for the viewer to determine the magnitude of the data points.

All charts have a chart area (the entire background area of the chart) and a plot area. The plot area shows the actual chart, and in this example, the plot area has a different background color.

Charts can have additional parts or fewer parts, depending on the chart type. For example, a pie chart has slices and no axes. A three-dimensional (3-D) chart may have walls and a floor. You can also add many other types of items to a chart. For example, you can add a trend line or display error bars. In other words, after you create a chart, you have a great deal of flexibility in customizing the chart.

Creating a Chart

Creating a chart is fairly simple:

1. Make sure that your data is appropriate for a chart.

2. Select the range that contains your data.

3. **Choose Insert ⇨ Charts, select a chart type, and then click a subtype.** Excel creates the chart and places it in the center of the window.

4. (Optional) **Use the commands in the Chart Tools contextual tabs to change the look or layout of the chart or add or delete chart elements.**

Tip
You can create a chart with a single keystroke. Select the range to be used in the chart and then press Alt+F1 (for an embedded chart) or F11 (for a chart on a chart sheet). Excel displays the chart of the selected data, using the default chart type. The default chart type is a column chart; however, you can customize this. Start by creating a chart of the type that you want to be the default type. Select a chart and choose Chart Tools ⇨ Design ⇨ Type ⇨ Change Chart Type. In the Change Chart Type dialog box, select the type you'd like as default, and then click the Set As Default Chart button. ∎

Hands On: Creating and Customizing a Chart

This section contains a step-by-step example of creating a chart and applying some customizations. If you've never created a chart, this is a good opportunity to get a feel for how it works.

Figure 18-4 shows a worksheet with a range of data. This data is customer survey results by month, broken down by customers in three age groups. In this case, the data resides in a table (created by choosing Insert ⇨ Tables ⇨ Table), but that's not a requirement to create a chart.

FIGURE 18-4

The source data for the hands-on chart example.

	A	B	C	D	E
1	**Customer Satisfaction by Age Group**				
2	*Percent 'Very Satisfied' by customer age*				
3					
4	Month ▾	< 30 ▾	30-49 ▾	50+ ▾	
5	Jan	42%	46%	75%	
6	Feb	39%	51%	76%	
7	Mar	29%	38%	73%	
8	Apr	33%	39%	75%	
9	May	48%	53%	70%	
10	Jun	51%	57%	78%	
11					
12					

Selecting the Data

The first step is to select the data for the chart. Your selection should include such items as labels and series identifiers (row and column headings). For this example, select the range A4:D10. This range includes the category labels but not the title (which is in A1).

Tip

If your chart data is in a table (or is in a rectangular range separated from other data), you can select just a single cell. Excel will usually select the range for the chart accurately (i.e., the entire table). ∎

Note

The data that you use in a chart doesn't need to be in contiguous cells. You can press Ctrl and make a multiple selection. The initial data, however, must be on a single worksheet. If you need to plot data that exists on more than one worksheet, you can add more series after the chart is created. In all cases, however, data for a single chart series must reside on one sheet. ∎

Choosing a Chart Type

After you select the data, select a chart type from the Insert ⇨ Charts group. Each control in this group is a drop-down list, which lets you further refine your choice by selecting a subtype.

For this example, choose Insert ⇨ Charts ⇨ Column ⇨ Clustered Column. In other words, you're creating a column chart, using the clustered column subtype. Excel displays the chart shown in Figure 18-5.

FIGURE 18-5

A clustered column chart.

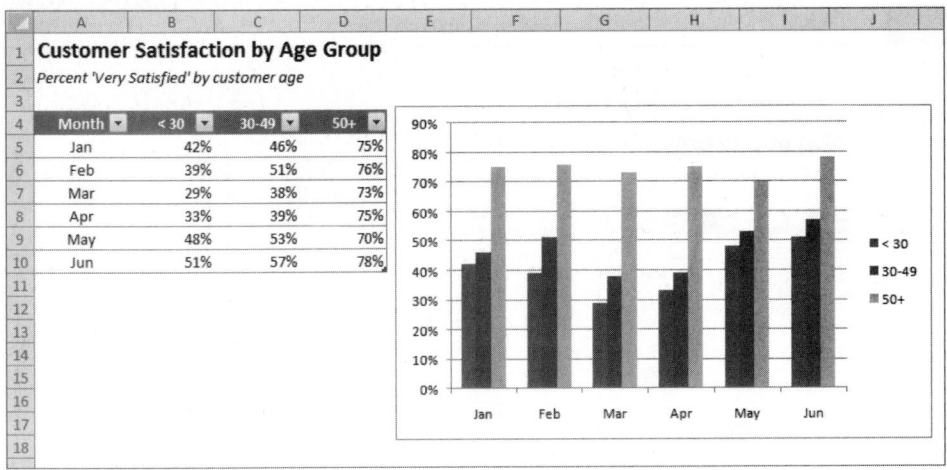

You can move the chart by dragging any of its borders. You can also resize it by dragging one of its corners.

Experimenting with Different Layouts

The chart looks pretty good, but it's just one of several predefined layouts for a clustered column chart.

To see some other configurations for the chart, select the chart and apply a few other layouts in the Chart Tools ⇨ Design ⇨ Chart Layouts group.

Note

Every chart type has a set of layouts that you can choose from. A layout contains additional chart elements, such as a title, data labels, axes, and so on. You can add your own elements to your chart, but often, using a predefined layout saves time. Even if the layout isn't exactly what you want, it may be close enough that you need to make only a few adjustments. ■

Figure 18-6 shows the chart after selecting a layout that adds a chart title and moves the legend to the bottom. The chart title is a text element that you can select and edit (the figure shows the generic title). For this example, *Customer Satisfaction by Age Group* would be a good title.

The chart, after selecting a different layout.

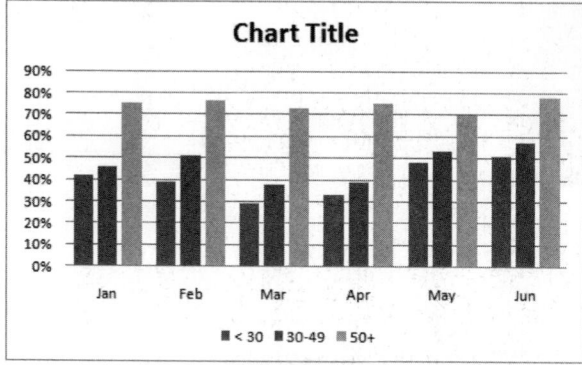

Tip

You can link the chart title to a cell so the title always displays the contents of a particular cell. To create a link to a cell, click on the chart title, type an equal sign (=), click on the cell, and press Enter. Excel displays the link in the Formula bar. In the example, the content of cell A1 is perfect for the chart title. ∎

Experiment with the Chart Tools ⇨ Layout tab to make other changes to the chart. For example, you can remove the grid lines, add axis titles, relocate the legend, and so on. Making these changes is easy and fairly intuitive.

Trying Another View of the Data

The chart, at this point, shows six clusters (months) of three data points in each (age groups). Would the data be easier to understand if you plotted the information in the opposite way?

Try it. Select the chart and then choose Chart Tools ⇨ Design ⇨ Data ⇨ Switch Row/Column. Figure 18-7 shows the result of this change. This chart also utilizes a different layout, which provides more separation between the three clusters.

Note

The orientation of the data has a drastic effect on the look of your chart. Excel has its own rules that it uses to determine the initial data orientation when you create a chart. If Excel's orientation doesn't match your expectation, it's easy enough to change. ∎

The chart, after changing the row and column orientation and choosing a different layout.

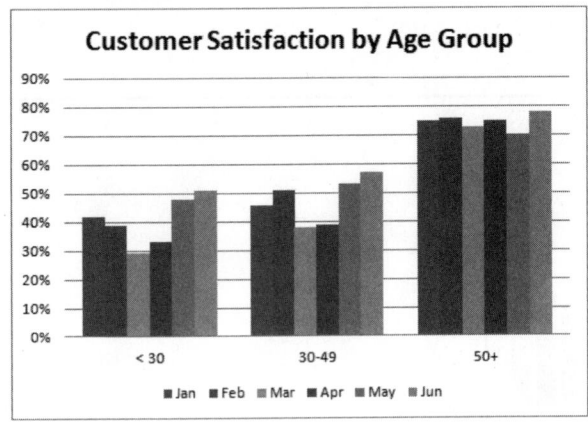

The chart with this new orientation reveals information that wasn't so apparent in the original version. The <30 and 30–49 age groups both show a decline in satisfaction for March and April. The 50+ age group didn't have this problem, however.

Trying Other Chart Types

Although a clustered column chart seems to work well for this data, there's no harm in checking out some other chart types. Choose Design ➪ Type ➪ Change Chart Type to experiment with other chart types. This command displays the Change Chart Type dialog box, shown in Figure 18-8. The main categories are listed on the left, and the subtypes are shown as icons. Select an icon and click OK, and Excel displays the chart using the new chart type. If you don't like the result, select Undo.

Tip
You can also change the chart type by selecting the chart and using the controls in the Insert ➪ Charts group. ■

Figure 18-9 shows a few different chart type options using the customer satisfaction data.

Trying Other Chart Styles

If you'd like to try some of the prebuilt chart styles, select the chart and choose Chart Tools ➪ Design ➪ Chart Styles gallery. You'll find an amazing selection of different colors and effects, all available with a single mouse click.

FIGURE 18-8

Use this dialog box to change the chart type.

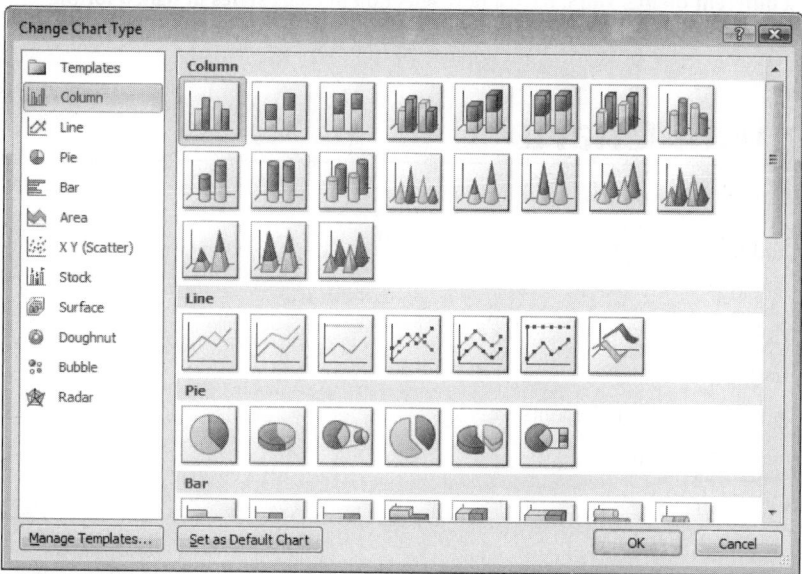

FIGURE 18-9

The customer satisfaction chart, using four different chart types.

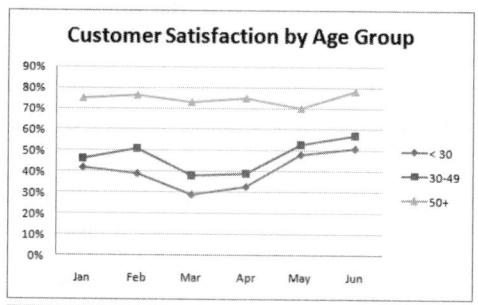

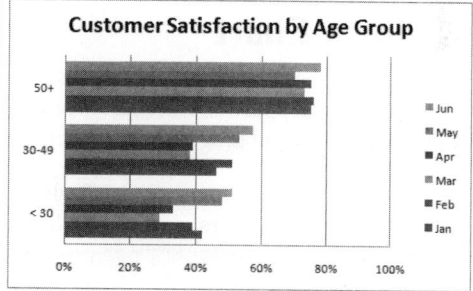

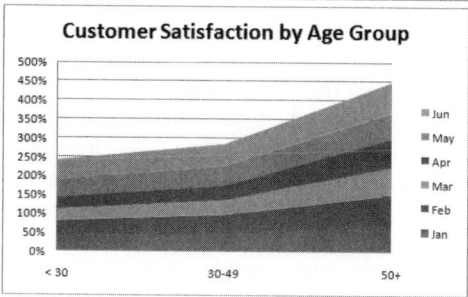

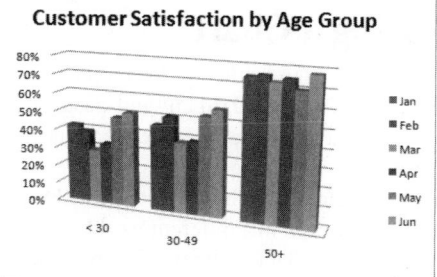

Tip

The styles displayed in the gallery depend on the workbook's theme. When you choose Page Layout ⇨ Themes ⇨ Themes to apply a different theme, you'll have a new selection of chart styles designed for the selected theme. ∎

Working with Charts

This section covers some common chart modifications:

- Resizing and moving charts
- Copying a chart
- Deleting a chart
- Adding chart elements
- Moving and deleting chart elements
- Formatting chart elements
- Printing charts

Note

Before you can modify a chart, the chart must be activated. To activate an embedded chart, click on it. Doing so activates the chart and also selects the element that you click. To activate a chart on a chart sheet, just click on its sheet tab. ∎

Resizing a Chart

If your chart is embedded, you can freely resize it with your mouse. Click on the chart's border. Handles (gray dots) appear on the chart's corners and edges. When the mouse pointer turns into a double arrow, click and drag to resize the chart.

When a chart is selected, choose Chart Tools ⇨ Format ⇨ Size to adjust the height and width of the chart. Use the spinners, or type the dimensions directly into the Height and Width controls.

Moving a Chart

To move a chart to a different location on a worksheet, click on the chart and drag one of its borders. You can use standard cut-and-paste techniques to move an embedded chart. In fact, this is the only way to move an embedded chart from one worksheet to another. Select the chart and choose Home ⇨ Clipboard ⇨ Cut (or press Ctrl+X). Then activate a cell near the desired location and choose Home ⇨ Clipboard ⇨ Paste (or press Ctrl+V). The new location can be in a different worksheet or even in a different workbook. If you paste the chart to a different workbook, it will be linked to the data in the original workbook.

To move an embedded chart to a chart sheet (or vice versa), select the chart and choose Chart Tools ⇨ Design ⇨ Location ⇨ Move Chart to display the Move Chart dialog box. Choose New Sheet, and provide a name for the chart sheet (or use the Excel-proposed name).

Copying a Chart

To make an exact copy of an embedded chart on the same worksheet, activate the chart, press and hold the Ctrl key, and drag. Release the mouse button, and a new copy of the chart is created.

To make a copy of a chart sheet, use the same procedure, but drag the chart sheet's tab.

You also can use standard copy-and-paste techniques to copy a chart. Select the chart (an embedded chart or a chart sheet) and choose Home ⇨ Clipboard ⇨ Copy (or press Ctrl+C). Then activate a cell near the desired location and choose Home ⇨ Clipboard ⇨ Paste (or press Ctrl+V). The new location can be in a different worksheet or even in a different workbook. If you paste the chart to a different workbook, it will be linked to the data in the original workbook.

Deleting a Chart

To delete an embedded chart, press Ctrl and click on the chart (to select the chart as an object). Then press Delete. When the Ctrl key is pressed, you can select multiple charts and then delete them all with a single press of the Delete key.

To delete a chart sheet, right-click on its sheet tab and choose Delete from the shortcut menu. To delete multiple chart sheets, select them by pressing Ctrl while you click the sheet tabs.

Adding Chart Elements

To add new elements to a chart (such as a title, legend, data labels, or gridlines), use the controls on the Chart Tools ⇨ Layout tab. These controls are arranged into logical groups, and they all display a drop-down list of options.

Moving and Deleting Chart Elements

Some elements within a chart can be moved: titles, legend, and data labels. To move a chart element, simply click on it to select it. Then drag its border.

The easiest way to delete a chart element is to select it and then press Delete. You can also use the controls on the Chart Tools ⇨ Layout tab to turn off the display of a particular chart element. For example, to delete data labels, choose Chart Tools ⇨ Layout ⇨ Labels ⇨ Data Labels ⇨ None.

Note

A few chart elements consist of multiple objects. For example, the data labels element consists of one label for each data point. To move or delete one data label, click once to select the entire element, and then click a second time to select the specific data label. You can then move or delete the single data label. ∎

Formatting Chart Elements

Many users are content to stick with the predefined chart layouts and chart styles. For more precise customizations, Excel allows you to work with individual chart elements and apply additional formatting. You can use the Ribbon commands for some modifications, but the easiest way to format chart elements is to right-click on the element and choose Format from the shortcut menu. The exact command depends on the element you select. For example, if you right-click on the chart's title, the shortcut menu command is Format Chart Title.

The Format command displays a stay-on-top tabbed dialog box with options for the selected element. Changes that you make are displayed immediately, but in some cases you need to deactivate the control by pressing Tab to move to the next control. You can keep this dialog box displayed while you work on the chart. When you select a new chart element, the dialog box changes to display the properties for the newly selected element.

Note

In Excel 2007, the designers removed the ability to double-click on a chart element to display the corresponding Format dialog box. In response to user complaints, double-clicking on a chart element has been reinstated in Excel 2010. ∎

Figure 18-10 shows the Format Axis dialog box, which is displayed by right-clicking on the vertical axis and selecting Format Axis from the shortcut menu — or by simply double-clicking on the vertical axis.

Tip

If you apply formatting to a chart element and decide that it wasn't such a good idea, you can revert to the original formatting for the particular chart style. Right-click on the chart element, and choose Reset to Match Style from the shortcut menu. To reset the entire chart, select the chart area when you issue the command. ∎

Printing Charts

Printing embedded charts is nothing special — you print them the same way that you print a worksheet. As long as you include the embedded chart in the range that you want to print, Excel prints the chart as it appears onscreen. When printing a sheet that contains embedded charts, it's a good idea to preview first (or use Page Layout view) to ensure that your charts do not span multiple pages. If you created the chart on a chart sheet, Excel always prints the chart on a page by itself.

Tip

If you activate an embedded chart and choose File ⇨ Print and then click the Print button, Excel prints the chart on a page by itself and does *not* print the worksheet. ∎

If you don't want a particular embedded chart to appear on your printout, use the Properties tab of the Format Chart Area dialog box. To display this dialog box, double-click on the background area of the chart. In the Properties tab of the Format Chart Area dialog box, clear the Print Object checkbox.

FIGURE 18-10

Each chart element has a formatting dialog box. This one is used to format a chart axis.

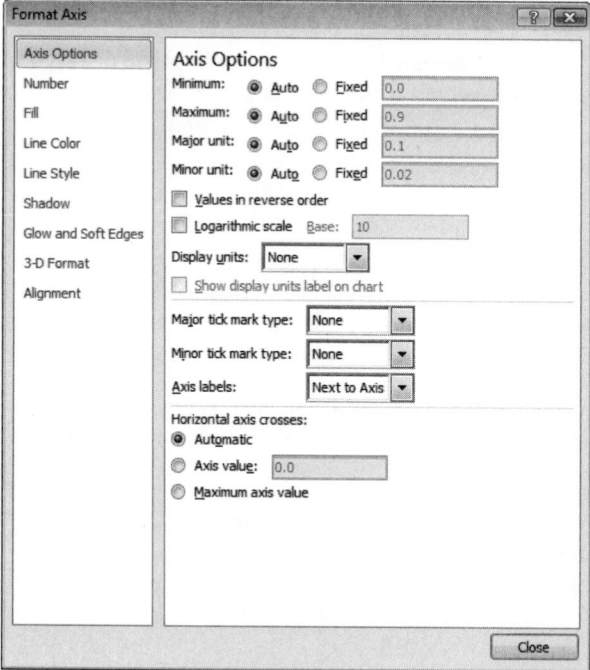

Understanding Chart Types

People who create charts usually do so to make a point or to communicate a specific message. Often, the message is explicitly stated in the chart's title or in text contained within the chart. The chart itself provides visual support.

Choosing the correct chart type is often a key factor in the effectiveness of the message. Therefore, it's often well worth your time to experiment with various chart types to determine which one conveys your message best.

In almost every case, the underlying message in a chart is some type of comparison. Examples of some general types of comparisons include the following:

- **Compare Item to Other Items.** A chart may compare sales in each of a company's sales regions.

- **Compare Data over Time.** A chart may display sales by month and indicate trends over time.

- **Make Relative Comparisons.** A common pie chart can depict relative proportions in terms of pie "slices."
- **Compare Data Relationships.** An XY chart is ideal for this comparison. For example, you might show the relationship between marketing expenditures and sales.
- **Frequency Comparison.** You can use a common histogram, for example, to display the number (or percentage) of students who scored within a particular grade range.
- **Identify "Outliers" or Unusual Situations.** If you have thousands of data points, creating a chart may help identify data that is not representative.

Choosing a Chart Type

A common question among Excel users is, "How do I know which chart type to use for my data?" Unfortunately, this question has no cut-and-dried answer. Perhaps the best answer is a vague one: "Use the chart type that gets your message across in the simplest way."

Figure 18-11 shows the same set of data plotted by using six different chart types. Although all six charts represent the same information (monthly "Website Visitors"), it looks quite different from one chart to another.

The column chart (upper left) is probably the best choice for this particular set of data because it clearly shows the information for each month in discrete units. The bar chart (upper right) is similar to a column chart, but the axes are swapped. Most people are more accustomed to seeing time-based information extend from left to right rather than from top to bottom.

The line chart (middle left) may not be the best choice because it seems to imply that the data is continuous — that points exist in between the 12 actual data points. This same argument may be made against using an area chart (middle right).

The pie chart (lower left) is simply too confusing and does nothing to convey the time-based nature of the data. Pie charts are most appropriate for a data series in which you want to emphasize proportions among a relatively small number of data points. If you have too many data points, a pie chart can be impossible to interpret.

The radar chart (lower right) is clearly inappropriate for this data. People aren't accustomed to viewing time-based information in a circular direction!

Fortunately, changing a chart's type is easy, so you can experiment with various chart types until you find the one that represents your data accurately, clearly, and as simply as possible.

FIGURE 18-11

The same data plotted using six different chart types.

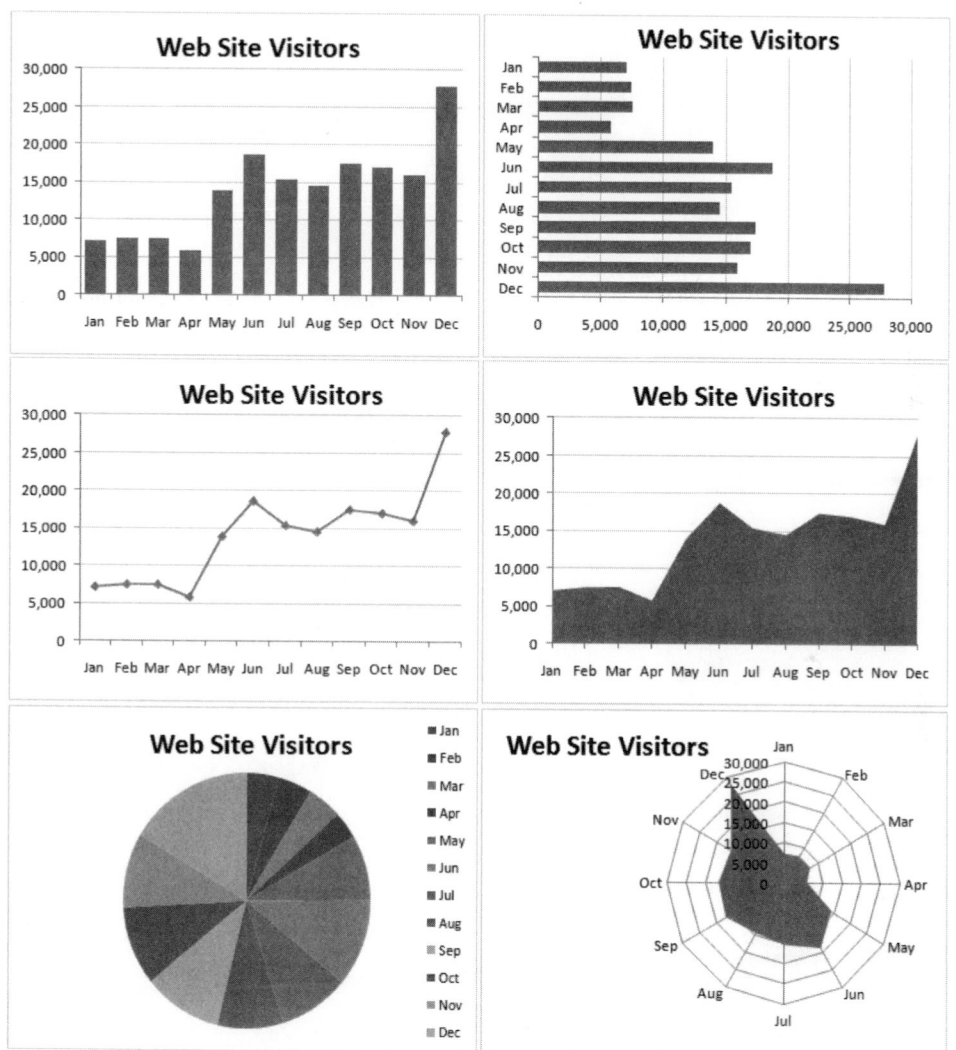

Summary

This chapter introduced Excel charts, including the differences between embedded charts and separate chart sheets, and parts of a chart. You learned how to create a chart; move, resize, and copy a chart; and how to work with chart elements. For many uses, the information in this chapter is sufficient to create a wide variety of charts.

Communicating Data Visually

This chapter explores conditional formatting, one of Excel's most versatile features. You can apply conditional formatting to a cell so that the cell looks different, depending on its contents. Microsoft made significant enhancements to conditional formatting in Excel 2007, and it's now a useful tool for visualizing numerical data. You'll find a few more conditional formatting improvements in Excel 2010.

This chapter also introduces sparklines and presents examples that demonstrate how they can be used in your worksheets. A sparkline looks like a small chart within a single cell.

About Conditional Formatting

Conditional formatting enables you to apply cell formatting selectively and automatically, based on the contents of the cells. For example, you can set things up so that all negative values in a range have a light-yellow background color. When you enter or change a value in the range, Excel examines the value and checks the conditional formatting rules for the cell. If the value is negative, the background is shaded. If not, no formatting is applied.

Conditional formatting is a useful way to quickly identify erroneous cell entries or cells of a particular type. You can use a format (such as bright-red cell shading) to make particular cells easy to identify.

Figure 19-1 shows a worksheet with nine ranges, each with a different type of conditional formatting rule applied. Here's a brief explanation of each:

- **Greater than 10.** Values greater than 10 are highlighted with a different background color. This rule is just one of many numeric value related rules that you can apply.

IN THIS CHAPTER

Understanding Excel's Conditional Formatting feature

Using the graphical conditional formats

Using conditional formatting formulas

Reviewing tips for using conditional formatting

Introducing the new sparklines graphics feature

Adding sparklines to a worksheet

Customizing sparklines

Making a sparkline display only the most recent data

- **Above Average.** Values that are higher than the average value are highlighted.
- **Duplicate Values.** Values that appear more than one time are highlighted.
- **Words that Contain X.** If the cell contains X (upper- or lowercase), the cell is highlighted.
- **Data Bars.** Each cell displays a horizontal bar, proportional to its value.
- **Color Scale.** The background color varies, depending on the value of the cells. You can choose from several different color scales or create your own.
- **Icon Set.** One of several icon sets. It displays a small graphic in the cell. The graphic varies, depending on the cell value.
- **Icon Set.** Another icon set, with all but one icon hidden.
- **Custom Rule.** The rule for this checkerboard pattern is based on a formula:

```
=MOD(ROW(),2)=MOD(COLUMN(),2)
```

FIGURE 19-1

This worksheet demonstrates a few conditional formatting rules.

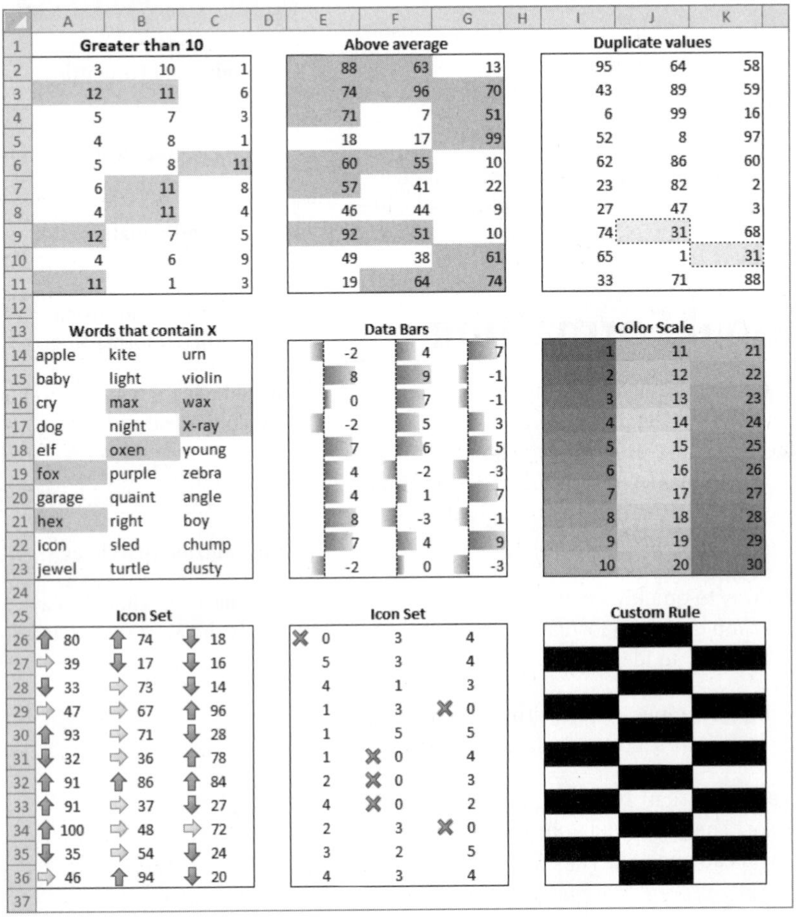

Greater than 10				Above average				Duplicate values		
3	10	1		88	63	13		95	64	58
12	11	6		74	96	70		43	89	59
5	7	3		71	7	51		6	99	16
4	8	1		18	17	99		52	8	97
5	8	11		60	55	10		62	86	60
6	11	8		57	41	22		23	82	2
4	11	4		46	44	9		27	47	3
12	7	5		92	51	10		74	31	68
4	6	9		49	38	61		65	1	31
11	1	3		19	64	74		33	71	88

Words that contain X				Data Bars				Color Scale		
apple	kite	urn		-2	4	7		1	11	21
baby	light	violin		8	9	-1		2	12	22
cry	max	wax		0	7	-1		3	13	23
dog	night	X-ray		-2	5	3		4	14	24
elf	oxen	young		7	6	5		5	15	25
fox	purple	zebra		4	-2	-3		6	16	26
garage	quaint	angle		4	1	7		7	17	27
hex	right	boy		8	-3	-1		8	18	28
icon	sled	chump		7	4	9		9	19	29
jewel	turtle	dusty		-2	0	-3		10	20	30

Icon Set				Icon Set				Custom Rule
80	74	18		0	3	4		
39	17	16		5	3	4		
33	73	14		4	1	3		
47	67	96		1	3	0		
93	71	28		1	5	5		
32	36	78		1	0	4		
91	86	84		2	0	3		
91	37	27		4	0	2		
100	48	72		2	3	0		
35	54	24		3	2	5		
46	94	20		4	3	4		

Specifying Conditional Formatting

To apply a conditional formatting rule to a cell or range, select the cells and then use one of the commands from the Home ⇨ Styles ⇨ Conditional Formatting drop-down list to specify a rule. The choices are as follows:

- **Highlight Cell Rules.** Example rules include highlighting cells that are greater than a particular value, between two values, contain specific text string, a date, or have duplicate values.

- **Top Bottom Rules.** Examples include highlighting the top 10 items, the items in the bottom 20 percent, and items that are above average.

- **Data Bars.** Applies graphic bars directly in the cells, proportional to the cell's value.

- **Color Scales.** Applies background color, proportional to the cell's value.

- **Icon Sets.** Displays icons directly in the cells. The icons depend on the cell's value.

- **New Rule.** Enables you to specify other conditional formatting rules, including rules based on a logical formula.

- **Clear Rules.** Deletes all the conditional formatting rules from the selected cells.

- **Manage Rules.** Displays the Conditional Formatting Rules Manager dialog box, in which you create new conditional formatting rules, edit rules, or delete rules.

Excel 2010 Improvements

If you've used conditional formatting in Excel 2007, you'll find several improvements in Excel 2010:

- Data bars display proportionally.
- Data bars can display in a solid color with a border. Previously, data bars were displayed with a gradient.
- Data bars handle negative values much better.
- You can specify minimum and maximum values for data bars.
- You can create customized icon sets.
- Hiding one or more icons in an icon set is easy.

Formatting Types You Can Apply

When you select a conditional formatting rule, Excel displays a dialog box specific to that rule. These dialog boxes have one thing in a common: a drop-down list with common formatting suggestions.

Figure 19-2 shows the dialog box that appears when you choose Home ⇨ Styles ⇨ Conditional Formatting ⇨ Highlight Cells Rules ⇨ Between. This particular rule applies the formatting if the value in the cell falls *between* two specified values. In this case, you enter the two values (or specify cell references) and then use choices from the drop-down list to set the type of formatting to display if the condition is met.

FIGURE 19-2

One of several different conditional formatting dialog boxes.

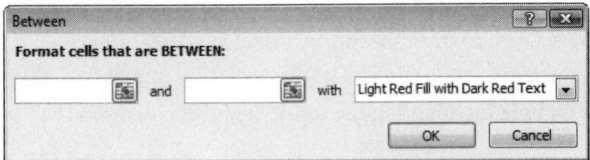

The formatting suggestions in the drop-down list are just a few of thousands of different formatting combinations. If none of Excel's suggestions are what you want, choose the Custom Format option to display the Format Cells dialog box. You can specify the format in any or all of the four tabs: Number, Font, Border, and Fill.

Note

The Format Cells dialog box used for conditional formatting is a modified version of the standard Format Cells dialog box. It doesn't have the Alignment and Protection tabs, and some of the Font formatting options are disabled. The dialog box also includes a Clear button that clears any formatting already selected. ■

Making Your Own Rules

For do-it-yourself types, Excel provides the New Formatting Rule dialog box, shown in Figure 19-3. Access this dialog box by choosing Home ⇨ Styles ⇨ Conditional Formatting ⇨ New Rules.

Use the New Formatting Rule dialog box to re-create all the conditional format rules available via the Ribbon, as well as new rules. First, select a general rule type from the list at the top of the dialog box. The bottom part of the dialog box varies, depending on your selection at the top. After you specify the rule, click the Format button to specify the type of formatting to apply if the condition is met. An exception is the first rule type, which doesn't have a Format button (it uses graphics rather than cell formatting).

Here is a summary of the rule types:

- **Format All Cells Based on Their Values.** Use this rule type to create rules that display data bars, color scales, or icon sets.

- **Format Only Cells That Contain.** Use this rule type to create rules that format cells based on mathematical comparisons (greater than, less than, greater than or equal to, less than or equal to, equal to, not equal to, between, not between). You can also create rules based on text, dates, blanks, non-blanks, and errors. This rule type is very similar to how conditional formatting was set up in previous versions of Excel.

- **Format Only Top or Bottom Ranked Values.** Use this rule type to create rules that involve identifying cells in the top *n*, top *n* percent, bottom *n*, and bottom *n* percent.

- **Format Only Values That Are Above or Below Average.** Use this rule type to create rules that identify cells that are above average, below average, or within a specified standard deviation from the average.

- **Format Only Unique or Duplicate Values.** Use this rule type to create rules that format unique or duplicate values in a range.

- **Use a Formula to Determine Which Cells to Format.** Use this rule type to create rules based on a logical formula. See "Creating Formula-Based Rules," later in this chapter.

FIGURE 19-3

Use the New Formatting Rule dialog box to create your own conditional formatting rules.

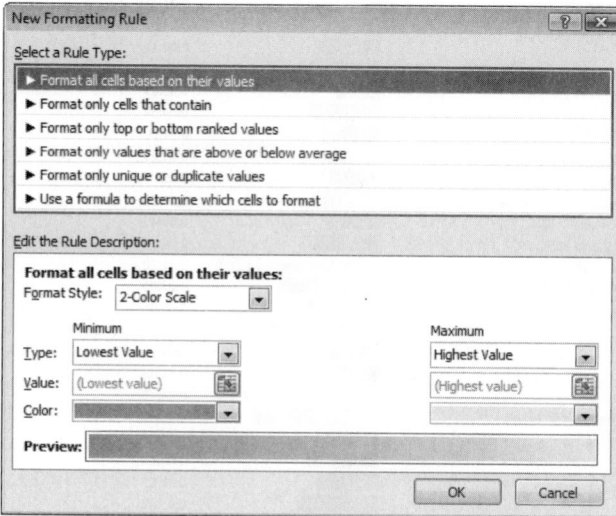

Conditional Formats That Use Graphics

This section describes the three conditional formatting options that display graphics: data bars, color scales, and icon sets. These types of conditional formatting can be useful for visualizing the values in a range.

Using Data Bars

The *data bars* conditional format displays horizontal bars directly in the cell. The length of the bar is based on the value of the cell, relative to the other values in the range.

Note

The Data Bars feature has improved significantly in Excel 2010. Data bars now display proportionally (just like a bar chart), and there is now an option to display data bars in a solid color (no more forced color gradient) and with a border. In addition, negative values can now display in a different color, and appear left of an axis. ■

A Simple Data Bar

Figure 19-4 shows an example of data bars. It's a list of tracks on Bob Dylan albums, with the length of each track in column D. I applied data bar conditional formatting to the values in column D. You can tell at a glance which tracks are longer.

FIGURE 19-4

The length of the data bars is proportional to the track length in the cell in column D.

	A	B	C	D
11	Bob Dylan	Another Side of Bob Dylan	Spanish Harlem Incident	0:02:24
12	Bob Dylan	Another Side of Bob Dylan	To Ramona	0:03:52
13	Bob Dylan	Blonde On Blonde	4th Time Around	0:04:36
14	Bob Dylan	Blonde On Blonde	Absolutely Sweet Marie	0:04:57
15	Bob Dylan	Blonde On Blonde	I Want You	0:03:08
16	Bob Dylan	Blonde On Blonde	Just Like A Woman	0:04:54
17	Bob Dylan	Blonde On Blonde	Leopard-Skin Pill-Box Hat	0:04:00
18	Bob Dylan	Blonde On Blonde	Most Likely You Go Your Way (And I'll Go Mine)	0:03:29
19	Bob Dylan	Blonde On Blonde	Obviously 5 Believers	0:03:36
20	Bob Dylan	Blonde On Blonde	One Of Us Must Know (Sooner Or Later)	0:04:56
21	Bob Dylan	Blonde On Blonde	Pledging My Time	0:03:49
22	Bob Dylan	Blonde On Blonde	Rainy Day Women #12 And #35	0:04:38
23	Bob Dylan	Blonde On Blonde	Sad Eyed Lady Of the Lowlands	0:11:20
24	Bob Dylan	Blonde On Blonde	Stuck Inside Of Mobile With the Memphis Blues Again	0:07:05
25	Bob Dylan	Blonde On Blonde	Temporary Like Achilles	0:05:06
26	Bob Dylan	Blonde On Blonde	Visions Of Johanna	0:07:34
27	Bob Dylan	Blood On The Tracks	Buckets Of Rain	0:03:22
28	Bob Dylan	Blood On The Tracks	Idiot Wind	0:07:49
29	Bob Dylan	Blood On The Tracks	If You See Her, Say Hello	0:04:49
30	Bob Dylan	Blood On The Tracks	Lily Rosemary And The Jack Of Hearts	0:08:53
31	Bob Dylan	Blood On The Tracks	Meet Me In The Morning	0:04:22
32	Bob Dylan	Blood On The Tracks	Shelter From The Storm	0:05:02
33	Bob Dylan	Blood On The Tracks	Simple Twist Of Fate	0:04:19
34	Bob Dylan	Blood On The Tracks	Tangled Up In Blue	0:05:42
35	Bob Dylan	Blood On The Tracks	You're A Big Girl Now	0:04:36
36	Bob Dylan	Blood On The Tracks	You're Gonna Make Me Lonesome When You Go	0:02:55
37	Bob Dylan	Bringing it All Back Home	Bob Dylan's 115th Dream	0:06:33
38	Bob Dylan	Bringing it All Back Home	Gates of Eden	0:05:44

Tip

When you adjust the column width, the bar lengths adjust accordingly. The differences among the bar lengths are more prominent when the column is wider. ■

Excel provides quick access to 12 data bar styles via Home ➪ Styles ➪ Conditional Formatting ➪ Data Bars. For additional choices, click the More Rules option, which displays the New Formatting Rule dialog box. Use this dialog box to

- Show the bar only (hide the numbers).
- Specify Minimum and Maximum values for the scaling.

- Change the appearance of the bars.
- Specify how negative values and the axis are handled.
- Specify the direction of the bars.

Note

Oddly, the colors used for data bars are not theme colors. If you apply a new document theme, the data bar colors do not change. ∎

Using Data Bars in Lieu of a Chart

Using data bars conditional formatting can sometimes serve as a quick alternative to creating a chart. Figure 19-5 shows a three-column table of data (created by using Insert ➪ Tables ➪ Table), with data bars conditional formatting applied in the third column. The third column of the table contains references to the values in the second column. The conditional formatting in the third column uses the Show Bars Only option, so the values are not displayed.

FIGURE 19-5

This table uses data bars conditional formatting.

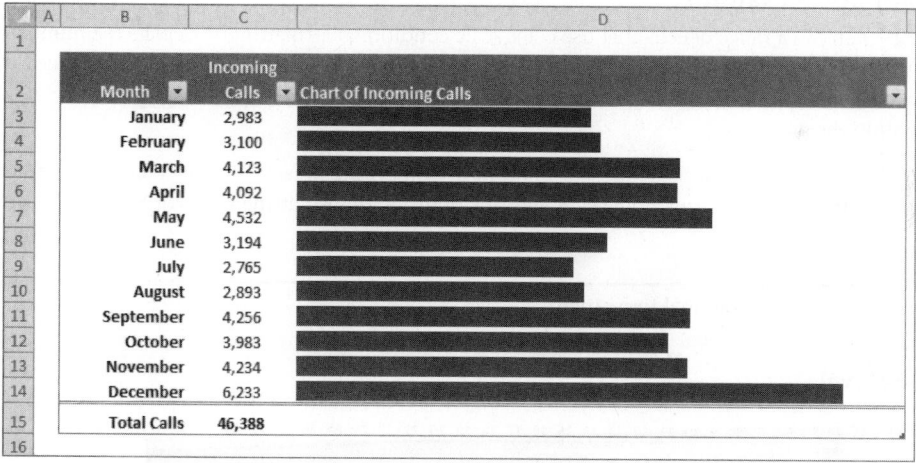

Figure 19-6 shows an actual bar chart created from the same data. The bar chart takes about the same amount of time to create and is a lot more flexible. But for a quick-and-dirty chart, data bars are a good option — especially when you need to create several such charts.

Using Color Scales

The *color scale* conditional formatting option varies the background color of a cell based on the cell's value, relative to other cells in the range.

FIGURE 19-6

A real Excel bar chart (not conditional formatting data bars).

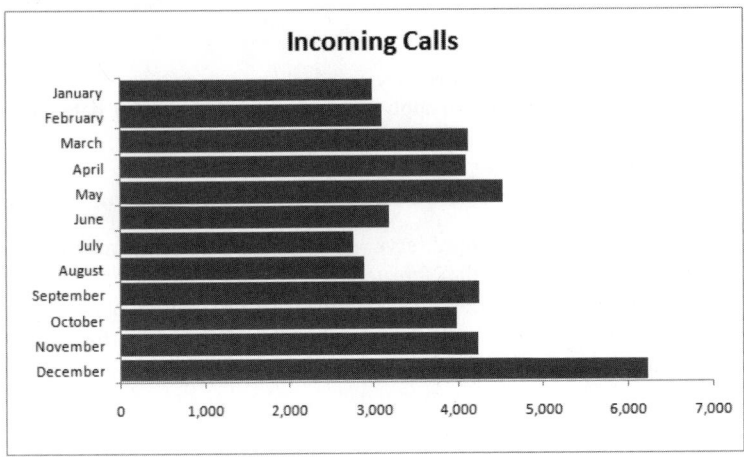

A Color Scale Example

Figure 19-7 shows a range of cells that use color scale conditional formatting. It depicts the number of employees on each day of the year. This is a three-color scale that uses red for the lowest value, yellow for the midpoint, and green for the highest value. Values in between are displayed using a color within the gradient.

Excel provides four 2-Color Scale presets and four 3-Color Scale presets, which you can apply to the selected range by choosing Home ➪ Styles ➪ Conditional Formatting ➪ Color Scales.

FIGURE 19-7

A range that uses color scale conditional formatting.

	1	2	3	4	5	6	7	8	9	10	11	12	13	14	15	16	17	18	19	20	21	22	23	24	25	26	27	28	29	30	31
Daily Staffing Level																															
January	80	80	80	80	80	80	80	79	79	79	79	79	79	80	82	82	82	82	82	82	82	82	82	82	84	84	84	84	84	84	84
February	84	84	84	84	84	84	84	84	83	83	83	82	82	82	82	82	82	82	82	82	82	82	82	82	85	85	85				
March	85	85	85	85	85	85	85	85	85	85	85	85	86	86	86	86	86	86	86	86	86	86	86	86	86	86	86	86	86	86	86
April	88	88	88	88	88	88	88	88	88	88	88	88	88	88	89	89	89	89	89	88	88	88	88	88	88	88	88	88	88	88	
May	88	88	88	88	88	88	88	88	88	88	89	89	89	89	89	89	89	89	89	89	89	89	89	89	89	92	92	92	92	92	92
June	92	92	92	92	92	92	92	92	92	92	92	92	91	91	91	91	91	91	91	91	91	91	92	92	92	92	92	92	92	92	
July	92	92	92	92	92	92	92	92	92	92	92	93	95	95	95	95	96	98	98	98	96	94	94	94	94	94	92	92	92	92	92
August	92	92	92	92	91	90	90	90	90	91	92	92	92	92	92	92	92	92	92	92	92	92	92	92	92	92	92	92	92	92	92
September	92	93	93	93	93	93	93	93	93	93	93	93	93	93	93	94	94	94	94	94	94	94	94	94	94	94	95	95	95		
October	95	95	95	95	95	95	94	94	94	94	94	95	95	95	95	95	96	96	96	96	96	96	96	96	96	96	96	97	97	97	97
November	97	97	97	97	97	97	97	96	96	96	96	97	97	97	99	99	99	99	99	99	99	99	99	99	99	99	99	99	99	99	
December	101	101	101	101	101	101	101	102	102	102	102	102	102	102	102	102	102	101	101	101	101	101	101	101	101	101	101	101	101	101	101

To customize the colors and other options, choose Home ⇨ Styles ⇨ Conditional Formatting ⇨ Color Scales ⇨ More Rules. This command displays the New Formatting Rule dialog box, shown in Figure 19-8. Adjust the settings, and watch the Preview box to see the effects of your changes.

FIGURE 19-8

Use the New Formatting Rule dialog box to customize a color scale.

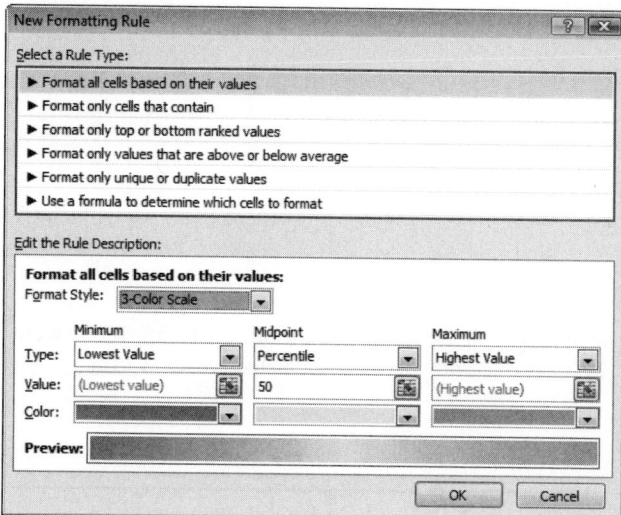

Using Icon Sets

Yet another conditional formatting option is to display an icon in the cell. The icon displayed depends on the value of the cell.

To assign an icon set to a range, select the cells and choose Home ⇨ Styles ⇨ Conditional Formatting ⇨ Icon Sets. Excel provides 20 icon sets to choose from. The number of icons in the sets ranges from three to five. You cannot supply your own icons.

An Icon Set Example

Figure 19-9 shows an example that uses an icon set. The symbols graphically depict the status of each project, based on the value in column C.

By default, the symbols are assigned using percentiles. For a three-symbol set, the items are grouped into three percentiles. For a four-symbol set, they're grouped into four percentiles. And for a five-symbol set, the items are grouped into five percentiles.

If you would like more control over how the icons are assigned, choose Home ⇨ Styles ⇨ Conditional Formatting ⇨ Icon Sets ⇨ More Rules to display the New Formatting Rule dialog box. To modify an existing rule, choose Home ⇨ Styles ⇨ Conditional Formatting ⇨ Manage Rules. Then select the rule to modify and click the Edit Rule button.

FIGURE 19-9

Using an icon set to indicate the status of projects.

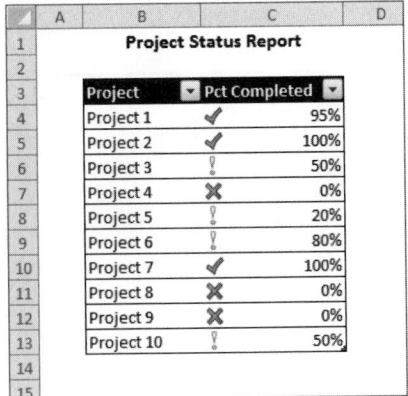

Figure 19-10 shows how to modify the icon set rules such that only projects that are 100 percent completed get the check mark icons. Projects that are 0 percent completed get the X icon. All other projects get no icon.

FIGURE 19-10

Changing the icon assignment rule.

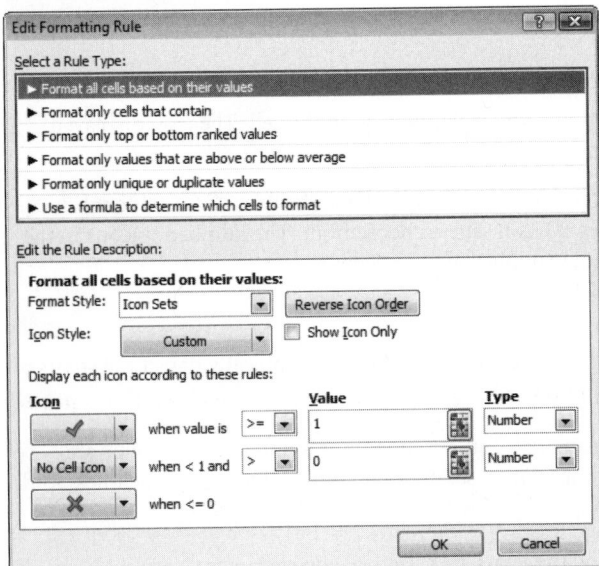

Figure 19-11 shows the project status list after making this change.

FIGURE 19-11

Using a modified rule and eliminating an icon makes the table more readable.

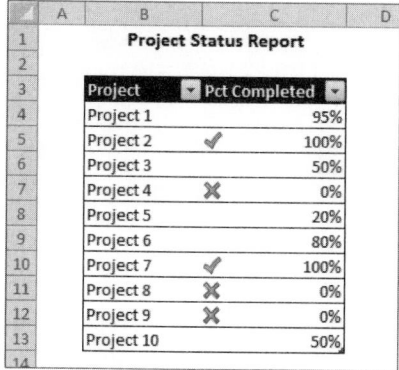

Another Icon Set Example

Figure 19-12 shows a table that contains two test scores for each student. The Change column contains a formula that calculates the difference between the two tests. The Trend column uses an icon set to display the trend graphically.

This example uses the icon set named *3 Arrows*, and I customized the rule:

- **Up Arrow.** When the value is >= 5
- **Level Arrow.** When the value is < 5 and >–5
- **Down Arrow.** When the value is <= –5

In other words, a difference of no more than five points in either direction is considered an even trend. An improvement of at least five points is considered a positive trend, and a decline of five points or more is considered a negative trend.

Note

The Trend column contains a formula that references the Change column. I used the Show Icon Only option in the Trend column, which also centers the icon in the column. ∎

In some cases, using icon sets can cause your worksheet to look very cluttered. Displaying an icon for every cell in a range might result in visual overload. You can hide icons by choosing No Cell Icon as the Icon choice in the Edit Formatting Rule dialog box.

FIGURE 19-12

The arrows depict the trend from Test 1 to Test 2.

	A	B	C	D	E
1					
2	Student	Test 1	Test 2	Change	Trend
3	Amy	59	65	6	⬆
4	Bob	82	78	-4	⇨
5	Calvind	98	92	-6	⬇
6	Doug	56	60	4	⇨
7	Ephraim	98	89	-9	⬇
8	Frank	67	75	8	⬆
9	Gretta	78	81	3	⇨
10	Harold	87	92	5	⬆
11	Inez	56	85	29	⬆
12	June	87	72	-15	⬇
13	Kenny	87	88	1	⇨
14	Lance	92	92	0	⇨
15	Marvin	82	73	-9	⬇
16	Noel	98	100	2	⇨
17	Opie	84	73	-11	⬇
18	Paul	94	93	-1	⇨
19	Quinton	68	92	24	⬆
20	Rasmus	91	90	-1	⇨
21	Sam	85	86	1	⇨
22	Ted	72	92	20	⬆
23	Ursie	80	82	2	⇨
24	Valerie	77	78	1	⇨
25	Wally	64	45	-19	⬇
26	Xerxes	59	63	4	⇨
27	Yolanda	89	99	10	⬆
28	Zippy	85	82	-3	⇨
29					

Creating Formula-Based Rules

Excel's Conditional Formatting feature is versatile, but sometimes it's just not quite versatile enough. Fortunately, you can extend its versatility by writing conditional formatting formulas.

The examples later in this section describe how to create conditional formatting formulas for the following:

- To identify text entries
- To identify dates that fall on a weekend
- To format cells that are in odd-numbered rows or columns (for dynamic alternate row or column shading)

- To format groups of rows (e.g., shade every two groups of rows)
- To display a sum only when all precedent cells contain values

Some of these formulas may be useful to you. If not, they may inspire you to create other conditional formatting formulas.

To specify conditional formatting based on a formula, select the cells and then choose Home ⇨ Styles ⇨ Conditional Formatting ⇨ New Rule. This command displays the New Formatting Rule dialog box. Click the rule type Use a Formula to Determine Which Cells to Format, and you can specify the formula.

You can type the formula directly into the box, or you can enter a reference to a cell that contains a logical formula. As with normal Excel formulas, the formula you enter here must begin with an equal sign (=).

Note

The formula must be a logical formula that returns either TRUE or FALSE. If the formula evaluates to TRUE, the condition is satisfied, and the conditional formatting is applied. If the formula evaluates to FALSE, the conditional formatting is not applied. ■

Understanding Relative and Absolute References

If the formula that you enter into the Conditional Formatting dialog box contains a cell reference, that reference is considered a *relative reference*, based on the upper-left cell in the selected range.

For example, suppose that you want to set up conditional formatting that applies shading to cells in range A1:B10 only if the cell contains text. None of Excel's default conditional formatting options can do this task, so you need to create a formula that will return TRUE if the cell contains text and FALSE otherwise. Follow these steps:

1. Select the range A1:B10 and ensure that cell A1 is the active cell.
2. Choose Home ⇨ Styles ⇨ Conditional Formatting ⇨ New Rule to display the New Formatting Rule dialog box.
3. Click the Use a Formula to Determine Which Cells to Format rule type.
4. Enter the following formula in the Formula box:

   ```
   =ISTEXT(A1)
   ```
5. Click the Format button to display the Format Cells dialog box.
6. From the Fill tab, specify the cell shading that will be applied if the formula returns TRUE.
7. Click OK to return to the New Formatting Rule dialog box (see Figure 19-13). Make sure that the formula is working correctly and that you see a preview of your selected formatting.
8. If the preview looks correct, click OK to close the New Formatting Rule dialog box.

FIGURE 19-13

Creating a conditional formatting rule based on a formula.

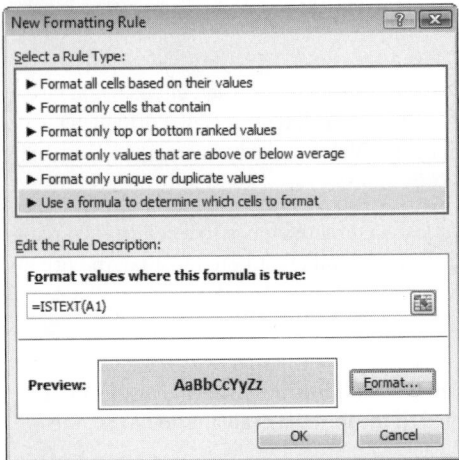

Notice that the formula entered in Step 4 contains a relative reference to the upper-left cell in the selected range.

Generally, when entering a conditional formatting formula for a range of cells, you'll use a reference to the active cell, which is typically the upper-left cell in the selected range. One exception is when you need to refer to a specific cell. For example, suppose that you select range A1:B10 and you want to apply formatting to all cells in the range that exceed the value in cell C1. Enter this conditional formatting formula:

```
=A1>$C$1
```

In this case, the reference to cell C1 is an *absolute reference;* it will not be adjusted for the cells in the selected range. In other words, the conditional formatting formula for cell A2 looks like this:

```
=A2>$C$1
```

The relative cell reference is adjusted, but the absolute cell reference is not.

Conditional Formatting Formula Examples

Each of these examples uses a formula entered directly into the New Formatting Rule dialog box, after selecting the Use a Formula to Determine Which Cells to Format rule type. You decide the type of formatting that you apply conditionally.

Identifying Weekend Days

Excel provides several conditional formatting rules that deal with dates, but it doesn't let you identify dates that fall on a weekend. Use this formula to identify weekend dates:

```
=OR(WEEKDAY(A1)=7,WEEKDAY(A1)=1)
```

This formula assumes that a range is selected and that cell A1 is the active cell.

Displaying Alternate-Row Shading

The conditional formatting formula that follows was applied to the range A1:D18, as shown in Figure 19-14, to apply shading to alternate rows.

```
=MOD(ROW(),2)=0
```

FIGURE 19-14

Using conditional formatting to apply formatting to alternate rows.

	A	B	C	D	E
1	430	470	843	319	
2	283	788	119	658	
3	821	426	265	269	
4	921	809	382	186	
5	282	287	289	712	
6	727	885	0	126	
7	395	83	836	351	
8	121	922	541	798	
9	885	426	109	234	
10	455	66	177	919	
11	562	794	743	145	
12	109	847	116	310	
13	748	65	740	259	
14	524	293	537	541	
15	475	71	831	370	
16	472	522	823	414	
17	467	608	963	278	
18	484	667	758	426	
19					

Alternate row shading can make your spreadsheets easier to read. If you add or delete rows within the conditional formatting area, the shading is updated automatically.

This formula uses the ROW function (which returns the row number) and the MOD function (which returns the remainder of its first argument divided by its second argument). For cells in even-numbered rows, the MOD function returns 0, and cells in that row are formatted.

For alternate shading of columns, use the COLUMN function instead of the ROW function.

Creating Checkerboard Shading

The following formula is a variation on the example in the preceding section. It applies formatting to alternate rows and columns, creating a checkerboard effect.

```
=MOD(ROW(),2)=MOD(COLUMN(),2)
```

Shading Groups of Rows

Here's another row-shading variation. The following formula shades alternate groups of rows. It produces four rows of shaded rows, followed by four rows of unshaded rows, followed by four more shaded rows, and so on.

```
=MOD(INT((ROW()-1)/4)+1,2)
```

Figure 19-15 shows an example.

FIGURE 19-15

Conditional formatting produces these groups of alternate shaded rows.

	A	B	C	D	E
1	250	589	585	878	
2	660	865	956	473	
3	229	322	298	669	
4	200	69	282	248	
5	387	584	924	119	
6	304	604	445	486	
7	122	887	534	809	
8	797	846	482	148	
9	846	99	384	234	
10	339	499	736	228	
11	78	574	216	33	
12	481	177	127	566	
13	881	772	437	408	
14	697	459	342	786	
15	474	541	216	634	
16	71	719	764	96	
17	15	805	966	180	
18	415	76	568	752	
19	573	492	165	483	
20	355	795	811	667	
21	623	942	122	23	
22	589	195	966	588	
23					

For different sized groups, change the 4 to some other value. For example, use this formula to shade alternate groups of two rows:

```
=MOD(INT((ROW()-1)/2)+1,2)
```

Displaying a Total Only When All Values Are Entered

Figure 19-16 shows a range with a formula that uses the SUM function in cell C6. Conditional formatting is used to hide the sum if any of the four cells above is blank. The conditional formatting formula for cell C6 (and cell C5, which contains a label) is

```
=COUNT($C$2:$C$5)=4
```

FIGURE 19-16

The sum is displayed only when all four values have been entered.

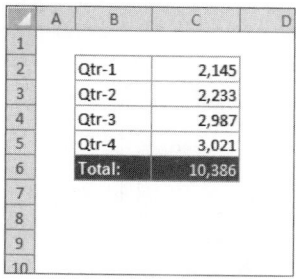

This formula returns TRUE only if C2:C5 contains no empty cells.

Figure 19-17 shows the worksheet when one of the values is missing.

FIGURE 19-17

A missing value causes the sum to be hidden.

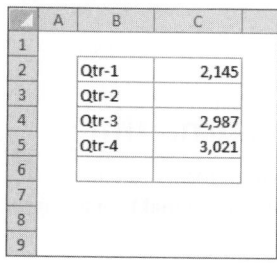

Working with Conditional Formats

This section describes some additional information about conditional formatting that you may find useful.

Managing Rules

The Conditional Formatting Rules Manager dialog box is useful for checking, editing, deleting, and adding conditional formats. First, select any cell in the range that contains conditional formatting. Then choose Home ➪ Styles ➪ Conditional Formatting ➪ Manage Rules.

You can specify as many rules as you like by clicking the New Rule button. As you can see in Figure 19-18, cells can even use data bars, color scales, and icon sets all at the same time — although I can't think of a good reason to do so.

FIGURE 19-18

This range uses data bars, color scales, and icon sets.

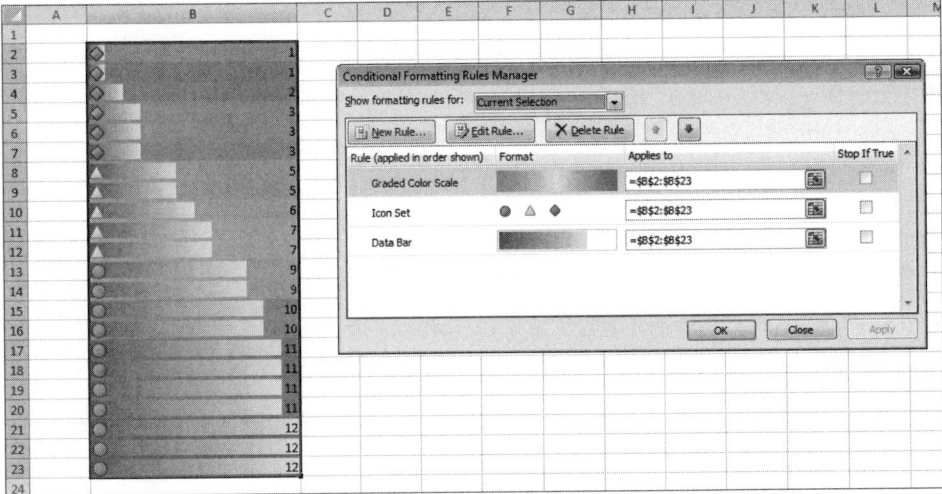

Copying Cells That Contain Conditional Formatting

Conditional formatting information is stored with a cell much like standard formatting information is stored with a cell. As a result, when you copy a cell that contains conditional formatting, you also copy the conditional formatting.

Tip

To copy only the formatting (including conditional formatting), use the Paste Special dialog box and select the Formats option. Or, use Home ➪ Clipboard ➪ Paste ➪ Formatting (R). ■

If you insert rows or columns within a range that contains conditional formatting, the new cells have the same conditional formatting.

Deleting Conditional Formatting

When you press Delete to delete the contents of a cell, you do not delete the conditional formatting for the cell (if any). To remove all conditional formats (as well as all other cell formatting), select the cell. Then choose Home ➪ Editing ➪ Clear ➪ Clear Formats. Or, choose Home ➪ Editing ➪ Clear ➪ Clear All to delete the cell contents and the conditional formatting.

To remove only conditional formatting (and leave the other formatting intact), use Home ➪ Styles ➪ Conditional Formatting ➪ Clear Rules.

Locating Cells That Contain Conditional Formatting

You can't tell, just by looking at a cell, whether it contains conditional formatting. You can, however, use the Go To dialog box to select such cells.

1. **Choose Home ➪ Editing ➪ Find & Select ➪ Go To Special.**
2. **In the Go To Special dialog box, select the Conditional Formats option.**
3. **To select all cells on the worksheet containing conditional formatting, select the All option; to select only the cells that contain the same conditional formatting as the active cell, select the Same option.**
4. **Click OK.** Excel selects the cells for you.

Note

The Excel Find and Replace dialog box includes a feature that allows you to search your worksheet to locate cells that contain specific formatting. This feature does *not* locate cells that contain formatting resulting from conditional formatting. ■

Introducing Sparklines

One of the new features in Excel 2010 is sparkline graphics. A sparkline is a small chart displayed in a single cell. A sparkline allows you to quickly spot time-based trends or variations in data. Because they are so compact, sparklines are often used in a group.

Although sparklines look like miniature charts (and can sometimes take the place of a chart), this feature is completely separate from the charting feature. For example, charts are placed on a worksheet's draw layer, and a single chart can display several series of data. A sparkline is displayed inside a cell and displays only one series of data. See Chapter 18 for information about charts.

Note

Sparklines are new to Excel 2010. If you create a workbook that uses sparklines and that workbook is opened using a previous version of Excel, any cells containing a sparkline will be empty. ■

Sparkline Types

Excel 2010 supports three types of sparklines. Figure 19-19 shows examples of the three types of sparkline graphics, displayed in column H. Each sparkline depicts the six data points to the left.

- **Line.** Similar to a line chart. As an option, the line can display with a marker for each data point. The first group in Figure 19-19 shows line sparklines, with markers. A quick glance reveals that with the exception of Fund Number W-91, the funds have been losing value over the 6-month period.

- **Column.** Similar to a column chart. The second group in Figure 19-19 shows the same data displayed with column sparklines.

- **Win/Loss.** A "binary" type chart that displays each data point as a high block or a low block. The third group shows win/loss sparklines. Notice that the data is different. Each cell displays the change from the previous month. In the sparkline, each data point is depicted as a high block (win) or a low block (loss). In this example, a positive change from the previous month is a win, and a negative change from the previous month is a loss.

FIGURE 19-19

Three groups of sparklines.

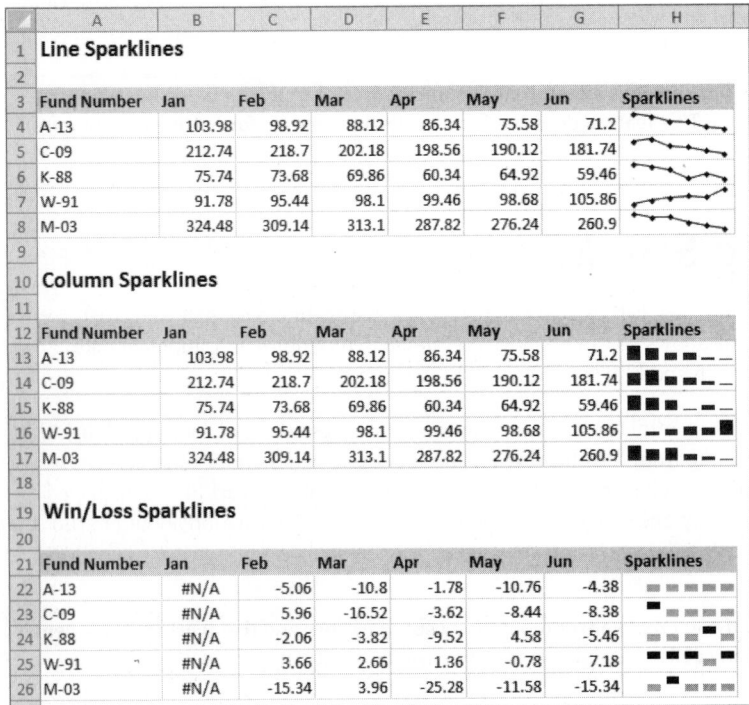

Why Sparklines?

If the term *sparkline* seems odd, don't blame Microsoft. Edward Tufte coined the term *sparkline*, and in his book, *Beautiful Evidence* (Graphics Press, 2006), he described it as

> sparklines: Intense, simple, word-sized graphics

In the case of Excel, sparklines are cell-sized graphics. As you see in this chapter, sparklines aren't limited to lines.

Creating Sparklines

Figure 19-20 shows some data to be summarized with sparklines. To create sparkline graphics, follow these steps:

1. **Select the data that will be depicted.** If you are creating multiple sparklines, select all the data. In this example, start by selecting the range B4:M12.

FIGURE 19-20

Data to be summarized with sparklines.

	A	B	C	D	E	F	G	H	I	J	K	L	M
1	**Average Monthly Precipitation (Inches)**												
2													
3		Jan	Feb	Mar	Apr	May	Jun	Jul	Aug	Sep	Oct	Nov	Dec
4	ASHEVILLE, NC	4.06	3.83	4.59	3.5	4.41	4.38	3.87	4.3	3.72	3.17	3.82	3.39
5	BAKERSFIELD, CA	1.18	1.21	1.41	0.45	0.24	0.12	0	0.08	0.15	0.3	0.59	0.76
6	BATON ROUGE, LA	6.19	5.1	5.07	5.56	5.34	5.33	5.96	5.86	4.84	3.81	4.76	5.26
7	BILLINGS, MT	0.81	0.57	1.12	1.74	2.48	1.89	1.28	0.85	1.34	1.26	0.75	0.67
8	DAYTONA BEACH, FL	3.13	2.74	3.84	2.54	3.26	5.69	5.17	6.09	6.61	4.48	3.03	2.71
9	EUGENE, OR	7.65	6.35	5.8	3.66	2.66	1.53	0.64	0.99	1.54	3.35	8.44	8.29
10	HONOLULU,HI	2.73	2.35	1.89	1.11	0.78	0.43	0.5	0.46	0.74	2.18	2.26	2.85
11	ST. LOUIS, MO	2.14	2.28	3.6	3.69	4.11	3.76	3.9	2.98	2.96	2.76	3.71	2.86
12	TUCSON, AZ	0.99	0.88	0.81	0.28	0.24	0.24	2.07	2.3	1.45	1.21	0.67	1.03
13													

2. **With the data selected, choose Insert ⇨ Sparklines, and click one of the three sparkline types: Line, Column, or Win/Loss.** Excel displays the Create Sparklines dialog box, as shown in Figure 19-21.

3. **Specify the location for the sparklines.** Typically, you'll put the sparklines next to the data, but that's not a requirement. Most of the time, you'll use an empty range to hold the sparklines. However, Excel does not prevent you from inserting sparklines into cells that already contain data. The sparkline location that you specify must match the source

data in terms of number of rows or number of columns. For this example, specify N4:N12 as the Location Range.

4. **Click OK.** Excel creates the sparklines graphics of the type you specified.

The sparklines are linked to the data, so if you change any of the values in the data range, the sparkline graphic will update.

FIGURE 19-21

Use the Create Sparklines dialog box to specify the data range and the location for the sparkline graphics.

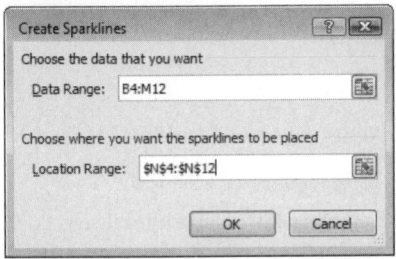

Figure 19-22 shows column sparklines for the precipitation data.

FIGURE 19-22

Column sparklines summarize the precipitation data for nine cities.

	A	Jan	Feb	Mar	Apr	May	Jun	Jul	Aug	Sep	Oct	Nov	Dec	N
1	**Average Monthly Precipitation (Inches)**													
2														
3		Jan	Feb	Mar	Apr	May	Jun	Jul	Aug	Sep	Oct	Nov	Dec	
4	ASHEVILLE, NC	4.06	3.83	4.59	3.5	4.41	4.38	3.87	4.3	3.72	3.17	3.82	3.39	
5	BAKERSFIELD, CA	1.18	1.21	1.41	0.45	0.24	0.12	0	0.08	0.15	0.3	0.59	0.76	
6	BATON ROUGE, LA	6.19	5.1	5.07	5.56	5.34	5.33	5.96	5.86	4.84	3.81	4.76	5.26	
7	BILLINGS, MT	0.81	0.57	1.12	1.74	2.48	1.89	1.28	0.85	1.34	1.26	0.75	0.67	
8	DAYTONA BEACH, FL	3.13	2.74	3.84	2.54	3.26	5.69	5.17	6.09	6.61	4.48	3.03	2.71	
9	EUGENE, OR	7.65	6.35	5.8	3.66	2.66	1.53	0.64	0.99	1.54	3.35	8.44	8.29	
10	HONOLULU, HI	2.73	2.35	1.89	1.11	0.78	0.43	0.5	0.46	0.74	2.18	2.26	2.85	
11	ST. LOUIS, MO	2.14	2.28	3.6	3.69	4.11	3.76	3.9	2.98	2.96	2.76	3.71	2.86	
12	TUCSON, AZ	0.99	0.88	0.81	0.28	0.24	0.24	2.07	2.3	1.45	1.21	0.67	1.03	
13														

Tip

Most of the time, you'll create sparklines on the same sheet that contains the data. If you want to create sparklines on a different sheet, start by activating the sheet where the sparklines will be displayed. Then, in the Create Sparklines dialog box, specify the source data either by pointing or by typing the complete sheet reference (e.g., Sheet1A1:C12). The Create Sparklines dialog box lets you specify a different sheet for the Data Range, but not for the Location Range. ∎

Understanding Sparkline Groups

Most of the time, you'll probably create a group of sparklines — one for each row or column of data. A worksheet can hold any number of sparkline groups. Excel remembers each group, and you can work with the group as a single unit. For example, you can select one sparkline in a group and then modify the formatting of all sparklines in the group. When you select one sparkline cell, Excel displays an outline of all the other sparklines in the group.

You can, however, perform some operations on an individual sparkline in a group:

- Change the sparkline's data source. Select the sparkline cell and choose Sparkline Tools ⇨ Design ⇨ Sparkline ⇨ Edit Data ⇨ Edit Single Sparkline's Data. Excel displays a dialog box that lets you change the data source for the selected sparkline.

- Delete the sparkline. Select the sparkline cell and choose Sparkline Tools ⇨ Design ⇨ Group ⇨ Clear ⇨ Clear Selected Sparklines.

Both operations are available from the shortcut menu that appears when you right-click on a sparkline cell.

You can also ungroup a set of sparklines by selecting any sparkline in the group and choosing Sparkline Tools ⇨ Design ⇨ Group ⇨ Ungroup. After you ungroup a set of sparklines, you can work with each sparkline individually.

Customizing Sparklines

When you activate a cell that contains a sparkline, Excel displays an outline around all the sparklines in its group. You can then use the commands on the Sparkline Tools ⇨ Design tab to customize the group of sparklines.

Sizing Sparkline Cells

When you change the width or height of a cell that contains a sparkline, the sparkline adjusts accordingly. In addition, you can insert a sparkline into merged cells.

Figure 19-23 shows the same sparkline, displayed at four sizes resulting from column width, row height, and merged cells.

Handling Hidden or Missing Data

By default, if you hide rows or columns that are used in a sparkline graphic, the hidden data does not appear in the sparkline. Also, missing data is displayed as a gap in the graphic.

To change these settings, choose Sparkline Tools ⇨ Design ⇨ Sparkline ⇨ Edit Data ⇨ Hidden and Empty Cells. In the Hidden and Empty Cell Settings dialog box that appears (see Figure 19-24), specify how to handle hidden data and empty cells.

FIGURE 19-23

A sparkline at various sizes.

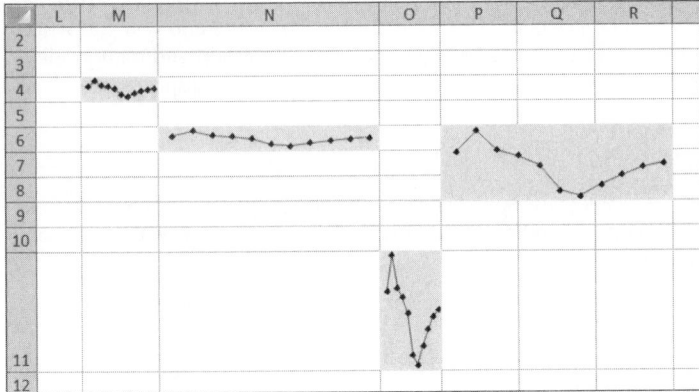

FIGURE 19-24

The Hidden and Empty Cell Settings dialog box.

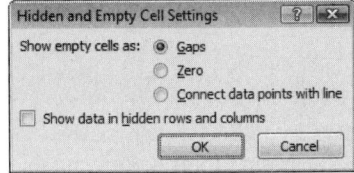

Changing the Sparkline Type

As mentioned earlier, Excel supports three sparkline types: Line, Column, and Win/Loss. After you create a sparkline or group of sparklines, you can easily change the type by selecting the sparkline and clicking on one of the three icons in the Sparkline Tools ⇨ Design ⇨ Type group. If the selected sparkline is part of a group, all sparklines in the group are changed to the new type.

Tip

If you've customized the appearance, Excel remembers your customization settings for each type if you switch among sparkline types. ∎

Changing Sparkline Colors and Line Width

After you've created a sparkline, changing the color is easy. Use the controls in the Sparkline Tools ⇨ Design ⇨ Style group.

Note

Colors used in sparkline graphics are tied to the document theme. Thus, if you change the theme (by choosing Page Layout ⇨ Themes ⇨ Themes), the sparkline colors will change to the new theme colors. See Chapter 6 for more information about document themes. ∎

For Line sparklines, you can also specify the line width. Choose Sparkline Tools ⇨ Design ⇨ Style ⇨ Sparkline Color ⇨ Weight.

Highlighting Certain Data Points

Use the commands in the Sparkline Tools ⇨ Design ⇨ Show group to customize the sparklines to highlight certain aspects of the data. The options are as follows:

- **High Point.** Apply a different color to the highest data point in the sparkline.
- **Low Point.** Apply a different color to the lowest data point in the sparkline.
- **Negative Points.** Apply a different color to negative values in the sparkline.
- **First Point.** Apply a different color to the first data point in the sparkline.
- **Last Point.** Apply a different color to the last data point in the sparkline.
- **Markers.** Show data markers in the sparkline. This option is available only for Line sparklines.

You control the color of the highlighting by using the Marker Color control in the Sparkline Tools ⇨ Design ⇨ Style group. Unfortunately, you cannot change the size of the markers in Line sparklines.

Figure 19-25 shows some Line sparklines with various types of highlighting applied.

FIGURE 19-25

Highlighting options for Line sparklines.

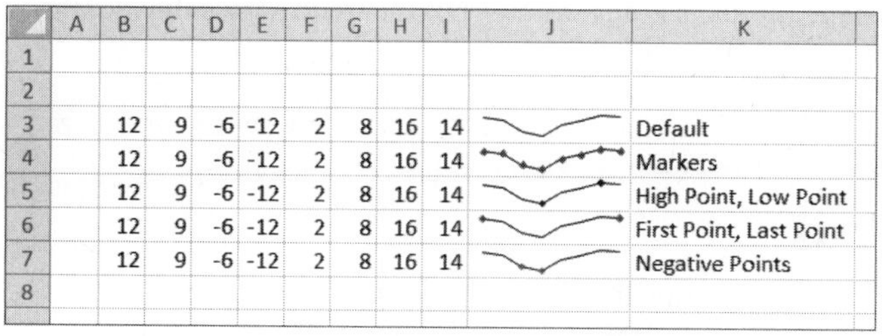

Adjusting Sparkline Axis Scaling

When you create one or more sparklines, by default they all use automatic axis scaling. In other words, the minimum and maximum vertical axis values are determined automatically for each sparkline in the group, based on the numeric range of the data used by the sparkline.

The Sparkline Tools ➪ Design ➪ Group ➪ Axis command lets you override this automatic behavior and control the minimum and maximum values for each sparkline, or for a group of sparklines. For even more control, you can use the Custom Value option and specify the minimum and maximum for the sparkline group.

Figure 19-26 shows two groups of sparklines. The group at the top uses the default axis settings (Automatic for Each Sparkline). Each sparkline shows the 6-month trend for the product, but there is no indication of the magnitude of the values.

FIGURE 19-26

The bottom group of sparklines shows the effect of using the same axis minimum and maximum values for all sparklines in a group.

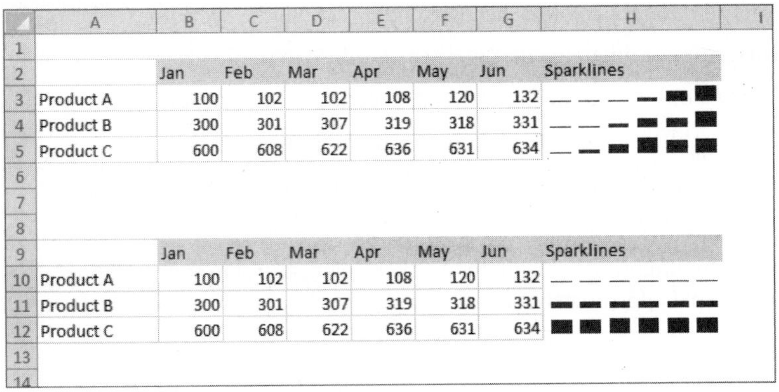

	Jan	Feb	Mar	Apr	May	Jun	Sparklines
Product A	100	102	102	108	120	132	
Product B	300	301	307	319	318	331	
Product C	600	608	622	636	631	634	

	Jan	Feb	Mar	Apr	May	Jun	Sparklines
Product A	100	102	102	108	120	132	
Product B	300	301	307	319	318	331	
Product C	600	608	622	636	631	634	

For the sparkline group at the bottom (which uses the same data), I changed the vertical-axis minimum and maximum to use the Same for All Sparklines setting. With these settings in effect, the magnitude of the values across the products is apparent — but the trend across the months within a product is not apparent.

The axis scaling option you choose depends on what aspect of the data you want to emphasize.

Specifying a Date Axis

Normally, data displayed in a sparkline is assumed to be at equal intervals. For example, a sparkline might display a daily account balance, sales by month, or profits by year. But what if the data isn't at equal intervals?

Figure 19-27 shows data, by date, along with a sparklines graphic created from column B. Notice that some dates are missing, but the sparkline shows the columns as if the values were spaced at equal intervals.

The sparkline displays the values as if they are at equal time intervals.

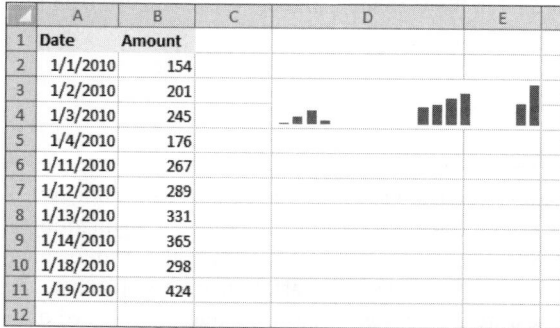

	A	B	C	D	E
1	**Date**	**Amount**			
2	1/1/2010	154			
3	1/2/2010	201			
4	1/3/2010	245			
5	1/4/2010	176			
6	1/11/2010	267			
7	1/12/2010	289			
8	1/13/2010	331			
9	1/14/2010	365			
10	1/18/2010	298			
11	1/19/2010	424			
12					

To better depict the data, the solution is to specify a date axis. Select the sparkline and choose Sparkline Tools ⇨ Design ⇨ Group ⇨ Axis ⇨ Date Axis Type. Excel displays a dialog box, asking for the range that contains the dates. In this example, specify range A2:A11. Click OK, and the sparkline displays gaps for the missing dates (see Figure 19-28).

After specifying a date axis, the sparkline shows the values accurately.

	A	B	C	D	E
1	**Date**	**Amount**			
2	1/1/2010	154			
3	1/2/2010	201			
4	1/3/2010	245			
5	1/4/2010	176			
6	1/11/2010	267			
7	1/12/2010	289			
8	1/13/2010	331			
9	1/14/2010	365			
10	1/18/2010	298			
11	1/19/2010	424			
12					

Auto-updating Sparklines

If a sparkline uses data in a normal range of cells, adding new data to the beginning or end of the range does *not* force the sparkline to use the new data. You need to use the Edit Sparklines dialog box to update the data range (choose Sparkline Tools ⇨ Design ⇨ Sparkline ⇨ Edit Data). But, if the sparkline data is in a column within a table (created by using Insert ⇨ Tables ⇨ Table), then the sparkline will use new data that's added to the end of the table.

Figure 19-29 shows an example. The sparkline was created using the data in the Rate column of the table. When you add the new rate for September, the sparkline will automatically update its Data Range.

FIGURE 19-29

Creating a sparkline from data in a table.

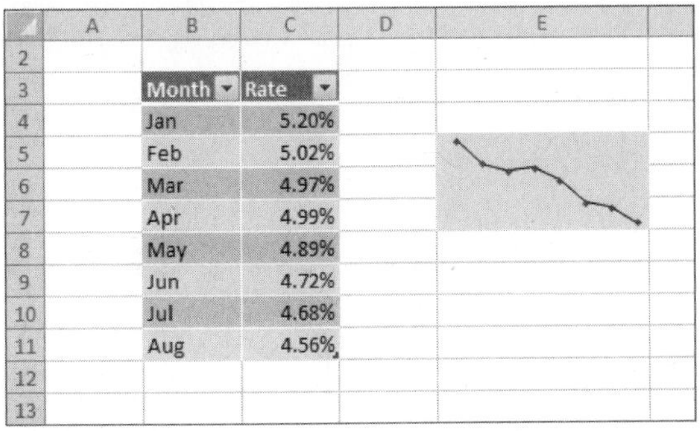

	A	B	C	D	E	
2						
3		Month	Rate			
4		Jan	5.20%			
5		Feb	5.02%			
6		Mar	4.97%			
7		Apr	4.99%			
8		May	4.89%			
9		Jun	4.72%			
10		Jul	4.68%			
11		Aug	4.56%			
12						
13						

Note

If you like the idea of sparklines — and you'd like to have access to other sparkline types — check out some add-ins that provide more sparklines for Excel. These products provide many additional sparkline types, and most provide many additional customization options. Search the Web for *sparklines excel*, and you'll find several add-ins to choose from. ∎

Summary

In this chapter, you learned about other features you can use to communicate the meaning of Excel data in a visual way. You learned how to use conditional formatting to apply highlighting or icons to cells that meet specified criteria, to identify cells with top or bottom values, and to apply data bars or color scales to compare the relative values in data. You also learned how to create and format sparklines, the new Excel 2010 feature that creates a cell-sized graphic of related data.

Part IV

Persuading and Informing with PowerPoint

A First Look at PowerPoint 2010

PowerPoint 2010 is a member of the Microsoft Office 2010 suite of programs. A *suite* is a group of programs designed by a single manufacturer to work well together. Like its siblings — Word (the word processor), Excel (the spreadsheet), Outlook (the personal organizer and e-mail manager), and Access (the database) — PowerPoint has a well-defined role. It creates materials for presentations.

A *presentation* is any kind of interaction between a speaker and an audience, but it usually involves one or more of the following visual aids: 35mm slides, overhead transparencies, computer-based slides (either local or at a website or other network location), hard-copy handouts, and speaker notes. PowerPoint can create all of these types of visual aids, plus many other types that you'll learn about as you go along.

Because PowerPoint is so tightly integrated with the other Microsoft Office 2010 components, you can easily share information among them. For example, if you have created a graph in Excel, you can use that graph on a PowerPoint slide. It goes the other way, too. You can, for example, take the outline from your PowerPoint presentation and copy it into Word, where you can dress it up with Word's powerful document formatting commands. Virtually any piece of data in any Office program can be linked to any other Office program, so you never have to worry about your data being in the wrong format. PowerPoint also accepts data from almost any other Windows-based application and can import a variety of graphics, audio, and video formats.

In this chapter, you'll get a big-picture introduction to PowerPoint 2010, and then we'll fire up the program and poke around a bit to help you get familiar with the interface. You'll find out how to use the tabs and panes, and how to get help and updates from Microsoft.

What's New in PowerPoint 2010?

PowerPoint 2010 is very much like PowerPoint 2007 in its basic functionality. It uses a tabbed Ribbon across the top, rather than a traditional menu system, and employs dialog boxes and a Quick Access Toolbar in the same ways that 2007 did.

This doesn't mean that there aren't changes and improvements, though! The following sections outline the major differences you will see when you upgrade from PowerPoint 2007 to PowerPoint 2010.

Backstage View

The File tab in the upper-left corner of the PowerPoint window replaces the Office button from PowerPoint 2007. Clicking it opens a full-screen File menu system, also known as the *Backstage view.*

From Backstage view, you can select file operations such as saving and printing, customizing the interface, and sharing your work with others. Figure 20-1 shows the Backstage view. To leave Backstage view, click any other tab.

FIGURE 20-1

Backstage view (or the File menu) provides access to various file management and customization commands.

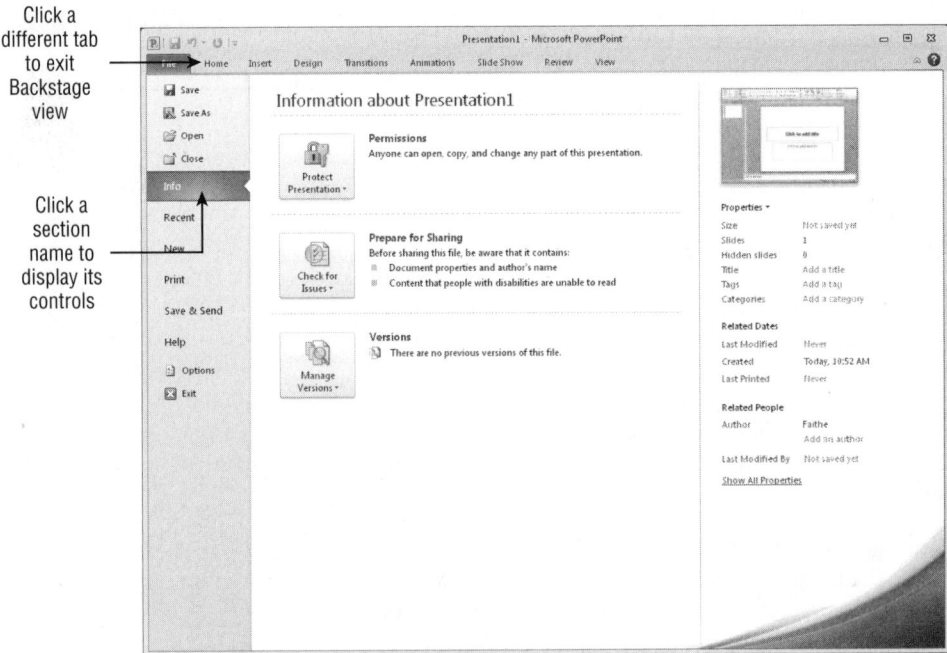

Better Support for Video Import and Editing

One of the features most asked for in PowerPoint has been support for more video file formats, and PowerPoint 2010 has delivered it. PowerPoint 2010 supports a wide variety of formats including QuickTime, Flash, Windows Media, and MP4. You can now also link video clips from online sources such as YouTube.

Not only can you import motion video from a larger variety of sources than in earlier versions, but you can also edit videos directly from within PowerPoint. For example, you can change the brightness and contrast of a video, trim it to show only certain parts, add a bookmark in the video clip (which you can then hyperlink to, to jump to a particular spot in the video quickly), and more. Figure 20-2 shows the Format tab in PowerPoint 2010's Video Tools.

FIGURE 20-2

Enhanced video tools enable you to modify the video clip without leaving PowerPoint.

Output to Video and DVD

Another feature in high demand has been the ability to output a presentation directly to popular video formats. In the past, people have had to resort to third-party solutions, but PowerPoint 2010 includes this capability built in. You can now output your presentation to Windows Media Video (.wmv) format, which can be played back by Windows Media Player or a variety of other utilities.

Collaboration

Collaborating with others on a draft presentation is now easier to do. PowerPoint now includes a Compare feature that includes revision tracking. With revision tracking you can see who has made what changes to the presentation, and review each change individually to accept or reject it, as shown in Figure 20-3.

Other Changes

Besides the major changes you've learned about in the preceding sections, there are also several smaller but still important improvements, including the following:

- New photo editing tools allow you to apply artistic filters to pictures, remove backgrounds, and crop with more precision.

- New transition effects are available in PowerPoint 2010, and they are now easier to apply, thanks to the new Transitions tab on the Ribbon.

- You can now insert math equations into a presentation with the Microsoft Office Equation Editor. Equation editing was revamped in some of the other Office applications in Office 2007, but PowerPoint is only now getting the new and improved equation interface.

- You can customize the Ribbon by adding, removing, and rearranging commands and tabs. This is a new feature across all of the Office 2010 applications, and very welcome to power users who like to control their working environment onscreen.

- Presentation broadcasting is much improved in PowerPoint 2010 because of its integration with the Web-based PowerPoint Live service.

FIGURE 20-3

You can track changes to a presentation draft to organize the work of multiple collaborators.

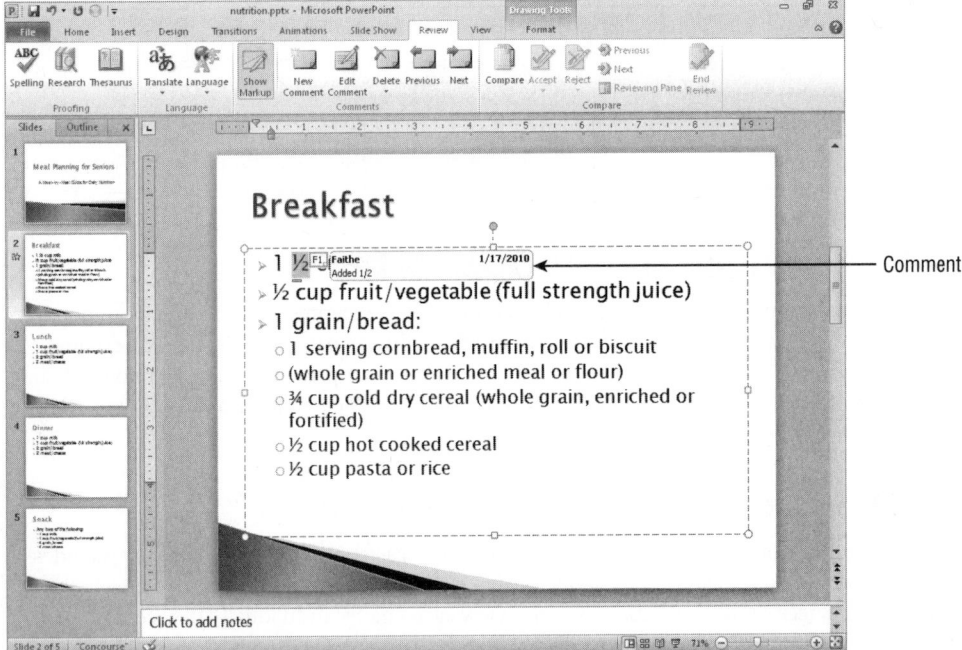

Learning Your Way around PowerPoint

Now that you have seen some of the potential uses for PowerPoint and toured the new features, let's get started using the program.

PowerPoint is one of the easiest and most powerful presentation programs available. You can knock out a passable presentation in a shockingly short time by skimming through the chapters in this part of the book, or you can spend some time with PowerPoint's advanced features to make a complex presentation that looks, reads, and works exactly the way you want.

Starting and Exiting PowerPoint

You can start PowerPoint just like any other program in Windows: from the Start menu. Follow these steps:

1. **Click the Start button.** The Start menu opens.
2. **Click All Programs.**
3. **Click Microsoft Office.**
4. **Click Microsoft PowerPoint 2010.** The program starts.

If you have opened PowerPoint before, a shortcut to it might appear in the Recently Used Programs list, which is directly above the All Programs command on the Start menu. If you use other applications more frequently than PowerPoint, PowerPoint may scroll off this list and you therefore have to access it via the All Programs menu.

Tip

If you don't want to worry about PowerPoint scrolling off the list of the most frequently used programs on the Start menu, right-click PowerPoint's name on the Start menu and choose Pin to Start Menu. PowerPoint will then appear on the list at the top of the left column of the Start menu, as shown in Figure 20-4. To remove it from there later, right-click on it and choose Unpin from Start Menu. ∎

FIGURE 20-4

A shortcut to PowerPoint might appear on the top level of the Start menu.

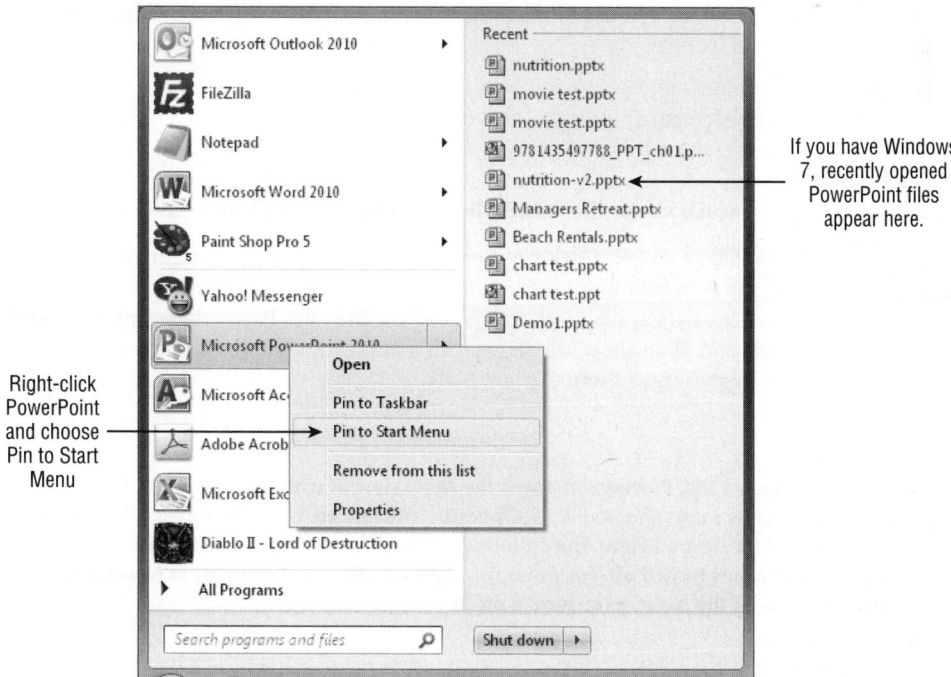

If you have Windows 7, recently opened PowerPoint files appear here.

Right-click PowerPoint and choose Pin to Start Menu

When you are ready to leave PowerPoint, select File ⇨ Exit or click the Close (X) button in the top-right corner of the PowerPoint window. (The File tab is the orange tab in the top-left corner.) If you have any unsaved work, PowerPoint asks if you want to save your changes. Because you have just been playing around in this chapter, you probably do not have anything to save yet. (If you do have something to save, see Chapter 3 to learn more about saving.) Otherwise, click No to decline to save your changes, and you're outta there.

Changing the View

A *view* is a way of displaying your presentation onscreen. PowerPoint comes with several views because at different times during the creation process, it is helpful to look at the presentation in different ways. For example, when you add a graphic to a slide, you need to work closely with that slide, but when you rearrange the slide order, you need to see the presentation as a whole.

PowerPoint offers the following views:

- **Normal.** A combination of several resizable panes, so you can see the presentation in multiple ways at once. Normal is the default view.
- **Slide Sorter.** A light-table-type overhead view of all the slides in your presentation, laid out in rows, suitable for big-picture rearranging.
- **Notes Page.** A view with the slide at the top of the page and a text box below it for typed notes. (You can print these notes pages to use during your speech.)
- **Slide Show.** The view you use to show the presentation onscreen. Each slide fills the entire screen in its turn.
- **Reading View.** A simplified version of Slide Show view, which appears in a window rather than full-screen. This view is new in PowerPoint 2010.

Cross-Reference
This chapter covers only the five regular views. The Master views are discussed in Chapter 22. ■

There are two ways to change a view: Click a button on the View tab in the Presentation Views group, or click one of the view buttons in the bottom-right corner of the screen, as shown in Figure 20-5. All of the views are available in both places except Notes Page, which you can access only from the View tab; and Slide Show, which you can access only from the buttons or from the Slide Show tab (From Beginning or From Current Slide).

Tip
When you save, close, and reopen a file, PowerPoint opens the same view in which you left the file. To have the files always open in a particular view, choose File ⇨ Options ⇨ Advanced, open the Open All Documents Using This View list, and select the desired view. The options on this list include some custom versions of Normal view that have certain panes turned off. For example, you can open all documents in Normal–Outline and Slide view to always start with the Notes pane turned off. ■

FIGURE 20-5

Select a view from the View tab or from the viewing controls in the bottom-right corner of the screen.

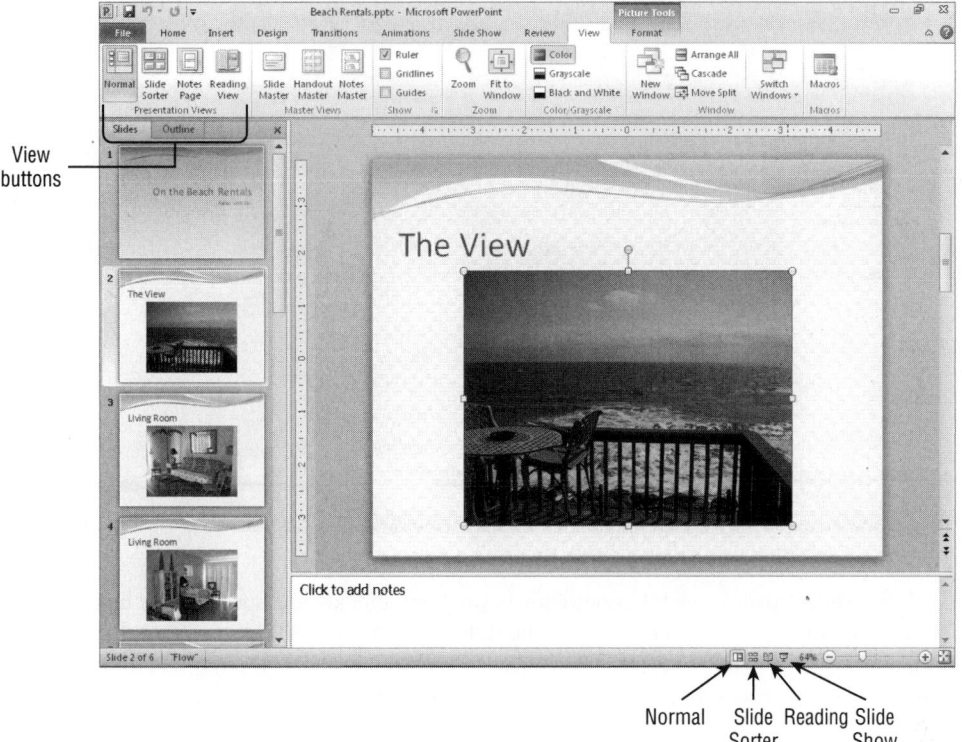

Normal View

Normal view, shown in Figure 20-6, is a very flexible view that contains a little bit of everything. In the center is the active slide, below it is a Notes pane, and to its left is a dual-use pane with two tabs: Slides and Outline. (Figure 20-5 shows the Slides tab, and Figure 20-6 shows the Outline tab.) When the Outline tab is selected, the text from the slides appears in an outline form. When the Slides tab is selected, thumbnail images of all the slides appear (somewhat like Slide Sorter view, which you will see later in this chapter).

Each of the panes in Normal view has its own scroll bar, so you can move around in the outline, the slide, and the notes independently of the other panes. You can resize the panes by dragging the dividers between the panes. For example, to give the Notes area more room, point the mouse pointer at the divider line between it and the Slide area so that the mouse pointer becomes a double-headed arrow, and then hold down the left mouse button as you drag the line up to a new spot.

FIGURE 20-6

Normal view, the default, offers access to the outline, the slide, and the notes all at once.

Slides/Outline pane

Slide pane

Notes pane

The Slides/Outline pane is useful because it lets you jump quickly to a specific slide by clicking on it. For example, you can click on any of the slide thumbnails on the Slides tab to display it in the Slide pane, as shown in Figure 20-5. You can also click on some text anywhere in the outline to jump to the slide containing that text, as shown in Figure 20-6.

Tip

In Microsoft Word, an Outlining tab is available when you are working on an outline. In PowerPoint, some of those same tools are available, but in a different location. You can right-click anywhere in the Outline pane to access those tools on a shortcut menu, such as expanding and collapsing outline levels and reordering items. ■

You can turn the Slides/Outline pane off completely by clicking the X button in its top-right corner. This gives maximum room to the Slides pane. When you turn it off, the Notes pane disappears too. To get the extra panes back, reapply Normal view.

Slide Sorter View

If you have ever worked with 35mm slides, you know that it can be helpful to lay the slides out on a big table and plan the order in which to show them. You rearrange them, moving this one here, that one there, until the order is perfect. You might even start a pile of backups that you will not show in the main presentation, but will hold back in case someone asks a pertinent question. That's exactly what you can do with Slide Sorter view, as shown in Figure 20-7. It lays out the slides in miniature, so you can see the big picture. You can drag the slides around and place them in the perfect order. You can also return to Normal view to work on a slide by double-clicking the slide.

FIGURE 20-7

Use Slide Sorter view for a birds-eye view of the presentation.

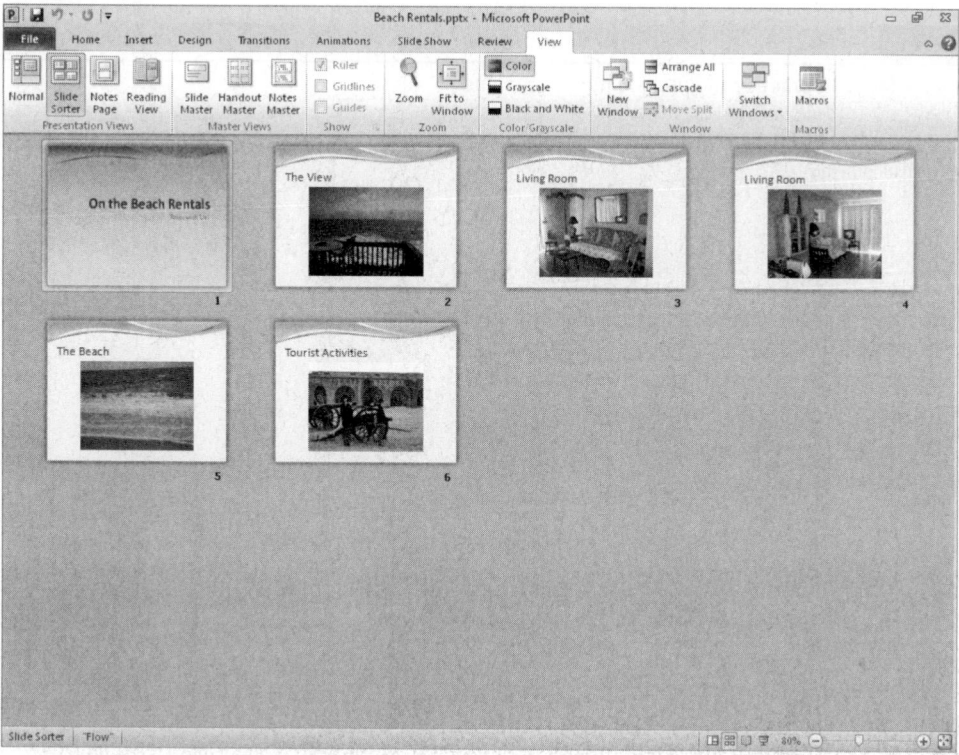

Slide Show View

When it's time to rehearse the presentation, nothing shows you the finished product quite as clearly as Slide Show view does. In Slide Show view, the slide fills the entire screen. You can move from slide to slide by pressing the Page Up or Page Down keys, or by using one of the other movement methods available (see Figure 20-8).

Cross-Reference
You learn about these other movement methods in Chapter 26. ■

You can right-click in Slide Show view to display a menu that enables you to control the show without leaving it. To leave the slide show, choose End Show from the menu or just press the Esc key.

Tip
When entering Slide Show view, the method you use determines which slide you start on. If you use the Slide Show View button in the bottom-right corner of the screen, the presentation will start with whatever slide

you have selected. (You can also press Shift+F5 to do this, or choose Slide Show ⇨ From Current Slide.) If you use the Slide Show ⇨ From Beginning command, or press F5, the presentation will start at the beginning. ∎

Slide Show view lets you practice the presentation in real life.

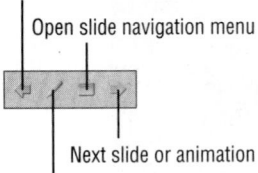

Previous slide or animation

Open slide navigation menu

Next slide or animation

Open pointer control menu

Notes Page View

When you give a presentation, your props usually include more than just your brain and your slides. You typically have all kinds of notes and backup material for each slide — figures on last quarter's sales, sources to cite if someone questions your data, and so on. In the old days of framed overhead transparencies, people used to attach sticky notes to the slide frames for this purpose and hope that nobody asked any questions that required diving into the 4-inch-thick stack of statistics they brought.

Today, you can type your notes and supporting facts directly in PowerPoint 2010. As you saw earlier, you can type them directly into the Notes pane below the slide in Normal view. However, if you have a lot of notes to type, you might find it easier to work with Notes Page view instead.

Notes Page view is accessible only from the View tab. In this view, you see a single slide (uneditable) with an editable text area below it called the *notes placeholder*, which you can use to type your notes. See Figure 20-9. You can refer to these notes as you give an onscreen presentation, or you can print Notes Pages to stack neatly on the lectern next to you during the big event. If your Notes Pages run off the end of the page, PowerPoint even prints them as a separate page. If you have trouble seeing the text you're typing, zoom in on it, as described in the next section.

Zooming In and Out

If you need a closer look at your presentation, you can zoom the view in or out to accommodate almost any situation. For example, if you have trouble placing a graphic exactly at the same vertical level as some text in a box next to it, you can zoom in for more precision. You can view your work at various magnifications onscreen without changing the size of the surrounding tools or the size of the print on the printout.

FIGURE 20-9

Notes Page view offers a special text area for your notes, separate from the slides.

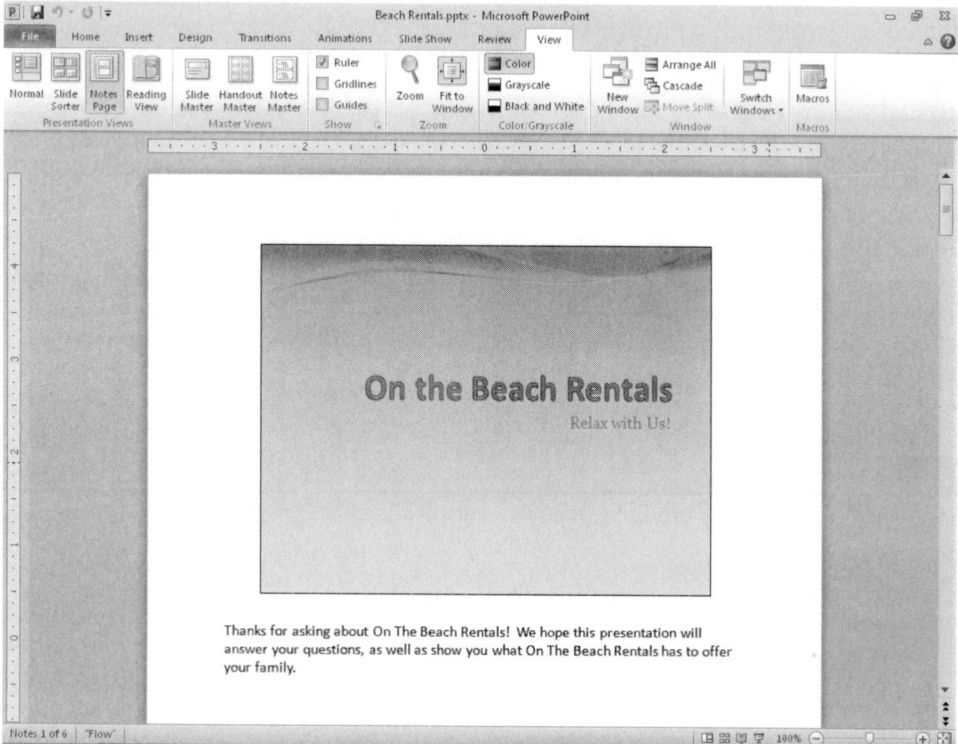

In Normal view, each of the panes has its own individual zoom. To set the zoom for the Slides/Outline pane only, for example, select it first; then choose a zoom level. Or to zoom only in the main workspace (the Slide pane), click it first. In a single-pane view such as Notes Page or Slide Sorter, a single zoom setting affects the entire work area.

The larger the zoom number, the larger the details on the display. A zoom of 10 percent would make a slide so tiny that you couldn't read it. A zoom of 400 percent would make a few letters on a slide so big they would fill the entire pane.

The easiest way to set the zoom level is to drag the Zoom slider in the bottom-right corner of the PowerPoint window, or click its plus or minus buttons to change the zoom level in increments, as shown in Figure 20-10.

To resize the current slide so that it is as large as possible while still fitting completely in the Slides pane, click the Fit Slide to Current Window button, or choose View ➪ Zoom ➪ Fit to Window.

FIGURE 20-10

Zoom in or out to see more or less of the slide(s) at once.

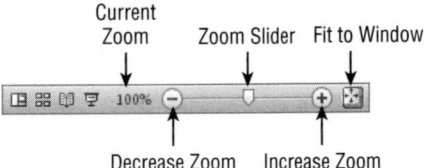

Another way to control the zoom is with the Zoom dialog box. Choose View ➪ Zoom ➪ Zoom to open it. (You can also open that dialog box by clicking the percent sign (%) next to the Zoom slider in the lower-right corner of the screen.) Make your selection, as shown in Figure 20-11, by clicking the appropriate button, and then click OK. Notice that you can type a precise zoom percentage in the Percent text box. You can specify any percentage you like, up to 400 percent. (Some panes and views will not go higher than 100%.)

FIGURE 20-11

You can zoom with this Zoom dialog box rather than the slider if you prefer.

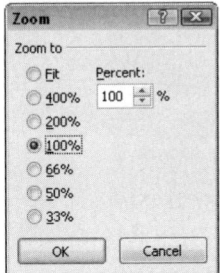

Enabling Optional Display Elements

PowerPoint has many optional screen elements that you may (or may not) find useful, depending on what you're up to at the moment. The following sections describe them.

Ruler

Vertical and horizontal rulers around the Slide pane can help you place objects more precisely. To toggle them on or off, select or deselect the Ruler check box on the View tab, as shown in Figure 20-12. Rulers are available only in Normal and Notes Page views.

The rulers help with positioning no matter what content type you are working with, but when you are editing text in a text frame, they have an additional purpose as well. The horizontal ruler shows the frame's paragraph indents and any custom tab stops, and you can drag the indent markers on the ruler just as you can in Word.

Note
The ruler's unit of measure is controlled from the Regional Settings in the Control Panel in Windows. ∎

Tip
The vertical ruler is optional. To disable it while retaining the horizontal ruler, choose File ⇨ Options, click Advanced, and in the Display section, clear the Show Vertical Ruler check box. ∎

FIGURE 20-12

Gridlines and the ruler help align objects on a slide.

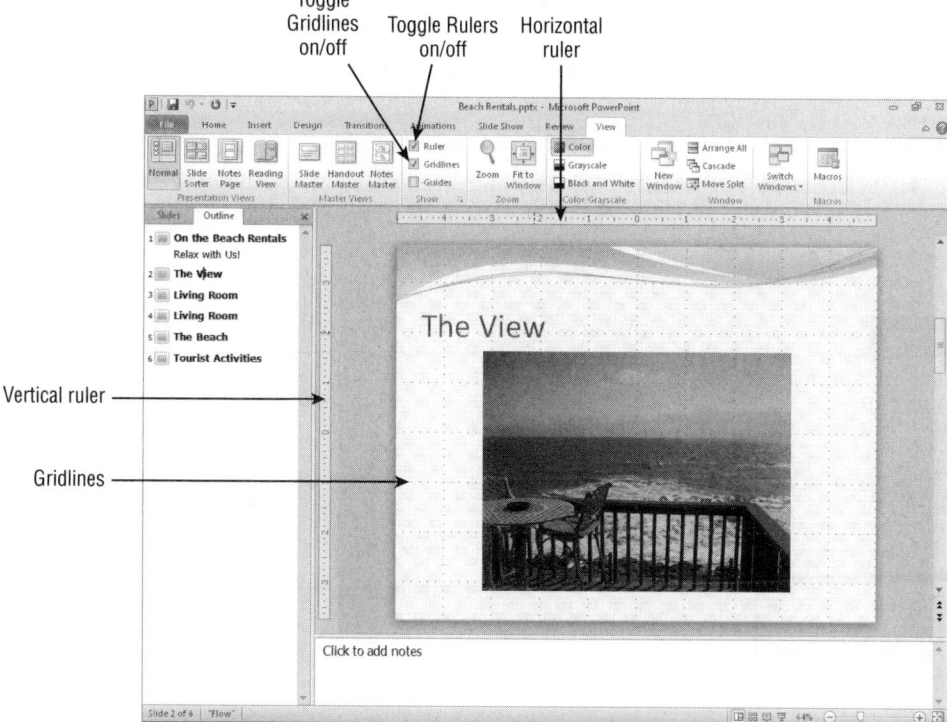

Gridlines

Gridlines are nonprinting dotted lines at regularly spaced intervals that can help you line up objects on a slide. Figure 20-12 shows gridlines (and the ruler) enabled.

To turn gridlines on or off, use either of these methods:

- Press Shift+F9.
- On the View tab, in the Show group, select or deselect the Gridlines check box.
- Choose Home ⇨ Drawing ⇨ Arrange ⇨ Align ⇨ View Gridlines.

There are many options you can set for the gridlines, including whether objects snap to it, whether the grid is visible, and what the spacing should be between the gridlines. To set grid options, follow these steps:

1. **On the Home tab, in the Drawing group, choose Arrange ⇨ Align ⇨ Grid Settings, or right-click the slide background and choose Grid and Guides.** The Grid and Guides dialog box opens (see Figure 20-13).

2. **In the Snap To section, select or deselect these check boxes:**
   - **Snap Objects to Grid.** Specifies whether objects will automatically align with the grid.
   - **Snap Objects to Other Objects.** Specifies whether objects will automatically align with other objects.

3. **In the Grid Settings section, enter the amount of space between gridlines desired.**

4. **Select or deselect the Display Grid on Screen check box to display or hide the grid.** (Note that you can make objects snap to the grid without the grid being displayed.)

5. **Click OK.**

FIGURE 20-13

Set grid options and spacing.

Guides

Guides are like gridlines except they are individual lines, rather than a grid of lines, and you can drag them to different positions on the slide. As you drag a guide, a numerical indicator appears to let you know the ruler position, as shown in Figure 20-14. Use the Grid and Guides dialog box shown in Figure 20-14 to turn guides on/off, or press Alt+F9.

FIGURE 20-14

Guides are movable, nonprinting lines that help with alignment.

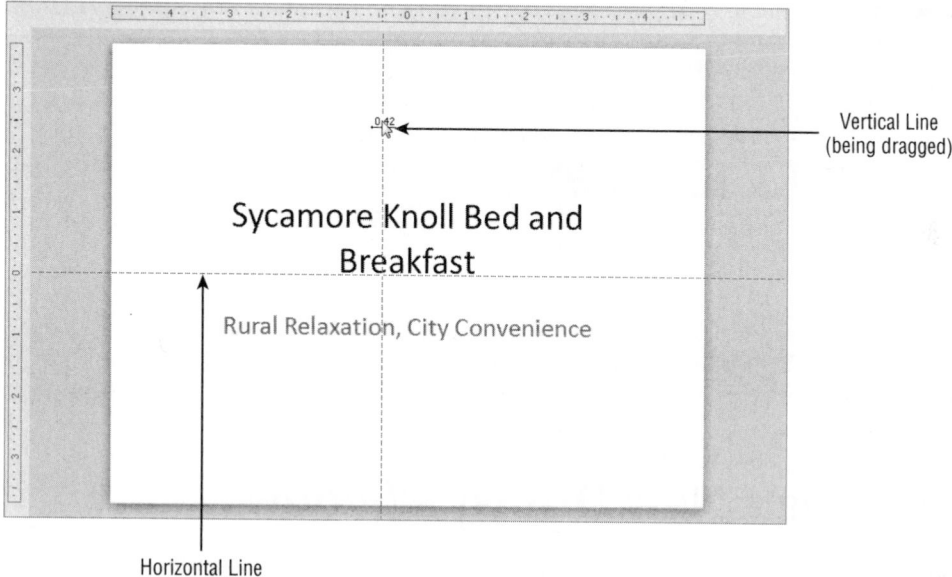

You can create additional sets of guide lines by holding down the Ctrl key while dragging a guide (to copy it). You can have as many horizontal and vertical guides as you like, all at positions you specify.

Color/Grayscale/Pure Black and White Views

Most of the time you will work with your presentation in color. However, if you plan to print the presentation in black and white or grayscale (e.g., on black-and-white handouts), you should check to see what it will look like without color.

Tip

This Color/Grayscale/Pure Black and White option is especially useful when you are preparing slides that will eventually be faxed, because a fax is pure black and white in most cases. Something that looks great on a color screen could look like a shapeless blob on a black-and-white fax. It doesn't hurt to check. ∎

Click the Grayscale or the Pure Black and White button in the Color/Grayscale group on the View tab to switch to one of those views. When you do so, a Grayscale or Black and White tab becomes available, as shown in Figure 20-15. From its Setting group, you can fine-tune the grayscale or black-and-white preview. Choose one that shows the object to best advantage; PowerPoint will remember that setting when printing or outputting the presentation to a grayscale or black-and-white source.

FIGURE 20-15

Select a grayscale or a black-and-white preview type.

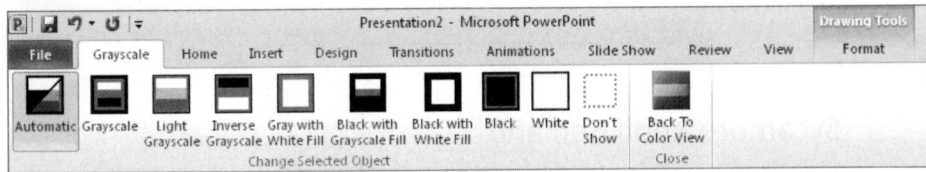

When you are finished, click the Back to Color View button on the Grayscale tab. Changing the Black and White or Grayscale settings doesn't affect the colors on the slides; it only affects how the slides will look and print in black and white or grayscale.

Opening a New Display Window

Have you ever wished you could be in two places at once? Well, in PowerPoint, you actually can. PowerPoint provides a way to view two spots in the presentation at the same time by opening a new window.

To display a new window, display the View tab and click New Window in the Window group. Then use Arrange All or Cascade to view both windows at once.

You can use any view with any window, so you can have two slides in Normal view at once, or Slide Sorter and Notes Page views, or any other combination. Both windows contain the same presentation, so any changes you make in one window are reflected in the other window.

Arranging Windows

When you have two or more windows open, whether they are for the same presentation or different ones, you need to arrange them for optimal viewing. You saw earlier in this chapter how to resize a window, but did you know that PowerPoint can do some of the arranging for you?

When you want to arrange the open windows, do one of the following:

- **Tile.** On the View tab, click Arrange All in the Window group to tile the open windows so there is no overlap.

- **Cascade.** On the View tab, click Cascade in the Window group to arrange the open windows so that the title bars cascade from upper-left to lower-right on the screen. Click on a title bar to activate a window.

These commands do not apply to minimized windows. If you want to include a window in the arrangement, make sure you restore it from its minimized state first.

Switching among Windows

If you have more than one window open and can see at least a corner of the window you want, click on it to bring it to the front. If you have one of the windows maximized, on the other hand, or if another window is obscuring the one you want, click Switch Windows (in the Window group on the View tab), and select the window you want to view.

Summary

This chapter provided an introduction to PowerPoint. You learned about PowerPoint 2010's new features and how to control the view of the PowerPoint window. In the next chapter, you'll learn about creating a presentation.

Creating a Presentation, Slides, and Text

I f you're an experienced Windows and PowerPoint user, starting new presentations and saving files may be second nature to you. If so — great! You may not need this chapter. On the other hand, if you aren't entirely certain about some of the finer points, such as saving in different formats or locations, stick around.

In this chapter, you'll learn how to create, save, and reopen presentation files, and how to build a simple text-based presentation by creating new slides and entering text on them. You'll learn how to import content from other programs, and how to create, size, and position text boxes to hold the text for your presentation.

Starting a New Presentation

You can start a blank presentation from scratch, or you can base the new presentation on a template or on another presentation. Using a template or existing presentation can save you some time. However, if you have a specific vision you're going for, starting a presentation from scratch gives you a clean canvas to work from.

Starting a Blank Presentation from Scratch

When you start PowerPoint, a new blank presentation begins automatically with one slide. Just add your content to it, add more slides if needed, change the formatting (as you'll learn in upcoming chapters), and go for it.

Starting a new presentation

Saving your work

Closing and reopening presentations

Creating new slides

Inserting content from external sources

Managing slides

Using content placeholders

Creating text boxes manually

Working with text boxes

If you need to start another blank presentation, follow these steps:

1. **Choose File ⇨ New.** The 21 available templates and themes appear, upon which you can base the new work, as shown in Figure 21-1.

2. **Blank Presentation is already selected.** Click Create.

Select Blank Presentation from Backstage view.

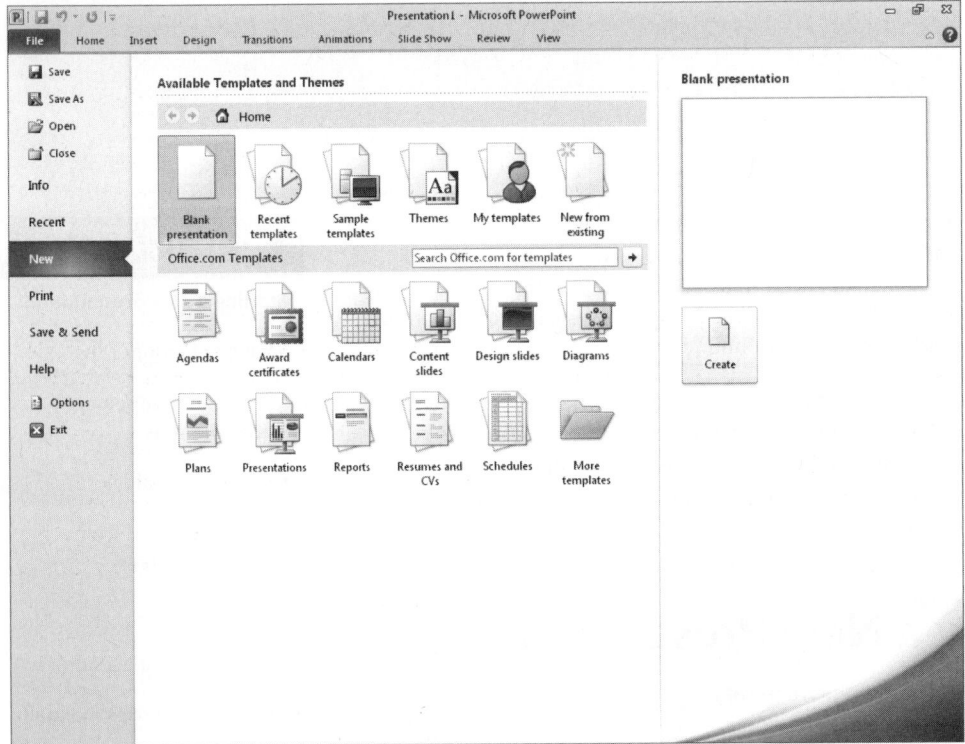

Tip
Press the Ctrl+N shortcut key to start a new blank presentation. ■

Starting a Presentation from a Template or Theme

A *template* is a file that contains starter settings — and sometimes starter content — upon which you can base new presentations. Templates vary in their exact offerings, but can include sample slides, a background graphic, custom color and font themes, and custom positioning for object placeholders.

When selecting a template, you can choose from these categories:

- **Sample Templates.** Microsoft-provided templates and presentations that come pre-installed with PowerPoint

- **Themes.** Microsoft-provided theme files, which are the same as the themes that you can later apply to a presentation from the Design tab

- **My Templates.** Templates that you have created and saved yourself, and templates that you previously downloaded from Office.com

- **Office.com Templates.** Microsoft-provided templates that you download from Microsoft on an as-needed basis

- **Recent Templates.** Shortcuts to recently used templates. This lets you easily re-choose the same template you have used before.

- **New from Existing.** Shortcuts to existing presentations, which you can use as a basis for new ones. This is useful when you want to create a new version of a presentation without interfering with the original.

Note

Notice in Figure 21-1 that, in addition to Sample Templates, there are *Themes*. Themes are not templates, but they are similar. Chapter 1 explains the difference. You can start a new presentation based on a theme as an alternative to using a template. Such a presentation starts with defined color, font, and effect settings, but no sample slides. ∎

Using a Sample Template

There are only a few sample templates stored on your hard disk because Microsoft assumes that most people have an always-on Internet connection these days. Each sample template demonstrates a special-purpose type of presentation, such as a photo album, pitchbook, or quiz show. If you are interested in standard corporate presentation templates, you might prefer to look at the online offerings instead.

Follow these steps to start a presentation based on a sample template:

1. **Choose File ⇨ New.** Icons for the various types of samples appear.
2. **Click Sample Templates.** Icons for the installed sample templates appear.
3. **Click a template to see a preview of it.**
4. **Select the template you want and click Create.** A new presentation opens based on that template.

Using an Online Template

The bulk of the templates for presentations are available online. You can access the library of online templates without leaving PowerPoint. Follow these steps:

1. **Choose File ⇨ New.**
2. **In the Office.com Templates section, click the category of template you want.**

3. **Depending on the category you choose, a subcategory list might appear in the center pane.** If it does, click the subcategory that you want. For example, if you choose "More Categories," you'll find an Office 2007 Document Themes category.

4. **Click a template to see a preview of it.**

5. **Select the template that you want and click Download.** A new presentation opens based on that template.

Tip

Spend some time exploring the templates available via the Office.com Templates section. There are many categories here! For example, Design Slides has templates that don't contain any sample content — just design elements. ■

Using a Saved Template

When you start a new presentation with an online template, as in the preceding section, PowerPoint copies that template to your hard disk so that you can reuse it in the future without connecting to the Internet. It is stored, along with any custom templates you have created, in the My Templates folder.

To access these downloaded and custom templates, follow these steps:

1. **Choose File ➪ New.**

2. **Click My Templates.** A New Presentation dialog box appears that contains templates that you have downloaded or created, as shown in Figure 21-2.

3. **Click OK.** A new presentation opens based on that template.

Tip

To quickly access templates you have previously used, choose Recent Templates, and then double-click the template to reuse. To remove an item from the Recently Used Templates list, right-click the item and choose Remove Template. To clear the whole list at once, right-click on any entry and choose Remove All Recent Templates. ■

Basing a New Presentation on an Existing One

If you already have a presentation that's similar to the new one you need to create, you can base the new presentation on the existing one.

Follow these steps to use an existing presentation as a template:

1. **Choose File ➪ New.**

2. **Click New from Existing.** The New from Existing Presentation dialog box opens, as shown in Figure 21-3.

FIGURE 21-2

Choose a previously used or custom template.

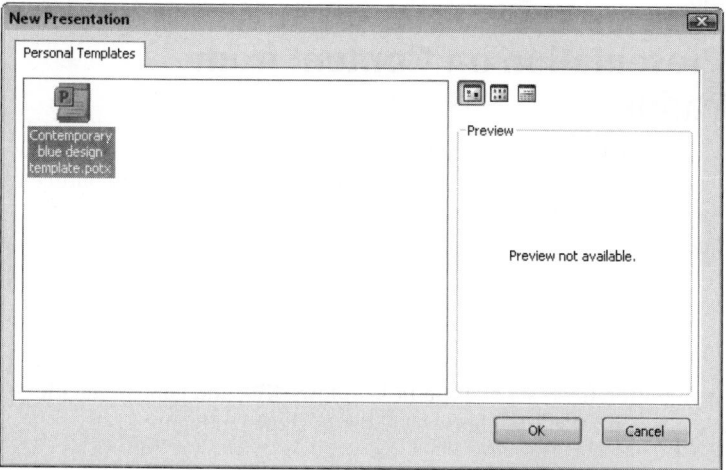

FIGURE 21-3

Select an existing presentation to use as a template.

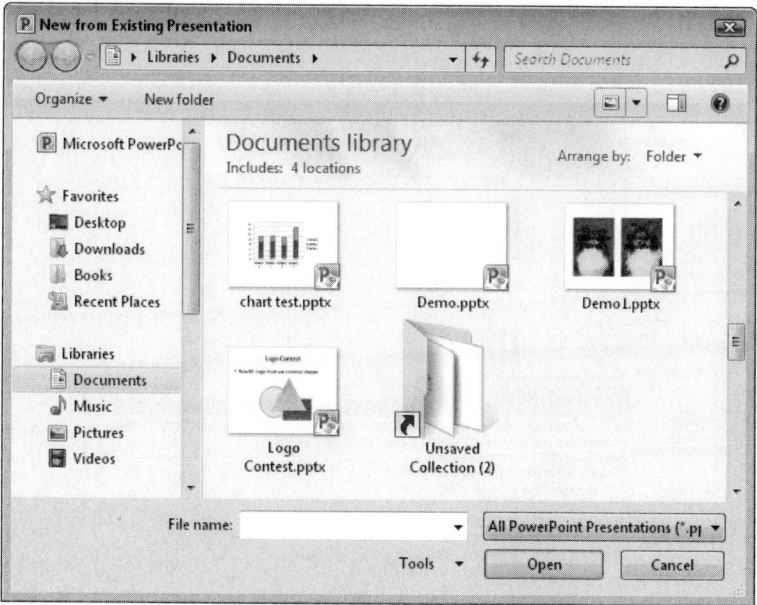

3. **Navigate to the location containing the existing presentation and select it.** When you select a presentation, the Open button changes to a Create New button.

4. **Click Create New.**

Basing a New Presentation on Content from Another Application

PowerPoint can open files in several formats other than its own, so you can start a new presentation based on some work you have done elsewhere. For example, you can open a Word outline in PowerPoint. The results might not be very attractive — but you can fix that later with some text editing, slide layouts, and design changes.

To open a file from another application, do the following:

1. **Choose File ➪ Open.** The Open dialog box appears.

2. **Click the File Type button (or Files of Type in Windows XP), and choose the file type**. For example, to open a text file, choose All Files as shown in Figure 21-4.

FIGURE 21-4

Select a data file from some other program as the basis of a new presentation.

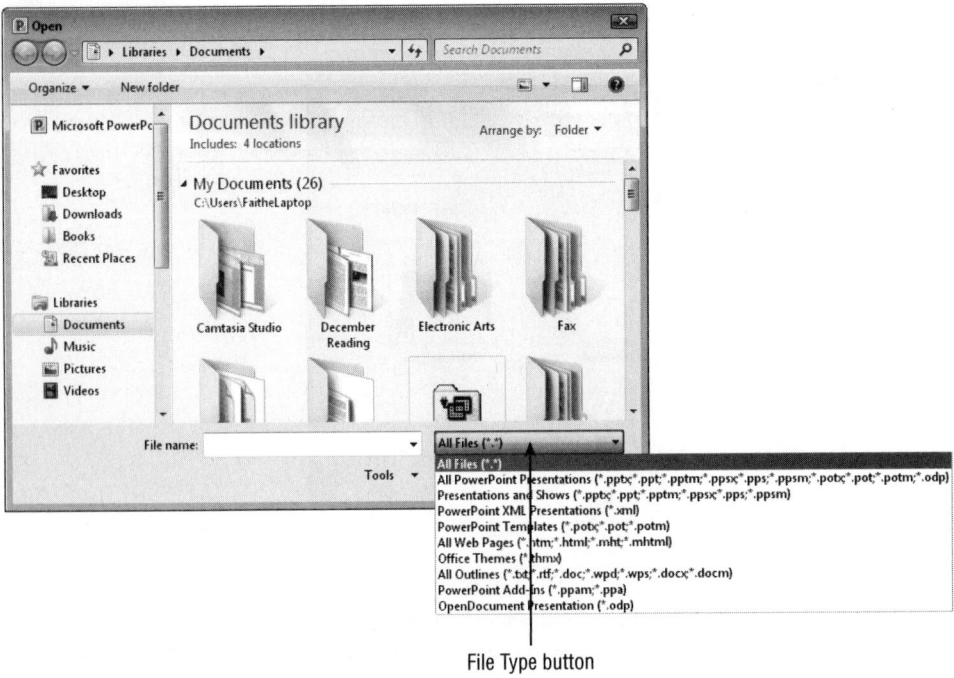

File Type button

3. Select the desired file, and then click Open.

4. Save your work as a PowerPoint file by choosing File ➪ Save As.

Saving Your Work

PowerPoint is typical of most Windows programs in the way that it saves and opens files. The entire PowerPoint presentation is saved in a single file, and any graphics, charts, or other elements are incorporated into that single file.

The first time you save a presentation, PowerPoint opens the Save As dialog box, prompting you for a name and location. Thereafter, when you save that presentation, PowerPoint uses the same settings and does not prompt you for them again.

Saving for the First Time

If you haven't previously saved the presentation you are working on, Save and Save As do the same thing: They open the Save As dialog box. From there, you can specify a name, file type, and file location. Follow these steps:

1. Choose File ➪ Save. The Save As dialog box appears.

2. Enter a filename in the File Name box, as shown in Figure 21-5.

Note

If you have Windows Vista, the Save As dialog box might not show the existing content of the current location by default. To view it, click the Browse Folders arrow in the bottom-left corner of the dialog box. ■

Cross-Reference

To save in a different location, see the section, "Changing Drives and Folders." To save in a different format, see the section, "Saving in a Different Format." ■

3. Click Save. Your work is saved.

Filenames can be up to 255 characters. For practical purposes, however, keep the names short. You can include spaces in the filenames and most symbols except <, >, ?, *, /, and \. However, if you plan to post the file on a network or the Internet at some point, you should avoid using spaces; use the underscore character instead to simulate a space, if necessary. Filenames that use exclamation points have also reportedly caused problems, so beware of that. Generally, it is best to avoid punctuation marks in filenames.

Tip

If you want to transfer your presentation file to a different computer and show it from there, and that other computer does not have the same fonts as your PC, you should embed the fonts in your presentation so that the desired fonts are available on the other PC. To embed fonts from the Save As dialog box, click the Tools button, choose Save Options, and select the Embed Fonts in the File check box. This option makes the saved file larger than normal, so choose it only when necessary. For more information on advanced saving features, see the section "Specifying Save Options." ■

FIGURE 21-5

Save your work by specifying a name for the presentation file.

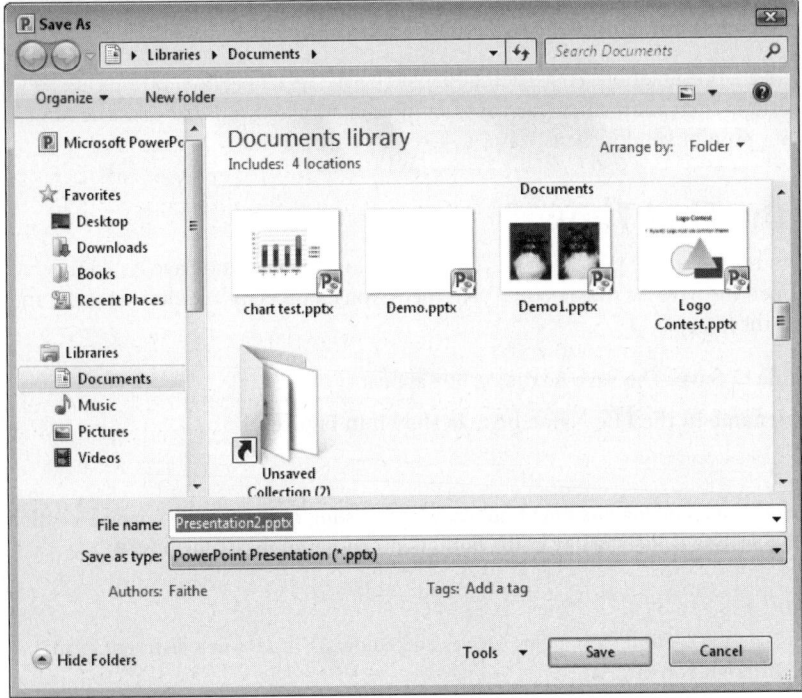

Saving Subsequent Times

After you have saved a presentation once, you can resave it with the same settings (same file type, name, and location) in any of the following ways:

- Choose File ⇨ Save.
- Press Ctrl+S.
- Click the Save button on the Quick Access Toolbar.

If you need to save your presentation under a different name, as a different file type, or in a different location, use the Save As command instead. This reopens the Save As dialog box, as in the preceding steps, so that you can save differently. The originally saved copy will remain under the original name, type, and location.

Tip

If you frequently use Save As, you may want to place a button for it on the Quick Access Toolbar. To do this, right-click the Save As command and choose Add to Quick Access Toolbar. ■

Changing Drives and Folders

By default, all files in PowerPoint (and all of the Office applications) are saved to the Documents folder or library (or My Documents under Windows XP) for the current user. Each user has his or her own version of this folder, so that each person's documents are kept separate depending on who is logged in to the PC.

The Documents folder is a convenient save location for beginners, because they never have to worry about changing the drive or folder. However, more advanced users will sometimes want to save files to other locations. These other locations can include flash drives, other hard disks on the same PC, hard disks on other PCs in a network, hard disks on web servers on the Internet, or writeable CDs.

Tip

Each user has a My Documents folder in his or her own profile. The actual location of that folder depends on the Windows version. For example, in Windows Vista or Windows 7, the path would be C:\Users\ *username*\My Documents. In Windows XP, the path would be C:\Documents and Settings*username*\ My Documents. If your usual PowerPoint files seem to be missing at some point, make sure you are logged in under your usual username.

If you are using Windows 7, the Documents shortcut in the Libraries list actually refers to a library rather than a single folder, and multiple folders may be associated with the Documents library. No matter — just navigate to the location you want to use. ■

Note

Throughout all of the Office programs, the dialog boxes that save and open files are different depending on the operating system you are using. ■

Changing the Save Location (Windows 7)

In Windows 7, the storage locations, and the interface for accessing these locations, are different from earlier versions of Windows.

The navigation pane on the left side of the Save As dialog box is home to several collapsible/ expandable categories. Double-click on a category to open it and then make selections from within it (see Figure 21-6). You can choose from the following categories:

- **Favorites.** Shortcuts for popular locations such as Downloads and Desktop appear in the Favorites list, and you can also add your own shortcuts here.

Tip

Add your own favorite locations to the Favorites list by dragging their icons into it. ■

FIGURE 21-6

In Windows 7, the Save As dialog box contains several shortcuts for navigation in the left pane.

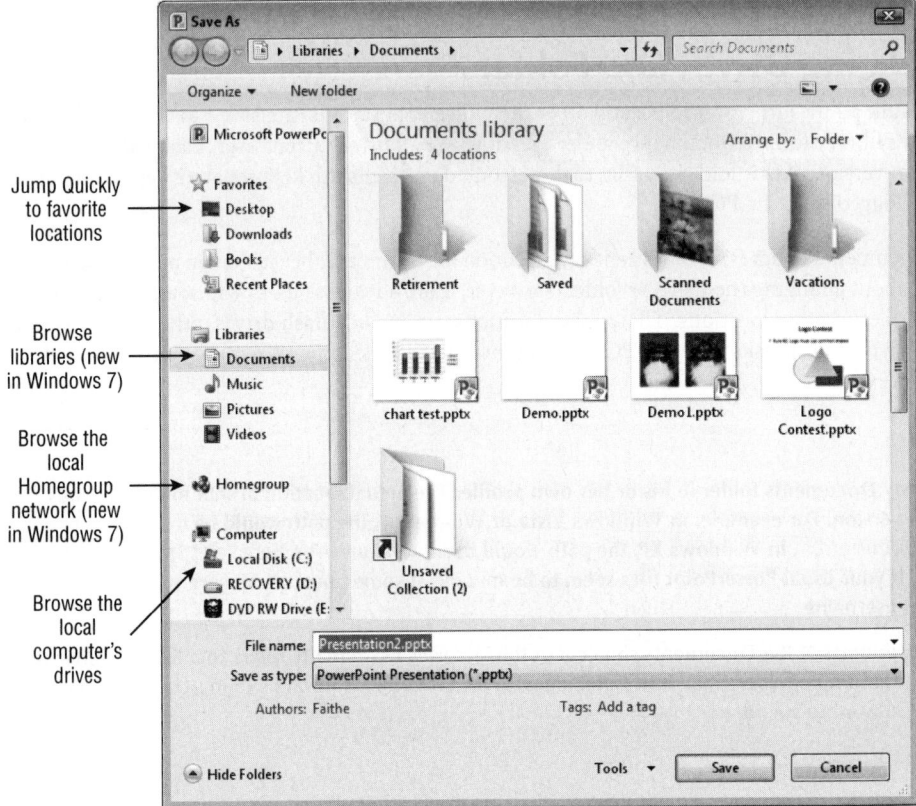

- **Libraries.** *Libraries* are virtual folders that organize locations by the types of files they contain. This is a new feature in Windows 7. Double-click Libraries and then click through a category such as Documents or Pictures.

- **Homegroup.** Windows 7 has a new home networking feature called *Homegroup*; if you use it to set up your network, you can browse other network computers by clicking here.

- **Computer.** Browse the complete drive and folder listing for your local PC here.

You can also navigate via the address bar (this applies to both Windows 7 and Windows Vista). The address bar shows the path to the currently displayed location. You can jump directly to any of those levels by clicking the name there. This is similar to the "Up One Level" feature from Windows XP style dialog boxes, except you are not limited to going up a single level at a time — you can go directly up to any level. You can also click the right-pointing arrow to the right of any level to see a menu of other folders within that location, and jump to any of them from the menu, as shown in Figure 21-7.

FIGURE 21-7

Click an arrow on the address bar to see a menu of locations at the chosen level within the current path.

Changing the Save Location (Windows Vista)

Windows Vista's Save As dialog box offers some navigation locations that are slightly different from the ones in Windows 7, as shown in Figure 21-8. Here's a summary:

FIGURE 21-8

Jump to a desired location using the Favorite Links and/or Folders lists.

Favorite link list

Folder list   Address bar

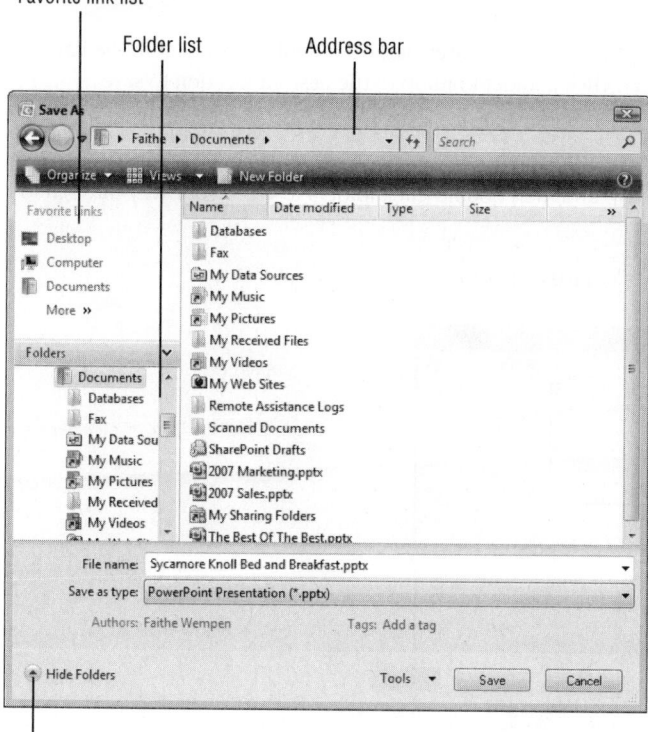

Click here to expand and
contract the dialog box

- **Favorite Links List.** This area displays shortcuts for popular locations such as Documents and Desktop. Double-click a shortcut here to jump to the desired location.

- **Folders List.** This area displays a folder tree of locations, similar to the folder list in a Windows Explorer window, or to the Computer listing in the Windows 7 version of the dialog box. See Figure 21-8. To display the Folders list if it does not already appear, click the up-arrow to the right of Folders (below the Favorite Links list). To hide the Folders list, click the down-arrow (which replaces the up-arrow).

Tip

Drag the divider line between the Favorite Links and Folders lists to adjust their relative sizes. Drag the vertical divider line between the lists and the file listing to make the Favorite Links and Folders panes wider or narrower. You can also enlarge the whole Save As dialog box, if necessary, by dragging its border. ■

Changing the Save Location (Windows XP)

Under Windows XP, the Save In list shows the top-level locations on the system, including each drive, My Documents, and My Network Places. Open the list, as shown in Figure 21-9, and select the location in which you want to start. Then double-click folder icons in the file listing to drill down to the location in which you want to save. To go back up one level, click the Up One Level button. See Figure 21-9.

Along the left side of the Save As dialog box is the Places Bar. It's roughly equivalent to the Favorite Links list in Windows Vista. You can click a folder to jump to the desired location to save a file.

FIGURE 21-9

Select a top-level location from the Save In list, and then double-click folders to work your way through to the desired location.

Up One Level button

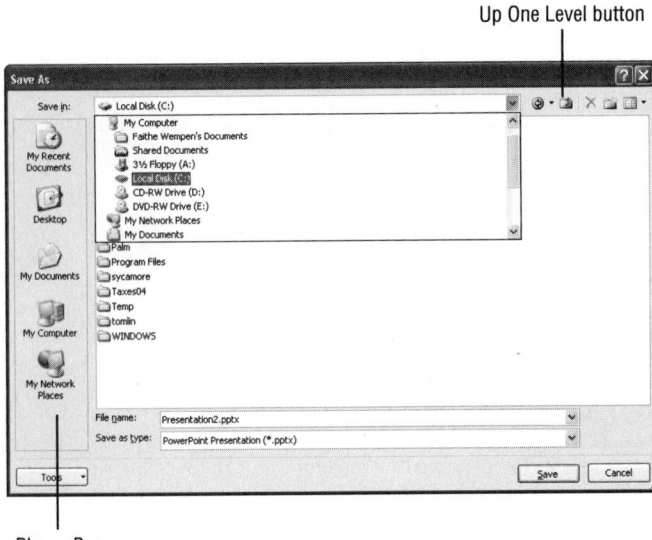

Places Bar

Tip

If you consistently want your PowerPoint files saved into a different folder, change the default file location. Choose File ⇨ Options and click Save. Then type a new file location in the Default File Location text box. You cannot browse for it; you must know the full path name. Separate the parts of the path with \ symbols, like this: `C:\Books\PowerPoint\PPBible`. ∎

Saving in a Different Format

PowerPoint 2007, and higher, has an XML-based file format. XML (eXtensible Markup Language) is a text-based coding system similar to HTML that describes formatting by using inline bracketed codes and style sheets. XML-based data files are smaller than the data files from earlier PowerPoint versions, and they support all of the latest PowerPoint features. For best results, use this format whenever possible.

There are also several variants of this format for specialty uses. For example, there's a macro-enabled version with a `.pptm` extension. There are also *show* variants (`.ppsx` and `.ppsm`) that open in Slide Show view by default, and template variants (`.potx` and `.potm`) that function as templates.

However, not everyone has PowerPoint 2007 or higher. You can download a compatibility pack for earlier PowerPoint versions that will allow them to accept the new files, but you can't assume that everyone who has an earlier version of PowerPoint will download it. Therefore, you might need to save presentations in other file formats in order to share files with other people.

The available formats are shown in Table 21-1. In the Save As dialog box, open the Save As type drop-down list and select the desired format, as shown in Figure 21-10.

TABLE 21-1

PowerPoint 'Save As' Formats

Format Presentations	Extension	Usage Notes
PowerPoint Presentation	`.pptx`	The default; use in most cases. Can open only in PowerPoint 2007 or 2010 (or in an earlier version with compatibility pack installed).
PowerPoint Macro-Enabled Presentation	`.pptm`	Same as above, except it supports the storage of VBA or macro code
PowerPoint 97–2003 Presentation	`.ppt`	A backward-compatible format for sharing files with users of PowerPoint 97, 2000, 2002 (XP), or 2003
PDF	`.pdf`	Produces files in Adobe PDF format, which is a hybrid of a document and a graphic. It shows each page exactly as it will be printed, and yet allows the user to mark up the pages with comments and to search the document text. You must have a PDF reader such as Adobe Acrobat to view PDF files.

continued

TABLE 21-1 *(continued)*

Format Presentations	Extension	Usage Notes
XPS Document	`.xps`	Much the same as PDF except it's a Microsoft format. Windows Vista and higher comes with an XPS viewer application.
PowerPoint Template	`.potx`	A 2007-format template file
PowerPoint Macro-Enabled Template	`.potm`	A 2007-format template file that supports the storage of VBA or macro code
PowerPoint 97–2003 Template	`.pot`	A backward-compatible template file, also usable with PowerPoint 97, 2000, 2002 (XP), or 2003
PowerPoint Show	`.ppsx`	Just like a regular PowerPoint file, except it opens in Slide Show view by default; useful for distributing presentations to the audience on disk
PowerPoint Macro-Enabled Show	`.ppsm`	Same as above, except it supports the storage of VBA or macro code
PowerPoint 97–2003 Show	`.pps`	Same as a regular backward-compatible presentation file, except it opens in Slide Show view by default
PowerPoint Add-in	`.ppam`	A file that contains executable code (usually VBA) that extends PowerPoint's capabilities
PowerPoint 97–2003 Add-in	`.ppa`	Same as above, except the add-in is backward-compatible
PowerPoint XML Presentation	`.xml`	A presentation in XML format, suitable for integrating into an XML information storage system

Graphics/Other		
Windows Media Video	`.wmv`	A video version of the presentation (new in PowerPoint 2010)
Office Theme	`.thmx`	Somewhat like a template, but it contains only theme settings (fonts, colors, and effects). Use this if you don't want to save any of the content. Theme files can be used to supply the colors, fonts, and effects to Word and Excel files too.
GIF Graphics Interchange Format	`.gif`	Static graphic. GIFs are limited to 256 colors.
JPEG File Interchange Format	`.jpg`	Static graphic. JPG files can be very small, making them good for Web use. A lossy format, so picture quality may not be as good as with a lossless format.

Format Presentations	Extension	Usage Notes
PNG Portable Network Graphics Format	.png	Static graphic. Similar to GIF, except without the color depth limitation. Uses lossless compression; takes advantage of the best features of both GIF and JPG.
TIFF Tagged Image File Format	.tif	Static graphic. TIF is a high-quality file format suitable for slides with high-resolution photos. A lossless compression format.
Device Independent Bitmap	.bmp	Static graphic. BMP is the native format for Windows graphics, including Windows background wallpaper.
Windows Metafile	.wmf	Static graphic. A vector-based format, so it can later be resized without distortion. Not Mac-compatible.
Enhanced Windows Metafile	.emf	Enhanced version of WMF; not compatible with 16-bit applications. Also vector-based and non-Mac-compatible.
Outline/RTF	.rtf	Text and text formatting only; excludes all non-text elements. Only text in slide placeholders will be converted to the outline. Text in the Notes area is not included.
PowerPoint Picture Presentation	.pptx	Saves all the slides as pictures and puts them into a new blank presentation.
OpenDocument Presentation	.odp	A presentation that conforms to the new OpenDocument standard for exchanging data between applications

Tip

If you consistently want to save in a different format from PowerPoint 2010, choose File ⇨ Options and click Save. Then, choose a different format from the Save Files in This Format drop-down list. This makes your choice the default in the Save As type drop-down list in the Save As dialog box. Not all of the formats are available here; your choices are PowerPoint Presentation (the default), PowerPoint Macro-Enabled Presentation, PowerPoint Presentation 97–2003, and OpenDocument Presentation. ∎

Table 21-1 lists many choices, but don't let that overwhelm you. You have three main decisions to make:

- **PowerPoint 2007/2010 Format or backward-compatible with PowerPoint 97–2003.** Unless compatibility is essential, go with the newer format because you get access to all of the new features. (See Table 21-2 to learn what you'll lose with backward-compatibility.) If you use a backward-compatible format, some of the features described in this book work differently or aren't available at all.

- **Macro-Enabled or Not.** If you plan to record and store macros, use a macro-enabled format; if not, use a file format that does not include macro support, for a slightly safer file (because a file cannot carry viruses if it can't carry macro code).

- **Regular Presentation or PowerPoint Show.** The *show* variant starts the presentation in Slide Show view when it is loaded in PowerPoint; that's the only difference between it and a regular presentation. You can build your presentation in a regular format, and then save in show format right before distribution. PowerPoint shows can be opened and edited in PowerPoint the same as any other file.

FIGURE 21-10

Choose a different format, if necessary, from the Save As type drop-down list.

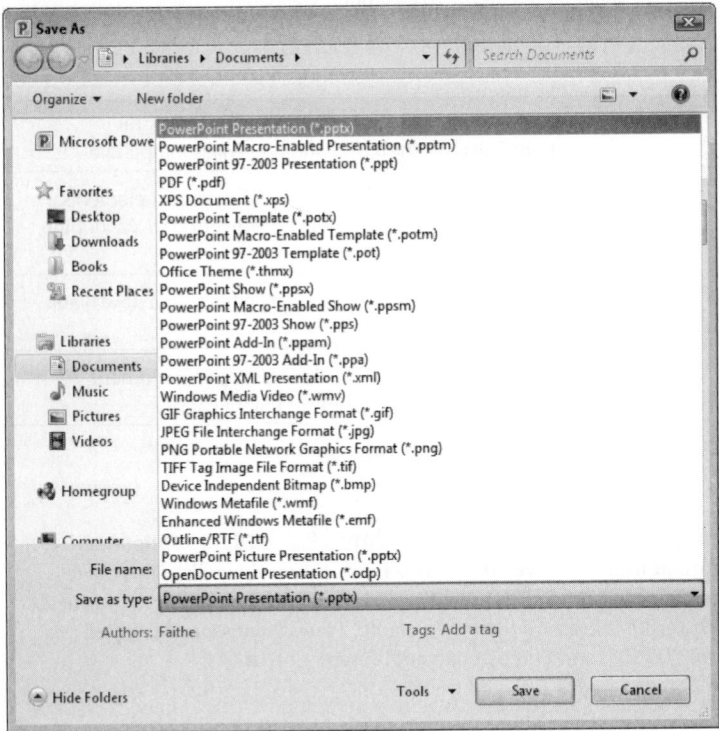

Most of the other choices from Table 21-1 are special-purpose and not suitable for everyday use. The following sections explain some of those special file types.

TABLE 21-2

PowerPoint 2010 Features Not Supported in the PowerPoint 97–2003 File Format

Feature	Issues
SmartArt Graphics	Converted to uneditable pictures
Charts (except Microsoft Graph charts)	Converted to editable OLE objects, but the chart might appear different
Custom Slide Layouts	Converted to multiple masters
Drop Shadows	Soft shadows converted to hard shadows
Equations	Converted to uneditable pictures
Heading and body fonts	Converted to non-theme formatting
New effects: • 2-D or 3-D WordArt text • Gradient outlines for shapes or text • Strikethrough and double-strikethrough • Gradient, picture, and texture fills on text • Soft edges, reflections, some types of shadows • Most 3-D effects	Converted to uneditable pictures
Themes	Converted to non-theme formatting
Theme colors	Converted to non-theme colors
Theme effects	Converted to non-theme effects
Theme fonts	Converted to non-theme fonts

Saving Slides as Graphics

If you save your presentation in one of the graphic formats shown in the Graphics/Other section of Table 21-1, the file ceases to be a presentation and becomes a series of unrelated graphics files, one per slide. If you choose one of these formats, you're asked whether you want to export the current slide only or all slides. If you choose all slides, PowerPoint creates a new folder in the selected folder with the same name as the original presentation file and places the graphics files in it.

Tip

The Picture Presentation format, new in PowerPoint 2010, does something unique: It converts each slide to an image and then places the images in a new presentation file. This is one way to make sure that your slides are not edited by anyone who uses the presentation. ■

Saving Slide Text Only

If you want to export the text of the slides to some other application, consider the Outline/RTF format, which creates an outline similar to what you see in the Outline pane in PowerPoint. This file can then be opened in Word or any other application that supports RTF text files. Only text in placeholders is exported, though, not text in manually inserted text boxes.

Specifying Save Options

The Save options enable you to fine-tune the saving process for special needs. For example, you can use Save options to embed fonts, to change the interval at which PowerPoint saves AutoRecover information, and more.

There are two ways to access the Save options:

- Choose File ➪ Options and click Save.
- From the Save As dialog box, click Tools ➪ Save Options.

The PowerPoint Options dialog box appears, as shown in Figure 21-11.

Then set any of the options desired. Click OK when you are finished.

Table 21-3 summarizes the Save options. One of the most important features described in Table 21-3 is AutoRecover, which is turned on by default. This means that if a system error or a power outage causes PowerPoint to terminate unexpectedly, you do not lose all of the work you have done. The next time you start PowerPoint, it opens the recovered file and asks if you want to save it.

Caution

AutoRecover is *not* a substitute for saving your work the regular way. It does not save in the same sense that the Save command does; it only saves a backup version as PowerPoint is running. If you quit PowerPoint normally, that backup version is erased. The backup version is available for recovery only if PowerPoint terminates abnormally (e.g., because of a system lockup or a power outage). ■

FIGURE 21-11

Set Save options to match the way you want PowerPoint to save your work.

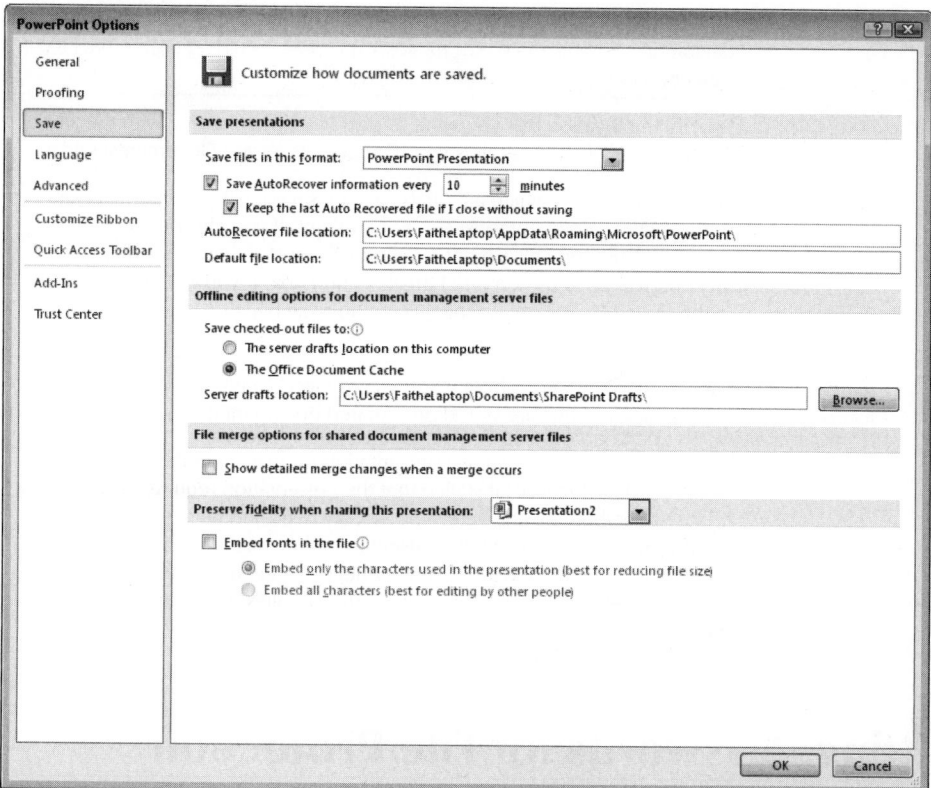

TABLE 21-3

Save Options

Feature	Purpose
Save Files in This Format	Sets the default file format to appear in the Save As dialog box. Your choices are a regular presentation, a macro-enabled presentation, or a 97–2003 backward-compatible presentation.
Save AutoRecover Info Every __ Minutes	PowerPoint saves your work every few minutes so that if the computer has problems and causes PowerPoint to terminate abnormally, you do not lose much work. Lower this number to save more often (for less potential data loss) or raise it to save less often (for less slowdown/delay related to repeated saving).

continued

TABLE 21-3   *(continued)*

Feature	Purpose
AutoRecover File Location	Specify the location in which AutoRecover drafts should be saved. By default, it is `C:\Users\`*`username`*`\AppData\Roaming\Microsoft\PowerPoint`.
Default File Location	Specify the location that you want to start from when saving with the Save As dialog box. By default, it is your Documents (or My Documents) folder.
Save Checked-Out Files To	Sets the location in which any drafts will be saved that you have checked out of a Web Server library such as SharePoint. If you choose The Server Drafts Location on This Computer, then you must specify what that location will be in the Server Drafts Location box. If you choose to save to the Office Document Cache, it's not an issue because every save goes immediately back to the server.
Show Detailed Changes When a Merge Occurs	Shows full information about what was changed when you merge two PowerPoint files that are stored on a shared document management server.
Embed Fonts in the File	Turn this on if you are saving a presentation for use on a different PC that might not have the fonts installed that the presentation requires. You can choose to embed the characters in use only (which minimizes the file size, but if someone tries to edit the presentation they might not have all of the characters out of the font that they need), or to embed all characters in the font set. Unlike the others, this setting applies only to the current presentation file.

Setting Passwords for File Protection

If a presentation contains sensitive or confidential data, you can encrypt the file and protect it with a password. *Encryption* is a type of "scrambling" done to the file so that nobody can see it, either from within PowerPoint or with any other type of file-browsing utility.

You can enter two separate passwords for a file: the Open password and the Modify password. Use an Open password to prevent unauthorized people from viewing the file at all. Use a Modify password to prevent people from making changes to the file.

You can use one, both, or neither of the password types. For example, suppose you have a personnel presentation that contains salary information. You might use an Open password and distribute that password to a few key people in the Human Resources Department who need access to it. But then you might use a Modify password to ensure that none of those people make any changes to the presentation as they are viewing it.

For the Open password, you can specify an encryption method and strength. Many encryption codes are available, and the differences between them are significant mostly to high-end technical users. However, if you do have a preference, you can choose it when you choose the Open password.

To manage a file's passwords and other security settings, follow these steps:

1. **Begin to save the file as you normally would from the Save As dialog box.**

2. **In the Save As dialog box, click Tools, and choose General Options.** The General Options dialog box opens, as shown in Figure 21-12.

FIGURE 21-12

Set a password to prevent unauthorized access.

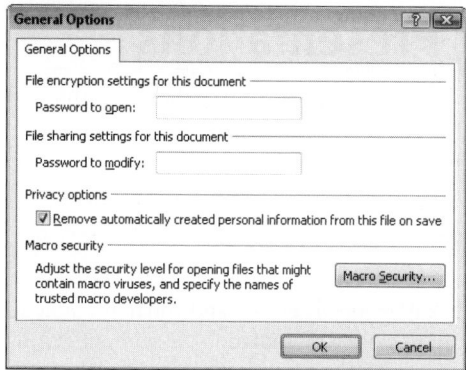

3. **If you want an Open password, enter it in the Password to Open box.**

4. **If you want a Modify password, enter it in the Password to Modify box.** (You don't have to use both an Open and a Modify password; you can use just one or the other if you like.)

5. (Optional) **If you want your personal information stripped from the file, such as your name removed from the Author field of the Properties box, select the Remove Automatically Created Personal Information from This File on Save check box.**

6. (Optional) **If desired, adjust the macro security level for PowerPoint (all files, not just this one) by clicking the Macro Security button and making changes to the settings in the Trust Center.** Then click OK to return to the General Options dialog box.

7. **Click OK.**

8. **If you specified a password in Step 3, a confirmation box appears for it.** Retype the same password and click OK.

9. **If you specified a password in Step 4, a confirmation box appears for it.** Retype the same password and click OK.

10. **Continue saving as you normally would.**

When you (or someone else) open the file, a Password prompt appears. The Open password must be entered to open the presentation file. The Modify password will not work. After that hurdle, if you have set a separate Modify password, a prompt for that appears. Your choices are to enter the

Modify password, to cancel, or to click the Read-Only option to open the presentation in read-only mode.

Caution

If you add a Modify password to a PPTX file and then save it as a PPTX file, it can be opened *and* edited in PowerPoint 2003 or earlier with the compatibility pack installed that allows opening of PPTX files. However, if you save the file in PowerPoint 2010 as a PowerPoint 97–2003 file (PPT file), it cannot be edited in earlier versions. ∎

Closing and Reopening Presentations

You can have several presentation files open at once and switch freely between them, but this can bog down your computer's performance somewhat. Unless you are doing some cut-and-paste work, it's best to have only one presentation file open — the one you are actively working on. It's easy to close and open presentations as needed.

Closing a Presentation

When you exit PowerPoint, the open presentation file automatically closes, and you're prompted to save your changes if you have made any. If you want to close a presentation file without exiting PowerPoint, follow these steps:

1. **Choose File ⇨ Close.** If you have not made any changes to the presentation since the last time you saved, you're done.

2. **If you have made any changes to the presentation, you're prompted to save them.** If you don't want to save your changes, click Don't Save, and you're done.

3. **If you want to save your changes, click Save.** If the presentation has already been saved once, you're done.

4. **If the presentation has not been saved before, the Save As dialog box appears.** Type a name in the File Name text box and click Save.

Opening a Presentation

To open a recently used presentation, choose File ⇨ Recent. Although only five files appear in Figure 21-13, up to 22 can appear by default.

Tip

To pin a certain file to the Recent list so that it never scrolls off, click the push-pin icon to the right of the file's name.

You can increase or decrease the number of recently used files that appear on the Recent list. Choose File ⇨ Options, click Advanced, and in the Display section, set the Number of Documents in the Recent Documents list.

You can right-click an entry on the Recent Files list for additional options, such as Open as Copy. ∎

FIGURE 21-13

Open the presentation via the Recent choice after clicking File.

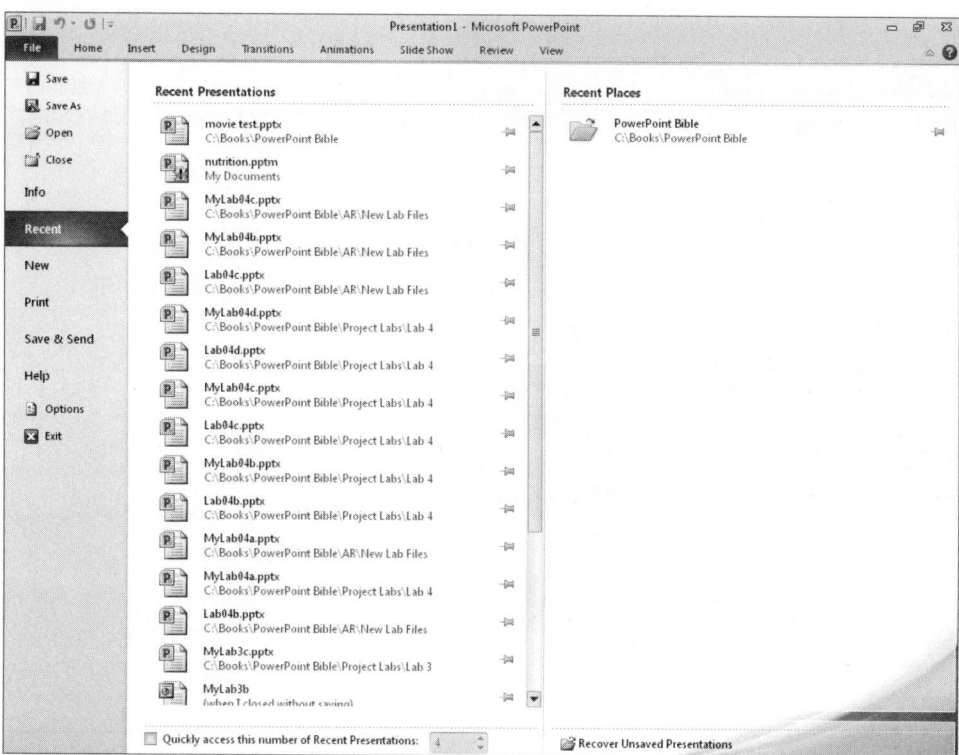

If the presentation you want to open does not appear on the Recent list, follow these steps to find and open it:

1. **Choose File ➪ Open.** The Open dialog box appears.
2. **Choose the file you want.** If necessary, change the location to find the file.
3. **Click Open.** The presentation opens.

To open more than one presentation at once, hold down the Ctrl key as you click each file you want to open. Then, click the Open button and they all open in their own windows.

The Open button in the Open dialog box has its own drop-down list from which you can select commands that open the file in different ways. See Figure 21-14, and refer to Table 21-4 for an explanation of the available options.

FIGURE 21-14

The Open button's menu contains several special options for opening a file.

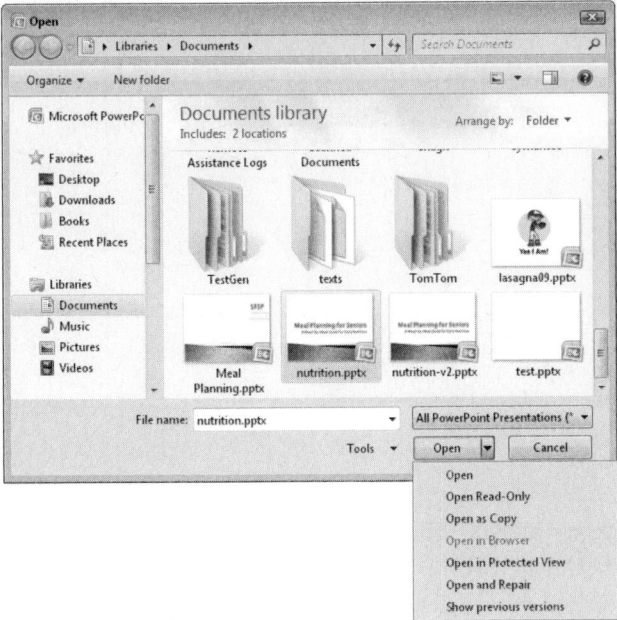

TABLE 21-4

Open Options

Open Button Setting	Purpose
Open	The default; simply opens the file for editing.
Open Read-Only	Allows changes but prevents those changes from being saved under the same name.
Open as Copy	Opens a copy of the file, leaving the original untouched.
Open in Browser	Applicable only for Web-based presentations; opens it for viewing in a Web browser. PowerPoint 2010 does not save in Web format, so it applies only to Web-based presentations created in earlier versions of PowerPoint.
Open in Protected View	Opens the file in an uneditable view. This option not only prevents you from saving any changes to the file, but it also prevents you from *making* changes.
Open and Repair	Opens the file, and identifies and repairs any errors it finds in it.
Show Previous Versions	Applicable only if the presentation file is stored on an NTFS volume under Windows Vista or Windows 7. See the next section for details.

Opening a File from a Different Program

Just as you can save files in various program formats, you can also open files from various programs. PowerPoint can detect the type of file and convert it automatically as you open it, so you do not have to know the exact file type. (For example, if you have an old PowerPoint file with a .ppt extension, you don't have to know what version it came from.) The only problem is with files that don't have extensions that PowerPoint automatically recognizes. In that case, you must change the File Type setting in the Open dialog box to All Files so that the file to be opened becomes available on the file list, as shown in Figure 21-15. This change is valid for only this one use of the Open dialog box; the file type reverts to All PowerPoint Presentations, which is the default, the next time you open it.

FIGURE 21-15

To open files from different programs, change the File Type setting to All Files.

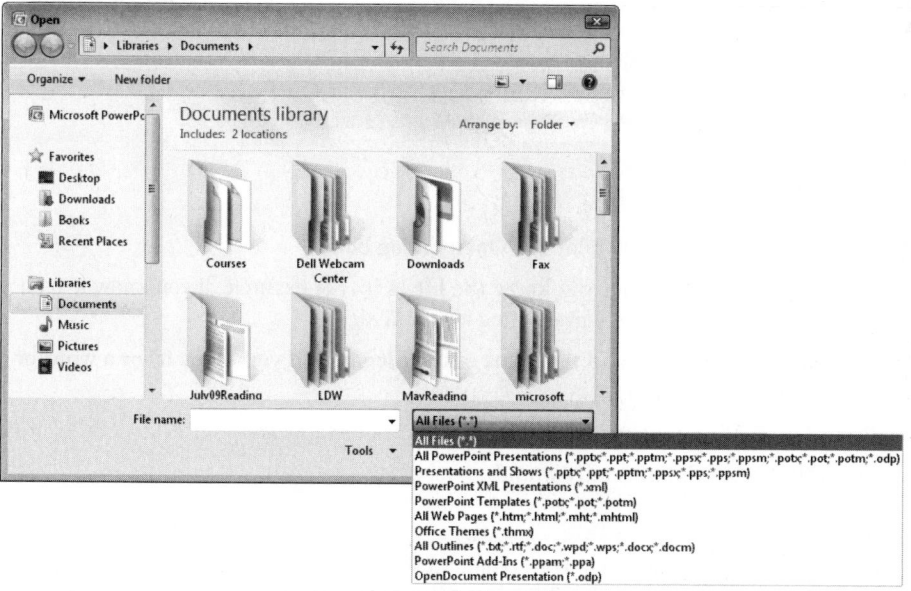

Caution

PowerPoint opens only presentation files and text-based files such as Word outlines. If you want to include graphics from another program in a PowerPoint presentation, insert them using the Picture command on the Insert tab. Do not attempt to open them with the Open dialog box. ■

Finding a Presentation File to Open

If you have forgotten where you saved a particular presentation file, you're not out of luck. The Open dialog box (under Windows Vista and Windows 7) includes a Search box that can help you locate it, as shown in Figure 21-16.

FIGURE 21-16

Use the Search box in the Open dialog box (Windows Vista and Windows 7 only) to look for a file.

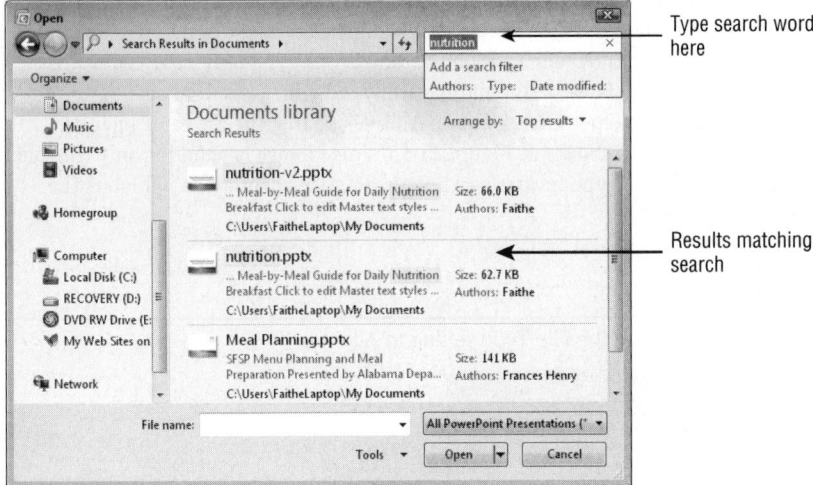

To search for a file, follow these steps:

1. Choose File ➪ Open to display the Open dialog box.

2. **Navigate to a location that you know the file is in.** For example, if you know it is on the C: drive, display the top-level listing for the C: drive.

3. **Click in the Search box and type part of the filename (if you know it) or a word or phrase used in the file.**

4. **Press Enter.** A list of files that match that specification appears.

5. **Open the file as you normally would.**

Note
You can also use the Search utility from outside of PowerPoint. In Windows Vista and Windows 7, click Start and use the Search text box. Although the Search utilities are different in each version of Windows, they all can find a file by name, content, author, date, or many other properties. ∎

Creating New Slides

Different templates start a presentation with different numbers and types of slides. A blank presentation has only a single slide, and you must create any others that you want.

There are several ways to create new slides. For example, you can type new text in the outline and then promote it to slide status, or you can add slides with the New Slide button that is on the

Home tab. You can also copy existing slides, either within the same presentation or from other sources. The following sections outline these procedures in more detail.

Creating New Slides from the Outline Pane

As discussed in Chapter 20, the Outline pane shows the text from the presentation's slides in a hierarchical tree, with the slide titles at the top level (the slide level) and the various levels of bulleted lists on the slides displaying as subordinate levels. Text that you type in the Outline pane appears on the slide, and vice versa.

Note

The Outline pane doesn't actually show all of the text in all cases; see "Creating a Text Box Manually" later in this chapter to find out why text in some text boxes does not appear in the Outline pane. ∎

Follow these steps to create a new slide from the Outline pane:

1. **Switch to Normal view and display the Outline pane if it does not already appear.**

2. **Right-click the existing line on the Outline pane that the new slide should follow.**

3. **Click New Slide.** A new line appears in the Outline pane, with a slide symbol to its left.

4. **Type the title for the new slide.** The title appears both in the Outline pane and on the slide.

You can also create a new slide by starting a new line in the Outline pane and then promoting it to slide level by pressing Shift+Tab. Follow these steps to insert a new slide in this way:

1. **Position the insertion point at the end of the last line of the slide that the new slide should follow, and press Enter to start a new line.**

2. **Press Shift+Tab to promote the new line to the highest level (press it multiple times if needed), so that a slide icon appears to its left.**

3. **Type the title for the new slide.** The title appears both in the Outline pane and on the slide.

After creating the slide, you can continue creating its content directly in the Outline pane. Press Enter to start a new line, and then use Tab to demote, or Shift+Tab to promote, the line to the desired level. You can also right-click the text and choose Promote or Demote. Promoting a line all the way to the top level changes the line to a new slide title.

Creating a Slide from the Slides Pane

Here's a very quick method for creating a new slide, based on the default layout. It doesn't get much easier than this:

1. **In Normal view, in the Slides pane, click the slide that the new slide should follow.**

2. **Press Enter.** A new slide appears using the Title and Content layout. You can also right-click the slide that the new one should follow and choose New Slide.

The drawback to creating a slide in either of these ways is that you cannot specify the layout. To choose a layout other than the default one, see the next section.

Creating a Slide from a Layout

A *slide layout* is a layout guide that tells PowerPoint what placeholder boxes to use on a particular slide and where to position them. Although slide layouts can contain placeholders for text, they also contain graphics, charts, tables, and other useful elements. After you create a new slide with placeholders, you can click a placeholder to open whatever controls you need to insert that type of object.

Cross-Reference

See the section, "Using Content Placeholders," for more information on inserting objects. ■

When you create new slides using the outline method described in the preceding section, the new slides use the Title and Content layout, which consists of a slide title and a single, large placeholder box for content. If you want to use another layout, such as a slide with two adjacent but separate frames of content, you must either switch the slide to a different layout after its creation (using the Layout menu on the Home tab), or you must specify a different layout when you initially create the slide.

To specify a certain layout as you are creating a slide, follow these steps:

1. **In Normal or Slide Sorter view, select or display the slide that the new one should follow.** You can select a slide by clicking its thumbnail image in Slide Sorter view or on the Slides pane in Normal view. You can also move the insertion point to the slide's text in the Outline pane.

2. **On the Home tab, do one of the following:**
   - To add a new slide using the default Title and Content layout, click the top (graphical) portion of the New Slide button in the Slides group.
   - To add a new slide using another layout, click the bottom (text) portion of the New Slide button in the Slides group and then select the desired layout from the menu, as shown in Figure 21-17.

Tip

The layouts that appear on the menu come from the Slide Master. To customize these layouts, click Slide Master on the View tab. You will learn more about the Slide Master and about changing layouts in Chapter 22. ■

Copying Slides

Another way to create a new slide is to copy an existing one in the same presentation. This is especially useful when you are using multiple slides to create a progression because one slide is typically identical to the next slide in a sequence, except for a small change. (You can also build effects within a single slide using PowerPoint's animation effects, as you will learn in Chapter 25.)

FIGURE 21-17

Create a new slide, based on the layout of your choice.

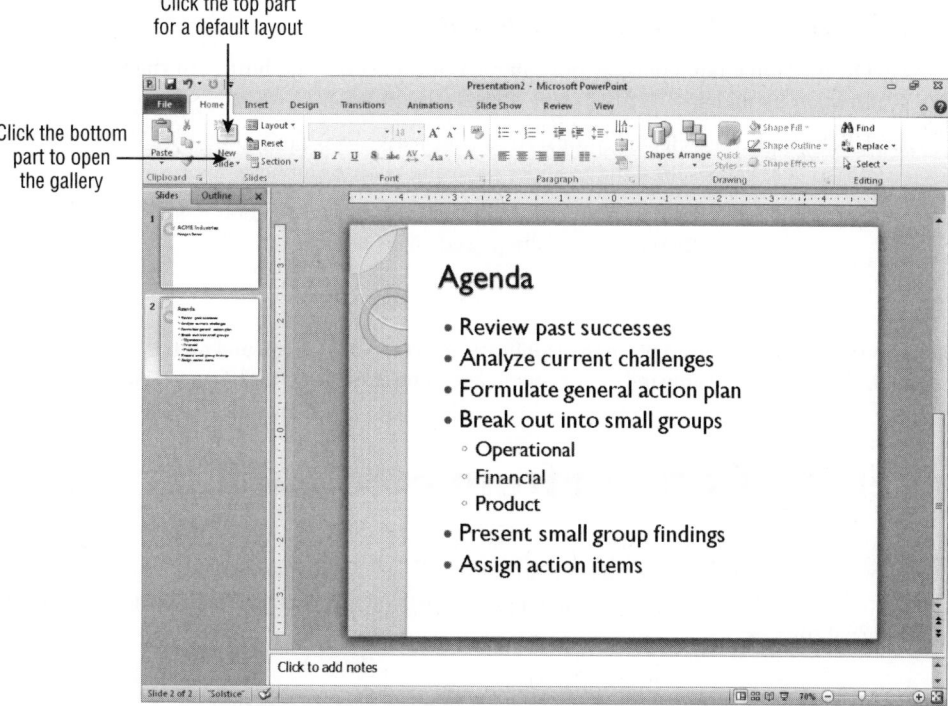

There are several ways to copy one or more slides. One way is to use the Windows Clipboard, as in the following steps:

1. **Select the slide or slides that you want to copy.** See "Selecting Slides" later in this chapter for more information about selecting slides.

Caution

If you select from the Outline pane, make sure that you click the icon to the left of the slide's title so that the entire slide is selected; if you select only part of the text on the slide, then only the selected part is copied. ∎

2. **Press Ctrl+C.** You can also click the Copy button on the Home tab, or right-click the selection and click Copy.

3. **Select the slide that the pasted slide or slides should follow.** Alternatively, in the Outline pane, click to place the insertion point where you want the insertion.

4. **Press Ctrl+V.** You can also click the Paste button on the Home tab, or right-click the destination and click Paste.

PowerPoint also has a Duplicate Slides command that does the same thing as a copy-and-paste command. Although it may be a little faster, it gives you less control as to where the pasted copies will appear:

1. **Select the slide or slides to be duplicated.**

2. **On the Home tab, click the bottom part of the New Slide button in the Slides group to open its menu.**

3. **Click Duplicate Selected Slides.** As an alternative, you can right-click a slide (or a group of selected slides) in the Slides pane and choose Duplicate Slide.

PowerPoint pastes the slides immediately after the last slide in the selection. For example, if you selected Slides 1, 3, and 6, then the copies are placed after Slide 6.

Tip

To make duplication even faster, you can place the Duplicate Selected Slides command on the Quick Access Toolbar. To do that, right-click the command on the menu, and choose Add to Quick Access Toolbar. ∎

Inserting Content from External Sources

Many people find that they can save a lot of time by copying text or slides from other programs or from other PowerPoint presentations to form the basis of a new presentation. There's no need to reinvent the wheel each time! The following sections look at various ways to bring in content from external sources.

Copying Slides from Other Presentations

There are several ways to copy slides from other presentations. You can:

- Open the presentation, save it under a different name, and then delete the slides that you don't want, leaving a new presentation with the desired slides ready for customization.

- Open two PowerPoint windows side-by-side and drag-and-drop slides between them.

- Open two PowerPoint presentations, copy slides from one of them to the Clipboard (Ctrl+C), and then paste them into the other presentation (Ctrl+V).

- Use the Reuse Slides feature in PowerPoint, as described next.

To reuse slides from other presentations with the Reuse Slides feature, follow these steps:

1. **On the Home tab, click the lower portion of the New Slide button in the Slides group to open its menu.**

2. **Click Reuse Slides.** The Reuse Slides pane appears.

3. **Click Open a PowerPoint File.**

   OR

   Click the Browse button and then click Browse File.

4. **In the Browse dialog box, select the presentation from which you want to copy slides, and click Open.** Thumbnail images of the slides in the presentation appear in the Reuse Slides pane, as shown in Figure 21-18.

5. (Optional) **If you want to keep the source formatting when copying slides, select the Keep Source Formatting check box at the bottom of the task pane.**

6. (Optional) **To see an enlarged image of one of the slides, move the mouse pointer over it.**

FIGURE 21-18

Choose individual slides to copy to the current presentation.

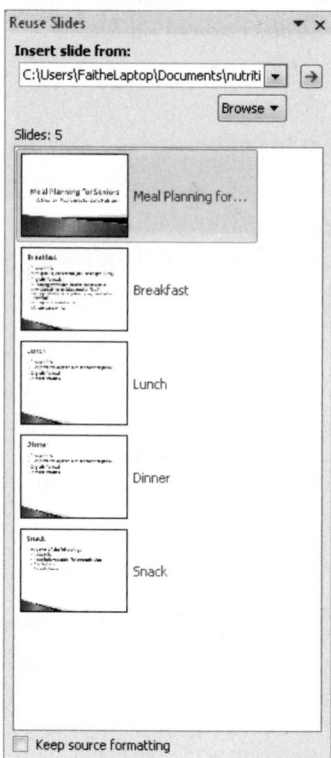

7. **Do one of the following:**
   - To insert a single slide, click it.

- To insert all slides at once, right-click any slide and choose Insert All Slides.
- To copy only the theme (not the content), right-click any slide and choose Apply Theme to All Slides, or Apply Theme to Selected Slides.

Inserting New Slides from an Outline

All of the Microsoft Office applications work well together, so it's easy to move content between them. For example, you can create an outline for a presentation in Microsoft Word and then import it into PowerPoint. PowerPoint uses the heading styles that you assigned in Word to decide which items are slide titles and which items are slide content. The top-level headings (Heading 1) form the slide titles.

To try this out, open Word, switch to Outline view (from the View tab), and then type a short outline of a presentation. Press Tab to demote, or Shift+Tab to promote, a selected line. Then save your work, go back to PowerPoint, and follow these steps to import it:

1. **On the Home tab, click the lower portion of the New Slide button in the Slides group to open its menu.**

2. **Click Slides from Outline.** The Insert Outline dialog box opens.

3. **Select the file containing the outline text that you want to import.**

4. **Click Insert.** PowerPoint imports the outline.

If there were already existing slides in the presentation, they remain untouched. (This includes any blank slides, and so you might need to delete the blank slide at the beginning of the presentation after importing.) All of the Heading 1 lines from the outline become separate slide titles, and all of the subordinate headings become bullet points in the slides.

Tips for Better Outline Importing

Although PowerPoint can import any text from any Word document, you may not always get the results that you want or expect. For example, you may have a document that consists of a series of paragraphs with no heading styles applied. When you import this document into PowerPoint, it might look something like Figure 21-19.

Figure 21-19 is a prime example of what happens if you don't prepare a document before you import it into PowerPoint. PowerPoint makes each paragraph its own slide and puts all of the text for each one in the title placeholder. It can't tell which ones are actual headings and which ones aren't because there are no heading styles in use. The paragraphs are too long to fit on slides, and so they are truncated off the tops of the slides. Extra blank lines are interpreted as blank slides. Quite a train wreck, isn't it? Figure 21-19 also illustrates an important point to remember: Regular paragraph text does not work very well in PowerPoint. PowerPoint text is all about short, snappy bulleted lists and headings. The better that you prepare the outline before importing it, the less cleanup you will need to do after importing. Here are some tips:

- Non-headings in Word do not import into PowerPoint unless you use no heading styles at all in the document (as in Figure 21-19). Apply heading styles to the text that you want to import.

- Stick with basic styles only in the outline: for example, just Heading 1, Heading 2, and so on.
- Delete all blank lines above the first heading. If you don't, you will have blank slides at the beginning of your presentation.
- Strip off as much manual formatting as possible from the Word text, so that the text picks up its formatting from PowerPoint. To strip off formatting in Word, select the text and press Ctrl+Spacebar.
- Do not leave blank lines between paragraphs. These will translate into blank slides or blank bulleted items in PowerPoint.
- Delete any graphic elements, such as clip art, pictures, charts, and so on. They will not transfer to PowerPoint anyway and may confuse the import utility.

FIGURE 21-19

A Word document consisting mainly of plain paragraphs makes for an unattractive presentation.

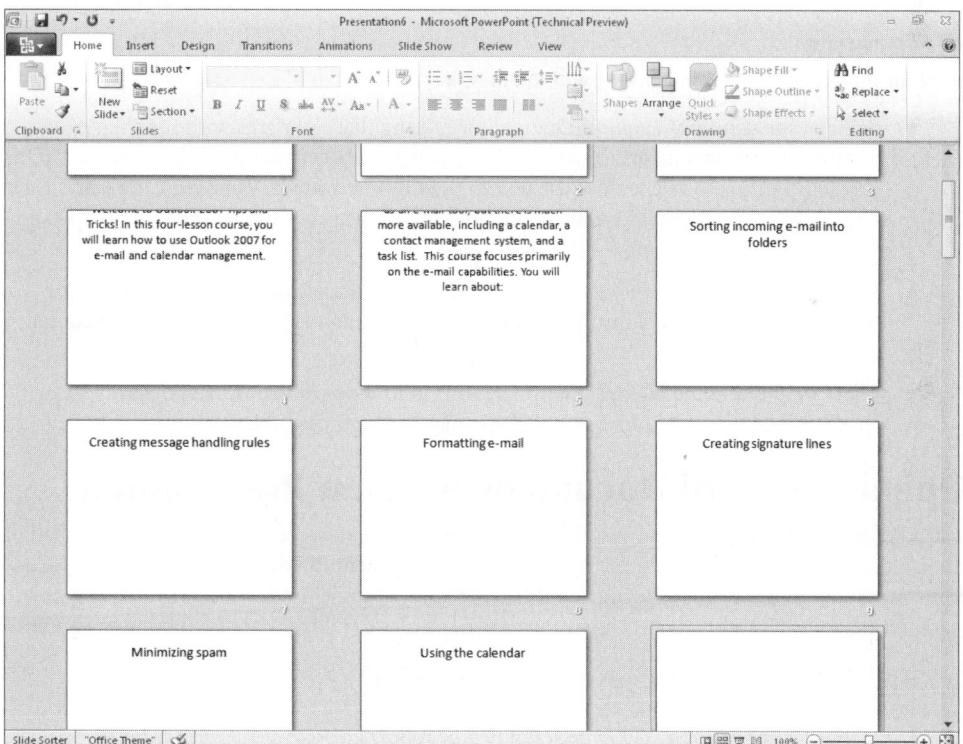

Importing from Other Text-Based Formats

In addition to Word, PowerPoint also imports from plain-text files, from WordPerfect (5.x or 6.x), from Microsoft Works, and from web pages. The procedure is the same as in the preceding steps. If the file does not appear in the Insert Outline dialog box, change the file type to the desired file type.

If you are setting up a plain-text file for import, you obviously won't have the outlining tools from Word at your disposal. Instead, you must rely on tabs. Each line that should be a title slide should start at the left margin; first-level bullet paragraphs should be preceded by a single tab; second-level bullets should be preceded by two tabs, and so on.

Post-Import Cleanup

After importing text from an outline, there will probably be a few minor corrections that you need to make. Run through this checklist:

- The first slide in the presentation might be blank. If it is, then delete it.

- The Title Slide layout may not be applied to the first slide; apply that layout, if necessary. (You can use the Layout list on the Home tab.)

- A theme may not be applied; choose one from the Design tab, if necessary, or format your slide masters and layouts as desired.

Cross-Reference
See Chapter 22 for more information on working with themes. ■

- Some of the text might contain manual formatting that interferes with the theme formatting and creates inconsistency. Remove any manual formatting that you notice. (One way to do this is to select all of the text in the Outline pane by pressing Ctrl+A and then stripping off the manual formatting by pressing Ctrl+Spacebar or by clicking the Reset button in the Slides group on the Home tab.)

- If some of the text is too long to fit comfortably on a slide, change to a different slide layout, such as a two-column list, if necessary. You might also need to split the content into two or more slides.

- There might be some blank bullet points on some slides (if you missed deleting all of the extra paragraph breaks before importing). Delete these bullet points.

Opening a Word Document as a New Presentation

Instead of importing slides from a Word document or other text-based document, as described in the preceding section, you can simply open the Word document in PowerPoint. PowerPoint starts a new presentation file to hold the imported text. This saves some time if you are starting a new presentation anyway, and you don't have any existing slides to merge with the incoming content.

To open a Word document in PowerPoint, follow these steps:

1. **Choose File ⇨ Open.** The Open dialog box appears.

2. **Change the file type to All Outlines.**

3. **Select the document.**

4. **Click Open.** The document outline becomes a PowerPoint presentation, with all Heading 1 paragraphs becoming title slides.

Caution

You can't open or insert a Word outline in PowerPoint if it is currently open in Word. This limitation is an issue only for Word files, not plain text or other formats. ∎

Importing Text from Web Pages

PowerPoint accepts imported text from several web-page formats, including HTML and MHTML (Single File Web Page). It is helpful if the data is in an orderly outline format or if it was originally created from a PowerPoint file, because there will be less cleanup needed.

There are several ways to import from a web page:

- Open a web-page file as you would an outline (see the preceding section), but set the file type to All Web Pages.

- Insert the text from the web page as you would a Word outline (in the Home tab, click Slides ⇨ New Slide arrow ⇨ Slides from Outline).

- Reuse slides from a Web presentation as you would from any other presentation (in the Home tab, click Slides ⇨ New Slide arrow ⇨ Reuse Slides).

Caution

You should use one of the above methods rather than pasting HTML text directly into PowerPoint. This is because when you paste HTML text, you might get additional HTML tags that you don't want, including cross-references that might cause your presentation to try to log onto a Web Server every time you open it. ∎

When importing from a web page, don't expect the content to appear formatted the same way that it was on the web page. We're talking strictly about text import here. The formatting on the web page comes from HTML tags or from a style sheet, neither of which you can import. If you want an exact duplicate of the web page's appearance, take a picture of the page with the Shift+Print Screen command, and then paste it into PowerPoint (Ctrl+V) as a graphic.

If you are importing an outline from an MHTML-format web page that contains pictures, the pictures are also imported into PowerPoint. If importing from a regular HTML file, you cannot import the pictures.

Tip

If you need to show a live Web page from within PowerPoint, try Shyam Pillai's free Live Web add-in, found at www.mvps.org/skp/liveweb.htm. ∎

Managing Slides

After inserting a few slides into a presentation, and perhaps building some content on them, you might decide to make some changes, such as rearranging, deleting, and so on. The following sections explain how to manage and manipulate the slides in a presentation.

Selecting Slides

Before you can issue a command that acts on a slide or a group of slides, you must select the slides that you want to affect. You can do this from either Normal or Slide Sorter view, but Slide Sorter view makes it easier because you can see more slides at once. From Slide Sorter view, or from the Slides pane in Normal view, you can use any of these techniques to select slides:

- To select a single slide, click it.
- To select multiple slides, hold down the Ctrl key as you click each one. Figure 21-20 shows Slides 1, 3, and 6 selected, as indicated by the shaded border around the slides.

FIGURE 21-20

Select slides in Slide Sorter view by holding down the Ctrl key and clicking each slide.

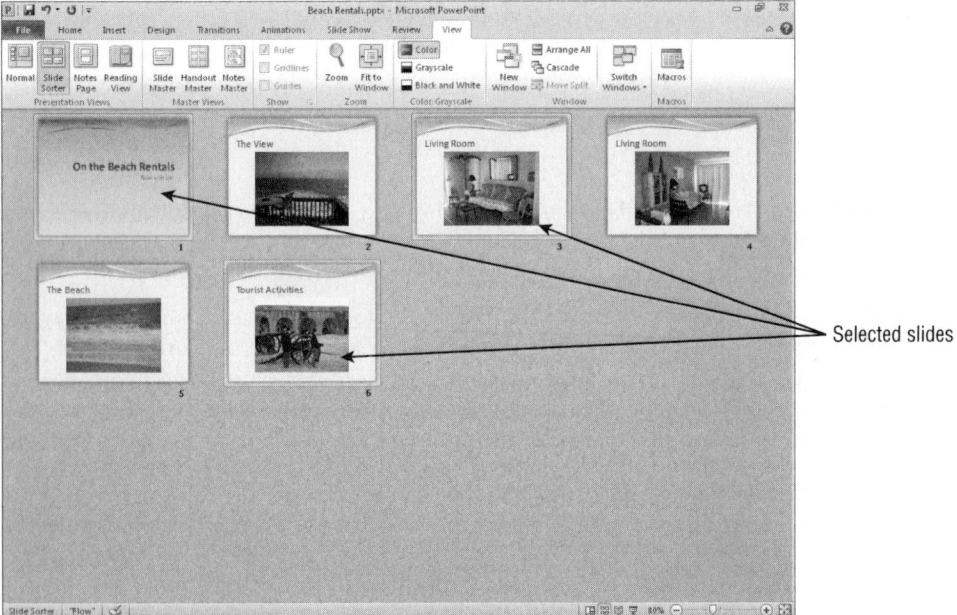

- To select a contiguous group of slides (e.g., Slides 1, 2, and 3), click the first slide, and then hold down the Shift key as you click the last one. All of the slides in between are selected as well.

To cancel the selection of multiple slides, click anywhere outside of the selected slides.

To select slides from the Outline pane in Normal view, click the slide icon to the left of the slide's title; this selects the entire slide, as shown in Figure 21-21. It's important to select the entire slide and not just part of its content before issuing a command such as Delete, because otherwise, the command only affects the portion that you selected.

FIGURE 21-21

Select slides in the Outline pane by clicking the slide icon to the left of the slide title.

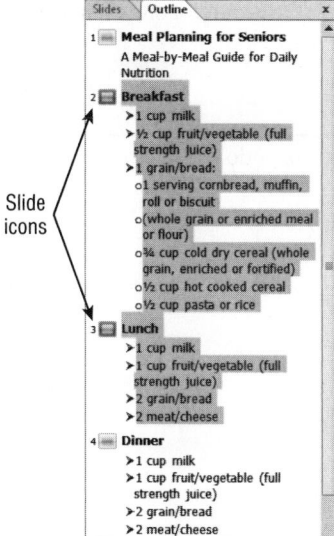

Slide
icons

Deleting Slides

You may want to get rid of some of the slides, especially if you created your presentation using a template that contained a lot of sample content. For example, the sample presentation may be longer than you need, or you may have inserted your own slides instead.

Select the slide or slides that you want to delete, and then do either of the following:

- Right-click the selection and choose Delete Slide.
- Press the Delete key on the keyboard.

Undoing Mistakes

Here's a command that can help you in almost all of the other chapters in this book: undoing. The Undo command allows you to reverse past actions. For example, you can use it to reverse all of the deletions that you made to your presentation in the preceding section. The easiest way to undo a single action is to click the Undo button on the Quick Access Toolbar or press Ctrl+Z. You can click it as many times as you like; each time you click it, you undo one action.

Tip

By default, the maximum number of Undo operations is 20, but you can change this. Choose File ➪ Options, then click Advanced, and in the Editing Options section, change the Maximum Number of Undos setting. Keep in mind that if you set the number of undos too high, it can cause performance problems in PowerPoint. ■

You can undo multiple actions at once by opening the Undo button's drop-down list, as shown in Figure 21-22. Just drag the mouse across the actions that you want to undo (you don't need to hold down the mouse button). Click when the desired actions are selected, and presto, they are all reversed. You can select multiple actions to undo, but you can't skip around. For example, to undo the fourth item, you must undo the first, second, and third ones, as well.

FIGURE 21-22

Use the Undo button to undo your mistakes and the Redo button to reverse an Undo operation.

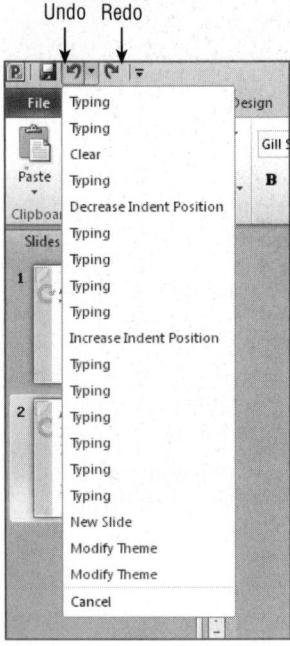

The Redo command is the opposite of Undo. If you make a mistake with the Undo button, you can fix the problem by clicking the Redo button. Like the Undo button, it has a drop-down list, and so you can redo multiple actions at once.

The Redo command is available only immediately after you use the Undo command. If Redo isn't available, a Repeat button appears in its place. The Repeat command enables you to repeat the last action that you performed (and it doesn't have to be an Undo operation). For example, you can repeat some typing, or some formatting. Figure 21-23 shows the Repeat button.

Rearranging Slides

The best way to rearrange slides is to do so in Slide Sorter view. In this view, the slides in your presentation appear in thumbnail view, and you can move them around on the screen to different positions, just as you would manually rearrange pasted-up artwork on a table. Although you can also do this from the Slides pane in Normal view, you are able to see fewer slides at once. As a result, it can be more challenging to move slides around, for example, from one end of the presentation to another. To rearrange slides, use the following steps:

1. **Switch to Slide Sorter view.**

2. **Select the slide that you want to move.** You can move multiple slides at once if you like.

3. **Drag the selected slide to the new location.** The mouse pointer changes to a little rectangle next to the pointer arrow as you drag. A vertical line also appears where the slide will go if you release the mouse button at that point, as shown in Figure 21-24.

4. **Release the mouse button.** The slide moves to the new location.

FIGURE 21-23

The Repeat button appears when Redo is not available and enables you to repeat actions.

Repeat

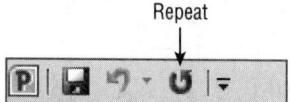

FIGURE 21-24

As you drag a slide, its new position is indicated by a vertical line.

Vertical line
shows
destination

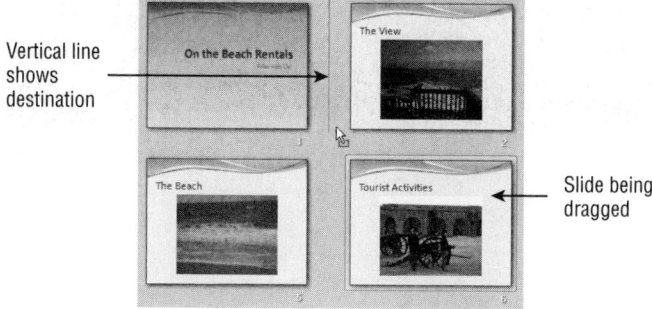

Slide being
dragged

You can also rearrange slides in the Outline pane in Normal view. This is not quite as easy as using Slide Sorter view, but it's more versatile. Not only can you drag entire slides from place to place, but you can also move individual bullets from one slide to another.

Follow these steps to move content in the Outline pane:

1. **Switch to Normal view and display the Outline pane.**

2. **Position the mouse pointer over the slide's icon.** The mouse pointer changes to a four-headed arrow.

3. **Click on the icon.** PowerPoint selects all of the text in that slide.

4. **Drag the slide's icon to a new position in the outline and then release the mouse button.** All of the slide's text moves with it to the new location.

There are also keyboard shortcuts for moving a slide up or down in the Outline pane that may be faster than clicking the toolbar buttons. You can press the Alt+Shift+up-arrow key to move a slide up, and the Alt+Shift+down-arrow key to move a slide down.

These shortcuts work equally well with single bullets from a slide. Just click to the left of a single line to select it, instead of clicking the Slide icon in Step 3.

Using Content Placeholders

Now that you know something about inserting and managing entire slides, let's take a closer look at the content within a slide. The default placeholder type is a multipurpose content placeholder, as shown in Figure 21-25.

FIGURE 21-25

A content placeholder can contain a variety of different elements.

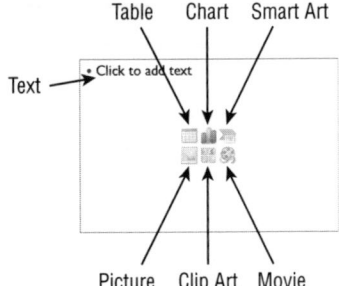

Inserting Content into a Placeholder

To type text into a content placeholder, click inside the placeholder box and start typing. You can enter and edit text as you would in any word-processing program. To insert any other type of content into a placeholder, click one of the icons shown in Figure 21-25. A dialog box opens to help you select and insert that content type.

A content placeholder can hold only one type of content at a time. If you click in the placeholder and type some text, the icons for the other content types disappear. To access them again, you must delete all of the text from the placeholder.

Placeholders versus Manually Inserted Objects

You can insert content on a slide independently of a placeholder by using the Insert tab's buttons and menus. This technique allows you to insert an item in its own separate frame on any slide, to coexist with any placeholder content.

Creating Text Boxes Manually

The difference between a placeholder-inserted object and a manually inserted one is most significant with text boxes. Although you might think that all text boxes are all alike, there are actually some significant differences between placeholder text boxes and manually inserted ones.

Here are some of the characteristics of a text placeholder:

- You cannot create new text placeholder boxes on your own, except in Slide Master view.

Cross-Reference
You learn how to use Slide Master view to create your own layouts that contain custom text placeholders in Chapter 22. ■

- If you delete all of the text from a text placeholder, the placeholder instructions return (in Normal view).
- A text placeholder box has a fixed size on the slide, regardless of the amount or size of text that it contains. You can resize it manually, but if you reapply the layout, the placeholder box snaps back to the original size.
- AutoFit is turned on by default in a text placeholder, so that if you type more text than will fit or resize the frame so that the existing text no longer fits, the text shrinks in size.
- The text that you type in a text placeholder box appears in the Outline pane.

A manual text box, on the other hand, is one that you create yourself using the Text Box tool in the Text group of the Insert tab. Here are some characteristics of a manual text box:

- You can create a manual text box anywhere, and you can create as many as you like, regardless of the layout.
- If you delete all of the text from a manual text box, the text box remains empty or disappears completely. No placeholder instructions appear.
- A manual text box starts out small vertically and expands as you type more text into it.
- A manual text box does not use AutoFit by default; the text box simply becomes larger to make room for more text.
- You cannot resize a manual text box so that the text that it contains no longer fits; PowerPoint refuses to make the text box shorter vertically until you delete some text from it. (However, you can decrease its horizontal width.)
- Text typed in a manual text box does not appear in the Outline pane.

Figure 21-26 shows two text placeholders (one empty) and a text box. Notice that the empty placeholder contains filler text to help you remember that it is there. Notice also that only the text from the placeholder appears in the Outline pane; the text box text does not. Empty text boxes and placeholders do not show up in Slide Show view, so you do not have to worry about deleting any unneeded ones.

FIGURE 21-26

Two text placeholders and a text box

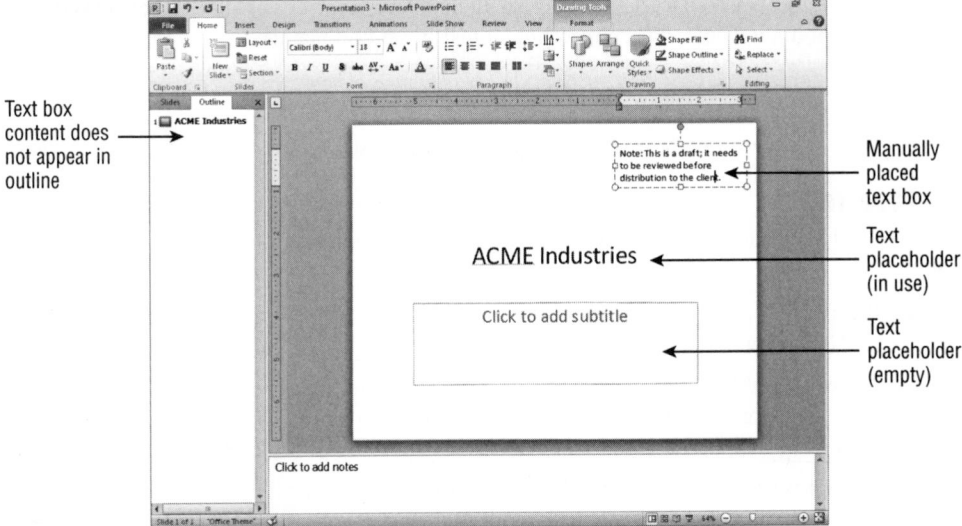

When Should You Use a Manual Text Box?

Graphical content such as photos and charts can work well either in placeholders or as manually inserted objects. However, when it comes to text, you should stick with placeholders as often as possible. Placeholder text appears in the Outline pane, whereas text in a manually inserted text box does not. When the bulk of a presentation's text is in manually created text boxes, the outline becomes less useful because it doesn't contain the presentation text. In addition, when you change to a different formatting theme that includes different positioning for placeholders — for example, to accommodate a graphic on one side — the manual text boxes do not shift. As a result, they might end up overlapping the new background graphic with unattractive results. In a case such as this, you would need to go through each slide manually and adjust the positioning of each text box.

However, there are times when a manually created text box is preferable or even necessary. For example, suppose that you have a schematic diagram of a machine and you need to label some of the parts. Manually placed text boxes are perfect for these little snippets of text that are scattered over the surface of the picture. Manual text boxes are also useful for warnings, tips, and any other information that is tangential to the main discussion. Finally, if you want to vary the placement of the text on each slide (consciously circumventing the consistency provided by layouts) and you want to precisely position each box, then manual text boxes work well because they do not shift their position when you apply different themes or templates to the presentation.

Tip

If you insert text in a placeholder and then change the slide's layout so that the slide no longer contains that placeholder (e.g., if you switch to Title Only or Blank layout), the text remains on the slide, but it becomes an orphan. If you delete the text box, then it simply disappears; a placeholder does not reappear. However, it does not become a manual text box because its content still appears in the Outline pane, whereas a manual text box's content does not. ■

Creating a Text Box Manually

To manually place a text box on a slide, follow these steps:

1. **If necessary, reposition the existing placeholders or objects on the slide to make room for the new text box.**

2. **On the Insert tab, click Text Box in the Text group.** The mouse pointer turns into a vertical line. You can alternately use the Text Box icon in any of the Shapes galleries, such as the one on the Insert tab.

3. **Do either of the following:**

   - To create a text box that automatically enlarges itself horizontally as you type more text but does not automatically wrap text to the next line, click once where you want the text to start, and begin typing.

   - To create a text box with a width that you specify and that automatically wraps text to the next line and grows in height as needed, click-and-drag to draw a box where you want the text box to be. Its height will initially snap back to a single line's height, regardless of the height that you initially draw; however, it will grow in height as you type text into it.

4. **Type the text that you want to appear in the text box.**

Working with Text Boxes

Text boxes (either placeholder or manual) form the basis of most presentations. Now that you know how to create them and how to place text in them, let's take a look at how to manipulate the boxes themselves.

Selecting Text Boxes

On the surface, this topic might seem like a no-brainer. Just click it, right? Well, almost. A text box has two possible *selected* states. One state is that the box itself is selected, and the other is that the insertion point is within the box. The difference is subtle, but it becomes clearer when you issue certain commands. For example, if the insertion point is in the text box and you press Delete, PowerPoint deletes the single character to the right of the insertion point. However, if you select the entire text box and press Delete, PowerPoint deletes the entire text box and everything in it.

To select the entire text box, click its border. You can tell that it is selected because the border appears as a solid line. To move the insertion point within the text box, click inside the text box. You can tell that the insertion point is there because you can see it flashing inside, and also because the box's border now consists of a dashed line. Figure 21-27 shows the difference between the two borders.

FIGURE 21-27

The border of a text box is different when the box itself is selected (left) and when the insertion point is in the box (right).

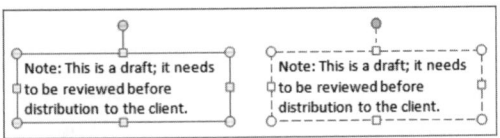

In the rest of this book, when you see the phrase "select the text box," it means that the *box* itself should be selected, and the insertion point should not appear in it. For most of the upcoming sections, it does not make any difference, although in a few cases it does.

Tip

When the insertion point is flashing in a text box, you can press Esc to select the text box itself. ■

You can select more than one text box at once by holding down the Shift key as you click additional text boxes. This technique is useful when you want to select more than one text box, for example, so that you can format them in the same way, or so that you can resize them by the same amount.

Sizing a Text Box

The basic techniques for sizing text boxes in PowerPoint are the same for every object type (for that matter, they are also the same as in other Office applications). To resize a text box, or any object, follow these steps:

1. **Position the mouse pointer over a selection handle for the object.** The mouse pointer changes to a double-headed arrow. If you want to resize proportionally, make sure that you use a corner selection handle, and hold down the Shift key as you drag.

2. **Drag the selection handle to resize the object's border.**

Caution

Allowing PowerPoint to manage placeholder size and position through layouts ensures consistency among your slides. When you start changing the sizes and positions of placeholders on individual slides, you can end up creating consistency problems, such as headings that aren't in the same spot from slide to slide, or company logos that shift between slides. ■

You can also set a text box's size from the Size group on the Drawing Tools Format tab. When the text box is selected, its current dimensions appear in the Height and Width boxes, as shown in Figure 21-28. You can change the dimensions within these boxes.

FIGURE 21-28

You can set an exact size for a text box from the Drawing Tools Format tab's Size group.

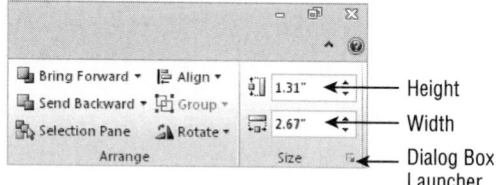

You can also set the size of a text box from the Size and Position dialog box:

1. **Click the Dialog Box Launcher in the Size group on the Drawing Tools Format tab, as shown in Figure 21-28.** The Format Shape dialog box opens with the Size tab displayed.

2. **On the Size tab, set the height and width for the text box, as shown in Figure 21-29.** To keep the size proportional, select the Lock Aspect Ratio check box in the Scale section before you start adjusting the height or width.

3. (Optional) **Click Close to close the dialog box.**

Tip

The Format Shape dialog box is *non-modal*. This means that you can leave it open and continue to work on your presentation. It also means that any changes that you make in this dialog box are applied immediately; there is no Cancel button in the dialog box to cancel your changes. To reverse a change, you can use the Undo command (Ctrl+Z). ■

Positioning a Text Box

To move an object, simply drag it by any part of its border other than a selection handle. Select the object, and then position the mouse pointer over a border so that the pointer turns into a four-headed arrow. Then drag the object to a new position. With a text box, you must position the mouse pointer over a border and not over the inside of the frame; with all other object types, you don't have to be that precise; you can move an object by dragging anywhere within it.

FIGURE 21-29

You can adjust the size of the text box from the Format Shape dialog box.

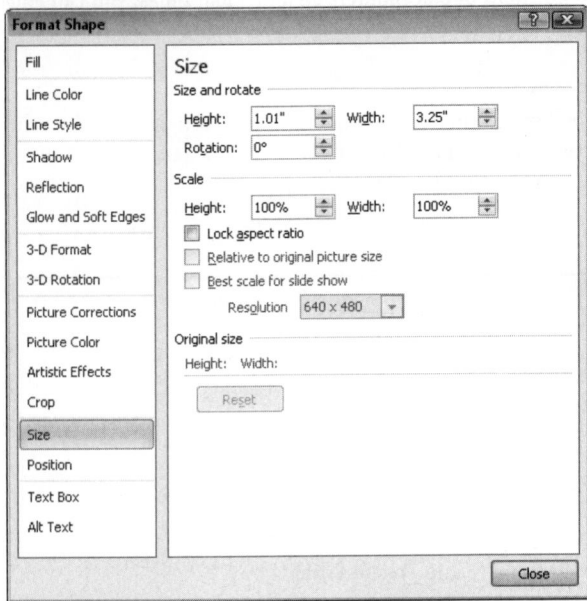

To set an exact position, use the Format Shape dialog box:

1. **Click the Dialog Box Launcher in the Size group on the Drawing Tools Format tab, as shown in Figure 21-28.** The Format Shape dialog box opens.

2. **On the Position tab, shown in Figure 21-30, set the horizontal and vertical position, and the point from which it is measured.** By default, measurements are from the top-left corner of the slide.

3. (Optional) **Click Close to close the dialog box.**

Changing a Text Box's AutoFit Behavior

When there is too much text to fit in a text box, there are three things that may happen:

- **Do Not AutoFit.** The text and the box can continue at their default sizes, and the text can overflow out of the box or be truncated.

- **Shrink Text on Overflow.** The text can shrink its font size to fit in the text box. This is the default setting for placeholder text boxes.

- **Resize Shape to Fit Text.** The text box can enlarge to the size needed to contain the text. This is the default setting for manual text boxes.

FIGURE 21-30

You can adjust the position from the Format Shape dialog box.

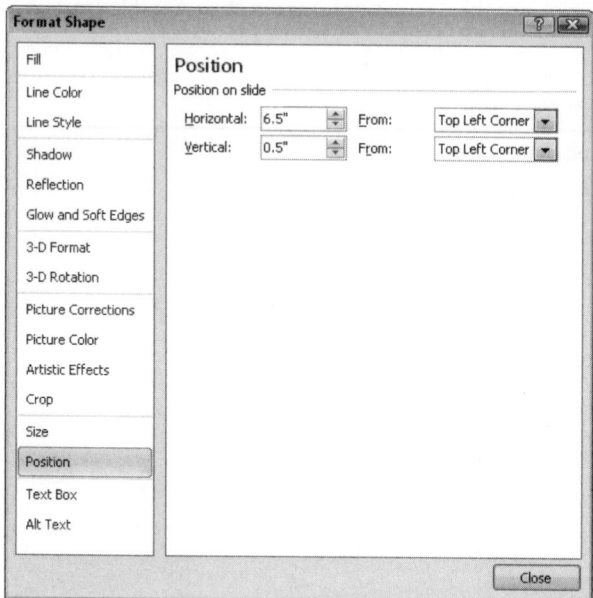

Whenever there is too much text in a placeholder box, the AutoFit icon appears in the bottom-left corner. Click that icon to display a menu, as shown in Figure 21-31. From that menu, you can turn AutoFit on or off. Depending on the text box type, you might not have all the menu items shown in Figure 21-31.

FIGURE 21-31

You can use the AutoFit icon's menu to change the AutoFit setting for a text box.

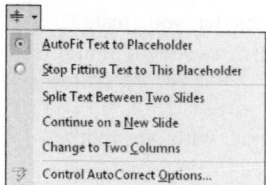

With a manual text box, the AutoFit icon does not appear, and so you must adjust the AutoFit behavior in the text box's properties. The following method works for both manual and place-holder boxes:

1. Right-click the border of the text box and choose Format Shape.

2. Click Text Box.

3. In the AutoFit section, choose one of the AutoFit options, as shown in Figure 21-32.

4. Click Close.

FIGURE 21-32

You can set AutoFit properties in the Format Shape dialog box.

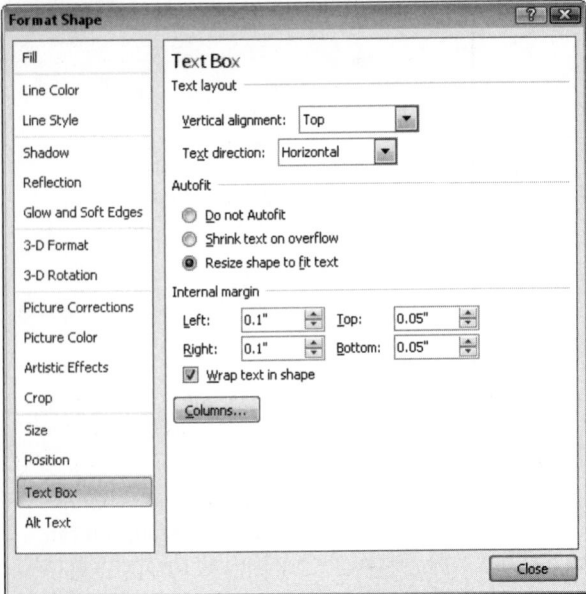

One other setting that also affects AutoFit behavior is the Wrap Text in Shape option. This on/off toggle enables text to automatically wrap to the next line when it reaches the right edge of the text box. By default, this setting is On for placeholder text boxes and for manual text boxes that you create by dragging. However, it is Off by default for manual text boxes that you create by clicking. You can change the setting by displaying the text box's properties, as shown in Figure 21-32, and selecting or deselecting the Wrap Text in Shape check box.

Table 21-5 summarizes the various AutoFit behaviors and how they interact with one another.

TABLE 21-5

AutoFit and Resize Shape to Fit Text Behaviors

Setting	Default For	When Wrap Text in Shape Is On	When Wrap Text in Shape Is Off
Do Not Autofit	n/a	Text overflows at bottom of text box.	Text overflows at right of text box only.
Shrink Text on Overflow	Placeholders	Text shrinks to fit.	Text shrinks to fit.
Resize Shape to Fit Text	Manual text boxes	Text box expands vertically only (default for manual text that you create by dragging).	Text box expands vertically and horizontally (default for manual box that you create by text box clicking). However, if you clicked to create the text box initially, the width keeps expanding until you press Enter.

Summary

This chapter made you a master of files. You can now confidently create new presentations, and save, open, close, and delete PowerPoint presentation files. You can also save files in different formats, search for missing presentations, and lots more. This is rather utilitarian knowledge and not very much fun to practice, but later you will be glad you took the time to learn it, when you have important files you need to keep safe.

In this chapter, you also learned how to create new slides, either from scratch or from outside sources. You learned how to select, rearrange, and delete slides, and how to place content on a slide. Along the way, you learned the difference between a content placeholder and a manually inserted object, and how to create your own text boxes, move and resize objects, and find or replace text. These are all very basic skills, and perhaps not as interesting as some of the more exciting topics to come, but mastering them will serve you well as you build your presentations.

In the next chapter, you'll learn about themes and layouts, two of the innovative features in PowerPoint 2010 that make it such an improvement over earlier versions. You'll find out how a theme differs from a template and how it applies font, color, and effect formatting to a presentation. You will then apply layouts and create your own custom layouts and themes.

Working with Layouts, Themes, and Masters

Most presentations consist of multiple slides, so you'll need a way of ensuring consistency among them. Not only will you want each slide (in most cases) to have the same background, fonts, and text positioning, but you will also want a way of ensuring that any changes you make to those settings later automatically populate across all your slides.

To accomplish these goals, PowerPoint offers layouts, themes, and masters. Layouts determine the positioning of placeholders; themes assign color, font, and background choices; and masters transfer theme settings to the slides and provide an opportunity for repeated content, such as a logo, on each slide. In this chapter you learn how to use layouts, themes, and masters to create a presentation that is attractive, consistent, and easy to manage.

Understanding Layouts and Themes

As you learned in Chapter 21, a *layout* is a positioning template. The layout used for a slide determines what content placeholders will appear and how they will be arranged. For example, the default layout, called *Title and Content*, contains a placeholder for a title across the top of the slide and a multipurpose placeholder for body content in the center.

A *theme* is a group of design settings. It includes color settings, font choices, object effect settings, and, in some cases, also a background graphic. In Figure 22-1, the theme applied is called *Concourse*, and it is responsible for the colored swoop in the corner, the color of that swoop, and the fonts used on the slide. A theme is applied to a *Slide Master*, which is a sample slide and not part of the regular presentation, existing only behind-the-scenes to provide its settings to the real slides. It holds the formatting that you want to be consistent among all the slides in the presentation (or at least a group of them, because a presentation can have multiple Slide Masters). Technically, you do not apply a theme to a slide; you apply a theme to a Slide Master, and then you apply a Slide Master to a slide. That's because a Slide Master can actually contain some additional elements besides the formatting of the theme such as extra graphics, dates, footer text, and so on.

FIGURE 22-1

In Slide Master view, notice that each layout has its own customizable layout master.

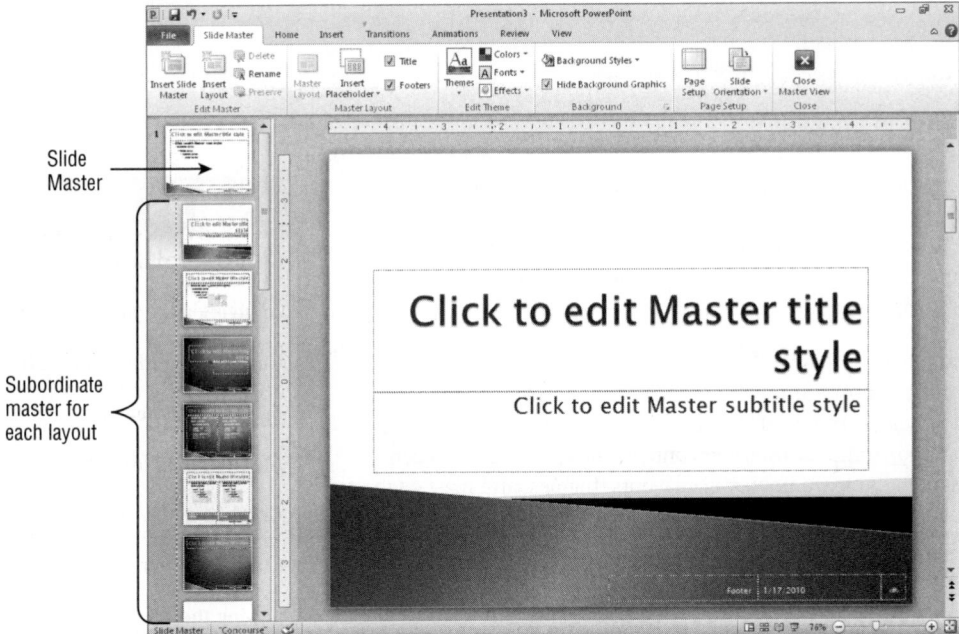

Themes versus Templates

PowerPoint 2007 and 2010 handle themes, layouts, and Slide Masters very differently from earlier versions, and this can take some getting used to if you're upgrading from PowerPoint 2003 or earlier.

In PowerPoint 2003 and earlier, you applied a design template (not a theme) to the Slide Master. A *design template* was a regular PowerPoint template file (.pot extension) with color choices, font choices, and background graphics. You could have multiple Slide Masters in a single presentation, so you could base some slides on a different design template from others. PowerPoint 2007 and 2010 still use templates, but the primary means of changing the presentation's look and feel is to apply different themes to the Slide Master rather than different templates to the presentation as a whole. A template with multiple Slide Masters can carry multiple themes.

A theme is both simpler and more complex than a template. It is simpler because it cannot hold some of the things a real template can hold. A theme can provide only font, color, effect, and background settings to the presentation. (It can also provide slide layouts, but let's postpone that discussion for a bit.) On the other hand, a theme can also do more than a PowerPoint template; you can apply a theme saved as a separate file to other Office applications, so you can share its color, font, and effect settings with Word or Excel, for example.

Where Themes Are Stored

A theme is an XML file (or a snippet of XML code embedded in a presentation or template file). A theme can come from any of these sources:

- **Built-In.** Some themes are embedded in PowerPoint itself and are available from the Themes Gallery on the Design tab regardless of the template in use.

- **Custom (Automatically Loaded).** The default storage location for theme files in Windows Vista or Windows 7 is `C:\Users\`*username*`\AppData\Roaming\Microsoft\ Templates\Document Themes`, where *username* is your login name. For Windows XP, it is `C:\Documents and Settings\`*username*`\Application Data\Microsoft\ Templates\Document Themes`. All themes (and templates containing themes) stored here are automatically displayed among the gallery of theme choices on the Design tab, in a Custom category.

- **Inherited from Starting Template.** If you start a presentation using a template other than the default blank one, that template might have one or more themes included in it.

- **Stored in Current Presentation.** If you modify a theme in Slide Master view while you are working on a presentation, the modified code for the theme is embedded in that presentation file.

- **Stored in a Separate File.** If you save a theme (using any of a variety of methods you'll learn later in this chapter), you create a separate theme file with a `.thmx` extension. These files can be shared among other Office applications, so you can standardize settings such as font and color choices across applications. (Some of the unique PowerPoint portions of the theme are ignored when you use the theme in other applications.)

Themes, Layouts, and Slide Master View

In PowerPoint 2010, the Slide Master has separate layout masters for each layout, and you can customize and create new layouts. For example, Figure 22-1 shows Slide Master view (View ➪ Master Views ➪ Slide Master). Notice along the left side that there is a different, separately customizable layout master for each available layout, all grouped beneath the Slide Master. Any changes you make to the Slide Master trickle down to the individual layout masters, but you can also customize each of the individual layout masters to override a trickle-down setting.

For example, on a particular layout you can choose to omit the background graphic to free up its space on the slide for extra content.

A *master* is a set of specifications that govern formatting and appearance. PowerPoint actually has three masters: the Slide Master (for slides), the Handout Master (for handouts), and the Notes Master (for speaker notes). This chapter deals only with the Slide Master.

Cross-Reference

For more on the Handout and Notes Masters, see Chapter 25. ■

The *Slide Master* holds the settings from a theme and applies them to one or more slides in your presentation. A Slide Master is not exactly the same thing as a theme because a theme can also be external to PowerPoint and used in other programs, but there's a rough equivalency there. A Slide Master is the representation of a particular theme applied to a particular presentation.

Note

Which themes appear in Slide Master view? The ones you have applied to at least one slide in the presentation, plus any custom themes copied from another presentation (see the section, "Copying a Theme from Another Presentation" for more details) and any themes inherited from the template used to create the presentation. The built-in themes do not show up here unless they are in use. ■

When you make changes to a Slide Master, those changes trickle down to the individual layout masters associated with it. When you make changes to an individual layout master, those changes are confined to that layout in that master only.

To enter Slide Master view, choose View ⇨ Master Views ⇨ Slide Master. A Slide Master tab appears. To exit from Slide Master view, choose Slide Master ⇨ Close ⇨ Close Master View, or select a different view from the View tab.

Changing a Slide's Layout

As you construct your presentation, you may find it useful to change a slide's layout. For example, you might want to switch from a slide that contains one big content placeholder to one that has two side-by-side placeholders, to compare/contrast two lists, drawings, or diagrams.

Many of the layouts PowerPoint provides contain multipurpose placeholders that accept various types of content. For example, the default layout, called *Title and Content*, has placeholders for a slide title plus a single type of content — text, a table, a chart, a picture, a piece of clip art, a SmartArt diagram, or a movie. You choose the layout you want based on the number and arrangement of the placeholders, and not the type of content that will go into them.

When you change to a different layout, you change the type and/or positioning of the placeholders on it. If the previous placeholders had content in them, that content shifts to a new location on the slide to reflect the different positioning for that placeholder type. If the new layout does not contain a placeholder appropriate for that content, the content remains on the slide but becomes orphaned. This means it is a free-floating object, outside of the layout. You need to manually position an orphaned object if it's not in the right spot. However, if you later apply a different layout that does contain a placeholder for the orphaned object, it snaps back into that placeholder.

To switch a slide to a different layout, follow these steps:

1. **Select the slide or slides to affect.**
2. **On the Home tab, click Layout in the Slides group.** A menu of layouts appears, as shown in Figure 22-2.
3. **Click the desired layout.**

FIGURE 22-2

Switch to a different layout for the selected slide(s).

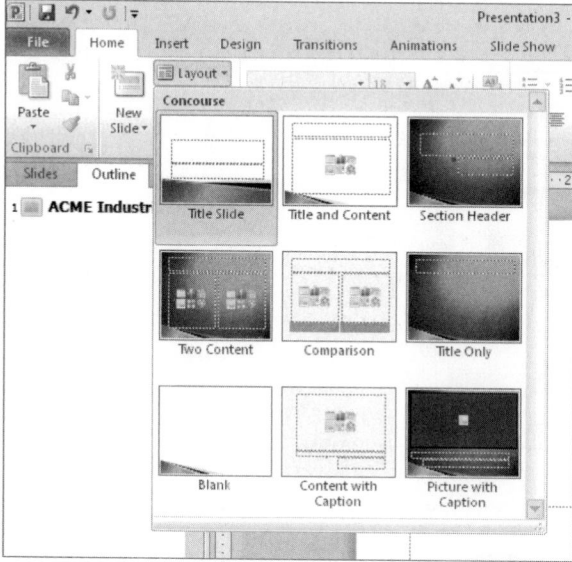

Cross-Reference

If you want to modify a built-in layout or create your own layouts, see "Customizing and Creating Layouts" later in this chapter. ■

When a presentation has more than one Slide Master defined, separate layouts appear for each of the Slide Master themes. Figure 22-3 shows the Layout menu for a presentation that has two Slide Masters.

FIGURE 22-3

When there are multiple Slide Masters, each one's layout is separate.

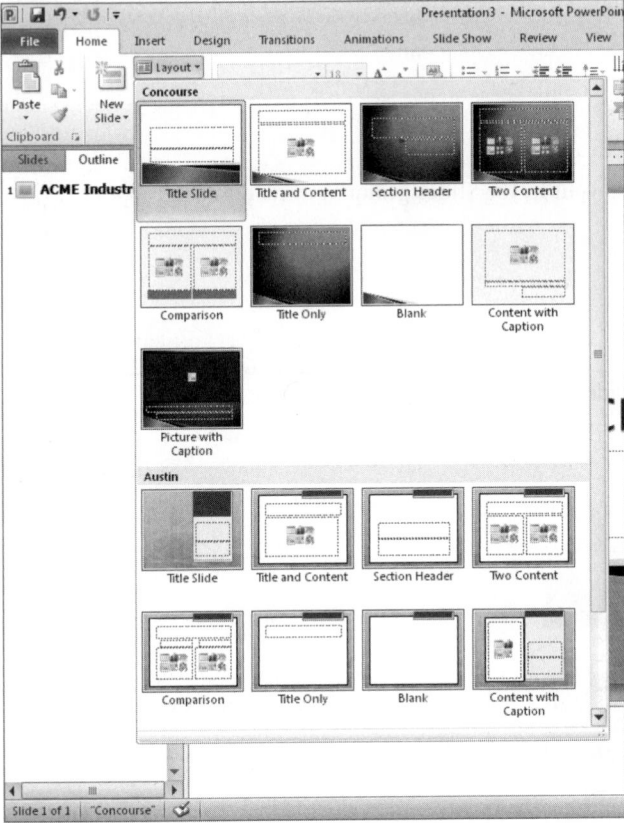

Applying a Theme

As you learned in "Understanding Layouts and Themes" at the beginning of this chapter, themes are the PowerPoint 2010 way of applying different designs to the presentation. A theme usually includes a background graphic, color and font choices, and graphic effect settings. A theme can also include custom layouts. The method for applying a theme depends on whether that theme is already available in the current presentation or not. Some themes are built into PowerPoint so that they are always available; other themes are available only when you use certain templates or when you specifically apply them from an external file. The following sections explain each of those possibilities.

Note

Themes, also called design themes, contain a combination of colors, fonts, effects, backgrounds, and layouts. There are also more specialized themes: color themes, font themes, and effect themes. When this book uses the term *theme* alone, it's referring to a design theme. Where there is potential for confusion, the book calls it a *design theme* to help differentiate it from the lesser types of themes. ■

Applying a Theme from the Gallery

A *gallery* in PowerPoint is a menu of samples from which you can choose. The Themes Gallery is a menu of all of the built-in themes plus any additional themes available from the current template or presentation file.

To select a theme from the gallery, follow these steps:

1. (Optional) **If you want to affect only certain slides, select them.** (Slide Sorter view works well for this.)

2. **On the Design tab, in the Themes group, if the theme you want appears, click it, and skip the rest of these steps.** If the theme you want does not appear, you will need to open the gallery. To do so, click the More button (down arrow with the line over it), as shown in Figure 22-4.

FIGURE 22-4

Open the Themes Gallery by clicking the More button.

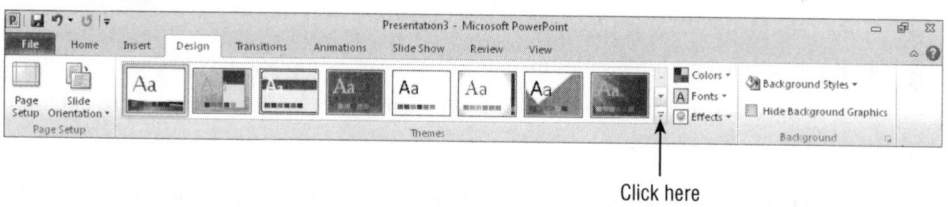

Click here

The Themes Gallery opens, as shown in Figure 22-5. The gallery is divided into sections based on the source of the theme. Themes stored in the current presentation appear at the top; custom themes you have added appear next. Built-in themes appear at the bottom.

Tip

You can drag the bottom-right corner of the menu to resize the gallery. To filter the gallery so that only a certain category of theme appears, click the down-arrow to the right of All Themes at the top, and select a category from the menu that appears. ■

FIGURE 22-5

Select the desired theme from the menu.

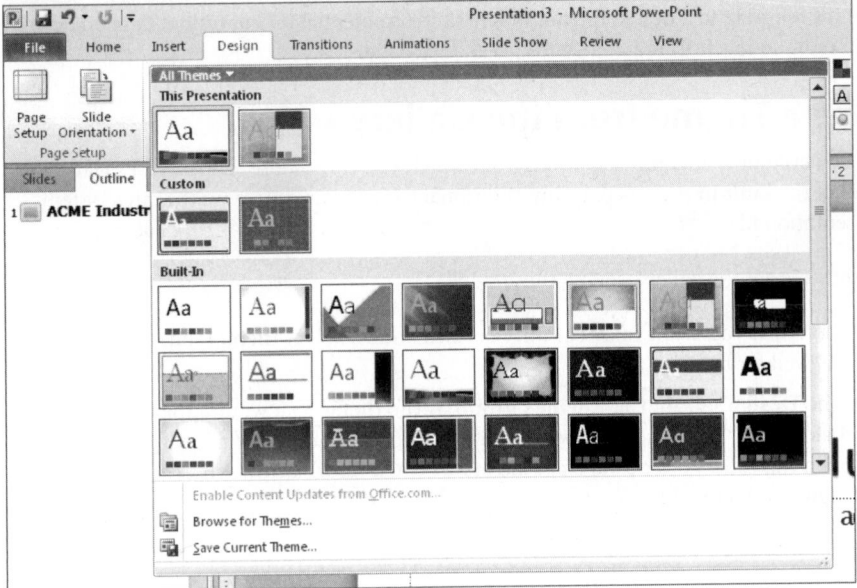

3. **Click the theme you want to apply.**

   - If you selected multiple slides in Step 1, the theme is applied only to them.
   - If you selected a single slide in Step 1, the theme is applied to the entire presentation.

Tip

To override the default behavior in Step 3 so that you can apply a different theme to a single slide, right-click instead of clicking in Step 3 and choose Apply to Selected Slide(s) from the shortcut menu. ■

Applying a Theme from a Theme or Template File

You can open and use externally saved theme files in any Office application. This makes it possible to share color, font, and other settings between applications to create consistency between documents of various types. You can also save and load themes from templates.

Cross-Reference

To create your own theme files, see "Creating a New Theme" later in this chapter. ■

To apply a theme to the presentation from a theme or template file, follow these steps:

1. **On the Design tab, open the Themes Gallery (see Figure 22-5) and click Browse for Themes.** The Choose Theme or Themed Document dialog box opens.

2. **Navigate to the folder containing the file and select it.**

3. **Click Apply.**

Note

Any custom themes you might have previously saved are located by default in `C:\Users\`*`username`*`\` `AppData\Roaming\Microsoft\Templates\Document Themes` **(in Windows Vista or Windows 7) or** `C:\Documents and Settings\`*`username`*`\Application Data\Microsoft\Templates\Document Themes` **(in Windows XP). However, you don't need to navigate to that location to open a theme file because all themes stored here are automatically included in the gallery already.** ■

Changing Colors, Fonts, and Effects

In addition to overall themes, which govern several types of formatting, PowerPoint also provides many built-in color, font, and effect themes that you can apply separately from your choice of overall theme. So, for example, you can apply a theme that contains a background design you like, and then change the colors and fonts for it.

In the following sections, you'll learn how to apply some of these built-in color, font, and effect settings to a presentation without changing the overall theme. Then later in the chapter, you will learn how to save these customized settings as new themes and even how to create your own custom color and font settings in a theme.

Understanding Color Placeholders

To understand how PowerPoint changes colors via a theme, you must know something about how it handles color placeholders in general. PowerPoint uses a set of color placeholders for the bulk of its color formatting. Because each item's color is defined by a placeholder, and not as a fixed color, you can easily change the colors by switching to a different color theme. This way if you decide, for example, that you want all the slide titles to be blue rather than green, you make the change once and it is applied to all slides automatically.

A group of colors assigned to preset placeholders is a *color theme*. PowerPoint contains 20+ built-in color themes that are available regardless of the overall theme applied to the presentation. Because most design themes use placeholders to define their colors, you can apply the desired design theme to the presentation and then fine-tune the colors afterward by experimenting with the built-in color themes.

How many color placeholders are there in a color theme? There are actually 12, but sometimes not all of them are available to be applied to individual objects. When you choose a color theme (Design ⇨ Themes ⇨ Colors), the gallery of themes from which you choose shows only the first eight colors of each color theme. It doesn't matter so much here because you can't apply individual colors from there anyway. When selecting colors from a color picker (used for applying fill and border color to specific objects), as in Figure 22-6, there are 10 theme swatches. And when you define a new custom color theme, there are 12 placeholders to set up. The final two are for visited and unvisited hyperlinks; these colors aren't included in a color picker.

FIGURE 22-6

PowerPoint uses color pickers such as this one to enable you to easily apply color placeholders to objects.

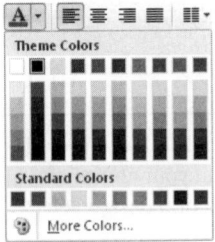

Switching Color Themes

After applying the overall theme you want, you might want to apply different colors. To switch to a different color theme, follow these steps:

1. (Optional) **To apply a different color theme to a Slide Master other than the default one, open Slide Master view (View ⇨ Master Views ⇨ Slide Master) and click the desired Slide Master.** Otherwise, the color change will apply to all slides that use the default Slide Master. The default Slide Master is the first one listed in Slide Master view.

2. **On the Design tab (or the Slide Master tab if in Slide Master view), click Colors.** A gallery of color themes opens.

3. (Optional) **Point to a color theme and observe the preview on the slide behind the list.**

4. **Click the desired color theme.** See Figure 22-7.

Cross-Reference

You can also create custom color themes; see the section, "Creating a Custom Color Theme," later in this chapter for details. ∎

FIGURE 22-7

Select the desired theme from the list.

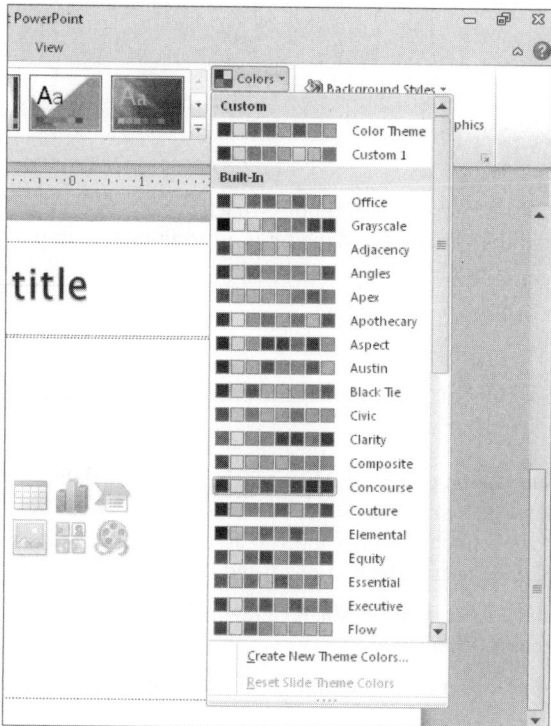

Understanding Font Placeholders

By default in most themes and templates, textbox fonts are not set to a specific font, but to one of two designations: Heading or Body. Then a *font theme* defines what specific fonts to use. To change the fonts across the entire presentation, all you have to do is apply a different font theme.

A *font theme* is an XML-based specification that defines a pair of fonts: one for headings and one for body text. Then that font is applied to the textboxes in the presentation based on their statuses of Heading or Body. For example, all of the slide titles are usually set to Heading, and all of the content placeholders and manual textboxes are usually set to Body.

In a blank presentation (default blank template), when you click inside a slide title placeholder box, you see *Calibri (Headings)* in the Font group on the Home tab. Figure 22-8 shows that the current font is Calibri, but that it is being used only because the font theme specifies it. You could change the font theme to Verdana/Verdana, for example, and then the font designation for that box would appear as *Verdana (Headings)*.

When some text is using a font placeholder rather than a fixed font, (Headings) or (Body) appears after its name in the Font group on the Home tab.

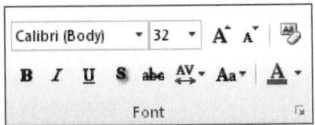

In some font themes, the same font is used for both headings and body. In a default blank presentation both fonts are Calibri, for example, and the Verdana/Verdana set is an additional example. In many other font themes, though, the heading and body fonts are different.

Switching Font Themes

After applying an overall theme, you might decide you want to use different fonts in the presentation. To switch to a different font theme, follow these steps:

1. (Optional) **To apply a different font theme to a Slide Master other than the default one, open Slide Master view (View ⇨ Master Views ⇨ Slide Master) and click the desired Slide Master.** Otherwise, the font change will apply to all slides that use the default Slide Master. The default Slide Master is the first one listed in Slide Master view.

2. **On the Design tab (or Slide Master tab, if in Slide Master view), click Fonts in the Themes group.** A gallery of font themes opens.

3. (Optional) **Point to a font theme and observe the change on the slide behind the list.**

4. **Click the desired font theme.** See Figure 22-9.

Changing the Effect Theme

Effect themes apply to several types of drawings that PowerPoint can construct, including SmartArt, charts, and drawn lines and shapes. They make the surfaces of objects formatted with three-dimensional (3-D) attributes look like different textures (more or less shiny-looking, colors more or less deep, etc.).

To change the effect theme, follow these steps:

1. **In the Themes group on the Design tab, click Effects.** A gallery of effect themes opens.

2. (Optional) **Point to a theme and observe the Live Preview on the slide behind the list.** (This works only if you have an object on that slide that is affected by the effect theme; see the sidebar, "Setting Up a Graphic on Which to Test Effect Themes," to set up such an object.)

3. **Click the desired effect theme.** See Figure 22-10.

FIGURE 22-9

Select the font theme you want for your slide.

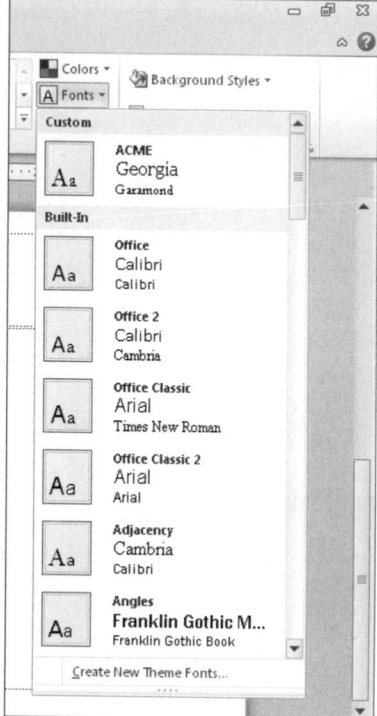

Setting Up a Graphic on Which to Test Effect Themes

Because you haven't worked with any of these graphics yet in this book, you haven't had an opportunity to try them out yet. Effect themes are most evident when you use colorful 3-D graphics, so do the following to construct a dummy diagram that you can use to try out effect themes:

1. **In the Illustrations group on the Insert tab, click SmartArt.**

2. **Click Cycle, click the top-left diagram, and click OK.**

3. **On the SmartArt Tools Design tab, click Change Colors, and click the first sample under Colorful.**

4. **On the SmartArt Tools Design tab, open the SmartArt Styles Gallery and click the first sample under 3-D.**

Now you have a diagram on which you can see the effect themes applied.

FIGURE 22-10

Select the desired effect theme.

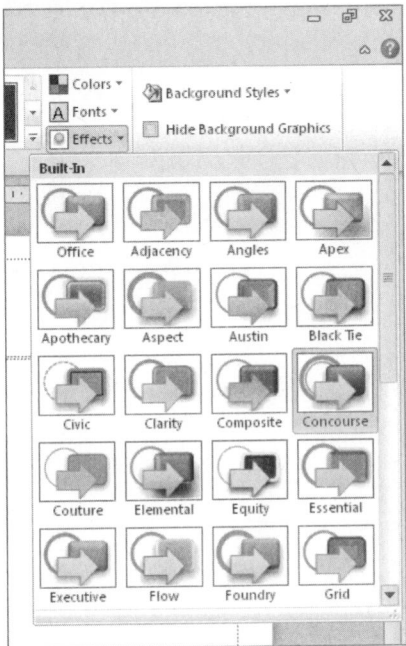

Creating and Managing Custom Color and Font Themes

You can define your own custom color themes and font themes and save them for reuse in other presentations. By default, these are saved in the personal folders for the logged-in user on the local PC, and they remain available to that user regardless of the theme or template in use.

These custom color and font themes are also included if you save the overall theme as a separate theme file (.thmx), as you will learn to do later in this chapter, so that you can take those settings to another PC or send them to some other user.

Creating a Custom Color Theme

A *custom color theme* defines specific colors for each of the 12 color placeholders (including the two that you can't directly use — the ones for hyperlinks). To create a custom color theme, first apply a color theme to the current presentation that is as close as possible to the color theme you want. This makes it easier because you have to redefine fewer placeholders. Then follow these steps:

1. **In the Themes group on the Design tab, open the Colors list and choose Create New Theme Colors.** The Create New Theme Colors dialog box opens.

2. **Type a name for the new color theme in the Name box, replacing the default name (Custom 1, or other number if there is already a Custom 1).**

3. **Click a color placeholder and open its menu.** See Figure 22-11.

Select the color for the chosen placeholder.

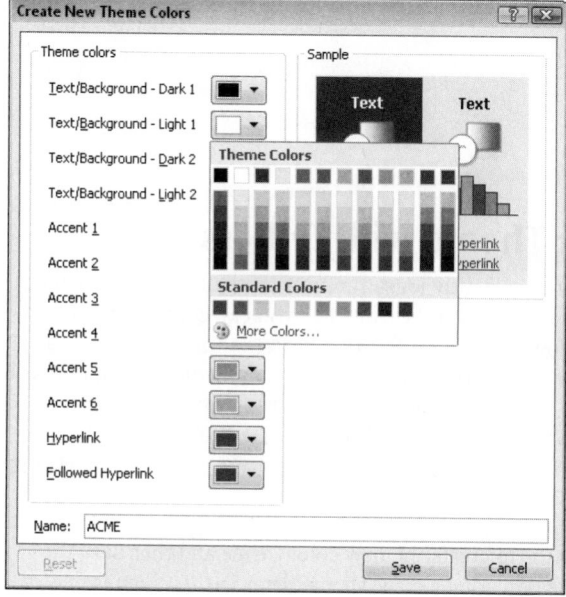

4. **Click a color.** Alternatively, you can click More Colors, select a color from the Colors dialog box (see Figure 22-12), and click OK. The Colors dialog box has two tabs: The Standard tab has color swatches, and the Custom tab enables you to define a color numerically by its RGB (Red Green Blue) or HSL (Hue Saturation Lightness).

5. **Redefine any other colors as needed.**

6. **Click Save.** The color theme is saved and now appears at the top of the Colors Gallery, in the Custom area.

Choose a custom color if none of the standard colors is appropriate.

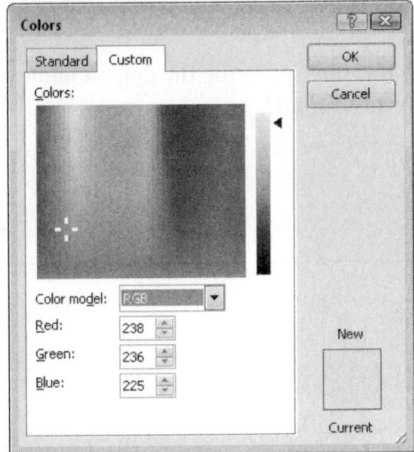

Sharing a Custom Color Theme with Others

A custom color theme is available only to the currently logged-in user on the PC upon which it is created. If you want to share it with another user on the same PC, you can copy it into his or her user folder in Windows Vista or Windows 7: C:\Users*username*\AppData\Roaming\ Microsoft\Templates\Document Themes\Theme Colors, where *username* is that user's login name. In Windows XP, use C:\Documents and Settings*username*\Application Data\Microsoft\Templates\Document Themes\Theme Colors. The default color themes are located in C:\Program Files\Microsoft Office\Document Themes 14\Theme Colors, regardless of the operating system version.

Another way to share a custom color theme is to create the new color theme and then save the (overall) theme to a theme file (.thmx). See "Creating a New Theme" later in this chapter. The resulting theme file will contain the custom colors, as well as the usual theme content.

Deleting a Custom Color Theme

A custom color theme remains until you delete it from the Theme Colors folder for your user profile. To delete a theme color, use Windows Explorer to navigate to C:\Users*username*\ AppData\Roaming\Microsoft\Templates\Document Themes\Theme Colors, and you'll find an .xml file for each of your custom color themes. Delete the files for the color themes that you want to delete. You can also right-click the color theme in the gallery, click Edit, and then click the Delete button in the Edit Theme Colors dialog box.

Tip

If you don't want to delete a custom color theme but you don't want it showing up on your Colors menu in PowerPoint all the time, move the file to a folder outside of the Document Themes folder hierarchy. For example, create an *Unused Themes* folder on your hard disk and move it there until you need it. When you want to use the custom color theme again, move the file back to its original location. ∎

If you don't want to exit from PowerPoint to delete the color theme, you can take advantage of the fact that you can use most dialog boxes in PowerPoint that save or open files to manage files in general. Follow these steps:

1. **Open any dialog box that saves or opens files.** For example, on the Design tab, open the Themes Gallery and choose Browse for Themes.

2. **Navigate to the location of the color themes.** `C:\Users\`*username*`\AppData\Roaming\Microsoft\Templates\Document Themes\Theme Colors`. (See earlier examples of the path if you're using a different operating system.)

3. **Open the File Type list and choose All Files so that all of the files appear.**

4. **Select the file for the color theme that you want to delete and press the Delete key on the keyboard.**

5. **Click Cancel to close the dialog box.**

Creating a Custom Font Theme

You can create your own custom font themes, which are then available in all presentations. A custom font theme defines two fonts: one for headings and one for body text. To create a custom font theme, follow these steps:

1. **In the Themes group on the Design tab, open the Fonts list and choose Create New Theme Fonts.** The Create New Theme Fonts dialog box opens, as shown in Figure 22-13.

2. **Type a name for the new font theme in the Name box, replacing the default text there.**

3. **Open the Heading Font drop-down list, and select the desired font for headings.**

4. **Open the Body Font drop-down list, and select the desired font for body text.**

5. **Click Save.** The font theme is saved and now appears at the top of the Fonts list, in the Custom area.

Sharing a Custom Font Theme with Others

A custom font theme is available only to the currently logged-in user on the PC upon which it is created. If you want to share it with another user on the same PC, you can copy it into his or her user folder. In Windows Vista or Windows 7, use `C:\Users\`*username*`\AppData\Roaming\Microsoft\Templates\Document Themes\Theme Fonts`. In Windows XP, use

C:\Documents and Settings*username*\Application Data\Microsoft\Templates\
Document Themes\Theme Fonts.

FIGURE 22-13

Create a new custom font theme by specifying the fonts to use.

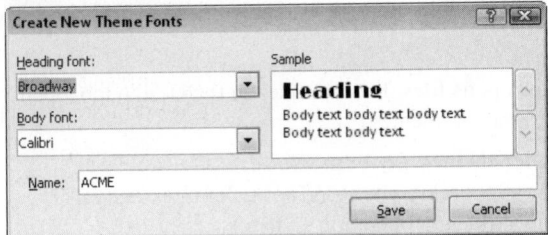

You can also share a custom font theme by creating it and then saving the (overall) theme as a new theme (.thmx) file. Then you can share that theme file with others via e-mail, disk, or other distribution methods.

Cross-Reference
To save your theme as a new theme, see the section, "Creating a New Theme." ∎

Deleting a Custom Font Theme

A custom font theme remains until you delete it from the Theme Fonts folder for your user profile. To delete a font theme, use Windows Explorer to navigate to this folder in Windows Vista or Windows 7: C:\Users*username*\AppData\Roaming\Microsoft\Templates\Document Themes\Theme Fonts. In Windows XP, use C:\Documents and Settings*username*\Application Data\Microsoft\Templates\Document Themes\Theme Fonts.

Delete the files for the font themes that you want to delete.

You can also delete the theme from within PowerPoint by browsing for the file with any dialog box that saves or opens files, or by right-clicking the font theme in the gallery, clicking Edit, and then clicking Delete in the Edit Theme Fonts dialog box.

Cross-Reference
Deleting a custom font theme from a dialog box is essentially the same as deleting a custom color theme. See the section, "Deleting a Custom Color Theme," for more details. ∎

Changing the Background

The *background* is the color, texture, pattern, or image that is applied to the entire slide (or Slide Master), upon which everything else sits. By its very definition, it applies to the entire surface of the slide; you cannot have a partial background. However, you can have a background graphic overlaid on top of the background. A *background graphic* is a graphic image placed on the Slide Master that complements and works with the background.

It's important to understand the distinction between a background and a background graphic because even though most themes contain both, they are set up differently, and making the change you want to the overall appearance of your slides often involves changing both. For example, Figure 22-14 shows the Concourse theme applied to a Slide Master. The slide background is pure white, and a blue-and-black background graphic is overlaid on it.

A slide's background is separate from its background graphic(s) if any are present.

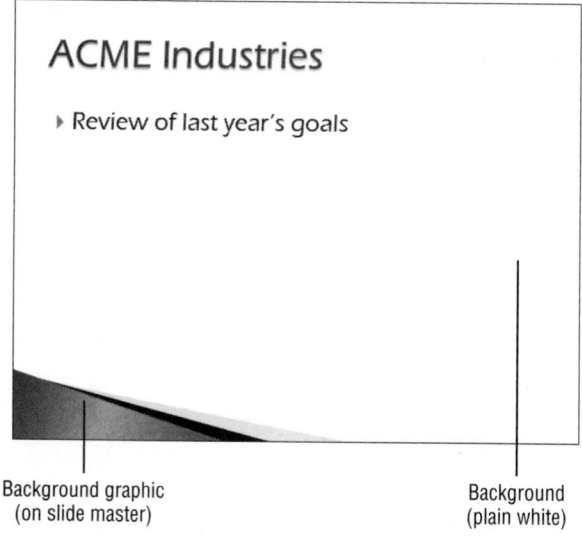

Background graphic
(on slide master)

Background
(plain white)

Most themes consist of both background formatting (even if it is just a solid color) and a background graphic. The background graphics included in the built-in themes in PowerPoint are unique to those themes and not available as separate graphics outside of them. So, for example, if you want the colored swoop shown in Figure 22-14, the only way to get it is to apply the Concourse theme. Because the decorative background graphics are unique to each theme, many people choose a theme based on the desired background graphic and then customize the Slide Master's appearance to modify the theme as needed.

Tip

To use a background graphic from one template with the look-and-feel of another, apply the first theme to a slide, and then in Slide Master view copy the background graphic to the clipboard. Then apply the second theme and paste the graphic from the clipboard into the Slide Master. ■

Applying a Background Style

Background styles are preset background formats that come with the built-in themes in PowerPoint. Depending on the theme you apply, different background styles are available. These background styles all use the color placeholders from the theme, so their color offerings change depending on the color theme applied.

To apply a background style, follow these steps:

1. (Optional) **To affect only certain slides, select them.** (Or, to affect certain layouts, go into Slide Master view and choose the layouts.)

2. **In the Background group on the Design tab, click Background Styles.** A gallery of styles appears, as shown in Figure 22-15.

FIGURE 22-15

Apply a preset background style.

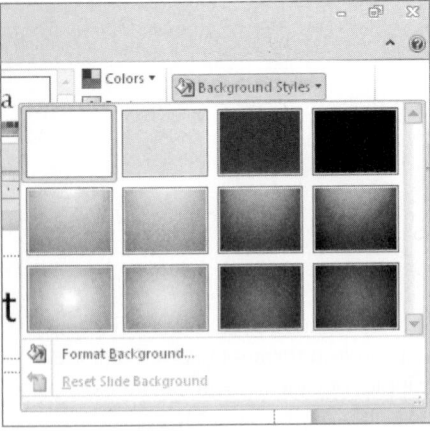

3. **Click the desired style to apply it to the entire presentation.** Alternatively, you can right-click the desired style and choose Apply to Selected Slides.

You cannot customize background styles or add your own custom background styles; there are always 12 of them, and they are always determined by the theme. If you need a different background, you can choose Format Backgrounds and then customize the background settings as described in the following sections.

Applying a Background Fill

A custom background fill can include solid colors, gradients, textures, or graphics. This section covers how to specify your own background fill, which involves the following steps:

1. (Optional) **To affect only certain slides, select them.** (Or, to affect certain layouts, go into Slide Master view and choose the layouts.)

2. **In the Background group on the Design tab, click Background Styles.** The Background Styles Gallery opens.

3. **Click Format Background.** The Format Background dialog box opens.

4. **Choose the option button that best describes the type of fill you want.** See Figure 22-16.

FIGURE 22-16

Select a background fill type, and configure the options for the type you chose.

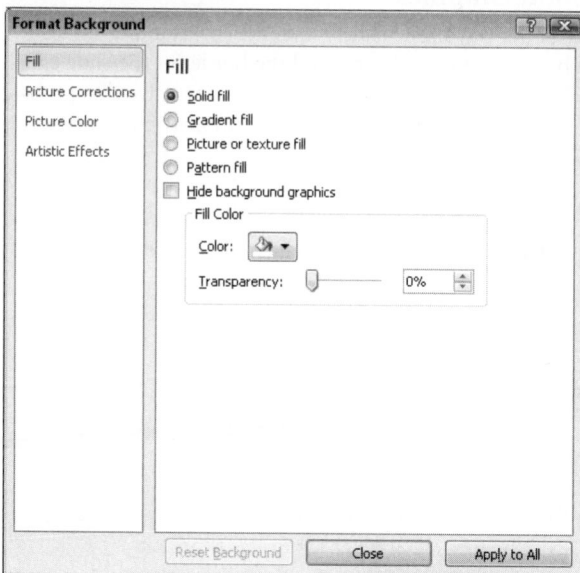

5. **Set the options for the fill type that you chose.** For example, in Figure 22-16, click the Color button and choose a solid color. The changes you make apply immediately.

6. (Optional) **To apply the change to all slides, click Apply to All.** Otherwise, the change will apply only to the slides you selected in Step 1.

7. (Optional) **To apply a different background to some other slides, select them and repeat Steps 4 and 5.** The Format Background dialog box is non-modal, so its changes are applied immediately and you can select things in the presentation file without closing it.

8. Click Close to exit the dialog box.

Working with Background Graphics

In the preceding steps, one of the fill types you could choose was Picture or Texture Fill. This type of fill covers the entire background with the picture or texture that you specify.

This is not a background graphic, however. A *background graphic* is an object or a picture overlaid on top of the background on the Slide Master. It complements the background, and it might or might not cover the entire background.

Note
Some theme-provided background graphics actually consist of multiple shapes grouped together. You can ungroup them so that you can modify or remove only a portion of the background graphic. ■

Displaying and Hiding Background Graphics

Sometimes a background graphic can get in the way of the slide's content. For example, on a slide that contains a large chart or diagram, a background graphic around the border of the slide can overlap the content. You don't have to delete the background graphic entirely to solve this problem — you can turn it off for individual slides. To hide the background graphics on one or more slides, follow these steps:

1. Select the slide or slides to affect.

2. In the Background group on the Design tab, select the Hide Background Graphics checkbox.

Deselect the checkbox to redisplay the background graphics later as needed.

Deleting Background Graphics

The background graphics reside on the Slide Master, so to remove one, you must use Slide Master view. Follow these steps:

1. **In the Master Views group on the View tab, click Slide Master.** The Slide Master view opens.

2. Select the Slide Master or layout master that contains the graphic to delete.

3. Click the background graphic to select it.

4. Press the Delete key on the keyboard.

Tip

Some background graphics are on the Slide Master itself, and others are on individual layout masters. The background graphics on the Slide Master trickle down to each of its layout masters, but can't be selected/ deleted from the individual layout masters.

To use a background graphic only on certain layouts, cut it from the Slide Master to the Clipboard (Ctrl+X), and then paste it individually onto each layout master desired (Ctrl+V). Alternatively, turn on the background graphic for the Slide Master and then use Hide Background Graphics on individual layout masters that should not contain it. ■

Adding Your Own Background Graphics

You can add your own background graphics, either to the Slide Master or to individual layout masters. This works just like adding any other graphic to a slide, except you add it to the master instead of to an individual slide.

Inserting pictures is covered in greater detail in Chapter 24, but here are the basic steps for adding a background graphic:

1. Display the Slide Master or layout master upon which you want to place the background graphic.

2. Do any of the following:

   - In the Images group on the Insert tab, click Picture. Select a picture to insert and click Open.

   - In the Images group on the Insert tab, click Clip Art. Search for a piece of clip art to use, and insert it on the master.

   - In any application (including PowerPoint), copy any graphic to the Clipboard by pressing Ctrl+C; then display the master and paste the graphic by pressing Ctrl+V.

Tip

Most of the background graphics that come with the built-in themes are either semi-transparent or use one of the placeholder colors for their fill. Therefore, changing the color theme also changes the color of the background graphic. Keep that in mind if you are creating your own background graphics; it's better to use theme colors or transparency than to use fixed colors that might clash with a color theme that you later apply. ■

Working with Placeholders

As a review, to enter Slide Master view, display the View tab and click Slide Master in the Master Views group. One or more Slide Masters appear in the left pane, with its own subordinate layout masters. A Slide Master has five preset placeholders that you can individually remove or move around. Figure 22-17 points them out on a Slide Master with the Concourse theme applied, but they might be in different locations in other themes:

FIGURE 22-17

Each Slide Master contains these placeholders (or can contain them).

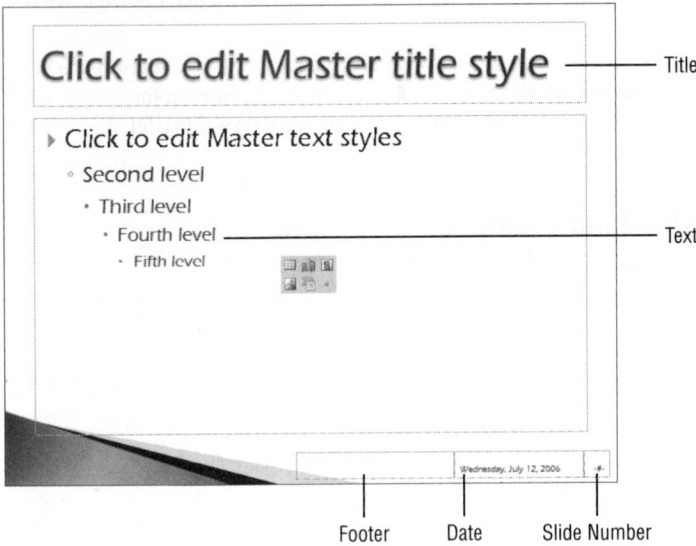

Click to edit Master title style ——— Title

▸ Click to edit Master text styles
  ◦ Second level
    • Third level
      • Fourth level ——————————— Text
        • Fifth level

Wednesday, July 12, 2006

Footer   Date   Slide Number

- **Title.** The placeholder for the title on each slide
- **Text.** The main content placeholder on each slide
- **Date.** The box that displays the current date on each slide
- **Slide Number.** The box that displays the slide number on each slide
- **Footer.** A box that displays repeated text at the bottom of each slide

These elements are all enabled by default, but the Footer is empty by default so it is not visible on individual slides unless you type some text into it in Slide Master view or add text to it using Insert Header and Footer. Each of these elements trickles down to the layout masters beneath it, so formatting, moving, or deleting one of these elements from the Slide Master also changes it on each of the layouts. See Figure 22-17 for an example of the various placeholders.

Formatting a Placeholder

You can format the text in each of the placeholders on the Slide Master just like any regular text, and that formatting carries over to all slides and layouts based on it. For example, if you format the code in the Slide Number box with a certain font and size, it will appear that way on every slide that uses that Slide Master. You can also format the placeholder boxes just like any other textboxes. For example, you can add a border around the Page Number's box, and/or fill its background with color.

Tip

If you want to make all of the text in a heading all-caps or small-caps, use the Font dialog box. From the Home tab, click the Dialog Box Launcher in the Font group and select the Small Caps or All Caps checkbox there. ∎

Moving, Deleting, or Restoring Placeholders

You can move each of the placeholders on the Slide Master or an individual layout master. For example, you might decide you want the Footer box at the top of the slide rather than the bottom, or that you want to center the slide number at the bottom of the slide:

- To move a placeholder, click it to select it and then drag its border.

- To delete one of the placeholders on the Slide Master, select its box and press the Delete key on the keyboard. Deleting it from the Slide Master deletes it from all of the associated layouts as well.

- To remove all three of the footer placeholders at once (Date, Footer, and Slide Number), display the Slide Master tab and deselect the Footers checkbox.

- To restore deleted placeholders on the Slide Master, display the Slide Master tab and select the Footers checkbox. If any of the footer placeholders (Date, Footer, or Slide Number) were previously deleted, they reappear.

Caution

Restored placeholders might not appear in the same spots as they did originally; you might need to move them. To put the placeholders back to their original locations, reapply the theme from the Themes button in the Edit Theme group on the Slide Master tab. ∎

Here are some more details you should remember about deleting and restoring:

- On an individual layout master, you can quickly delete and restore the Title and Footer placeholders by selecting or deselecting the Title and Footers checkboxes on the Slide Master tab. The *footer* that this checkbox refers to is actually all three of the bottom-of-the-slide elements: the actual footer, the Date box, and the Slide Number box.

- You can also individually delete the placeholders from a layout master, the same as you can on a Slide Master. Just select a placeholder box and press the Delete key.

- You can restore all of the placeholders, except Text, by selecting the aforementioned checkboxes on the Slide Master tab. Whenever any of the three footer boxes are missing, the Footers checkbox becomes cleared, and you can restore the missing box or boxes by reselecting the checkbox.

- You cannot restore the Text placeholder, however, on an individual layout master. You must re-create it with the Insert Placeholder command.

Cross-Reference

For more on the Insert Placeholder command, see the section, "Customizing and Creating Layouts." ∎

Displaying the Date, Number, and Footer on Slides

Even though the placeholders for Date, Number, and Footer might appear on the Slide Master, they do not appear on the actual slides in the presentation unless you enable them. This might seem counterintuitive at first, but it's actually a benefit. PowerPoint enables you to turn the date, number, and footer on and off without having to delete, re-create, or reformat their placeholders. You can decide at the last minute whether you want them to display or not, and you can choose differently for different audiences and situations.

You can control all three areas from the Header and Footer dialog box. To open it, in the Text group of the Insert tab, click Header and Footer. (Clicking Date and Time or clicking Number opens the same dialog box.) Then on the Slide tab, select the checkboxes for each of the three elements that you want to use, as shown in Figure 22-18.

FIGURE 22-18

Choose which footer elements should appear on slides.

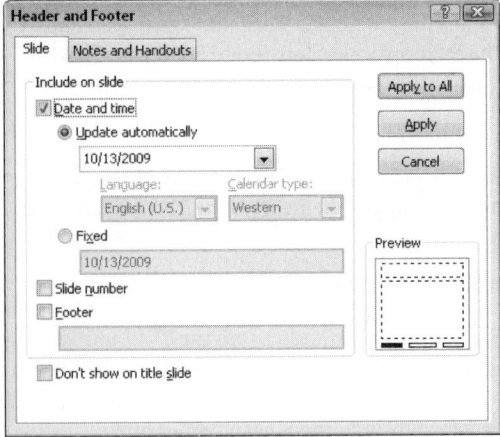

Date and Time

You can set Date and Time either to Update Automatically or to Fixed:

- **Update Automatically.** This pulls the current date from the computer's clock and formats it in whatever format you choose from the drop-down list. You can also select a language and a Calendar Type (although this is probably not an issue unless you are presenting in some other country than the one for which your version of PowerPoint was developed).

- **Fixed.** This prints whatever you enter in the Fixed textbox. When Fixed is enabled it defaults to today's date in the m/dd/yyyy format.

Tip

In addition to (or instead of) placing the date on each slide, you can insert an individual instance of the current date or time on a slide, perhaps as part of a sentence. To do so, position the insertion point inside a textbox or placeholder and then, on the Insert tab, click Date and Time. Select the format you want from the dialog box that appears and click OK. ■

Slide Number

The Slide Number option shows the slide number on each slide, wherever the Number placeholder is positioned. You can format the Number placeholder on the master slide with the desired font, size, and other text attributes.

By default, slide numbering starts with 1. You can start with some other number if you like by following these steps:

1. **Close Slide Master view if it is open.** To do so, click the Close Master View button in the Close group on the Slide Master tab.
2. **On the Design tab, click Page Setup in the Page Setup group.** The Page Setup dialog box opens.
3. **In the Number Slides From box, increase the number to the desired starting number.**
4. **Click OK.**

Tip

You can insert the slide number on an individual slide, either instead of or in addition to the numbering on the Slide Master. Position the insertion point, and then on the Insert tab, click Slide Number. If you are in Slide Master view, this places a code on the Slide Master for the slide number that looks like this: ⟨#⟩. If you are on an individual slide, it inserts the same code, but the code itself is hidden and the actual number appears. ■

Footer

The footer is blank by default. Select the Footer checkbox, and then enter the desired text in the Footer box. You can then format the footer text from the Slide Master as you would any other text. You can also enter the footer text in the Header and Footer dialog box's Footer textbox.

Don't Show on Title Slide

The Don't Show on Title Slide checkbox in the Header and Footer dialog box suppresses the date/time, page number, and footer on slides that use the Title Slide layout. Many people like to hide those elements on title slides for a cleaner look and to avoid repeated information (e.g., if the current date appears in the subtitle box on the title slide).

Customizing and Creating Layouts

In addition to customizing the Slide Master (including working with its preset placeholder boxes, as you just learned), you can fully customize the individual layout masters.

A layout master takes some of its settings from the Slide Master with which it is associated. For example, by default, it takes its background, fonts, theme colors, and preset placeholder positioning from the Slide Master. But the layout master also can be individually customized; you can override the Slide Master's choices for background, colors, and fonts; and you can create, modify, and delete various types of content placeholders.

Understanding Content Placeholders

You can insert seven basic types of content on a PowerPoint slide: Text, Picture, Chart, Table, Diagram, Media (video or sound), and Clip Art. A placeholder on a Slide Master or layout master can specify one of these types of content that it will accept, or you can designate it as a Content placeholder, such that it will accept any of the seven types. Most of the layouts that PowerPoint generates automatically for its themes use the Content placeholder type because it offers the most flexibility. By making all placeholders Content placeholders rather than a specific type, PowerPoint can get by with fewer separate layout masters because users will choose the desired layout based on the positioning of the placeholders, not their types.

A Content placeholder appears as a text placeholder with a small palette of icons in the center, one for each of the content types. Each content placeholder can hold only one type of content at a time, so as soon as the user types some text into the Content placeholder or clicks one of the icons in the palette and inserts some content, the placeholder becomes locked into that one type of content until the content is deleted from it.

Note

If a slide has a placeholder that contains some content (any type), selecting the placeholder and pressing Delete removes the content. To remove the placeholder itself from the layout, select the empty placeholder and press Delete. If you then want to restore the placeholder, reapply the slide layout to the slide. ■

You can move and resize a placeholder on a layout master as you would any other object. Drag a selection handle on the frame to resize it, or drag the border of the frame (not on a selection handle) to move it.

Cross-Reference

The Content placeholders were identified back in Chapter 21. You can also see Chapter 21 for more on moving and resizing an object. ■

Adding a Custom Placeholder

You can add a custom placeholder to an individual layout master. This makes it easy to build your own custom layouts.

To add a custom placeholder, follow these steps:

1. In Slide Master view, select the layout master to affect.

2. In the Master Layout group on the Slide Master tab, click the bottom part of the Insert Placeholder button to open its menu.

3. **Click Content to insert a generic placeholder, or click one of the specific content types.** See Figure 22-19. The mouse pointer becomes a cross-hair.

FIGURE 22-19

Create a new placeholder on a slide.

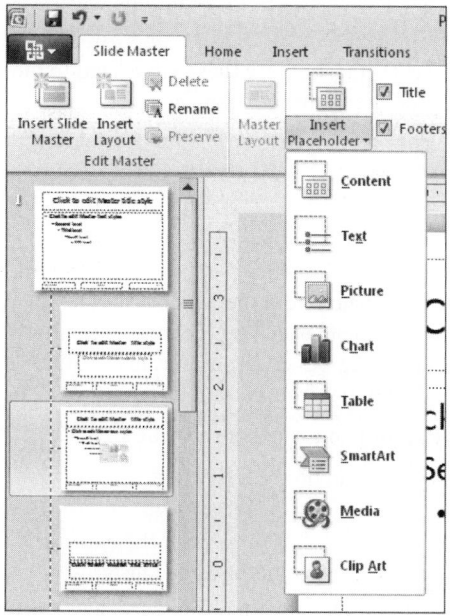

4. **Drag on the slide to draw a placeholder box of the size and position desired.** A blue box appears showing where the placeholder box will go. When you release the mouse button, the new placeholder appears on the slide.

Deleting and Restoring a Custom Placeholder

To delete a custom placeholder, select it and press the Delete key, just as you learned to do earlier with the preset placeholders.

The difference between custom and preset placeholders is not in the deleting, but rather in the restoring. You can immediately undo a deletion with Ctrl+Z, but you cannot otherwise restore a deleted custom placeholder from a layout master. PowerPoint retains no memory of the content placeholders on individual layouts. Therefore, you must re-create any content placeholders that you have accidentally deleted.

Tip

To restore one of the built-in layouts, copy it from another Slide Master. See the sections "Duplicating and Deleting Layouts" and "Copying Layouts between Slide Masters" later in this chapter. ■

Overriding the Slide Master Formatting for a Layout

You can apply formatting to a layout in almost exactly the same ways as you apply formatting to a regular slide or to a Slide Master. Only a few things are off-limits:

- You cannot apply a different theme to individual layouts under a common Slide Master. To use a different theme for some slides, you have to create a whole new Slide Master (covered later in this chapter).

- You cannot apply a different font, color, or effect theme, because these are related to the main theme and the Slide Master. If you need different fonts or colors on a certain layout, specify fixed font formatting for the text placeholders in that layout, or specify fixed color choices for objects.

Cross-Reference

For more on Slide Masters, see the section, "Managing Slide Masters." ■

- You cannot delete a background graphic that is inherited from the Slide Master; if you want it only on certain layouts, delete it from the Slide Master, and then paste it individually onto each layout desired, or select Hide Background Graphics from the Slide Master tab and then deselect Hide Background Graphics from certain layouts.

- You cannot change the slide orientation (Portrait or Landscape) or the slide size.

So what *can* you do to an individual layout, then? Plenty. You can do the following:

- Apply a different background.

- Reposition, resize, or delete preset placeholders inherited from the Slide Master.

- Apply fixed formatting to text placeholders, including different fonts, sizes, colors, attributes, indents, and alignment.

- Apply formatting using theme colors and theme fonts.

- Apply fixed formatting to any placeholder box, including different fill and border styles and colors.

- Create manual textboxes and type any text you like into them. You might do this to include copyright notice on certain slide layouts, for example.

- Insert pictures or clip art that should repeat on each slide that uses a certain layout.

Creating a New Layout

In addition to modifying the existing layouts, you can create your own brand-new layouts, defining the exact placeholders you want. To create a new layout, follow these steps:

1. **From Slide Master view, click the Slide Master with which to associate the new layout.**

2. **Click Insert Layout in the Edit Master group of the Slide Master tab.** A new layout appears. Each new layout you create starts with preset placeholders inherited from the Slide Master for Title, Footer, Date, and Slide Number.

3. (Optional) **Delete any of the preset placeholders that you don't want.**

4. Insert new placeholders as needed.

5. (Optional) Name the layout.

Cross-Reference
To insert a placeholder, see the section, "Adding a Custom Placeholder," earlier in this chapter. To name the layout, see the next section, "Renaming a Layout." ∎

Note
The new layout is part of the Slide Master, but not part of the theme. The theme is applied to the Slide Master, but at this point their relationship ends; and changes that you make to the Slide Master do not affect the existing theme. To save your custom layout(s), you have two choices: You can save the presentation as a template, or you can save the theme as a separate file. You learn more about saving themes in "Managing Themes" later in this chapter. ∎

Renaming a Layout

Layout names can help you determine the purpose of a layout if it is not obvious from viewing its thumbnail image.

To change the name of a layout, or to assign a name to a new layout you've created, follow these steps:

1. **In Slide Master view, right-click the layout and choose Rename Layout.** The Rename Layout dialog box opens.

2. **Type a new name for the layout, replacing the existing name.**

3. **Click Rename.**

Duplicating and Deleting Layouts

You might want to copy a layout to get a head start on creating a new one. To copy a layout, right-click the layout in Slide Master view and choose Duplicate Layout. A copy of the layout appears below the original.

If you are never going to use a certain layout, you might as well delete it; every layout you can delete makes the file a little bit smaller. To delete a layout, right-click the layout in Slide Master view and choose Delete Layout.

Caution
You might have a couple of layouts at the bottom of the list that use vertical text. These are for users of Asian languages. They show up in the New Slide and Layout galleries on the home tab if you have certain Asian languages enabled on your system. Don't delete them if you will sometimes need to create Asian-language slides. ∎

Copying Layouts between Slide Masters

When you create additional Slide Masters in the presentation, any custom layouts you've created for the existing Slide Masters do not carry over. You must manually copy them to the new Slide Master.

To copy a layout from one Slide Master to another, follow these steps:

1. **In Slide Master view, select the layout to be copied.**
2. **Press Ctrl+C.**
3. **Select the Slide Master under which you want to place the copy.**
4. **Press Ctrl+V.**

You can also copy layouts between Slide Masters in different presentations. To do so, open both presentation files, and then perform the previous steps. The only difference is that after Step 2, you must switch to the other presentation's Slide Master view.

Managing Slide Masters

Let's review the relationship one more time between Slide Masters and themes. A *theme* is a set of formatting specs (colors, fonts, and effects) that can be used in PowerPoint, Word, or Excel. Themes are not applied directly to slides — they are applied to Slide Masters, which govern the formatting of slides. The Slide Masters exist within the presentation file itself. You can change them by applying different themes, but they are essentially built in to the presentation file.

When you change to a different theme for all of the slides in the presentation, your Slide Master changes its appearance. You can tweak that appearance in Slide Master view. As long as all of the slides in the presentation use the same theme, you need only one Slide Master. However, if you apply a different theme to some of your slides, you need another master, because a master can have only one theme applied to it at a time. PowerPoint automatically creates the additional master(s) for you, and they are all available for editing in Slide Master view.

If you later reapply a single theme to all of the slides in the presentation, you do not need multiple masters anymore, so the unused one is automatically deleted. In addition to all this automatic creation and deletion of Slide Masters, you can also manually create and delete Slide Masters on your own. Any Slide Masters that you create manually are automatically preserved, even if they aren't always in use. You must manually delete them if you don't want them anymore.

In the following sections, you learn how to create and delete Slide Masters manually, and how to rename them. You also learn how to lock one of the automatically created Slide Masters so that PowerPoint does not delete it if it falls out of use.

Creating and Deleting Slide Masters

To create another Slide Master, click Insert Slide Master on the Slide Master tab. It appears below the existing Slide Master(s) in the left pane of Slide Master view. From there, just start customizing it. You can apply a theme to it, modify its layouts and placeholders, and all the usual things you can do to a Slide Master. Another way to create a new Slide Master is to duplicate an existing one. To do this, right-click the Slide Master and choose Duplicate Master.

To delete a Slide Master, select it in Slide Master view (make sure you select the Slide Master itself, not just one of its layouts) and press the Delete key. If any of that Slide Master's layouts were applied to any slides in the presentation, those slides automatically convert to the default Slide Master's equivalent layout. If no exact layout match is found, PowerPoint does its best: It uses its default Title and Content layout and includes any extra content as orphaned items.

Renaming a Slide Master

Slide Master names appear as category headings on the Layout list as you are selecting layouts. For example, in Figure 22-20, the Slide Master names are *Apex* and *Check*.

FIGURE 22-20

Slide Master names form the category titles on the Layout list.

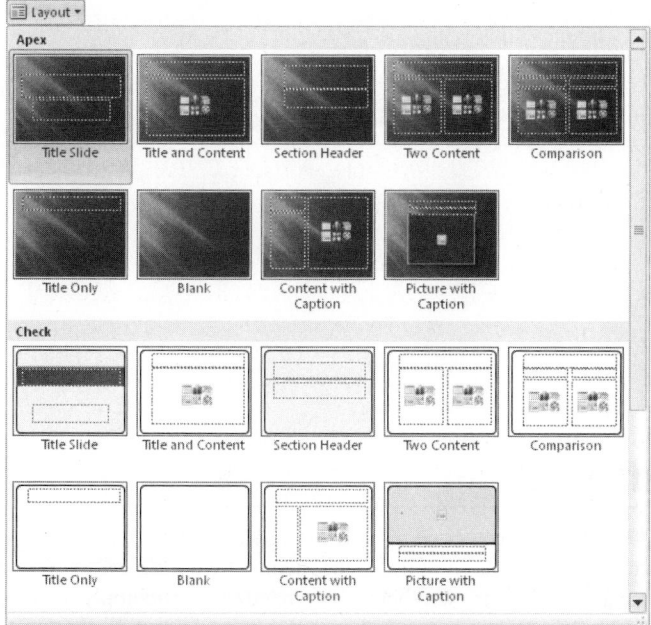

To rename a Slide Master, follow these steps:

1. **In Slide Master view, right-click the Slide Master and choose Rename Master.** The Rename Master dialog box opens.

2. **Type a new name for the master, replacing the existing name.**

3. **Click Rename.**

Preserving a Slide Master

Unless you have created the Slide Master yourself, it is temporary. Slide Masters come and go as needed, as you format slides with various themes. To lock a Slide Master so that it doesn't disappear when no slides are using it, right-click the Slide Master and choose Preserve Master. A check mark appears next to Preserve Master on its right-click menu, indicating that it is saved. To un-preserve it, select the command again to toggle the check mark off. See Figure 22-21.

FIGURE 22-21

The Preserve Master command saves a Slide Master so that PowerPoint cannot automatically delete it.

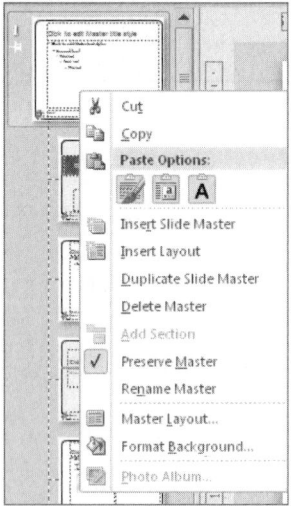

Managing Themes

As you learned earlier in the chapter, themes are applied to Slide Masters to create the background, color, font, and effect formatting for a presentation. Some themes are built into PowerPoint, and you can also create and save your own themes as separate files and apply them to other presentations or even to other Office documents, such as in Word and Excel. In this section, you learn how to create new themes, manage theme files, and apply themes across multiple presentations.

Creating a New Theme

To create a new theme, first format a Slide Master exactly the way you want, including any custom layouts, backgrounds, colors, and font themes. Then save the Slide Master's formatting as a new theme by following these steps:

1. **On the Slide Master or the Design tab, click Themes, and click Save Current Theme.** The Save Current Theme dialog box opens.

   The default location shown in the Save Current Theme dialog box under Windows Vista or Windows 7 is `C:\Users\`*username*`\AppData\Roaming\Microsoft\Templates\Document Themes`. For Windows XP, it is `C:\Documents and Settings\`*username*`\Application Data\Microsoft\Templates\Document Themes`.

2. **Type a name for the theme file in the File Name textbox.**

3. **Click Save.** The new theme is saved to your hard disk.

The new theme is now available from the Themes button's menu in all presentations you create while logged in as the same user on the same PC. All of its formatting is available, including any custom color or font themes it includes. You can use it in other programs too; in Word or Excel, choose Page Layout ➪ Themes.

Renaming a Theme

You can rename a theme file by renaming the `.thmx` file from Windows Explorer, outside of PowerPoint. You can also rename a theme file from inside PowerPoint by using any dialog box that saves or opens files. For example, to use the Choose Theme or Themed Document dialog box to rename a theme, follow these steps:

1. **From the Design or Slide Master tab, click Themes, and choose Browse for Themes.** The Choose Theme or Themed Document dialog box opens.

2. **Navigate to the folder containing the theme file to rename.**

   By default, theme files are stored under Windows Vista or Windows 7 in `C:\Users\`*username*`\AppData\Roaming\Microsoft\Templates\Document Themes`. For Windows XP, it is `C:\Documents and Settings\`*username*`\Application Data\Microsoft\Templates\Document Themes`.

3. **Right-click the theme file and choose Rename.**

4. **Type the new name for the theme and press Enter.**

5. **Click Cancel to close the dialog box.**

Deleting a Theme

A custom theme file continues appearing on the Themes Gallery indefinitely. If you want to remove it from there, you must delete it from the Document Themes folder, or move it to some other location for storage. To delete a theme, follow these steps:

1. **From the Design or Slide Master tab, click Themes, and choose Browse for Themes.** The Choose Theme or Themed Document dialog box opens.

2. **Navigate to the folder containing the theme files.**

In Windows Vista or Windows 7, it is `C:\Users\`*`username`*`\AppData\Roaming\Microsoft\Templates\Document Themes`. In Windows XP, it is `C:\Documents and Settings\`*`username`*`\Application Data\Microsoft\Templates\Document Themes`.

3. **Right-click the theme file and choose Delete.**

4. **At the Delete File confirmation box, click Yes.**

5. **Click Cancel to close the dialog box.**

Copying a Theme from Another Presentation

A presentation file *contains* themes, in that the themes are applied to its Slide Masters. (That's also how a template contains themes.) As you learned earlier, you can preserve a Slide Master in Slide Master view so that it doesn't get deleted automatically when there are no slides based on it; by creating new Slide Masters, applying themes to them, and then preserving them, you can create a whole library of themes in a single presentation or template file. Then to make this library of themes available in another presentation, you simply base the new presentation on that existing presentation (or template).

However, if you did not initially base the new presentation on the template or presentation that contains the theme you want, you can apply the theme from it after the fact. One way to do this is to copy-and-paste (or drag-and-drop) the Slide Master from one file's Slide Master view to the other's.

Follow these steps to copy a Slide Master (and thereby copy its theme) to another presentation:

1. **Open both presentations.**

2. **In the presentation that contains the theme, enter Slide Master view (View ⇨ Master Views ⇨ Slide Master).**

3. **Select the Slide Master (top slide in the left pane) and press Ctrl+C to copy it.**

4. **Switch to the other presentation (View ⇨ Window ⇨ Switch Windows).**

5. **Enter Slide Master view (View ⇨ Master Views ⇨ Slide Master).**

6. **Press Ctrl+V to paste the Slide Master (and its associated theme and layouts).**

Summary

In this chapter you learned how themes and Slide Masters make it easy to apply consistent formatting in a presentation, and how layout masters are associated with Slide Masters and provide consistent layouts for the slides based on them. You learned how to create, edit, rename, and delete themes, masters, and layouts, and how to copy themes between presentations.

Now that you know how to format entire presentations using themes, the next chapter explains how to create charts and tables on slides.

Working with Tables and Charts

You can type tabular data — in other words, data in a grid of rows and columns — directly into a table, or import it from other applications. You can also apply formatting that makes tabular data easier to read and more attractive. When you need to create a quick chart that has no external source, PowerPoint's charting tool works perfectly. The PowerPoint 2010 charting interface is based on the one in Excel, so you don't have to leave PowerPoint to create, modify, and format professional-looking charts.

In this chapter, you'll learn how to create and manage PowerPoint tables and how to create charts that present numeric data in a visual format.

Creating a New Table

A table is a great way to organize little bits of data into a meaningful picture. For example, you might use a table to show sales results for several salespeople or to contain a multicolumn list of team member names.

Note

Text from a table does not appear in the presentation's outline. ∎

There are several ways to insert a table, and each method has its purpose. The following sections explain each of the table creation methods.

A table can be part of a content placeholder or it can be a separate, free-floating item. If the active slide has an available placeholder that can accommodate a table and there is not already content in that placeholder, the table is placed in it. Otherwise, the table is placed as an independent object on the slide and is not part of the layout.

Tip

Depending on what you want to do with the table, it could be advantageous in some cases to not have the table be part of the layout. For example, perhaps you want the table to be a certain size and to not change when you apply a different theme. To ensure that the table is not part of the layout, start with a slide that uses a layout that contains no table-compatible placeholder, such as Title Only. ■

Creating a Table with the Insert Table Dialog Box

To create a basic table with a specified number of rows and columns, you can use the Insert Table dialog box. You can open it in either of two ways (see Figure 23-1):

- In a content placeholder, click the Table icon.
- In the Tables group of the Insert tab, choose Table ➪ Insert Table.

In the Insert Table dialog box shown in Figure 23-2, specify a number of rows and columns and click OK. The table then appears on the slide.

Open the Insert Table dialog box from either the Table menu or a content placeholder.

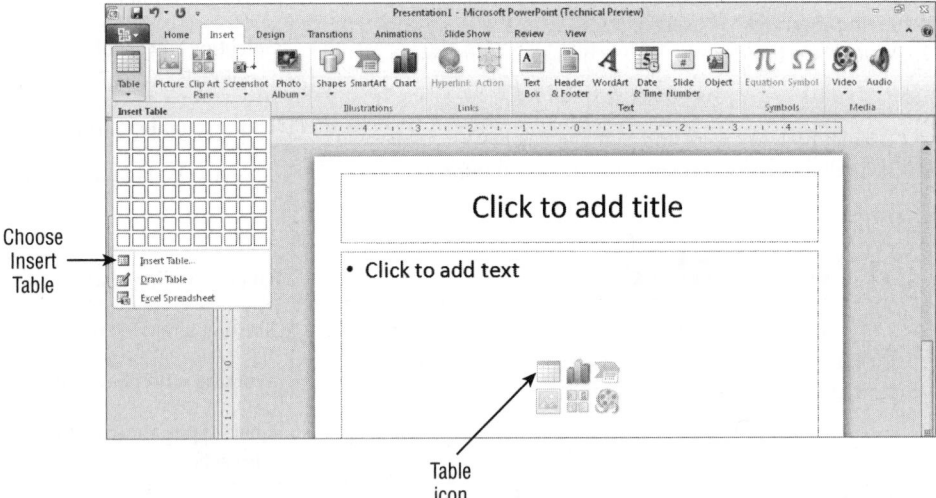

Choose Insert Table

Table icon

Enter the number of rows and columns to specify the size of the table that you want to create.

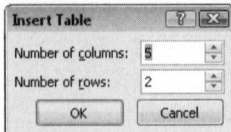

Creating a Table from the Table Button

When you opened the Table button's menu (see Figure 23-1) in the preceding section, you probably couldn't help but notice the grid of white squares. Another way to create a table is to drag across this grid until you select the desired number of rows and columns. The table appears immediately on the slide as you drag, so you can see how it will look, as shown in Figure 23-3.

FIGURE 23-3

Drag across the grid in the Table button's menu to specify the size of the table that you want to create.

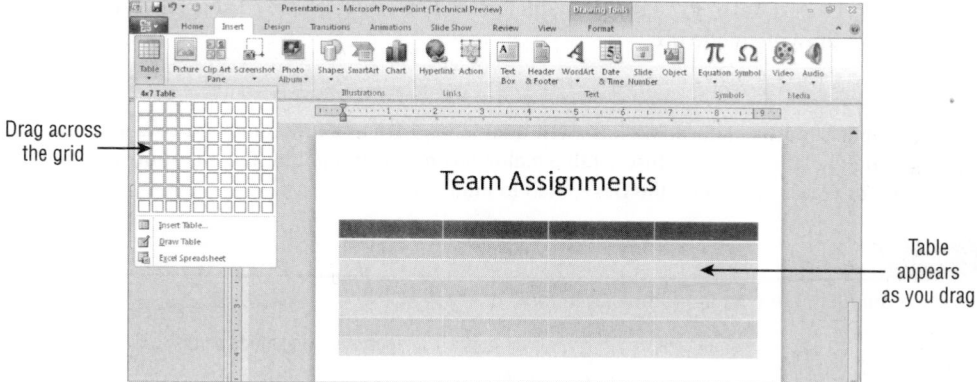

Drag across
the grid

Table
appears
as you drag

Other than the method of specifying rows and columns, this method is identical to creating a table via the Insert Table dialog box, because the same issues apply regarding placeholders versus free-floating tables. If a placeholder is available, PowerPoint uses it.

Note

When you create a table with this method and the preceding one, the table is automatically formatted with one of the preset table styles. You learn how to change this later in the chapter. ■

Drawing a Table

I've saved the most fun method for last. Drawing a table enables you to use your mouse pointer like a pencil to create every row and column in the table in exactly the positions you want. You can even create unequal numbers of rows and columns. This method is a good one to use whenever you want a table that is nonstandard in some way — different row heights, different column widths, different numbers of columns in some rows, and so on. To draw a table, follow these steps:

1. **In the Tables group of the Insert tab, click Table, and choose Draw Table.** The mouse pointer turns into a pencil.

2. **Drag to draw a rectangle representing the outer frame of the table.** Then release the mouse button to create the outer frame and to display the Table Tools Design tab.

3. **On the Table Tools Design tab, click Draw Table in the Draw Borders group to re-enable the Pencil tool if it is not already enabled.**

4. **Drag to draw the rows and columns you want.** You can draw a row or column that runs all the way across or down the table's frame, or you can stop at any point to make a partial row or column. See Figure 23-4. When you begin to drag vertically or horizontally, PowerPoint locks into that mode and keeps the line exactly vertical or horizontal and straight. (Exception: It allows you to draw a diagonal line between two corners of existing cells.)

5. (Optional) **To erase a line, click the Eraser button in the Draw Borders group of the Table Tools Design tab, and then click the line to erase.** Then click the Draw Table button on the Design tab to return the mouse pointer to its drawing (pencil) mode.

6. **When you finish drawing the table, press Esc or click Draw Table again to toggle the drawing mode off.**

Tip

If you need a table that is mostly uniform but has a few anomalies, such as a few combined cells or a few extra divisions, create the table using the Insert Table dialog box or the grid on the Table button, and then use the Draw Table and/or Eraser buttons on the Design tab to modify it. ∎

FIGURE 23-4

You can create a unique table with the Draw Table tool.

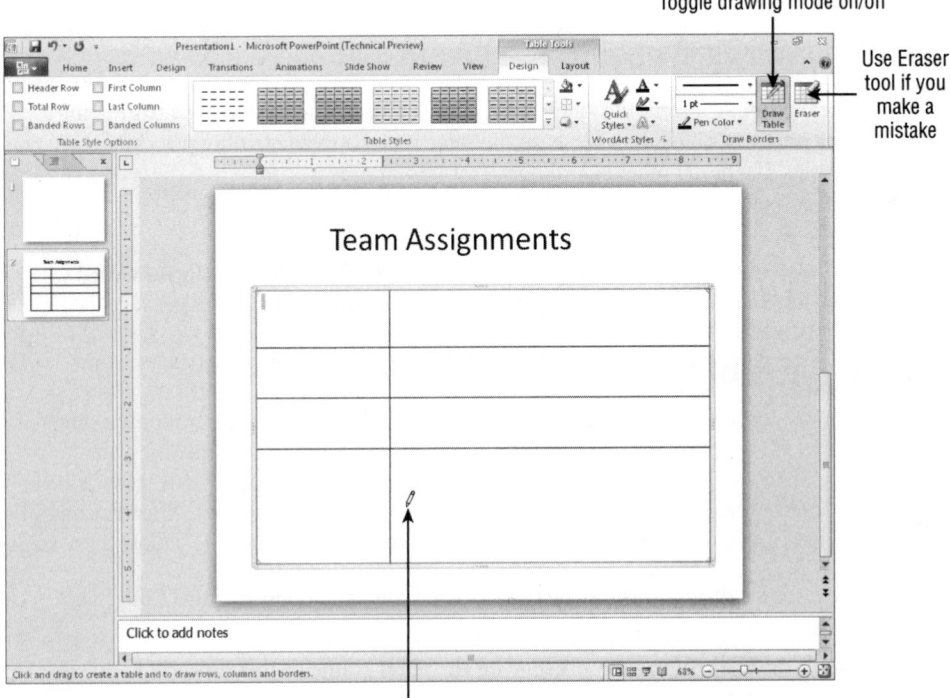

Toggle drawing mode on/off

Use Eraser tool if you make a mistake

Drag pencil to draw a line

Moving Around in a Table

Each cell is like a little textbox. To type in a cell, click in it and type. It's pretty simple! You can also move between cells with the keyboard. Table 23-1 lists the keyboard shortcuts for moving the insertion point in a table.

TABLE 23-1

Moving the Insertion Point in a Table

To Move to	Press This
Next cell	Tab
Previous cell	Shift+Tab
Next row	Down arrow
Previous row	Up arrow
Tab stop within a cell	Ctrl+Tab
New paragraph within the same cell	Enter

Selecting Rows, Columns, and Cells

If you want to apply formatting to one or more cells or issue a command that acts upon them such as Copy or Delete, you must first select the cells to be affected, as shown in Figure 23-5:

- **A Single Cell.** Move the insertion point by clicking inside the desired cell. At this point, any command acts on that individual cell and its contents, not the whole table, row, or column. Drag across multiple cells to select them.

- **An Entire Row or Column.** Click any cell in that row or column, and then open the Select button's menu in the Table group on the Table Tools Layout tab and choose Select Column or Select Row. Alternatively, position the mouse pointer above the column or to the left of the row, so that the mouse pointer turns into a black arrow, and then click to select the column or row. (You can drag to extend the selection to additional columns or rows when you see the black arrow.)

There are two ways to select the entire table — or rather, two senses in which the entire table can be *selected*:

- **Select All Table Cells.** When you select all of the cells, they all appear with shaded backgrounds, and any text formatting command that you apply at that point affects all of the text in the table. To select all cells, do one of the following:
  - Drag across all of the cells in the entire table.
  - Click inside the table, and then press Ctrl+A.

- **Select the Entire Table.** When you do this, the table's frame is selected, but the insertion point is not anywhere within the table and cells do not appear with a shaded background. You do this kind of selection before moving or resizing the table, for example. To select the entire table, do one of the following:

  - Choose Select Table from the Select button's menu, shown in Figure 23-5.

  - Click the frame of the table.

  - Click inside the table, and then press Esc once.

  - Right-click the table and choose Select Table.

- **Drag a Marquee around the Table.** You can use the mouse to drag a marquee (a box) around the table. This is also called *lassoing*. When you release the mouse button, everything inside the area is selected.

FIGURE 23-5

Select a row or column with the Select button's menu, or click above or to the left of the column or row.

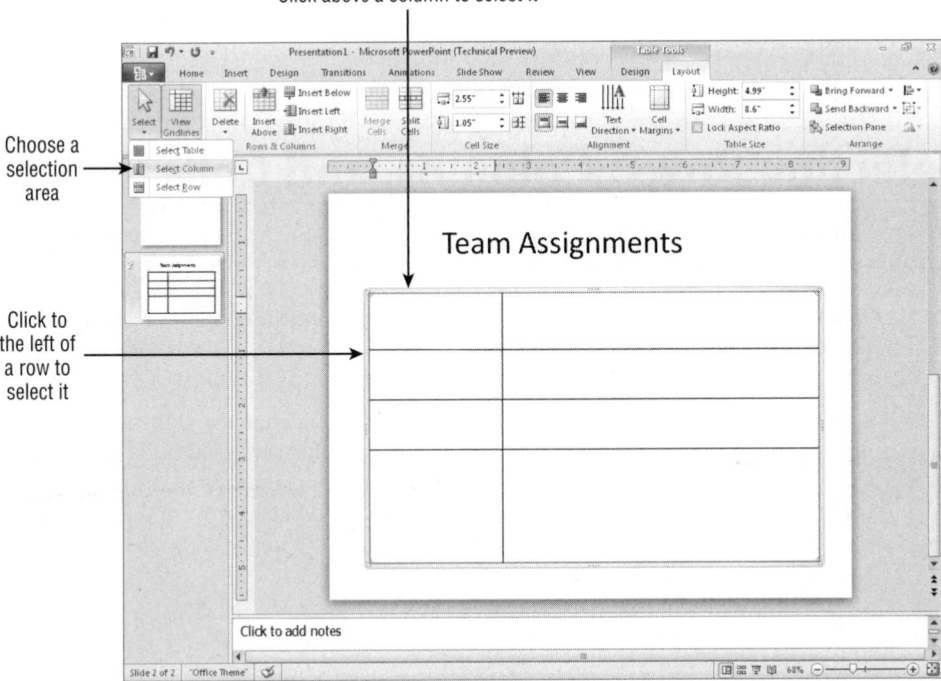

Editing a Table's Structure

Now that you've created a table, let's look at some ways to modify the table's structure, including resizing the entire table, adding and deleting rows and columns, and merging and splitting cells.

Resizing the Overall Table

As with any other framed object in PowerPoint, dragging the table's outer frame resizes it. Position the mouse pointer over one of the selection handles (the dots on the sides and corners) so that the mouse pointer becomes a double-headed arrow, and drag to resize the table. See Figure 23-6.

FIGURE 23-6

To resize a table, drag a selection handle on its frame.

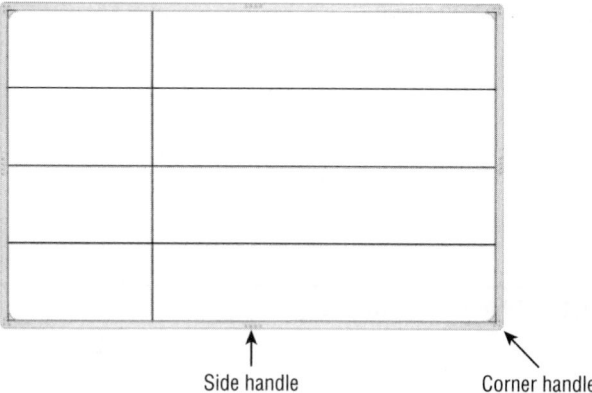

Side handle   Corner handle

Note

If you drag when the mouse pointer is over any other part of the frame, so that the mouse pointer becomes a four-headed arrow, you move the table rather than resize it. ■

To maintain the aspect ratio (height-to-width ratio) for the table as you resize it, hold down the Shift key as you drag a corner of the frame. If maintaining the aspect ratio is not critical, you can drag either a corner or a side.

All of the rows and columns maintain their spacing proportionally to one another as you resize them. However, when a table contains text that would no longer fit if its row and column were shrunken proportionally with the rest of the table, the row height does not shrink fully; it shrinks as much as it can while still displaying the text. The column width *does* shrink proportionally, regardless of cell content.

You can also specify an exact size for the overall table frame by using the Table Size group on the Table Tools Layout tab, as shown in Figure 23-7. From there you can enter Height and Width values. To maintain the aspect ratio, select the Lock Aspect Ratio checkbox before you change either the Height or Width settings.

Inserting or Deleting Rows and Columns

Here's an easy way to create a new row at the bottom of the table: Position the insertion point in the bottom-right cell and press Tab. Need something more complicated than that?

The Table Tools Layout tab contains buttons in the Rows & Columns group for inserting rows or columns above, below, to the left, or to the right of the selected cell(s), as shown in Figure 23-8. By default, each button inserts a single row or column at a time, but if you select multiple existing ones beforehand, these commands insert as many as you've selected. For example, to insert three new rows, select three existing rows and then click Insert Above or Insert Below.

FIGURE 23-7

Set a precise height and width for the table from the Table Size group.

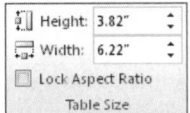

FIGURE 23-8

Insert rows or columns by using these buttons on the Table Tools Layout tab.

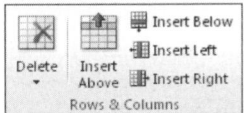

Alternatively, you can right-click any existing row or column, point to Insert, and choose one of the commands on the submenu. These commands are the same as the names of the buttons in Figure 23-8.

Caution

Adding new rows can increase the overall vertical size of the table frame to the point where it runs off the bottom of the slide. You might need to adjust the overall frame size after adding rows. On the other hand, inserting columns does not change the overall frame size; it simply resizes the existing columns so that they all fit and are all a uniform size (unless you have manually adjusted any of them to be a custom size). ■

To delete a row or column (or more than one of each), select the row(s) or column(s) that you want to delete, and then open the Delete button's menu on the Layout tab and choose Delete Rows or Delete Columns.

Note

You cannot insert or delete individual cells in a PowerPoint table. (This is unlike in Excel, where you can remove individual cells and then shift the remaining ones up or to the left.) ■

Merging and Splitting Cells

If you need more rows or columns in some spots than others, you can use the Merge Cells and Split Cells commands. Here are some ways to merge cells:

- Click the Eraser button in the Draw Borders group on the Table Tools Design tab, and then click the line you want to erase. The cells on either side of the deleted line are merged.

- Select the cells that you want to merge and click Merge Cells in the Merge group on the Table Tools Layout tab.

- Select the cells to merge, right-click them, and choose Merge Cells.

Here are some ways to split cells:

- Click the Draw Table button in the Draw Borders group on the Table Tools Design tab, and then drag to draw a line in the middle of a cell to split it.

- Select the cell that you want to split, right-click it, and choose Split Cells. In the Split Cells dialog box (see Figure 23-9), select the number of pieces in which to split in each direction, and click OK.

- Select the cell to split, and then click Split Cells in the Merge group on the Table Tools Layout tab. In the Split Cells dialog box (see Figure 23-9), select the number of pieces in which to split in each direction, and click OK.

FIGURE 23-9

Specify how the split should occur.

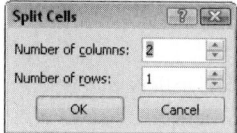

Applying Table Styles

The quickest way to format a table attractively is to apply a table style to it. When you insert a table using any method except drawing it, a table style is applied to it by default; you can change to some other style if desired, or you can remove all styles from the table, leaving it plain black-and-white.

When you hover the mouse pointer over a table style, a Live Preview of it appears in the active table. The style is not actually applied to the table until you click the style to select it, however.

If the style you want appears on the Table Tools Design tab without opening the gallery, you can click on it from there. If not, you can scroll row-by-row through the gallery by clicking the up/down arrow buttons, or you can open the gallery's full menu, as shown in Figure 23-10.

FIGURE 23-10

Apply a table style from the gallery.

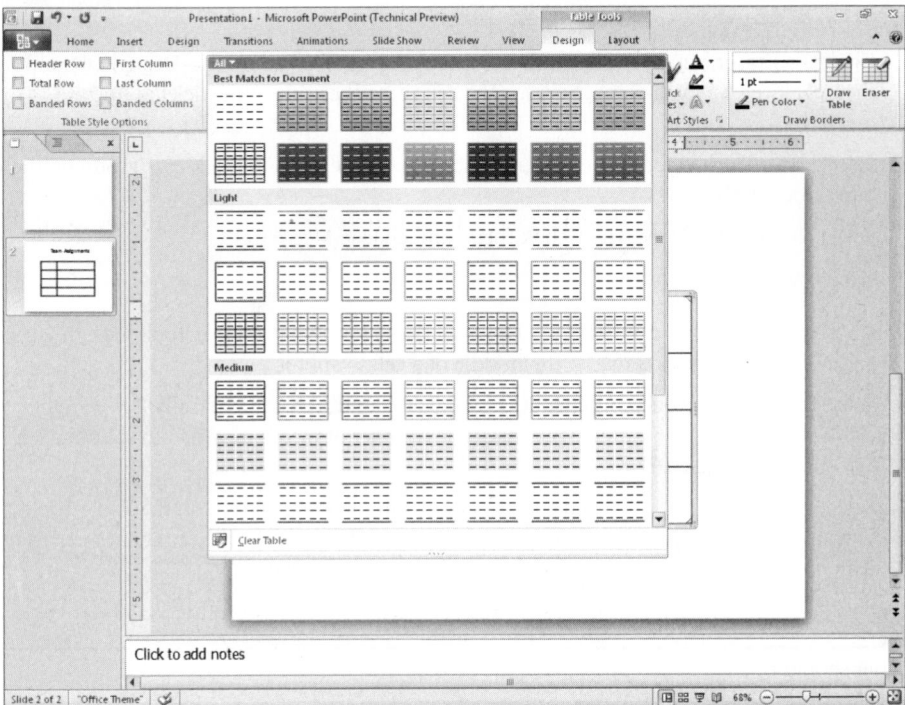

To remove all styles from the table, choose Clear Table from the bottom of the gallery menu. This reverts the table to default settings: no fill, and plain, black 1-point borders on all sides of all cells.

The table styles use theme-based colors, so if you change to a different presentation theme or color theme, the table formatting might change. (Colors, in particular, are prone to shift.)

By default, the first row of the table (a.k.a. the header row) is formatted differently from the others, and every other row is shaded differently. (This is called *banding*.) You can control how different rows are treated differently (or not) from the Table Style Options group on the Table Tools Design tab. There is a checkbox for each of six settings:

- **Header Row.** The first row
- **Total Row.** The last row
- **First Column.** The leftmost column
- **Last Column.** The rightmost column

- **Banded Rows.** Every other row formatted differently
- **Banded Columns.** Every other column formatted differently

Caution

With some of the styles, there is not a whole lot of difference between some of the settings. For example, you might have to look very closely to see the difference between First Column being turned on or off; ditto with Last Column and Total Row. ■

Tip

You can right-click one of the thumbnails in the Table Style Gallery and choose Set as Default to change the default table style. ■

Formatting Table Cells

Although table styles provide a rough cut on the formatting, you might want to fine-tune your table formatting as well. In the following sections, you learn how to adjust various aspects of the table's appearance.

Changing Row Height and Column Width

You might want a row to be a different height or a column a different width from others in the table. To resize a row or column, follow these steps:

1. **Position the mouse pointer on the border below the row or to the right of the column that you want to resize.** The mouse pointer turns into a line with arrows on each side of it.

2. **Hold down the mouse button as you drag the row or column to a new height or width.** A dotted line appears showing where it will go.

3. **Release the mouse button.**

You can also specify an exact height or width measurement using the Height and Width boxes in the Cell Size group on the Table Tools Layout tab. Select the row(s) or column(s) to affect, and then enter sizes in inches or use the increment buttons, as shown in Figure 23-11.

FIGURE 23-11

Set a precise size for a row or column.

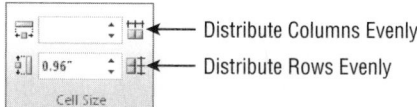

— Distribute Columns Evenly

— Distribute Rows Evenly

The Distribute Rows Evenly and Distribute Columns Evenly buttons in the Cell Size group (see Figure 23-11) adjust each row or column in the selected range so that the available space is occupied evenly among them. This is handy especially if you have drawn the table yourself rather than allowing PowerPoint to create it initially. If PowerPoint creates the table, the rows and columns are already of equal height and width by default.

You can also double-click between two columns to size the column to the left so that the text fits exactly within the width.

Table Margins and Alignment

Remember, PowerPoint slides do not have any margins per se; everything is in a *frame*. An individual cell does have internal margins, however.

You can specify the internal margins for cells using the Cell Margins button in the Alignment group on the Table Tools Layout tab, as follows:

1. **Select the cells to which the setting should apply.** To apply settings to the entire table, select the entire table.

2. **In the Alignment group on the Table Tools Layout tab, click the Cell Margins button.** A menu of margin presets opens.

3. **Click one of the presets or choose Custom Margins, and then follow these steps:**

   3a. In the Cell Text Layout dialog box, set the Left, Right, Top, and Bottom margin settings, as shown in Figure 23-12.

   3b. Click OK.

FIGURE 23-12

You can set the internal margins on an individual cell basis for each side of the cell.

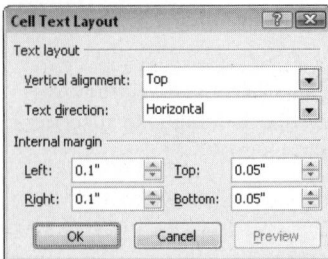

Applying Borders

The border lines around each cell are very important because they separate the data in each cell. By default (without a table style), there's a 1-point border around each side of each cell, but you can make some or all borders thicker, a different line style (e.g., dashed), or a different color, or remove them altogether to create your own effects. Here are some ideas:

- To make items appear to *float* in multiple columns on the slide (i.e., to make it look as if they are not really in a table at all — just lined up extremely well), remove all table borders.

- To create a header row at the top without using the Quick Style Options, make the border beneath the first row of cells darker or thicker than the others.

- To make certain rows or columns appear as if they are outside of the table, turn off their borders on all sides except the side that faces the other cells.

- To make certain items appear as if they have been crossed off a list, format those cells with diagonal borders. This creates the effect of an X running through each cell. These diagonal lines are not really borders in the sense that they don't go around the edge of the cell, but they're treated as borders in PowerPoint.

When you apply a top, bottom, left, or right border, those positions refer to the entire selected block of cells if you have more than one cell selected. For example, suppose you select two adjacent cells in a row and apply a left border. The border applies only to the leftmost of the two cells. If you want the same border applied to the line between the cells too, you must apply an inside vertical border.

To apply a border, follow these steps:

1. **Select the cell(s) that you want to affect.**
2. **In the Draw Borders group on the Table Tools Design tab, select a line style, width, and color from the Pen Style, Pen Weight, and Pen Color drop-down lists, as shown in Figure 23-13.**

Tip
Try to use theme colors rather than fixed colors whenever possible, so that if you change to a different color theme later, the colors you choose now won't clash because they will update automatically. ∎

3. **Open the Borders button's menu in the Table Styles group, and choose the sides of the selected area to which the new settings should apply.** See Figure 23-14. For example, to apply the border to the bottom of the selected area, click Bottom Border. If you want to remove all borders from all sides, choose No Border from the menu.
4. **If necessary, repeat Step 3 to apply the border to other sides of the selection.** Some of the choices on the Borders button's menu apply to only one side; others apply to two or more at once.

Applying Fills

When you apply a table style, as you learned earlier in the chapter, the style specifies a background color — or in some cases, multiple background colors depending on the options you choose for special treatment of certain rows or columns.

FIGURE 23-13

Use the Draw Borders group's lists to set the border's style, thickness, and color.

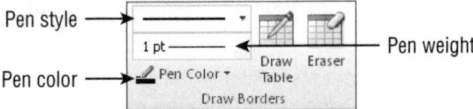

FIGURE 23-14

Select the side(s) to apply borders to the chosen cells.

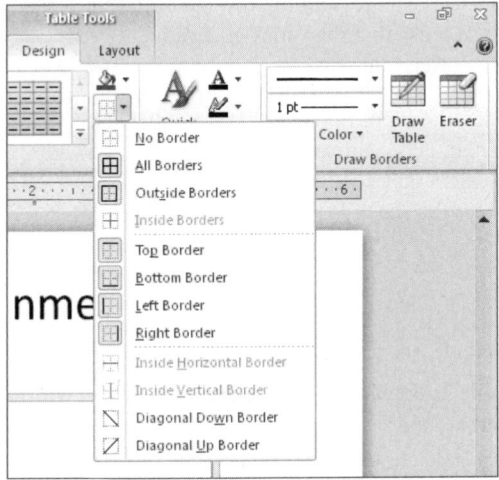

You can also manually change the fill for a table to make it either a solid color or a special fill effect. You can apply this fill to individual cells, or you can apply a background fill for the entire table.

Filling Individual Cells

Each individual cell has its own fill setting; in this way a table is like a collection of individual object frames, rather than a single object. To set the fill color for one or more cells, follow these steps:

1. **Select the cell(s) to affect, or to apply the same fill color to all cells, select the table's outer frame.**

2. **In the Table Styles group on the Table Tools Design tab, click the down-arrow next to the Shading button to open its palette.**

3. **Select the desired color or fill effect.** See Figure 23-15.

Tip

For a semi-transparent color fill, first apply the fill and then right-click the cell and choose Format Shape. In the Format Shape dialog box, drag the Transparency slider. For some types of fills, you can also set the transparency when you initially apply the fill. ■

FIGURE 23-15

Apply a fill effect to the selected cell(s).

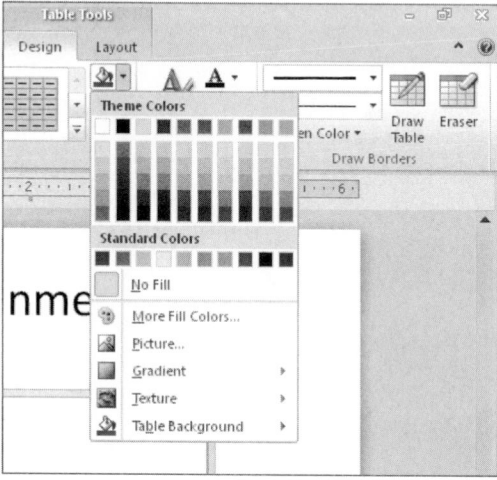

Applying an Overall Table Fill

You can apply a solid color fill to the entire table that is different from the fill applied to the individual cells. The table's fill color is visible only in cells in which the individual fill is set to No Fill (or a semi-transparent fill, in which case it blends).

To apply a fill to the entire table, open the Shading button's menu and point to Table Background, and then choose a color, as shown in Figure 23-16.

To test the new background, select some cells and choose No Fill for their fill color. The background color appears in those cells. If you want to experiment further, try applying a semi-transparent fill to some cells, and see how the color of the background blends with the color of the cell's fill.

Filling a Table with a Picture

When you fill one or more cells with a picture, each cell gets its own individual copy of it. For example, if you fill a table with a picture of a koala and the table has six cells, you get six koalas, as shown in Figure 23-17.

FIGURE 23-16

Apply a fill to the table's background.

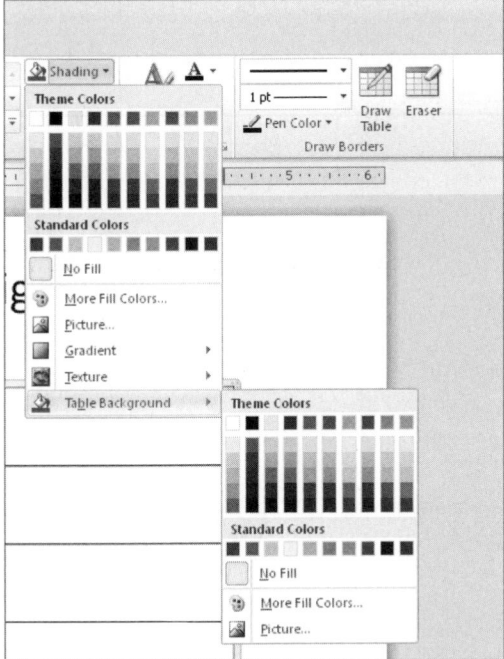

FIGURE 23-17

When you apply a picture fill to a table, each cell gets its own copy.

If you want a single copy of the picture to fill the entire area behind the table, there several ways you can do this.

One is to set the picture to be tiled like a texture. Follow these steps:

1. **Select the cells, and then right-click the selection and choose Format Shape.**

2. **Click Fill, and then click Picture or Texture Fill.**

3. **Click the File button, select the picture file, and click Insert.**

4. **Select the Tile Picture as Texture checkbox, as shown in Figure 23-18.**

FIGURE 23-18

Set the picture to be tiled as a texture.

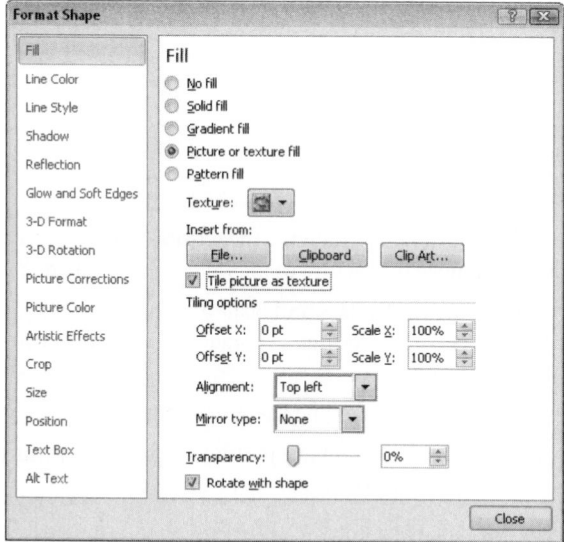

Another way to do this is to choose a picture fill from the Shading options for the table. To do that:

1. **Select the cell(s) you want to affect.**

2. **Choose Table Tools Design ⇨ Table Styles ⇨ Shading ⇨ Picture.** The Insert Picture dialog box opens.

3. **Click Insert.** The picture is inserted in the table cell.

At this point, the picture fills the table without regard for cell borders, but it probably doesn't fill it exactly. Depending on the original size of the graphic and the size of the table, you probably either see a truncated version of the picture or a tiled version that does not match up with the cell borders. Figure 23-19 shows an example of a picture that is too large.

FIGURE 23-19

This picture is too large for the table fill.

To adjust the picture, use the Tiling Options in the Format Shape dialog box, as shown in Figure 23-18:

- Adjust the position of the picture within the table by changing the Offset X and Offset Y values. These are measured in points and move the picture to the right (X) and down (Y).

- Change the sizing of the picture by adjusting the Scale X and Scale Y values. The smaller the number, the smaller the picture — but don't go too small or the picture will start to tile (unless that's what you want, of course).

- Change the way the picture aligns in the table by changing the Alignment.

- (Optional) Set a mirror type if desired so that if you do have multiple copies tiled within the frame, each copy is flipped horizontally and/or vertically. (This is not common.)

It can take some time to get the picture optimally adjusted so that it exactly fits in the allotted space. Figure 23-20 shows an example.

If all of that seems like more than you want to mess with, there is an alternative method: Make the table transparent and place the picture behind it on the slide. Here's how:

1. **Place the picture on the slide by choosing Insert ⇨ Images ⇨ Picture.**

2. **Select the picture and choose Picture Tools Format ⇨ Arrange ⇨ Send Backward arrow ⇨ Send to Back.** (If the picture is the only object on the slide, this command is unavailable, but the command is unnecessary in that case.)

3. **Create a plain, unformatted table on top of the picture.**

4. **Set the table's fill to No Fill if it is not already transparent.**

5. **Resize the table and the picture as needed so they are both the same size.** You might need to crop the picture to keep the right aspect ratio.

The picture now fills the table background as a single copy.

Applying a Shadow to a Table

You can apply a shadow effect to a table so that it appears *raised* off the slide background. You can make it any color you like, and adjust a variety of settings for it.

Note

If the cells have no fill, the shadow will apply to the gridlines, not to the table as a whole object. ■

Here's a very simple way to apply a shadow to a table:

1. Select the table's outer frame.
2. Choose Table Tools Design ➪ Table Styles ➪ Effects ➪ Shadow.
3. Click the shadow type you want.

Here's an alternative method that gives a bit more control:

1. Select the table's outer frame, and then right-click the frame and choose Format Shape.
2. Click Shadow, and then choose a preset and a color, as shown in Figure 23-21.
3. (Optional) If desired, drag any of the sliders to fine-tune the shadow.
4. Click Close to close the Format Shape dialog box when you are finished.

Applying a 3-D Effect to a Table

PowerPoint does not enable you to apply 3-D effects to tables, so you have to fudge that by creating the 3-D effect with rectangles and then overlaying a transparent table on top of the shapes. As you can see in Figure 23-22, it's a pretty convincing facsimile.

FIGURE 23-21

Apply a shadow to a table.

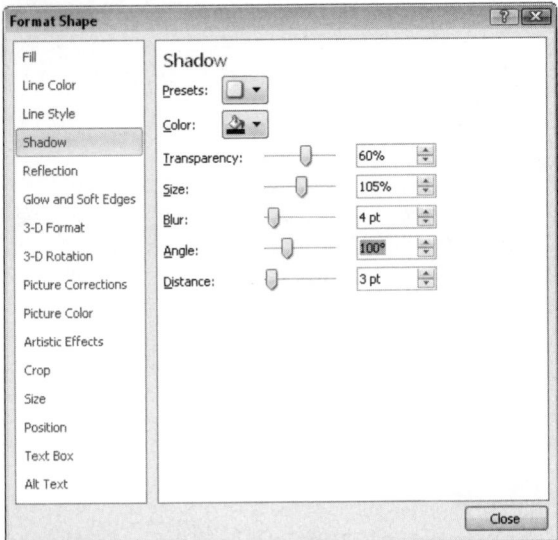

FIGURE 23-22

This 3-D table is actually a plain table with a 3-D rectangle behind it.

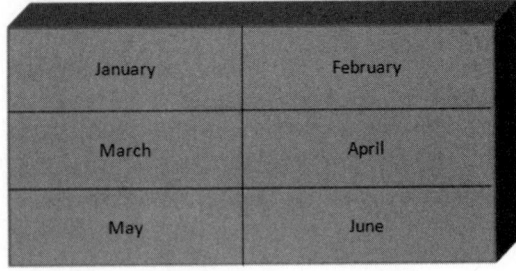

Here's the basic procedure:

1. **Create a rectangle from the Shapes choice of the Illustrations group on the Insert tab, and apply a 3-D effect to it (from the Drawing Tools Format tab's Shape Styles ⇨ Shape Effect ⇨ 3-D Rotation).** Use any effect you like. To create the traditional *box* appearance as in Figure 23-22, apply the second Oblique preset and then in the 3-D Format options, increase the Depth setting to about 100 points.

2. **Size the rectangle so that its face is the same size as the table.**

3. On the Drawing Tools Format tab, choose Arrange ➪ Backward ➪ Send to Back to send the rectangle behind the table.

4. Set the table's fill to No Fill if it is not already transparent.

5. (Optional) Set the table's outer frame border to None to make its edges appear to blend with the edges of the rectangle. To do that, open the Borders button's menu on the Table Tools Design tab and select Outside Border to toggle that off.

Changing Text Alignment

If you followed the preceding steps to create the effect shown in Figure 23-22, you probably ran into a problem: Your text probably didn't center itself in the cells. That's because, by default, each cell's vertical alignment is set to Top, and horizontal alignment is set to Left.

Although the vertical and horizontal alignments are both controlled from the Alignment group on the Table Tools Layout tab, they actually have two different scopes. Vertical alignment applies to the entire cell as a whole, whereas horizontal alignment can apply differently to individual paragraphs within the cell. To set vertical alignment for a cell, follow these steps:

1. **Select one or more cells to affect.** To affect only one cell, you do not have to select it; just click inside it.

2. **On the Table Tools Layout tab, in the Alignment group, click one of the vertical alignment buttons: Align Top, Center Vertically, or Align Bottom.** See Figure 23-23.

FIGURE 23-23

Set the vertical and horizontal alignment of text from the Alignment group.

Horizontal alignment

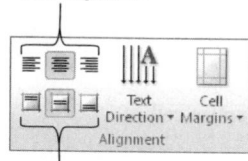

Vertical alignment

To set the horizontal alignment for a paragraph, follow these steps:

1. **Select one or more paragraphs to affect.** If you select multiple cells, all paragraphs within those cells are affected. If you click in a cell without selecting anything, the change only affects the paragraph in which you clicked.

2. **On the Table Tools Layout tab, in the Alignment group, click one of the horizontal alignment buttons: Align Left, Align Center, or Align Right.** See Figure 23-23. You can also use the paragraph alignment buttons on the Home tab for horizontal alignment, or the buttons on the Mini toolbar.

Tip

The horizontal alignments all have keyboard shortcuts: Ctrl+L for left, Ctrl+E for center, and Ctrl+R for right. ■

Changing Text Direction

The default text direction for table cells is Horizontal, which reads from left to right (at least in countries where that's how text is read). Figure 23-24 shows the alternatives.

You can set types of text direction.

To change the text direction for a cell, follow these steps:

1. **Select the cell(s) to affect.** To affect only a single cell, move the insertion point into it.
2. **On the Table Tools Layout tab in the Alignment group, click Text Direction.**
3. **Select a text direction from the menu that appears.**

Note

You cannot set text direction for individual paragraphs; the setting applies to the entire cell. ■

Understanding Charts

PowerPoint 2010's charting feature is based on the same Escher 2.0 graphics engine as is used for drawn objects. Consequently, most of what you have learned about formatting objects in earlier chapters (about Word) also applies to charts. For example, you can apply shape styles to the individual elements of a chart, and apply WordArt styles to chart text. However, there are also many chart-specific formatting and layout options, as you will see throughout this chapter.

Parts of a Chart

The sample chart shown in Figure 23-25 contains these elements:

- **Data Series.** Each different bar color represents a different *series*: Q1, Q2, and Q3.
- **Legend.** Colored squares in the Legend box describe the correlation of each color to a data series.
- **Categories.** The North, South, East, and West labels along the bottom of the chart are the *categories*.
- **Category Axis.** The horizontal line running across the bottom of the chart is the *category axis*, also called the *horizontal axis*.
- **Value Axis.** The vertical line running up the left side of the chart, with the numbers on it, is the *value axis*, also called the *vertical axis*.
- **Data Points.** Each individual bar is a *data point*. The numerical value for that data point corresponds to the height of the bar, measured against the value axis.
- **Walls.** The *walls* are the areas behind the data points. On a 3-D chart, as shown in Figure 23-25, there are both back and side walls. On a 2-D chart, there is only the plot area behind the chart.
- **Floor.** The *floor* is the area on which the data points sit. A floor appears only in a 3-D chart.

FIGURE 23-25

Parts of a chart

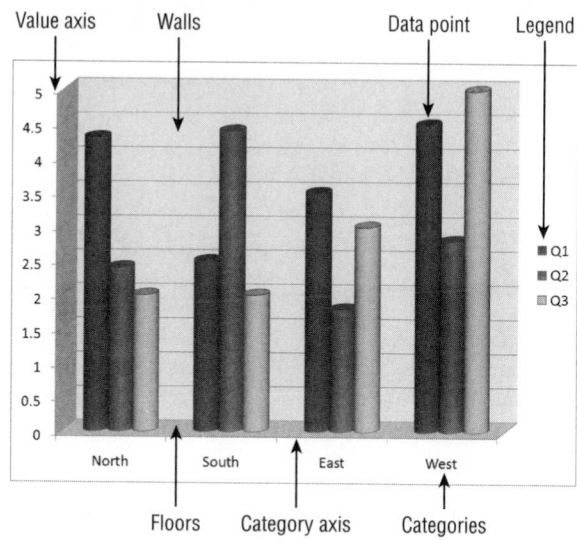

PowerPoint 2010 versus Legacy Charts

The Charts feature in PowerPoint 2010 shown in Figure 23-26 (which is the same as in PowerPoint 2007) is very powerful and flexible. It is based on the charting feature in Excel. Earlier versions of PowerPoint (2003 and earlier) used a much simpler charting utility called *Microsoft Graph*.

FIGURE 23-26

The PowerPoint 2010 charting interface

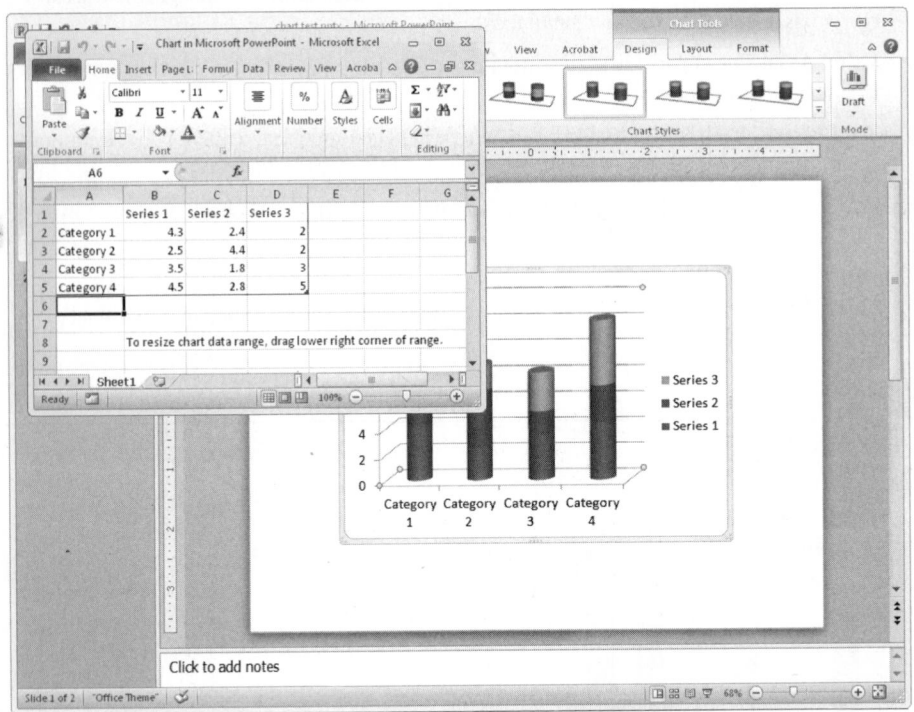

If you create a chart in a PowerPoint 2010 presentation and then save the file as a PowerPoint 97–2003 presentation, it does not take away your ability to access the PowerPoint 2010 charting interface as long as you are working in PowerPoint 2007 or 2010. The chart is still saved as a PowerPoint 2010 object in the 2003 file, but it also contains a 2003 version of itself, for backward compatibility.

If you want to make sure that the chart appears exactly as you created it in PowerPoint 2003, even if it is edited there, then you should insert the chart initially using Microsoft Graph, rather than the PowerPoint 2010 charting tools. To do this, insert a Microsoft Graph object by following these steps:

1. **On the Insert tab, click Object in the Text group.** The Object dialog box opens.

2. **Click Create New.**

3. **On the Object Type list, click Microsoft Graph Chart.**

4. **Click OK.** The Microsoft Graph window opens within PowerPoint, complete with a 2003-style menu bar from which you can access all of the same controls that were available in PowerPoint 2003's charting interface. The Microsoft Graph window is shown in Figure 23-27.

FIGURE 23-27

Microsoft Graph from within PowerPoint 2010

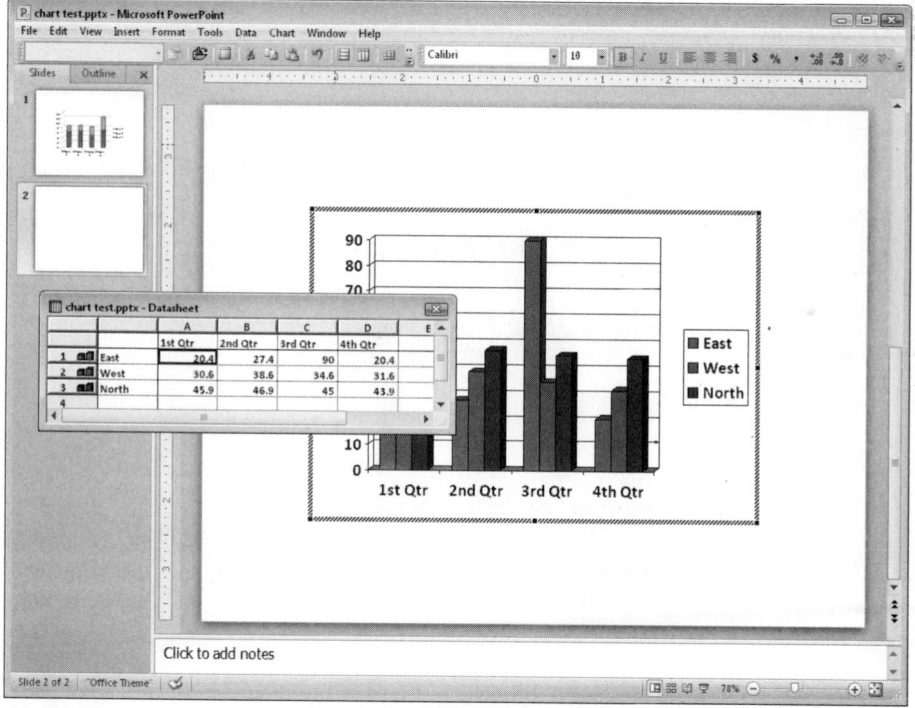

Tip

When you double-click to edit a Microsoft Graph chart within a PowerPoint 2010 presentation file, a message appears asking whether you want to Convert, Convert All, or Edit Existing. If you choose to convert (this chart or all charts) to 2010 format, you can use the new charting tools. If you choose Edit Existing, Microsoft Graph opens. ■

Starting a New Chart

The main difficulty with creating a chart in a non-spreadsheet application such as PowerPoint is that there is no data table from which to pull the numbers. Therefore, PowerPoint creates charts using data that you have entered in an Excel window. By default, it contains sample data, which you can replace with your own data.

You can place a new chart on a slide in two ways: You can either use a chart placeholder from a layout, or you can place one manually.

If you are using a placeholder, click the Insert Chart icon on the placeholder. If you are placing a chart manually, follow these steps:

1. **In the Illustrations group on the Insert tab, click Chart.** The Insert Chart dialog box opens, as shown in Figure 23-28.

FIGURE 23-28

Select the desired chart type.

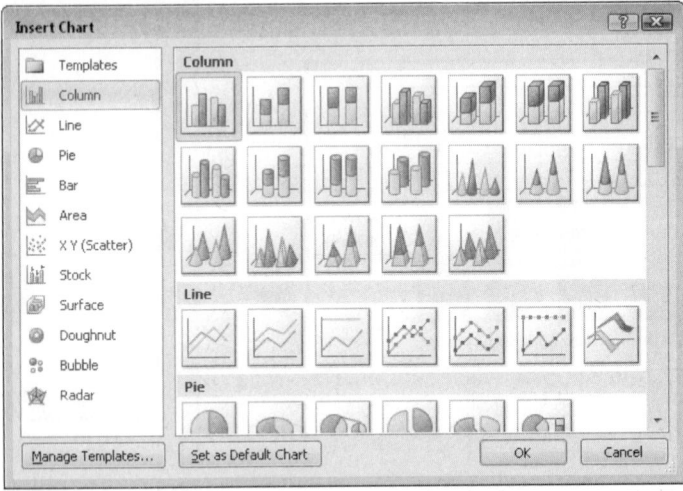

2. **Click the desired chart type.** See Table 23-2 for an explanation of the chart types. Figures 23-29 and 23-30 show examples of some of the chart types.
3. **Click OK.** The chart appears on the slide, and an Excel datasheet opens with sample data.
4. **Modify the sample data as needed.** To change the range of cells that appear in the chart, see the section, "Redefining the Data Range," later in this chapter. If you want, you can then close the Excel window to move it out of the way.

Note

A chart inserted into PowerPoint is an *embedded* object; it exists only within PowerPoint, even though it is created using Excel's tools. ∎

Note

After you have closed the Excel window, you can open it again by clicking Edit Data in the Data group on the Chart Tools Design tab. ∎

FIGURE 23-29

Examples of chart types, from top left, clockwise: column, line, bar, and pie

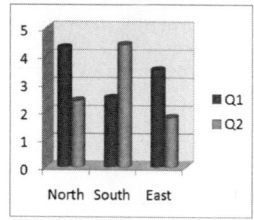
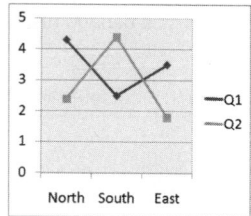
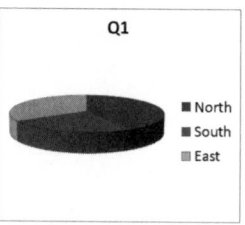
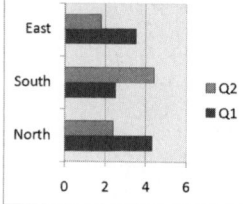

TABLE 23-2

Chart Types in PowerPoint 2010's Charting Tool

Type	Description
Column	Vertical bars, optionally with multiple data series. Bars can be clustered, stacked, or based on a percentage, and either 2-D or 3-D.
Line	Shows values as points and connects the points with a line. Different series use different colors and/or line styles.
Pie	A circle broken into wedges to show how parts contribute to a whole. This de-emphasizes the actual numeric values. In most cases, this type is a single series only.
Bar	Just like a column chart, but horizontal.
Area	Just like a column chart, but with the spaces filled in between the bars.

continued

TABLE 23-2	(continued)
Type	**Description**
XY (Scatter)	Shows values as points on both axes, but does not connect them with a line. However, you can add trend lines.
Stock	A special type of chart that is used to show stock prices.
Surface	A 3-D sheet that is used to illustrate the highest and lowest points of the data set.
Doughnut	Similar to a pie chart, but with multiple concentric rings, so that multiple series can be illustrated.
Bubble	Similar to a scatter chart, but instead of fixed-size data points, bubbles of varying sizes are used to represent a third data variable.
Radar	Shows changes of data frequency in relation to a center point.

FIGURE 23-30

Examples of chart types, from top left, clockwise: area, scatter, donut, and surface

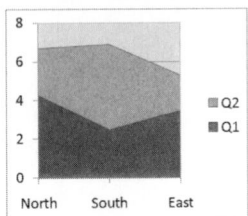 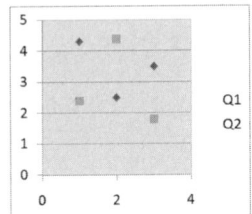

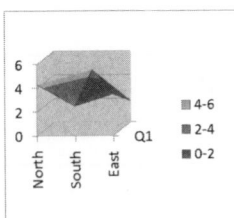 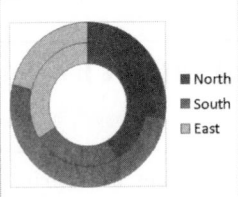

Note

At any point, you can return to your PowerPoint presentation by clicking anywhere outside of the chart on the slide. To edit the chart again, you can click the chart to redisplay the chart-specific tabs. ∎

Tip

If you delete a column or row by selecting individual cells and pressing Delete to clear them, the empty space that these cells occupied remains in the chart. To completely remove a row or column from the data range, select the row or column by clicking its header (letter for column; number for row) and clicking Delete on the Home tab in Excel. ∎

Working with Chart Data

After you create a chart, you might want to change the data range on which it is based, or how this data is plotted. The following sections explain how you can do this.

Plotting by Rows versus by Columns

By default, the columns of the datasheet form the data series. However, if you want, you can switch the data around so that the rows form the series. Figures 23-31 and 23-32 show the same chart plotted both ways so that you can see the difference.

Note

What does the term *data series* mean? Take a look at Figures 23-31 and 23-32. Notice that there is a legend next to each chart that shows what each color (or shade of gray) represents. Each of these colors, and the label associated with it, is a *series*. The other variable (the one that is not the series) is plotted on the chart's horizontal axis. ∎

FIGURE 23-31

A chart with the columns representing the series

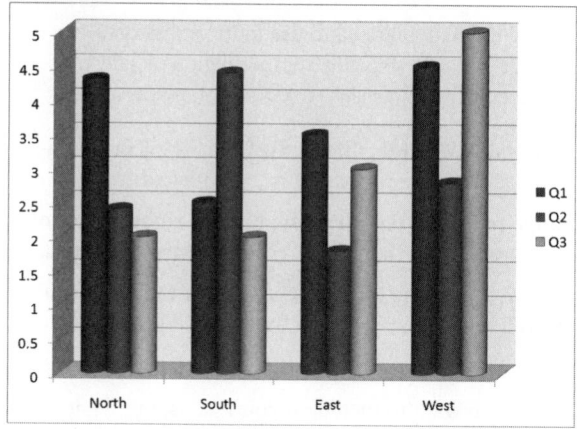

To switch back and forth between plotting by rows and by columns, click the Switch Row/ Column button on the Chart Tools Design tab.

Tip

A chart can carry a very different message when you arrange it by rows versus by columns. For example, in Figure 23-31, the chart compares the quarters. The message here is about improvement — or lack thereof — over time. Contrast this to Figure 23-32, where the series are the regions. Here, you can compare one region to another. The overriding message here is about competition — which division performed the best in each quarter? It's easy to see how the same data can convey very different messages; make sure that you pick the arrangement that tells the story that you want to tell in your presentation. ∎

FIGURE 23-32

A chart with the rows representing the series

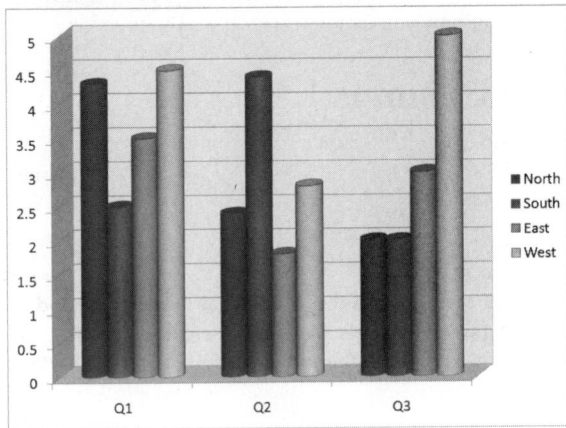

Redefining the Data Range

After you have created your chart, you may decide that you need to use more or less data. Perhaps you want to exclude a month or quarter of data, or to add another region or salesperson. To add or remove a data series, you can simply edit the datasheet. To do so, follow these steps:

1. **In the Data group on the Chart Tools Design tab, click Edit Data.** The Excel datasheet appears. A blue outline appears around the range that is to be plotted.

2. (Optional) **To change the data range to be plotted, drag the bottom-right corner of the blue outline.** For example, in Figure 23-33, the West division is being excluded.

   You can also enlarge the data range by expanding the blue outline. For example, you could enter another series in column E in Figure 23-33 and then extend the outline to encompass column E.

The preceding steps work well if the range that you want to include is contiguous, but what if you wanted to exclude a row or column that is in the middle of the range? To define the range more precisely, follow these steps:

1. **In the Data group on the Chart Tools Design tab, click Select Data.** The Select Data Source dialog box opens, along with the Excel datasheet, as shown in Figure 23-34.

2. **Do any of the following:**
   - To remove a series, select it from the Legend Entries (Series) list and click Remove.

- To add a series, click Add, and then drag across the range on the datasheet to enter it into the Edit Series dialog box; then click OK to accept it.

- To edit a series, select it in the Legend Entries (Series) list and click Edit. Then drag across the range or make a change in the Edit Series dialog box, and click OK.

3. (Optional) **To redefine the range from which to pull the horizontal axis labels, click the Edit button in the Horizontal (Category) Axis Labels section.** A dotted outline appears around the current range; drag to redefine that range and click OK.

4. (Optional) **To redefine how empty or hidden cells should be treated, click the Hidden and Empty Cells button.** In the Hidden and Empty Cell Settings dialog box that appears, choose whether to show data in hidden rows and columns, and whether to define empty cells as gaps in the chart or as zero values. Then click OK. The Hidden and Empty Cell Settings dialog box is shown in Figure 23-35.

5. **When you are finished editing the settings for the data ranges, click OK to close the Select Data Source dialog box.**

6. (Optional) **Close the Excel datasheet window, or leave it open for later reference.**

FIGURE 23-33

You can redefine the range for the chart by dragging the blue outline on the datasheet.

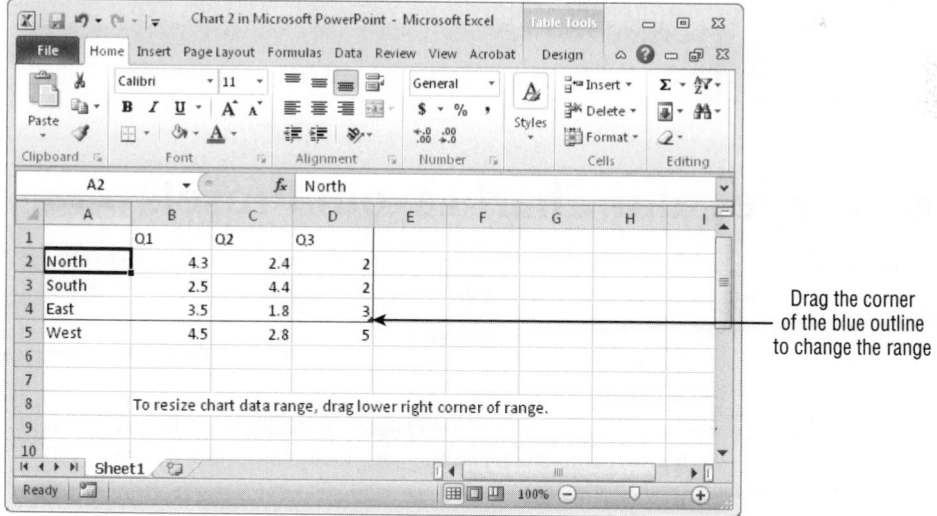

Drag the corner of the blue outline to change the range

FIGURE 23-34

To fine-tune the data ranges, you can use the Select Data Source dialog box.

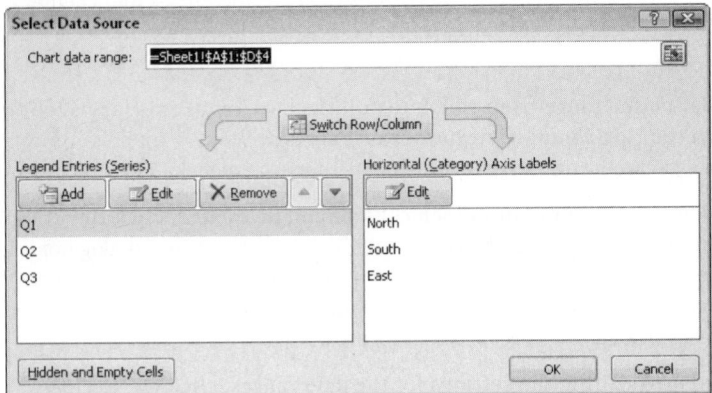

FIGURE 23-35

Specify what should happen when the data range contains blank or hidden cells.

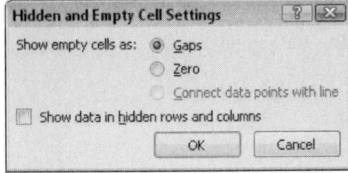

Chart Types and Chart Layout Presets

The default chart is a column chart. However, there are a lot of alternative chart types to choose from. Not all of them will be appropriate for your data, of course, but you may be surprised at the different spin on the message that a different chart type presents.

Caution

Many chart types come in both 2-D and 3-D models, and you can choose which chart type looks most appropriate for your presentation. However, try to be consistent. For example, it looks nicer to stay with all 2-D or all 3-D charts rather than mixing the types in a presentation. ∎

You can revisit your choice of chart type at any time by following these steps:

1. Select the chart, if needed, so that the Chart Tools Design tab becomes available.

2. In the Type group, click Change Chart Type.

3. Select the desired type, just as you did when you originally created the chart. Figure 23-28 shows the chart types.

4. Click OK.

This is the basic procedure for the overall chart type selection, but there are also many options for fine-tuning the layout. The following sections explain these options.

Tip

To change the default chart type, after selecting a chart from the Change Chart Type dialog box, click the Set as Default Chart button. ■

PowerPoint provides a limited number of preset chart layouts for each chart type. You can choose these presets from the Chart Layouts group in the Chart Tools Design tab. They are good starting points for creating your own layouts, which you will learn about in this chapter.

To choose a layout, click the down-arrow in the Chart Layouts group and select one from the gallery, as shown in Figure 23-36. Although you cannot add your own layouts to these presets, you can create chart templates, which are basically the same thing with additional formatting settings. This chapter also covers chart template creation.

FIGURE 23-36

You can choose one of the preset layouts that fits your needs.

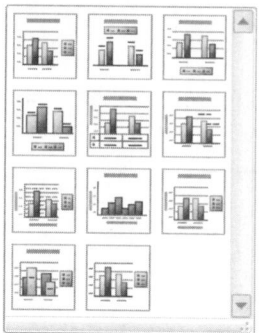

Working with Labels

On the Chart Tools Layout tab, the Labels group provides buttons for controlling which labels appear on the chart. Figure 23-37 points out the various labels that you can use.

Each of these label types has a button on the Layout tab that opens a drop-down list that contains some presets. The drop-down list also contains a "More" command for opening a dialog box that contains additional options. For example, the drop-down list for the Chart Title button contains a More Title Options command, as shown in Figure 23-38.

Tip

You can add data labels to a series by right-clicking on a series and choosing Add Data Labels. You can also format label text from the MiniBar, which may be easier than using the Home tab's controls. ∎

FIGURE 23-37

Labels help to make it clear to the audience what the chart represents.

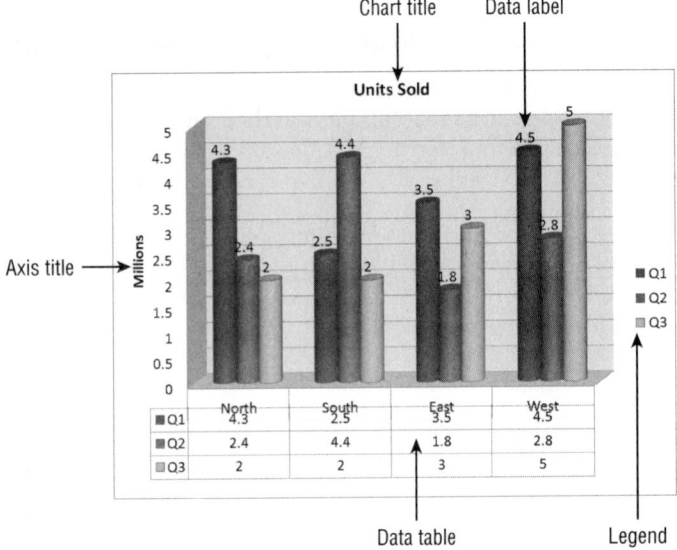

FIGURE 23-38

Each type of label has its own button that displays a drop-down list.

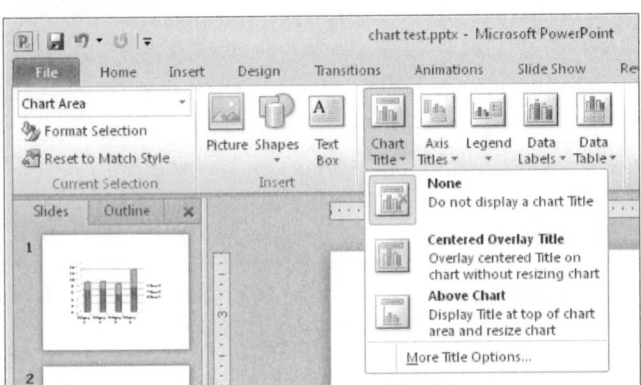

You can format the label text, just as you can format any other text. To do this, select the text and then use the Font group on the Home tab. This allows you to choose a font, size, color, alignment, and so on.

You can also format the label box by right-clicking it and choosing Format Name, where *name* is the type of label that the box contains. In some cases, the dialog box that appears contains only standard formatting controls that you would find for any object, such as Fill, Border Color, Border Styles, Shadow, 3-D Format, and Alignment. These controls should already be very familiar to you from earlier sections in this chapter. In other cases, in addition to the standard formatting types, there is also a unique section that contains extra options that are specific to the content type. For example, for the Legend, there is a Legend Options section in which you can set the position of a legend.

The following sections look at each of the label types more closely. These sections will not dwell on the formatting that you can apply to them (fonts, sizes, borders, fills, etc.) because this formatting is the same for all of them, as it is with any other object. Instead, they concentrate on the options that make each label different.

Working with Chart Titles

A *chart title* is text that typically appears above the chart — and sometimes overlapping it — that indicates what the chart represents. Although you would usually want either a chart title *or* a slide title, but not both, this could vary if you have multiple charts or different content on the same slide.

You can select a basic chart title, either above the chart or overlapping it, from the Chart Title drop-down list, as shown in Figure 23-38. You can also drag the chart title around after placing it. For more options, you can choose More Title Options to open the Format Chart Title dialog box. However, in this dialog box there is nothing that specifically relates to chart titles; the available options are for formatting (Fill, Border Color, etc.), as for any textbox.

Working with Axis Titles

An *axis title* is text that defines the category or the unit of measurement on an axis. For example, in Figure 23-37, the vertical axis title is *Millions*.

Axis titles are defined separately for the vertical and the horizontal axes. Click the Axis Titles button on the Layout tab, and then select either Primary Horizontal Axis Title or Primary Vertical Axis Title to display a submenu that is specific to that axis. When you turn on an axis title, a textbox appears containing the default placeholder text, "Axis Title." Click in this textbox and type your own label to replace it, as shown in Figure 23-39. If you've plotted any data on a secondary axis, you'll see Secondary Horizontal Axis Title and Secondary Vertical Axis Title options as well.

Tip
You can easily select all of the placeholder text by clicking in the textbox and pressing Ctrl+A. ■

For the horizontal axis title, the options are simple: either None or Title Below Axis. You can choose More Primary Horizontal Axis Title Options, but again, as with the regular title options, there are no unique settings in the dialog box — just general formatting controls.

FIGURE 23-39

An axis title describes what is being measured on the axis.

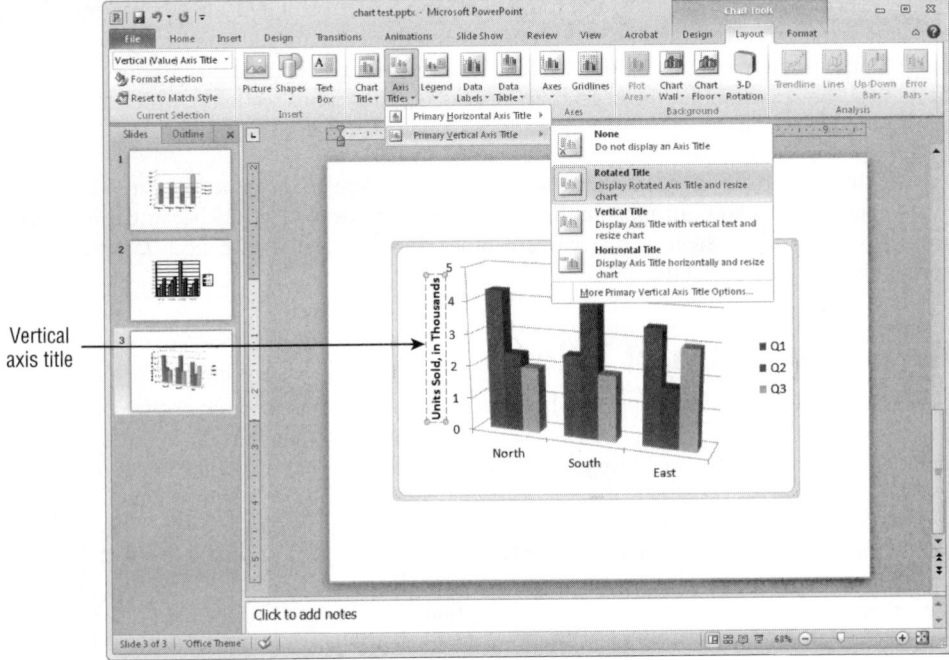

Vertical axis title

For the vertical axis title, you can choose from among the following options, as shown in Figure 23-40:

- **Rotated Title.** The title appears vertically along the vertical axis, with the letters rotated 90 degrees (so that their bases run along the axis).

- **Vertical Title.** The title appears vertically along the vertical axis, but each letter remains unrotated, so that the letters are stacked one on top of the other.

- **Horizontal Title.** The title appears horizontally, like regular text, to the left of the vertical axis.

Each type of vertical axis shrinks the chart somewhat when you activate it, but the Horizontal Title format shrinks the chart more than the others because it requires more space to the left of the chart.

Caution

If you turn off an axis title by setting it to None and then turn it back on again, you will need to retype the axis title; it returns to the generic placeholder text. ∎

If the chart does not resize itself automatically when you turn on the Vertical Axis Title, you might need to adjust the chart size manually. Click the chart, so that selection handles appear around the inner part of the chart (*plot area*), as shown in Figure 23-41. Then drag the left side-selection handle inward to decrease the width of the chart to make room for the vertical axis label.

You can select these vertical axis titles, from left to right: Rotated Title, Vertical Title, and Horizontal Title.

5	5	5
4.5	4.5	4.5
4	M 4	4
3.5	i 3.5	3.5
3	l 3	3
Millions 2.5	l 2.5	Millions 2.5
2	i 2	2
1.5	o n 1.5	1.5
1	s 1	1
0.5	0.5	0.5
0	0	0

You can adjust the size of the plot area to make more room for the vertical axis title.

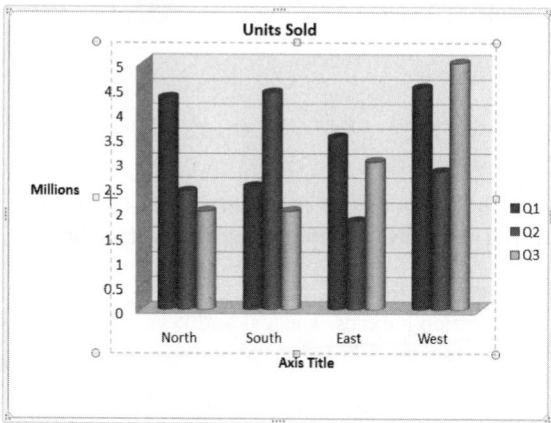

Working with Legends

The *legend* is the little box that appears next to the chart (or sometimes above or below it). It provides the key that describes what the different colors or patterns mean. For some chart types and labels, you may not find the legend to be useful. If it is not useful for the chart that you are working on, you can turn it off by clicking the Legend button on the Chart Tools Layout tab Labels group and then clicking None. You can also just click it and press Delete. Turning off the legend makes more room for the chart, which grows to fill the available space. To turn the legend back on, click the Legend button again and select the position that you want for it, as shown in Figure 23-42.

FIGURE 23-42

You can select a legend position, or turn the legend off altogether.

Caution

Hiding the legend is not a good idea if you have more than one series in your chart, because the legend helps people to distinguish which series is which. However, if you have only one series, a legend might not be useful. ■

To resize a legend box, you can drag one of its selection handles. The text and keys inside the box do not change in size, although they may shift in position.

When you right-click on the legend and choose Format Legend, or when you choose More Legend Options from the Legend drop-down list on the Layout tab, the Format Legend dialog box opens with the Legend Options displayed, as shown in Figure 23-43. From here, you can choose the legend's position in relation to the chart and whether or not it should overlap the chart. If it does not overlap the chart, the plot area will be automatically reduced to accommodate the legend.

Note

The controls on the Legend Options tab refer to the legend's position in relation to the chart, not to the position of the legend text within the legend box. You can drag the legend wherever you want it on the chart after placing it. ■

FIGURE 23-43

You can set legend options in the Format Legend dialog box.

Adding Data Labels

Data labels show the numeric values (or other information) that are represented by each bar or other shape on the chart. These labels are useful when the exact numbers are important or where the chart is so small that it is not clear from the axes what the data points represent.

To turn on data labels for the chart, click the Data Labels button in the Labels group on the Chart Tools Layout tab. The options available depend on whether it's a 2-D or 3-D chart, and on what type of chart it is (bar, pie, column, etc.). Figure 23-44 shows the options for a 3-D pie chart.

Data labels show the values by default, but you can also set them to display the series name and the category name, or any combination of the three. The data labels can also include the legend key, which is a colored square. To quickly add data labels to a chart, right-click the chart and choose Add Data Labels.

To set data label options, choose More Data Label Options from the Data Labels drop-down menu, to access the Format Data Labels dialog box, as shown in Figure 23-45. For a 3-D chart, the Label Position section does not appear.

FIGURE 23-44

You can display or hide data labels using the Data Labels button.

FIGURE 23-45

You can set data label options using the Format Data Labels dialog box.

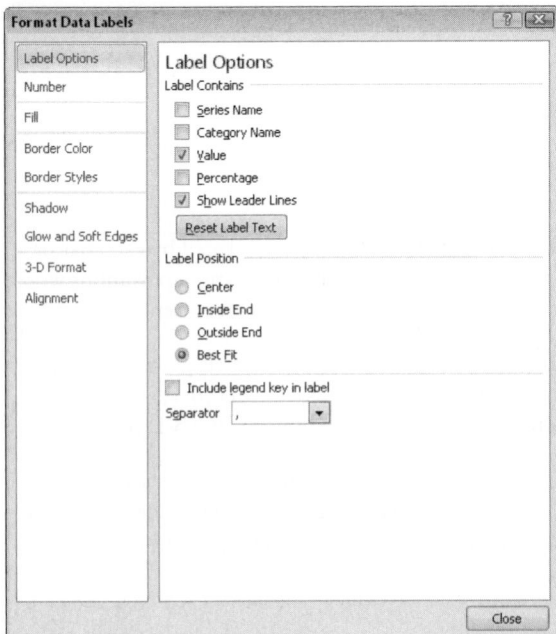

Tip

To turn the data labels on or off for a particular data point or data series, select it and then select the None or Show option in the Data Labels drop-down menu. This is useful when you want to highlight a particular value or set of values. ∎

Adding a Data Table

Sometimes the chart tells the full story that you want to tell, but other times the audience may benefit from seeing the actual numbers on which you have built the chart. In these cases, it is a good idea to include the data table with the chart. A data table contains the same information that appears on the datasheet.

To display the data table with a chart, click the Data Table button in the Labels group on the Chart Tools Layout tab, as shown in Figure 23-46, and choose to include a data table either with or without a legend key.

To format the data table, choose More Data Table Options from the Data Table drop-down menu. From the Format Data Table dialog box that appears, you can set data table border options, as shown in Figure 23-47. For example, you can display or hide the horizontal, vertical, and outline borders for the table from here.

FIGURE 23-46

Use a data table to show the audience the numbers on which the chart is based.

FIGURE 23-47

Use the Data Table Options to specify which borders should appear in the data table.

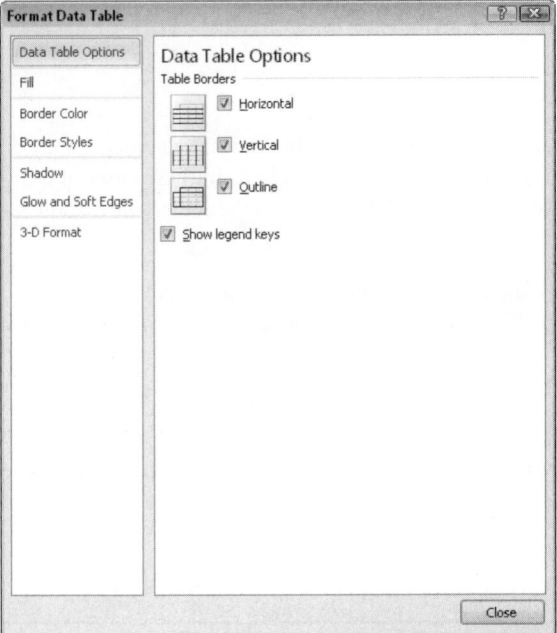

Controlling the Axes

No, *axes* are not the tools that chop down trees. *Axes* is the plural of *axis*, and an *axis* is the side of the chart containing the measurements against which your data is plotted.

You can change the various axes in a chart in several ways. For example, you can make an axis run in a different direction (such as from top-to-bottom instead of bottom-to-top for a vertical axis), and you can turn the text on or off for the axis and change the axis scale.

Using Axis Presets

You can select some of the most popular axis presets using the Axes button in the Axes group on the Chart Tools Layout tab. As with the axis titles that you learned about earlier in this chapter, there are separate submenus for horizontal and vertical axes. Figure 23-48 shows the options for horizontal axes, and Figure 23-49 shows those for vertical axes.

FIGURE 23-48

Presets for horizontal axes

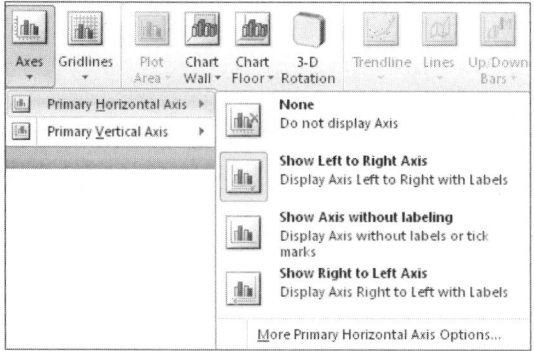

FIGURE 23-49

Presets for vertical axes

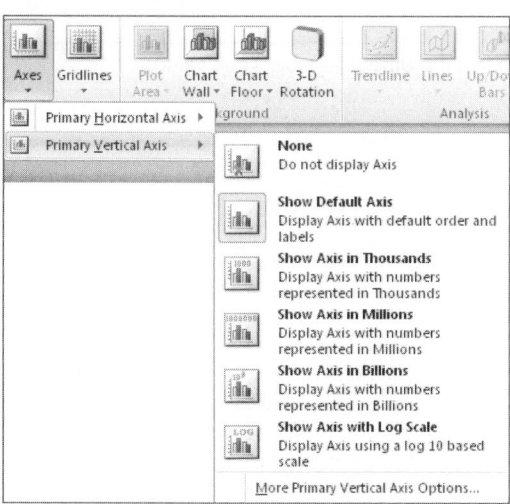

Setting Axis Scale Options

The *scale* determines which numbers will form the start point and endpoint of the axis line. For example, take a look at the chart in Figure 23-50. The bars are so close to one another in value that it is difficult to see the difference between them. Compare this chart to one showing the same data in Figure 23-51, but with an adjusted scale. Because the scale is smaller, the differences now appear more dramatic.

FIGURE 23-50

This chart does not show the differences between the values very well.

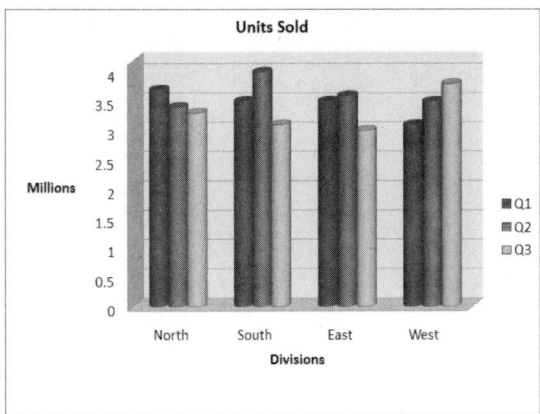

FIGURE 23-51

A change to the values of the axis scale makes it easier to see the differences between values.

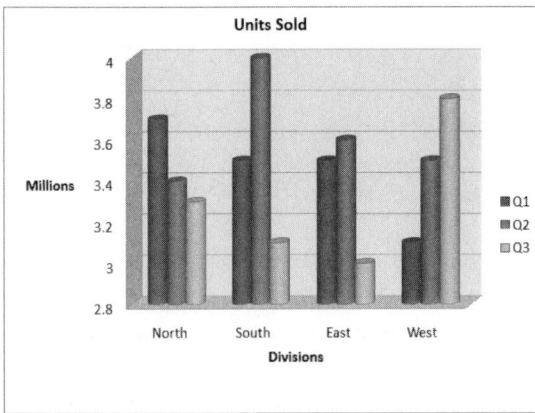

Tip

You will probably never run into a case as dramatic as the difference between Figures 23-50 and 23-51 because PowerPoint's charting feature has an automatic setting for the scale that is turned on by default. However, you may sometimes want to override this setting for a different effect, such as to minimize or enhance the difference between data series. This is a good example of "making the data say what you want." For example, if you wanted to make the point that the differences between three months were insignificant, then you would use a larger scale. If you wanted to highlight the importance of the differences, then you would use a smaller scale. ■

To set the scale for an axis, follow these steps:

1. **On the Chart Tools Layout tab, choose Axes ➪ Axes ➪ Primary Vertical Axis ➪ More Primary Vertical Axis Options.** The Format Axis dialog box opens, displaying the Axis Options, as shown in Figure 23-52.

FIGURE 23-52

You can set axis options in the Format Axis dialog box, including the axis scale.

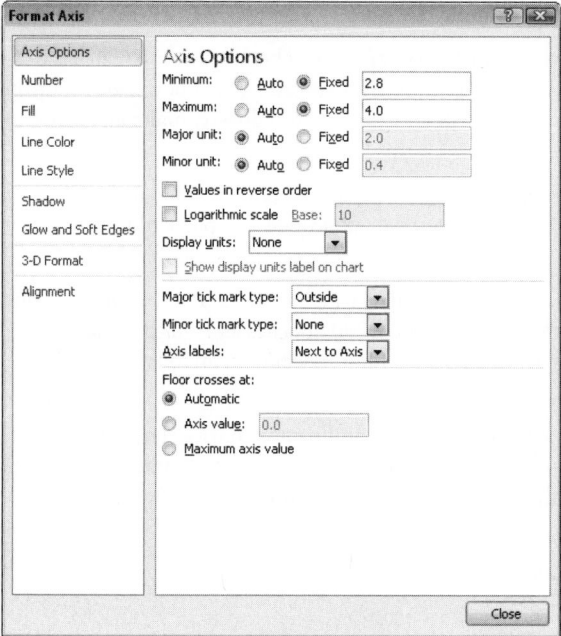

2. **Drag the Format Axis dialog box to the side so that you can see the results on the chart.**

3. **If you do not want the automatic value for one of the measurements, click Fixed and enter a different number in its textbox.**

   - **Minimum.** Minimum is the starting number. The usual setting is 0, as shown in Figure 23-50, although in Figure 23-51, it is set to 2.8.

   - **Maximum.** Maximum is the top number. This number is 4 in both Figures 23-50 and 23-51.

   - **Major Unit.** This determines the axis text. It is also the unit by which gridlines stretch out across the back wall of the chart. In Figure 23-50, gridlines appear at increments of 0.5 million units; in Figure 23-51, they appear in increments of 0.2 million units.

- **Minor Unit.** This is the interval of smaller gridlines between the major ones. Most charts look better without minor units because these units can make a chart look cluttered. You should leave this setting at Auto. You can also use this feature to place tick marks on the axes between the labels of the major units.

4. (Optional) **If you want to activate any of these special features, select their checkboxes.** Each of these checkboxes recalculates the numbers in the Minimum, Maximum, Major Unit, and Minor Unit textboxes.

- **Values in Reverse Order.** This checkbox turns the scale backward so that the greater values appear at the bottom or left.

- **Logarithmic Scale.** Rarely used by ordinary folks, this checkbox recalculates the Minimum, Maximum, Major Unit, and Minor Unit according to a power of 10 for the value axis, based on the range of data. (If this explanation doesn't make any sense to you, then you're not the target audience for this feature.)

- **Floor Crosses At.** When you select this feature, you can enter a value indicating where the axes should cross. You can specify an axis value of a particular number, or use the Maximum axis value.

5. (Optional) **You can set a display unit to simplify large numbers.** For example, if you set display units to Thousands, then the number 1,000 appears as *1* on the chart. If you then select the Show Display Units Label on Chart checkbox, an axis label will appear as *Thousands*.

6. (Optional) **You can set tick-mark types for major and minor marks.** These marks appear as little lines on the axis to indicate the units. You can use tick marks either with or without gridlines. (To set gridlines, use the Gridlines button's menu on the Chart Tools Layout tab.)

7. **If you are happy with the results, click Close.**

Setting a Number Format

You can apply a number format to axes and data labels that show numerical data. This is similar to the number format that is used for Excel cells; you can choose a category, such as Currency or Percentage, and then fine-tune this format by choosing a number of decimal places, a method of handling negative numbers, and so on.

To set a number format, follow these steps:

1. **Right-click the axis and choose Format Axis.**

2. **In the Format Axis dialog box that appears, click Number.** A list of number formats appears.

3. (Optional) **You can select the number format in two ways: the first way is to select the Linked to Source checkbox if you want the number format to be taken from the number format that is applied to the datasheet in Excel.** The second way is to click the desired number format in the Category list. Options appear that are specific to the

format that you selected. For example, Figure 23-53 shows the options for the Number type of format, which is a generic format.

4. **(Optional) You can fine-tune the numbering format by changing the code in the Format Code textbox.** The number signs (#) represent optional digits, while the zeroes represent required digits.

5. **Click Close to close the dialog box.**

Note

To see some examples of custom number formats that you might use in the Format Code textbox, choose Custom as the number format. ■

FIGURE 23-53

You can set a number format in the Format Axis dialog box.

Formatting a Chart

In the following sections, you learn about chart formatting. There is so much that you can do to a chart that this subject could easily take up its own chapter! For example, just like any other object, you can resize a chart. You can also change the fonts; change the colors and shading of bars, lines, or pie slices; use different background colors; change the 3-D angle; and much more.

Tip
The Format dialog box can remain open while you format various parts of the chart. Just click a different part of the chart behind the open dialog box (drag it off to the side if needed); the controls in the dialog box change to reflect the part that you have selected. ■

Clearing Manually Applied Formatting

PowerPoint uses Format dialog boxes that are related to the various parts of the chart. These dialog boxes are *non-modal*, which means that they can stay open indefinitely, that their changes are applied immediately, and that you don't have to close the dialog box to continue working on the document. Although this is handy, it is all too easy to make an unintended formatting change.

To clear the formatting that is applied to a chart element, select it and then, on the Format tab, click Reset to Match Style. This strips off the manually applied formatting from that element, returning it to whatever appearance is specified by the chart style that you have applied.

Formatting Titles and Labels

Once you add a title or label to your chart, you can change its size, attributes, colors, and font. Just right-click on the title that you want to format and choose Format Chart Title (or whatever kind of title it is; e.g., an axis label is called *Axis Title*). The Format Chart Title (or Format Axis Title) dialog box appears.

Note
The formatting covered in this section applies to the textbox, not to the text within it. If you need to format the fill, outline, or typeface, use the Mini toolbar (right-click to open it) or use the font tools on the Home tab. ■

The categories in this dialog box vary, depending on the type of text that you are formatting, but the following categories are generally available:

- **Fill.** You can choose No Fill, Solid Fill, Gradient Fill, Picture or Text Fill, or Automatic. When you select Automatic, the color changes to contrast with the background color specified by the theme.

- **Border Color.** You can choose No Line, Solid Line, or Automatic. When you select Automatic, the color changes to contrast with the background color specified by the theme.

- **Border Styles.** You can set a width, a compound type (i.e., a line made up of multiple lines), and a dash type.

- **Shadow.** You can apply a preset shadow in any color you want, or you can fine-tune the shadow in terms of transparency, size, angle, and so on. You might need to apply a fill to the box in order for the shadow to appear. This shadow is for the textbox, not for the text within it; use the Font group on the Home tab to apply the text shadow, or the shadows available for WordArt.

- **3-D Format.** You can define 3-D settings for the textbox, such as Bevel, Depth, Contour, and Surface.

- **Alignment.** You can set vertical and horizontal alignment, angle, and text direction, as well as control AutoFit settings for some types of text.

Note

Alignment is usually not relevant in a short label or title textbox. The textbox is usually exactly the right size to hold the text, and so there is no other way for the text to be aligned. Therefore, no matter what alignment you choose, the text looks very much the same. ∎

From the Home tab or the Mini toolbar, you can also choose all of the text effects that you learned about earlier in this book, such as font, size, font style, underline, color, alignment, and so on.

Applying Chart Styles

Chart styles are presets that you can apply to charts in order to add colors, backgrounds, and fill styles. The Chart Styles Gallery, shown in Figure 23-54, is located on the Chart Tools Design tab, which appears when you select a chart.

FIGURE 23-54

You can apply a chart style using the Chart Styles Gallery.

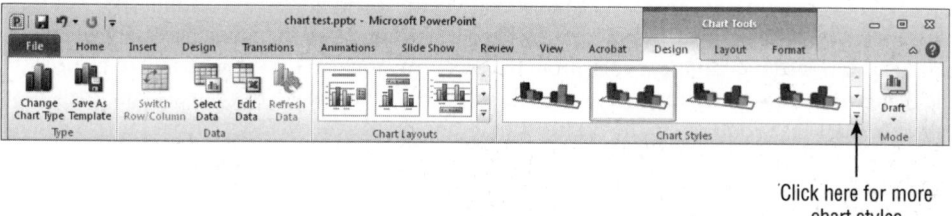

Click here for more
chart styles

Chart styles are based on the themes and color schemes in the PowerPoint Design tab. When you change the theme or the colors, the chart style choices also change.

Note

You cannot add to the presets in the Chart Styles Gallery, but you can save a group of settings as a template. To do this, use the Save As Template command on the Chart Tools Design tab. ∎

Formatting the Chart Area

Your next task is to format the big picture: the *chart area*. The *chart area* is the big frame that contains the chart and all of its elements: the legend, the data series, the data table, the titles, and so on.

The Format Chart Area dialog box has many of the same categories as for textboxes — such as fill, border color, border styles, shadow, and 3-D format — and it also adds 3-D rotation if you are working with a 3-D chart. You can choose to rotate and tilt the entire chart, just as you did with drawn shapes earlier in this book.

Formatting the Legend

When you use a multi-series chart, the value of the legend is obvious — it tells you which colors represent which series. Without the legend, your audience will not know what the various bars or lines mean. You can do all of the same formatting for a legend that you can for other chart elements. Just right-click on the legend, choose Format Legend from the shortcut menu, and then use the tabs in the Format Legend dialog box to make your modifications. The available categories are Fill, Border Color, Border Styles, and Shadow, as well as the Legend options mentioned earlier in this chapter.

Tip

If you select one of the individual keys in the legend and change its color, the color on the data series in the chart changes to match. This is especially useful with stacked charts, where it is sometimes difficult to select the data series that you want. ■

Formatting Gridlines and Walls

Gridlines help the reader's eyes move across the chart. Gridlines are related to the axes, which you learned about earlier in this chapter. Although both vertical and horizontal gridlines are available, most people use only horizontal ones. *Walls* are nothing more than the space between the gridlines, formatted in a different color from the plot area. You can set the Walls fill to None to hide them. (Don't you wish tearing down walls was always that easy?) You can also use the Chart Wall and Chart Floor buttons in the Background group on the Chart Tools Layout tab.

Note

You can only format walls on 3-D charts; 2-D charts do not have them. To change the background behind a 2-D chart, you must format the plot area. ■

In most cases, the default gridlines that PowerPoint adds work well. However, you may want to make the lines thicker or a different color, or turn them off altogether.

Gridline presets are available from the Gridlines drop-down menu on the Layout tab. There are separate submenus for vertical and horizontal gridlines, as shown in Figure 23-55. You can also choose the More command for either of the gridlines submenus for additional options.

To change the gridline formatting, right-click on a gridline and choose Format Major Gridlines. You can then adjust the line color, line style, and shadow from the Format Major Gridlines dialog box.

Note

Gridline spacing is based on the major and minor units that you have set in the Format Axis dialog box (vertical or horizontal). To set this spacing, see the section, "Setting Axis Scale Options," earlier in this chapter. ■

FIGURE 23-55

You can apply gridline presets from the Gridlines drop-down menu.

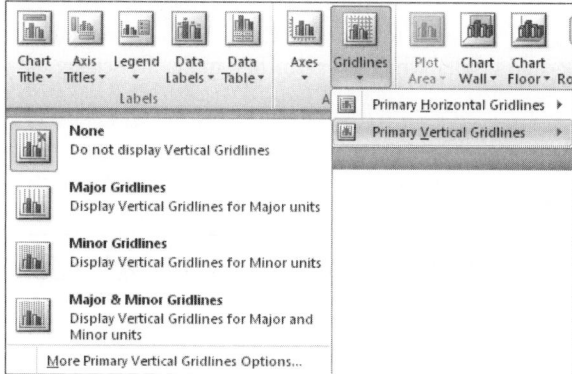

Formatting the Data Series

To format a data series, just right-click on the bar, slice, or chart element, and choose Format Data Series from the shortcut menu. Then, depending on your chart type, different tabs appear that you can use to modify the series appearance. Here are the ones for bar and column charts, for example:

- **Series Options.** This tab contains options that are specific to the selected chart type. For example, when working with a 3-D bar or column chart, the series options include Gap Depth and Gap Width, which determine the thickness and depth of the bars. For a pie chart, you can set the rotation angle for the first slice, as well as whether a slice is *exploded* or not.

- **Shape.** For charts involving bars and columns, you can choose a shape option such as Box, Full Pyramid, Partial Pyramid, Cylinder, Full Cone, or Partial Cone. The partial options truncate the top part of the shape when it is less than the largest value in the chart.

- **Fill.** You can choose a fill, including solid, gradient, or picture/texture.

- **Border Color.** The *border* is the line around the shape. You can set it to a Solid Line, No Line, or Automatic (i.e., based on the theme).

- **Border Styles.** The only option available on this tab for most chart types is Width, which controls the thickness of the border. For line charts, you can set arrow options and other line attributes.

- **Shadow.** You can add shadows to the data series bars or other shapes, just as you would add shadows to anything else.

- **3-D Format.** These settings control the contours, surfaces, and beveling for 3-D data series.

681

Other chart types have very different categories available. For example, a line chart has Marker Options, Marker Fill, Line Color, Line Style, Marker Line Color, and Marker Line Style, in addition to the generic Series Options, Shadow, and 3-D Format categories.

It is often easier to set up formatting for a chart using the tools on the Chart Tools Format tab. From here, you can choose preset shadows and bevels, which is easier than manually setting up 3-D effects.

Rotating a 3-D Chart

Three-dimensional charts have a 3-D Rotation option in the Format Chart Area dialog box. This feature works just the same as with other 3-D objects, where you can rotate the chart on the X-, Y-, and Z-axes. In addition, there are some extra chart-specific options, as shown in Figure 23-56. For example, you can set the chart to AutoScale, control its depth, and reset it to the default rotation.

FIGURE 23-56

You can adjust the 3-D rotation of a chart.

Summary

In this chapter, you learned the ins and outs of creating and formatting tables in PowerPoint including how to insert, draw, move, and resize the various cells of a table as well as how to add fills, styles, and effects. You also learned how to create and format charts using PowerPoint. You learned how to create charts, change their type and their data range, and use optional text elements on them such as titles, data labels, and so on. You also learned how to format charts. In the next chapter, you'll learn how to work with clip art, pictures, and diagrams.

Using SmartArt Diagrams, Clip Art, and Pictures

Just as charts and graphs can enliven a boring table of numbers, a SmartArt diagram can enliven a conceptual discussion. SmartArt helps the audience understand the interdependencies of objects or processes in a visual way, so they don't have to juggle that information mentally as you speak. Some potential uses include organizational charts, hierarchy diagrams, and flow charts. Similarly, the right clip art image or photo can highlight a concept or present a product with clarity that words cannot achieve.

In this chapter you will learn how to create and fine-tune SmartArt diagrams, and how to select and insert clip art into your presentations. You'll also learn how to integrate photos and images from other sources, including how to compress them so they take up less disk space.

Understanding SmartArt Types and Their Uses

SmartArt is a special class of vector graphic object that combines shapes, lines, and text placeholders. SmartArt is most often used to illustrate relationships between bits of text.

The SmartArt interface is similar regardless of the type of diagram you are creating. You can type directly into the placeholders on the diagram, or you can display a Text pane to the side of the diagram and type into that, much as you would type into an Outline pane to have text appear in a slide's text placeholder boxes (see Figure 24-1). You can also select some text, right-click on it, and choose Convert to SmartArt.

FIGURE 24-1

A typical SmartArt diagram being constructed.

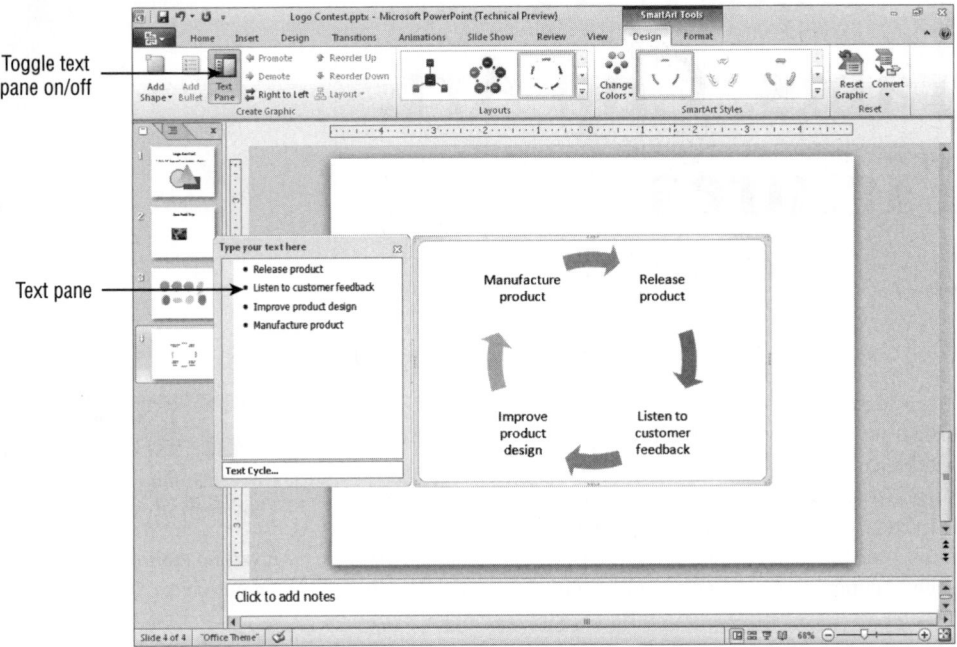

There are eight types of SmartArt diagrams in PowerPoint 2010, and each is uniquely suited for a certain type of data delivery: List, Process, Cycle, Hierarchy, Relationship, Matrix, Pyramid, and Picture.

List

A *List diagram* presents information in a fairly straightforward, text-based way, somewhat like a fancy outline. List diagrams are useful when information is not in any particular order or when the process or progression between items is not important. The list can have multiple levels, and you can enclose each level in a shape or not. Figure 24-2 shows an example.

Process

A *Process diagram* is similar to a list, but it has directional arrows or other connectors that represent the flow of one item to another. This adds an extra aspect of meaning to the diagram. For example, in Figure 24-3, the way the boxes are staggered and connected with arrows implies that the next step begins before the previous one ends.

FIGURE 24-2

A List diagram de-emphasizes any progression between items.

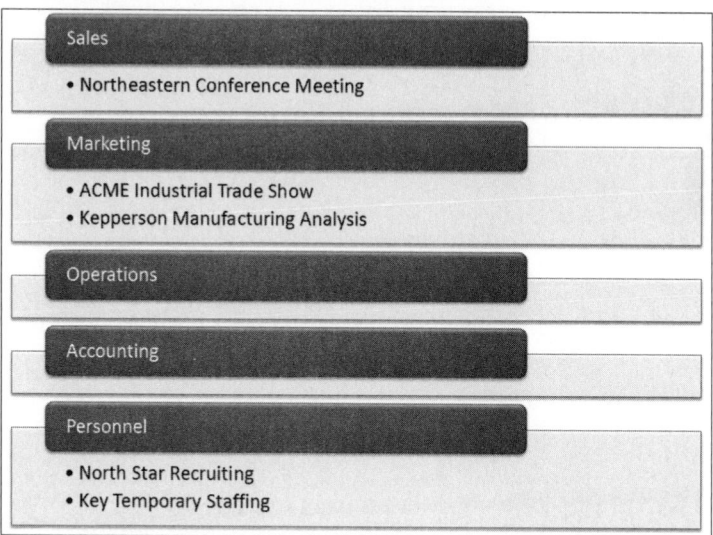

FIGURE 24-3

A Process diagram shows a flow from Point A to Point B.

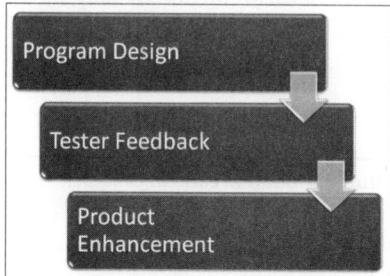

Cycle

A *Cycle diagram* also illustrates a process, but a repeating or recursive one — usually a process in which there is no fixed beginning or endpoint. You can jump into the cycle at any point. In Figure 24-4, for example, the ongoing process of product development and improvement is illustrated.

A Cycle diagram traces the steps of a repeating process.

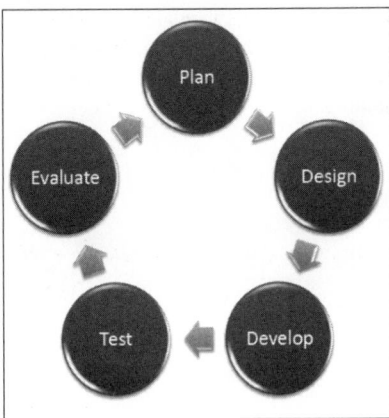

Hierarchy

A *Hierarchy diagram* is an organization chart. It shows structure and relationships between people or things in standardized levels. For example, it can show who reports to whom in a company's employment system. It is useful when describing how the organization functions and who is responsible for what. In Figure 24-5, for example, three organization levels are represented, with lines of reporting drawn between each level. Hierarchy diagrams can also run horizontally, for use in tournament rosters.

A Hierarchy diagram, also called an organization chart, explains the structure of an organization.

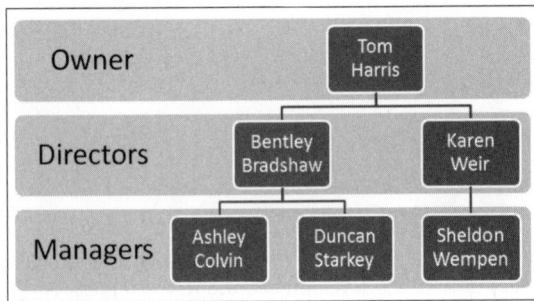

Tip

Should you include your company's organization chart in your presentation? That's a question that depends on your main message. If your speech is about the organization, you should. If not, show the organization structure only if it serves a purpose to advance your speech. Many presenters have found that an organization chart makes an excellent backup slide. You can prepare it and have it ready in case a question arises about the organization. Another useful strategy is to include a printed organization chart as part of the handouts you distribute to the audience, without including the slide in your main presentation. ■

Relationship

A *relationship diagram* graphically illustrates how parts relate to a whole. One common type of Relationship diagram is a Venn diagram, as shown in Figure 24-6, showing how categories of people or things overlap. Relationship diagrams can also break things into categories or show how parts contribute to a whole, as with a pie chart.

FIGURE 24-6

A Relationship diagram shows how parts relate to a whole.

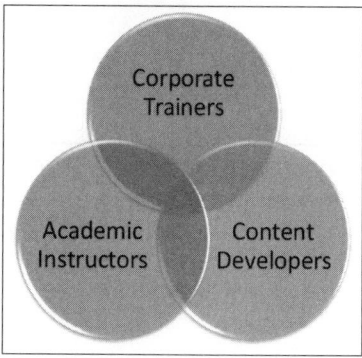

Matrix

A *Matrix diagram* also shows the relationship of parts to a whole, but it does so with the parts in orderly looking quadrants. You can use Matrix diagrams when you do not need to show any particular relationship between items, but you want to make it clear that they make up a single unit. See Figure 24-7 for an example.

Pyramid

A *Pyramid diagram* is just what the name sounds like — it's a striated triangle with text at various levels, representing not only the relationship between the items, but also that the items at the smaller part of the triangle are less numerous or more important. For example, the diagram in Figure 24-8 shows that there are many more workers than there are executives.

FIGURE 24-7

A Matrix diagram uses a grid to represent the contributions of parts to a whole.

FIGURE 24-8

A Pyramid diagram represents the progression between less and more of something.

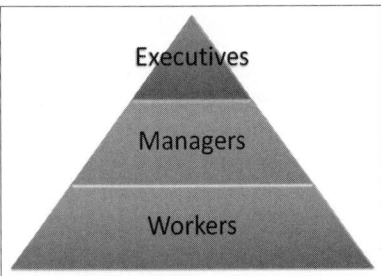

Tip

Notice in Figure 24-8 that the labels do not confine themselves to within the associated shape. If this is a problem, you might be able to make the labels fit with a combination of line breaks (Shift+Enter) and font changes. ■

Picture

The *Picture diagram* category is a collection of SmartArt diagram types from the other categories that include picture placeholders in them. You'll find List, Process, and other types of diagrams here; the Picture category simply summarizes them.

Inserting a Diagram

All SmartArt diagrams start out the same way — you insert them on the slide as you can any other slide object. That means you can either use a diagram placeholder on a slide layout or you can insert the diagram manually.

To use a placeholder, start with a slide that contains a layout with a diagram placeholder in it, or change the current slide's layout to one that does. Then click the Insert SmartArt Graphic icon in the placeholder, as shown in Figure 24-9. To insert from scratch, click the SmartArt button in the Illustrations group on the Insert tab.

FIGURE 24-9

Click the SmartArt icon in the placeholder on a slide.

Insert SmartArt Graphic

Another way to start a new diagram is to select some text and then right-click on the selection and choose Convert to SmartArt.

Any way you start it, the Choose a SmartArt Graphic dialog box opens, as shown in Figure 24-10. Select one of the SmartArt categories, click the desired SmartArt object, and click OK, and the diagram appears. From there it's just a matter of customizing.

Note

Some diagrams appear in more than one category. To browse all of the categories at once, select the All category. You can access additional diagrams by choosing the Office.com category. ∎

When you select a diagram, SmartArt Tools Design and Format tabs become available. You will learn what each of the buttons on them does as this chapter progresses. The buttons change depending on the type of diagram.

Editing SmartArt Text

All SmartArt has text placeholders, which are basically text boxes. You simply click in one of them and type. Then use the normal text-formatting controls (Font, Font Size, Bold, Italic, etc.) on the Home tab to change the appearance of the text, or use the WordArt Styles group on the Format tab to apply WordArt formatting.

FIGURE 24-10

Select the diagram type you want to insert.

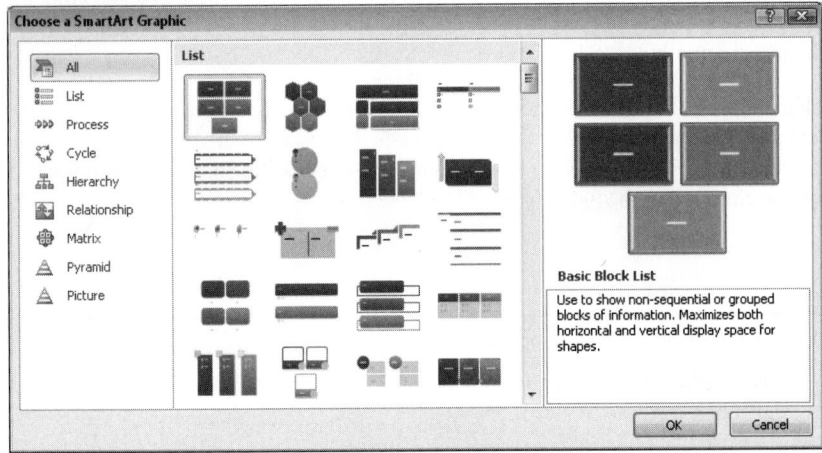

You can also display a Text pane, as shown in Figure 24-1, and type or edit the diagram's text there. The Text pane serves the same purpose for a diagram that the Outline pane serves for the slide as a whole.

Caution
The text in the Outline pane is not always in the order you would expect it to be for the diagram because it forces text to appear in linear form from a diagram that is not necessarily linear. It does not matter how the text appears in the Text pane because only you see that. What matters is how it looks in the actual diagram. ■

Here are some tips for working with diagram text:

- To leave a text box empty, just don't type anything in it. The [Text] prompts do not show up in a printout or in Slide Show view.

- To promote a line of text, press Shift+Tab; to demote it, press Tab in the Text pane.

- Text wraps automatically, but you can press Shift+Enter to insert a line break if necessary.

- In most cases, the text size shrinks to fit the graphic in which it is located. There are some exceptions to that, though; for example, at the top of a pyramid, the text can overflow the tip of the pyramid.

- All of the text is the same size, so if you enter a really long string of text in one box, the text size in all of the related boxes shrinks too. You can manually format parts of the diagram to change this behavior, as you will learn later in the chapter.

- If you resize the diagram, its text resizes automatically.

Modifying SmartArt Structure

The structure of the diagram includes how many boxes it has and where they are placed. Even though the diagram types are all very different, the way you add, remove, and reposition shapes in them is surprisingly similar across all types.

Note

When you add a shape, you add both a graphical element (a circle, a bar, or other) and an associated text placeholder. The same applies to deletion; removing a shape also removes its associated text placeholder from the diagram. ■

Inserting and Deleting Shapes

To insert a shape in a diagram, follow these steps:

1. **Click a shape that is adjacent to where you want the new shape to appear.**

2. **In the Create Graphic group on the SmartArt Tools Design tab, click Add Shape.**

You can either click the top part of the Add Shape button to add a shape of the same level and type as the selected one, or you can click the bottom part of the button to open a menu from which you can choose other variants. The choices on the menu depend on the diagram type and the type of shape selected. For example, in Figure 24-11, you can insert a shape into a diagram either before or after the current one (same outline level).

FIGURE 24-11

Add a shape to the diagram.

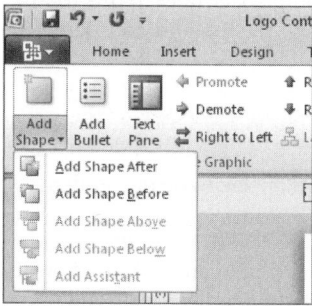

To delete a shape, click it to select it in the diagram, and then press the Delete key on the keyboard. You might need to delete subordinate shapes before you can delete the main shape.

Note

Not all diagram types can accept different numbers of shapes. For example, the four-square matrix diagram is fixed at four squares. ■

Adding Bullets

In addition to adding shapes to the diagram, you can add bullets — that is, subordinate text to a shape. To do so, click the Add Bullet button in the Create Graphic group of the SmartArt Tools Design tab. Bullets appear indented under the shape's text in the Text pane, as shown in Figure 24-12.

FIGURE 24-12

Create subordinate bullet points under a shape.

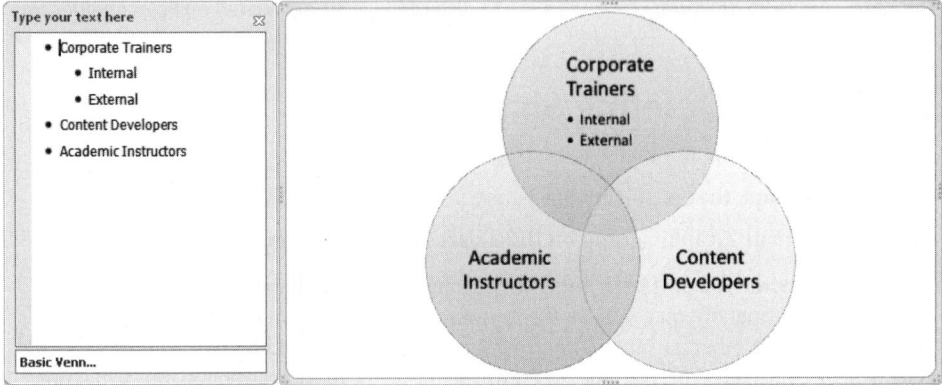

Promoting and Demoting Text

The difference between a shape and a bullet is primarily a matter of promotion and demotion in the Text pane's outline. The Text pane works just as the regular Outline pane does in this regard; you can promote with Shift+Tab or demote with Tab. You can also use the Promote and Demote buttons in the Create Graphic group on the SmartArt Tools Design tab.

Changing the Flow Direction

Each diagram flows in a certain direction. A Cycle diagram flows either clockwise or counter-clockwise. A Pyramid diagram flows either up or down.

If you realize after typing all of the text that you should have made the SmartArt diagram flow in the other direction, you can change it by clicking the Right to Left button in the Create Graphic group on the SmartArt Tools Design tab. It is a toggle; you can switch back and forth freely.

Reordering Shapes

Not only can you reverse the overall flow of the diagram, but you can also move around individual shapes. For example, suppose you have a diagram that illustrates five steps in a process and you realize that Steps 3 and 4 are out of order. You can move one of them without having to retype all of the labels.

The easiest way to reorder the shapes is to select one and then click the Move Down or Move Up button on the SmartArt Tools Design tab.

If you have more complex reordering to do, you might prefer to work in the Text pane instead, cutting and pasting text like this:

1. **Display the Text pane if it does not already appear.** You can either click the arrow button to the left of the diagram or click the Text Pane button in the Create Graphic group on the SmartArt Tools Design tab.

2. **Select some text to be moved in the Text pane.**

3. **Press Ctrl+X to cut it to the Clipboard.**

4. **Click in the Text pane at the beginning of the line above which it should appear.**

5. **Press Ctrl+V to paste.**

Repositioning Shapes

You can individually select and drag each shape to reposition it on the diagram. Any connectors between it and the other shapes are automatically resized and extended as needed. For example, in Figure 24-13, notice how the arrows that connect the circles in the cycle diagram have elongated as one of the circles has moved out.

FIGURE 24-13

When you move pieces of a diagram, connectors move and stretch as needed.

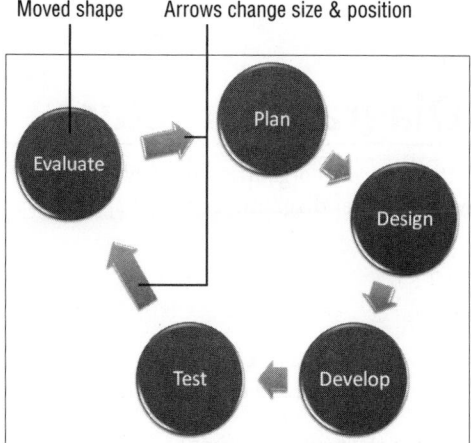

695

Resetting a Graphic

After making changes to a SmartArt diagram, you can return it to its default settings with the Reset Graphic button in the Reset group on the SmartArt Tools Design tab. This strips off everything, including any SmartArt styles and manual positioning, and makes it exactly as it was when you inserted it except it keeps the text that you've typed.

Changing to a Different Diagram Layout

The layouts are the diagram types. When you insert a SmartArt diagram, you choose a type, and you can change that type at any time later.

To change the layout type, use the Layouts Gallery on the SmartArt Tools Design tab, as shown in Figure 24-14. You can open the gallery and click the desired type, or click More Layouts at the bottom of its menu to redisplay the same dialog box as in Figure 24-10, from which you can choose any layout.

FIGURE 24-14

Switch to a different diagram layout.

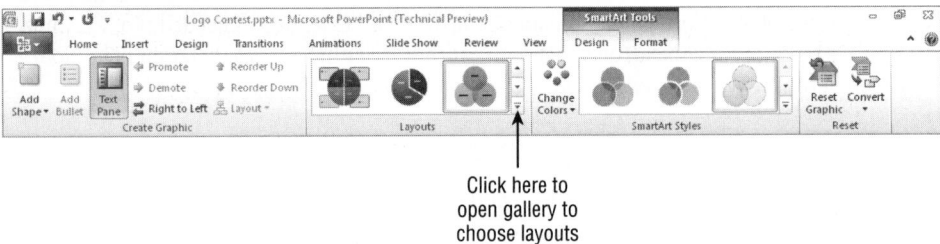

Click here to
open gallery to
choose layouts

Modifying a Hierarchy Diagram Structure

Hierarchy diagrams (organization charts) show the structure of an organization. They have some different controls for changing their structure compared to other diagrams, so this chapter looks at them separately.

Inserting and Deleting Shapes

The main difference when inserting an organization chart shape (i.e., a box into which you will type a name) is that you must specify which existing box the new one is related to and how it is related.

For example, suppose you have a supervisor already in the chart and you want to add some people to the chart who report to him. You would first select his box on the chart, and then insert the new shapes with the Add Shape button. For a box of the same level, or of the previously inserted level, click the top part of the button; for a subordinate or other relationship, open the button's menu. See Figure 24-15. The chart can only have one box at the top level, however, just as a company can have only one CEO.

FIGURE 24-15

Add more shapes to a hierarchy diagram.

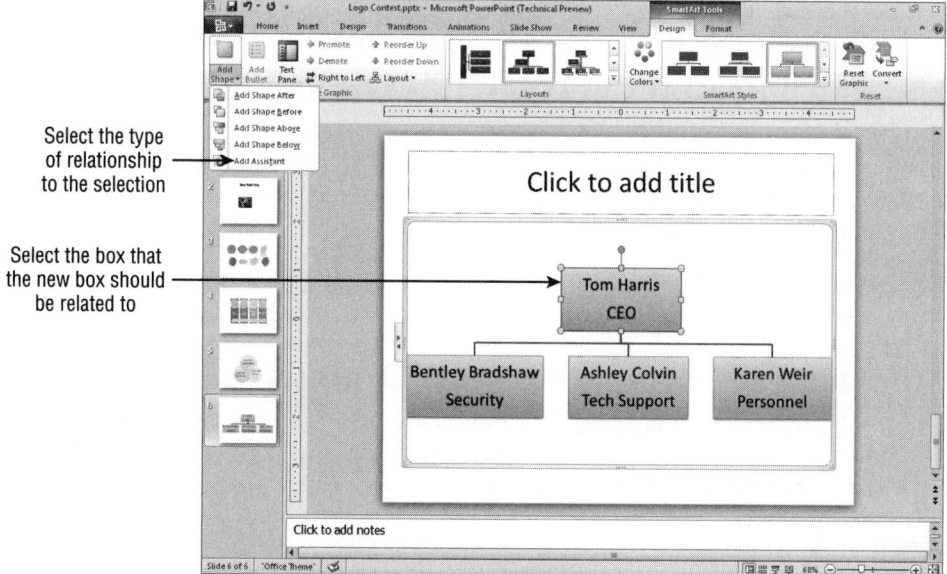

When you insert a new shape in a hierarchy diagram, four of the options are the same as with any other diagram, and one is new: Add Shape After and Add Shape Before insert shapes of the same level as the selected one, and Add Shape Above and Add Shape Below insert a superior and subordinate level, respectively. The new option, Add Assistant, adds a box that is neither subordinate nor superior, but a separate line of reporting, as shown in Figure 24-16.

FIGURE 24-16

An Assistant box in a hierarchy chart.

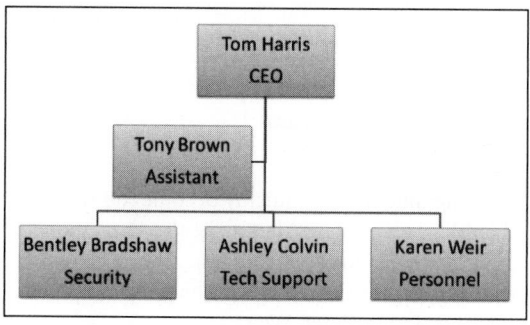

Note

An *assistant* is a person whose job is to provide support to a certain person or office. An executive secretary is one example. In contrast, a *subordinate* is an employee who may report to a manager but whose job does not consist entirely of supporting that manager. Confused? Don't worry about it. You don't have to make a distinction in your organization chart. Everyone can be a subordinate (except the person at the top of the heap, of course). ∎

To delete a shape, select it and press the Delete key, as with all of the other diagram types.

Changing a Person's Level in the Organization

As the organization changes, you might need to change your chart to show that people report to different supervisors. The easiest way to do that is to move the text in the Text pane, the same way as you learned in the section, "Reordering Shapes," earlier in this chapter. To promote someone, select his or her box and press Shift+Tab.

To change who someone reports to, select his or her box and press Ctrl+X to cut it to the Clipboard. Then select the box of the person they now report to, and press Ctrl+V to paste.

Controlling Subordinate Layout Options

When subordinates report to a supervisor, you can list the subordinates beneath that supervisor in a variety of ways. In standard layout, each subordinate appears horizontally beneath the supervisor, as shown in Figure 24-17.

FIGURE 24-17

This is the standard layout for a branch of an organization chart.

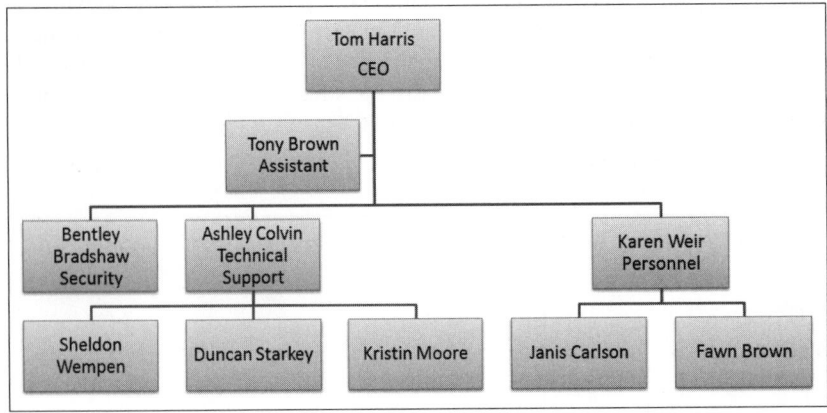

However, in a large or complex organization chart, the diagram can quickly become too wide with the standard layout. Therefore, there are "hanging" alternatives that make the chart more vertically oriented. The alternatives are Both, Left Hanging, and Right Hanging. They are just what their names sound like. Figure 24-18 shows examples of Left Hanging (the people reporting to Ashley Colvin) and Right Hanging (the people reporting to Karen Weir).

FIGURE 24-18

Hanging layouts make the chart more vertically oriented.

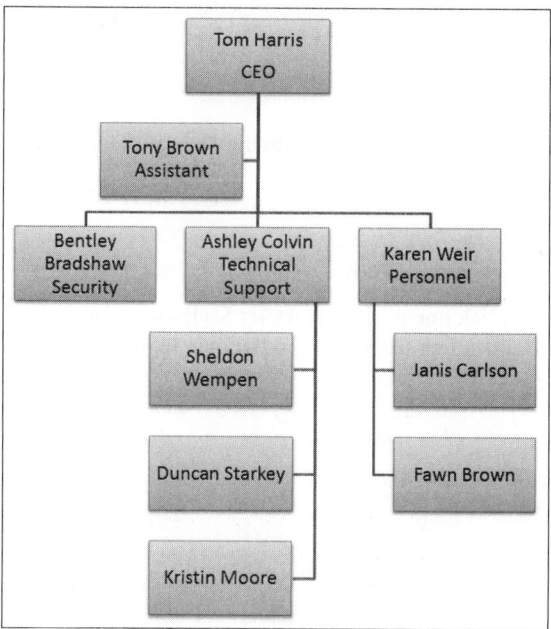

The layout is chosen for individual branches of the organization chart, so before selecting an alternative layout, you must click on the supervisor box whose subordinates you want to change. To change a layout, follow these steps:

1. **Click the box for the supervisor whose layout you want to change.**

2. **In the Create Graphic group on the SmartArt Tools Design tab, click the Layout button.** A menu of layout options appears.

3. **Choose one of the layouts (Standard, Both, Left Hanging, or Right Hanging).**

Note

If the Layout button's menu does not open, you do not have a box selected in a Hierarchy diagram. ∎

Formatting a Diagram

You can format a diagram either automatically or manually. Automatic formatting is the default, and many PowerPoint users don't even realize that manual formatting is a possibility. The following sections cover both.

Applying a SmartArt Style

SmartArt Styles are preset formatting specifications (border, fill, effects, shadows, etc.) that you can apply to an entire SmartArt diagram. They make it easy to apply surface texture effects that make the shapes look reflective or appear to have three-dimensional (3-D) depth or perspective.

Note

SmartArt Styles do not include color changes. Those are separately controlled with the Change Colors button in the SmartArt Styles group on the SmartArt Tools Design tab. ■

To apply a SmartArt Style, follow these steps:

1. Select the diagram so that the SmartArt Tools Design tab becomes available.
2. On the SmartArt Tools Design tab, click one of the SmartArt Styles samples (see Figure 24-19), or open the gallery and select from a larger list (see Figure 24-20).

FIGURE 24-19

Select a SmartArt Style.

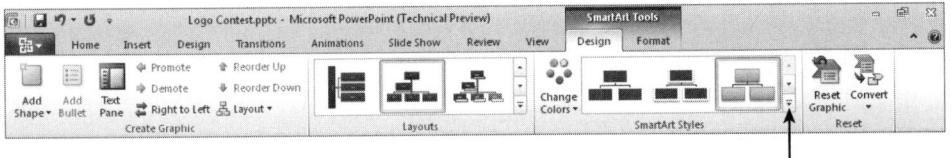

Click here to open the
gallery to select styles

FIGURE 24-20

Open the SmartArt Style Gallery for more choices.

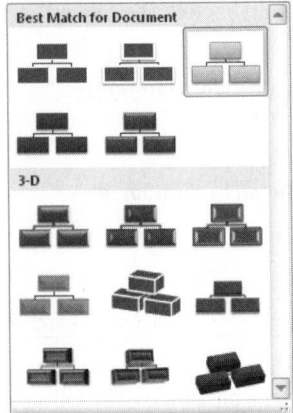

Changing SmartArt Colors

After you apply a SmartArt Style, as in the preceding section, you might want to change the colors used in the diagram.

The easiest way to apply colors is to use the Change Colors button's menu in the SmartArt Styles group on the SmartArt Tools Design tab. You can select from a gallery of color schemes. As shown in Figure 24-21, you can choose a Colorful scheme (one in which each shape has its own color), or you can choose a monochrome color scheme based on any of the current presentation color theme's color swatches.

FIGURE 24-21

Select a color scheme from the Change Colors button's menu.

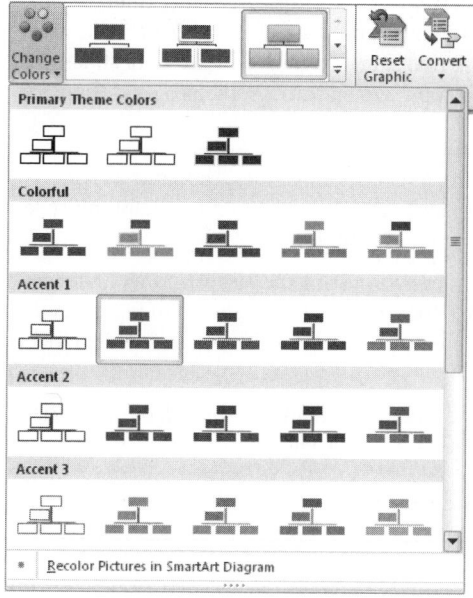

Notice the command at the bottom of the menu in Figure 24-21: Recolor Pictures in SmartArt Graphic. You can toggle this button on or off. When the button is toggled on, it applies a color tint to any pictures that are part of the diagram.

Manually Applying Colors and Effects to Individual Shapes

In addition to formatting the entire diagram with a SmartArt Style, you can also format individual shapes using Shape Styles. Here are the steps:

1. **Select a shape in a SmartArt diagram.**

2. On the SmartArt Tools Format tab, select a shape style from the Shape Styles Gallery.

3. (Optional) **Fine-tune the style by using the Shape Fill, Shape Outline, and/or Shape Effects buttons, and their associated menus, in the Shape Styles group.**

Manually Formatting the Diagram Text

WordArt formatting works the same in a SmartArt diagram as it does everywhere else in PowerPoint. Use the WordArt Styles Gallery and controls on the SmartArt Tools Format tab to apply text formatting to individual shapes, or select the entire diagram to apply the changes to all shapes at once.

Making a Shape Larger or Smaller

In some diagram types, it is advantageous to make certain shapes larger or smaller than the others. For example, if you want to emphasize a certain step in a process, you can create a diagram where that step's shape is larger. Then you can repeat that same diagram on a series of slides, but with a different step in the process enlarged on each copy, to step through the process. There are several options for this:

- You can manually resize a shape by dragging its selection handles, the same as with any other object. However, this is imprecise and can be a problem if you want multiple shapes to be enlarged, because they won't be consistently so.

- You can set a precise size for the entire diagram by adjusting the height and width measurements in the Size group on the SmartArt Tools Format tab, as shown in Figure 24-22. However, if different shapes are already different sizes, and you want to resize them in proportion, this won't help.

- You can use the Larger or Smaller buttons on the Format tab to bump up or down the sizes of one or more shapes slightly with each successive click.

FIGURE 24-22

Change the size of the diagram or an individual shape.

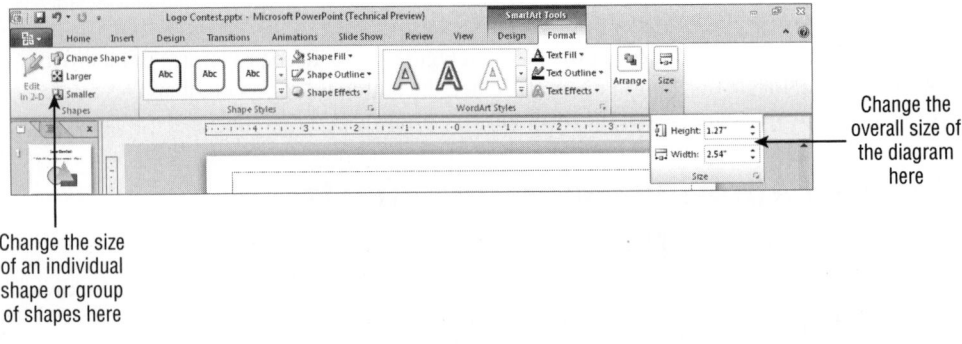

Change the overall size of the diagram here

Change the size of an individual shape or group of shapes here

Resizing the Entire SmartArt Graphic Object

When you resize the entire SmartArt object as a whole, everything within its frame changes size proportionally. There are several ways to do this:

- Drag a corner selection handle on the SmartArt graphic's outer frame.

- Use the Size controls on the SmartArt Tools Format tab to enter a precise height and width.

- Right-click on the outer frame of the SmartArt graphic and choose Size and Position. The Format Shape dialog box opens, as shown in Figure 24-23; on the Size tab, enter a height and width in inches, or scale it by a percentage in the Scale box. Select the Lock Aspect Ratio check box if you want to maintain the proportions.

FIGURE 24-23

Right-click on the graphic and choose Size and Position to open this dialog box.

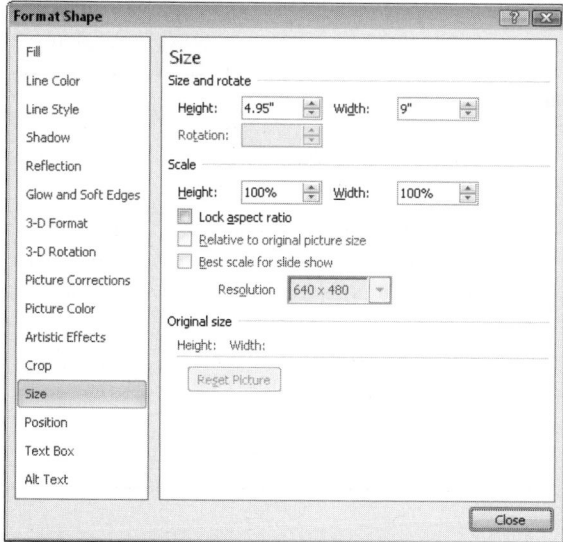

Editing in 2-D

If you choose one of the 3-D selections from the SmartArt Style gallery, the text might become a bit hard to read and edit when you are working with the diagram at a small zoom percentage. There are a couple of ways around this:

- Right-click on a shape and choose Edit Text. The face of the shape appears in two dimensions (2-D) temporarily, making it easier to edit the text.

- Click the Edit in 2-D button in the Shapes group on the SmartArt Tools Format tab. The entire diagram appears in 2-D temporarily.

Caution

Even though the face of the shape appears in 2-D, which you think would make it easier to read, in some diagram types and styles, the text might still be fuzzy and hard to read. You might be better off editing it in the Text pane. ∎

Changing the Shapes Used in the Diagram

Each SmartArt layout has its own defaults that it uses for the shapes, but you can change these manually. On the SmartArt Tools Format tab, click Change Shape in the Shapes group to open a palette of shapes, then click on the desired shape to apply to the selected shape. You can also access this from the right-click menu.

Each shape is individually configurable. If you simply select the entire diagram, the Change Shape button is not available; you must select each shape you want to change. Hold down the Shift key as you click on each one to be selected. Figure 24-24 shows a diagram that uses some different shapes.

FIGURE 24-24

You can apply different shapes within a SmartArt diagram.

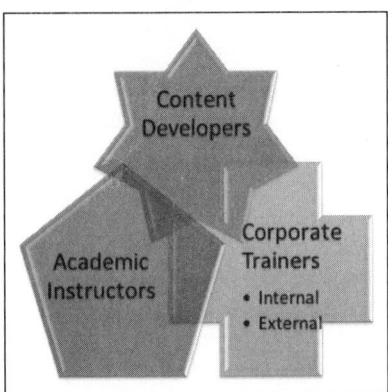

Saving a SmartArt Diagram as a Picture

SmartArt diagrams work only within Office applications, but you can easily export one for use in any other application. It is exported as a graphic (by default a .png file), which you can then import into any application that accepts graphics. To save a diagram as a picture, follow these steps:

1. **Select the outer frame of the SmartArt graphic object.**

2. **Right-click the frame and choose Save as Picture.** The Save as Picture dialog box opens.

3. (Optional) **Open the Save as Type list and select a different file type if desired.**

Tip

PowerPoint can save graphics in GIF, JPEG, TIFF, PNG, BMP, WMF, and EMF formats. Different formats have different qualities and advantages. EMF and WMF can be ungrouped, but not the other formats. EMF does not result in a quality loss when resized, but most of the others do. JPG doesn't use a transparent background, but PNG does. ∎

Choosing Appropriate Clip Art

Clip art is pre-drawn art that comes with PowerPoint or that is available from other sources (such as through the Internet). There are thousands of images that you can use royalty-free in your work, without having to draw your own. For example, suppose you are creating a presentation about snow-skiing equipment. Rather than hiring an artist to draw a picture of a skier, you can use one of PowerPoint's stock drawings of skiers and save yourself a bundle.

Being an owner of a Microsoft Office product entitles you to the use of the huge clip art collection that Microsoft maintains on its website, and if you are connected to the Internet while you are using PowerPoint, PowerPoint can automatically pull clips from that collection as easily as it can from your own hard drive. You also can use the Clip Organizer to catalog and organize artwork in a variety of other formats, including photos that you scan, photos that you take with your digital camera, and drawings and pictures that you acquire from the Internet and from other people.

Don't just use any old image! You must never use clip art simply because you can; it must be a well-thought-out decision. Here are some tips for using clip art appropriately:

- **Use for Fun.** Use cartoonish images only if you specifically want to impart a light-hearted, fun feel to your presentation.

- **Use One Style.** The clip art included with Office has many styles of drawings, ranging from simple black-and-white shapes to very complex, shaded color drawings and photographs. Try to stick with one type of image rather than bouncing among several drawing styles.

- **Use Only One Piece per Slide.** Also, do not use clip art on every slide, or it becomes overpowering.

- **Avoid Repetition.** Don't repeat the same clip art on more than one slide in the presentation unless you have a specific reason to do so.

- **Avoid Clip Art with Bad News.** If your message is very serious or you are conveying bad news, don't use clip art. It looks frivolous in these situations.

- **Better None than Bad.** If you can't find clip art that is exactly right for the slide, then don't use any. It is better to have none than to have an inappropriate image.

- **Buy Appropriate Art.** If clip art is important and Office doesn't have what you want, you can buy more. Don't try to struggle along with the clips that come with Office if it isn't meeting your needs; impressive clip art collections are available at reasonable prices at your local computer store, as well as online.

About the Clip Organizer

The *Clip Organizer* is a Microsoft utility that you access from within an Office application such as PowerPoint. It organizes and catalogs artwork of various types. The primary type is clip art, but it can also hold sounds, videos, and photos. All of the Microsoft-provided clip art is automatically included in the Clip Organizer, including links to online Microsoft clip art; you can also add your own clips from your hard disk. Most of the Microsoft clip art is online, rather than stored locally, so you will need Internet access to use it.

The Clip Organizer has two main interfaces. When you use the Clip Art command on the Insert tab, you work with the Clip Art task pane, and clips that you select are inserted onto the active slide, as shown in the section, "Inserting Clip Art on a Slide." When you use the Clip Organizer utility separately, you must copy and paste the clip art into the presentation using the Clipboard.

Depending on what you are inserting, you might also encounter other interfaces that access the Clip Organizer, such as interfaces for choosing custom bullet characters, which are also stored as clip art.

Inserting Clip Art on a Slide

You can insert clip art on a slide either with or without a content placeholder. If you use a content placeholder, PowerPoint inserts the clip art wherever the placeholder is; if you don't, PowerPoint inserts the clip art at the center of the slide. (You can move it afterward, of course.)

Tip
Some clip art files in Microsoft Office applications have a `.wmf` extension, which stands for *Windows Metafile*. WMF is a vector graphic format, which means that it is composed of mathematical formulas rather than individual pixels. This allows you to resize it without distortion and keeps the file size very small. Some other clip art files are Enhanced Metafile (`.emf`) files, which are like WMF files but with some improvements. The Clip Organizer can also organize *bitmap* graphic files (i.e., graphics composed of individual pixels of color), as you'll see later in this chapter. However, there are some editing activities through PowerPoint that you can perform only on WMF and EMF files. ■

To find and insert a piece of clip art, follow these steps:

1. (Recommended) **If you want to include Web collections when searching for clip art, make sure that you are connected to the Internet.** Otherwise, you are limited to the clip art on your local hard disk.

2. **In the Images group on the Insert tab, click Clip Art.** The Clip Art pane appears. Alternatively, you can click the Clip Art icon in a content placeholder.

3. **Make sure that the Include Office.com Content check box is checked in the Clip Art pane.**

4. **In the Search For text box, type the subject keyword that you want to search for.**

5. (Optional) **Narrow down the types of results that you want, using the Results Should Be list.** For example, select only Illustrations (not photographs, videos, or audio) to find only clip art.

6. **Click Go.** The matching clip art appears, as shown in Figure 24-25.

The clip art that matches your search specifications appears in the task pane.

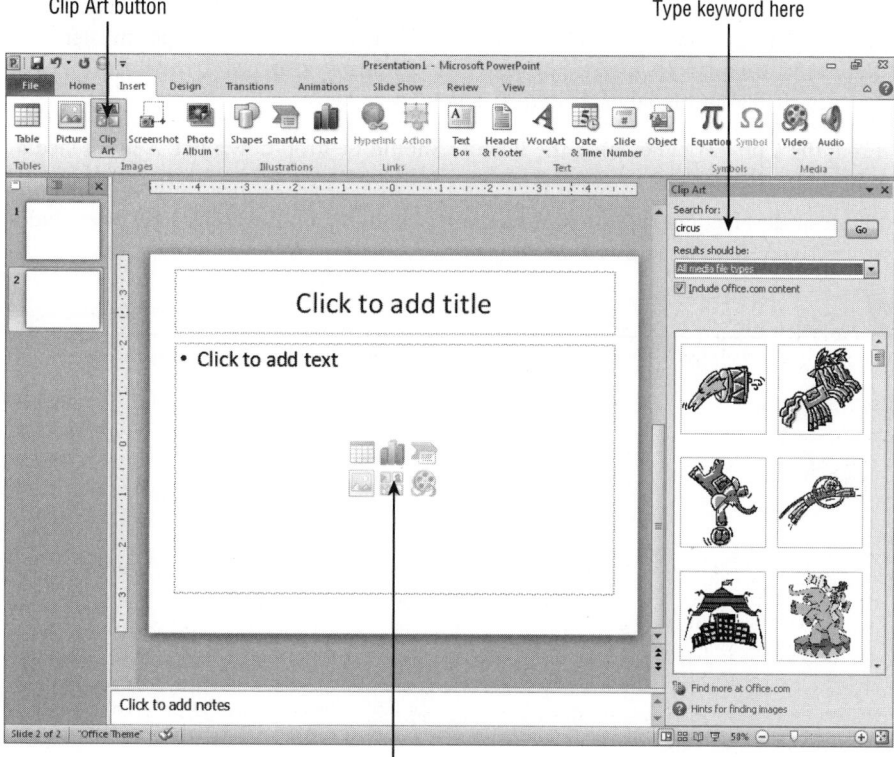

Clip Art button

Type keyword here

Clip Art placeholder icon

7. **Click the clip art that you want to insert.** It appears on the slide.

8. **Edit the image, for example, by resizing or moving it, as explained later in this chapter.**

Clip Art Search Methods

Now that you've seen the basic process for searching for a clip by keyword, let's look at some ways to fine-tune those results so that you can more easily find what you want.

Using Multiple Keywords

If you enter multiple keywords in the Search For text box of the Clip Art pane, only clips that contain all of the entered keywords appear in the search results. You can simply type the words separated by spaces; you do not have to use any special symbols or punctuation in order to use multiple keywords.

Specify Which Media File Types to Find

Besides true clip art (WMF and EMF files), you can also find videos, audio clips, and photographs using the Clip Art pane. You can learn more about each of these media types in later chapters, but let's take a quick look here at how to include them in searches. To filter results by media type (or to enable additional media types), follow these steps:

1. **From the Clip Art pane, open the Results Should Be drop-down list.** A list of media types appears.

2. **Select or deselect check boxes for media types that you want to include or exclude, respectively.** See Figure 24-26.

FIGURE 24-26

Narrow the search for a clip to certain file types by only selecting check boxes for the media types that you want.

Note
You can drag the left edge of the Clip Art task pane to the left to widen the pane so you can see more clips at once. ■

Work with Found Clips

Each of the clips found by the clip art search has its own menu. You can open the menu by right-clicking on the clip, or by pointing at it with the mouse, so that an arrow button appears to its right, and then clicking that arrow. Figure 24-27 shows an example menu.

FIGURE 24-27

Right-click on a clip or click its arrow button for a menu of commands that apply to that clip.

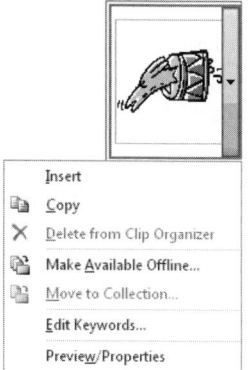

The commands available include:

- **Insert.** Inserts the clip on the active slide. This is the same as clicking the clip, which also inserts it.

- **Copy.** Copies the clip to the Clipboard. You can then paste it (Ctrl+V) onto any slide.

- **Delete from Clip Organizer.** Available only if the clip is stored on your hard disk; removes it from your hard disk. The clip may still be available online, so it may continue to show up in searches if you allow Office.com to be searched. See "Deleting Clips from the Clip Organizer" later in this chapter.

- **Make Available Offline.** Stores a copy of the clip on your hard disk. This enables you to re-access it when you are not connected to the Internet, and also to change the clip's properties and keywords. See the section, "Making Clips Available Offline," later in this chapter.

- **Move to Collection.** Available only if the clip is stored on your hard disk; it places the clip in another clip collection. See the section, "Moving Clips between Collections," later in this chapter.

- **Edit Keywords.** Available only if the clip is stored on your hard disk. It enables you to change the keywords assigned to the clip, which affects what searches it can be found with.

- **Preview/Properties.** Opens the Preview/Properties dialog box, from which you can see a complete list of the clip's keywords, determine its filename and size, and see a large-size preview of it. See Figure 24-28. This information is read-only if the clip is online; some of it can be changed if the clip is stored on your hard disk.

FIGURE 24-28

Examine a clip's properties in the Preview/Properties dialog box.

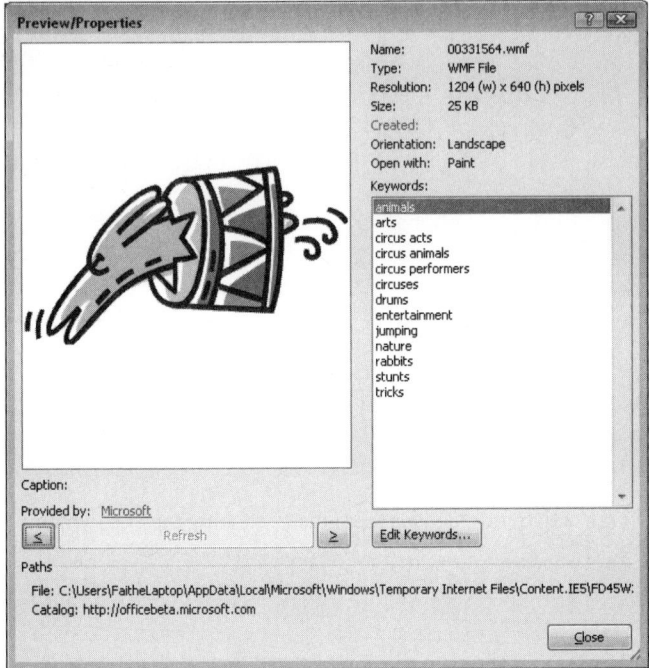

Working with Clip Art Collections

The Clip Organizer is an external utility (separate from PowerPoint) that manages clips, including enabling you to organize them into various collections and categories and making them available when you are offline. You can use the Clip Organizer to browse entire clip collections by subject, regardless of keyword. It also manages clips of other types, including bitmap images (such as scanned photos), sounds, and video clips. In the following sections, you'll learn how to browse, categorize, and organize clips in the Clip Organizer, as well as how to add clips to it.

Opening and Browsing the Clip Organizer

To open the Clip Organizer, choose Start ➪ All Programs ➪ Microsoft Office ➪ Microsoft Office 2010 Tools ➪ Microsoft Clip Organizer.

Clip art is stored in *collections*, which are logical groupings of artwork arranged by subject or location. The Collection List pane lists the three default collections:

• **Office Collections.** These are the clips that came with Microsoft Office 2010.

- **My Collections.** These include any clips that you have marked as favorites, as well as any uncategorized clips. They also include any clips that you have added through the Clip Organizer, any downloaded clips, and any clips shared from a network drive.

- **Web Collections.** These are clip collections that are available online via Microsoft. This is by far the largest collection, but you must be connected to the Internet in order to access it. All of the clips from this collection appear with a little globe icon in the corner when you preview them in the task pane.

Within each of these collections are nested folders, or subcollections, containing clips. To expand or collapse a folder, double-click on it, or click the plus or minus sign to its left. Figure 24-29 shows the three top-level collections, with My Collections expanded.

FIGURE 24-29

You can browse clip art by collection, as well as by category within a collection.

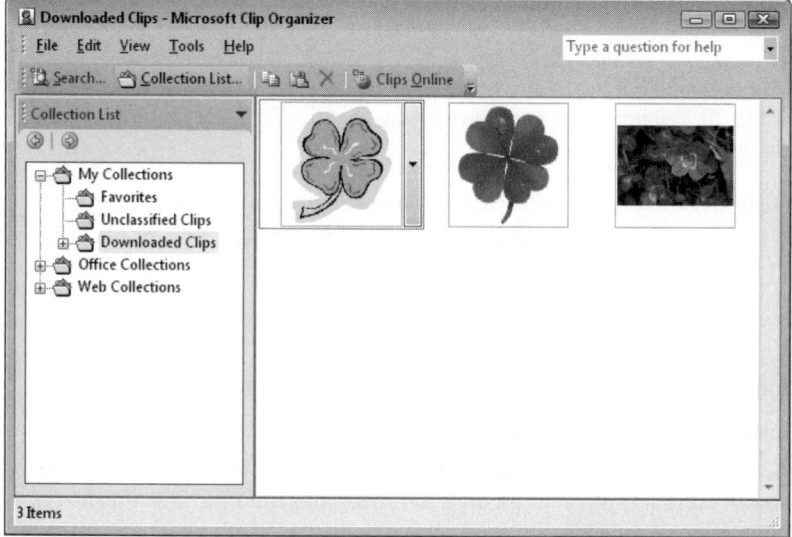

Note

The physical location of the Office Collections clips is `C:\Program Files\Microsoft Office\ MEDIA\CAGCAT10` **(paths listed in this chapter may be slightly different based on your operating system). However, users don't normally need to know this because PowerPoint manages the locations of the clip art automatically.** ■

The My Collections group contains these collections by default:

- **Favorites.** This is where clips are placed when you make them available offline. (This is covered in the section, "Making Clips Available Offline.")

- **Unclassified Clips.** This is where clips are placed when they are manually added to the Clip Organizer.

- **Downloaded Clips.** This category appears only if you have downloaded one or more clips from Office.com. If you have, all the downloaded clips appear here. Downloading clips is covered in the section, "Browsing for More Clips on Office.com."

You can add more folders to My Collections, as well as more clips. It is the only collection that you can modify. Office Collections contains collections that Microsoft provides and stores on your hard disk. The Web Collections group contains collections that you access through the Internet.

Using the Clip Organizer to Insert Clip Art

As you saw at the beginning of this chapter, when you insert clip art from the Clip Art pane, you cannot browse for it. You can only search based on keywords. If you would rather peruse the available clip art in a more leisurely fashion, you can open the Clip Organizer to do so.

The Clip Organizer is not really designed for easy insertion of clips into a presentation, but it is possible to do this using the Clipboard. To select a clip from the Clip Organizer for insertion in your presentation, do the following:

1. **Open the Clip Organizer, as you learned to do in the previous section.**

2. **Make sure that Collection List, and not Search, is selected on the toolbar.** Click Collection List if necessary.

3. **Click the collection that you want to browse.** The Clip Organizer displays the available clips.

4. **When you find the clip that you want to insert, right-click on it and choose Copy.**

5. **Close or minimize the Clip Organizer.**

6. **Display the slide in PowerPoint on which you want to place the clip, and then press Ctrl+V to paste.** Alternatively, you can drag-and-drop clips from the Clip Organizer window onto a PowerPoint slide.

Creating and Deleting Folders

Each folder in the Clip Organizer represents a collection (or a subcollection within a collection). The folders that you create are placed in the My Collections group, and you can place clips into a collection or subcollection by dragging and dropping them into the desired folder. To create a folder in the Clip Organizer, follow these steps:

1. **Choose File ⇨ New Collection.** The New Collection dialog box opens, as shown in Figure 24-30.

2. **In the Name text box, type a name for the new collection.**

3. **To create a top-level collection, click My Collections.** To create a folder within a collection, click on that collection within My Collections.

4. **Click OK.** The Clip Organizer creates the new folder.

To delete a folder, right-click on it and choose Delete *foldername*, where *foldername* is the name of the folder.

FIGURE 24-30

You can create new collection folders.

Moving Clips between Collections

A clip can exist in multiple collections simultaneously; only one copy actually exists on your hard disk, but pointers to it can appear in multiple places. When you drag a clip from one collection to another, you are actually making a copy of its pointer to the new location. The shortcut to the clip is not removed from the original collection. You can delete a clip from a collection by right-clicking on it and choosing Delete, or pressing the Delete key.

Cataloging Clips

There are probably images elsewhere on your PC that you would like to use in PowerPoint besides the Microsoft Office clip art collection. For example, perhaps you have some scanned photos or some clip art that you have downloaded from a website that offers free clips. If you need to use this downloaded clip art only once or twice, you can simply insert it with the Picture button on the Insert tab. However, if you want to use the clip art more often, you can add it to your Clip Organizer. Adding to the Clip Organizer gives you the advantage of being able to search for the image by keyword, which is useful if you have hundreds of photographs to keep organized.

You can include images in all image formats in the Clip Organizer, not just the default format that PowerPoint's clip art uses. The image formats that PowerPoint supports are shown in Table 24-1.

TABLE 24-1

PowerPoint Image Formats

BMP	EPS	PCX
CDR	FPX	PNG
CGM	GIF	RLE
DIB	JPG/JPEG/JPE/JFIF	TGA
DRW	MIX	TIF/TIFF
DXF	PCD	WMF
EMF	PCT/PICT	WPG

The Clip Organizer is not only for clip art, but also for scanned and digital camera photos, video clips, and sound clips. It can accept many sound and video formats.

Adding a clip to the Clip Organizer does not physically move the clip; it simply creates a link to it in the Clip Organizer so that the clip is included when you search or browse for clips.

Note

Any clips that you add are placed in My Collections; you cannot add clips to the Office Collections or Web Collections categories. ∎

Caution

Some earlier versions of Office stored the local collection of clip art in a different place. For example, Office XP stored this collection in C:\Program Files\Common Files\Microsoft Shared\Clipart\ Catcat50. By default, the clip art in this old location does not appear in the collections for Office 2003 and higher. The only way to import it into the Clip Organizer is by manually cataloging it, as described next. ∎

To add one or more clips, do the following:

1. **From the Clip Organizer window, choose File ⇨ Add Clips to Organizer ⇨ On My Own.** The Add Clips to Organizer window appears.

2. **Navigate to the clips that you want to add.** They can be in a local, network, or Internet location.

3. **Select the clips.** To select more than one clip, hold down the Shift key to select a contiguous group or the Ctrl key to select a noncontiguous group.

4. **Click the Add To button.** A list of the existing collections in the Clip Organizer appears, as shown in Figure 24-31.

FIGURE 24-31

You can specify the location to which you want to add the clips.

5. **Select the collection in which you want to place the new clips, and click OK.**

    If you would rather create a new clip collection:

    5a. Click My Collections and then click New.

    5b. Type a name for the new collection.

    5c. Click OK. Then select the new folder on the list and click OK.

6. **Click the Add button.** The Clip Organizer adds the clips to the specified collection.

Working with CIL or MPF Files

Occasionally, you might encounter a file that claims to be clip art but that has a `.cil` or `.mpf` extension. Both of these are clip art *package* formats that Microsoft has used to bundle and transfer clip art at one time or another. MPF is the newer format for Office XP and higher; CIL is the older format for Office 97 and 2000.

These packages are executable, which means that executing them copies the art to the Clip Organizer. When you find one of these files, you can choose to run it rather than save it to immediately extract its clips, or you can download the file and then double-click it to extract the clip art from it later.

Deleting Clips from the Clip Organizer

To remove a graphic — or even an entire folder — from your Clip Organizer, right-click on it and choose Delete. This does not delete the pictures from the hard disk; it simply removes their references from the Clip Organizer. You can also delete individual clips in the same way.

Making Clips Available Offline

Most of the clips that appear in the Clip Organizer are not on your local hard disk; they are online. This means that you do not have access to them when you are not connected to the Internet. If you find some clip art in the Clip Organizer that you want to have available offline, you can add the clip to your local hard disk, as follows:

1. **In the Clip Organizer or the Clip Art pane, open the menu of the clip that you want (the arrow to its right) and choose Make Available Offline.** The Copy to Collection dialog box opens.

   If the Make Available Offline command is not present, it means that this clip is already on your local hard disk.

2. **Select the collection in which you want to place the clip.** (You can also click New to create a new collection.) Then click OK.

Browsing for More Clips on Office.com

When you browse for clip art while connected to the Internet, the Office.com clip art automatically appears. However, you can also visit the Office.com website to browse the clip art directly.

To open a Web browser window for the Office.com clip art gallery, do one of the following:

- Open a Web browser window, navigate to `http://office2010.microsoft.com`, and click the Images link.
- From the Clip Organizer window, click the Clips Online toolbar button.
- From the Clip Art task pane, click Find More at Office.com.

Either way, the same web page displays (provided you have Internet access). It contains information about clip art, links to art collections, featured clips, and more. It is constantly changing, but Figure 24-32 shows how it looked on the day I visited.

If you have a full-time Internet connection, there is little reason to download clips to your hard disk from the Office.com website because your clip art search by keyword will always include this website. However, if your Internet connection is not always active, you might want to download the clips you need in advance so that they will be available when you need them.

To copy clips from the Office.com website to your hard disk for later use, follow these steps:

1. **From the web page shown in Figure 24-32, type a keyword in the Search box and press Enter.**
2. **In the list of clips that the site finds, point to a clip that you want.** A pop-up menu for it appears, as shown in Figure 24-33.
3. **Click Add to Collection.** The clip appears in a Collection pop-up, in the upper-right corner of the page. See Figure 24-34. You can hover the mouse over Unsaved Collection to make this pop-up reappear if it goes away.

FIGURE 24-32

Visit the Office.com clip art web page for more information and more clip art.

Type search keywords here

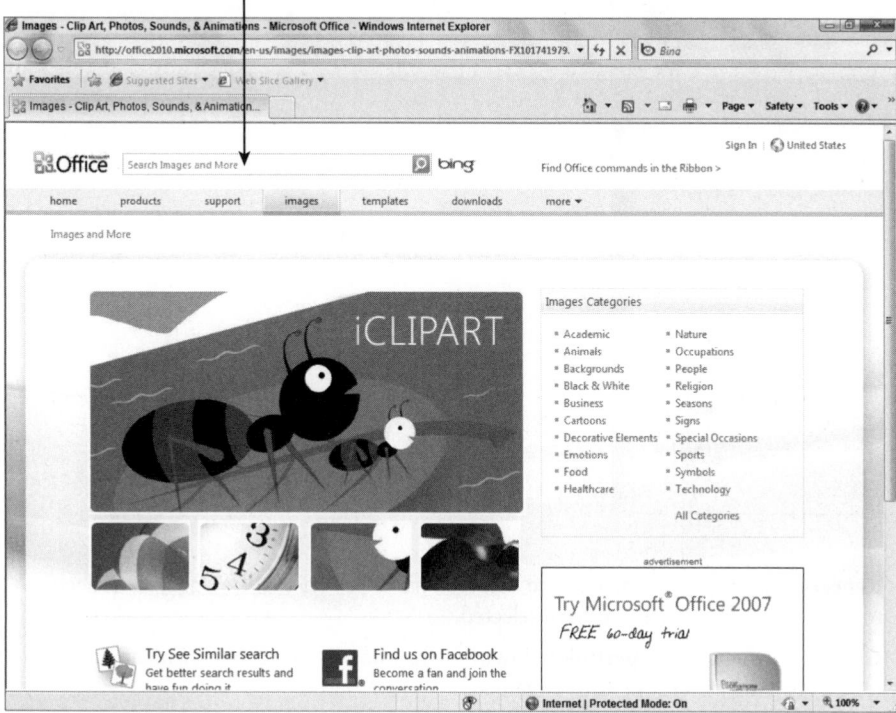

FIGURE 24-33

Point at a found clip to display its menu.

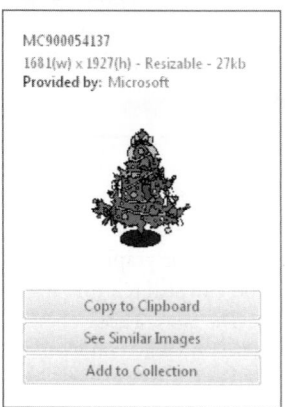

FIGURE 24-34

The clip or clips that you have selected appear here.

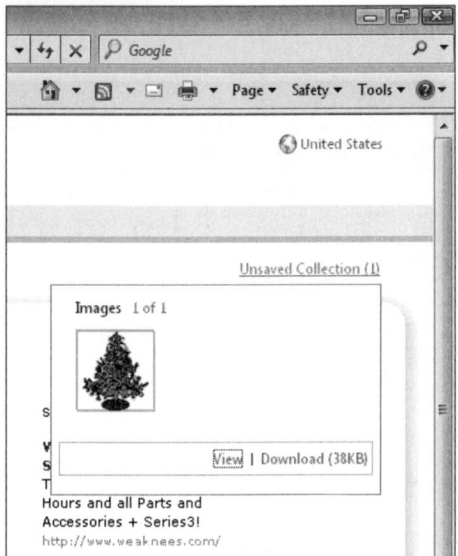

4. **Repeat Steps 2 and 3 as needed to select more clips.** Then click Unsaved Collection to display all of the clips you have selected.

5. **Click the Download hyperlink below the clip images.** The clips download, and links for them are created in the Clip Organizer.

6. **If the Save As dialog box appears prompting you to save a link to the collection, click Save.** This creates links to the clips in your Pictures library, so you can access them from outside of the Clip Organizer. Close the Pictures library window if it opens.

7. **Switch back to the Clip Organizer window.** The new clips now appear there, in the Downloaded Clips folder. They are now ready for you to use.

Understanding Raster Graphics

There are two kinds of graphics in the computer world: vector and raster. As you learned earlier in this book, *vector graphics* (clip art, drawn lines and shapes, etc.) are created with mathematical formulas. Some of the advantages of vector graphics are their small file size and the fact that they can be resized without losing any quality. The main disadvantage of a vector graphic is that it doesn't look *real*. Even when an expert artist draws a vector graphic, you can still tell that it's a drawing, not a photograph. For example, perhaps you've seen the game *The Sims*. Those characters and objects are 3-D vector graphics. They look pretty good, but there's no way you would mistake them for real people and objects.

In this chapter, you'll be working with raster graphics. A *raster graphic* is made up of a very fine grid of individual colored pixels (*dots*). The grid is sometimes called a *bitmap*. Each pixel has a unique numeric value representing its color. Figure 24-35 shows a close-up of a raster image. You can create raster graphics from scratch with a "paint" program on a computer, but a more common way to acquire a raster graphic is by using a scanner or digital camera as an input device.

FIGURE 24-35

A raster graphic, normal size (right) and zoomed in to show individual pixels (left).

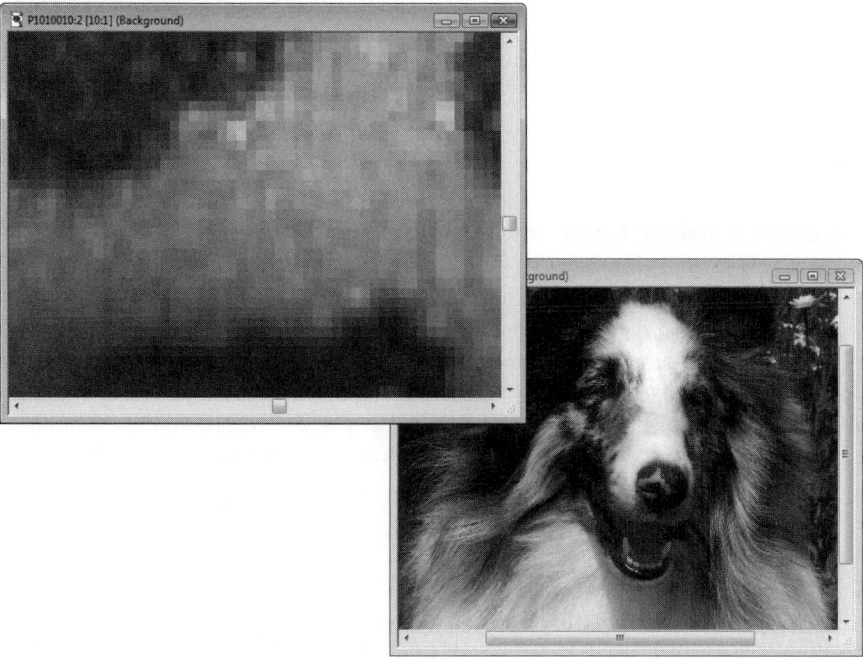

Note

The term *bitmap* is sometimes used to refer generically to any raster graphic, but it is also a specific file format for raster graphics, with a BMP extension. This is the default format for the Paint program that comes with Windows XP and Windows XP desktop wallpaper. (The Windows 7 and Windows Vista versions of Paint use a different format, `.png`, as the default.) ■

Because there are so many individual pixels and each one must be represented numerically, raster graphics are much larger than vector graphics. They take longer to load into the PC's memory, take up more space when you store them as separate files on disk, and make your PowerPoint presentation file much larger. You can compress a raster graphic so that it takes up less space on disk, but the quality may suffer. Therefore, it's best to use vector graphics when you want simple lines, shapes, or cartoons and reserve raster graphics for situations in which you need photographic quality.

The following sections explain some of the technical specifications behind raster graphics; you'll need this information to make the right decisions about the way you capture the images with your scanner or digital camera, and the way you use them in PowerPoint.

Resolution

The term *resolution* has two subtly different meanings. One is the size of an image, expressed in the number of pixels of width and height, such as 800 × 600. The other meaning is the number of pixels per inch when the image is printed, such as 100 dots per inch (dpi).

If you know the resolution of the picture (i.e., the number of pixels in it) and the resolution of the printer on which you will print it (e.g., 300 dpi), you can figure out how large the picture will be in inches when you print it at its native size. Suppose you have a picture that is 900 pixels square, and you print it on a 300 dpi printer. This makes it 3 inches square on the printout (900/300 dpi = 3).

Resolution on Preexisting Graphics Files

When you acquire an image file from an outside source, such as downloading it from a website or getting it from a CD of artwork, its resolution has already been determined. Whoever created the file originally made that decision. For example, if the image was originally scanned on a scanner, whoever scanned it chose the scan resolution — that is, the dots per inch setting. That determined how many individual pixels each inch of the original picture would be carved up into. At a 100 dpi scan, each inch of the picture is represented by 100 pixels vertically and horizontally. At 300 dpi, each inch of the picture is broken down into three times that many.

If you want to make a graphic take up less disk space, you can use an image-editing program to change the image size, or you can crop off one or more sides of the image.

Caution

If you crop or decrease the size of an image in an image-editing program, save the changes under a different filename. Maintain the original image in case you ever need it for some other purpose. Decreasing the image resolution decreases its dpi setting, which decreases its quality. You might not notice any quality degradation onscreen, but you will probably notice a difference when you are printing the image at a large size. That's because the average monitor displays only 96 dpi, but the average printer prints at 600 dpi or higher.

PowerPoint slides do not usually need to be printed at a professional-quality resolution, so image quality on a PowerPoint printout is not usually an issue. However, if you use the picture for something else later, such as printing it as a full-page color image on photo paper, then a high-resolution file can make a difference. ∎

Resolution on Graphics You Scan Yourself

When you create an image file yourself by using a scanner, *you* choose the resolution, expressed in dots per inch, through the scanner software. For example, suppose you scan a 4-inch by 6-inch photo at 100 dpi. The scanner will break down each 1-inch section of the photo horizontally and vertically into 100 separate pieces and decide on a numeric value that best represents the color of each piece. The result is a total number of pixels of $4 \times 100 \times 6 \times 100$, or 240,000 pixels. Assuming that each pixel requires 3 bytes of storage, the fill becomes approximately 720 KB in size. The actual size varies slightly depending on the file format.

Now, suppose you scan the same photo at 200 dpi. The scanner breaks down each 1-inch section of the photo into 200 pieces, so that the result is $4 \times 200 \times 6 \times 200$, or 960,000 pixels. Assuming again that 1 pixel required 3 bytes for storage (24 bits), the file will be approximately 2.9 MB in size. That's a big difference.

The higher the resolution in which you scan, the larger the file becomes, but the details of the scan also become finer. However, unless you are zooming in on the photo, you cannot tell a difference between 100 dpi and a higher resolution. That's because most computer monitors display at 96 dpi, so any resolution higher than that does not improve the output.

Let's look at an example. In Figure 24-36 you can see two copies of an image open in a graphics program. The same photo was scanned at 75 dpi (left) and 150 dpi (right). However, the difference between them is not significant when the two images are placed on a PowerPoint slide, as shown in Figure 24-37. The lower-resolution image is at the top left, but there is no observable difference in the size at which they are being used.

FIGURE 24-36

At high magnification, the difference in dots per inch for a scan is apparent.

75 dpi   150 dpi

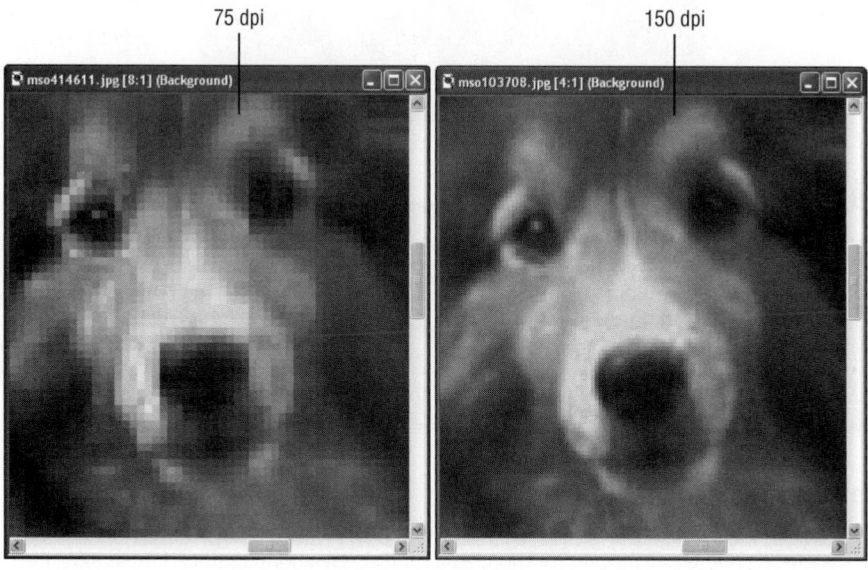

FIGURE 24-37

When the image is used at a normal size, there is virtually no difference between a high-resolution and low-resolution scan.

75 dpi

150 dpi

Scanners and Color Depth

If you are shopping for a scanner to scan images to include in a presentation, you will probably notice that they're advertised with higher numbers of bits than the graphics formats support. This is for error correction. If there are extra bits, it can throw out the bad bits to account for *noise* and still end up with a full set of good bits. Error correction in a scan is a rather complicated process, but fortunately your scanner driver software takes care of it for you.

Resolution on Digital Camera Photos

Top-quality digital cameras today take very-high-resolution pictures and are much higher than you will need for an onscreen PowerPoint presentation. At a typical size and magnification, a high-resolution graphic file is overkill; it needlessly wastes disk space. Therefore, you may want to adjust the camera's image size so that it takes lower-resolution pictures for your PowerPoint show.

If you think you might want to use those same pictures for some other purpose in the future, such as printing them in a magazine or newsletter, then go ahead and take them with the camera's highest setting, but you should compress them in PowerPoint or resize them in a third-party image-editing program. See the section, "Compressing Images," later in this chapter to learn how.

Color Depth

Color depth is the number of bits required to describe the color of a single pixel in the image. For example, in 1-bit color, a single binary digit represents each pixel. Each pixel is either black (1) or white (0). In 4-bit color, there are 16 possible colors because there are 16 combinations of 1s and 0s in a four-digit binary number. In 8-bit color there are 256 combinations.

For most file formats, the highest number of colors you can have in an image is 16.7 million colors, which is 24-bit color (also called *true color*). It uses 8 bits each for red, green, and blue.

There is also 32-bit color, which has the same number of colors as 24-bit, but adds 8 more bits for an alpha channel. The *alpha channel* describes the amount of transparency for each pixel. This is not so much an issue for single-layer graphics, but in multilayer graphics, such as the ones you can create in high-end graphics programs like Photoshop, the extent to which a lower layer shows through an upper one is important.

Tip

For a great article on alpha channel usage in PowerPoint by Geetesh Bajaj, go to `www.indezine.com/products/powerpoint/ppalpha.html`. ∎

A color depth of 48 bits is fairly new, and it's just like 24-bit color except it uses 16 rather than 8 bits to define each of the three channels: red, green, and blue. It does not have an alpha channel bit. Forty-eight-bit color depth is not really necessary, because the human eye cannot detect the small differences it introduces. Of the graphics formats that PowerPoint supports, only PNG and TIFF support 48-bit color depth.

Normally, you should not decrease the color depth of a photo to less than 24-bit unless there is a major issue with lack of disk space that you cannot resolve any other way. To decrease the color depth, you would need to open the graphic file in a third-party image-editing program and use the command in that program for decreasing the number of colors. Before going through that, try compressing the images in the presentation (see the section, "Compressing Images," later in the chapter) to see if that solves the problem.

File Format

Many scanners scan in JPEG format by default, but most also support TIF, and some also support other formats. Images you acquire from a digital camera are almost always JPEG. Images from other sources may be any of dozens of graphics formats, including PCX, BMP, GIF, or PNG.

Different graphic formats can vary tremendously in the size and quality of the image they produce. The main differentiators between formats are the color depth they support and the type of compression they use (which determines the file size).

Remember earlier how I explained that each pixel in a 24-bit image requires 3 bytes? (That's derived by dividing 24 by 8 because there are 8 bits in a byte.) Then you multiply that by the height, and then by the width, to determine the image size. Well, that formula was not completely accurate because it does not include compression. *Compression* is an algorithm (basically a math formula) that decreases the amount of space that the file takes up on the disk by storing the data about the pixels more compactly. A file format will have one of these three states in regard to compression:

- **No Compression.** The image is not compressed.
- **Lossless Compression.** The image is compressed, but the algorithm for doing so does not throw out any pixels so there is no loss of image quality when you resize the image.
- **Lossy Compression.** The image is compressed by recording less data about the pixels, so that when you resize the image there may be a loss of image quality.

Table 24-2 provides a brief guide to some of the most common graphics formats. Generally speaking, for most onscreen presentations, JPEG should be your preferred choice for graphics because it is compact and Web-accessible (although PNG is also a good choice and uses lossless compression).

TABLE 24-2

Popular Graphics Formats

Extension	Pronunciation	Compression	Maintains Transparency	Notes
JPEG or JPG	*Jay-peg*	Yes	No	Stands for *Joint Photographic Experts Group.* Very small image size. Uses lossy compression. Common on the Web. Up to 24-bit.
GIF	*gif* or *jif*	Yes	No	Stands for *Graphic Interchange Format.* Limited to 8-bit (256 colors). Uses proprietary compression algorithm. Allows animated graphics, which are useful on the Web. Color depth limitation makes this format unsuitable for photos.

Extension	Pronunciation	Compression	Maintains Transparency	Notes
PNG	*ping*	Yes	Yes	Stands for *Portable Network Graphic*. An improvement on GIF. Up to 48-bit color depth. Lossless compression, but smaller file sizes than TIF. Public domain format.
BMP	*B-M-P* or *bump* or *bitmap*	No	No	Default image type for Windows XP. Up to 24-bit color. Used for some Windows wallpaper and other Windows graphics.
PCX	*P-C-X*	Yes	No	There are three versions: 0, 2, and 5. Use version 5 for 24-bit support. Originally introduced by a company called ZSoft; sometimes called *ZSoft Paintbrush format*.
TIF or TIFF	*tiff*	Optional	Yes	Stands for *Tagged Image File Format*. Supported by most scanners and some digital cameras. Up to 48-bit color. Uses lossless compression. Large file size but high quality.

Tip

If you are not sure what format you will eventually use for an image, scan it in TIF format and keep the TIF copy on your hard disk. You can always save a copy in JPEG or other formats when you need them for specific projects. The TIF format's compression is lossless, so it results in a high-quality image. ∎

Importing Image Files into PowerPoint

Most of the choices you make regarding a raster image's resolution, color depth, and file type are done outside of PowerPoint. Consequently, by the time you're ready to put them into PowerPoint, the hard part is over.

Assuming that you have already acquired an image, use the following steps to insert it into PowerPoint:

1. **Display the slide on which you want to place the image.**
2. **If the slide has a content placeholder for Insert Picture from File, as in Figure 24-38, click it.** Otherwise, click Picture on the Insert tab. The Insert Picture dialog box opens.

FIGURE 24-38

You can insert a picture by using the Insert Picture from File content placeholder icon.

Insert Picture
from File

3. **Select the picture to import.** See Figure 24-39. You can switch the view by using the View (or Views) button in the dialog box to see thumbnails or details if either is effective in helping you determine which file is which.
4. **Click Insert.** The picture is inserted.

FIGURE 24-39

Select the picture to be inserted.

Click here to change
the view if needed

Tip

If you have a lot of graphics in different formats, consider narrowing down the list that appears by selecting a specific file type from the File Type list. By default, it is set to All Pictures, as in Figure 24-39. ∎

Linking to a Graphic File

If you have a sharp eye, you may have noticed that the Insert button in Figure 24-39 has a drop-down list associated with it. That list has these choices:

- **Insert.** The default, inserts the graphic but maintains no connection.
- **Link to File.** Creates a link to the file, but does not maintain a local copy of it in PowerPoint.
- **Insert and Link.** Creates a link to the file, and also inserts a local copy of its current state, so if the linked copy is not available in the future, the local copy will still appear.

Use Link to File whenever you want to insert a pointer rather than the original. When the presentation opens, it pulls in the graphic from the disk. If the graphic is not available, it displays an empty frame with a red X in the corner in the graphic's place. Using Link to File keeps the size of the original PowerPoint file very small because it doesn't actually contain the graphics — it only links to them. However, if you move or delete the graphic, PowerPoint won't be able to find it anymore.

The important thing to know about this link in the Link to File feature is that it is not the same thing as an OLE link. This is not a dynamic link that you can manage. It is a much simpler link and much less flexible. You can't change the file location to which it is linked, for example; if the location of the graphic changes, you must delete it from PowerPoint and reinsert it.

Tip

If you are building a graphic-heavy presentation on an older computer, you might find that it takes a long time to move between slides and for each graphic to appear. You can take some of the hassle away by using Link to File instead of inserting the graphics. Then temporarily move the graphic files to a subfolder so PowerPoint can't find them. It displays the placeholders for the graphics on the appropriate slides, and the presentation file is much faster to page through and edit. Then when you are ready to finish up, close PowerPoint and move the graphics files back to their original locations so PowerPoint can find them again when you reopen the presentation file. ∎

Acquiring Images from a Scanner

If you have a compatible scanner attached to your PC, you can scan a picture directly into the Clip Organizer, and from there import it into PowerPoint. You can also use the scanner's interface from outside of PowerPoint (and outside of the Clip Organizer).

Note

Earlier versions of PowerPoint had direct access to the Scanner and Camera Wizard, but PowerPoint 2010 does not have this. The only way to access the Scanner and Camera Wizard in Office 2010 applications is via the Clip Organizer. ∎

To scan an image from the Microsoft Clip Organizer, follow these steps:

1. **Open the Clip Organizer utility (Start ⇨ All Programs ⇨ Microsoft Office ⇨ Microsoft Office 2010 Tools ⇨ Microsoft Clip Organizer).**

2. **Choose File ⇨ Add Clips to Organizer ⇨ From Scanner or Camera.** The Insert Picture from Scanner or Camera dialog box opens.

3. **Choose the scanner from the Device list, as shown in Figure 24-40.**

FIGURE 24-40

Select the device and the basic properties.

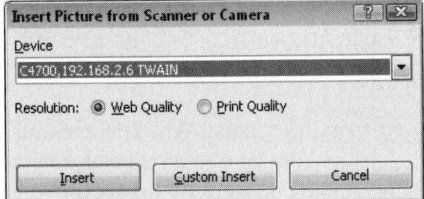

Note

In Step 3, more than one choice may be available for your scanner on the Device list, even if you have only one scanner. If you have a choice between a driver that has the word TWAIN in the name and one that doesn't, avoid the TWAIN one. TWAIN is an older, backward-compatible scanner interface that offers fewer features, and you won't see the feature-rich Custom Insert dialog box; instead, you'll see a much simpler dialog box if you click Custom Insert, which provides fewer customization options. ■

4. **Choose a resolution: Web (low) or Print (high).** Lower resolution means smaller file size and fewer pixels overall comprising the image. Low resolution is the best choice for onscreen presentations.

5. **Click Insert to scan with the default settings, or click Custom Insert, make changes to the settings, and click Scan.**

The Custom Insert option opens the full controls for the scanner. They vary depending on the model; the box for an HP scanner is shown in Figure 24-41.

Here are some of the things you can do in the Custom Insert dialog box:

- **Choose a Scanning Mode.** Color Picture, Grayscale Picture, or Black and White Picture or Text. This option determines the color depth. Color is full 24-bit color. Grayscale is 256 shades of gray (8-bit, single color). Black and white is single-bit scanning that produces an extremely small file similar to a fax.

- **Preview the Scan.** Click the Preview button to do a test scan and then drag the black squares in the preview area to adjust what portion of the image is saved when you do the "real scan" by clicking the Scan button.

- **Choose a Paper Source.** If your scanner has a document feeder, you have that choice on the Paper Source drop-down list in addition to Flatbed (the default).

- **Adjust the Quality of the Scanned Picture.** Click the Adjust the Quality of the Scanned Picture hyperlink to open an Advanced Properties dialog box. From there you can drag the Brightness and Contrast sliders and choose a resolution setting (dots per inch). The default depends on your scanner, but is probably 150 or 200 dpi.

Custom insert options are available when scanning into the Clip Organizer.

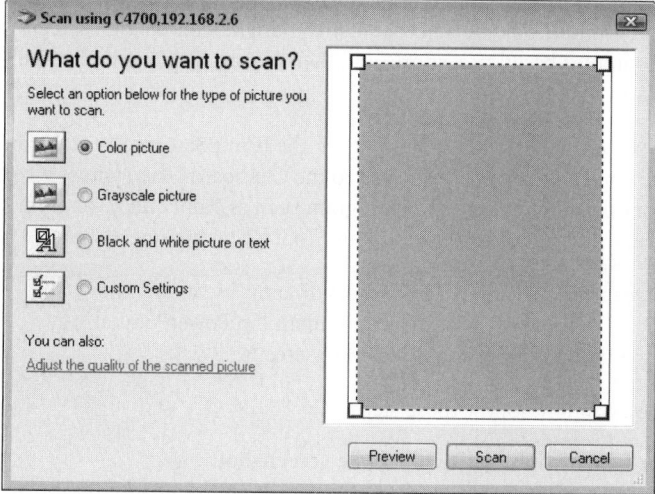

Tip

The default resolution (dpi) setting is appropriate in most cases in which you are using the image at approximately the same size as the original, but if you are concerned about file size, you can reduce this to 100 dpi without a noticeable loss of image quality onscreen. If you plan on using the image at a large size, like full screen, and the image was originally a very small hard copy, then scan at a higher resolution. ■

Acquiring Images from a Digital Camera

There are a lot of ways to transfer images from a digital camera in Windows. You can connect most cameras to the PC via a USB port and treat them as a removable drive, from which you can drag-and-drop pictures into a folder on your hard disk. You can also remove the memory card from the camera and use a card reader, and in some cases you can even insert a memory card into a printer and print the images directly.

With all of these methods available, inserting directly from the camera into the Clip Organizer is probably not your first choice. However, if you want to try it, use the same method as with the scanner. Then just follow the prompts to select and insert the picture.

Note

When you hear digital cameras referred to in *megapixels* that means a million pixels in total — the height multiplied by the width. For example, a 1,152-pixel by 864-pixel image is approximately 1 megapixel (995,328 pixels, to be exact). Most digital cameras take pictures at 10 to 15 megapixels these days, which is overkill for use in a PowerPoint show. Most cameras have settings you can change that control the image size, though, so you can reduce the image size on the camera itself. You can also resize the picture after transferring it to the computer. ■

Capturing and Inserting Screenshots

A *screenshot* is a picture that you take of your computer screen using Windows itself (or a screen capture utility). Most of the images in this book are screenshots. You might want to take screenshots to illustrate the steps in a computer-based procedure, and then create a PowerPoint presentation that teaches others to perform that procedure.

Windows has always had a basic screenshot capability built into it: the [Print Screen] key. You can press [Print Screen] at any time to copy an image of the screen to the Clipboard. Then you can paste it directly onto your slide, or open a graphics editing program such as Paint and paste from the Clipboard to save the file. Windows 7 also offers the Snipping Tool for taking screenshots.

In PowerPoint 2010, you can also capture and insert screenshots directly, bypassing the Clipboard and an outside graphics program. The Screenshot command in PowerPoint also enables you to capture individual windows rather than the entire screen.

To capture a screenshot of an open window, follow these steps:

1. **Display the slide upon which you want to place the screenshot.**
2. **Choose Insert ➪ Images ➪ Screenshot.** A menu appears showing thumbnails of the available windows. See Figure 24-42.
3. **Click the thumbnail image of the window you want to capture.** The image is immediately inserted as a new picture on the active slide.

Note

The Screenshot command does not show every open window as a thumbnail; it shows each tab of Internet Explorer, and each open Office application window except for PowerPoint itself. If you want to capture a window other than the ones shown in the thumbnails, you must use the Screen Clipping command. ■

If the window you want does not appear on the thumbnails list or if you want different cropping, use the Screen Clipping command instead. Follow these steps:

1. **Display the window that you want to capture.**
2. **Using the taskbar, switch to PowerPoint.**
3. **Choose Insert ➪ Images ➪ Screenshot ➪ Screen Clipping.** The PowerPoint window is minimized, and the window immediately beneath it appears, with a whitewash overlay on it.
4. **Drag to define the rectangular area you want to crop, as shown in Figure 24-43.** When you release the mouse button, the defined area appears in PowerPoint as a new image.

FIGURE 24-42

Capture a window using the Screenshot command.

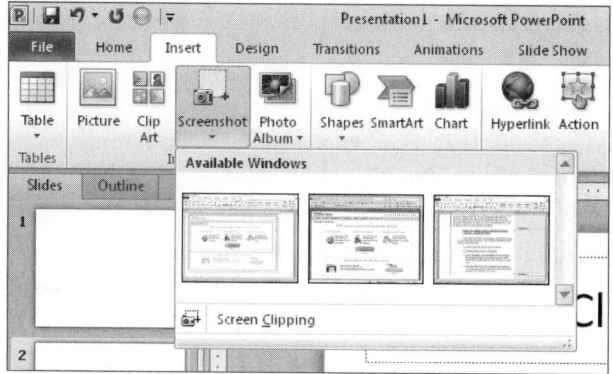

FIGURE 24-43

Drag to define an area of the screen to be captured.

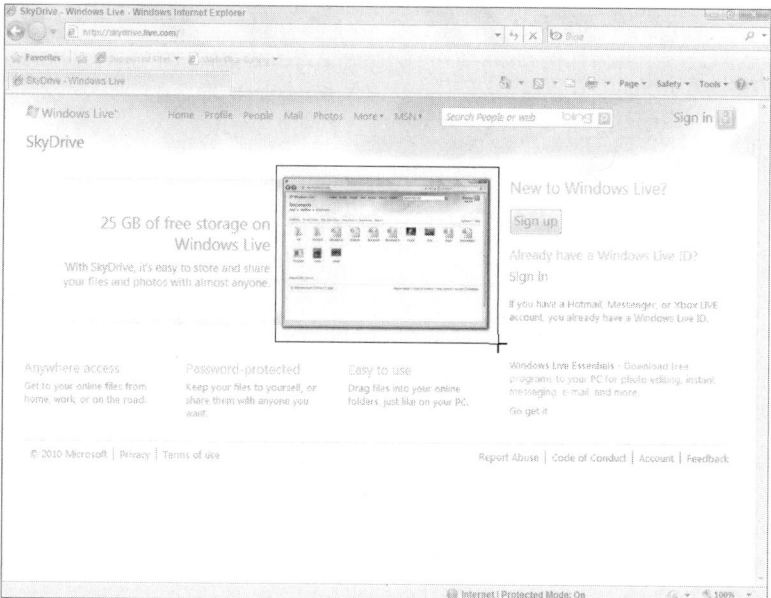

Tip

If you need better cropping than you can get with the preceding steps, use the cropping techniques in the following section to fine-tune the crop after insertion into PowerPoint.

If you need more robust screen capture capabilities, consider an application that is specifically designed for screen captures such as SnagIt (snagit.com). ■

Sizing and Cropping Photos

After placing a picture on a slide, you will probably need to adjust its size, and/or crop it, to make it fit in the allotted space the way you want it. The following sections explain these techniques.

Sizing a Photo

Sizing a photo is just like sizing any other object. Drag its selection handles. Drag a corner to maintain the aspect ratio, or drag a side to distort it. (Distorting a photo is seldom a good idea, though, unless you're after some weird funhouse effect.)

You can also specify an exact size for a photo the same as with drawn objects. Right-click on the photo and choose Size and Position to set a size in the Format Picture dialog box on the Size tab (see Figure 24-44). Alternatively, you can display the Picture Tools Format tab, and then use the Height and Width boxes in the Size group, also shown in Figure 24-44.

FIGURE 24-44

Size a photo via either the dialog box or the Format tab.

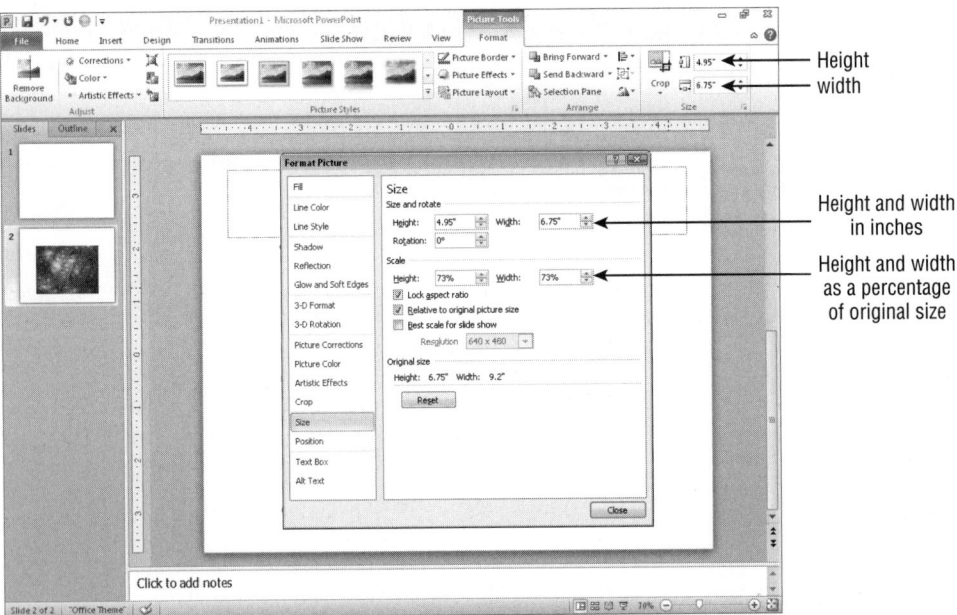

The most straightforward way to specify the size is in inches in the Height and Width boxes, either in the dialog box or on the tab. These measurements correspond to the markers on the onscreen ruler in Normal view. The size of a slide varies depending on how you have it set up (by using the Page Setup tab), but an average slide size is 10 inches wide by 7.5 inches tall. You can also size the photo using the Scale controls in the Size and Position dialog box, in which you adjust the size based on a percentage of the original size.

Note

The Scale is based on the original size, not the current size. So, for example, if you set the Height and Width to 50 percent, close the dialog box, and then reopen it and set them each to 75 percent, the net result will be 75 percent of the original, not 75 percent of the 50 percent. However, you can override this by deselecting the Relative to Original Picture Size check box (see Figure 24-44). ■

If you are setting up a presentation for the primary purpose of showing full-screen graphics, you can use the Best Scale for Slide Show check box (see Figure 24-44). This enables you to choose a screen resolution, such as 640 × 480 or 800 × 600, and size the pictures so that they will show to the best advantage in that resolution. Choose the resolution that corresponds to the display setting on the PC upon which you will show the presentation. To determine what the resolution is on the PC, right-click on the Windows desktop and choose Screen Resolution (Windows 7), or right-click on the Windows desktop, choose Properties, and then look up the resolution under Settings (Windows XP and Windows Vista).

Tip

When possible, develop your presentation at the same Windows screen resolution as the PC upon which you present the show. Many digital projectors display at 1,024 × 768. ■

Cropping a Photo

Cropping is for those times when you want only a part of the image. For example, you might have a great photo of a person or animal, but there is extraneous detail around it, as shown in Figure 24-45. You can crop away all but the important object in the image with a cropping tool.

Tip

Here's something important to know: Cropping and sizing a picture in PowerPoint does not reduce the overall size of the PowerPoint presentation file. When you insert a picture, PowerPoint stores the whole thing at its original size and continues to store it that way regardless of any manipulations you perform on it within PowerPoint. That's why it's recommended throughout this chapter that you do any editing of the photo in a third-party image program *before* you import it into PowerPoint. However, there's a work-around. If you use the Compress Pictures option (covered later in this chapter), it discards any cropped portions of the images. That means the file size decreases with the cropping, and that you can't reverse the cropping later. ■

You can crop two sides at once by cropping at the corner of the image, or crop each side individually by cropping at the sides. To crop an image, do the following:

1. Select the image, so the Picture Tools Format tab becomes available.

2. Click the Crop button in the Size group on the Picture Tools Format tab. Your mouse pointer changes to a cropping tool, and crop marks appear on the picture (see Figure 24-45).

3. Position the pointer over one of the black markers on the image frame, and drag toward the center until the image is cropped the way you want.

4. **Repeat Step 3 for each side.** Then click the Crop button again, or press Esc, to turn cropping off.

5. **Resize the cropped image, if needed.**

FIGURE 24-45

This picture can benefit from cropping.

Figure 24-46 shows the result of cropping and resizing the image from Figure 24-45.

To undo a crop, re-enter cropping mode by clicking the Crop button again, and then drag the side(s) back outward again. Or you can simply reset the photo, as described in the following section.

New in PowerPoint 2010, you can also crop to a shape, or crop to a particular aspect ratio (i.e., ratio of height to width).

Cropping to a shape crops the picture so that it fits inside one of the drawing shapes that PowerPoint provides, such as a star, triangle, or arrow. (This feature was called *Picture Shape* in PowerPoint 2007 and was accessed differently.)

To crop to a shape, follow these steps:

1. **Select the picture.**

2. **On the Picture Tools Format tab, click the down-arrow under the Crop button in the Size group, and point to Crop to Shape.** A palette of shapes appears, as shown in Figure 24-47.

3. **Click the shape to which you want the picture cropped.**

FIGURE 24-46

The picture has been improved by cropping and resizing it.

FIGURE 24-47

You can crop a picture to a shape.

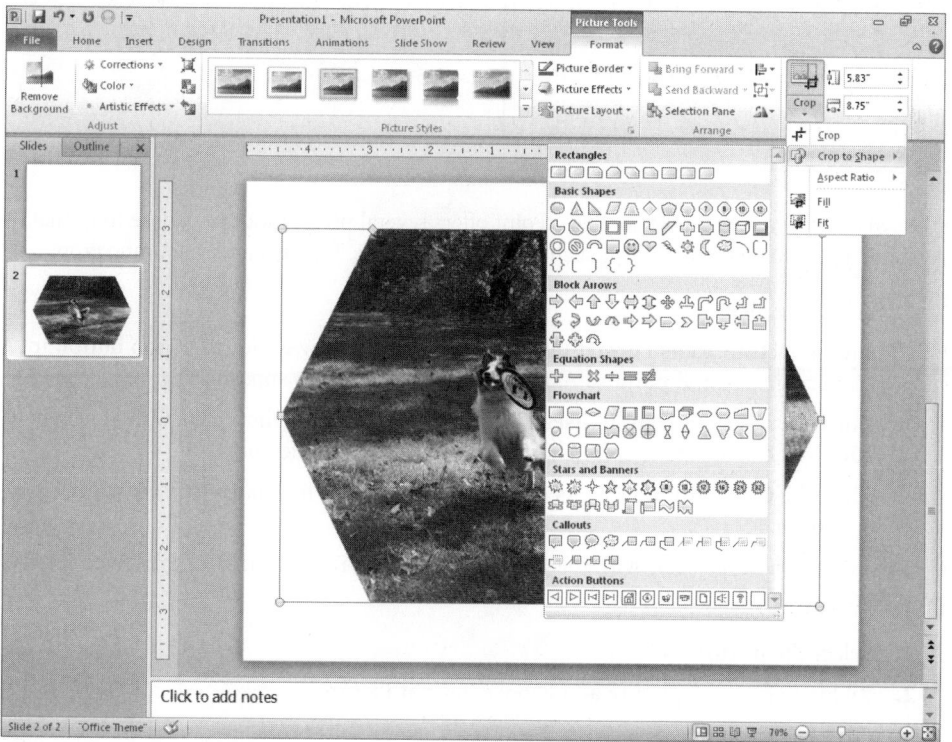

Tip

After cropping to a shape, you'll notice the central part of the image might not be exactly centered within the shape. To adjust the centering of the picture within the crop area, right-click on the picture and choose Format Picture. Click the Crop tab, and then adjust the values in the Picture Position section, as shown in Figure 24-48. ■

FIGURE 24-48

Set a precise amount of cropping in the Format Picture dialog box.

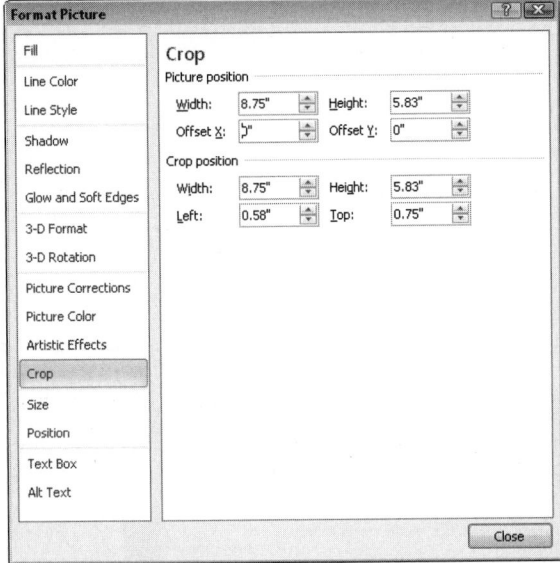

You can also crop to an aspect ratio. PowerPoint offers several preset ratios to choose from that correspond to common picture sizes, such as 2:3, 3:4, and 3:5. To apply an aspect ratio crop:

1. Select the picture.
2. On the Picture Tools Format tab, click the down-arrow under the Crop button in the Size group, and point to Aspect Ratio. A list of ratios appears.
3. Click the ratio you want to use. Crop marks appear on the image. New in PowerPoint 2010, you can see the rest of the picture as you crop, for reference.
4. Click the Crop button or press Esc on your keyboard to finalize the cropping operation.

You can also crop *by the numbers* with the Crop settings in the Format Picture dialog box. Here's how to do that:

1. Select the picture.
2. Right-click on the picture and choose Format Picture.
3. Click the Crop tab.

4. Use the controls under Picture Position (see Figure 24-48) to manually enter cropping amounts for each side.

5. Click Close.

Note

To crop from the bottom, decrease the Height setting; to crop from the right, decrease the Width setting. The Left and Top settings crop from those sides, respectively. ■

Caution

You cannot uncrop after compressing the picture (assuming you use the default compression options that include deleting cropped areas of pictures). By default, saving compresses and makes crops permanent, so be sure to undo any unwanted cropping before you save. ■

Resetting a Photo

Once the picture is in PowerPoint, any manipulations you do to it are strictly on the surface. They change how the picture appears on the slide but don't change how the picture is stored in PowerPoint. Consequently, you can reset the picture back to its original settings at any time (provided you have not compressed the picture). This resetting also clears any changes you make to the image's size, contrast, and brightness (which are discussed in the next section).

Resetting a photo is different depending on what aspects of it you want to reset. In the Format Picture dialog box, many of the tabbed sections have a Reset button. Click the Reset button that applies to what you want to reset. For example, to reset the cropping and sizing of a photo, use the Reset Picture button and drop-down list in the Adjust group of the Picture Tools format tab.

Compressing Images

Having an image that is too large (i.e., too high a resolution or dpi) is not a problem quality-wise. You can resize it in PowerPoint to make it as small as you like; just drag its selection handles. There will be no loss of quality as it gets smaller.

However, as mentioned earlier in the chapter, inserting a picture file that is much larger than necessary can increase the overall size of the PowerPoint file, which can become problematic if you plan to distribute the presentation in a form where space or bandwidth is an issue.

To avoid problems with overly large graphics files, you can compress the images to reduce their resolution and remove any cropped portions. You can do this from within PowerPoint or with a third-party utility.

Reducing Resolution and Compressing Images in PowerPoint

PowerPoint offers an image compression utility that compresses all of the pictures in the presentation in a single step and reduces their resolution to the amount needed for the type of output you specify (e-mail, Screen, or Print).

Picture resolution is measured in PowerPoint in pixels per inch, or ppi. This roughly translates to dots per inch (dpi) on a printout. A computer screen shows 96 pixels per inch, so you do not need higher resolution than that if you are only showing your presentation onscreen. However, if you are distributing the presentation in other forms, a higher resolution might be appropriate.

To reduce resolution and compress images, do the following:

1. **Click on a picture, so that the Picture Tools Format tab appears.**
2. **Click the Compress Pictures button in the Adjust group.** The Compress Pictures dialog box appears, as shown in Figure 24-49.

FIGURE 24-49

Click OK to compress with the default settings.

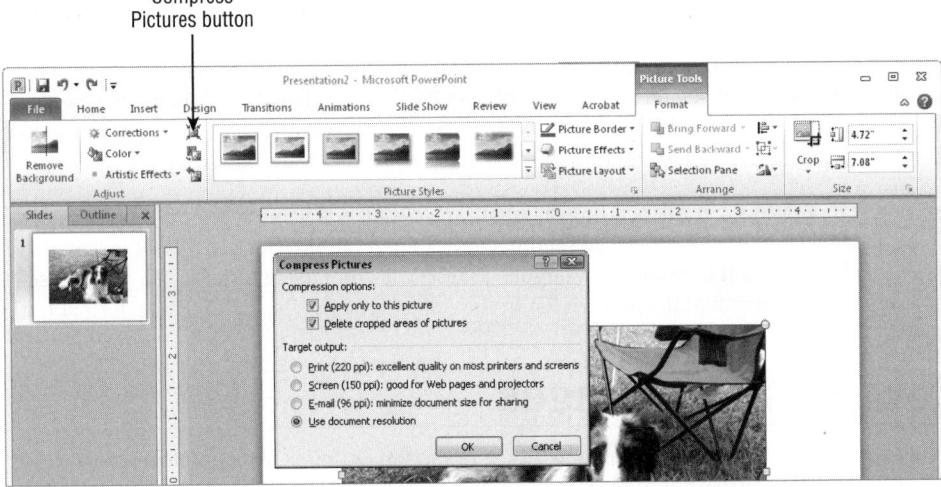

Compress
Pictures button

3. (Optional) **If you do not want to compress all of the pictures, select the Apply Only to This Picture check box.**
4. (Optional) **If you wish to save additional space by deleting the cropped-out areas of pictures, select the Delete Cropped Areas of Pictures check box.**
5. **Select the desired amount of compression:**
   - **Print (220 ppi).** Choose this if you are printing the presentation on paper; it keeps the photos at a resolution where they will look crisp on a printout.
   - **Screen (150 ppi).** Choose this if you are displaying the presentation using a projector or distributing it via the Internet. Some projectors have a higher resolution than a monitor.

- **E-mail (96 ppi).** Choose this if you are e-mailing the presentation to others, because this lower setting results in a smaller file that will transmit more easily via e-mail.

- **Use Document Resolution.** Use this to match the resolution of the pictures to the resolution defined in the PowerPoint Options (File ⇨ Options ⇨ Advanced).

6. **Click OK to perform the compression.**

Caution

Almost all e-mail servers have limits on the file sizes they will accept, so keeping the PowerPoint file as small as possible when distributing via e-mail is a good idea. If you send someone an e-mail with a large file attached to it, the server may reject the message, but you might not get an error message back from the server at all, or you might not get one for several days. ■

Reducing Resolution with a Third-Party Utility

Working with resolution reduction from an image-editing program is somewhat of a trial-and-error process, and you must do each image separately.

You can approximate the correct resolution by simply *doing the math*. For example, suppose you have a 10-inch by 7.5-inch slide. Your desktop display is set to 800 × 600. So your image needs to be 800 pixels wide to fill the slide. Your image is a 5-inch by 3-inch image, so if you set it to 200 dpi, that gives you 1,000 pixels, which is a little larger than you need but in the ballpark.

Summary

In this chapter, you learned how to create SmartArt diagrams and use clip art and pictures in your presentation. You learned how to select a diagram type, how to rearrange shapes in a diagram, and how to apply formatting. You learned how to insert and manage clip art, how to organize your clips in the Clip Organizer, and how to find more clips online. This chapter taught you about the technical specs for graphics that determine their file size, quality, and flexibility; and you learned how to insert them into your presentations. You will probably find lots of creative uses for diagrams, clip art, and pictures now that you know how you can make the most of them!

In the next chapter, you'll learn how to make your presentation even more lively and useful by adding animations and transitions, and by creating the support materials that you'll use for presenting.

Building Animation Effects, Transitions, and Support Materials

You invest hard work in creating presentation content so that you can deliver your important message to an audience. When you are delivering a live presentation — also called a *slide show* — you need to make sure that your speaking manner and the presentation have enough zip to hold the audience members' interest. This chapter teaches you how to add that zip with transitions and animation effects, and how to print the support materials you'll need to ensure that the audience can follow along.

Understanding Animation and Transitions

In PowerPoint, *animation* is the way that individual objects enter or exit a slide. On a slide with no animation, all of the objects on the slide simply appear at the same time when you display it. (Boring, eh?) However, you can apply animation to the slide so that the bullet points fly in from the left, one at a time, and the graphic drops down from the top afterward.

A *transition* is another kind of animation. A *transition* refers to the entry or exit of the entire slide, rather than of an individual object on the slide.

Here are some ideas for using animation effectively in your presentations:

- Animate parts of a chart so that the data appears one series at a time. This technique works well if you want to talk about each series separately.

- Set up questions and answers on a slide so that the question appears first, and then, when you click the question, the answer appears.

- Dim each bullet point when the next one comes into view, so that you are, in effect, highlighting the current one.

- Make an object appear and then disappear. For example, you might have an image of a lightning bolt that flashes on the slide for 1 second and then disappears, or a picture of a racecar that drives onto the slide from the left and then immediately drives out of sight to the right.

- Rearrange the order in which objects appear on the slide. For example, you could make numbered points appear from the bottom up for a Top Ten list.

Assigning Transitions to Slides

Transitions determine how you get from Slide A to Slide B. Back in the old slide projector days, there was only one transition: the old slide was pushed out, and the new slide dropped into place. However, with a computerized presentation, you can choose from all kinds of fun transitions, including wipes, blinds, fly-ins, and much more. These transitions are almost exactly like the animations, except that they apply to the whole slide (or at least the *background* — the base part of the slide — if the slide's objects are separately animated).

Note

The *transition effect* for a slide refers to how the slide *enters*, and not how it exits. As a result, if you want to assign a particular transition while moving from Slide 1 to Slide 2, you would assign the transition effect to Slide 2. ■

The individual transitions are hard to describe in words; it is best if you just view them onscreen to understand what each one does. You should try out several transitions before making your final selection.

Setting Transition Effects and Timings

The default transition effect is None. One slide replaces another with no special effect. If you want something flashier than that, you must choose it from the Transitions tab.

As you are setting up the transition effect, you have a choice of allowing it to occur manually (i.e., On Click) or automatically. Generally speaking, if there is a live person controlling and presenting the show, transitions should be manual. With manual transitions, the presenter must click the mouse to move to the next slide, just like clicking the advance button on a 35mm slide projector. This might sound distracting, but it helps the speaker to maintain control of the show. If someone in the audience asks a question or wants to make a comment, the show does not continue on blindly, but pauses to accommodate the delay.

However, if you are preparing a self-running presentation, such as for a kiosk, automatic transitions are a virtual necessity. In the following section, you will learn how to set the timing between slides.

Chapter 25: Building Animation Effects, Transitions, and Support Materials

To assign a transition effect and control its timing, follow these steps:

1. **View or select the slide in Normal or Slide Sorter view.** If you use Slide Sorter view, you can more easily select multiple slides to which you can apply the transition.

2. (Optional) **On the Transitions tab, in the Transition to This Slide group, click the transition you want to use.** Open the gallery to see additional transitions if needed. See Figure 25-1. The effect is previewed on the slide.

   If you do not want a transition effect, do not choose a transition; instead leave the default transition (None) selected.

FIGURE 25-1

Select a transition.

Click here for
more transitions

3. **Click Effect Options, and select any options for the chosen effect transition as desired.** The effects listed will be different depending on the transition you chose.

4. **In the Timing group, mark or clear the check boxes for:**
   - **On Mouse Click.** Transitions when you click the mouse.
   - **Automatically.** Transitions after a specified amount of time has passed. (Enter the time, in seconds, in the associated text box.)

Note

It is perfectly OK to leave the On Mouse Click check box selected, even if you choose automatic transitions — in fact, this is a good idea. There may be times when you want to manually advance to the next slide before the automatic transition time has elapsed, and leaving this option selected allows you to do so. ■

Caution

You will probably want to assign automatic transitions to either all or none of the slides in the presentation, but not a mixture of the two. This is because mixed transition times can cause confusion when some of the slides automatically advance and others do not. However, there may be situations in which you need to assign different timings and effects to the various slides' transitions. ∎

5. (Optional) **Adjust the Duration setting to specify how quickly the transition effect will occur.** This is not the timing between slides, but rather the timing from the beginning to the end of the transition effect itself. For example, for a Fade transition, it determines how fast the fade occurs.

6. (Optional) **If you want a sound associated with the transition, select it from the Sound drop-down list.** See the next section for details.

7. (Optional) **If you want these same transition settings to apply to all slides in the presentation, click Apply to All.**

Any automatically advancing transitions that you have set appear with the timings beneath each slide in Slide Sorter view, as shown in Figure 25-2.

FIGURE 25-2

You can view slide timings in Slide Sorter view.

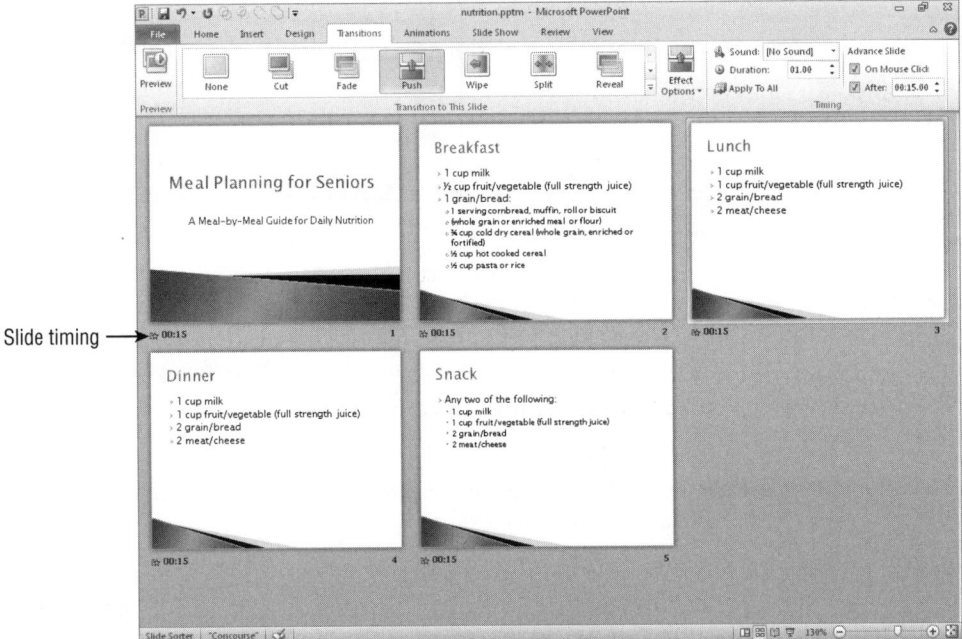

More about Transition Sounds

In the transition Sound menu in the Timing group of the Transitions tab, shown in Figure 25-3, you can choose from among PowerPoint's default sound collection, or you can choose any of the following:

● **No Sound.** Does not assign a sound to the transition.

- **Stop Previous Sound.** Stops any sound that is already playing. This usually applies where the previous sound was very long and was not finished when you moved on to the next slide, or in cases in which you used the Loop Until Next Sound transition (see below).

- **Other Sound.** Opens a dialog box from which you can select another WAV sound file stored on your system.

- **Loop Until Next Sound.** An on/off toggle that sets whatever sound you select to loop continuously either until another sound is triggered or until a slide appears that has Stop Previous Sound set for its transition.

FIGURE 25-3

Select a transition sound.

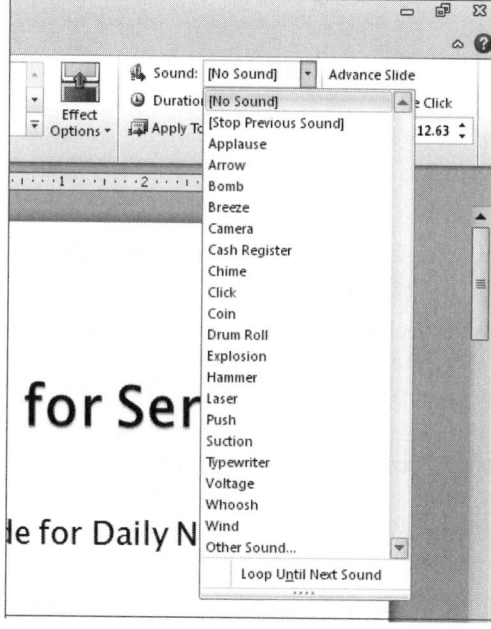

Caution
Sounds associated with transitions can get annoying to your audience very quickly. Don't use them gratuitously. ∎

Rehearsing and Recording Transition Timings

The trouble with setting the same automatic timings for all slides is that not all slides deserve or need equal time onscreen. For example, some slides may have more text than others, or more complex concepts to grasp. To allow for the differences, you can manually set the timings for each slide, as described in the preceding section. However, another way is to use the Rehearse Timings feature to run through your presentation in real time, and then to allow PowerPoint to set the timings for you, based on that rehearsal.

Note

When you set timings with the Rehearse Timings feature, PowerPoint ignores any hidden slides. If you later unhide these slides, they are set to advance automatically. You need to individually assign them an Automatically After transition time, as described earlier in the chapter. ∎

To set transition timings with the Rehearse Timings feature, follow these steps:

1. **In the Set Up group on the Slide Show tab, click Rehearse Timings.** The slide show starts with the Recording toolbar in the upper-left corner, as shown in Figure 25-4.

FIGURE 25-4

Use the Recording toolbar to set timings for automatic transitions.

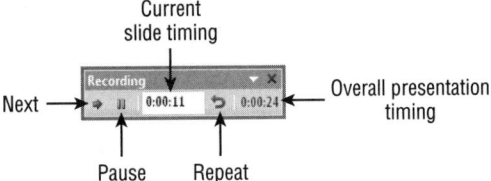

Note

If you want to record voice-over narration as you rehearse and record the timings, click Record Slide Show in Step 1 instead of Rehearse Timings. (Have your microphone ready to go before you do that.) ∎

2. **Click through the presentation, displaying each slide for as long as you want it to appear in the actual show.** To move to the next slide, you can click on the slide, click the Next button in the Recording toolbar (right-pointing arrow), or press Page Down.

   When setting timings, it may help to read the text on the slide, slowly and out loud, to simulate how an audience member who reads slowly would proceed. When you have read all of the text on the slide, pause for one or two more seconds and then advance. If you need to pause the rehearsal at any time, click the Pause button. When you are ready to resume, click the Pause button again.

   If you make a mistake on the timing for a slide, click the Repeat button to begin timing this slide again from 00:00.

Tip

If you want a slide to display for a fairly long time, such as 30 seconds or more, you might find it faster to enter the desired time in the Current Slide Timing text box on the Recording toolbar, rather than waiting the full amount of time before advancing. To do this, click in the text box, type the desired time, and press Tab. You must press the Tab key after entering the time — do not click the Next button — or PowerPoint will not apply your change. ∎

3. **When you reach the final slide, a dialog box appears, asking whether you want to keep the new slide timings.** Click Yes.

Tip

If you want to temporarily discard the rehearsed timings, deselect the Use Timings check box on the Slide Show tab. This turns off all automatic timings and allows the show to advance through mouse-clicks only. To clear timings altogether, choose Slide Show ➪ Set Up ➪ Record Slide Show ➪ Clear ➪ Clear Timings on All Slides. ∎

Animating Slide Content

Whereas transitions determine how a slide (as a whole) enters the screen, animations determine what happens to the slide's content after that point. You might animate a bulleted list by having each bullet point fade in one-by-one, for example, or you might make a picture gradually grow or shrink to emphasize it. The effects you can create are limited only by your imagination.

Animation gives you full control over how the objects on your slides appear, move, and disappear. You can not only choose from the full range of animation effects for each object, but you can also specify in what order the objects appear and what sound is associated with their appearance.

Understanding Animations

The Animations tab provides many settings and shortcuts for creating animation events. An *event* is an animation occurrence, such as an object entering or exiting the slide. An event can also consist of an object on the slide moving around in some way (spinning, growing, changing color, etc.).

Each animation event appears as a separate entry in the Animation pane. You can display or hide the Animation pane by choosing Animations ➪ Advanced Animation ➪ Animation Pane at any time.

When you animate bulleted lists and certain other types of text groupings, the associated events may be collapsed or expanded in the Animation pane. For example, in Figure 25-5, an animated bulleted list's events are collapsed.

Notice the following in Figure 25-5:

- The event has a mouse icon to its left. That indicates that the animation is set to occur On Click.

- It has a green star on it. Green means entrance; this is an entrance effect. (Yellow means emphasis, and red means exit effect.) A line instead of a star means that it is a motion path (covered later in this chapter).

- It has a double down-pointing arrow below it. That indicates that there are collapsed animation events beneath it.

Tip

To assign meaningful names to slide objects so it's easier to tell what you are working with when animating, choose Home ➪ Editing ➪ Select ➪ Selection Pane. Then in that pane, you can edit each object's name. ∎

FIGURE 25-5

The animation events for a bulleted list are collapsed.

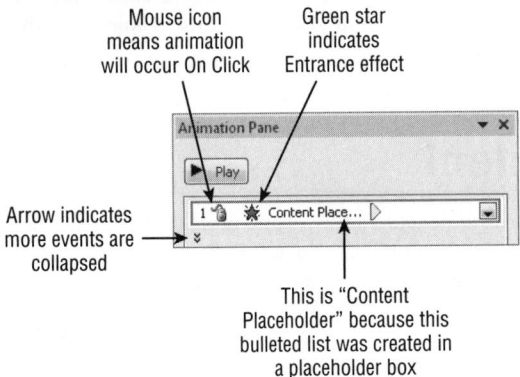

Mouse icon means animation will occur On Click

Green star indicates Entrance effect

Arrow indicates more events are collapsed

This is "Content Placeholder" because this bulleted list was created in a placeholder box

In Figure 25-6, the events are expanded. To expand or collapse a group of events, click the double up-pointing or down-pointing arrow. Notice the following in Figure 25-6:

- Each event has a mouse icon to its left. That indicates that each one requires a separate mouse click to activate.
- Each bulleted list item on the slide has a number next to it that corresponds to one of the numbered animation events in the Animation pane.

FIGURE 25-6

The events are expanded.

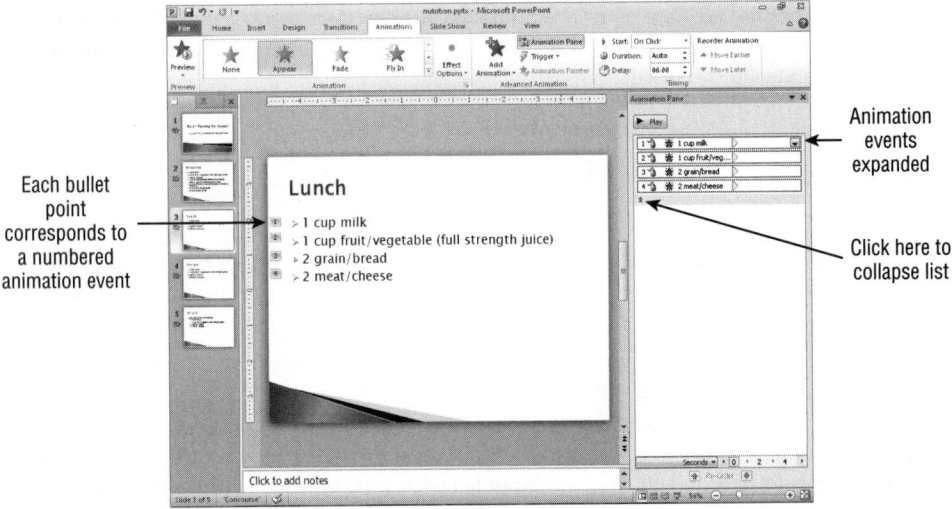

Each bullet point corresponds to a numbered animation event

Animation events expanded

Click here to collapse list

Choosing an Animation Effect

There are four categories of custom animation effects. Each effect has a specific purpose, as well as a different icon color:

- **Entrance (Green).** The item's appearance on the slide is animated. Either it does not appear right away when the rest of the slide appears, or it appears in some unusual way (such as flying or fading), or both.

- **Emphasis (Yellow).** The item is already on the slide and is modified in some way. For example, it may shrink, grow, wiggle, or change color.

- **Exit (Red).** The item disappears from the slide before the slide itself disappears, and you can specify that it does so in some unusual way.

- **Motion Paths (Gray).** The item moves on the slide according to a preset path. Motion paths are discussed later in the chapter.

Within each of these broad categories there are a multitude of animations. Although the appearance of the icons may vary, the colors (on the menus from which you choose them, and on the effects listed in the Animation pane) always match the category.

Different effect categories have different choices. For example, the Emphasis category, in addition to providing movement-based effects, also has effects that change the color, background, or other attributes of the object.

You can choose animation effects in any of these ways (all from the Animations tab) after selecting the object to be animated:

- Click one of the animation samples in the Animations group.

- Click the Add Animation button in the Advanced Animation group, and choose an effect from the menu that appears.

- Click the down-arrow to open the gallery in the Animations group, and choose an effect from the gallery that appears. (This menu is identical to the one provided by the Add Animation button.) See Figure 25-7.

- Click the Add Animation button in the Advanced Animation group, and then choose one of the "More" commands at the bottom, depending on the type of animation you want. For example, you might want More Entrance Effects. This opens a dialog box with a full listing of the effects of that type, as shown in Figure 25-8.

Note
Use the Animation Gallery to change an existing animation or to apply animation to an object that is not already animated. Add Animation can be used to add more animation to an object that is already animated, as well as to animate objects that are not already animated. ∎

FIGURE 25-7

Choose an animation effect to apply.

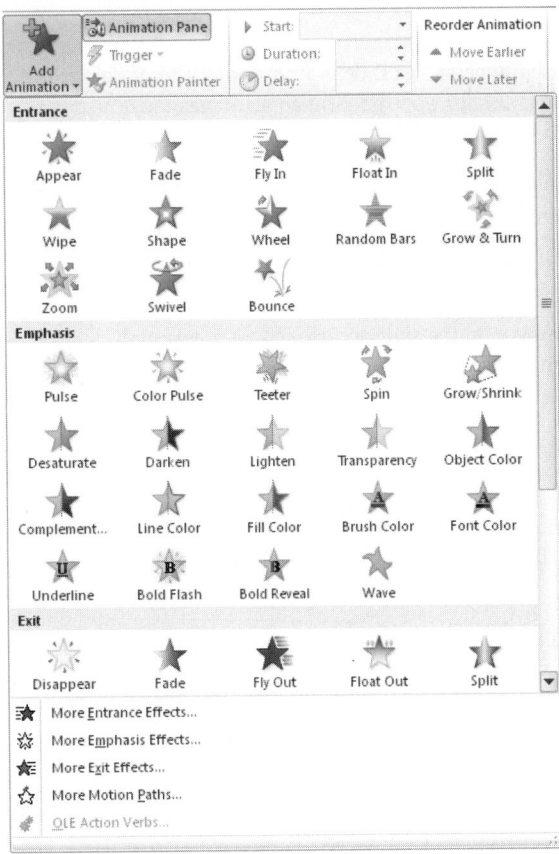

Animating Parts of a Chart

If you create a chart using PowerPoint's charting tool, then you can display the chart all at once or apply a custom animation effect to it. For example, you can make the chart appear by series (divided by legend entries), by category (divided by X-axis points), or by individual element in a series or category. Figures 25-9 and 25-10 show progressions based on series and category.

FIGURE 25-8

The More command opens a dialog box of effects for the chosen type.

FIGURE 25-9

In this progression, the chart is appearing by series.

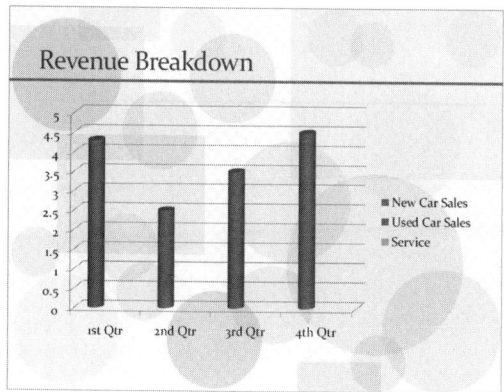

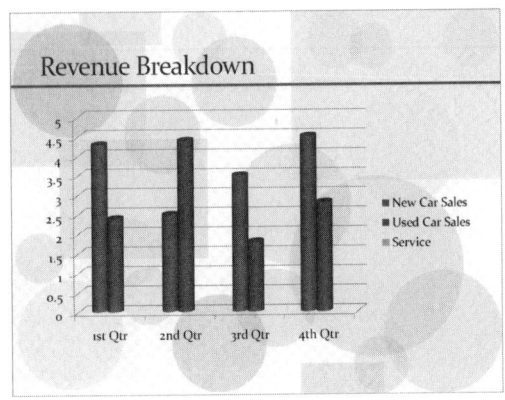

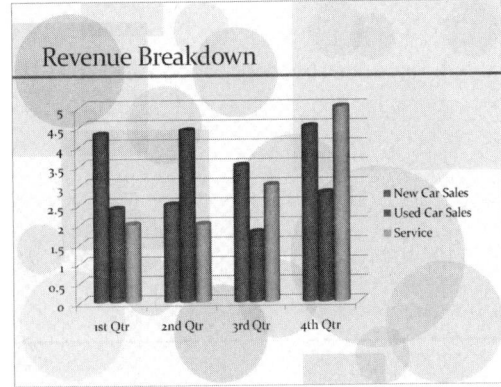

FIGURE 25-10

Here, the chart is appearing by category.

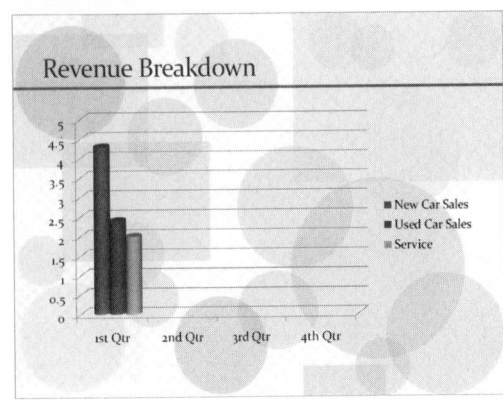

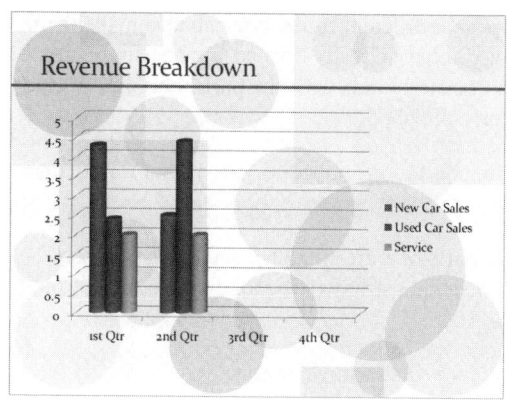

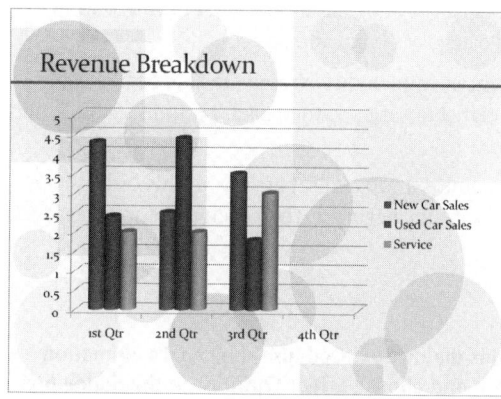

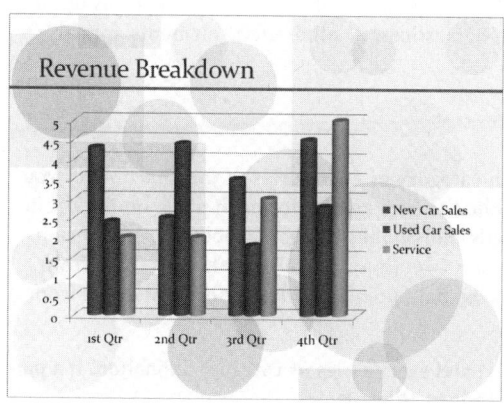

Along with making various parts of the chart appear at different times, you can also make them appear using any of the animated techniques that you have already learned, such as flying in, dropping in, fading in, and so on. You can also associate sounds with the parts, and dim them or change them to various colors when the animation is finished.

To animate a chart, you must first set up the entire chart to be animated, just as you would any other object on a slide.

Then, to set up the selected chart so that different parts of it are animated separately, choose Animations ⇨ Animation ⇨ Effect Options, and then choose any of the following options from the Sequence section of the menu (see Figure 25-11):

- **As One Object.** The entire chart is animated as a single object.
- **By Series.** In a multi-series chart, all of series 1 enters at once (all the bars of one color), then all of series 2 enters at once, and so on.
- **By Category.** All the bars for the first category appear at once (an entire grouping of multi-colored bars), then the second category's bars, and so on.
- **By Element in Series.** Each data point is animated separately, in this order: each point (from bottom to top, or left to right) in series 1, then each point in series 2, and so on.
- **By Element in Category.** Each data point is animated separately, in this order: each point (from bottom to top, or left to right) in category 1, then each point in category 2, and so on.

Tip

You can also set up chart animation from the Effect Options dialog box. Collapse the chart's animation in the Animation pane (if needed), and then right-click on it and choose Effect Options. In the dialog box that appears, click the Chart Animation tab, and make your selection there. The choices are exactly the same as on the menu in Figure 25-11, plus there is one additional check box: Start Animation by Drawing the Chart Background, which is on by default. It animates the grid and legend. If you deselect this option, these items appear immediately on the slide, and the data bars, slices, or other chart elements appear separately from them. ∎

Tip

You do not have to use the same animation effect for each category or each series of the chart. After you set up the chart to animate each piece individually, individual entries appear for each piece on the list in the Animation pane. You can expand this list and then apply individual settings to each piece. For example, you could have some data bars on a chart fly in from one direction, and other data bars fly in from another direction. You can also reorder the pieces so that the data points build in a different order from the default order.

Not all animation effects are available for every type of chart and every series or category animation. If a particular animation is not working, try a simpler one, such as Fade or Wipe. ∎

You can animate the chart by series, by category, or by individual data points.

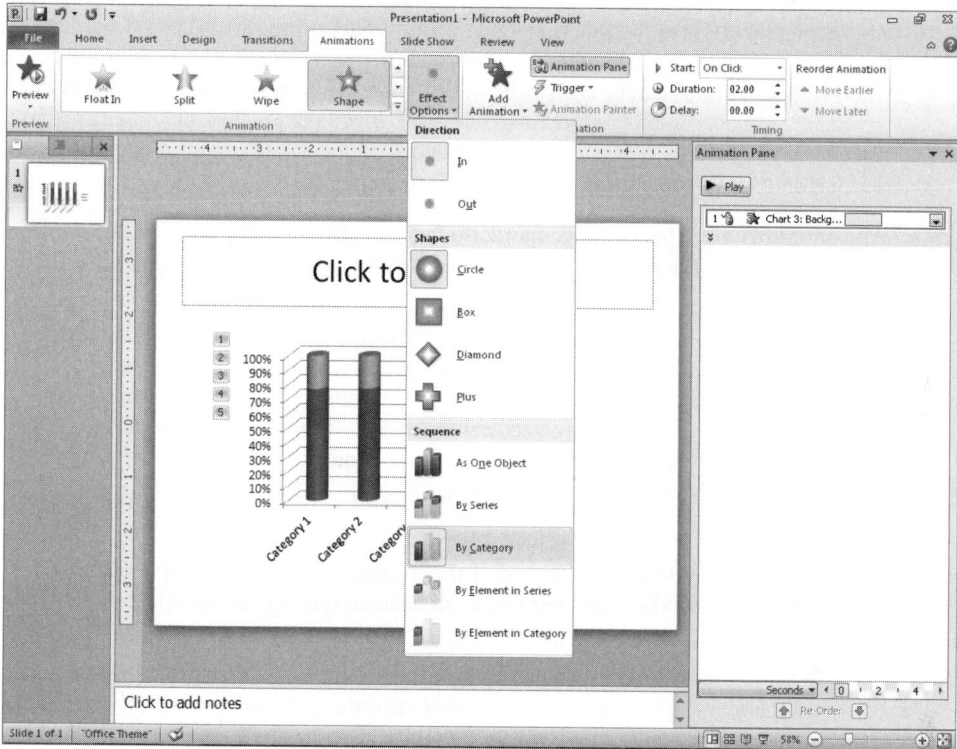

The When and How of Handouts

If you are presenting a live show, the centerpiece of your presentation is your slides. Whether you show them using a computer screen, a slide projector, or an overhead projector, the slides — combined with your own dazzling personality — make the biggest impact. But if you rely on your audience to remember everything you say, you may be disappointed. With handouts, the audience members can follow along with you during the show and even take their own notes. They can then take the handouts home with them to review the information again later.

Presentation professionals are divided about how and when to use handouts most effectively. Here are some of the many conflicting viewpoints. I can't say who is right or wrong, but each of these statements brings up issues that you should consider. The bottom line is that each of them is an opinion on how much power and credit to give to the audience; your answer may vary depending on the audience you are addressing.

- **You should give handouts at the beginning of the presentation. The audience can absorb the information better if they can follow along on paper.**

  This approach makes a lot of sense. Research has proven that people absorb more facts if presented with them in more than one medium. This approach also gives your audience free will; they can listen to you or not, and they still have the information. It's their choice, and this can be extremely scary for less-confident speakers. It's not just a speaker confidence issue in some cases, however. If you plan to give a lot of extra information in your speech that's not on the handouts, people might miss it if you distribute the handouts at the beginning because they're reading ahead.

- **You shouldn't give the audience handouts because they won't pay as close attention to your speech if they know that the information is already written down for them.**

  This philosophy falls at the other end of the spectrum. It gives the audience the least power and shows the least confidence in their ability to pay attention to you in the presence of a distraction (handouts). If you truly don't trust your audience to be professional and listen, this approach may be your best option. However, don't let insecurity as a speaker drive you prematurely to this conclusion. The fact is that people won't take away as much knowledge about the topic without handouts as they would if you provide handouts. So, ask yourself if your ultimate goal is to fill the audience with knowledge or to make them pay attention to you.

- **You should give handouts at the end of the presentation so that people will have the information to take home but not be distracted during the speech.**

  This approach attempts to solve the dilemma with compromise. The trouble with it, as with all compromises, is that it does an incomplete job from both angles. Because audience members can't follow along on the handouts during the presentation, they miss the opportunity to jot notes on the handouts. And because the audience knows that handouts are coming, they might nod off and miss something important. The other problem is that if you don't clearly tell people that handouts are coming later, some people spend the entire presentation frantically copying down each slide on their own notepaper.

Creating Handouts

To create handouts, you simply decide on a layout (a number of slides per page) and then choose that layout from the Print dialog box as you print. No muss, no fuss! If you want to get more involved, you can edit the layout in Handout Master view before printing.

Choosing a Layout

Assuming you have decided that handouts are appropriate for your speech, you must decide on the format for them. You have a choice of one, two, three, four, six, or nine slides per page.

- **1:** Places a single slide vertically and horizontally "centered" on the page.
- **2:** Prints two big slides on each page. This layout is good for slides that have a lot of fine print and small details or for situations in which you are not confident that the

reproduction quality will be good. There is nothing more frustrating for an audience than not being able to read the handouts!

- **3:** Makes the slides much smaller — less than one-half the size of the ones in the two-slide layout. But you get a nice bonus with this layout: lines to the side of each slide for note-taking. This layout works well for presentations where the slides are big and simple and the speaker is providing a lot of extra information that isn't on the slides. The audience members can write the extra information in the note-taking space provided.

- **4:** Uses the same size slides as the three-slide layout, but they are spaced out two-by-two without note-taking lines. However, there is still plenty of room above and below each slide, so the audience members still have lots of room to take notes.

- **6:** Uses slides the same size as the three-slide and four-slide layouts, but crams more slides on the page at the expense of note-taking space. Six-slide layouts are good for presentations with big, simple slides where the audience does not need to take notes. If you are not sure if the audience will benefit at all from handouts being distributed, consider whether choosing one of the six-slide layouts would be a good compromise. This also saves paper, which might be an issue if you need to make hundreds of copies.

- **9:** Makes the slides very tiny, almost like a Slide Sorter view, so that you can see nine at a time. The layouts with this many slides make them very hard to read unless the slide text is extremely simple. I don't recommend this layout in most cases, because the audience really won't get much out of such handouts.

Tip

One good use for the nine-slides model is as an index or table of contents for a large presentation. You can include a nine-slides-per-page version of the handouts at the beginning of the packet that you give to the audience members, and then follow it up with a two-slides-per-page version that they can refer to if they want a closer look at one of the slides. ∎

Finally, there is an Outline handout layout, which prints an outline of all of the text in your presentation — that is, all of the text that is part of placeholders in slide layouts; any text in extra text boxes you have added manually is excluded. It is not considered a handout when you are printing, but it is included with the handout layouts in the Handout Master. More on this type of handout later in the chapter.

Printing Handouts

When you have decided which layout is appropriate for your needs, print your handouts as follows:

1. (Optional) **If you want to print only one particular slide, or a group of slides, select the ones you want in either Slide Sorter view or in the slide thumbnails task pane on the left.**

2. **Select File ⇨ Print.** The Print options appear.

3. **Enter a number of copies in the Copies text box.** The default is 1. If you want the copies collated (applicable to multipage printouts only), make sure you mark the Collate check box.

4. **Set options for your printer or choose a different printer.** See the "Setting Printer-Specific Options" section later in this chapter for help with this.

5. **If you do not want to print all the slides, type the slide numbers that you want into the Slides text box.** Indicate a contiguous range with a dash. For example, to print Slides 1 through 9, type **1-9**. Indicate noncontiguous slides with commas. For example, to print Slides, 2, 4, and 6, type **2, 4, 6**. Or to print Slides 2 plus 6 through 10, type **2, 6-10**. To print them in reverse order, type the order that way, such as **10-6, 2**.

   Alternatively, you can click Print All Slides to open a menu of range choices, and choose one of these from its list:

   - **Print Selection.** Prints multiple slides you selected before you issued the Print command. It is not available if you did not select any slides beforehand.

   - **Print Current Slide.** Prints whatever slide you selected before you issued the Print command.

   - **Custom Range.** Prints the slide numbers that you type in the Slides text box. When you enter slide numbers in the Slides text box, this option gets selected automatically, so usually you don't have to select this option manually.

   - **Custom Show.** Prints a certain custom show you have set up. Each custom show you have created appears on the list. You won't see any custom shows if you haven't created any.

6. (Optional) **If you don't want to print hidden slides, click the same button again to reopen the menu and click Print Hidden Slides to toggle the check mark off next to that command.**

7. **Click Full Page Slides to open a menu of views you can print.**

8. **On the menu that appears, click the number and layout of handouts you want.** See Figure 25-12.

Note

In Step 8, you can choose to print an Outline if you prefer. An outline can be a useful handout for an audience in certain situations. ∎

9. (Optional) **Click the Color button, and select the color setting for the printouts:**

   - **Color.** This is the default. It sends the data to the printer assuming that color will be used. When you use this setting with a black-and-white printer, it results in slides with grayscale or black backgrounds. Use this setting if you want the handouts to look as much as possible like the onscreen slides.

   - **Grayscale.** Sends the data to the printer assuming that color will not be used. Colored backgrounds are removed, and if text is normally a light color on a dark background, that is reversed. Use this setting if you want PowerPoint to optimize the printout for viewing on white paper.

   - **Pure Black and White.** This format hides most shadows and patterns, as described in Table 25-1. It's good for faxes and overhead transparencies.

FIGURE 25-12

Choose which handout layout you want.

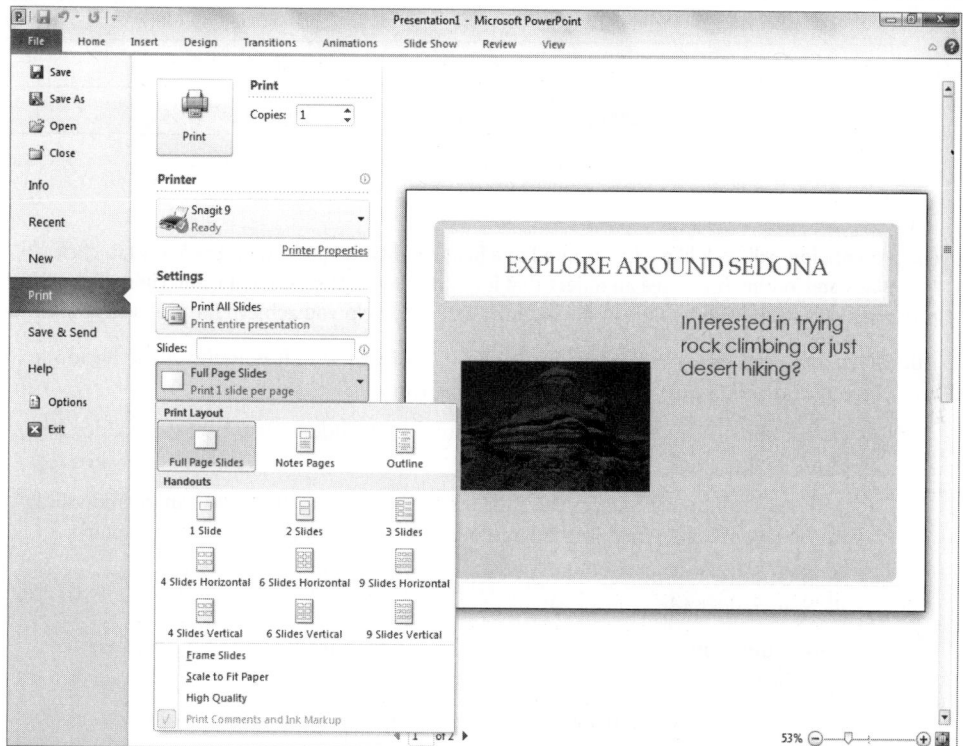

TABLE 25-1

Differences between Grayscale and Pure Black and White

Object	Grayscale	Pure Black and White
Text	Black	Black
Text Shadows	Grayscale	Black
Fill	Grayscale	Grayscale
Lines	Black	Black
Object Shadows	Grayscale	Black
Bitmaps	Grayscale	Grayscale

continued

Object	Grayscale	Pure Black and White
Clip Art	Grayscale	Grayscale
Slide Backgrounds	White	White
Charts	Grayscale	White

TABLE 25-1 *(continued)*

Tip

To see what your presentation will look like when printed to a black-and-white printer, on the View tab click Grayscale or Pure Black and White. If you see an object that is not displaying the way you want, right-click on it and choose Grayscale or Black and White. One of the options there may help you achieve the look you're after. ■

10. (Optional) **If desired, open the drop-down list from which you chose the handout layout and select any of these additional options:**

   - **Frame Slides.** Draws a black border around each slide image. Useful for slides being printed with white backgrounds.

   - **Scale to Fit Paper.** Enlarges the slides to the maximum size they can be and still fit on the layout (as defined in the Handout Master, covered later in this chapter).

   - **High Quality.** Optimizes the appearance of the printout in small ways, such as allowing text shadows to print.

   - **Print Comments and Ink Markup.** Prints any comments that you have inserted with the Comments feature in PowerPoint.

11. **Check the preview of your handouts, which appears at the right.** Make any necessary changes.

12. **Click Print.** The handouts print, and you're ready to roll!

Caution

Be aware of the cost of printer supplies for your specific printer. If you are planning to distribute copies of the presentation to a lot of people, it may be tempting to print all of the copies on your printer. But the cost per page of printing is fairly high, especially for some small-business-oriented inkjet printers. You will quickly run out of ink in your ink cartridge and have to spend $20 or more for a replacement. Consider whether it might be cheaper to print one original and take it to a copy shop. ■

Setting Printer-Specific Options

In addition to Print settings in PowerPoint that you learned about in the preceding section, there are controls you can set that affect the printer you have chosen.

Notice that a printer's name appears under the Printer heading in Figure 25-12. Click that printer's name to open a menu of additional printers you can select instead. These are the printers installed on your PC (either local or network).

Note

Some of the "printers" listed are not really physical printers but drivers that create other types of files. For example, Fax the file in a format that is compatible with the Fax driver included with Windows. It doesn't produce a hard copy printout. ∎

After selecting the desired printer, click the Printer Properties hyperlink beneath the name. A Properties dialog box opens that is specific to that printer. Figure 25-13 shows the box for my HP PhotoSmart C4700 printer, an all-in-one inkjet. Notice that there are three tabs: Printing Shortcuts, Features, and Advanced. The tabs may be different for your printer.

FIGURE 25-13

Each printer's options are slightly different, but the same types of settings are available on most printers.

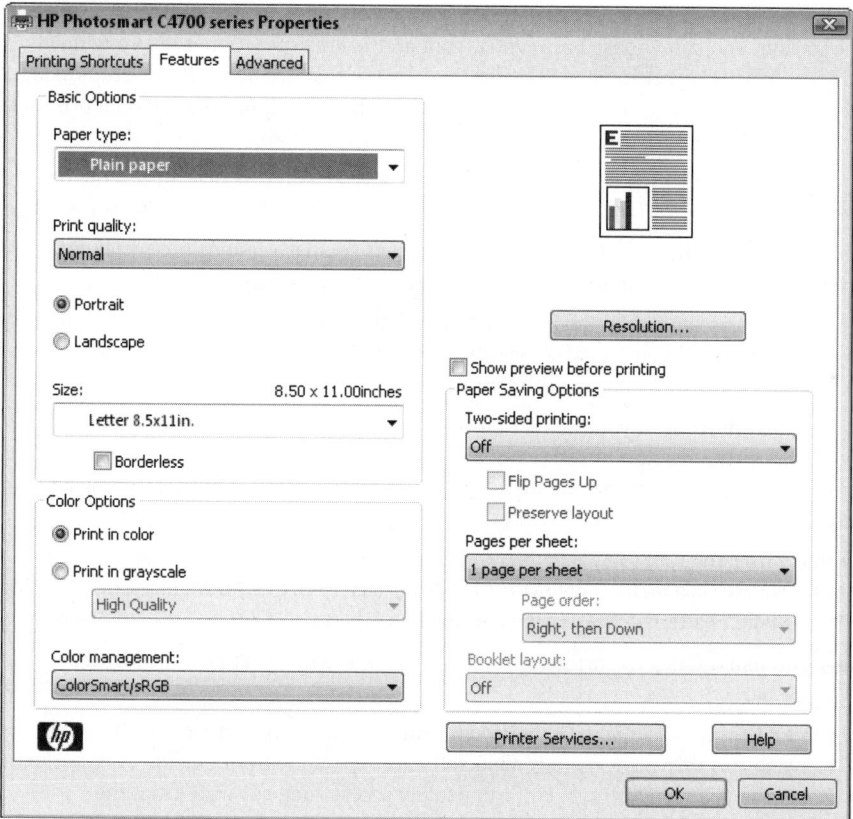

These settings affect how the printer behaves in all Windows-based programs, not just in PowerPoint, so you need to be careful not to change anything that you don't want globally changed. Here are some of the settings you may be able to change on your printer. (Not all of these are shown in Figure 25-13.)

- **Paper Size.** The default is Letter, but you can change to Legal, A4, or any of several other sizes.

- **Paper Source.** If your printer has more than one paper tray, you may be able to select Upper or Lower.

- **Paper Type.** Some printers print at different resolutions or with different settings depending on the type of paper (e.g., photo paper versus regular paper). You can choose the type of paper you are printing on.

- **Print Quality.** Some printers give you a choice of quality levels, such as Draft, Normal, and Best. Draft is the quickest; Best is the slowest and may use more ink.

- **Duplex or Print on Both Sides.** Some printers enable you to print on both sides of the paper. Some printers flip the paper over automatically, but most prompt you to flip it over manually.

- **Orientation.** You can choose between Portrait and Landscape. It's not recommended that you change this setting here, though; make such changes in the Page Setup dialog box in PowerPoint instead. Otherwise, you may get the wrong orientation on a printout in other programs.

- **Page Order.** You can choose Front to Back or Back to Front. This determines the order in which the pages print.

- **Pages per Sheet.** The default is 1, but you can print smaller versions of several pages on a single sheet. This option is usually only available on PostScript printers.

- **Copies.** This sets the default number of copies that should print. Be careful; this number is a multiplier. If you set two copies here and then set two copies in the Print dialog box in PowerPoint, you end up with four copies.

- **Graphics Resolution.** If your printer has a range of resolutions available, you may be able to choose the resolution you want. My printer lets me choose between 300 and 600 dpi; on an inkjet printer, choices are usually 360, 720, and 1,440 dpi. Achieving a resolution of 1,440 dpi on an inkjet printer usually requires special glossy paper.

- **Graphic Dithering.** On some printers, you can set the type of dithering that makes up images. *Dithering* is a method of creating shadows (shades of gray) from black ink by using tiny cross-hatch patterns. You may be able to choose between Coarse, Fine, and None.

- **Image Intensity.** On some printers, you can control the image appearance with a light/dark slide bar.

Some printers, notably inkjets, come with their own print-management software. If that's the case, you may have to run that print-management software separately from outside of PowerPoint for full control over the printer's settings. You can usually access such software from the Windows Start menu.

Using the Handout Master

Just as the Slide Master controls your slide layout, the Handout Master controls your handout layout. To view the Handout Master, shown in Figure 25-14, click Handout Master in the Master

Views group on the View tab. Unlike the Slide Master and Title Master, you can have only one Handout Master layout per presentation.

FIGURE 25-14

The Handout Master lets you define the handout layout to be printed.

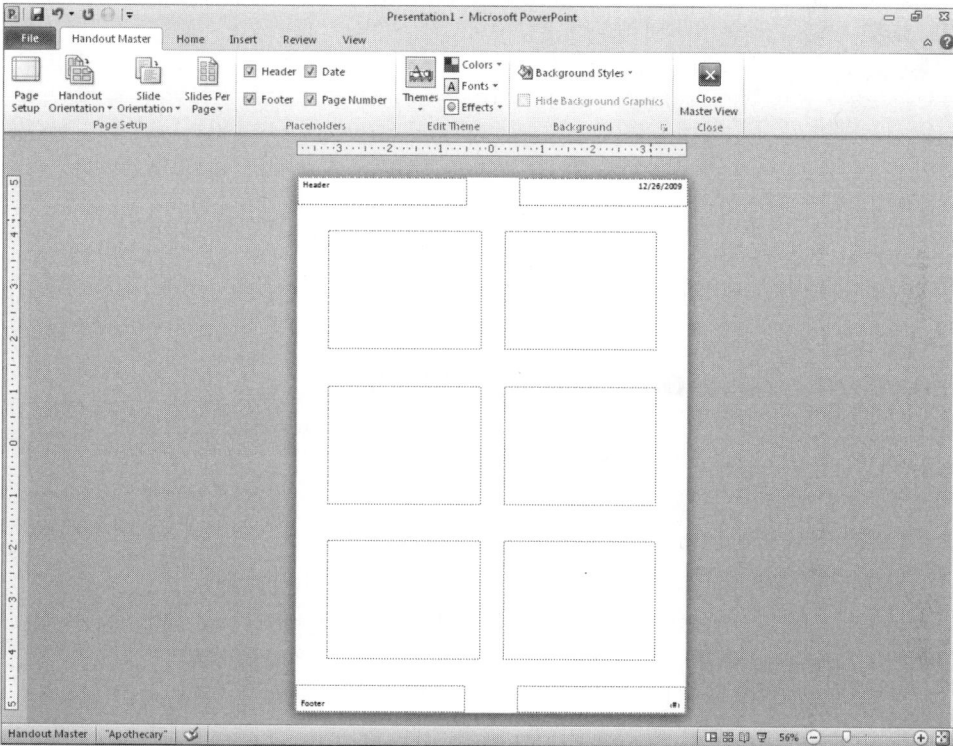

You can do almost exactly the same things with the Handout Master that you can with the Slide Master. The following sections describe some of the common activities.

Setting the Number of Slides per Page

You can view the Handout Master with various numbers of slides per page to help you see how the layout will look when you print it. However, the settings are not different for each number of slides per page; for example, if you apply a header or footer, or page background, for a three-slides-per-page layout, it also applies to all the others. To choose the number of slides per page to display as you work with the Handout Master, click the Slides Per Page button in the Page Setup group and then make your selection from its menu. See Figure 25-15.

FIGURE 25-15

Choose a number of slides per page.

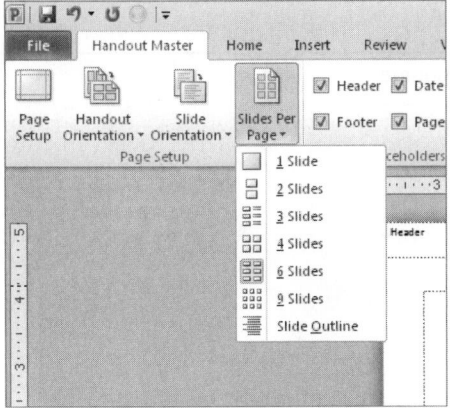

Using and Positioning Placeholders

The Handout Master has four placeholders by default: Header, Footer, Date, and Page Number, in the four corners of the handout, respectively:

- **Header.** Appears in the upper-left corner and is a blank box into which you can type fixed text that will appear on each page of the printout.

- **Footer.** Same thing as Header but appears in the lower-left corner.

- **Date.** Appears in the upper-right corner and shows today's date by default.

- **Page Number.** Appears in the lower-right corner and shows a code for a page number: <#>. This will be replaced by an actual page number when you print.

In each placeholder box, you can type text (replacing, if desired, the Date and Page codes already there in those). You can also drag the placeholder boxes around on the layout.

There are two ways to remove the default placeholders from the layout. Select the placeholder box and press Delete, or you can clear the check box for that element on the Handout Master tab, as shown in Figure 25-16.

Note

Because the Header and Footer are blank by default, there is no advantage to deleting these placeholders unless they have something in them you want to dispose of; having a blank box and having no box at all have the same result. ■

Tip

You can't move or resize the *slide* placeholder boxes on the Handout Master, nor can you change the margins. If you want to change the size of the slide boxes on the handout or change the margins of the page, consider exporting the handouts to Word and working on them there. ■

FIGURE 25-16

Turn on/off placeholder elements from the Handout Master tab.

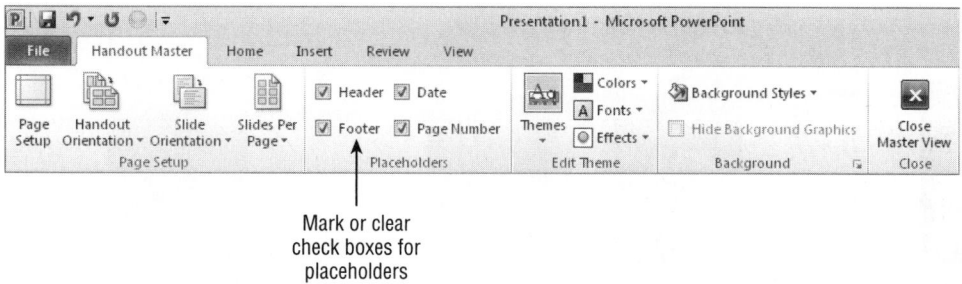

Mark or clear
check boxes for
placeholders

Setting Handout and Slide Orientation

Orientation refers to the direction on the page the material runs. If the top of the paper is one of the narrow edges, it's called *Portrait*; if the top of the paper is a wide edge, it's *Landscape*. Figure 25-17 shows the difference in handout orientation.

FIGURE 25-17

Portrait (left) and Landscape (right) handout orientation.

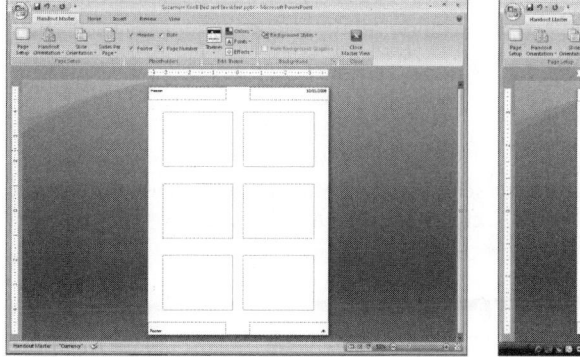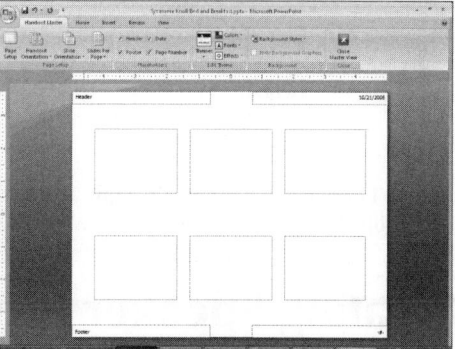

You can also set an orientation for the slides themselves on the handouts. This is a separate setting that does not affect the handout page in terms of the placement of the header, footer, and other repeated elements. Figure 25-18 shows the difference between Portrait and Landscape slide orientation on a Portrait handout.

To set either of these orientations, use their respective drop-down lists on the Handout Master tab, in the Page Setup group.

FIGURE 25-18

Landscape (left) and Portrait (right) slide orientation.

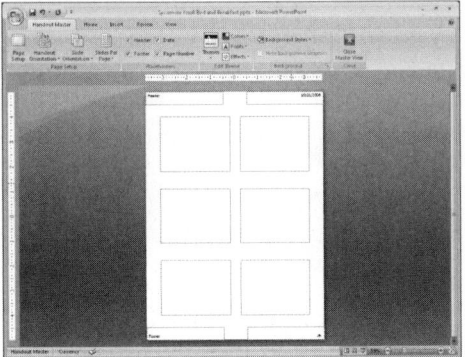 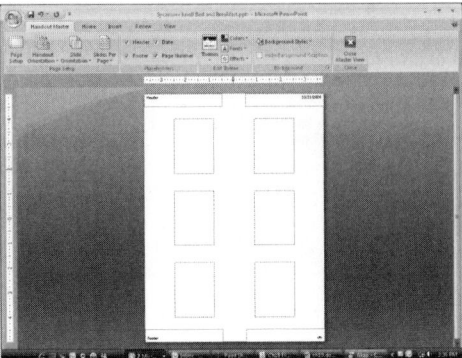

Formatting Handouts

You can manually format any text on a handout layout using the formatting controls on the Home tab, the same as with any other text. Such formatting affects only the text you select, and only on the layout you're working with. You can also select the entire placeholder box and apply formatting.

You can also apply Colors, Fonts, and/or Effects schemes from the Edit Theme group, as shown in Figure 25-19, much as you can do for the presentation as a whole. The main difference is that you cannot select an overall theme from the Themes button; all the themes are unavailable from the list while in Handout Master view. The settings you apply here affect only the *handouts*, not the presentation as a whole.

Note

You probably won't have much occasion to apply an Effects scheme to a handout layout because handouts do not usually have objects that use effects (i.e., drawn shapes, charts, or SmartArt diagrams). ■

Creating Speaker Notes

You probably want a different set of support materials for yourself from what you want for the audience. Support materials designed for the speaker's use are called *speaker notes*. In addition to small printouts of the slides, the speaker notes contain any extra notes or background information that you think you may need to jog your memory as you speak. Some people get very nervous when they speak in front of a crowd; speaker notes can remind you of the joke you wanted to open with or the exact figures behind a particular pie chart.

Only one printout format is available for speaker notes: the Notes Pages layout. It consists of the slide on the top half (the same size as in the two-slides-per-page handout) with the blank space below it for your notes to yourself.

FIGURE 25-19

FIGURE 25-19

Apply Color, Font, and/or Effect schemes from the Edit Theme group.

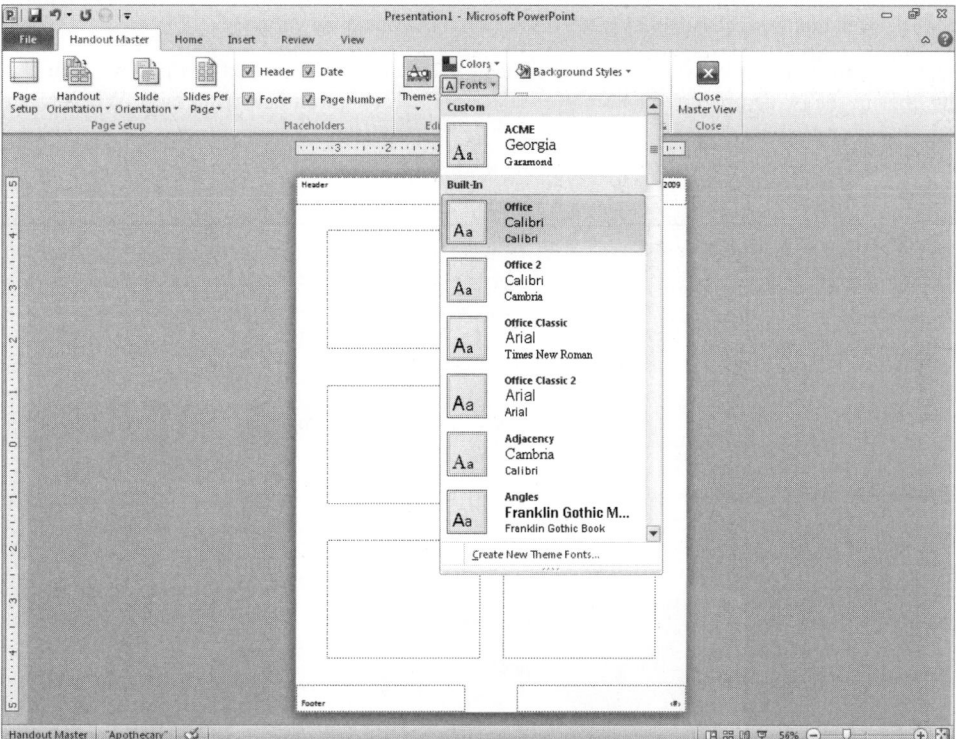

Speaker notes printed in PowerPoint are better than traditional note cards for several reasons. For one thing, you can type your notes right into the computer and print them out on regular paper. There's no need to jam a note card into a typewriter and use messy correction fluid or erasers to make changes. The other benefit is that each note page contains a picture of the slide, so it's not as easy to lose your place while speaking.

Typing Speaker Notes

You can type your notes for a slide in Normal view (in the Notes pane), or in Notes Page view. The latter shows the page more or less as it will look when you print your notes pages; this can help if you need to gauge how much text will fit on the printed page.

To switch to Notes Page view, in the Presentation Views group on the View tab, click Notes Page, as shown in Figure 25-20. Unlike some of the other views, there is no shortcut button for this view in the bottom-right corner of the PowerPoint window. Once you're in Notes Page view, you can zoom and scroll just like in any other view to see more or less of the page at once. You can scroll further to move from slide to slide, or you can move from slide to slide in the traditional ways (the Page Up and Page Down keys on the keyboard or the Next Slide or Previous Slide buttons onscreen).

Note

Use the Zoom control to zoom in or out until you find the optimal view so that the text you type is large enough to be clear, but small enough so that you can see across the entire width of the note area. I find that 100 percent works well on my screen at 1024 x 768 resolution, but yours may vary. ■

Just type your notes in the Notes area, the same as you would type any text box in PowerPoint. The lines in the paragraph wrap automatically. Press Enter to start a new paragraph. When you're done, move to the next slide.

FIGURE 25-20

Notes Page view is one of the best ways to work with your speaker notes.

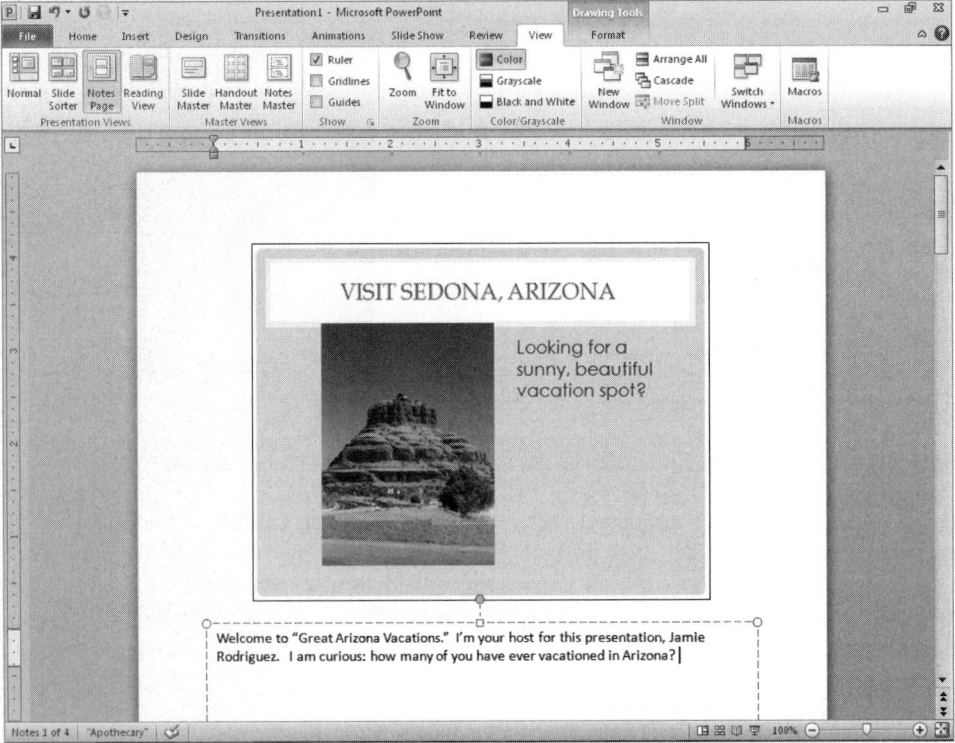

Changing the Notes Page Layout

Just as you can edit your handout layouts, you can also edit your notes page layout. Just switch to its Master and make your changes. Follow these steps:

1. **In the Master Views group on the View tab, click Notes Master.**

2. **Edit the layout, as you have learned to edit other masters.** See Figure 25-21. This can include:

- Moving placeholders for the slide, the notes, or any of the header or footer elements
- Changing the font used for the text in any of those areas
- Resizing the placeholder for the slide graphic
- Resizing the Notes pane
- Adding clip art or other graphics to the background
- Adding a colored, textured, or patterned background to the notes page

3. **When you are finished, click the Close Master View button to return to Normal view.**

FIGURE 25-21

You can edit the layout of the notes pages in Notes Master view.

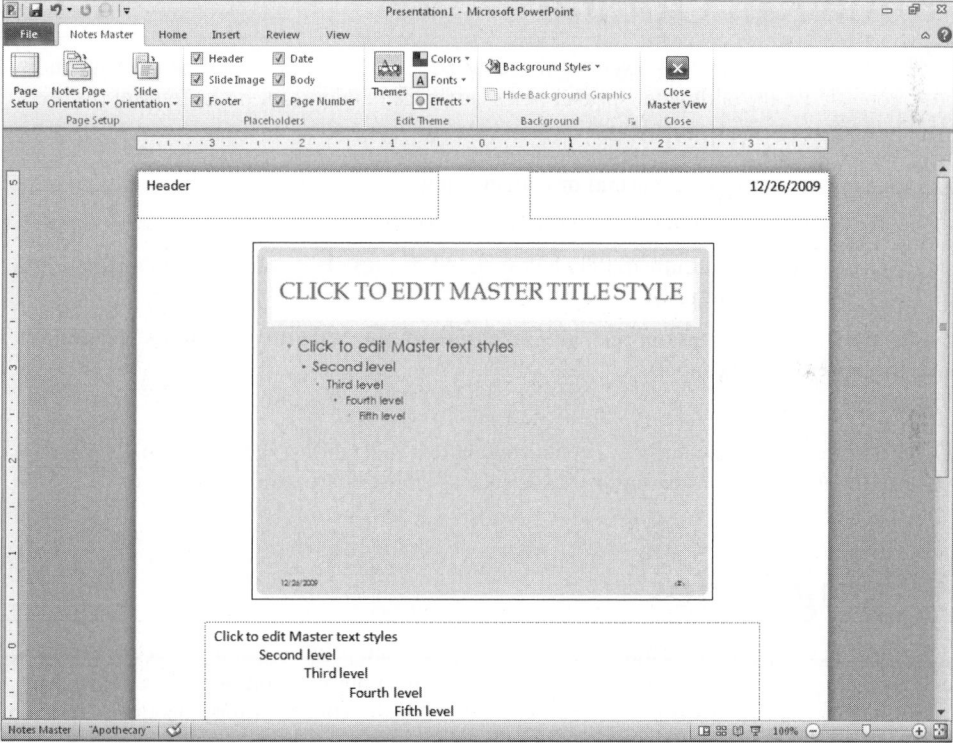

Printing Notes Pages

When you're ready to print your notes pages, follow these steps:

1. **Choose File ⇨ Print.** The Print controls appear.
2. **Click the button immediately below the Slides text box, and choose Notes Pages as the type of layout to print.**

3. Set any other options, just as you did when printing handouts earlier in the chapter. (If you need to choose which printer to use or to set the options for that printer, see the "Setting Printer-Specific Options" section earlier in this chapter.) There are no special options for notes pages.

4. Click Print. The notes pages print.

Caution
If you print notes pages for hidden slides, you may want to arrange your stack of pages after they're printed so that the hidden slides are at the bottom. That way you won't get confused when giving the presentation and can easily select one of the last notes pages should the need to display a hidden slide arise. ■

Printing an Outline

If text is the main part of your presentation, you might prefer to print an outline instead of mini-slides. You can use the outline for speaker notes, audience handouts, or both. To print the text from Outline view, follow these steps:

1. View the outline in Normal or Outline view.

2. Choose File ⇨ Print. The Print controls appear.

3. Click the button immediately below the Slides text box, and choose Outline as the type of layout to print.

4. Set any other print options, as you learned in the "Printing Handouts" section earlier in this chapter.

5. Click Print.

Be aware, however, that the outline will not contain text that you've typed in manually placed text boxes or any other non-text information, such as tables, charts, and so on.

Printing Slides

Of course, you can print your slides one per page rather than printing handouts or notes pages. You may print slides, for example, when you need to send a presentation to a client rather than presenting it in person. Printing presentation slides works just like printing a document from any other application:

1. Click File ⇨ Print or press Ctrl+P. The Print controls appear.

2. **Select the printer to use from the Printer drop-down list.** The printer becomes the current or active printer.

3. **On the button immediately below the Slides text box, make sure that Full Page Slides is selected.**

4. Specify what slides to print in the Slides text box.

5. Specify how many copies to print in the Copies text box.

6. If you're printing multiple copies, specify whether the copies should be Collated or Uncollated using the next-to-last drop-down list.

7. If you're using a color printer, make a choice from the bottom drop-down list to determine whether to print in color.

8. Click Print.

Summary

In this chapter, you learned how to animate the objects on your slides to create some great special effects, and how to create animated transitions from slide to slide. You also learned how to create support materials for a presentation, such as handouts and speaker notes, and how to format and fine-tune their formatting. Finally, you learned how to print notes pages and slides.

Preparing and Delivering a Live Presentation

I t's show time! Well, actually, I hope for your sake that it is not time for the show this very instant, because things will go much more smoothly if you can practice using PowerPoint's slide-show controls before you have to go live.

Presenting your slide show can be as simple or as complex as you make it. At the most basic level, you can start the show, move through it slide-by-slide with simple mouse-clicks or key presses, and then end the show. However, to take advantage of PowerPoint's extra slide-show features, you should spend a little time studying the following sections.

Note
The first part of this chapter assumes that you are showing your presentation on a PC that has PowerPoint 2010 installed; sections later in this chapter discuss other situations. ■

Starting and Ending a Show

To start a show, do any of the following:

- In the Start Slide Show group on the Slide Show tab, click either From Beginning or From Current Slide.
- Click the Slide Show View button in the bottom-right corner of the screen (to begin from the current slide).
- Press F5 (to begin from the beginning).
- Press Shift+F5 (to begin from the current slide).

Once the show is under way, you can control the movement from slide to slide as described in the section, "Moving from Slide to Slide."

To end the show, do any of the following:

- Right-click and choose End Show.
- Press Esc, – (minus), or Ctrl+Break.

If you want to temporarily pause the show while you have a discussion, you can blank the screen by pressing **W** or , (comma) for a white screen, or **B** or . (period) for a black screen. To resume the show, press any key.

Tip

If you set up the slide transitions to occur automatically at a certain time, you can stop or restart the show by pressing S or + (plus sign). However, this is more of an issue for self-running shows. ∎

Using the Onscreen Show Controls

When you display a slide show, the mouse pointer and show controls are hidden. To make them appear, you can move the mouse. When you do this, very faint buttons appear in the bottom-left corner of the slide show, as shown in Figure 26-1, and the mouse pointer also appears. You can toggle the pointer and these buttons on and off by pressing **A** or = (equal sign). Ctrl+H also hides the pointer and buttons. When you toggle this feature on, the following buttons appear:

FIGURE 26-1

Buttons appear in the bottom-left corner of a slide in Slide Show view. The third button opens a menu that controls navigation between slides.

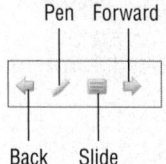

- **Back.** The leftmost button, Back, takes you back to the previous slide, or to the previous animation event if the present slide contains animation.
- **Pen.** Next to Back, the Pen button opens a menu for controlling the appearance of the pen or pointer. (I discuss this feature later in this chapter.)
- **Slide.** The Slide button displays a box icon and opens a menu for navigating between slides. You can also open the navigation menu, shown in Figure 26-2, by right-clicking anywhere on the slide.

FIGURE 26-2

Click the Slide button or right-click on the slide to open this menu.

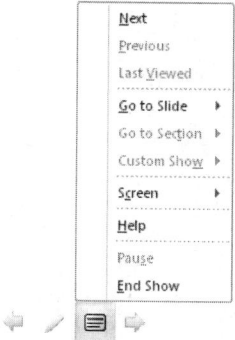

Tip

You can set up your show to move backward when you click the right-mouse button. Choose File ➪ Options, click Advanced, and in the Slide Show section deselect the Show Menu on Right Mouse Click check box. If you do that, you can't right-click to open the navigation menu, though. The control buttons in the lower-left corner of Slide Show view can be disabled via File ➪ Options ➪ Advanced ➪ Slide Show ➪ Show Popup Toolbar. ■

- **Forward.** Forward, the rightmost button, moves you to the next slide. Normally, you can just click to go to the next slide, but if you are using the pen (covered later in this chapter), then clicking it causes it to draw, rather than advance the presentation. In this situation, you can use the Forward button.

Note

Because the slide navigation menu that appears is identical whether you click the Slide button or right-click anywhere on the slide, this chapter only mentions the right-click method whenever you need to choose something from this menu. However, keep in mind that you can also click the Slide button if you prefer. ■

New in PowerPoint 2010 are media control shortcuts in Slide Show view, shown in Table 26-1.

TABLE 26-1

New Shortcuts on the Slide Show View

Shortcut	Function
Alt+P	Media Play/Pause.
Alt+Q	Media Stop Playback.

continued

TABLE 26-1 *(continued)*	
Shortcut	**Function**
Alt+Home	Go to previous bookmark in the media clip.
Alt+End	Go to next bookmark in the media clip.
Alt+Shift+left-arrow	Skip backward.
Alt+Shift+right-arrow	Skip forward.
Alt+U	Mute/Unmute media.

There are a lot of shortcut keys to remember when working in Slide Show view, and so PowerPoint provides a handy summary of these keys. To see them, right-click and choose Help, or press F1. The Slide Show Help dialog box appears, as shown in Figure 26-3. The dialog box has several tabbed pages; click a tab to browse for the shortcuts of interest to you. Click OK to close this dialog box when you are done.

FIGURE 26-3

The Slide Show Help dialog box provides a quick summary of the shortcut keys that are available during a presentation.

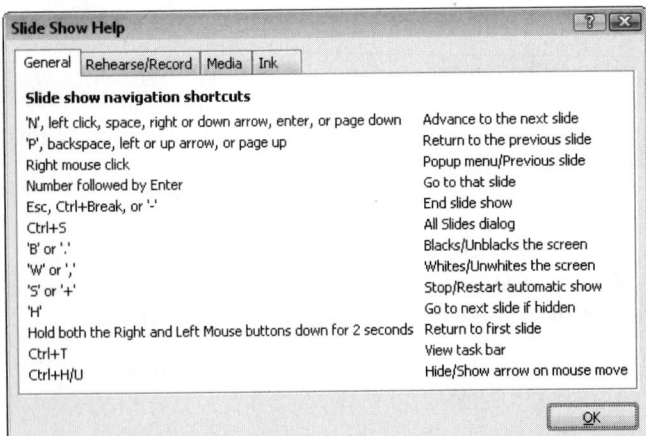

Moving from Slide to Slide

The simplest way to move through a presentation is to move to the next slide. To do so, you can use any of these methods:

- Press any of these keys: **N**, Spacebar, right-arrow, down-arrow, Enter, or Page Down.
- Click the left mouse button.

- Right-click and then choose Next.
- Click the right-pointing arrow button in the bottom-left corner of the slide.

If you have animated any elements on a slide, these methods advance the animation and do not necessarily move to the next slide. For example, if you have animated your bulleted list so that the bullets appear one at a time, then any of the actions in this list make the next bullet appear, rather than making the next slide appear. Only after all of the objects on the current slide have displayed does PowerPoint advance to the next slide. If you need to advance immediately to the next slide, you can use the instructions in the section, "Jumping to Specific Slides," later in this chapter.

To back up to the previous slide, use any of these methods:

- Press any of these keys: **P**, Backspace, left-arrow, up-arrow, or Page Up.
- Click the left-pointing arrow button on the bottom-left corner of the slide.
- Right-click and then choose Previous.

You can also go back to the last slide that you viewed. To do this, right-click and choose Last Viewed. Although you would think that the last slide viewed would be the same as the previous slide, this is not always the case. For example, if you jump around in the slide show — such as to a hidden slide — then the last slide viewed is not the previous slide in the show but the hidden slide that you have just viewed.

Jumping to Specific Slides

There are several ways to jump to a particular slide. One of the easiest ways is to select the slide by its title. To do so, follow these steps:

1. **During the slide show, right-click to display the shortcut menu.**

2. **Select Go to Slide.** A submenu appears, listing the titles of all of the slides in the presentation, as shown in Figure 26-4. Parentheses around the slide numbers indicate hidden slides.

3. **Click the slide title to which you want to jump.**

Tip

The slide titles on the menu shown in Figure 26-4 come from Title placeholders on the slides. If you want to show text on the list here but you don't want it to appear on the slide, type it in a Title placeholder and then drag the placeholder off the edge of the slide so it doesn't show in Slide Show view. ∎

You can also jump to a certain slide number by typing this number and pressing Enter. For example, to go to the third slide, you would type **3** and then press Enter. Another way is to press Ctrl+S to open an All Slides dialog box listing the titles of all of the slides in the presentation. You can click a slide to select it and then click Go To, as shown in Figure 26-5.

To jump back to the first slide in the presentation, hold down both the left and right mouse buttons for 2 seconds (or type **1** and press Enter).

FIGURE 26-4

You can go to a specific slide using the Go to Slide command on the menu.

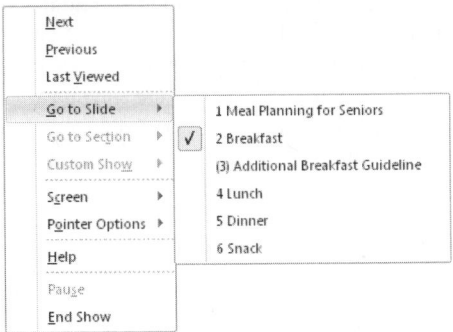

FIGURE 26-5

The All Slides dialog box lists the titles of all of the slides so that you can select the one that you want to go to.

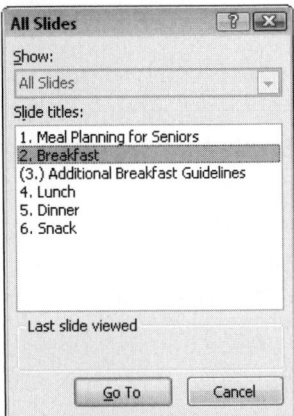

Blanking the Screen

Sometimes during a live presentation there may be a delay. Whether it is a chatty audience member with a complicated question, a fire drill, or just an intermission, you will want to pause the show.

If you have the slides set for manual transition, then whichever slide you stopped on remains on the screen until you resume. However, you may not want this. For example, it may be distracting to the audience, especially if the pause is to allow someone to get up and speak in front of the screen. A solution is to turn the screen into a blank expanse of black or white. To do so, type **W** or a **,** (comma), for white, or **B** or a **.** (period) for black. To return to the presentation, you can press the same key or press any key on the keyboard.

Tip

While the screen is completely black or white, you can draw on it with the Pen tool so that it becomes a convenient *scratch pad*. Any annotations that you make with the pen on the blank screen are not saved; when you resume the presentation, they are gone forever. (In contrast, you do have the opportunity to save any annotations you make on the slides themselves, as you will learn in the next section.) ■

Using the Onscreen Pen

Have you ever seen a coach in a locker room drawing out football plays on a chalkboard? Well, you can do the same thing in PowerPoint. You can have impromptu discussions of concepts that are illustrated on slides and punctuate the discussion with your own circles, arrows, and lines. Perhaps during the discussion portion of your presentation, you may decide that one point on the slide is not important. In this case, you can use the pen to cross it out. Conversely, a certain point may become really important during a discussion so that you want to emphasize it. In this case, you can circle it or underline it with the pen cursor.

You can choose your pen color as follows:

1. **Move the mouse or press A to make the buttons appear.**
2. **Click the Pointers button (the one that looks like a pen).** A menu appears. Alternatively, you can right-click and then choose Pointer Options to see this same menu.
3. **Select Ink Color and then click the color you want, as shown in Figure 26-6.**

Tip

To change the default pen color for the show, so that you do not always have to manually select the color you want, click Set Up Show on the Slide Show tab. Then, in the Pen Color drop-down list, choose the color you want. ■

FIGURE 26-6

You can select a pen type and an ink color for it.

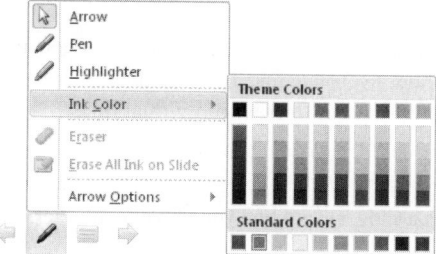

You can turn on the type of pen that you want, as follows:

1. **Click the Pointers button again.**

2. **Click the type of pen that you want:**

   - **Pen.** A thin solid line
   - **Highlighter.** A thick, semi-transparent line

Note

The onscreen buttons in the slide show continue to work while you have a pen enabled, but you have to click them twice to activate them — once to tell PowerPoint to temporarily switch out of the Pen mode, and then again to open the menu. ■

You can also turn on the default Pen by pressing Ctrl+P, and then return to the arrow again by pressing Ctrl+A or Esc.

After enabling a pen, just drag and draw on the slide to make your mark. You should practice drawing lines, arrows, and other shapes because it takes a while to master. Figure 26-7 shows an example of using the pen.

Caution

As you can see from Figure 26-7, the onscreen pen is not very attractive. If you know in advance that you are going to emphasize certain points, then you may prefer to build the emphasis into the presentation by making these points larger, bolder, or in different colors. You can also circle the points using an animated oval shape. ■

FIGURE 26-7

You can draw on the slide with the Pen tools.

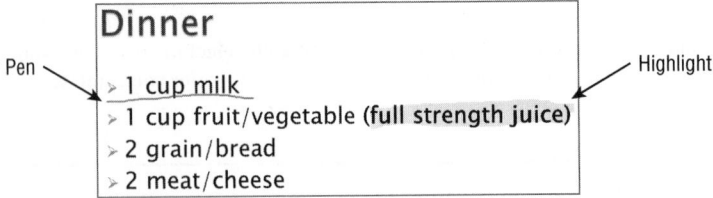

To erase your lines and try again, press **E** (for Erase), or open the Pointer menu (or right-click and choose Pointer Options) and choose Erase All Ink on Slide. To erase just a part of the ink, open the Pointer menu, choose Eraser, and then use the mouse pointer to erase individual lines.

Note

Unlike in some earlier versions of PowerPoint, drawings stay with a slide, even when you move to another slide. ■

When you exit Slide Show view after drawing on slides, a dialog box appears, asking whether you want to keep or discard your annotations. If you choose Keep, the annotations become drawn objects on the slides, which you can then move or delete, similar to a line drawn with the drawing tools.

To change the pen back to a pointer again, open the Pointer menu and choose Arrow, press Ctrl+A, or press Esc. The pen remains a pen when you advance from slide to slide.

Hiding Slides for Backup Use

You may not always want to show every slide that you have prepared. Sometimes it pays to prepare extra data in anticipation of a question that you think someone might ask, or to hold back certain data unless someone specifically requests it.

By hiding a slide, you keep it filed in reserve, without making it a part of the main slide show. Then, at any time during the presentation when (or if) it becomes appropriate, you can display that slide. *Hiding* refers only to whether the slide is a part of the main presentation's flow; it has no effect in any other view.

Tip

If you have only a handful of slides to hide, go ahead and hide them. However, if you have a large group of related slides to hide, consider creating a custom show for them instead. Custom shows are covered later in this chapter. ■

Hiding and Unhiding Slides

A good way to hide and unhide slides is in Slide Sorter view because an indicator appears below each slide to show whether it is hidden. This way, you can easily determine which slides are part of the main presentation. In the slide thumbnail pane in Normal view, hidden slides appear ghosted out.

Follow these steps to hide a slide:

1. **Switch to Slide Sorter view.**
2. **Select the slide or slides that you want to hide.** Remember, to select more than one slide, hold down the Ctrl key as you click the ones that you want.
3. **Click the Hide Slide button in the Set Up group on the Slide Show tab.** A gray box appears around the slide number and a diagonal line crosses through it, indicating that it is hidden.

To unhide a slide, select the slide and click the Hide Slide button again. The slide's number returns to normal. You can also right-click a slide and choose Hide Slide or Unhide Slide to toggle the hidden attribute on and off.

Tip

To quickly unhide all slides, select all of the slides (press Ctrl+A) and then click the Hide Slide button twice. The first click hides all of the remaining slides that were not already hidden, and the second click unhides them all. ∎

Showing a Hidden Slide during a Presentation

When you advance from one slide to the next during a show, hidden slides do not appear. (This is what being hidden is about, after all.) If you need to display one of the hidden slides, follow these steps:

1. In Slide Show view, right-click, or click the Slide icon in the bottom-left corner of the screen.

2. **Choose Go to Slide, and then choose the slide to which you want to jump.** Hidden slides show their slide numbers in parentheses, but you can access them like any other slide. Refer back to Figure 26-4, where the third slide is hidden.

Tip

If you already know the number of the hidden slide, then you can simply type the number on the keyboard and press Enter to display it. This also works with slides that are not hidden. ∎

Once you display a hidden slide, you can easily return to it later. When you move backward through the presentation (using the Backspace key, the left-arrow or up-arrow key, or the onscreen Back button), any hidden slides that you displayed previously are included in the slides that PowerPoint scrolls back through. However, when you move forward through the presentation, the hidden slide does not reappear, regardless of when you viewed it previously. You can always jump back to it again using the preceding steps. You can also set up hyperlinks to go to, and leave, hidden slides.

Using Custom Shows

Many slide shows have a linear flow: First you show Slide 1, and then Slide 2, and so on, until you have completed the entire presentation. This format is suitable for situations where you are presenting clear-cut information with few variables, such as a presentation about a new insurance plan for a group of employees. However, when the situation becomes more complex, a single-path slide show may not suffice. This is especially true when you are presenting a persuasive message to decision-makers; you want to anticipate their questions and needs for more information and have many backup slides, or even entire backup slide shows that are prepared in case questions arise. Figure 26-8 shows a flow chart for this kind of presentation.

Note

If you simply want to hide a few slides for backup use, then you do not need to create a custom show. Instead, you can just hide the slides. ∎

FIGURE 26-8

You can use custom shows to hide related groups of backup slides.

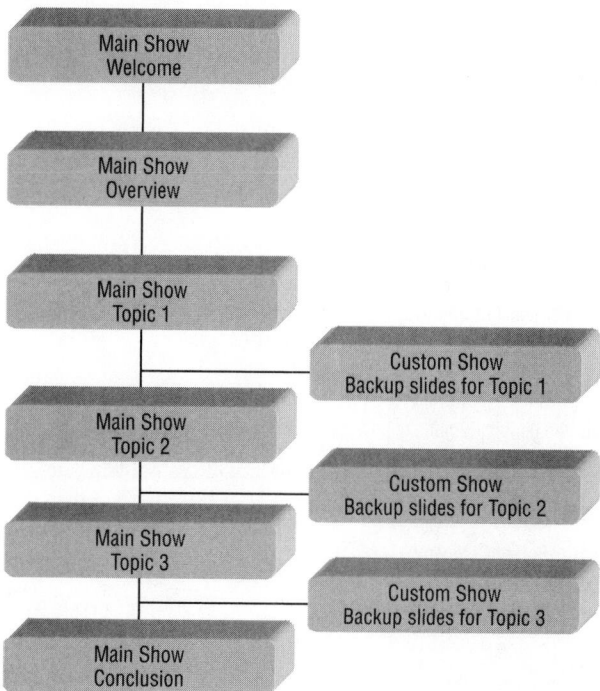

Another great use for custom shows is to set aside a group of slides for a specific audience. For example, you might need to present essentially the same information to employees at two different sites. In this case, you could create two custom shows within the main show, where each show includes slides that they both have in common, as well as slides that are appropriate for only one audience or the other. Figure 26-9 shows a flow chart for this kind of presentation.

Notice in Figure 26-9 that although some of the slides in the two custom shows are the same, they repeat in each custom show rather than jumping back to the main presentation. This is because it is much easier to jump to the custom show once and stay there, than it is to keep jumping into and out of the show.

Slides in a custom show remain a part of the main presentation. Placing a slide in a custom show does not exclude it from the regular presentation flow. However, you may decide that you no longer want to show the main presentation in its present form; you may just want to use it as a resource pool from which you can select slides for other custom shows. To learn how to set up PowerPoint so that a custom show starts rather than the main presentation when you enter Slide Show view, see the section, "Using a Custom Show as the Main Presentation," later in this chapter.

FIGURE 26-9

You can create custom shows that allow you to use the same presentation for multiple audiences.

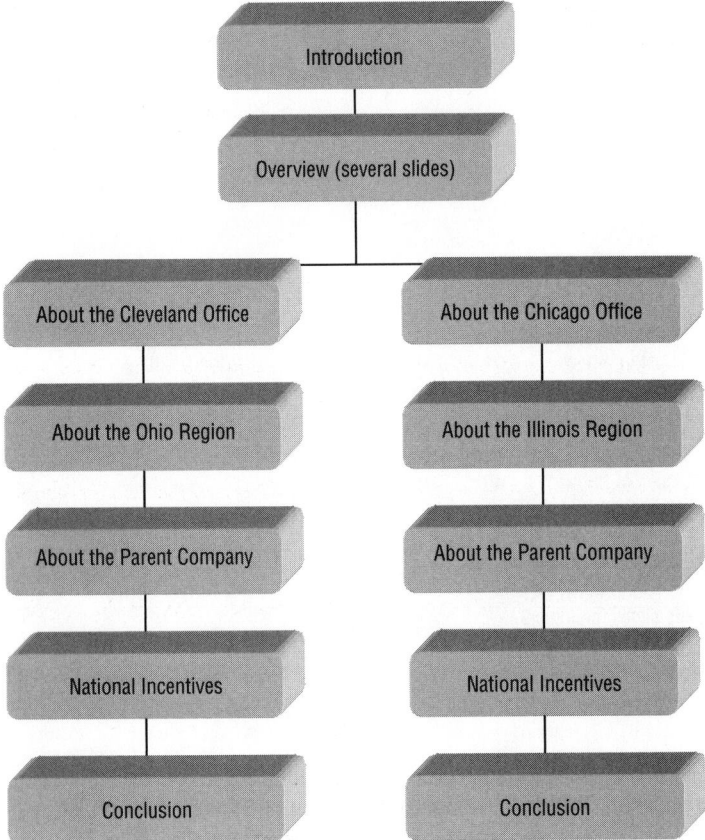

Ideas for Using Custom Shows

Here are some ideas to start you thinking about how and why you might want to include some custom shows in your presentation files:

- **Avoiding Duplication.** If you have several shows that use about 50 percent of the same slides and 50 percent different ones, then you can create all of the shows as custom shows within a single presentation file. This way, the presentations can share the 50 percent of the slides that they have in common.

- **Managing Change.** By creating a single presentation file with custom shows, you make it easy to manage changes. If any changes occur in your company that affect any of the common slides, then making the change once in your presentation file makes the change to each of the custom shows immediately.

- **Overcoming Objections.** You can anticipate client objections to your sales pitch and prepare several custom shows, each of which addresses a particular objection. Then, whatever reason your potential customer gives for not buying your product, you have a counteractive argument at hand.

- **Covering Your Backside.** If you think that you may be asked for specific figures or other information during a speech, you can have this information ready in a custom show (or on a few simple hidden slides, if there is not a lot of information) to display if needed. No more going through the embarrassment of having to say, "I'm not sure, but let me get back to you on that."

Creating Custom Shows

To create a custom show, first create all of the slides that should go into it. Start with all of the slides in the main presentation. Then follow these steps:

1. In the Start Slide Show group on the Slide Show tab, click **Custom Slide Show**, and then click **Custom Shows.** The Custom Shows dialog box opens.

Note

If no custom shows are defined yet, the Custom Shows command is the only item that appears on this menu. Otherwise, your existing custom shows appear on the menu, and you can run them from here. ∎

2. Click **New.** The Define Custom Show dialog box opens.

3. Type a name for your custom show in the Slide Show Name text box, replacing the default name.

4. In the Slides in Presentation pane, click the first slide that you want to appear in the custom show.

Tip

You can select multiple slides in Step 4 by holding down the Ctrl key as you click each one. However, be aware that if you do this, the slides move to the Slides in Custom Show pane in the order that they originally appeared. If you want them in a different order, copy each slide over separately, in the order that you want, or rearrange the order as described in Step 7. ∎

5. Click Add to copy the slide to the Slides in Custom Show pane, as shown in Figure 26-10.

6. Repeat Steps 4 and 5 for each slide that you want to include in the custom show.

7. If you need to rearrange the slides in the custom show, click the slide that you want to move in the Slides in Custom Show pane and then click the up-arrow or down-arrow button to change its position.

8. When you are finished building your custom show, click **OK.** The new show appears in the Custom Shows dialog box.

9. (Optional) **To test your custom show, click the Show button.** Otherwise, click Close to close the Custom Shows dialog box.

FIGURE 26-10

Use the Add button to copy slides from the main presentation into the custom show.

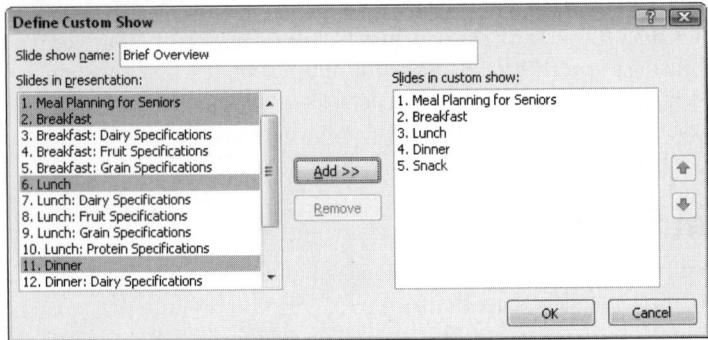

Editing Custom Shows

You can manage your custom shows from the Custom Shows dialog box, the same place in which you created them. This includes editing, deleting, or making a copy of a show. To change which slides appear in a custom show, and in what order, follow these steps:

1. **In the Start Slide Show group on the Slide Show tab, click Custom Slide Show and then click Custom Shows.** The Custom Shows dialog box appears, as shown in Figure 26-11.

FIGURE 26-11

You can select a custom show to edit, copy, or delete, and then click the appropriate button.

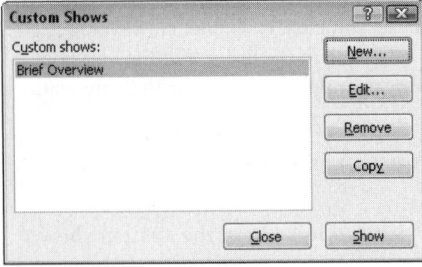

2. **If you have more than one custom show, then click the one that you want to edit.**
3. **Click Edit.** The Define Custom Show dialog box reappears, as shown in Figure 26-10.
4. **Add or remove slides, as needed.** To add a slide, select it in the left pane and click Add. To remove a slide, select it in the right pane and click Remove.

Note

Removing a slide from a custom show does not remove it from the overall presentation. ∎

5. Rearrange slides as needed with the up-arrow and down-arrow buttons.

6. (Optional) **You can change the custom show's name in the Slide Show Name text box.**

7. **Click OK.** PowerPoint saves your changes.

8. **Click Close to close the Custom Shows dialog box.**

Copying Custom Shows

A good way to create several similar custom shows is to create the first one and then copy it. You can then make small changes to the copies as necessary. To copy a custom show, follow these steps:

1. **In the Start Slide Show group on the Slide Show tab, click Custom Slide Show and then click Custom Shows.** The Custom Shows dialog box appears, as shown in Figure 26-11.

2. **If you have more than one custom show, then select the show that you want to copy.**

3. **Click Copy.** A copy of the show appears in the dialog box. The filename includes the words *Copy of* so that you can distinguish it from the original.

4. **Edit the copy, as explained in the preceding section, to change its name and content.**

5. **When you are finished, click Close to close the Custom Shows dialog box.**

Deleting Custom Shows

It is not necessary to delete a custom show when you do not want it anymore; it does not do any harm remaining in your presentation. Because custom shows do not display unless you call for them, you can simply choose not to display it. However, if you want to make your presentation more orderly, you can delete a custom show that you no longer want. Follow these steps:

1. **In the Start Slide Show group on the Slide Show tab, click Custom Slide Show and then click Custom Shows.** The Custom Shows dialog box appears, as shown in Figure 26-11.

2. **Select the show that you want to delete.**

3. **Click Remove.** The show disappears from the list.

4. **Click Close to close the Custom Shows dialog box.**

Displaying a Custom Show

To start your presentation with a custom show, on the Slide Show tab, click Custom Slide Show and then click the name of the custom show on the drop-down menu. The custom show runs.

You can also call up the custom show at any time during your main presentation. There are two ways to do this: You can navigate to the custom show with PowerPoint's regular presentation controls, or you can create a hyperlink to the custom show on your slide.

Navigating to a Custom Show

During a presentation, you can jump to any of your custom shows by following these steps:

1. **Open the shortcut menu in Slide Show view by right-clicking or by clicking the navigation button.**

2. **Choose Custom Show and then select the custom show that you want, as shown in Figure 26-12.** The custom show starts.

FIGURE 26-12

Choose the custom show that you want to jump to.

When you start a custom show, you are no longer in the main presentation. To verify this, open the shortcut menu again, choose Go to Slide, and check out the list of slides. This list shows only the slides that belong to the custom show.

Navigating Back to the Main Show

To return to the main show, follow these steps:

1. **Press Ctrl+S to open the All Slides dialog box.**

2. **Open the Show drop-down list and choose All Slides.**

3. **Select the slide that you want to go to.** You can choose from all of the slides in the entire presentation.

4. **Click Go To.**

Tip

To avoid having to click Ctrl+S to return to the main show, you can create a hyperlink or action button for a specific slide in your main show. ∎

Creating a Hyperlink to a Custom Show

Although you learn a lot about hyperlinks in upcoming chapters, here is a preview. *Hyperlinks* are hot links that you place on your slides. When you click a hyperlink, you jump the display to some other location. This is why they are called *hot*. A hyperlink can jump to an Internet location, a different spot in your presentation, an external file (such as a Word document), or just about anywhere else.

One way to gain quick access to your custom shows in a presentation is to create hyperlinks for them on certain key slides that act as jumping points. You can insert a text hyperlink into any text box, and its text becomes the marker that you click. For example, if you insert a hyperlink for a custom show called *Radio Spots*, then the hyperlink text could read *Radio Spots*. If you want to get fancier, you can select some existing text or an existing graphic object and then attach the hyperlink to it. For example, in Figure 26-13, I have inserted a clip art image of a radio and set it up to be a hyperlink to the custom show that provides details about the radio spots.

FIGURE 26-13

You can create hyperlinks on slides that display custom shows.

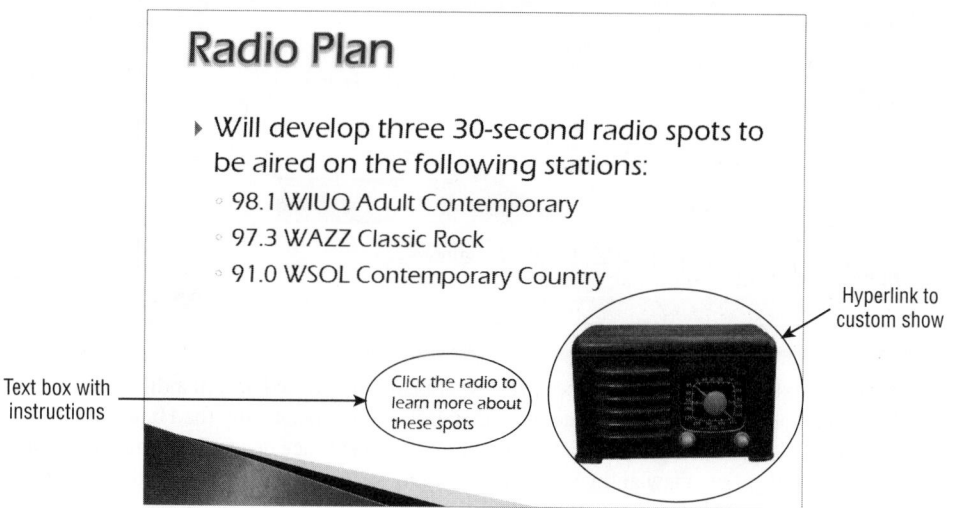

Follow these steps:

1. If you are attaching the hyperlink to another object (such as the radio in Figure 26-13) or some text, then select the object or text.

2. **In the Links group on the Insert tab, click Hyperlink.** The Insert Hyperlink dialog box appears.

3. **Click the Place in This Document icon along the left side of the dialog box.**

4. **In the Select a Place in This Document pane, scroll down to the Custom Shows list.**

5. **Click the custom show that you want to jump to with this hyperlink, as shown in Figure 26-14.**

6. (Optional) **If you want to return to the same spot that you left in the main presentation after viewing this custom show, then select the Show and Return check box.** If you do not select this option, the presentation will simply end when the custom show ends.

7. (Optional) **If you want to specify a ScreenTip for the hyperlink, click the ScreenTip button to create one.**

8. **Click OK.**

FIGURE 26-14

Choose one of your custom shows as the place to jump to when the user clicks the hyperlink.

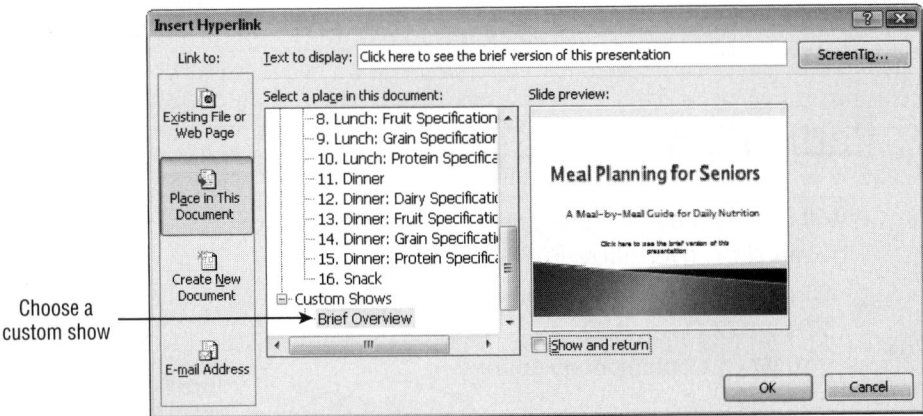

If you are using text for the hyperlink, the text now appears underlined and in a different color. This color is controlled by the color theme of your presentation (specifically the Hyperlink and Followed Hyperlink colors). If you are using a graphic, its appearance does not change. However, when you are in Slide Show view and you move the mouse pointer over the object, the pointer changes to a pointing hand, indicating that the object is a hyperlink.

Tip

If you do not want your linked text to be underlined or to change colors upon return, you can draw a rectangle with no border and 100 percent Transparent fill over the top of the text and link to the shape instead. Because this shape is on top of the text, you click it instead of the text. Keep in mind that you should probably create your link before changing the border and fill of the shape to no color! ■

Another way to use hyperlinks for custom shows is to set up the first few slides generically for all audiences and then to branch off into one custom show or another, based on user input. The diagram in Figure 26-8 is an example of this type of presentation. After the first two slides, you could set up a "decision" slide that contains two hyperlinks — one for Digital Products and one for Audio Products. The user would then click the hyperlink they want.

Tip

You can also create hyperlinks to custom shows by using action buttons. *Action buttons* are a special type of drawn shape that is designed specifically for creating hyperlinks within a presentation. ■

Using a Custom Show as the Main Presentation

If you have a complete show contained in one of your custom shows, you may sometimes want to show it as the default presentation. To do this, you must tell PowerPoint that you want to bypass the main presentation and start with the custom show.

The easiest way to show a custom show is to select it from the Custom Slide Show drop-down menu on the Slide Show tab. However, you can also set up a custom show to be the default show for the presentation by following these steps:

1. **In the Set Up group on the Slide Show tab, click Set Up Slide Show.** The Set Up Show dialog box appears.

2. **Open the Custom Show drop-down list and choose the show that you want to use, as shown in Figure 26-15.**

3. **Click OK.** Now, when you start the show, the custom show runs.

FIGURE 26-15

Use the Set Up Show dialog box to control which of your custom shows runs when you start the show.

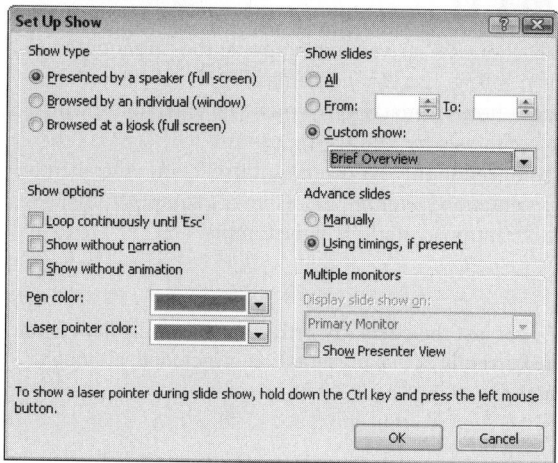

Tip

You do not have to set up a custom show to narrow down the list of slides that appear when you run your presentation. You can choose which slides you want to show by using the From and To text boxes in the Show Slides section, as shown in Figure 26-15. For example, to show Slides 5 to 10, you would type 5 in the From text box and 10 in the To text box. ∎

Giving a Presentation on a Different Computer

The computer upon which you create a presentation is usually not the same computer that you will use to show it. For example, you may be doing the bulk of your work on your desktop computer in your office in Los Angeles, but you need to use your laptop computer to give the presentation in Phoenix.

One way to transfer a presentation to another computer is simply to copy the PowerPoint file (the file with the .pptx extension) using a flash drive or other removable media. However, this method is imperfect because it assumes that the other computer has all of the fonts, sounds, and other elements that you need for every part of the show. This can be a dangerous assumption. For example, suppose that your presentation contains a link to some Excel data. If you do not also copy the Excel file, then you cannot update the data when you are on the road.

A better way to ensure that you are taking everything you need while traveling is to use the Package Presentation for CD feature in PowerPoint. This feature reads all of the linked files and associated objects and ensures that they are transferred along with the main presentation. You do not actually need to copy the presentation to a writeable CD, and you do not need a CD-R or CD-RW drive to use this feature. You can copy the presentation to anywhere you want, such as to a ZIP drive or a network location.

Copying a Presentation to CD

If you have a CD-R or CD-RW drive (or DVD-R or -RW drive), then copying the presentation to CD is an attractive choice. It produces a self-running disc that contains all the presentation files and their needed linked files, plus a web page (.html format) from which you can choose which presentation file to run. That web page also contains a hyperlink you can use to download the PowerPoint Viewer application if needed. (You need it only if PowerPoint itself is not installed on the PC upon which you want to view the presentation.) Figure 26-16 shows a sample web page for accessing a package that contains two different presentations, for example.

Tip

You can copy many presentation files onto a single CD, not just the currently active one. The only limit is the size of the disc (usually 650 to 700 MB). By default, the currently active presentation is included, although the following steps show you how to add other presentations. ∎

FIGURE 26-16

The Package for CD command generates a CD containing all data files needed to show the presentation plus a browser-based interface like the one shown here.

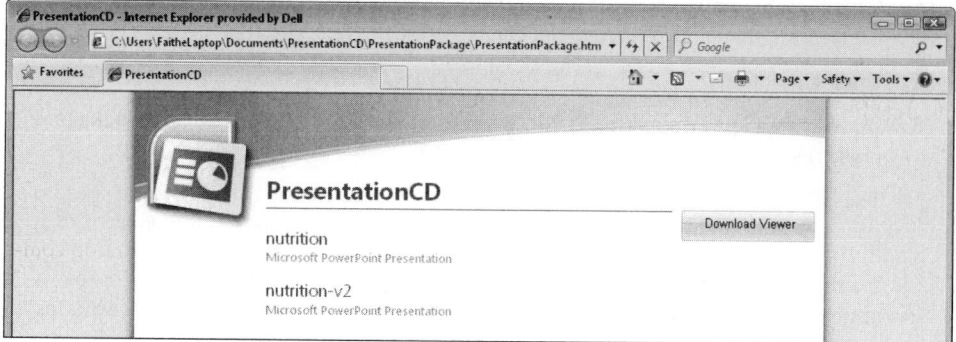

Here is the basic procedure, which is elaborated on in the following sections:

1. **Place a blank CD-R or CD-RW disc in your writeable CD or DVD drive.** If using a DVD drive, you can use recordable DVD media, instead.

2. **Finalize the presentation in PowerPoint.** If you are using a CD-R disc, keep in mind that this disc type is not rewriteable, and so you should ensure that the presentation is exactly as you want it.

3. **Choose File ⇨ Save & Send ⇨ Package Presentation for CD ⇨ Package for CD.** The Package for CD dialog box opens, as shown in Figure 26-17.

FIGURE 26-17

Use the Package for CD feature to place all of the necessary files for the presentation on a CD.

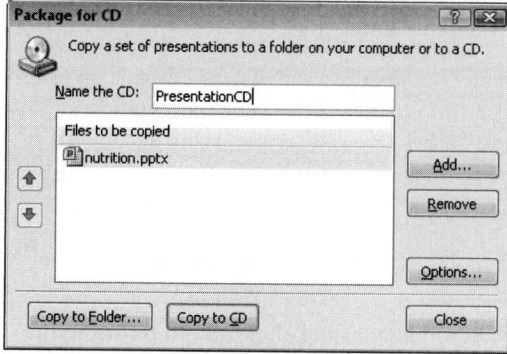

4. Type a name for the CD; this is similar to adding a volume label for the disc.

5. (Optional) **Add more files to the CD if you want.** See the next section, "Creating a CD Containing Multiple Presentation Files," for more details.

6. (Optional) **Set any options that you want.** See the section, "Setting Copy Options," later in this chapter, for more details.

7. Click Copy to CD.

8. **If a warning appears asking if you want to include linked files in your package, click Yes.**

    The CD-writing process may take several minutes, depending on the writing speed of your CD drive and the size of the presentation files that you are placing on it.

    If a message appears that the package will not include comments, revisions, or ink annotations, click Continue. This message appears only if your presentation contains any of those things.

9. **A message appears when the files are successfully copied to the CD, asking whether you want to copy the same files to another CD.** Click Yes or No. If you choose No, then you must also click Close to close the Package for CD dialog box.

The resulting CD automatically plays the presentations when you insert it in any computer. You can also browse the CD's contents to open the PowerPoint Viewer separately and use it to play specific presentations.

Caution
File corruption can occur on a CD drive during the writing process. After burning a CD, test it thoroughly by running the complete presentation from CD before you rely on the CD copy as the version that you take with you while traveling. ■

Creating a CD Containing Multiple Presentation Files

By default, the active presentation is included on the CD, but you can also add others, up to the capacity of your disc. For example, if you have several versions of the same presentation for different audiences, then a single CD can contain all of them. As you are preparing to copy the files using the Package for CD dialog box, shown in Figure 26-17, follow these steps to add more files:

1. **Click Add.** An Add dialog box opens, similar to the Open dialog box that you use to open PowerPoint files.

2. **Select the additional files that you want to include, and click Add to return to the Package for CD dialog box.** The list of files now appears, as shown in Figure 26-18, with extra controls.

FIGURE 26-18

When you specify multiple files for a CD, you can specify the order in which they should play.

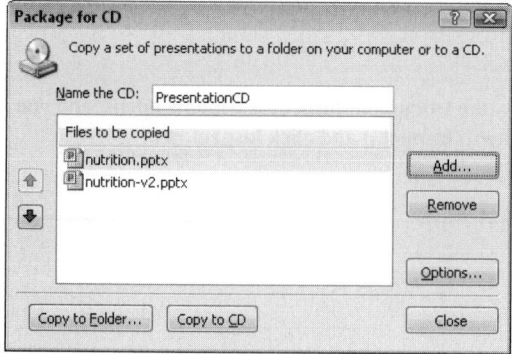

Note

You can select multiple files from the same location by holding down the Ctrl key as you click the ones you want. To include multiple files from different locations, repeat Steps 1 and 2 for each location. ∎

3. (Optional) **Rearrange the list by clicking a presentation and then clicking the up-arrow or down-arrow buttons to the left of the list.**

4. **If you need to remove a presentation from the list, click it and then click Remove.**

5. **Continue making the CD as you normally would.**

Setting Copy Options

The default copy options are suitable in most situations. However, you may sometimes want to modify them. To do this, open the Package Presentation for CD dialog box, and follow these steps:

1. **Click Options.** The Options dialog box opens, as shown in Figure 26-19.

2. **The Linked Files check box is selected by default; this option tells PowerPoint to include the full copies of all linked files.** You can deselect this option if you want; a static copy of the linked data will remain in the presentation, but the link will not work. You should leave this option selected if you have sounds or multimedia files in your presentation that are linked rather than embedded.

3. **The Embedded TrueType Fonts check box is also selected by default.** If you are sure that the destination computer contains all of the fonts that are used in the presentation, then deselect this option. This makes the presentation file slightly smaller. Remember, not all fonts can be embedded; this depends on the level of embedding allowed by the font's manufacturer.

4. **If you want to add passwords for the presentations, do so in the Enhance Security and Privacy section.** There are separate text boxes for opening and modifying passwords.

5. If you want to check the presentation for private information, such as your name or any comments, select the Inspect Presentations for Inappropriate or Private Information check box.

6. Click OK, and then write the CD as you normally would.

Note

If you select the check box in Step 5, as part of the process, the Document Inspector window opens, and you can use it to check the document for selected types of content. Inspect it and click Inspect. ■

FIGURE 26-19

You can set options for copying the presentations to CD.

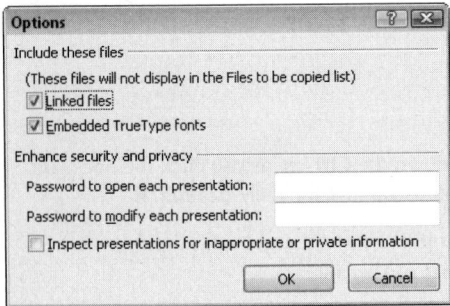

Copying a Presentation to Other Locations

Although it is not well known, you can also use the Package Presentation for CD feature to copy presentation files and their associated support files to any location you want. For example, you can transfer files to another computer on a network, or place them on a flash drive. To do so, follow these steps:

1. In the Package for CD dialog box, set up the package exactly the way you want it, including all of the presentation files and options. See the preceding sections for more information.

2. Click Copy to Folder. A Copy to Folder dialog box appears.

3. Type a name for the new folder to be created in the Folder Name text box.

4. Type a path for the folder in the Location text box, as shown in Figure 26-20.

5. Click OK.

6. If a warning appears about linked files, then click Yes or No as appropriate. PowerPoint copies the files to that location.

7. If a warning appears about comments or link annotations, click Continue.

8. Click Close to close the Package for CD dialog box.

FIGURE 26-20

You can copy presentation files and support files anywhere, not just to a CD.

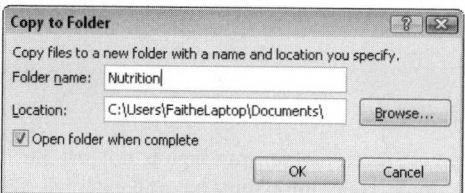

Working with Audiovisual Equipment

The first part of this chapter assumed that you were using a computer with a single monitor to show your presentation, but this may not always be the case. This section looks at the entire range of audiovisual options from which you can choose. There are many models of projection equipment in conference rooms all across the world, but most of them fall into one of these categories:

- **Noncomputerized Equipment.** This can include an overhead transparency viewer, a 35mm slide projector, or other older technology. You face two challenges if you need to work with this category of equipment: One is figuring out how the equipment works, because every model is different, and the other is producing attractive versions of your slides to work with them. There are companies that can produce 35mm slides from your PowerPoint files, or you can invest in a slide-making machine yourself. For transparencies, you simply print your slides on transparency film that is designed for your type of printer.

- **Single Computer with a Single Monitor.** If there is a computer with a monitor in the meeting room, then you can run your presentation on that computer. You can do this with the Package Presentation for CD feature that is discussed in the preceding sections, and then run the presentation directly from the CD, provided that the PC has PowerPoint or the PowerPoint Viewer on it.

- **Single Computer with a Dual-Monitor System.** On systems with dual monitors, one monitor is shown to the audience, and the other is for your own use. This is useful when you want to display your speaker notes on the monitor that the audience does not see. However, you might need to set up multi-monitor support in Windows so that you can view different displays on each monitor.

- **Projection System (LCD) or Large Monitor without a Computer.** If the meeting room has a large monitor but no computer, you will need to bring your own laptop computer and connect it to the monitor. Most of these systems use a standard VGA plug and cable.

The following sections look at some of these options in more detail.

Presenting with Two Screens

If you have two monitors — either your laptop computer screen and an external monitor, or two external monitors hooked up to the same computer — you can display the presentation on one of them and your own notes on the other one using Presenter View. This is a very handy setup!

Caution

To use two screens and Presenter View, you need the full version of PowerPoint on your laptop, not just the PowerPoint Viewer. You also need compatible hardware. For example, your laptop must have an external VGA port and a built-in video card that supports multiple monitors. If you have a desktop computer, you must have two separate video cards or a video card with two separate video ports. ■

Configuring Display Hardware for Multi-screen Viewing

First, you need to prepare your hardware. On a laptop computer, this means enabling both the built-in and the external monitor ports and connecting an external monitor. Some laptops toggle between internal, external, and dual monitors with an **Fn** key combination; refer to your laptop's documentation.

On a desktop computer, install a second video card and monitor, and then do the following to set them up in Windows:

1. **When Windows restarts after you install the second video card, right-click on the desktop and choose Personalize (Windows Vista or Windows 7) or Properties (Windows XP).**

2. **Click Display Settings (Windows Vista), or Display ⇨ Change Display Settings (Windows 7), or click the Settings tab (Windows XP).**

3. **A sample area displays two monitors.** Figure 26-21 shows Windows 7; other Windows versions are similar.

4. **The monitor that you use most of the time should be Monitor 1, and the other one should be Monitor 2.** To determine which is which, click Identify Monitors (Windows Vista, as in Figure 26-21) or the Identify button (Windows XP or Windows 7); large numbers appear briefly on each screen.

5. **If you need to swap the numbering of the monitors, click the one that should be the primary monitor and then select Make This My Main Display (Windows 7), This Is My Main Monitor (Windows Vista), or Use This Device as the Primary Monitor (Windows XP).** This option will be unavailable if the currently selected monitor is already set to be the primary one.

6. **Select the secondary monitor, and then select the Extend These Displays (Windows 7) or Extend My Desktop onto This Monitor check box (Windows Vista) or Extend the Desktop onto This Monitor check box (Windows XP).**

7. (Optional) If the monitors are not arranged in the sample area in the way that they are physically positioned on your desk, you can drag the icons for the monitors to where you want them.

8. (Optional) You can click on a monitor in the sample area to adjust its display settings.

Tip

You can also adjust the refresh rate for each monitor. To do this, make sure that you have selected the video card to which the monitor is attached, and then click the Advanced Settings button (Windows Vista or Windows 7) or the Advanced button (Windows XP). On the Monitor tab in the dialog box that appears, change the refresh rate. A higher refresh rate reduces screen flicker, but if you exceed the monitor's maximum supported rate, the display may appear distorted and the screen may be damaged. ■

9. Click OK. You are now ready to work with the two monitors in PowerPoint.

FIGURE 26-21

You must set up the second monitor in Windows before setting it up in PowerPoint.

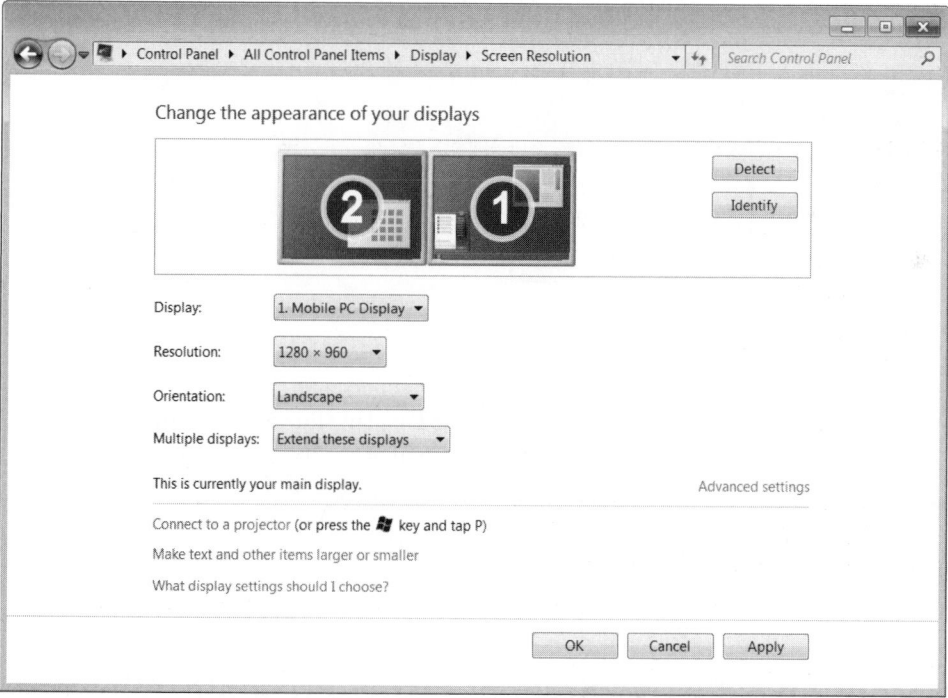

You can now drag items from your primary monitor to your secondary one. This can also be useful outside of PowerPoint as well. For example, you can have two applications open at once, each in its own monitor window.

Setting Up a Presentation for Two Screens

If you have two monitors available and configured as described in the preceding section, you can use the following steps to help PowerPoint recognize and take advantage of these monitors:

1. **Open the presentation in PowerPoint.**

2. **In the Set Up group on the Slide Show tab, click Set Up Slide Show.** The Set Up Show dialog box opens, as shown in Figure 26-22.

You can set up the show for multiple monitors in the Set Up Show dialog box.

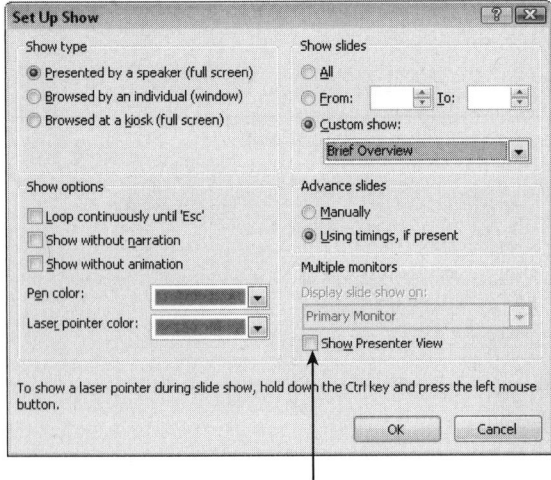

Enable Presenter View here

3. **In the Multiple Monitors section, open the Display Slide Show On drop-down list, and choose the monitor that the audience will see.** This list is not available if you do not have multiple monitors enabled (see the preceding section).

4. **Select the Show Presenter View check box.** This will give you a separate, very useful control panel on the other monitor during the show, as described in the next section.

5. **Click OK.** You are now ready to show the presentation using two separate displays — one for you and one for the audience.

Presenting with Two Screens Using Presenter View

Presenter View is a special view of the presentation that is available only on systems with more than one monitor, and only where you have selected the Show Presenter View check box in the Set Up Show dialog box, as described in the preceding section. This view provides many useful tools for managing the show behind-the-scenes, as shown in Figure 26-23. It appears automatically on the non-audience monitor when you enter Slide Show view, and includes the following features:

- At the bottom of the screen is a pane containing thumbnail images of each slide. You can jump to a slide by selecting it here. You can also move between slides by using the large left-arrow and right-arrow buttons.

- The speaker notes for each slide appear in the right pane. You cannot edit them from here, however. Zoom buttons appear below the Speaker Notes pane, so you can zoom in and out on the notes.

- A Time and Duration display appears below the current slide. It tells you the current time and how long you have been talking.

- The panes are adjustable by dragging the dividers between them, so you can have larger thumbnails, a smaller slide display, more or less room for notes, and so on.

FIGURE 26-23

Presenter View provides tools for helping you manage your slide show from a second monitor.

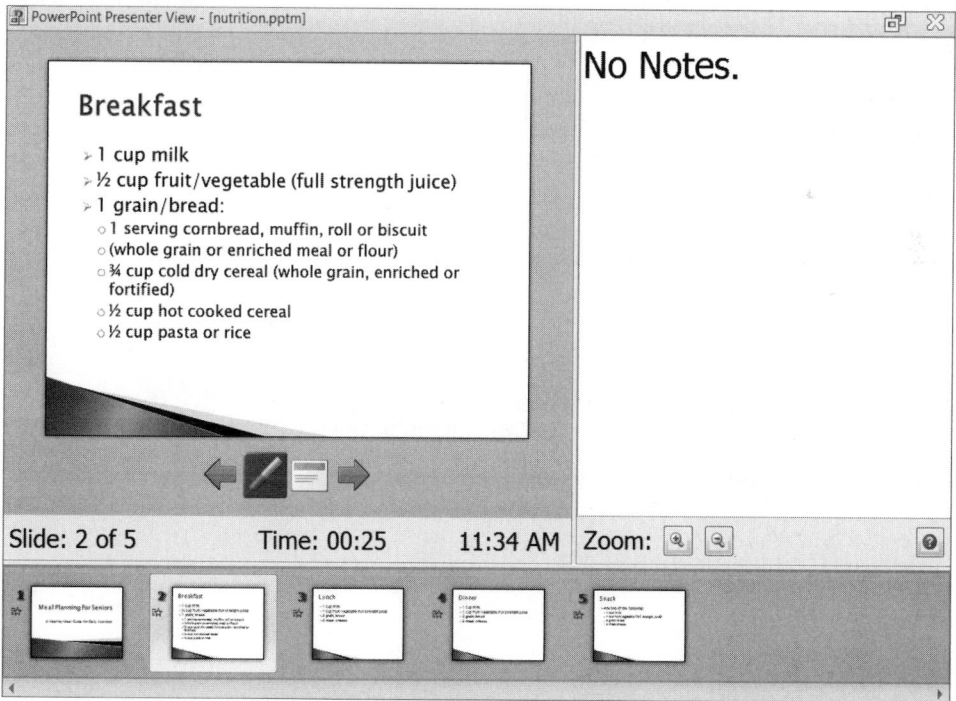

Presenter View does not have all of the features that you have learned about so far in Slide Show view. However, keep in mind that the audience's monitor is still active and available for your use!

Because you extended the desktop onto the second monitor, you can simply move the mouse pointer onto the audience's display and then use the buttons in the corner (or the right-click menu) as you normally would.

Summary

In this chapter, you learned how to prepare for a big presentation. You now know how to package a presentation and move it to another computer, how to set up single and multi-screen audiovisual equipment to work with your laptop, and how to control a presentation onscreen using your computer. You also know how to jump to different slides, how to take notes during a meeting, and how to assign action items. You're all set! All you need now is a nice starched shirt and a shoeshine.

Part V

Organizing Messages, Contacts, and Time with Outlook

Fundamentals of E-mail

Before you can send and receive e-mail using Outlook, you must set up at least one e-mail account, providing Outlook with the information it needs to connect to your online e-mail account. From there, you can compose, send, and receive messages. Outlook provides great tools for creating and organizing your messages, as well as options for customizing how it works with your messages. This chapter helps you learn the basics for all of those actions in Outlook.

Setting Up Your E-mail Accounts

Before you can use Outlook to send and receive e-mail, you must set up your e-mail account. You can have more than one account — you'll follow the same steps for each one. There are two parts to this.

First, your account must be set up on the server or at your ISP. This is not done in Outlook. If your account is at your workplace, it will likely have been set up by an IT person, and he or she will have provided you with the required information such as your e-mail address and login and password information. If you are setting up a home or small-business account, you may be doing this yourself. The details depend on your ISP, and as part of the process you will need to specify your credentials to gain access.

Second, you must set up your account in Outlook. This process provides Outlook with the information, such as your e-mail address or login/user name and password, that are needed to connect to your e-mail server and send and receive messages. If you are at work, you may be lucky enough to have an IT administrator set up Outlook for you, in which case you can skip this section. If you must do it yourself, the minimum information you need is your login and password. You may also need to know the addresses for your organization's or ISP's e-mail server. The URL looks much like a web page address and will be something like mail.hosting.com. Some mail accounts require two addresses, one for incoming mail and another for outgoing mail.

Outlook supports several different kinds of e-mail accounts including a Microsoft Exchange Server account. The account setup process differs depending on whether you have an Exchange account, a Web-based account such as Windows Live, or one of the other supported account types (POP and IMAP). All of these procedures are covered in the following sections.

E-mail Terminology

E-mail acronyms can be confusing! *POP* stands for Post Office Protocol, a technology for receiving e-mail. *You'll also see POP3 used; they mean the same thing.* *IMAP* stands for Internet Mail Access Protocol, another incoming mail technology. *SMTP* is Simple Mail Transfer Protocol, the almost universally used technology for sending e-mail.

Automatic E-mail Account Setup

Outlook can automatically configure some e-mail accounts, a feature called Auto Account Setup. This works for some but not all POP, IMAP, Exchange Server, or Web-based accounts. To use the automated e-mail account setup feature in many cases, you need to have your e-mail address and your password. (You may not even need that much information if your company server is set up to automate account setup.) Then, here are the steps to follow:

1. **Choose File ➪ Info, and then click the Add Account button to display the Add New Account dialog box.** The dialog box, shown in Figure 27-1, asks for three pieces of information:
   - Your name
   - Your e-mail address
   - Your password

2. **After you enter the information, click Next.** Outlook will try to connect to your e-mail server and set up the account.

Note
To use your Hotmail account with Outlook, you must install the Microsoft Office Outlook Hotmail Connector for Windows Live Hotmail. You can download the Hotmail Connector from the Office website and install it in advance of creating your account. Alternatively, after Step 2 of account setup, you will be prompted to download and install the Connector automatically. You must then restart Outlook and the account setup process. ■

FIGURE 27-1

The Add New Account dialog box.

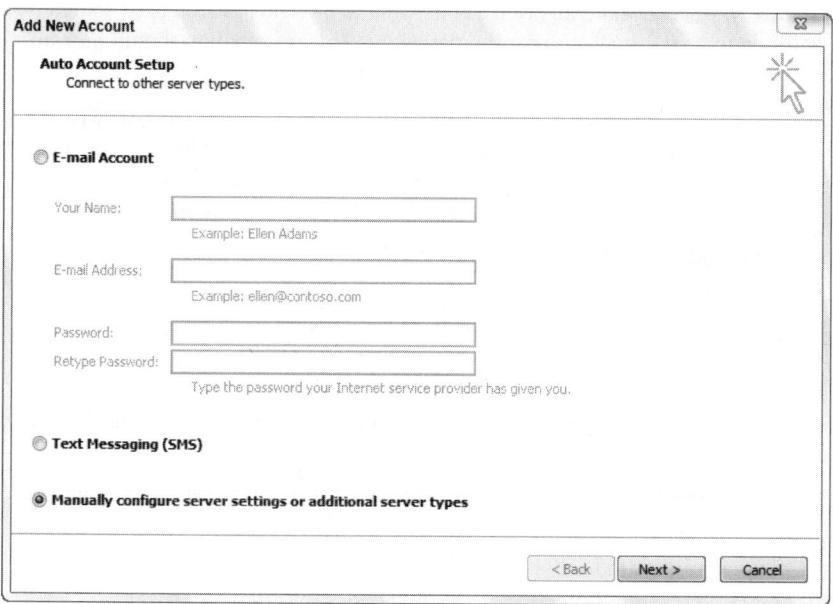

If you are continuing with automatic account setup, Outlook will attempt to connect to your e-mail server and set up the account. In most cases, this will work just as it is supposed to, and you will just click the Finish button in the Add New Account dialog box. The new account will be listed in the E-mail Accounts list, and you'll be able to start sending and receiving messages. However, this automated process does not always work. You may encounter one of the following situations:

- Outlook tells you that it cannot establish an encrypted connection to the server and offers to try again using an unencrypted connection. Click Next to proceed. The process will either complete properly or you'll encounter one of the other conditions in this list.

- Outlook cannot establish a connection to your account and asks you to verify the spelling of your e-mail address. Make any needed corrections and click Next to try again. The process will either complete properly or you'll encounter the final condition in this list.

- If the preceding steps fail, Outlook will require that you manually configure the server settings. This option will be automatically selected in the Add New E-mail Account dialog box. Click Next to continue. The manual account setup steps differ for the various account types and are covered in the following sections.

Manual E-mail Account Setup (POP and IMAP)

If automatic account setup does not work for your POP or IMAP account, you will have to perform the setup manually. It's a bit more involved but nothing to be afraid of. You need some information in addition to your e-mail address and password. This information should be available from your ISP or your IT person:

- The addresses of your incoming mail server and outgoing mail server. These may be the same but are usually different. For POP incoming mail servers, the address usually looks something like pop.example.com. For outgoing mail servers, it may look like mail.example.com or smtp.example.com. Your ISP will provide the correct information to enter.

- The user name and password for your account login.

When you have this information, you are ready to begin. You will arrive at this dialog box if automatic setup failed, so you can go to Step 4 in the following process.

Here are the steps to follow for manual account setup:

1. **Choose File ➪ Info, and then click the Add Account button to display the Add New Account dialog box.**

2. **Select the Manually Configure Server Settings or Additional Server Types option.**

3. **Click Next to display the dialog box shown in Figure 27-2.** This is where you select the type of account to set up.

FIGURE 27-2

Selecting the type of account to set up.

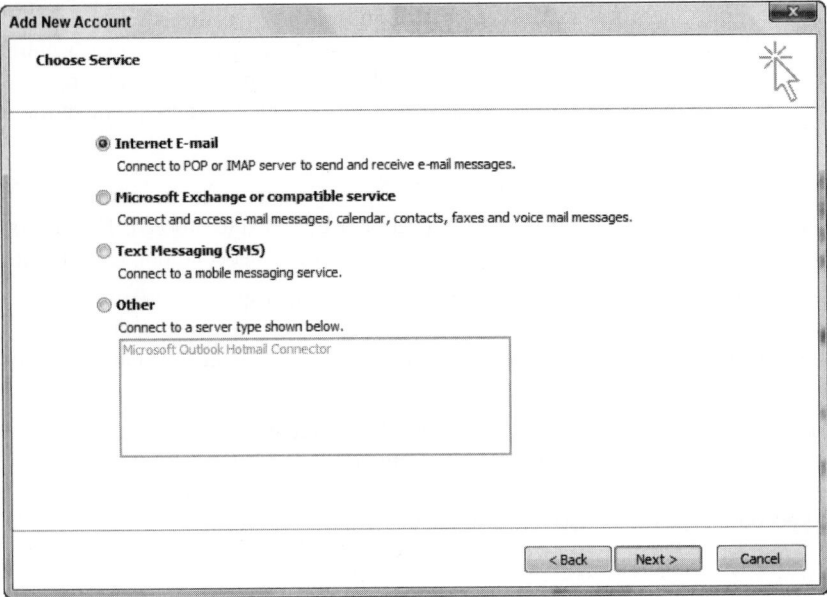

4. **Select the Internet E-mail option, and then click Next.** In the dialog box shown in Figure 27-3, enter all the requested information in the corresponding boxes, and be sure to select the type of e-mail server from the Account Type list. The Remember Password and Require Logon using Secure Password Authentication options are explained later in this chapter. Most people should leave these at their default settings. The More Settings button is also explained later in this chapter.

5. **After you have entered all the information, click the Test Account Settings button.** If the test works, click Next and then Finish to complete the account setup. If the test does not work, please refer to the next section ("If Your Account Settings Don't Work") for steps to resolve the problem.

Two options are available in the Add New Account dialog box. If you select the Remember Password option, Outlook will be able to log on automatically to your e-mail account as needed. Otherwise, you will be prompted for the password each time you send and receive e-mail.

Secure Password Authentication (SPA) is an additional level of security that some mail servers have implemented. If your server requires this, you should have been told and given any additional credentials required for login. You would need to check the Require Logon Using Secure Password Authentication (SPA) option shown in Figure 27-3.

FIGURE 27-3

Entering required information for manual POP or IMAP e-mail account setup.

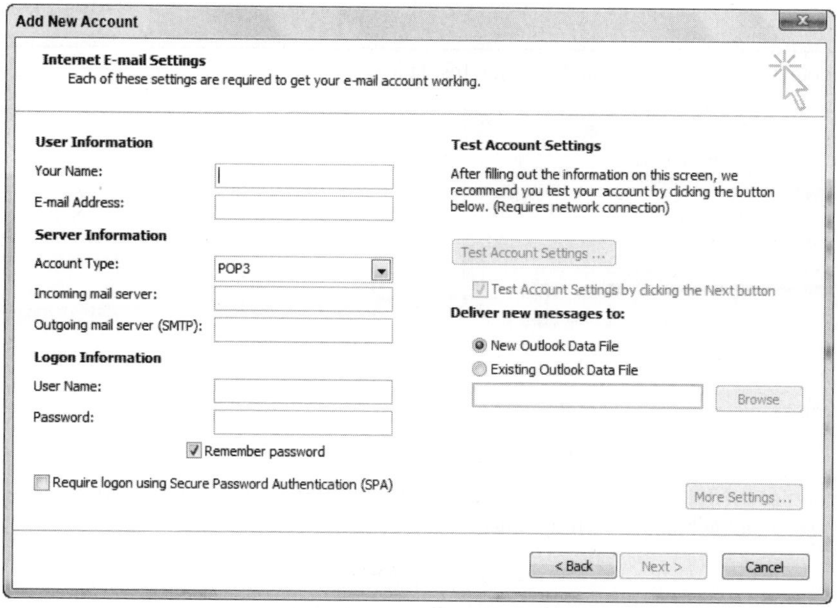

If Your Account Settings Don't Work

It's not uncommon for e-mail account settings to not work at first. When you click the Test Account Settings button, Outlook tries to log on to your incoming mail server and send a test message via your outgoing mail server. One or both of these tests may fail, and the results shown in the Test Account Settings dialog box (shown in Figure 27-4, which depicts a failed test) will tell you the results. Note also that this dialog box has an Errors tab, shown in Figure 27-5. The information on this tab may give you a clue as to where the problem lies. For example, if the problem is reported as "Your e-mail server rejected your login," the problem almost surely lies with the user name or password that you entered.

FIGURE 27-4

This dialog box displays the results of testing your e-mail account settings.

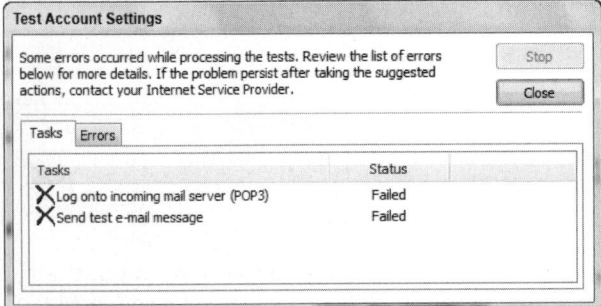

FIGURE 27-5

The Errors tab provides details on why the Account Settings Test failed.

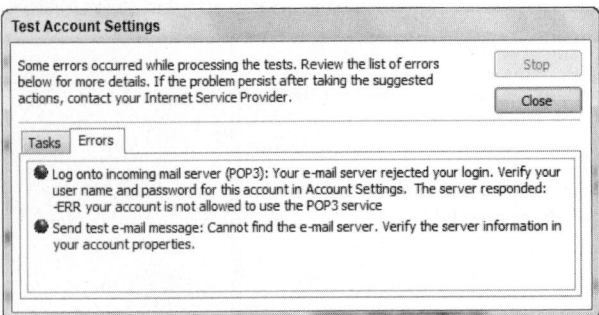

The most common cause of problems is simply mistyping some of the information required in the account setup dialog box. Everything must be 100 percent correct!

If the test failed in the outgoing mail server part, it most likely means that your outgoing mail server requires authentication. Setting this option is examined in the following section.

More Account Settings

The Add New Account dialog box, shown in Figure 27-3, has a button labeled More Settings. You may not need to make any changes here, but if you do, you can refer to this section for the details.

Clicking the More Settings button brings up the Internet E-mail Settings dialog box. This dialog box has four tabs for POP and IMAP accounts and a fifth for IMAP accounts only. The next sections look at these in turn.

General

The General tab, shown in Figure 27-6, has these three entries:

- **Mail Account.** This is the name Outlook uses to refer to the account, for example, in the Account list. The default is your e-mail address, but you can change it to anything you like, such as *Work E-mail* or *Windows Live Account*.

- **Organization.** If you enter your organization name here, it will be included in the headers of all e-mail messages you send. Recipients normally do not see these headers, and Outlook does not make use of this information in any way. Other e-mail programs may, however.

- **Reply E-mail.** When recipients receive an e-mail from you and reply by clicking the Reply button in their e-mail program, their reply message is sent to this address. By default, it is the e-mail address associated with the current e-mail account, but if you have more than one e-mail account, you can enter another address here.

Outgoing Server

The Outgoing Server tab, shown in Figure 27-7, lets you specify authentication — that is, login — settings for your outgoing mail server. By default, this option is turned off because many outgoing mail servers do not require authentication. If yours does, select the My Outgoing Server (SMTP) Requires Authentication box, and then select other options and enter information as follows:

- **Use Same Settings as My Incoming Mail Server.** Outlook will log on to your outgoing mail server using the same user name and password that you specified for your incoming mail server. This is the most commonly used setting.

- **Log on Using.** Select this option if your outgoing server requires different credentials than for retrieving your mail. Then enter your User Name and Password in the corresponding fields. The Remember Password and Require Secure Password Authentication (SPA) options work the same as was described for them in the previous section, "Manual E-mail Account Setup (POP and IMAP)."

- **Log on To Incoming Mail Server before Sending Mail.** Select this option only if your incoming mail server is the same as your outgoing mail server. You will know that this is the case when you are given the same address for both servers and enter this address for both during account setup.

FIGURE 27-6

The General tab in the Internet E-mail Settings dialog box.

Connection

The Connection tab lets you specify details of how Outlook connects to your e-mail server. To set these options, you need to know how your computer is connected to the Internet. If you are at work, you almost surely connect via a local area network (LAN). If you are at home and have a cable modem or DSL connection, including wireless connections, this is also a LAN. A dial-up or phone line connection is an older connection technology that is still in use by many people.

If you are connected via a LAN, select the Connect Using My Local Area Network (LAN) option. If you select this option, you can also select the Connect via Modem When Outlook Is Offline option. Doing so causes Outlook to use a dial-up connection (assuming that one is available) to connect when the LAN is not available.

If you connect via a modem (phone line), select the Connect Using My Phone Line option. You may already have a dial-up connection defined in Windows. If not, you must define one before you can use Outlook for e-mail. Defining a dial-up network connection is a process that is part of the Windows operating system, not Outlook, and is beyond the scope of this book. If you select this option, you then must select the defined dial-up connection that you want to use in the

Modem section of the dialog box. You can use the Add button to add a new dial-up connection and the Properties button to examine and modify the properties of an existing connection.

FIGURE 27-7

The Outgoing Server tab in the Internet E-mail Settings dialog box.

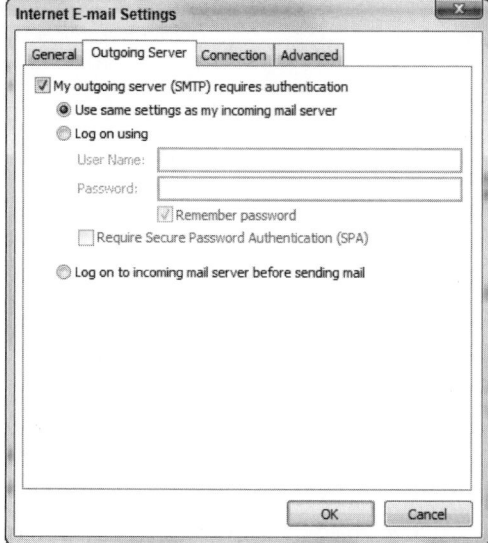

Advanced

The Advanced tab contains options that most people will never need to change. You may not be "most people," however, so I explain these settings here. Note that the options available on this tab differ slightly for POP and IMAP accounts. Figure 27-8 shows the tab for POP accounts.

The advanced settings that are common to both POP and IMAP accounts are the following:

- **Server Port Numbers, Incoming Server.** The default values are 110 for POP servers and 143 for IMAP servers. For security reasons, many corporate servers are set up on different ports, so if yours is, you can enter the correct port numbers here.

- **Server Port Numbers, Outgoing Server.** Regardless of whether your incoming server is POP or IMAP, your outgoing server will use SMTP, and the default port number is 25. Do not change this unless you know that your outgoing mail server uses a different port.

- **Server Timeouts.** This is the amount of time that Outlook will wait for the mail server to respond when retrieving or sending e-mail. The default setting of 1 minute works fine in most cases. If you find Outlook timing out, it probably means that you are working over a slow connection or that your server is often busy. Try a longer time-out setting to resolve this problem.

FIGURE 27-8

The Advanced tab for POP accounts in the Internet E-mail Settings dialog box.

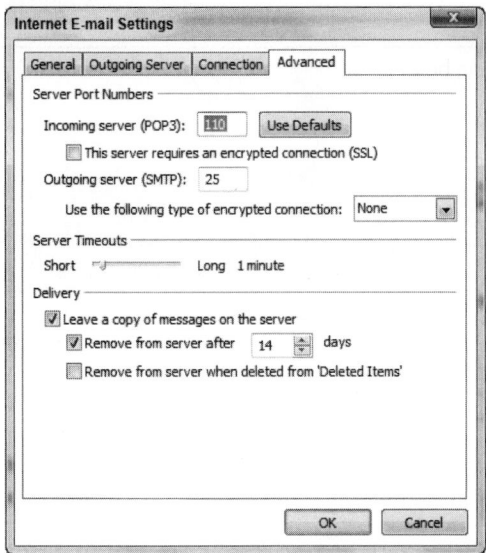

POP accounts also include the This Server Requires An Encrypted Connection (SSL) setting. Turn this option on for the incoming or outgoing mail server, or both, if required.

If you are working with an IMAP account, there is one unique option, Root Folder Path, which specifies the root folder of the mailbox. Normally, you can leave this blank and Outlook will use the default root folder on the server. If you need to specify a different root folder, enter it here.

If you are working with a POP account, you have several settings available that control how Outlook handles messages on the server:

- **Leave a Copy of Messages on the Server.** By default, messages that you have received are removed from the server as soon as they are downloaded to Outlook. Turn this option on if you want Outlook to leave the messages on the server after download. This can be useful if you want to retrieve your messages later from another computer.

- **Remove from Server After . . . Days.** Specifies how long messages are to be retained on the server after they have been downloaded.

- **Remove from Server When Deleted from Deleted Items.** A message is retained on the server until you permanently delete it in Outlook.

To work with message handling settings for an IMAP account, use the Sent Items and Deleted Items tabs in the Internet E-mail Settings dialog box.

Manual E-mail Account Setup (Exchange Server)

If automatic account setup does not work for your Exchange account, you must exit Outlook and set up the account through the Windows Control Panel. Although some of the dialog boxes look the same, you cannot set up an Exchange account manually while Outlook is running. To complete this setup, you need to know the DNS address of your Exchange server (typically), the user name that has been set up for you, and your password.

Downloading an Exchange Profile

Some Exchange account providers give you the option of downloading an Exchange profile file to your computer. When you run this file, it sets up the Exchange profile for you. If available, this is an easy and error-free way to set up an Exchange profile.

These are the steps to set up an Exchange account:

1. **Make sure that Outlook is not running.**

2. **Select the Control Panel from the Windows Start menu.**

3. **In Windows 7 or Windows Vista, type Mail in the search box in the upper-right corner of the Control Panel window.**

4. **Click or Double-click the Mail icon to display the Mail Setup dialog box.**

5. **Click the E-mail Accounts button to open the Account Settings dialog box.** This is the same dialog box that you can use when editing accounts from within Outlook, a topic you'll learn about shortly.

6. **On the E-mail tab, click the New button to display the Add New E-mail Account dialog box.**

7. **Make sure that the E-mail Account option is selected and then click Next.**

8. **In the next dialog box, select the Manually Configure Server Settings or Additional Server Types option, and then click Next.**

9. **In the next dialog box, select the Microsoft Exchange or Compatible Service option, and then click Next.**

10. **In the next dialog box, shown in Figure 27-9, enter your Exchange Server address and User Name, and then click Next.**

11. **If a dialog box appears asking whether you want to continue, click OK.**

12. **Click Finish.**

After setting up your account, you can start Outlook. You will be prompted for the Exchange account password. If the connection is established, Outlook displays "Connected to Microsoft Exchange" at the right end of the status bar (which is at the bottom of the Outlook window).

FIGURE 27-9

Entering information about your Exchange server and user name.

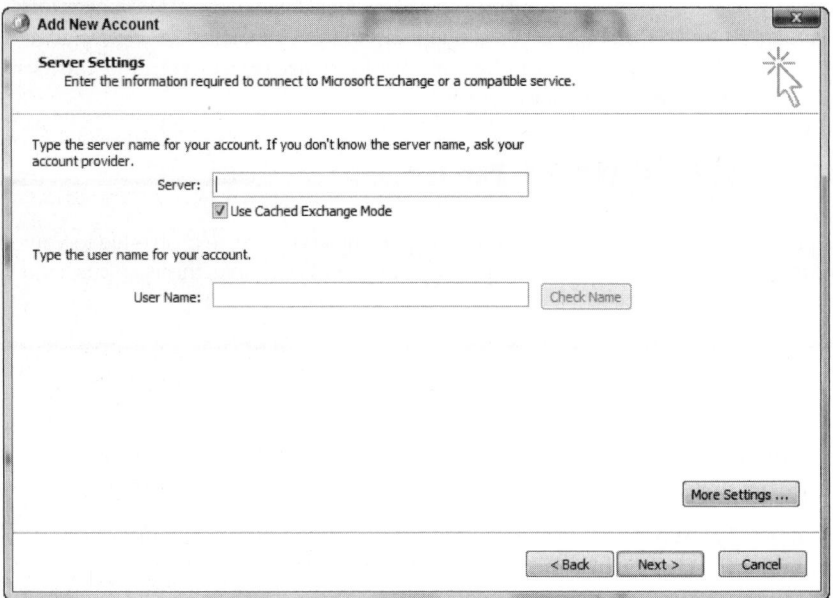

More Exchange Accounts

Outlook 2010 supports up to three Exchange accounts on a single profile.

Manual E-mail Account Setup (Web)

You may have a Web-based e-mail account if you have signed up for Windows Live or Hotmail. Other e-mail providers may also have Web-based accounts that are compatible with Outlook. If so, they will have provided you with the information you need to set up the account when you signed up.

Web-based mail accounts are designed primarily for Web use — that is, you will use a browser such as Internet Explorer to log on to your e-mail account and read and send messages. However, it can be useful to set up an Outlook account, too, so that you can download and read mail in Outlook and use the program's various features to organize your messages. Be aware that not all Web e-mail accounts are compatible with Outlook, and for some, such as Gmail, you have to enable an account option. For others, such as Yahoo! Mail in the U.S., you have to sign up for a premium mail service.

To set up your Web e-mail account in Outlook, you need your e-mail address and password. You will also need to know the address (URL) of the mail server and your user name. Then, follow these steps:

1. **Choose File ⇨ Info, and then click the Add Account button to display the Add New Account dialog box.**

2. **Select the Manually Configure Server Settings or Additional Server Types option.**

3. **Click Next.**

4. **In the next dialog box that appears, make sure that the Internet E-mail option is selected; then click Next.**

5. **In the next dialog box that appears, enter your name, e-mail address, server information, user name, and password.** Figure 27-10 shows example entries. Make sure that POP3 is selected in the Account Type list.

6. **Click Next to complete account setup as for other account types.**

FIGURE 27-10

Entering information for manual Web mail account setup.

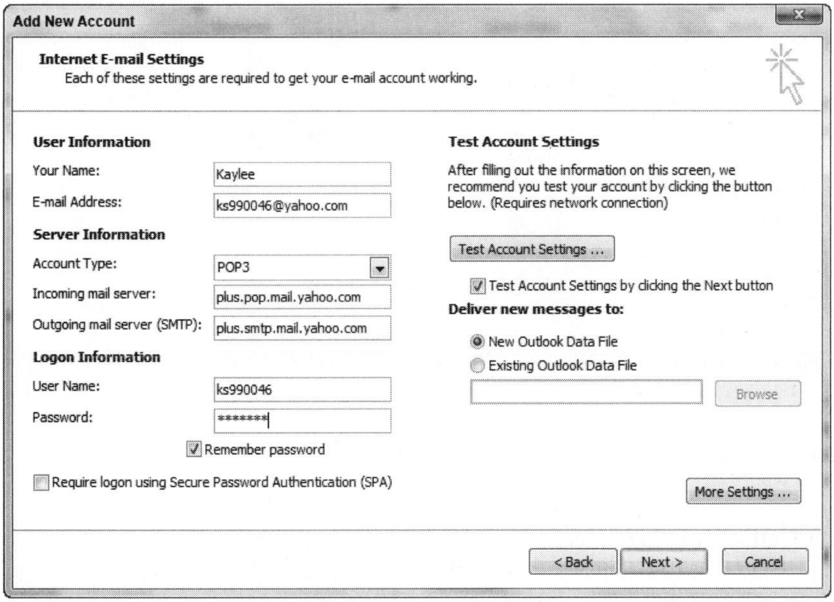

Modifying Account Settings

If you should need to change your account settings, the procedure is similar to setting up the account in the first place. Choose File ➪ Info, click the Account Settings button, and then click Account Settings to display the Account Settings dialog box. Make sure that the E-mail tab is displayed, as shown in Figure 27-11. Select the account of interest (necessary only if you have more than one) and then click the Change button. You are taken through one or more dialog boxes where you can view and change the settings for this account. The settings depend on the type of account and were explained earlier in this chapter in the section on setting up e-mail accounts.

FIGURE 27-11

Work with settings for existing accounts here.

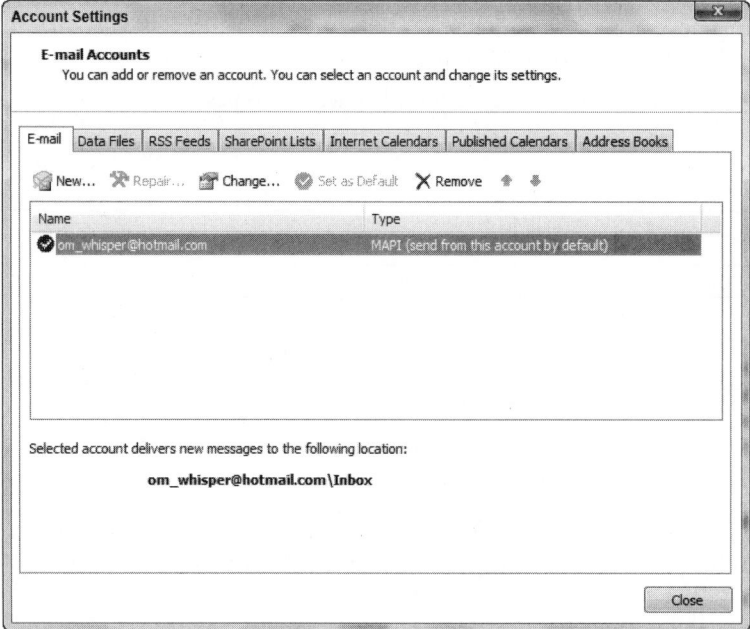

You can take several other actions with e-mail accounts in the Account Settings dialog box, as follows:

- **Repair.** Outlook tries to connect to your e-mail provider and refresh your account settings. This is the first step to try if an e-mail account has suddenly stopped working.

- **Remove.** Deletes the account.

- **Set as Default.** If you have two or more e-mail accounts, this option makes the selected account the default.

What exactly is the default e-mail account? It's the account that is used to send e-mail messages that you create from scratch. When you create an e-mail message by replying to a message you have received, it is sent using the account that the message was received through. Note, however, that when you are composing an e-mail message, you can always change the account that the message is to be sent from. This feature is explained in the next chapter.

Using Outlook Profiles

An *Outlook profile* stores information about a user's accounts and settings. All Outlook users have at least one profile, and for many people that is all that is needed. In some circumstances, multiple profiles can be useful. This section explains how to create and use profiles in Outlook.

Understanding Profiles

In the first part of this chapter, you learned how to set up your e-mail accounts. Later chapters in this part of the book deal with configuring other aspects of Outlook such as RSS feeds and the screen appearance. All this information constitutes your profile. The vast majority of users never need more than one profile, but in some situations they can be useful, such as the following:

- If you want to completely segregate two or more types of information, such as work and personal, you can create a profile for each.

- If you want to keep your regular POP and IMAP e-mail accounts separate from an Exchange account.

- If more than one person uses the same computer, each person can have his or her own profile.

The third reason is usually a moot point because modern versions of Windows provide for different user accounts for logging onto Windows, which automatically gives each user his or her own Outlook profile. If, however, you want more than one person to use the same Windows logon and have separate Outlook data, you can use profiles.

Please note that creating an Outlook profile is not the same as creating a separate personal folder file. Although a given Outlook profile can have one or more personal folder files, each profile's folders are usually kept separate from other profiles.

Creating a New Profile

When you first install Outlook, a wizard walks you through the steps of creating a profile. To create a new profile, you do not use Outlook, but rather the Windows Control Panel, as follows:

1. **Select the Control Panel from the Windows Start menu.**

2. **In Windows 7 and Windows Vista, type** Mail **in the search box in the upper-right corner.** Click or double-click the Mail icon. The Mail Setup–Outlook dialog box appears.

3. **Click the Show Profiles button to open the Mail dialog box.** This dialog box lists the existing profiles; the default profile is named *Outlook*.

4. Click the Add button to open the New Profile dialog box.

5. Enter a name for the new profile and click OK.

6. **Follow the onscreen prompts to set up your e-mail account.** This procedure is covered earlier in this chapter.

Other actions you can take in the Mail dialog box are the following:

- **Remove.** Removes the selected profile from the system.

- **Properties.** Lets you view and edit the properties of the profile including the e-mail account settings and data files.

- **Copy.** Makes a copy of the selected profile under a new name. This is useful if you want a new profile that has some of the same settings as an existing one. Create a copy, then edit it as needed.

- **Prompt for A Profile to Be Used.** If this option is selected and you have more than one profile, Outlook will prompt you to select the profile you want to use each time the program starts.

- **Always Use This Profile.** Select the profile that you want Outlook to use from the list.

Switching Profiles

You cannot switch from one profile to another while Outlook is running. If you selected the Prompt for a profile option (as explained in the preceding section), quit Outlook and restart it; then select the desired profile when prompted.

If you selected the Always Use This Profile option (also explained in the preceding section), you must perform the following steps:

1. Quit Outlook.

2. Open the Control Panel from the Windows Start menu.

3. In the Control Panel, open Mail.

4. Click the Show Profiles button.

5. Select the Prompt for a profile to be used option.

6. Close all dialog boxes.

7. Restart Outlook.

Composing and Sending Messages

Outlook's e-mail features are sophisticated and comprehensive. Underneath all that power, however, are the fundamental tasks of composing, sending, and reading messages. This section explains the basics of composing and sending e-mail messages.

Quick Compose and Send

Outlook provides much flexibility when it comes to creating and formatting e-mail messages. Often, however, all you want to do is to quickly create and send a basic message. Here's how:

1. **Click the Mail button in the Navigation pane.**

2. **On the Home tab, click the New E-mail button in the New group to create a new, blank e-mail message.** The new message appears, as shown in Figure 27-12.

3. **Type the recipient's address in the To field, or click the To button and select a recipient from your Address Book.**

4. **Type the message subject in the Subject field.**

5. **Type the body of the message in the main section of the message window.**

6. **Click the Send button.**

FIGURE 27-12

A blank e-mail message ready to be composed and sent.

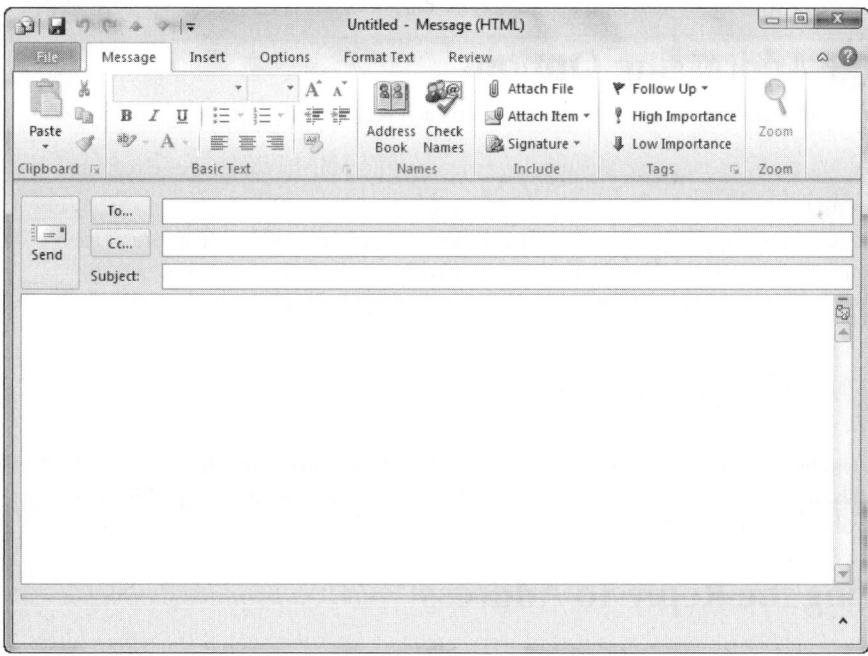

That's all there is to it. Depending on Outlook's Send and Receive options, your message is sent immediately or placed in the Outbox to be sent the next time a Send or Receive is performed. If you want to be sure that the message is sent immediately, press F9.

Sending a Message

When you click the Send button to send an e-mail message, Outlook places the message in the Outbox. This is one of the mail folders displayed in the Navigation pane. Depending on your connection status and Outlook option settings, the message may be transmitted to your e-mail provider immediately, or it may wait until you are online or until a timed Send/Receive occurs. In either case, once the message is sent, it is removed from the Outbox folder and a copy is saved in the Sent Items folder unless your settings do not call for a copy to be retained.

You can also create a new e-mail message using settings other than the defaults by clicking New Items in the New group, and then pointing to E-mail Message Using. Then, in the submenu, do one of the following:

- To create a message based on stationery, select More Stationery to select from all available stationery.

- To create a message in a format (HTML, Rich Text, or plain text) other than the default, select the desired format.

Message Addressing Options

An e-mail message can have multiple recipients, and each recipient can be one of three types:

- **To.** The main message recipient(s). Every message usually has at least one recipient in the To field.

- **Cc (Carbon Copy).** Generally you use Cc when a person needs to be aware of the content of the message but is not a primary recipient — that is, does not need to respond or take action. All recipients of a message can see who is in the Cc list.

- **Bcc (Blind Carbon Copy).** This is like Cc, but the names and e-mail addresses of Bcc recipients are not visible to any other recipients of the message.

Tip

By default, an e-mail window does not display the Bcc field with the other addressing information; it displays just the To and Cc fields. If you want the Bcc field displayed, click the Options tab at the top of the message window and click the Show Bcc button. ∎

Changing the Reply To Address

By default, the Reply To address that is part of every e-mail message you send is the reply address that you specified when you set up the e-mail account. There may be situations in which you want replies to a message that you send directed to a different e-mail address. To do so, follow these steps:

1. In the message window, click the **Direct Replies To** button in the **More Options group** of the Options tab on the Ribbon. Outlook will open the Message Options dialog box.

2. Under Delivery Options, make sure that the **Have Replies Sent To** option is checked.

3. Enter the desired reply address in the adjacent box, or click the Select Names button to choose from your Address Book.

4. Click Close.

Entering Recipients Manually

You can type recipients directly into the To, Cc, and Bcc fields. To enter more than one recipient in a field, use a semicolon as a separator between addresses.

By default, Outlook's AutoComplete feature is turned on for all recipient fields. As you start entering an address or name, Outlook displays suggestions based on what you have entered in the past. The suggestions come from a list of names and e-mail addresses that you have entered previously. Outlook will narrow the list as you enter more of the name or address. If the recipient you want is displayed, select it by clicking. You can also highlight it with the up- and down-arrow keys and press Enter. Otherwise, just continue typing in the full name or address.

When Outlook is first installed, the AutoComplete list is empty, so it may seem to not be working. As you continue to use Outlook, however, it will become a useful tool. Names that you use less frequently move to the bottom of the list and eventually disappear.

Entering Recipients from Your Contacts (Address Book)

Any recipients you have added as Contacts (see Chapter 29) are listed in your Address Book and can be added to an e-mail message with a few clicks. If you refer back to Figure 27-12, you can see that the e-mail window has To and Cc buttons next to the corresponding fields. If the Bcc field is visible, it will have an adjacent Bcc button. Click on any of these buttons to open the Select Names dialog box, shown in Figure 27-13.

Deleting AutoComplete Items

If someone changes his or her e-mail address, you may find that old, invalid address still appearing on the AutoComplete list. When the list is displayed and you see an address that you no longer want, use the down-arrow key to highlight it; then press Delete.

If you have more than one Address Book, you should select it from the Address Book drop-down list. The default Address Book, which is adequate for many Outlook users, is called *Contacts*. The entries in the selected Address Book are displayed in an alphabetized list. Then, add recipients to your message as follows:

- Select a single recipient by clicking it. Select multiple recipients by holding down Ctrl while clicking.

- Add the selected recipient(s) to the To, Cc, or Bcc field by clicking on the corresponding button.

- Add the selected recipients to the active field by pressing Enter. The active field is the one corresponding to the button you clicked — To, Cc, or Bcc — to display the Select Names dialog box.

- Add a single recipient to the active field by double-clicking on the recipient in the list.

- To remove a recipient from the To, Cc, or Bcc field, click it — the entire name will become highlighted — and press Delete.

When you are finished adding recipients, click the OK button to return to the message.

FIGURE 27-13

Selecting e-mail recipients from your Address Book.

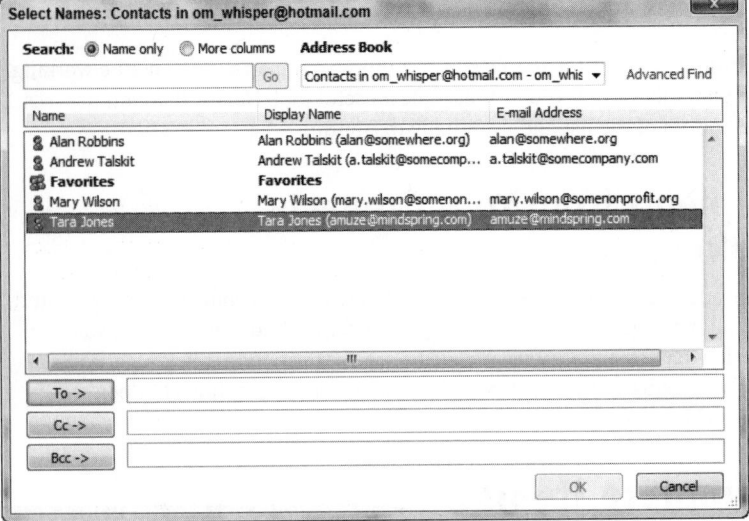

Sending Attachments

An *attachment* is a file that you send along with an e-mail message. When the recipient receives the message, he or she can save the file to disk and open it. Attachments can be a very useful way to pass documents around — whether you're sending photos of the kids to other family members or distributing a Word document to your colleagues for review.

You should be aware of some concerns with attachments. One has to do with file size. Most e-mail accounts limit the size of attachments that can accompany an e-mail message. The limit varies between different accounts, but 10 MB is a common figure. Even if your account allows you to send large attachments, the recipient's account may prohibit receiving them.

Another concern about attachments relates to security. Certain types of files can harm your computer by introducing a virus or by other means. Outlook and other e-mail client programs block potentially harmful attachments based on the filename extension, which indicates the type of file. For example, executable program files use the .exe extension and are blocked by Outlook.

One approach to dealing with both of these concerns is to use a file-archiving utility to compress your files into a ZIP or other kind of archive. Compression not only reduces the file size but also may enable you to send certain types of files that might be blocked on the receiving end.

What kinds of files can you send and receive as attachments? Any image file is okay, including those with the .jpg, .gif, .png, and .tif extensions. So are text files (.txt extension), XML files (.xml extension), PDF files, and most Microsoft Office documents: Word (.doc and .docx extensions), Excel (.xls and .xlsx extensions), and PowerPoint (.ppt and .pptx extensions). ZIP archives (.zip extension) are OK, too.

When you are composing an e-mail message, you attach a file as follows:

1. **If necessary, click the Message tab on the Ribbon in the message window.**
2. **Click the Attach File button (with a paper clip icon) in the Include group.** Outlook opens the Insert File dialog box, which looks like any other dialog box for opening or saving files.
3. **If necessary, navigate to the folder containing the file.**
4. **Click on the name of the file to attach.** To attach multiple files from the same folder, hold down the Ctrl key while clicking.
5. **Click the Insert button.**

After you have attached one or more files, the message displays an Attached line in the header, as shown in Figure 27-14. The attached files are listed here along with the file size. If you change your mind and want to remove a file, click on its name in the Attached box and press Delete.

Sending and Receiving

Outlook's default is to send and receive messages on all accounts when the program first starts and then every 30 minutes. If you want to send or receive manually, click the Send/Receive button on the toolbar or press F9.

FIGURE 27-14

The names of attached files are displayed in the message header.

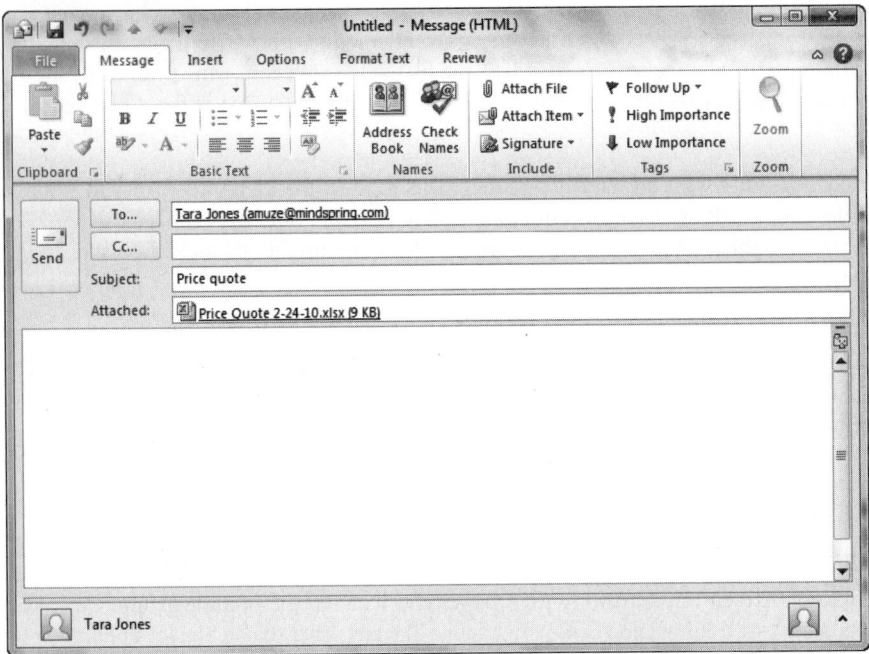

Reading and Replying to Messages

When Outlook receives an e-mail message, it places it in your Inbox folder by default, as shown in Figure 27-15. By default, messages are sorted by the time and date they were received. You can see that the sender, the subject, the time and date received, and the message size are displayed. Please also note the following:

- A message that you have not yet read is displayed in bold type with a closed envelope icon; see, for example, the top message in the figure. A message that has been read is displayed in normal type with an open envelope icon; see the bottom message in the figure.

- If the message includes one or more attachments, a paper clip icon is displayed.

Reading a Message

To read a message, click on it in the Inbox. The message opens in the Reading Pane at the right (by default), as shown in Figure 27-16.

Tip

You also can open a message in its own window by double-clicking on the message. ■

While you have an e-mail message open, you can carry out the following actions:

- Print the message by clicking File and then clicking the Print button.
- Close the message and delete it by clicking the Delete button in the Delete group of the Home tab on the Ribbon. Outlook moves the message to the Deleted Items folder.

Other actions that you can take with an e-mail message are covered later in this chapter.

FIGURE 27-15

Messages that you receive are placed in your Inbox folder.

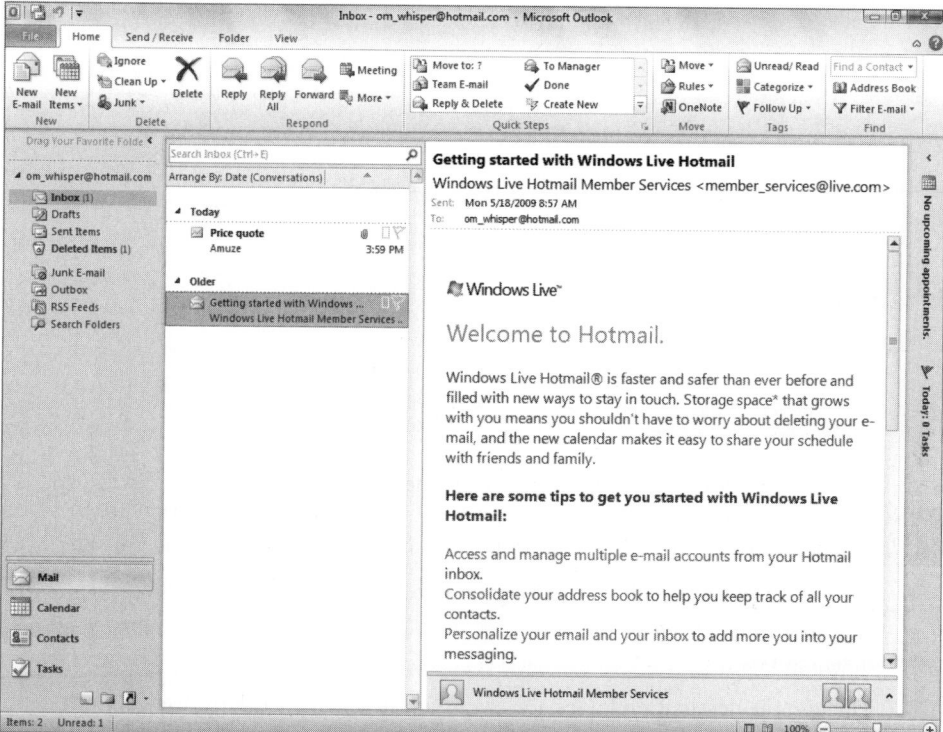

Note

If you are working with a web-based e-mail account such as a Hotmail account, you may see additional folders including a Sync Issues folder appear in the list of folders, after you have added content that is synched with the online account. If you are working with an IMAP or POP e-mail account, the Quick Steps group on the Home tab may be condensed to a single column, and a Send/Receive group with a Send/Recieve All folders button may appear at far right on the tab.

FIGURE 27-16

Reading an e-mail message.

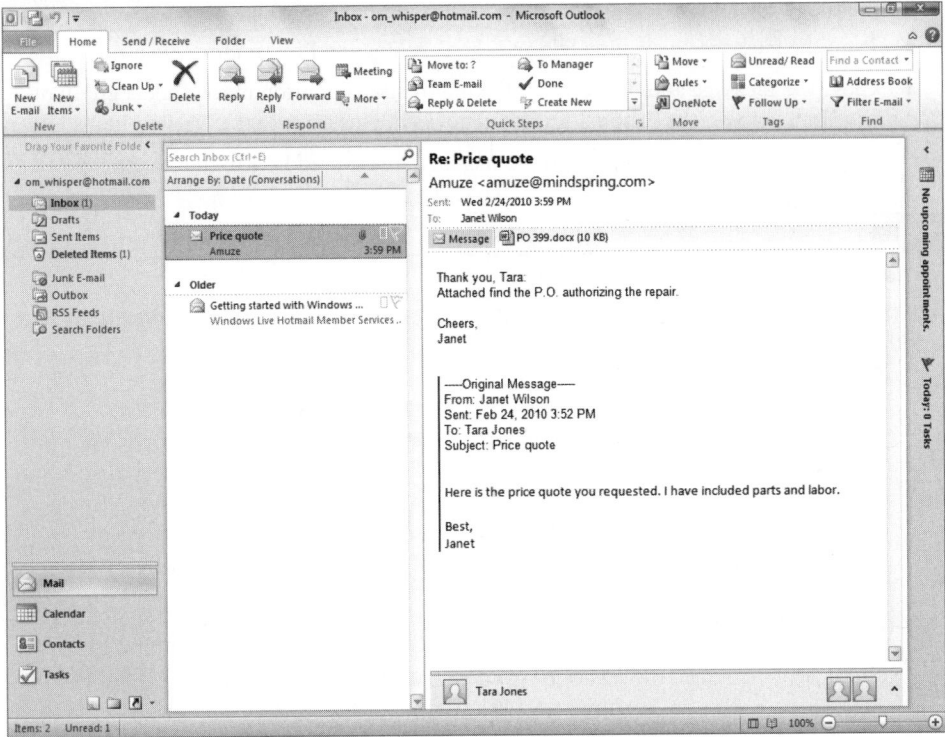

You can also move the message from the Inbox to another folder. Doing so is useful when you want to organize received e-mail messages. (You'll learn more about working with Outlook folders later in the chapter.) The basic steps for moving an open message are the following:

1. **Click the Move button in the Move group on the Home tab of the Ribbon.**

2. **Select Other Folder from the menu.** Outlook displays the Move Items dialog box, as shown in Figure 27-17.

3. **Click on the destination folder.** Or, to create a new folder, click the New button. Details on creating a new folder are presented later in the chapter.

4. **Click OK.** The message is closed and moved to the specified folder.

When you are moving an e-mail message to another folder, you are given the opportunity to create a new folder. When you click the New button in the Move Item dialog box, Outlook opens the Create New Folder dialog box. Then, follow these steps:

1. **Enter the name for the new folder in the Name box.**

2. **Make sure that Mail and Post Items is selected in the Folder Contains list.**

3. **Click the location for the new folder in the list.** The new folder is created as a subfolder to the item you select here.

4. **Click OK to close the dialog box and return to the Move Items dialog box.** The new folder is selected in the list.

5. **Click OK to complete moving the mail message.**

Moving an e-mail message to another folder.

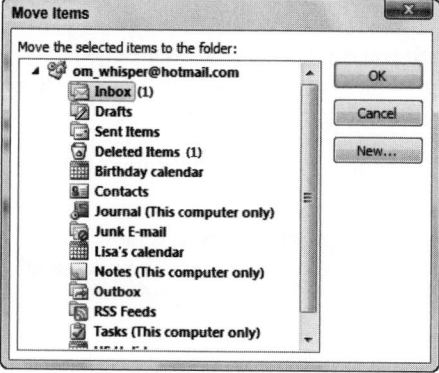

Marking Messages as Read or Unread

Messages that have not been read are displayed in bold font and with a closed envelope icon. When you open a message, it is marked as read and displayed in normal font with an open envelope icon. You can control how a message is flagged. Perhaps you open a message and then are called away; you might want to mark it as unread so that you will be sure to look at it again later.

If the message is open in its own window, simply click the Mark Unread button in the Tags group on the Message tab of the Ribbon. If no message is open, you can select a message in the Inbox (or whatever mail folder you are in) and then click Unread/Read in the Tags group of the Home tab or right-click the message and click Mark as Unread.

Using the Reading Pane

You already learned that Outlook's Reading Pane lets you view the contents of a message without opening it. When the Reading Pane is displayed, it shows the contents of whatever message is selected in the Inbox (or whatever other mail folder you are working in).

The Reading Pane can be displayed at the bottom of the screen instead of the default position at the right. To control the display of the Reading Pane, choose View ➪ Layout ➪ Reading Pane, and then select Right, Bottom, or Off.

Using Outlook as a Hub for Your Social Networks

As of this writing, Microsoft was working hard to finish integrating a new feature called the *Outlook Social Connector*. The Outlook Social Connector displays information and updates from your social networks such as LinkedIn. It appears in a small pane called the *People Pane* at the bottom of the Reading Pane. Use the People Pane button in the People Pane group of the View tab to set up your social network settings and control the display of the People Pane.

Other Actions for Received Messages

When you are viewing a message that you have received, you can take several other actions besides those already described with the message. Each of these actions is available via the Home tab on the ribbon:

- **Create Rule.** Lets you create a rule for handling similar messages. Rules are covered in Chapter 28.

- **Block Sender.** Adds the message sender to your Blocked Senders list and moves the message to the Junk e-mail folder. You'll find more details on dealing with junk e-mail in Chapter 28.

- **Categorize.** Assign the message to an Outlook category.

- **Follow Up.** Flag the message for follow-up, or create a reminder associated with the message.

- **Related.** Find other messages from the same sender or that are related by subject or content.

Replying to and Forwarding Messages

Replying to and forwarding messages are two very useful things you can do with e-mail using Outlook. When a mail message is open, you have three buttons in the Respond group of the Message tab of the Ribbon. These same buttons are also found in the Respond group of the Home tab when a message window is not open:

- **Reply.** Creates a new message addressed to the person who sent you the original message. By default, the new message contains the entire original message, and the subject of the new message is "Re:" followed by the subject of the original message.

- **Reply to All.** Same as Reply except the new message is also addressed to all people in the To and Cc lines of the original message.

- **Forward.** Creates a new, unaddressed message. The new message quotes the entire original message, includes any attachments that were sent with the original message, and the subject is "FW:" followed by the subject of the original message.

At this point, the new message is ready for editing. You can add your own text to the body of the message, add or remove recipients (you must add at least one recipient when forwarding), add attachments, and so on. When you're finished, click Send.

Another message forwarding option is to select Forward as Attachment from the Actions menu. A new e-mail message is created with the original message attached as a separate file rather than being inserted into the body of the new message.

In Outlook 2010, messages appear as threaded conversations by default. You can click on the white triangle beside a topic to expand it and see specific messages in the thread, as shown in Figure 27-18. Make sure you click on the right message in the list before clicking one of the Reply buttons. You then can click the black triangle beside the message topic to collapse the list.

FIGURE 27-18

Viewing a conversation.

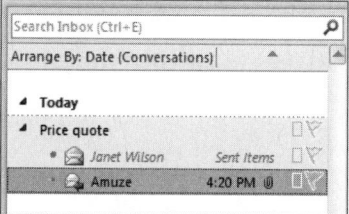

Working with Received Attachments

Outlook lets you save attachments to disk and also lets you view attachments without opening them in their native application. The viewing option is available for many attachment types including most image files, Word documents, and Excel workbooks.

Saving Attachments

When a received message includes one or more attachments, it will have a small, paper clip icon displayed next to the message. There are two ways to save attachments. The first method is easiest. Right-click the attachment in the Reading Pane, and click Save As. Then use the Save Attachment dialog box to finish the save.

The second method also lets you save attachments without opening the message:

1. **Select the message in the Inbox (or whatever mail folder you are working in) or open the message by double-clicking on it.**

2. **Choose File ⇨ Save Attachments from the Ribbon.**

Outlook opens the Save All Attachments dialog box, shown in Figure 27-19.

Note

When you reply (or reply all) to a message, any attachments that came with the original message are not included. When you forward a message, however, attachments are included. ■

3. If you want to save just some of the attachments, select them by clicking and Ctrl+clicking (to select more than one individual attachment) or Shift+clicking (to select a group of adjacent attachments).

4. Click OK.

5. Navigate to the folder where you want the attachment saved.

6. Click Save.

FIGURE 27-19

Saving all message attachments simultaneously.

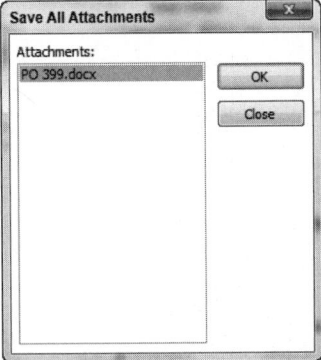

Viewing Attachments

When a message that you receive includes one or more attachments, they are listed below the message details (both in the Reading Pane and when the message is open). You also see a Message button next to the attachment names. You can take the following actions:

- Click on an attachment name to view the attachment.
- Click the Message button to return to the message.

Figure 27-20 shows these elements along with an attachment that is being viewed.

Opening Attachments

You usually open an attachment in its native application by saving the attachment to disk, as described previously, and then starting the application and opening the file as usual. You can, however, open an attachment directly from Outlook by following these steps:

1. Open the message or display it in the Reading Pane.

2. Right-click on the attachment name.

3. Select Open from the shortcut menu.

Depending on the file type, Outlook may display a warning dialog box asking whether you want to open or save the file. Click Open, and the attachment is opened in its native application.

FIGURE 27-20

Viewing an attachment.

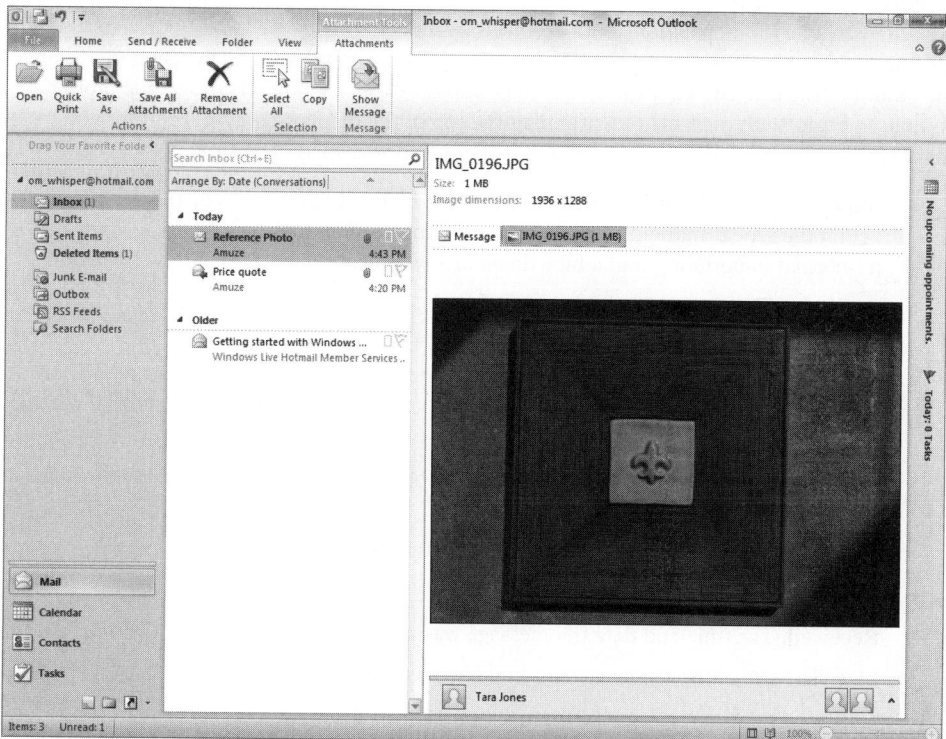

The reason for the cautionary dialog box in Step 3 is security. Some kinds of files, such as Word documents and Excel workbooks, have the potential to contain malicious macro code that can harm your system. This code is harmless unless the file is opened, so you may want to save it to disk first and run a virus scan before opening it.

If you do open an attachment this way, you can work with it in the application as you normally would, including saving to disk.

Native Applications

A native, or default, application is an application that is registered on your system for working with a particular kind of file. Usually, only one application can be *native*, such as Microsoft Word for Word files and Excel for Excel files. For other kinds of files, such as image files, you may select from several possibilities, depending on what's installed on your system. For example, on my system, PhotoShop is registered as the native application for most image files, but on your system it might be Paint Shop Pro or Corel Draw.

Understanding the Inbox Display

The message list in the Inbox, or any other Outlook folder that contains e-mail messages, provides you with a lot of information about the messages it contains. Some icons appear to the right of the message name in the default view. If you change to the Preview view (by using the Change View button in the Current View group of the Group tab), the list expands to include more columns, or fields, with each field identified at the top of the display. It's important for you to understand the meaning of the icons and fields in the Inbox display. They are:

- **Importance (Exclamation Point Icon).** A red exclamation point is displayed in this field if the sender marked the message as having high importance. Nothing is displayed for normal importance, and a blue down arrow indicates messages of Low Importance.

- **Reminder (Bell Icon).** A bell is displayed in this field if the message has been associated with a reminder.

- **Read (Page Icon).** Displays a closed or open envelope for unread and read messages, respectively. Also displays various icons for special messages such as alerts and meeting requests.

- **Attachment (Paper Clip Icon).** Displays a paper clip icon if the message includes one or more attachments.

- **From.** The name or e-mail address of the message sender.

- **Subject.** The message subject.

- **Received.** The time and date the message was received.

- **Size.** The size of the message including any attachments.

- **Categories.** If the message has been assigned to a category, the category name and icon are displayed here.

- **Follow-Up (Flag Icon).** Displays a flag indicating the follow-up status of the message. A clear flag indicates no follow-up status. Various colored flags indicate other follow-up statuses, such as due tomorrow or due next week. A checkmark indicates complete.

In the Preview view, you can sort the messages in the Inbox by any of the fields that are displayed. Simply click on the field heading to sort by that field in ascending order; click a second time to sort in descending order. If the field heading is wide enough, it displays an upward- or downward-pointing arrow to show you that the messages are sorted by that field in ascending or descending order, respectively.

The default Compact view enables you to open the Arrange By menu at the top and choose the desired order.

Understanding Files and Folders

Most computer users are familiar with the idea of a *file*. A *file* is a unit of storage on a disk that contains data, such as a word processing document, a spreadsheet, or a digital photograph.

Outlook uses files to store all of its information, ranging from e-mail account settings and user options to all of its e-mail messages, appointments, tasks, and other items. In fact, for a single-user setup Outlook uses a single file called an *Outlook Personal Folders file* to store just about everything.

Most computer users are also familiar with the concept of a *folder* (sometimes referred to as a *directory*). Folders are used to divide a hard disk into discrete storage areas; can you imagine the confusion if all your files were stored in the same location? Outlook uses folders, too, but they are not the same as disk folders. They serve the same purpose — to help organize the items that are stored — but they exist within the Outlook Personal Folders file and not as separate folders on your hard disk.

Outlook folders come in different types based on the kind of item they are designed to hold. For example, your Inbox is a folder, and it is intended to hold e-mail messages, but you cannot store a contact there.

Outlook Data Files

For most Outlook users, program data and items are stored in an Outlook Personal Folders file. This is true if you are using a POP, an IMAP, or an HTML e-mail account. The file has the .pst extension and is by default named *Outlook.pst*. The folder on your hard disk where this file is normally kept is as follows:

- **Windows XP and Windows Server 2003.** `C:\Documents and Settings\user\Local Settings\Application Data\Microsoft\Outlook`

- **Windows Vista.** `C:\Users\user\AppData\Local\Microsoft\Outlook`

- **Windows 7.** `C:\Users\user\My Documents\Outlook Files`

Here, `user` is the name you have used to log on to Windows. If the computer is configured for more than one user, each will have his or her own separate and independent Outlook Personal Folders file.

You can have more than one Personal Folders file, but only one is designated as the default, which means that Outlook uses it to store account settings, messages, and other items. Additional PST files are used for special purposes such as archiving old items. You cannot change the storage location of the default PST file.

Offline Folders File

If you use a Microsoft Exchange e-mail account rather than, or in addition to, an IMAP, a POP, or an HTML account, you may have an Offline Folders file (which has the .ost extension). Normally, Exchange keeps copies of your messages and other items on the server, but you can configure Outlook to keep a local copy of the items on your system, in the Offline Folders file. Doing so allows you to work with your Outlook items when a connection to the Exchange server is not available.

Hidden Folders?

The folder where the Outlook data file is kept may be *hidden*, which means that it normally does not show up in Windows Explorer or My Computer. To see hidden folders and files, you must change a view option by choosing Options from the Tools menu (in My Computer or Explorer, not Outlook) in Windows XP, or by choosing Organize Folder and Search Options in Vista or Windows 7.

Working with Outlook Folders

Outlook folders let you organize all the myriad items that you work with in Outlook. Outlook comes with a default set of folders that is a good starting point, but many users find these folders insufficient. This section shows you how to create new folders and work with folders and folder items.

As mentioned earlier, Outlook folders are designed to hold a specific type of item. The choices are as follows:

- **Calendar Folders.** Calendar folders hold appointments and other scheduling items.
- **Mail Folders.** Mail folders hold e-mail messages.
- **Contacts Folders.** Contacts folders hold contact information.
- **Journal Folders.** Journal folders hold journal entries.
- **Task Folders.** Task folders hold task items.
- **Notes Folders.** Notes folders hold notes.

You cannot move an item into a folder of the wrong type, such as moving an e-mail message into a Contacts folder. The one exception to this rule is the Deleted Items folder, which can hold any type of item.

Note
Note that RSS feed items are treated like e-mail messages by Outlook when it comes to folder types. ■

Outlook's Default Folders

When installed, Outlook has a set of default folders that are located at the top level in your Personal Folders file. You cannot rename, move, or delete these default folders. They are as follows:

- **Calendar.** Holds calendar items (appointments, etc.).
- **Contacts.** Holds your contacts.

- **Deleted Items.** Holds any and all items you have deleted before they are permanently deleted. See the section "Deleting Items and Using the Deleted Items Folder," later in this chapter.

- **Drafts.** Holds e-mail messages you have started composing but not yet sent.

- **Inbox.** Holds received e-mails.

- **Journal.** Holds your journal items.

- **Junk E-mail.** Holds e-mail that has been flagged as junk (spam).

- **Notes.** Holds your notes.

- **Outbox.** Holds e-mails that you have sent but that have not yet been transferred to your e-mail server.

- **RSS Feeds.** Holds content from your subscribed RSS feeds.

- **Sent Items.** Holds copies of e-mail messages that you have sent.

Creating a New E-mail Folder

E-mail folders get their own section because Outlook treats them a bit differently from other folders. To be more specific, you cannot organize e-mail folders into groups, but rather you have to organize them hierarchically when you create them.

When you create a new e-mail folder, you can place it at the top level — the same level as Outlook's default folders. You can also put it within an existing folder. You can put folders within folders to essentially any level and thereby organize your e-mail messages in the way that best suits you.

Look at the example in Figure 27-21, which shows Outlook's default e-mail folders. You can see that they are all at the same level within Personal Folders.

FIGURE 27-21

The organization of Outlook's default e-mail folders.

Suppose that you want to organize e-mails from your clients by creating an e-mail folder for each client. For this example, I assume that you have three clients: Acme, Consolidated, and National.

One approach is to create three new folders at the top level. The resulting structure is shown in Figure 27-22. This is the only approach that's allowed for Web-based accounts.

FIGURE 27-22

New e-mail folders can be created at the top level of the folder hierarchy.

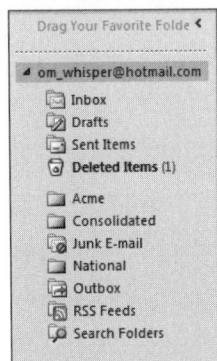

Another approach is to use the ability to create folders within other folders, resulting in a hierarchy of folders that is structured according to the folder contents. This approach can be implemented by creating a Clients folder at the top level and then creating Acme, Consolidated, and National subfolders within the Clients folder. This structure is shown in Figure 27-23. Note that a folder that contains other folders — Clients, in this case — displays an adjacent arrow icon that you can click to show or hide the subfolders.

FIGURE 27-23

New e-mail folders can also be created in a hierarchical structure by placing folders within other folders.

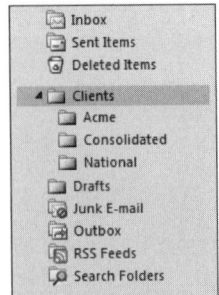

In any event, you do not have to decide all the details of your e-mail folder structure ahead of time because you can always move the folders around if needed.

Now you can get to the details of creating a new e-mail folder. Here are the steps to follow:

1. **If necessary, click the Mail button at the bottom of the Navigation pane to display the mail folders.**

2. **If you want the new folder at the top level, right-click on your account name (which by default is your e-mail address, unless you've changed it to another name).** Otherwise, right-click on the folder that you want the new folder in.

3. **Select New Folder from the shortcut menu.** Outlook displays the Create New Folder dialog box (Figure 27-24). The location for the new folder is shaded in the folder display — Inbox, for example, in the figure. You can, if necessary, change the location at this point.

4. **Type the name of the new folder in the Name box.**

5. **Make sure that Mail and Post Items is selected in the Folder contains list.**

6. **Click OK.**

The new folder is created, and you can start using it to store mail items.

FIGURE 27-24

Creating a new folder to hold e-mail items.

Creating a New Non–E-mail Folder

Non–e-mail folders — those for tasks, calendar, journal, and contacts — are handled a bit differently than mail folders. You can only create folders for some items for the default mail account, so if you are using multiple accounts, make sure that you have set the appropriate account as the default.

The following steps show how to create a non–e-mail folder:

1. **Click the appropriate button in the Navigation pane corresponding to where you want to add a new folder — Calendar, Contacts, and so on.**

2. **Click the Folder tab in the Ribbon.**

3. **For Contacts and Tasks, click New Folder in the New group.** For Calendar, click New Calendar in the New Group. Outlook displays the Create New Folder dialog box (refer to Figure 27-24). The folder for the type of item you selected in Step 1 — Calendar, for example — is highlighted in the folder list.

4. **Enter the name of the new folder in the Name box.**

5. **Make sure that the Folder contains list displays the appropriate type of item for the folder you are creating.**

6. **Click OK.**

After you create a non–e-mail folder, it is displayed near the top of the Navigation pane along with other folders, including the default one, for that type of item. Figure 27-25 shows an example for Tasks after creating two new task folders called *Work Related* and *Personal*.

Caution
You can create new Task folders if you want, but be forewarned that task items you move from the default task folder to a new folder are not updated if you have assigned the task to someone else and receive accept, decline, or progress update messages. ∎

FIGURE 27-25

User-created folders for non–e-mail items are displayed along with the default folder in the Navigation pane.

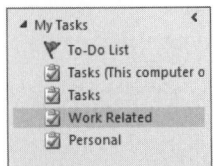

Changing the Default E-mail Account

To change the default e-mail account:

1. **Choose File ⇨ Info from the main Outlook window, click the Account Settings button, and then click Account Settings to display the Account Settings dialog box.**

2. **If necessary, click the E-mail tab.** The current default account is indicated in the account list by "(send from this account by default)."

3. **Click another account in the list.**
4. **Click the Set as Default button.**
5. **Click Close.**

Organizing Folders in Groups

Outlook folders that are not e-mail folders can be organized into groups. This is similar in concept to organizing e-mail folders by their location in the folder hierarchy, but the procedures are a bit different.

By default, every category of non–e-mail item has a single group with a name such as *My Contacts*, *My Tasks*, and so on. If you create new folders, they are displayed as part of this default group. For example, Figure 27-26 shows the Contact folders after adding four new folders to the default Contacts folder. They are all part of the default My Contacts group (which can be expanded or collapsed using the adjacent arrow).

FIGURE 27-26

All folders for non–e-mail items are initially part of the default group, which is My Contacts in this figure.

By creating new groups, you can organize these folders as desired. In this example, there are five Contacts folders, and you might want to arrange them as follows:

- The Contacts folder, for miscellaneous contacts, remains in the My Contacts group.
- The Personal Contacts and Family Contacts go into a new group named *Personal*.
- The Work Contacts and Freelance Contacts folders go into a new group called *Work*.

The result of this reorganization is shown in Figure 27-27. Now you can expand and contract individual groups to find just the items you need.

Creating a New Group

To create a new group, right-click on an existing group (e.g., My Contacts in Figure 27-27) and select New (*Object Name*) Group, such as New Task Group, from the shortcut menu. Then, type in the name for the group and press Enter.

FIGURE 27-27

You can organize folders into separate groups.

A newly created group is empty, as you might expect. To move a folder to it, point at the folder, press and hold the left mouse button, and drag it to the destination folder.

To create a new folder within a group, follow the procedures earlier in this chapter for creating a new folder; then move it to the desired group.

Working with Groups

You can take the following actions with a group by right-clicking on it and selecting one of the following options from the shortcut menu:

- Rename Group
- Delete Group
- Arrange by Name — order the folders in the group alphabetically.
- Move Up/Down in List — change the position of the group in the list.

Additional actions you can take with groups are covered in the next section.

Working with Folders, Groups, and Items

This section covers the everyday tasks that you need to perform with your folders, groups, and Outlook items to keep them organized.

Viewing Folder Contents

When you switch from one type of item to another — for example, from viewing mail items to viewing contact items — Outlook automatically displays the contents of one folder, usually the default one, in the main Outlook window. To view the contents of another folder (also called *opening the folder*):

- Click the folder to display its contents in the main window.

- Right-click on the folder and select Open in New Window to view the folder's contents in a new window.

You can open as many new windows as you want. When you close a window, Outlook continues running as long as at least one window is open.

Moving or Copying Items

Outlook lets you move or copy items between folders. For some types of items, only moving is allowed. To move or copy one or more items, you must first select them, as follows:

- To select a single item, click on it.
- To select multiple contiguous items, click on the first item and then hold down the Shift key and click on the last item.
- To select multiple noncontiguous items, click on the first item and then hold down the Ctrl key and click on each additional item.
- To select all items in the folder, press Ctrl+A. You can then deselect individual items with Ctrl+click.
- To deselect multiple items, release any key and click on any non-selected item.

Now you can move or copy the selected items in one of several ways:

- Drag the item or group of items to the destination folder and drop.
- Click the Move button in the Move Group of the Home tab. In the menu that appears, select the destination folder to which you want to move the item or click Copy to Folder to specify another folder to copy the item, instead.

Moving, Copying, Deleting, and Renaming Folders

As you fine-tune your Outlook organization, you may want to move folders to new locations. Depending on the type of folder, you may be able to copy a folder as well. E-mail folders can be moved to a new location in the folder hierarchy, whereas other folders can be moved from one group to another.

- To move an e-mail folder, point and click and then drag it to the new location. For example, Figure 27-28 shows how you move the National folder from its location in the Clients folder to a new location in the Key Clients folder.
- To move a non–e-mail folder, point at it and drag it from the current group to the new group.
- To delete a folder, right-click on it and select Delete Folder in the shortcut menu.
- To rename a folder, right-click on it and select Rename Folder in the shortcut menu; then type in the new name and press Enter.

FIGURE 27-28

Moving an e-mail folder to a new location.

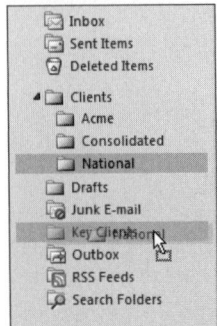

Deleting Items and Using the Deleted Items Folder

When you delete a folder or an Outlook item, it does not get deleted immediately. Rather, it goes to the Deleted Items folder. This is a safety feature that allows users to recover from accidental deletions. You can "delete" items in the usual way (select them and press Delete) or you can drag them to the Deleted Items folder.

Undeleting Items

If an item has not been permanently deleted — that is, if it is still in the Deleted Items folder — you can *undelete* it by moving it back to its original folder (or another folder of the same type).

When you delete an item from the Deleted Items folder, it is truly gone for most e-mail users. Most people prefer to delete items from this folder manually by selecting one or more items and pressing Delete. To delete all items from the Deleted Items folder, choose Empty Deleted Items Folder from the Tools menu. You can also tell Outlook to automatically empty the Deleted Items folder whenever the program exits, as follows:

1. Choose File ⇨ Options to open the Outlook Options dialog box.
2. Click Advanced in the list at the left (shown in Figure 27-29).
3. Select the Empty Deleted Items Folder When Exiting Outlook option.
4. Click OK.

FIGURE 27-29

Setting options for emptying the Deleted Items folder.

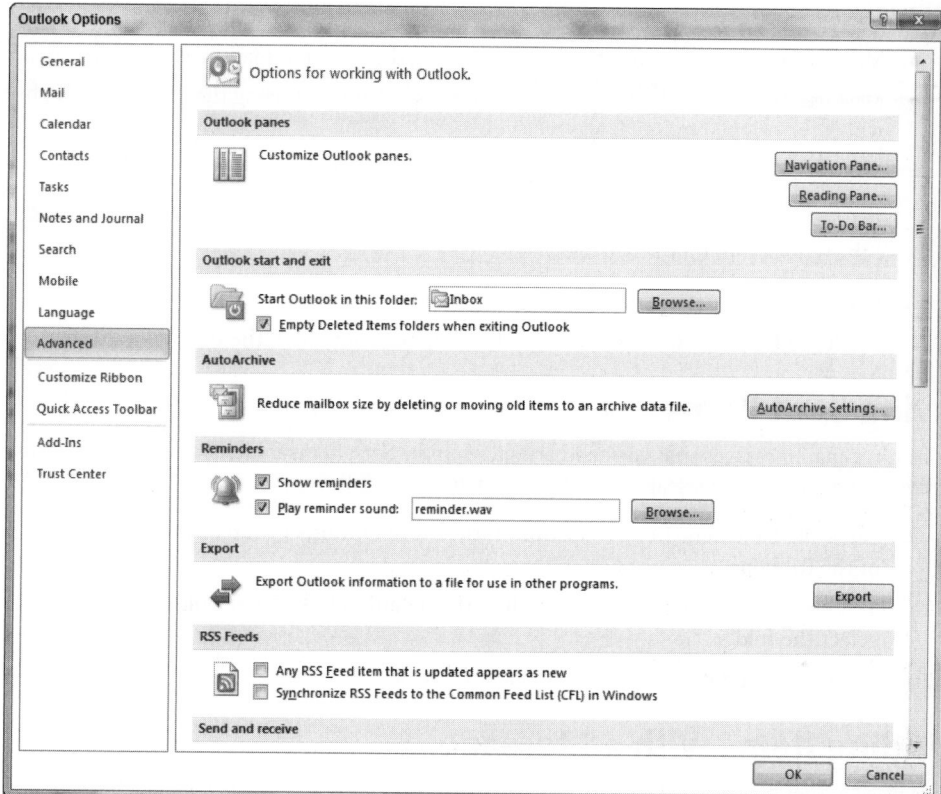

Setting Options for an Individual E-mail Message

Although you can create and send e-mail messages using all of Outlook's default settings, you would be missing a lot of flexibility and convenience if you did so. The various e-mail options that Outlook offers let you use e-mail in the way that is most convenient and productive for you. These options fall into two categories: those that apply to a single message and those that apply globally. This section explains a variety of options available for individual e-mail messages that you create.

Changing the Send Account

This topic is relevant only if you have two or more e-mail accounts. By default, messages are sent as follows:

- Messages you create from scratch are sent using the default e-mail account.
- Messages that are replies to a message you received are sent using the account through which the original message was received.
- Messages you forward are sent using the account through which the original message was received.

To change the send account for a message:

1. **Create the new message.** A new message window appears.
2. **Click the From button above the To button, and then click the desired account.**

Saving Sent Items

By default, e-mail messages that you send are saved in the Sent Items folder. You can change this location for an individual message in its Message window as follows:

1. **Click the Save Sent Item To button in the More Options group of the Options tab of the Ribbon.**
2a. **To save the item to a folder other than the default, click Other Folder and then select the folder.**
2b. **To not save the item at all, click Do Not Save.**

Sending Items with a Message

You learned earlier how you can attach a file to a message. Outlook also lets you attach certain items, specifically calendars and business cards, to a message.

Sending a Calendar

Sending calendar information with a message can be useful to let colleagues know when you are and are not available for a meeting. To send calendar information with an e-mail message, click the Attach Item button in the Include section of the Message tab on the Ribbon, and then click Calendar. Outlook displays the Send a Calendar via E-mail dialog box, shown in Figure 27-30. You make entries in this dialog box to specify the calendar information that will be sent, as follows:

1. **If you have more than one calendar, select the calendar to use from the Calendar list.**
2. **Select the date range from the Date Range list. Predefined ranges include Today, Tomorrow, and Next 7 Days.** Select Specify Dates from the list to enter a custom date range.

3. **From the Detail list, select the level of calendar detail that you want included in the message.** The choices are the following:

   - **Availability Only.** Time is shown as Free, Busy, Tentative, or Out of Office.

   - **Limited Details.** In addition to availability, this option includes the subjects of calendar items.

   - **Full Details.** In addition to availability, this option includes the full detail of calendar items.

4. **Select the Show Time within My Working Hours Only option to limit the sent calendar information to these hours.** By default, they are 8:00 a.m. to 5:00 p.m. Monday–Friday. Click the Set Working Hours link to change this setting.

5. **Click the Show button to display three additional options.** Two of them relate to what information is included in the message. These options are relevant only if you selected Limited Details or Full Details. The third option determines the format of the sent calendar: Daily Schedule or List of Events. See the main text for information on these two layouts.

6. **Click OK to close the dialog box and insert the calendar information in the message.**

FIGURE 27-30

Sending calendar information in an e-mail message.

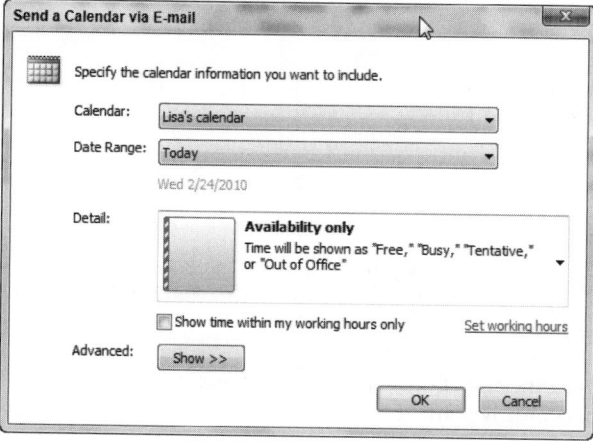

When calendar information is inserted into an e-mail message, at the top is a calendar of the month or months involved with the relevant days highlighted and underlined, as shown for February 24–March 2 in Figure 27-31. The recipient can click these days to go to the detail section for that day.

FIGURE 27-31

This part of the calendar information includes links to individual days.

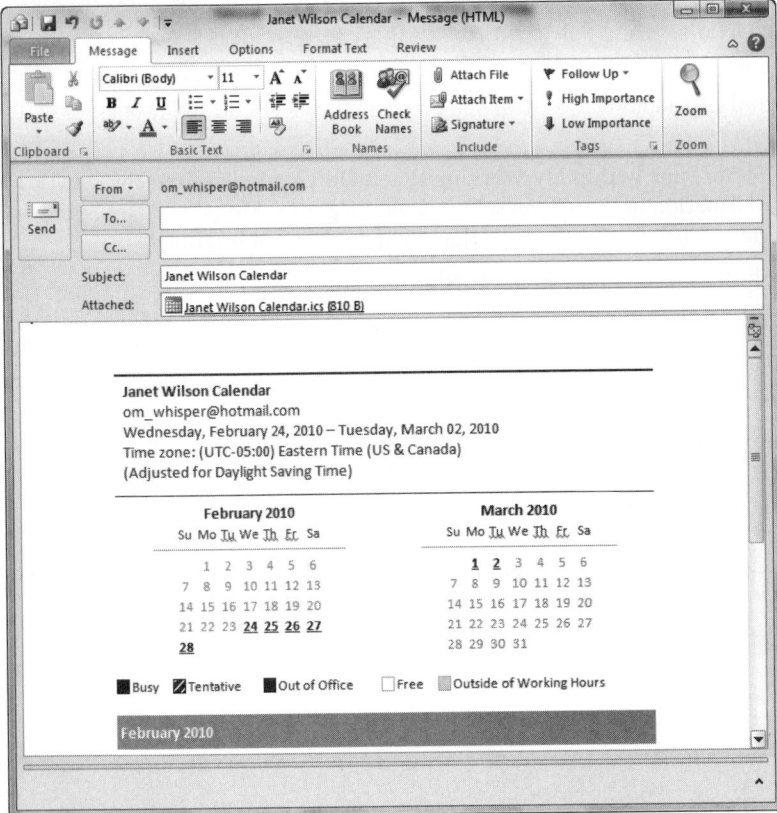

If the calendar information was sent using the Daily Schedule option, the message recipient can scroll down to see details about the schedule. You can see that blocks of time during each day are marked as Free, Busy, and so on.

If the calendar information was sent using the List of Events option, the message lists specific calendar events only — free time is not explicitly marked.

Sending a Business Card

A *business card* is just what it sounds like — an electronic representation of the information normally found on a paper business card. Every entry in a Contacts list automatically has a business card created for it. You can insert these cards into e-mail messages to send contact information to e-mail recipients. When you do so, a visual representation of the business card is added to the message, and a VCF file is attached to the message. The recipient can use the VCF file to quickly add the contact information to his or her own Contacts list.

To send a business card with an e-mail message from the Message window:

1. **Click the Attach Item button in the Include group of the Message tab on the Ribbon and point to Business Card.** The menu that is displayed lists recently sent business cards.

2. **Select the card you want to send, or select Other Business Cards to select from your Contacts list.**

3. **If you selected Other Business Cards, Outlook displays the Insert Business Card dialog box, as shown in Figure 27-32.**

4. **If you have more than one Address Book, select the desired one from the Look in list.**

5. **Click the contact whose business card you want to include.** The card is previewed in the lower part of the dialog box.

6. **If you want to include more than one card, hold down Ctrl while clicking.**

7. **Click OK.**

FIGURE 27-32

Selecting a business card to include in an e-mail message.

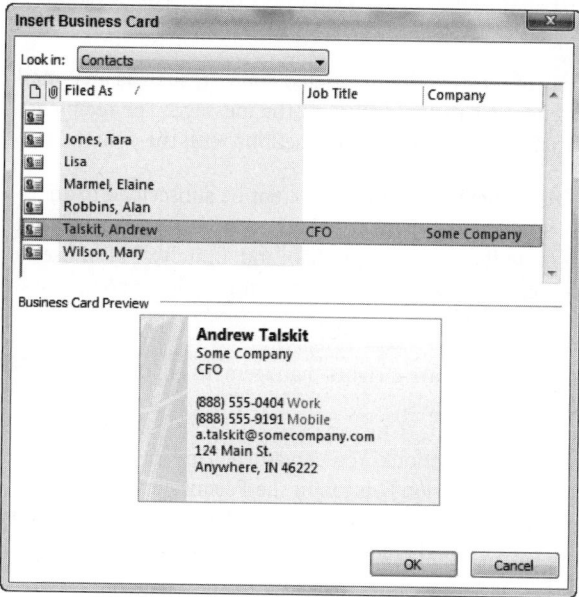

Your Own Business Card

If you create an entry for yourself in your Contacts list, you can send your own business card with e-mail messages.

Setting Message Importance and Sensitivity

An e-mail message can be flagged as having low importance or high importance. Normal is the default. The recipient's e-mail program may indicate the importance of a message in some way. For example, Outlook displays an exclamation point next to the message in the Inbox if it is marked as having high importance. Many e-mail clients, including Outlook, also allow recipients to sort their received messages by importance.

To mark a message with high importance, click the High Importance button (a red exclamation point) in the Tags group of the Message tab on the Ribbon. To change a message to low importance, click the Low Importance button (a downward-pointing arrow).

Setting Message Restrictions

Message restrictions, or permissions, let you restrict who can view your e-mail messages and what they can do with them (e.g., Can the message be forwarded?). This feature, which is applicable to all Office documents as well as e-mail messages, is part of Information Rights Management (IRM).

IRM is based on the concept of credentials. To create rights-restricted content, such as an e-mail message, you must possess appropriate credentials to associate with the message. The recipient must also possess the appropriate credentials to view or take other actions with the content.

IRM requires that both the creator and the recipient of restricted content be subscribed to an IRM server. Many people use the Windows Right Management (WRM) service, which at present is free (but with no guarantee that Microsoft will continue the service indefinitely). WRM uses a Windows Live ID as a means of verifying identities and validating credentials. Some companies use their own IRM server or one provided by a third party.

The steps described in this section assume that you have a rights management client installed on your computer and have set up the necessary credentials.

By default, e-mail messages are created with no restrictions. You can add a "Do Not Forward" restriction by clicking the down arrow on the Permissions button in the Permission group on the Options tab of the Ribbon and selecting Do Not Forward from the menu. This restriction permits recipients to view the message if they have the required credentials, but not to forward, print, or copy the message.

You may be asked which credentials to use for this message (an individual can possess multiple credentials). When a message you are composing is restricted, it displays a banner below the Ribbon describing the restrictions, as shown in Figure 27-33.

FIGURE 27-33

A message that has restrictions applied displays a notification of that fact below the Ribbon.

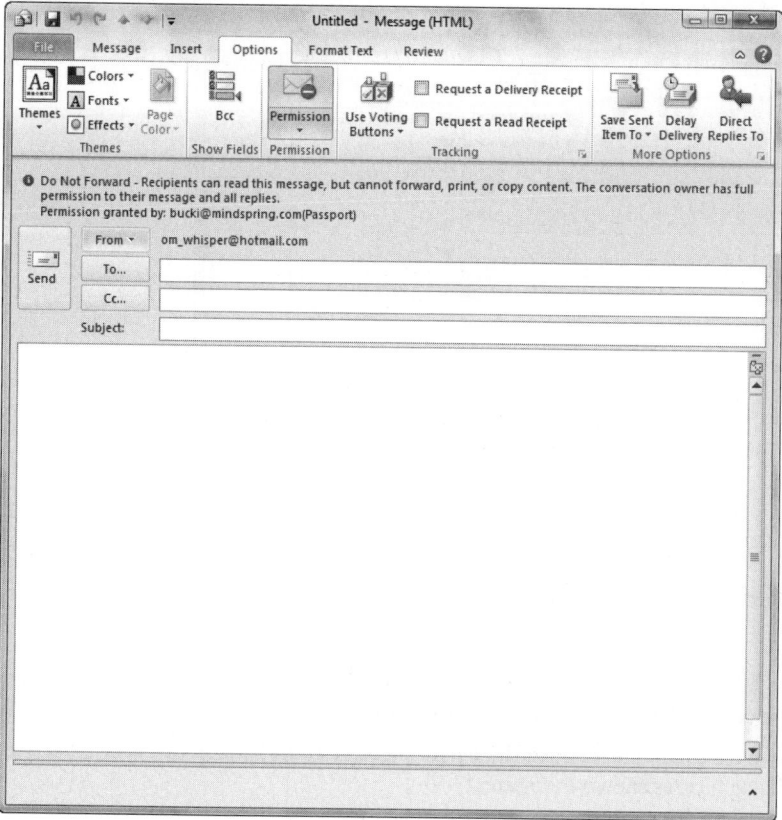

If you attach a document, workbook, or presentation to a message, the restricted permissions of the message are applied to the attachments as well. If the attachment has already had restrictions set in the originating program (Word, Excel, or PowerPoint), those restrictions also remain in effect.

You may also have custom restrictions available to you. In a company, the IT department may have defined a restriction level that restricts contents to people on the company network. Your IT person can provide you with information on custom restrictions if they are in use in your organization.

Flagging a Message for Follow-up

Sometimes, when you send a message, you would like to be reminded to follow up on the message — for example, to make sure that you have received a reply. You can flag a message for follow-up and, optionally, have Outlook remind you. Here's how:

1. **Click the Follow Up button in the Tags group on the Message tab of the Ribbon.**
   Outlook displays the menu shown in Figure 27-34.

FIGURE 27-34

Flagging a message for follow-up.

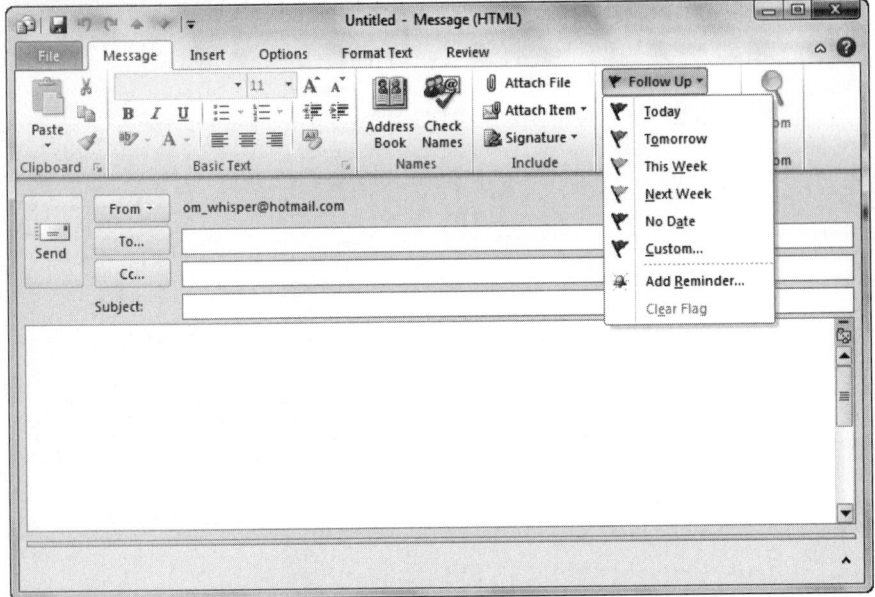

2. **To flag for follow-up at one of the predefined times (e.g., tomorrow or next week), choose the corresponding command on the menu.**

3. **To specify a custom time, choose the Custom command.** Outlook displays the Custom dialog box, as shown in Figure 27-35.

4. **Make sure that the Flag for Me option is selected.**

5. **From the Flag To list, select the type of follow-up (e.g., Follow Up, Reply, etc.).**

6. **Enter the desired Start and Due dates in the corresponding fields.** Click the down arrow next to each field to select from a calendar.

7. **If you want Outlook to remind you of this item, select the Reminder option and then enter the date and time in the adjacent fields.**

8. **Click OK.**

You can also flag a message for the recipient. All you need to do is select Flag for Recipients from the Follow Up menu (Figure 27-34) and then enter the relevant information in the lower part of the Custom dialog box (Figure 27-35).

When an Outlook user receives a message with such a flag, the flag status column in the Inbox displays a special icon indicating that follow-up information is included with the message. The user can right-click this icon to add the message to his or her to-do list. E-mail programs other than Outlook may ignore this information or handle it differently.

FIGURE 27-35

Specifying a custom follow-up interval.

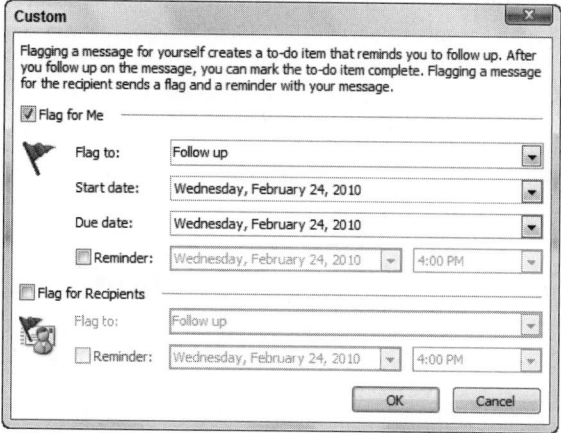

Assigning a Message to a Category

Outlook's categories are a powerful tool for organizing all kinds of information. When you create a message, you can assign it to a category. Then you can find the message — the saved copy of the sent message, that is — based on this category. To assign a category to a message:

1. **Click the Tags group Dialog Box Launcher in the Tags group of the Message tab on the Ribbon to display the Message Options dialog box.**

2. **At the lower left of the dialog box, click the Categories button.**

3. **Select the desired category from the menu.** Or, click Clear All Categories to remove any category assignment from the message.

Requesting Delivery and Read Receipts

When you send a message, you can request delivery or read receipts (or both) by selecting the corresponding option in the Tracking group of the Options tab of the Ribbon. A delivery receipt is generated when the message is delivered to the recipient, and a read receipt is generated when the message is opened by the recipient. The receipt consists of an e-mail message back to you that contains the date and time that the original message was delivered or read.

Delivery and read receipts sound like a great idea, but their usefulness in practice is limited. The delivery receipt must be generated by the e-mail server software, and sometimes this feature is turned off by the server administrator to reduce the load on the server. Even if you do receive a delivery receipt, there is no guarantee that the recipient has read the message. Likewise, the read receipt is sent by Outlook (or whatever other e-mail program the recipient is using), and the user may have this feature turned off.

When you have sent a message and requested a receipt, Outlook automatically processes the receipt when and if it arrives (unless you have turned this feature off under Tracking Options, as explained later in this chapter). When you open the message in the Sent Items folder, the Message tab of the Ribbon displays a Show group with Message and Tracking buttons. Click the Tracking button to view the details of any receipts that have been received for this message. Click the Message button to return to the message text.

Be aware that if Outlook has not yet received and processed any receipt for a message, the Tracking button is not available on the Message tab of the Ribbon.

Delaying Delivery and Setting Message Expiration

If you do not want a message delivered right away, you can specify a "Do not deliver before" date. If you are sending a message that is relevant for only a limited period, you can set an expiration date for the message. When the recipient receives the message, that message will behave normally until the expiration date, after which it will display in the Inbox (or whatever folder it is in) with a line through it. The recipient can still open the message, but the strikethrough provides a visual indication that the message has expired. Other e-mail programs may handle message expiration differently.

Set these two options from the message window, as follows:

1. **Click the Delay Delivery button in the More Options group of the Options tab of the Ribbon in the Message window.** Outlook displays the Properties dialog box (Figure 27-36).

2. **In the Delivery Options section, select the Do Not Deliver Before option.**

3. **Enter the desired date and time in the adjacent fields.**

4. **In the Delivery Options section of the dialog box, select the Expires After option.**

5. **Enter the desired expiration date and time in the adjacent fields.**

6. **Click the Close button.**

If you are using a Microsoft Exchange e-mail account, the message is sent to the server and held there until the specified date and time. If you are using another kind of e-mail account, the message is held in Outlook's Outbox until the first send operation that occurs after the specified date and time.

FIGURE 27-36

Delaying the delivery of a message.

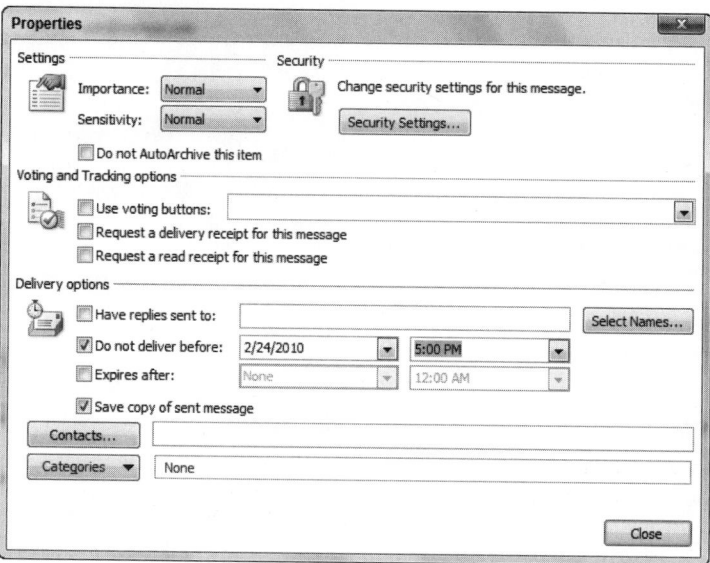

Setting Global E-mail Options

Many of Outlook's options apply globally to all messages and to e-mail in general. You select these options using several dialog boxes that display the options in related groups. This section follows the same organization.

To view and change e-mail preferences:

1. **Choose File ⇨ Options from the main Outlook window to display the Outlook Options dialog box.**
2. **Click the desired section in the list at the left.** For example, Figure 27-37 shows the Mail options.
3. **Set options in this dialog box as explained in the following sections.**
4. **Click OK.**

FIGURE 27-37

Setting global e-mail preferences.

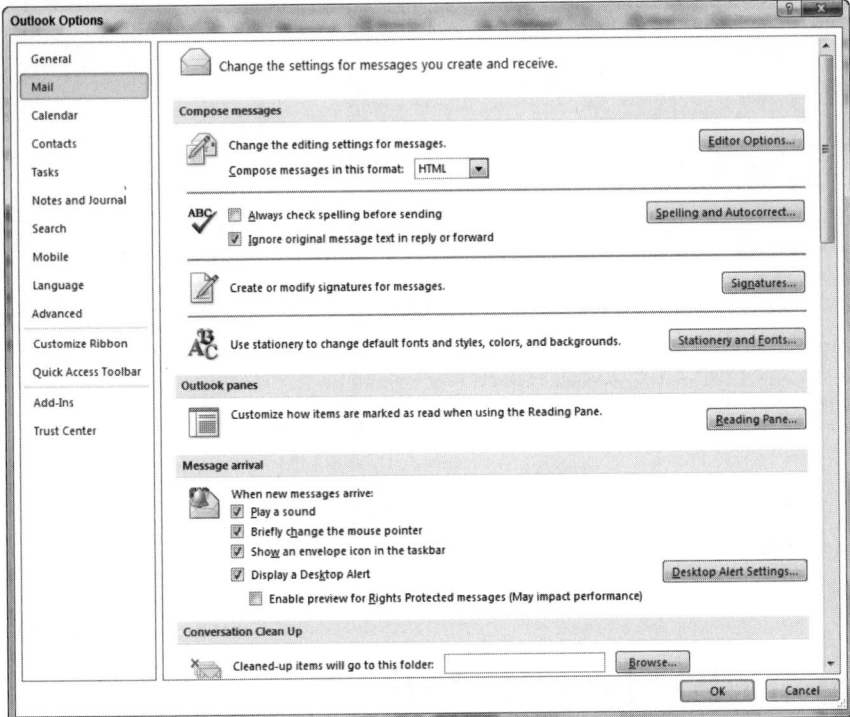

Some key options in the Mail section of the Outlook Options dialog box include:

- **Compose Messages in This Format.** Select the default message format.

- **Save Copies of Messages in the Sent Items Folder.** When you send a message, a copy is saved in the Sent Items folder.

- **Automatically Save Items That Have Not Been Sent after This Many Minutes.** Messages that you have started composing but have not sent are saved in the Drafts folder.

- **Save to This Folder.** Specifies the folder when Outlook automatically saves items (e.g., messages that you have started composing but have not sent yet).

- **When New Message Arrives.** Determines whether Outlook plays a sound or displays some type of alert when a message arrives.

- **Set Default Importance and Sensitivity Levels.** Specifies the default importance and sensitivity levels for new messages that you create.

- **Tracking Options.** View and set tracking options in this section.

The On Replies and Forwards section of this section determines what Outlook does when you reply to a message or forward a message. You set each independently, but the options are essentially the same, as follows:

- **Do Not Include Original Message.** Replies are sent without the original message. This is not applicable to forwarded messages.

- **Attach Original Message.** Replies and forwards are sent with the original message included as an attachment.

- **Include Original Message Text.** Replies and forwards are sent with the original message included as part of the new message.

- **Include and Indent Original Message Text.** Replies and forwards are sent with the original message included as part of the new message, indented with respect to the other parts of the message.

- **Prefix Each Line of the Original Message.** Replies and forwards are sent with the original message included as part of the new message, with each line of the original message prefixed by what is entered in the Prefix Each Line With field (by default, this is the > sign).

Summary

This chapter explained the fundamentals of setting up your e-mail account and sending and receiving e-mail messages. It also covered sending attachments, dealing with attachments that you receive, and using the Inbox. Outlook data consists of items such as e-mail messages, appointments, and contacts. These items are organized into folders that are, in most cases, specialized to hold a single type of item. Folders, in turn, are stored in a Personal Folders file that also contains your account information and other Outlook settings. This chapter showed you how to work with items, folders, and data files to keep your Outlook information organized, accessible, and backed up. It seems that Outlook has an overwhelming number of e-mail options. Fortunately, most options can be left with their default settings and changed only when you have a specific reason to do so. As you become more familiar with Outlook, you'll gain a better understanding of how to set options to maximize your convenience and productivity.

Processing and Securing E-mail

J unk e-mail, often called *spam*, is a problem for most e-mail users. It can range from a minor annoyance for a home user to a major problem for a large organization, clogging mail servers and reducing the efficiency of employees. Fortunately, Outlook provides you with tools that greatly reduce the spam problem. You also can use message rules to process incoming e-mail, cutting down on the amount of time you spend moving messages around or deleting them. Computer security has unfortunately become a very important topic. With the almost universal use of the Internet and e-mail, it's easier than ever for various kinds of malicious software such as viruses to spread. Security issues also include message privacy and verification of people's identities. Because e-mail is the favored means of spreading such malware, Outlook users have to be particularly vigilant. This chapter explains the various tools that Outlook provides to make you more efficient in dealing with spam and managing messages, and to enhance your security.

Understanding Junk E-mail Filtering

Junk e-mail filtering works based on two principles. The first is the content of the message — certain keywords and phrases are considered likely to be spam. The other is the identity of the sender. You can define a *safe list* — people whose messages are never treated as spam regardless of content. Likewise, you can define a *blocked list* — people whose messages are always treated as spam regardless of content. In either case, messages that Outlook flags as spam are placed in the Junk E-mail folder rather than the Inbox.

IN THIS CHAPTER

Understanding junk e-mail filtering

Setting junk e-mail options

Defining blocked and allowed lists

Understanding e-mail rules

Defining a new rule

Looking at some rule examples

Managing e-mail rules

Protecting against viruses

Understanding Outlook's attachment blocking

Implementing macro security

Using certificates and digital signatures

Encrypting and digitally signing messages

Why doesn't Outlook just delete spam messages? The fact is that content-based spam filtering is not perfect, and legitimate messages are sometimes caught as spam. Some people like to quickly scan their Junk E-mail folder before permanently deleting the messages just to make sure that a legitimate message has not been caught. However, if you want spam to be deleted automatically, you can tell Outlook to do this. See the next section, "Setting Junk E-mail Options," for details.

Third-Party Anti-Spam Software

Several anti-spam programs on the market work in conjunction with Outlook to catch spam. These programs may provide more sophisticated filtering options and other features. If you are using one of these programs, you may want to turn Outlook's spam filtering off. You do not have to, however; leaving it on does no harm and may, in fact, catch spam that the other program misses.

Setting Junk E-mail Options

You set Outlook's filtering and handling of junk e-mail in the Junk E-mail Options dialog box, as follows:

1. Click the Junk button in the Delete group of the Home tab in the main Outlook window, and then click Junk E-mail Options to display the Junk E-mail Options dialog box.

2. If necessary, click the Options tab (shown in Figure 28-1).

3. Choose option settings as described in the following list.

4. Click OK.

The first option in this dialog box determines the level of filtering based on message content. You have four levels to choose from:

- **No Automatic Filtering.** Messages are not filtered based on their content.

- **Low.** Only obvious spam is treated as such. Some spam will get through to your Inbox.

- **High.** More stringent spam rules are applied when message content is scanned. Some legitimate messages may be treated as spam.

- **Safe Lists Only.** Only messages from senders on your safe lists (explained later in this chapter) are allowed through; all other messages are treated as spam regardless of their content.

Setting options for junk e-mail filtering

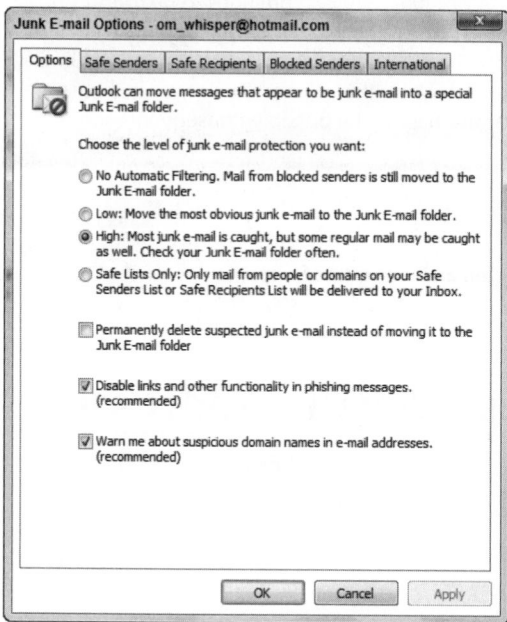

The other options in this dialog box are as follows:

- **Permanently Delete.** Messages that Outlook considers to be spam are deleted rather than moved to the Junk E-mail folder. You may not want to use this option unless you are sure that legitimate messages are not mistakenly being tagged as spam.

- **Disable Links and Other Functionality in Phishing Messages.** Phishing messages (see the "Phishing" sidebar) usually contain links to web pages where you are asked for confidential information such as passwords. If this option is selected, Outlook disables these links.

- **Warn Me about Suspicious Domain Names in E-mail Addresses.** A spoofed domain name is one that is not what it appears to be. For example, a link might display www.microsoft.com but actually be a link to another domain. If this option is selected, Outlook warns you about possible spoofed domain names in a message.

Phishing

Phishing is a particularly dangerous kind of junk e-mail. A *phishing message* pretends to be from a company you do business with, for example, PayPal or eBay. The message asks you to take some seemingly legitimate action, such as resetting your password. When you follow the link to a website, the site looks just like the real thing, but it is not — it's a fake website set up by the phisher. The result is that some unscrupulous person now has your password, and you can imagine the possible consequences.

Note

Is spam related to viruses? Not directly, although viruses often arrive as part of a spam message (but can come with a legitimate message, too). ■

Blocking and Allowing Specific Addresses

A very useful tool in the fight against spam is Outlook's ability to define lists of e-mail addresses and domains that are always blocked or always allowed through.

Defining Safe Senders

A *safe sender* is a person, or more precisely an e-mail address, whose e-mail messages are always considered to be OK — not spam — regardless of the content. Sometimes a Safe Senders list is called a *white list*. You can create a Safe Senders list based on your contacts and by entering individual addresses. You can also specify entire domains as safe — for example, all messages from Microsoft.com would be considered to be safe. Here are the steps to follow:

1. Click the Junk button in the Delete group of the Home tab in the main Outlook window, and then click Junk E-mail Options to display the Junk E-mail Options dialog box.

2. Click the Safe Senders tab (shown in Figure 28-2).

3. To add an address or domain to the list, click the Add button.

4. Enter the address (e.g., someone@microsoft.com) or the domain (e.g., microsoft.com or @microsoft.com).

5. Click OK to add the address or domain to the safe list.

6. To edit or remove a safe list entry, highlight it in the list and then click the Edit or Remove button.

7. Click OK.

The other two options in this dialog box are self-explanatory. Having the Also Trust E-mail from My Contacts option selected saves you the effort of entering these addresses manually.

FIGURE 28-2

Defining your Safe Senders list

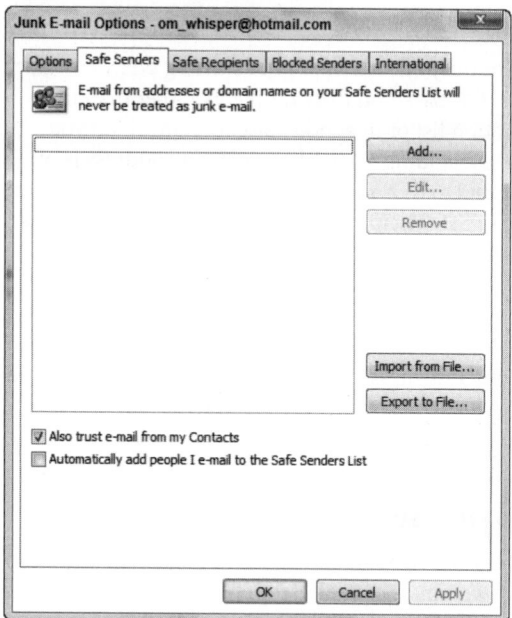

The Import and Export tools are useful if you want to transfer a safe list between Outlook and another e-mail program, or pass your safe list to a friend or colleague. The import/export format is a plain-text file with one address per line.

Blocking/Allowing Individual Senders

The shortcut menu is a fast way to add addresses to your safe and blocked lists. All you have to do is right-click on the message in the Inbox (or whatever folder it is in), choose Junk in the shortcut menu, and then choose the desired action from the submenu. If you have opened a message, you can use the commands in the Junk list in the Delete group of the Message tab on the Ribbon to perform the same commands:

- **Block Sender.** Adds the message sender to your Blocked Senders list.
- **Never Block Sender.** Prevents messages from the sender from being placed in the Junk E-mail folder.
- **Never Block Sender's Domain.** Prevents messages from all senders from a particular domain from being placed in the Junk E-mail folder.
- **Never Block This Group or Mailing List.** Prevents messages addressed to the same group or mailing list used in the message from being placed in the Junk E-mail folder.

- **Not Junk.** This command is available only if the message is in your Junk E-mail folder. Click to move the message to the Inbox and add the sender to your Safe Senders list.

Defining Safe Recipients

The Safe Recipients list, located on another tab in the Junk E-mail Options dialog box, is similar to the Safe Senders list, but it marks messages as OK based on their *recipients* rather than their sender. This is useful when you are on a distribution list or in another situation in which you receive e-mails that are sent to a list of recipients, including you. When an e-mail address is on the Safe Recipients list, any message sent to you *and* to that address will never be treated as spam, regardless of the message sender and content. The Safe Recipients tab works exactly the same as the Safe Senders tab, described in the previous section.

Defining Blocked Senders

A *blocked sender* is an e-mail address or domain whose messages are always treated as spam. The Blocked Senders tab in the Junk E-mail Options dialog box works exactly like the Safe Senders tab as described earlier.

International Junk E-mail Options

You may receive some e-mails that appear to be gibberish — random, meaningless characters. These messages occur when a sender's e-mail program uses a different character encoding than the one you are using. For example, a person in China likely uses Chinese encoding to create a message in Chinese characters. If your e-mail reader is set to use, say, English encoding, the message displays as gibberish. Outlook lets you block messages that use specified character encodings. It also lets you block e-mails from certain countries based on the top-level domain of the sender's address. Here are the steps to follow:

1. Click the Junk button in the Delete group of the Home tab in the main Outlook window, and then click Junk E-mail Options to display the Junk E-mail Options dialog box.

2. Click the International tab.

3. To block top-level domains, click the Blocked Top-Level Domains button to display a list of domains (Figure 28-3).

Note

The top-level domain of an e-mail address is the part after the last period. People in the United States are used to seeing top-level domains such as .com, .org, and .edu that indicate the type or organization. In the rest of the world, however, the top-level domain usually identifies the country of origin — for example, .ca for Canada, .cn for China, and .fr for France. ∎

4. Select the domains you want to block, and then click OK.

5. To block character encodings, click the Blocked Encodings List to display a list of encodings (Figure 28-4).

6. Select the character encodings you want to block, and then click OK.

7. Click OK to close the Junk E-mail Options dialog box.

FIGURE 28-3

Specifying top-level domains to block

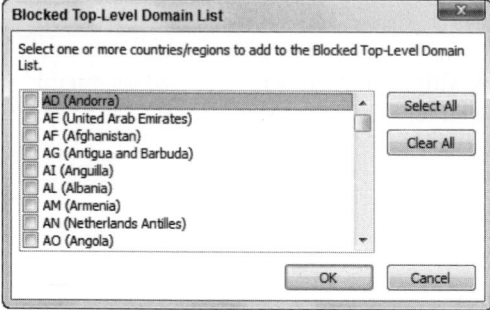

FIGURE 28-4

Specifying character encodings to block

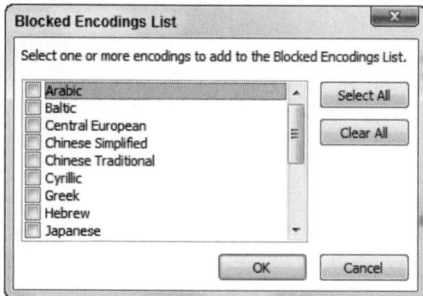

Understanding E-mail Rule Basics

Outlook lets you automate the handling of e-mail messages with *rules*. A *rule* can perform actions such as moving messages from a specific person to a designated folder or deleting messages with certain words in the subject. Rules can also display alerts, play sounds, and move InfoPath forms and RSS feed items. Rules can help you save time and stay organized.

Outlook e-mail rules are all similar in that they specify a *condition* and an *action*. A rule can be defined to apply to e-mail messages when they arrive, which is most common, and to messages as you send them. The Rules Wizard, through which you create rules, provides a set of partially defined rules for commonly needed actions — all you need to do is fill in the details. This wizard also provides the capability to define a rule completely from scratch, a feature you'll use if one of the existing rule templates does not meet your needs.

Creating a New Rule

To create a new e-mail rule, click the Rules button in the Move group of the Home tab in the Outlook window, and then click Manage Rules & Alerts. Outlook displays the Rules and Alerts dialog box, in which you should select the E-mail Rules tab. If you have any rules already defined, they are listed here. You can work with existing rules as described later in this chapter. To create a new rule, click the New Rule button to display the Rules Wizard, as shown in Figure 28-5.

FIGURE 28-5

The first step in defining a new rule

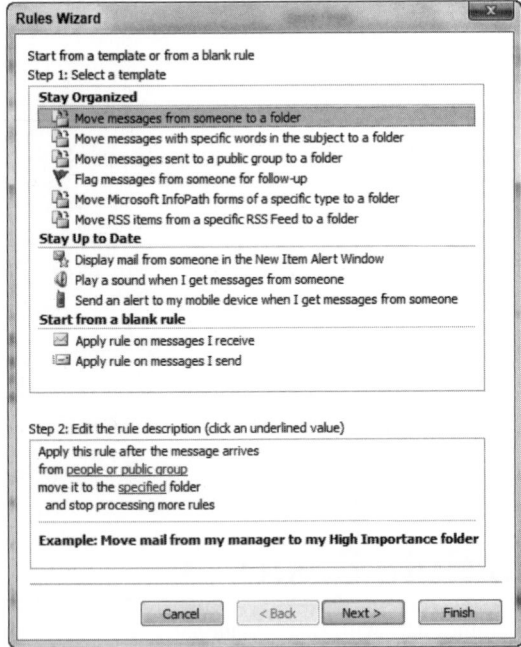

You can see that this dialog box has two parts, Step 1: Select a Template at the top and Step 2: Edit the Rule Description at the bottom. The following sections look at these in turn.

Selecting a Rule Template

The first step, selecting a template, of this dialog box is divided into three subsections, each containing two or more templates:

- **Stay Organized:** Templates that move, delete, or flag messages or other items
- **Stay Up to Date:** Templates for alerting you when messages arrive
- **Start from a Blank Rule.** Templates that are empty and let you define a rule from scratch

The remainder of this section deals with the first two of these categories. Starting from a blank rule is covered separately later in this chapter.

When you click on an item in the Select a Template section, the Step 2: Edit the Rule Description section displays the rule definition along with an example. Editing the definition is covered next.

Editing a Rule Description

A rule definition contains underlined elements that represent the parts of the rule that you can edit. Figure 28-5, for example, shows a definition with two editable elements: *people or public group* and *specified*. When you click such an underlined element, Outlook opens a dialog box in which you can specify the details. In this example:

- Click People or Public Group to open a dialog box in which you can select the people, distribution lists, or both from your Address Book. The rule will be applied to messages from the selected people.
- Click Specified to select a folder to which matching messages will be moved.

After you have made selections for the editable rule items, the rule displays the selected information. An example is shown in Figure 28-6, in which the rule is defined to move messages from "Alan Robbins" to the "Clients" folder. Note that these elements of the rule are still underlined and can be clicked on to make changes as needed.

Finishing the Rule

At this point, the rule is ready to use. You can click Finish in the Rules Wizard dialog box to save the rule. In some cases, you may want to fine-tune the rule; if so, click the Next button. Fine-tuning a rule is essentially the same as creating a rule from a blank template, which is covered in the next section.

FIGURE 28-6

A completed rule definition displays the details that you have specified

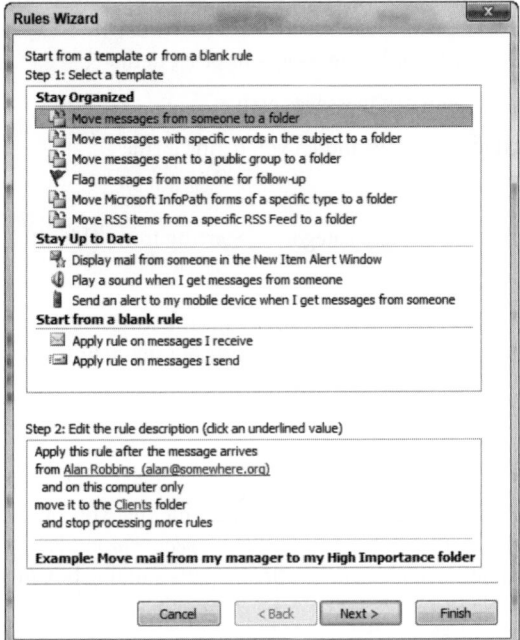

Creating a Rule from a Blank Template

If the rule templates that Outlook provides do not suit your needs, you can create a rule from a blank template. In the first step of the Rules Wizard, shown earlier in Figure 28-5, you must select one of the following from the Start from a Blank Rule section:

- **Apply Rule on Messages I Receive.** Creates a rule that works with messages you receive.

- **Apply Rule on Messages I Send.** Creates a rule that works with messages you send.

After making your selection, click the Next button. Outlook displays the next Rules Wizard step as shown in Figure 28-7. You use this dialog box to specify the conditions for the rule. You can have more than one condition for a rule. When you do, all conditions must be met for a message to be processed. The steps to follow are:

1. Click the box next to a description to place a checkmark in the box and add the condition to the rule description.

2. If the condition requires it, click the underlined element in the description to specify the details.

3. Repeat Steps 1 and 2 if needed to add conditions to the rule.

FIGURE 28-7

Selecting conditions for a rule

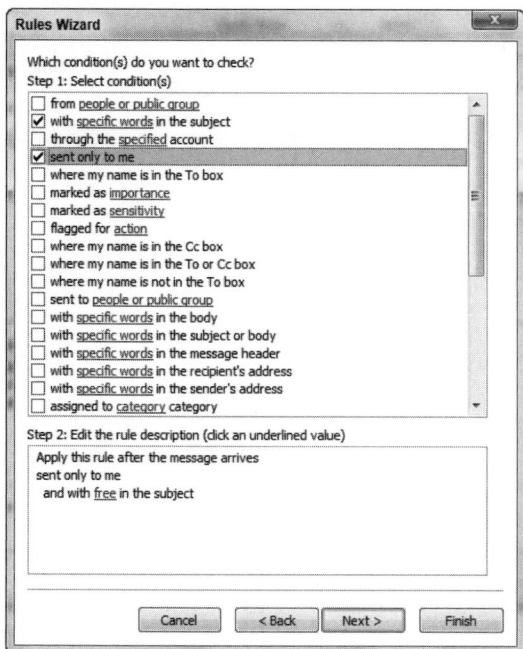

4. **Click the Next button to proceed to the next Wizard step, where you will define the rule's action.** This dialog box is shown in Figure 28-8.

5. **Select the action that you want to be part of the rule.**

6. **If necessary, click any underlined element in the action to specify the details.**

7. **Click Next to display the next Wizard step, where you specify any exceptions to the rule (Figure 28-9).** An exception lets you modify a rule, as in this example: "If the message subject contains the word *free*, delete it unless the message is marked High Importance." Exceptions are optional, and they are added the same way as conditions and actions.

8. **Click Next to go to the final step of the Wizard (Figure 28-10).** In this dialog box, you specify a name for the rule and have the opportunity to edit the rule by clicking underlined elements in the rule description. You can also set the following options:

   - **Run This Rule Now on Messages Already in "*Account.*"** Apply the rule to messages already in your mailbox.

   - **Turn on This Rule.** Enable the rule for newly received or sent messages.

   - **Create This Rule on All Accounts.** Apply the rule for all your e-mail accounts (relevant only if you have multiple accounts).

9. **Click Finish to complete the rule definition and return to the Rules and Alerts dialog box.**

FIGURE 28-8

Selecting an action for a rule

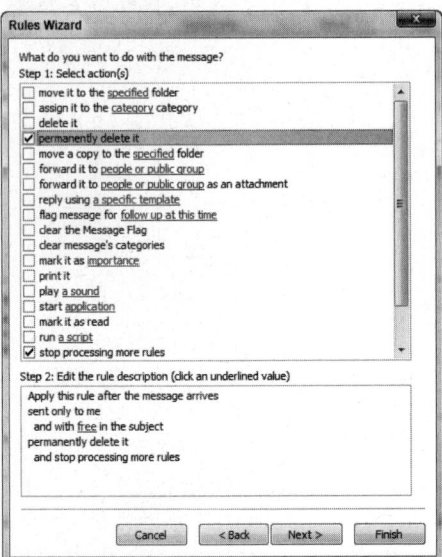

FIGURE 28-9

Specifying exceptions for a rule

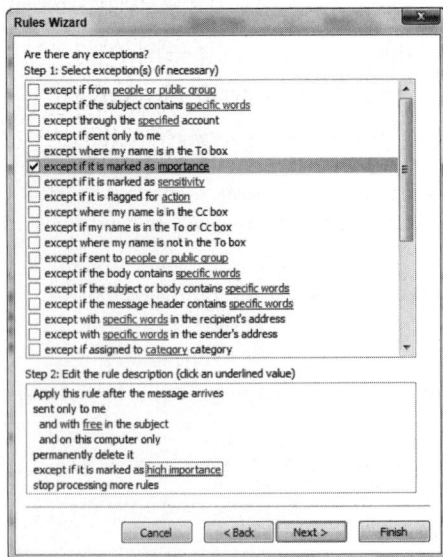

FIGURE 28-10

The final step of the Rules Wizard

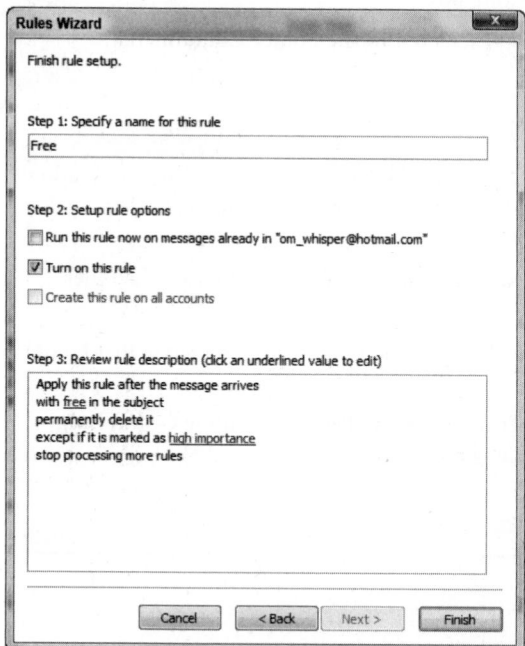

Some Rule Examples

Outlook e-mail rules are admittedly rather complex. It may help you to understand them if you follow the steps required to define a few different kinds of rules.

Rule Example 1

This first rule example shows you how to define a rule that moves all messages from a certain domain to a specified folder. It would be useful if, for example, you are doing some contracting work for a company and are interacting with several people there. This rule moves all e-mail that you receive from anyone at that company into one folder, helping you to stay organized.

The first step is to create the folder:

1. **In the mail Navigation pane, click on the location where you want to place the new folder.** You can click on a mailbox if you want the new folder to be at the top level in that mailbox. You can also click on an existing folder to create the new folder within that folder.

2. **Click the Folder tab on the Ribbon, and then click New Folder in the New Group.** Outlook displays the Create New Folder dialog box.

3. **Enter the new folder name in the Name box.**

4. **Make sure that Mail and Post Items is selected in the Folder Contains list.**

5. **Click OK.**

Now that you have created the folder, you can proceed to defining the rule:

1. **Click the Rules button in the Move group of the Home tab in the Outlook window, and then click Manage Rules & Alerts.** Outlook displays the Rules and Alerts dialog box, with the E-mail Rules tab selected.

2. **On the E-mail Rules tab, click the New Rule button.** Outlook displays the Rules Wizard dialog box.

3. **In the Stay Organized section, click the Move Messages from Someone to a Folder template.**

4. **In the Edit the Rule Description section, click the People or Public Group link.** Outlook displays the Rule Address dialog box (Figure 28-11).

FIGURE 28-11

Specifying an address to be part of a new e-mail rule

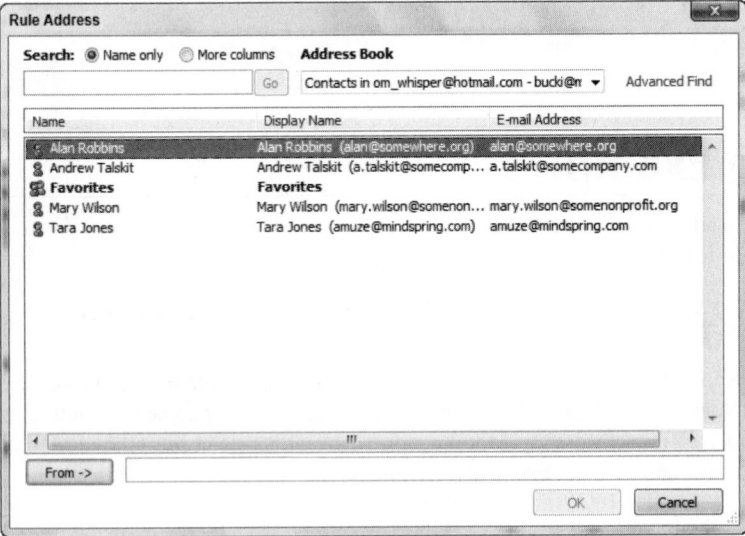

5. **If you wanted to move messages from a single individual who is in your Contacts list, you could click that person's entry in the list and then click the From button.** Because we want to move all messages from a domain, enter **acme.com** in the From box.

6. Click OK.

7. **Click Cancel in the dialog box claiming not to recognize "acme.com" because it is not a complete e-mail address.** This is OK; closing this dialog box returns you to the Rules Wizard.

8. **In the Edit the Rule Description section, click the *specified* link.** Outlook displays the Rules and Alerts dialog box.

9. **Select the desired destination folder and then click OK.** Note that if you had not created the new folder earlier, you could do it now by clicking the New button in this dialog box.

10. **Back in the Rules Wizard dialog box, click the Finish button to close the Rules Wizard and return to the Rules and Alerts dialog box.**

After you create a rule, you will see it listed in the Rules and Alerts dialog box. It is assigned a default name based on the information in the rule. You can, if desired, change the rule name as explained later in this chapter in the section on managing rules.

Rule Example 2

This rule example shows you how you can use a rule to help guard against spam. Let's say that you receive many junk e-mails offering to sell you prescription medication online. However, the subject of the message is often disguised, so you want to define a rule that looks for the word *prescription* in both the subject and the body of the message, and if the word is found, Outlook deletes the message.

But there's a wrinkle — you do in fact get some meds from a legitimate online drug store, and you do not want e-mails from that store to be caught — so the rule will have to include an exception. Here are the steps for creating this rule:

1. **Click the Rules button in the Move group of the Home tab in the Outlook window, and then click Manage Rules & Alerts.** Outlook displays the Rules and Alerts dialog box, with the E-mail Rules tab selected.

2. **On the E-mail Rules tab, click the New Rule button.** Outlook displays the Rules Wizard dialog box.

3. **In the Start from a Blank Rule section, select the Apply Rule on Messages I Receive template.**

4. **Click Next to display a list of conditions.**

5. **Select With Specific Words in the Subject or Body.**

6. **In the lower part of this dialog box, click the *Specific Words* link to open the Search Text dialog box (Figure 28-12).**

7. **Enter prescription in the upper box, and then click Add to add the word to the list.** If you wanted to search for more than one word, you would repeat this step as needed.

8. **Click OK to return to the Rules Wizard dialog box.**

9. **Click Next to display a list of actions.**

10. **Select the Delete It action.** Doing so tells Outlook to move matching messages to the Deleted Items folder. You can also select the Permanently Delete It action, which does precisely what it says.

11. **Click Next to display a list of exceptions.**

12. **Select the Except if from *People or Public Group* exception.**

13. **In the lower part of the dialog box, click the *People or Public Group* link to display the Rule Address dialog box.**

14. **If the legitimate online pharmacy's address is in your Contacts list, you can add it using the From button.** Otherwise, just type it in the From box and then click OK.

15. **Back in the Rules Wizard dialog box, click Finish to complete your rule definition.**

FIGURE 28-12

Use this dialog box to specify words that will be searched for in a message.

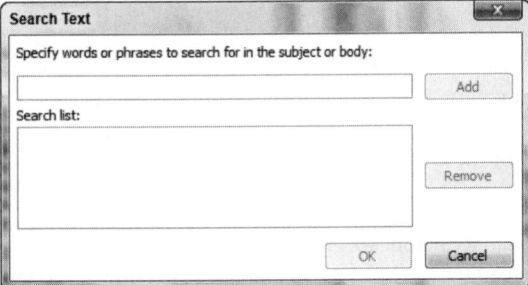

Rule Example 3

Our final rule example shows you how to process messages that you send. Suppose that your major client is Acme Corporation and you have created an Outlook category specifically for items that are related to Acme. You want all messages you send to Acme to be placed in this category automatically. Here's how:

1. **Click the Rules button in the Move group of the Home tab in the Outlook window, and then click Manage Rules & Alerts.** Outlook displays the Rules and Alerts dialog box, with the E-mail Rules tab selected.

2. **On the E-mail Rules tab, click the New Rule button.** Outlook displays the Rules Wizard dialog box.

3. In the Start from a Blank Rule section, select the Apply Rule on Messages I Send template.

4. Click Next to display a list of conditions.

5. Select Sent to *People or Public Group*.

6. In the lower part of the dialog box, click the *People or Public Group* link to open the Rule Address dialog box.

7. Enter acme.com in the To box and then click OK.

8. Click Cancel in the dialog box claiming not to recognize "acme.com" because it is not a complete e-mail address. You will return to the Rules Wizard.

9. Click Next to display a list of actions.

10. Select the Assigned to *Category* Category option.

11. In the lower part of the dialog box, click the *Category* link to open the Color Categories dialog box (Figure 28-13).

FIGURE 28-13

Selecting a category to assign sent messages to

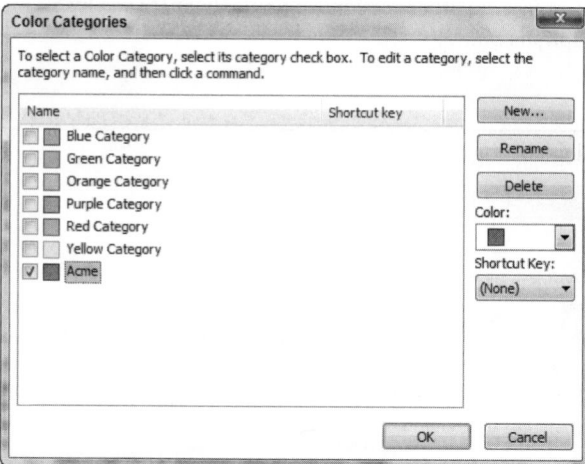

12. Select the desired category — in this case, it would be Acme — then click OK to return to the Rules Wizard dialog box.

13. Back in the Rules Wizard dialog box, click Finish to complete your rule definition.

Managing Rules

When you select Rules ➪ Manage Rules & Alerts from the Move group of the Home tab, the E-mail Rules tab in the Rules and Alerts dialog box lists all the rules that are defined (Figure 28-14). If you have more than one rule, they are applied in top-down order. The actions you can take in this dialog box are the following:

- To edit a rule, click on it and then click the Change Rule button. Then select Edit Rule Settings or Rename Rule from the menu.

- To change a rule's position in the list, click on it and then click the up- or down-arrow button.

- To copy a rule, click on it and then click the Copy button. Outlook will make a copy of the rule, which you can then rename and modify as desired.

- To delete a rule, click on it and then click the Delete button.

- To run rules, click the Run Rules Now button. Then, in the dialog box that is displayed, select the rules to run and the folder(s) and messages to apply the rules to (Figure 28-15).

- To deactivate a rule, click the adjacent box to remove the checkmark.

- To import or export your rules from or to other versions of Outlook, or for use by a friend or colleague, click the Options button.

FIGURE 28-14

You manage your e-mail rules in the Rules and Alerts dialog box.

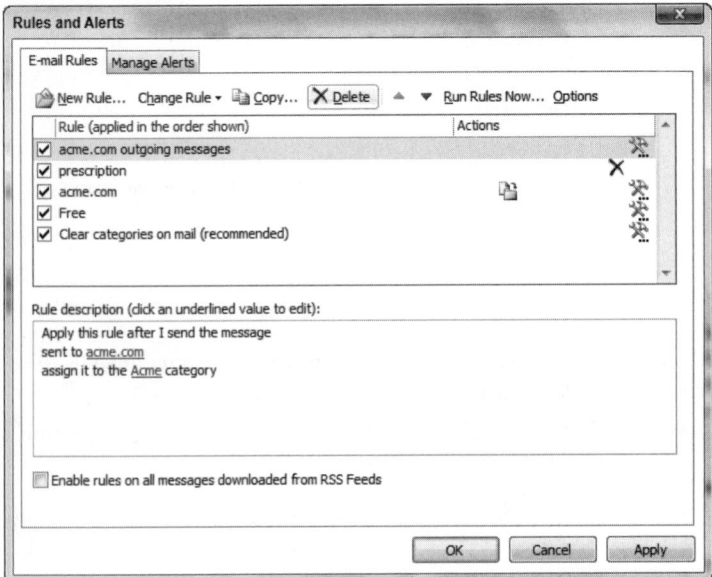

FIGURE 28-15

Running rules manually

Protecting against Viruses

Everyone has heard about *viruses*, malicious software elements that infect and harm computer systems. Technically, a *virus* is a piece of software that not only infects a computer system but also actively spreads itself to other systems usually by means of a host file, similarly to biological viruses that cause colds and other human illnesses. The term is often used more broadly to include other kinds of *malware* — a generic term for harmful software — that do not fit the strict definition of a virus, such as worms and Trojan horses.

Viruses range from the merely annoying to the truly disastrous, but they all have one thing in common — you do not want them on your system! Because viruses often spread by means of e-mail, Outlook provides you with some defenses against them.

It's important to understand that Outlook itself does not have any anti-virus capabilities. An anti-virus program is specialized to detect and remove viruses and will have a way to automatically download the latest virus definitions so that it can stay up-to-date. Symantec, Zone Alarm, and McAfee are three of the better-known publishers of anti-virus software. Microsoft also offers a free anti-virus program called Microsoft Security Essentials, and there are other decent freeware and shareware antivirus programs available. Most systems have anti-virus software installed, and part of protecting yourself against viruses that come with e-mail is to make sure that your anti-virus program is configured properly. Specifically, you should set the anti-virus program's options so that it always scans incoming e-mail and attachments for viruses before they get to Outlook. It's also advisable to set the program to scan outgoing e-mail and attachments in order to prevent you from inadvertently spreading a virus that you have been infected with through other means (such as a floppy disk).

On-demand E-mail Scan

If you have an Outlook-compatible anti-virus program installed, you may find that it has added a command or option for working with the anti-virus program. The details of how the virus scan works and how you set options depend on the specific anti-virus program that you have installed. Please refer to that program's documentation for more information. However, the possible commands fall into two categories:

- **Scan for Viruses.** Opens your anti-virus program and performs an immediate virus scan of e-mail items according to the program options. Use this command when you are not sure that the anti-virus program's automatic scanning is enough.
- **E-mail Scan Properties.** Opens your anti-virus program's Options dialog box, in which you can specify the details of how the program scans e-mail items for viruses.

People worry about getting viruses via e-mail, and I think it's a good idea to reassure them that messages from you are safe. I include a brief note at the bottom of every e-mail that I send that states, "This e-mail message and any attachments have been scanned for viruses by XXX" (where XXX is the name of the anti-virus program that I use).

Protection against Phishing Attacks

Phishing is a technique where you receive an e-mail that appears to be from a legitimate company. The message asks you to click a link to go to the company's website to renew your password or some such thing. Although the site looks legitimate, it is, in fact, a cleverly designed front that lets unscrupulous people get hold of your password. Outlook provides anti-phishing protections, such as the ability to disable links in phishing messages.

Dealing with Attachments

One of the most common ways for viruses to spread is by means of e-mail attachments. However, all attachments are not equal in their ability to spread a virus. Certain file types are potentially very dangerous, such as executable programs, batch files, and installation files. Others, such as image and music files, are generally safe.

Automatically Blocked Attachments

Because of the potential danger posed by some file types, Outlook blocks certain kinds of attachments that are sent to you; you receive the message with a notification that an unsafe attachment has been blocked. This blocking is built into Outlook and cannot be turned off or changed. Some of the more common blocked file types are listed in Table 28-1. You can search Outlook Help for *blocked file types* to see the whole list, which includes many file types you may not be familiar with.

Outlook also catches these file types on the way out — that is, if you try to send them as an attachment. They aren't necessarily blocked, but Outlook reminds you that the recipient may not be able to receive them (and definitely won't if he or she uses Outlook) and asks you if you want to proceed.

TABLE 28-1

File Types That Are Blocked by Outlook

Extension	File Type
ASP	Active Server Page
BAS	BASIC source code
BAT	Batch processing
CER	Internet Security Certificate file
CHM	Compiled HTML help
CMD	DOS CP/M command file, or a command file for Windows NT
COM	Command
EXE	Executable file
.GADGET	Windows Vista gadget
HLP	Windows Help file
JSE	JScript encoded script file
MSC	Microsoft Management Console Snap-in control file (Microsoft)
MSI	Windows Installer File (Microsoft)
MSP	Windows Installer Update
OPS	Office Profile settings file
PIF	Windows Program Information file (Microsoft)
PST	Exchange Address Book file, Outlook Personal Folder File (Microsoft)
TMP	Temporary file/folder

continued

TABLE 28-1	*(continued)*
Extension	**File Type**
URL	Internet location
VB	VBScript file or any Visual Basic source
VBE	VBScript encoded script file
VBS	VBScript script file, Visual Basic for Applications script
WS	Windows script file
WSC	Windows script component
WSF	Windows script file
WSH	Windows Script Host settings file

Blocked File Types and Exchange

If you use an Exchange account for e-mail, these same file types are blocked by default. However, the Exchange administrator can modify the list if needed.

Other Attachment Types

Some other file types are not on the blocked list even though they have the potential to carry viruses. These file types are not blocked because they are very commonly sent as attachments. They include Microsoft Word documents (.docx), Excel workbooks (.xlsx), and PowerPoint files (.pptx). When you receive this kind of file as an attachment, it's important for you to be aware of the potential for harm. Even if you have anti-virus software, you cannot be sure that it will catch every virus, particularly because new ones are created regularly.

The general rule is to not open any such file unless you trust the source. It is also wise to have macro security set to a safe level, as described elsewhere in this chapter.

Sending Blocked File Types

Many people have perfectly legitimate reasons for sending blocked file types as attachments. You have two ways to get around Outlook's restrictions to do this:

1. **Change the file's extension.** For example, if you want to forward a compiled HTML Help file named *MyHelp.CHM*, change the file extension to something that Outlook won't block, such as *MyHelp.TXT*. In your message, instruct the file recipient to change the file extension back before using the file.

2. **Put the file in a ZIP or other kind of archive.** This kind of file is permitted by Outlook. You need to instruct the recipient as to how the file can be extracted, of course.

Sending Zip Files as Attachments

When you create a Zip file, you have the option of protecting it with a password. Although doing so can provide security against unauthorized access to the Zip file's contents, it can prevent anti-virus software from checking the Zip file's contents for viruses.

Also note that Zip files and other archives are often blocked by corporate mail servers as a security measure. You can use suggestion number one above to try to bypass this issue.

Macro Security

A *macro* is a sequence of program commands that have been recorded and saved and can be executed with a single command. Outlook has its own macro capabilities. More germane to the topic of security, however, are the macros in programs such as Microsoft Word and Excel. Such macros are part of the document file and as such are included when the file is sent as an e-mail attachment. (However, you can identify files that contain macros because the file name extension changes, from .docx to .docm for a Word document, for example.) A malicious macro can be set to execute automatically when the file is opened and can potentially wreak havoc on your system and data files. Such viruses are called *macro viruses*.

Anti-virus programs catch most macro viruses, and the precaution of not opening attachments from unknown sources is another layer of protection. The final layer of protection against macro viruses is the macro security level in your programs.

Macro security applies to all Office programs, and it is set in the Trust Center. The Trust Center is an Office component, not specifically part of Outlook or any other any program. On Outlook, you access the Trust Center by clicking File, then clicking Options to open the Outlook Options dialog box. Then, in the list on the left, click Trust Center. Finally, click the Trust Center Settings button, and click Macro Settings in the list at the left to display the macro security settings shown in Figure 28-16.

You can see that the options mention "signed macros." *Digital signing* is a way that the person who creates a macro can "sign" it so that the recipient can be assured that it comes from a trusted source. You'll learn more about digital signatures later in this chapter. You can choose from four levels of macro security, described here from the strictest to the least strict:

- **Disable All Macros Without Notification.** No macros, whether signed or not, are ever run.

- **Notifications for Digitally Signed Macros, All Other Macros Disabled.** For a signed macro, the program displays a notification message and asks you whether it should be run. Unsigned macros are never run. This is the default macro security level.

- **Notifications for All Macros.** The program displays a notification message for any macro, signed or unsigned, and asks you whether it should be run.

- **Enable All Macros.** All macros are run without a notification message. For reasons that are probably obvious, this level is not recommended.

The default level of macro security for all Office programs is recommended. You can always set a lower level temporarily if you want to run some unsigned macros from a trusted source.

FIGURE 28-16

Setting macro security in the Trust Center

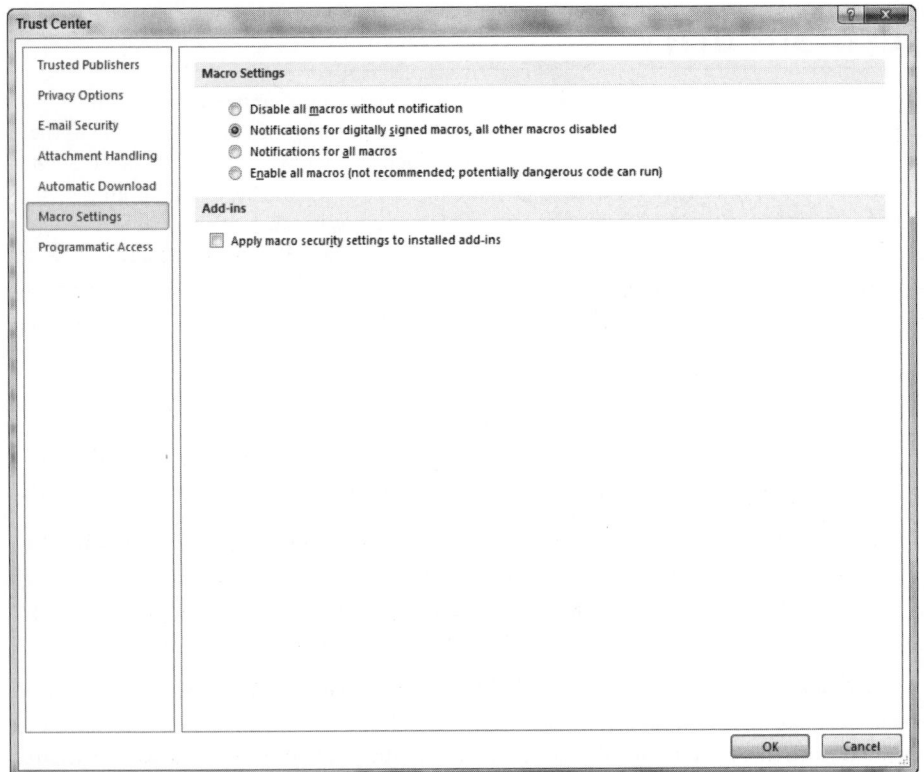

Using Certificates and Digital Signatures

A *certificate*, also known as a *digital ID*, provides a higher level of security with Outlook. You can use a certificate to send encrypted e-mails so that only the intended recipient can view the contents. You can also use them to sign messages to prevent tampering and prove your identity. Finally, you can use a digital ID in lieu of a user name and password to access certain restricted websites, although this use is not relevant to Outlook.

Digital IDs are based on the technique of a *public/private key pair*. These are two long numbers that are related to each other. You can use either key of the pair to encrypt data, and only people who have the other key of the pair are able to un-encrypt the data. When you have a digital signature, you keep your private key secret and make your public key freely available. Here's how it works:

- To send an encrypted message to people, you use their public key to encrypt it. Only they can decrypt the message because no one else has their private key.

- To prove your identity, encrypt some data using your private key. When recipients of a message decrypt the data using your public key, if the data is intact they will know that you must have encrypted it because nobody else has your private key.

Digital certificates have expiration dates, typically one year after they are issued.

Obtaining a Digital ID

If you are using Outlook at work, your employer may provide a digital ID to you that you'll import as described in the next section. Otherwise, you can get your own. Digital IDs are provided by independent companies for a small fee. A digital ID is linked to a specific e-mail address and cannot be used with other addresses.

To get your own digital ID:

1. **Click the File tab, click Options, and then click Trust Center in the list at the left.**

2. **Click the Trust Center Settings button.**

3. **Select E-mail Security from the list on the left side of the Trust Center window to display the E-mail Security page (Figure 28-17).**

4. **Click the Get a Digital ID button.** Your Web browser opens and displays a Microsoft page that lists companies that sell digital IDs.

5. **Select the company you want, and follow the prompts to register for and pay for your digital ID.**

After you complete the ordering process, the issuing company will send you an e-mail containing instructions for installing the digital ID.

Using the Trust Center to get a digital ID

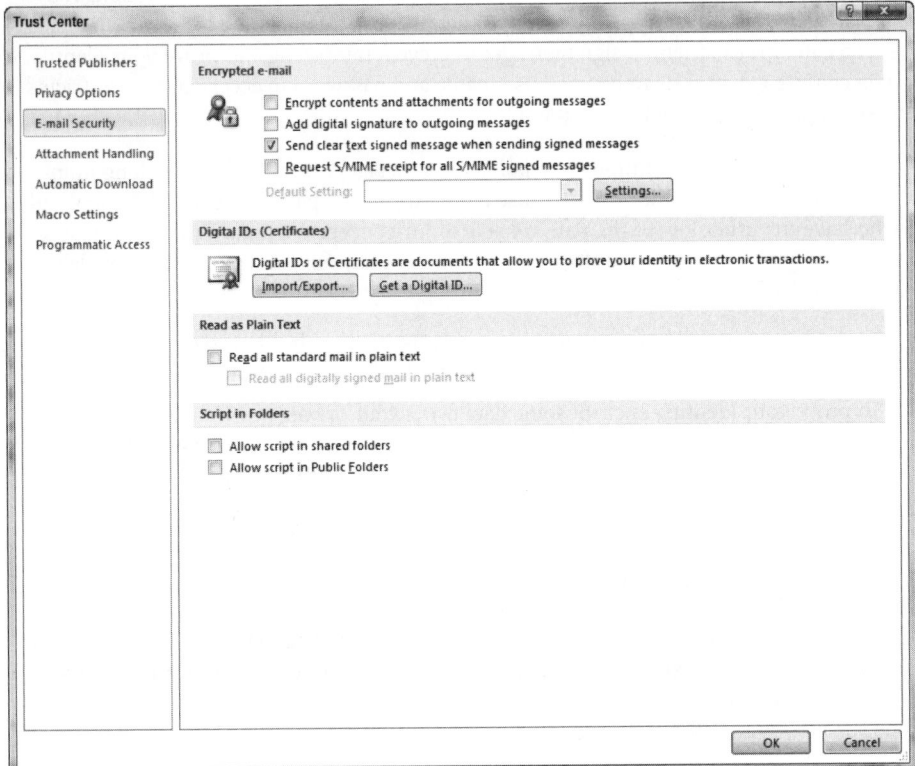

Importing/Exporting Digital IDs

Digital IDs can be provided to you in a file as well as obtained over the Web, as described in the previous section. Your employer may provide you with an ID in a file; you can also export an existing ID to a file for backup purposes or to install it on multiple computers, such as both a personal and a work computer. These files are password protected for security reasons.

To import a digital ID:

1. **Click the File tab, click Options, and then click Trust Center in the list at the left.**

2. **Click the Trust Center Settings button.**

3. **Select E-mail Security from the list on the left.**

4. **Under Digital IDs, click the Import/Export button to display the Import/Export Digital ID dialog box (Figure 28-18).**

FIGURE 28-18

The Import/Export Digital ID dialog box

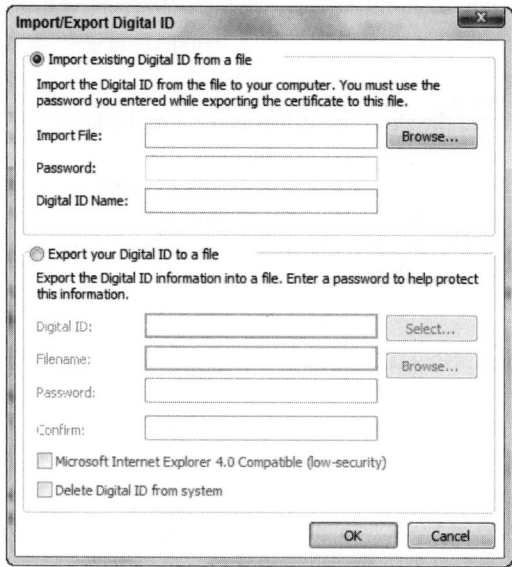

5. Select the Import Existing Digital ID from a File option.

6. Enter the name of the file in the Import File box, or use the Browse button to locate it. Digital ID files have the .epf, .pfx, or .p12 extension.

7. Enter the file password in the Password box.

8. Enter a name of your choosing for the certificate in the Digital ID Name box.

9. Click OK.

Exporting a digital ID uses the same dialog box as shown in Figure 28-18, except you must select the Export option. Then, follow these steps:

1. If you have more than one digital ID, use the Select button to choose the ID to export.

2. Enter the export filename in the Filename box, or use the Browse button to select an export location.

3. Enter and confirm the password in the boxes provided.

4. Select the Microsoft Internet Explorer 4.0 Compatible option only if you will use the exported ID with older versions of Internet Explorer.

5. Select Delete Digital ID from System if you want to completely delete the ID rather than export it.

6. Click OK.

Receiving Digitally Signed Messages

When you receive a digitally signed message, the only difference is that the message says "Signed By XXXX" (where XXXX is the sender's e-mail address) in the header, just below the subject line. You can use such a message to add the sender's public key to your Contacts list, as explained in the next section.

Just because a message is signed does not mean that the signature is legitimate. On the same line that "Signed By XXXX" is displayed, Outlook displays a red ribbon icon, as shown in Figure 28-19, to indicate that the signature is valid. If the signature is not valid, the message "There are problems with the signature" is displayed, and you can click a button to view the details. A digital signature could be invalid because it has expired, the issuing authority has revoked it, or the server that verifies the certificate is invalid.

FIGURE 28-19

The red ribbon icon indicates that the digital signature in a message is valid.

Obtaining Other People's Public Keys

To send an encrypted message to people, you must have their public key. You can get this from a signed message that an intended recipient sent you. That recipient's certificate will be added to his or her entry in Contacts, and it will be available for you to use to send encrypted e-mail. Follow these steps to send an encrypted e-mail message:

1. **Select or open the digitally signed message.**

2. **Right-click on the sender's name or address in the From box.**

3. **Choose Add to Outlook Contacts from the shortcut menu.**

4. **If the contact already exists in your Contacts folder, Outlook notifies you.** Select Update Information of Selected Contact.

You can view a contact's certificates by opening the contact and clicking the Certificates button in the Show section of the Ribbon. Outlook displays a list of the contact's certificates, if there are any, as shown in Figure 28-20. You can take the following actions by clicking the buttons at the right side of this window:

- **Properties.** View the certificate details, including the name of the issuing company and its expiration date.

- **Set as Default.** If the contact has more than one certificate, this command sets the one that will be used as the default for encrypting messages to the contact.

- **Import.** This option lets you import a person's certificate from a file. Certificate files have the .p7c or .cer extension.

- **Export.** This option lets you export the certificate to a file. Doing so can be useful when you want to transfer a contact's certificate to another computer.

- **Remove.** This option deletes the certificate from the contact information.

FIGURE 28-20

Viewing a contact's digital certificates

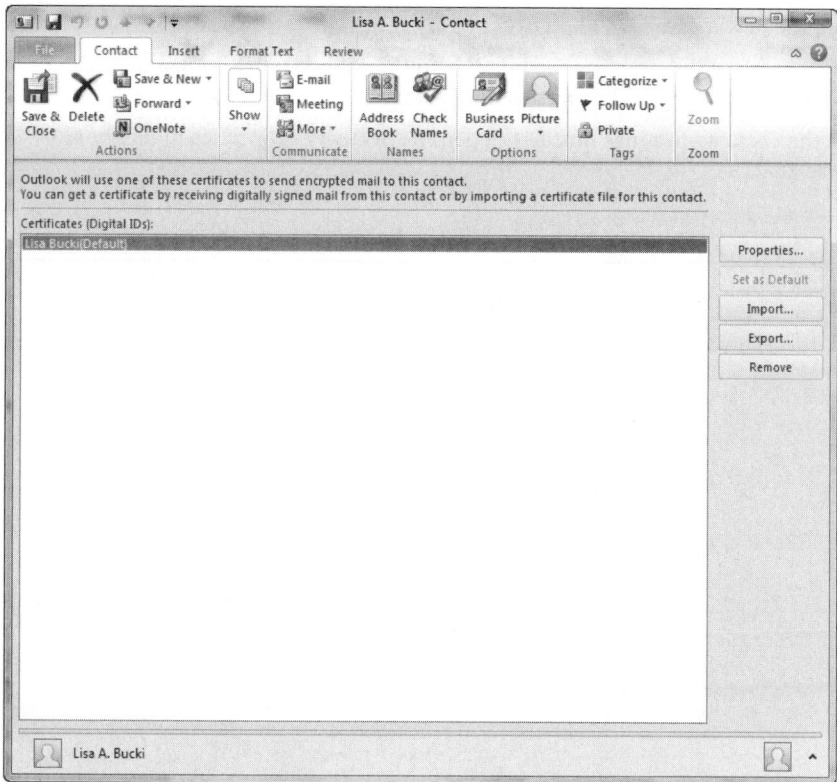

Encrypting and Digitally Signing Messages

It's important to understand that encrypting a message and signing a message are two different things, as follows:

- **Encrypting.** Encrypting uses the recipient's public key to encrypt the message and attachments so that only the recipient can read them.

- **Signing.** Signing uses your digital ID to mark a message so that recipients can verify that it really came from you.

A message can be signed, encrypted, or both.

Encrypting Messages

You can send an encrypted message to anyone for whom you have the public key — in other words, you have that recipient's certificate as part of his or her contact information. You can encrypt single messages or specify that all messages be encrypted (when possible).

To encrypt a single message:

1. **Create the new message.**
2. **In the message window, click the File tab on the Ribbon, click Info, and click Properties to display the Properties dialog box.**
3. **Click the Security Settings button to open the Security Properties dialog box (Figure 28-21).**

FIGURE 28-21

The Security Properties dialog box

4. **Select the Encrypt Message Contents and Attachments option.**
5. **Click OK; then, click Close to return to the message.**
6. **Compose and send the message as usual.**

Of course, messages can be encrypted only when they are going to one or more recipients for whom you have a certificate. If you request encryption for a message going to people for whom you do not have a certificate, Outlook displays a message and gives you the option of sending the message without encryption.

You can also tell Outlook to encrypt all outgoing messages and attachments. Of course, this capability affects only messages that you send to people whose public key you have. To tell Outlook to encrypt all outgoing messages and attachments, follow these steps:

1. **In the main Outlook window, click the File tab, click Options, and then click Trust Center in the list at the left.**

2. **Click the Trust Center Settings button.**

3. **Select E-mail Security from the list on the left.**

4. **Select the Encrypt Contents and Attachments for Outgoing Messages option.**

5. **Close the open dialog boxes.**

Digitally Signing Messages

As with encryption, you can apply digital signatures to individual outgoing messages or to all of them.

To add a digital signature to an individual message:

1. **Create, compose, and address a new e-mail message as usual.**

2. **In the message window, click the File tab on the Ribbon, click Info, and click Properties to display the Properties dialog box.**

3. **Click the Security Settings button to open the Security Properties dialog box (shown previously in Figure 28-21).**

4. **Select the Add Digital Signature to the Message option.**

5. **Click OK; then, click Close to return to the message.**

To add a digital signature to all outgoing messages:

1. **In the main Outlook window, click the File tab, click Options, and then click Trust Center in the list at the left.**

2. **Click the Trust Center Settings button.**

3. **Click E-mail Security.**

4. **In the Encrypted E-mail section, select the Add Digital Signature to Outgoing Messages option.**

5. **Click OK twice.**

HTML Message Dangers

Because HTML messages can contain script and ActiveX controls, they are a potential source of virus attacks. Outlook blocks links and a lot of functionality automatically, and may move a message to the Junk E-mail folder, as well. As shown in Figure 28-22, Outlook displays a notification in the message header when there is blocked content. The notification tells you how to restore the content. For example, you may be instructed to click the notification to download and view blocked pictures.

FIGURE 28-22

Many features in HTML messages are automatically disabled.

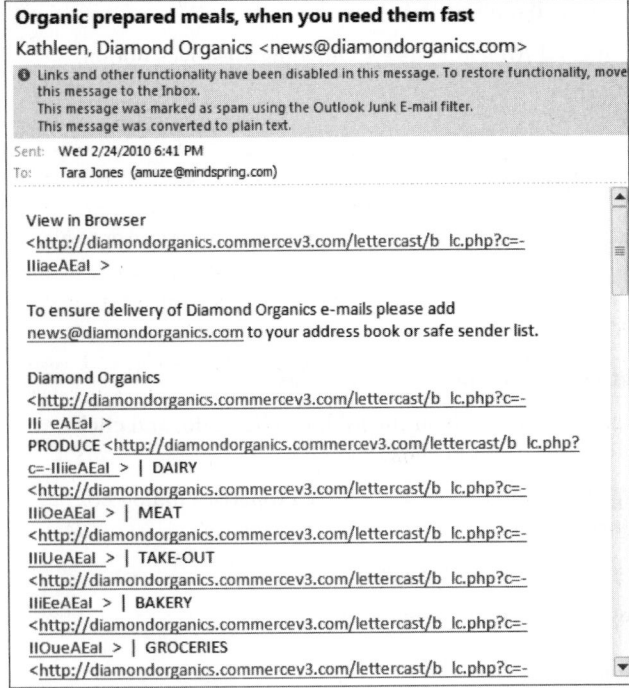

To guard against HTML viruses that make it past your anti-virus software, you can tell Outlook to display HTML messages as plain text. Because scripts and ActiveX controls are not activated until the HTML is displayed, this prevents them from doing harm.

To guard against malicious HTML messages:

1. **In the main Outlook window, click the File tab, click Options, and then click Trust Center in the list at the left.**

2. Click the Trust Center Settings button.

3. Click E-mail Security.

4. Under Read as Plain Text, select Read All Standard Mail in Plain Text (this means unsigned messages).

5. If you want to include digitally signed messages, select Read All Digitally Signed Mail in Plain Text.

Tip

Click Automatic Download in the list at the left to work with settings for other types of downloaded content. ∎

6. Click OK twice.

Summary

Spam, or junk e-mail, is a serious problem for most e-mail users. Outlook provides you with some powerful tools to detect and filter spam. By understanding these tools and using them efficiently, you can greatly reduce the negative impact that spam has on your productivity. E-mail rules are another way that Outlook helps you save time and stay organized. You may be hesitant to spend the time to define a rule, but in the long run they will be well worth the effort. Of course, rules are probably not warranted for situations that arise only occasionally, but most people who rely on e-mail in their work will find plenty of good uses for them. Ignore e-mail security at your own risk. In today's interconnected world, it is all too easy for viruses and other malicious software to spread. Fortunately, Outlook provides you with several tools that help you to protect yourself against these threats.

Working with Contacts

Outlook's Contacts feature is much more than a simple address book. It provides you with powerful tools not only to store but also to find and use information about your business and personal contacts.

Understanding Outlook Contacts

Outlook's Contacts feature is one of its most powerful features. At heart, the Contacts feature is just an address book, but what an address book! Of course, it covers the basics of organizing names, addresses, and phone numbers, but it can do so much more. Many people use Contacts primarily as a way to store people's e-mail addresses for ease of sending e-mails. This is important, but if that's all you use Contacts for, you are really missing out. For example, you should know that you can use Outlook Contacts to:

- Create electronic business cards so that you can send your or other people's contact information by e-mail.

- Store multiple phone numbers, e-mail addresses, and postal addresses for an individual.

- Perform an automated mail merge, creating a mailing to some or all of your contacts.

- Automatically dial a contact's phone number (if your computer is equipped with a modem).

- Store a photograph as part of a contact's information.

- Define custom fields to store whatever information you need as part of a contact.

- View a map of the location of a contact's address.

After you understand all the power of Outlook Contacts, you can use as many or as few of its features as you like.

Note

Personal Address Books, a feature available in earlier versions of Outlook, is no longer supported. ■

The Contacts Window

When you click the Contacts button at the bottom of the Navigation pane, the top part of the pane displays the name of your Address Book. Usually, this name is *My Contacts*. If you have more than one address book, they are all displayed here. Using multiple address books is covered later in this chapter; most people have and need only one.

By default, Contacts appear in Business Card view, as shown in Figure 29-1. Use the Change View button in the Current View group of the Group tab on the Ribbon to select how information will be displayed in the Contacts window. You have four view choices:

- Business Card
- Card
- Phone
- List

Simply click on the view that you want, and the Contacts window changes immediately.

FIGURE 29-1

Business Card view is one of several different ways to view contacts.

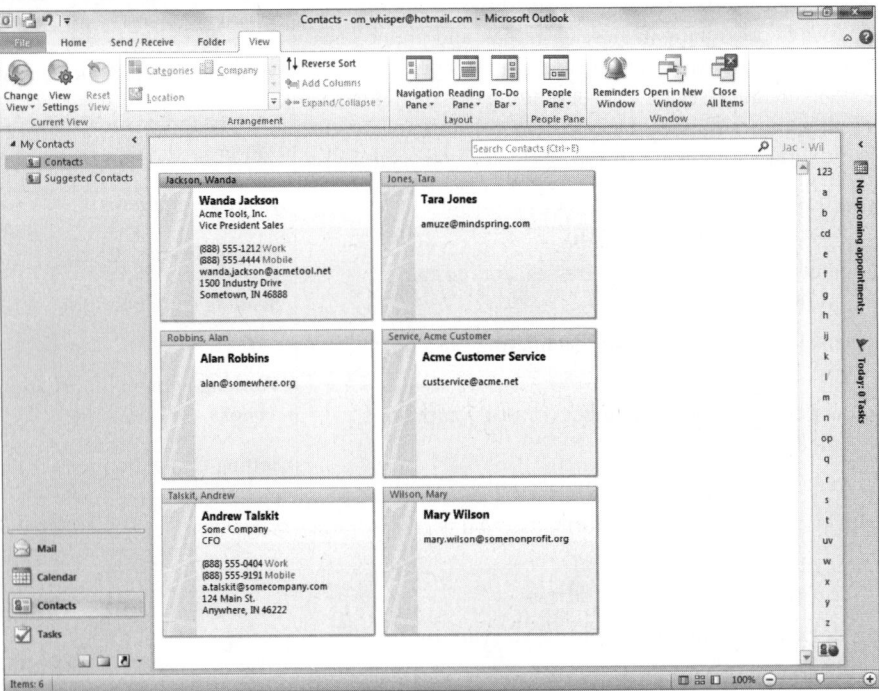

You can create groups to further organize your contacts or customize the view. The next sections look at these.

Adding a New Contact Group

By default, an Address Book is not subdivided. As the number of contacts grows, you may find it useful to define groups to organize contacts in a way that makes them easier to find and use.

Note that Contacts groups are different from the folder groups introduced in Chapter 27. A folder group enables you to store a completely separate list of contacts. You create the folder group and drag contacts from the list into the group.

You create a Contact group, in contrast, so that you can easily send a message to the list of recipients defined in the group. You might have Family and Work Team groups, for example. You could then choose the Family group to send an e-mail to all your family members, and use the Work Team group to e-mail messages to your team members at work.

To define a group, follow these steps:

1. **Make sure that Contacts is selected in the Navigation pane.**

2. **In the New group of the Home tab on the Ribbon, click the New Contact Group button.** The Contact Group window opens.

3. **Type the name for the group in the Name textbox.**

4. **In the Members group of the Contact Group tab of the Ribbon, click the Add Members button, and then click Outlook Contacts.** The Select Members window opens.

5. **Select the contact(s) to add to the group in the list, and click the Members button.** The members appear in the textbox beside the button, as shown in Figure 29-2.

FIGURE 29-2

Adding contacts to a new group

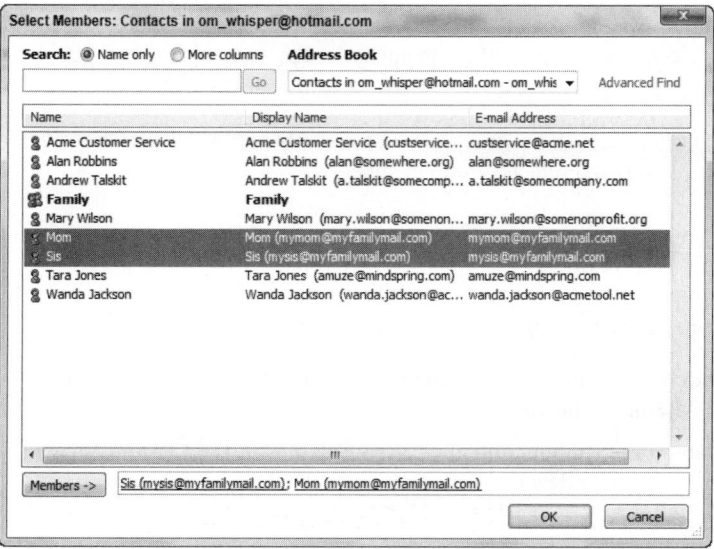

6. After you finish adding all members as desired, click OK.

7. In the Actions group of the Contact Group tab of the Ribbon, click Save & Close. Outlook adds the new group in the list of contacts (Figure 29-3).

FIGURE 29-3

The list of contacts now includes a group called *Family*.

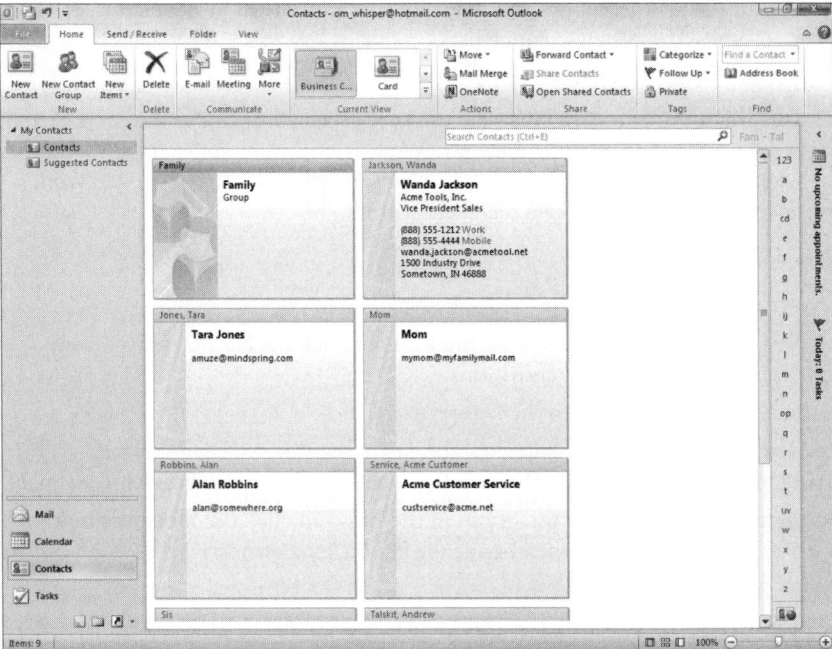

Note that the contacts you add to the group continue to appear in the overall list of contacts, as before.

After you have created one or more additional groups, you can simply double-click on a group to reopen it to change its name or add and remove group members.

Customizing a Contacts View

The different views that Outlook provides for contacts can be customized to suit your needs. You cannot, however, create a new view from scratch. To customize a view:

1. Click the View tab on the Ribbon, click Change View in the Current View group, and then click the name of the view to customize.

2. Click the View tab on the Ribbon, and click View Settings in the Current View group. Outlook displays the Advanced View Settings dialog box (Figure 29-4).

FIGURE 29-4

Customizing a Contacts view

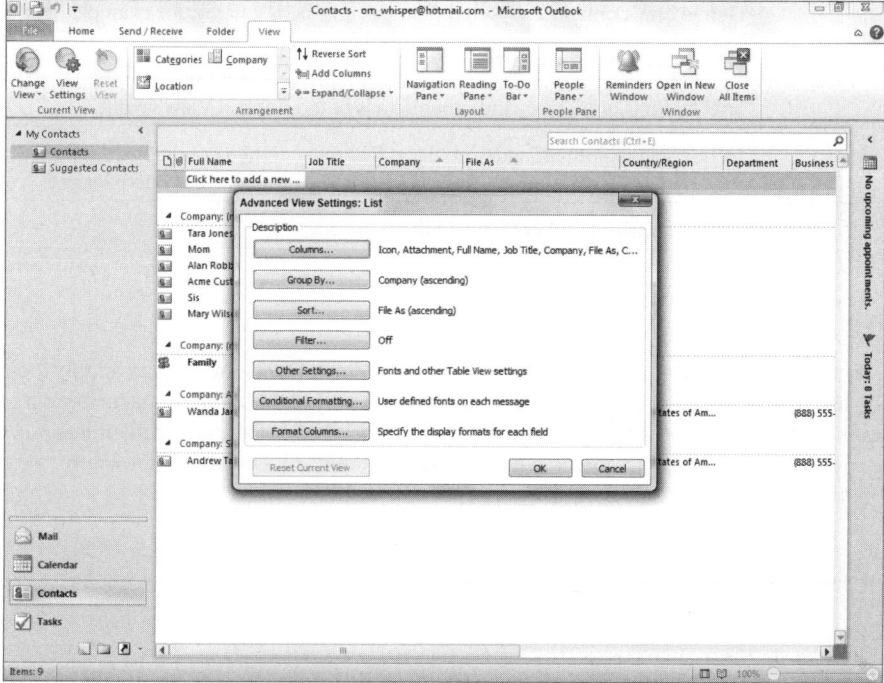

3. **Click on one of the buttons to change related view settings (explained in more detail in the text).** The text next to each button describes the purpose of each.

4. **If necessary, click Reset Current View to return the view to its original default settings.**

5. **Click OK to save your changes and close the dialog box.**

Depending on the view you are customizing, you may have only some of the buttons in the Advanced View Settings dialog box available because certain aspects of a view are not relevant to some views. The aspects of the view that you change with the different buttons are described in Table 29-1.

TABLE 29-1

Components of Customizing a Contacts View

Button	Action
Columns	Specify which fields (items of information) are included in the view.
Group By	Define grouping for the displayed contacts based on one or more fields. For example, you can group contacts by company or state.

continued

TABLE 29-1	(continued)
Button	**Action**
Sort	Define how contacts are sorted. You can sort by last name, for example.
Filter	Display only those contacts that meet your defined criteria.
Other Settings	Specify fonts, grid lines, and other details of the Contact View layout.
Conditional Formatting	Define special formatting for contacts that meet certain conditions, such as for a contact associated with an overdue task or one that has been flagged.
Format Columns	Define formatting for columns in the view.

Finding Contacts

As your Contacts list grows, you may find it helpful to search for contacts rather than simply look through the list hoping to find what you are looking for. At the top right of the Contacts list is a search field in which you type the text that you are looking for. Outlook automatically filters the contacts to show only those that match what you have entered. An example is shown in Figure 29-5. If no matches occur, a message to that effect is displayed.

FIGURE 29-5

Searching for contacts

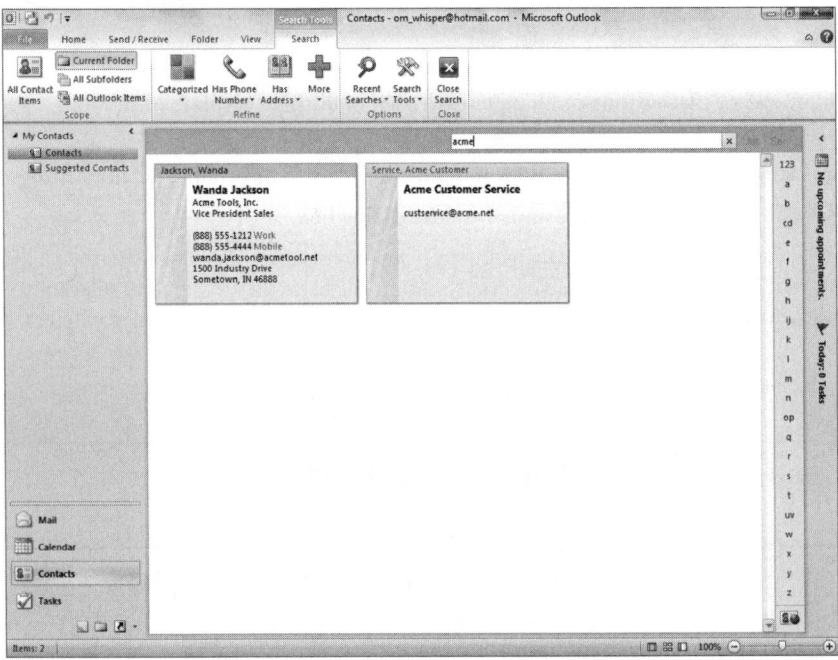

After conducting a search, click the X next to the Search box to clear the search and return to displaying all contacts.

Tip

In some Contacts views, Outlook displays a column of index buttons at the right side of the Contacts window; the first of these buttons is labeled *123*, followed by buttons labeled *A* through *Z*. Click on one of these buttons to scroll the Contacts display to entries that begin with the specified letter. ■

The search I have just described searches all the contact fields for the text you entered. If you want to search in specific fields, you can perform an Advanced Search by clicking in the Search box, clicking the Search Tools button in the Options group of the Search Tools Search tab that appears, and then clicking Advanced Find. Outlook displays the Advanced Find window, as shown in Figure 29-6.

FIGURE 29-6

Performing an Advanced Search in Contacts

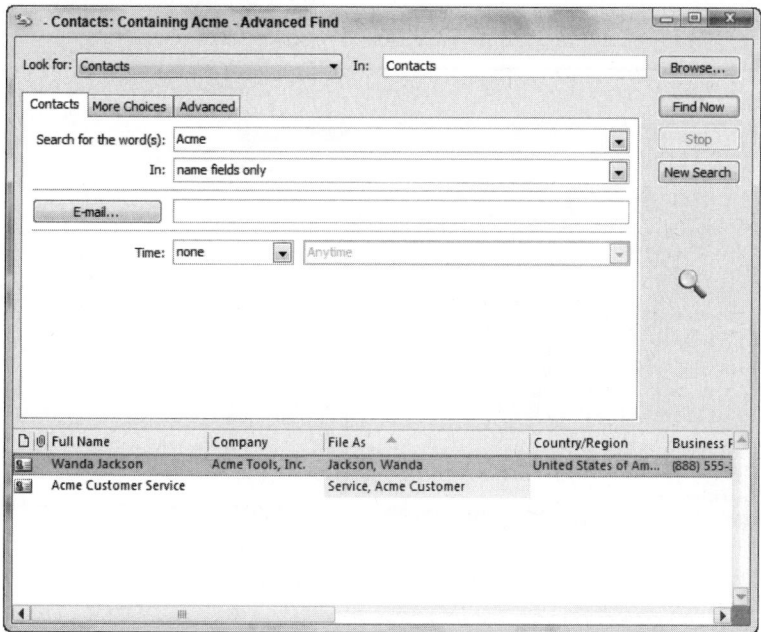

Following are ways to use these tools.

- On the Contacts tab, type the text to search for in the Search for the Word(s) textbox, and then use the In drop-down list to select the field to search.
- Click the More Choices tab to add additional criteria, such as selecting a category to search by.

- To include more fields in the search, click the Advanced tab and use the Field and Add to List buttons to select the desired fields.
- Click Find Now to perform the search. The search results appear at the bottom of the window. Close the window when you finish with the search.

Adding Contacts

Outlook provides you with several ways to add information to the Contacts list.

Adding a Contact Manually

To add a new contact in Contacts, click the New Contact button in the New group of the Ribbon.

Outlook displays a new, blank contact window, as shown in Figure 29-7. Type in the information — only a name is required, and you can use or not use the other fields as you desire — and then click Save & Close in the Actions group on the Contact tab on the Ribbon. If you want to save this contact and enter another, click Save & New. Most of the fields on the contact form are self-explanatory, but I provide full details about the form later in this chapter.

FIGURE 29-7

A blank Contact window

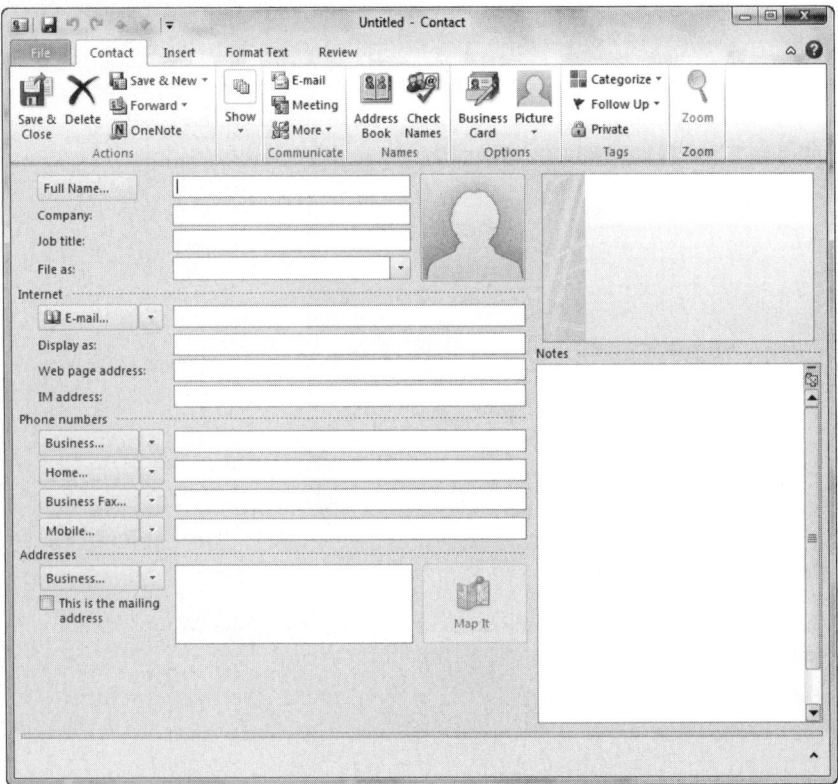

Adding a Contact from a Received E-mail

When you have opened a received e-mail, the From field displays the name or the e-mail address (or both) of the sender. It also displays any other recipients — other than you, that is — in the To and Cc fields. You can add the From person or any of the other To or Cc people to your Contacts list by right-clicking on them and choosing Add to Outlook Contacts from the shortcut menu. Outlook opens a new Contact window with the available information filled in. This information includes only the person's e-mail address and perhaps name. You can add additional information to the Contact form, if desired, and then click Save & Close.

Adding a Contact from an Outlook Contact

The heading of this section may seem confusing, but it makes more sense when you understand that an Outlook user can send a contact as an attachment to an e-mail message. The technique for doing this is covered later in this chapter, in the section, "Sending Contact Information by E-mail."

If you receive a contact in an e-mail message, it appears as an attachment identified by a small Business Card icon and the contact's name, as shown in Figure 29-8. If you double-click on the attachment, Outlook opens a new Contact form with the contact's information entered. You can edit the information if needed and then save it to your list of contacts.

FIGURE 29-8

When you receive an Outlook contact attached to an e-mail message, it is identified by a small Business Card icon.

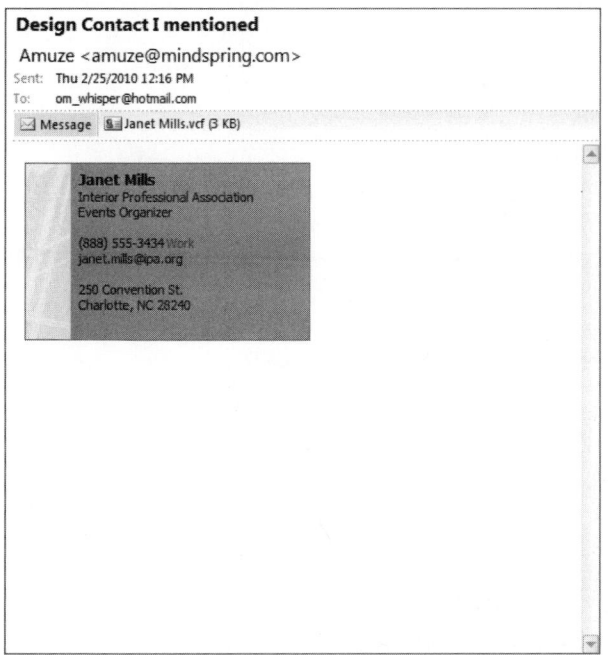

A *vCard file* is a special file format designed to send contact information. Outlook can read vCard files that you may receive from people using other e-mail software.

Sending an E-mail to a Contact or Group

Part of the point of developing the list of contacts and creating groups is to make it even easier to make sure you're addressing e-mail to the correct person(s). To create an e-mail message from Contacts:

1. **In the list of contacts, click on the contact or group to which you want to send an e-mail.** You can Ctrl+click to select multiple contacts that are not in a group.

2. **On the Home tab, click E-mail in the Communicate group.** Outlook opens a new message window, as shown in Figure 29-9.

3. **Complete and send the message as you normally would.**

When you address an e-mail message to a group, the group name is displayed in the To or Cc field of the message with an adjacent + sign, as shown in Figure 29-9. If you click this + sign, the list is expanded to display its individual members just as though you had added them individually to the To or Cc field. This feature can be useful if you want to send a message to everyone on the list except one or two people; you can expand the Distribution list and delete those few individuals from the To or Cc field of the message.

FIGURE 29-9

A group in the To field of an e-mail message

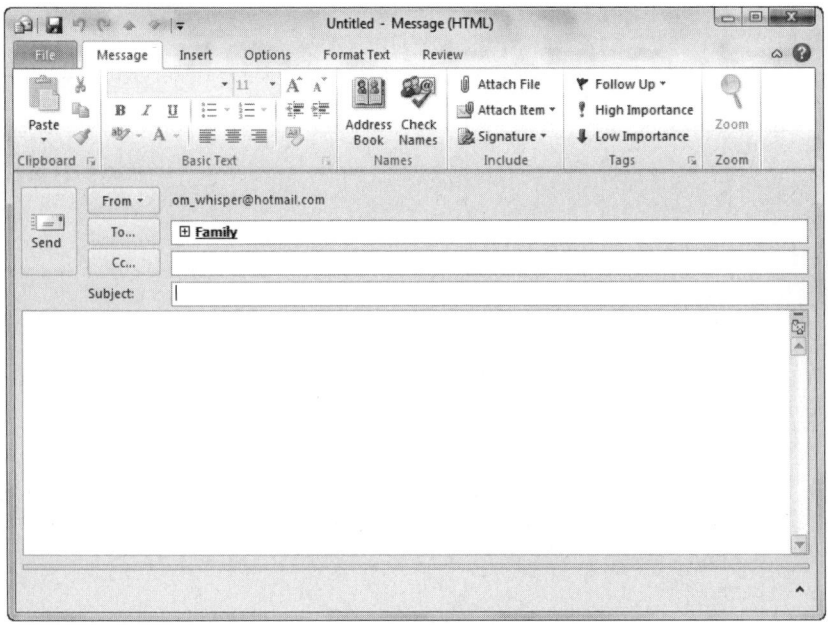

More about Contacts

Outlook Contacts function as much more than as the contents of a simple address book. This section covers additional details and capabilities of Outlook Contacts.

The Contact Window

The Contact window (refer to Figure 29-7) that appears when you create a contact or that you can reopen at any time by double-clicking on the contact provides places for you to enter many different kinds of information about a contact. The only field that is required is the name; you can use all, some, or none of the other fields, as you like. Some of the elements on the Contacts window may deserve an explanation, as provided in the following sections.

Quick E-mail

When a contact is open, click the E-mail button in the Communicate group of the Contact tab on the Ribbon to create a new e-mail message addressed to the contact.

Full Name

You can simply enter a contact's name in the Full Name field in the usual way, for example, **John Q. Public**. You can also click the adjacent Full Name button to bring up the Check Full Name dialog box, shown in Figure 29-10. Here you can specify a title such as *Dr.* or *Mrs.* and a suffix such as *Jr.* or *Sr.*

FIGURE 29-10

The Check Full Name dialog box lets you enter more details for a contact's name.

Note the option in this dialog box: Show This Again When Name Is Incomplete or Unclear. When this option is on (the default), Outlook opens this dialog box automatically when you enter an incomplete name such as *Fred* in the Full Name field.

The File As field determines how a contact will be filed in the Address Book. The default is last name first ("Public, John Q."), but you can also choose to file a contact first name first.

Phone Numbers

The Phone Numbers section of the Contacts window provides spaces for four numbers. By default, these are labeled as Business, Home, Business Fax, and Mobile, but you can change which numbers are displayed in a particular Phone Number field by clicking the adjacent down-arrow and selecting from the list. Some of the choices available are Home Fax, Pager, and Assistant. Outlook can save a phone number for each designation, but only four numbers are displayed on the Contacts window at one time. When you open the list of designations, those for which you have entered a phone number are checked.

Next to each Phone Number field is a button with the field's designation on it. If you click on one of these buttons, Outlook opens the Check Phone Number dialog box, shown in Figure 29-11. Here you can enter additional details for the phone number if desired.

FIGURE 29-11

The Check Phone Number dialog box lets you enter more details for a contact's phone number.

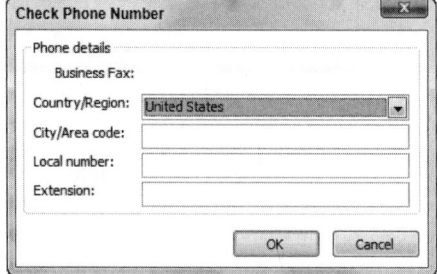

Addresses

The Addresses section of the Contacts window can store up to three addresses designated as Home, Business, and Other. Select the one to display by clicking the down-arrow adjacent to the Address box. Click the adjacent button to open the Check Address dialog box (Figure 29-12), in which you can enter or edit address details. By default, Outlook displays this dialog box auto-matically if you enter an address that appears to be incomplete or unclear.

One of the addresses for a contact can be designated as the mailing address by selecting the corresponding option. Outlook uses this address when you are doing a mail merge using Outlook contact data. Mail merge is discussed later in this chapter.

Picture

You can associate a picture with a contact by clicking the Picture button in the Options group of the Contact tab in the Contacts window and then clicking Add Picture. Outlook displays a dialog box that lets you browse for the picture file. The picture file can be the person's picture, a company logo, or just a unique image that you want to use to identify the person. When you have associated a picture with a contact, it displays on the picture button and on the contact's Business Card, as shown in Figure 29-13. To remove or change the picture, right-click on it and choose from the shortcut menu.

FIGURE 29-12

The Check Address dialog box lets you enter more details for a contact's address.

FIGURE 29-13

You can associate a picture with a contact.

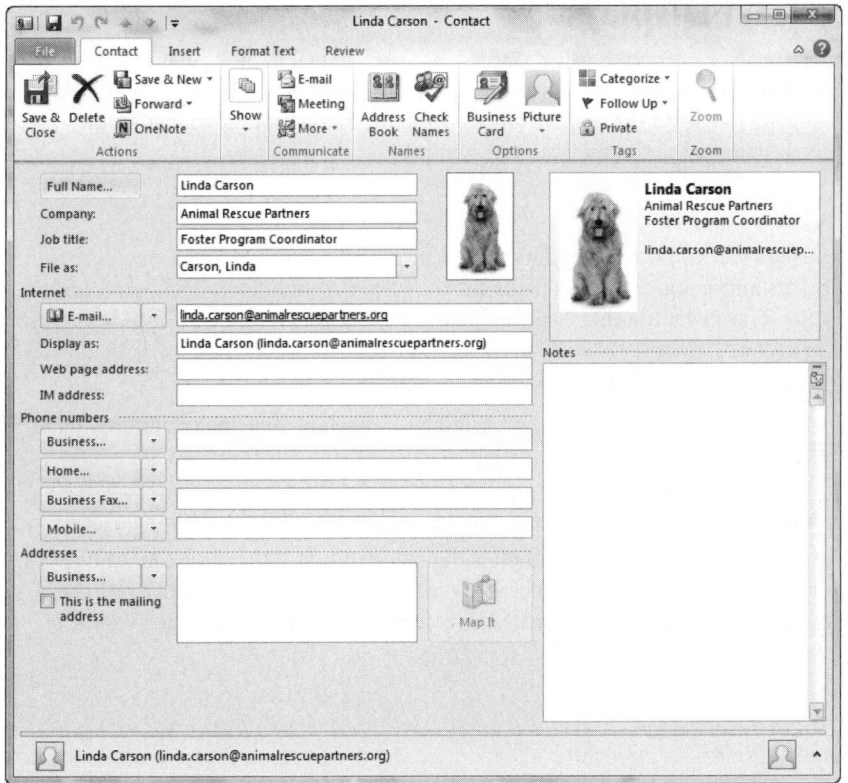

E-mail Addresses

Outlook can store as many as three e-mail addresses for a contact, designated as *E-mail*, *E-mail 2*, and *E-mail 3*. You select which one to display on the Contact window using the arrow adjacent to the E-mail button.

If you create an e-mail message to a contact by clicking the E-mail button on the Contact tab of the Ribbon in a Contact window, Outlook creates a message addressed to all the e-mail addresses for that contact. If you click the To button on an e-mail message, the list of contacts displays each e-mail separately, and you can choose the one to use.

The Display As field determines how the contact is displayed in a message's To or Cc field. By default, Outlook displays the contact's name followed by the e-mail address in parentheses, but you can edit this to display as desired — for example, just the person's name.

Notes

The Notes section on a Contact window is for entry of any arbitrary information that you want to save with the contact. Simply click in the box and enter or edit as usual. You can use the tools on the Format Text tab of the Ribbon to apply formatting to the Notes text, if desired.

Other Contact Displays

The default display for an open contact, called *General*, has been shown in the figures throughout this chapter so far. This is the display that you will probably use most often. Several other displays, or views, are available; you select the display to view from the Show drop-down list on the Contact tab of the Ribbon in the Contact message window.

Details View

The Details view gives you access to secondary information about a contact. This view is shown in Figure 29-14. This information includes fields such as Department, Office, Nickname, and Spouse/Partner. You may never use this view, but it's available if you need it.

Activities View

When you use the Activities view in the Contact window, it displays all items pertaining to the contact, such as e-mails and tasks.

Certificates View

One of the security features available in Outlook is digital certificates. A contact can send you a certificate, and you can then use this certificate to send encrypted mail to that person. The Certificates display lets you view and work with the certificate(s) that you have for a contact. Digital certificates are covered in Chapter 28.

FIGURE 29-14

The Details view for a contact

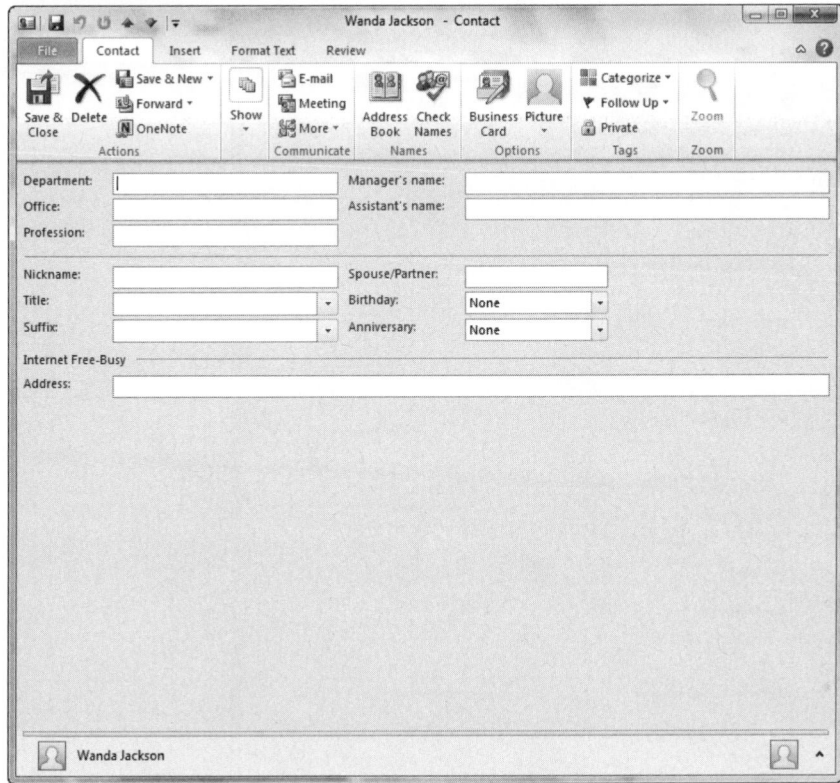

All Fields View

The All Fields view lets you view all or selected subsets of the data associated with a contact. The amount of information — number of fields — that an individual contact can hold is quite impressive and is way too much to display fully in any other contact view. The All Fields display also lets you define your own custom fields for a contact and to change the properties of some fields.

The All Fields display is shown in Figure 29-15. Near the top is the Select From list, in which you choose which fields to display in the window. You can display all fields as well as one of several defined subsets, such as All Contact Fields or All Mail Fields.

FIGURE 29-15

The All Fields view for a contact

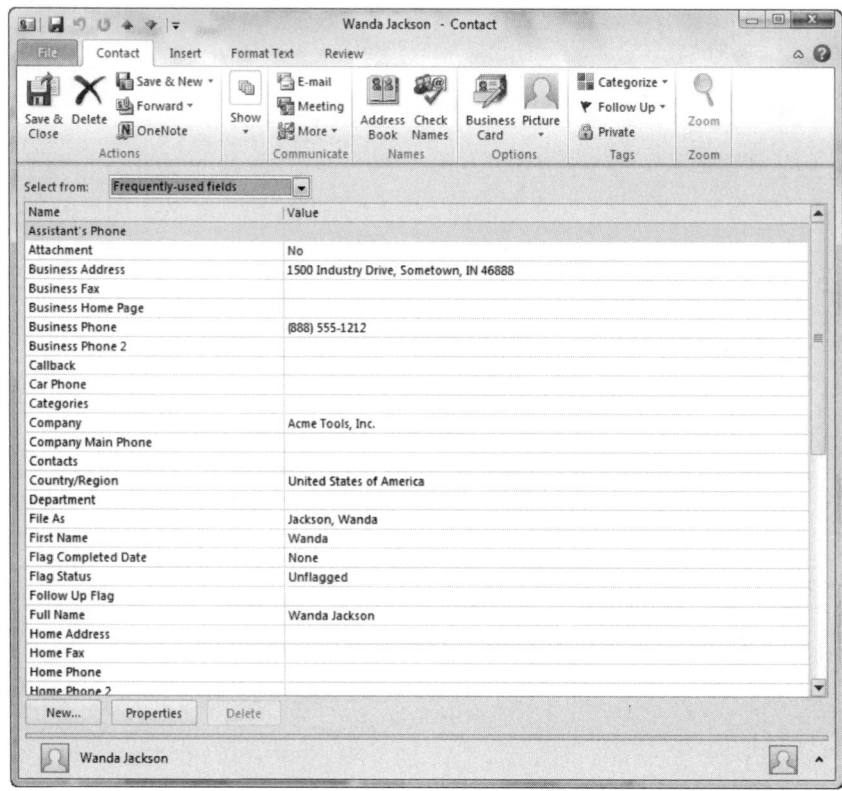

Some fields can be edited in this view by clicking in the Value column and making the desired changes. Other fields are generated internally by Outlook and cannot be edited.

You can add a custom field to the contact by clicking the New button at the bottom of the window. Outlook displays the New Column dialog box (Figure 29-16), in which you enter a name for the field (which cannot duplicate an existing field name). You also select the data type for the field. Your choices are Text, Number, Percent, Currency, Yes/No, and Date/Time. For certain data types, you can also select a format from the Format list. When you are finished, click OK, and the custom field will be added to the All Fields display.

You can change the properties of a field by clicking on it in the list and then clicking the Properties button. This is relevant only for user-defined fields; the properties of Outlook's built-in fields are locked.

FIGURE 29-16

Defining a new field for a contact

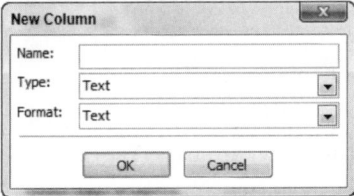

Editing the Business Card

Outlook creates a Business Card for each contact based on a default template. As you have seen in previous examples in the chapter, this template includes name, company, title, phone numbers, e-mail and postal addresses, and a photo (assuming that these elements are part of the contact).

To edit the Business Card for a contact, first double-click on the contact to open its Contact window. Then, click the Business Card button in the Options group of the Contact tab on the Ribbon. Outlook opens the Edit Business Card dialog box, shown in Figure 29-17.

FIGURE 29-17

Editing the Business Card for an individual contact

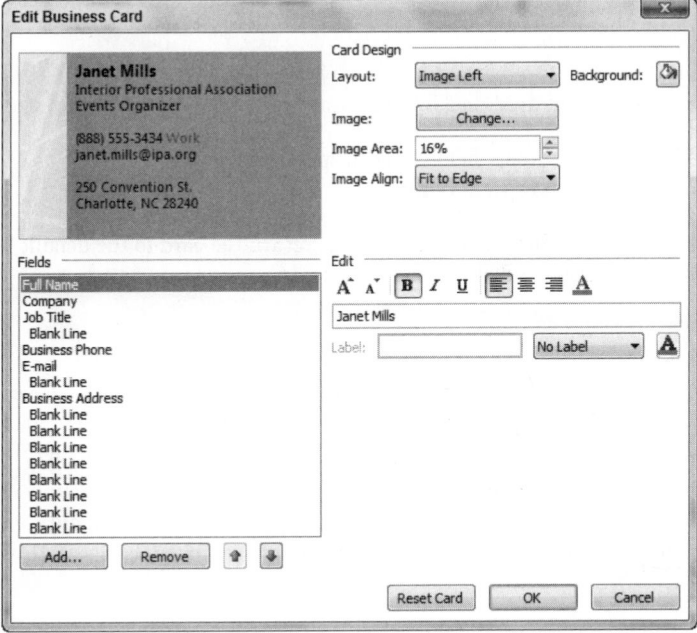

The top-left section of this dialog box previews how the Business Card will look with your edits. The top-right section defines the overall layout of the card:

- **Layout.** Specifies the image location. You can also omit the image or use it as the card background.
- **Background.** Lets you select a background color for the card.
- **Image.** Lets you specify a different image when you click the Change button.
- **Image Area.** Determines how much of the card is occupied by the image. The maximum is 50 percent.
- **Image Align.** Determines how the image is positioned within the image area.

The lower-left section of the Edit Business Card dialog box lets you specify the data fields that are included on the card and their order. You can do the following:

- Click Add and then select from the menu to add a field to the card.
- Click Remove to remove the selected field from the card.
- Click the up- or down-arrow to change the position of the selected field.

The lower-right section of this dialog box is for text formatting. When a field is selected in the Fields list, use the tools here to do the following:

- Increase or decrease font size.
- Make font bold, italic, or underlined.
- Align text left, center, or right.
- Change font color.

Oddly enough, you cannot change the font used on a Business Card; you can change only its size.

The Label section lets you add a label to any data field. You can specify the text of the label, its color, and whether it is displayed to the left or right of the item.

Click the Reset Card button to undo any edits you have made and return the card to the default appearance. Click OK to save your changes and close the dialog box.

Dialing the Phone

If your computer is equipped with a modem, you can have Outlook dial the phone for you based on the number associated with a contact. Then you can pick up your handset and complete the call as usual. You must have the modem and handset on the same line, which can be inconvenient if you use the modem to access the Internet. If your Internet connection is via cable modem or DSL or via a second telephone line, you may want to dedicate an old modem as a dedicated dialer on your voice line. The speed of the modem is not relevant in this application.

When a contact is open in its own window, click the More button in the Communicate group of the Contact tab, and point to the Call choice to display the submenu shown in Figure 29-18.

This menu lists all the phone numbers for the current contact. Select the one to dial, and Outlook opens the New Call dialog box (Figure 29-19) with the selected phone number entered.

FIGURE 29-18

Using Outlook to dial the phone

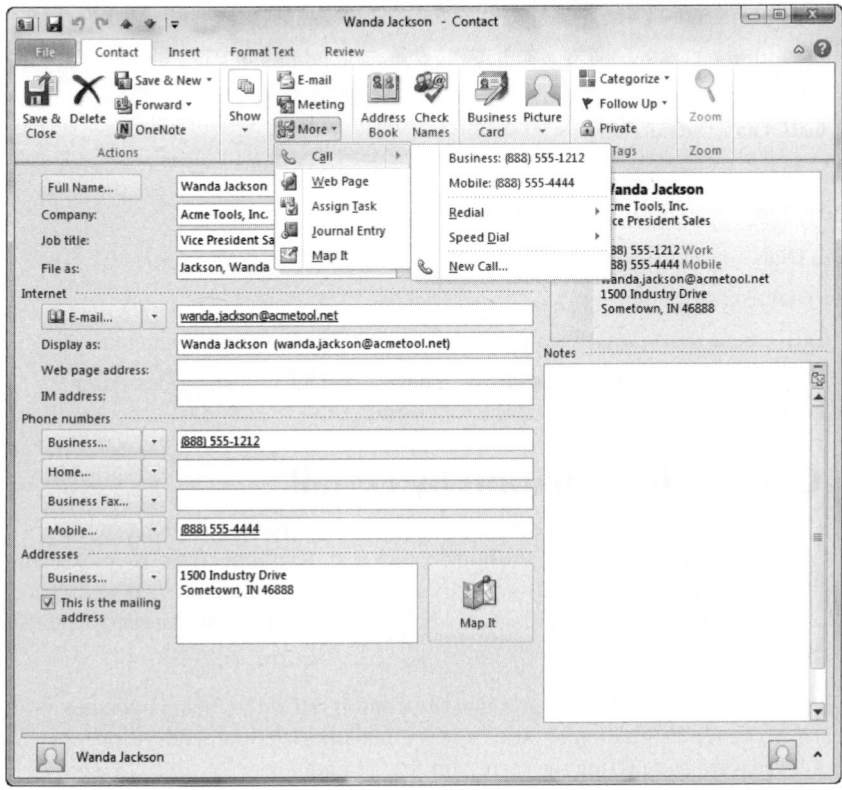

FIGURE 29-19

The New Call dialog box

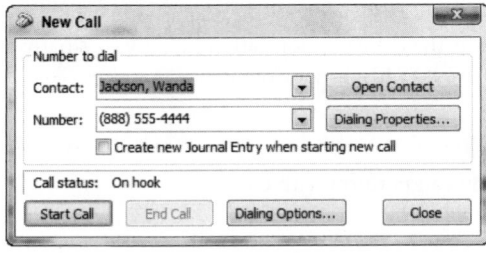

The settings and commands in this dialog box are as follows.

- **Dialing Properties.** Opens the Dialing Properties dialog box, in which you define rules for dialing from your computer. You should not have to change these because they will have been set up when you installed and configured your modem.

- **Create New Journal Entry When Starting New Call.** Creates an Outlook Journal Entry for the call, noting the number called and the time and date of the call.

- **Dialing Options.** Lets you set speed dialer options and add names and numbers to the Speed Dial list.

- **Start Call.** Dials the number.

- **End Call.** Hangs up.

The Call submenu has several other commands, as follows:

- **Redial.** Dials a recently called number.

- **Speed Dial.** Dials a number on your Speed Dial list.

- **New Call.** Opens the New Call dialog box without any phone number entered.

Outlook can also make Instant Messenger calls. If you have specified an Instant Messenger address for the contact, this option appears on the Call menu.

Sending Contact Information by E-mail

Sending contact information attached to an e-mail message can be very useful. Doing so lets recipients enter the information in their address books quickly and without errors. If you keep an entry for yourself in your Address Book, you can easily send your own information as well. You saw in Chapter 27 how to send Business Cards from Mail in Outlook. You also can send a contact directly in an open Contact window.

When you have a contact open, the Actions group of the Contact tab of the Ribbon includes a Forward button. You can use this button to create a new e-mail message and send the open contact in one of three ways by selecting the corresponding command:

- **As a Business Card.** Outlook creates a new message with the contact inserted in the message body as a Business Card and attached to the message as a vCard file.

- **In Internet Format (vCard).** Outlook creates a new message with the contact attached to the message as a vCard file.

- **As an Outlook Contact.** Outlook creates a new message with the contact attached to the message as an Outlook item. This sends the contact information in Outlook's native format, so the recipient can open it and save it to his or her Contacts.

Other Contact Actions

This section describes some of the other actions you can perform with contacts.

Viewing a Map of the Contact's Address

If a contact has a valid address entered, you can click the Map It button to the right of the Contact's address in the Contact window to open a Web browser and view a map of the specified location. This feature is powered by the Windows Live Local website, which provides other services such as driving directions and business search.

Inviting the Contact to a Meeting

To invite the contact to a meeting, click the Meeting button in the Communicate group of the Contact tab on the Ribbon. Outlook creates a new meeting request addressed to the contact, as shown in Figure 29-20. You can specify the subject and location, enter the date and start and end times, and include a message. You can also add other recipients to the request.

FIGURE 29-20

Sending a meeting request to a contact

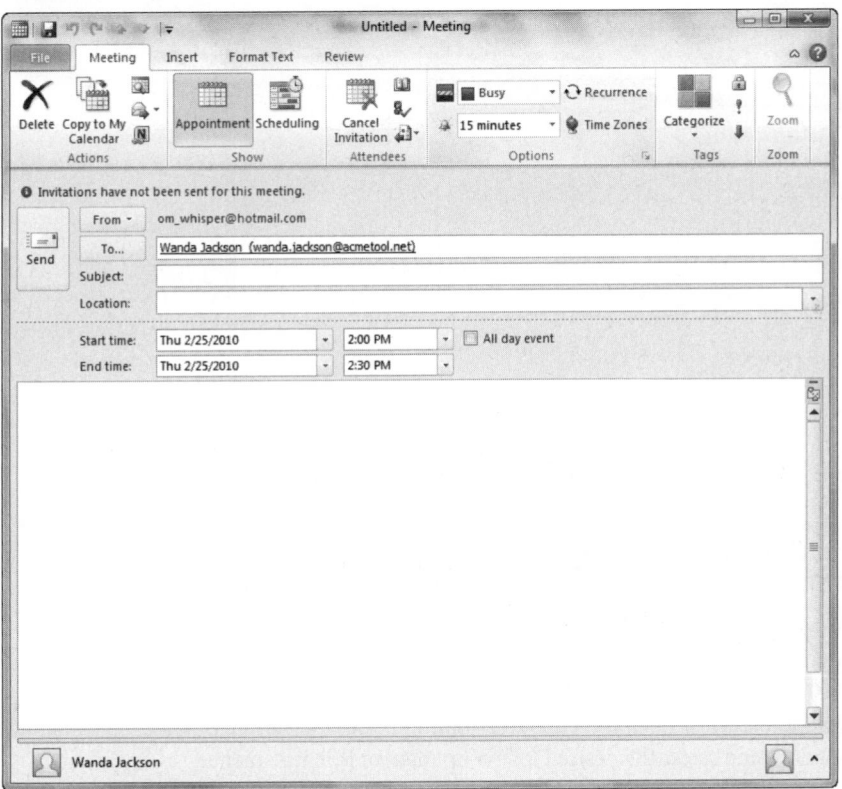

Assigning a Task to a Contact

To assign a new task to a contact, click the More button in the Communicate group on the Contact tab in the Contact window, and then click Assign Task. Outlook opens a Task window, as shown in Figure 29-21, in which you can enter details of the task and save it. You learn more about tasks, including assigning an existing task to a contact, in Chapter 30.

FIGURE 29-21

Assigning a task to a contact

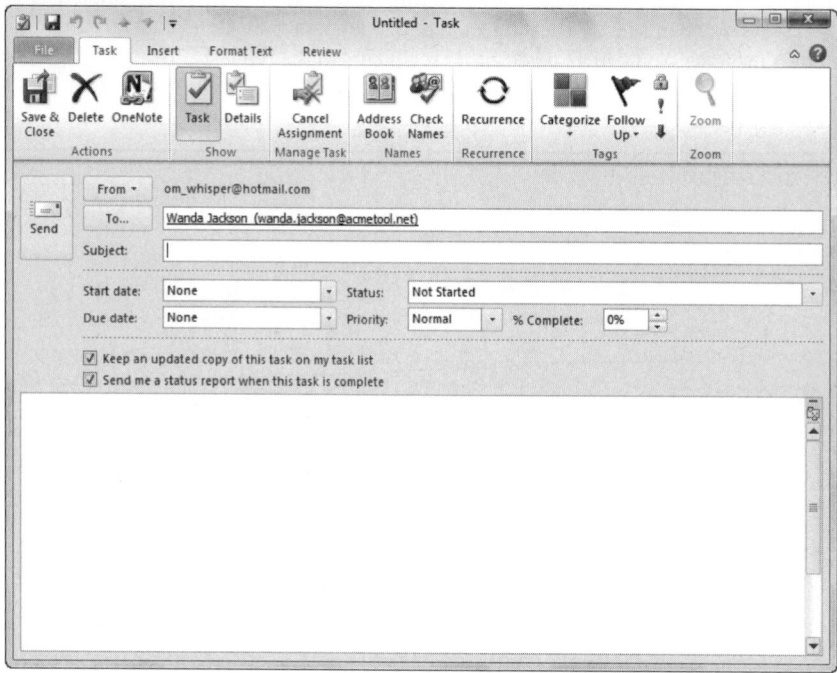

Viewing the Contact's Web Page

If you have entered a web page URL for a contact, clicking the Web Page button on the Contact ribbon launches your default Web browser and displays the web page.

Tagging a Contact for Follow-up

To tag a contact for follow-up, click the Follow Up button in the Tags group of the Contact tab in the Contact window, and select the desired follow-up interval from the menu.

Use the Shortcut Menus

Many of the actions that you can take with contacts that are described in this section can be accessed without opening the contact. In the Contacts window, simply right-click on the contact and choose from the shortcut menu. You can use this technique to send a contact, call a contact, or assign a follow-up flag or category to a contact.

Performing a Mail Merge from Your Contacts

Mail merge is a technique that lets a form letter be addressed and sent to many different individuals. It can also be used to create mailing labels, envelopes, and catalogs such as a mailing list. Microsoft Office has merge tools built into several of its applications, most notably Word and Outlook.

When would you use Outlook to perform a mail merge? Only when the names and addresses that you want to use are in your Outlook Address Book. In this situation, using Outlook is often the simplest approach. Even so, some factors may mitigate against using Outlook for a merge and instead using the more advanced mail merge tools available in other Office applications. For example, Outlook cannot separate documents by zip code to get reduced mailing rates, and it would not be a good choice for a large merge that will create thousands of documents.

Note
You need to have Microsoft Word installed on your system to perform a mail merge. ■

The first step in performing a mail merge is usually to filter your contacts so that only the ones you want included are shown. You can do this by using Outlook's search capability or by customizing the Contacts view, both of which are covered earlier in this chapter. However, you can skip this step and select the contacts to include later. Then, follow these steps:

1. In the main Outlook window, click Contacts in the Navigation pane.
2. Click Mail Merge in the Actions group of the Home tab. Outlook displays the Mail Merge Contacts dialog box, as shown in Figure 29-22.
3. Make entries in this dialog box as described in the list that follows these steps.
4. Click OK to open Word to complete the merge.

FIGURE 29-22

Performing a mail merge with Outlook contacts

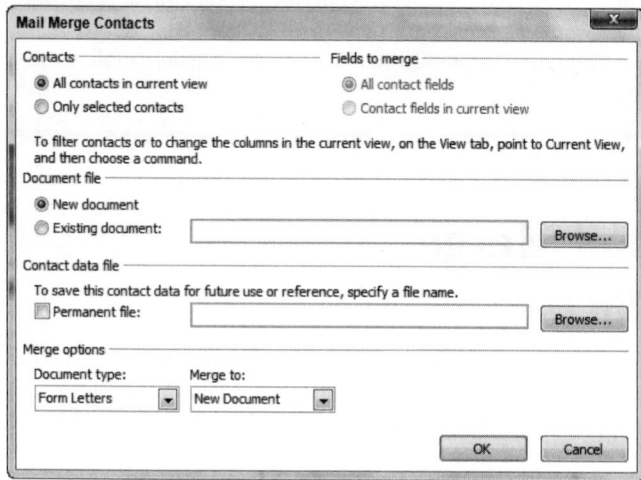

The options in the Mail Merge Contacts dialog box are as follows:

- **Contacts.** Select All Contacts in Current View to include all displayed contacts in the merge. Select Only Selected Contacts to select contacts to include later.

- **Fields to Merge.** Specifies whether only visible contact fields or all contact fields will be available for the merge. These options may or may not be available depending on the current Contacts view.

- **Document File.** Specifies whether the merge will use a new or an existing Word document. If you choose the latter option, use the Browse button to locate the document to use.

- **Contact Data File.** You can select this option to save the merge contact data in a separate Word document. Typically, this option is used to create a record of the people who were included in the mailing.

- **Document Type.** You can merge to form letters, mailing labels, envelopes, or a catalog.

- **Merge To.** Specify whether the merge output goes to a Word document, to the printer, or to e-mail, as follows:

  - **New Document.** Merge creates a Word document that you can edit as needed before creating the final output.

  - **Printer.** The merged document is created and sent directly to the default printer.

  - **E-mail.** The merged documents are created as e-mail messages and placed in your Outbox.

In most situations, the remainder of the merge process is carried out in Word. Please consult your Word documentation for more information.

Working with Multiple Address Books

The majority of Outlook users have only a single address book. This is all that most people usually need. In some situations, you may have two or more address books. This can happen if you create more than one Outlook data file. Each data file will have its own address book, and you will have access to the one in whichever Outlook data file is open. You might want to use more than one Outlook data file if you want to keep your personal e-mail completely separate from your work e-mail. Chapter 27 has more about working with Outlook data files.

Another situation in which you will have more than one address book is when you have both a regular (i.e., SMTP/POP) e-mail account and a Microsoft Exchange account set up in Outlook. The regular account will have its own address book, and the Exchange account will have another, separate one. You will have both available to you at the same time in Outlook; they are listed at the top of the Navigation pane when Contacts are active, and you can choose to view one or the other. When you add a contact, it is added to whichever address book is active.

Setting Contact Options

Outlook has some global options that affect the way contacts work. To view and change these options:

1. **In the main Outlook window, click File, and then click Options.** The Outlook Options dialog box opens.
2. **Click Contacts in the list at the left to display the Contact Options dialog box (Figure 29-23).**
3. **Set options as described in the list that follows these steps.**
4. **Click OK.**

The options that are available for contacts are as follows:

- **Default Full Name Order.** Specifies how contacts are sorted when you order them based on full name. You can choose First Middle Last, Last First, or First Last1 Last2.
- **Default File As Order.** Specifies how contacts are sorted when you order them based on the File As field. Your choices are Last First, First Last, Company, Last First (Company), Company (Last, First).
- **Check for Duplicate When Saving New Contacts.** Outlook warns you if you try to enter a new contact with the same name as an existing contact.

FIGURE 29-23

Setting global options for contacts

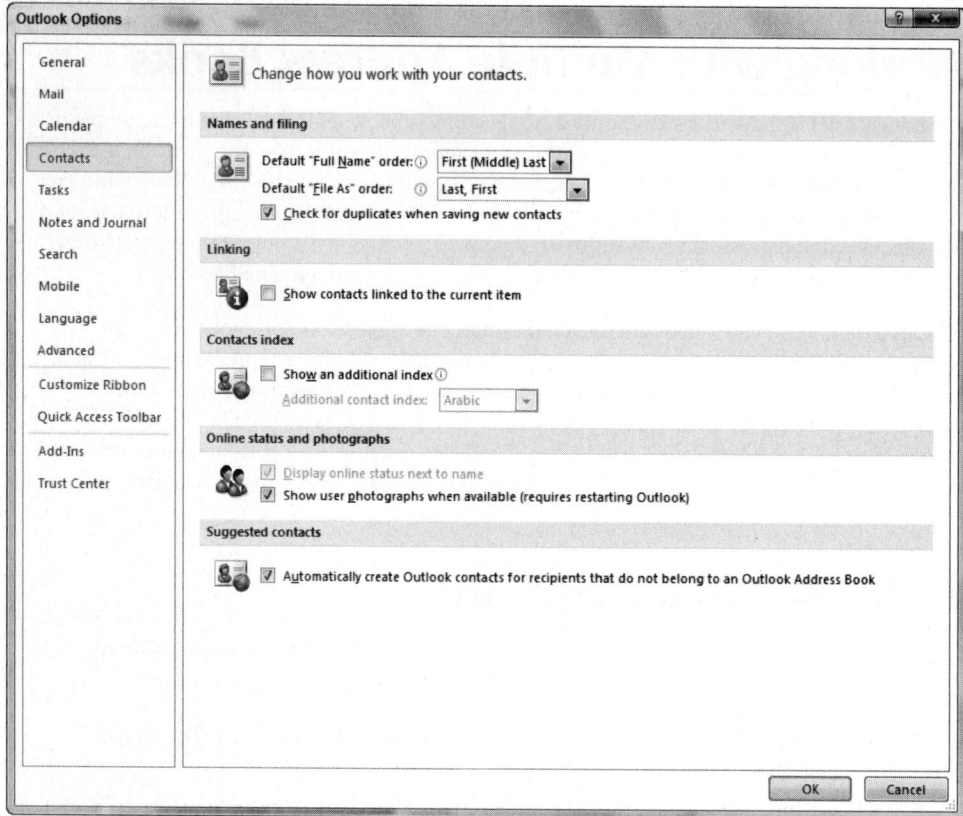

- **Show Contact Linking on All Forms.** Controls whether all information linked to a contact (tasks, for example) is displayed.
- **Show an Additional Index.** Outlook displays a second set of index buttons at the right edge of the Contacts window using the language you select from the list.

Summary

The Outlook Contacts feature is a powerful tool for managing and using information about people. It goes way beyond the basic address book to store just about any kind of information about a person you can imagine. What's more, it makes it easy to find and use that information in various ways. Many people find the Contacts feature to be one of Outlook's most useful tools.

Working with Appointments and Tasks

A calendar is something you usually hang on the wall. It has a page for each month and a picture of a puppy, lighthouse, or famous painting. If that's what you think, then you haven't used the Outlook Calendar! Outlook provides a sophisticated calendar that helps you manage your time efficiently. In today's busy world, few of us have any shortage of things to do. A list of tasks always seems to be waiting for our attention, particularly in a high-pressure business or professional environment. This chapter covers the Outlook Calendar and Task (To-Do list) features, which can help you stay on time and on track with whatever you do.

Understanding the Outlook Calendar

At its heart, the Outlook Calendar stores and displays *appointments*. An *appointment* is just what it sounds like — a scheduled event with a title and a time and date specified for the beginning and end of the event. Outlook distinguishes between two types of appointments:

- A regular appointment has a specific start time and stop time. It is usually on the same day but does not have to be.

- An all-day event does not have specific start and stop times but rather takes up all of one or more days.

Scheduling appointments may not sound so special, and in fact it's not. But it's the way that Outlook lets you organize, use, and share your appointments that makes the Calendar so useful.

Using the Calendar

To show the Calendar, click the Calendar button in the Navigation pane. The View window shows the Calendar itself, and we'll get to that in a moment. The top section of the Navigation pane shows a small calendar of the current month, called the *Date Navigator*, which has several useful features, as shown in Figure 30-1 and described in the following list:

- Today's date is enclosed in a box — the 25th in Figure 30-1.

FIGURE 30-1

In Calendar view, the Navigation pane displays the Date Navigator.

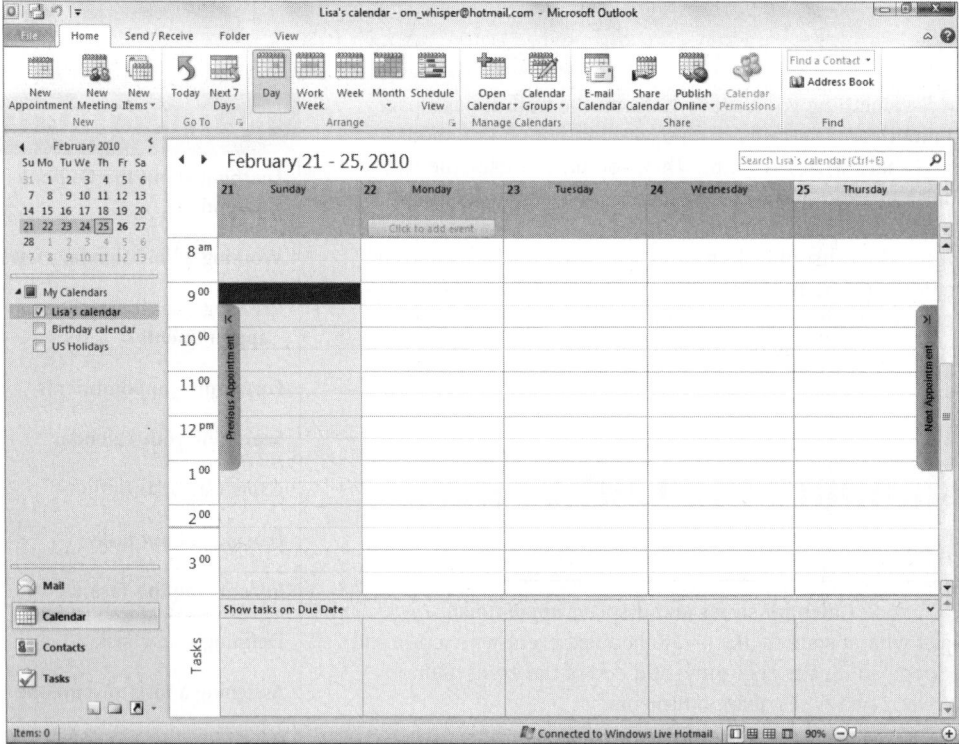

- The day(s) that are displayed in the larger Calendar view are highlighted in the small calendar. In Figure 30-1, these encompass the 21st through the 25th.
- Days on which there is at least one appointment are in bold.
- The arrows to the left and right of the month and year can be clicked on to move to the previous or next month, updating the Calendar view as well.
- You can click any day number to change the Calendar view accordingly.

Note

If the Date Navigator is not displayed in the Navigation pane, it is probably because it is displayed in the To-Do bar. The Date Navigator is displayed in one place or the other, not both. You learn about the To-Do bar later in this chapter. ■

A Word about the Default Calendars

If you have set up a single POP e-mail account in Outlook, in the Navigation pane you will see the My Calendars Calendar group, with a single calendar named *Calendar* stored in it. However, if you set up a Web-based e-mail account, it may set up multiple calendars in the My Calendars group, as shown in the figures in this chapter. Make sure that you have selected the desired calendar in the Navigation pane when you start adding appointments. Also, if you have multiple e-mail accounts installed, you will see multiple calendars; to see which e-mail account a calendar goes with, click on the calendar in the Navigation pane, and look at the Outlook Window title bar.

Working with Calendar Views

When the Calendar is displayed, you can choose between viewing a single day (the default), a workweek, a week, or an entire month. Choose Week view to view the entire week or just the workweek (Monday–Friday). In Month view you can set the level of detail display to low, medium, or high. You select your view using either the View tab or the choices in the Arrange group on the Home tab. Outlook displays the date or date range displayed as well as buttons that move the calendar forward or backward by one of whatever unit (day, week, or month) is displayed above the calendar (see Figure 30-2).

Finding Today

No matter what day, week, or month you are viewing in the Calendar, you can always go directly to the current day by clicking the Today button in the Go To group on the Home tab of the Ribbon.

Using the Calendar Day View

When the Calendar is displaying a single day, it looks as shown in Figure 30-3. Times of the day are listed at the left edge of the window, and each appointment is displayed in its assigned time slot. Use the scroll bar to bring different times into view. Any all-day events for the day are displayed at the top of the window.

Click on an appointment to select it; it displays with a black border and small handles (boxes) on the top and bottom borders. You can:

- Point at the appointment and drag to move it to a different time slot.
- Point at one of the handles and drag it to change either the start or end time.

If you double-click on an appointment, it opens for editing, as explained later in this chapter.

FIGURE 30-2

The Outlook Calendar can display a day, a week, or a month at a time.

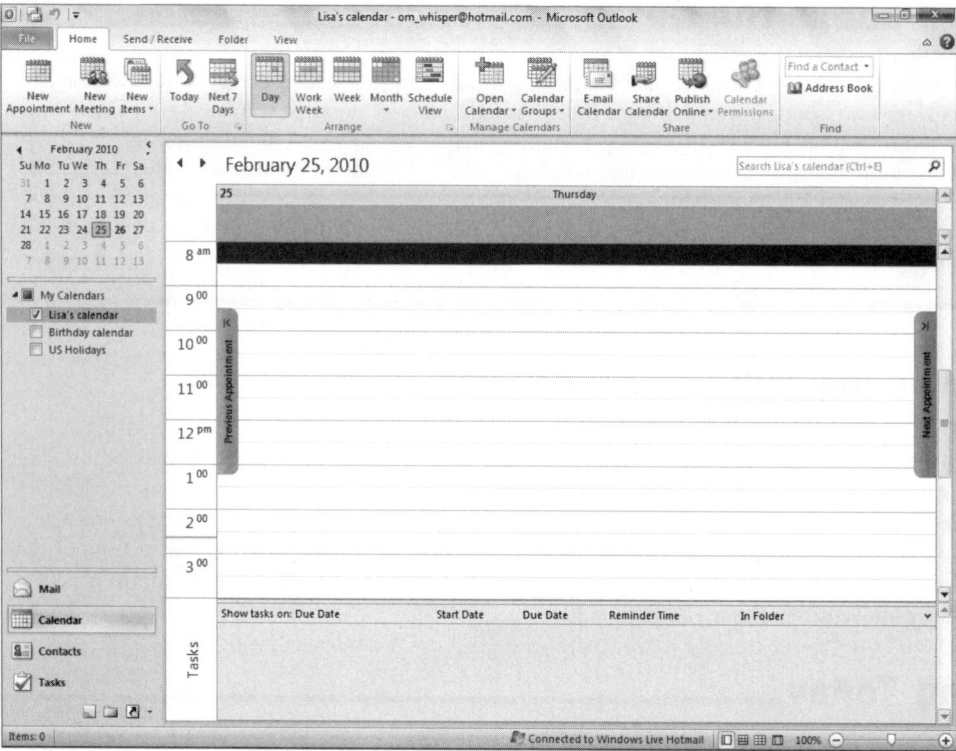

Using the Calendar Work Week and Week Views

The Calendar Work Week view is shown in Figure 30-4. You can display the full seven-day week by selecting the Week view, instead.

In essence, the Week view consists of five or seven single-day views side-by-side, and you can perform the same actions as described for the Day view. You can also drag an appointment to a different day.

You can display the Reading pane with a view if you want to see details about a selected appointment, as shown at the right in Figure 30-4. This feature can be useful when the Calendar itself is too crowded to show these details for each appointment. To toggle the Reading pane on or off, click the View tab, click Reading Pane in the Layout group, and click the desired position. Clicking Off hides the Reading pane, which is the default setting.

FIGURE 30-3

The Outlook Calendar displaying a single day's appointments

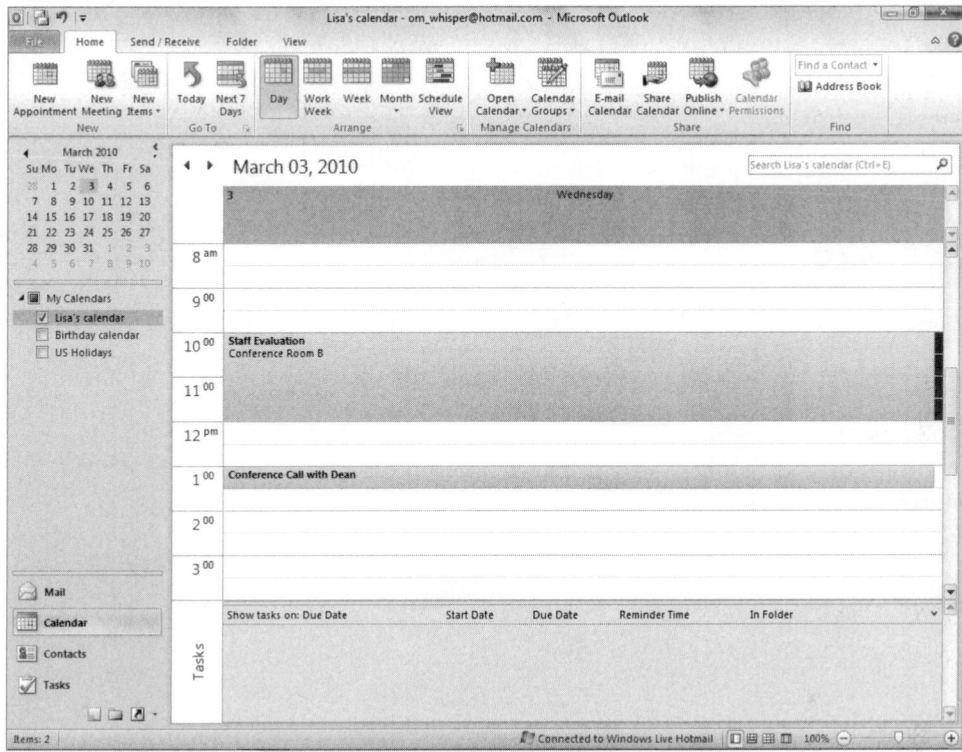

Using the Calendar Month View

The Month view shows an entire month of appointments, as shown in Figure 30-5. Appointments for each day are displayed in order but without time details. If an all-day event exists for the day, it is displayed at the top with a line around it — for example, the "Staff Retreat" appointment on the 8th and 9th, shown in Figure 30-5. If a day has more appointments than can be shown, a small down-arrow is displayed. Click on the arrow to open the single-day display, where you can view all appointments for that date.

Figure 30-5 shows the Month display with the High option selected for details, which is the default setting. You can also select Low or Medium details, as follows:

- **Low.** Shows only all-day events. Appointments with specific start and stop times are not displayed.

- **Medium.** All-day events are displayed as usual. Appointments with specific start and stop times are displayed as shaded lines or rectangles with the position and thickness of the line or rectangle indicating the approximate time and duration of the appointment.

The Outlook Calendar displaying an entire workweek's appointments

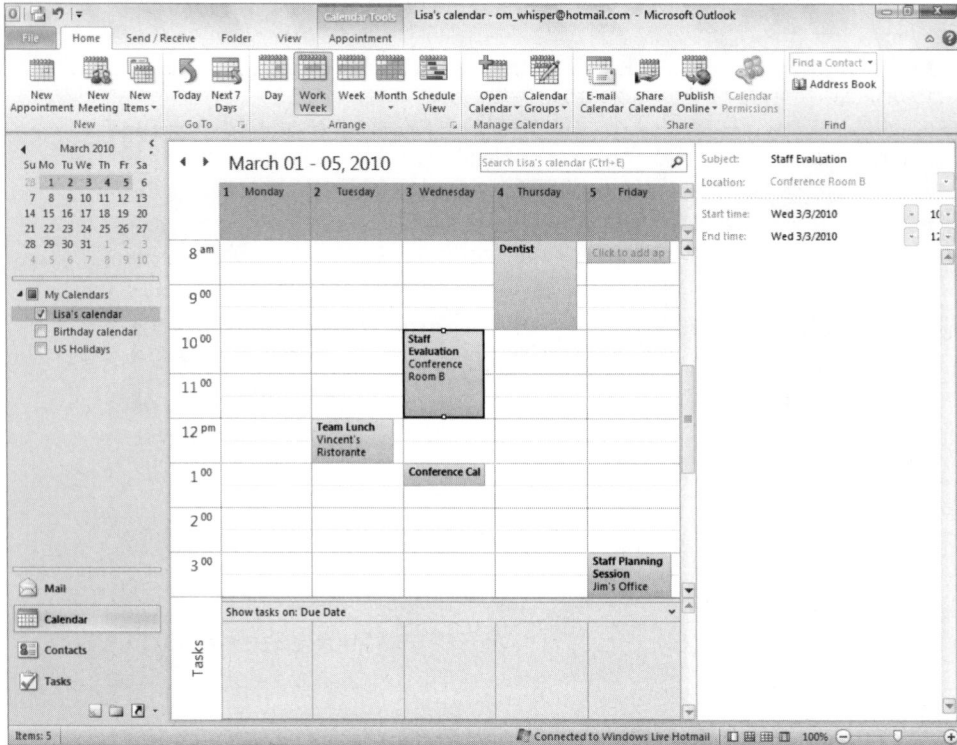

Using the To-Do Bar with Appointments

Outlook's To-Do bar can be useful for working with Calendar items. To display the To-Do bar, click To-Do Bar in the Layout group of the View tab, then choose Normal. The To-Do bar is shown in Figure 30-6.

The To-Do bar can display three items:

- The Date Navigator, a small monthly calendar whose features are explained earlier in this chapter. If the Date Navigator is displayed in the To-Do bar, it will not be displayed in the Navigation pane.

- A list of appointments for the current week
- A list of tasks. Tasks are not directly related to the Calendar and will be explained later in this chapter.

FIGURE 30-5

The Outlook Calendar displaying a month's appointments

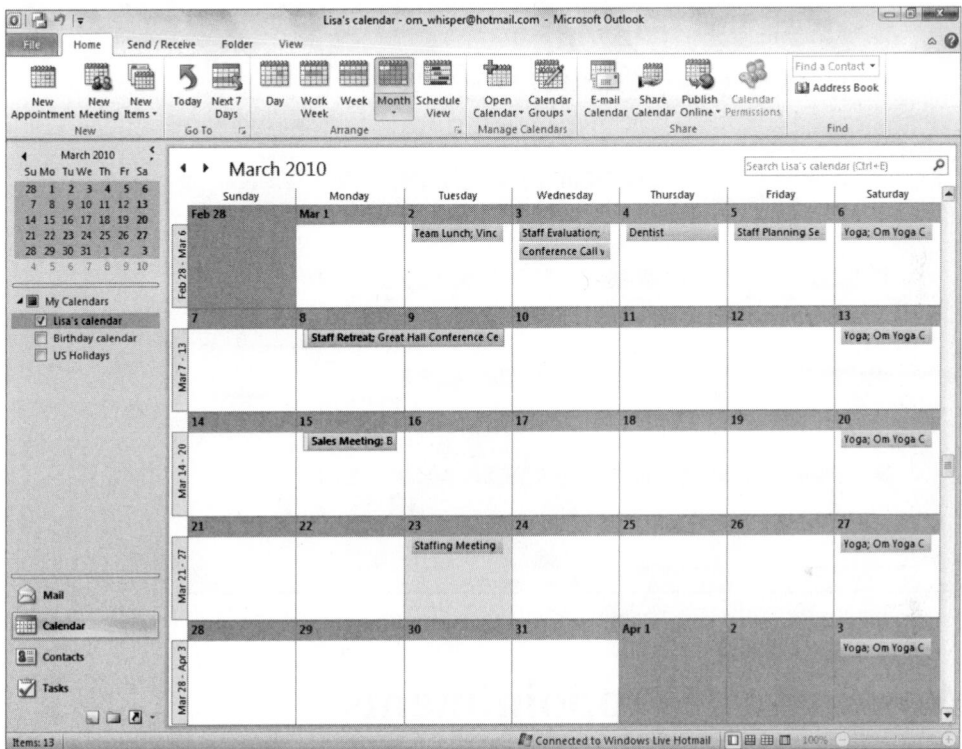

You can control what is displayed on the To-Do bar. You can display one, two, or all of the items in the preceding list. To change the To-Do bar display, right-click above the Task List in the To-Do bar, and then select or deselect the individual items — Date Navigator, Appointments, and Task List — on the shortcut menu. You can also select Options from this menu to display the To-Do Bar Options dialog box, shown in Figure 30-7. Here you can turn the display of individual items on or off as well as specify how many months are displayed in the Date Navigator and how many appointments are displayed.

FIGURE 30-6

The To-Do bar can display the Date Navigator and upcoming appointments.

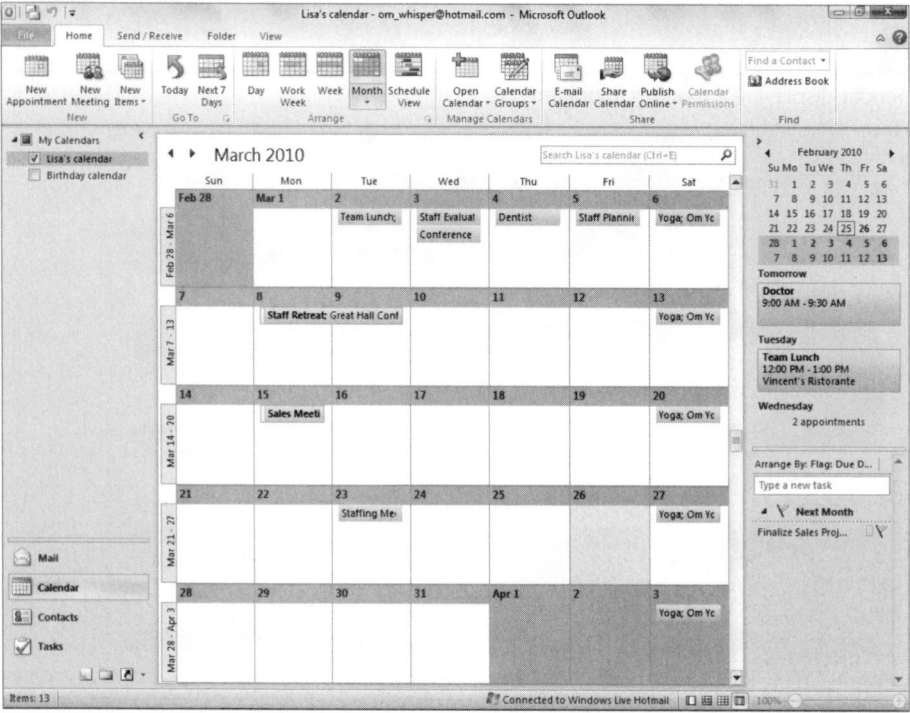

Working with Appointments

An Outlook appointment can be very simple, or you can use Outlook's tools to add various features and options to an appointment. The following sections start with the basics of creating a simple appointment and then look at the various options.

Creating a Simple Appointment

To create a simple appointment, make sure that Outlook is displaying the Calendar. Then do one of the following:

- Click the New Appointment button in the New Group of the Home tab on the Ribbon. Outlook opens a new appointment form for whatever day is selected in the Calendar.

- Double-click on a day on the Calendar. Outlook opens a new appointment form for that day.

- If working in Day, Work Week, or Week view, you can click on a specific time on a specific day to specify that the appointment should start at that time.

FIGURE 30-7

FIGURE 30-7

Setting To-Do bar display options

The Appointment window is shown in Figure 30-8 before any information has been entered. Then, follow these steps:

FIGURE 30-8

An Outlook Appointment window

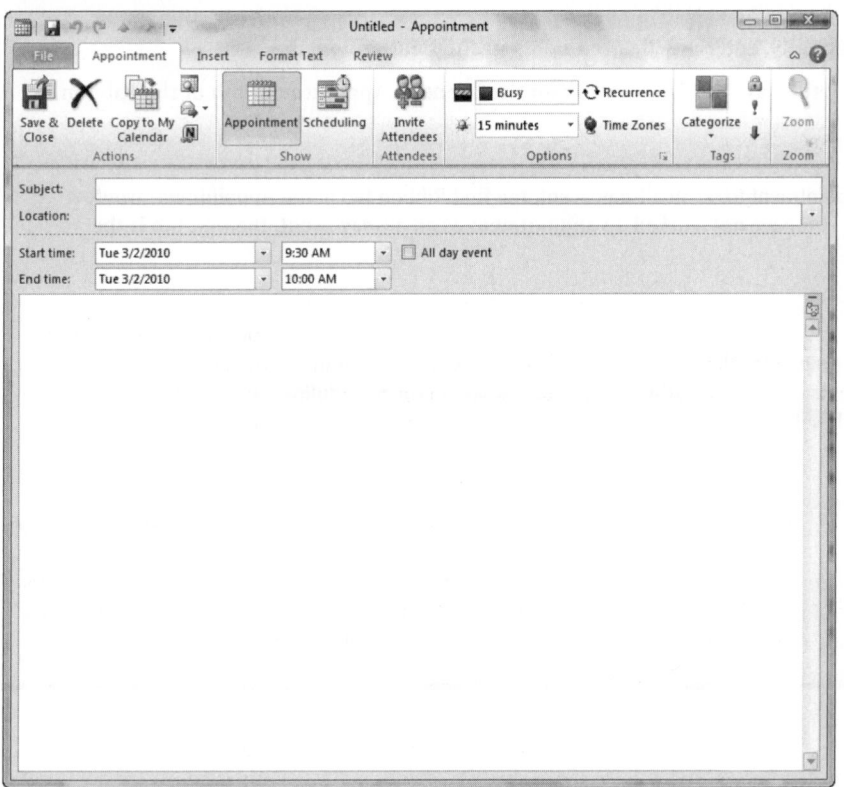

1. **At a minimum, you must enter a Subject for the appointment.** The Subject is the title of the appointment and is displayed in the Calendar — or at least part of it will be, depending on the length.

2. **Optionally, enter a Location for the appointment.** If you click on the arrow adjacent to the Location field, Outlook displays a list of previously used locations from which you can select. Otherwise, just type the location into the field. If space allows, the location displays along with the appointment subject in the Calendar.

3. **If necessary, adjust the start or stop date (or both) by clicking on the arrow next to the displayed date and selecting from the calendar that Outlook displays.** An appointment can span two or more days, if needed.

4. **If the appointment is an all-day event, make sure that the All Day Event option is selected.** An all-day event marks one or more entire days as Busy, with no specific start and stop times.

5. **If the appointment is not an all-day event, make sure that the All Day Event option is not selected.** Outlook enables the fields for the start and stop times. If you double-clicked on a date in Month view, you will need to clear this check box before you can change times for the appointment.

6. **To select a start or stop time, click on the adjacent arrow and select from the list that is displayed (Figure 30-9).**

7. **Optionally, enter any desired notes in the field provided.**

8. **Click the Save & Close button on the Event or Appointment tab of the Ribbon.**

Note

If you've marked an appointment to be an all-day event, the first Ribbon tab in the Appointment window is the Event tab. When you have not marked an appointment as an all-day event, the first tab is the Appointment tab. ■

Caution

When you create an appointment that is an all-day event, Outlook does not mark the time as Busy but rather keeps it marked as Free. If you want an all-day event to display on the Scheduling page as either Tentative or Busy, you must explicitly select this option in the Options section of the Event tab of the Ribbon. ■

Dealing with Conflicts

You are free to schedule overlapping appointments if you want. When an overlap exists, Outlook displays a small message about it above the Subject text box in the Appointment window. So check that area carefully when you are creating new appointments if you want to avoid conflicts.

Selecting the stop time for an appointment

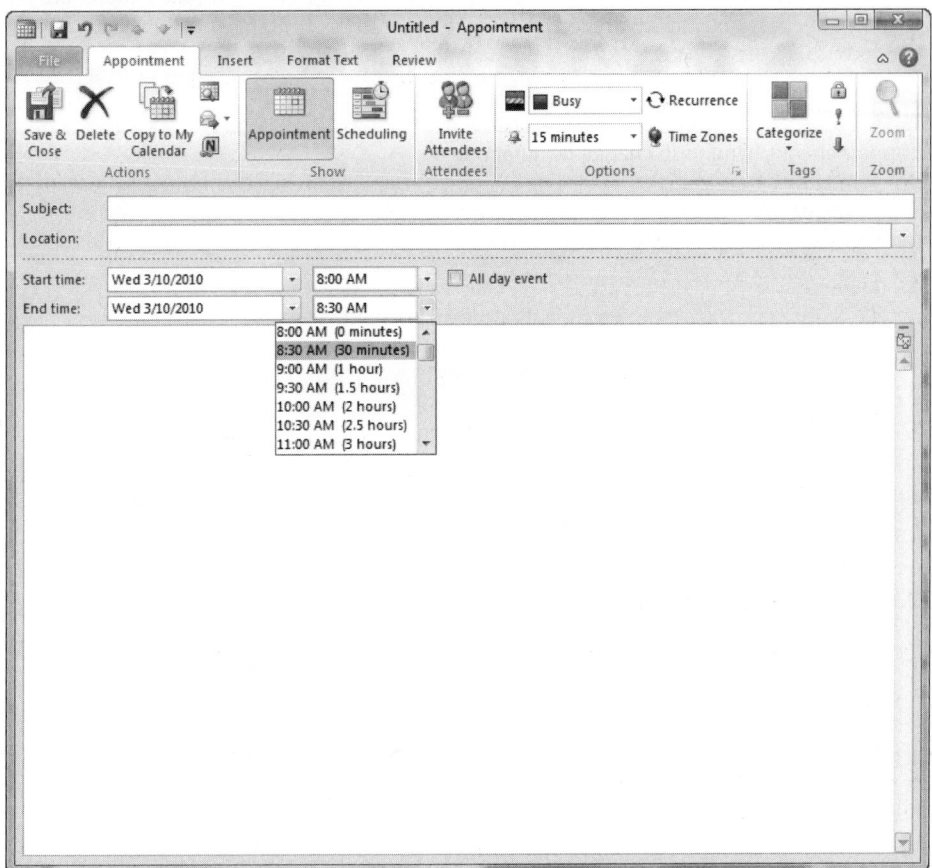

Editing and Deleting Appointments

To edit an appointment, double-click on it in the current Calendar view to open the Appointment window. Make any needed changes, and click the Save & Close button on the Event or Appointment tab of the Ribbon.

To delete an appointment, click it in Calendar view to select it; then, press Delete.

If you simply want to change the duration of an appointment, you can do so without opening the appointment form. When you select the appointment in the Calendar by clicking on it, it displays small, square handles on its border, as shown in Figure 30-10. For a regular appointment, the handles will be at the top and bottom, as shown in the figure. Drag the top or bottom handle to change the appointment's start or stop time, respectively. For an all-day event, the handles are on the left and right edges and can be dragged to change the start or stop time.

FIGURE 30-10

Drag a selected appointment's handles to change its duration.

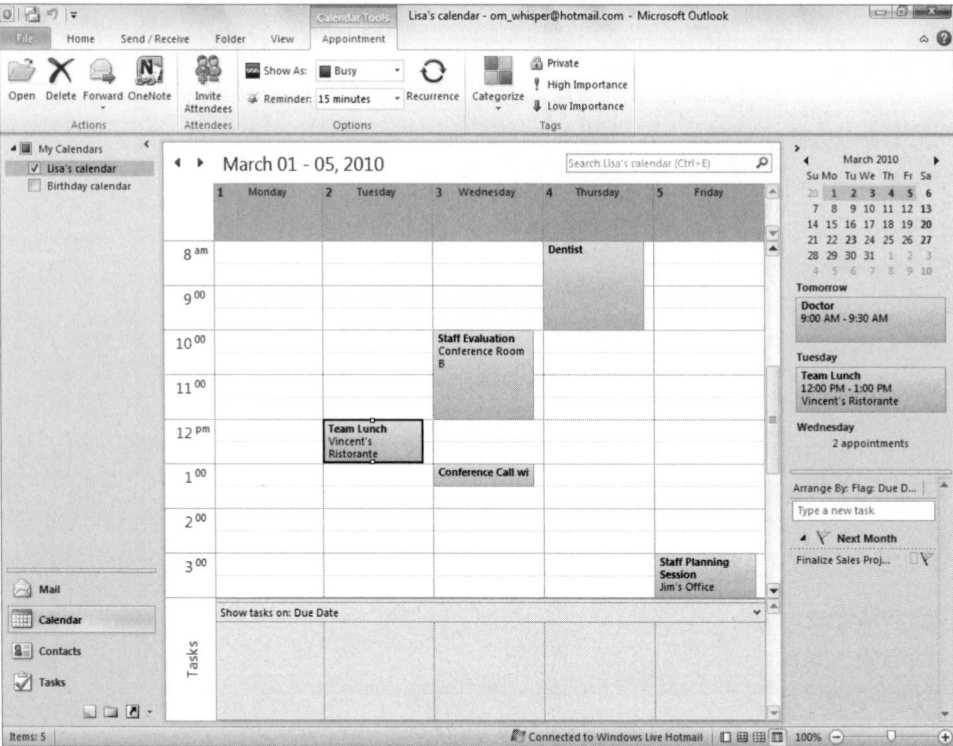

You can also change an appointment's time, date, or both without changing its duration; do so by pointing at the appointment and dragging it to the new position on the Calendar.

Appointment Options

When you create an appointment, there are several optional features you may want to use. They are described in the following sections.

Scheduling Recurring Events

Some events occur on a regular basis. Perhaps you have a chiropractor appointment at 10:00 a.m. every Monday, or a company strategy meeting on the first Tuesday of each month. You can enter such appointments only once and have Outlook create all the recurrences automatically. Here's how:

1. **Use the techniques described earlier in this chapter to create an appointment for the first instance, but do not save and close it.**

2. **In the Appointment window, click the Recurrence button in the Options group of the Event or Appointment tab of the Ribbon.** Outlook displays the Appointment Recurrence dialog box, as shown in Figure 30-11.

Defining a recurring appointment

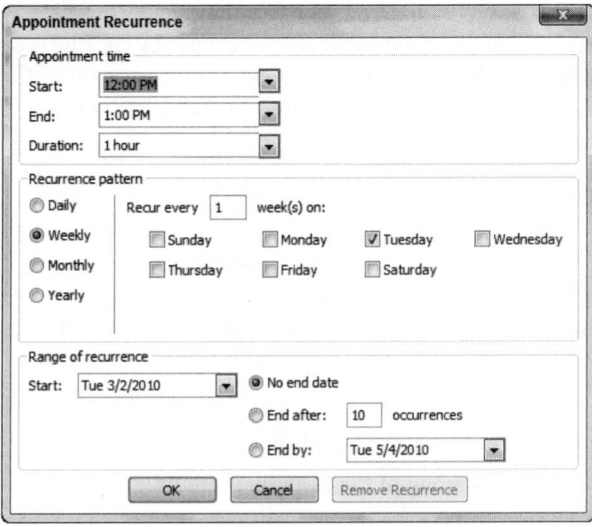

3. **In the Appointment Time section of the dialog box, make sure that the Start time and End time are correct.**

4. **In the Recurrence Pattern section, select Daily, Weekly, Monthly, or Yearly.**

5. **Depending on the option selected in the previous step, enter other recurrence details:**

   - **Daily.** Specify how often the appointment recurs (e.g., every two days) or that it occurs every weekday.

   - **Weekly.** Specify how often the appointment recurs (e.g., every week) and then on which day or days.

   - **Monthly.** Specify how often the appointment recurs (e.g., every three months) and on which day. You can select a day by number, such as the 15th of every month. You can also select a day by the day of week, such as the second Tuesday of the month.

6. **Under Range of Recurrence, enter the starting date and then specify when the recurrences end.** Your choices are the following:

   - No end date

   - End after a certain number of occurrences

   - End by a specified date

7. **Click OK to return to the Appointment window.**

8. **Complete any additional appointment details as needed.**

9. **Click Save & Close.**

When you double-click an existing recurring appointment for editing, you can click Open This Occurrence or Open the Series and then click OK to indicate whether to edit one or all of the appointments. You can then click the Recurrence button to open the Appointment Recurrence dialog box to modify the recurrence pattern. You can also remove the recurrence by clicking the Remove Recurrent button in this dialog box. Outlook removes all instances of the appointment from the Calendar except the next one. Note that changing the schedule for a single occurrence unlinks it from the overall recurring appointment.

If you try to delete a recurring appointment, Outlook gives you the option of deleting all occurrences of the appointment or just the current one.

Using Appointment Reminders

Outlook can remind you of an appointment by displaying a dialog box and playing a sound. You can specify how much advance notice you get and change the sound that is played. You can also turn reminders off. To set a reminder, follow these steps:

1. **Create the appointment, or open an existing one for editing.**

2. **Click the Reminder list in the Options group of the Event or Appointment tab of the Ribbon (Figure 30-12).**

3. **Select the desired duration of the advance warning, from 0 minutes to 2 weeks.** The default is 15 minutes before the start time, although you can change this in Calendar Options (covered later in this chapter). Select None for no reminder.

4. **Reopen the menu and select Sound to change the sound that is played when a reminder is displayed.** Deselect the Play This Sound option if you do not want a sound played (a dialog box is displayed).

5. **Click OK to return to the Appointment window.**

When a reminder comes due, Outlook plays the sound (if one was specified for the appointment) and displays the dialog box shown in Figure 30-13. If more than one reminder is due, they will all be listed. The actions you can take are the following:

- Click Dismiss to dismiss the selected reminder.

- If more than one reminder is listed, click Dismiss All to dismiss all listed reminders.

FIGURE 30-12

Specifying the reminder interval for an appointment

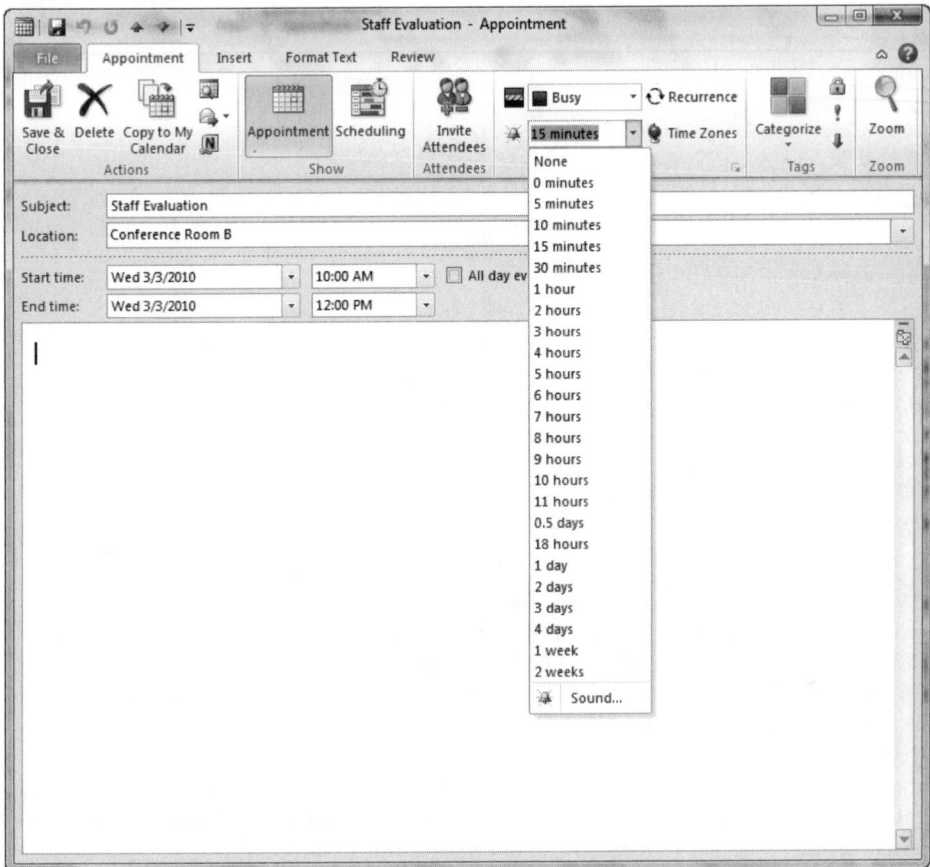

- Click Open Item to open the corresponding appointment.
- Click Snooze to be reminded again in the specified time, selected from the adjacent list. You can, for example, choose to be reminded 5 minutes before the appointment start time, or 10 minutes from the current time.

Note

Dismissing a reminder does not affect the appointment itself, which remains in your calendar. ■

Using Other Time Zones

By default, Outlook appointments use the time zone that your system is set up to use. At times, you may want to use another time zone — for example, if you are in New York and your client says, "Call me at 8:00 a.m. my time." You may not know the number of hours difference, but as long as you know her time zone you are all set.

FIGURE 30-13

The Appointment Reminder dialog box

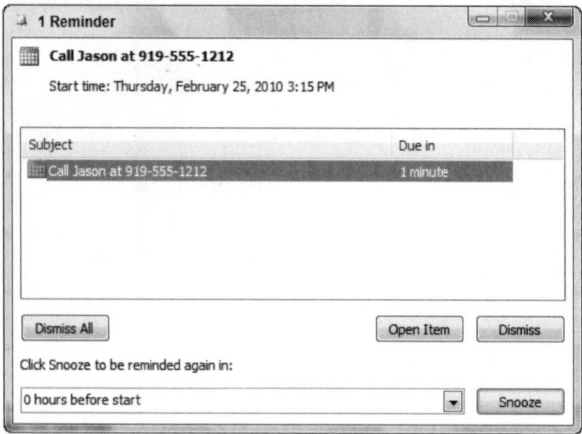

When you have the Appointment window open, click the Time Zones button in the Options group of the Event or Appointment tab of the Ribbon to display time zone selectors next to the start and end time fields (Figure 30-14). Change either the start or end time zone to the desired setting; the other will change to the same thing. Now the start and stop times you enter will be interpreted as being in the selected time zone, and the appointment will be displayed in the correct local time slot. For example, if you are in the Eastern time zone and enter an appointment from 8:00 a.m. to 9:00 a.m. in the Pacific time zone, the appointment will display between 11:00 and 12:00 a.m. on your Calendar because the Pacific zone is three hours behind the Eastern zone.

Forwarding an Appointment

Outlook lets you forward an appointment to an e-mail recipient. Forwarding is different from inviting an attendee to a meeting (covered in the next chapter). You have two ways to forward an Outlook appointment:

- Open the appointment, and click the Forward button in the Actions group of the Event or Appointment tab of the Ribbon.
- Right-click on the appointment in the Calendar, and select Forward from the shortcut menu.

In either case, Outlook creates a new e-mail message with the appointment attached as an Outlook item and the title of the appointment inserted in the Subject field. You then address and complete the e-mail message as usual. If you are using Outlook with an Exchange Server account, the appointment itself is forwarded without being attached to an e-mail message.

Basing an appointment on a different time zone from the one you are in

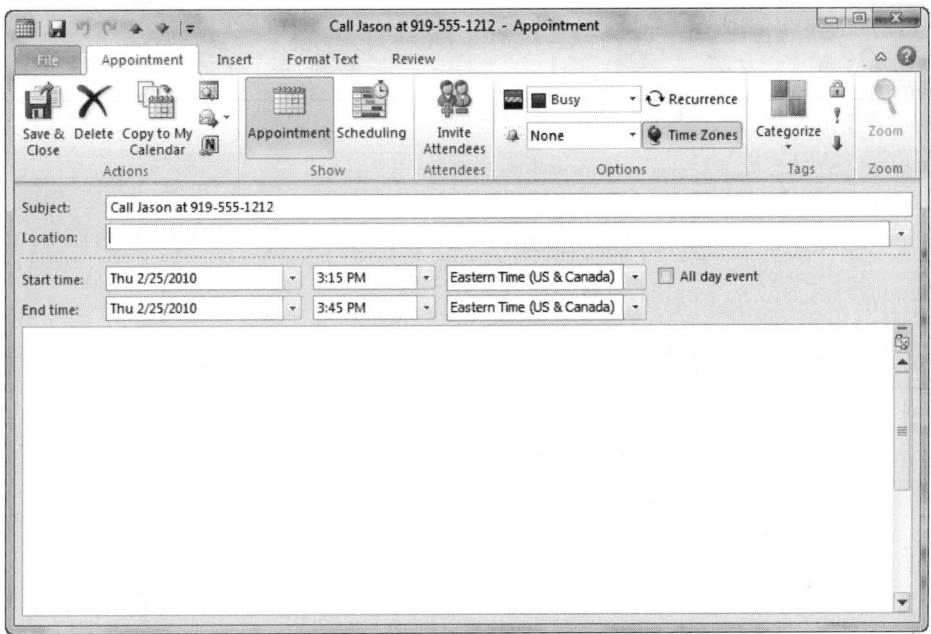

When the recipients receive a forwarded appointment, they can double-click on the attachment to open it. It opens in an Appointment window, and users can save it to their calendars or discard it as desired. Of course, recipients must be using Outlook or another program that supports the Outlook appointment format.

Another forwarding option for appointments is the iCalendar format. This is a widely supported format for calendar information and is supported by Outlook as well as many other scheduling programs. If you are not sure that all your recipients are using Outlook, using this format may be needed when forwarding an appointment. To do so, follow these steps:

1. **In an open appointment, click on the arrow next to the Forward button in the Actions group of the Event or Appointment tab.**

2. **Choose Forward as iCalendar from the menu. Outlook creates a new e-mail message with the iCalendar attached.**

3. **Complete and send the message as usual.**

Assigning Appointments to Categories

As with most Outlook items, an appointment can be assigned to a category. Outlook comes with six predefined and color-coded categories. Initially they are named according to their color, but you can change these to more meaningful names such as "Professional Development," as in the example shown in Figure 30-15. The first time you apply a category color, you are prompted to enter a name for the category.

The color-coded categories appear in the Appointment window.

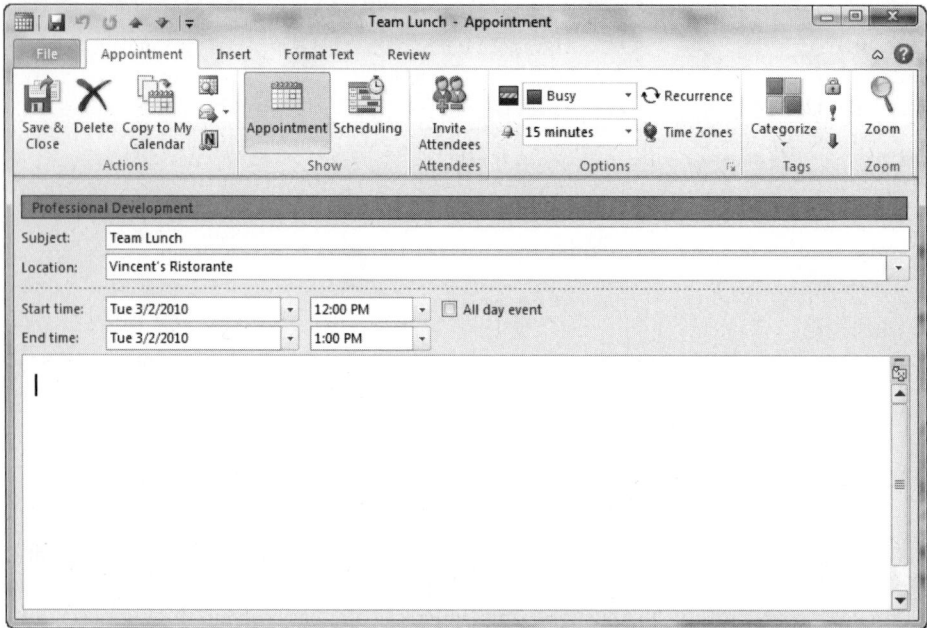

You have two ways to assign an appointment to a category:

- With the appointment open, click the Categorize button in the Options group of the Event or Appointment tab of the Ribbon, and select the desired category from the list that is displayed. Select Clear All Categories to remove any assigned categories from the appointment.

- In the Calendar, right-click on the appointment and select Categorize from the shortcut menu. Then, select the desired category.

An appointment, as is true of other Outlook items, can be assigned to more than one category. In the Calendar, a categorized appointment is displayed in the color of the assigned category.

Setting Appointment Importance

By default, all appointments that you create are assigned normal importance. You can assign either low or high importance to an open appointment by clicking on the corresponding button in the Options group of the Event or Appointment tab of the Ribbon. Then you can use this importance level as a criterion when using the Search feature in your Calendar, as discussed elsewhere in this chapter.

Marking an Appointment as Private

Outlook gives you the ability to publish your calendar so that other people can view your schedule. This topic is covered elsewhere in this chapter. You may at times want to mark an appointment as Private so that other people viewing your calendar cannot see the details. They can still see that you are busy during the period of the appointment but will not have access to details about the appointment.

To mark an open appointment as Private, click the Private (padlock) button in the Options group of the Event or Appointment tab of the Ribbon.

Determining How an Appointment Displays on the Scheduling Page

Outlook's Scheduling page provides a view of your schedule and the schedules of other people whose calendars you have imported. It is a very useful tool for finding time that is free for all the people you want to attend a meeting.

An appointment in your calendar can display in one of several ways on the Scheduling page: Busy, Tentative, Out of Office, or Free. This display affects your own Scheduling page as well as that of other people with whom you are sharing your calendar. When you create an appointment, you can specify how it will display. (The default is Busy except for all-day events, as mentioned earlier in this chapter.) To do so, click the Show As list on the Options group of the Event or Appointment tab on the Ribbon, and select from the list (Figure 30-16).

Why Display an Appointment as Free?

It may seem strange that Outlook gives you the option of displaying an appointment as Free on the Scheduling page. It makes sense however, when you realize that some appointments are not critical and can easily be changed. You can just as easily get that haircut tomorrow as you can today. By displaying such appointments as Free, you do not prevent other people from scheduling a meeting at that time when they view your schedule.

FIGURE 30-16

Specifying how an appointment displays on the Scheduling page

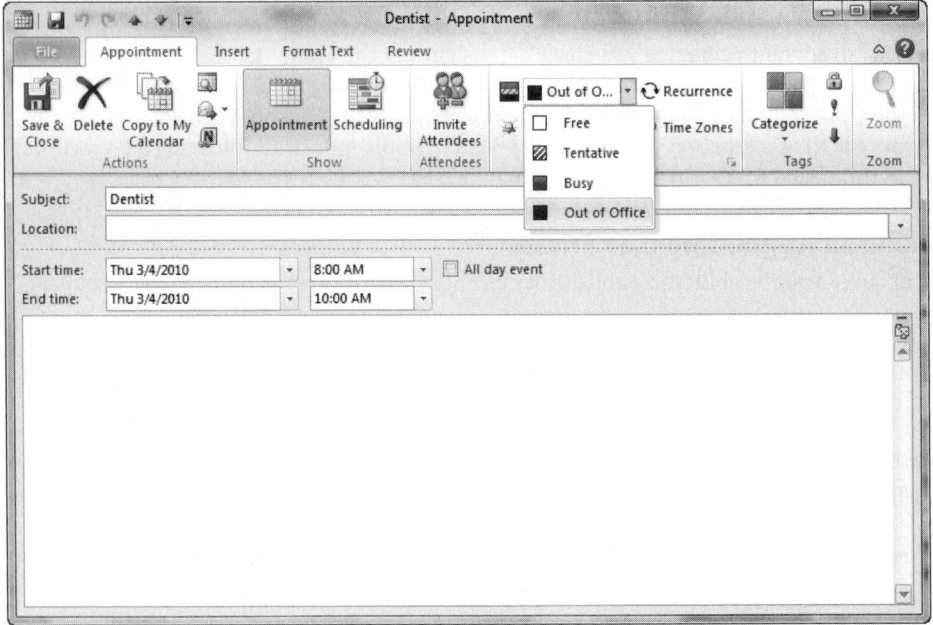

Searching the Calendar

As your Calendar becomes filled with appointments past and future, it will become difficult if not impossible to find information by simply scrolling through the Calendar. You can use the Search feature to filter the Calendar to show just the information you want. For example, you can filter to show only appointments within a certain month assigned to a specific category.

For a basic search, enter your search term in the Search Calendar box at the top right of the Calendar display (Figure 30-17). You can also click on the down arrow to select from previously used search terms. Outlook automatically searches as you enter the term and displays only matching appointments (or a message, if it finds no matching entries). Click the X that is adjacent to the Search box to cancel the search and return to displaying all Calendar items.

If you need more control over the search, click on the magnifying glass at the right end of the Search box without typing anything. Outlook displays the Search Tools Search contextual tab, as shown in Figure 30-18. You can use one of the choices in the Refine group to narrow the search results. Or, you can click Search Tools in the Options group, and then click Advanced Find to open the Advanced Find dialog box. It works just like the one for Contacts described in Chapter 29. Click the Close Search button in the Close group at the right end of the tab to finish working with the search features.

FIGURE 30-17

Performing a basic search of the Calendar

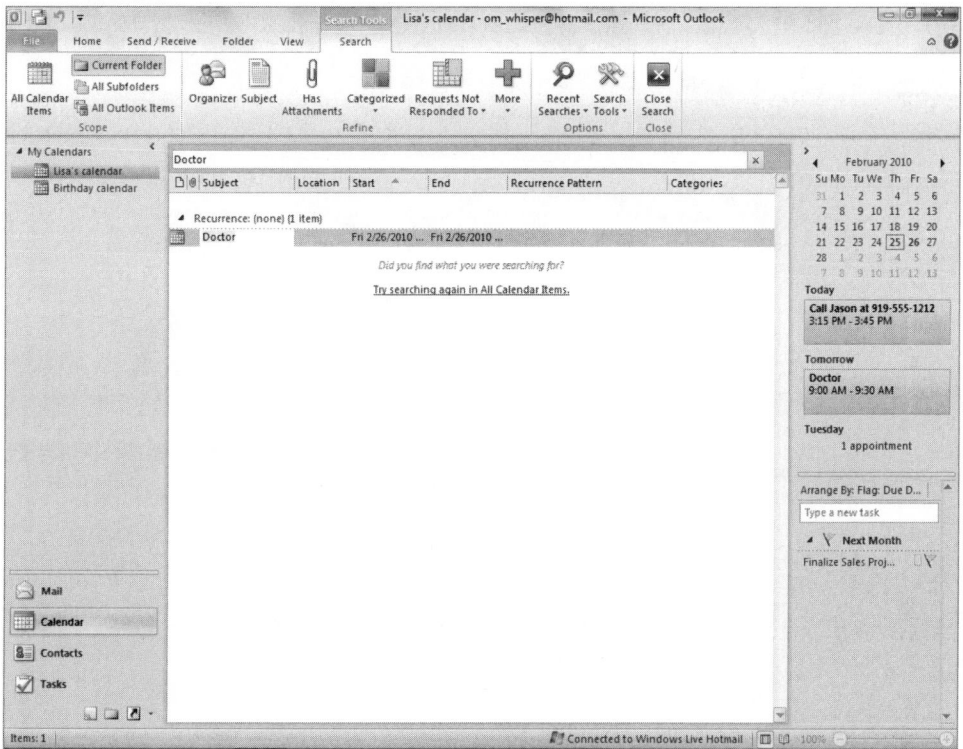

Setting Calendar Options

The Outlook Calendar comes with default settings for many aspects of its operation. As you become familiar with the Calendar, you may want to make changes to these settings to customize the Calendar for the way you work. You access Calendar Options by choosing File on the Ribbon and clicking Options. In the Options dialog box, click Calendar in the list at the left. The Calendar section of options is shown in Figure 30-19. The various options available here are divided into several sections.

The first section of Calendar options has to do with how Outlook defines the workweek, as follows:

- **Calendar Work Week.** Select days that you want to be considered part of the workweek, and deselect those that you do not.

- **First Day of Week.** Select the day that Outlook uses as the first day of the week for Calendar displays.

FIGURE 30-18

Tools for performing an advanced search of the Calendar

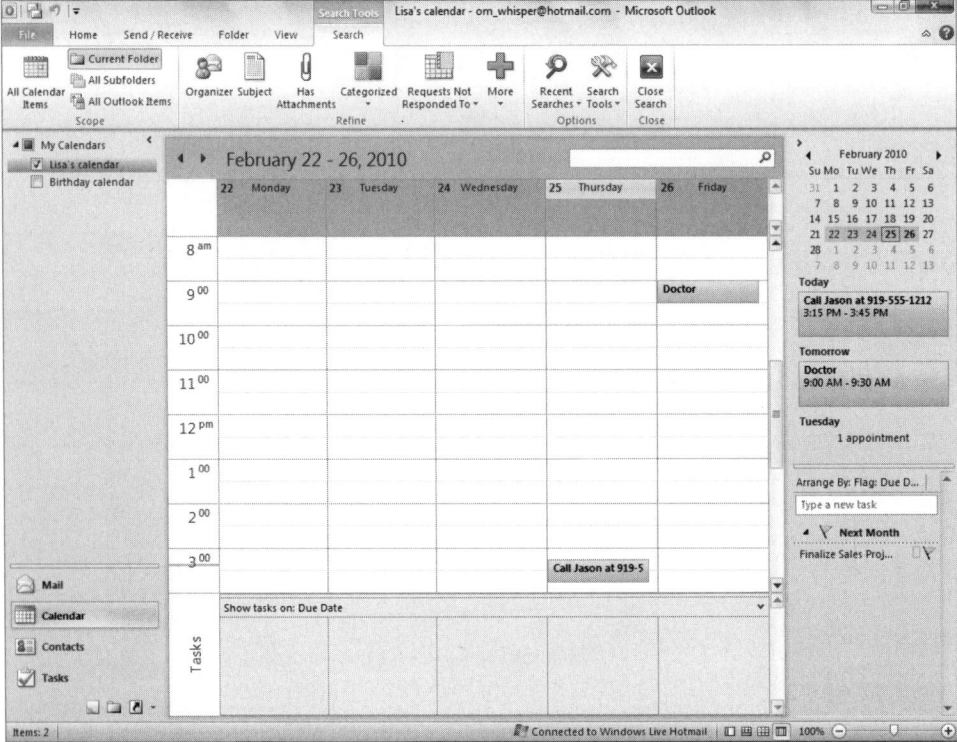

- **Start Time/End Time.** Select the times of day that Outlook uses for the start and stop of the workday.

- **First Week of Year.** Select how Outlook determines the first week of the year. The options are Starts on Jan 1 (the week that contains Jan 1), the first week with four days in the new year, and the first week that is entirely in the new year.

The next section of the Calendar Options dialog box includes options for a variety of features:

- **Default Reminders.** By default, Outlook reminds you of appointments 15 minutes before the start time (you can change this for individual appointments, of course). To change the default lead time, select it from the drop-down list. You can select any time from 0 minutes to two weeks. If you do not want a default reminder for messages, deselect the Default Reminder option.

- **Allow Attendees to Propose New Times for Meetings.** People you invite to meetings are allowed to respond by proposing a new time for the meeting.

- **Use This Response When Proposing a New Meeting Time.** Select from the list to specify whether new meeting times that you propose are marked as Tentative, Accept, or Decline.

- **Add Holidays.** Lets you copy holidays for one or more specific countries onto your calendar. You select the country or countries from a list.

Finally, this dialog box has a few advanced options, as follows:

- **Enable an Alternate Calendar.** Lets you display an alternate calendar in parallel with the default one using the language and calendar structure you select.

- **When Sending Meeting Requests...** Sends meeting requests in the more widely supported iCalendar format instead of Outlook's proprietary format.

FIGURE 30-19

The Calendar section of the Preferences tab in the Options dialog box

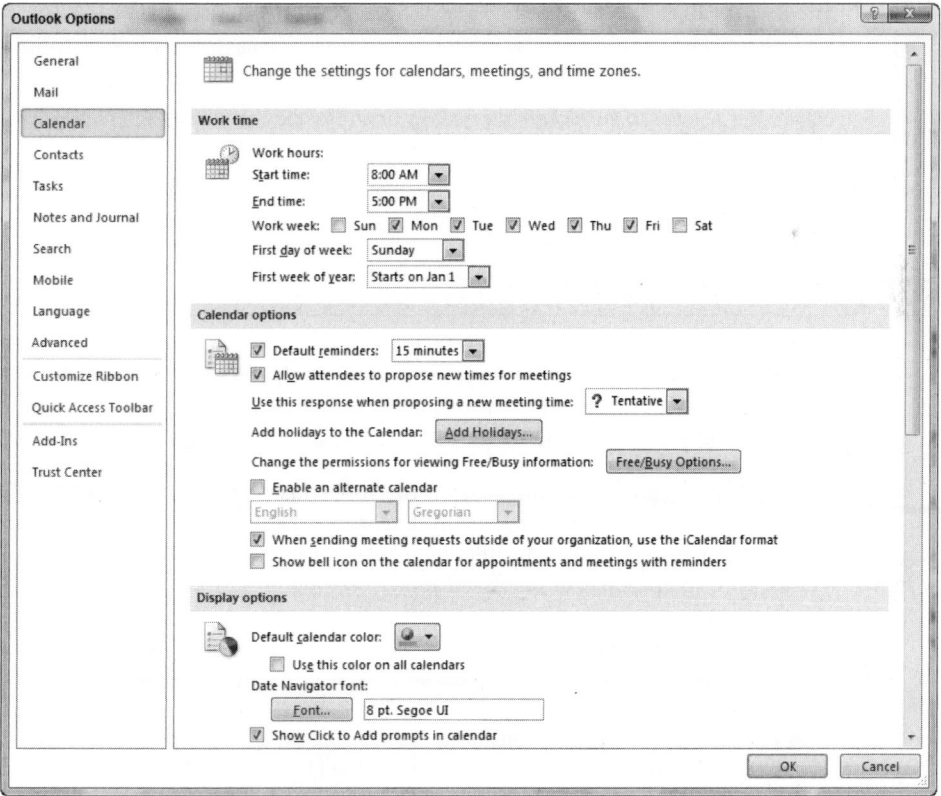

- **Free/Busy Options.** Sets options for publishing your calendar. These options were covered earlier in this chapter.

- **Default Calendar Color.** Select the color to use for the calendar display.

- **Time Zones.** Sets the default time zone for your calendar and also permits you to display a second, alternate time zone in the Calendar.

Understanding Tasks

A *task* is similar to an appointment in that it is something you must do. It is different in that it does not have a specific date or time associated with it, although it may well have a due date by which it is supposed to be completed. In this sense, Outlook tasks are pretty much like a paper to-do list that you stick on the fridge. When you look a little deeper, however, you'll find that tasks can do so much more:

- You can be reminded of a task at a specified time and date.

- You can specify different priorities for different tasks.

- You can assign a task to someone else and send that person a message with the required information.

- You can assign a status to a task (not started, in progress, etc.) as well as a percent completed value.

- You can send a status report on a task to other people.

Using the Tasks Feature

To switch to working with Tasks in Outlook, click the Tasks button in the Navigation pane. The default Tasks view, shown in Figure 30-20, displays active tasks — those not yet completed. They are arranged by due date initially, although you can change the sort order by clicking the column headings (To-Do Title, Status, etc.) at the top of the list.

Strictly speaking, the display shown in Figure 30-20 is the To-Do List — that is, uncompleted tasks. If you want to display all tasks, including completed ones, click the Change View button in the Current group of the Home tab, and click either Simple List or Detailed (Figure 30-21). This view shows all tasks, with completed ones displayed and crossed out.

No Due Date?

Although most tasks have a Due Date, it is not required. Tasks that do not have a Due Date are displayed in their own section, "No Due Date," when tasks are organized by Due Date.

FIGURE 30-20

The default Tasks view displays a list of all your active tasks.

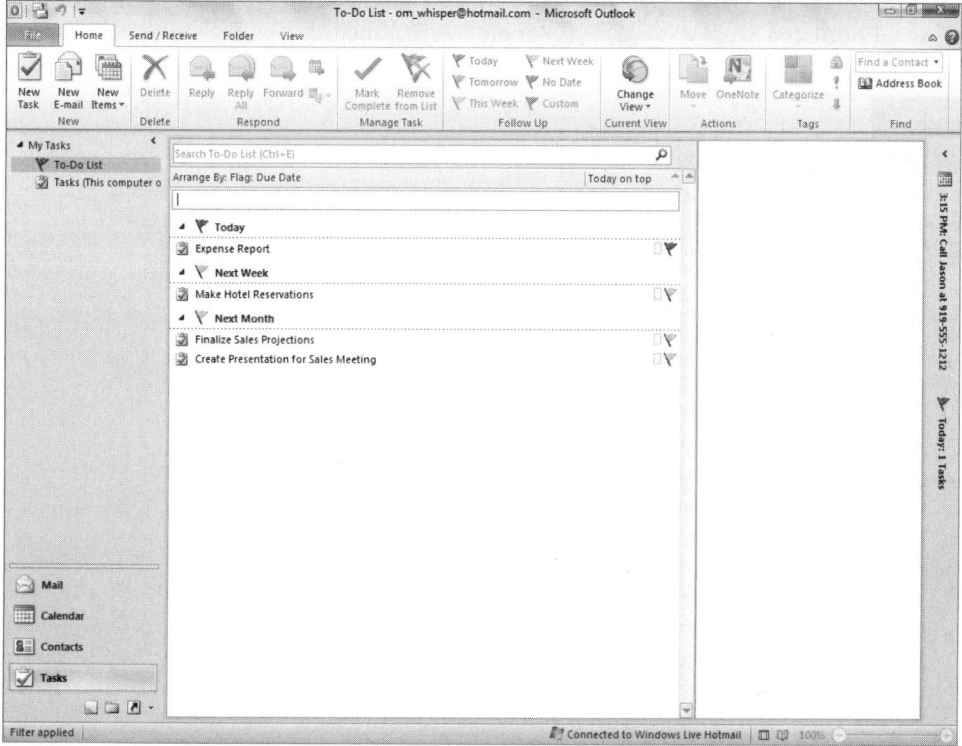

While you are viewing tasks, you can open a single task by double-clicking on it. You can also perform certain actions with the task by right-clicking on it and selecting from the shortcut menu. These actions are the following:

- Mark a task as complete.

- Assign the task to someone.

- Add a follow-up to the task.

- Assign a category to the task.

You learn more about these actions later in this chapter when you learn how to create a new task.

Outlook provides you with several other ways to view your tasks. You can switch to a different view by selecting the desired view using the Change View button on the Home tab. The views are as follows:

- **Detailed.** Similar to Simple List but with more details about each task

- **Simple List.** A list of all tasks including completed ones (same as clicking Tasks, as described earlier)

- **To-Do List.** Displays active tasks in a simplified, easy-to-use format.

- **Prioritized.** Displays tasks with a priority setting applied.

FIGURE 30-21

You can also display all tasks, including completed ones.

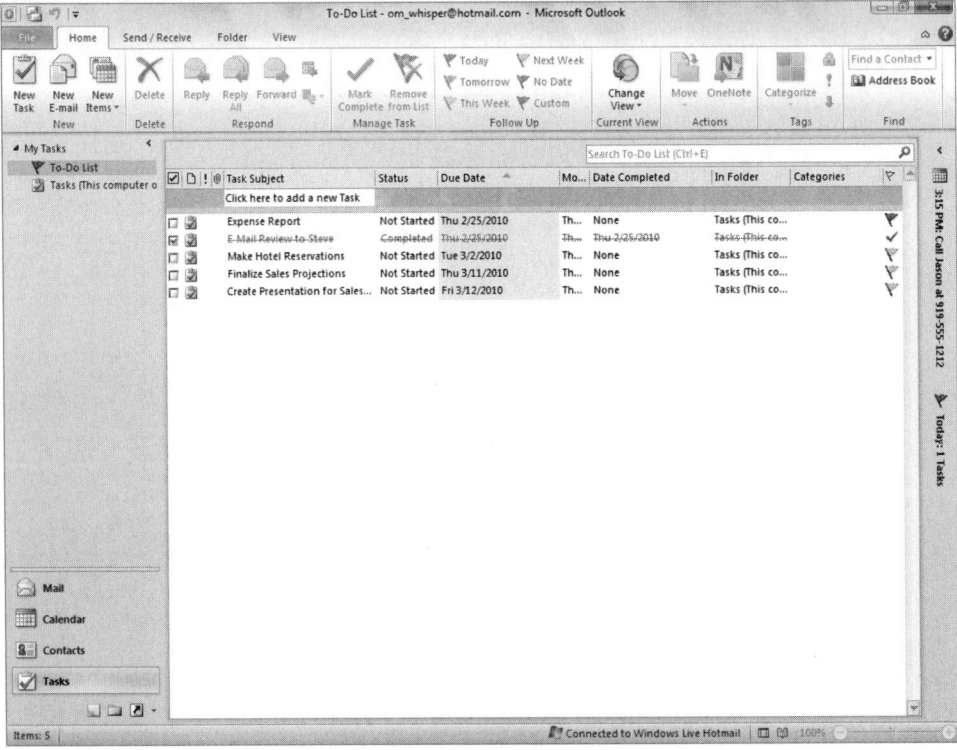

- **Active.** Tasks not marked as completed

- **Completed.** Tasks that have been marked as completed

- **Today.** Shows tasks due to be completed today.

- **Next 7 Days.** Tasks due within the next seven days.

- **Overdue.** Tasks whose due date has passed but are not marked as completed.

- **Assigned.** Tasks organized by the person they are assigned to.

- **Server Tasks.** Lists tasks and whom each task has been assigned to.

Creating a New Task

To create a new task, click the New Task button in the New group on the Home tab of the Ribbon. (You can also press Ctrl+Shift+K.) Outlook creates a new task and displays it as shown in Figure 30-22.

FIGURE 30-22

Creating a new task

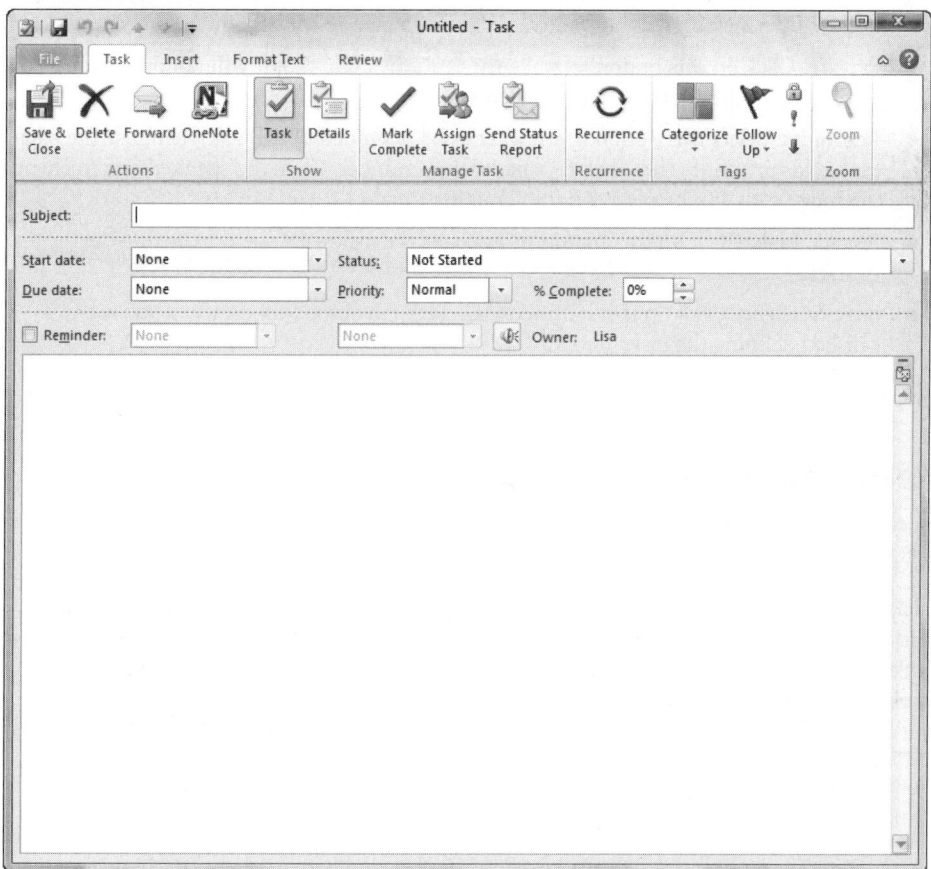

The only required entry in this window is the Subject, which will be the title of the task that is displayed in Task view. The other task information in the window is explained here and in the following sections:

- **Start Date.** If you want to specify a start date for the task, click on the adjacent down-arrow, and select the date from the Calendar.

- **Due Date.** Click on the adjacent down-arrow, and select the task's due date from the Calendar.

- **Status.** By default, this is set as Not Started. If necessary, you can open this list and select In Progress, Completed, Waiting on Someone Else, or Deferred.

- **Priority.** The default is Normal; you can also select Low or High.

- **% Complete.** If the task is already partially complete, use the up and down arrows to specify the correct value in this field.

- **Categorize.** Click on this button to assign the task to an Outlook category.

- **Follow Up.** Click on this button to assign a follow-up to the task.

- **Private.** Click on this button to make the task private so that it will not be viewable by other people when you share your calendar.

- **Reminder.** Select this option if you want to be reminded of the task; then, use the adjacent fields to specify the date and time of the reminder. Click the speaker icon to change the sound that will be played at the reminder time.

- **Assign Task.** Click on this button to associate the task with one or more of your contacts.

- **Save & Close.** Click on this button on the Task tab of the Ribbon when you are finished defining the task.

Other aspects of creating a new task are explained in the following sections.

Entering Task Details

If you click the Details button in the Show group of the Task tab of the Ribbon, Outlook displays the Details window for the task. This window is shown in Figure 30-23.

The fields available in the Details window let you keep track of additional information related to a task. You can specify the completion date, enter information about the time spent on the task, identify a company associated with the task, track mileage, and enter billing information. Outlook does not track this information for you but just provides these detail fields for you to enter it in.

The lower section of the Details window is relevant only if the task has been assigned to someone; this window is explained in the next section.

When you have finished entering details for the task, click the Task button in the Show group of the Task tab on the Ribbon to return to the regular Task window. You can also click Save & Close if you have finished defining the task.

Assigning a Task

Outlook lets you assign a task to someone else. Doing so can be useful in a variety of situations, such as when you are heading a committee and need to delegate various jobs to the committee members. By using Outlook's Assign Task command, you can track progress and be notified when each task has been completed.

FIGURE 30-23

Entering details for a new task

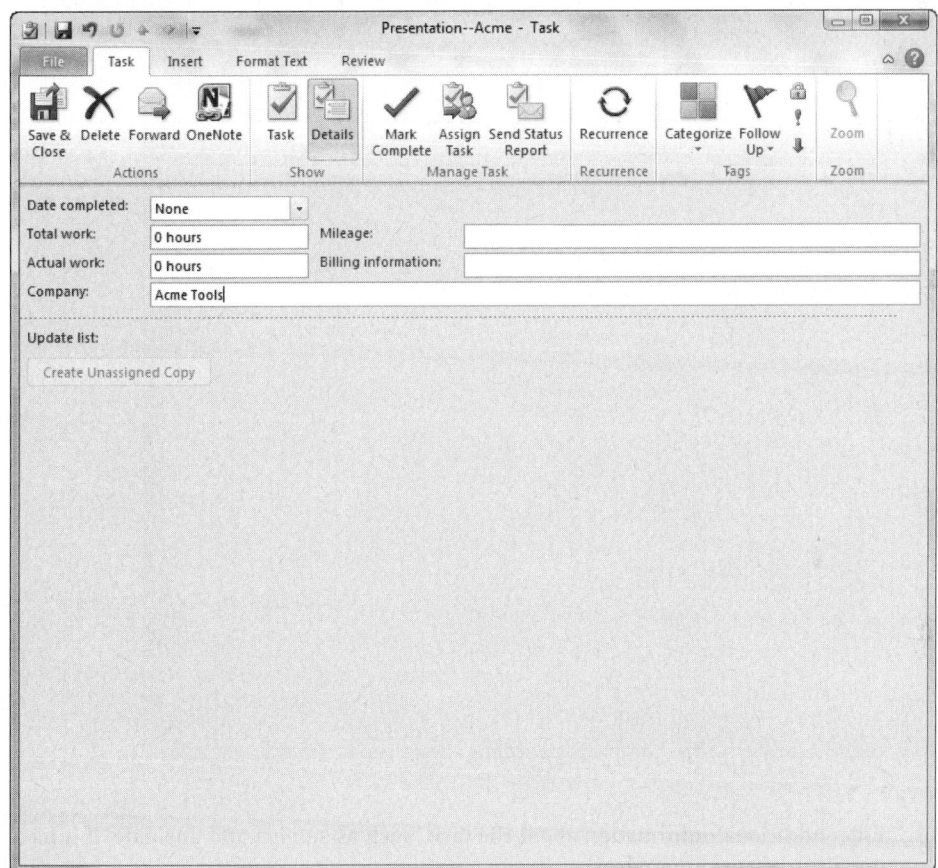

To assign a task, create the task as described earlier in this chapter. You can also open an existing task and, as long as you are the owner of the task, assign it to someone else. Here's how:

1. **Click the Assign Task button in the Manage Task group of the Task tab of the Ribbon.** Outlook displays the window shown in Figure 30-24. This is actually just the regular Task window with a few extra elements.

2. **In the To field, enter the e-mail address of the person to whom you are assigning the task.** You can also click the To button and select from your contacts.

FIGURE 30-24

Assigning a task to someone else

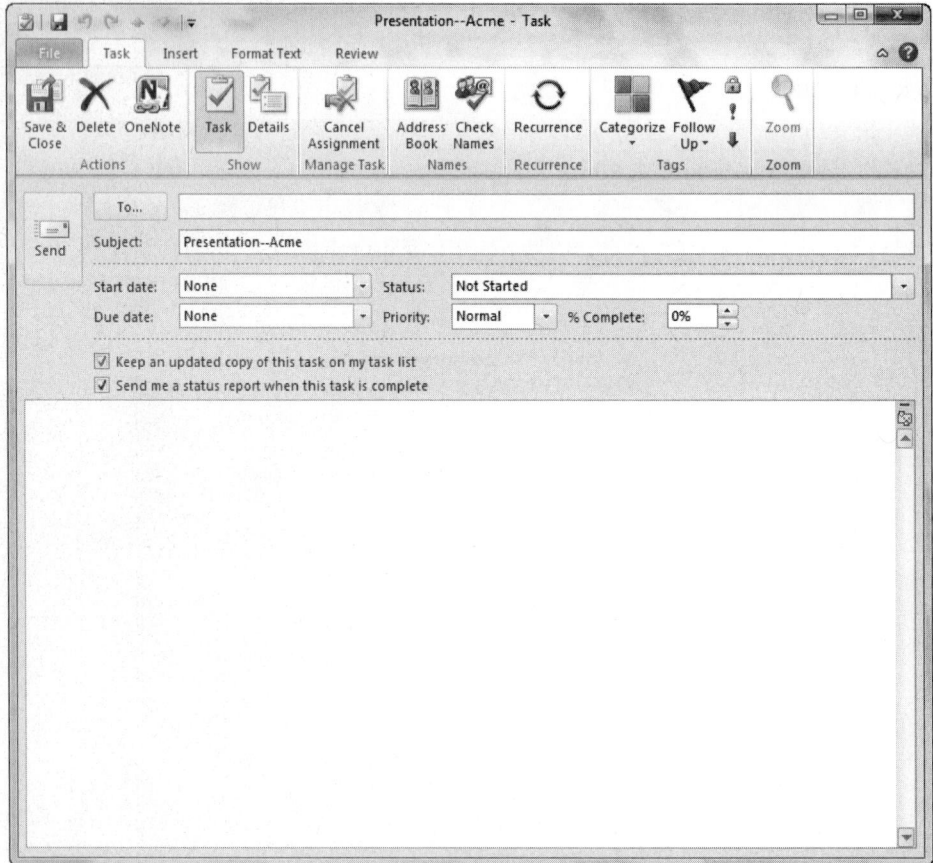

3. Enter additional information about the task, such as subject and due date, if it has not already been entered.

4. Select or deselect the two available options (explained next).

5. Click the Send button.

Two options are available when you assign a task to someone else, as follows:

- **Keep an Updated Copy of This Task on My Task List.** You receive automatic updates when the person to whom you assign the task updates its status.

- **Send Me a Status Report When This Task Is Complete.** You receive an automatic notification when the person to whom you assign the task marks it as Completed.

When you send a task assignment, the recipient receives an e-mail message containing information about the assignment and permitting the recipient to either accept or decline the assignment. You learn more about this and other aspects of task assignments later in this chapter, in the section, "Working with Assigned Tasks."

Specifying Task Recurrence

Like appointments, tasks can have a defined recurrence. For example, you may have to review each month's sales figures by the end of the next month. Rather than enter a new task each month, you can define a task that recurs each month.

To define a recurring task, create the task as usual, and before saving and closing it, click the Recurrence button in the Options group of the Task tab of the Ribbon. Outlook opens the Task Recurrence dialog box, as shown in Figure 30-25.

Assigning Recurring Tasks

When you assign a recurring task, a copy of the task remains in your Task List but cannot be updated automatically. However, if you requested a status report when the task is complete, you receive a status report for each occurrence of the task that is completed.

FIGURE 30-25

Defining a recurring task

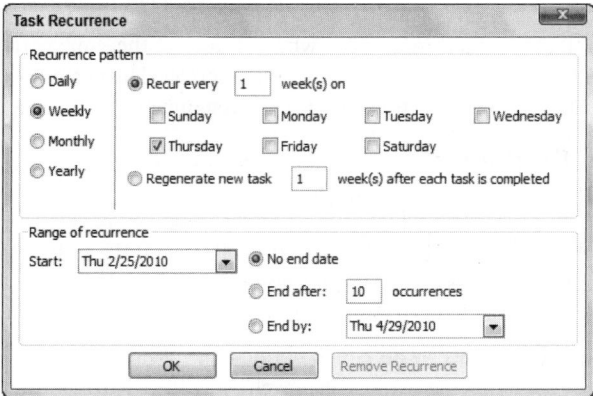

The four basic patterns of recurrence are Daily, Weekly, Monthly, and Yearly. When you choose the basic pattern in the top left of the dialog box, the remainder of the options change to reflect what's available:

- **Daily.** You can choose every so many days or every weekday.

- **Weekly.** You specify how often (every week, every two weeks, etc.) and the day or days of the week.

- **Monthly.** You specify which day of the month, either as a number (e.g., the 25th of each month) or a day of the week (e.g., the first Thursday).

- **Yearly.** You specify a specific date (e.g., June 12) or a day of a month (e.g., the first Monday in June).

In all cases, you also specify a start date and when the recurring task ends.

Working with Assigned Tasks

Working with assigned tasks, whether you are the person doing the assigning or the person accepting the assignment, can be a bit confusing. After you understand it, however, the tool can be very useful.

Receiving a Task Assignment

When someone sends you a task assignment, you receive an e-mail message asking you to respond to the assignment request. There are three buttons of importance on the Task tab of the Ribbon in the message window:

- **Accept.** Accepts the assignment, adds it to your Task List, and notifies the person who sent you the assignment that you have accepted.

- **Decline.** Declines the assignment and notifies the person who sent you the assignment that you have declined.

- **Assign Task.** Lets you assign the task to a third person, who will receive the same notification and can accept, decline, or assign the task to yet another person. The person who originally assigned the task to you will be notified of the reassignment.

Receiving Accept/Decline Notifications

When you send a task assignment to someone, one of three things will happen:

- **The person may accept the task.** You receive a message to that effect, and the task is automatically updated to reflect that the task was accepted and is now owned by that person.

- **The person may decline the task.** You receive an e-mail notification. When you open this e-mail, you can take one of the following two actions by clicking the corresponding button on the toolbar:

  - **Return the task to your Task List.** You regain ownership of the task.

  - **Assign task.** Assign the task to someone else.

- **The person you assigned the task to may assign it to someone else.** That person, in turn, can accept, decline, or reassign the task.

About Task Ownership

A task has, at any given moment, one and only one owner. *Owning* a task means that you can assign it to someone else. Here's how ownership works:

- When you create a task, you are the original owner.
- When you assign the task to someone, that person becomes the temporary owner.
- The person who receives the assignment can do one of three things: (1) accept the task and become the owner; (2) decline the task and return ownership to the sender; or (3) assign the task to a third person, who then becomes the temporary owner.

If you assign a task to someone and that person declines, ownership passes back to you only when you reclaim ownership by returning the task to your Task List. It does not happen automatically.

Assigning a Task to Multiple People

Although Outlook does not prevent you from assigning a task to two or more people, you cannot keep an updated copy of the task in your Task List. For this reason, it is better to divide a multiperson task into parts and assign each part, as a separate task, to an individual person.

Task Status Reports

When you have accepted a task assignment, you own that task and no one but you can change the task even though it may be on someone else's Task List. You can then, as you work on the task, open it and update the status and percentage completed of the task; you can also mark it as Completed. When you do so and save the modified task, an update is sent to the person who assigned you the task (assuming that the Keep an Updated Copy of This Task on My Task List option was selected when you were sent the assignment). By default, this update does not appear in the task assigner's Inbox but is processed automatically, and the updated information is available the next time the task assigner views the task.

Likewise, if the Send Me a Status Report When This Task Is Complete option was selected when you were sent the assignment, the person who assigned the task receives an automatic update when you mark the task as Completed. Although Task Complete updates are processed automatically, they appear in the person's Inbox.

A task can have more than one prior owner. Suppose, for example, that person A created the task and sent a task request to person B. Then, person B sent a task request to person C, who accepted the task. C is the owner of the task, and both A and B are prior owners and will receive status updates.

Sending a Status Report Manually

Sometimes you may want to send a status report or comments about a task manually. Here are two situations in which doing so might be desirable:

- The original task request (when you were assigned the task) did not include a request for automatic status updates.

- You were not assigned the task; it is simply a task that you created but want to keep other people updated about.

To send a status report manually, open and save the task and click the "Send Status Report" button in the Manage Task group of the Task tab of the Ribbon. Outlook creates an e-mail message with information about the task status in the body of the message. You can add text as needed. If the task was assigned to you, the To field already contains the addresses of the task's prior owners. You can add additional recipients if desired.

Other Ways of Viewing Tasks

The most flexible way to view your tasks is by using the Task view, as explained earlier in this chapter. You can also have Outlook display tasks on the To-Do bar and in Calendar view.

Viewing Tasks on the To-Do Bar

You can display active tasks on the To-Do bar along with the Date Navigator and upcoming appointments. They are displayed at the bottom, as shown in Figure 30-26.

If you do not see your tasks on the To-Do bar, you may need to change the To-Do bar display by right-clicking it and then selecting Task List from the shortcut menu.

Viewing Tasks on the Calendar

The Outlook Calendar can display the daily Task List along with your appointments. The daily Task List is displayed below the Appointment section of the Calendar, as shown in Figure 30-27. You have three options as to how the daily Task List is displayed:

- **Normal.** This is shown in the figure, with task subjects, categories, and follow-up flags.

- **Minimized.** This displays the number of active tasks for the displayed time period without any details.

- **Off.** This does not display the list.

To switch between daily Task List views, display the Outlook Calendar, click the View tab, and then choose Daily Task List in the Layout group. Then, select the desired view from the next menu. The Arrange By choices on this menu also let you specify whether to display tasks by due date (the default) or start date, and whether to show completed tasks.

FIGURE 30-26

Viewing the daily Task List on the To-Do bar.

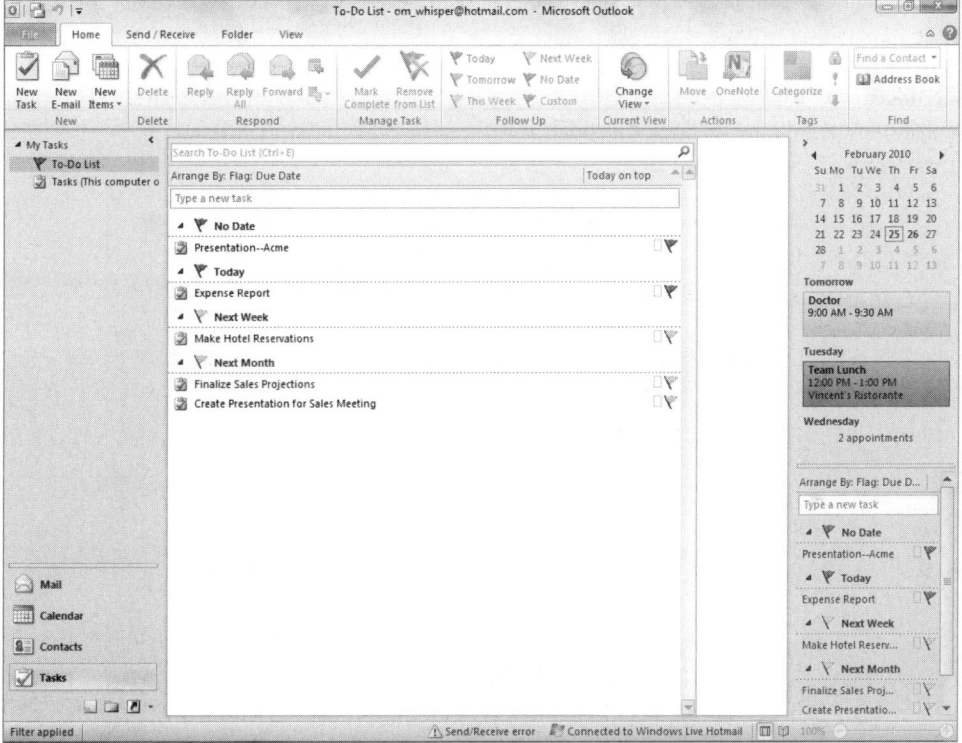

Setting Task Options

Outlook offers several options that relate to the way tasks and task assignments work. To view and change these options, select Options from the File to display the Outlook Options dialog box, then click Tasks at the left. The Tasks choices are shown in Figure 30-28. The first two options determine the colors used to display overdue tasks and completed tasks; the default colors are red and dark gray, respectively. The other options are as follows:

- **Set Reminders on Tasks with Due Dates.** If selected, Outlook automatically sets a reminder for all tasks that you create with a due date.

- **Keep My Task List Updated.** If selected, Outlook maintains updated copies of tasks you have assigned on your task list.

- **Send Status Report.** If selected, Outlook automatically sends a status report when you mark as Completed a task that you have been assigned.

FIGURE 30-27

Viewing the daily Task List on the Outlook Calendar.

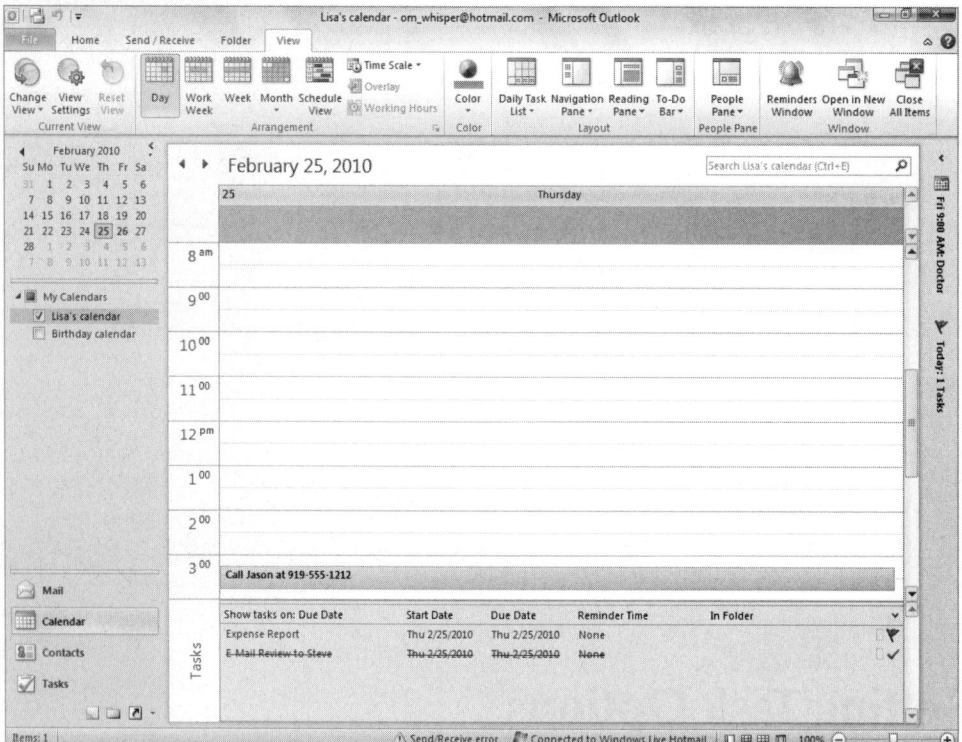

FIGURE 30-28

The Task Options dialog box

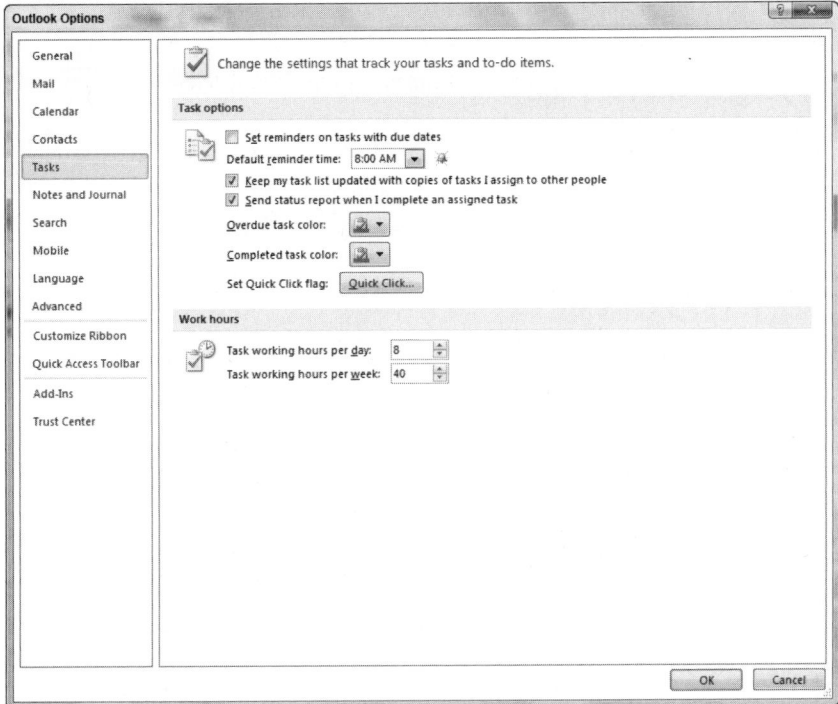

Summary

Outlook's Calendar is a powerful and flexible tool for keeping track of your appointments and other time commitments. Much more than a simple date book, the Outlook Calendar can do things such as remind you of an upcoming appointment.

Outlook provides some powerful tools for keeping track of your tasks. Although a task does not have a specific period of time associated with it (unlike an appointment), it can have a due date. By listing your tasks and optionally reminding you of when they are due, Outlook can greatly reduce the chance that you'll forget to do something important. Outlook even lets you assign tasks to other people and track their progress, a truly valuable tool for a manager or team leader.

Part VI

Designing Publications with Publisher

Introducing Publisher

Desktop publishing made creating printed publications easier and faster but for years it remained the bailiwick of graphic art and design superheroes. The software was expensive and difficult to master and provided little in the way of design help for mere mortals.

Microsoft Publisher was one of the first programs to make publication design affordable and doable for Joe Blow and Jill Blow computer users. From its first version, Publisher offered an easy layout, simple tools, a variety of styles and graphics, and attractive templates for publication designs. This chapter shows you how to use Publisher 2010 to choose a publication template and add text and graphics to complete a publication.

The Publisher Workspace

The 2010 version of Publisher now features the Ribbon interface added in the core Office applications in its 2007 incarnation. Even if you've used Publisher previously, reading this chapter and the next will help you become familiar with the new 2010 version.

Each time you start Publisher, the program prompts you to create a new publication file by selecting a template. You can either create a new publication as described in the next section, click on a tab on the Ribbon to go to a default blank document, or click the Open command to open a publication you created previously. In any case, Publisher displays a publication and the Ribbon in its workspace (Figure 31-1).

You can design your publications by adding text, graphic objects, and other elements to the white page area. When the publication has multiple pages,

IN THIS CHAPTER

Learning how to get around in Publisher

Choosing and using a publication design

Typing text or inserting it from a file

Working with text AutoFlow and flowing text between frames

Formatting text

Inserting and formatting pictures

Drawing your own shapes and lines

Adding and editing a table

you can move between pages by pressing Ctrl+Page Up and Ctrl+Page Down, or by clicking on the icon for a page in the Page Navigation pane, on the left side of the workspace. The gray area that appears around the page is called the *scratch area*. This area serves as a holding space for any objects you might want to pull off the page and reuse elsewhere. For example, you can drag a graphic off one page to the scratch area, display another page, and then drag the graphic onto that page.

FIGURE 31-1

The Publisher workspace offers a variety of tools for creating publications.

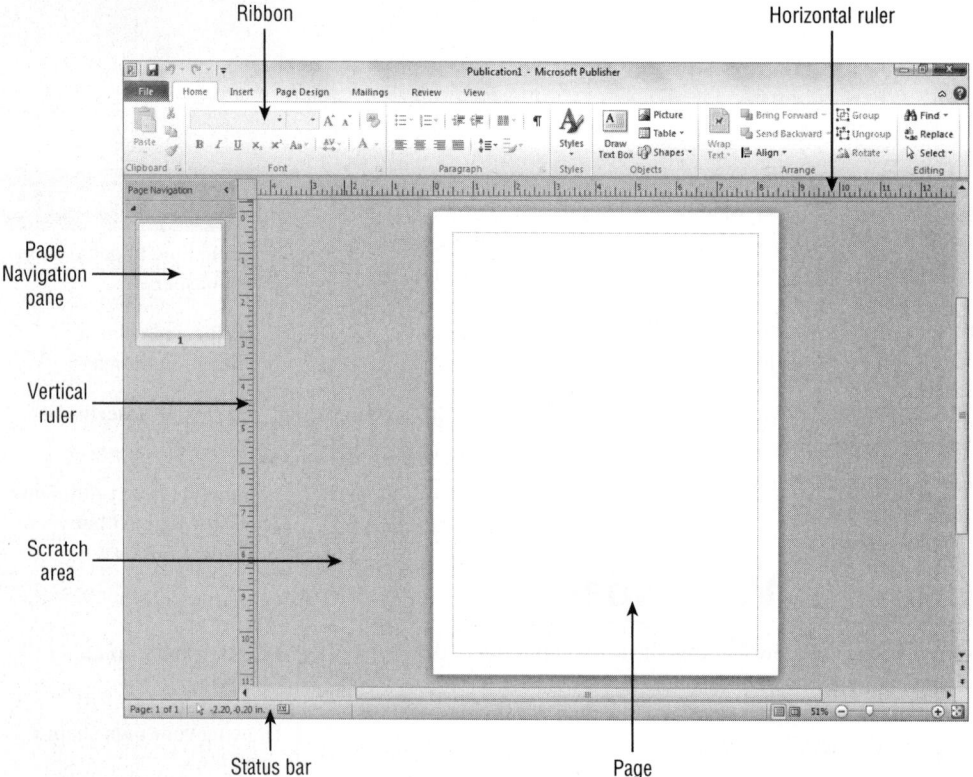

The *vertical* and *horizontal rulers* enable you to align objects on a page with precision. As you drag an object, a moving marker appears on each ruler to indicate the mouse position, and the position measurements appear in the status bar. By default, when you drag an object and release the mouse, the object will snap into alignment with any green ruler guides that you have displayed or added. You can turn this snap feature on or off using the Guides check box in the Layout group of the Page Design tab. You can display built-in ruler guides for arranging objects by clicking the Guides button in the Layout group of the Page Design tab, and then clicking one of the thumbnails under Built-In Ruler Guides on the gallery that appears. You can also create custom ruler guides by dragging them from either ruler, as shown in the example in Figure 31-2. Then, drag objects to align with your guides.

Note

You also can use the Size settings, described later in the chapter, to size and position objects. ■

FIGURE 31-2

Drag from either ruler to create a guide.

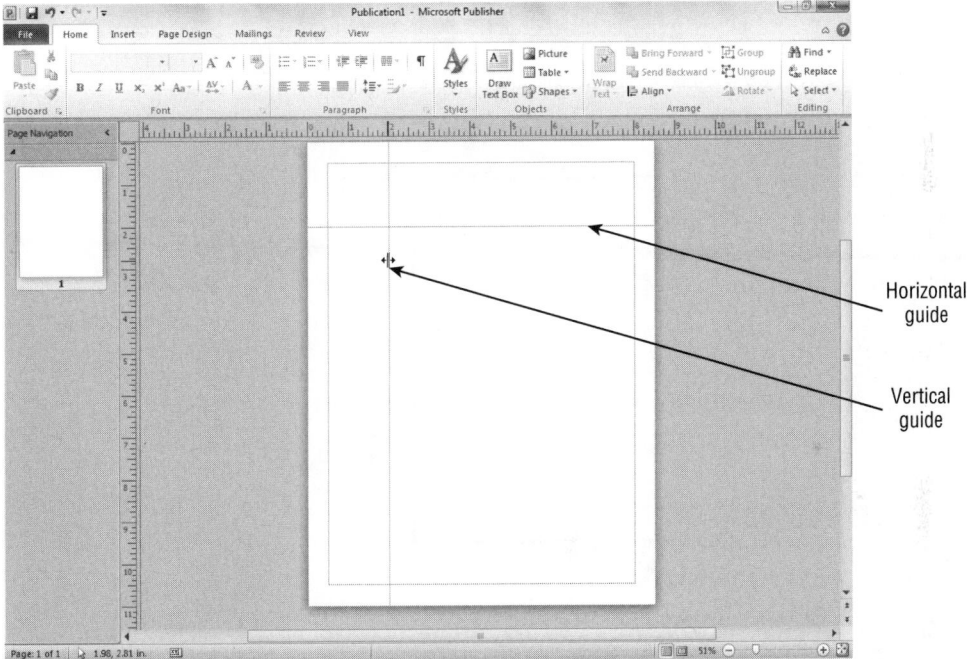

The Ribbon in Publisher offers a variety of buttons, galleries, and lists that you can use to add and work with publication content and publication files. Publisher displays these seven Ribbon tabs onscreen by default:

- **File.** As in the other Office 2010 applications, the File tab displays the Backstage view, with choices for creating, managing, sharing, and printing files.

- **Home.** This tab includes buttons for adding and formatting text, copying and pasting, working with object positioning, and finding and replacing.

- **Insert.** This tab enables you to insert pages, create tables, insert different types of illustrations such as clip art, use building blocks to create content, add business information or insert text from another document, add hyperlinks, and work with headers and footers.

● **Page Design.** This tab enables you to change the page template, modify the margins, and set the color and font scheme. For example, Figure 31-3 shows a template applied to a previously blank document.

FIGURE 31-3

Use the Page Design tab to change templates and choose other page settings.

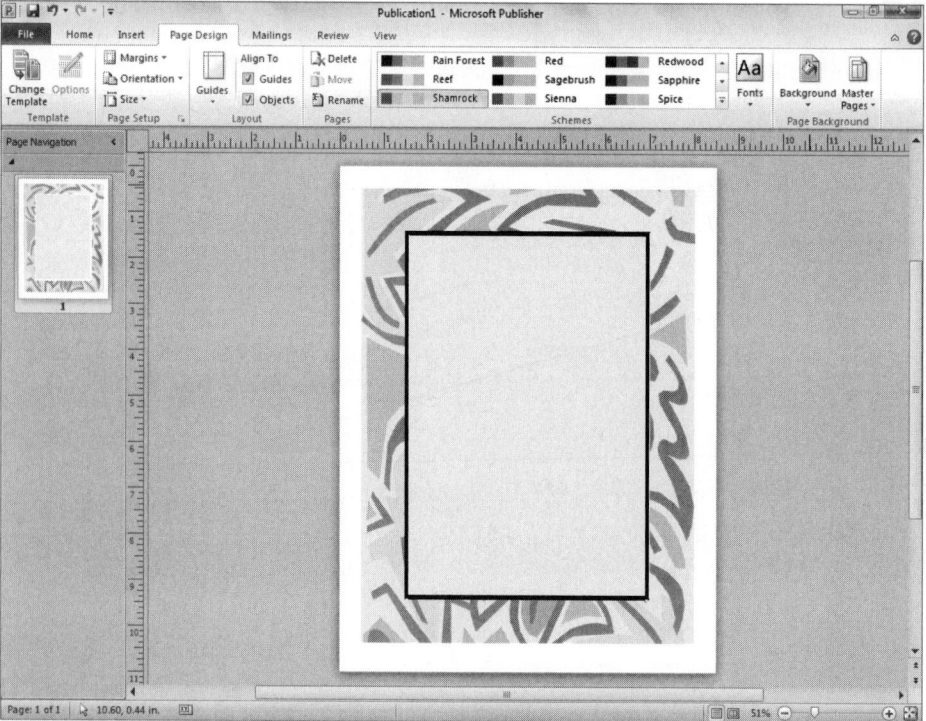

● **Merge.** This tab enables you to merge data from a list to make custom copies of a document, as in Word 2010.

● **Review.** This tab offers choices for spell checking the document, performing content research, substituting words with the thesaurus, and changing language settings.

● **View.** This tab offers the options for changing how the document appears onscreen, including the settings for hiding and redisplaying specific screen elements such as guides and rulers.

Tip

Remember, to see the function of any Ribbon button or list, point to it with the mouse to display a pop-up ScreenTip identifying what the button or list does. ■

As in other Office applications, with Publisher one or more contextual tabs may appear depending on what item you've selected in the document. For example, you might see the Drawing Tools Format or Text Box Tools Format tabs. You can use the choices on contextual tabs as needed to format and edit the selected object.

Using a Template to Create a Publication

Any time you start Publisher or select the File ➪ New command (Ctrl+N), Publisher displays the Available Template choices (Figure 31-4) in the Backstage view so that you can navigate to and select a template to use to create a new publication file.

FIGURE 31-4

Publisher enables you to select a template from various publication types arranged by category.

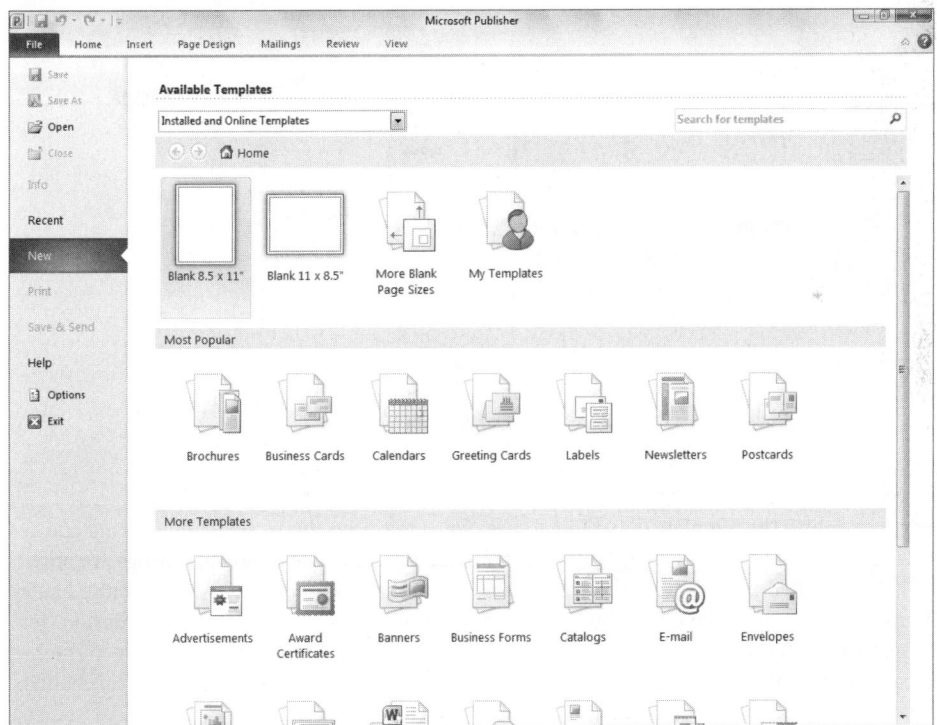

Scroll down, click an icon under a category such as Most Popular, and Publisher displays the templates for that document type. Click on the desired template to see a preview in the upper-right corner, as shown in Figure 31-5. If you want to see more template choices, you can simply scroll down. Use the drop-down list just below Available Templates to control whether Publisher displays templates from Office.com, only templates installed on your computer, or both.

FIGURE 31-5

Browse, preview, and select a template.

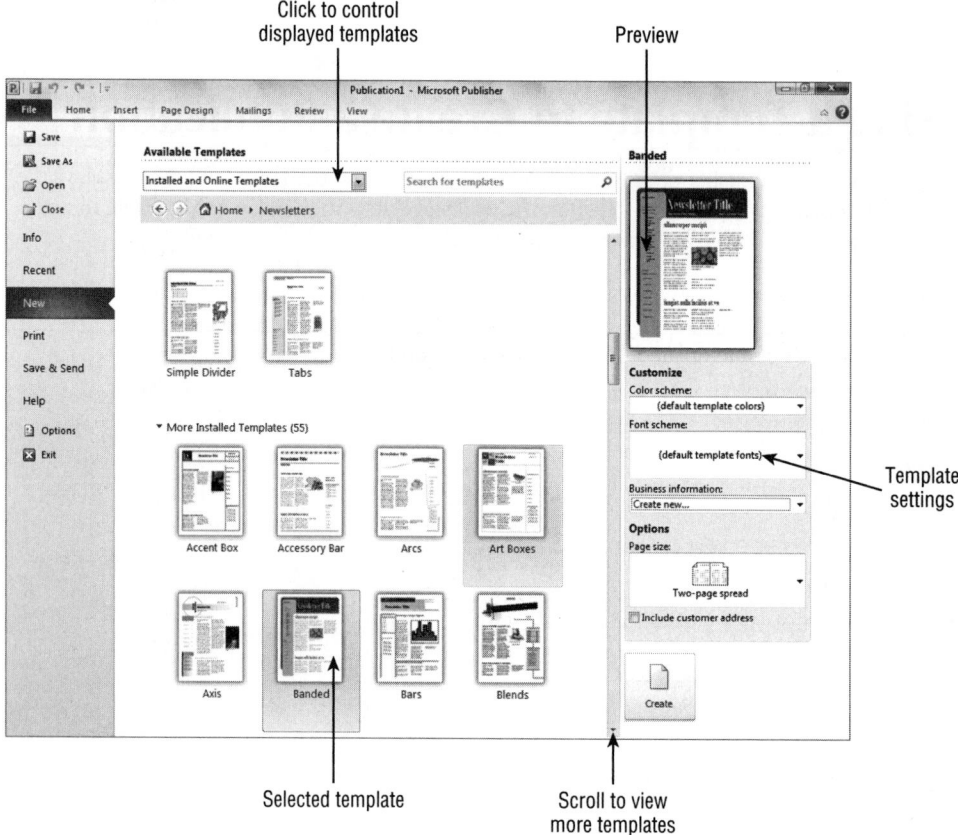

Click to control
displayed templates

Preview

Template
settings

Selected template

Scroll to view
more templates

When you've found the template you'd like to use, you can set up the template by making choices in the Customize and Options areas below the template preview. The template settings are only available for installed templates. Online templates do not display any options. After you've made the desired choices, click the Create button (for installed templates) or the Download button (for online templates) in the lower-right corner to create the new publication. It will appear in the workspace, as in the example shown in Figure 31-6, so that you can begin replacing placeholder information with the unique information for your publication.

Notice that the new publication file has a placeholder name, *Publication2*, as seen in the example in Figure 31-6. Remember to use the File ➪ Save command (Ctrl+S) or click the Save button on the Quick Access Toolbar to name the publication and specify a save location for it. Press Ctrl+S periodically to save changes as you make them in the file, and use the File ➪ Open command (Ctrl+O) or click the Open button on the Standard toolbar to reopen any existing publication.

FIGURE 31-6

The new document based on the template appears.

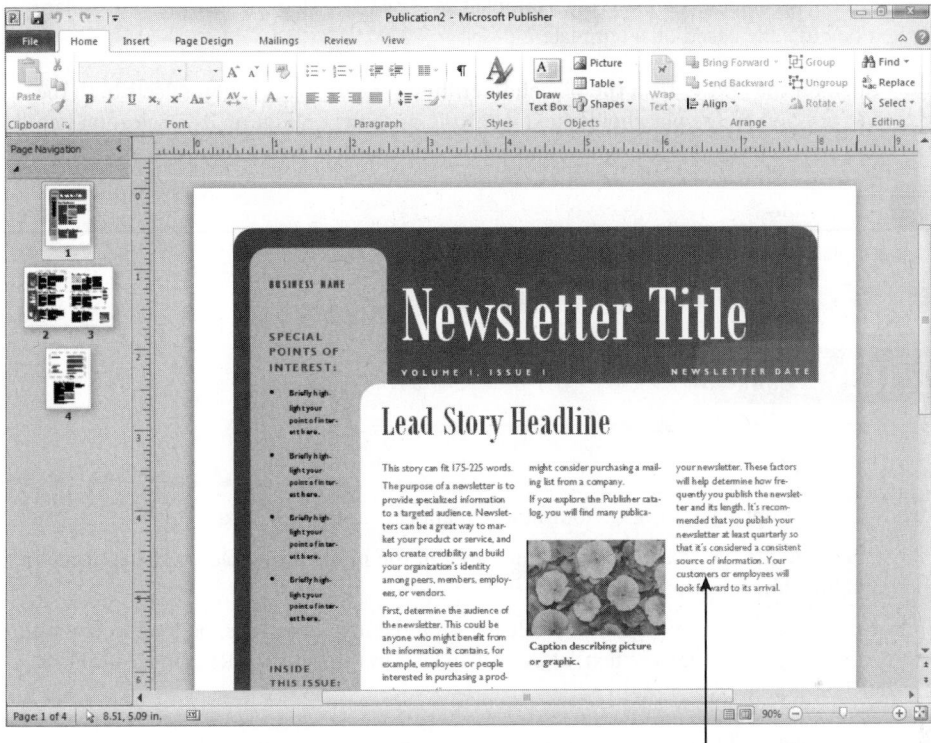

Text boxes with
instructions

Note

You can click Recent in the Backstage view and then click on one of the publications listed to reopen a recently used file. ∎

Working with Text

In Publisher, you add text into a text box. When you move the mouse over a text box, a dashed boundary displays to define where the text will appear. (Clicking in the text box changes to a solid boundary with selection handles.) If you created your publication from a template, the template design provided placeholder text boxes within the publication, as in the example shown in Figure 31-6. In that case, you can simply use an existing text box to add the text. You also can create your own text boxes as required for your publication design.

Typing Text in a Placeholder

Adding text into a placeholder text box requires that you select the placeholder and then type the text within the placeholder to replace the example text. Use these steps to add text into a placeholder text box in a file based on a template:

1. **Click on the text within the placeholder.** In most cases, this action selects both the text box and all the placeholder text within it, as shown in Figure 31-7. Selection handles appear around the text box, and the placeholder text is highlighted.

FIGURE 31-7

Click the text in a template text box to select both the text box and the example text.

2. **Type the replacement text.** Your new text appears in the text box.
3. **Click outside the text box on a blank area of the publication.** Doing so deselects the text box, finishing your entry.

Text boxes do not resize automatically in Publisher, so if the text you add is too long to fit within the text box, you need to resize the text, as described later in the section, "Resizing, AutoFlow, and Linked Text Boxes."

Many of the templates have automated placeholders that automatically insert business information stored in the business information set in Publisher. If you have not yet specified information for the business information set, choose File ➪ Info ➪ Edit Business Information. Enter the information in the Create New Business Information Set dialog box, click Save, and then click Update Publication. You can use the Business Information drop-down list in the Text group of the Insert tab to select a business information component and add that item to the publication at the insertion point. Business information items may have their own placeholders in publications. When you point to such an item, you can click on the option button that appears and then click on a choice in the shortcut menu to decide how to work with the information.

Tip

When you click in a text box, you can press the Del key to delete it from the publication. ■

Creating a Placeholder and Adding Text

Whether you used a template as the basis for your publication or created the publication from scratch, you can add a new text box to place text in any location that you like in the publication. To add a text box, use the Draw Text Box tool, which is available on two of the Ribbon tabs.

1. **Click the Draw Text Box button in the Objects group of the Home tab or the Text group on the Insert tab.**

2. **Drag diagonally on the publication page to create a text box in the desired size and shape** (Figure 31-8). When you release the mouse button, the blinking insertion point appears within the text box.

FIGURE 31-8

Drag to define the size and shape for the text box.

Draw Text Box button

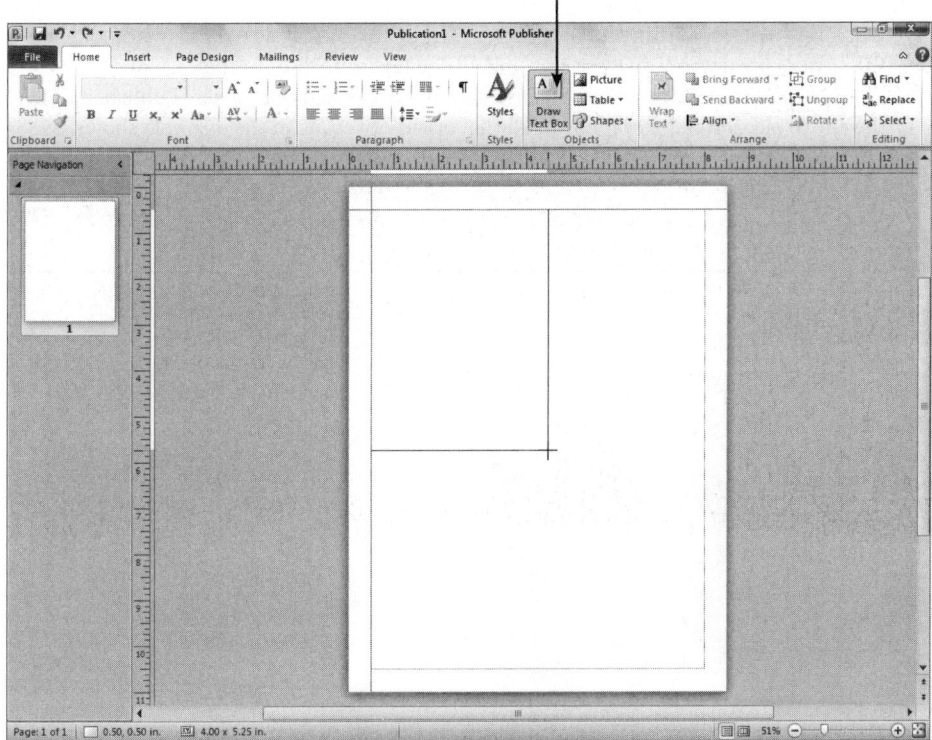

3. **Type the text.** Your new text appears in the text box.

4. **Click outside the text box on a blank area of the publication.** Doing so deselects the text box, finishing your entry.

Tip
The text that you add into a text box is also called a *story*. ∎

Inserting a Text File

Often, writing text and designing a publication are two separate activities assigned to two different people within an organization or group, especially for a publication that requires a lot of text, such as a newsletter or catalog. The person handling the writing assignment typically uses Word, WordPad, or another word processing program to write and edit the text, because a word processing program is the better tool for that purpose.

You need not worry about retyping text supplied by a colleague. Instead, you can insert word processing files [in popular formats including Word, WordPerfect, plain text (.txt), or Rich Text Format (.rtf)] directly into a text placeholder. The steps for doing so, which follow, combine the process for adding text into a text box and for opening a file:

1. **Click on the text within the placeholder.** If the text box is a template placeholder, this action selects both the text box and all the text within it. In the case of a placeholder for a newsletter story or other situation with linked text boxes, Publisher selects the entire placeholder story within all the linked boxes, as in the example shown in Figure 31-9.

FIGURE 31-9

Publisher selects the entire story in linked text boxes.

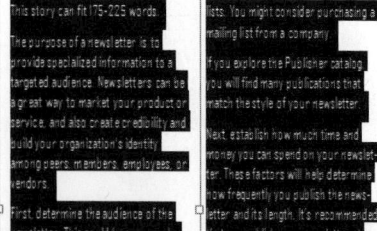

High Goals Are the Right Goals

Caption describing picture or graphic.

2. **Click the Insert tab, and click Insert File in the Text group.** The Insert Text dialog box appears.

3. **Navigate to the folder holding the word processing file to insert.** The dialog box lists the files with readable text formats stored in that folder, as depicted in Figure 31-10.

FIGURE 31-10

Insert a text file from a word processing program to avoid retyping the information.

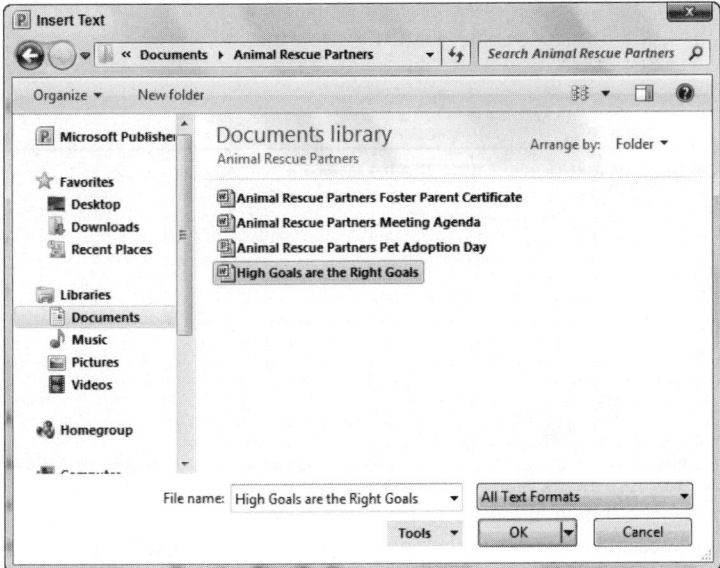

Tip

Click All Text Formats and then select Recover Text from Any File to list all the folder's files in the dialog box. ∎

4. **Click on the name of the text file to insert, and then click OK.** The text from the inserted file appears in the placeholder you selected in Step 1.

Depending on the file format of the inserted file and whether any text and style formatting was applied in the original document, you may need to change the formatting of the text after inserting the file. The later section titled "Formatting Text" discusses some of the formatting methods you can use.

Note

If the writer for a publication that you're creating uses an older or unsupported word processing program, have the writer use the Save As or Export command in the program to save the file that you need to use as a plain-text or Rich Text Format file. Even PowerPoint can save files in RTF format. ∎

Resizing, AutoFlow, and Linked Text Boxes

Publisher does not resize a text box if the text you type or a file you insert is too lengthy. When the number of words you've typed or placed into a text box exceeds the number the box can hold and you haven't allowed text to overflow into a linked text box, or there aren't any subsequent linked text boxes, a Text in Overflow button shown near the lower-right corner of the text box in Figure 31-11 appears. When you see that button, you can drag one of the handles on the text box to enlarge the box to display the text in its entirety. You also can flow the text into another text box, as described later in this section.

FIGURE 31-11

The Text in Overflow button cues you that the text doesn't fit in the text box.

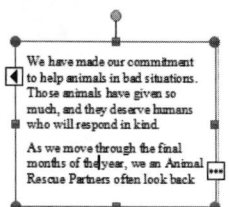

If you insert a file into a text box and the file's contents are too large for the text box, Publisher displays a message box like the one shown in Figure 31-12. If you click Yes, Publisher automatically flows the extra text into subsequent frames in the publication until all the text has been placed, a feature called *AutoFlow*. If you click No, you can handle the extra text by resizing the text box manually. Alternatively, you can link the text box to another of your choice, thus choosing exactly which text box will receive the flowed text. Linking text boxes enables you to control how a story flows from one text box to another.

FIGURE 31-12

Publisher enables you to AutoFlow extra text from an inserted file into other text boxes in the publication.

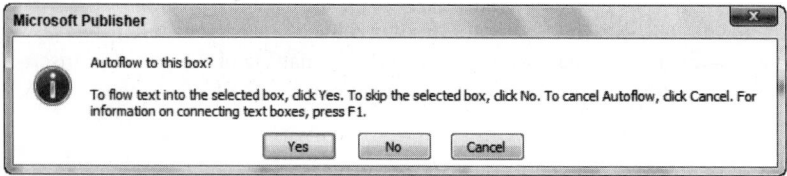

Tip

You can set up some text boxes to resize text so that it can, to some degree, fit itself within the existing boundary of a text box. To toggle this autofit feature on and off, right-click on the text box and click either Best Fit or Shrink Text on Overflow. If those options aren't active, click Format Text Box in the shortcut menu, instead. Click the Text Box tab in the Format Text Box dialog box, and then click Best Fit or Shrink Text On Overflow under Text Autofitting. Click OK to apply the change. ■

To link two text boxes so that the overflow text flows from one to the other:

1. **Click on the text box that holds the overflow text.** The Text in Overflow button appears below the text box.

2. **Click the Create Link button in the Linking group of the Text Box Tools Format tab.** The mouse pointer changes to a pitcher appearance.

3. **Move the mouse pointer over the text box into which you want to flow the overflow text.** As shown in Figure 31-13, the mouse pointer changes to a "pouring" appearance to indicate that it is in position to add the overflow text into the text box.

FIGURE 31-13

Linking text boxes flows text between them.

4. **Click on the text box to link.** The overflow text appears in the box. If a Text in Overflow button appears below the newly linked text box, it holds still more overflow text that you can display by resizing or linking to another text box.

Note

When text overflows the initial text box where you insert it, Publisher often creates a new page in the document and AutoFlows the text into it. If that's not the outcome you want, click the first text box where you added the text or file and click the Break button in the Linking group of the Text Box Tools Format tab. Then link to the text box where you do want to place the overflow text as described above. ∎

Other special buttons appear when you click on a linked text box. You may see the Go To Previous Text Box button above a linked text box. Clicking on that button selects the previous text box. When a Go To Next Text Box button appears below a linked text box, you can click on the button to select the next text box in sequence.

Formatting Text

Some text formatting in Microsoft Publisher works similarly to Word and PowerPoint, and you can refer to earlier chapters about those programs to learn more about fonts, font sizes, alignments, and the type of text formats that you can apply. Click in the text box that has the text to format, drag over text within the text box to make a more specific selection to format or press Ctrl+A to select the entire story, and then use the choices in the Font and Paragraph groups of the Home tab to apply the desired changes. For example, you can click the Bold button to apply bold-face or click the Bullets button to convert the text to a bulleted list.

Often, text that you've imported from another file will have its own formatting applied rather than adhere to the formatting established by the publication template. In this case, you can work with the Styles gallery to apply template formatting to the text:

1. **Click in the text box that holds the text to format.**

2. **Drag over text within the text box or press Ctrl+A to select the entire story.** The Ctrl+A shortcut even selects text in linked text boxes, making this a convenient shortcut when you need to reformat a larger volume of text distributed across multiple frames.

3. **Click Styles in the Styles group of the Home tab to open the drop-down gallery of styles.**

4. **Click on the desired style (Figure 31-14).** Publisher applies the style to the selected text.

FIGURE 31-14

Applying a template style saves formatting legwork.

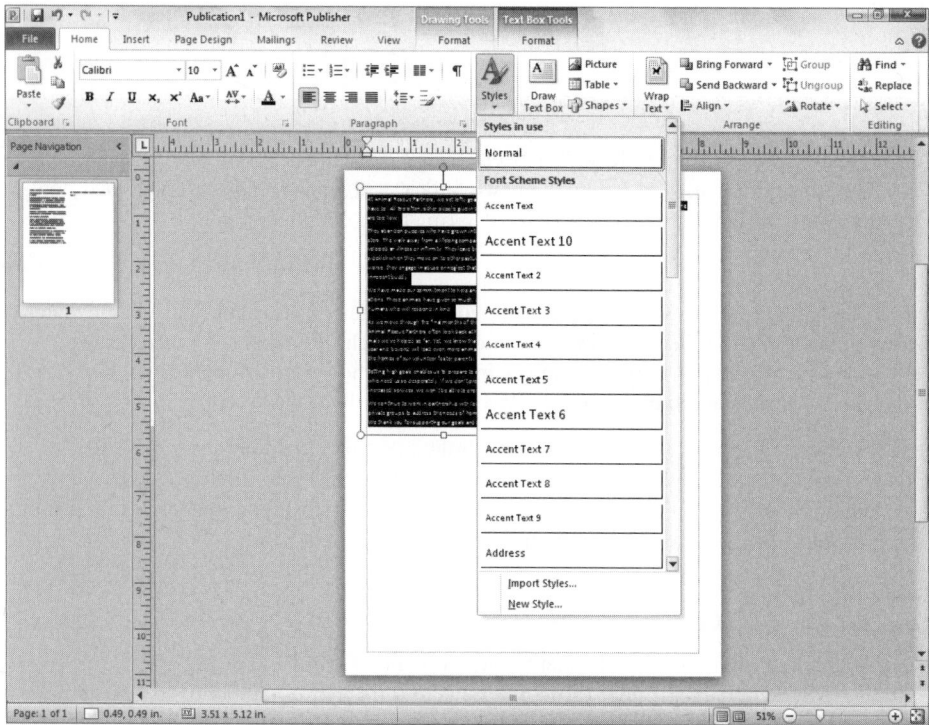

Note

Many of the body text styles automatically include spacing between paragraphs, so if you've pressed Enter to add space between paragraphs when creating your text — either in Publisher or in a word processing program — you may want to remove those extra hard returns after applying body text styles in Publisher. ∎

One feature that Publisher 2010 shares with some other Microsoft Office 2010 applications is the ability to apply a new font scheme to the publication. Changing the font scheme changes the entire set of styles in the publication to styles that use different fonts, sizes, and so on. By making one choice in a task pane, you can update the look of all the text in the entire publication. Here's how to choose a new font scheme via the Format Publication task pane:

1. **Click the Page Design tab, and then click Fonts in the Schemes group.** The gallery of built-in font schemes appears.

2. **Scroll the list of schemes (Figure 31-15), and click on the new scheme to apply.** Publisher updates the fonts throughout the document for any text to which you've previously applied styles. If you want to return to the default font scheme for the template, choose the top font scheme choice.

FIGURE 31-15

Applying a font scheme updates all the document styles to use new formatting.

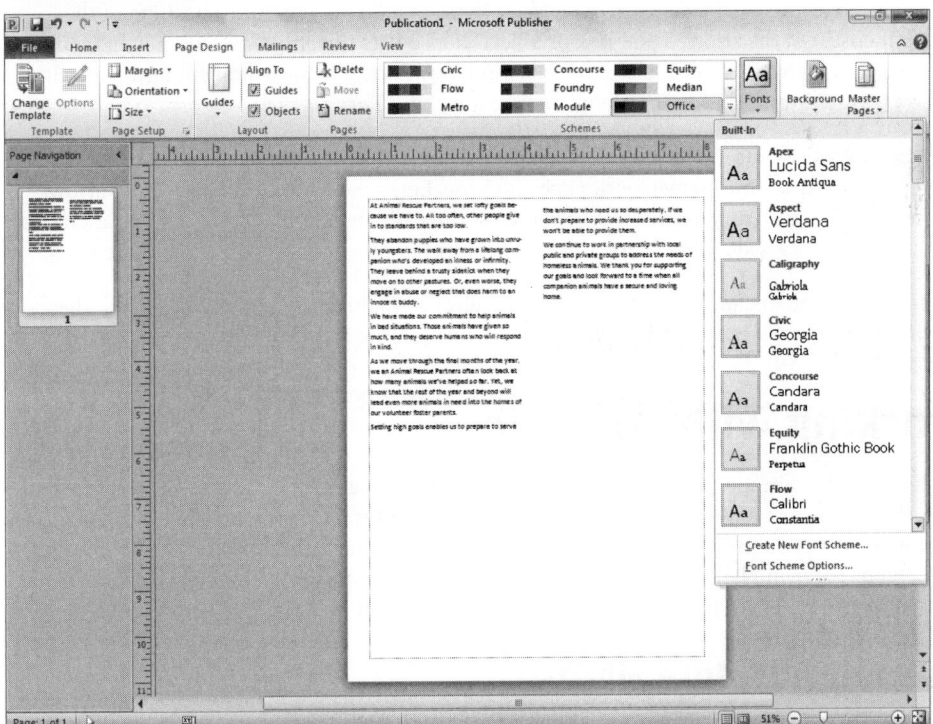

The Measurement Task Pane

One nice benefit of Publisher's templates is that they have already been set up with great precision. All the text boxes, graphics, and other elements have been sized and aligned to exact dimensions. If you want to be as precise with your own publication — such as making sure that text boxes have the same width or sizing of certain types of graphics (for inserted pictures, use the Format Picture dialog box instead) to fit exactly within a column — you can use the Measurement task pane (Figure 31-16).

View and change numerous dimensions for a selected object or text using the Measurement task pane.

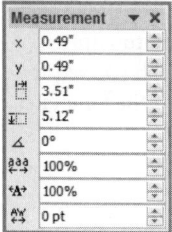

The Measurement task pane displays the exact *x* (horizontal) and *y* (vertical) position of the upper-left corner of the selected text box or object. It also lists the object's width, height, and rotation angle (if any). If you've selected text within a text box, the Measurement task pane also displays text settings including Tracking, Text Scaling, and Kerning.

To change any of the settings for the selected object or text, you can enter a new value in the applicable text box on the Measurement task pane and press Enter, or you can use the spinner arrow buttons to change the entry. In this way, if you want three different text boxes in a publication to be exactly 2.205 inches wide, you can use the Measurement task pane to set that width dimension.

To display and hide the Measurement task pane, select a graphic object or text box, click the Drawing Tools Format tab, and then click Measurement in the Size group.

Working with Graphics

Graphics bring publication stories to life. If you're a realtor creating a flyer to describe a terrific house that you have for sale, anyone who sees your flyer will *really* know how fabulous the house is if you include pictures of the granite countertops in the kitchen, the luxurious bathroom, and the gorgeous patio and landscaping in the backyard. Publisher makes it easy to add pictures and other graphic elements to punch up a story and really sell your message.

Inserting a Picture File

Digital cameras and scanners are virtually as cheap as film cameras once were. Even the typical home or small business generally has a digital camera and users who take and transfer dozens of digital pictures to the computer's hard disk. Microsoft Publisher enables you to place pictures in formats commonly captured by digital cameras, such as JPEG and TIFF, as well as numerous other graphics formats created with drawing and painting programs, directly into a publication.

This process does not require a picture placeholder, so when you're ready to insert a digital picture file into a publication, follow this process:

1. **Display the page in the publication on which you'd like to insert the picture.** Clicking on a page icon in the status bar takes you there.

2. **Choose Insert ➪ Illustrations ➪ Picture.** The Insert Picture dialog box appears.

3. **Navigate to the folder holding the file to insert.** The dialog box lists the files with readable graphics formats stored in that folder.

Tip
Click All Pictures and then select a particular format to list only picture files using that format. ∎

4. **Click on the name of the text file to insert, and then click Insert.** The inserted picture file appears on the page.

After you insert the picture, you can resize and position it as needed. You can drag the handles that appear on the corners and sides of the picture (Figure 31-17) to resize it, or move the mouse within the picture and drag to move it. You also can use the Measurement toolbar as described earlier to set the picture's size and position. When you finish sizing the picture, click outside it to deselect it.

FIGURE 31-17

Resize and move the inserted picture as needed.

Caution
If you plan to have your publication professionally printed, you need to use high-resolution pictures to get good results. If you crop a portion of a digital camera shot and then size it at a large size in the publication, those changes might result in a low-resolution graphic that prints with a fuzzy or blocky appearance. If you

have any doubts about how an image might print, ask the print shop to inspect your publication file for such problems *before* proceeding with your print order. ∎

Inserting a Clip Art Image

If you don't have your own digital pictures but want to flesh out your publication with some images, you can take advantage of the Clip Art available in Office and via Office.com. The Clip Art task pane enables you to search for the type of picture you want, such as a flower, boat, or person. You enter a word or phrase describing the type of clip art you want, and Publisher by default searches for matches both in installed clip art and online. Follow these steps when you want to insert a clip art graphic into a publication:

1. **Display the page in the publication on which you'd like to insert the clip art.** Clicking on a page icon in the status bar takes you there.

2. **Select Insert ⇨ Illustrations ⇨ Clip Art.** The Clip Art task pane appears.

3. **Type the descriptive word or phrase in the Search For text box at the top of the pane; then, click Go.** Thumbnail images of matching clip art appear in the task pane, as shown in Figure 31-18.

FIGURE 31-18

Find and insert clip art using the Clip Art task pane.

Note

The first time you search for clip art, a prompt may appear to ask whether you want to search online clips by default. Click Yes to do so. ∎

4. **Scroll down to review all the available choices.**

5. **Click the clip art media object to place on the publication.** It appears on the page you specified in Step 1. You can then resize the picture as needed to fit with the other contents in your publication, and click outside the picture to deselect it.

Changing a Placeholder Picture

Many publication templates include placeholder graphics that provide suggested sizes and locations where you can insert your own pictures or alternative clip art images. When you insert the replacement picture or clip art graphic, Publisher automatically resizes the replacement image to fit within the frame for the existing image.

To replace a placeholder image, right-click on it to display a shortcut menu. (If the picture frame is grouped with a text frame for a caption, right-click on the group first and click Ungroup. Then select the image itself and right-click on it.) Select Change Picture in the shortcut menu that appears, and then select Change Picture again in the submenu that appears. From there, the process works just like the steps you've already learned for inserting a picture or clip art object.

Formatting Pictures

You can adjust numerous settings to fine-tune a picture and its placement, including settings such as an added fill color or outline, size and rotation, layout and text wrapping, and brightness and contrast. The available settings vary somewhat depending on whether the selected picture is a digital image file or clip art graphic, and whether the picture is inserted on its own or is within a frame that's grouped with other objects.

The settings for formatting a picture appear in the Format Picture dialog box. To display the dialog box, right-click on the picture (right-click on the grouped object first and click Ungroup, if needed, and then select the picture alone), and then select Format Picture. Change settings on the tabs in the Format Picture dialog box (Figure 31-19) as needed, and then click OK to apply your choices to the picture.

Tip

The *rotation handle* is the green handle that appears at the top center of a selected picture, clip art object, or other drawn object. Drag it to rotate the selected object. ∎

Drawing Lines and Shapes

You also can enhance a publication by drawing shapes using the Shapes choices in the Illustrations group of the Insert tab. For example, you might draw an arrow to point to an important piece of information or draw a banner AutoShape to layer behind headline text.

FIGURE 31-19

The tabs in this dialog box offer numerous settings for fine-tuning the appearance of a picture.

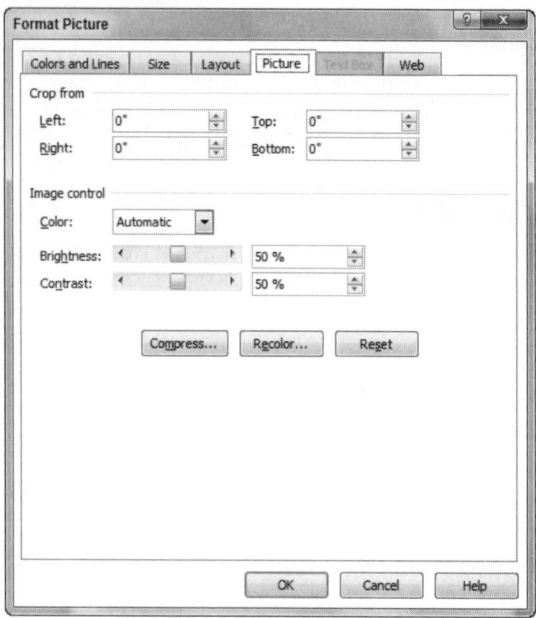

To draw the shape, click Insert, and then click the Shapes button in the Illustrations group. Click on the desired shape in the gallery that appears. If you click the AutoShapes button, a menu appears. Click on a shape category in the menu, and then click the specific AutoShape you want to draw in the submenu that appears, as shown in Figure 31-20.

After you've selected the desired line or shape, drag on the publication page to draw the object. Keep these hints in mind when you draw and work with shapes:

- Drag in the desired direction to create a line or arrow. If you want to help the line snap to vertical, horizontal, or a 45-degree angle, press the Shift key when your line is close to the desired angle.

- Drag diagonally to draw an oval, rectangle, or other shape. Press and hold Shift as you drag to constrain the shape to proportional dimensions; doing so results in a perfect circle or square, or an AutoShape that fits within a perfect circle or square.

- Some shapes include a special yellow handle when selected. You can use this handle to reshape the object, such as dragging to increase the three-dimensional (3-D) angle of the shape.

- Right-click on a shape and then select Format AutoShape to display the Format AutoShape dialog box, where you can change shape settings, as for a picture. One cool thing you can do is insert a picture within a shape or AutoShape. To do so, click the

Fill Effects in the Fill area of the Colors and Lines tab. Click the Picture tab in the Fill Effects dialog box that appears, and then use the Select Picture button to open the Select Picture dialog box. Navigate to and select the desired picture file, click Insert, and then click OK twice to fill the shape.

- Right-click on a shape, and click Add Text to insert text within it.

- To be able to reuse a shape that you've formatted, right-click on it and choose Save as Building Block. Specify the desired information in the Create New Building Block dialog box, and then click OK. You can then use the gallery you specified in the dialog box to insert the shape from the Building Blocks group of the Insert tab.

FIGURE 31-20

You can select one of dozens of shapes to draw.

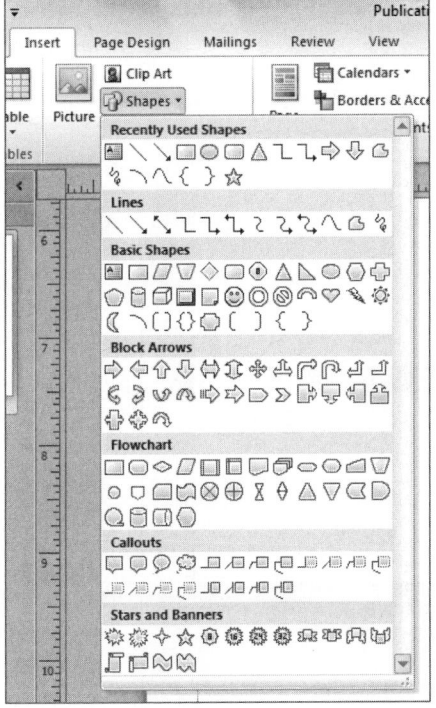

Working with Tables

When you need to organize information in a series of rows and columns, you don't have to draw and arrange a text box for each bit of data. You can instead create a table, which has cells formed by the intersections of rows and columns. When you create a table using these steps, you specify the number of rows and columns and pick the initial table design:

1. **Display the page in the publication on which you'd like to insert the table.** Clicking on a page icon in the status bar takes you there.

2. **Click the Insert tab, and then click the Table button in the Tables group.** A table grid appears below the button.

3. **Drag diagonally on the grid to specify the table's size in rows and columns.** When you release the mouse button, the table appears on the page.

4. **Open the Table Formats gallery of the Table Tools Design tab, and move the mouse pointer over a format.** As shown in Figure 31-21, moving the mouse pointer over one of the formats before clicking on it displays a live preview of the selected formatting on the table.

FIGURE 31-21

Create a table by specifying rows, columns, and format.

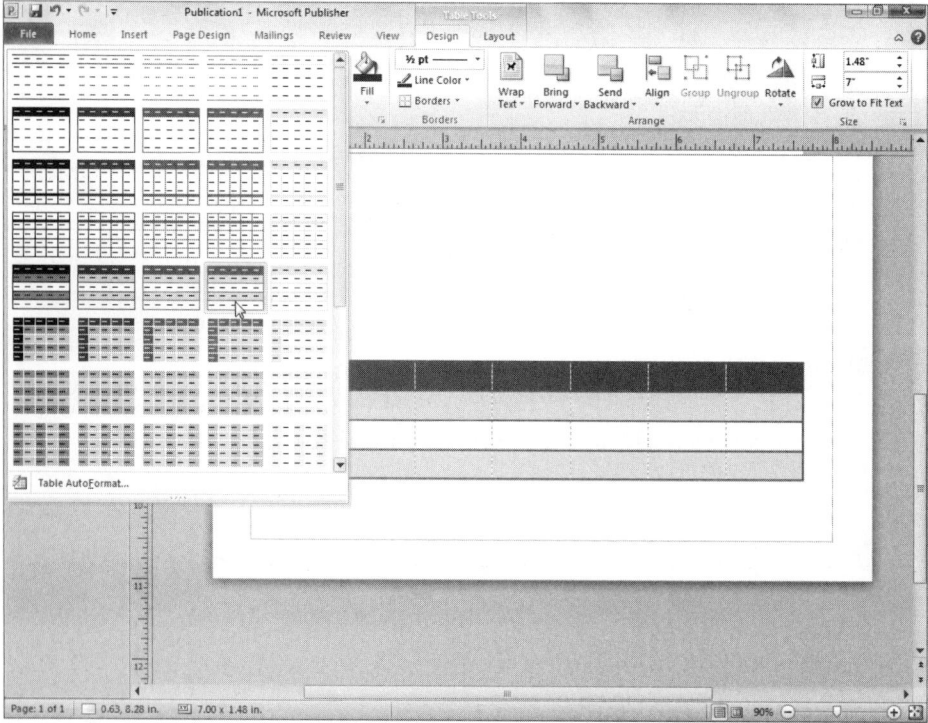

5. **Click on the format.** The formatting appears on the table. You can then move and resize the table as needed.

Tip

You also can create a table using the Create Table dialog box. Click the Insert tab, click Table in the Tables group, and then click Insert Table. After you make your choices and click OK, Publisher automatically places the table on the current publication page, where you can move and resize it as needed. ■

Entering and Editing Table Data

When the new table appears, the insertion point appears in the upper-left cell. Simply type the entry for each cell, and press Tab to move on to the next cell. If you type more text than the cell can initially handle, Publisher wraps the text to the next line and increases the row height as needed. You can press Shift+Tab to back up to a previous cell as needed.

To edit the entry in any particular table cell, click on the cell and then make the desired changes by selecting and replacing text or using editing keys such as Backspace. When you finish entering and editing table text, click outside the table to deselect it.

You can then click on a table at any time to reselect it.

Working with the Table Format

As with other objects you've seen in this chapter, you can right-click on a table and then click Format Table to open the Format Table dialog box. Note that the settings on the Colors and Lines tab apply only to the selected cell — the cell upon which you right-clicked to open the dialog box. If you want to work with colors and fills for more than one cell, you have to select those cells before right-clicking and selecting Format Table. To select cells, first click on the table. Then drag over the cells to select. You also can move the mouse pointer outside the table boundary above a column or to the left of a row that you want to select. When the mouse pointer changes to a black arrow pointing to the row or column, clicking the mouse selects the entire row or column. Also note that the Format Table dialog box includes a Cell Properties tab, on which you can change the vertical text alignment, margins, and text rotation for the selected cells.

One last table skill that's handy to know is how to resize the width of a table column. To do so, point to the right border of the column until you see the resizing pointer, which appears in the Tuesday row in Figure 31-22. Then drag left or right to fix the column width as desired.

FIGURE 31-22

Drag to adjust table column width.

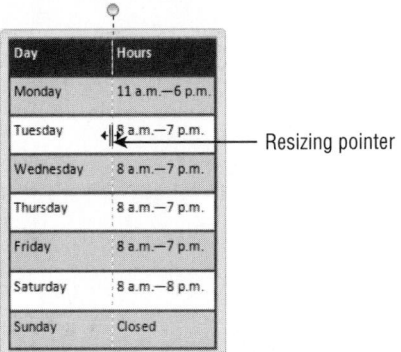

Resizing pointer

Summary

Making it through this chapter provided you with the basic know-how for creating a publication in Microsoft Publisher. You learned to work with the Ribbon tabs and other features of the Publisher workspace, as well as how to create a blank file or a file based on a template supplied with Publisher or on Office.com. You learned how to add text into a text box supplied by a template; how to create a text box and type in text; how to insert text from a word processing file; and how to format your text with formatting tools, styles, and a font scheme. You learned how to use the Measurement toolbar to format objects, as well as how to insert, create, and change graphics and tables to enhance the publication's appearance and supplement the message delivered in the text.

Designing Dazzling Publications with Publisher

S tarting your design with one of Publisher's templates virtually guarantees that you will create a nice-looking publication. You know your message and your audience best, so you can improve on a template by adding graphics and changing aspects of the overall document design. You can use special graphic features that emphasize or decorate text, add predesigned objects such as coupons, and work with page options such as the color scheme for the publication. From there, you can fine-tune objects and page settings and then wrap up and print the publication. This chapter shows you how to do all that to add your own razzle-dazzle to a publication.

Adding Special Effects

One of the advantages of using Publisher to design your publications is that Publisher makes laying out and designing document text easier. Linked text boxes give you much control over where information appears in a document. Beyond dealing with that aspect of text design, Publisher also provides you with tools to dress up text to catch your reader's eye — BorderArt, drop caps, WordArt, and special new text formatting choices and effects.

BorderArt

You learned in Chapter 31 that you can right-click on an inserted picture, clip art, or table object and select a format command that opens a formatting dialog box. Similarly, you can right-click on any text box in a publication and click Format Text Box to open the Format Text Box dialog box (Figure 32-1). You can use the tabs in this dialog box to add fills and outlines to the text box, and more. In addition, you can click the BorderArt button on the Colors and Lines tab to open the BorderArt dialog box.

FIGURE 32-1

Overall text box formatting settings appear in the Format Text Box dialog box.

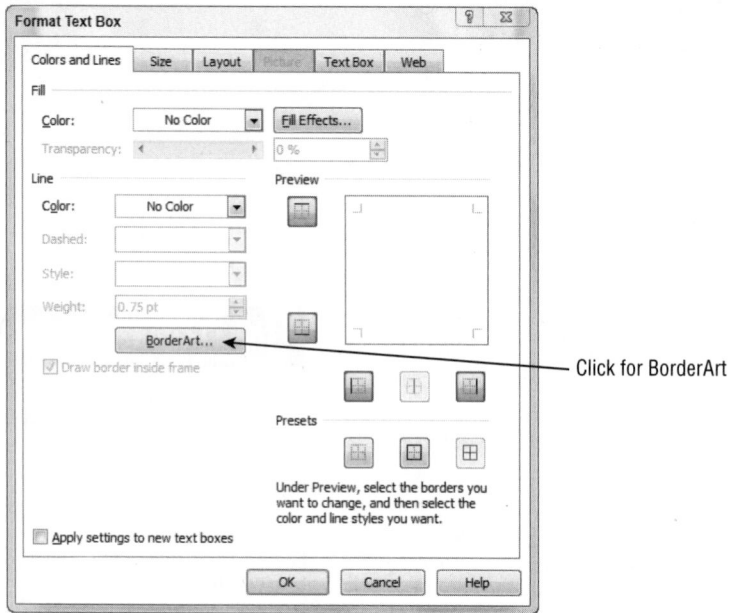

Click for BorderArt

Rather than placing a plain-colored line around your text box, BorderArt applies a border made up of small graphics. The graphics range from geometric forms that apply a formal, decorative feel to items that set a fun mood or tone, such as ladybugs or candy corn. The available BorderArt designs fit any number of occasions, making them ideal to use in almost any of your publications, including invitations and greeting cards, for example.

As shown in Figure 32-2, you can preview any border by selecting it in the Available Borders list at the left side of the dialog box. The border design appears in the Preview area at the right, using its default settings. By default, Publisher stretches the border graphics to fill the border area a little more completely. If you prefer to turn off this feature, click the Don't Stretch Pictures option button near the lower-left corner of the dialog box. Each border has an automatic size, shown in the Preview. If you want to control the border width yourself, click to uncheck the Always Apply at Default Size check box before continuing.

When you've selected the BorderArt and changed any settings as needed, click OK to close the BorderArt dialog box and return to the Format Text Box dialog box. Change the Weight entry on the Colors and Lines tab to set the border width if needed. You also can modify the border color in the Line area, but you may not want to do so if the BorderArt graphics already include great colors. Click OK to close the dialog box and finish applying the BorderArt. As shown in the party invitation in Figure 32-3, the BorderArt can make even simple text pop from the page.

FIGURE 32-2

You can preview a border in the BorderArt dialog box.

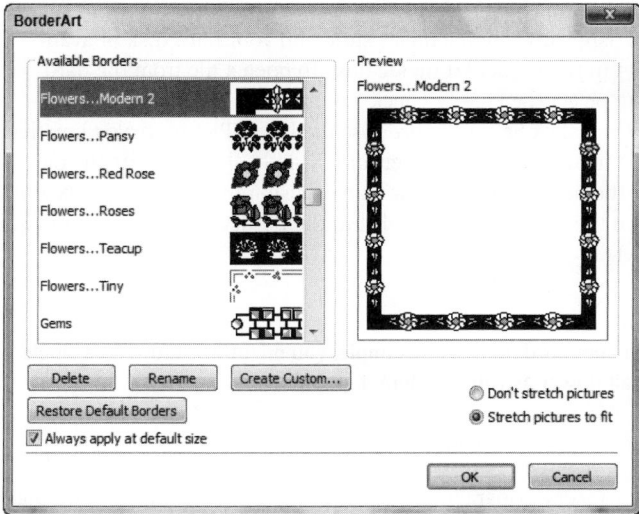

FIGURE 32-3

Party time! Seasonal or theme-oriented BorderArt works well for greeting cards and invitations.

Tip

To center text both horizontally and vertically as in Figure 32-3, select the text box. Click the Text Box Tools Format tab, and click the Align Center button in the Alignment group. ■

You can create your own BorderArt using any graphic image stored on your hard disk or available as clip art. Click Create Custom in the BorderArt dialog box. To open a file from the hard disk, click the Use Clip Organizer to Select the Picture check box in the Create Custom Border dialog box to clear the check box. Then click Select Picture. Use the Insert Picture dialog box that appears to select a picture or clip art image; then click Insert or OK. Publisher converts the picture into a border. Type a name for the new border into the Name Custom Border dialog box and click OK. The new border appears in the Available Borders list in the BorderArt dialog box until you select the border and click Delete.

Tip

Choose small, simple pictures to convert to custom border art. For example, you might want to crop a single flower out of a larger picture and use that small flower as your BorderArt graphic. ■

Drop Caps

Formatting the first letter or word of a story or paragraph as a *drop cap* draws the eye to that spot in your publication. Setting up a letter or word as a drop cap increases its size, causing it to stand above the first line of text or have the first few lines wrap around it, or both. The drop cap style you choose might also use a contrasting color or other text formatting to give it a fancy appearance. Figure 32-4 shows a story with a drop cap applied.

FIGURE 32-4

Attract readers to a story by setting the first paragraph off with a drop cap.

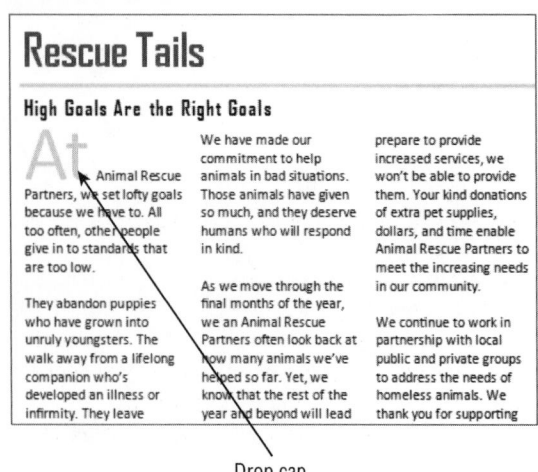

Drop cap

Follow these steps to create a drop cap in a story:

1. **Select the text box and then click in the paragraph where you want to add the drop cap.**

2. **Click the Text Box Tools ⇨ Format tab, and then click Drop Cap in the Typography group.** The Drop Cap gallery appears, as shown in Figure 32-5.

FIGURE 32-5

Make sure that the drop cap fits your text by checking the Preview.

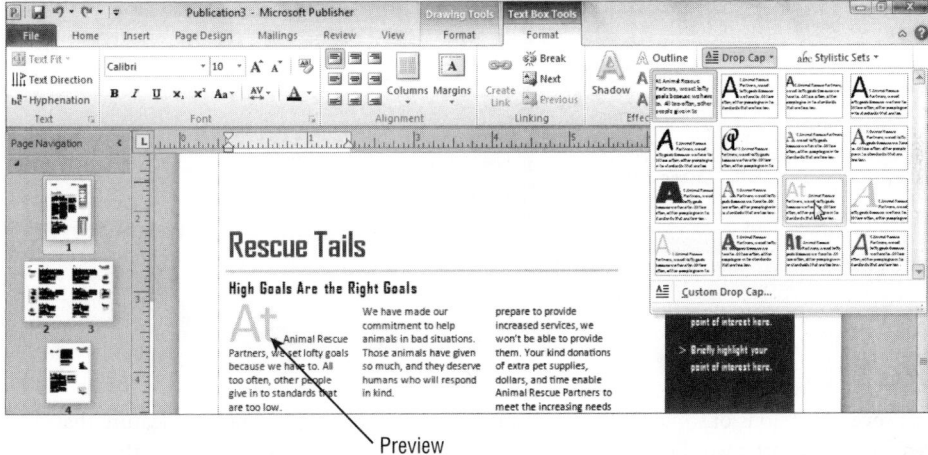

Preview

3. **Scroll the available drop cap choices as needed and move the mouse over a drop cap style.** Live Preview in the document shows how the drop cap will look when applied to the paragraph, as in the example in Figure 32-5.

4. **Click on a drop cap style to apply it.**

Note

Clicking the No Drop Cap choice at the upper left in the gallery removes the drop cap from the paragraph. ∎

If none of the available drop cap styles is quite what you're looking for, you can click Custom Drop Cap at the bottom of the Drop Cap gallery to open the Drop Cap dialog box to display the settings for creating your own custom drop cap or for customizing a drop cap that you've already applied, as shown in Figure 32-6. You can work with the drop cap position, size, and text appearance. As you try on various setting combinations, the Preview at the right shows you how your paragraph will look with the custom drop cap. Click OK to apply the custom drop cap and close the dialog box.

FIGURE 32-6

For a truly custom drop cap, work with the settings here.

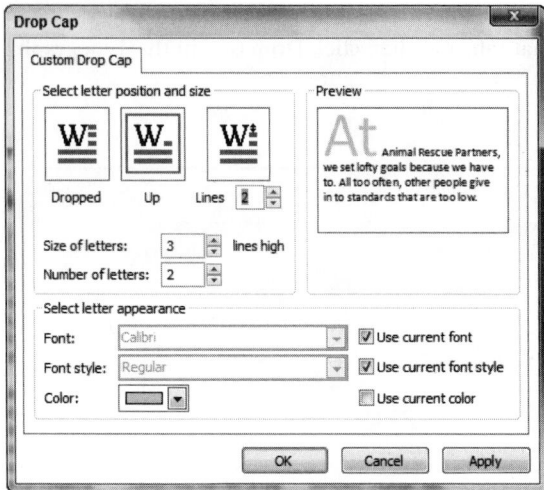

WordArt

The last several versions of some Office applications have all included *WordArt*, a feature that enables you to convert a word or phrase to a colorful graphic object. For example, rather than have "just" a title for your newsletter, you can create a WordArt object that really pops, like the example shown in Figure 32-7.

FIGURE 32-7

No mere text attracts attention the way that WordArt can.

To create a WordArt object in a publication, follow these steps:

1. **Display the page in the publication upon which you'd like to insert the WordArt.** Clicking on a page icon in the Page Navigation pane takes you there.

2. **Choose Insert ⇨ Text ⇨ WordArt.** The WordArt gallery (Figure 32-8) appears.

FIGURE 32-8

Give some text WordArt style — simple, wavy, shadowed, vertical, or 3D.

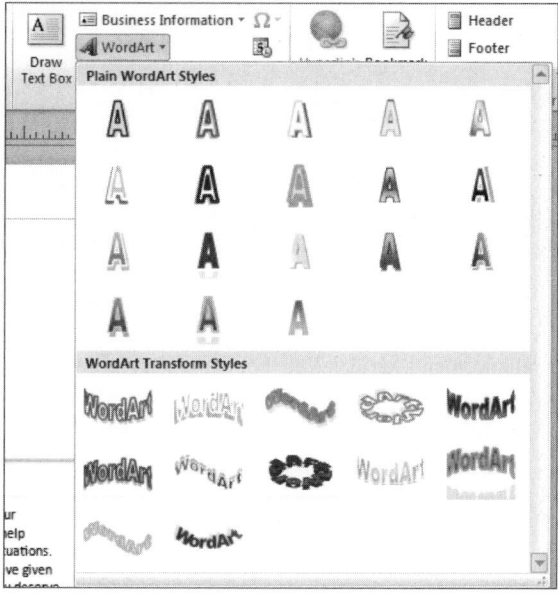

3. **Click on a WordArt style.** The Edit WordArt Text dialog box appears.

4. **Type the WordArt text, and adjust its font, size, and attributes as needed.**

5. **Click OK.** The WordArt object appears on the publication, where you can size and position it as desired.

Tip

Keep WordArt text brief. Decorative text created with WordArt can be difficult to read in large quantities. ■

When you select any WordArt object, the WordArt toolbar appears. It offers buttons for editing the WordArt's text, changing the WordArt's style and shape, and more. Work with the settings here as needed to finish designing and positioning the WordArt object.

Text Effects and Typography Tools

The Text Box Tools Format contextual tab, shown in Figure 32-9, offers some text enhancement settings that were not available in previous versions. The Effects group offers Shadow, Outline, Engrave, and Emboss treatments that you can add to selected text. These effects should be used sparingly because they can affect readability, so they are probably best reserved for headlines, advertisements, titles, and other situations in which you need to emphasize a word or phrase.

FIGURE 32-9

Use the settings in the Effects and Typography groups to enhance text.

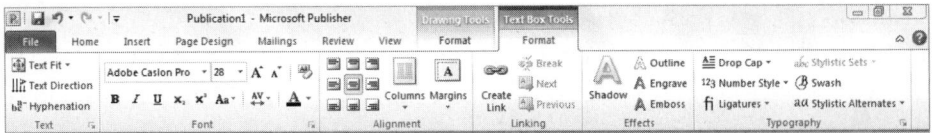

The choices that become available in the Typography group (with the exception of the Drop Cap command) will depend on the font applied to the selected text. Some fonts following newer font standards offer advanced typography features. You can take advantage of these features when present by using the Number Style, Ligatures, Stylistic Sets, Swash, and Stylistic Alternates choices in the Typography group. You can experiment with the various choices in this group in combination with different fonts to see what typographic enhancements are possible. For example, Figure 32-10 shows two ligatures.

FIGURE 32-10

The connections in the *fl* and *fi* letter pairs are ligatures.

flash fission

Using Building Blocks

Publications often include special elements not typically found in ordinary business documents. For example, a new product brochure might include a coupon. A flyer might need phone number tear-off tabs along the bottom. A newsletter might need a masthead with certain information or a volunteer sign-up form. Building these types of elements from scratch by layering graphics, text boxes, and borders could be time-consuming, but you don't have to bother. Instead, you can add any of a number of predesigned items from the building blocks galleries to your publication and then customize the item with your own text.

Follow these steps to add a building block object to a publication:

1. **Display the page in the publication upon which you'd like to insert the Design Gallery object.** Clicking on a page icon in the Page Navigation pane takes you there.

2. **Click the Insert tab on the Ribbon, and then click on the button for one of the galleries — Page Parts, Calendars, Borders & Accents, or Advertisements — in the Building Blocks group.** The specified gallery opens.

3. **Scroll down the gallery to review all the choices, and then click on the desired object.** The object appears on the publication page, where you can move and resize it, as well as update it with your own text if required. Figure 32-11 shows an example coupon building block.

FIGURE 32-11

Inspire your readers to action with building block objects.

Updating a Publication

Not only can you change settings for the text and objects in a publication, you also can make many changes to upgrade the publication itself. You can change the background fill for the pages, change how the page information is arranged, and choose another color scheme.

To make some publication-wide design changes, work with the Format Publication task pane. To make other publication-wide changes, use Format menu commands.

Changing the Background

Many publication designs purposely do not have a background color. That's because for years few computer printers could print *bleeds* — in which color prints all the way to the edge of the page. Some color printers now can handle bleeds. If that applies in your case or if you're sending the publication for commercial printing (or you don't really care if your background doesn't print all the way to the edges of the page), you can apply a background to your publication. You also may want to add a background if you're using Publisher to design a web page.

Caution

Printing a bleed can add significantly to your costs because the printer will have to trim away paper stock around the edges of each page. Be sure you know whether your print shop charges more for bleeds. ∎

To apply or remove a background, click the Page Design tab on the Ribbon, and then click Background in the Page Background group. The Background gallery appears (Figure 32-12). The available choices depend on the color scheme applied to the document. Click on a specific background choice to apply it. The publication immediately previews the background choice. To remove any applied background, redisplay the gallery and click the blank area directly below No Background at the top.

FIGURE 32-12

Pump up your pages with a background color or pattern.

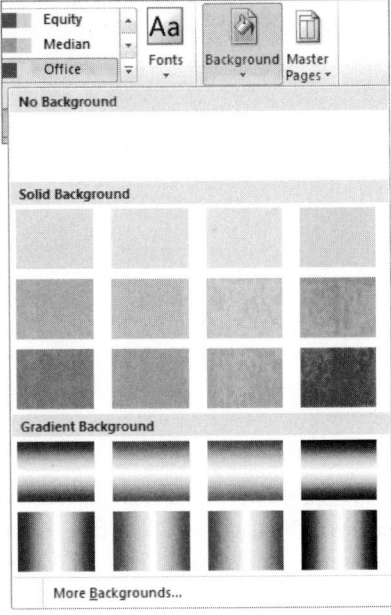

Changing Page Settings

The Page Design tab offers a variety of settings for changing the layout of the page or pages in your publication. For example, you can use the choices in the Page Setup group to specify Margins, Page Orientation, and Page Size. These choices now work the same as they do in Word, so you can refer to Chapter 8 to learn more.

Publications based on a template may have other page choices available. For a newsletter, for example, you might be able to specify the number of columns per page.

To change the options for a publication page, first display the page to change. Click the Page Design tab, and then click the Options button in the Template group. In the Page Content dialog box that appears, select the options that you want and click OK.

Changing Colors

In addition to an overall font scheme, every publication has an overall color scheme. The color scheme defines a main color and several accent colors for use throughout the publication. It's best to stick with the colors in the scheme for the text and objects as this helps keep the publication design coherent.

To choose another color scheme for your publication, click the Page Design tab on the Ribbon, and then click the More button in the Schemes group to open the Color Schemes gallery, as shown in Figure 32-13. Click on the desired color scheme. When you do so, Publisher automatically replaces the previous main and accent colors with those from the new scheme, so you can see the impact of the change on your publication. You can continue applying other color schemes until you've found one that suits your needs.

FIGURE 32-13

Bring new colors into your publication by choosing another color scheme here.

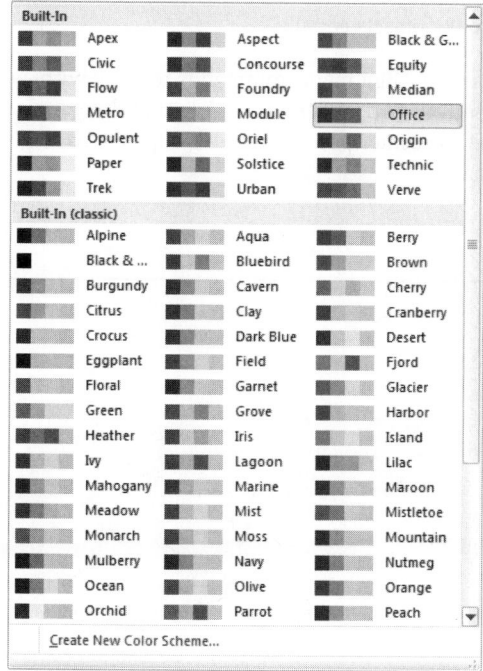

Fine-Tuning Objects

If you can't find just the right building block object or other object settings to meet your needs, or if you just like noodling around with design possibilities in your publications, you may find yourself creating and positioning many objects. Although you can drag with the mouse and use tools such as ruler guides to help you size and position objects, other shortcuts might be more appropriate in some cases. This section shows you some more tricks — aligning and grouping objects, and wrapping and hyphenating text.

Aligning Objects

Aligning objects can be a little frustrating, especially if you have a finicky mouse or are working with a notebook touchpad to drag objects. You can use the arrow keys to move a selected object, but each press of a key merely nudges the object a very small distance in the indicated direction. Plus, if you're trying to do something trickier such as align multiple selected objects, you have no precise way to do it with the mouse.

Use the commands on the Arrange group of the Home tab to align multiple selected objects. After you Shift+click to select the desired objects, click Align in the Arrange group, and then select one of the commands on the menu that appears to align the objects' left, center, and right horizontal dimensions, or top, middle, and bottom vertical dimensions. You also can use the Distribute Horizontally or Distribute Vertically choice to space the objects equally.

Figure 32-14 shows an example of how you can use the Align menu commands to work with publication objects. After selecting both objects, both the Align Center and Align Middle commands were selected. These commands placed the center point of the dog clip art image right over the center point of the beveled frame shape.

FIGURE 32-14

Move objects into position using alignment commands.

You also can keep your eyes peeled for pink alignment guidelines that may appear as you move around objects. These appear to indicate when you have reached an alignment point, such as centering an object on a column. For good alignment, release the object when you see one of these guides.

Tip

If you need to replace a picture that you've already formatted and positioned, select it, and then use the Change Picture button in the Adjust Group of the Picture Tools Format tab. ■

Tip

To control how an object layers when positioned with other objects, right-click on the object, point to the Order command, and click one of the choices in the submenu that appears. For example, the Bring to Front command positions the selected object in front of (on top of) all other stacked objects. ■

Grouping Objects

After you've placed multiple objects into the position you want, such as in the example in Figure 32-14, you should group the objects so that you can move them around as a unit without accidentally misaligning one or more of them. When you use Shift+click to select multiple objects, the Group choice in the Arrange group of the Home tab becomes active. You can use that button or right-click on the object and click Group, as shown in Figure 32-15. To ungroup a selected group, click the Ungroup button in the Arrange group of the Home tab, or right-click on the group and click Ungroup.

FIGURE 32-15

Use the Group command to make the selected objects stick together as a single unit.

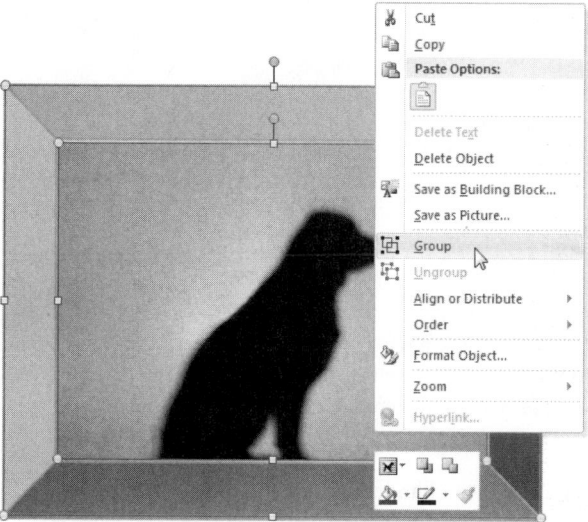

Note

You can still select an individual object within a group, such as to work with the object's formatting settings. First click on the group and then click on the individual object. Selection handles with X marks in them appear around the selected object within the group. ■

Wrapping and Hyphenating Text

Your text will read much better if you make sure that you've chosen the right text-wrapping settings for objects and have chosen whether to use hyphenation in a story.

You can apply one of several text-wrapping styles to objects, typically shapes or picture objects that you want to appear within the text. Wrapping style options include Square, Tight, Through, Top and Bottom, and None. For example, Figure 32-16 illustrates the Tight wrapping style used for a grouped object. To choose a wrapping setting, click the Drawing Tools Format tab, click Wrap Text in the Arrange group, and then click on a wrapping option.

FIGURE 32-16

The right wrapping setting makes sure that text remains readable when it flows around the object.

If you're wrapping text tightly around an object or have a narrow text box with large text, Publisher may by default hyphenate words to try to fill the space as well as possible. Many readers prefer not to see hyphens because they become tiring to read in longer stories. You can use these steps to turn the automatic hyphenation off in any story:

1. **Click in the story for which you'd like to change hyphenation settings.**

2. **Select Text Box Tools ⇨ Format ⇨ Text ⇨ Hyphenation (Ctrl+Shift+H).**
   The Hyphenation dialog box shown in Figure 32-17 opens.

FIGURE 32-17

Control hyphenation in any story by using this dialog box.

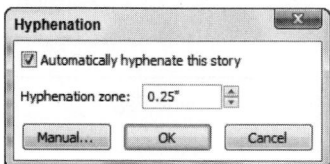

3. **Click the Automatically Hyphenate This Story check box to clear the check.**

4. **Click OK.** Publisher removes the hyphenation from the story you selected in Step 1.

Working with Pages

Many publications you create will be multipage documents, either to hold all the information that you want to present, as for a newsletter, or to come out in the proper format when folded, as for a greeting card. You can add any number of pages as needed to any publication.

Adding Pages

The Page Navigation pane at the left side of Publisher shows a numbered icon for each page in the publication. To go to another page, just click on the icon for that page. You can insert more pages as needed to expand the contents of the publication.

If you want to insert a new page before or after a particular page that's already in the publication, click on the icon for that page in the status area. Then click the Insert tab of the Ribbon, click the down arrow portion of the Page button in the Pages group, and click Insert Page (Ctrl+Shift+N).

Note

Using Ctrl+Shift+N will automatically insert a page after the currently selected page. It will not give you any additional options. ■

The Insert Page dialog box that appears varies depending on the type of publication you're working in. For example, when you're inserting a page in a file that was created as a blank publication, the dialog box looks like the one shown in Figure 32-18. Specify how many pages to insert and whether to insert before or after the current page; choose any other options you want, and then click OK. Publisher will choose the appropriate left-hand or right-hand layout for the inserted page.

If you are inserting a page in a file that was based on a more complicated template, such as a newsletter, Publisher assumes that you want to insert pages consistent with the layout of the existing pages and may even assume that you want to insert a pair of facing pages, so it displays a dialog box like the one shown in Figure 32-19. You can either use the drop-down list at the top of the dialog box to choose another type of page, as shown for Right-Hand Page at the top of Figure 32-19, or you can click the More button to display the Insert Page dialog box as shown in Figure 32-18. After you make your choice, click OK to insert the page(s).

FIGURE 32-18

If you started with a blank publication, Publisher assumes that you want to insert more blank pages.

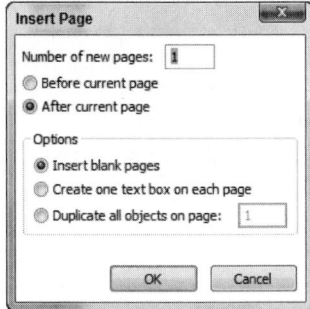

FIGURE 32-19

In other types of publications, Publisher assumes that you want to insert pages that follow the template design.

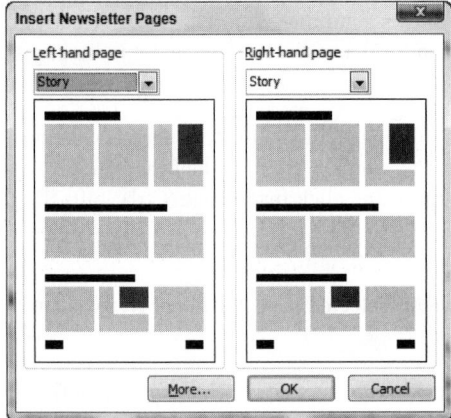

To create an exact duplicate of the current page, use the Insert Duplicate Page command (Ctrl+Shift+U) on the Page menu in the Pages group of the Insert tab.

Tip

To delete a page, right-click on its icon in the Page Navigation pane, and then click Delete in the shortcut menu. ■

Numbering Pages

As a courtesy to your readers, you should always include page numbers for multipage documents. Including page numbers has the added benefit of giving anyone printing the document a heads-up about the order in which to place the pages. The process for adding page numbers places them in the header or footer area (above or below the rest of the text) in the position that you specify.

Select Page Number in the Header & Footer group of the Insert tab to open a gallery of page number position choices (Figure 32-20). Click on one of the choices to finish adding the page numbers.

FIGURE 32-20

You can add page numbers in the position you specify.

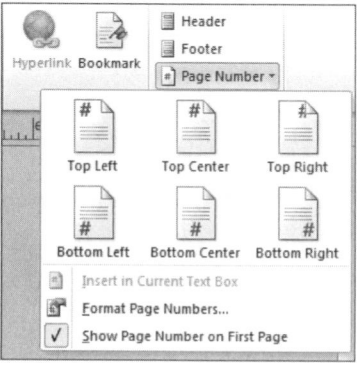

Checking and Printing

Printing your publication can be a thrilling moment — or an absolute dud if you discover that you've missed something and have to go back and fix it. So before you print, take the time to use the Design Checker. After that, it's off to the printer!

Note
Always remember to save your final changes to the publication before printing by pressing Ctrl+S or selecting File ⇨ Save. ∎

Using the Design Checker

Publisher's Design Checker checks a publication for boo-boos such as empty text boxes and spacing errors. Running the Design Checker so that you can uncover and fix these errors saves you toner, paper, and printing time. Among the problems Design Checker looks for are text in overflow areas, disproportional pictures, empty frames, covered objects, objects partially off the page, objects in nonprinting regions, blank space at the top of the page, spacing between sentences, and (for web sites) a page unreachable by hyperlinks.

Select File ⇨ Info ⇨ Run Design Checker to run Design Checker. When it finishes, results appear in the Design Checker task pane, as shown in Figure 32-21. To correct each error, click on the error in the list. Publisher displays the location where the error occurs so that you can correct it.

FIGURE 32-21

Yep, Design Checker caught a number of errors in this publication.

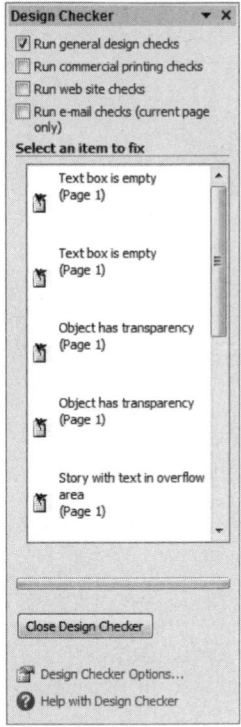

Tip

It's usually a good idea to run a spelling check before printing. Publisher's spell check works just like the ones in other Office applications, so just press F7 to start the process. ∎

If you plan to have the document commercially printed, click the Run Commercial Printing Checks check box at the top of the Design Checker task pane to check that option. The Design Checker then immediately displays any errors that might cause a problem at a commercial printer, such as the publication's being in the wrong color mode. When you click on this type of error, a drop-down arrow appears beside it. Click on that error to display a drop-down menu with options for correcting or learning more about the error.

Printing

When you're satisfied that your publication is as near to perfect as you can make it, you're ready to print. Printing is pretty much the same as in any Office application, choose File ⇨ Print or press Ctrl+P. Review the preview in the Backstage view carefully, and then select a printer, a range of pages to print, and the number of copies you want. Click Print to finish and send the job to the printer.

Preparing for Outside Printing

Sometimes you want to be able to send your publication to a print shop for printing on a professional press rather than on your own printer. Publisher can help you prepare your files for that purpose.

Give Your Printer and Yourself a Break

Small print shops labor every day to deal with errors in Publisher files, from wrong output colors to unneeded spot colors to other poor document design and setup problems. If you're unwilling or unable to take the time to learn about and fix these types of issues, please be willing to pay your service bureau (print shop) a fair fee for fixing them. The following are always good practices for working with a print shop to get your publication file printed right:

- Know and adhere to the print shop's requirements.
- If you have questions but want to do the work yourself, consult Publisher's extensive help on this subject and ask the printer for tips.
- Most print shops will review a file for problems before printing it. Sending your file for such an advanced checkup provides time to fix problems.
- Be professional. A professional admits to errors and is willing to learn and change. If you keep submitting bad files to the print shop, you'll keep getting poorly printed materials.

To start preparing a publication for commercial printing, choose File ⇨ Save & Send ⇨ Save for a Commercial Printer. At the right side of the Backstage view, make the choices you want from the top and bottom drop-down lists, which specify the overall type of printer and whether the preparation process will create just a Publisher file or both a Publisher file and a PDF file. (Some printers prefer that you submit your files as PDF files.) Generally speaking, you should choose either Commercial Press or High Quality Printing from the top drop-down list. If you choose Custom, Publisher opens a Publish Options dialog box (Figure 32-22), where you can choose more specific options, such as the resolution at which pictures should print. If you click Print Options in that dialog box, the Print Options dialog box offers even more choices, such as adding crop marks and whether to allow bleeds. Click OK after you make your choices in each of these dialog boxes.

FIGURE 32-22

FIGURE 32-22

The settings here are important for commercial printing and advanced print jobs of your own.

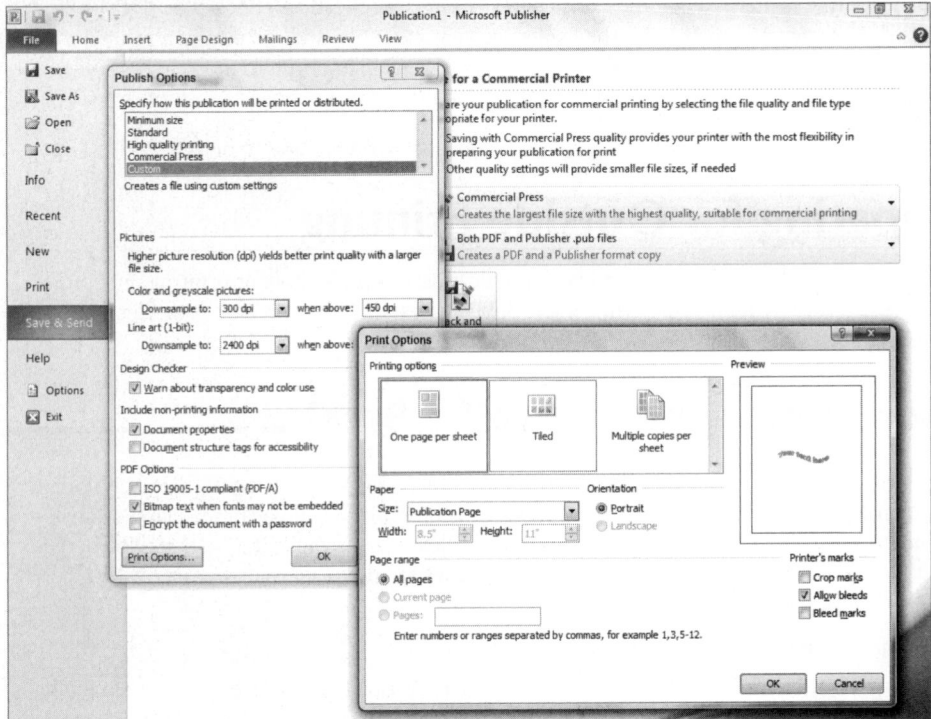

Tip

To create a more standard PDF file, say to e-mail to a colleague as a proof for the publication, click Create PDF/XPS Document after choosing File ⇨ Save & Send. You also can publish to HTML (web page) format from this location. ∎

Once you've selected the needed output settings, click the Pack and Go Wizard button. Specify where you want to save the file(s), click Next, and follow the prompts to finish the process of preparing your files for offsite professional printing, including embedding fonts, including linked graphics, creating links for embedded graphics, compressing your publication, and adding an unpacking utility for uncompressing it when it gets to its destination. In most cases, you will want to pack the files on a CD-R or DVD-R disc, unless your printer allows you to upload files to its location over the Internet or enables you to submit them on a USB flash drive.

Summary

This final *Office 2010 Bible* chapter about Microsoft Publisher gave you the information you need to improve the content and design for a publication, add missing elements, and finalize and print the publication. The chapter showed you how to use special effects such as BorderArt, drop caps, and WordArt; how to add a building block object; and how to change overall page and publication design settings such as the color scheme. You learned how to better align objects and wrap text around them, as well as how to group them. You worked with pages and page numbering before seeing how to check the design and print. Finally, the chapter introduced you to good practices for preparing a publication for commercial printing.

Part VII

Managing Information with Access and OneNote

An Introduction to Database Development

I n this chapter, you learn the concepts and terminology of databases
and how to design the tables that your Access application's forms and
reports will use.

Database development is quite unlike most other ways in which you work
with computers. Unlike Microsoft Word or Excel, where the approach to
working with the application is easy to understand, good database development requires prior knowledge. A beginning user opening Access for the
first time likely has no idea where to start. Although the opening user interface helps you create your first database, from that point on, you're pretty
much on your own. Unlike Word or Excel, you can't just start typing things
in at the keyboard and see any results.

The fundamental concept underlying Access databases is that data is stored
in *tables*. *Tables* are composed of rows and columns of data, much like an
Excel worksheet. In a properly designed database, each table represents
a single type of entity, such as a customer or a list of products. Each row
within a table describes a single instance of the entity, such as one customer
or an individual product. Each column in an Access table contains a single
type of data, such as text or date/time.

As you work with Access, you'll spend considerable time designing and
refining the tables in your Access applications. Table design and implementation are two processes that distinguish database development from most
other computer activities you may pursue.

After you understand the basic concepts and terminology, the next important lesson to learn is good database design. Without a good design, you
may have to constantly rework your tables, queries will be difficult to
write, and you may not be able to extract the information you want from

your database. Throughout this section of the book, you learn how to use the basic components of Access applications, including queries, forms, and reports. You also learn how to design and implement each of these objects. Although the CollectibleMiniCars case study shown in this chapter provides invented examples, the concepts illustrated by this simple application are not fictitious.

Some of this chapter's concepts are somewhat complex, especially to people new to Access or database development.

Cross-Reference

If your goal is to get right into Access, you might want to skip to Chapter 34 and read about building tables. If you're fairly familiar with Access but new to designing and creating tables, read the current chapter before starting to create tables. ■

The Database Terminology of Access

Before examining the table examples in this book, it's a good idea to have a firm understanding of the terminology used when working with databases — especially Access databases. Microsoft Access follows most, but not all, traditional database terminology. The terms *database*, *table*, *record*, *field*, and *value* indicate a hierarchy from largest to smallest. These same terms are used with virtually all database systems, so you should learn them well.

Databases

Generally, the word database is a computer term for a collection of information concerning a certain topic or business application. Databases help you organize this related information in a logical fashion for easy access and retrieval. Some older database systems used the term database to describe individual tables. But current usage of *database* applies to all the elements of a database system.

Databases aren't only for computers. There are also manual databases; we sometimes refer to these as *manual filing systems* or *manual database systems.* These filing systems usually consist of people, papers, folders, and filing cabinets — paper is the key to a manual database system. In a real manual database system, you probably have in/out baskets and some type of formal filing method. You access information manually by opening a file cabinet, taking out a file folder, and finding the correct piece of paper. Users fill out paper forms for input, perhaps by using a keyboard to input information that is printed on forms. You find information by manually sorting the papers or by copying information from many papers to another piece of paper (or even into an Excel spreadsheet). You may use a spreadsheet or calculator to analyze the data or display it in new and interesting ways.

An *Access database* is nothing more than an automated version of the filing and retrieval functions of a paper filing system. Access databases store information in a carefully defined structure. Access tables store a variety of different kinds of data, from simple lines of text (such as name and address) to complex data such as pictures, sounds, or video images. Storing data in a precise format enables a database management system (DBMS) like Access to turn data into useful information.

Tables serve as the primary data repository in an Access database. Queries, forms, and reports provide access to the data, enabling a user to add or extract data, and presenting the data in useful ways. Most developers add macros or Visual Basic for Applications (VBA) code to forms and reports to make their Access applications easier to use.

A relational database management system (RDBMS), such as Access, stores data in *related tables*. For example, a table containing employee data (names and addresses) may be related to a table containing payroll information (pay date, pay amount, and check number). *Queries* allow the user to ask complex questions (such as, "What is the sum of all paychecks issued to Jane Doe in 2012?") from these related tables, with the answers displayed as onscreen forms and printed reports.

In fact, one of the fundamental differences between a relational database and a manual filing system is that, in a relational database system, data for a single individual person or item may be stored in separate tables. For example, in a patient management system, the patient's name, address, and other contact information is likely to be stored in a different table from the table holding patient treatments. In fact, the treatment table holds all treatment information for all patients, and a patient identifier (usually a number) is used to look up an individual patient's treatments in the treatment table.

In Access, a database is the overall container for the data and associated objects. It's more than the collection of tables, however — a database includes many types of objects, including queries, forms, reports, macros, and code modules.

Access works with a single database at a time. As you open an Access database, the objects (tables, queries, etc.) in the database are presented for you to work with. You may open several copies of Access at the same time and simultaneously work with more than one database, if needed.

Many Access databases contain hundreds, or even thousands, of tables, forms, queries, reports, macros, and modules. With a few exceptions, all the objects in an Access database reside within a single file with an extension of `.accdb`, `.accde`, or `.adp`.

Tables

A table is just a container for raw information (called *data*), similar to a folder in a manual filing system. Each table in an Access database contains information about a single entity, such as a customer or product list, and the data in the table is organized into rows and columns.

Figure 33-1 shows the products table (named tblProducts) from the CollectibleMiniCars database application. The products table is typical of the tables found in Access applications. Each row defines a single product. In Figure 33-1, the row containing information on the die-cast model of a 2003 Volkswagen Beetle is selected.

FIGURE 33-1

The CollectibleMiniCars products table (tblProducts)

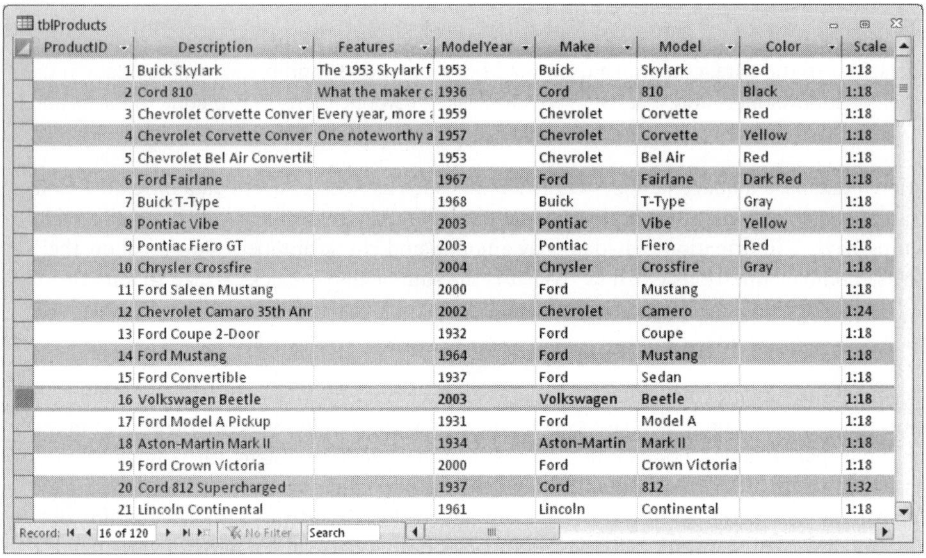

ProductID	Description	Features	ModelYear	Make	Model	Color	Scale
1	Buick Skylark	The 1953 Skylark f	1953	Buick	Skylark	Red	1:18
2	Cord 810	What the maker c	1936	Cord	810	Black	1:18
3	Chevrolet Corvette Conver	Every year, more ;	1959	Chevrolet	Corvette	Red	1:18
4	Chevrolet Corvette Conver	One noteworthy a	1957	Chevrolet	Corvette	Yellow	1:18
5	Chevrolet Bel Air Convertit		1953	Chevrolet	Bel Air	Red	1:18
6	Ford Fairlane		1967	Ford	Fairlane	Dark Red	1:18
7	Buick T-Type		1968	Buick	T-Type	Gray	1:18
8	Pontiac Vibe		2003	Pontiac	Vibe	Yellow	1:18
9	Pontiac Fiero GT		2003	Pontiac	Fiero	Red	1:18
10	Chrysler Crossfire		2004	Chrysler	Crossfire	Gray	1:18
11	Ford Saleen Mustang		2000	Ford	Mustang		1:18
12	Chevrolet Camaro 35th Anr		2002	Chevrolet	Camero		1:24
13	Ford Coupe 2-Door		1932	Ford	Coupe		1:18
14	Ford Mustang		1964	Ford	Mustang		1:18
15	Ford Convertible		1937	Ford	Sedan		1:18
16	Volkswagen Beetle		2003	Volkswagen	Beetle		1:18
17	Ford Model A Pickup		1931	Ford	Model A		1:18
18	Aston-Martin Mark II		1934	Aston-Martin	Mark II		1:18
19	Ford Crown Victoria		2000	Ford	Crown Victoria		1:18
20	Cord 812 Supercharged		1937	Cord	812		1:32
21	Lincoln Continental		1961	Lincoln	Continental		1:18

Record: 16 of 120 ▶ No Filter | Search

In the section, "A Five-Step Design Method," later in this chapter, you'll learn a successful technique for planning Access tables.

In fact, it's very important that you begin to think of the objects managed by your applications in abstract terms. Because each Access table defines an entity, you have to learn to think of the table *as* the entity. As you design and build Access databases, or even when working with an existing application, you must think of how the tables and other database objects represent the specific entities (people, products, etc.) managed by your database and how the entities relate to one another.

After you create a table, you view the table in a spreadsheet-like form, called a *datasheet*, comprising rows and columns (known as *records* and *fields*, respectively — see the following section, "Records and Fields"). Figure 33-2 shows the Datasheet view of the customers table (named tblCustomers) in the CollectibleMiniCars application. Although a datasheet and a spreadsheet are superficially similar, a datasheet is a very different type of object.

Cross-Reference

Chapter 34 discusses Access datasheets and the differences between datasheets and spreadsheets. ■

The customers table represents people who work with CollectibleMiniCars. Notice how the table is divided into horizontal (left-to-right) rows and vertical (top-to-bottom) columns of data. Each row (or *record*) defines a single customer, while each column (or *field*) represents one type of information associated with the customers.

FIGURE 33-2

A table displayed as a datasheet

tblCustomers							
Custon ▾	Company ▾	Address ▾	City ▾	Stat ▾	ZipCo ▾	Phone ▾	
⊞	1 Fun Zone	105 S Dubuque Street	Iowa City	IA	52240-	(319) 352-0725	
⊞	2 Exelon Shoppe	123 South Street	Newington	NH	12301-	(603) 555-6887	
⊞	3 Southwest Softies	Rt 9	Pine Plains	NY	12567-	(518) 555-6699	
⊞	4 Pinnacle Playables	560 Broadway	Salem	NH	03079-	(603) 555-4422	
⊞	5 Toys in the Baseme	100 Elm Street	Sunnyville	GA	12305-	(478) 555-8822	
⊞	6 Rockin And Rollin	60 Newbury Rd	Carlsen	NY	10554-	(212) 555-9639	
⊞	7 Mary's Merchandis	95 south Main Street	Summerville	CT	06028-	(860) 555-1285	
⊞	8 World's Best Toys	54 Oak Street	New Town	NY	10555-	(212) 555-7774	
⊞	9 Carmen's Collectib	15 Hatter Drive	Allison	PA	15413-	(724) 555-9874	
⊞	10 Red Hat Hattery	1600 Mountain Rd	Montclair	CA	91763-	(909) 555-6666	
⊞	11 Adorable Stuff	93 Prospect Ave	Bell Gardens	CA	90202-	(323) 555-4777	
⊞	12 All Your Needz	8 River Run	Island Lake	IL	60042-	(847) 555-1234	
⊞	13 Terriffic Toys	64 Highland Street	Sale Creek	GA	31784-	(912) 555-4567	
⊞	14 Regis Toys	15 Mineral Drive	Iron Springs	AZ	86330-	(520) 555-6888	
⊞	15 Top End Toys	60 State Street	Salado	TX	76571-	(254) 555-1236	
⊞	16 Coventry Collectib	15 Main Street	Elsa	TX	78543-	(956) 555-4544	
⊞	17 The Toy Box	15 Long Ave	Greenleaf	ID	83626-	(208) 555-6914	
⊞	18 Zoomy Collectible:	55 West North Street	Knox	IN	46534-	(219) 555-3666	
⊞	19 Paul's Best Toys	54 Plains Rd	Turon	KS	67583-	(316) 555-7778	
⊞	20 Midwest Collectibl	16 South Hill Road	Truxton	MO	63381-	(636) 555-9560	

Record: I◄ ◄ 1 of 32 ► ►I ►☒ No Filter Search

For example, the top row in `tblCustomers` contains data describing the customer called *Fun Zone*, including their address and phone number. Each bit of information describing Fun Zone is a field (`CompanyName`, `Address`, `Phone`, etc.). Fields are combined to form a record, and records are grouped to build the table. (Each row in a table constitutes a record.)

Each field in an Access table includes many properties that specify the type of data contained within the field and how Access should handle the field's data. These properties include the name of the field (`Company`) and the type of data in the field (`Text`). A field may include other properties as well. For example, the Address field's `Size` property tells Access the maximum number of characters allowed for the address.

Cross-Reference
You learn much more about fields and field properties in Chapter 34. ∎

Records and Fields

As Figure 33-2 shows, the datasheet is divided into rows (called records) and columns (called fields), with the first row (the heading on top of each column) containing the names of the fields in the database. In Figure 33-2, the fields are named `CustomerID`, `Company`, `Address`, `City`, `State`, and so on. Each row is a single record containing fields that are related to that record. In a manual system, the rows are individual forms (sheets of paper), and the fields are equivalent to the blank areas on a printed form that you fill in.

Note

When working with Access, the term *field* is used to refer to an attribute stored in a record. In many other database systems, including SQL Server, *column* is the expression you'll hear most often in place of *field*. Field and column mean the same thing. The exact terminology used relies somewhat on the context of the database system underlying the table containing the record. ∎

Values

At the intersection of a record and a field is a *value* — the actual data element. For example, Fun Zone, the company name in the first record, represents one data value. Certain rules (discussed in Chapter 34) govern how data is contained in an Access table. For example, in a properly designed database, the Fun Zone record occurs only once because each row in a table must be unique in some way. A table may contain more than one company named Fun Zone, but *something* about each company (such as the address) must be different. If rows in a table are not unique, Access has no way to distinguish between the duplicate rows, and the data can't be trusted or managed properly.

Relational Databases

Microsoft Access is a relational database development system. Access data is stored in related tables, wherein data in one table (such as customers) is related to data in another table (such as orders). Access maintains the relationships between related tables, making it easy to extract a customer and all the customer's orders, without losing any data or pulling order records not owned by the customer.

Note

In the following sections (in fact, in the rest of this book), you'll see references to things such a "the customers table" or "the tblCustomers table." In the former, "the customers table" refers to the database table containing customer data, while "the tblCustomers table" (or just "tblCustomers") refers to the database table *named* tblCustomers. Different developers have different ways of naming things. For example, in my database, I may use tblCustomers as the name of the customers table, whereas another person might use *Customers* as the name for the same table. When working with a database it's very important to understand exactly *which* object is referenced by a name or description. ∎

Multiple tables simplify data entry and reporting by decreasing the input of redundant data. By defining two tables for an application that uses customer information, for example, you don't need to store the customer's name and address every time the customer purchases an item.

After you've created the tables, they need to be related to each other. For example, if you have a customers table (tblCustomers) and a sales table (tblSales), you must relate tblCustomers to tblSales in order to see all the sales records for a customer. If you had only one table, you would have to repeat the customer name and address for each sale record. Using two tables lets you look up information in tblCustomers for each sale by using the related fields CustomerID (in tblCustomers) and CustomerID (in tblSales). This way, when a customer changes address, for example, the address changes only in one record in tblCustomers. When sales information is onscreen, the correct contact address is always visible.

Separating data into multiple tables within a database makes the system easier to maintain because all records of a given type are within the same table. By taking the time to segment data properly into multiple tables, you experience a significant reduction in design and work time. This process is known as *normalization*.

Later in this chapter, in the section, "A Five-Step Design Method," you can work through a case study for CollectibleMiniCars that consists of five tables.

Why Create Multiple Tables?

The prospect of creating multiple tables almost always intimidates beginning database users. Most often, beginners want to create one huge table that contains all the information they need — for example, a customer table with all the sales placed by the customer plus the customer's name, address, and other information. After all, if you've been using Excel to store data so far, it may seem quite reasonable to take the same approach when building tables in Access.

A single large table for all customer information quickly becomes difficult to maintain. You have to input the customer information for every sale a customer makes (repeating the name and address information over and over again in every row). The same is true for the items purchased for each sale when the customer has purchased multiple items as part of a single purchase. This makes the system more inefficient and prone to data-entry mistakes. The information in the table is inefficiently stored — certain fields may not be needed for each sales record, and the table ends up with a lot of empty fields.

You want to create tables that hold the minimum of information while still making the system easy to use and flexible enough to grow. To accomplish this, you need to consider making more than one table, with each table containing fields that are only related to the focus of that table. Then, after you create the tables, you link them so that you're able to glean useful information from them. Although this process sounds extremely complex, the actual implementation is relatively easy.

Access Database Objects and Views

If you're new to databases (or even if you're an experienced database user), you need to understand a few key concepts before starting to build Access databases. The Access database contains six types of top-level objects, which consist of the data and tools that you need to use Access:

- **Table.** Holds the actual data.
- **Query.** Searches for, sorts, and retrieves specific data.
- **Form.** Lets you enter and display data in a customized format.

- **Report.** Displays and prints formatted data.
- **Macro.** Automates tasks without programming.
- **Module.** Contains programming statements written in the Visual Basic for Applications (VBA) programming language.

Datasheets

Datasheets are one of the many ways in which you can *view* data in Access. Although not a permanent database object, a datasheet displays a table's content in a row-and-column format similar to that of a Microsoft Excel worksheet. An Access datasheet displays a table's information in a raw form, without transformations or filtering. The Datasheet view is the default mode for displaying all fields for all records. (Figures 33-1 and 33-2 earlier in this chapter are Datasheet views of Access tables.)

You scroll through the datasheet using the directional keys on your keyboard. You can also display related records in other tables while in a datasheet. In addition, you can make changes to the displayed data.

Caution
Be careful when you're making changes or allowing a user to modify data in Datasheet view. When a datasheet record is updated, the data in the underlying table is permanently changed. ∎

Queries

Queries extract information from a database. A query selects and defines a group of records that fulfill a certain condition. Most forms and reports are based on queries that combine, filter, or sort data before it's displayed. Queries are often called from macros or VBA procedures to change, add, or delete database records.

Examples of queries are when a person at the sales office tells the database, "Show me all customers, in alphabetical order by name, who are located in Massachusetts and bought something over the past six months," or "Show me all customers who bought Chevrolet car models within the past six months, and display them sorted by customer name and then by sale date."

Instead of asking the question in English words, a person uses the query by example (QBE) method. When you enter instructions into the Query Designer window and run the query, the query translates the instructions into Structured Query Language (SQL) and retrieves the desired data.

Cross-Reference
Chapter 36 discusses the Query Designer window and building queries. ∎

In the first example, the query first combines data from tblSales and tblCustomers, using CustomerID as a link between the tables. Next, it retrieves the customer name, address, and any other data you want to see. Access then filters the records, selecting only those in which the sales date is within six months of the current date. The query sorts the resulting records by the customer's name. Finally, the resulting records are displayed as a datasheet. Figure 33-3 shows just such a query in Design view. In this figure, the user is requesting all customers who've placed an order in the previous six months.

Building a typical Access query

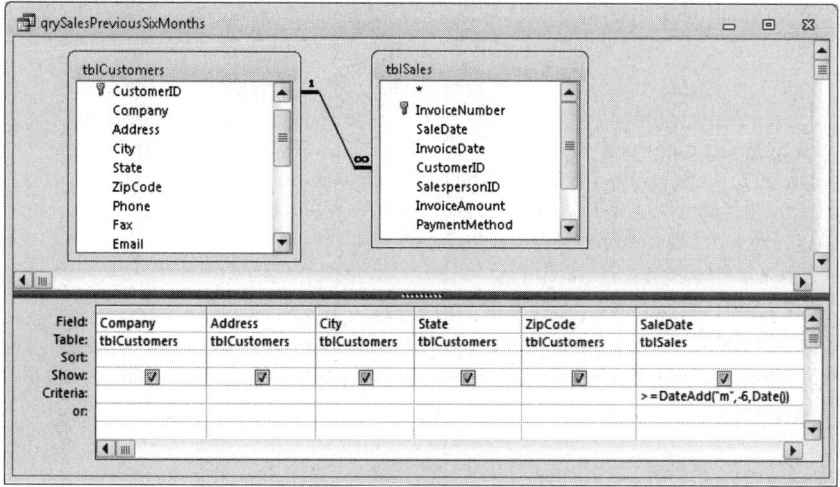

After you run a query, the resulting set of records may be used in a form that is displayed onscreen or printed on a report. In this way, user access is limited to the data that meets the criteria in the returned records.

Data-Entry and Display Forms

Data-entry forms help users get information into a database table quickly, easily, and accurately. Data-entry and display forms provide a more structured view of the data than what a datasheet provides. From this structured view, database records can be viewed, added, changed, or deleted. Entering data through the data-entry forms is the most common way to get data into a database table.

Data-entry forms restrict access to certain fields within the table. Forms can also check the validity of your data before it's added to the database table.

Most users prefer to enter information into data-entry forms rather than into Datasheet views of tables. Forms often resemble familiar paper documents and can aid the user with data-entry tasks. Forms make data entry easy to understand by guiding the user through the fields of the table being updated.

Read-only screens and forms are often used for inquiry purposes. These forms display certain fields within a table. Displaying some fields and not others means that you can limit a user's access to sensitive data while allowing access to other fields within the same table.

Reports

Reports present your data in printed format. Access supports several different types of reports. A report may list all records in a given table (such as a customers table) or may contain only the records meeting certain criteria, such as "all customers living in Arizona." You do this by basing the report on a query that selects only the records needed by the report.

Reports often combine multiple tables to present complex relationships among different sets of data. An example is printing an invoice. The customers table provides the customer's name and address (and other relevant data) and related records in the sales table to print the individual line-item information for each product ordered. The report also calculates the sales totals and prints them in a specific format. Additionally, you can have Access output records into an *invoice report*, a printed document that summarizes the invoice.

Tip
When you design your database tables, keep in mind all the types of information that you want to print. Doing so ensures that the information you require in your various reports is available from within your database tables. ■

Database Objects

To create *database objects*, such as tables, forms, and reports, you first complete a series of *design* tasks. The better your design is, the better your application will be. The more you think through your design, the faster and more successfully you can complete any database system. The design process is not some necessary evil, nor is its intent to produce voluminous amounts of documentation. The sole intent of designing an object is to produce a clear-cut path to follow as you implement it.

A Five-Step Design Method

Figure 33-4 is a version of a common design method modified especially for use with Microsoft Access. This five-step method is a top-down approach, starting with the overall system design and ending with the forms design.

These five design steps, along with the database system illustrated by the examples in this book, give you a good understanding of Access and provide a great foundation for creating database applications — including tables, queries, forms, reports, macros, and simple VBA modules.

The time you spend on each step depends entirely on the circumstances of the database you're building. For example, sometimes users give you an example of a report they want printed from their Access database, and the sources of data on the report are so obvious that designing the report takes a few minutes. Other times, particularly when the users' requirements are complex or the business processes supported by the application require a great deal of research, you may spend many days on Step 1.

FIGURE 33-4

The five-step design flowchart. This design methodology is particularly well-suited for Access databases.

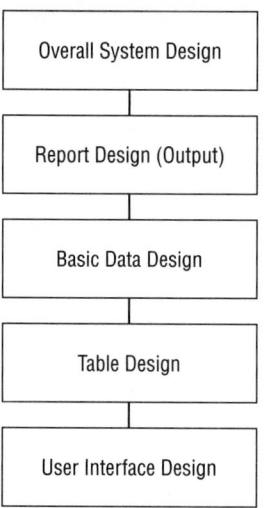

As you read through each step of the design process, *always* look at the design in terms of outputs and inputs. Although you see actual components of the system (products, customers, and transactions), remember that the focus of this chapter is how to move through each step. As you watch the CollectibleMiniCars database being designed, pay particular attention to the *design process*, not the actual system.

Step 1: The Overall Design — From Concept to Reality

All software developers face similar problems, the first of which is determining how to meet the needs of the end user. It's important to understand the overall user requirements before zeroing in on the details.

The five-step design method shown in Figure 33-4 helps you to create the system that you need, at an affordable price (measured in time or dollars). The CollectibleMiniCars database, for example, allows the client to sell items (vehicles and parts) to customers and supports the following tasks:

1.   Entering and maintaining customer information (name, address, and financial history)

2.   Entering and maintaining sales information (sales date, payment method, total amount, customer identity, and other fields)

3. Entering and maintaining sales line-item information (details of items purchased)

4. Viewing information from all the tables (sales, customers, sales line items, and payments)

5. Asking all types of questions about the information in the database

6. Producing a monthly invoice report

7. Producing a customer sales history

8. Producing mailing labels and mail-merge reports

These eight tasks have been described by the users. You may also need to consider additional tasks as you start the design process.

Most of the information that is necessary to build the system comes from the users. This means that you need to sit down with them and learn how the existing process works. To accomplish this, you must do a thorough *needs analysis* of the existing system and how you might automate it.

One way to accomplish this is to prepare a series of questions that give insight to the client's business and how the client uses his or her data. For example, when considering automating any type of business, you may consider asking these questions:

- What reports and forms are currently used?

- How are sales, customers, and other records currently stored?

- How are billings processed?

As you ask these questions and others, the client will probably remember other things about the business that you should know.

A walk-through of the existing process is also helpful to get a feel for the business. You may have to go back several times to observe the existing process and how the employees work.

As you prepare to complete the remaining steps, keep the client involved — let the users know what you're doing, and ask for input on what to accomplish, making sure it's within the scope of the users' needs.

Step 2: Report Design

Although it may seem odd to start with reports, in many cases, users are more interested in the printed output from a database than they are in any other aspect of the application. Reports often include every bit of data managed by an application. Because reports tend to be comprehensive, reports are often the best way to gather important information about a database's requirements. In the case of the CollectibleMiniCars database, the printed reports contain detailed and summarized versions of most of the data in the database.

After you've defined the CollectibleMiniCars' overall systems in terms of what must be accomplished, you can begin report design.

When you see the reports that you'll create in this section, you may wonder, "Which comes first — the chicken or the egg?" Does the report layout come first, or do you first determine the data items and text that make up the report? Actually, these items are considered at the same time.

It isn't important how you lay out the data in a report. The more time you take now, however, the easier it will be to construct the report. Some people go so far as to place gridlines on the report so that they know exactly where they want each bit of data to be.

The reports in Figures 33-5 and 33-6 were created with two different purposes. The report in Figure 33-5 displays information about the CollectibleMiniCars products, while the report in Figure 33-6 is an invoice with billing and customer information. The design and layout of each report are driven by the report's purpose and the data it contains.

Cross-Reference

You can read more about the reports in Chapter 37. ∎

FIGURE 33-5

A product information report

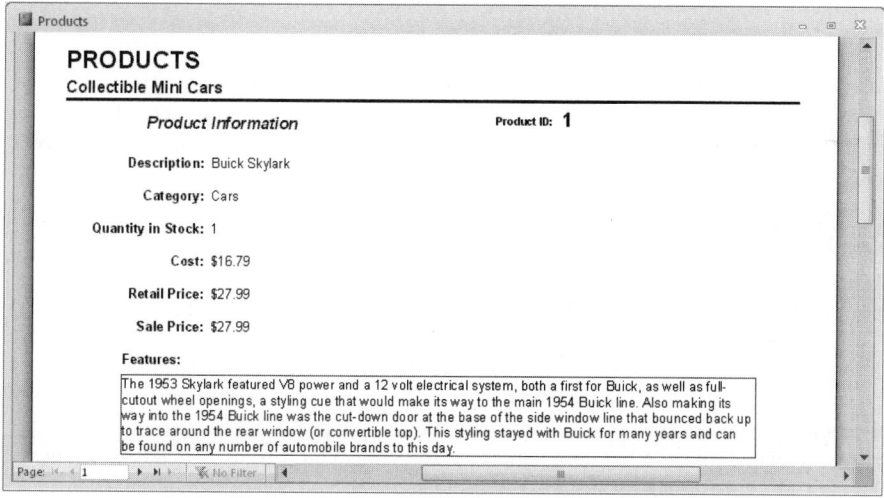

Step 3: Data Design

The next step in the design phase is to take an inventory of all the information needed by the reports. One of the best methods is to list the data items in each report. As you do so, take careful note of items that are included in more than one report. Make sure that you keep the same name for a data item that is in more than one report, because the data item is really the same item.

FIGURE 33-6

A sales invoice report containing sales information

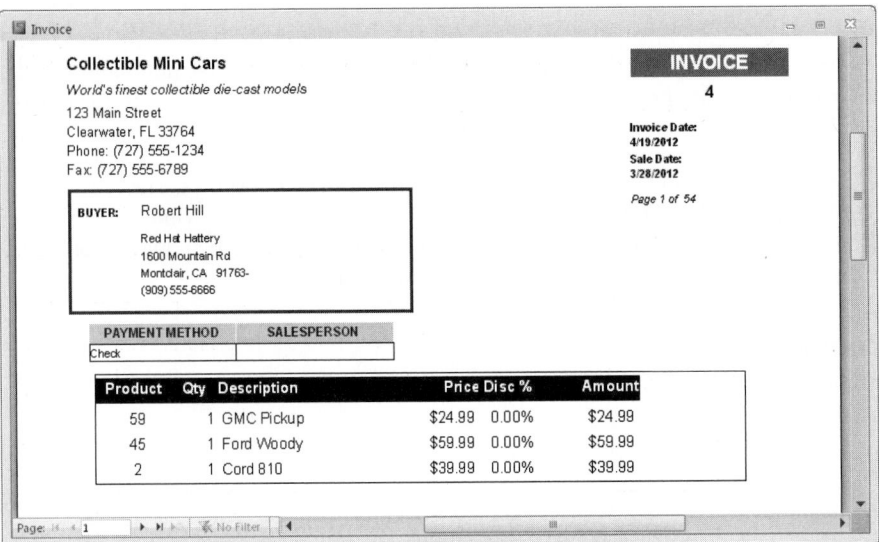

Another method is to separate the data items into a logical arrangement. Later, these data items are grouped into table structures and then mapped onto data-entry screens (forms). You should enter customer data, for example, as part of a customers table process, not as part of a sales entry.

Customer Information

First, look at each report you've roughed out for your database. For the CollectibleMiniCars database, start with the customer data and list the data items, as shown in Table 33-1.

As you can see by comparing the type of customer information needed for each report, there are many common fields. Most of the customer data fields are found in both reports. Table 33-1 shows only some of the fields that are used in each report — those related to customer information. Because the related row and the field names are the same, you can easily make sure that you have all the data items. Although locating items easily is not critical for this small database, it becomes very important when you have to deal with large tables containing many fields.

Sales Information

After extracting the customer data, you can move on to the sales data. In this case, you need to analyze only the Invoice report for data items that are specific to the sales. Table 33-2 lists the fields in the report that contain information about sales.

TABLE 33-1

Customer-Related Data Items Found in the Reports

Customers Report	Invoice Report
Customer Name	Customer Name
Street	Street
City	City
State	State
ZIP Code	ZIP Code
Phone Number	Phone Number
E-Mail Address	
Web Site Information	
Discount Rate	
Customer Since	
Last Sales Date	
Sales Tax Rate	
Credit Information (four fields)	

TABLE 33-2

Sales Data Items Found in the Reports

Invoice Report	Line Item Data
Invoice Number	
Sales Date	
Invoice Date	
Payment Method	
Salesperson	
Discount (overall for sale)	
Tax Location	
Tax Rate	

continued

TABLE 33-2 *(continued)*

Invoice Report	Line Item Data
Product Purchased (multiple lines)	Product Purchased
Quantity Purchased (multiple lines)	Quantity Purchased
Description of Item Purchased (multiple lines)	Description of Item Purchased
Price of Item (multiple lines)	Price of Item
Discount for each item (multiple lines)	Discount for Each Item
Payment Type (multiple lines)	
Payment Date (multiple lines)	
Payment Amount (multiple lines)	
Credit Card Number (multiple lines)	
Expiration Date (multiple lines)	

As you can see when you examine the type of sales information needed for the report, a few items (fields) are repeating (e.g., the Product Purchased, Quantity Purchased, and Price of Item fields). Each invoice can have multiple items, and each of these items needs the same type of information — the number ordered and the price per item. Many sales have more than one purchased item. Also, each invoice may include partial payments, and it's possible that this payment information will have multiple lines of payment information, so these repeating items can be put into their own grouping.

Line-Item Information

You can take all the individual items that you found in the sales information group in the preceding section and extract them to their own group for the invoice report. Table 33-2 shows the information related to each line item.

Looking back at the report in Figure 33-6, you can see that the data from Table 33-2 doesn't list the calculated field amount. The amount is dynamically calculated as the report prints, rather than storing the value in the database.

Tip
Unless a numeric field needs to be specifically stored in a table, simply recalculate it when you run the report (or form). You should avoid creating fields in your tables that can be created based on other fields — calculated data can be easily created and displayed in a form or report. ■

Step 4: Table Design

Now for the difficult part: You must determine what fields are needed for the tables that make up the reports. When you examine the multitude of fields and calculations that make up the many documents you have, you begin to see which fields belong to the various tables in the database.

(You already did much of the preliminary work by arranging the fields into logical groups.) For now, include every field you extracted. You'll need to add others later (for various reasons), although certain fields won't appear in any table.

It's important to understand that you don't need to add every little bit of data into the database's tables. For example, users may want to add vacation and other out-of-office days to the database to make it easy to know which employees are available on a particular day. However, it's very easy to burden an application's initial design by incorporating too many ideas during the initial development phases. Because Access tables are so easy to modify later on, it's probably best to put aside noncritical items until the initial design is complete. Generally speaking, it's not difficult to accommodate user requests after the database development project is under way.

After you've used each report to display all the data, it's time to consolidate the data by purpose (e.g., group the data into logical groups) and then compare the data across those functions. To take this step, first, look at the customer information, and combine all its different fields to create a single set of data items. Then you do the same thing for the sales information and the line-item information. Table 33-3 compares data items from these three groups of information.

TABLE 33-3

Comparing the Data Items

Customer Data	Invoice Data	Line Items
Customer Company Name	Invoice Number	Product Purchased
Street	Sales Date	Quantity Purchased
City	Invoice Date	Description of Item Purchased
State	Payment Method	Price of Item
ZIP Code		Discount for Each Item
Phone Numbers (two fields)	Discount (overall for this sale)	Taxable?
E-Mail Address	Tax Rate	
Web Site	Payment Type (multiple lines)	
	Payment Date (multiple lines)	
Discount Rate	Payment Amount (multiple lines)	
Customer Since	Credit Card Number (multiple lines)	
Last Sales Date	Expiration Date (multiple lines)	
Sales Tax Rate		
Credit Information (four fields)		

Consolidating and comparing data is a good way to start creating the individual table definitions for CollectibleMiniCars, but you have much more to do.

As you learn more about how to perform database design, you also learn that the customer data must be split into two groups. Some of these items are used only once for each customer, while other items may have multiple entries. An example is the Sales column — the payment information can have multiple lines of information.

You need to further break these types of information into their own columns, thus separating all related types of items into their own columns — an example of the *normalization* part of the design process. For example, one customer can have multiple contacts with the company. One customer may make multiple payments toward a single sale. Of course, I've already broken the data into three categories: customers, invoices, and sales line items.

Keep in mind that one customer may have multiple invoices, and each invoice may have multiple line items on it. The Invoice category contains information about individual sales, and the Line Items category contains information about each invoice. Notice that these three columns are all related; for example, one customer can have multiple invoices, and each invoice may require multiple detail lines (*line items*).

The relationships between tables can be different. For example, each sales invoice has one and only one customer, while each customer may have multiple sales. A similar relationship exists between the sales invoice and the line items of the invoice.

Database table relationships require a unique field in both tables involved in a relationship. A unique identifier in each table helps the database engine to join and extract related data properly.

Only the sales table has a unique identifier (InvoiceNumber), which means that you need to add at least one field to each of the other tables to serve as the link to other tables, for example, adding a CustomerID field to tblCustomers, adding the same field to the invoice table, and establishing a relationship between the tables through CustomerID in each table. The database engine uses the relationship between customers and invoices to connect customers with their invoices. Relationships between tables is done through *key* fields.

With an understanding of the need for linking one group of fields to another group, you can add the required key fields to each group. Table 33-4 shows two new groups and link fields created for each group of fields. These linking fields, known as *primary keys* and *foreign keys*, are used to link these tables together.

The field that uniquely identifies each row in a table is the *primary key*. The corresponding field in a related table is the *foreign key*. In our example, CustomerID in tblCustomers is a primary key, while CustomerID in tblInvoices is a foreign key.

Let's assume that a certain record in tblCustomers has 12 in its CustomerID field. Any records in Invoices with 12 as its CustomerID is "owned" by Customer 12.

TABLE 33-4

Tables with Keys

Customers Data	Invoice Data	Line Items Data	Sales Payment Data
CustomerID	InvoiceID	InvoiceID	InvoiceID
Customer Name	CustomerID	Line Number	Payment Type
Street	Invoice Number	Product Purchased	Payment Date
City	Sales Date	Quantity Purchased	Payment Amount
State	Invoice Date	Description of Item Purchased	Credit Card Number
ZIP Code	Payment Method	Price of Item	Expiration Date
Phone Numbers (two fields)	Salesperson	Discount for Each Item	
E-Mail Address			
Web Site Information			
Discount Rate			
Customer Since			
Last Sales Date			
Sales Tax Rate	Tax Rate		

With the key fields added to each table, you can now find a field in each table that links it to other tables in the database. For example, Table 33-4 shows CustomerID in both the customers table (where it's the primary key) and the invoice table (where it's a foreign key).

You've identified the core of the three primary tables for your system, as reflected by the first three columns in Table 33-4. This is the general, or first, cut toward the final table designs. You've also created an additional table to hold the sales payment data. Normally, payment details (such as the credit card number) are not part of a sales invoice.

Taking time to properly design your database and the tables contained within it is arguably the most important step in developing a database-oriented application. By designing your database efficiently, you maintain control of the data — eliminating costly data-entry mistakes and limiting your data entry to essential fields.

Although this book is not geared toward teaching database theory and all its nuances, this is a good point to briefly describe the art of database normalization. You should know that *normalization* is the process of breaking data down into constituent tables. Earlier in this chapter you read about how many Access developers add dissimilar information, such as customers, invoice data, and invoice line items, into one large table. A large table containing dissimilar data quickly becomes unwieldy and hard to keep updated. Because a customer's phone number appears in every row containing that customer's data, multiple updates must be made when the phone number changes. To avoid such problems, best practice calls for separating each type of data (invoice versus customer contact information, for example) into separate tables.

Step 5: Form Design

After you've created the data and established table relationships, it's time to design your forms. *Forms* are made up of the fields that can be entered or viewed in Edit mode. Generally speaking, your Access screens should look a lot like the forms used in a manual system.

When you're designing forms, you need to place three types of objects onscreen:

- Labels and text box data-entry fields. The fields on Access forms and reports are called *controls*.

- Special controls (multiple-line text boxes, option buttons, list boxes, check boxes, business graphs, and pictures)

- Graphical objects to enhance the forms (colors, lines, rectangles, and three-dimensional effects)

Ideally, if the form is being developed from an existing printed form, the Access data-entry form should resemble the printed form. The fields should be in the same relative place on the screen as they are in the printed counterpart to make it easier for users familiar with the paper form to transition to using the onscreen form.

Labels display messages, titles, or captions. *Text boxes* provide an area where you can type or display text or numbers that are contained in your database. *Check boxes* indicate a condition and are either unchecked or checked. Other types of controls available with Access include list boxes, combo boxes, option buttons, toggle buttons, and option groups.

Cross-Reference
Chapter 35 covers the various types of form controls available in Access. ∎

Summary

This chapter introduces the concepts and considerations driving database development. There is no question that data is important to users. Most companies simply can't operate without their customer and product lists, accounts receivable and accounts payable, and payroll information. Even very small companies must efficiently manage their business data.

Good database design means much more than sitting down and knocking together a few tables. Very often, poor database design habits come back to haunt developers and users in the form of missing or erroneous information on screens and printed reports. Users quickly tire of reentering the same information over and over again, and business managers and owners expect database applications to *save* time and money, not contribute to a business's overhead.

The next chapter introduces you to how to create tables, an integral skill in good database design.

Creating Access Tables

I n this chapter, you learn how to create a new Access database and
its tables. You establish the database container to hold your tables,
forms, queries, reports, and code that you build as you learn Access.
Finally, you create the actual tables used by the CollectibleMiniCars
database.

Getting Started with Access

As you open Access 2010, the default startup screen, called the *Backstage
view*, is revealed (see Figure 34-1). I'll examine the Backstage in more detail
later in this chapter, but you should understand the major components of
the user interface (UI) as you get started using Access 2010. Even experienced Access developers are surprised at how different Access 2010 looks
from previous versions.

Each time you open Access, the welcome screen may look different,
depending on whether Office.com offers new templates and you've elected
to have Office update automatically. In an effort to provide a high level
of support for Microsoft Office users, Microsoft has equipped each of
the Office applications with the ability to communicate directly with
Microsoft's Web Servers to access new Office.com content.

The center of the screen is dominated by the Office.com templates,
which are described in the next section. The right side of the screen
contains a list of recently opened databases, while the left side of the
screen contains a number of tabs for revealing other options for working
with Access.

FIGURE 34-1

The opening Access screen provides several ways to start working with Access.

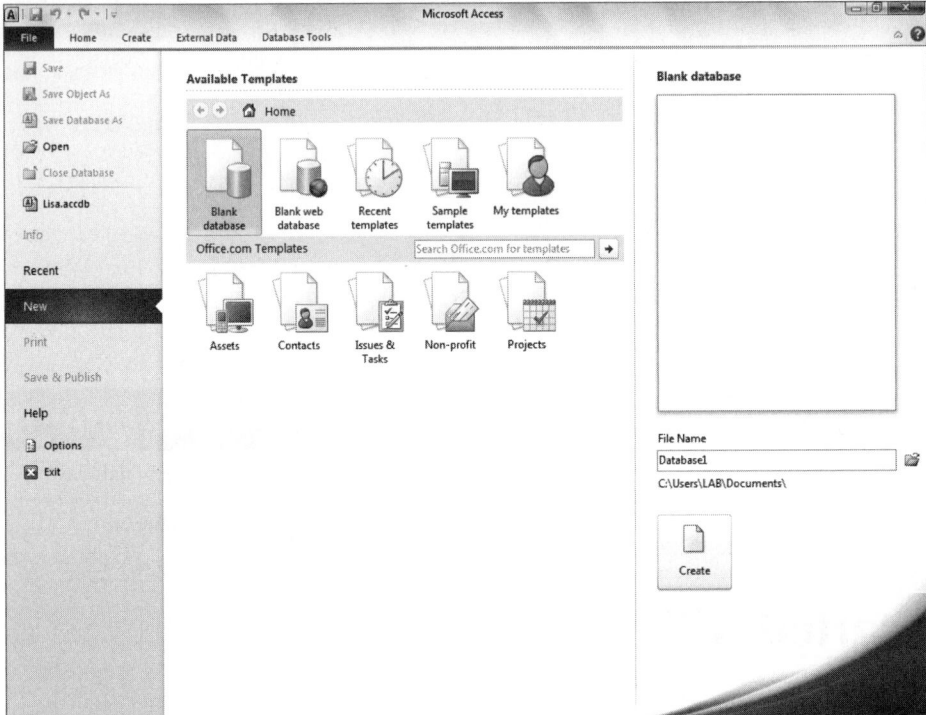

The Templates Section

As just noted, the Office.com templates section shown in the Backstage view when you start Access lists categories of online templates available via the Office.com web site.

I'll show you how to create a new database in the "Creating a Database" section of this chapter. In the meantime, let's take a look at the purpose of online templates. Microsoft has long been concerned that building Access databases is too difficult for many people. Not everyone takes the time to understand the rules governing database design or to learn the intricacies of building tables, queries, forms, and reports.

Microsoft established the online templates repository as a way to provide beginners and other busy people with the opportunity to download partially or completely built Access applications. The template databases cover many common business requirements such as inventory control and sales management. You might want to take a moment to explore the online templates. They fall in categories including Assets, Contacts, and Issues & Tasks, as shown in Figure 34-1. You can navigate to and download a template rather than creating a blank database from scratch. Just follow the onscreen prompts to do so.

The Office Backstage View

Our main interest at the moment is the rectangular button (labeled *File*) in the upper-left corner of the main Access screen. This button opens the Office Backstage view (shown in Figure 34-1), which is the gateway to various options for creating, opening, or configuring Access databases. The Backstage is shared by all the Office 2010 applications, and it features similar options in Access, Word, Excel, and Outlook. The Backstage options include activities that are used infrequently when you're working within the main Access window, but that are necessary for saving, printing, or maintaining Access databases. Putting these options into the Backstage area means that they don't have to appear anywhere on the Ribbon as you're working with Access.

In Figure 34-2, the Recent choice is selected. Notice that a list of recently opened databases appears to the right of commands in the Backstage. Near the bottom of the Recent Databases list is a Quickly Access This Number of Recent Databases text box for selecting the number of databases you'd like to see in the Recent databases list. Each database in the list is accompanied by a button that lets you pin the database to the recent list so that it's always available as you work with Access.

FIGURE 34-2

Click the File tab and then Recent to access recently opened databases.

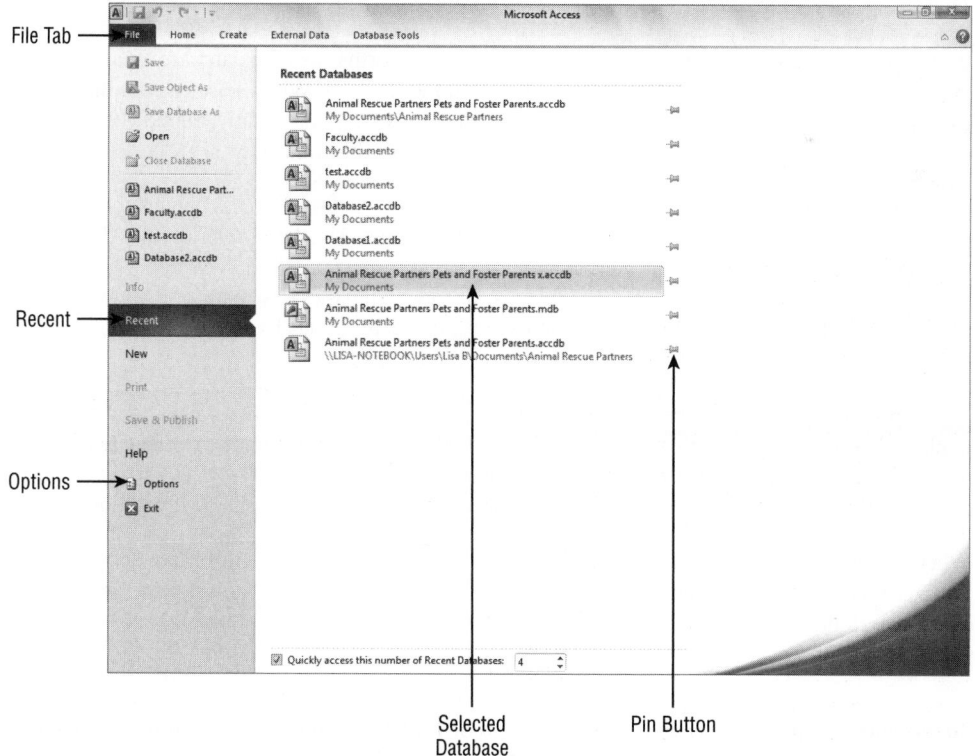

Instead of discussing each of the other Backstage commands at the moment, I'll cover each command in detail as we work through the Access user interface. For the moment, notice the New command near the middle of the menu on the left side of the Backstage. You'll use this choice to create a new Access database in the next section.

Note

Some confusion exists over the name of the rectangular button you see in the upper-left corner of the main Access window. Most users call this button the *File tab,* and the drop-down that appears when this button is clicked, the *File menu.* However, in Access 2007, Microsoft referred to this button as the *Microsoft Office Button.* In Access 2010, the button's name has returned to its earlier name, and it's once again called the *File button or tab.* As mentioned earlier, the screen you see when the File tab is clicked in Access 2010 is the Backstage — it's no longer referred to as the *File menu.* ■

Creating a Database

There are many ways to create a new database file. Selecting the New choice in the Backstage area opens the new database screen (refer to Figure 34-1). This is where you either create an entirely new database or open a new database based on a template (for more on templates, see "The Templates Section," earlier in this chapter). You can even create a new database from the design of an existing Access file.

In the Backstage, clicking the Blank Database button transforms the new database area at the right side of the new database screen as shown in Figure 34-3. When selecting the Blank Database button, the preview area above the File Name box is, quite literally, blank. (If you selected a template, instead, you would see a preview of it in this area.)

Enter the name of the new database in the File Name box. By default, Access creates the new database file in the default folder specified in Access Options. (The Access options are discussed throughout this book.) By default, Access selects your Documents (Windows 7 and Windows Vista) or My Documents (Windows XP) folder as the new database's destination. If you want to use a different folder, use the Browse button (it looks like a Windows Explorer folder) to the right of the File Name box to browse to the location you want to use.

Access provides a default name of Database1.accdb or just Database1 for new databases. Replace this placeholder name with a name that you'll recognize, and then click the Create button. For example, Figure 34-4 shows a new database named CollectibleMiniCars.accdb. (Entering the extension .accdb is optional — Access automatically supplies it if you don't.)

When the new database is created, Access automatically opens it for you. In Figure 34-4, notice that Access opens the new database with a blank table already added to the database, ready to be filled in with fields and other design details.

Note

Access 2010 recognizes all previous versions of Access database files. By default, the 2007 format (with an .accdb extension) is used, but you can specify Access 2000, 2002–2003, or 2007 as the default format.

Choose File ⇨ Options ⇨ General, select the Default File Format option, and choose whichever format you prefer. For example, if much of your Access 2010 work is performed on Access 2000 databases, you should choose the 2000 format to preserve backward compatibility. Users still working with Access 2000 aren't able to open Access files created in the .accdb format.

If you choose to use an older Access database format, you won't be able to use the features that are only supported by the .accdb format. ■

FIGURE 34-3

Enter the name of the new database in the File Name box.

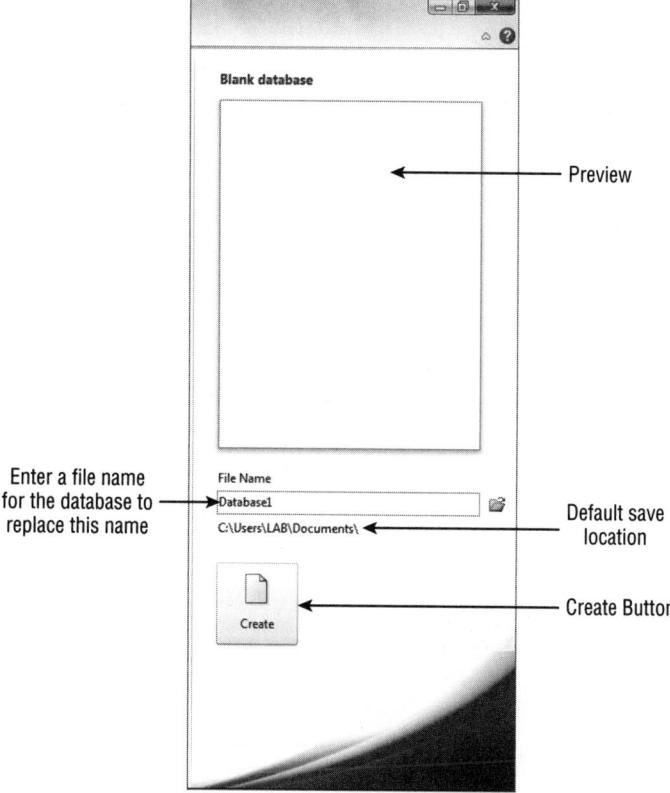

Access 2010 works directly with Access 2000, 2002–2003, and Access 2007. accdb databases. Earlier Access database files (such as Access 97 or 95) must be converted to 2000, 2002–2003, or 2007 before they can be used in Access 2010. Access examines the database file you're opening and, if the file must be converted, presents you with the Database Enhancement dialog box (shown in Figure 34-5).

Clicking Yes in the Database Enhancement dialog box opens a second dialog box (not shown), which asks for the name of the converted database. Clicking No in the Database Enhancement dialog box opens the older database in read-only mode, enabling you to view, but not modify, objects in the database; this process is sometimes referred to as *enabling* the database. Choosing to enable a database using an older format is sometimes necessary when you must understand the design of an old database, but users are still working with the old database and it can't be upgraded to Access 2010 format.

FIGURE 34-4

The new CollectibleMiniCars database is created.

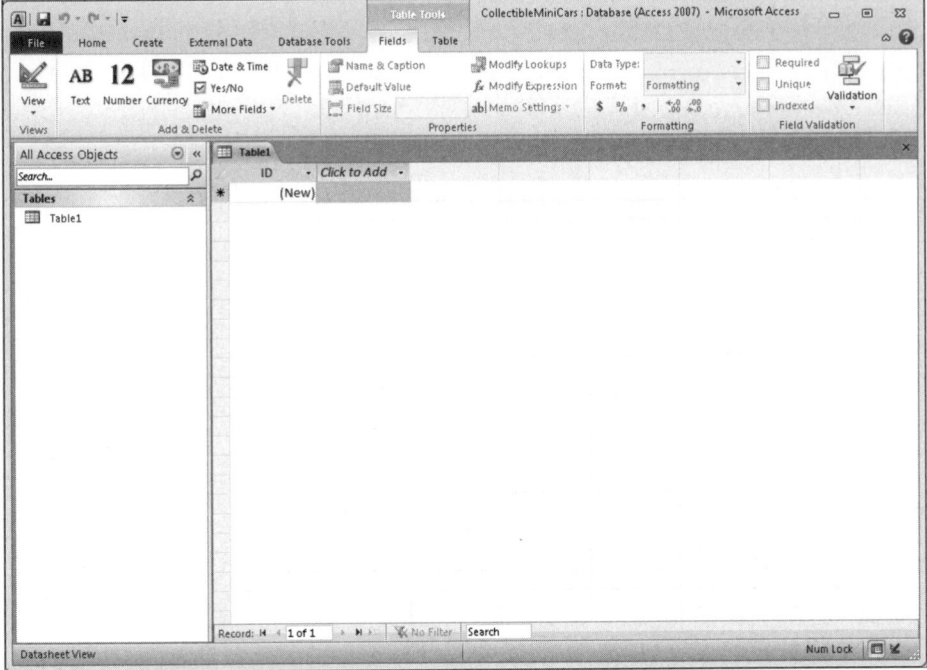

FIGURE 34-5

Opening an older Access data file invokes the Database Enhancement dialog box.

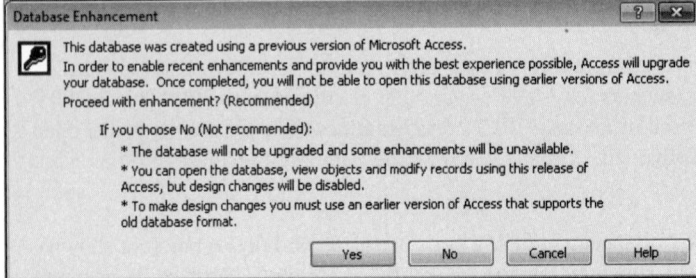

If you're following the examples in this book, note that `CollectibleMiniCars.accdb` is the name of the database file shown in some of this chapter's figures. This database is for the hypothetical business Collectible Mini Cars.

Understanding How Access Works with Data

Microsoft Access works with data in numerous ways. For simplicity, most of the examples in this book use data stored in local tables. A local table is contained within the Access `.accdb` file that's open in front of you. This is how you've seen examples so far.

In many professionally developed Microsoft Access applications, the actual tables are kept in a database (usually called the *back end*) separate from the other interface objects (forms, reports, queries, pages, macros, and modules). The back-end data file stays on a file server on the network, and each user has a copy of the front-end database (containing the forms and reports) on his computer. This is done to make the application more maintainable. By separating the data and their tables into another database, maintenance work (building new indexes, updating reports, etc.) is more easily done without affecting the remainder of the system.

For example, you may be working with a multiuser system and find a problem with a form or report in the database. If all the data and interface objects are in the same database, you have to shut down the system while repairing the broken form or report — other users can't work with the application while you repair the form or report.

By separating data from other objects, you can fix the errant object while others are still working with the data. After you've fixed the problem, you can deliver the new changes to everyone, and they'll import the form or report into their local databases. Splitting a database also makes it much easier to back up an application's data without affecting the application's user interface.

You may want to first develop your application with the tables within the `.accdb` database. Then, later, you can use the Database Splitter Wizard to automatically move the tables in your `.accdb` file to a separate Access `.accdb` file.

The Access 2010 Environment

The initial Access screen, after creating a new database, is shown in Figure 34-4. Across the top of the screen is the Access Ribbon, which was new in Access 2007 and replaces the toolbars and menus seen in previous versions of Access. The Ribbon is divided into several groups. The chapters covering Access in this part of the book will discuss the groups and the controls in each group as needed.

The Navigation Pane

The Navigation pane, at the left of the screen, is your primary navigation aid when working with Access. By default, the list is filled with the names of tables in the current database, but it can also display other types of objects if you click on the drop-down list in the Navigation pane's title bar to reveal the navigation options (shown in Figure 34-6).

FIGURE 34-6

Choosing an alternate display for the Navigation pane.

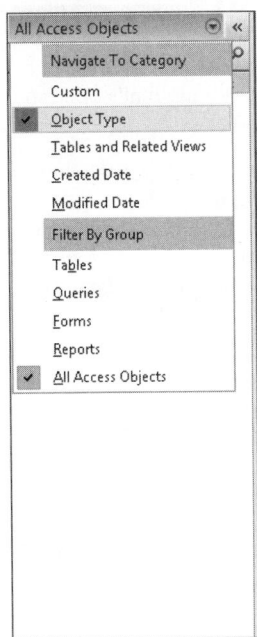

The Navigation pane shows queries, forms, reports, and other Access object types. It can even display a combination of different types of objects.

Here are the navigation options:

- **Custom.** The Custom option creates a new tab in the Navigation pane. This new tab is titled *Custom Group 1* by default and contains objects that you drag-and-drop into the tab's area. Items added to a custom group still appear in their respective "object type" view, as described in the next bullet.

Tip

Custom groups are a great way to group dissimilar objects (like tables, queries, and forms) that are functionally related. For example, you could create a Customers custom group, and add all the database objects related to customer activities. Items contained in a custom group can appear in other groups as well. ■

- **Object Type.** The Object Type setting is most similar to previous versions of Access. When selected, Object Type transforms the selection list to display the usual Access object types: tables, queries, forms, reports, and so on.

- **Tables and Related Views.** The Tables and Related Views setting requires a bit of explanation. Access tries very hard to keep the developer informed of the hidden connections between objects in the database. For example, a particular table may be used in a number of queries or referenced from a form or report. In previous versions of Access, these relationships were very difficult to determine, and no effective tool was built into Access helping you understand these relationships.

  Figure 34-7 shows how the Tables and Related Views works. The Categories group has been expanded to show that nine other objects in the Northwind Traders database are all related to the Categories table. This information helps a developer understand that changing the Categories table affects many other objects in the database.

  In addition to the Categories group, there are several other table-related groups, such as Customers, Employees, Order Details, and so on.

FIGURE 34-7

The Tables and Related Views setting is a powerful tool for analyzing an Access database.

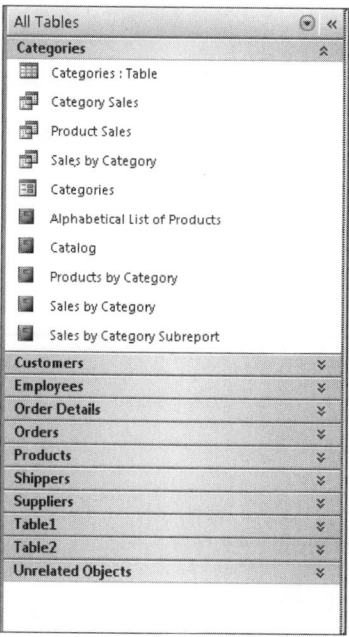

- **Created Date and Modified Date.** These options group the database objects by either the created date or the modified date. These settings are useful when you need to know *when* an object was either created or last modified.

- **Filter By Group.** The Filter By Group option filters the selected object type (table, form, etc.) by a number of grouping options. The grouping option is determined by the navigation category chosen in Navigate To Category at the top of the Navigation pane (refer to Figure 34-6). For example, selecting Created Date changes the options under Filter By Group to the following options: Today, Yesterday, Last Week, Two Weeks Ago, and so on.

Tip

The Filter By Group option is really only helpful when you have a fairly large number of objects in your Access database. If you have an Access database containing several hundred different forms, you'll find it very useful to filter by forms that were modified within the last week or so. But when there are only a few objects in a database, the Filter By Group option has little effect. ∎

- **Tables, Queries, Forms, and Reports.** These are the major types of Access objects. You filter the objects shown in the Navigation pane by selecting a single object type. Some Access databases contain dozens of each type of object, and these options enable you to view only a single type of object (such as Tables) in the Navigation pane.

- **All Access Objects.** By default, the Navigation pane shows all objects in the current database. Select All Access Objects when you have been working with one of the filtered views and want to see every object in the database.

The Ribbon

The Access Ribbon occupies the top portion of the main Access screen. The Ribbon replaces the menus and toolbars seen in previous versions of Access. The Ribbon's appearance changes depending on what task you're working on in the Access environment. Figure 34-8 shows the Home Ribbon tab you see when you're working with Access tables in Datasheet view. A different Ribbon appears when working with forms or reports in Design view.

FIGURE 34-8

The Home tab of the Access 2010 Ribbon.

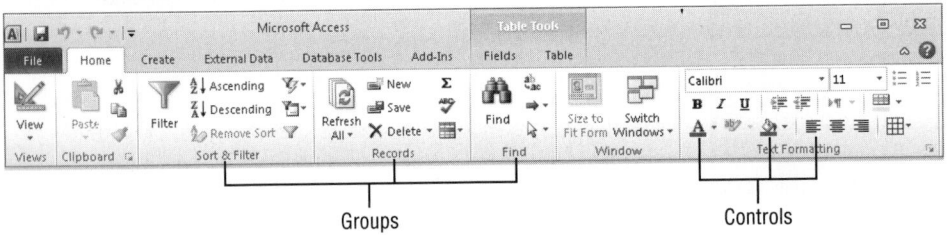

The Ribbon is divided into various groups, each containing any number of controls. The Sort & Filter group, for example, includes options for sorting a datasheet's contents in ascending or descending order, whereas the Find group contains commands for searching through records within the datasheet.

The other groups on the Ribbon — Views, Clipboard, Records, Window, and Text Formatting — contain controls that perform other tasks commonly associated with Access datasheets. For example, the View control in the Views group changes the Datasheet view of the table to Design view, making it easy to update the table's design.

Instead of explaining each of the groups and controls within groups on the Ribbon, I'll introduce you to each relevant Ribbon command in the proper context in this chapter and the chapters that follow.

Other Relevant Features of the Access Environment

The Access environment includes a number of other important features. In the far-right lower corner are two buttons that enable you to quickly change the selected object in the middle of the screen from Design view to the object's Normal view. For example, in the case of an Access table, the Normal view is to display the table as a datasheet, while a report's Normal view is to display the report in Print Preview.

Figure 34-9 illustrates one of the more interesting changes for Access 2007 and 2010, the tabbed interface. A common complaint among some developers with earlier versions of Access was the fact that, when multiple objects were simultaneously opened in the Access environment, the objects would often overlap and obscure each other, making it difficult to navigate between the objects. For example, in Access 2000, you might have a form open in Design view and, at the same time, a table open in Datasheet view. Invariably, one of these objects would overlap the other, and, depending on how large the object was, could completely obscure the other object.

Microsoft has added a tabbed document interface to Access, preventing objects from obscuring other objects that are open at the same time. In Figure 34-9, the Northwind Employees form is currently in use. Three other database objects (the Employees table, the Orders form, and the Invoices report) are also opened in the Access work area. Clicking on a tab associated with an object activates the tab and brings the object to the top.

When an object such as the Employees form is put into Design view by right-clicking on the tab and selecting Design View from the shortcut menu, the form view is replaced with the Form Designer (shown in Figure 34-10). The Access environment is highly adaptable to whichever tasks you're currently performing in your database.

Tip
If you decide that you don't care for the tabbed interface, click the File tab, and select Options near the bottom of the Backstage list. Then select the Current Database tab, and change the Document Window Options from Tabbed Documents to Overlapping Windows. ∎

Creating a New Table

Creating database tables is as much art as it is science. Acquiring a good working knowledge of the user's requirements is a fundamental step for any new database project.

In this chapter, I show you the steps required to create basic Access tables. In the following sections, you'll study the process of adding tables to an Access database, including the relatively complex subject of choosing the proper data type to assign to each field in a table.

FIGURE 34-9

The tabbed interface is a welcome addition to Access.

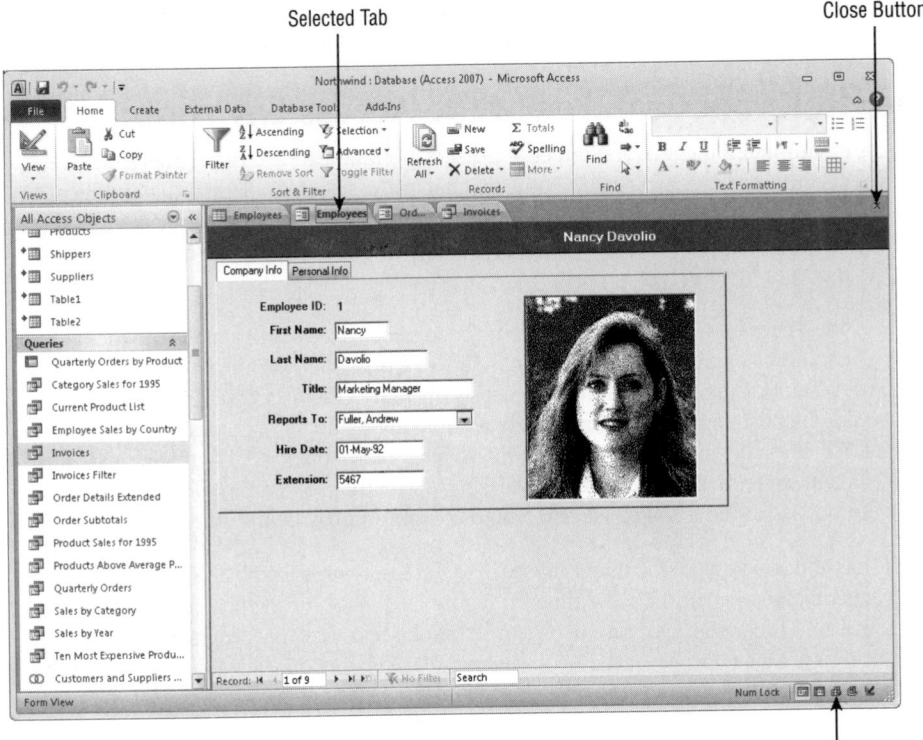

It's always a good idea to plan tables on paper first, before you use the Access tools to add tables to the database. Many tables, especially small ones, really don't require a lot of forethought before adding them to the database. After all, not much planning is required to design a table holding lookup information, such as the names of cities and states. However, more complex entities, such as customers and products, usually require considerable thought and effort to implement properly.

Although you can create the table interactively without any forethought, carefully planning a database system is a good idea. You can make changes later, but doing so wastes time; generally, the result is a system that's harder to maintain than one that you've planned well from the beginning.

In the following sections, I explore the new, blank table when you create a new database. It's important to understand the steps required to add new tables to an Access database. Because the steps required to add tables have changed so dramatically from earlier versions of Access, even experienced Access developers will want to read the following sections.

FIGURE 34-10

The Access environment adapts to your workflow.

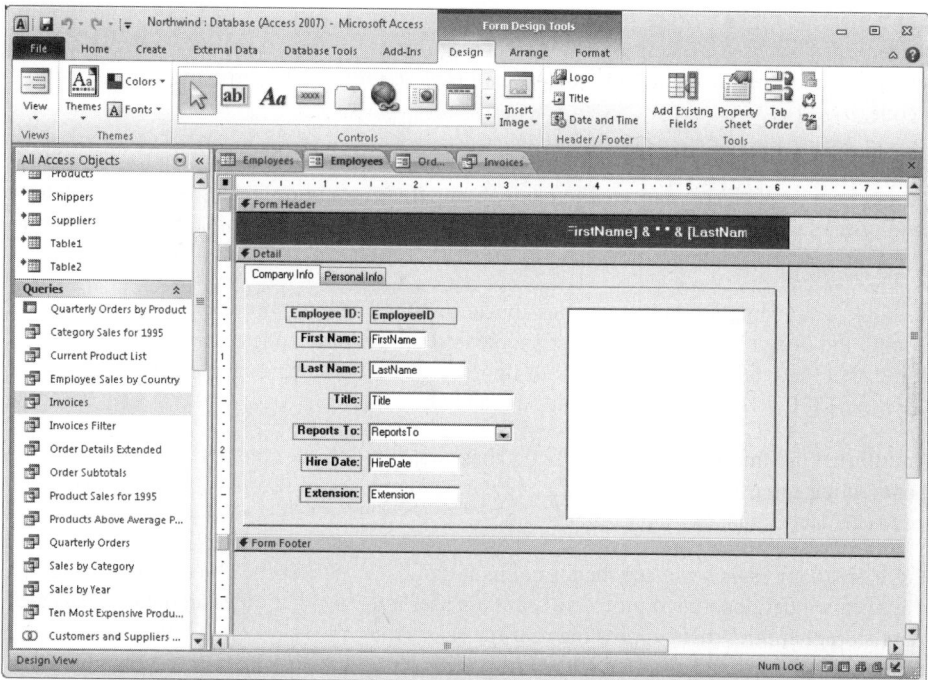

The Importance of Naming Conventions

Most Access developers eventually adopt a naming convention to help identify database objects. Most naming conventions are relatively simple and involve nothing more than adding a prefix indicating an object's type to the object's name. For example, an Employees form might be named frmEmployees.

As your databases grow in size and complexity, the need to establish a naming convention for the objects in your databases increases. Even with the Name AutoCorrect option turned on (click the File tab and choose Options ➪ Current Database ➪ Name AutoCorrect), Access only corrects the most obvious name changes. Changing the name of a table breaks virtually every query, form, and report that uses the information from that table. Your best defense is to adopt reasonable object names, use a naming convention early on as you begin building Access databases, and stick with the naming convention throughout the project.

Access imposes very few restrictions on the names assigned to database objects. Therefore, it's entirely possible to have two distinctly different objects (e.g., a form and a report, or a table and a macro) with the same name. (You can't, however, have a table and a query with the same name, because tables and queries occupy the same namespace in the database.)

Although simple names like *Contacts* and *Orders* are adequate, as a database grows in size and complexity, you might be confused about which object a particular name refers to. For example, later in this book, you'll read about manipulating database objects through code and macros. When working with Visual Basic for Applications (VBA), the programming language built into Access, there must be no ambiguity or confusion between referenced objects. Having both a form and a report named *Contacts* might be confusing to you *and* to your code.

The simplest naming convention is to prefix object names with a three- or four-character string indicating the type of object carrying the name. Using this convention, tables are prefixed with tbl and queries with qry. The generally accepted prefixes for forms, reports, macros, and modules are frm, rpt, mcr, and bas or mod, respectively.

In this book, most compound object names appear in mixed case: tblBookOrders, tblBookOrderDetails, and so on. Most people find mixed-case names easier to read and remember than names that appear in all-uppercase or all-lowercase characters (such as TBLBOOKORDERDETAILS or tblbookorderdetails).

Also, at times, I use informal references for database objects. For example, the formal name of the table containing contact information in the previous examples is tblContacts. An informal reference to this table might be "the Contacts table."

In most cases, your users never see the formal names of database objects. One of your challenges as an application developer is to provide a seamless user interface that hides all data-management and data-storage entities that support the user interface. You can easily control the text that appears in the title bars and surfaces of the forms, reports, and other UI components to hide the actual names of the data structures and interface constituents.

Take advantage of the long object names that Access permits to give your tables, queries, forms, and reports descriptive, informative names. There is no reason why you should confine a table name to ConInfo when tblContactInformation is handled just as easily and is much easier to understand.

Descriptive names can be carried to an extreme, of course. There's no point in naming a form frmUpdateContactInformation if frmUpdateInfo does just as well. Long names are more easily misspelled or misread than shorter names, so use your best judgment when assigning names.

Finally, although Access lets you use spaces in database object names, you should avoid spaces at all costs. Spaces don't add to readability and can cause major headaches, particularly when upsizing to client/server environments or using Object Linking and Embedding (OLE) automation with other applications. Even if you don't anticipate extending your Access applications to a client/server or incorporating OLE or Dynamic Data Exchange (DDE) automation into your applications, get into the habit of not using spaces in object names.

The Table Design Process

Designing a table is a multistep process. By following the steps in order, your table design can be created readily and with minimal effort:

1. Create the new table.

2. Enter field names, data types, properties, and (optionally) descriptions.

3. Set the table's primary key.

4. Create indexes for appropriate fields.

5. Save the table's design.

Generally speaking, some tables are never really finished. As users' needs change or the business rules governing the application change, you might find it necessary to open an existing table in Design view. This book, like most books on Access, describes the process of creating tables as if every table you'll ever work on is brand-new. The reality, however, is that most of the work that you'll do on an Access application will be performed on preexisting objects in the database. Some of those objects you've added yourself, while other objects may have been added by another developer at some time in the past. However, the process of maintaining an existing database component is exactly the same as creating the same object from scratch.

Tip

Just a quick note about modifying tables once they're built: Adding a *new* field to a table almost never causes problems. Existing queries, forms, and reports, and even VBA code, will continue using the table as before. After all, these objects won't reference the new field because the field was added *after* their creation. Therefore, you can add a new field and incorporate the field where needed in your application, and everything will work as expected.

The trouble comes when you remove or rename a field in a table. Even with AutoCorrect turned on, Access won't update field-name references in VBA code, in control properties, and in expressions throughout the database. Changing an existing field (or any other database object, for that matter) is always a bad idea. You should always strive to provide your tables, fields, and other database objects with good, strong, descriptive names when you add them to the database, instead of planning to go back later and fix them. ∎

Adding a New Table to the Database

Begin by selecting the Create tab on the Ribbon at the top of the Access screen. The Create tab (shown in Figure 34-11) contains all the tools necessary to create not only tables, but also forms, reports, and other database objects.

There are two main ways to add new tables to an Access database, both of which are invoked from the Tables group on the Create tab:

- **Clicking on the Table Button.** Adds a complete new table to the database.
- **Clicking on the Table Design Button.** Adds a table in Design view to the database.

For this example, I'll be using the Table Design button, but first, let's take a look at the Table button.

FIGURE 34-11

The Create tab contains tools necessary for adding new objects to your Access database.

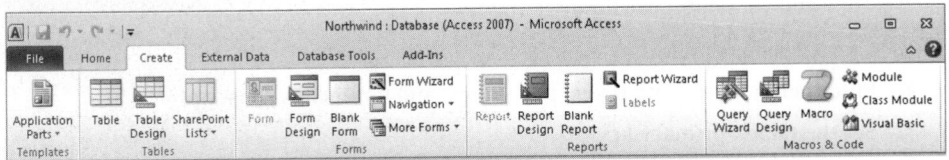

Clicking the Table button adds a new table to the Access environment. The new table appears in Datasheet view in the area to the right of the Navigation pane, as shown in Figure 34-12. Notice that the new table appears in Datasheet view, with an ID column already inserted, and a Click to Add column to the right of the ID field.

FIGURE 34-12

The new table in Datasheet view.

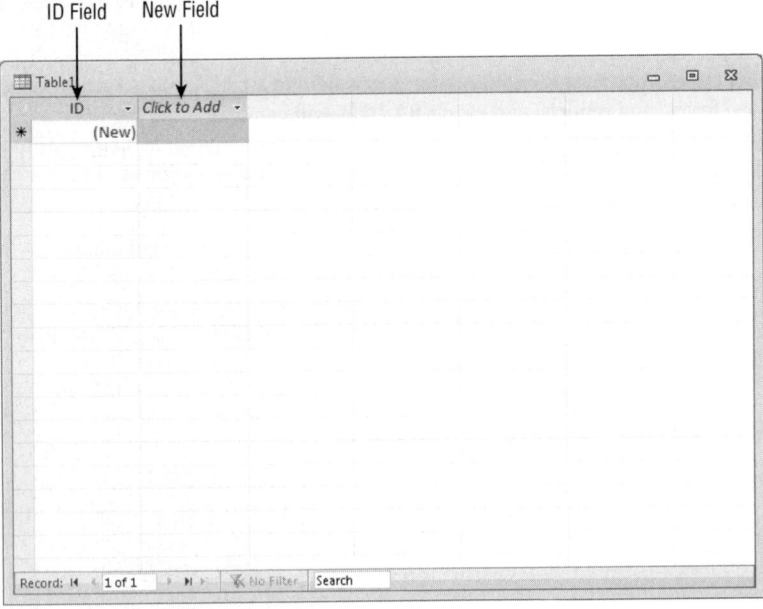

The Click to Add column is intended to permit users to quickly add tables to an Access database. All that you have to do is begin entering data in the new column. You assign the field a name by right-clicking on the field's heading, selecting Rename Column, and entering a name for the field. In other words, building an Access table can be very much like creating a spreadsheet in Microsoft Excel.

Note
This approach was usually referred to as "creating a table in Datasheet view" in previous versions of Microsoft Access. ∎

Once you've added the new column, the tools in the Fields Ribbon tab allow you to set the specific data type for the field, and its formatting, validation rules, and other properties.

There are good reasons *not* to use the Datasheet view method of building tables. Relational database systems such as Access are constructed by breaking data into constituent entities, and then building a table for each entity. The tables in an Access database should carefully and accurately reflect the entities they describe. Seemingly small issues, such as deciding which data type to assign to a field, have a dramatic impact on the utility, performance, and integrity of the database and its data.

Every table added to an Access database, and the fields added to tables, should have a purpose in the overall database design. Even when adding tables using the Table button, it's far too easy to add tables that don't fit well into the database's design.

The second method of adding new tables is to click the Table Design button in the Tables group on the Create tab. Access opens a new table in Design view, allowing you to add fields to the table's design. Figure 34-13 shows a new table's design after a few fields have been added. The Table Design view provides a somewhat more deliberate approach to building Access tables.

FIGURE 34-13

A new table added in Design view.

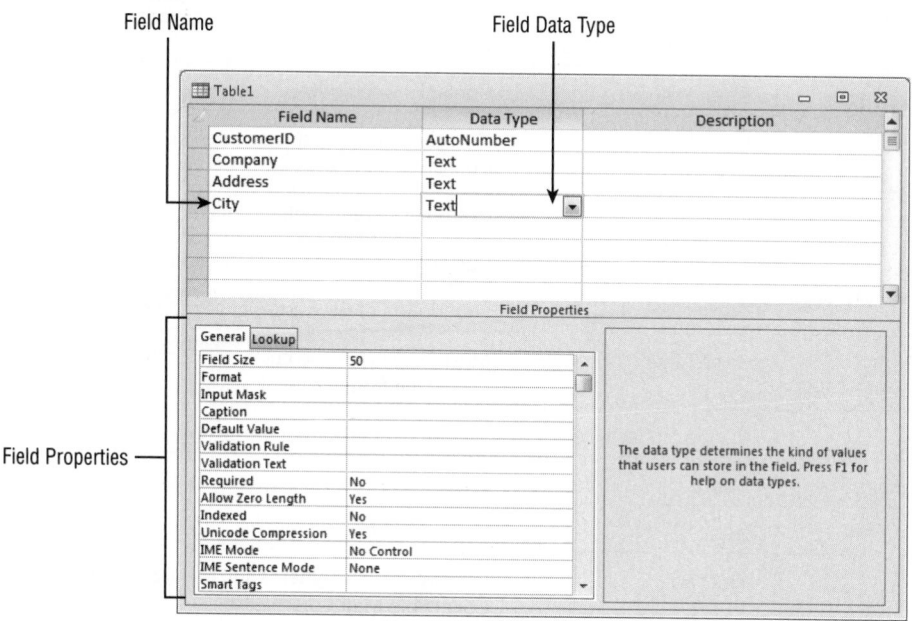

The Table Designer is quite easy to understand, and each column is clearly labeled. At the far left is the Field Name column, where you input the names of the fields that you add to the table. You assign a data type to each field in the table and (optionally) provide a description for the field.

For this chapter's example, we'll create the Customers table for the CollectibleMiniCars application. The basic design of this table is outlined in Table 34-1. I cover the details of this table's design in the "Creating tblCustomers" section, later in this chapter.

TABLE 34-1

The CollectibleMiniCars Customers Table

Field Name	Data Type	Description
CustomerID	AutoNumber	Primary key
Company	Text 50	Contact's employer or other affiliation
Address	Text 50	Contact's address
City	Text 50	Contact's city
State	Text 50	Contact's state
ZipCode	Text 50	Contact's zip code
Phone	Text 50	Contact's phone
Fax	Text 50	Contact's fax
Email	Text 100	Contact's e-mail address
WebSite	Text 100	Contact's web address
OrigCustDate	DateTime	Date the contact first purchased something from Collectible Mini Cars
CreditLimit	Currency	Customer's credit limit in dollars
CurrentBalance	Currency	Customer's current balance in dollars
CreditStatus	Text	Description of the customer's credit status
LastSalesDate	DateTime	Most recent date the customer purchased something from Collectible Mini Cars
TaxRate	Number (Double)	Sales tax applicable to the customer
DiscountPercent	Number (Double)	Customary discount provided to the customer
Notes	Memo	Notes and observations regarding this customer
Active	Yes/No	Whether the customer is still buying or selling to Collectible Mini Cars

Some of the fields in Table 34-1 are rather generous in the amount of space allocated for the field's data. For example, it's unlikely that anyone's name will occupy 50 characters, but there is no harm in providing for very long names. Access only stores as many characters as are actually entered into a text field (plus an extra character about the entry's length). Therefore, allocating 50 characters doesn't actually use 50 characters for every name in the database.

Looking once again at Figure 34-13, you see that the Table Design window consists of two areas:

- **The Field Entry Area.** Use the field entry area, at the top of the window, to enter each field's name and data type. You can also enter an optional description.

- **The Field Properties Area.** The area at the bottom of the window is where the field's properties are specified. These properties include field size, format, input mask, and default value, among others. The actual properties displayed in the properties area depend on the data type of the field. You learn much more about these properties in the "Assigning Field Data Types" section, later in this chapter.

Tip

You can switch between the upper and lower areas of the Table Designer by pressing F6. ∎

Using the Table Tools Design Tab

The Table Tools Design tab on the Access Ribbon (shown in Figure 34-14) contains many controls that assist in creating a new table definition.

The Table Tools Design tab of the Ribbon.

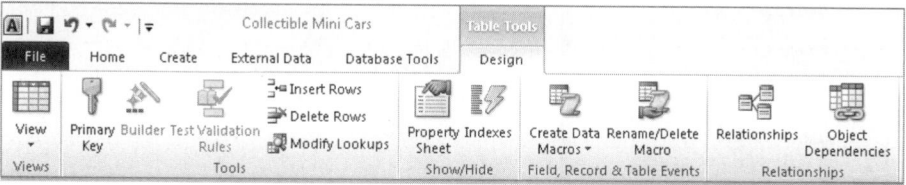

The controls in the Table Tools Design tab affect the important table design considerations. Only a few of the controls shown in Figure 34-14 are described in the following sections. You'll learn much more about the other buttons in the "Creating tblCustomers" section, later in this chapter.

Primary Key Button

Click the Primary Key button to designate which of the fields in the table you want to use as the table's primary key. Traditionally, the primary key appears at the top of the list of fields in the table, but it could appear anywhere within the table's design. Moving a field is easy: Simply left-click on the gray selector to the left of the field's name to highlight the field in the Table Design view, and drag the field to its new position.

Insert Rows Button

Although it makes very little difference to the database engine, many developers are fussy about the sequence of fields in a table. Also, particularly when assigning an index or composite index to a table, you want the fields to be next to each other in the table's field list.

The Insert Rows button inserts a blank row just *above* the position occupied by the insertion point. For example, if the insertion point is currently in the second row of the Design view, clicking the Insert Row button inserts an empty row in the second position, moving the existing second row to the third position.

Delete Rows Button

Conversely, the Delete Rows button removes a row from the table's design. Be careful, however, because Access doesn't ask you to confirm the deletion before actually removing the row.

Property Sheet Button

The Property Sheet button opens the table's Property Sheet (shown in Figure 34-15). These properties enable you to specify important table characteristics, such as a validation rule to apply to the entire table or an alternative sort order for the table's data.

FIGURE 34-15

The Property Sheet.

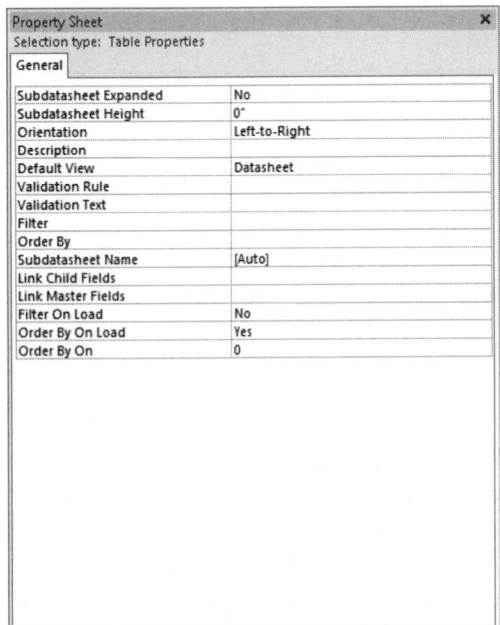

Indexes Button

Indexes are discussed in much more detail in the "Indexing Access Tables" section, later in this chapter. Clicking the Indexes button opens the Indexes dialog box (shown in Figure 34-18, later in this chapter), enabling you to specify the details of indexes on the fields in your table.

Working with Fields

Fields are created by entering a field name and a field data type in the upper entry area of the Design view. The optional Description property indicates the field's purpose. The description appears in the status bar at the bottom of the screen during data entry and may be useful to people working with the application. After entering each field's name and data type, you can further specify how each field is used by entering properties in the property area.

Naming a Field

A field name should be descriptive enough to identify the field to you as the developer, to the user of the system, and to Access. Field names should be long enough to quickly identify the purpose of the field, but not overly long. (Later, as you enter validation rules or use the field name in a calculation, you'll want to save yourself from typing long field names.)

To enter a field name, position the pointer in the first row of the Table Design window under the `Field Name` column. Then type a valid field name, observing these rules:

- Field names can be from 1 to 64 characters.
- Field names can include letters, numbers, and many special characters.
- Field names can't include a period (.), exclamation point (!), brackets ([ ]), or accent grave (`).
- You can't use low-order ASCII characters — for example, Ctrl+J or Ctrl+L (ASCII values 0 through 31).
- You can't start with a blank space.
- You can't use a double quotation mark (") in the name of a Microsoft Access project file.

You can enter field names in uppercase, lowercase, or mixed case. If you make a mistake while typing the field name, position the cursor where you want to make a correction, and type the change. You can change a field name at any time, even if the table contains data.

Note

Access is not case-sensitive, so the database itself doesn't distinguish between `tblCustomers` or `TblCustomers`. Choosing uppercase, lowercase, or mixed-case characters is entirely your decision and should be aimed at making your table names descriptive and easy to read.

After your table is saved, if you change a field name that is also used in queries, forms, or reports, you have to change it in those objects as well. One of the leading causes of errors in Access applications stems from changing the names of fundamental database objects such as tables and fields, but neglecting to make all the changes required throughout the database. Overlooking a field name reference in the control source of a control on the form or report, or deeply embedded in VBA code somewhere in the application, is far too easy. ∎

Specifying a Data Type

The next step is to actually create your tables and define your fields for those tables. You must also decide what type of data each of your fields will hold. In Access, you can choose any of several data types (these data types are detailed in the "Assigning Field Data Types" section, later in this chapter):

- **Text.** Alphanumeric characters; up to 255 characters.
- **Memo.** Alphanumeric characters; very long strings up to 65,535 characters.
- **Number.** Numerical values of many types and formats. The different numerical options are described in the "Number Data Type" section, later in this chapter.
- **Date/Time.** Date and time data.
- **Currency.** Monetary data.
- **AutoNumber.** Automatically incremented numeric counter.
- **Yes/No.** Logical values — Yes/No, True/False.
- **OLE Object.** Pictures, graphs, sound, video, word processing, and spreadsheet files.
- **Hyperlink.** A field that links to a picture, graph, sound, video, word processing, or spreadsheet file.

One of these data types must be assigned to each of your fields. You may also want to specify the Field Size property for the Text fields, or accept the default of 255 characters. The Field Size property specifies the maximum number of characters that a Text data type field may contain.

Specifying Data Validation Rules

The last major design decision concerns data validation, which becomes important as users enter data. You want to make sure that only good data (data that passes certain defined tests) gets into your system. You have to deal with several types of data validation. You can test for known individual items, stipulating that the Gender field can accept only the values Male, Female, or Unknown, for example. Or you can test for ranges, specifying that the value of Weight must be between 0 and 1,500 pounds. The validation settings are amongst the field properties.

Assigning Field Data Types

After you name a field, you must decide what type of data the field holds. Before you begin entering data, you should have a good grasp of the data types that your database uses. Access supports 10 basic data types (see Table 34-2). Some data types (such as Number) have several options. After you choose the data type, choose properties as needed on the General tab below. For example, for many Text fields, you will want to change the Field Size property. The available properties differ depending on the selected data type.

TABLE 34-2

Data Types Available in Microsoft Access

Data Type	Type of Data Stored	Storage Size
Text	Alphanumeric characters	255 characters or less
Memo	Alphanumeric characters	65,535 characters or less
Number	Numeric values	1, 2, 4, or 8 bytes, 16 bytes for Replication ID (GUID)
Date/Time	Date and time data	8 bytes
Currency	Monetary data	8 bytes
AutoNumber	Automatic number increments	4 bytes, 16 bytes for Replication ID (GUID)
Yes/No	Logical values: Yes/No, True/False	1 bit (0 or –1)
OLE Object	Pictures, graphs, sound, video	Up to 1 GB (disk space limitation)
Hyperlink	Link to an Internet resource	64,000 characters or less
Attachment	A special field that enables you to attach external files to an Access database	Varies by attachment
Lookup Wizard	Displays data from another table	Generally 4 bytes

Figure 34-16 shows the Data Type drop-down list used to select the data type for the field you just created.

Here are the basic rules to consider when choosing the data type for new fields in your tables:

- **The data type should reflect the data stored in the field.** For example, you should select one of the numeric data types to store numbers like quantities and prices. Do not store data like phone numbers or Social Security numbers in numeric fields, however. Your application won't be performing numeric operations like addition or multiplication on phone numbers, and this data should not be stored in numeric fields. Instead, use text fields for common data, such as Social Security numbers and phone numbers.

Note

Numeric fields never store leading zeros. Putting a zip code such as *02173* into a numeric field means that only the last four digits (2173) are actually stored. ∎

- **Consider the storage requirements of the data type you've selected.** Although you can use a Long Integer data type in place of a Simple Integer or Byte Value, the storage requirements of a Long Integer (4 bytes) is twice that of a Simple Integer. This means that twice as much memory is required to use and manipulate the number, and twice as much disk space is required to store its value. Whenever possible, use Byte or Integer data types for simple numeric data.

- **Will you want to sort or index the field?** Because of their binary nature, Memo and OLE Object fields can't be sorted or indexed. Use Memo fields sparingly. The overhead required to store and work with Memo fields is considerable.

- **Consider the impact of data type on sorting requirements.** Numeric data sorts differently from text data. Using the numeric data type, a sequence of numbers will sort as expected: 1, 2, 3, 4, 5, 10, 100. The same sequence stored as text data will sort like this: 1, 10, 100, 2, 3, 4, 5. If it's important to sort text data in a numeric sequence, you'll have to first apply a conversion function to the data before sorting.

Tip

If it's important to have text data representing numbers sort in the proper order, you might want to prefix the numerals with zeros (001, 002, etc.). Then the text values will sort in the expected order: 001, 002, 003, 004, 005, 010, 100. ∎

FIGURE 34-16

The Data Type drop-down list.

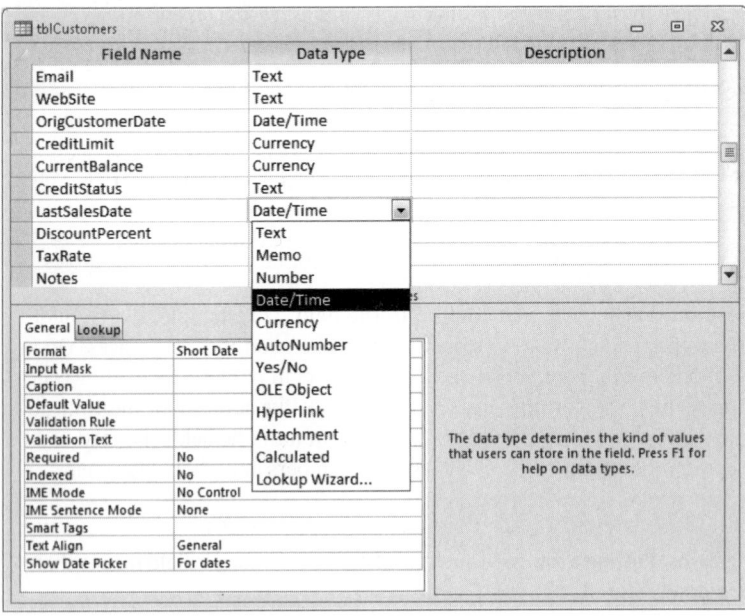

- **Is the data text or date data?** When working with dates, you're almost always better off storing the data in a Date/Time field than as a Text field. Text values sort differently from date data (dates are stored internally as numeric values), which can upset reports and other output that rely on chronological order.

Don't be tempted to store dates in one Date/Time field and times in another Date/Time field. The Date/Time field is specifically designed to handle *both* dates and times, and, as you'll see throughout this book, it's quite easy to display only the date or time portion of a Date/Time value.

A Date/Time field is also meant to store a discrete date and time, and not a time interval. If keeping track of durations is important, you should use two Date/Time fields — one to record the start and the other at the end of a duration.

- **Keep in mind the reports that will be needed.** You won't be able to sort or group memo or OLE data on a report. If it's important to prepare a report based on memo or OLE data, add a Tag field like a date or sequence number, which can be used to provide a sorting key, to the table.

Text Data Type

The Text data type holds information that is simply characters (letters, numbers, punctuation, etc.). Names, addresses, and descriptions are all text data, as are numeric data that is not used in a calculation (such as telephone numbers, Social Security numbers, and zip codes).

Although you specify the size of each Text field in the property area, you can enter no more than 255 characters of data in any Text field. Access uses variable length fields to store text data. If you designate a field to be 25 characters wide and you use only 5 characters for each record, then only enough room to store 5 characters is used in your database.

You'll find that the .accdb database file might quickly grow quite large, but text fields are not the usual cause. However, it's good practice to limit Text field widths to the maximum you believe is likely for the field. Names can be quite tricky because fairly long names are common in some cultures. However, it's a safe bet that a postal code might be less than 12 characters, while a U.S. state abbreviation is always 2 characters. By limiting a Text field's width, you also limit the number of characters users can enter when the field is used in a form.

Memo Data Type

The Memo data type holds a variable amount of data from 0 to 65,535 characters for each record. So, if one record uses 100 characters, another requires only 10, and yet another needs 3,000, you use only as much space as each record requires.

You don't specify a field size for the Memo data type. Access allocates as much space as necessary for the memo data.

Number Data Type

The Number data type enables you to enter *numeric* data — that is, numbers that will be used in mathematical calculations or represent scalar quantities such as inventory counts.

Note

If you have data that will be used in monetary calculations, you should use the Currency data type, which performs calculations without rounding errors. ∎

The exact type of numeric data stored in a number field is determined by the Field Size property. Table 34-3 lists the various numeric data types, their maximum and minimum ranges, the decimal points supported by each numeric data type, and the storage (bytes) required by each numeric data type.

TABLE 34-3

Numeric Field Settings

Field Size Setting	Range	Decimal Places	Storage Size
Byte	0 to 255	None	1 byte
Integer	–32,768 to 32,767	None	2 bytes
Long Integer	–2,147,483,648 to 2,147,483,647	None	4 bytes
Double	-1.797×10^{308} to 1.797×10^{308}	15	8 bytes
Single	-3.4×10^{38} to 3.4×10^{38}	7	4 bytes
Replication ID	N/A	N/A	16 bytes
Decimal	1–28 precision	15	8 bytes

Caution

Many errors are caused by choosing the wrong numeric type for number fields. For example, notice that the maximum value for the Integer data type is 32,767. I once saw a database that ran perfectly for several years and then started crashing with overflow errors. It turned out that the overflow was caused by a particular field being set to the Integer data type, and when the company occasionally processed very large orders, the 32,767 maximum was exceeded.

Be aware that overflow may occur simply by adding two numbers together or performing any mathematical operation that results in a value too large to be stored in a field. Some of the most difficult bugs occur only when circumstances (such as adding or multiplying two numbers) cause an overflow condition at run time. ∎

Design your tables very conservatively, and allow for larger values than you ever expect to see in your database. This is not to say that using the Double data type for all numeric fields is a good idea. The Double data type is very large (8 bytes) and might be somewhat slow when used in calculations or other numeric operations. Instead, the Single data type is probably best for most floating-point calculations, and Long Integer is a good choice where decimal points are irrelevant.

Date/Time Data Type

The Date/Time data type is a specialized number field for holding dates or times (or dates *and* times). When dates are stored in a Date/Time field, it's easy to calculate days between dates and other calendar operations. Date data stored in Date/Time fields sorts and filters properly as well. The Date/Time data type holds dates from January 1, 100, to December 31, 9999.

Currency

The Currency data type is another specialized number field. Currency numbers are not rounded during calculations and preserve 15 digits of precision to the left of the decimal point and 4 digits to the right. Because Currency fields use a fixed-decimal-point position, they're faster in numeric calculations than doubles.

AutoNumber

The AutoNumber field is another specialized Number data type. When an AutoNumber field is added to a table, Access automatically assigns a long integer (32-bit) value to the field (beginning at 1) and increments the value each time a record is added to the table. Alternatively (determined by the New Values property), the value of the AutoNumber field is a random integer that is automatically inserted into new records.

Only one AutoNumber field can appear in a table. Once assigned to a record, the value of an AutoNumber field can't be changed programmatically or by the user. AutoNumber fields are equivalent to the Long Integer data type and occupy 4 bytes, but they display only positive values. The range of possible values for AutoNumber fields is from 1 to 4,294,967,296 — more than adequate as the primary key for most tables.

Note

Only one AutoNumber **field can be added to an Access table. Generally speaking, it's better to use** AutoNumber **fields where their special characteristics are needed by an application.** ∎

Yes/No

Yes/No fields accept only one of two possible values. Internally stored as 1 (Yes) or 0 (No), the Yes/No field is used to indicate yes/no, on/off, or true/false. A Yes/No field occupies a single bit of storage.

OLE Object

The OLE Object field stores OLE data, highly specialized binary objects such as Microsoft Word documents, Excel spreadsheets, sound or video clips, and images. The OLE object is created by an application that Windows recognizes as an OLE Server, and can be linked to the parent application or embedded in the Access table. OLE objects can only be displayed in bound object frames in Access forms and reports. OLE objects can be as large as 1 GB or more in size. OLE fields can't be indexed.

Attachment

The Attachment data type was introduced Access 2007. In fact, the Attachment data type is one of the reasons Microsoft changed the format of the Access data file. The older .mdb format is unable to accommodate attachments.

The Attachment data type is relatively complex, compared to the other type of Access fields, and requires a special type of control when displayed on Access forms.

Hyperlink Data Type

The Hyperlink data type field holds combinations of text and numbers stored as text and used as a hyperlink address. It can have up to three parts:

- The text that appears in a control (usually underlined).
- The Internet address — the path to a file or web page.
- Any subaddress within the file or page. An example of a subaddress is a picture on a web page. Each part of the hyperlink's address is separated by the pound sign (#).

Access hyperlinks can even point to forms and reports in other Access databases. This means that you can use a hyperlink to open a form or report in an external Access database and display the form or report on the user's computer.

Lookup Wizard

The Lookup Wizard data type inserts a field that enables the end user to choose a value from another table, from the results of a SQL statement, or from a list of values that you enter for the lookup. The values may also be presented as a combo box or list box. When you choose the Lookup Wizard data type, the wizard starts and leads you through the process of defining the lookup list or selecting the table.

When you add a lookup field, a combo box or list box is automatically created in the table. The list box or combo box also appears on a query datasheet that contains the field and can be added to forms.

Entering a Field Description

The field description is completely optional; you use it only to help you remember a field's uses or to let another developer understand the field's purpose. Often, you don't use the Description column at all, or you use it only for fields whose purpose is not obvious. If you enter a field description, it appears in the status bar whenever you use that field in Access — in the datasheet or in a form. The field description can help clarify a field whose purpose is ambiguous or give the user a more complete explanation of the appropriate values for the field during data entry.

Creating a Table

Working with the different data types, you should be ready to create a table, such as the tblCustomers example mentioned earlier. This example table includes a field that could be used to link this table to two other tables (tblSales and tblContactLog) in the CollectibleMiniCars database.

Using AutoNumber Fields

Access gives special consideration to `AutoNumber` fields. You can't change a previously defined field from another type to `AutoNumber` if any data has been added to the table. If you try to change an existing field to `AutoNumber`, you'll see an error that says:

```
Once you enter data in a table, you can't change the data type of
any field to AutoNumber, even if you haven't yet added data to that
field.
```

You'll have to add a new `AutoNumber` field and begin working with it instead of changing an existing field to `AutoNumber`.

Completing tblCustomers

With `tblCustomers` in Design view, you're ready to finalize its design. Table 34-1, shown earlier in this chapter, lists the field definitions for `tblCustomers`. Enter the field names and data types as shown in Table 34-1. The next few pages explain how to change existing fields (which includes rearranging the field order, changing a field name, and deleting a field).

Here are the steps for adding fields to a table structure:

1. Click the cell in the `Field Name` column in the row where you want the field to appear.

2. Enter the field name and press Enter or Tab to move to the `Data Type` column.

3. Select the field's data type from the drop-down list in the `Data Type` column.

4. If desired, add a description for the field in the `Description` column.

Repeat each of these steps to create each of the data entry fields for `tblCustomers`. You can press the down-arrow (↓) key to move between rows, or use the mouse and click on any row. Pressing F6 switches the focus from the top to the bottom of the Design window, and vice versa.

Setting the Primary Key

Every table should have a *primary key* — one or a combination of fields with a unique value for each record. (This principle is called *entity integrity* in the world of database management.) In `tblCustomers`, the `CustomerID` field is the primary key. Each customer has a unique `CustomerID` value so that the database engine can distinguish one record from another. `CustomerID` 17, for example refers to one and only one record in the customers table. If you don't specify a primary key (unique value field), Access can create one for you.

Choosing a Primary Key

Without the `CustomerID` field, you'd have to rely on another field or combination of fields for uniqueness. You couldn't use the `Company` field because two customers could easily have the same company name. In fact, you couldn't even use the `Company` and `City` fields together (in a multifield key), for the same reason — it's entirely possible that two customers with the same name exist in the same city. You need to come up with a field or combination of fields that makes every record unique.

The easiest way to solve this problem is to add an `AutoNumber` field to serve as the table's primary key. The primary key in `tblCustomers` is `CustomerID`, an `AutoNumber` field.

If you don't designate a field as a primary key, Access can add an `AutoNumber` field and designate it as the table's primary key. `AutoNumber` fields make very good primary keys because Access creates the value for you, the number is never reused within a table, and you can't change the value of an `AutoNumber` field.

Good primary keys:

- Uniquely identify each record.
- Cannot be null.
- Must exist when the record is created.
- Must remain stable — you should never change a primary key value once it's established.
- Should be simple and contain as few attributes as possible.

In addition to uniquely identifying rows in a table, primary keys provide other benefits:

- A primary key is always an index.
- An index maintains a presorted order of one or more fields that greatly speeds up queries, searches, and sort requests.
- When you add new records to your table, Access checks for duplicate data and doesn't allow any duplicates for the primary key field.
- By default, Access displays a table's data in the order of its primary key.

By designating a field such as `CustomerID` as the primary key, data is displayed in a meaningful order. In our example, because the `CustomerID` field is an `AutoNumber`, its value is assigned automatically by Access in the order that a record is put into the system.

Although all the tables in the CollectibleMiniCars application use `AutoNumber` fields as their primary keys, you should be aware of the reasons why `AutoNumber` fields make such excellent primary keys.

The ideal primary key, then, is a single field that is immutable and guaranteed to be unique within the table. For these reasons, the CollectibleMiniCars database uses the `AutoNumber` field exclusively as the primary key for all tables.

Creating the Primary Key

The primary key can be created in any of three ways. With a table open in Design view:

- Select the field to be used as the primary key and click the Primary Key button (the key icon) in the Tools group in the ribbon's Design tab.

- Right-click on the field to display the shortcut menu and select Primary Key.
- Save the table without creating a primary key, and allow Access to create an `AutoNumber` field automatically.

After you designate the primary key, a key icon appears in the gray selector area to the left of the field's name to indicate that the primary key has been created.

Creating Composite Primary Keys

You can designate a combination of fields to be used as a table's primary key. Such keys are often referred to as *composite primary keys*. As indicated in Figure 34-17, select the fields that you want to include in the composite primary key, then click on the key icon in the Tools Ribbon tab. It helps, of course, if the fields lie right next to each other in the table's design.

FIGURE 34-17

Creating a composite primary key.

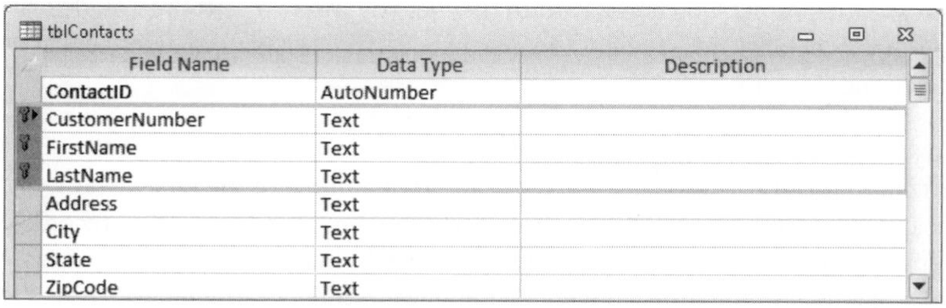

	Field Name	Data Type	Description	
	ContactID	AutoNumber		
	CustomerNumber	Text		
	FirstName	Text		
	LastName	Text		
	Address	Text		
	City	Text		
	State	Text		
	ZipCode	Text		

tblContacts

Composite primary keys are primarily used when the developer strongly feels that a primary key should be composed of data that occurs naturally in the database. There was a time when all developers were taught that every table should have a *natural primary key* (data that occurs naturally in the table).

The reason that composite primary keys are seldom used these days is because developers have come to realize that data is highly unpredictable. Even if your users promise that a combination of certain fields will never be duplicated in the table, things have a way of turning out differently than planned. Using a *surrogate primary key* (a *surrogate primary key* is a key field that does not naturally occur in the table's data, such as a Social Security Number or Employee ID), such as an `AutoNumber`, separates the table's design from the table's data. The problem with natural primary keys is that, eventually, given a large enough data set, the values of fields chosen as the table's primary key are likely to be duplicated.

Furthermore, when using composite keys, maintaining relationships between tables becomes more complicated because the fields comprising the primary key must be duplicated in all the tables containing related data. Using composite keys simply adds to the complexity of the database without adding stability, integrity, or other desirable features.

Indexing Access Tables

Data is rarely, if ever, entered into tables in a meaningful order. Usually, records are added to tables in random order (with the exception of time-ordered data). For example, a busy order-entry system will gather information on many different customer orders in a single day. Most often, this data will be used to report orders for a single customer for billing purposes or for extracting order quantities for inventory management. The records in the Orders table, however, are in chronological order, which is not necessarily helpful when preparing reports detailing customer orders. In that case, you'd rather have data entered in customer ID order.

To further illustrate this concept, consider the Rolodex card file that many people use to store names, addresses, and phone numbers. Assume for a moment that the cards in the file were fixed in place. You could add new cards, but only to the end of the card file. This limitation would mean that "Jones" might follow "Smith," which would, in turn, be followed by "Baker." In other words, there is no particular order to the data stored in this file.

An unsorted Rolodex like this would be very difficult to use. You'd have to search each and every card looking for a particular person, a painful and time-consuming process. Of course, this is not how you use address card files. When you add a card to the file, you insert it into the Rolodex at the location where it *logically* belongs. Most often, this means inserting the card in alphabetical order, by last name, into the Rolodex.

Records are added to Access tables as described in the fixed card file example earlier. New records are always added to the end of the table, rather than in the middle of the table, where they may logically belong. However, in an order-entry system, you'd probably want new records inserted next to other records on the same customer. Unfortunately, this isn't how Access tables work. The *natural order* of a table is the order in which records were added to the table. This order is sometimes referred to as *entry order* or *physical order* to emphasize that the records in the table appear in the order in which they were added to the table.

Using tables in natural order is not necessarily a bad thing. Natural order makes perfect sense if the data is rarely searched or if the table is very small. Also, there are situations in which the data being added to the table is highly ordered to start with. If the table is used to gather sequential data (like readings from an electric meter) and the data will be used in the same sequential order, there is no need to impose an index on the data.

But for situations in which natural order does not suffice, Microsoft Access provides *indexing* to help you find and sort records faster. You specify a *logical* order for the records in a table by creating an *index* on that table. Access uses the index to maintain one or more internal sort orders for the data in the table. For example, you may choose to index the LastName field that will frequently be included in queries and sorting routines.

Microsoft Access uses indexes in a table as you use an index in a book: To find data, Access looks up the data's location in the index. Most often, your tables will include one or more *simple indexes*. A *simple index* is one that involves a single field in the table. Simple indexes may arrange the table's records in ascending or descending order. Simple indexes are created by setting the field's `Indexed` property to one of the following values:

- `Yes (Duplicates OK)`
- `Yes (No Duplicates)`

By default, Access fields are not indexed, but it's hard to imagine a table that doesn't require some kind of index. The next section discusses why indexing is important to use in Access tables.

The Importance of Indexes

Microsoft's data indicates that more than half of all tables in Access databases contain *no* indexes. This number doesn't include the tables that are improperly indexed — it includes only those tables that have no indexes at all. It appears that a lot of people don't appreciate the importance of indexing the tables in an Access database.

Because an index means that Access maintains an internal sort order on the data contained in the indexed field, you can see why performance is enhanced by an index. You should index virtually every field that is frequently involved in queries or is frequently sorted on forms or reports.

Without an index, Access must search each and every record in the database looking for matches. This process is called a *table scan* and is analogous to searching through each and every card in a Rolodex file to find all the people who work for a certain company. Until you reach the end of the deck, you can't be sure you've found every relevant card in the file.

As mentioned earlier in this chapter, a table's primary key field is always indexed. This is because the primary key is used to locate records in the table. Indexing the primary key makes it much easier for Access to find the required tables in either the current table or a foreign table related to the current table. Without an index, Access has to search all records in the related table to make sure it has located all the related records.

Tip

The performance losses due to un-indexed tables can have a devastating effect on the overall performance of an Access application. Anytime you hear a complaint about the performance of an application, consider indexing as a possible solution. ■

Multiple-Field Indexes

Multiple-field indexes (also called *composite indexes*) are easy to create. In Design view, click on the Indexes toolbar button or select the Indexes command on the View menu. The Indexes dialog box (shown in Figure 34-18) appears, allowing you to specify the fields to include in the index.

Enter a name for the index (`CityState` in Figure 34-18) and tab to the `Field Name` column. Use the drop-down list to select the fields to include in the index. In this example, `City` and `State` are combined as a single index. Any row appearing immediately below this row that does not contain an index name is part of the composite index. Access considers both these fields when creating the sort order on this table, speeding queries and sorting operations that include both the City and State fields.

FIGURE 34-18

Multiple-field (composite) indexes can enhance performance.

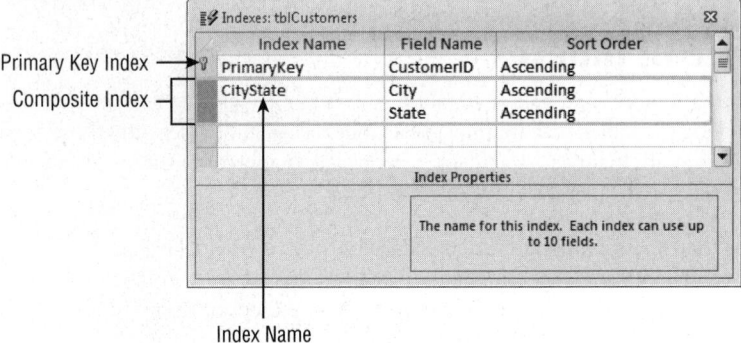

Index Name

As many as 10 fields can be included in a composite index. As long as the composite index is not used as the table's primary key, any of the fields in the composite index can be empty.

Figure 34-19 shows how to set the properties of an index. The cursor is placed in the row in the Indexes dialog box containing the name of the index. Notice the three properties appearing below the index information in the top half of the Indexes dialog box.

FIGURE 34-19

It's easy to set the properties of an index.

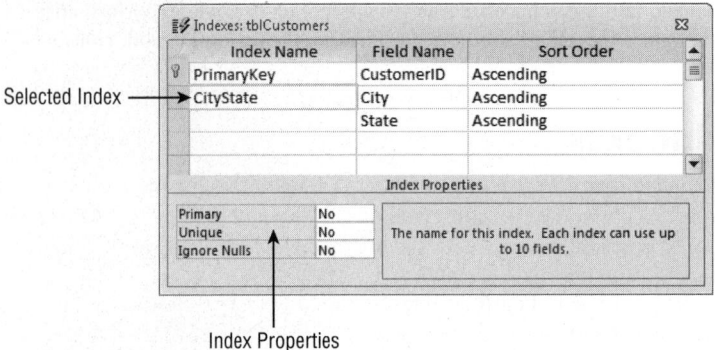

Index Properties

The index properties are quite easy to understand (these properties apply to single-field and composite indexes equally):

- **Primary.** When set to `Yes`, Access uses this index as the table's primary key. More than one field can be designated as the primary key, but keep the rules governing primary keys in mind, particularly those requiring each primary key value to be unique and that no field in a composite primary key can be empty. The default for the `Primary` property is `No`.

- **Unique.** When set to `Yes`, the index must be unique within a table. A Social Security Number field is a good candidate for a unique index because the application's business rules may require one and only one instance of a Social Security Number in the table. In contrast, a last name field should not be uniquely indexed, because many last names, like *Smith* and *Jones*, are very common, and having a unique index on the last name field will only cause problems.

    When applied to composite keys, the *combination* of field values must be unique — each field within the composite key can duplicate fields found within the table.

- **Ignore Nulls.** If a record's `Index` field contains a `Null` value (which happens in a composite index only if all fields in the composite index are `Null`), the record's index won't contribute anything to the overall indexing. In other words, unless a record's index contains some kind of value, Access doesn't know where to insert the record in the table's internal index sort lists. Therefore, you might want to instruct Access to ignore a record if the index value is `Null`. By default, the `Ignore Nulls` property is set to `No`, which means that Access inserts records with a `Null` index value into the indexing scheme along with any other records containing `Null` index values.

You should test the impact of the index properties on your Access tables and use the properties that best suit the data handled by your databases.

A field can be both the primary key for a table and part of a composite index. You should index your tables as necessary to yield the highest possible performance without worrying about over-indexing or violating some arcane indexing rules. For example, in a database such as CollectibleMiniCars, the invoice number in `tblSales` is frequently used in forms and reports, and should be indexed. In addition, there are many situations in which the invoice number is used in combination with other fields, such as the sales date or salesperson ID. You should consider adding composite indexes combining the invoice number with sales date, and salesperson ID, to the Sales table.

When to Index Tables

Depending on the number of records in a table, the extra overhead of maintaining an index may not justify creating an index beyond the table's primary key. Although data retrieval is somewhat faster than it is without an index, Access must update index information whenever you enter or change records in the table. In contrast, changes to un-indexed fields do not require extra file activity. You can retrieve data from un-indexed fields as easily (although not as *quickly*) as from indexed fields.

Generally speaking, it's best to add secondary indexes when tables are quite large, and when indexing fields other than the primary key speeds up searches. Even with large tables, however, indexing can slow performance if the records in tables will be changed often or new records will be added frequently. Each time a record is changed or added, Access must update all the indexes in the table.

Given all the advantages of indexes, why not index everything in the table? What are the drawbacks of indexing too many fields? Is it possible to over-index tables?

First, indexes increase the size of the Access database somewhat. Unnecessarily indexing a table that doesn't really require an index eats up a bit of disk space for each record in the table. More important, indexes extract a performance hit for each index on the table every time a record is added to the table. Because Access automatically updates indexes each time a record is added (or removed), the internal indexing must be adjusted for each new record. If you have 10 indexes on a table, Access makes 10 adjustments to the indexes each time a new record is added or an existing record is deleted, causing a noticeable delay on large tables (particularly on slow computers).

Sometimes changes to the data in records cause adjustments to the indexing scheme. This is true if the change causes the record to change its position in sorting or querying activities. Therefore, if you're working with large, constantly changing data sets that are rarely searched, you may choose *not* to index the fields in the table, or to minimally index by indexing only those few fields that are likely to be searched.

As you begin working with Access tables, you'll probably start with the simplest one-field indexes and migrate to more complex ones as your familiarity with the process grows. Do keep in mind, however, the trade-offs between greater search efficiency and the overhead incurred by maintaining a large number of indexes on your tables.

It's also important to keep in mind that indexing does not modify the physical arrangement of records in the table. The natural order of the records (the order in which the records were added to the table) is maintained after the index is established.

Note

A compact-and-repair cycle on an Access database forces Access to rebuild the indexes in all the tables and physically rearranges tables in primary key order in the `.accdb` file. The maintenance operations ensure that your Access databases operate at maximum efficiency. ■

Printing a Table Design

You can print a table design by clicking the Database Documenter button in the Analyze group on the Ribbon's Database Tools tab. The Analyze group contains several tools that make it easy to document your database objects. When you click the Database Documenter button, Access shows you the Documenter dialog box, which lets you select objects to print. In Figure 34-20, tblCustomers is selected in the Documenter's Tables tab.

FIGURE 34-20

The Documenter dialog box.

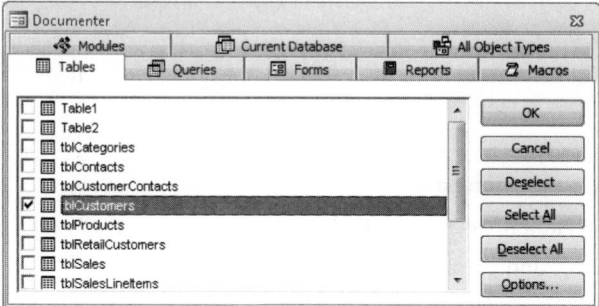

You can also set various options for printing. When you click the Options button, the Print Table Definition dialog box appears, enabling you to select which information from the table design to print. You can print the various field names, all their properties, the indexes, and even network permissions.

After you select which data you want to view, Access generates a report. You can view the report in a Print Preview window or send it to a printer. You may want to save the report within the database as part of the application's documentation.

Tip
The Database Documenter creates a table of all the objects and object properties you specify. You can use this utility to document such database objects as forms, queries, reports, macros, and modules. ■

Saving the Completed Table

You can save the completed table design by choosing File ➪ Save or by clicking the Save button in the Quick Access Toolbar (QAT) in the upper-left corner of the Access environment. If you're saving the table for the first time, Access asks for its name. Table names can be up to 64 characters long and follow standard Access object-naming conventions — they may include letters and numbers, cannot begin with a number, and can't include punctuation. You can also save the table when you close it.

If you've saved this table before and you want to save it with a different name, choose File ➪ Save Object As, and enter a different table name. This action creates a new table design and leaves the original table with its original name untouched. If you want to delete the old table, select it in the Navigation pane and press the Delete key.

Manipulating Tables

As you add many tables to your database, you may want to use them in other databases or make copies of them as backups. In many cases, you may want to copy only the table's design and not include all the data in the table. You can perform many table operations in the Navigation pane, including renaming, deleting, and copying tables. You perform these tasks by direct manipulation or by using menu items.

Renaming Tables

Rename a table by following these steps:

1. Select the table name in the Navigation pane.
2. Click once on the table name, and press F2.
3. Type the new name of the table and press Enter.

You can also rename the table by right-clicking on its name in the Navigation pane and selecting Rename from the shortcut menu. After you change the table name, it appears in the Tables list, which re-sorts the tables in alphabetical order.

Caution
If you rename a table, you must change the table name in any objects in which it was previously referenced, including queries, forms, and reports. ■

Deleting Tables

Delete a table by selecting the table in the Navigation pane and pressing the Delete key. Another method is to right-click on the table and select Delete from the shortcut menu. Like most delete operations, you have to confirm the delete by clicking Yes in a confirmation box.

Copying Tables in a Database

The copy and paste options in the Clipboard group on the Home tab allow you to copy any table in the database. When you paste the table back into the database, the Paste Table As dialog box appears, asking you to choose from three options:

- **Structure Only.** Clicking the Structure Only button creates a new table, an empty table with the same design as the copied table. This option is typically used to create a temporary table or an archive table to which you can copy old records.
- **Structure and Data.** When you click Structure and Data, a complete copy of the table design and all its data is created.
- **Append Data to Existing Table.** Clicking the Append Data to Existing Table button adds the data of the selected table to the bottom of another table. This option is useful for combining tables, such as when you want to add data from a monthly transaction table to a yearly history table.

Follow these steps to copy a table:

1. **Right-click on the table name in the Navigation pane and choose Copy from the shortcut menu, or click the Copy button in the Clipboard group on the Home tab.**

2. **Choose Paste from the shortcut menu, or click the Paste button in the Clipboard group on the Home tab.**

3. **Enter the name of the new table.**

   When you're appending data to an existing table (see the next step), you must type the name of an existing table.

4. **Choose one of the Paste options — Structure Only, Structure and Data, or Append Data to Existing Table — from the Paste Table As dialog box.**

5. **Click OK to complete the operation.**

Figure 34-21 shows the Paste Table As dialog box where you make these decisions.

FIGURE 34-21

Pasting a table opens the Paste Table As dialog box.

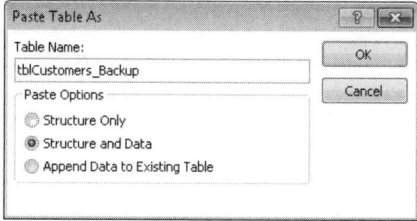

Copying a Table to Another Database

Just as you can copy a table within a database, you can copy a table to another database. There are many reasons why you may want to do this. Maybe you share a common table among multiple systems, or you may need to create a backup copy of your important tables within the system.

When you copy tables to another database, the relationships between tables are not copied. Access copies only the table design and the data to the other database. The method for copying a table to another database is essentially the same as for copying a table within a database:

1. **Right-click on the table name in the Navigation pane and choose Copy from the shortcut menu, or click the Copy button in the Clipboard group on the Home tab.**

2. **Open the other Access database and choose Edit Paste from the shortcut menu, or click the Copy button in the Clipboard group on the Home tab.**

3. Provide the name of the new table, and choose one of the Paste options (Structure Only, Structure and Data, or Append Data to Existing Table).

4. Click OK to complete the operation.

Adding Records to a Database Table

Adding records to a table is as simple as double-clicking on the table in the Navigation pane to open the table in Datasheet view. Once the table is opened, enter values for each field, pressing Tab to move between fields. Figure 34-22 shows adding records in Datasheet mode to the table.

FIGURE 34-22

Using Datasheet view to add records to a table.

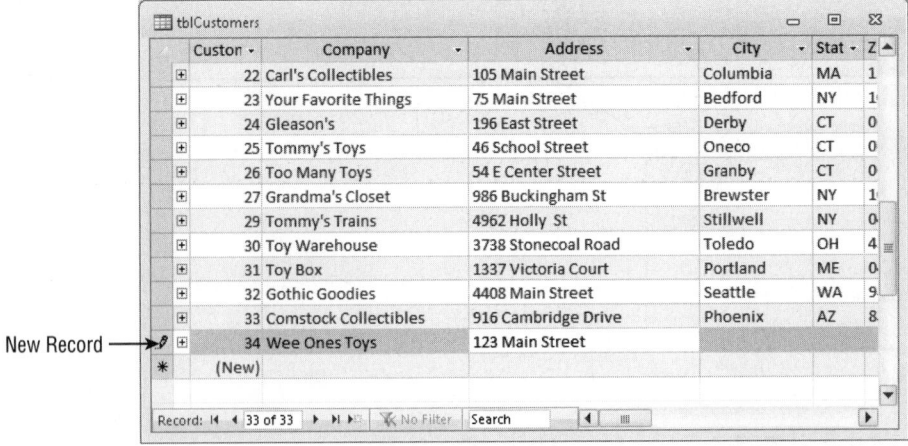

You can enter information into all fields except `CustomerID`. `AutoNumber` fields automatically provide a number for you.

Although you can add records directly into the table through the Datasheet view, it isn't the most efficient way. Adding records using forms is better because code behind a form can dynamically provide default values (perhaps based on data already added to the form) and communicate with the user during the data-entry process.

Opening a Datasheet

Follow these steps to open a datasheet from the Database window:

1. Click Tables in the Navigation pane.

2. Double-click on the table name you want to open (in this example, `tblProducts`).

An alternative method for opening the datasheet is to right-click on the table and select Open in the shortcut menu.

Caution

If you're in any of the design windows, click on the Datasheet View command in the Ribbon's View group to view your data in a datasheet. ■

Moving within a Datasheet

You easily move within the Datasheet window using the mouse to indicate where you want to change or add to your data — just click on a field within a record. In addition, the Ribbons, scroll bars, and Navigation buttons make it easy to move among fields and records. Think of a datasheet as a spreadsheet without the row numbers and column letters. Instead, columns have field names, and rows are unique records that have identifiable values in each cell.

Table 34-4 lists the navigational keys you use for moving within a datasheet.

TABLE 34-4

Navigating in a Datasheet

Navigational Direction	Keystrokes
Next field	Tab
Previous field	Shift+Tab
First field of current record	Home
Last field of current record	End
Next record	Down-arrow ($\downarrow$)
Previous record	Up-arrow ($\uparrow$)
First field of first record	Ctrl+Home
Last field of last record	Ctrl+End
Scroll up one page	PageUp
Scroll down one page	PageDown

Using the Navigation Buttons

The *Navigation buttons* (shown in Figure 34-23) are the six controls located at the bottom of the Datasheet window, which you click to move between records. The two leftmost controls move you to the first record or the previous record in the datasheet. The three rightmost controls position you on the next record, last record, or new record in the datasheet. If you know the record number (the row number of a specific record), you can click the record-number box, enter a record number, and press Enter.

FIGURE 34-23

The Navigation buttons of a datasheet.

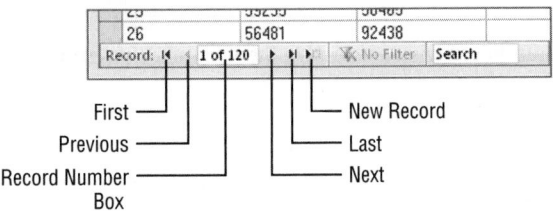

Note

If you enter a record number greater than the number of records in the table, an error message appears stating that you can't go to the specified record. ∎

Entering New Data

All the records in your table are visible when you first open it in Datasheet view. If you just created your table, the new datasheet doesn't contain any data. Figure 34-24 shows an empty datasheet and the Table Tools Fields tab. When the datasheet is empty, the first row contains an asterisk (*) in the record selector — indicating it's a new record.

FIGURE 34-24

An empty datasheet. Notice that the first record is blank and has an asterisk in the record selector.

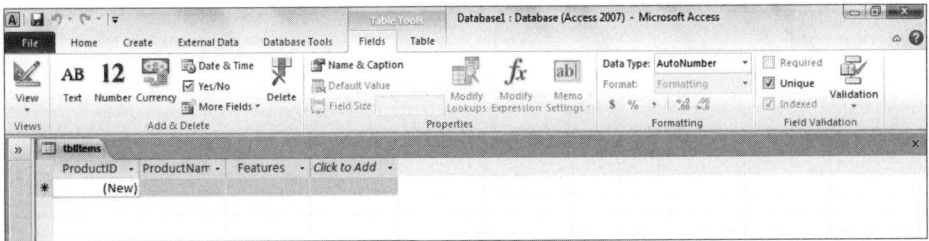

The Table Tools Fields tab includes virtually all the tools needed to build a complete table. You can specify the data type, default formatting, indexing, field and table validation, and other table construction tasks from the controls in the Table Tools Fields tab.

The new row appears at the bottom of the datasheet when the datasheet already contains records. Click the New Record command in the Ribbon's Record group, or click the New Record button in the group of navigation buttons at the bottom of the datasheet to move the insertion point to the new row — or simply click on the last row, which contains the asterisk. The asterisk turns into a pencil when you begin entering data, indicating that the record is being edited. A new row — containing an asterisk — appears below the one you're entering data into. The new-record pointer always appears in the last row of the datasheet. Figure 34-25 shows adding a new record to tblProducts.

FIGURE 34-25

Entering a new record into the Datasheet view of tblProducts.

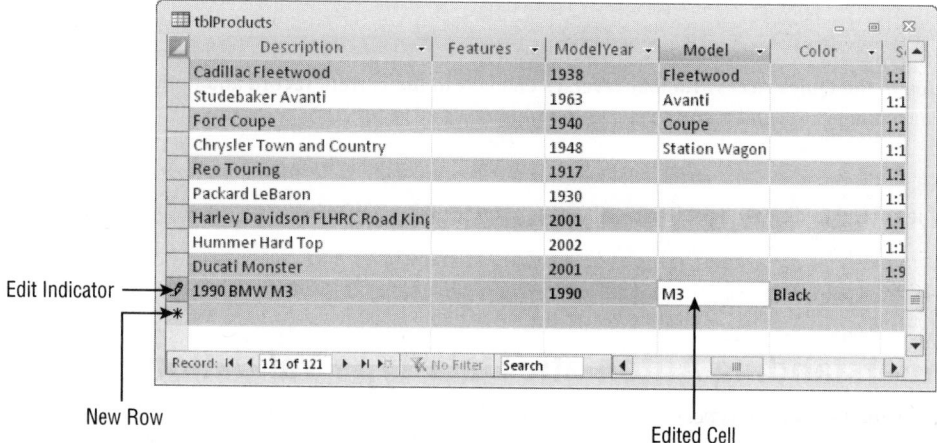

To add a new record to the open Datasheet view of tblProducts, follow these steps:

1. **Click the New Record button.**
2. **Type in values for all fields of the table, moving between fields by pressing the Enter key or the Tab key.**

When adding or editing records, you might see three different record pointers:

- **Record Being Edited.** A pencil icon
- **Record Is Locked (multiuser systems).** A padlock icon
- **New Record.** A pencil icon

Caution

If the record contains an AutoNumber **field, Access shows the name** (*New*) **in the field. You can't enter a value in this type of field; instead, simply press the Tab or Enter key to skip this field. Access automatically puts the number in when you begin entering data.** ∎

Saving the Record

Moving to a different record saves the record you're editing. Tabbing through all the fields, clicking on the Navigation buttons, clicking Save in the Ribbon's Record group, and closing the table all write the edited record to the database. You'll know the record is saved when the pencil disappears from the record selector.

To save a record, you must enter valid values into each field. The fields are validated for data type, uniqueness (if indexed for unique values), and any validation rules that you've entered into the `Validation Rule` property. If your table has a primary key that's not an `AutoNumber` field, you'll have to make sure you enter a unique value in the primary key field to avoid an error message. One way to avoid this error message while entering data is to use an `AutoNumber` field as the table's primary key.

Tip

The Undo button in the Quick Access Toolbar reverses changes to the current record and to the last saved record. After you change a second record, you can't undo the saved record. ■

Tip

You can save the record to disk without leaving the record by pressing Shift+Enter. ■

Now you know how to enter, edit, and save data in a new or existing record. In the next section, you learn how Access validates your data as you make entries into the fields.

Understanding Automatic Data-Type Validation

Access validates certain types of data automatically. Therefore, you don't have to enter any data-validation rules for these data types when you specify table properties. The data types that Access automatically validates include the following:

- Number/Currency
- Date/Time
- Yes/No

Access validates the data type when you move off the field. When you enter a letter into a `Number` or `Currency` field, you don't initially see a warning not to enter these characters. However, when you tab out or click on a different field, you get a warning like the one shown in Figure 34-26. This particular warning lets you choose to enter a new value or change the column's data type to `Text`. You'll see this message if you enter other inappropriate characters (symbols, letters, etc.), enter more than one decimal point, or enter a number too large for the specified numeric data type.

Access validates `Date/Time` fields for valid date or time values. You'll see a warning similar to the one shown in Figure 34-26 if you try to enter a date such as **14/45/05**, a time such as **37:39:12**, or an invalid character in a `Date/Time` field.

`Yes/No` fields require that you enter one of these defined values:

- Yes. **Yes, True, –1,** or a number other than 0 (which displays as –1)
- No. **No, False, Off,** or 0

Of course, you can define your own acceptable values in the `Format` property for the field, but generally these values are the only acceptable ones. If you enter an invalid value, the warning appears with the message to indicate an inappropriate value.

Tip

Display a check box in `Yes/No` fields to prevent users from entering invalid data. ■

FIGURE 34-26

The warning Access displays when you enter data that doesn't match the field's data type. Access gives you a few choices to correct the problem.

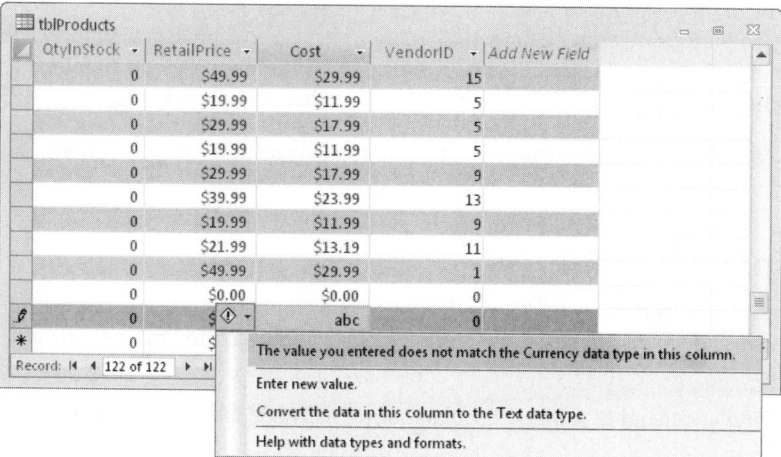

Navigating Records in a Datasheet

Wanting to make changes to records after you've entered them is not unusual. You might want to change records for several reasons:

- You receive new information that changes existing values.

- You discover errors in existing values.

- You need to add new records.

When you decide to edit data in a table, the first step is to open the table — if it isn't already open. From the list of tables in the Navigation pane, double-click on `tblProducts` to open it in Datasheet view. If you're already in Design view for this table, click the "Datasheet View" button to switch views.

When you open a datasheet in Access that has related tables, a column with a plus sign (+) is added to indicate the related records, or subdatasheets. Click on a row's plus sign to open the subdatasheet for the row.

Moving between Records

You can move to any record by scrolling through the records and positioning your cursor on the desired record. With a large table, scrolling through all the records might take a while, so you'll want to use other methods to get to specific records quickly.

Use the vertical scroll bar to move between records. The scroll-bar arrows move one record at a time. To move through many records at a time, drag the scroll box or click the areas between the scroll thumb and the scroll-bar arrows.

Tip

Watch the scroll tips when you use scroll bars to move to another area of the datasheet. Access does not update the record-number box until you click a field. ■

Use the five Navigation buttons (refer to Figure 34-23) to move between records. You simply click these buttons to move to the desired record. If you know the record number (the row number of a specific record), click the record-number box, enter a record number, and press Enter.

Also use the Go To command in the Home tab's Find group to navigate to the First, Previous, Next, Last, and New records.

Finding a Specific Value

Although you can move to a specific record (if you know the record number) or to a specific field in the current record, usually you'll want to find a certain value in a record. You can use one of these methods for locating a value in a field:

- Select the Find command (a pair of binoculars) from the Home tab's Find group.
- Press Ctrl+F.
- Use the Search box at the bottom of the Datasheet window.

The first two methods display the Find and Replace dialog box. To limit the search to a specific field, place your cursor in the field you want to search before you open the dialog box. Change the Look In combo box to the table name to search the entire table for the value.

Tip

If you highlight the entire record by clicking the record selector (the small gray box next to the record), Access automatically searches through all fields. ■

The Find and Replace dialog box lets you control many aspects of the search. Enter the value you want to search for in the Find What combo box — which contains a list of recently used searches. You can enter a specific value or choose to use three types of wildcards:

- * (any number of characters)
- ? (any one character)
- # (any one number)

To look at how these wildcards work, suppose that you want to find all the rows with *Ford* at the beginning of the Description field in tblProducts. Using **Ford*** in the Find What box will find rows beginning with *Ford*. Then, suppose that you want to search for values ending with *Mustang*; you'd use ***Mustang**. If you want to search for any value that begins with *Ford*, ends with *Mustang*, and contains any number of characters in between, use **Ford*Mustang**.

The Match drop-down list contains three choices that eliminate the need for wildcards:

- **Any Part of Field.** If you select Any Part of Field, Access searches to see whether the value is contained anywhere in the field. This search finds *Ford* anywhere in the field, including values like Ford Mustang, 2008 Ford F-150, and Ford Galaxy 500.

- **Whole Field.** The default is Whole Field, which finds fields containing exactly what you've entered. For example, the Whole Field option finds *Ford* only if the value in the field being searched is exactly Ford, and nothing else.

- **Start of Field.** A search for *Ford* using the Start of Field option searches from the beginning of the field and returns all the rows containing Ford as the first four characters of the description.

In addition to these combo boxes, you can use two check boxes at the bottom of the Find and Replace dialog box:

- **Match Case.** Match Case determines whether the search is case-sensitive. The default is not case-sensitive (not checked). A search for *SMITH* finds smith, SMITH, or Smith. If you check the Match Case check box, you must then enter the search string in the exact case of the field value. (The data types Number, Currency, and Date/Time don't have any case attributes.)

  If you've checked Match Case, Access doesn't use the value Search Fields As Formatted (the second check box), which limits the search to the actual values displayed in the table. (If you format a field for display in the datasheet, you should check the box.)

- **Search Fields As Formatted.** The Search Fields As Formatted check box, the selected default, finds only text that has the same pattern of characters as the text specified in the Find What box. Clear this box to find text regardless of the formatting. For example, if you're searching the Cost field for a value of $16,500, you must enter the comma if Search Fields As Formatted is checked. Uncheck this box to search for an unformatted value (*16500*).

Caution

Checking Search Fields As Formatted may slow the search process. ∎

The search begins when you click the Find Next button. If Access finds the value, the cursor highlights it in the datasheet. To find the next occurrence of the value, click the Find Next button again. The dialog box remains open so that you can find multiple occurrences. Choose one of three search direction choices (Up, Down, or All) in the Search drop-down list to change the search direction. When you find the value that you want, click Close to close the dialog box.

Use the Search box at the bottom of the Datasheet window to quickly search for the first instance of a value. When using the Search box, Access searches the entire datasheet for the value in any part of the field. If you enter **FORD** in the Search box, the datasheet moves to the closest match as you type each letter. First, it finds a field with *F* as the first character, then it finds *FO*, and so on. Once it finds the complete value, it stops searching. To find more than one instance, use the Find Next button in the upper-left corner of the Find and Replace dialog box.

Changing Values in a Datasheet

If the field that you're in has no value, you can type a new value into the field. When you enter new values into a field, follow the same rules as for a new-record entry.

Manually Replacing an Existing Value

Generally, you enter a field with either no characters selected or the entire value selected. If you use the keyboard (Tab or arrow keys) to enter a field, you select the entire value. (You know that the entire value is selected when it's displayed in reverse video.) When you begin to type, the new content replaces the selected value automatically.

When you click in a field, the value is not selected. To select the entire value with the mouse, use any of these methods:

- Click just to the left of the value when the cursor is shown as a large plus sign.
- Click to the left of the value, hold down the left mouse button, and drag the mouse to select the whole value.
- Click in the field and press F2.

Tip

You may want to replace an existing value with the value from the field's `Default Value` **property. To do so, select the value and press Ctrl+Alt+spacebar. To replace an existing value with that of the same field from the preceding record, press Ctrl+' (single quote mark). Press Ctrl+; (semicolon) to place the current date in a field.** ∎

Caution

Pressing Ctrl+– (minus sign) deletes the current record. ∎

If you want to change an existing value instead of replacing the entire value, use the mouse and click in front of any character in the field to activate Insert mode; the existing value moves to the right as you type the new value. If you press the Insert key, your entry changes to Overstrike mode; you replace one character at a time as you type. Use the arrow keys to move between characters without disturbing them. Erase characters to the left by pressing Backspace, or to the right of the cursor by pressing Delete.

Table 34-5 lists editing techniques.

TABLE 34-5

Editing Techniques

Editing Operation	Keystrokes
Move the insertion point within a field	Right-arrow (→) and left-arrow (←) keys
Insert a value within a field	Select the insertion point and type new data

Editing Operation	Keystrokes
Select the entire field	F2
Replace an existing value with a new value	Select the entire field and type a new value
Replace a value with the value of the previous field	Ctrl+' (single quote mark)
Replace the current value with the default value	Ctrl+Alt+Spacebar
Insert a line break in a Text or Memo field	Ctrl+Enter
Save the current record	Press Shift+Enter or move to another record
Insert the current date	Ctrl+; (semicolon)
Insert the current time	Ctrl+: (colon)
Add a new record	Ctrl++ (plus sign)
Delete the current record	Ctrl+– (minus sign)
Toggle values in a check box or option button	Spacebar
Undo a change to the current field	Press Esc or click the Undo button
Undo a change to the current record	Press Esc or click the Undo button a second time after you undo the current field

Fields That You Can't Edit

Some fields can't be edited, such as:

- **AutoNumber Fields.** Access maintains AutoNumber fields automatically, calculating the values as you create each new record. AutoNumber fields can be used as the primary key.

- **Calculated Fields.** Forms or queries may contain fields that are the result of expressions. These values are not actually stored in your table and are not editable.

- **Locked or Disabled Fields.** You can set certain properties in a form to prevent editing for a specific field.

- **Fields in Multiuser Locked Records.** If another user locks the record, you can't edit any fields in that record.

Summary

This chapter has covered the important topics of creating new Access databases and adding tables to Access databases. Although I've covered these topics from the perspective of creating brand-new databases and tables, the operations you performed in this chapter are identical to the maintenance procedures you perform on existing databases and tables.

The next chapter drills into the very important topics of creating and using forms.

Creating and Entering Data with Basic Access Forms

Forms provide the most flexible way for viewing, adding, editing, and deleting your data. They're also used for switchboards (forms with buttons that provide navigation), for dialog boxes that control the flow of the system, and for messages. Controls are the objects on forms such as labels, text boxes, buttons, and many others. In this chapter, you will learn how to create different types of forms. I also fill you in on the types of controls that are used on a form. This chapter also discusses form and control properties, and how you determine the appearance and behavior of an Access interface through setting or changing property values.

The forms you add to an Access database are a critical aspect of the application you create. In most situations, users should not be permitted direct access to tables or query datasheets. It's far too easy for a user to delete information or incorrectly input data into the table. Forms provide a valuable tool for managing the integrity of a database's data. Because forms can contain VBA code or macros, a form can verify data entry or confirm deletions before they occur. Also, a properly designed form can reduce training requirements by helping the user understand what kind of data is required by displaying a message as the user tabs into a control. Or, a form can provide default values or perform calculations based on data input by the user or retrieved from a database table.

Adding a Form

Use the Forms group on the Create tab of the Ribbon to add forms to your database. The commands in the Forms group — shown in Figure 35-1 — let you create the following different types of forms and ways to work with Access forms:

IN THIS CHAPTER

Creating different types of forms

Understanding controls

Adding controls to a form

Working with the Property Sheet

Viewing and modifying data in Form view

Printing the forms

- **Form.** Creates a new form that lets you enter information for one record at a time. You must have a table, query, form, or report open or selected to use this command. When you click on the Form button with a table or query highlighted in the Navigation pane, Access binds the new form to the data source and opens the form in Layout view.

FIGURE 35-1

Use the Forms group on the Ribbon's Create tab to add new forms to your database.

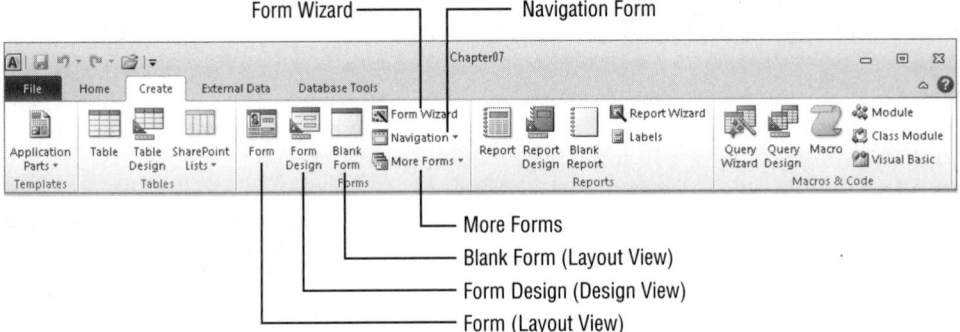

- **Form Design.** Creates a new blank form and displays it in Design view. If a table or query is selected in the Navigation pane when the Form Design button is clicked, the new form is automatically bound to the data source.

- **Blank Form.** Instantly creates a blank form with no controls. The new form is not bound to a data source, and it opens in Layout view. You must specify a data source (table or query) and build the form by adding controls from the data source's Field List.

- **Form Wizard.** Access features a simple wizard to help you get started building forms. The Form Wizard asks for the data source, provides a screen for selecting fields to include on the form, and lets you choose from several very basic layouts for the new form.

- **Navigation Form.** The Access navigation form is a specialized form intended to provide user navigation through an application. Navigation forms are discussed in detail later in this chapter.

Note

The navigation form is new to Access 2010. ∎

- **More Forms.** The More Forms button in the Forms group drops down a gallery containing a number of other form types:

  - **Multiple Items.** This is a simple tabular form that shows multiple records bound to the selected data source.

  - **Datasheet.** Creates a form that is displayed as a datasheet.

- **Split Form.** Creates a split form, which shows a datasheet in the upper, lower, left, or right area of the form; and a traditional form in the opposite section for entering information on the record selected in the datasheet.

- **Modal Dialog.** Provides a template for a modal dialog form. A modal dialog form (often called a *dialog box*) stays on the screen until the user provides information requested by the dialog or is dismissed by the user.

- **PivotChart.** Instantly creates a PivotChart form.

- **PivotTable.** Creates a form consisting of a PivotTable.

If any of the terminology in the preceding bullets is new to you, don't worry — each of these terms is discussed in detail in this chapter. Keep in mind that the Access Ribbon and its contents are very context-dependent, so every item may not be available at the time you access the Create tab.

Creating a New Form

Like many other aspects of Access development, Access provides multiple ways of adding new forms to your application. The easiest is to select a data source, such as a table, and click the Form command in the Create Ribbon tab. Another is to use the Form Wizard and allow the Wizard to guide you through the process of specifying a data source and other details of the new form.

Using the Form Command

Use the Form command in the Ribbon's Form group to automatically create a new form based on a table or query selected in the Navigation pane.

Note

This process was called *AutoForm* in previous versions of Access. ∎

To create a form based on a table, follow these steps:

1. **Select the table in the Navigation pane.**
2. **Select the Create tab on the Ribbon.**
3. **Click on the Form command in the Form group.**

Access creates a new form containing all the fields from the table displayed in Layout view, shown in Figure 35-2. Layout view lets you see the form's data while changing the layout of controls on the form. (The form shown in Figure 35-2 is from the example database shown in Chapter 34.)

The new form is opened in Layout view, which is populated with all the controls in the underlying data source. Layout view gives you a good idea how the controls appear relative to one another, but it can't be used for resizing controls or moving controls about on the form. Right-click on the form's title bar and select Design View to rearrange controls on the form.

FIGURE 35-2

Use the Form command to quickly create a new form with all the fields from a table or query.

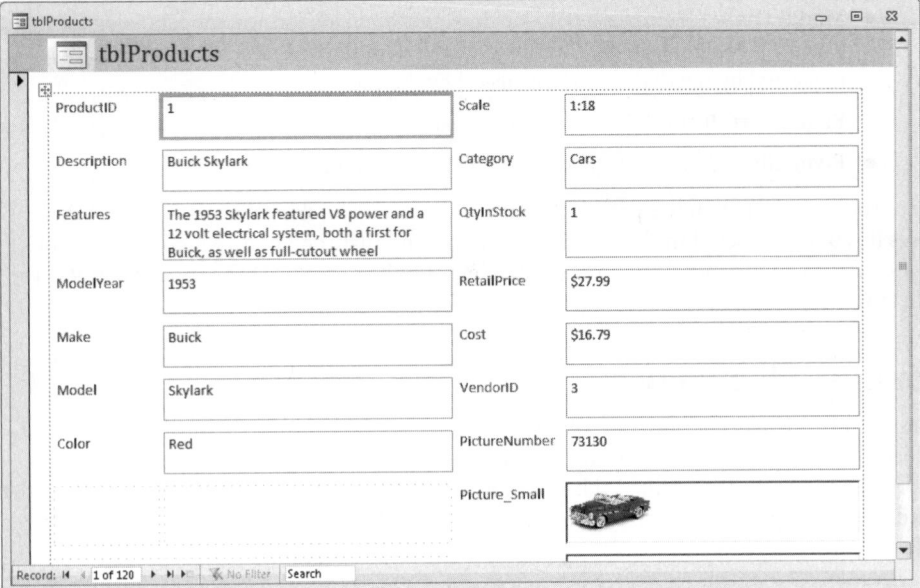

The Form Design button in the Forms group does essentially the same thing as the Form button, except that no controls are added to the form's design surface and the form is opened in Design view. Form Design is most useful when you're creating a new form that might not use all the fields in the underlying data source, and you want more control over control placement from the start.

Similarly, the Blank Form option opens a new empty form, but this time in Layout view. You add controls to the form's surface from the Field List, but you have little control over control placement. The Blank Form option is most useful for quickly building a form with bound controls with little need for precise placement. A new blank form can be produced in less than a minute.

Using the Form Wizard

Use the Form Wizard command in the Forms group to create a form using a wizard. The Form Wizard visually walks you through a series of questions about the form that you want to create and then creates it for you automatically. The Form Wizard lets you select which fields you want on the form, the form layout (Columnar, Tabular, Datasheet, Justified), the form style (Access 2003, Access 2010, Apex, etc.), and the form title.

To start the Form Wizard based on a table, follow these steps:

1. Select the table in the Navigation pane.

2. Select the Create tab on the Ribbon.

3. Click on the Form Wizard button in the Forms group.

Access starts the Form Wizard shown in Figure 35-3.

FIGURE 35-3

Use the Form Wizard to create a form with the fields you choose.

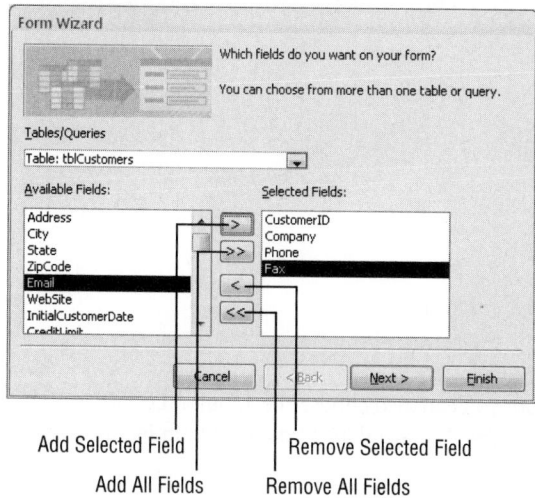

```
Add Selected Field            Remove Selected Field
   Add All Fields           Remove All Fields
```

The Wizard is initially populated with fields from the table you selected in Step 1, but you can choose another table or query with the Tables/Queries drop-down list above the field selection area. Use the buttons in the middle of the form to add and remove fields to the Available Fields and Selected Fields list boxes.

Note

You can also double-click on any field in the Available Fields list box to add it to the Selected Fields list box. ■

The series of buttons at the bottom of the form lets you navigate through the other steps of the Wizard. The types of buttons available here are common to most Wizard dialog boxes:

- **Cancel.** Cancel the Wizard without creating a form.
- **Back.** Return to the preceding step of the Wizard.
- **Next.** Go to the next step of the Wizard.
- **Finish.** End the Wizard using the current selections.

Caution

If you click Next or Finish without selecting any fields, Access tells you that you must select fields for the form before you can continue. ■

Clicking Next opens the second Wizard dialog box (shown in Figure 35-4), where you specify the overall layout and appearance of the new form.

FIGURE 35-4

Select the overall layout for the new form.

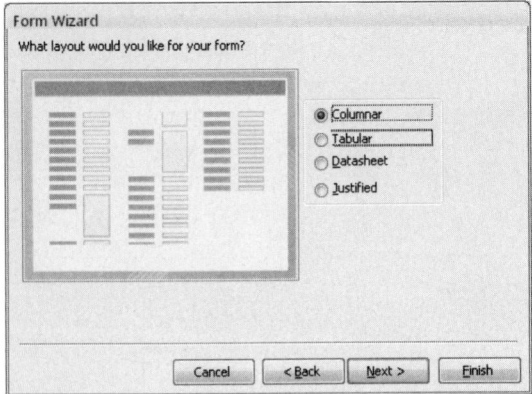

The Columnar layout is the Wizard default, but you can also choose the Tabular, Datasheet, or Justified options. Clicking Next takes you to the last Wizard dialog box (shown in Figure 35-5), where you provide a name for the new form.

FIGURE 35-5

Saving the new form.

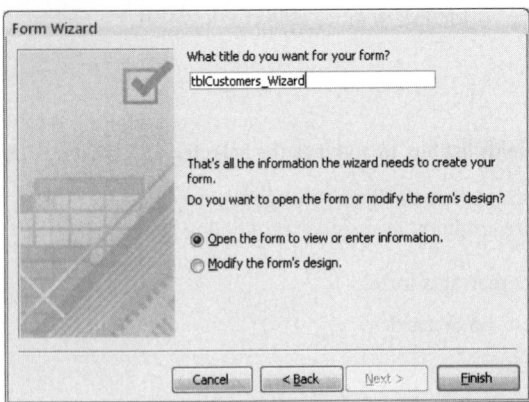

The main advantage of using the Form Wizard is that it binds the new form to a data source and adds controls for the selected fields. In most cases, however, you still have considerable work to do after the Form Wizard has finished.

Looking at Special Types of Forms

When working with Access, the word *form* can mean any of several different things, depending on context. This section discusses several different ways that forms are used in Access and presents an example of each usage.

Navigation Forms

Access 2010 introduces an entirely new form intended specifically as a navigation tool for users. Navigation forms include several tabs that provide instant access to any number of other forms in a form/subform arrangement. The Navigation Ribbon button offers a number of button placement options (shown in Figure 35-6). Horizontal Tabs is the default.

FIGURE 35-6

The Navigation button provides several tab placement options.

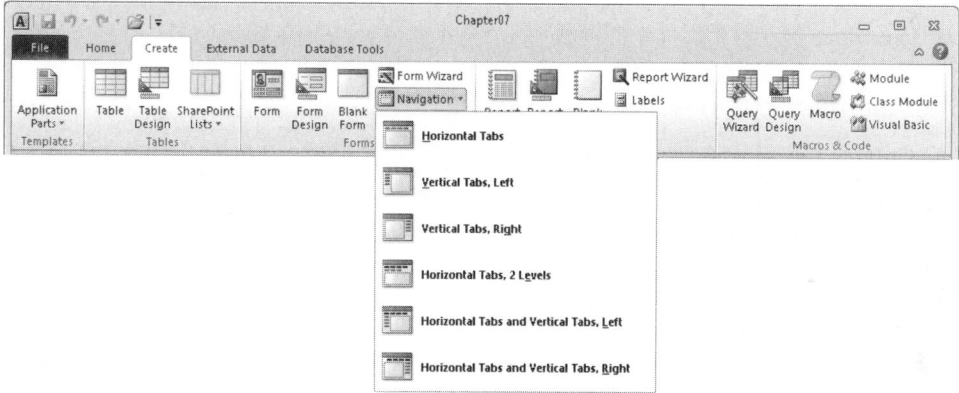

Selecting a tab placement in the Navigation drop-down list opens the new navigation form in Design view (see Figure 35-7). The new form includes a row of tabs along the top and a large area under the tabs for embedding subforms. You type the tab's label (say, *Products*) directly into the tab or add it through the tab's Caption property. As you complete the tab's label, Access adds a new, blank tab to the right of the current tab.

In Figure 35-7, the Horizontal Tabs option was selected when choosing a navigation form template. The alternatives to Horizontal Tabs (Vertical Tabs, Left, Vertical Tabs, Right, and so on) are shown in Figure 35-6.

The tab's Property Sheet (shown in Figure 35-8) includes the Navigation Target Name property for specifying the Access form to use as the tab's subform. Select a form from the drop-down list in the Navigation Target Name property, and Access creates the association to the subform for you.

FIGURE 35-7

The navigation form features a large area for embedding subforms.

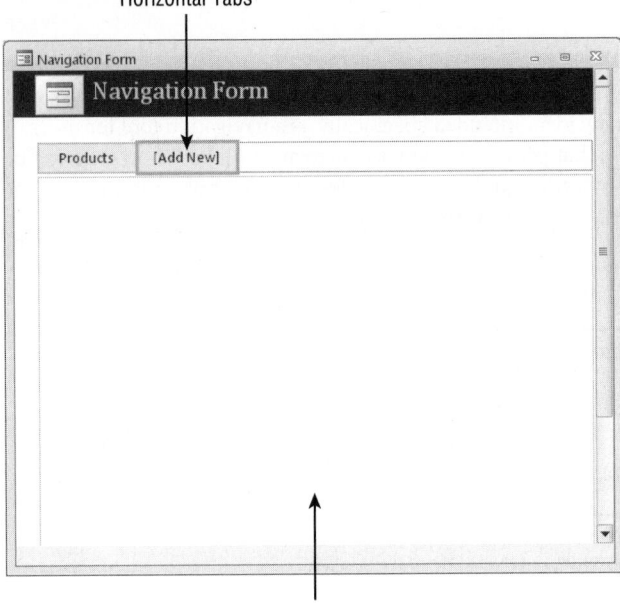

Horizontal Tabs

Subform Area

The completed navigation form is shown in Figure 35-9. The auto-generated navigation form makes extravagant use of screen space. There are several things that could be done to enhance this form, such as removing the navigation form's header section and reducing the empty space surrounding the subform. Example form frmProducts is shown in Figure 35-9.

Multiple Items Forms

Click the More Forms button in the Forms group of the Create tab and then click the Multiple Items button to create a tabular form based on a table or query selected in the Navigation pane. A tabular form is much like a datasheet, but it's much more attractive than a plain datasheet.

Cross-Reference

Chapter 34 discusses datasheets in detail. ■

Because the tabular form is truly an Access form, you can convert the default text box controls on the form to combo boxes, list boxes, and other advanced controls. Because tabular forms display multiple records at one time, they're very useful when you're reviewing or updating multiple records. To create a multiple items form based on a table, follow these steps:

1. Select the table in the Navigation pane.

2. Select the Create tab on the Ribbon.

3. Click the More Forms button in the Forms group and click Multiple Items.

FIGURE 35-8

Use the Navigation Target Name property to specify the tab's subform.

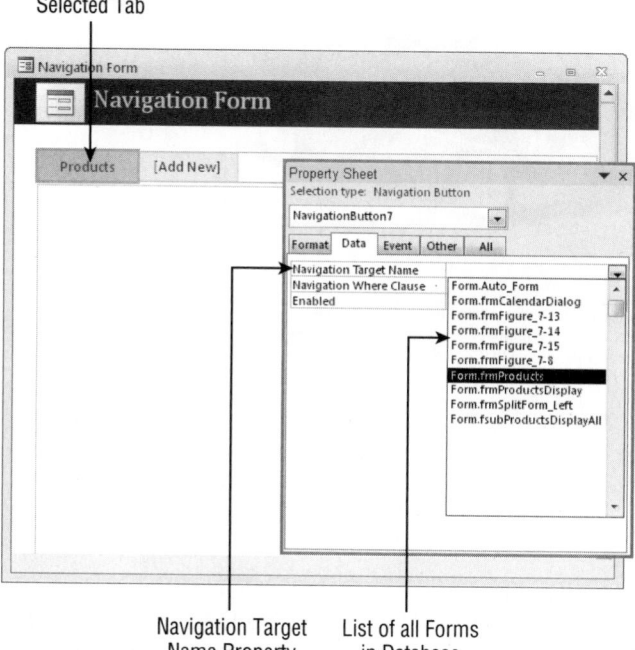

Access creates a new multiple items form based on the table you selected in Step 1 displayed in Layout view (as shown in Figure 35-10). Although the form looks similar to a datasheet, you can only resize the rows and columns in Design view and Layout view.

FIGURE 35-9

A navigation form is a quick and easy way to provide basic navigation features.

Tabs   Navigation Form Header

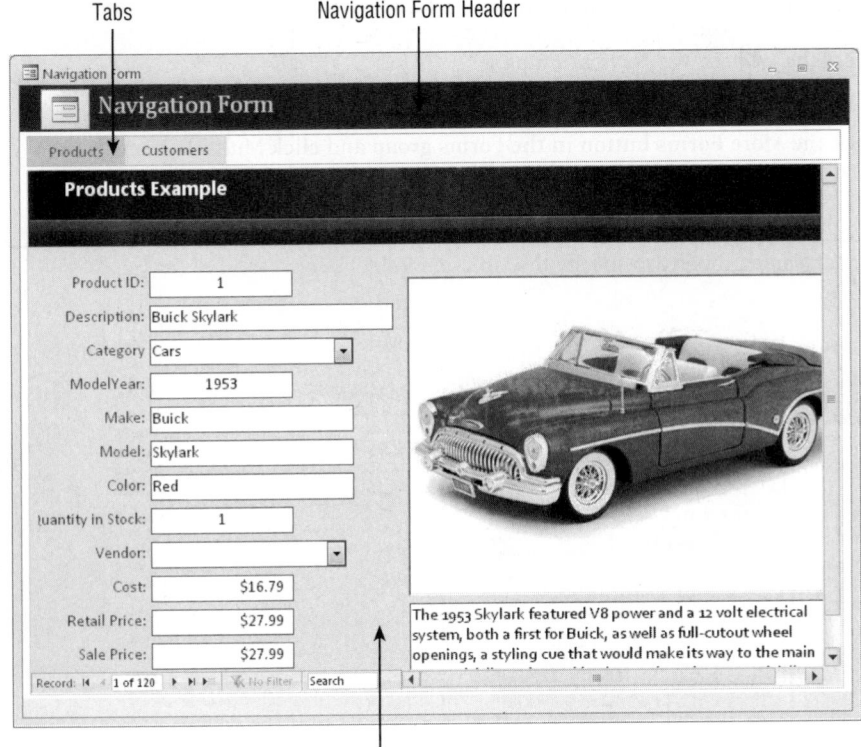

Subform Area

Split Forms

Click the More Forms button in the Forms group of the Create tab, and then click the Split Form button, to create a split form based on a table or query selected in the Navigation pane. The Split Form feature gives you two views of the data at the same time, letting you select a record from a datasheet in the upper section and edit the information in a form in the lower section.

To create a split form based on a table, follow these steps:

1. **Select the table in the Navigation pane.**
2. **Select the Create tab on the Ribbon.**
3. **Click the More Forms button in the Forms group and then click Split Form.**

Access creates a new split form based on the table you selected in Step 1, displayed in Layout view (shown in Figure 35-11). Resize the form and use the splitter bar in the middle to make the lower section completely visible.

FIGURE 35-10

Create a multiple items form when you want to see data similar to Datasheet view.

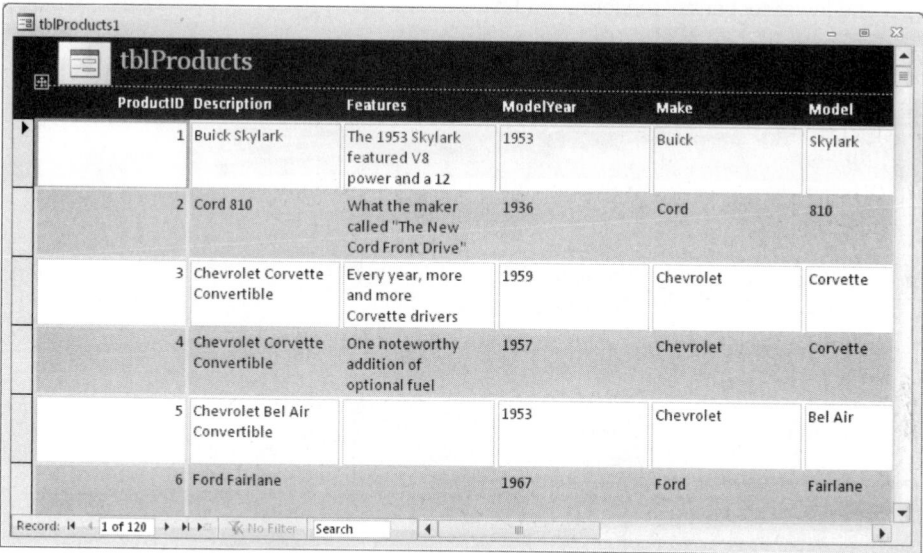

The Split Form Orientation property determines whether the datasheet is on the top, bottom, left, or right of the form area. The default is as shown in Figure 35-11, with the datasheet area on the bottom.

Datasheet Forms

Click the More Forms button in the Forms group of the Create tab and then click the Datasheet button to create a form that looks like a table or query's datasheet. A datasheet form is useful when you want to see the data in a row-and-column format, but you want to limit which fields are displayed and editable.

To create a datasheet form based on a table, follow these steps:

1. Select the table in the Navigation pane.
2. Select the Create tab on the Ribbon.
3. Click the Form group's More Forms button and then click Datasheet.

You can view any form you create as a datasheet by selecting Datasheet view from the Ribbon's View drop-down. A datasheet form appears in Datasheet view by default when you open it.

Tip

You can prevent users from viewing a form as a datasheet by setting the form's properties. You'll learn more about form properties in the "Understanding Properties" section, later in this chapter. ■

FIGURE 35-11

Create a split form when you want to select records from a list and edit them in a form. Use the splitter bar to resize the upper and lower sections of the form.

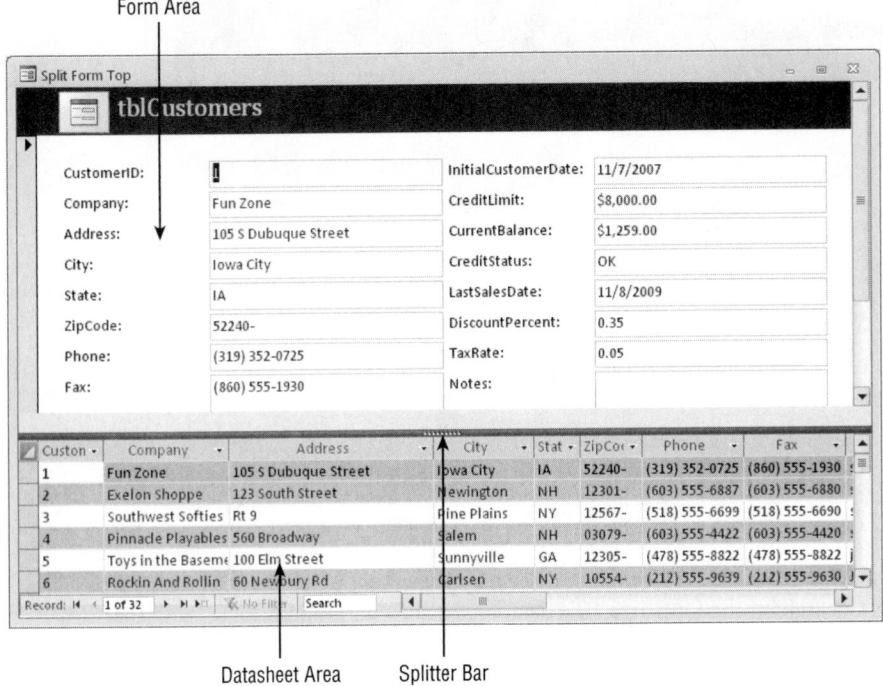

Form Area

Datasheet Area   Splitter Bar

Resizing the Form Area

The white area of the form is where you work. This is the size of the form when it's displayed. Resize the white area of the form by placing the mouse pointer on any of the area borders and dragging the border of the area to make it larger or smaller. Figure 35-12 shows a blank form in Design view being resized.

Saving Your Form

You can save the form at any time by clicking on the Save button in the Quick Access Toolbar (QAT). When you're asked for a name for the form, give it a meaningful name (e.g., frmProducts, frmCustomers, frmProductList). Once you've given the form a name, you won't be prompted the next time you click Save.

FIGURE 35-12

Design view of a blank form. Resize the form area by dragging the bottom-right corner.

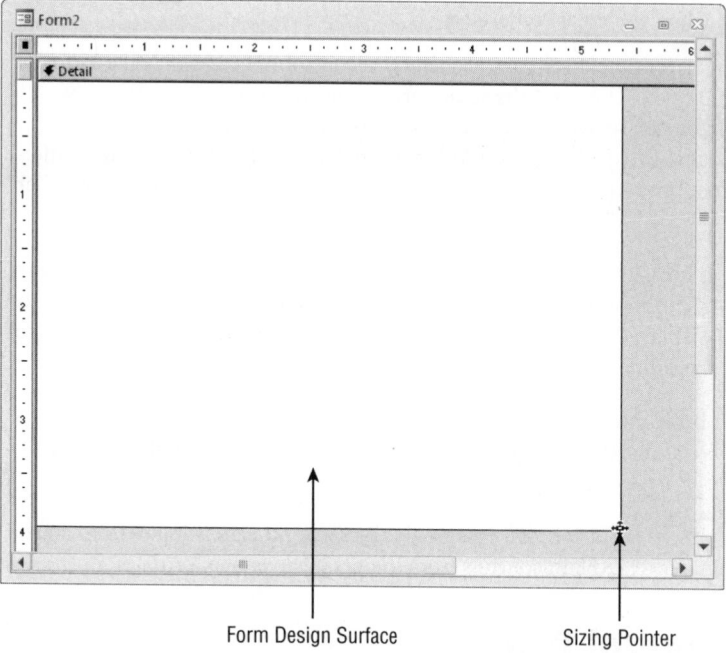

Form Design Surface   Sizing Pointer

When you close a form after making changes, Access asks you to save it. If you don't save a form, all changes since you opened the form (or since you last clicked Save) are lost. You should frequently save the form while you work if you're satisfied with the results.

Tip

If you're going to make extensive changes to a form, you might want to make a copy of the form. For example, if you want to work on the form frmProducts, you can copy and then paste the form in the Navigation pane, giving it a name like *frmProductsOriginal*. Later, when you've completed your changes and tested them, you can delete the original copy. ■

Working with Controls

Controls and properties form the basis of forms and reports. It's critical to understand the fundamental concepts of *controls* and of *properties* before you begin to apply them to custom forms and reports.

Note

Although this chapter is about forms, you'll learn that forms and reports share many common characteristics, including controls and what you can do with them. As you learn about controls in this chapter, you'll be able to apply nearly everything you learn when you create reports. ■

The term *control* has many definitions in Access. Generally, a control is any object on a form or report, such as a label or text box. These are the same sorts of controls used in any Windows application, such as Access, Excel, or Web-based HTML forms, or those that are used in any language, such as .NET, Visual Basic, C++, or C#. Although each language or product has different file formats and different properties, a text box in Access is similar to a text box in any other Windows product.

You enter data into controls and display data using controls. A control can be bound to a field in a table (when the value is entered in the control, it's also saved in some underlying table field), or data can be unbound and displayed in the form but not saved when the form is closed. A control can also be an object, such as a line or rectangle.

Some controls that aren't built into Access are developed separately — these are ActiveX controls. ActiveX controls extend the basic feature set of Access and are available from a variety of vendors.

Whether you're working with forms or reports, essentially the same process is followed to create and use controls. In this chapter, I explain controls from the perspective of a form.

The Different Control Types

Forms and reports contain many different types of controls. You can add these controls to forms using the Controls group on the Design tab (under the Form Design Tools tab), shown in Figure 35-13. Hovering the mouse over the control displays a ScreenTip telling you what the control is.

FIGURE 35-13

The Design tab (under Form Design Tools) lets you add and customize controls in a form's Design view.

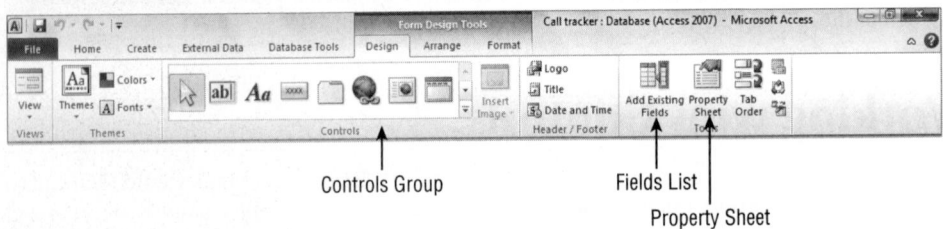

Controls Group   Fields List
                        Property Sheet

Table 35-1 briefly describes the basic Access controls.

TABLE 35-1

Controls in Access Forms

Control	What It Does
Text Box	Displays and allows users to edit data.
Label	Displays static text that typically doesn't change.
Button	Also called a *command button*. Calls macros or runs VBA code when clicked.
Combo Box	A drop-down list of values. Combo boxes include a text box at the top for inputting values that are not included in the drop-down list.
List Box	A list of values that is always displayed on the form or report.
Subform/Subreport	Displays another form or report within the main form or report.
Line	A graphical line of variable thickness and color, which is used for separation.
Rectangle	A rectangle can be any color or size or can be filled in or blank; the rectangle is used for emphasis.
Image	Displays a bitmap picture with very little overhead.
Option Group	Holds multiple option buttons, check boxes, or toggle buttons.
Check Box	A two-state control, shown as a square that contains a check mark if it's on and an empty square if it's off.
Option Button	Also called a *radio button*, this button is displayed as a circle with a dot when the option is on.
Toggle Button	This is a two-state button — up or down — which usually uses pictures or icons instead of text to display different states.
Tab Control	Displays multiple pages in a file-folder-type interface.
Page	Adds a page on the form or report. Additional controls are added to the page, and multiple pages may exist on the same form.
Chart	This chart displays data in a graphical format.
Unbound Object Frame	This frame holds an OLE object or embedded picture that isn't tied to a table field and can include graphs, pictures, sound files, and video.
Bound Object Frame	This frame holds an OLE object or embedded picture that is tied to a table field.
Page Break	This is usually used for reports and indicates a physical page break.
Hyperlink	This control creates a link to a web page, a picture, an e-mail address, or a program.
Attachment	This control manages attachments for the Attachment data type. Attachment fields (see Chapter 34) provide a way to *attach* external files (such as music or video clips or Word documents) to Access tables.

The Use Control Wizards button, revealed by expanding the Controls group by clicking on the More button in the lower-right corner of the group, doesn't add a control to a form. Instead, the Use Control Wizards button determines whether a wizard is automatically activated when you add certain controls. The Option Group, Combo Box, List Box, Subform/Subreport, Bound and Unbound Object Frame, and Command Button controls all have wizards to help you when you add a new control. You can also use the ActiveX Controls button (also found at the bottom of the expanded Controls group) to display a list of ActiveX controls, which you can add to Access.

There are three basic categories of controls: bound, unbound, and calculated.

Bound Controls

Bound controls are controls that are bound to a field in the data source underlying the form. When you enter a value into a bound control, Access automatically updates the field in the current record. Most of the controls used for data entry can be bound. Controls can be bound to most data types, including Text, Date/Time, Number, Yes/No, OLE Object, and Memo fields.

Unbound Controls

Unbound controls retain the entered value, but they don't update any table fields. You can use these controls for text label display, for controls such as lines and rectangles, or for holding unbound OLE objects (such as bitmap pictures or your logo) that aren't stored in a table but on the form itself. Very often, VBA code is used to work with data in unbound controls and directly update Access data sources.

Calculated Controls

Calculated controls are based on expressions, such as functions or calculations. Calculated controls are unbound because they don't directly update table fields. An example of a calculated control is =[SalePrice] - [Cost]. This control calculates the total of two table fields for display on a form but is not bound to any table field. The value of an unbound calculated control may be referenced by other controls on the form or used in an expression in another control on the form or in VBA in the form's module.

Adding a Control

You add a control to a form in one of three ways:

- By clicking a button in the Design tab's Controls group and drawing a new unbound control on the form: Use the control's ControlSource property to bind the new control to a field in the form's data source.

- By dragging a field from the Field List to add a bound control to the form: Access automatically chooses a control appropriate for the field's data type and binds the control to the selected field.

- By double-clicking a field in the Field List to add a bound control to the form: Double-clicking works just like dragging a field from the Field List to the form. The only difference is that, when you add a control by double-clicking a field, Access decides where to add the new control to the form. Usually the new control is added to the right of the most recently added control, and sometimes below it.

Using the Controls Group

When you use the buttons in the Controls group to add a control, you decide which type of control to use for each field. The control you add is unbound (not attached to the data in a table field) and has a default name such as Text21 or Combo11. After you create the control, you decide what table field to bind the control to, enter text for the label, and set any properties. You'll learn more about setting properties later in this chapter.

You can add one control at a time using the Controls group. To create three different unbound controls, perform these steps:

1. With a blank form open in Design view, click the Text Box button (ab|) in the Controls group.
2. Move the mouse pointer to the Form Design window, and drag the new control onto the form's surface in its initial size and position.
3. Click the Option button in the Controls group, click on the form's surface, and drag the Option button to its initial position and size on the form.
4. Click the Check Box button in the Controls group and add it to the form as you added the other controls.

When you're done, you'll see new controls like the ones shown in Figure 35-14.

FIGURE 35-14

Unbound controls added from the Controls group.

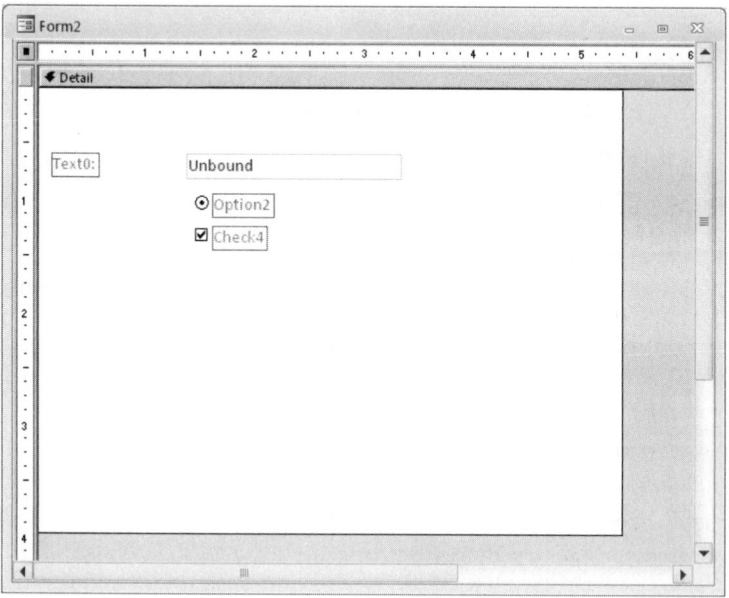

Tip

Clicking the Form Design window with a control selected creates a default-size control. If you want to add multiple controls of the same type, double-click on the icon in the Controls group to lock it down, and then draw as many controls as you want on the form. Click the selector control (the arrow) to unlock the control and return to normal operation. ■

Using the Field List

The Field List displays a list of fields from the table or query the form is based on. Open the Field List by clicking the Add Existing Fields button in the Tools group on the Ribbon's Design tab (refer to Figure 35-13).

Drag fields from the Field List and drop them on the form to create bound controls. Select and drag them one at a time, or select multiple fields by using the Ctrl key or Shift key:

- To select multiple contiguous fields, hold down the Shift key and click the first and last fields that you want.

- To select multiple noncontiguous fields, hold down the Ctrl key and click each field that you want.

By default, the Field List, shown in Figure 35-15, appears docked on the right of the Access window. The Field List window is movable and resizable and displays a vertical scroll bar if it contains more fields than can fit in the window.

FIGURE 35-15

Click Add Existing Fields in the Tools group to show the Field List.

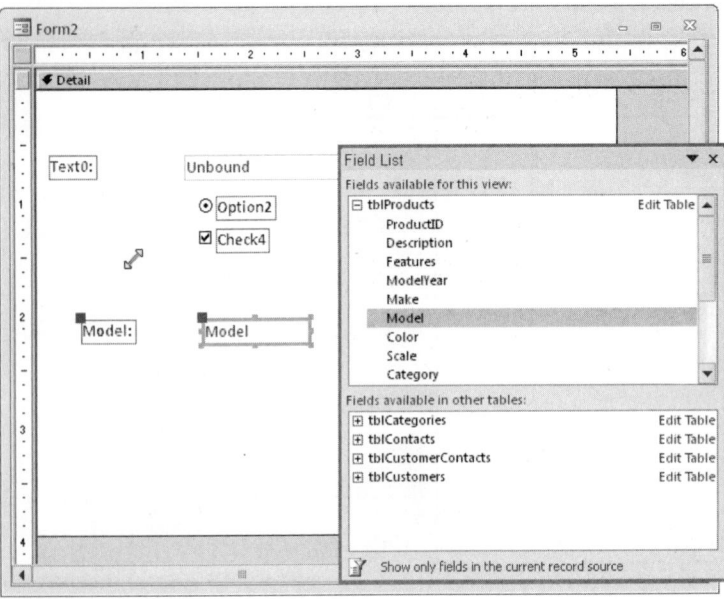

Most often, dragging a field from the Field List adds a bound text box to the Design window. If you drag a Yes/No field from the Field List window, Access adds a check box. Optionally, you can select the type of control by selecting a control from the Controls group and dragging the field to the Design window.

Caution

When you drag fields from the Field List pane, the first control is placed where you release the mouse button. Make sure that you have enough space to the left of the control for the labels. If you don't have enough space, the labels slide under the controls. ∎

You gain several distinct advantages by dragging a field from the Field List pane:

- The control is automatically bound to the field.

- Field properties inherit table-level formats, Status-bar text, and data-validation rules and messages.

- The label control and label text are created with the field name as the caption.

- The label control is attached to the field control, so they move together.

Figure 35-16 shows an example in which the Description, Category, RetailPrice, and Cost fields were added from the Field List window to the form. Double-clicking a field also adds it to the form.

FIGURE 35-16

Drag fields from the Field List to add bound controls to the form.

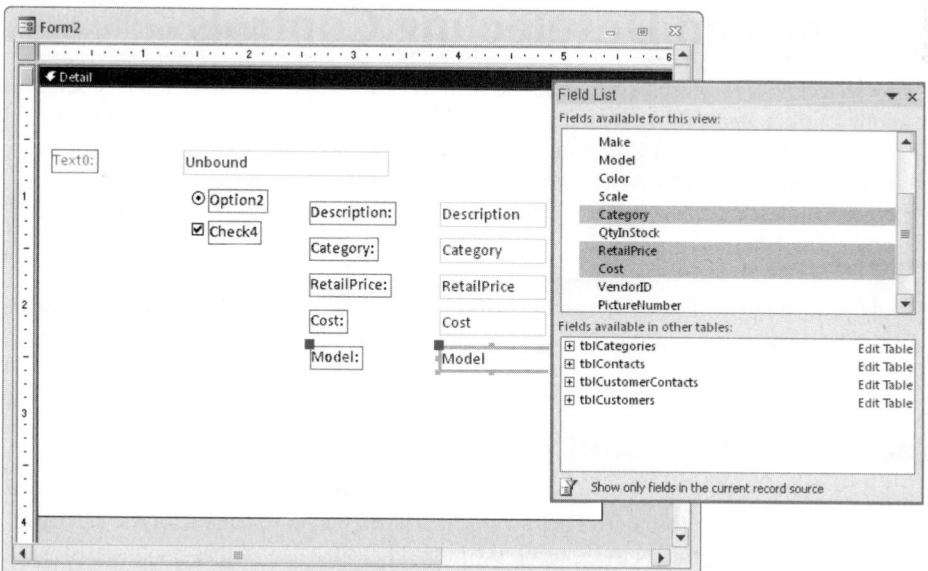

You can see four new controls in the form's Design view — each one consists of a Label control and a Text Box control (Access attaches the Label control to the text box automatically). You can work with these controls as a group or independently, and you can select, move, resize, or delete them. Notice that each control has a label with a caption matching the field name, and the Text Box control displays the bound field name used in the text box. If you want to resize just the control and not the label, you must work with the two controls (label and associated text box) separately.

Close the Field List by clicking the Add Existing Fields command in the Tools group of the Form Design Tools Design tab or the Close button on the Field List.

Tip

In Access, you can change the type of control after you create it; then you can set all the properties for the control. For example, suppose that you add a field as a Text Box control and you want to change it to a List Box. Right-click on the control and select Change To from the shortcut menu to change the control type. However, you can change only from some types of controls to others. You can change almost any type of control to a Text Box control, while option buttons, toggle buttons, and check boxes are interchangeable, as are List Box and Combo Box controls. ■

In the "Understanding Properties" section, later in this chapter, you learn how to change the control names, captions, and other properties. Using properties speeds the process of naming controls and binding them to specific fields. If you want to see the differences between bound and unbound controls, switch to Form view using the View command in the Home tab's Views group. Some fields you add will display data because they're bound to the source table. Other controls don't display data because they aren't bound to any data source.

Selecting and Deselecting Controls

After you add a control to a form, you can resize it, move it, or copy it. The first step is to select one or more controls. Depending on its size, a selected control might show from four to eight handles around the control — at the corners and midway along the sides. The move handle in the upper-left corner is larger than the other handles, and you use it to move the control. You use the other handles to size the control. Figure 35-17 displays some selected controls and their moving and sizing handles.

The Select command (which looks like an arrow) in the Controls group must be chosen in order for you to select a control. If you use the Controls group to create a single control, Access automatically reselects the pointer as the default.

Selecting a Single Control

Select any individual control by clicking anywhere on the control. When you click on a control, the sizing handles appear. If the control has an attached label, the move handle for the label also appears in the upper-left corner of the control. If you select a label control that is associated with another control, all the handles for the label control are displayed, and only the move handle appears in the associated control.

A conceptual view of selecting controls and their moving and sizing handles.

Moving Handle

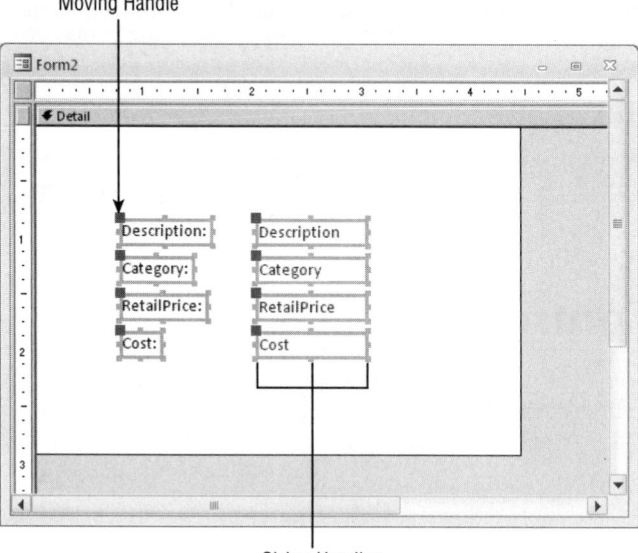

Sizing Handles

Selecting Multiple Controls

You select multiple controls in these ways:

- Click each control while holding down the Shift key.
- Drag the pointer through or around the controls that you want to select.
- Click and drag in the ruler to select a range of controls.

Figure 35-17 shows the result of selecting the multiple bound controls graphically. When you select multiple controls by dragging the mouse, a rectangle appears as you drag the mouse. Be careful to drag the rectangle only through the controls you want to select. Any control you touch with the rectangle or enclose within it is selected. If you want to select labels only, make sure that the selection rectangle only encloses the labels.

Tip

If you find that controls are not selected when the rectangle passes through the control, you may have the global selection behavior property set to Fully Enclosed. This means that a control is selected only if the selection rectangle completely encloses the entire control. Change this option by clicking the File tab and selecting Options. Then select Object Designers, and set the Forms/Reports Selection behavior to `Partially Enclosed`. ■

Tip

By holding down the Shift or Ctrl key, you can select several noncontiguous controls. This lets you select controls on totally different parts of the screen. Click on the form in Design view and then press Ctrl+A to select all the controls on the form. Press Shift or Ctrl and click on any selected control to remove it from the selection. ■

Deselecting Controls

Deselect a control by clicking an unselected area of the form that doesn't contain a control. When you do so, the handles disappear from any selected control. Selecting another control also deselects a selected control.

Manipulating Controls

Creating a form is a multistep process. The next step is to make sure that your controls are properly sized and moved to their correct positions. The Arrange tab (under Form Design Tools) of the Ribbon — shown in Figure 35-18 — contains commands used to assist you in manipulating controls.

FIGURE 35-18

The Arrange tab (under Form Design Tools) lets you work with moving and sizing controls, as well as manipulate the overall layout of the form.

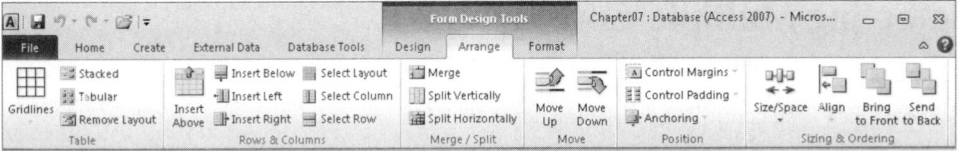

Resizing a Control

You resize controls using any of the smaller handles in the upper, lower, and right edges of the control. The sizing handles in the control corners let you drag the control larger or smaller in both width and height — and at the same time. Use the handles in the middle of the control sides to size the control larger or smaller in one direction only. The top and bottom handles control the height of the control; the left and right handles change the control's width.

When the mouse pointer touches a corner handle of a selected control, the pointer becomes a diagonal double arrow. You can then drag the sizing handle until the control is the desired size. If the mouse pointer touches a side handle in a selected control, the pointer changes to a horizontal or vertical double-headed arrow. Figure 35-19 shows the Description control being resized. Notice the double-headed arrow in the corner of the Description control.

Resizing a control.

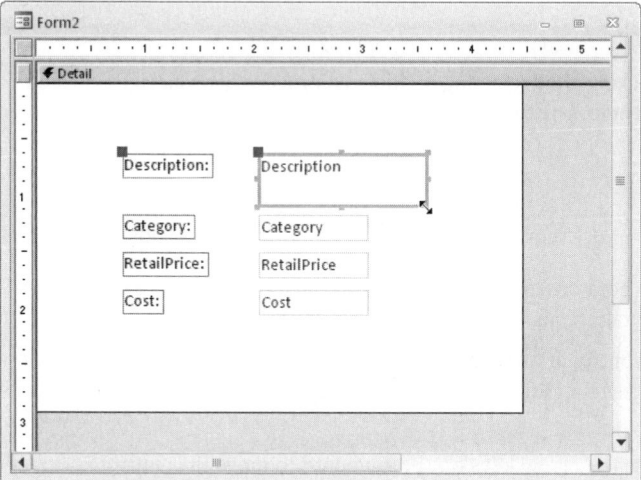

Tip

You can resize a control in very small increments by holding the Shift key down while pressing the arrow keys (up, down, left, and right). This technique also works with multiple controls selected. Using this technique, a control changes by only 1 pixel at a time (or moves to the nearest grid line if Snap to Grid is selected in the Layout tab's Control Layout group). ∎

When you double-click on any of the sizing handles, Access resizes a control to best fit the text contained in the control. This feature is especially handy if you increase the font size and then notice that the text is cut off either at the bottom or to the right. For label controls, note that this best-fit sizing adjusts the size vertically and horizontally, although text controls are resized only vertically. This is because when Access is in Form Design mode, it can't predict how much of a field to display — the field name and field contents can be radically different. Sometimes Access doesn't correctly resize the label and you must manually change its size.

Sizing Controls Automatically

The Size/Space drop-down list in the Sizing & Ordering group on the Arrange tab has several commands that help the arrangement of controls:

- **To Fit.** Adjusts control height and width for the font of the text they contain.
- **To Tallest.** Makes selected controls the height of the tallest selected control.

- **To Shortest.** Makes selected controls the height of the shortest selected control.

- **To Grid.** Moves all sides of selected controls in or out to meet the nearest points on the grid.

- **To Widest.** Makes selected controls the width of the widest selected control.

- **To Narrowest.** Makes selected controls the height of the narrowest selected control.

Tip
You can access many commands by right-clicking after selecting multiple controls. When you right-click on multiple controls, a shortcut menu displays choices to size and align controls. ∎

Moving a Control

After you select a control, you can easily move it, using any of the following methods:

- Click on the control and hold down the mouse button; the mouse pointer changes to a four-directional arrow. Drag the mouse to move the control to a new location.

- Click once to select the control and move the mouse over any of the highlighted edges; the mouse pointer changes to a four-directional arrow. Drag the mouse to move the control to a new location.

- Select the control and use the arrow keys on the keyboard to move the control. Using this technique, a control changes by only 1 pixel at a time (or moves to the nearest grid line if "To Grid" is selected when you right-click on the control).

Figure 35-20 shows a Label control that has been separately moved to the top of the Text Box control. The four-directional arrow pointer indicates that the controls are ready to be moved together. To see this pointer, the control(s) must already be selected.

Press Esc before you release the mouse button to cancel a moving or a resizing operation. After a move or resizing operation is complete, click the Undo button on the Quick Access Toolbar to undo the changes, if needed.

Aligning Controls

You might want to move several controls so that they're all aligned. The Align menu in the Sizing & Ordering group on the Form Design Tools Arrange tab contains the following alignment commands:

- **Left.** Aligns the left edge of the selected controls with the leftmost selected control.

- **Right.** Aligns the right edge of the selected controls with the rightmost selected control.

- **Top.** Aligns the top edge of the selected controls with the topmost selected control.

- **Bottom.** Aligns the bottom edge of the selected controls with the bottommost selected control.

- **To Grid.** Aligns the top-left corners of the selected controls to the nearest grid point.

FIGURE 35-20

Moving a control.

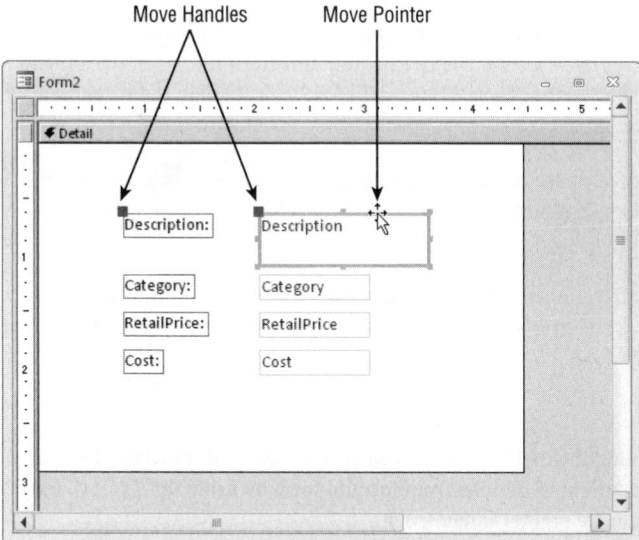

You can align any number of selected controls by selecting an align command. When you choose one of the align commands, Access uses the control that is the closest to the desired selection as the model for the alignment. For example, suppose that you have three controls and you want to left-align them. They're aligned on the basis of the control farthest to the left in the group of the three controls.

Figure 35-21 shows several sets of controls. The first set of controls is not aligned. The label controls in the middle set of controls have been left-aligned, while the Text Box controls in the right-side set have been right-aligned.

FIGURE 35-21

An example of unaligned and aligned controls on the grid.

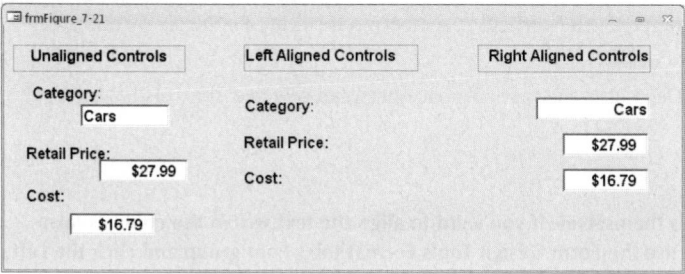

Each type of alignment must be done separately. In this example, you can left-align all the labels or right-align all the text boxes at once.

The sizing grid has been turned off in Figure 35-21. By default, Access displays a series of small dots across the entire surface of a form while it's in Design view. The grid can assist you in aligning controls. Hide or display the grid by selecting the Grid command from the Size/Space menu in the Sizing & Ordering group in the Arrange tab. You can also hide or display the ruler using the Ruler command in the same menu.

Use the To Grid command in the Size/Space menu to align controls to the grid as you draw or place them on a form. This also aligns existing controls to the grid when you move or resize them.

As you move or resize existing controls, Access lets you move only from grid point to grid point. When To Grid is off, Access ignores the grid and lets you place a control anywhere on the form or report.

Tip

You can temporarily turn To Grid off by pressing the Ctrl key before you create a control (or while sizing or moving it). You can change the grid's fineness (number of dots) from form to form by using the Grid X and Grid Y form properties. (Higher numbers indicate greater fineness.) ■

The Size/Space menu in the Sizing & Ordering group on the Form Design Tools Arrange tab also contains commands to adjust spacing between controls. The spacing commands adjust the distance between controls on the basis of the space between the first two selected controls. If the controls are across the screen, use horizontal spacing; if they're down the screen, use vertical spacing. The spacing commands are as follows:

- **Equal Horizontal.** Makes the horizontal space between selected controls equal. You must select three or more controls in order for this command to work.
- **Increase Horizontal.** Increases the horizontal space between selected controls by one grid unit.
- **Decrease Horizontal.** Decreases the horizontal space between selected controls by one grid unit.
- **Equal Vertical.** Makes the vertical space between selected controls equal. You must select three or more controls in order for this command to work properly.
- **Increase Vertical.** Increases the vertical space between selected controls by one grid unit.
- **Decrease Vertical.** Decreases the vertical space between selected controls by one grid unit.

Tip

Aligning controls aligns only the controls themselves. If you want to align the text within the controls (also known as *justifying the text)*, you must use the Form Design Tools Format tab's Font group and click the Left, Right, or Center buttons. ■

Modifying the Appearance of a Control

To modify the appearance of a control, select the control and click on commands that modify that control, such as the options in the Font or Controls group. Follow these steps to change the text color and font of a label:

1. **Click the label on the form.**
2. **In the Form Design Tools Format tab's Font group, change Font Size as desired and apply other attributes, such as clicking the Bold button and changing the Font Color to blue.**
3. **Resize the label so the larger text fits.**

Note
You can double-click on any of the sizing handles to autosize the label. ∎

To modify the appearance of multiple controls at once, select the controls and click on commands to modify the controls, such as commands in the Font or Controls group.

As you click on the commands, the controls' appearances change to reflect the new selections (shown in Figure 35-22). The fonts in each control increase in size, become bold, and turn blue. Any changes you make apply to all selected controls.

FIGURE 35-22

Changing the appearance of multiple controls at the same time.

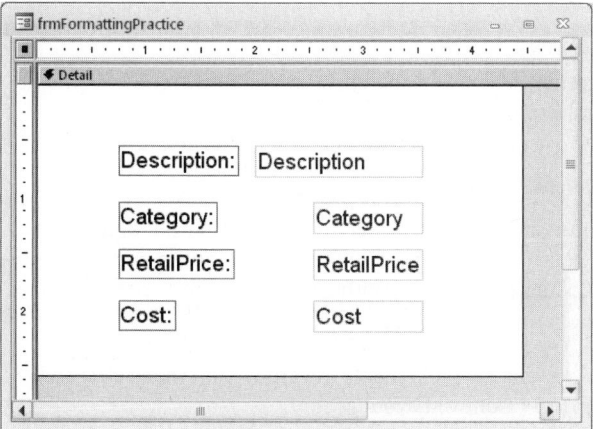

When multiple controls are selected, you can also move the selected controls together. When the mouse pointer changes to the four-directional arrow, drag to move the selected controls. You can also change the size of all the controls at once by resizing one of the controls in the selection. All the selected controls increase or decrease by the same number of units.

Grouping Controls

If you routinely change properties of multiple controls, you might want to group them together. To group controls together, select the controls by holding down the Shift key and clicking them or dragging the selection box through them. After the desired controls are selected, select the Group command from the Form Design Tools Arrange tab's Size/Space menu in the Sizing & Ordering group. A box appears around the selected controls, as shown in Figure 35-23, indicating that they're grouped together.

Grouping multiple controls together.

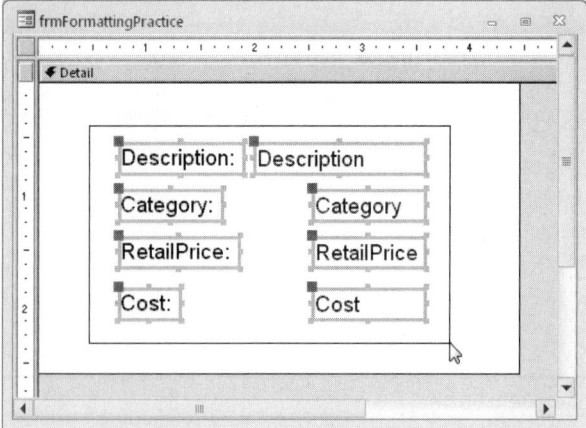

After you've grouped the controls together, whenever you click on any of the controls inside the group, the entire group is selected. Double-click on a control to select just that one control. After a single control in the group is selected, you can click on any other control to select it.

To resize the entire group, put your mouse on the side you want to resize. After the double arrow appears, drag until you reach the desired size. Every control in the group changes in size. To move the entire group, drag the group to its new location. With grouped controls, you don't have to select all the controls every time you change something about them.

To remove a group, select the group by clicking any field inside the group, and then select the Ungroup command from the Layout Ribbon's Control Layout group.

Attaching (and Reattaching) a Label to a Control

If you accidentally delete a label from a control, you can reattach it. To create and then reattach a label to a control, follow these steps:

1. Click the Label button in the Controls group of the Form Design Tools Design tab.

2. Place the mouse pointer in the Form Design window.

3. Press and hold down the mouse button where you want the control to begin; drag the mouse to size the control.

4. Type Description: (or the desired name) and click outside the control.

5. Select the new Label control.

6. Select Cut from the Home tab's Clipboard group.

7. Select the Text Box control.

8. Select Paste from the Home tab's Clipboard group to attach the Label control to the Text Box control.

Another way to attach a label to a control is to click on the informational icon next to the label, as shown in Figure 35-24. This informational icon lets you know that this label is unassociated with a control. Select the Associate Label with a Control command from the menu, and then select the control you want to associate the label with.

Associating a label with a control.

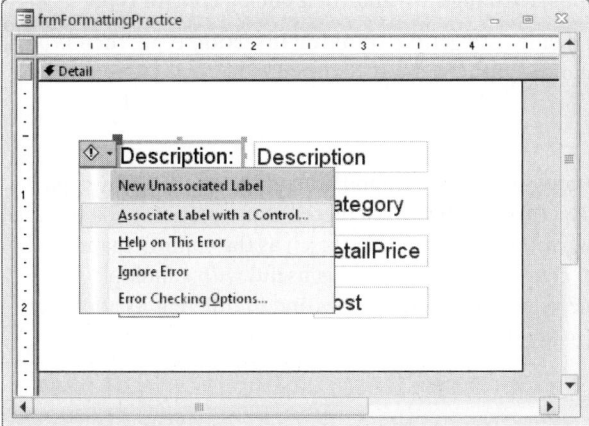

Changing a Control's Type

In Figure 35-25, the Complete control is a check box. Although there are times you may want to use a check box to display a Boolean (yes/no) data type, there are other ways to display the value, such as a toggle button. A toggle button is raised if it's true and depressed (or at least very unhappy) if it's false.

FIGURE 35-25

Become a magician and turn a check box into a toggle button.

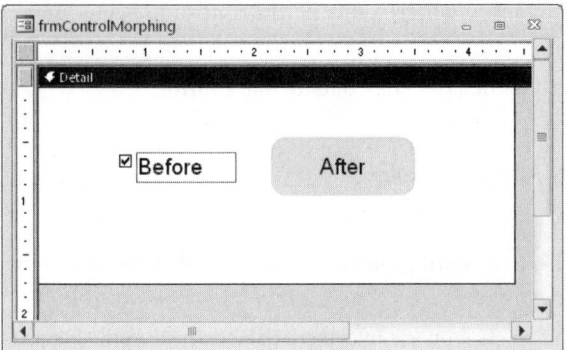

Use these steps to turn a check box into a toggle button:

1. **Select the Label control (just the Label control, not the control itself) for the control to change.**

2. **Press Delete to delete the Label control because it isn't needed.**

3. **Right-click on the control, choose Change To, and then click a control type.**

4. **Resize the control and click inside it to get the blinking insertion type; then type a new caption (such as** After **shown on the right of Figure 35-25).**

Copying a Control

You can create copies of any control by copying it to the Clipboard and then pasting the copies where you want them. If you have a control for which you've entered many properties or specified a certain format, you can copy it and revise only the properties (such as the control's name and bound field name) to make it a different control. This capability is useful with a multiple-page form when you want to display the same values on different pages and in different locations, or when copying a control from one form to another.

Deleting a Control

You can delete a control by simply selecting it in the form's Design view and pressing the Delete key on your keyboard. The control and any attached labels will disappear. You can bring them back by immediately selecting Undo from the Quick Access Toolbar. You can also select Cut from the Home tab's Clipboard group or Delete from the Home tab's Records group.

You can delete more than one control at a time by selecting multiple controls and pressing Delete. You can delete an entire group of controls by selecting the group and pressing Delete.

If you have a control with an attached label, you can delete only the label by clicking the label itself and then selecting one of the delete methods. If you select the control, both the control and the label are deleted.

Understanding Properties

Properties are named attributes of controls, fields, or database objects that are used to modify the characteristics of a control, field, or object. Examples of these attributes are the size, color, appearance, or name of an object. A property can also modify the behavior of a control, determining, for example, whether the control is read-only or editable and visible or not visible.

Properties are used extensively in forms and reports to change the characteristics of controls. Each control on the form has properties. The form itself also has properties, as does each of its sections. The same is true for reports; the report itself has properties, as does each report section and individual control. The Label control also has its own properties, even if it's attached to another control.

Everything that you do with the Ribbon commands — from moving and resizing controls to changing fonts and colors — can be done by setting properties. In fact, all these commands do is change properties of the selected controls.

Displaying the Property Sheet

Properties are displayed in a *Property Sheet* (sometimes called a *Property Window*). To display the Property Sheet for a control, follow these steps:

1. **In Design view, click on the control to select it.**
2. **Click the Property Sheet command in the Form Design Tools Design tab's Tools group, or press F4 to display the Property Sheet.**

The screen should look like the one shown in Figure 35-26. In Figure 35-26, the Description text box control has been selected and the Format tab in the Property Sheet is being scrolled to find the margin properties associated with a text box.

Because the Property Sheet is a window, it can be undocked, moved, and resized. It does not, however, have Maximize or Minimize buttons.

There are several ways to display a control's Property Sheet if it's not visible:

- Select a control and click the Property Sheet command in the Design tab's Tools group.
- Double-click on any control.
- Right-click on any control and select Properties from the pop-up menu.
- Press F4 while any control is selected.

FIGURE 35-26

Change an object's properties with the Property Sheet.

Selected Control   Tabs

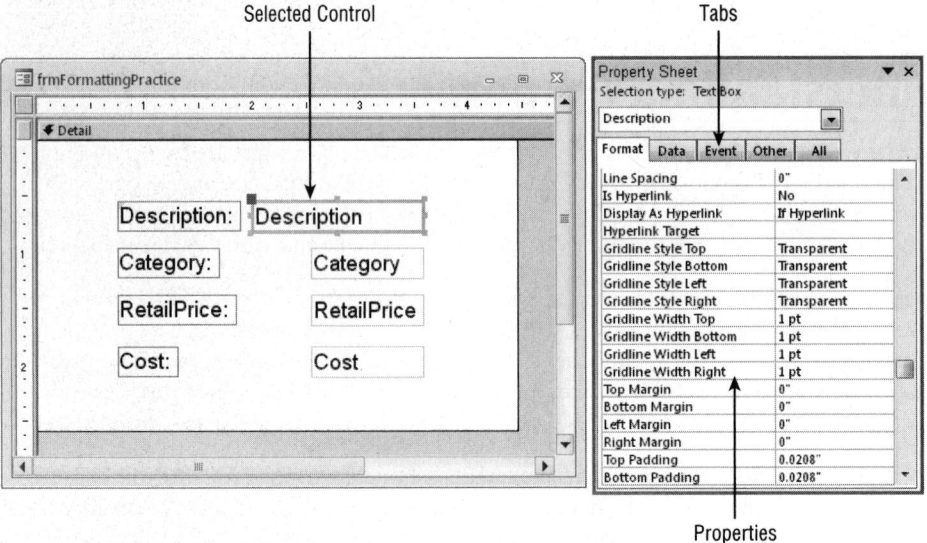

Properties

Getting Acquainted with the Property Sheet

With the Property Sheet displayed, click on any control in Design view to display the properties for that control. Select multiple controls to display similar properties for the selected controls. The vertical scroll bar lets you move between various properties.

The Property Sheet has an All tab that lets you see all the properties for a control. Or you can choose another tab to limit the view to a specific group of properties. The specific tabs and groups of properties are as follows:

- **Format.** These properties determine how a label or value looks: font, size, color, special effects, borders, and scroll bars.

- **Data.** These properties affect how a value is displayed and the data source it is bound to: control source, input masks, validation, default value, and other data-type properties.

- **Event.** Event properties are named events, such as clicking a mouse button, adding a record, pressing a key for which you can define a response (in the form of a call to a macro or a VBA procedure), and so on.

- **Other.** Other properties show additional characteristics of the control, such as the name of the control or the description that displays in the Status bar.

Figure 35-26 shows the Property Sheet for the Description text box. The first column lists the property names; the second column is where you enter or select property settings or options.

Changing a Control's Property Setting

There are many different methods for changing property settings, including the following:

- Enter or select the desired value in a Property Sheet.
- For some properties, double-clicking the property name in the Property Sheet cycles through all the acceptable values for the property.
- Change a property directly by changing the control itself, such as changing its size.
- Use inherited properties from the bound field or the control's default properties.
- Enter color selections for the control by using the Ribbon commands.
- Change label text style, size, color, and alignment by using the Ribbon commands.

You can change a control's properties by clicking on a property and typing the desired value.

In Figure 35-27, you see a down-arrow and a button with three dots to the right of the Control Source property entry area. Some properties display a drop-down arrow in the property entry area when you click in the area. The drop-down arrow tells you that Access has a list of values from which you can choose. If you click the down-arrow in the Control Source property, you find that the drop-down list displays a list of all fields in the data source — tblProducts. Setting the Control Source property to a field in a table creates a bound control.

FIGURE 35-27

Setting a control's Control Source property.

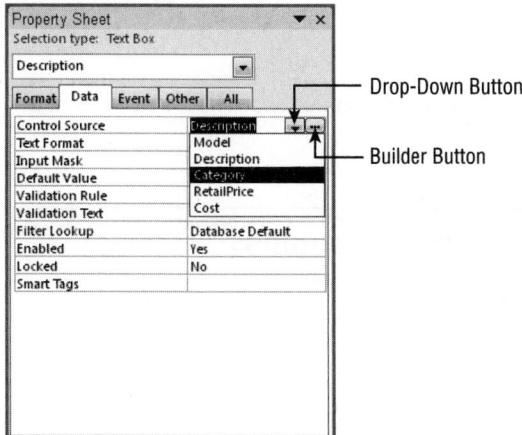

1111

Some properties have a list of standard values such as Yes or No; others display varying lists of fields, forms, reports, or macros. The properties of each object are determined by the control itself and what the control is used for.

A nice feature in Access is the ability to cycle through property choices by repeatedly double-clicking on the choice. For example, double-clicking on the Display When property alternately selects Always, Print Only, and Screen Only.

The Builder button contains an ellipsis (...) and opens one of the many builders in Access — including the Macro Builder, the Expression Builder, and the Module Builder. When you open a builder and make some selections, the property is filled in for you. You'll learn about builders later in this book.

Each type of object has its own property window and properties. These include the form itself, each of the form sections, and each of the form's controls. You display each of the Property windows by clicking on the object first. The Property window will instantly change to show the properties for the selected object.

Naming Control Labels and Their Captions

You might notice that each of the data fields has a Label control and a Text Box control. Normally, the label's Caption property is the same as the text box's Name property. The text box's Name property is usually the same as the table's field name — shown in the Control Source property. Sometimes the label's Caption is different because a value was entered into the Caption property for each field in the table.

When creating controls on a form, it's a good idea to use standard naming conventions when setting the control's Name property. Name each control with a prefix followed by a meaningful name that you'll recognize later (e.g., *txtTotalCost*, *cboState*, *lblTitle*). Table 35-2 shows the naming conventions for form and report controls.

Note
You can find a very complete, well-established naming convention online at www.xoc.net/standards. ∎

TABLE 35-2

Form/Report Control-Naming Conventions

Prefix	Object
frb	Bound object frame
cht	Chart (graph)
chk	Check box
cbo	Combo box

Prefix	Object
cmd	Command button
ocx	ActiveX custom control
det	Detail (section)
gft[n]	Footer (group section)
fft	Form footer section
fhd	Form header section
ghd[n]	Header (group section)
hlk	Hyperlink
img	Image
lbl	Label
lin	Line
lst	List box
opt	Option button
grp	Option group
pge	Page (tab)
brk	Page break
pft	Page footer (section)
phd	Page header (section)
shp	Rectangle
rft	Report footer (section)
rhd	Report header (section)
sec	Section
sub	Subform/subreport
tab	Tab control
txt	Text box
tgl	Toggle button
fru	Unbound object frame

The properties displayed in Figure 35-27 are the specific properties for the Description text box. The first two properties, `Name` and `Control Source`, are set to `Description`.

The `Name` is simply the name of the field itself. When a control is bound to a field, Access automatically assigns the `Name` property to the bound field's name. Unbound controls are given names such as *Field11* or *Button13*. However, you can give the control any name you want.

With bound controls, the `Control Source` property is the name of the table field to which the control is bound. In this example, *Description* refers to the field with the same name in the table `tblProducts`. An unbound control has no control source, whereas the control source of a calculated control is the actual expression for the calculation, as in the example `=[SalePrice] - [Cost]`.

Entering Records in Form View

Form view is where you actually view and modify data. Working with data in Form view is similar to working with data in a table or query's Datasheet view. Form view presents the data in a user-friendly format, which you create and design.

Figure 35-28 shows a form displayed in Form view. This view has many of the same elements as Datasheet view.

FIGURE 35-28

A form in Form view.

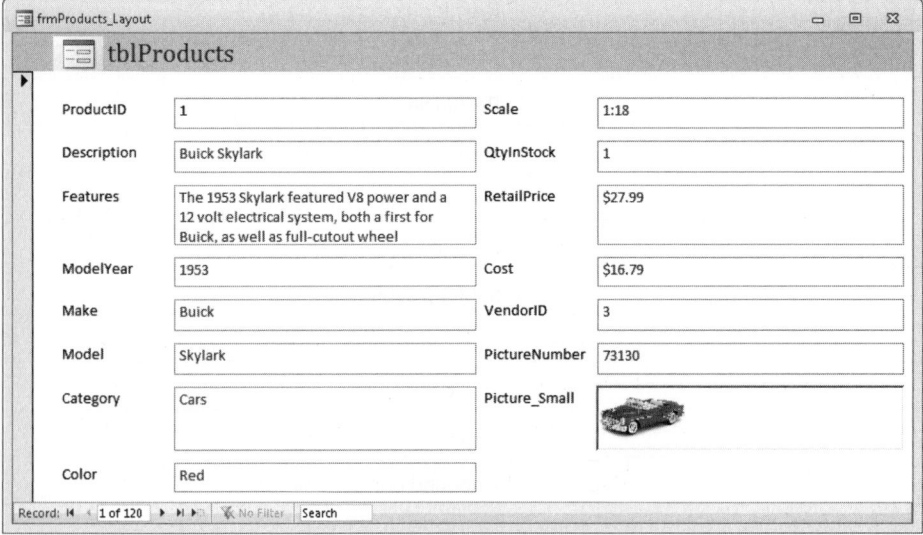

If the form contains more fields than can fit onscreen at one time, Access automatically displays a horizontal and/or vertical scroll bar that you can use to see the remainder of the data. You can also see the rest of the data by pressing the Page Down key. If you're at the bottom of a form or the entire form fits on the screen without scrolling, and you press Page Down, you'll move to the next record.

The status bar at the bottom of the window displays the active field's Description property that you defined when you created the table (or form). If no Description exists for a field, Access displays "Form View" in the status bar. Generally, error messages and warnings appear in dialog boxes in the center of the screen (rather than in the status bar). The navigation controls, search box, and view shortcuts are found at the bottom of the screen. These features let you move from record to record, quickly find data, or switch views.

The Form View Ribbon Appearance

The Home tab (shown in Figure 35-29) adjusts to enable you to work with the data in Form view. The Home tab for Form view has some familiar objects on it, as well as some new ones. This section provides an overview of the Form view's Home tab. Keep in mind that the Access Ribbon and its controls are very context-sensitive. Depending on your current task, one or more of the commands may be grayed out or not visible. Although this behavior can be confusing, Microsoft's intent is to simplify the Ribbon as much as possible to allow you to focus on the task at hand, and not have to deal with irrelevant commands as you work.

FIGURE 35-29

The Ribbon's Home tab for Form view.

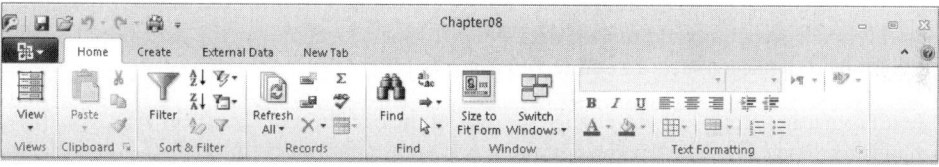

At the far left is the Views group, which allows you to switch among the following views, which you can see by clicking the button's down-arrow:

- **Form View.** Form view lets you manipulate data on the form.

- **Datasheet View.** Datasheet view shows the data in the row-and-column format.

- **PivotTable View.** PivotTable view lets you display a form's data as a pivot table.

- **PivotChart View.** PivotChart view lets you display a form's data as pivot charts.

- **Layout View.** Layout view lets you change the form's design while viewing data.

- **Design View.** Design view permits you to make changes to the form's design.

The Clipboard group contains the Cut, Copy, Paste, and Format Paint commands. These commands work like the same commands in other applications (like Word and Excel). The Clipboard is a resource provided by Windows and is shared by virtually all Windows applications. Items you copy or cut from Excel, for example, can be pasted into Access if the context is appropriate. For example, you could copy a VBA procedure from an Excel worksheet and paste it into an Access VBA code module because the contexts are the same. But you could not copy an Excel spreadsheet and paste it into Access, because Access has no way of working with an Excel spreadsheet.

The Paste command's down-arrow gives you three choices:

- **Paste.** The Paste button inserts whatever item has been copied to the Windows Clipboard into the current location in Access. Depending on the task you're working on, the pasted item might be plain text, a control, a table or form, or some other object.

- **Paste Special.** Paste Special gives you the option of pasting the contents of the Clipboard in different formats (Text, CSV, Records, etc.).

- **Paste Append.** Paste Append pastes the contents of the Clipboard as a new record — as long as a record with a similar structure was copied to the Clipboard. Obviously, Paste Append remains disabled for any operation that does not involve copying and pasting a database table record.

The Sort & Filter group lets you change the order of the records, and, based on your criteria, limit the records shown on the form.

The Records group lets you save, delete, or add a new record to the form. It also contains commands to show totals, check spelling, freeze and hide columns, and change the row height and cell width while the form is displayed in Datasheet view.

The Find group lets you find and replace data and go to specific records in the datasheet. Use the Select command to select a record or all records.

The Text Formatting group lets you change the look of the datasheet in Datasheet view. Use these commands to change the font, size, bold, italic, color, and so on. Use the Align Left, Align Right, and Align Center commands to justify the data in the selected column. Click the Gridlines option to toggle gridlines on and off. Use Alternate Fill/Back Color to change the colors of alternating rows, or make them all the same. When modifying text in a Memo field with the Text Format property set to Rich Text, you can use these commands to change the fonts, colors, and so on.

Navigating between Fields

Navigating a form is nearly identical to moving around a datasheet. You can easily move around the form by clicking on the control that you want and making changes or additions to your data. Because the form window displays only as many fields as can fit onscreen, you need to use various navigational aids to move within your form or between records.

Table 35-3 displays the navigational keys used to move between fields within a form.

TABLE 35-3

Navigating in a Form

Navigational Direction	Keystrokes
Next field	Tab, right-arrow (→) or down-arrow (↓) key, or Enter
Previous field	Shift+Tab, left-arrow (←), or up-arrow (↑)
First field of current record	Home or Ctrl+Home
Last field of current record	End or Ctrl+End
Next page	Page Down or Next Record
Previous page	Page Up or Previous Record

If you have a form with more data that can fit on the screen at one time, a vertical scroll bar displays. You can use the scroll bar to move to different pages on the form. You can also use the Page Up and Page Down keys to move between form pages. You can move up or down one field at a time by clicking the scroll-bar arrows. With the scroll-bar button, you can move past many fields at once.

Moving between Records in a Form

Although you generally use a form to display one record at a time, you still need to move between records. The easiest way to do this is to use the navigation buttons, as shown in Figure 35-30.

FIGURE 35-30

The navigation buttons of a form.

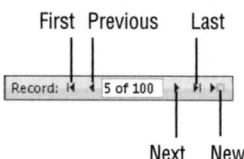

The navigation buttons are the six controls located at the bottom-left corner of the Form window. The two leftmost controls move you to the first record and the previous record in the form. The three rightmost controls position you on the next record, last record, or new record in the form. If you know the record number (the row number of a specific record), you can click the Record Number box, enter a record number, and press Enter.

The record number displayed in the Navigation controls is just an indicator of the current record's position in the recordset and changes every time you filter or sort the records. To the right of the record number is the total number of records in the current view. The record count may not be the same as the number of records in the underlying table or query. The record count changes when you filter the data on the form.

Changing Values in a Form

Earlier in this book, you learned datasheet techniques to add, change, and delete data within a table. These techniques are the same ones you use on an Access form. Table 35-4 summarizes these techniques.

TABLE 35-4

Editing Techniques

Editing Technique	Keystrokes
Move insertion point within a control.	Press the right-arrow (→) and left-arrow (←) keys.
Insert a value within a control.	Select the insertion point and type new data.
Select the entire contents of a control.	Press F2.
Replace an existing value with a new value.	Select the entire field and enter a new value.
Replace a value with value of the preceding field.	Press Ctrl+' (single quotation mark).
Replace the current value with the default value.	Press Ctrl+Alt+Spacebar.
Insert the current date into a control.	Press Ctrl+; (semicolon).
Insert the current time into a control.	Press Ctrl+: (colon).
Insert a line break in a Text or Memo control.	Press Ctrl+Enter.
Insert a new record.	Press Ctrl++ (plus sign).
Delete the current record.	Press Ctrl+– (minus sign).
Save the current record.	Press Shift+Enter or move to another record.
Toggle values in a check box or option button.	Spacebar
Undo a change to the current control.	Press Esc or click the Undo button.
Undo a change to the current record.	Press Esc or click the Undo button a second time after you undo the current control.

Controls That You Can't Edit

Some controls, including the following, can't be edited:

- **Controls Displaying AutoNumber Fields.** Access maintains AutoNumber fields automatically, calculating the values as you create each new record.

- **Calculated Controls.** Access may use calculated controls in forms or queries. Calculated values are not actually stored in your table.

- **Locked or Disabled Fields.** You can set certain form and control properties to prevent changes to the data.

- **Controls in Multiuser Locked Records.** If another user locks the record, you can't edit any controls in that record.

Working with Pictures and OLE Objects

OLE (Object Linking and Embedding) objects are not part of an Access database. OLE objects commonly include pictures but may be any number of other data types, such as links to Word documents, Excel spreadsheets, and audio files. You can also include video files such as .mpg or .avi files.

In Datasheet view, you can't view a picture or an OLE object without accessing the OLE server (such as Word, Excel, or the Windows Media Player). In Form view, however, you can size the OLE control area to be large enough to display a picture, business graph, or other OLE objects. You can also size Text Box controls on forms so that you can see the data within the field — you don't have to zoom in on the value, as you do with a datasheet field.

The Access OLE control supports many types of objects. As with a datasheet, you have two ways to enter OLE fields into a form:

- Copy the object (such as an .mp3 file) to the Clipboard and paste it from the controls in the Ribbon's Clipboard group.

- Right-click on the OLE control and click Insert Object from the shortcut menu to display the Insert Object dialog box, shown in Figure 35-31.

Use the Insert Object dialog box to add a new object to the OLE field, or add an object from an existing file. The Create from File option button adds a picture or other OLE object from an existing file.

When displaying a picture in an OLE control, set the Size Mode property to control how the image representing the OLE object is displayed. The settings for this property are as follows:

- **Clip.** Keeps the image at its original size and cuts off parts of the picture that don't fit in the control.

- **Zoom.** Fits the image in the control and keeps it in its original proportion, which may result in extra white space.

- **Stretch.** Sizes image to fit exactly between the frame borders. The stretch setting may distort the picture.

FIGURE 35-31

The Insert Object dialog box.

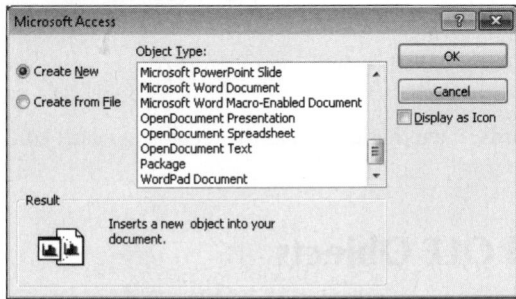

Entering Data in a Memo Field

The Features field in the form shown in Figure 35-28 is a Memo data type. This type of field contains up to 65,535 bytes of text. The first two sentences of data appear in the text box. When you click in this text box, a vertical scroll bar appears, allowing you to view all the data in the control.

Better yet, you can resize the Memo control in the form's Design view if you want to make it larger to show more data. With the Memo field's text box selected, you can press Shift+F2 and display a Zoom dialog box, as shown in Figure 35-32, to see more data. The text in the Zoom dialog box is fully editable. You can add new text or change text already in the control.

Entering Data in a Date Field

A Date/Time data field is formatted to accept and show date values. When you click in the text box for this type of field, a Date Picker icon automatically appears next to it, as shown in Figure 35-33. Click the Date Picker to display a calendar from which you can choose a date.

If the Date Picker doesn't appear, switch to Design view and change the control's Show Date Picker property to For dates. Set the Show Date Picker property to Never if you don't want to use the Date Picker.

Using Option Groups

Option groups let you choose from several option buttons (sometimes called *radio buttons*). *Option buttons* let you select one value while deselecting all the other values. Option groups work best when you have a small number of mutually exclusive choices to select from. Figure 35-34 shows an option group next to the Follow-Up Date text box. Option groups also work with toggle buttons and check boxes.

FIGURE 35-32

The Zoom dialog box.

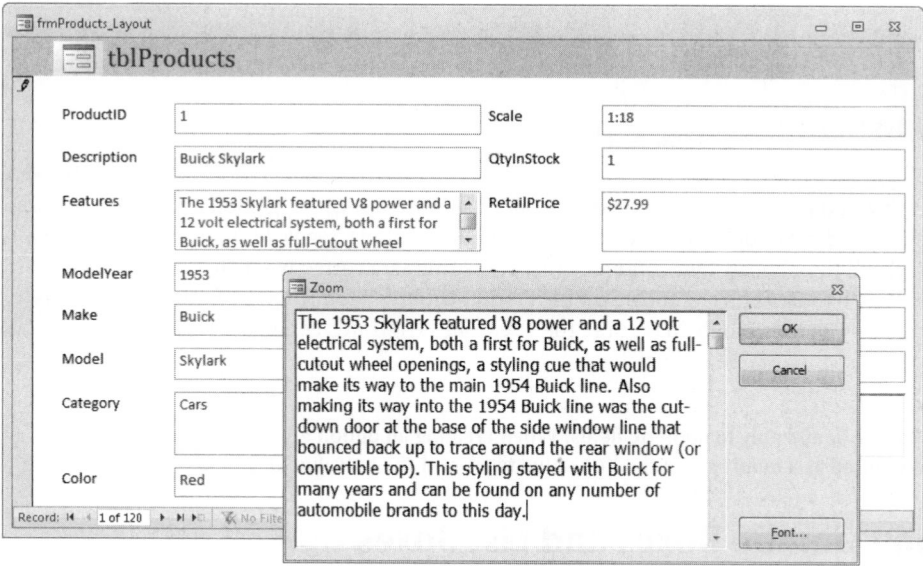

FIGURE 35-33

Using the Date Picker control.

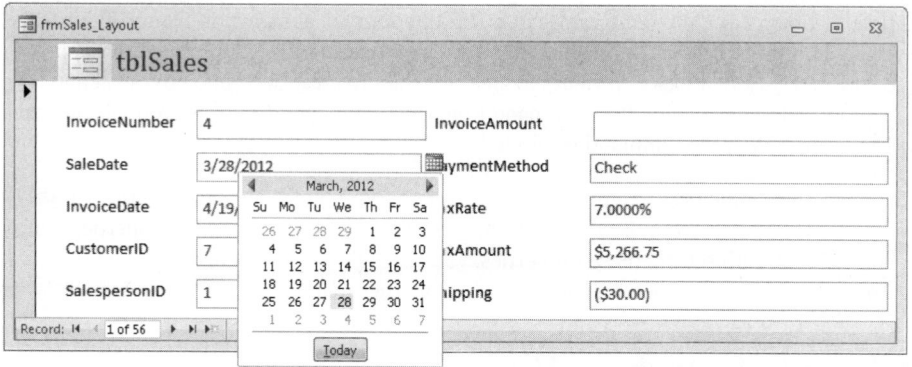

FIGURE 35-34

Using an option group to select a mutually exclusive value.

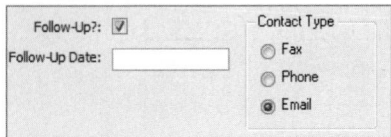

The easiest and most efficient way to create option groups is with the Option Group Wizard. You can use it to create option groups with multiple option buttons, toggle buttons, or check boxes. When you're through, all your control's property settings are correctly set. To create an option group, switch to Design view and select the Option Group button from the Form Design Tools Design tab's Controls group. Make sure the Use Control Wizards command is selected.

Tip

Option groups can be bound only to numeric fields. When creating an option group for a Yes/No field (which is actually stored as a number), set the Yes value to -1 and the No value to 0.

Using Combo Boxes and List Boxes

Access has two types of controls — list boxes and combo boxes — for showing lists of data from which a user can select. The list box is always open and ready for selection, whereas the combo box has to be clicked to open the list for selection. Also, the combo box enables you to enter a value that is not on the list and takes up less room on the form.

Because combo boxes are very efficient use of space on the surface of a form, you may want to use (for example) a combo box containing values from tblCustomers, as shown in Figure 35-35. The easiest way to do this is with the Combo Box Wizard. This Wizard walks you through the steps of creating a combo box that looks up values in another table. To create a combo box, switch to Design view and select the Combo Box command from the Design tab's Controls group. Make sure that the Use Control Wizards command is selected.

After you create the combo box, examine the Row Source Type, Row Source, Column Count, Column Heads, Column Widths, Bound Column, List Rows, and List Width properties. Once you become familiar with setting these properties, you can right-click on a text box, choose Change To ⇨ Combo Box, and set the combo box's properties manually.

Switching to Datasheet View

With a form open, switch to Datasheet view by using one of these methods:

- Click the Datasheet View command in the Home tab's Views group.
- Click the Datasheet View button in the View Shortcuts section at the bottom-right of the Access window.

- Right-click on the form's title bar — or any blank area of the form — and choose Datasheet View from the pop-up menu.

FIGURE 35-35

Using a combo box to select a value from a list.

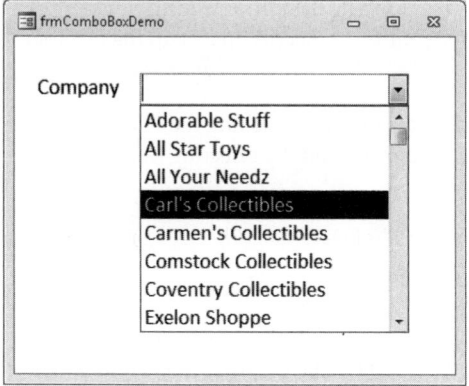

The datasheet is displayed with the cursor on the same field and record that it occupied while in the form. Moving to another record and field and then redisplaying the form in Form view causes the form to appear with the cursor on the field occupied in Datasheet view.

To return to Form view — or any other view — select the desired view from the Views group, the View Shortcuts, or the pop-up menu.

Saving a Record

Access automatically saves each record when you move off it. Pressing Shift+Enter or selecting Save from the Ribbon's Records group saves a record without moving off it. Closing the form also saves a record.

Caution

Because Access automatically saves changes as soon as you move to another record, you may inadvertently change the data in the underlying tables. And, because you can't undo changes to an Access database, there is no easy way to revert to the record's previous state. ■

Printing a Form

You can print one or more records in your form exactly as they appear onscreen. (You'll learn how to produce formatted reports in Chapter 37.) The simplest way to print is to click the File tab, click Print, and then click Quick Print in the Backstage view to send the print job to the default printer.

Printing a form is like printing anything else. Windows is a WYSIWYG ("What You See Is What You Get") environment, so what you see on the form is what you get in the printed hard copy. If you added page headers or page footers, they would be printed at the top or bottom of the page. The printout contains any formatting that you specified in the form (including lines, boxes, and shading) and converts colors to grayscale if you're using a monochrome printer.

The printout includes as many pages as necessary to print all the data. If your form is wider than a single printer page, you need multiple pages to print your form. Access breaks up the printout as necessary to fit on each page.

You can control more aspects of printing from the Backstage view by clicking the File tab, clicking on Print, and then clicking Print again. Customize your printout by selecting from several options:

- **Print Range.** Prints the entire form or only selected pages or records.
- **Copies.** Determines the number of copies to be printed.
- **Collate.** Determines whether copies are collated.

You can also click the Properties button and set options for the selected printer or select a different printer. The Setup button allows you to set margins and print headings.

Tip

Although you may have a form ready to print, you may not be sure whether that information will print on multiple pages or fit on a single page. Click the Print Preview choice in the Backstage view to display the Print Preview window. The default view is the first page to show in single-page preview. Use the Print Preview tab commands to select different views and zoom in and out. Click Print in the Print group to print the form to the printer. Click the Close Print Preview command in the Close Preview group to return to Form view. ■

Summary

In this chapter, you learned how to add different types of forms to your database using the Create Ribbon's Form group. You learned about the different types of controls and how to add them to the form. Then you learned how to move and resize these controls.

You also learned how properties are the building blocks of an object. The Property Sheet contains every attribute of the control, from where it's located on the form to what data it displays to what font it's displayed in. You learned how to display the Property Sheet and how to change a few properties, including the Name property, using naming conventions.

You also learned that you can enter database data in Form view. You learned how to navigate between fields and records and how to use controls such as options groups and combo boxes to facilitate data entry. Finally, you learned how to print a form.

Selecting Data with Queries

Q ueries are an essential part of any database application. Queries are the tools that enable you and your users to extract data from multiple tables, combine it in useful ways, and present it to the user as a datasheet, on a form, or as a printed report.

You may have heard the old cliché, "Queries convert data to information." To a certain extent, this statement is true — that's why it's a cliché. The data contained within tables is not particularly useful because, for the most part, the data in tables appears in no particular order. Also, in a properly normalized database, important information is spread out among several different tables. Queries are what draw these various data sources together and present the combined information in such a way that users can actually work with the data.

In this chapter, you'll learn how to create and enhance queries. Using the Sales (`tblSales`), Customers (`tblCustomers`), Contacts (`tblContacts`), Sales Line Items (`tblSalesLineItems`), Categories (`tblCategories`), and Products (`tblProducts`) example tables, you'll see how to create several types of queries for the CollectibleMiniCars example database.

The data returned by Access queries is often used to populate forms and reports. As you read this chapter, keep in mind that the transformations and conversions imposed on data returned by a query apply whether the data is viewed in a datasheet, in a form, or in a report. One of the underlying principles of queries is that the work performed by a query is independent of how the query's data is used. In many cases, it makes more sense to include logic such as transformations, combinations, and sorting in a query, instead of performing these actions at the form or report level.

Understanding Queries

A database's primary purpose is to store and extract information. Information can be obtained from a database immediately after the data is added, or days, weeks, or even years later. Of course, retrieving information from database tables requires knowledge of how the database is designed.

For example, consider printed reports kept in a traditional filing cabinet, arranged by date and by a sequence number that indicates when the report was produced. To find a specific report, you must know its year and sequence number. In a good filing system, you might have a cross-reference book to help you find a specific report. This book might have all reports categorized alphabetically by type of report and, perhaps, by date. Such a book can be helpful, but if you know only the report's topic and approximate date, you still have to search through all the sections of the book to find out where to get the report.

Unlike manual filing systems, databases like Microsoft Access quickly and easily retrieve information to meet virtually any criteria you specify.

This is the real power of a database — the capacity to examine the data in more ways than you can imagine. Queries, by definition, ask questions about the data stored in the database. Most queries are used to drive forms, reports, and graphical representations of the data contained in a database.

What Queries Are

Let's start with the basics. The word *query* comes from the Latin word *quaerere*, which means "to ask or inquire." Over the years, the word *query* has become synonymous with *quiz, challenge, inquire,* or *question.*

A *Microsoft Access query* is a question that you ask about the information stored in Access tables. You build queries with the Access Query tools, and then save them as new objects in the Access database. Your query can be a simple question about data in a single table, or it can be a more complex question about information stored in several tables. After you submit the question, Microsoft Access returns only the information you requested.

Using queries this way, you might ask the CollectibleMiniCars database to show you only trucks that were sold in the year 2012. To see the types of trucks sold for the year 2012, you need information from three tables: tblSales, tblSalesLineItems, and tblProducts. Figure 36-1 shows just such a query in the Access Query Designer. Although it might look complex, it's actually very simple and easy to understand.

After you create and run a query, Microsoft Access retrieves and displays the requested records as a datasheet. This set of records returned by a query is called a *recordset.* As you've seen in Chapters 1 and 2, a datasheet looks just like a spreadsheet, with rows of records and columns of data. The Datasheet view of the recordset can display many records simultaneously.

FIGURE 36-1

A typical three-table select query

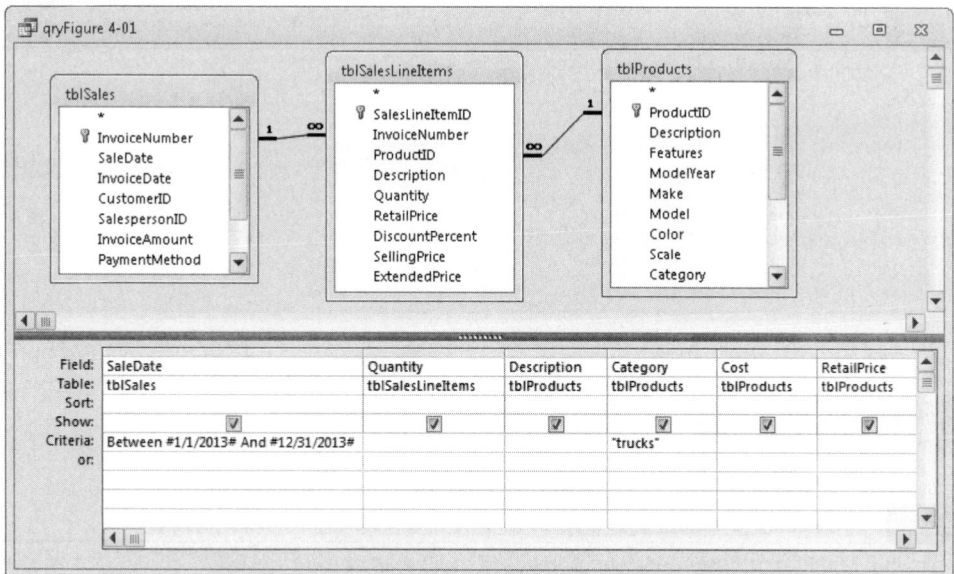

You can easily filter information from a single table using the Search and Filter capabilities of a table's Datasheet view (Filter by Selection and Filter by Form).

Cross-Reference

I discuss datasheets in detail in Chapter 34. ∎

Clicking the Datasheet View button on the Ribbon runs the query and returns the records shown in Figure 36-2. This query is relatively easy to design when you understand how to use the Access Query Designer. This simple query has many elements that demonstrate the power of the Access query engine: sorting a result set of records, specifying multiple criteria, and even using a complex Or condition in one of those fields.

You can build very complex queries using the Access Query Designer. Suppose, for example, that you want to send a notice to all previous buyers of multiple products in the past year. This type of query requires getting information from four tables: tblCustomers, tblSales, tblSalesLineItems, and tblProducts. The majority of the information you need is in tblCustomers and tblProducts.

In this case, you want Access to show you a datasheet of all customer names and addresses meeting the query's criteria ("multiple products purchased in 2012"). In this case, Access retrieves customer names and cities from tblCustomers and then obtains the number of products from the `tblProducts` table, and the year of sale from the `tblSales` table. Figure 36-3 shows this relatively complex query.

FIGURE 36-2

The results of the query shown in Figure 36-1

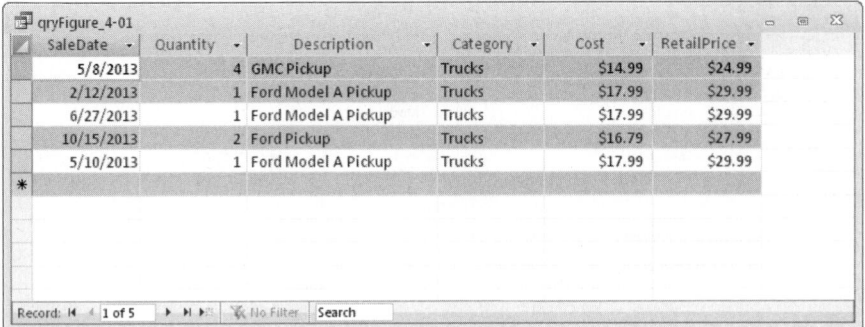

FIGURE 36-3

A more complex query returning customers who purchased more than one car in 2012

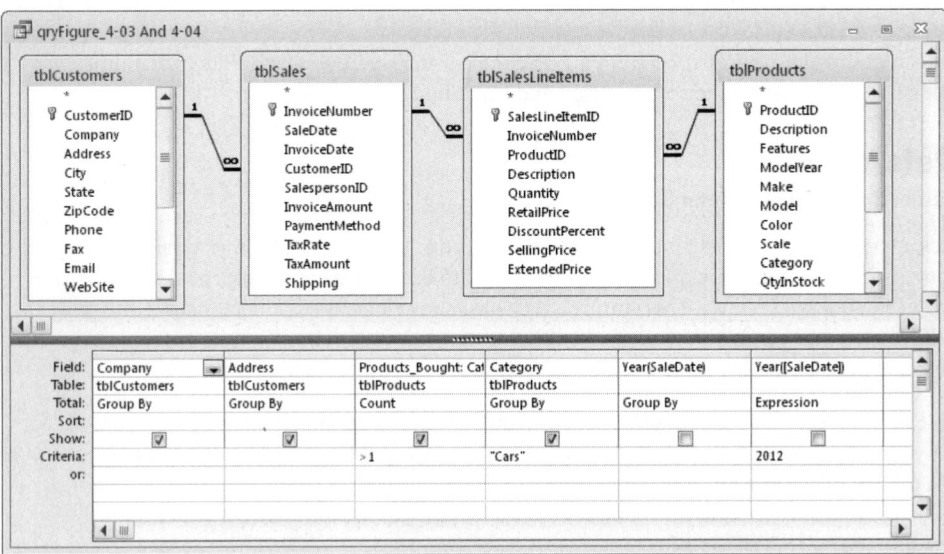

Access takes the information specified by the criteria, combines it, and displays it in a single datasheet. This datasheet is the result of a query that draws from `tblCustomers`, `tblSales`, `tblSalesLineItems`, and `tblProducts`. The database query performs the work of assembling all the information for you. Figure 36-4 shows the resulting datasheet.

FIGURE 36-4

The resulting datasheet of the query shown in Figure 36-3

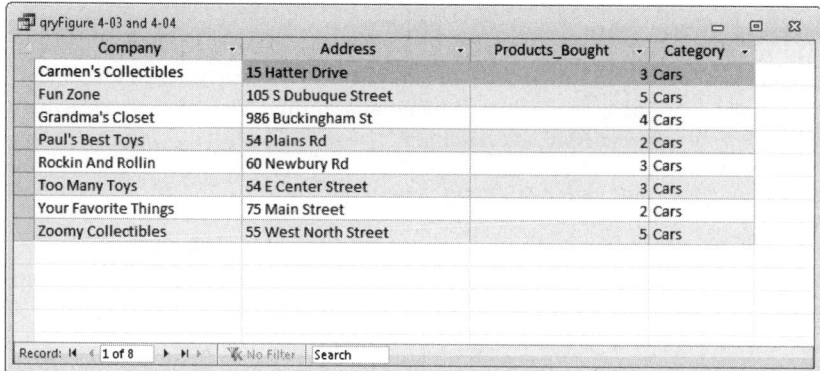

Company	Address	Products_Bought	Category
Carmen's Collectibles	15 Hatter Drive	3	Cars
Fun Zone	105 S Dubuque Street	5	Cars
Grandma's Closet	986 Buckingham St	4	Cars
Paul's Best Toys	54 Plains Rd	2	Cars
Rockin And Rollin	60 Newbury Rd	3	Cars
Too Many Toys	54 E Center Street	3	Cars
Your Favorite Things	75 Main Street	2	Cars
Zoomy Collectibles	55 West North Street	5	Cars

Record: 1 of 8 — No Filter — Search

In Figure 36-4, notice that you can't tell which table provided the data in each column. In most cases, your users won't know, nor will they care, where the data they see in an application comes from. In this case, you know that the data is taken from four different tables, but the complexity of the query is hidden from users. Access does an excellent job of connecting users to data, as this query example shows.

Types of Queries

Access supports many different types of queries, grouped into six basic categories:

- **Select.** The most common type of query is the select query. As its name implies, a *select query* selects information from one or more tables, creating a recordset. Generally speaking, the data returned by a select query is updatable and is often used to populate forms and reports.

- **Total.** A *total query* is a special type of select query. Total queries provide sums or other calculations (such as count) from the records returned by a select query. Selecting this type of query adds a Total row in the query by example (QBE) grid.

- **Action.** An *action query* (Make Table, Delete, Update, or Append) enables you to create new tables or change data in existing tables. Action queries affect many records as a single operation.

- **Crosstab.** A *crosstab query* can display summary data in cross-tabular form like a spreadsheet, with row and column headings based on fields in the table. The individual cells of the recordset are computed or calculated from data in the underlying tables.

- **Specialized Queries.** There are three specialized query types — union, pass-through, and data definition. These queries are used for advanced database manipulation, such as working with client/server SQL databases like SQL Server or Oracle. You create these queries by writing SQL statements that are specific to the server database.

- **Top(n).** *Top(n) queries* enable you to specify a number or percentage of records you want returned from any type of query (select, total, etc.).

What Queries Can Do

Queries are flexible. They allow you to look at your data in virtually any way you can imagine. Most database systems are continually evolving and changing over time. Very often, the original purpose of a database is very different from its current use.

Here is just a sampling of what you can do with Access queries:

- **Choose Tables.** You can obtain information from a single table or from many tables that are related by some common data. Suppose you're interested in seeing the customer name along with the items purchased by each type of customer. When using several tables, Access combines the data as a single recordset.

- **Choose Fields.** Specify which fields from each table you want to see in the recordset. For example, you can select the customer name, ZIP code, sales date, and invoice number from `tblCustomers` and `tblSales`.

- **Provide Criteria.** Record selection is based on selection criteria. For example, you might want to see records for only a certain category of products.

- **Sort Records.** You might want to sort records in a specific order. For example, you might need to see customer contacts sorted by last name and first name.

- **Perform Calculations.** Use queries to perform calculations such as averages, totals, or counts of data in records.

- **Create Tables.** Create a brand-new table based on data returned by a query.

- **Display Query Data on Forms and Reports.** The recordset you create from a query might have just the right fields and data needed for a report or form. Basing a form or report on a query means that, every time you print the report or open the form, you see the most current information contained in the tables.

- **Use a Query as a Source of Data for Other Queries (Subquery).** You can create queries that are based on records returned by another query. This is very useful for performing ad hoc queries, where you might repeatedly make small changes to the criteria. In this case, the second query filters the first query's results.

- **Make Changes to Data in Tables.** Action queries modify multiple rows in the underlying tables as a single operation. Action queries are frequently used to maintain data, such as archiving stale records or deleting obsolete information.

What Queries Return

Access combines a query's records and, when executed, displays them in a datasheet by default. The set of records returned by a query is commonly called (oddly enough) a *recordset*. A *recordset* is a dynamic set of records. The recordset returned by a query is not stored within the database, unless you have directed Access to build a table from those records.

When using an action query, the query's recordset is gone when the query ends. Action queries perform an action on the records specified by the query's design, but no records are returned to display on a form or report.

When you save a query, only the structure of the query is saved, not the returned records. Consider these benefits of not saving the recordset to a physical table:

- A smaller amount of space on a storage device (usually a hard disk) is needed.
- The query uses updated versions of records.

Every time the query is executed, it reads the underlying tables and re-creates the recordset. Because recordsets themselves are not stored, a query automatically reflects any changes to the underlying tables made since the last time the query was executed — even in a real-time, multi-user environment. Depending on your needs, a query's recordset can be viewed as a datasheet, or in a form or report. When a form or report is based on a query, the query's recordset is re-created and bound to the form or report each time it's opened.

Creating a Query

After you create your tables and place data in them, you're ready to work with queries. To begin a query, choose the Create tab on the Ribbon, and click on the Query Design button in the Queries group. Access opens the Query Designer in response.

Figure 36-5 shows two windows. The underlying window is the Query Designer. Floating on top of the Designer is the Show Table dialog box. The Show Table dialog box is modal, which means that you must do something in the dialog box before continuing with the query. Before you continue, you add the tables required for the query. In this case, tblProducts is highlighted and ready to be added.

The Show Table dialog box (refer to Figure 36-5) displays all tables and queries in your database. Double-click on a table such as tblProducts to add it to the query design, or highlight the table in the list and click the Add button. Close the Show Table dialog box after adding the table. Figure 36-6 shows tblProducts added to the query.

To add additional tables to the query, right-click anywhere in the upper portion of the Query Designer and select Show Table from the shortcut menu that appears. Alternatively, drag tables from the Navigation pane to the upper portion of the Query Designer. There is also a Show Table button on the Design Ribbon tab.

Removing a table from the Query Designer is easy. Just right-click on the table in the Query Designer and select Remove Table from the shortcut menu.

FIGURE 36-5

The Show Table dialog box and the Query Design window

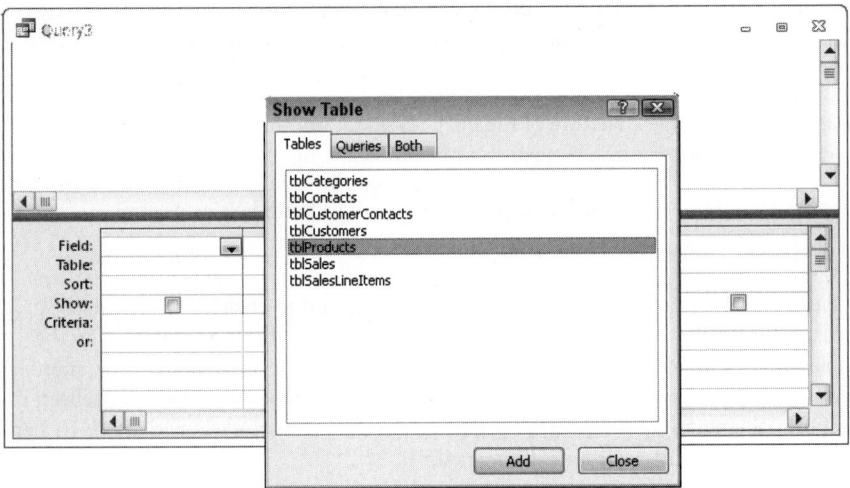

FIGURE 36-6

The Query Design window with tblProducts added

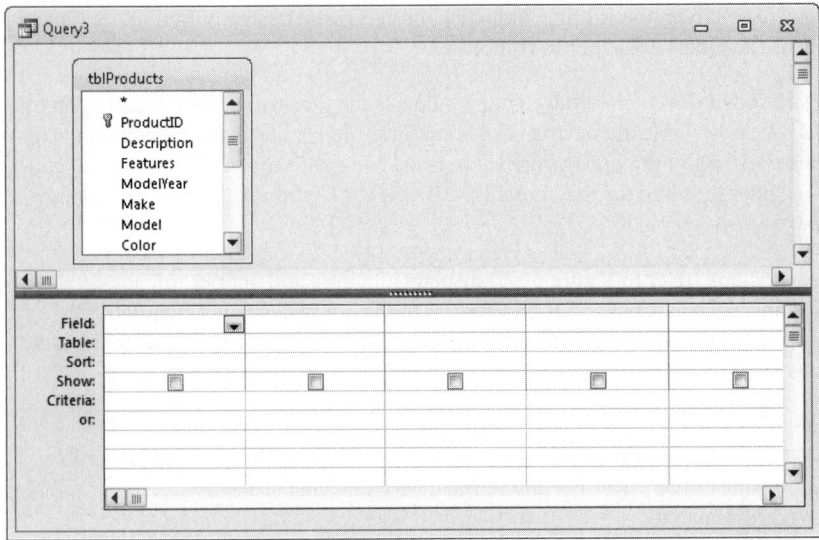

The Query window has three primary views:

- **Design View.** Design view is where you create the query.

- **Datasheet View.** Datasheet view displays the records returned by the query.
- **SQL View.** The SQL view window displays the SQL statement behind a query.

The Field List window (or, more simply, the *Field List*) contains the names of all the fields in the selected table or query. A Field List can be resized by clicking on the edges and dragging it to a different size. You may want to resize a Field List so that all of a table's fields are visible.

The Query Designer consists of two sections:

- **The Table/Query Pane (Top).** This is where tables or queries and their fields are added to the query's design.
- **The Query by Example (QBE) Design Grid (Bottom).** The QBE grid holds the field names involved in the query and any criteria used to select records. Each column in the QBE grid contains information about a single field from a table or query contained within the upper pane.

The two window panes are separated horizontally by a pane-resizing bar (refer to Figure 36-6). Use the mouse to move the bar up or down to change the relative sizes of the upper and lower panes.

Switch between the upper and lower panes by clicking the desired pane or by pressing F6 to switch panes. Each pane has horizontal and vertical scroll bars to help you move around.

You actually build the query by dragging fields from the upper pane to the QBE grid.

Figure 36-6 displays an empty QBE grid at the bottom of the Query Designer. The QBE grid has six labeled rows:

- **Field.** This is where field names are entered or added.
- **Table.** This row shows the table the field is from. This is useful in queries with multiple tables.
- **Sort.** This row enables sorting instructions for the query.
- **Show.** This row determines whether to display the field in the returned recordset.
- **Criteria.** This row consists of the criteria that filter the returned records.
- **Or.** This row is the first of a number of rows to which you can add multiple query criteria.

You learn more about these rows as you create queries in this chapter.

The Query Tools Design tab (shown in Figure 36-7) contains many different buttons specific to building and working with queries. Although each button is explained as it's used in the chapters of this book, here are the main buttons:

- **View.** Switches between the Datasheet view and Design view in the Query window. The View drop-down control also enables you to display the underlying SQL statement behind the query.

- **Run.** Runs the query. Displays a select query's datasheet, serving the same function as selecting Datasheet View from the View button. However, when working with action queries, the Run button performs the operations (append, make table, etc.) specified by the query.

- **Select.** Clicking the Select button opens a new select query in the Query Designer.

- **Make Table, Append, Update, and Crosstab.** Each of these buttons specifies the type of query you're building. In most cases, you transform a select query into an action query by clicking one of these buttons.

- **Show Table.** Opens the Show Table dialog box.

- **Save (in the Quick Access Toolbar).** Saves the query. It's a good idea to save your work often, especially when creating complex queries.

The remaining buttons are used for creating more advanced queries, printing the contents of the query, and displaying a query's Property Sheet.

FIGURE 36-7

The Query Tools Design Tab

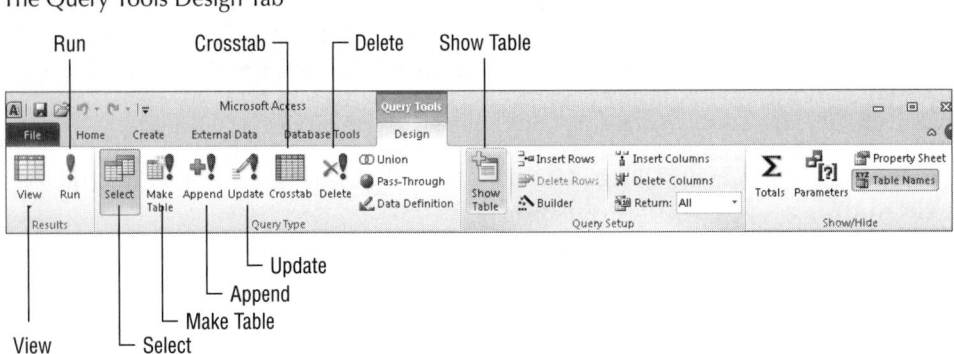

Adding Fields

There are several ways to add fields to a query. You can add fields one at a time, select and add multiple fields, or select all the fields in a Field List.

Adding a Single Field

You can add a single field in several ways. One method is to double-click the field name in the table in the top pane of the Query Designer. The field name immediately appears in the first available column in the QBE pane. Alternatively, drag a field from a table in the top pane of the Query Designer, and drop it on a column in the QBE grid. Dropping a field between two fields in the QBE grid pushes other fields to the right.

Another way to add fields to the QBE grid is to click on an empty field cell in the QBE grid, and select the field's name from the drop-down list in the cell, or type the field's name into the cell. Figure 36-8 shows selecting the Cost field from the drop-down list. Once the field is selected, simply move to the next field cell and select the next field you want to see in the query.

FIGURE 36-8

Adding fields in the QBE grid. Clicking the down-arrow in the Field box reveals a drop-down list from which you select a field.

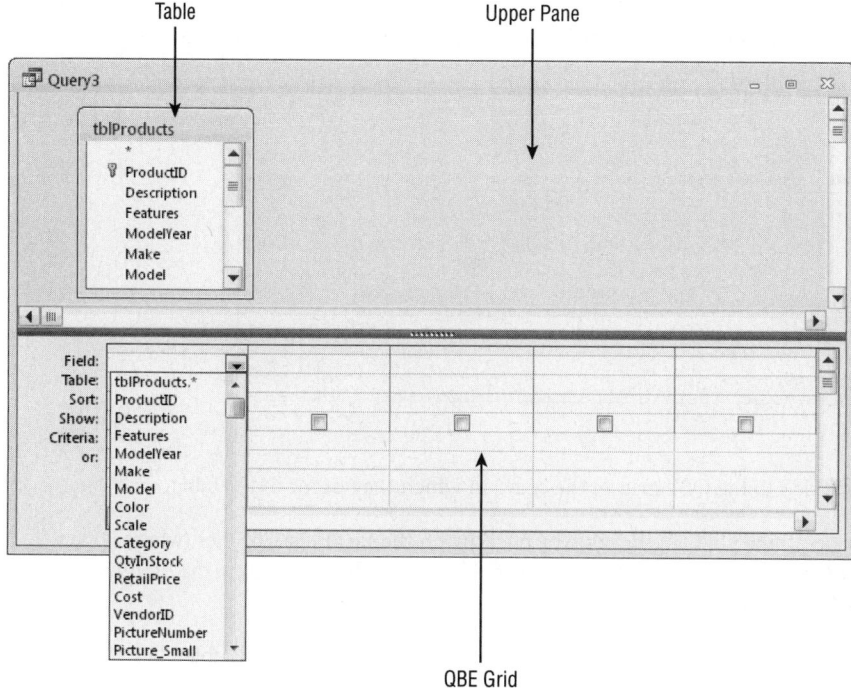

Each cell in the Table row of the QBE grid contains a drop-down list of the tables contained in the upper pane of the Query Designer.

After selecting the fields, run the query by clicking the Datasheet button or the Run button in the Results group of the Query Tools Design tab. Click the Design View button on the Home tab to return to the Query Design window.

Adding Multiple Fields

You can add multiple fields in a single action by selecting the fields from the Field List window and dragging them to the QBE grid. The selected fields don't have to be contiguous (one after the other). Hold down the Ctrl key while selecting multiple fields. Figure 36-9 illustrates the process of adding multiple fields.

FIGURE 36-9

Selecting multiple fields to add to the QBE grid

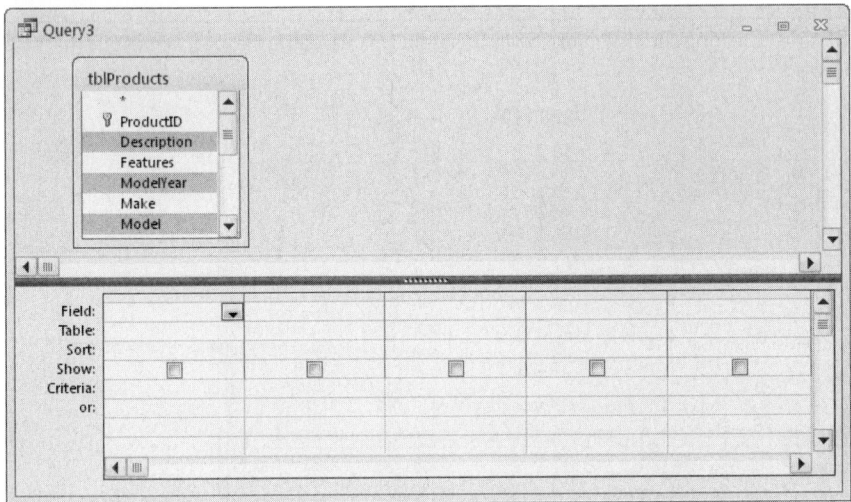

The fields are added to the QBE grid in the order in which they occur in the table.

You can also add all the fields in the table by clicking on the Field List's header (where it says *tblProducts* in Figure 36-10) to highlight all the fields in the table. Then drag the highlighted fields to the QBE grid.

Alternatively, drag the asterisk (*) from the Field List to the QBE grid (or double-click the asterisk to add it to the QBE grid). Although this action doesn't add all the fields to the QBE grid, the asterisk directs Access to include all fields in the table in the query.

Unlike selecting all the fields, the asterisk places a reference to all the fields in a single column. When you drag multiple columns, as in the preceding example, you drag names to the QBE grid. If you later change the design of the table, you also have to change the design of the query. The advantage of using the asterisk for selecting all fields is that changes to the underlying tables don't require changes to the query. The asterisk means to select all fields in the table, regardless of the field names or changes in the number of fields in the table.

The downside of using the asterisk to specify all fields in a table is that the query, as instructed, returns all the fields in a table, regardless of whether every field is used on a form or report. Retrieving unused data can be a very inefficient process. Very often, performance problems can be traced to the asterisk returning many more fields than necessary to a form or report.

FIGURE 36-10

Adding the asterisk to the QBE grid selects all fields in the table

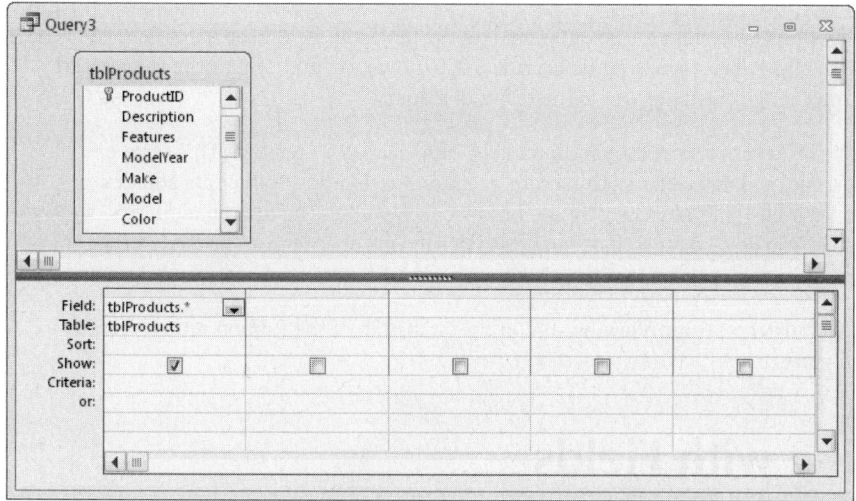

Displaying the Recordset

Click the Run button or the Datasheet button in the Results group of the Query Tools Design tab to view the query's results (see Figure 36-11).

FIGURE 36-11

The Datasheet view of the query

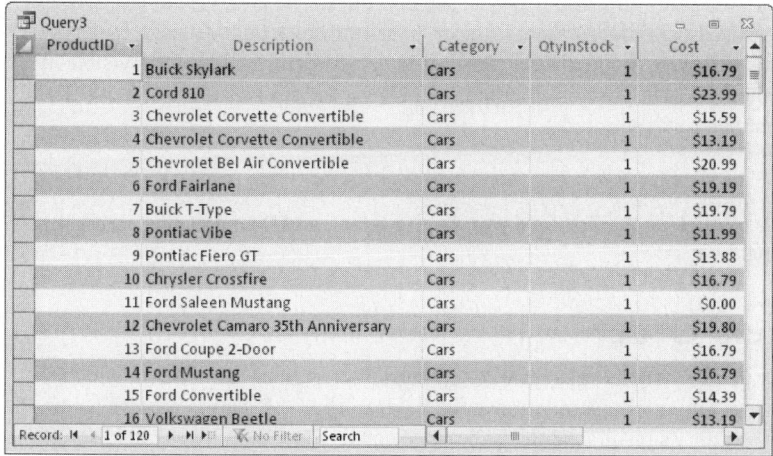

Filtering, sorting, rearranging, and searching within a datasheet is quite easy. My simple select query didn't transform the data in any way, so the data shown in Figure 36-11 is completely editable. I can modify existing data, delete rows, and even add new records to this data set, if I want.

When you're working with data in the datasheet, all the table and field properties defined at the table level are in effect. Therefore, validation rules, default values, and other properties assert themselves even though the datasheet is the result of a query.

Earlier versions of Access referred to an updatable datasheet as a *Dynaset*. This term emphasized the fact that the datasheet was dynamically linked to its underlying data sources. However, the term has fallen by the wayside because, very often, the data in a query's datasheet is not updatable. You'll see data transformations later in this chapter and in many other chapters in this book.

At any time, clicking the Design View button on the Home tab of the Ribbon returns you to Query Design view.

Working with Fields

Sometimes you'll want to work with the fields you've already selected — rearranging their order, inserting a new field, or deleting an existing field. You may even want to add a field to the QBE grid without showing it in the datasheet. Adding a field without showing it enables you to sort on the hidden field, or to use the hidden field as a criterion.

Selecting a Field in the QBE Grid

Before you can move a field's position, you must first select it. To select it, you will work with the field selector row.

The *field selector* is the thin, gray area at the top of each column in the QBE grid at the bottom of the Query Designer. Each column represents a field. To select the Category field, move the mouse pointer until a small selection arrow (in this case, a dark downward arrow) is visible in the selector row and then drag the column. Figure 36-12 shows the selection arrow above the Category column just before it's selected.

Tip
Select multiple contiguous fields by clicking the first field you want to select, and then dragging across the field selector bars of the other fields. ■

Changing Field Order

The left-to-right order in which fields appear in the QBE grid determines the order in which they appear in Datasheet view. You might want to move the fields in the QBE grid to achieve a new sequence of fields in the query's results. With the fields selected, you can move the fields on the QBE design by simply dragging them to a new position.

FIGURE 36-12

Selecting a column in the QBE grid. The pointer changes to a downward-pointing arrow when you move over the selection row.

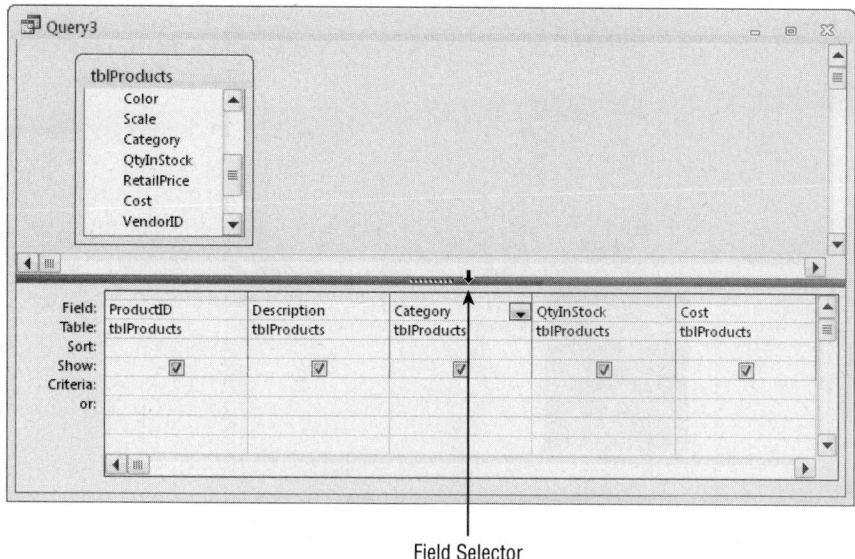

Field Selector

Left-click on a field's selector bar, and, while holding down the left mouse button, drag the field into a new position in the QBE grid.

Figure 36-13 shows the Category field highlighted. As you move the selector field to the left, the column separator between the fields ProductID and Description changes (gets wider) to show you where Category will go.

Tip
The field order in a query is irrelevant to how the data appears on a form or report. Normally, you'll arrange the controls on a form or report in response to user requirements. ■

Resizing Columns in the QBE Grid

The QBE grid generally shows five or six fields in the viewable area of your screen. The remaining fields are viewed by moving the horizontal scroll bar at the bottom of the window.

You might want to shrink some fields to be able to see more columns in the QBE grid. You adjust the column width to make them smaller (or larger) by moving the mouse pointer to the margin between two fields and dragging the column resizer left or right (see Figure 36-14).

Tip
An easier way to resize columns in the QBE grid is to double-click on the line dividing two columns in the grid. Access autosizes the column to fit the data displayed in the column. ■

Moving the Category field to between ProductID and Description. Notice the QBE field icon below the arrow near the Description column

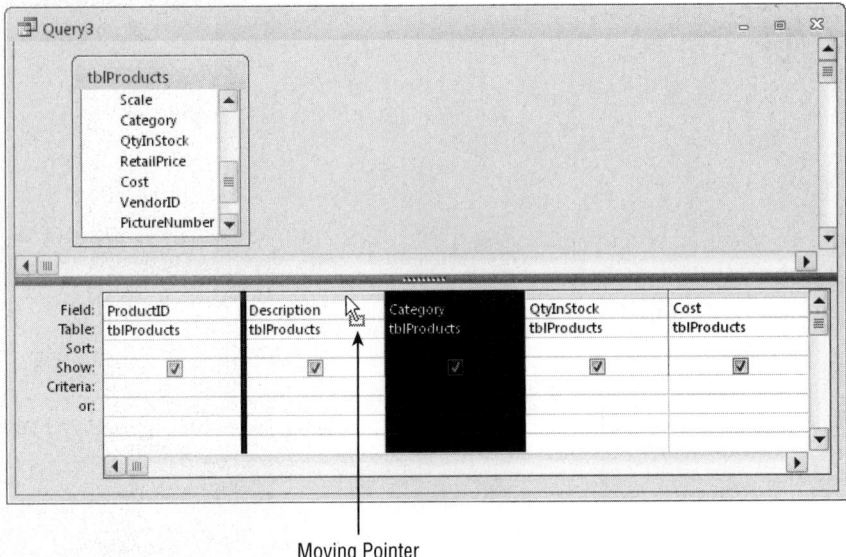

Moving Pointer

Resizing columns in the QBE grid

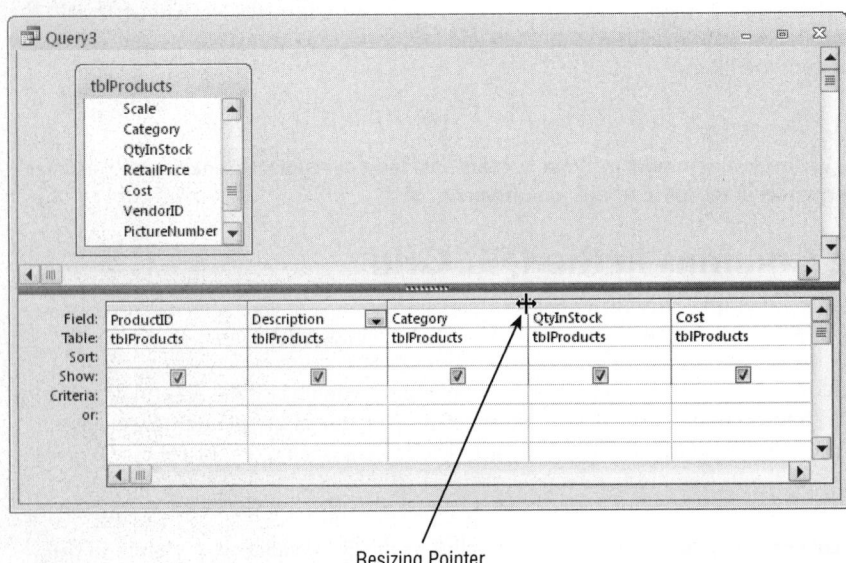

Resizing Pointer

The width of a column in the QBE grid has no effect on how the field's data is displayed in a datasheet, form, or report. The column width in the QBE grid is just a convenience to you, the developer. Also, QBE column width is not preserved when you save and close the query.

Removing a Field

Remove a field from the QBE grid by selecting the field (or fields) and pressing the Delete key. You can also right-click on a field's selector bar and choose Cut from the shortcut menu.

Inserting a Field

Insert new fields in the QBE grid by dragging a field from a Field List window in the tables pane above the QBE grid and dropping it onto a column in the QBE grid. The new column is inserted to the left of the column on which you dropped the field. Double-clicking a field in a Field List adds the new column at the far-right position in the QBE grid.

Providing an Alias for the Field Name

To make the query datasheet easier to read, you can provide aliases for the fields in your query. An alias becomes the field's heading in the query's datasheet, but it doesn't affect the field's name or how the data is stored and used by Access. Aliases are sometimes useful to help users better understand the data returned by a query. Data in queries is often transformed by performing simple operations such as combining a person's first and last name as a single field. In these situations, aliases are very useful because they provide an easily recognizable reference to the transformed data.

In this example, I create a query using the fields from the tblProducts table (refer to Figure 36-13). Follow these steps to establish an alias for the ProductID and Description fields:

1. Click to the left of the *P* of the ProductID column in the top row of the QBE grid.
2. Type ProductNumber: to the left of ProductID.
3. Click to the left of the *D* in the Description column and enter ProductDescription: to the left of the field name.

When you run the query, the aliases you created appear as the column headings. Figure 36-15 shows both the query in Design view and the query's datasheet. Notice that the ProductID and Description columns sport their new aliases instead of their respective field names.

Use aliases with caution. Because an alias masks the name of the field underlying a datasheet, it's easy to become confused about which column headings are aliases and which are field names. It is a complete waste of time looking for a field named *ProductDescription*, based on a datasheet column heading. It would be nice if Access somehow distinguished between aliases and field names in Datasheet view, but the only way to know for sure is to examine the query's design. Also, the alias is how the field is named when used in a form or report.

FIGURE 36-15

Aliases can help users understand data

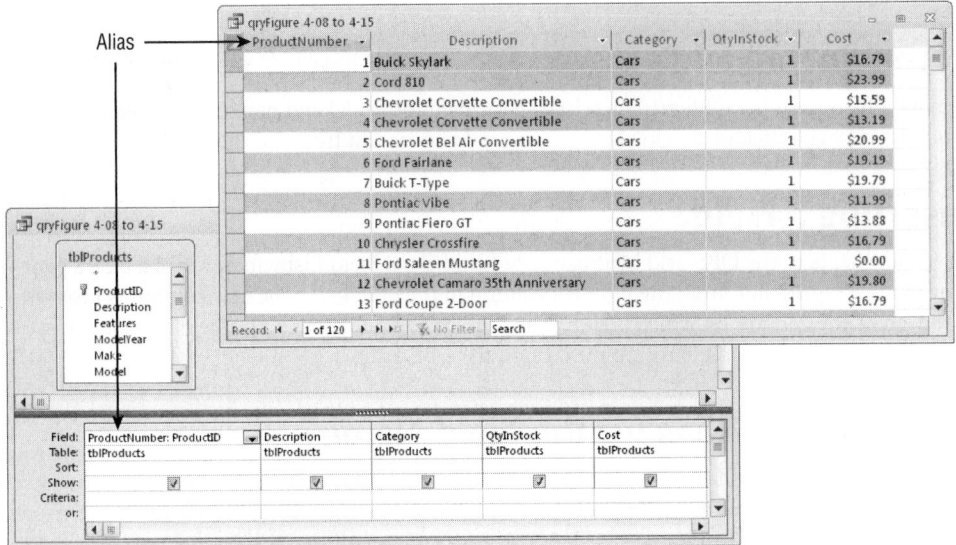

Showing a Field

While you're performing queries, you might want to show only *some* of the fields in the QBE grid. Suppose, for example, you've chosen FirstName, LastName, Address, City, and State. Then you decide that you want to temporarily look at the same data, without the State field. You could start a new query adding all the fields except State, or you could simply *turn off* the State field by unchecking the Show checkbox in the State column (see Figure 36-16).

By default, every field you add to the QBE grid has its Show checkbox selected.

In Figure 36-17 notice that the State field does not appear in the query's results. In many cases, especially with a query such as the one illustrated in Figure 36-16, you don't need to see a field that is used as the query's criterion. You already know that every record returned by the query will have *CT* in the State field, so you can save a little screen space and a tiny bit of time to run the query by removing the State field from the query results.

Access still considers the State field because it contains the query's criterion, but otherwise the field is ignored.

A common reason to hide a field in the query is because the field is used for sorting, but its value is not needed in the query. For example, consider a query involving the invoices from the CollectibleMiniCars database. For a number of reasons, the users might want to see the invoices sorted by the order date, even though the actual order date is irrelevant for this particular purpose. Simply include the OrderDate field in the QBE grid, set the sort order for the OrderDate field, and uncheck its Show box. Access sorts the data by the OrderDate field even though the field is not shown in the query's results.

Caution

If you save a query that has an unused field (its Show box is unchecked and no criterion or sort order is applied to the field), Access eliminates the field from the query as part of the query-optimization process. The next time you open the query, the field won't be included in the query's design. ■

FIGURE 36-16

The Show checkbox is unchecked for the State field

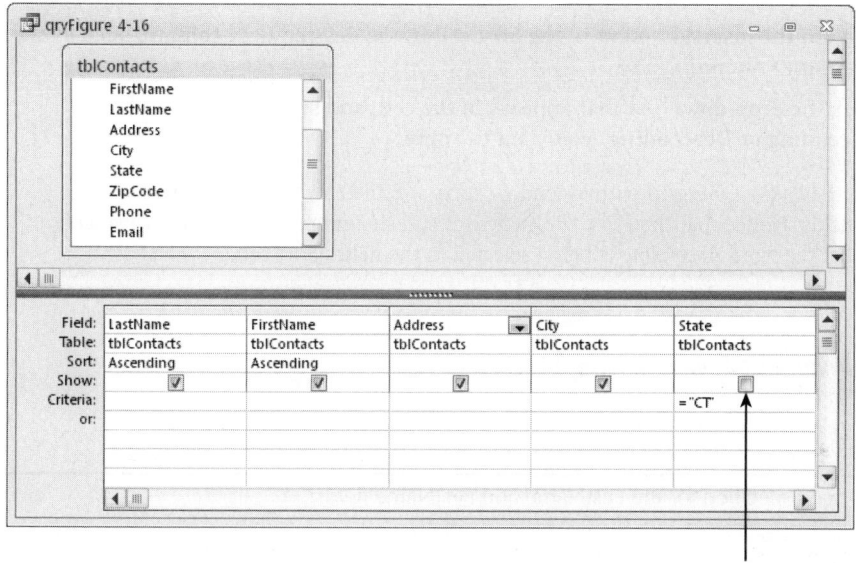

Unchecked Show Box

FIGURE 36-17

The unchecked field does not appear in the query's results

Changing the Sort Order

When viewing a recordset, you often want to display the data in a sorted order. You might want to sort the recordset to make it easier to analyze the data (e.g., to look at all the tblProducts sorted by category).

Sorting places the records in alphabetical or numerical order. The sort order can be ascending (0 to 9 and A to Z) or descending (9 to 0 and Z to A). You can sort on a single field or multiple fields.

You input sorting directions in the Sort row in the QBE grid. To specify a sort order on a particular field (such as LastName), perform these steps:

1. **Position the insertion point in the Sort cell in the desired field column, such as the LastName column.**

2. **Click the drop-down list that appears in the cell, and select the sort order (Ascending or Descending) you want to apply.**

Figure 36-18 shows the QBE grid with ascending sorts specified for the LastName and FirstName fields. Notice that the FirstName field is still showing the sort options available. Also notice that the word *Ascending* is being selected in the field's Sort cell.

Note
You can't sort on a Memo or an OLE object field. ∎

FIGURE 36-18

An ascending sort has been specified for the LastName and FirstName fields.

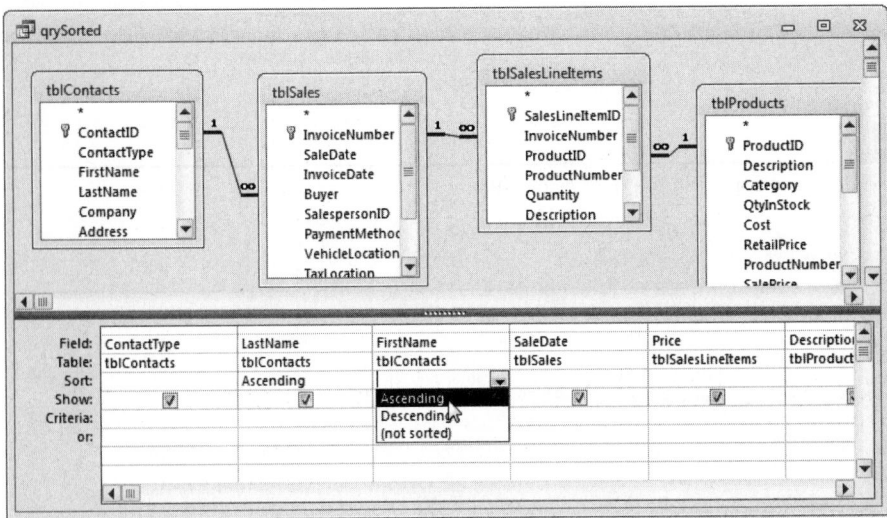

The left-to-right order in which fields appear in the QBE grid is important when sorting on more than one field. Not only do the fields appear in the datasheet in left-to-right order, but they're sorted in the same order; this is known as *sort order precedence*. The leftmost field containing sort criteria is sorted first, the first field to the right containing sort criteria is sorted next, and so on. In the example shown in Figure 36-18, the LastName field is sorted first, and then the FirstName field.

Figure 36-19 shows the results of the query shown in Figure 36-18. Notice that the data is sorted by LastName, and then by FirstName. This is why *Ann Bond* appears before *John Bond*, and *Cindy Casey* appears before *Debbie Casey* in the query's data.

FIGURE 36-19

The order of the fields in the QBE grid is critical when sorting on multiple fields.

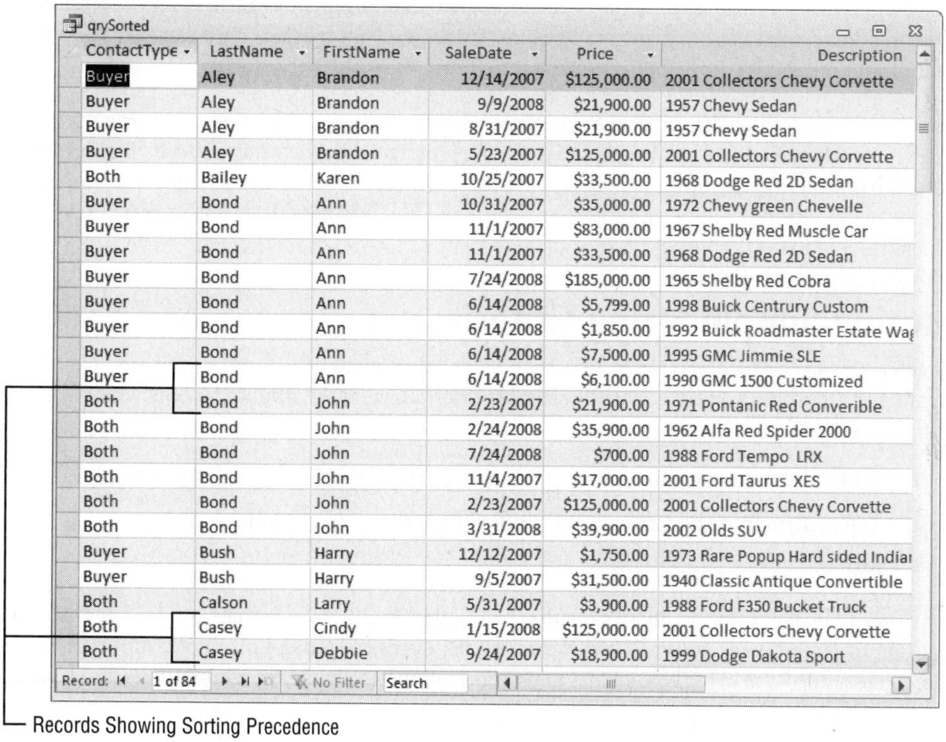

Records Showing Sorting Precedence

Displaying Only Selected Records

So far, most of the queries described in this chapter return all the records in the example tblCustomers and tblProducts tables. Most often users want to work only with records conforming to some criteria. Otherwise, too many records may be returned by a query, causing serious performance issues. For example, you might want to look only at customers who have not bought any products within the last six months. Access makes it easy for you to specify a query's criteria.

Understanding Selection Criteria

Selection criteria are filtering rules applied to data as it's extracted from the database. Selection criteria instruct Access which records to display from the recordset. A typical criterion might be "all sellers," or "only those vehicles that are not trucks," or "products with retail prices greater than $75."

Selection criteria limit the records returned by a query. Selection criteria aid the user by selecting only the records a user wants to see, and ignoring all the others.

You specify criteria in the Criteria row of the QBE grid. You designate criteria as an expression. The expression can be as a simple example (like "trucks" or "not trucks"), or it can take the form of complex expressions using built-in Access functions.

Proper use of query criteria is critical to an Access database's success. In most cases, the users have no idea what data is stored in a database's tables and accept whatever they see on a form or report as truthfully representing the database's status. Poorly chosen criteria might hide important information from the application's users, leading to bad business decisions or serious business issues later on.

Entering Simple String Criteria

Character-type criteria are applied to Text-type fields. Most often, you'll enter an example of the text you want to retrieve. Here is a small example that returns only product records where the product type is "Cars":

1. Add tblProducts and choose the Description, Category, and Cost fields.

2. Type CARS into the Criteria cell under the Category column.

3. Run the query.

Only cars are displayed in the query's results (see Figure 36-20). Notice that you did not enter an equal sign or place quotes around the sample text, yet Access added double quotes around the value. Access, unlike many other database systems, automatically makes assumptions about what you want.

Figure 36-20 shows both the query design and the datasheet resulting from the query. This figure also illustrates one reason you might want to hide a column in a query. There's no point in displaying *Cars* in every row in the third column. In fact, because this query only returns information about cars, the user can very well assume that every record references a car, and there's no need to display a product category in the query. Unchecking the Category field's Show box in the query's design removes Category from the datasheet, making the data easier to understand.

FIGURE 36-20

Specifying "Cars" as the query's criterion

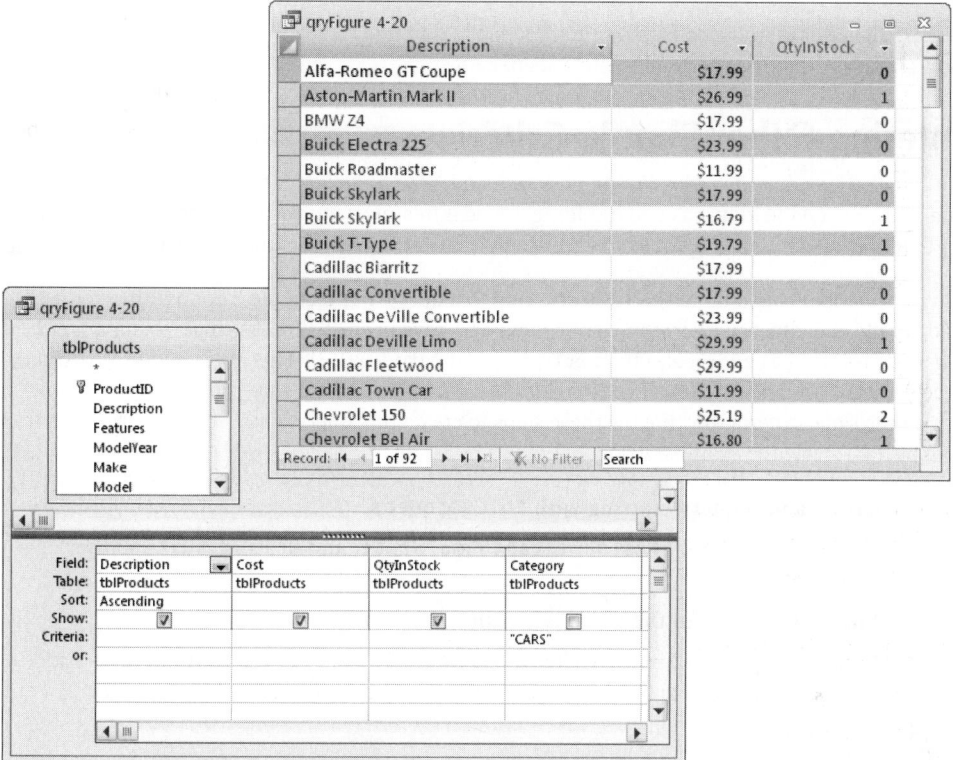

You could enter the criteria expression in any of these other ways:

CARS   =   CARS   "CARS"   =   "Cars"

By default, Access is *not* case-sensitive, so any form of the word *cars* works just as well as this query's criterion.

Figure 36-20 is an excellent example for demonstrating the options for various types of simple character criteria. You could just as well enter **Not Cars** in the Criteria column, to return all products that are not cars (trucks, vans, etc.).

Generally, when dealing with character data, you enter equalities, inequalities, or a list of acceptable values.

This capability is a powerful tool. Consider that you have only to supply an example, and Access not only interprets it but also uses it to create the query recordset. This is exactly what *query by example* means: You enter an example and let the database build a query based on the example.

To erase the criteria in the cell, select the contents and press Delete, or select the contents and right-click Cut from the shortcut menu that appears.

Entering Other Simple Criteria

You can also specify criteria for Numeric, Date, and Yes/No fields. Simply enter the example data in the criteria field just as you did for text fields. In almost every case, Access understands the criteria you enter and adjusts to correctly apply the criteria to the query's fields.

It is also possible to add more than one criterion to a query. For example, suppose that you want to look only at contacts who live in Connecticut and have been customers since January 1, 2012 (where OrigCustDate is greater than or equal to January 1, 2012). This query requires criteria in both the State and OrigCustDate fields. To do this, it's critical that you place both examples on the same criteria row. Follow these steps to create this query, with tblCustomers as the example table with the example fields:

1. **Create a new query starting with tblCustomers.**
2. **Add ContactType, FirstName, LastName, State, and OrigCustDate to the QBE grid.**
3. **Enter "ct" or "CT" in the Criteria cell in the State column.**
4. **Enter >= 01/01/2012 in the Criteria cell in the OrigCustDate column.** Access adds pound sign characters (#) around the date in the Criteria box.
5. **Run the query.**

Figure 36-21 shows how the query should look.

Access displays records of customers who live in Connecticut and who became customers after January 1, 2012.

Access uses comparison operators to compare Date fields to a value. These operators include less than (<), greater than (>), equal to (=), or a combination of these operators.

Notice that Access automatically adds pound sign (#) delimiters around the date value. Access uses these delimiters to distinguish between date and text data. The pound signs are just like the quote marks Access added to the "Cars" criteria. Because OrigCustDate is a DateTime field, Access understands what you want and inserts the proper delimiters for you.

Be aware that Access interprets dates according to the Regional and Language Options (Windows XP) or the Region and Language settings (Windows 7) in the Windows Control Panel. For example, in most of Europe and Asia, *#5/6/2012#* is interpreted as "June 5, 2012," whereas in the United States, this date is "May 6, 2012." It is very easy to construct a query that works perfectly but returns the wrong data because of subtle differences in regional settings.

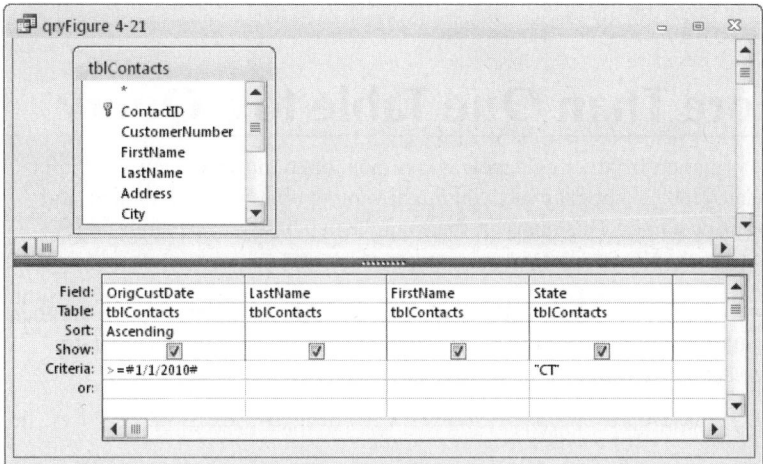

FIGURE 36-21

Specifying text and date criteria in the same query

Printing a Query's Recordset

After you create your query, you can easily print all the records in the recordset. Although you can't specify a type of report, you can print a simple matrix-type report (rows and columns) of the recordset created by your query.

You do have some flexibility when printing a recordset. If you know that the datasheet is set up just as you want, you can specify some options as you follow these steps:

1. **If you aren't in the Datasheet view, run the query by clicking the Run button in the Results group on the Ribbon.**

2. **Choose File ⇨ Print from the Query Datasheet window's Ribbon.**

3. **Specify the print options that you want in the Print dialog box and click OK.**

The printout reflects all layout options in effect when you print the data set. Hidden columns don't print, and gridlines print only if the Gridlines option is on. The printout reflects the specified row height and column width.

Saving a Query

To save your query, click the Save button in the Quick Access Toolbar at the top of the Access screen. Access asks you for the name of the query if this is the first time the query has been saved.

After saving the query, Access returns you to the mode you were working in. Occasionally, you'll want to save and exit the query in a single operation. To do this, click the "Close Window" button in the upper-right corner of the Query Designer. Access always asks you to confirm saving the changes before it actually saves the query.

Adding More Than One Table to a Query

Using a query to get information from a single table is common; often, however, you need information from several related tables. For example, you might want to obtain a buyer's name and product purchased by the customer. This query in the example database requires four tables: tblCustomers, tblSales, tblSalesLineItems, and tblProducts.

After you create the tables for your database and decide how the tables are related to one another, you're ready to build multiple-table queries to obtain information from several related tables. A multi-table query presents data as if it existed in one large table.

The first step in creating a multi-table query is to add the tables to the Query window:

1. **Create a new query by clicking the "Query Design" button in the Create Ribbon tab.**
2. **Add the tables (tblCustomers, tblSales, tblSalesLineItems, and tblProducts, for example) by double-clicking each table's name in the Show Table dialog box.**
3. **Click the Close button in the Show Table dialog box.**

Note
You can also add each table by highlighting the table in the list separately and clicking Add. ∎

Figure 36-22 shows the top pane of the Query Design window with the four example tables added. Because the relationships were set at table level, the join lines are automatically added to the query.

Note
You can add more tables, at any time, by choosing Query Setup ⇨ Show Table from the Query Tools Design tab. ∎

FIGURE 36-22

The Query Design window with four tables added. Notice that the join lines are already present.

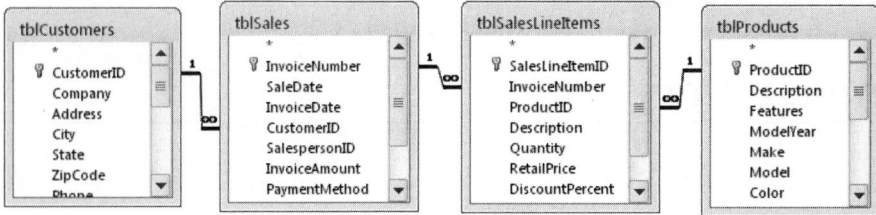

You add fields from more than one table to the query in exactly the same way as you do when you're working with a single table. You can add fields one at a time, multiple fields as a group, or all the fields from a table.

Caution

If you type a field name in an empty field cell that has the same name in more than one table, Access enters the field name from the first table that it finds containing the field name. ∎

Selecting a field from the drop-down list in the field cell first adds the table's name, followed by a period and the field name. For example, the `ProductID` in `tblSalesLineItems` is displayed as `tblSalesLineItems.ProductID`. This helps you select the correct field name. Using this method, you can select a common field name from a specific table.

Tip

The easiest way to select fields is still to double-click the field names in the top half of the Query Designer. To do so, you might have to resize the Field List windows to see the fields that you want to select. ∎

Working with the Table Pane

The upper (table) pane of the Query Designer contains information that is important to your query. Understanding the Table pane and how to work with Field Lists is critically important to building complex queries.

Looking at the Join Line

A *join line* connects tables in the Query Designer (refer to Figure 36-22). The join line connects the primary key in one table to the foreign key in another table. The join line represents the relationship between two tables in the Access database. In this example, a join line goes from `tblSales` to `tblCustomers`, connecting `ContactID` in the `tblCustomers` table to the `Buyer` field in `tblSales`. The join line is added by Access because relationships were set in the Relationship Builder.

If referential integrity is set on the relationship, Access uses a somewhat thicker line for the join connecting to the table in the Query Designer. A one-to-many relationship is indicated by an infinity symbol (∞) on the many-side table end of the join line.

Access auto-joins two tables if the following conditions are met:

- Both tables have fields with the same name.
- The same-named fields are the same data type (text, numeric, etc.).
- One of the fields is a primary key in its table.

Manipulating Field Lists

Each Field List begins at a fixed size, which shows a number of fields and several leading characters of each field name. Each Field List window is resizable and can be moved within the Query Designer. If there are more fields than will show in the Field List window, a scroll bar enables you to scroll through the fields.

Note
After a relationship is created between tables, the join line remains between the two fields. As you move through a table selecting fields, the line moves relative to the linked fields. For example, if you scroll downward, toward the bottom of the window in tblCustomers**, the join line moves upward with the customer number, eventually stopping at the top of the Table window. ■**

When you're working with many tables, these join lines can become confusing as they cross or overlap. As you scroll through the table, the line eventually becomes visible, and the field it is linked to becomes obvious.

Moving a Table

Move the Field Lists by grabbing the title bar of a Field List window (where the name of the table is) with the mouse and dragging the Field List window to a new location. You may want to move the Field Lists for a better working view or to clean up a confusing query diagram.

You can move and resize the Field Lists anywhere in the top pane. Access saves the arrangement when you save and close the query. Generally speaking, the Field Lists will appear in the same configuration the next time you open the query.

Removing a Table

You might need to remove tables from a query. Use the mouse to select the table you want to remove in the top pane of the Query window and press the Delete key. Or right-click on the Field List window and choose Remove Table from the shortcut menu.

Removing a table from a query's design does not remove the table from the database, of course.

Caution
When you remove a table from a query design, join lines to that table are deleted as well. There is no warning or confirmation before removal. The table is simply removed from the screen, along with any of the table's fields added to the QBE grid. Be aware, however, that deleted tables referenced in calculated fields will not be removed. The *phantom* **table references may cause errors when you try to run the query. ■**

Adding More Tables

You might decide to add more tables to a query or you might accidentally delete a table and need to add it back. You accomplish this task by clicking on the Show Table button on the Query Setup group in the Query Tools Design tab of the Ribbon. The Show Table dialog box appears in response to this action.

Viewing Table Names

When you're working with multiple tables in a query, the field names in the QBE grid can become confusing. You might find yourself asking, for example, just which table the Description field is from.

Access automatically maintains the table name that is associated with each field displayed in the QBE grid. Figure 36-23 shows the Query Designer with the name of each table displayed under the field name in the QBE grid.

FIGURE 36-23

The QBE grid with table names displayed. Notice that it shows all four table names.

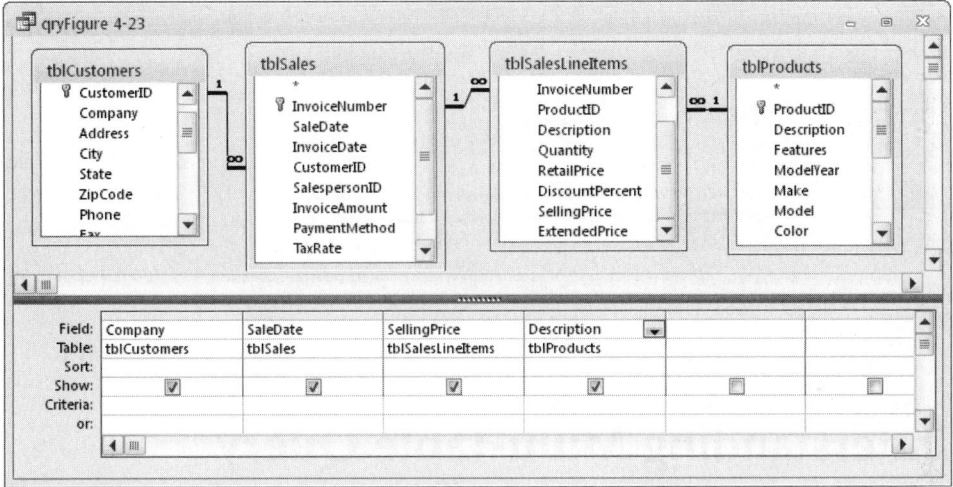

After you add fields to a query, you can run the query. Figure 36-24 shows the data returned by the query in Figure 36-23.

Adding Multiple Fields

The process of adding multiple fields in a multi-table query is identical to adding multiple fields in a single-table query. When you're adding fields from several tables, you must add them from one table at a time. The easiest way to do this is to select multiple fields and drag them together down to the QBE grid.

Select multiple contiguous fields by clicking on the first field of the list and then clicking on the last field while holding down the Shift key. You can also select noncontiguous fields in the list by holding down the Ctrl key while clicking on individual fields.

Caution

Selecting the asterisk (*) does have one drawback: You can't specify criteria on the asterisk column itself. You have to add an individual field from the table and enter the criterion. If you add a field for a criterion (when using the asterisk), the query displays the field twice — once for the asterisk field and a second time for the criterion field. Therefore, you might want to deselect the Show cell of the criterion field. ■

The Datasheet view of data from multiple tables

Understanding Multi-Table Query Limitations

When you create a query with multiple tables, there are limits to which fields can be edited. Generally, you can change data in a query's recordset, and your changes are saved in the underlying tables. The main exception is a table's primary key — a primary key value can't be edited if referential integrity is in effect and if the field is part of a relationship.

To update a table from a query, a value in a specific record in the query must represent a single record in the underlying table. This means that you can't update a field that transforms data, such as combining first and last names. Each field in a transformed recordset usually represents multiple fields in the underlying tables. There is no way to change the data in a transformed field and have it reflected in the underlying tables.

In Access, the records in your tables might not always be updateable. Table 36-1 shows when a field in a table is updateable. As Table 36-1 shows, queries based on one-to-many relationships are updateable in both tables (depending on how the query was designed).

TABLE 36-1

Rules for Updating Queries

Type of Query or Field	Updateable	Comments
One table	Yes	
One-to-one relationship	Yes	
Results contain Memo field.	Yes	Memo field updateable
Results contain a hyperlink.	Yes	Hyperlink updateable
Results contain an OLE object.	Yes	OLE object updateable
One-to-many relationship	Usually	Restrictions based on design methodology (see text)
Many-to-one-to-many relationship	No	Can update data in a form or data access page if Record Type = Recordset.
Two or more tables with no join line	No	Must have a join to determine updateability
Crosstab	No	Creates a snapshot of the data.
Totals query (Sum, Avg, etc.)	No	Works with grouped data creating a snapshot.
Unique Value property is Yes	No	Shows unique records only in a snapshot.
SQL-specific queries	No	Union and pass-through work with ODBC data.
Calculated field	No	Will recalculate automatically.
Read-only fields	No	If opened read-only or on read-only drive (CD-ROM)
Permissions denied	No	Insert, replace, or delete are not granted.
ODBC tables with no unique identifier	No	A unique identifier must exist.
Paradox table with no primary key	No	A primary key file must exist.
Locked by another user	No	Can't be updated while a field is locked by another

Overcoming Query Limitations

Table 36-1 shows that there are times when queries and fields in tables are not updateable. As a general rule, any query that performs aggregate operations or uses an Open DataBase Connectivity (ODBC) data source is not updateable; most other queries can be updated. When your query has more than one table and some of the tables have a one-to-many relationship, some fields might not be updateable (depending on the design of the query).

Updating a Unique Index (Primary Key)

If a query uses two tables involved in a one-to-many relationship, the query must include the primary key from the one-side table. Access must have the primary key value so that it can find the related records in the two tables.

Replacing Existing Data in a Query with a One-to-Many Relationship

Normally, all the fields in the many-side table (such as the `tblSales` table) are updateable in a one-to-many query. All the fields (except the primary key) in the one-side table (`tblCustomers`) can be updated. Normally, this is sufficient for most database application purposes. Also, the primary key field is rarely changed in the one-side table because it is the link to the records in the joined tables.

Updating Fields in Queries

If you want to add records to both tables of a one-to-many relationship, include the foreign key from the many-side table and show the field in the datasheet. After doing this, records can be added starting with either the one-side or the many-side table. The one-side table's primary key field is automatically copied to the many-side table's join field.

If you want to add records to multiple tables in a form (forms were covered in Chapter 35), remember to include all (or most) of the fields from both tables. Otherwise, you won't have a complete set of the record's data on your form.

Summary

This chapter has taken on the major topic of building select queries. Without a doubt, query creation is a daunting task, and one that takes a lot of practice. Even simple queries can return unexpected results, depending on the characteristics of the join between tables and the criteria used to filter data in the underlying tables.

Queries are an integral and important part of any Access database application. Queries drive forms, reports, and many other aspects of Access applications.

Users always assume that the data they see in a form or report is correct. Most often, data in a form or report is provided by a query. As you read in this chapter, it's quite easy to produce a query that returns only part of the data expected by users, or transforms data in unpredictable ways. You should always carefully test your queries and verify that they're working as expected.

Your best bet for mastering Access queries is to try increasingly difficult queries and to always check your work. In the case of improperly joined tables, Access queries almost always under-report the data in the tables. You'll discover the missing records only by carefully examining the data to ensure that your query is working properly.

Presenting Data with Access Reports

I t's hard to underestimate the importance of reports in database applications. Many people who never work with an Access application in person use reports created by Access. A lot of maintenance work on database projects involves creating new and enhancing existing reports. Access is well known and respected for its powerful reporting features.

Reports provide the most flexible way of viewing and printing summarized information. They display information with the desired level of detail, while enabling you to view or print your information in many different formats. You can add multilevel totals, statistical comparisons, and pictures and graphics to a report.

In this chapter, you learn to use the Report Wizard as a starting point. You also learn how to create reports and what types of reports you can create with Access.

Introducing Reports

Reports present a customized view of your data. Report output is viewed onscreen or printed to provide a hard copy of the data. Very often reports provide summaries of the information contained in the database. Data can be grouped and sorted in any order and can be used to create totals that perform statistical operations on data. Reports can include pictures and other graphics as well as memo fields in a report. If you can think of a report you want, Access probably supports it.

Identifying the Different Types of Reports

A few basic types of reports are used by most businesses:

- **Tabular Reports.** These reports print data in rows and columns with groupings and totals. Variations include summary and group/total reports.

- **Columnar Reports.** These reports print data and can include totals and graphs.

- **Mailing-Label Reports.** These reports create multicolumn labels or snaked-column reports.

Tabular Reports

Tabular reports are similar to tables displaying data in rows and columns. Figure 37-1 is a typical tabular report (rptProductsSummary) displayed in Print Preview.

FIGURE 37-1

A tabular report (rptProductsSummary) displayed in Print Preview

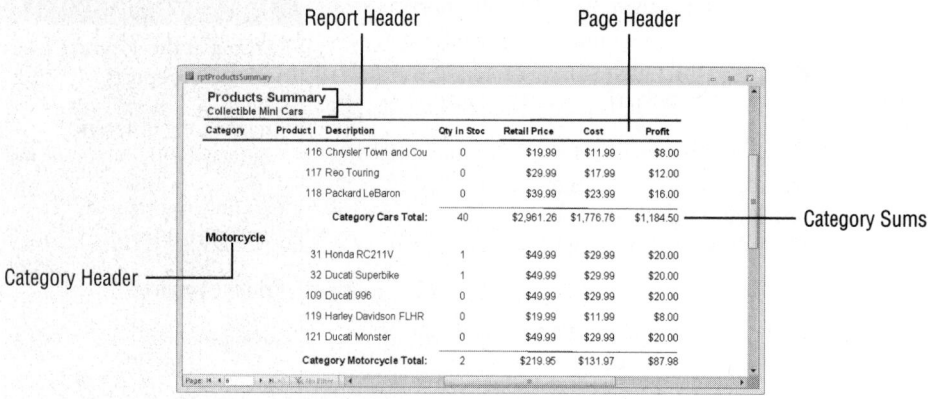

Unlike forms or datasheets, tabular reports often group data by one or more fields. Often, tabular reports calculate and display subtotals or statistical information for numeric fields in each group. Some reports include page totals and grand totals. You can even have multiple snaked columns so that you can create directories (such as telephone books). These types of reports often use page numbers, report dates, or lines and boxes to separate information. Reports may have color and shading and display pictures, business graphs, and memo fields. A special type of summary tabular report can have all the features of a detail tabular report but omit record details.

Columnar Reports

Columnar reports generally display one or more records per page, but they do so vertically. Columnar reports display data very much as a data-entry form does, but they're used strictly for viewing data and not for entering data. Figure 37-2 shows part of a columnar report (named Products) in Print Preview.

FIGURE 37-2

A columnar report showing report controls distributed throughout the entire page

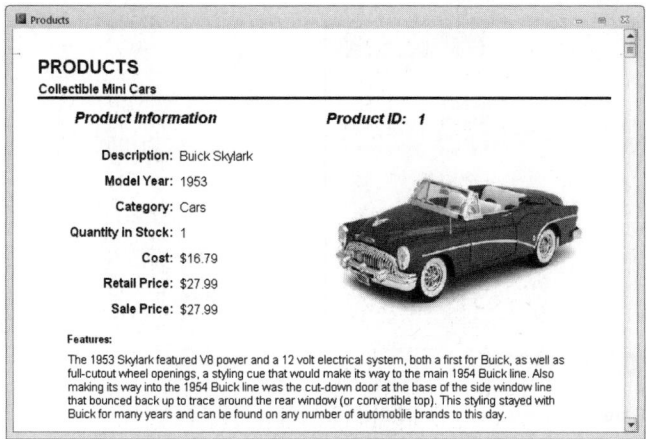

Another type of columnar report displays one main record per page (like a business form) but can show many records within embedded subforms. An invoice is a typical example. This type of report can have sections that display only one record and at the same time have sections that display multiple records from the many side of a one-to-many relationship — and even include totals.

Figure 37-3 shows an invoice report (rptInvoice) from the CollectibleMiniCars database system in Report view.

In Figure 37-3, the information in the top portion of the report is on the *main* part of the report, whereas the product details near the bottom of the figure are contained in a subreport embedded within the main report.

Mailing-Label Reports

Mailing labels (shown in Figure 37-4) are also a type of report. Access includes a Label Wizard to help you create this type of report. The Label Wizard enables you to select from a long list of label styles. Access accurately creates a report design based on the label style you select. You can then open the report in Design mode and customize it as needed.

Distinguishing between Reports and Forms

The main difference between reports and forms is the intended output. Whereas forms are primarily for data entry and interaction with the users, reports are for viewing data (either onscreen or in hard-copy form). Calculated fields can be used with forms to display an amount based on other fields in the record. With reports, you typically perform calculations on groups of records, a page of records, or all the records included in the report. Anything you can do with a form — except input data — can be duplicated by a report. In fact, you can save a form as a report and then refine it in the Report Design window.

FIGURE 37-3

An invoice report (rptInvoice)

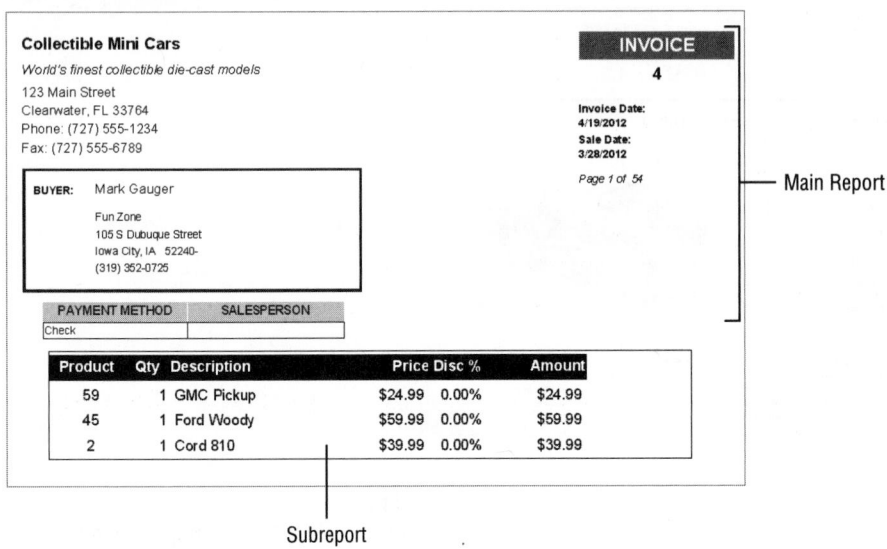

Main Report

Subreport

FIGURE 37-4

rptCustomerMailingLabels, a typical mailing-label report

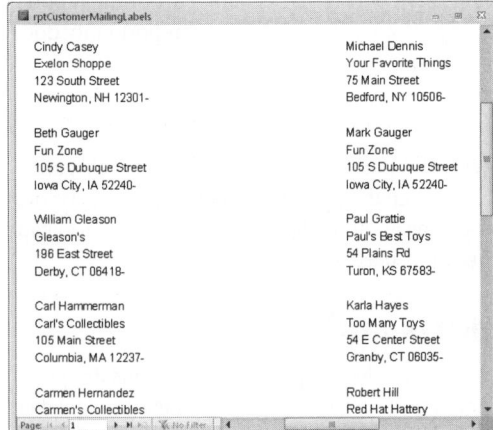

Creating a Report, from Beginning to End

The report process begins with your desire to view data, but in a way that differs from a form or datasheet display. The purpose of the report is to transform raw data into a meaningful set of information. The process of creating a report involves several steps:

1. Defining the report layout

2. Assembling the data

3. Creating the report with the Report Wizard

4. Printing the report

5. Saving the report

Defining the Report Layout

You should begin by having a general idea of the layout of your report. You can define the layout in your mind, on paper, or interactively using the Report Designer.

Tip
Very often, an Access report is expected to duplicate an existing paper report or form used by the application's consumers. ■

Assembling the Data

After you have a general idea of the report layout, assemble the data needed for the report. Access reports use data from two primary sources:

- A single database table
- A recordset produced by the query

You can join many tables in a query and use the query's recordset as the record source for your report. A query's recordset appears to an Access report as if it were a single table.

As you learned in Chapter 36, you use queries to specify the fields, records, and sort order of the records stored in tables. Access treats the recordset of data that results from running a query as if it were a single table (for processing purposes) in datasheets, forms, and reports. When the report is run, Access matches data from the recordset or table against the fields specified in the report and uses the data available at that moment to produce the report.

Note
Reports do not follow the sort order specified in an underlying query. Most often reports are sorted at the report level, either in the detail section or in a group section. Very often, it's a waste of time to sort data in a query that is used solely to populate a report because the data is resorted and rearranged by the report itself. ■

The following example illustrates how to use data from `tblProducts` to create a relatively simple tabular report.

Creating the Report with the Report Wizard

Access enables you to create virtually any type of report. Some reports, however, are easier to create than others, especially when a Report Wizard is used as a starting point. Like form wizards, the Report Wizard gives you a basic layout for your report, which you can then customize.

The Report Wizard simplifies laying out controls by stepping you through a series of questions about the report that you want to create. In this chapter, you use the Report Wizard to create tabular and columnar reports.

Creating a New Report

The Access Ribbon contains several commands for creating new reports for your applications. That Create tab includes a group called *Reports* containing several options such as Report, Labels, and Report Wizard. To get help creating a report, click the Report Wizard button in the Reports group of the Create tab. The first screen of the Report Wizard (shown in Figure 37-5) appears.

FIGURE 37-5

The first screen of the Report Wizard after selecting a data source and fields

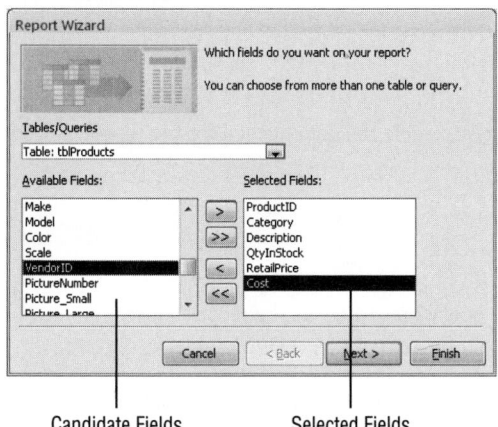

Candidate Fields   Selected Fields

In Figure 37-5, tblProducts has been selected as the data source for the new report. Under the Tables/Queries drop-down list is a list of available fields. When you click on a field in this list and click the right-pointing arrow, the field moves from the Available Fields list to the report's Selected Fields list. For this example, Product ID, Category, Description, QtyInStock, RetailPrice, and Cost were selected.

Tip

Double-clicking on any field in the Available Fields list adds it to the Selected Fields list. You can also double-click on any field in the Selected Fields list to remove it from the box. ■

You're limited to selecting fields from the original record source you started with. You can select fields from other tables or queries by using the Tables/Queries drop-down list in the Report Wizard. As long as you've specified valid relationships so that Access properly links the data, these fields are added to your original selection and you use them on the report. If you choose fields from unrelated tables, a dialog box asks you to edit the relationship and join the tables. Or you can return to the Report Wizard and remove the fields.

After you've selected your data, click Next to go to the next wizard dialog box.

Selecting the Grouping Levels

The next dialog box enables you to choose which field(s) to use for grouping data. Figure 37-6 shows the Category field selected as the data grouping field for the report. The field selected for grouping determines how data appears on the report, and the grouping fields appear as group headers and footers in the report.

Groups are most often used to combine data that is logically related. The classic example is grouping all products by product category. A very practical example is choosing to group on CustomerID so that each customer's sales history appears as a group on the report. You use the report's group headers and footers to display the customer name and any other information specific to each customer.

The Report Wizard lets you specify as many as four group fields for your report. You use the Priority buttons to change the grouping order on the report. The order you select for the group fields is the order of the grouping hierarchy.

Selecting the Category field as the grouping field and clicking the > button would specify a grouping based on category values. Notice that the preview changes to show Category as a grouping field in the example in Figure 37-6. Each of the other fields (ProductID, Description, QtyInStock, RetailPrice, and SalesPrice) selected for the report will appear within the Category groups.

FIGURE 37-6

Specifying the report's grouping

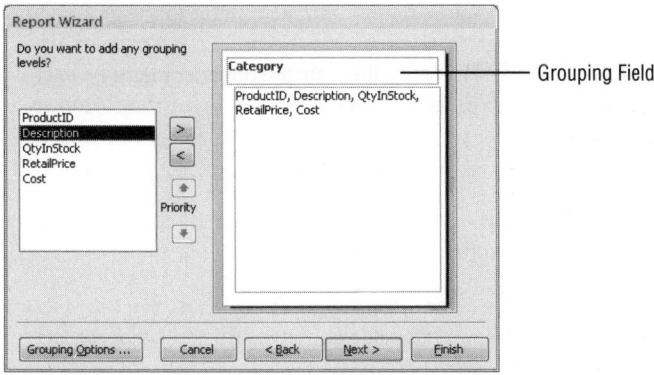

Defining the Group Data

After you select the group field(s), click the Grouping Options button at the bottom of the dialog box to display the Grouping Options dialog box, which enables you to further define how you want groups displayed on the report.

For example, you can choose to group by only the first character of the grouping field. This means that all records with the same first character in the grouping field are grouped. If you group a customers table on `CustomerName`, and then specify grouping by the first character of the `CustomerName` field, a group header and footer appears for all customers whose name begins with the same character. This specification groups all customer names beginning with the letter *A*, another group for all records with customer name beginning with *B*, and so on.

The Grouping Options dialog box enables you to further define the grouping. This selection can vary in importance, depending on the data type.

The Grouping Intervals list box displays different values for various data types:

- **Text.** Normal, 1st Letter, 2 Initial Letters, 3 Initial Letters, 4 Initial Letters, 5 Initial Letters
- **Numeric.** Normal, 10s, 50s, 100s, 500s, 1000s, 5000s, 10000s, 50000s, 100000s
- **Date.** Normal, Year, Quarter, Month, Week, Day, Hour, Minute

Normal means that the grouping is on the entire field. In this example, I used the entire `CustomerName` field.

Notice that the grouping options simplify creating reports grouped by calendar months, quarters, years, and so on. This means that you can easily produce reports showing sales, payroll, or other financial information needed for business reporting.

If you displayed the Grouping Options dialog box, click the OK button to return to the Grouping Levels dialog box, and then click the Next button to move to the Sort Order dialog box.

Selecting the Sort Order

By default, Access automatically sorts grouped records in an order meaningful to the grouping field(s). For example, after you've chosen to group by Customer Name, Access arranges the groups in alphabetical order by Customer Name. However, for your purposes, it might be useful to specify a sort within each group. As an example, your users might want to see the customer records sorted by Order Date in descending order so that the newest orders appear near the top for each customer group.

In the example shown in Figure 37-6, Access sorts data by the `Category` field. As Figure 37-7 shows, the data is also sorted by Description within each group.

Sort fields are selected by the same method you use for selecting grouping fields. You can select sorting fields that haven't been chosen for grouping. The fields chosen in this dialog box affect only the sorting order in the data displayed in the report's Detail section. Select Ascending or Descending sort by clicking the button to the right of each sort field.

FIGURE 37-7

Selecting the field sorting order

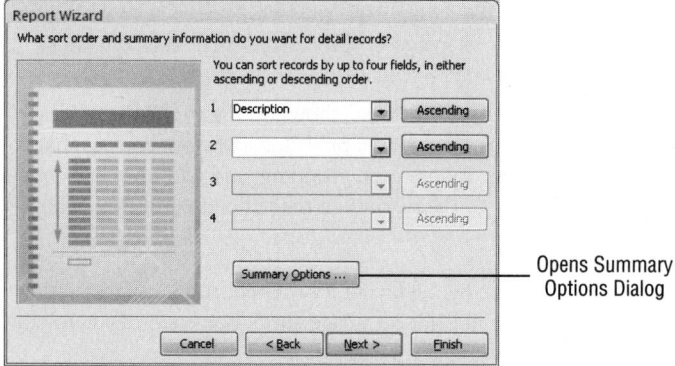

Opens Summary
Options Dialog

Selecting Summary Options

Near the bottom of the sorting screen of the Report Wizard is a Summary Options button. Clicking this button displays the Summary Options dialog box (shown in Figure 37-8), which provides additional display options for numeric fields. All the numeric and currency fields selected for the report are displayed and may be summed. Additionally, you can display averages, minimums, and maximums.

FIGURE 37-8

Selecting the summary options

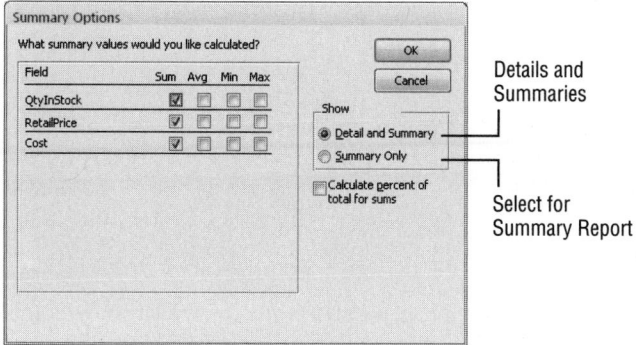

Details and
Summaries

Select for
Summary Report

You can also decide whether to show or hide the data in the report's Detail section. If you select Detail and Summary, the report shows the detail data, whereas selecting Summary Only hides the Detail section and shows only totals in the report.

Finally, checking the Calculate Percent of Total for Sums box adds the percentage of the entire report that the total represents below the total in the group footer. If, for example, you have three products and their totals are 15, 25, and 10, respectively, *30%*, *50%*, and *20%* show below their total (i.e., 50) — indicating the percentage of the total sum (100%) represented by their sum.

Clicking the OK button in this dialog box returns you to the sorting screen of the Report Wizard. There you can click the Next button to move to the next Wizard screen.

Selecting the Layout

Two more dialog boxes affect the look of your report. The first (shown in Figure 37-9) enables you to determine the basic layout of the data. The Layout area provides six layout choices that tell Access whether to repeat the column headers, indent each grouping, and add lines or boxes between the detail lines. As you select each option, the picture on the left changes to show how the choice affects the report's appearance.

You choose between Portrait (tall) and Landscape (wide) layout for the report in the Orientation area. Finally, the Adjust the Field Width so All Fields Fit on a Page check box enables you to cram a lot of data into a little area. (A magnifying glass may be necessary!)

Figure 37-9 shows Stepped and Portrait selected. After making your choices, click the Next button to move to the next dialog box.

FIGURE 37-9

Selecting the page layout

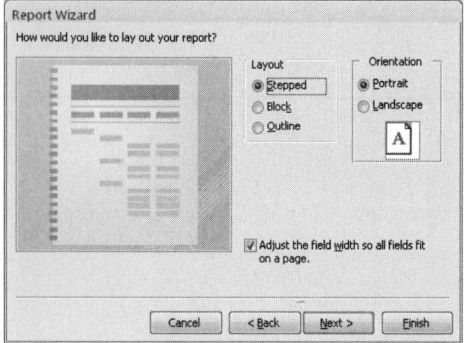

Opening the Report Design

The final Report Wizard screen contains a checkered flag, which lets you know that you're at the finish line. The first part of the screen enables you to enter a title for the report. This title appears only once, at the very beginning of the report, not at the top of each page. The report title also serves as the new report's name. The default title is the name of the table or query you initially specified as the report's data source. The example report just shown in Figure 37-10 is named *rptProducts_Wizard*.

Next, choose one of the option buttons at the bottom of the dialog box:

- Preview the report.
- Modify the report's design.

For this example, leave the default selection intact to preview the report. Click Finish and the report displays in Report view (see Figure 37-10).

rptProducts_Wizard displayed in Report view

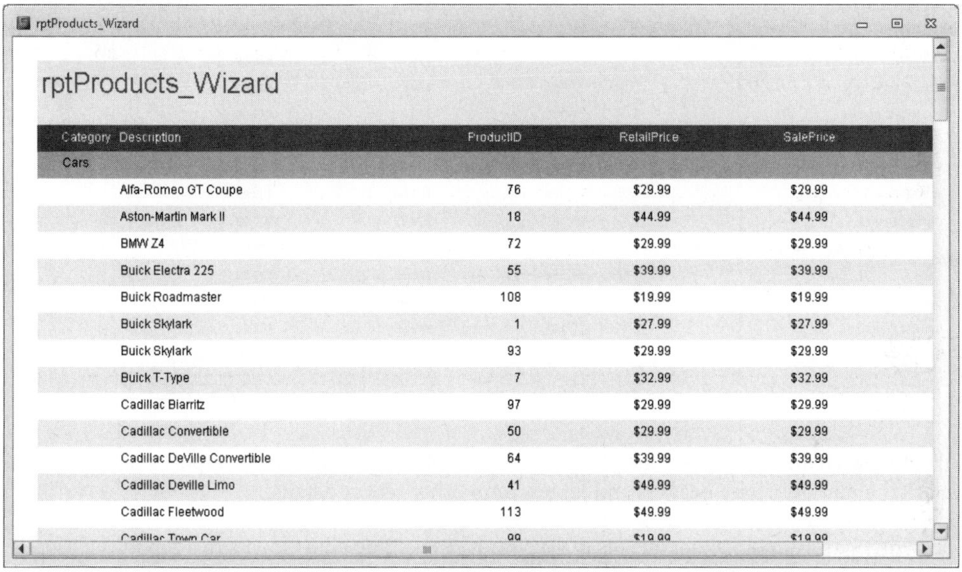

Report view provides an overall presentation of the report, but it doesn't show margins, page numbering, and how the report will look when printed on paper. To get a good idea of how the printed report will look, right-click on the report's title bar and select Print Preview from the shortcut menu.

Adjusting the Report's Layout

There are a few small issues with the report you see in Figure 37-10. For example, the Access Report Wizard has chosen the fonts and overall color scheme, which may not be what you had in mind.

The Report Wizard displays the new report in Report view. Right-click on the report's title bar or tab and select Layout View from the shortcut menu. Or click the View drop-down arrow in the Views group on the Home or Design tab, and click Layout View. The new report in Layout view is shown in Figure 37-11.

FIGURE 37-11

Layout view is useful for resizing controls in a columnar report

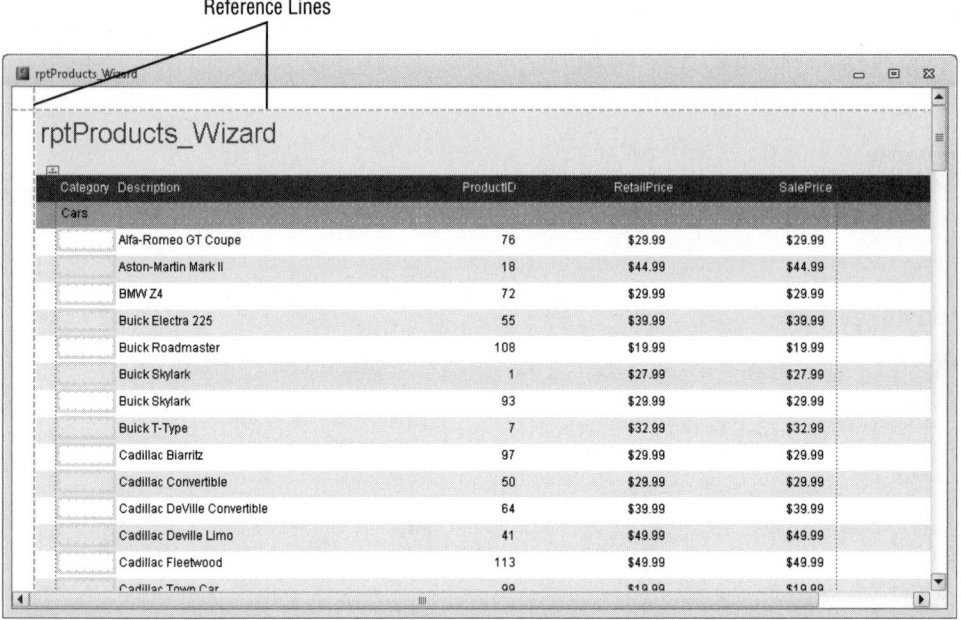

Layout view enables you to see the relative positions of the controls on the report's surface, as well as the margins, page headers and footers, and other report details.

The main constraint of Layout view is that you can't make fine adjustments to a report's design unless you put the report in Design view. Layout view is primarily intended to allow you to adjust the relative positions of controls on the report and is not meant for moving individual controls around on the report. For example, you can delete any item by clicking on the item and pressing the Delete key, or move the item to another location by dragging it on the report's area.

While in Layout view, you can also right-click on any control and select Properties from the shortcut menu. The Property Sheet allows you to modify the default settings for the selected control.

Choosing a Theme

After you adjust the layout, you can use controls in the Themes group on the Ribbon's Report Layout Tools Design tab (which appears while the report appears in Layout view) to change the report's colors, fonts, and overall appearance. The Themes button opens a gallery containing several dozen themes (see Figure 37-12).

Themes are an important concept in Access 2010. A *theme* sets the color scheme, selected font face, font colors, and font sizes for Access 2010 forms and reports. As you hover the mouse over the theme icons in the gallery, the report open in Layout view behind the gallery instantly changes to show you a Live Preview of how the report would look with the selected theme.

FIGURE 37-12

Choosing a theme for the report

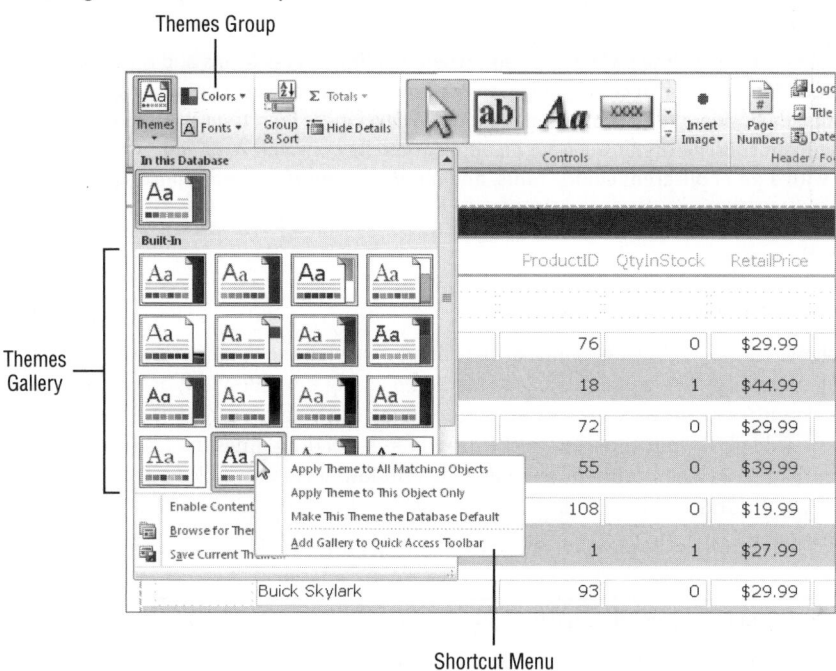

Each theme has a name, like *Office*, *Apex*, *Flow*, *Paper*, and *Metro*. Theme names are useful when you want to refer to a particular theme in the application's documentation or in an e-mail or other correspondence. Themes are stored in a file with a `.thmx` extension, usually in the `Program Files\Microsoft Office\Document Themes 14` folder, depending on your system's Windows and Office versions. Themes apply to all the Office 2010 documents (Word, Excel, and Access), making it easy to determine a style to apply to all of a company's Office output.

Note

Access 2007 users may be wondering what happened to the AutoFormat feature found in 2007. For a number of reasons, Microsoft decided to replace AutoFormat with themes in Office 2010. AutoFormat applied to individual controls, which meant a lot of work when building a complicated form or report. AutoFormat also tended to be all or nothing, making it difficult to apply an AutoFormat and then alter the colors and fonts applied to controls on a form or report. Themes are much more flexible. They even allow you to save a completed form or report as a new theme (see the Save Current Theme option at the bottom of the theme gallery in Figure 37-12). There was no way to create a custom AutoFormat in Access 2007. ■

As the shortcut menu in Figure 37-12 indicates, you can apply the selected theme just to the current report (Apply Theme to This Object Only), all reports (Apply Theme to All Matching Objects), or all forms and reports in the application (Make This Theme the Database Default). There's also an option to add the theme as a button to the Quick Access Toolbar (QAT), an extremely useful option for selectively applying the theme to other objects in the database.

Tip

It's very tempting to try out every reporting style and option when building Access forms and reports. Unfortunately, when carried too far, your Access application may end up looking like a scrapbook of design ideas rather than as a valuable business tool. Professional database developers tend to use a minimum of form and report styles and use them consistently throughout an application. Be considerate of your users and try not to overwhelm them with a lot of different colors, fonts, and other user interface and reporting styles. ■

For the purposes of this exercise, the Concourse theme was selected for the new products report shown in this chapter.

Using the Print Preview Window

Figure 37-13 shows the Print Preview window in a zoomed view of the example report. Display this view by right-clicking the report title bar or tab and clicking Print Preview, or by clicking the View drop-down arrow in the Views group on the Home or Design tab, and clicking Print Preview. This view displays your report with the actual fonts, shading, lines, boxes, and data that will be used on the report when printed to the default Windows printer. Clicking the left mouse button on the report's surface changes the view to a page preview that shows the entire page.

FIGURE 37-13

Displaying the example report in the zoomed preview mode

The Print Preview tab displays controls relevant to viewing and printing the report. It includes controls for adjusting the size, margins, page orientation (Portrait or Landscape), and other printing options. The print options are stored with the report when you save the report's design. The Print Preview tab also includes a Print button for printing the report and another button for closing Print Preview and returning to the report's previous view (Design, Layout, or Report view).

You can move around the page by using the horizontal and vertical scroll bars, or use the Page controls (at the bottom-left corner of the window) to move from page to page. The Page controls include DVD-like navigation buttons to move from page to page or to the first or last page of the report. You can also go to a specific page of the report by entering a value in the text box between the Previous and Next controls.

Right-clicking on the report and selecting the Multiple Pages option or using the controls in the Zoom group in the Print Preview tab lets you view more than one page of the report in a single view. Figure 37-14 shows a view of the report in the Print Preview's two-page mode. Use the navigation buttons (in the lower-left section of the Print Preview window) to move between pages, just as you would to move between records in a datasheet. The Print Preview window has a toolbar with commonly used printing commands.

FIGURE 37-14

Displaying multiple pages of a report in Print Preview's Multiple Pages mode

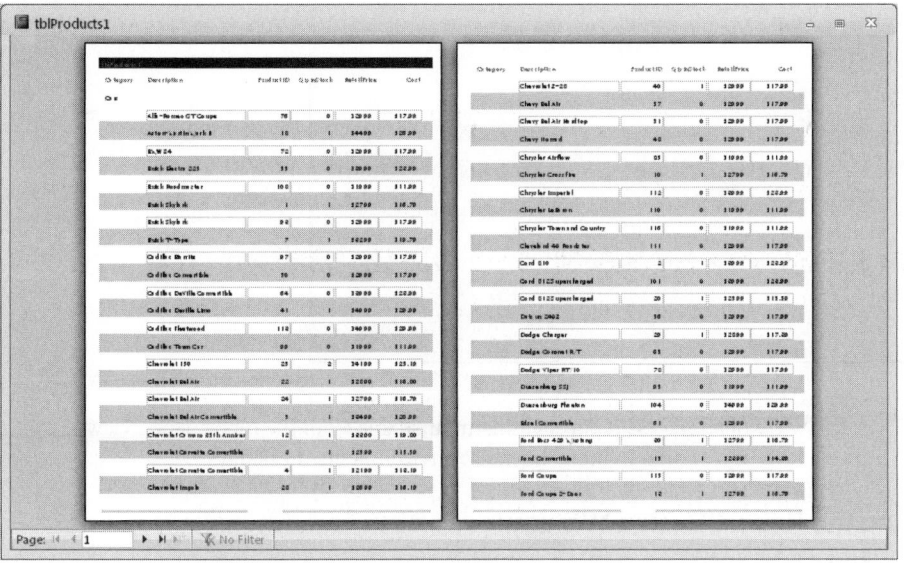

If, after examining the preview, you're satisfied with the report, click the Print button in the Print group of the Print Preview tab to print the report. If you're dissatisfied with the design, select the Close Print Preview button in the Close Preview group to switch to the Report Design window and make further changes.

Publishing in Alternate Formats

An important feature of the Print Preview tab is the ability to output the Access report in a number of common business formats, including PDF, XPS (XML Paper Specification), HTML, and other formats.

Clicking the PDF or XPS button in the Data group on the Print Preview tab opens the Publish as PDF or XPS dialog box (shown in Figure 37-15). This dialog box provides options for outputting in standard PDF format or in a condensed version (for use in a Web context). You also specify the destination folder for the exported file.

Access 2010 provides powerful options for publishing reports

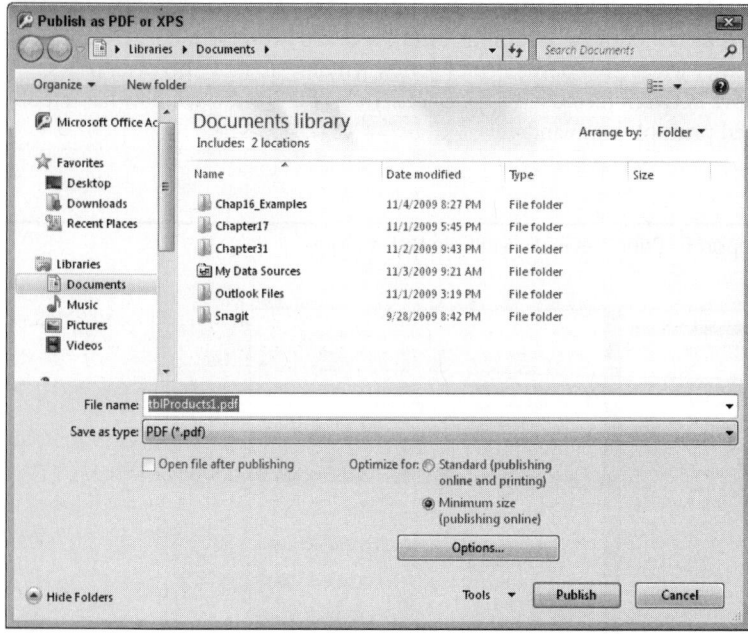

The PDF or XPS view of an Access report is indistinguishable from the report when viewed in Access. Either format is common in many business environments these days.

Viewing the Report Design Window

Right-clicking on the report's tab or title bar and selecting Design View opens the Access Report Designer on the report. As shown in Figure 37-16, the report design reflects the choices you made using the Report Wizard. Here, you can make changes such as working with fields and controls, adjusting section size, adding a background image or working with page setup. The Report

Design Tools contextual tab that appears in this view offers four subtabs — Design, Arrange, Format, and Page Setup — with the design tools you need.

The Report Design view

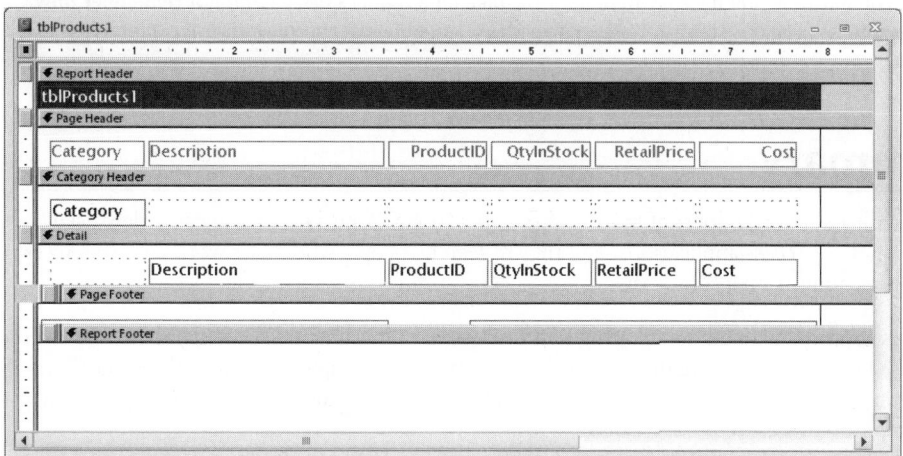

Return other views by using the View drop-down menu in the Views group of the Report Design Tools Design tab, and click the Save button on the QAT to save the changes made to the report.

Printing the Report

The final step in the process of creating a report is printing it. There are several ways to print your report:

- Choose File ➪ Print in the main Access window (with a report highlighted in the Navigation pane). Choosing File ➪ Print opens the report in the Backstage view, with a preview and print settings. You use this view to select the print range, number of copies, and print properties.

- Change to the Print Preview view, and click the Print button in the Print group of the Print Preview tab. Clicking the Print button here immediately sends the report to the default printer without displaying print settings.

Saving the Report

Save the report design at any time by choosing File ➪ Save, or File ➪ Save Object As from the Report Design window, or by clicking the Save button on the QAT. You also can choose File ➪ Save & Publish ➪ Save Object as to see choices for saving the report to another format. The first time you save a report (or any time you select Save As), a dialog box enables you to select or type a name.

Tip

You might find it useful to save a copy of a report before beginning maintenance work on the report. Reports tend to be pretty complicated, and it's easy to make a mistake on a report's design and not remember how to return the report to its previous state. A backup provides a valuable safeguard against accidental loss of a report's design. ∎

Summary

Reports are an important part of most Access applications. Reports are the most widely used feature of many Access applications, and they're seen by people who never work with the Access application running on a computer.

Access is endowed with an outstanding Report Designer. This chapter showed you how to use the Report Wizard, the easiest method for creating a report. The chapter also introduced the views you can use to make changes to the report design. Finally, you saw how to preview, print, and save a report.

Keeping Information at Hand with OneNote

O ne of the challenges in managing any project is how to bring together all the information so that it's at your fingertips. This typically includes notes, tracking tasks, creating data files, looking at Web information, and handling other activities in different programs. Storing all the files or having many open program windows onscreen has never been a satisfactory way to manage your project's information. Microsoft OneNote 2010 provides that elusive solution, enabling you to bring together notes and other types of information in an accessible way. If you're ready to see how you can be better organized and more effective at anything you do, read this chapter and learn how to use OneNote.

Who Needs OneNote and Why

OneNote is designed to function as a digital three-ring binder. With a three-ring binder, you can add and rearrange pages, write on pages, paste clipped articles on a page, or even punch holes in a magazine or report page to add it to the binder. You also can add plastic sleeves that expand the notebook's versatility, enabling you to include non-paper materials in the notebook.

OneNote brings the same type of versatility to tracking all sorts of digital information in a centralized location. You can add a variety of information to a OneNote notebook — notes, Outlook tasks, pictures, files, screen clips, audio or video recordings, details about a meeting, information copied from a web page, and much more. But, the best part is that you can see and use *all* the information at the same time — you don't have to open multiple files and arrange multiple windows.

These capabilities make OneNote a perfect tool for managing information related to specific projects or clients, research or study subjects, or topical areas of interest. Although OneNote's versatility can make it useful to anyone, users in the following types of situations will find OneNote an especially valuable tool:

- If you attend many meetings that generate ideas and action items, OneNote can be perfect for tracking these. Because OneNote enables you to organize information quickly and flexibly, you can easily add the notes and tasks you need. You also can jump right to the information you need as a meeting discussion changes.

- If you often handle research projects in which you bring together information from a variety of sources, OneNote provides a great central storage location for statistics, citations, and useful documents.

- If you like to brainstorm or capture ideas about a topic over time, OneNote helps you keep the information together so that the big picture comes together. You can even capture your ideas as an audio recording so that you're not slowed down by your typing skills.

- If you're a student and need to keep together notes and information for each class, OneNote enables you to collect all the notes and schedule information that you need to stay prepared.

- If you need to use your notes on multiple computers or share them with other users, OneNote enables you to place a notebook on a shared network location or even a USB thumb drive. In this way, OneNote gives you the opportunity to take your work with you or keep others involved.

Touring OneNote

OneNote divides information into *notebooks*, *sections*, and *pages*. You can start OneNote from the Start menu (Start ➪ All Programs ➪ Microsoft Office ➪ Microsoft OneNote 2010). Rather than represent a file, each notebook is a separate subfolder within the Documents\OneNote Notebooks folder within your Windows Vista or Windows 7 user folder.

Note

In Windows XP, the My Documents\My Notebooks folder holds the Notebook subfolders. ∎

Each section you add to a notebook appears as a file within the folder for the specific notebook, and that file stores the information for the pages in the section.

In the OneNote window, this arrangement translates to a Notebooks navigation bar at the left, where you can click on a notebook's button to display the sections for that notebook as seen in Figure 38-1. Tabs for the sections within the selected notebook appear above the page area. Clicking a section tab selects that section, displaying page tabs for the pages in the section at the right. Click on a page tab to display the contents of that page. OneNote also includes a Ribbon with tabs and choices, just as in the other Office applications.

Clicking selects a notebook, section, or page.

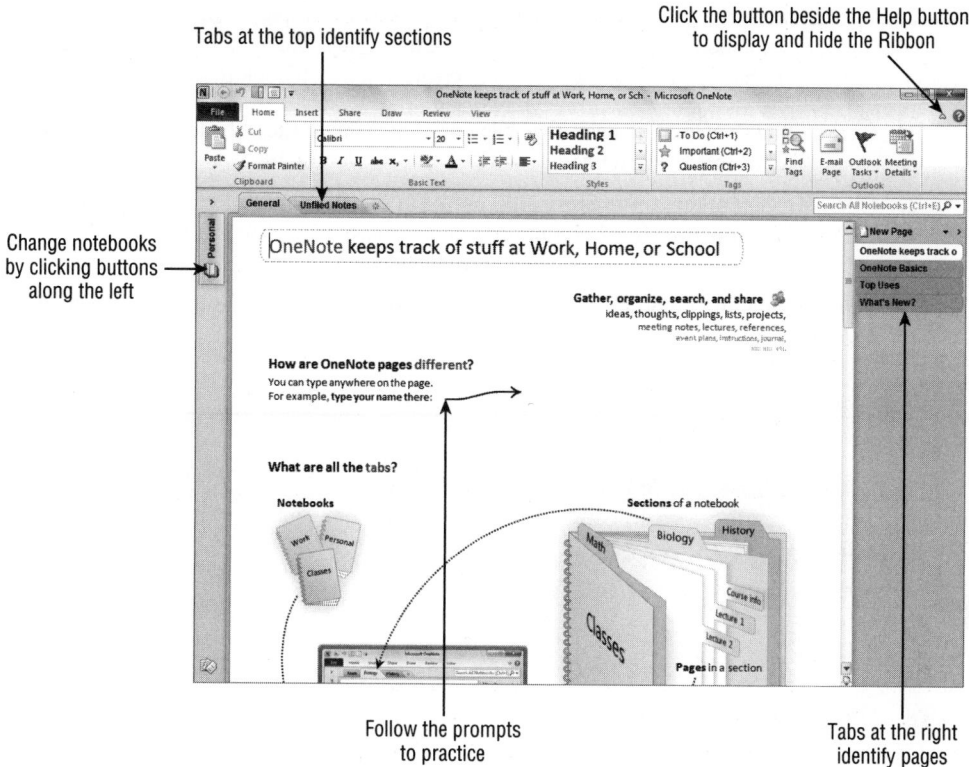

As Figure 38-1 also shows, by default, OneNote includes a notebook named *Personal* with descriptive instructions to help you get started. The help is organized on four separate pages that you can view by clicking on the page tabs at the right. Scroll down each page to read the useful information it offers.

As shown in Figure 38-1, the first page in the "Getting Started with OneNote" section even prompts you to practice by typing your name. You can use these practice prompts as desired. OneNote also now incorporates the Ribbon. The Ribbon is collapsed by default. To display it, click the down arrow button next to the Help button. Click the button again to re-collapse the Ribbon.

If you want to close any notebook, right-click on the notebook's name in the Notebooks Navigation bar and then click Close. You can reopen a notebook at any time by choosing

File ➪ Open ➪ Open Notebook, navigating to and selecting the notebook folder in the Open Notebook dialog box, and then clicking Open.

Creating a Notebook

You can create a notebook for any project, client, subject, research topic, or purpose that you want. Because each notebook represents a folder, you can create as many notebooks as your system has storage to handle. Follow these steps to create a new notebook in OneNote:

1. **Choose File ➪ New.** The Backstage view prompts you to select the location where you would like to store the notebook.

2. **Click My Computer in the Store Notebook On list to specify that you want to store the notebook on your local computer.** The Backstage view prompts you to name the notebook and specify a save location for it.

3. **Type a name for the notebook into the Name textbox.** Figure 38-2 shows the notebook creation in progress.

FIGURE 38-2

The Backstage view prompts you to name the new notebook.

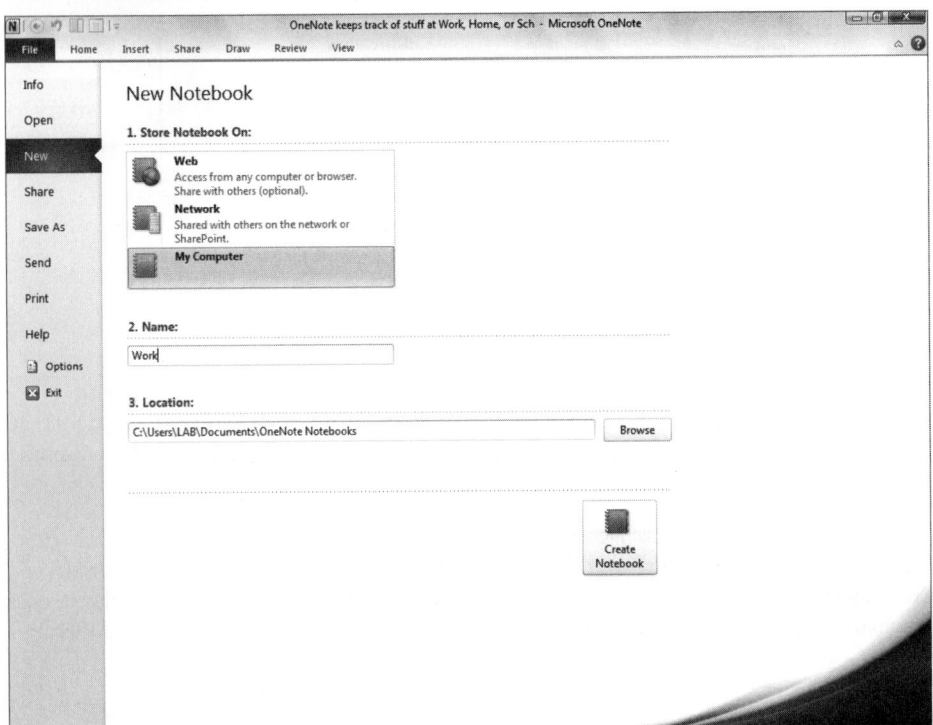

1178

4. **Click Create Notebook.** The new notebook appears onscreen, ready for your use.

The new notebook will have a single section called *New Section 1* that contains a single blank page called *Untitled Page*.

Note

You can rename a notebook later by right-clicking on the notebook and clicking Rename. Change the contents of the Display Name textbox as needed and then click OK. ■

Creating Shared or Online Notebooks

Rather than choosing to store the OneNote notebook on your computer, you can choose to store it on the Web or on a network in Step 2 of the preceding section. Saving the notebook on the Web in Windows Live SkyDrive enables you to access it from anywhere, including a different computer, and optionally share it with other users. (As of this writing, this feature isn't fully operational, but the link for working with it is present.) Click Web in Step 2, click the Windows Live link, and then follow the prompts on the Backstage view to sign in and create the notebook in Windows Live. Storing the notebook on a network enables you to share it with other users in your organization. In this case, you would click Network in Step 2, enter the notebook name in the Name textbox, choose a Network Location (which can be a SharePoint location), and then click Create Notebook. Use the File ➪ Share command to control sharing settings for a notebook.

Creating a Section

Each new section in a notebook works much like a tabbed divider added into a three-ring binder. The section sets off the pages within and provides a label for them. If you create a notebook for client information, for example, you might create a new section for each client. If you create a notebook for school studies, you might create a section for each class during the current semester.

To add a new section to a notebook:

1. **In the Notebooks Navigation bar, click the name of the notebook to which you want to add a section.** The contents of the selected notebook appear.

2. **Right-click on the notebook name and click New Section or click the New Section tab to the right of the rightmost section tab.** The new Section tab appears, with the temporary name highlighted, as shown in Figure 38-3.

3. **Type the name for the new section and press Enter.** The finished section appears, waiting for you to add pages, notes, and other content.

FIGURE 38-3

Type a name to replace the placeholder in the new section's tab.

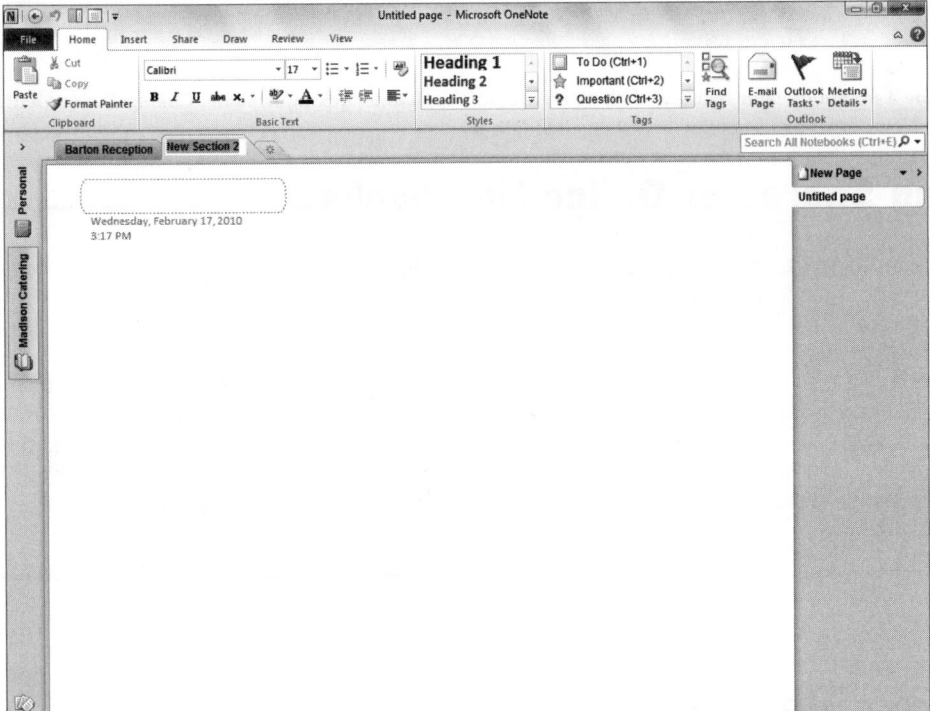

Creating a Page

Each new section you create includes, by default, a new, blank page called *Untitled Page*. You can add pages as needed to further organize the information in a notebook. For example, within a section for a client, you could have a page for each project you're handling for that client. Within a section for a class, you could have a page for each assignment, report, or exam. Because you can switch between pages simply by clicking a page tab, dividing your notes into more pages actually saves time because you can jump to the information you need by clicking a tab rather than having to scroll around in a lengthy document.

Use these steps to add a page:

1. **In the Notebooks Navigation bar, click on the name of the notebook to which you want to add a page.** The contents of the selected notebook appear.

2. **At the top of the notebook, click on the section tab for the section into which you want to add a page.** The tabs for the pages in the section appear at the right.

3. **Click the New Page button at the top of the page tabs area or press Ctrl+N.** The new Page tab appears.

4. **Type a new name for the page and then press Enter.** As shown in Figure 38-4, the name you type appears on both the Page tab and in a title area on the new page.

The page name appears on the Page tab and as a page title.

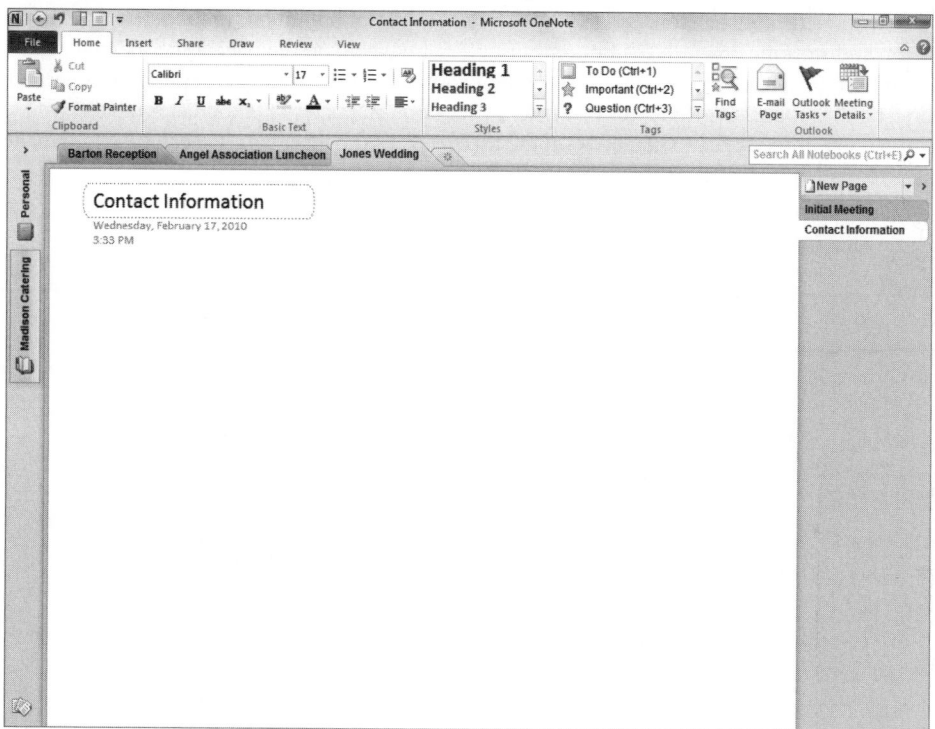

Note

You don't have to use the Save command to save your work in OneNote. The program automatically saves it for you. You can use the Save As command on the File tab to make a copy of the current notebook file. ∎

You also can use a template to create a page. There are dozens of templates for special purposes from taking lecture notes to keeping meeting notes, to creating a planner, to simply applying a nice design to a page. Click on the drop-down arrow beside the New Page choice above the page tabs at the right, and then click Page Templates. A Templates task pane appears. Click on the triangle beside any category to select it, and then click on a template. OneNote instantly inserts a page using that template design. Click the pane's Close (X) button to close it when you've finished.

Inserting Notes

Each new page you add to a notebook section is ready to go as a blank slate for your notes, doodles, tasks, and more. Adding notes to a notebook may be the feature you use the most. This section explains how OneNote trumps sticky notes in helping you capture key thoughts.

Plain Notes

You can add a note anywhere on a page in OneNote. You're not bound by the tradition of starting at the top and working down to the bottom. Just click anywhere on the page, type the note text (see Figure 38-5), and click outside the note when you've finished. You can press Enter as needed within a note, and pressing Tab after you enter at least one character of text creates table cells within the note. You also can click back on the note to place the insertion point within it to make changes to the note at any time.

FIGURE 38-5

Click and type a note anywhere on a page.

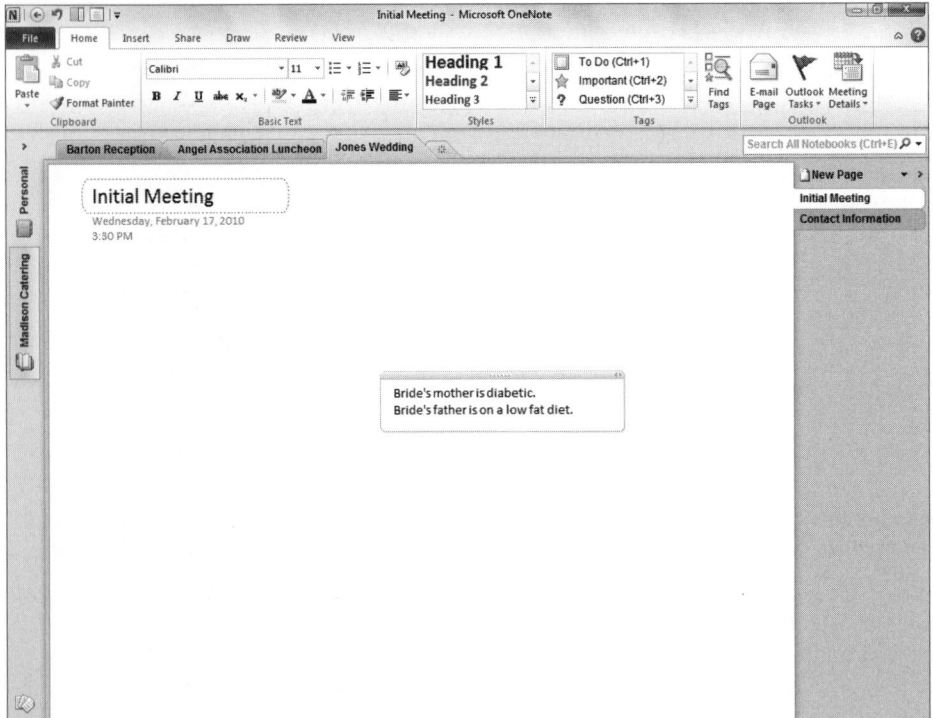

Tagged Notes

Tagging a note assigns a category and icon to the note, such as the To Do tag, Important tag, Question tag, Phone number tag, or Idea tag. The tag icon appears beside the note so that you can determine what kind of information a note contains just by scanning the page. You also can view tagged notes by group, as described later in this chapter.

First click in the note to tag. On the Home tab of the Ribbon, click the More button for the Tag This Note gallery in the Tags group, and then click the tag to apply from the drop-down list. You can assign a tag when you create a note or at any later time. To assign the tag when you create the note, click in the page to position the insertion point where you want the note to appear, click the More button in the Tags group, and then click the desired tag type in the menu. A *note container* with the tag icon appears. Type your note text, and then click outside the boundaries to finish.

To assign a tag to an existing note, click the note to display its note container. Then click More on the Tag This Note gallery in the Tags group of the Home tab, and click the tag type in the drop-down list (see Figure 38-6). Then click outside the note.

FIGURE 38-6

Tagging a note identifies the type of information the note contains.

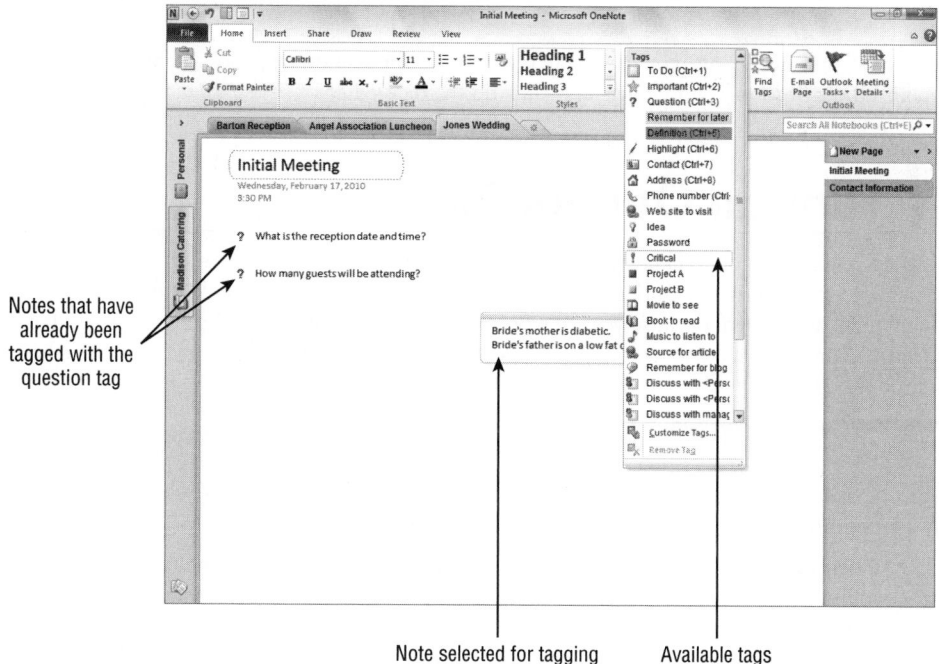

Notes that have already been tagged with the question tag

Note selected for tagging   Available tags

Extra Writing Space

Even though you certainly can make room for more information by creating a new page in a section, you also have the option of extending the space available in a page so that it can accommodate more notes or larger items. To add more writing space, click the Insert tab of the Ribbon, and click the Insert Space button in the Insert group. Drag down the page until the down-arrow pointer changes from a single arrow to a layered arrow. Then click on the page. OneNote adds more space on the page. If you scroll back up without adding anything to the new space, the extra space disappears.

Formatting Information

The addition of the Ribbon in OneNote makes formatting note content much easier. If you refer to Figure 38-6, you can see that the Home tab includes a Basic Text group with a variety of formatting settings. These settings work just as they do in Word. You can drag over text within a note container and then apply formatting to only the selected text. Or, you can click the note container title bar to select all of the note text, and then apply the desired formatting.

Note

OneNote 2010 offers basic formatting styles like those found in Word. Select the note text to which you want to apply the style, open the Styles gallery in the Styles group of the Home tab, and click the style to apply. ■

One other formatting change you can make is to change the section tab color. Right-click on the tab, point to the Section Color choice, and click on the desired color.

Inserting an Outlook Task

Talk about keeping you on track! Any Outlook task you add on a OneNote page automatically appears in your To-Do list in Outlook. If you, like many people, have ever failed to follow through on an action item because you didn't copy it from your meeting notes to your calendar, this feature alone will make you more productive. The Outlook tools do not appear on the Home tab of the Ribbon until you configure a profile in Outlook.

To add an Outlook Task into the notebook:

1. **Create a note that has the desired task title, and then drag over the title in the note container.**

2. **Click the Outlook Tasks button in the Outlook group of the Home tab.** A submenu or list of the flags that you can use to schedule the task — such as Today, Tomorrow, or This Week — appears.

3. **Click the desired flag.** The flag appears in the note container.

Note

If you click Custom, a Task window from Outlook opens so that you can enter a custom Start Date and Due Date to schedule the task in the Outlook To-Do List. ■

As shown in Figure 38-7, when you select the task in your Outlook To-Do list, Outlook identifies it as a task linked to OneNote. The two applications synchronize the task information. Marking the task as complete in Outlook, for example, identifies it as complete in OneNote, dimming the task flag for that note.

FIGURE 38-7

The selected task was created in OneNote and remains synchronized to the notebook.

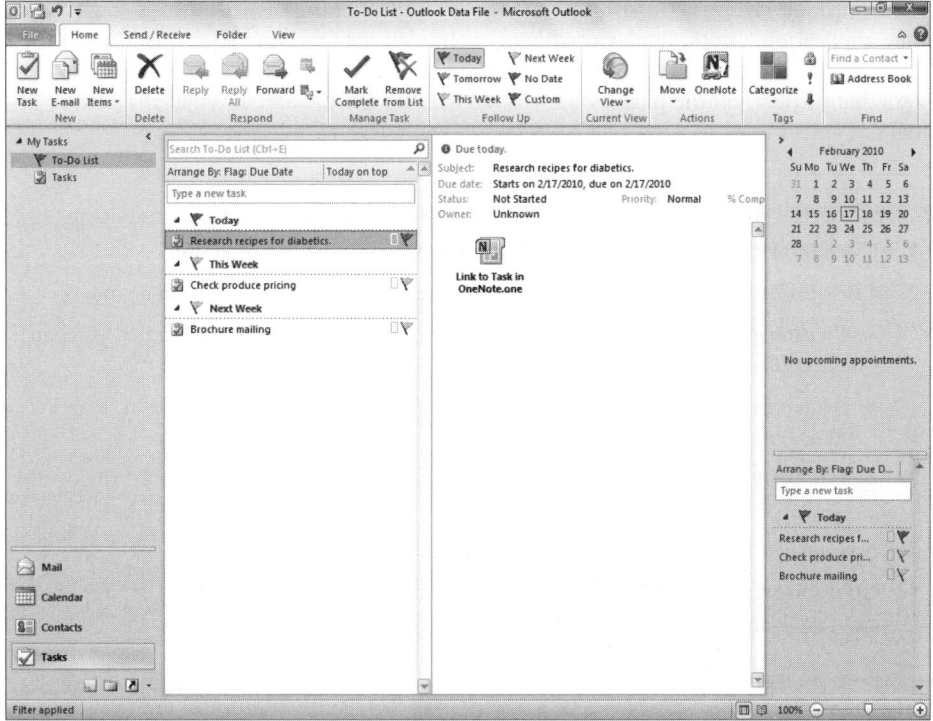

Tip

If you mark a task as complete in Outlook but want to reinstate it in OneNote, deselecting the task in Outlook won't work. You have to select the OneNote task, open the Outlook Tasks menu in the Outlook group of the Home tab, and click Delete Outlook Task, and then use the drop-down list again to reapply a task flag. You can then delete the original task in Outlook. ■

Inserting a Picture or File

If the contents you want to capture already exist in a file outside OneNote, you can insert the information. Inserting information works much the same as opening a file: You give a command, navigate to the folder holding the file to insert, and select and insert the file.

When you insert a picture, the image appears on the OneNote page, where you can move or resize it as desired. You might insert a picture that shows a look or idea that you're after, or that you want to use to illustrate some other document at a later time. (You can copy-and-paste the picture from OneNote.)

There are two different ways in which you can insert a file. A regular insert operation displays a hyperlinked icon for the file on the page. Double-clicking the icon opens the file in its home application. Or, to display the file's contents on the OneNote page, insert the file as a printout. In that case, a special OneNote print driver outputs a version of the file's contents that displays on the page along with an icon for the file and a hyperlink to the original document.

To insert a picture, file, or printout, use these steps:

1. Click in the page at the location where you want to insert the item.
2. Click the Insert tab and then click the command for the type of item to insert.
   - **Picture in the Images group.** Opens the Insert Picture dialog box so that you can select the picture to insert.
   - **Attach File in the Files group.** Opens the Choose a File or Set of Files to Insert dialog box so that you can select one or more files to insert.
   - **File Printout in the Files group.** Opens the Choose Document to Insert dialog box so that you can choose the file to "print" and display.
3. Navigate to the folder holding the desired file and select the file.
4. Click Insert. The picture, file icon, or "printed" file appears on the page. Figure 38-8 shows an example of each.

Inserting a Screen Clipping

Adding a screen clipping to OneNote literally enables you to take a picture of something on your computer screen and place it on a OneNote page. You might use this feature to capture information that appears onscreen during a Webcast or shared online work session. Or you can capture information from a web page, such as grabbing the headline and lead photo from a news site so that you remember where you saw the information. When you take a screen clipping from a web page, OneNote also inserts a hyperlink to the web page.

FIGURE 38-8

This page holds an icon for an inserted file, an inserted picture, and a "printout" of a file.

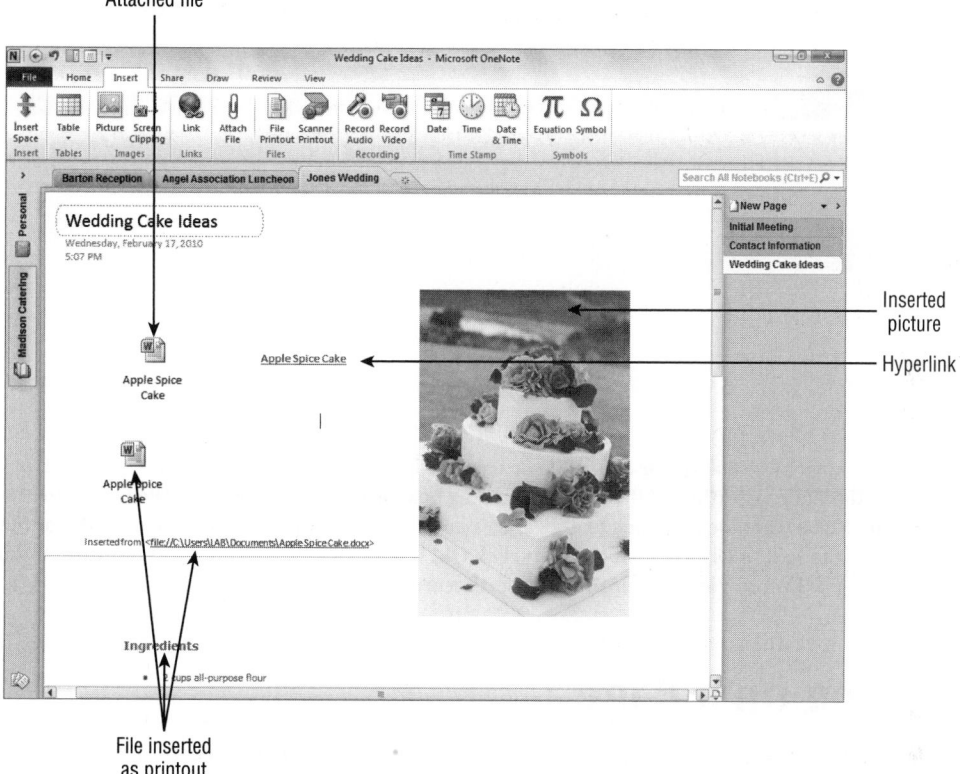

Attached file

Inserted picture

Hyperlink

File inserted as printout

Here's how to create a screen clip in OneNote:

1. **Click in the page at the location where you want to insert the item in OneNote.**

2. **Switch to the location from which you want to clip the screen.** For example, display the desktop or launch your Web browser and browse to the page that holds the information to clip.

3. **Switch back to OneNote.**

4. Choose **Insert ⇨ Images ⇨ Screen Clipping**. OneNote minimizes, and the location you selected in Step 2 appears. The screen appears grayed out to indicate that OneNote is waiting for you to make your clip selection.

5. **Drag diagonally to make the selection.** When you release the mouse, the clip appears in a note container along with any hyperlink, as in the example in Figure 38-9.

FIGURE 38-9

The screen clip appears as a new note.

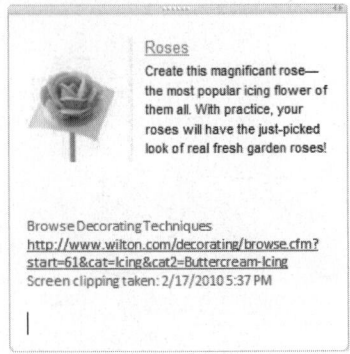

Note

If you want to insert a plain hyperlink rather than a file or screen clipping, choose Insert ➪ Links ➪ Link. Type the URL to link to in the Address textbox of the Hyperlink dialog box, or click the Browse for File button to select a file to link to. If you want the hyperlink to appear as a label or descriptive text rather than a URL or file path, make an entry in the Text to Display textbox. Then click OK. Use the Insert ➪ Recording ➪ Record Audio and Insert ➪ Recording ➪ Record Video commands to insert recorded content. ■

Writing on a Page

If you have a Tablet PC or a pen input device attached to your computer, you can choose a pen and then use the stylus to create a handwritten note, also called *ink*, like this:

1. **With the page on which you want to add the note selected, click the Draw tab on the Ribbon.**

2. **In the Tools group, click the More button for the pens gallery, and then click the desired pen.** The pen becomes active for the stylus.

3. **Write on the tablet with the stylus to create the note.** The note text appears on the page, as in the example in Figure 38-10.

4. **Click the Select & Type button in the Tools group to turn off the pen (stylus) input.** The stylus resumes working like a mouse.

Note

You also can use the ink feature with a regular mouse rather than a pen input device, but because writing with a mouse is rather difficult, you might change your mind after you try it. ■

FIGURE 38-10

FIGURE 38-10

Create handwritten notes on a Tablet PC or pen input device.

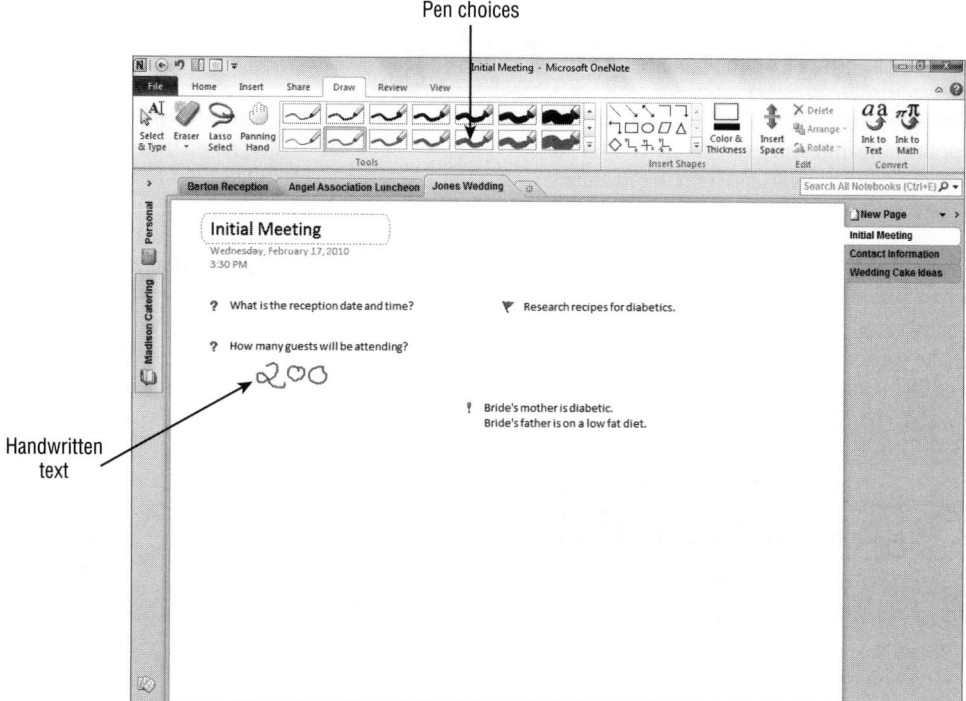

If you want to convert the handwritten note to text, move the mouse over the note so that the note container appears. Click (or tap) the top edge of the note container to select all the note contents. Then choose Draw ➪ Convert ➪ Ink to Text. Figure 38-11 shows a selected note container with some handwriting and the same note with the ink converted to text. Converting the note to text in this way makes it easier to edit later, if needed.

FIGURE 38-11

You can select a handwritten note and convert it to text.

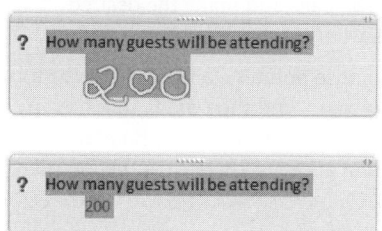

Tip
You also can create drawings on the page using a Tablet PC or pen input device. ■

Using Linked Note Taking

OneNote 2010 enables you to dock it to the side of the desktop so that you can work with other applications but still have access to OneNote. This makes it easier to take notes from other documents and the Internet. To dock or undock One Note, click the Dock to Desktop button on OneNote's Quick Access Toolbar (QAT).

When you dock OneNote, by default it enters a new mode called *Linked Note Taking*. When you add a note on any page while viewing a particular web page or location in a document such as a particular slide in a PowerPoint presentation, OneNote automatically creates a hyperlink back to the content you were viewing. As shown in Figure 38-12, an icon for the hyperlink appears beside the note container. Moving the mouse pointer over it displays information about the source, and clicking it redisplays the linked location.

Organizing, Finding, and Sharing

Just as you can rearrange, change, and view pages in a three-ring binder, your OneNote notes remain flexible so that you can update, change, rearrange, and use them exactly as you need to. You can search for notes or even publish them for use by others. This last section in the chapter explains how you can get the most out of all the content that you pile in to your OneNote notebooks.

Reorganizing

You can tackle any of a number of tasks to reorganize and rearrange information on a page, between sections, and between notebooks. These are the most common actions you will use to keep your notebook information up-to-date:

- **Rename a Section.** Right-click on the section tab, click Rename, type the new name, and press Enter.

- **Rename a Page.** Click in the title box at the top of the page and make the desired changes. The new name appears in the page tab, as well.

- **Move a Note on a Page.** Click the note, move the mouse pointer over the bar at the top of the note container until the four-headed arrow appears, and then drag. To move an icon, drag it. To move a picture or inserted file printout, place the mouse pointer over the picture or printout and click the select button that appears; then, drag the picture.

- **Move a section to another notebook.** Right-click on the section tab and click Move or Copy. In the Move or Copy Section dialog box that appears (Figure 38-13), click on the notebook into which you want to move the section, and then click the Move button.

Working with hyperlinked notes.

Click to dock and undock OneNote

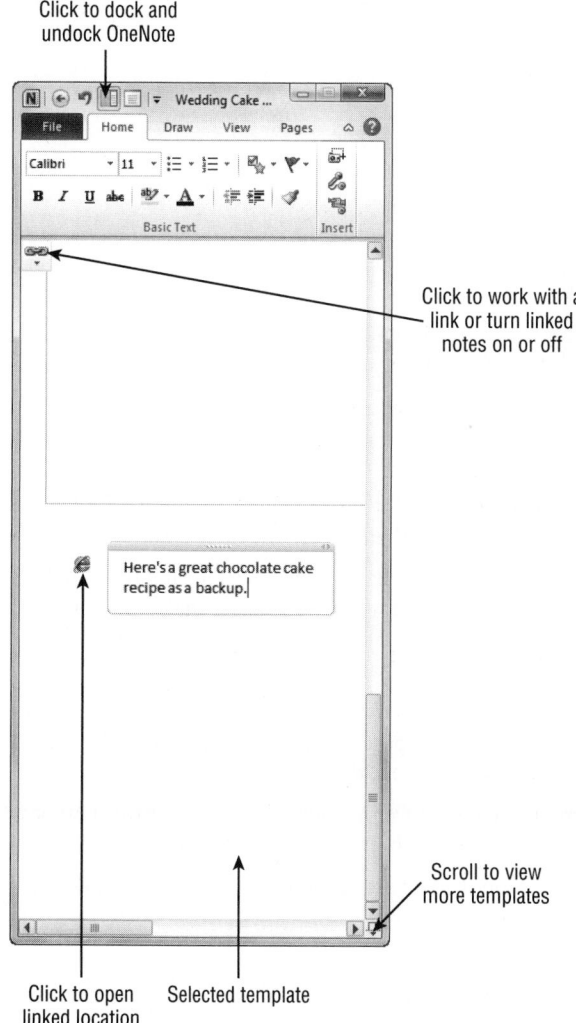

Click to work with a link or turn linked notes on or off

Here's a great chocolate cake recipe as a backup.

Scroll to view more templates

Click to open linked location

Selected template

FIGURE 38-13

You can move a section into another notebook.

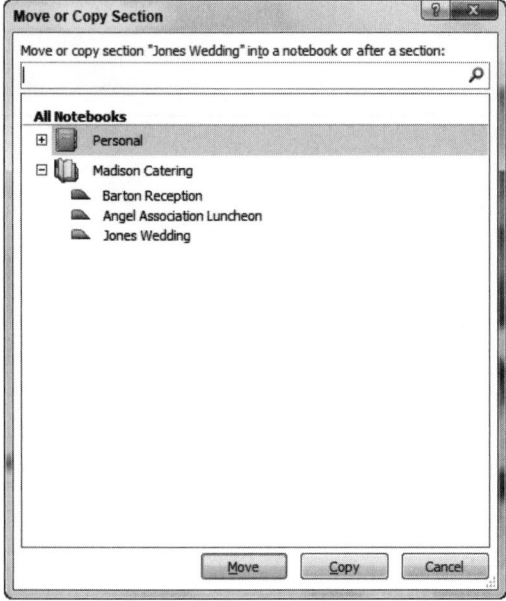

- **Move a section within the notebook.** Drag the section tab left or right until the black triangle appears in the desired destination, and then release the mouse button.

- **Move or copy a page to another section.** Right-click on the page tab, and then click Move or Copy. Select the desired section in the Move or Copy Pages dialog box that appears (it resembles the Move or Copy Section dialog box in Figure 38-13), click the section into which you want to move or copy the page, and then click the Move or Copy button.

- **Move a page within its own section.** Drag the page tab until the black triangle appears at the desired destination location, and then release the mouse button.

- **Delete a note or other item from the page.** Move the mouse pointer over the item or note container, and then click the select button that appears. Press Delete.

- **Delete a page or section.** Right-click on the page or section tab, and then click Delete.

Viewing Tagged Notes

Taking the time to tag notes pays off when you need to view key note information later. OneNote can display a Tags Summary task pane (Figure 38-14), which displays the tagged notes from all your open notebooks. To open the Tags Summary task pane, click Find Tags in the Tags group of the Home tab. To change how the task pane lists the notes, open the Group Tags By drop-down list at the top of the task pane, and then click the desired grouping: Tag Name, Section, Title, Date, or Note Text. You can even add a new page listing the tagged notes to the current notebook by clicking the Create Summary Page button at the bottom of the task pane. Click the task pane's Close (X) button when you finish viewing the tagged notes.

FIGURE 38-14

Viewing tagged notes can help you find key information stored in your notebooks.

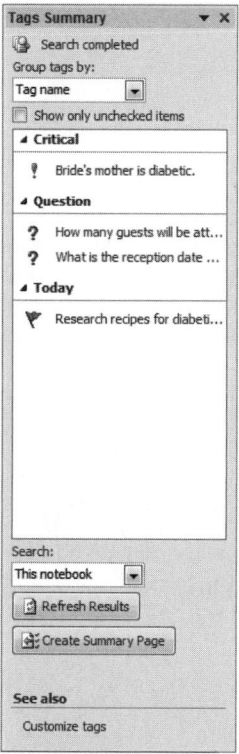

Searching Notes

When you want to find a particular note, type a search word or phrase into the Search All Notebooks textbox above the page tabs (Figure 38-15), and then press Enter. The Search feature highlights every item on the page that holds matching text. The search results also highlight the tab for every page that holds the matching text; click page tabs or the arrows in the Search textbox area to view additional matches. To close the search, click the red X (Exit Search and Clear Match Highlighting) button at the right end of the Search textbox area.

Search for notes by making an entry in the Search All Notebooks textbox.

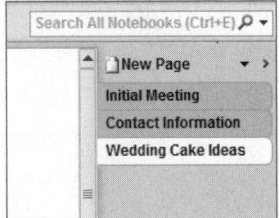

Saving Note Information for Others

You can use the Save As command to convert the current page, section, or notebook to another file format to share the information with others who need the information but don't necessarily need to have access to your OneNote notebook. You can select one of several formats: Single File Web Page (viewable with a Web browser), OneNote 2010 or 2007 Sections, Word Document (for Word 2010 and 2007 users), Word 97-2003 Document (for users of an older Word version), as well as the PDF and XPS formats.

Use this process to save information from the notebook in another file format:

1. **Select the notebook and section, and then select the pages to publish using the page tabs.** To select a single page, click on its tab. To select multiple pages, click on the first tab and then Ctrl+click to add other pages or Shift+click to select a range of pages.

2. **Choose File ⇨ Save As.** The Save As choices appear in Backstage view (Figure 38-16).

3. Click the information you want to save in the 1. Save Current list.

4. Click the desired file type in the 2. Select Format list.

5. **Click the Save As button.** The Save As dialog box appears.

6. Type a filename in the File Name textbox.

7. Select another folder to save to if needed.

8. **Click Save.** OneNote creates the file, which you can then e-mail or otherwise provide to the desired recipients. The recipient can then double-click on the file in Windows to open the file in its associated application.

Tip

If you also have Microsoft Office Word 2010 installed, you can publish any page as a blog entry. Choose File ⇨ Send ⇨ Send to Blog. If you aren't already signed up with a blogging provider, you will be prompted to do so. Otherwise, the prompts help you configure Office to post to your blogging provider. You also can use the File ⇨ Send command to e-mail the current page. ■

FIGURE 38-16

Saving notebook content in another format enables other users to view your notes.

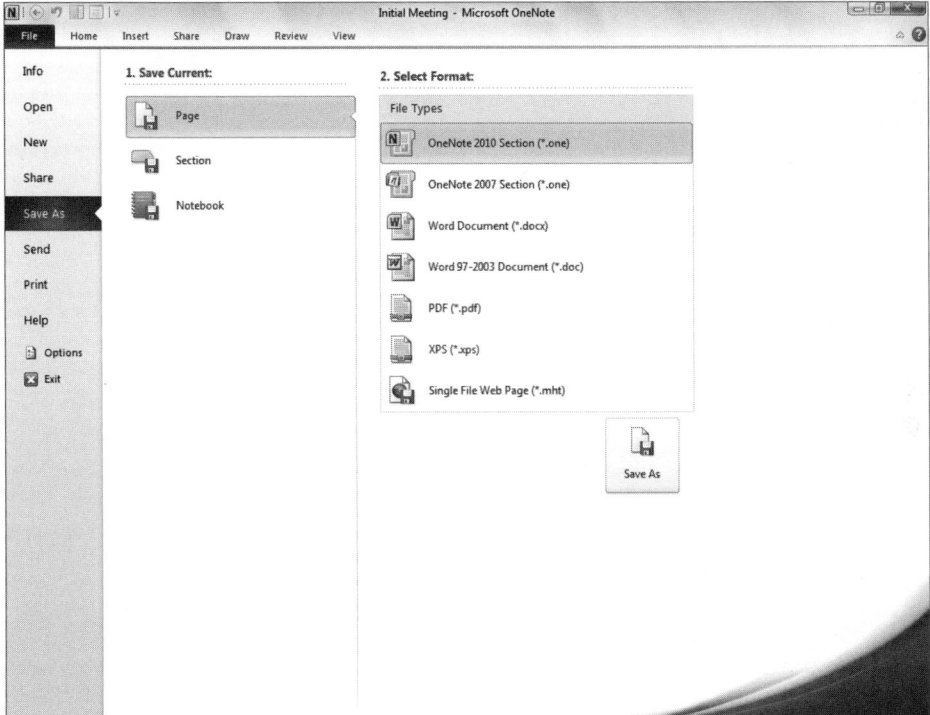

Summary

You're now well on your way to getting your life organized with Microsoft OneNote. This chapter explained the benefits of using OneNote and how OneNote organizes information. You saw how to create a notebook, sections, and pages to arrange information in the way that suits your needs. You learned how to add notes and tasks on a page, as well as how to insert a file, picture, or screen clipping and how to write on a page. You also learned how to create linked notes when OneNote is docked. From there, you learned how to take advantage of the content you've captured in OneNote by reorganizing and updating it, viewing and searching it, and saving information for others.

Part VIII

Sharing and Collaboration

SharePoint and SkyDrive

SharePoint Server is a program that helps businesses share access to files and information in a variety of ways. In essence, SharePoint is a special kind of website that provides controlled access to folders, documents, contact information, scheduling, and other resources related to documents and workflow management.

SharePoint Server works as a server that can be installed on your own company's computers. A *server* is a computer or computer program that provides services to client programs. Servers usually are connected to a network — such as the Internet or a local area network (LAN) — and are available to respond to client applications, such as your Web browser, Microsoft Outlook, and even Microsoft Word. For example, websites are located on servers, and they respond to your browser requests to display information. When you send or receive e-mail, different kinds of server programs are used to deliver e-mail between you and your correspondents.

If you or your company doesn't have its own servers connected to the Internet, you can purchase SharePoint hosting services, just as you can purchase a hosting plan for other websites and services. Increasingly, the same companies that provide ordinary Web hosting are also offering SharePoint hosting, sometimes bundled into hosting plans as cheap as $10 per month or lower. You can discover such plans by searching for "sharepoint hosting" online.

Word 2010 has features that are designed to work with SharePoint Server 2010. You can access these features directly, using the Share command from the File menu, or you can access them indirectly by saving a file to SharePoint Server or by opening a file that resides on SharePoint Server. All you need is a SharePoint Server server and a user account.

IN THIS CHAPTER

Creating a SharePoint document workspace from Word

Publishing documents to a SharePoint server

Checking documents out from a SharePoint server

Creating and reviewing workflow tasks from Word

Adding new files and folders to a SharePoint document workspace

What Happened to Workspace Management?

All the workspace management features that were accessible in Office 2007 have been moved to SharePoint Workspace. SharePoint Workspace takes on the role of providing workspace management for SharePoint Workspace and facilitating the creation of shared folders. See Chapter 40 for additional information.

If you're using a pre-2010 version of SharePoint Server, the enhanced collaboration features for Word 2010, such as co-authoring, are not supported. As of this writing, it remains to be seen whether co-authoring will be supported by Windows Live SkyDrive or Office Live Workspace.

Accessing Your SharePoint Server

Accessing SharePoint Server from Word can be as easy as opening a file. First, you'll need the URL (Internet address), your user name, and a password. Choose File ➪ Open, type or paste the SharePoint URL into the File Name text box, and press Enter. Yes, we know it's not a file. This is a shortcut method for navigating to a location. Or, rather than use the File Name text box, click in the location field at the top of the Open dialog box, replace the current location with the SharePoint server's URL, and press Enter.

Note
If you are connected to SharePoint 2010, you will have additional options not available to users of earlier versions of SharePoint. Even aside from server version differences, installation options and feature implementation vary considerably, so you might see more or fewer features than others using different installations of the same server version. ∎

Assuming you typed the URL correctly, you may be prompted for a user name and password, as shown in Figure 39-1.

Type your user name and password. Note that a SharePoint user name format may call for a site/domain name in all uppercase letters, a backslash, and your user name. Accessing the server from a different location on the Internet will require the more complex login (i.e., which includes the site/domain name, rather than just the user name), except in instances when using VPN or remote desktop will put you onto the same network as the SharePoint server.

Type your password, click Remember My Credentials if you like (unless your employer requires otherwise), and click OK. This opens the SharePoint site, which might resemble Figure 39-2, depending on your site's settings. SharePoint sites usually are organized into one or more libraries and document workspaces. A *library* is a collection of resources on a SharePoint site. Don't worry if your SharePoint site doesn't look like this one. Different organizations format sites differently, and appearances can vary wildly. A document workspace is a location on a SharePoint site that enables you to coordinate work on one or more documents with other team members.

Tip

Once you've navigated to your SharePoint library, you can drag the top SharePoint folder/library link from the location box (the address bar at the top of the file window) into the Favorites list. This can save you navigation and typing time in the future. Click in the Location box to select the address. Click on the folder icon at the left, then drag it down and drop it onto Favorites. The SharePoint link will now appear in your Favorites list. Note that you can drag subfolders to the Favorites area as well. ■

FIGURE 39-1

If you're the only user of your computer and not otherwise concerned about security, you can save time if you click Remember My Credentials.

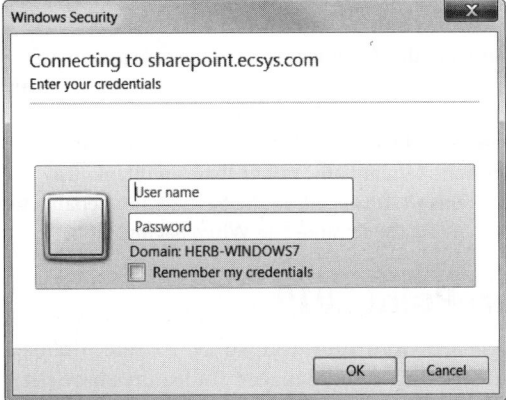

FIGURE 39-2

Access documents using a SharePoint library.

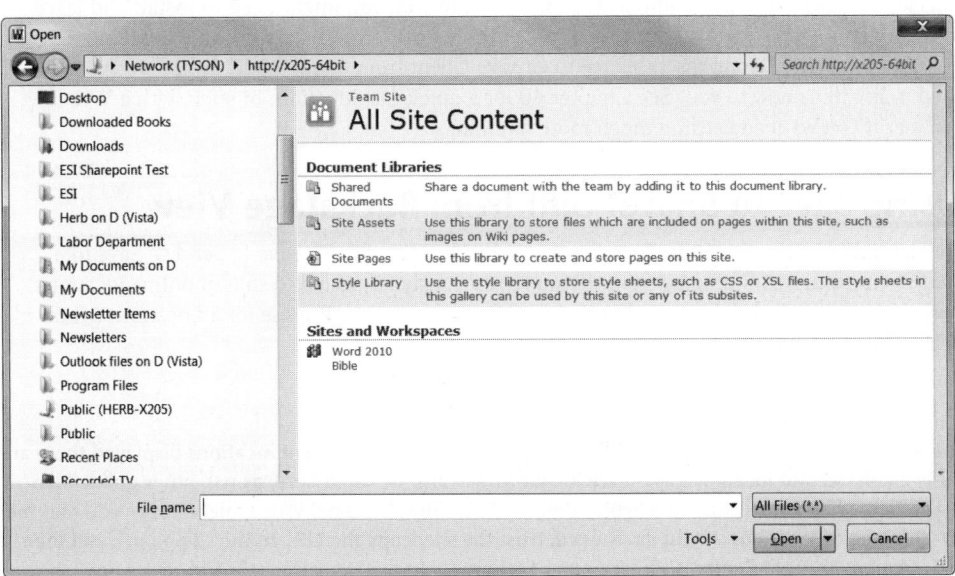

A document workspace provides several tools and facilities to share files, make updates available to team members, establish workflow by creating and managing tasks, and provide information about the status of documents and tasks. Unlike in Office 2007, many of those features no longer are found in Word, Excel, PowerPoint, and other main applications. Instead, those facilities are now accessible via either your Web browser or SharePoint Workspace.

There are other ways to log on to your SharePoint server. Once you have checked out a document from the library, anytime you open a local copy of that file, Word attempts to log you on to the server to check for updates, and the like. Using the URL, however, is a surefire direct route, especially when you're just getting started.

Note
With SharePoint you can either work from the file that is stored in the document workspace or work on a local copy. When you choose the latter route, you are notified of changes to the workspace copy, and you can choose when and whether to publish your changes. This approach can be a bit tedious because you often have to compare your changes to those of others so you can integrate and coordinate changes. As a result, it's usually ultimately more efficient if work on a given document is done sequentially, rather than simultaneously. Nonetheless, if you choose the local route, choose File ➪ Options ➪ Advanced. In the Save section, enable the option Copy Remotely Stored Files onto Your Computer and Update the Remote File When Saving. ■

Using Office 2010 with SharePoint 2010

If you were accustomed to working with SharePoint in Word 2007, you will notice some dramatic differences. The most important difference is that the document-management features have been removed from Word. You will now find those features in SharePoint Workspace 2010. If you need to create a local copy of a document workspace, that is no longer done from Word. You now perform that operation from SharePoint Workspace or from a Web browser.

This helps make Word less complicated. But it means that you might need to install and learn to use an entirely new application. Well, not entirely new, if you used Groove. SharePoint Workspace bears a strong resemblance to Groove Client from Office 2007. Still, if you've never used it, it will be new to you. See Chapter 40 for a quick introduction, or stick with a Web browser if you want something much more familiar.

Using Save to SharePoint from Backstage View

You can initiate access to SharePoint resources by choosing File ➪ Save & Send ➪ Save to SharePoint, as shown in Figure 39-3. If you've previously navigated to shared online locations, they will be shown under Recent Locations. Otherwise, choose Browse for a Location, which opens the Save As dialog box, shown in Figure 39-4.

Note
Although the selected Save & Send choice is called *Save to SharePoint*, the recent locations displayed there are not necessarily all SharePoint locations. SkyDrive locations will also be listed here, as will other online locations. Note also that when you access a particular online site for the first time, Word might notify you that the site is not in your trusted locations. If you do, indeed, trust the site, copy the URL to the Clipboard, and then choose File ➪ Options ➪ Trust Center ➪ Trust Center Settings ➪ Trusted Locations ➪ Add New Location.

Paste the URL into the Path text box, enable the Subfolders option (if appropriate), type a description, and click OK ⇨ OK ⇨ OK. This setting might not take effect until you close all Office 2010 applications. ∎

FIGURE 39-3

Use File ⇨ Save & Send ⇨ Save to SharePoint to save the current file to the document-management server (SharePoint site).

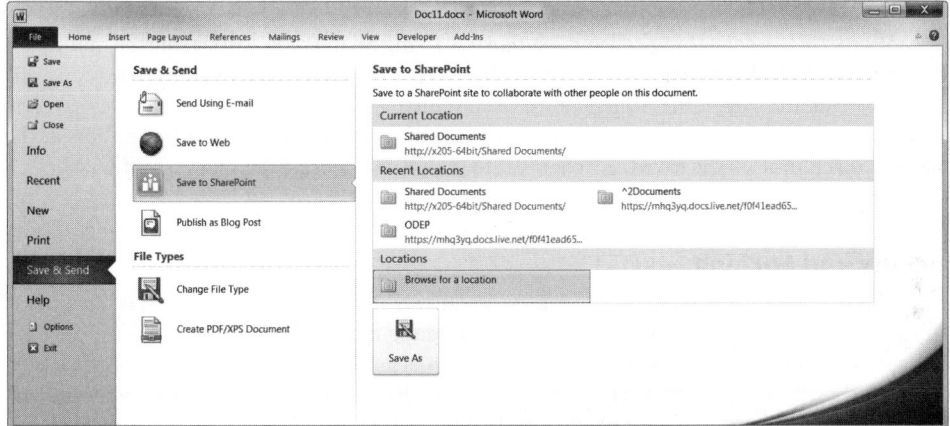

FIGURE 39-4

The Save As dialog box can be used to navigate to online storage locations.

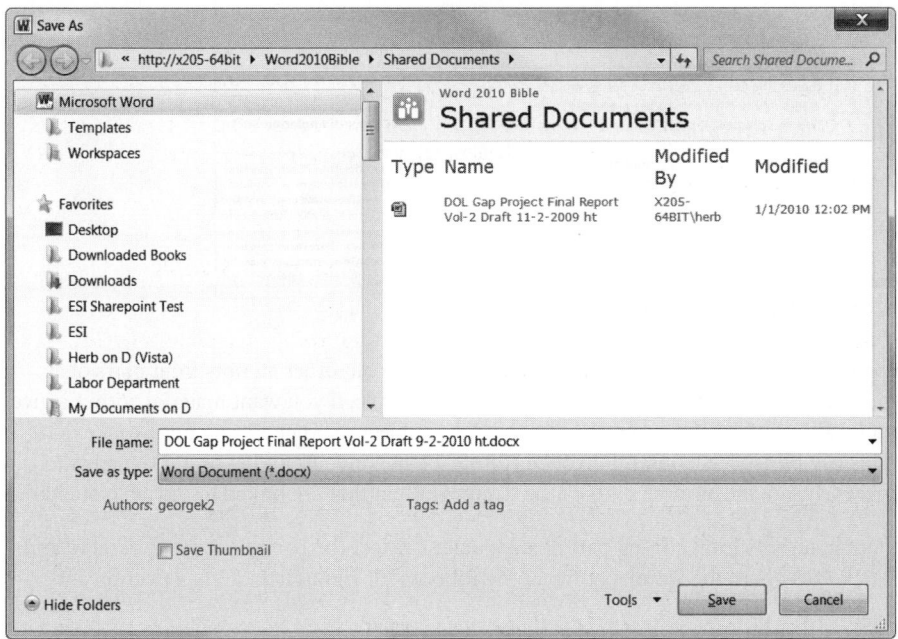

Type or paste the URL for the SharePoint site into the location field at the top of the Save As dialog box. Depending on the speed of your connection, Internet latency, and the speed of the server's connection, it may take a while for the location to appear. Once it does, type the name of the file and click Save. For the balance of the session, while that document is opened, each time you save it, it will be saved to the server.

Co-authoring

New to Word 2010 is something called *co-authoring*. Using SharePoint 2010 resources, multiple users can open and edit the same document at the same time, with different authors working on different parts at the same time. When you save your changes, not only are your changes saved to the copy of the file on the server, but Word also retrieves saved changes from other authors at the same time. Each time others save their changes, they will also receive the most recent changes saved by you.

Blocking and Locking

So, with all this saving going on, what happens when two authors are working on the same paragraph at the same time? It can't happen. That's because the moment you begin to edit a paragraph — by making any change — that paragraph is automatically locked from other authors, as shown in Figure 39-5. The dotted, light-blue left bracket shows that I am working on the current paragraph. The bracket would appear even if Track Changes were not being used.

FIGURE 39-5

Co-authoring indicators show which paragraphs currently are being edited.

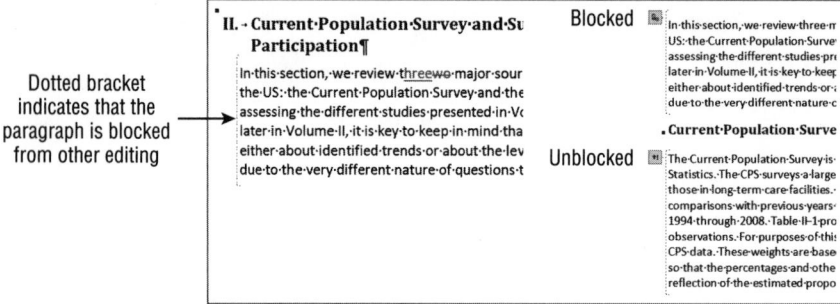

Dotted bracket indicates that the paragraph is blocked from other editing

In addition to automatic locking, you can preemptively lock out other authors from parts of a document you want to reserve. You might do this, for example, if you want material within a given document heading, subheading, and the like not to be subject to other editing until you're done with it. This can be especially useful if you're editing a table or chart and expect those edits to have ripple effects in one or more parts of the document text that are linked to the table or chart.

To block other authors from editing part of a document, select the part you want to reserve and choose Block Authors in the Developer tab of the Ribbon. Or right-click on the selection and choose Block Authors. To release a blocked section, right-click on the blocked part and choose Block Authors to toggle blocking off.

Note that the icon next to the paragraph changes but does not go away, as shown in Figure 39-5. This serves as a notice that changes might have been made to that paragraph. The icon and brackets do not go away until the document is saved to the server.

Co-authoring Indicators

When a document is being edited by multiple authors, the Number of Authors Editing item in the Status bar tells you how many. Note that this item does not become active unless at least two people currently are editing the document. To enable this indicator, right-click on the Status bar, and place a check next to Number of Authors Editing, as shown in Figure 39-6.

FIGURE 39-6

Enable the Number of Authors Editing indicator to display the number of authors on the Status bar.

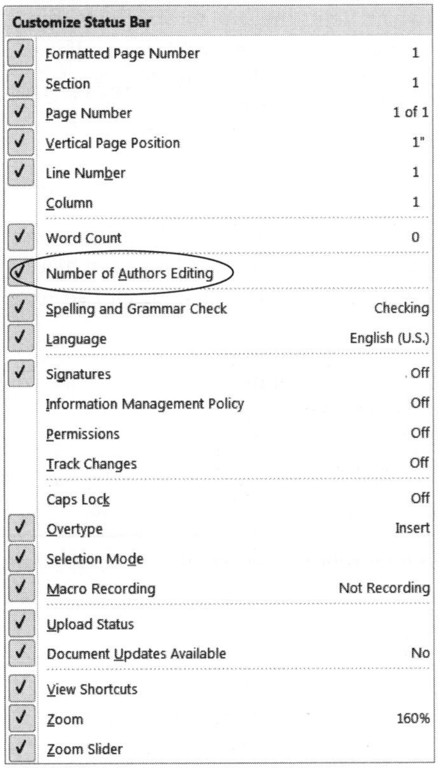

Customize Status Bar	
✓ Formatted Page Number	1
✓ Section	1
✓ Page Number	1 of 1
✓ Vertical Page Position	1"
✓ Line Number	1
Column	1
✓ Word Count	0
✓ Number of Authors Editing	
✓ Spelling and Grammar Check	Checking
✓ Language	English (U.S.)
✓ Signatures	. Off
Information Management Policy	Off
Permissions	Off
Track Changes	Off
Caps Lock	Off
✓ Overtype	Insert
✓ Selection Mode	
✓ Macro Recording	Not Recording
✓ Upload Status	
✓ Document Updates Available	No
✓ View Shortcuts	
✓ Zoom	160%
✓ Zoom Slider	

When multiple authors are editing, a multi-editing indicator appears, as shown in Figure 39-7. Click the indicator to see who is editing.

FIGURE 39-7

Click the Number of Authors Editing indicator to see who else is editing the current document.

Save to Web (SkyDrive)

Windows Live SkyDrive is a relatively new service that replaces Office Live Workspace. SkyDrive provides up to 25 GB of free online storage space, accessed through your Windows Live credentials. Files and folders can be shared, and co-authoring is supported. The down side, unfortunately, is that the maximum file size is 50 MB, which limits the uses for which you can employ SkyDrive. You won't find SkyDrive mentioned by name in Word's user interface. If you already have a SkyDrive account set up, to get there in Word, choose File ➪ Save & Send ➪ Save to Web. If you don't already have a SkyDrive account, then continue reading.

Creating a SkyDrive Account

Creating a SkyDrive account requires a Windows Live ID. To obtain one, use an Internet browser and go to http://home.live.com/. Click Sign Up and fill in the required information (noting that you can either create a live.com or hotmail.com e-mail address or click the Or Use Your Own E-mail Address link).

Once you have a Windows Live ID, you're ready to roll. Click the Sign In button and provide your Windows Live ID credentials (complete e-mail address and password) in the dialog box shown in Figure 39-8.

FIGURE 39-8

When logging into Windows Live, use your e-mail address rather than your display name.

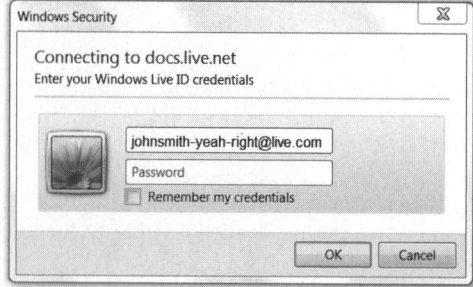

The first time you log in this way, Windows Live accesses your free 25-GB online storage account. By default, there are two top-level folders: Public and My Documents, both shown in Figure 39-9. Use Public for documents, pictures, and other files that you want to share with anybody who has a Windows Live ID. Use My Documents for more secure online storage. Use encryption and Digital Rights Management permissions for even more secure storage, or consider renting a safe-deposit box.

Caution

Is SkyDrive safe and secure? I don't know. While I have no qualms about putting vacation photos or test documents there for temporary storage, I would not put anything proprietary or personal there. It might be more secure than my own hard drive — or not. I just don't know. It's new, and being a neophobe, I don't trust anything that's new. If I absolutely needed to store something more sensitive there, I would use permissions and encryption. ∎

FIGURE 39-9

The Windows Live link and New button open a browser. Stick with Public, My Documents, and Save As to stay within Word.

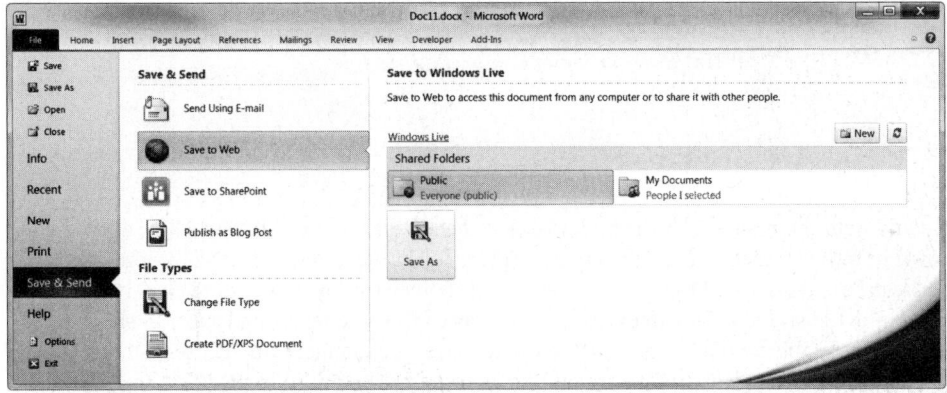

Accessing SkyDrive Documents

When you come to SkyDrive for the first time, it's useful to create some infrastructure for when you later return. Note the New button in Figure 39-9. It opens your Web browser, and from there you can enter a name for the folder and the desired Share With: settings (Everyone, My Network, Just Me, or Select people). However, it may be easier to double-click on either Public or My Documents, which will display a Windows Explorer–based file dialog box within Word. Here you can right-click in a blank area and choose New Folder to create a new folder. The name *New folder* is highlighted. Type a name for the folder and press Enter.

Adding a SkyDrive Shortcut to Your Favorites List

Even more useful than creating new folders, however, is putting down some breadcrumbs so you can find your way back easily. After you double-click Public or My Documents (or click Save

As), Word displays the Save As dialog box, and the current location is now the SkyDrive location. Dismiss the Save As dialog box and press Ctrl+O (or choose File ⇨ Open). Then click in the location field near the top of the dialog box, as shown in Figure 39-10.

FIGURE 39-10

For easy return, drag SkyDrive folder locations into the Favorites list.

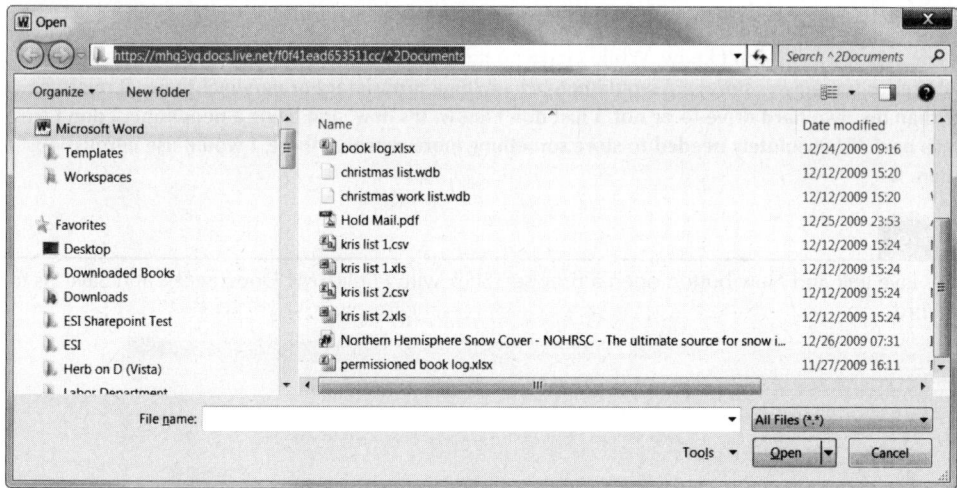

Click and hold the mouse over the folder icon at the left end of the SkyDrive URL, and drag it down into the Favorites area, as shown in Figure 39-11. Release the mouse button when the ScreenTip says Create Link in Favorites. (If the ScreenTip says something else, you might be dropping the shortcut into an existing folder instead.) If the resulting Favorites shortcut name is not suitably obvious, right-click on it and choose Rename. I find it useful to prepend "SkyDrive" to such shortcuts. If you like, you can create multiple shortcuts to different SkyDrive folders.

From now on, to access existing SkyDrive folders and documents, use the Favorites links in any dialog box based on Windows Explorer. Those links are available in all Office 2010 applications, as well as in Windows Explorer itself.

Note

As of this writing, Microsoft says that SkyDrive will support co-authoring for Office 2010 documents. It does not provide such support at the current time. When and if it does, refer to the earlier sections in this chapter on co-authoring in SharePoint to see how to use collaborative features. ∎

Release the mouse button when the ScreenTip says Create Link in Favorites.

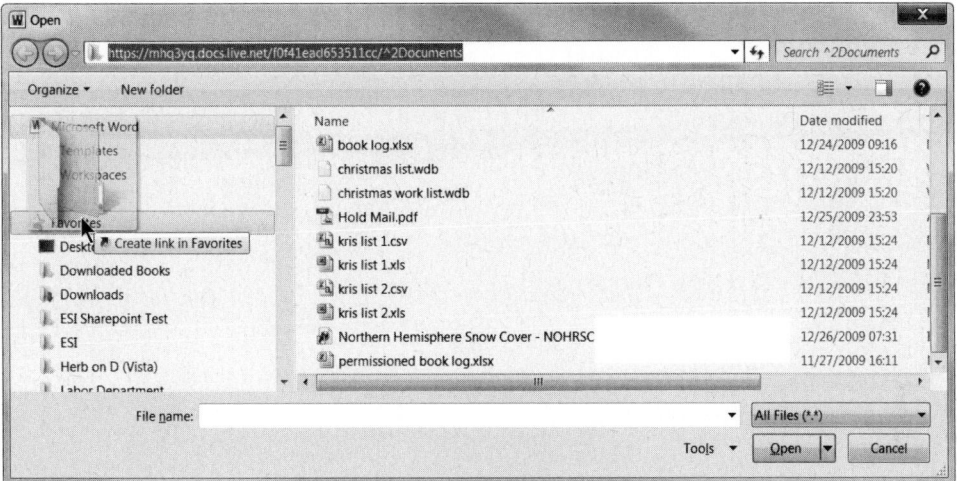

Summary

In this chapter, you've seen how SharePoint integrates with Word 2010 — sort of. You've learned how to initiate contact with a SharePoint site, save files to the SharePoint server, and open them. You've also seen how co-authoring allows you to work with other authors to avoid having to work with multiple versions of the same document. You've also seen how to access 25 GB of free online storage using Windows Live SkyDrive and your Windows Live ID. You should now be able to do the following:

- Save a document to your SharePoint site.
- Check out (open) a document from a SharePoint site.
- Block other authors from editing parts of a document you need to reserve.
- Find out who else is editing the current document.
- Set up a SkyDrive online storage account.
- Save and retrieve files stored on SkyDrive.

SharePoint Workspace

The SharePoint Workspace 2010 application is collaborative software that provides local access to documents stored or shared using SharePoint and Shared Folders. SharePoint Workspace replaces the Groove client from Office 2007. To a certain extent, it also replaces SharePoint Workspace and document-management functions that were built into previous versions of Word, Excel, and PowerPoint. It provides a third sharing mechanism, Shared Folders, which allows you to share folders among your own computers as well as with friends and colleagues.

Just when you thought integration was king, features integrated into Office get farmed out to another client application altogether. Rather than dwelling on that, let's just dive in and start using SharePoint Workspace. Please note that this book is called *The Office 2010 Bible* — not *The SharePoint Workspace 2010 Bible*. For that reason, I cover only the basics dealing with gaining access to documents — enough to whet your appetite, perhaps, or maybe just enough so you can determine whether the SharePoint Workspace client application has anything to offer you. For the calendar, discussions, and other features, consult the Help file or a detailed book about SharePoint Workspace 2010.

First, some definitions are in order. To begin with, let's distinguish between a *Microsoft SharePoint Workspace 2010 client* (the application) and a *SharePoint workspace*, which is a copy of all or part of a SharePoint site's content — which can include documents, a calendar (which, while enticing, is not actually supported by SharePoint Workspace), links, and other shared assets.

Yes, this overlapping and redundant terminology is confusing, but it's useful for understanding this chapter.

IN THIS CHAPTER

Groove versus SharePoint

SharePoint Workspace 2010 basics

Creating and deleting accounts

Creating and deleting workspaces

Sending workspace invitations

Working with workspace documents

To try for some clarity, I will use *SPW 2010* to refer to the client software, and I will refer to the local storage area as a *SharePoint workspace,* also called a SharePoint site.

A SharePoint workspace is logically parallel to a Groove workspace. Both kinds of workspaces can be created with SharePoint Workspace 2010. SharePoint Workspace 2010 can also be used to share folders without the overhead of SharePoint or Groove, that is, if all you need is access to files and folders with no need for any kind of coordination or control.

What's a workspace? A *workspace* is a set of (hopefully related) folders and files. Typically, a workspace contains a set of folders and files for working on a particular project or task. It might contain data, Word documents, Excel worksheets/spreadsheets, PowerPoint documents, resource documents, links, and any other assets you need to complete your part of a project or task.

You would typically use a SharePoint workspace to carve out a portion of a SharePoint site to which you need access wherever you are. Typically, this would allow you to use that material even when you are not connected to a SharePoint server or the Internet, as well as to access several other SharePoint tools, such as announcements, links, tasks, and team discussion. You might also prefer to use a SharePoint workspace when access to the server is slow, rather than waiting each time you need to access a document from the server. Then, when content changes — either on the server or on your own computer — you can synchronize your personal SharePoint workspace with the SharePoint server.

In the past, you would typically use a Groove workspace to synchronize a set of working files and documents between two or more computers and/or users. This allowed you, for example, to coordinate and synchronize files and other content you needed for a project (whether for work, home, or whatever) between your home desktop computer and a laptop you use while traveling, at the library, and so on. You can accomplish the same functions using a SharePoint workspace.

For business users who do not have access to a SharePoint server, a Groove workspace provided a substitute for some of the convenience of using a SharePoint server. Although a Groove workspace did not provide for co-authoring, it did let multiple users coordinate their work by automatically synchronizing content as it changed. Hence, if you were working on the Chapter 7 file and someone else was working on the Chapter 8 file, when each of you saved changes to his or her own copy of the respective file, the other person's copy was automatically updated on a regular schedule or when you explicitly chose to synchronize. Synchronization is handled automatically by SharePoint Workspace 2010.

In this chapter, you'll learn how to use SharePoint Workspace 2010 to create SharePoint workspaces, as well as shared folders. Although the chapter won't come anywhere close to exhausting SharePoint Workspace 2010's full range of features, if you've never before touched this new application, this chapter will give you a basic sense of how to use it and what it can do for you, an Office user.

Who Needs SharePoint Workspace 2010?

If you never collaborate or share documents with anybody — not even with yourself between two or more computers that you control — proceed to Chapter 41, which basically tells you how to collaborate with yourself while using different Office 2010 applications. SharePoint Workspace 2010 is for people who need to coordinate information that is stored and used on different computers — and for this discussion, *different computers* can refer to different partitions on the same computer when multiple copies of the same files need to be maintained.

If you do not know or care what SharePoint is and do not work in an environment that uses a SharePoint server to facilitate collaboration, then please feel free to concentrate on the sections of this chapter dealing with SharePoint workspaces and shared folders. No sense fretting over features you don't have.

On the other hand, if you frequently find yourself having to reconcile edits — tracked and otherwise — in multiple versions of the same document being edited by different people, you might want to go back and peruse Chapter 39. The collaborative benefits of co-authoring can put an end to a lot of frustration, and SharePoint might be a worthwhile investment for you or your employer.

Note
SharePoint Workspace 2010 is included in the Professional Plus editions of Office 2010. ■

Groove Workspaces versus SharePoint Workspaces

What is the difference between a Groove workspace and a SharePoint workspace? A Groove workspace does not provide the following:

- A local copy of SharePoint-based assets

- Check-in and check-out of documents (when preferred) so that multiple people can't edit at cross-purposes

- Co-authoring of the same document in real time, when taking complete ownership of a document isn't necessary or when co-authoring makes the work go more quickly and smoothly

- Server storage of shared resources and documents

- An enterprise-wide server location for managing a team project

Note
Some of these same needs — such as server-based storage of folders and other resources and co-authoring — might be met by SkyDrive. SharePoint provides greater control and more space, but could be overkill if your needs are met by SkyDrive, which is free. ■

Conversely, is SharePoint Workspace really what you need? Suppose, for example, that you — an individual user, and not part of a team — want to be able to edit a project's files from multiple locations, such as your work computer, your home computer, and your notebook computer. In addition, suppose some or all of those computers are sometimes offline. A SharePoint workspace enables you to do the following:

- Automatically (or on demand) synchronize a shared workspace in multiple locations when you are connected to the Internet.

- Work on documents even when you aren't connected to the Internet, and then synchronize the next time you're connected.

- Share a workspace with multiple peers who aren't on your work network or in the same Windows workgroup.

- Share multiple workspaces with multiple peers, including yourself when you're using a different computer.

Using the SharePoint Workspace 2010 Client

In order to use SharePoint Workspace 2010, you need an account. The first time you start SharePoint Workspace 2010, you are prompted to either create an account or to restore an existing account. (To create a new account later, right-click on the SharePoint Workspace 2010 icon in the system tray and choose New Account.) Assuming you want to create an account, click Next, type your name and e-mail address, and click Finish. (If you have an Account Configuration Code you probably aren't reading this chapter, and if you are you need to speak with your company's IT manager.)

Tip

Don't use the same name when creating multiple SharePoint Workspace 2010 accounts for yourself. Your name is used to identify the accounts. If you use the same name each time, you won't be able to tell which name is which account. Instead, include something about the e-mail address (if you're using different e-mail addresses) or about the computer you're using. ∎

Note

Accounts are *not* tied to Windows Live IDs. The e-mail address you provide here has nothing to do with Windows Live. Your e-mail address is simply one way that other SharePoint Workspace 2010 members can contact you. ∎

Deleting an Account

Deleting an account can be a little confusing because of the way information is presented. To delete an account, right-click on the SharePoint Workspace 2010 icon on the system tray, click the account name you want to delete, and then click Launchbar. In the Launchbar window, choose File ➪ Options ➪ General ➪ Preferences button ➪ Account tab. The lower part of the Account tab panel displays the name of your computer — not your SharePoint Workspace 2010 account name. That notwithstanding, this is the place to delete the account. It will not delete your computer name.

Caution

Deleting an account will delete any standard workspaces you have created and all data and files they contain (see "Workspaces," below). Back up anything you need to save before deleting an account. ■

Once you've backed up everything you need to save, under Delete Account from This Computer, click Delete. Notice the admonitions about what deleting does, and then click Yes to confirm the deletion. SharePoint Workspace 2010 deletes the account, leaving any other accounts you have untouched. Click OK to complete this mindless wanton destruction.

The SharePoint Workspace 2010 Interface

There are two main SharePoint Workspace 2010 windows: the Launchbar and the Workspace window. When you install SharePoint Workspace 2010 and configure it to start automatically, a SharePoint Workspace 2010 icon is added to the Windows notification area (also known as the system tray). To open SharePoint Workspace 2010, right-click on the SharePoint Workspace 2010 icon and click Launchbar. If you have multiple accounts, you will first need to click the account you wish to use.

The Launchbar, shown in Figure 40-1, is displayed in Workspace Folders view by default. Here it's displayed in Workspaces Type view, which you can select by choosing View and setting Workspaces to Type. This example lets you see that there are three types of workspaces currently set up: Groove Workspace, SharePoint Workspace, and Shared Folder (the latter isn't a workspace per se).

FIGURE 40-1

Use the Launchbar to access your Workspaces and Contacts lists.

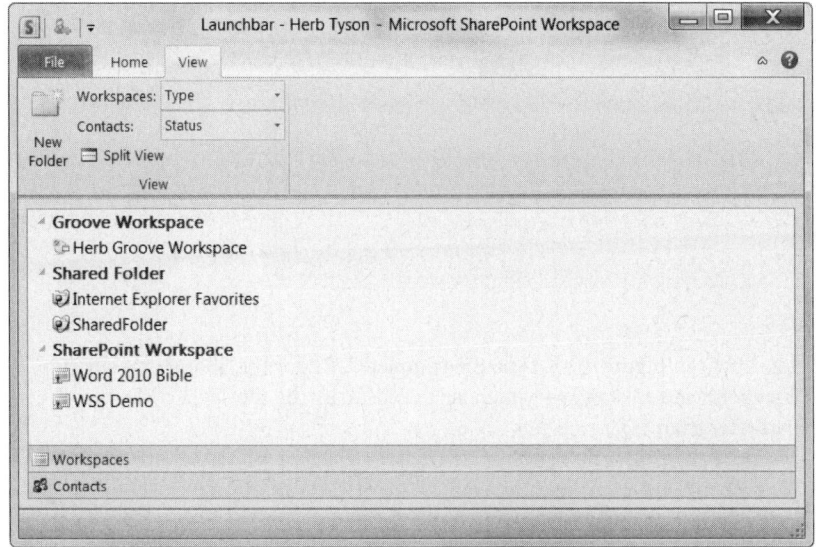

Use the Launchbar to create new workspaces, change workspace properties, control alerts, issue invitations, and add and remove contacts, among other things.

To display a Workspace window, right-click on the SharePoint Workspace 2010 icon in the system tray and choose Open Workspace. (Again, if you have multiple accounts, you will first need to click the desired account.) In Select Workspace, click on the workspace you want to open and then click OK. You will learn more about workspaces in "Workspaces," later in this chapter. The Workspace window enables you to do many of the same things as the Launchbar.

SharePoint Workspaces

To create a SharePoint workspace, display the Launchbar, and, in the Home tab, choose New ➪ SharePoint Workspace, as shown in Figure 40-2.

The Launchbar lets you create SharePoint and Groove workspaces as well as Shared Folders.

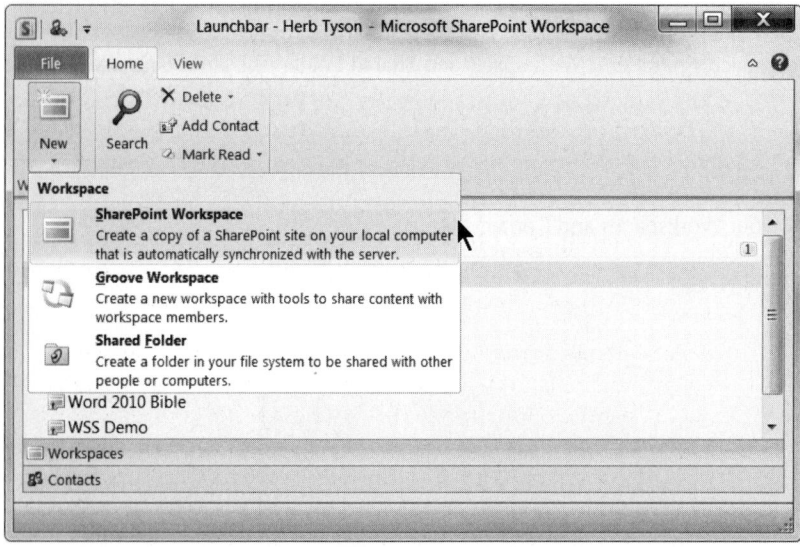

In the Location field, shown in Figure 40-3, type the complete URL for the SharePoint site (top-level SharePoint folder you want to copy) — which isn't necessarily the top-level URL — and then click Configure rather than OK.

Why? There are two "why" questions. First, "Why the top-level folder rather than just the basic URL?" Good question.

The basic URL refers to the entire SharePoint site. You usually will not want to sync the entire site because it's often a lot more than you need. Even if you're a pack rat like me and like having as much data as possible, sites sometimes contain hundreds of gigabytes of data — often more than your own hard disk capacity. Synchronizing that much information is very time- and bandwidth-consuming. It's much better to narrow it down just to what you're likely to need. If you need more, you can select it later on.

FIGURE 40-3

Specify the Location URL as narrowly as possible to save yourself work downstream.

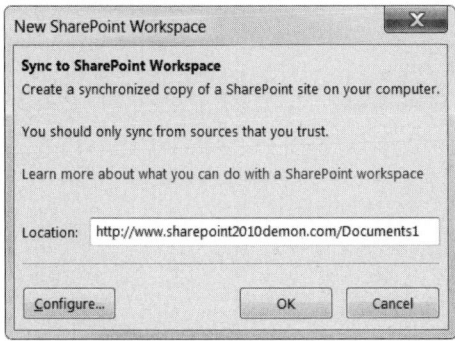

The second question is "Why click Configure rather than OK?" Good question. This gives you an opportunity to narrow down or expand your request if the initial URL wasn't precise or inclusive enough.

So click Configure. You will next be prompted for your user ID and password. If the SharePoint site is not on the same network as you, your ID will probably be in the form *DOMAIN/user*. Provide the information requested, choose to remember your password, if desired, and press Enter.

In the Configure Settings dialog box, shown in Figure 40-4, notice the Content field, which for most items says "No Content," and only for Documents says "All Content." That's because I specified the Document folder rather than the entire site. This particular site contains dozens of libraries — some with tens of thousands of huge files. To synchronize that much content could take several days, even at 25 Mbps. Worse, different libraries sometimes have their own separate passworded access. When synchronizing for the first time (even assuming you choose the Remember Password option), you might be prompted for your credentials dozens of times. Once *is* enough.

If desired, change the Content setting to All Content or Headers Only for any additional folders that strike your fancy. Click OK when you're ready. SharePoint Workspace 2010 now opens the SharePoint Workspace window, as shown in Figure 40-5. At the left, if Content is checked, you will see the types of content available via SharePoint Workspace (Documents, Lists, and Discussion). Under Available on Server, you see assets that are not available using SharePoint Workspace, including Calendar.

FIGURE 40-4

Being selective means faster synchronization and not being overburdened by too much local storage.

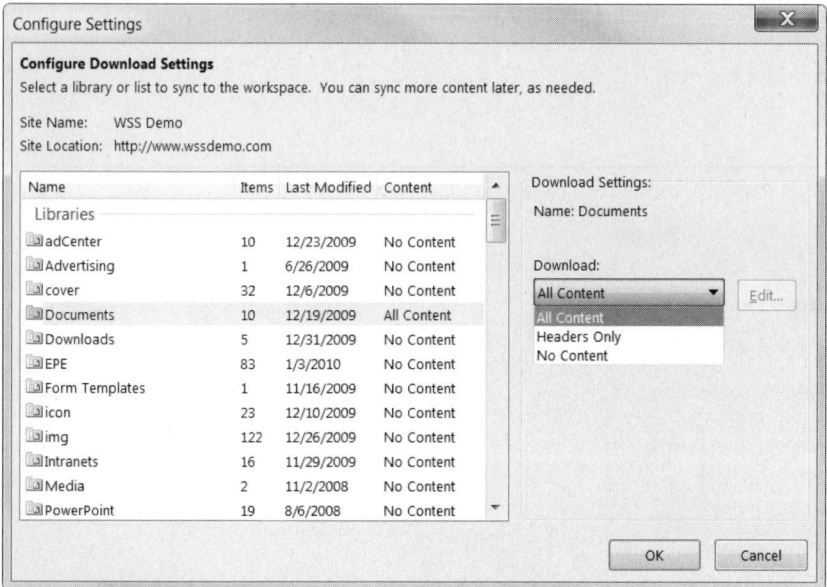

FIGURE 40-5

A SharePoint Workspace window will vary depending on your SharePoint Server implementation.

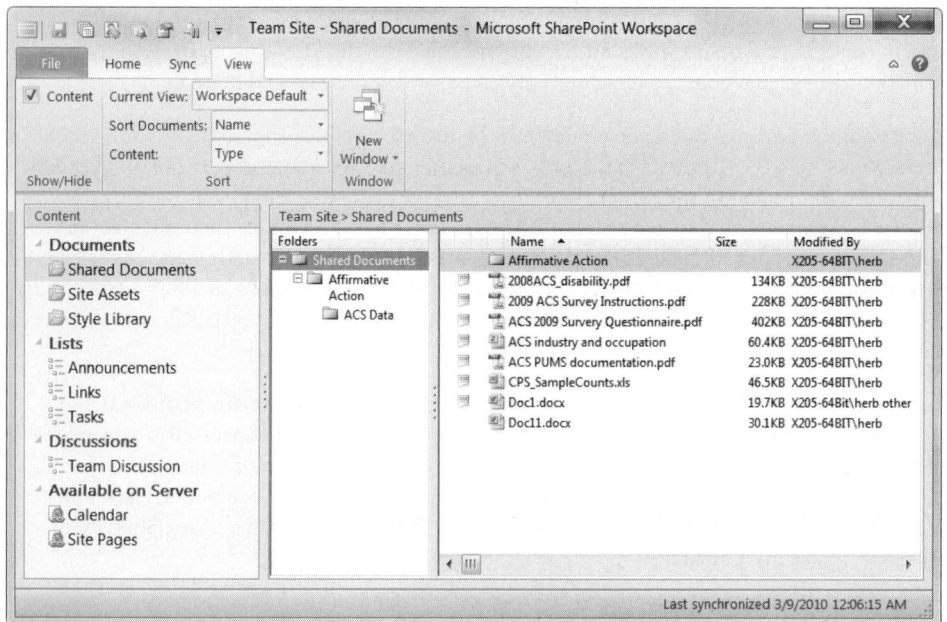

The available tools you see in the Workspace window will depend upon, among other things, the implementation of this particular server. Tools and implementation vary so widely that I could not hope to cover them in this brief introductory chapter. As the saying goes, if you have questions, consult your site administrator.

To open a SharePoint workspace later, right-click on the SharePoint Workspace 2010 icon in Windows' notification area, and choose Open Workspace. Click the desired target, and then click OK.

Deleting a SharePoint Workspace

When your need to maintain a local copy of SharePoint resources goes away, delete the copy. This will, among other things, reduce your own computer's need to synchronize your copy with the server's. This reduces bandwidth and overhead. This will also eliminate space on your own hard drive where your copy of the SharePoint workspace resides.

To delete a SharePoint workspace, click on it in the Launchbar and press the Delete key. Click Yes to confirm your desire to delete. Note that deleting the workspace does not have any effect on the SharePoint site itself or your access to it through a Web browser. Also, should the need arise, you can always carve out a new SharePoint workspace anytime you want — now that you know how.

Groove Workspaces

Unlike SharePoint, Groove workspaces do not provide shared or completely coordinated access to the same files. Instead, when computers are sharing a workspace, each computer has its own local copy of the files in the workspace. This might seem redundant, but what it lacks in storage thriftiness it makes up for in convenience. Moreover, for some of us, redundancy is a benefit, as long as the required storage is not excessive.

Note
If you are working in an enterprise, you might have access to additional facilities through Groove Server or SharePoint Server. Because implementation can vary substantially, it would be impossible for this chapter to accurately or adequately describe how you interact with the environment created by your IT department. Instead, this section focuses on the individual user's Groove workspace experience, and aspects common to all users of the SharePoint Workspace 2010 client application with respect to Groove workspaces. ■

Workspaces

To create a Groove workspace, in the Launchbar Home tab, choose New ⇨ Groove Workspace. In the New Groove Workspace dialog box, type a name for the workspace and click Create. (The Options button lets you choose 2010 or 2007 — it defaults to 2010.)

A Groove workspace contains three kinds of tools by default: Documents, Discussion, and Calendar (see Figure 40-6). Right-click on the blank area in the Content section and choose Add

New Tool to see a list of additional kinds of content you can add to the workspace. Note that the numeral 1 you see in a rounded green rectangle indicates that one user is active in the displayed workspace.

Adding Documents and Folders to a Groove Workspace

There are several ways to add documents and folders to a Groove workspace. The most natural way is by dragging and dropping, as shown in Figure 40-6. Note that when you drag items into a Groove workspace, you are not moving the files — you are copying them. The mouse pointer will gain a + sign to show that you are copying rather than moving.

Note

When you make changes to files in a workspace, only those copies are changed (and eventually any workspaces that are shared). If I copy files from C:\Consulting\CSS to my Groove workspace, the original files in C:\Consulting\CSS remain untouched. If I want my own files to be updated, I need to drag files from the workspace back into C:\Consulting\CSS.

Note also that if you use Windows Explorer to search your hard drive for the files that reside in a Groove workspace, you will not find them. That's because Groove workspace does not store them as files. Instead, they are stored in a database, and Windows Explorer does not know how to search SPW 2010's database. ■

FIGURE 40-6

A Groove workspace can contain various kinds of tools or content.

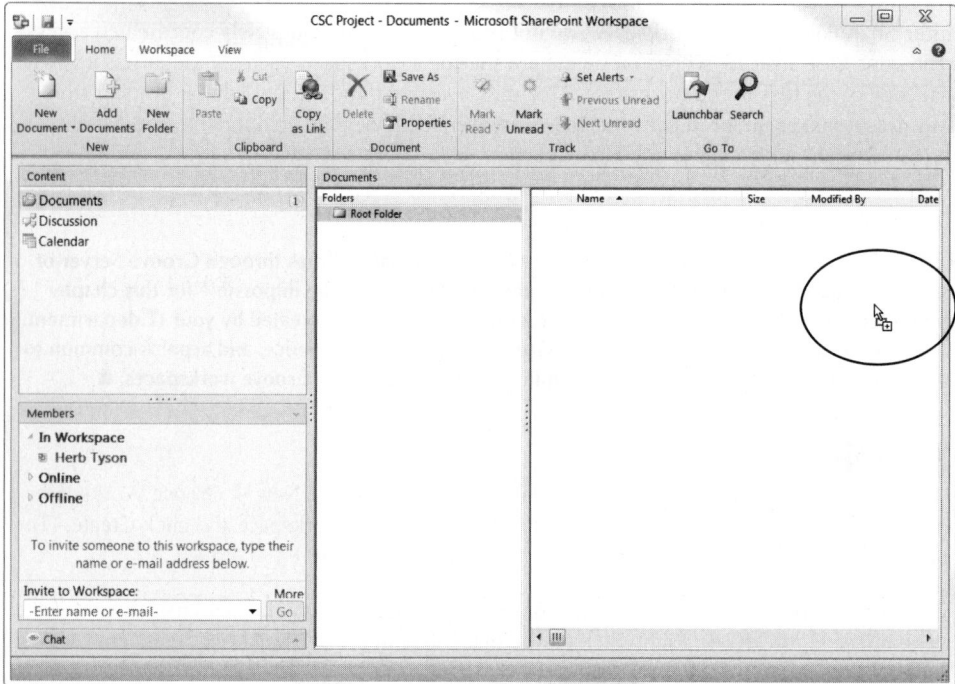

Because files and folders you copy to a Groove workspace are not tied in any way to the original files, if you delete the files in the workspace, the original files are not touched. This should reinforce for you, however, the idea that if you want any changes stored in *normal* file format, you will need to drag or otherwise copy them to the desired folder on your hard drive — outside of SharePoint Workspace 2010.

Deleting Workspaces

To delete a Groove workspace from your computer, select the workspace in the Launchbar and press the Delete key, or click Delete in the Home tab of the Ribbon (or right-click and click Delete). To delete all copies of that workspace from all your computers (i.e., all computers using your current SharePoint Workspace 2010 account), click the Delete tool's drop-down arrow and choose Delete from All Computers. This does not delete copies of the workspace that reside on other user accounts. To delete all copies of the Groove workspace everywhere, choose Delete for All Members.

Caution

Make regular file-system copies of anything you want saved before deleting a Groove workspace. Once you delete a Groove workspace, the delete cannot be undone. As long as the workspace still exists on any computer, however, you can re-create it. So, if there are no unsynchronized changes that resided only in your copy, you can effectively undo the delete, even though there is no Undo command. However, once you have deleted every copy of a Groove workspace, it cannot be undone, period (unless you have a backup copy of the folder structure where Groove keeps its database). Windows Explorer's own Undo command, however, will not do you any good in any of these situations. ■

Sending Workspace Invitations

To be of any real use, workspaces need to be used from different computers. One way to do that is to invite others, even if it's just yourself.

You can invite someone to use a Groove workspace either from the Launchbar or from a workspace's Workspace tab. To invite another user, in the Launchbar, click to select the workspace, and choose one of the Invite options shown in Figure 40-7. If you choose Invite to Workspace and the user isn't currently available, the invitation is sent by e-mail, so this option is generally most efficient for inviting other people.

In the To field, type the name or e-mail address of the contact. Set Role to Manager, Participant, or Guest. Consult the Help system to see precisely how each is defined by default, and how to change the levels of access granted to each for a particular workspace.

In the space provided, type a message. If the invitation will go by e-mail, you can decide what level of information and detail the invitees need, based on your assessment of his familiarity with Groove workspaces.

If you choose Invite My Other Computers, the workspace is automatically shared with your other computers where your current account is being used. Computers to which you've copied your Groove account information will automatically receive the shared folder information.

FIGURE 40-7

There are several ways to invite someone to a Groove workspace.

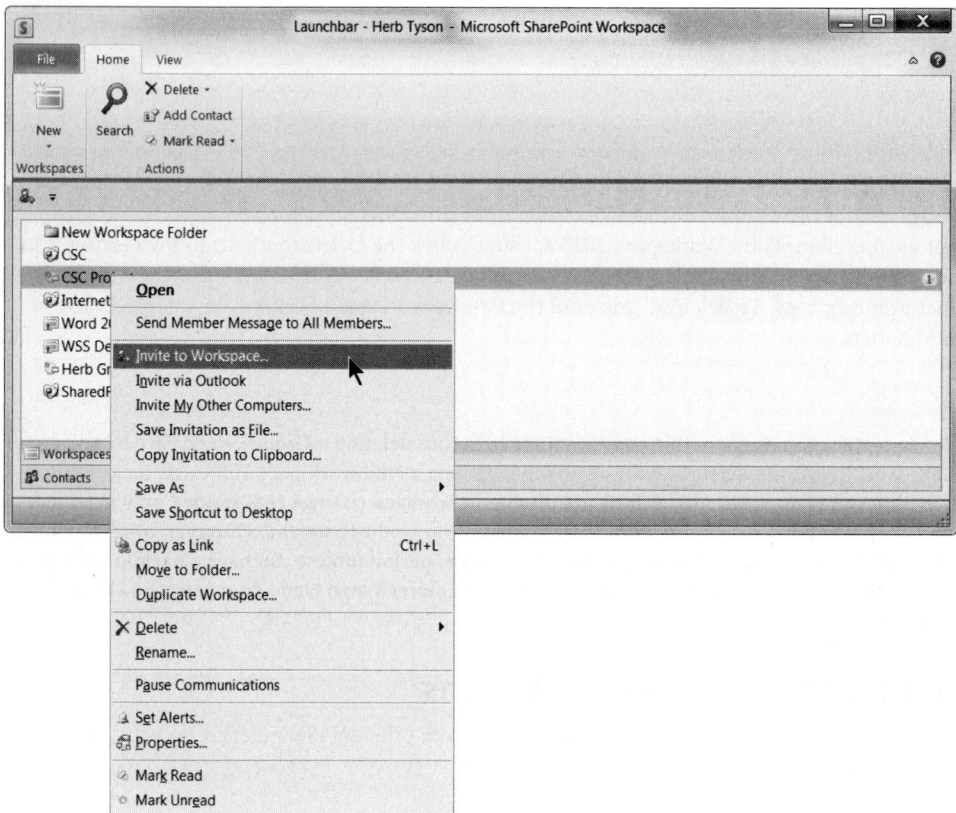

Canceling Pending Invitations

To cancel a membership, open the Groove workspace. In the Members panel, select the member you want to uninvite, and click Uninvite Member in the Workspace tab. To cancel all pending invitations, click Cancel All Invitations, also in the Workspace tab. You cannot cancel a pending individual invitation.

Accepting Workspace Invitations

You can receive a workspace invitation in either of two ways. If you are online and logged into Groove, the invitation shows up as a pop-up (or a pop-down, because it appears by the notification area), as shown in Figure 40-8. If the invitation disappears before you can get to it, hover the mouse over the SharePoint Workspace 2010 icon in the system tray to make the message reappear. Click the invitation link.

FIGURE 40-8

If you are logged into your SharePoint Workspace 2010 account, invitation links appear near the notification area.

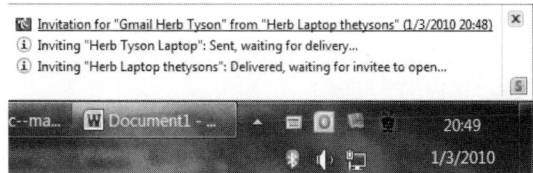

In Respond to Invitation, click Accept or Decline, as you wish, or Close to defer a decision. If you click Reply and send a reply, that is in effect a verbose acceptance.

If you're not logged into your SharePoint Workspace 2010 account, the invitation will arrive as an e-mail. The e-mail will contain a link for you to click to accept the invitation.

Caution

For some reason, the e-mail invitations sent by Groove sometimes contain broken links. Because of the way the lines are wrapped, part of the link can occur on a successive line, and fail to be included as part of the link. When that happens, copy the orphaned portion to the clipboard and then click the non-orphaned portion. When your browser appears, press Esc to stop it from loading the broken link. Paste the orphaned portion at the end of the URL shown, to complete it, and then press enter to load the link. ∎

Working with Groove Documents

As noted previously, Groove does not have facilities for version control or managing editing by multiple users at the same time. It does, however, check before saving changed files to the workspace. When you're working from a Groove workspace, if there are changes, SharePoint Workspace 2010 alerts you to that fact and asks if you want to save the changes to the Groove workspace.

If the new version conflicts with an existing version — that is, changes from another user who is logged into the same workspace — SharePoint Workspace 2010 alerts you to the conflict. You can then use either the Compare or Combine commands to resolve the different changes.

Shared Folders

The third kind of workspace, Shared Folders, is not displayed in a SharePoint Workspace 2010 window. Instead, it is displayed in a Windows Explorer window, with the Shared Folder Synchronization panel at the left, as shown in Figure 40-9.

If you turn the Synchronization panel off (by clicking the X in the upper-right corner), you can turn it back on for any folder — not just folders that have already been shared. If Windows Explorer's menu is not already displayed, choose Organize ➪ Layout ➪ Menu bar. In the menu, choose View ➪ Explorer Bar ➪ Groove Folder Synchronization to redisplay the Shared Folder Synchronization panel. Or, for folders that have already been shared with SharePoint Workspace 2010, simply double-click on the shared folder in the Launchbar.

FIGURE 40-9

SharePoint Workspace 2010 uses Windows Explorer to display shared folders.

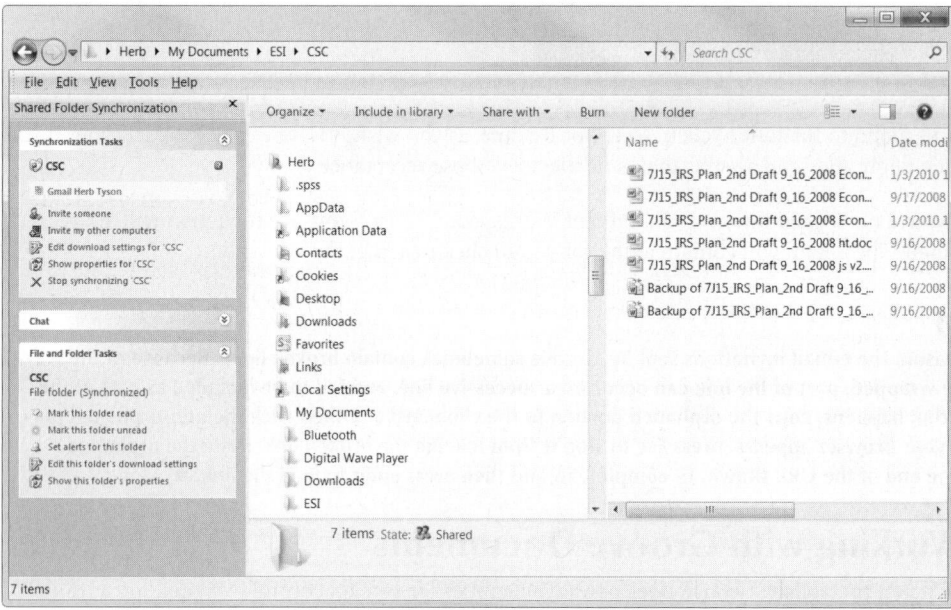

Once a folder has been shared, you can use the Shared Folder Synchronization panel controls to invite people or your other computer to share the folder. This is extremely intuitive, so you should peruse the options shown in the panel.

Caution

Unlike with a SharePoint workspace or a Groove workspace, when you're using a Shared Folder, SharePoint Workspace 2010 provides no file coordination. Because you're working on a local copy of each file, it is quite possible to edit that file at cross-purposes with someone else. This can lead to confusion when multiple users are editing the same file. If you are not averse to using a cloud-based server, you might consider using SkyDrive for such editing — assuming that SharePoint is not an option. When you share a folder on SkyDrive, co-authoring controls are available in Word 2010, making editing at cross-purposes less likely. ■

Deleting a Shared Folder

When you delete a Shared Folder workspace using SharePoint Workspace 2010, you aren't deleting the actual folder. Instead, you're simply telling SharePoint Workspace 2010 to stop synchronizing and sharing it. To do this, in the Launchbar, right-click on the folder and choose Delete ➪ From This Computer or For All Members. If you choose the former, you're only unsharing the folder on your own computer. If you choose the latter, you're unsharing for all members. In neither case, however, are any actual files deleted. All that is removed is the association with SharePoint Workspace 2010.

Summary

In this chapter, you've been introduced to SharePoint Workspace 2010. You now know how to create a SharePoint Workspace 2010 account, how to create and delete workspaces, and how to share a Groove workspace and folders. You should now be able to do the following:

- Use SharePoint Workspace 2010 to copy all or part of a SharePoint site to your computer for use offline.

- Use a Groove workspace to synchronize files on different computers you own.

- Use a Groove workspace to synchronize work performed by a project team, without using SharePoint.

- Send Groove workspace and Shared Folder invitations to contacts.

- Use the Shared Folder Synchronization panel in Windows Explorer to work with Shared Folders.

Integration with Other Office Applications

I n some ways, using Office 2010 is like using a single multipurpose program. Things mesh together almost seamlessly. For example, when you insert a chart into a Word 2010 document, the process starts Excel 2010, almost as if Excel were an extension of Word.

Although integration is now better than ever for many things you do in Office 2010, there are times when you really wonder if the left hand knows what the right hand is doing. For example, when copying cells from an Excel spreadsheet into a Word table, you might wonder why the default action would be Nest Table (which might, for example, paste a 10 × 10 selection into a single Word table cell).

In this chapter, you explore the ways in which OneNote, Excel, PowerPoint, and Outlook communicate with Word. Some things are perfectly intuitive, and others aren't. The casual PowerPoint user might never stumble on how to send outlines back and forth with Word. Do you ever wonder about the array of different picture options when copying images between Word and other programs? Which format should you use, and what are the consequences of using this one or that? How can pasting a 40K picture into a Word file add 900K to its size? In this chapter, the focus is on the less intuitive, to get you over some hurdles and stumbling blocks, and to make sense of some of those little mysteries that can make using Word seem like a struggle.

OneNote

Until you get in the swing of using OneNote for note taking and project tracking, you might still do some of that work in Word. You also might have documentation previously generated in Word that you want to transfer to OneNote, or OneNote information that you want to incorporate in a more formal document in Word. Transferring information between the two applications is a breeze, making it easy for you to choose the note taking tool that's appropriate for any given situation.

Printing from Word to OneNote

When you want to incorporate information from a Word document into OneNote, you "print" from Word to OneNote. Start by opening the document to print in Word. To send only a portion of the document to OneNote, select the information to transfer.

Choose File ➪ Print. In the Backstage view, open the Printer drop-down list, and click Send to OneNote 2010, the choice shown in Figure 41-1. If you selected part of the document to send, open the first Settings drop-down list, which initially shows Print All Pages, and click Print Selection. Then click the Print button near the top.

FIGURE 41-1

Printing a file from Word to OneNote

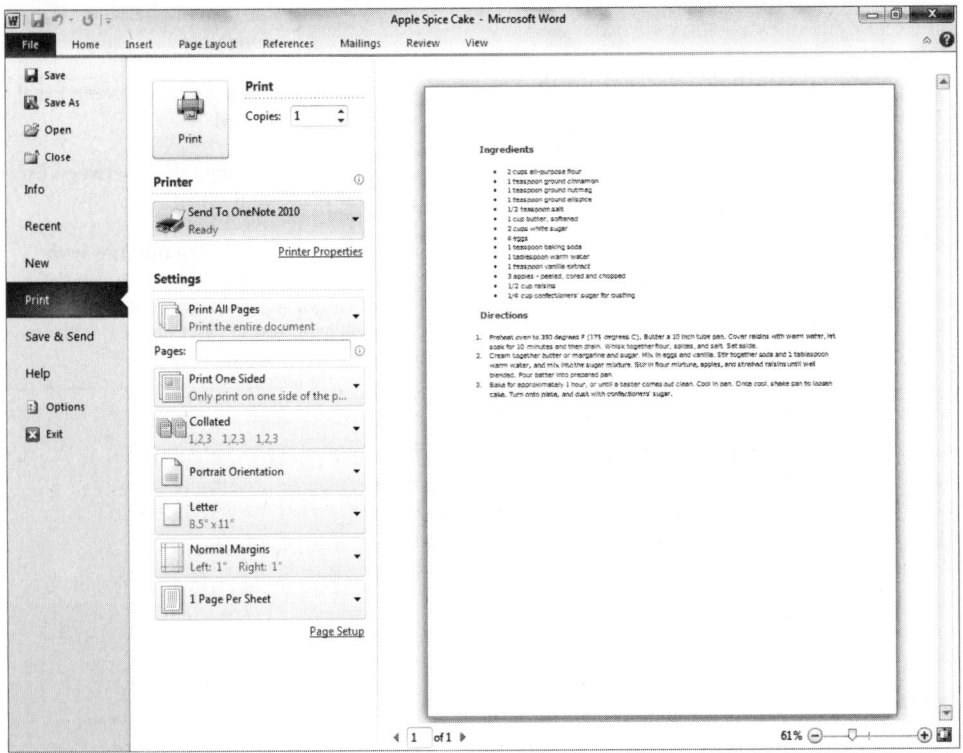

OneNote opens, and the Select Location in OneNote dialog box appears, as shown in Figure 41-2. Select one of the notebooks under Recent Picks, or use the folder tree under All Notebooks to choose a different destination. Then click OK. Word inserts the information as a page image on a new page tab in the specified notebook.

FIGURE 41-2

Selecting a Notebook destination for the "printed" Word information

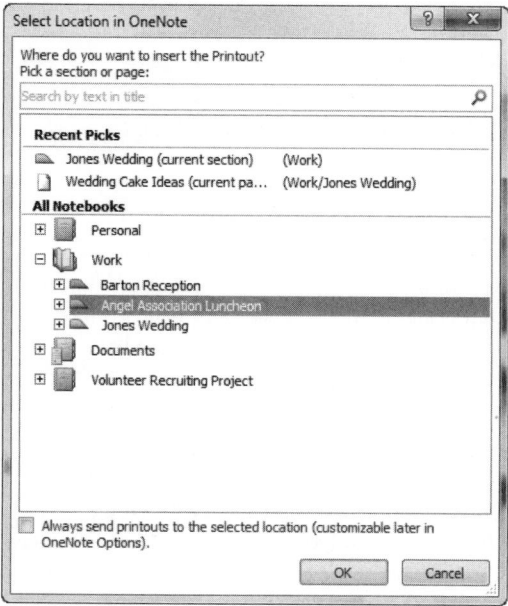

Sending from OneNote to Word

You can send a notebook page from OneNote to Word. The notebook page's information — notes, links, pictures, and more — are converted to an appropriate format and placed in a new Word document with as many pages as needed to include all the information. After selecting the page to send, choose File ➪ Send, and then click Send to Word.

Excel

Although sharing work between Word and Excel often works well, differences in how the two programs operate can produce confusing results. This can be addressed by becoming aware of those differences and working in a way that accommodates them and smoothes the way. This section looks at Word and Excel and ways to share text, data, tables, and graphics.

Using Excel Content in Word

Word offers a variety of different ways to share and exchange content with Excel:

- **Clipboard.** Copying content to the Clipboard, and then using Paste or Paste Special to insert the contents into Word or Excel. Commandment: When in doubt, use Paste Special.

- **Chart.** Using Office 2010's Chart feature to create a chart inside Word using Excel's facilities.

- **Object.** Using Insert ⇨ Text ⇨ Object ⇨ Object ⇨ Create New or Create from File to embed all or part of an Excel worksheet into a Word document.

- **File.** Using Insert ⇨ Text ⇨ Object ⇨ Text from File to insert content from an Excel worksheet into a Word file.

A common method that does not work, however, is drag-and-drop. You cannot select data or other content in Excel and drag it into Word. Attempting to drag a selection in Excel simply expands the selection. The reverse does work, however — dragging from Word into Excel — as you'll see shortly.

Clipboard

Excel's Clipboard works differently from the Clipboard in most other Office programs. Why? Nobody seems to know for certain, although theories abound. The best theory is that Excel is cell-based, requiring a different working mode. If you're not an Excel veteran, however, it's likely to bother you. When you select cells in an Excel worksheet, they are highlighted as shown in Figure 41-3. At this point, they are merely highlighted, and cannot be moved or otherwise acted upon. You also need to copy (or cut) the selection to the Clipboard, by pressing Ctrl+C, right-clicking and choosing Copy, and so on.

FIGURE 41-3

To move cells in Excel, it's not enough to select them; you have to copy them to the Clipboard.

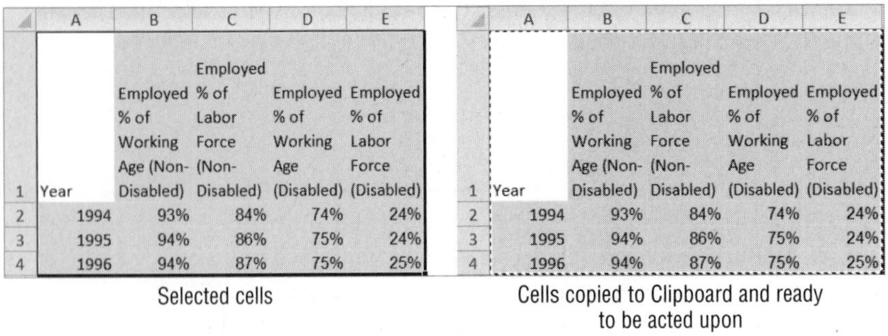

	A	B	C	D	E
			Employed		
		Employed	% of	Employed	Employed
		% of	Labor	% of	% of
		Working	Force	Working	Labor
		Age (Non-	(Non-	Age	Force
1	Year	Disabled)	Disabled)	(Disabled)	(Disabled)
2	1994	93%	84%	74%	24%
3	1995	94%	86%	75%	24%
4	1996	94%	87%	75%	25%

Selected cells

	A	B	C	D	E
			Employed		
		Employed	% of	Employed	Employed
		% of	Labor	% of	% of
		Working	Force	Working	Labor
		Age (Non-	(Non-	Age	Force
1	Year	Disabled)	Disabled)	(Disabled)	(Disabled)
2	1994	93%	84%	74%	24%
3	1995	94%	86%	75%	24%
4	1996	94%	87%	75%	25%

Cells copied to Clipboard and ready
to be acted upon

Even after you've copied the selection to the Clipboard, the Excel selection needs to remain high-lighted as shown (surrounded by a dashed outline). If you press Esc in Excel or double-click elsewhere (or perform any of a dozen or more other actions in Excel) the Paste button dies. Even if the data has actually been copied to the Clipboard, you still can't use the Paste button unless the selection is still active in Excel. More to the point, the Paste Special feature is no longer avail-able, and Paste Special often is the best way to deal with Excel data.

When the selection has been disturbed, and if the Clipboard was set up to automatically collect data, you can use the Clipboard pane itself to paste the selection into Word. However, the Paste Special options aren't available.

The Office Clipboard develops a terrible case of amnesia about Excel's data unless the selection is still active. Therefore, don't get distracted in the middle of trying to copy data from Excel to Word.

With the selection active in Excel, click where you want the data to appear in Word, click the Paste button's drop-down arrow, and choose Paste Special (or press Ctrl+Alt+V). The Paste Special dialog box, shown in Figure 41-4, appears. Notice that the default is HTML Format. Why is that the case, rather than Formatted Text (RTF), and does it make any difference?

FIGURE 41-4

When pasting a selection of cells from Excel into Word, you'll often have as many as eight options regard-ing how to paste.

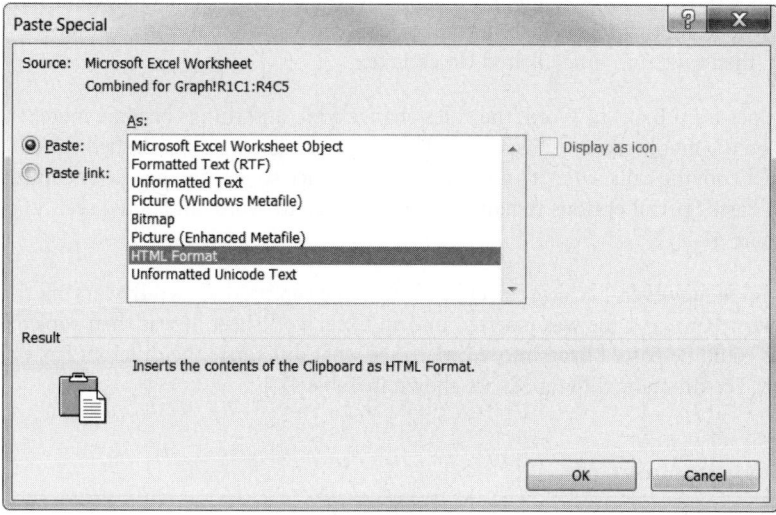

Nothing special was done in Excel to format the cells, so there's no compelling reason that HTML would have been chosen. That's simply the default. At the end of the day, both HTML and RTF retain both formatting and table structure, but there are differences. They might seem subtle, or they might seem substantial, depending on your needs. There also are differences among other options that might seemingly appear similar. Different Paste Special options are as follows:

- **Microsoft Office Excel Worksheet Object.** Inserts the selection as a complete mini-spreadsheet, complete with Excel facilities.

- **Formatted Text (RTF).** Inserts formatted text as a table, retaining the cell, column, and row formatting in effect in the Excel file. This option often misinterprets cell shading and other colors.

- **Unformatted Text.** Inserts plain text with no attributes. Tabs are used to separate text that originated in different cells.

- **Picture (Windows Metafile).** Inserts a `.wmf` picture file that does not retain the cell divisions in the resulting picture, that is, it's just a picture of the text (larger than either Bitmap or Enhanced Metafile).

- **Bitmap.** Inserts a picture file in a format smaller than either of the other two picture options.

- **Picture (Enhanced Metafile).** Inserts an `.emf` picture file that is essentially identical in appearance to the Windows Metafile, but is slightly smaller in size.

- **HTML Format.** Retains text formatting, but doesn't retain all of the table formatting. This usually results in a table that is smaller in width than the RTF table. This option inserts cell shading and colors more accurately than RTF.

- **Unformatted Unicode Text.** Usually, this yields the same result as unformatted text. Unicode goes well beyond ASCII and ANSI and provides for many more characters and languages. If you find that linguistic information is being lost when pasting as unformatted text, then switch to unformatted Unicode text.

When you copy graphics from Excel to Word, the rules change a bit, and things become more familiar. Right-click on the graphic and choose Copy. This time, you don't get the dashed selection because you're not copying cells — so it's a bit simpler, and once something has been copied to the Clipboard, the Paste Special options remain available. Switch to Word, and you'll see the options shown in Figure 41-5.

The simplicity stops there, however, because the choice you make can produce wildly varying file sizes. For example, a 40K `.jpg` file was inserted into an Excel worksheet. It was then copied to the Clipboard so it could be pasted back into Word, to see what difference the different Paste Special options make. The dramatic differences are shown in Table 41-1.

TABLE 41-1

Graphics Sizes When Using Different Paste Methods

Paste Special Method	File Extension	Size
Picture (Windows Metafile)	`.emf`	460K
Bitmap	`.bmp`	331K

Paste Special Method	File Extension	Size
Picture (Enhanced Metafile)	.emf	214K
Picture (GIF)	.gif	129K
Picture (PNG)	.png	821K
Picture (JPEG)	.jpg	47K
Microsoft Office Graphic Object (Default)	.gif	40K

FIGURE 41-5

When copying pictures from Excel to Word, no special handling is required.

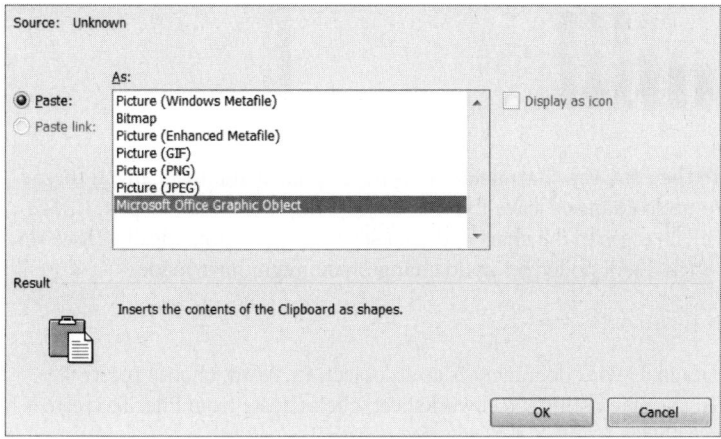

When using Paste Special, you might want to experiment to see which format gives you the best appearance in your document depending on how it's going to be presented (online versus on paper). However, based only on file size, Word's default option, Microsoft Office Graphic Object, is the best choice.

Chart

When you insert a chart, assuming that Excel 2010 is installed and available, Word starts Excel, uses a placeholder data set in an Excel worksheet, and creates a chart based on that data. The chart is embedded as an Excel object in Word. Use Excel to replace the data set with the data you want to use. The chart and all information taken from the data set are updated automatically.

For the record, though, this is not how charts typically are created in Word. Instead, you would begin the process in Excel, not Word, and would ultimately copy the resulting chart into Word.

Once the chart is in Word, additional formatting can be performed using the Chart Tools Design, Layout, and Format tabs. If you need to change the data, however, you use Excel, but don't start

Excel directly. Instead, click inside the chart, choose the Chart Tools Design tab, and then click Select Data or Edit Data in the Data group, as shown in Figure 41-6.

FIGURE 41-6

Clicking Edit Data in the Chart Tools Design tab selects and opens the data in Excel.

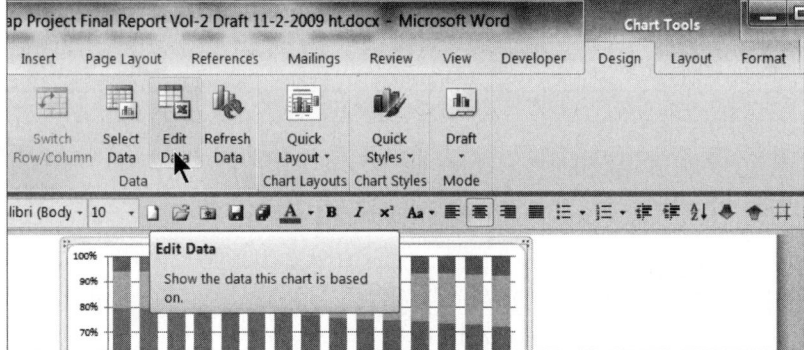

When you make changes to the data, the chart itself in Word is updated automatically. If there's a chance that you'll need to undo changes, leave Excel open. As long as it remains open, Ctrl+Z will work. If you close Excel, changes to the chart and data set are saved automatically. However, Excel really does close, so Ctrl+Z will no longer undo changes you might have made.

Object

A third way to use Excel data in a Word document is as an object. In Word, choose Insert ➪ Text ➪ Object ➪ Object. To use an existing Excel worksheet, click Create from File. To create a new Excel object, click Create New.

Create from File

Use the Browse button to navigate to the target file. Choose Link to File and/or Display as Icon, according to your needs, and click OK.

Note

Typically, you would use Display as Icon when the purpose is to provide access to the contents of the Excel file, rather than to display it. For example, suppose you have several tax tables that you want to provide to the reader. Some readers need one table, others need another, and so on. A document will be much less cluttered if users can click a link to open the data set of interest in Excel, rather than make all readers have to look through all of the data files to find the one they want. ■

Create New

In the Create New tab of the Object dialog box, select the desired type of Excel object, as shown in Figure 41-7. Choose Display as Icon, if desired (click Change Icon, if appropriate), and then click OK. Use Excel's tools to create the desired object, and then close Excel. When you close Excel, you will be prompted to save the changes in the Word document. Click Yes to save the changes; click No to keep working on the Excel object; or click No if you don't mind losing the work you've been doing.

Tip

Notice that when working in Excel this way, there is no way inside the Excel object to save your work. Saving is controlled within the Word process. If you would like to have an independent version of the Excel object that is accessible from Excel without using Word, copy the contents of the *objectized* Excel worksheet to the Clipboard, open the full Excel application, paste your work into it, and save it. ■

The Change Icon button appears only if Display as Icon is checked.

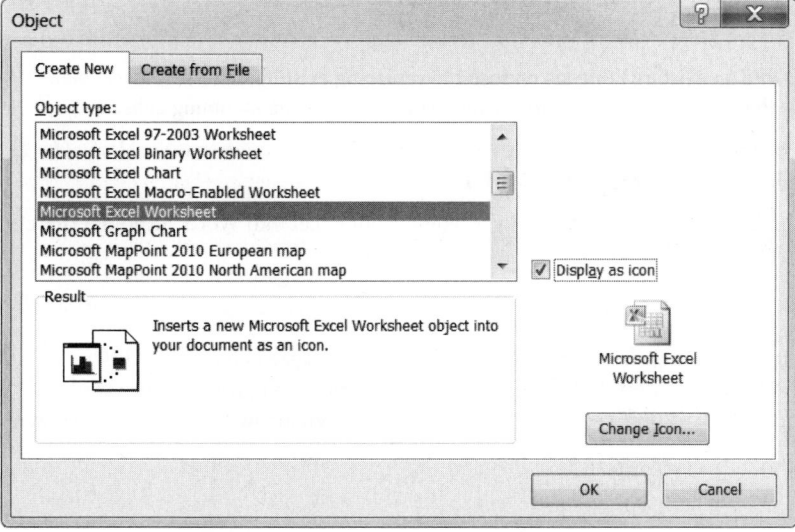

To insert the contents of the file, click Insert. To link to the contents, click the drop-down arrow next to Insert, and choose Insert as Link. Word now issues a confirmation dialog box. If you're sure the Excel file you're opening is safe, click Yes.

From Spreadsheet to Table

When you use one of the methods shown to insert formatted Excel data into Word, a Word table is created automatically. Sometimes, however, you need to insert data into a table that already exists. Typically, two problems can occur. First, sometimes the pasted cells don't go exactly where you want them to go. Second, no matter what you do, the formatting in the table never ends up exactly as you want.

To handle the first problem, the dimensions (rows and columns) of the source must be identical to the destination, and the destination cells must be selected. For example, if you are pasting a selection of cells that contains five rows and four columns, then the destination must also be 5 × 4, and you must select the destination cells. If you try to paste in the top-left cell (which seems logical, right?), Word will paste the entire selection into that cell, so you end up with a table within a table.

There is no perfect way to handle the second problem. Even if you choose the setting File ➪ Options ➪ Advanced ➪ Cut, Copy, and Paste ➪ Pasting from Other Programs to Match Destination Formatting or Keep Text Only, something in the formatting will be messed up — usually the spacing.

Your best bet, assuming that you're using a style, is to choose Paste Special ➪ Unformatted Text, and then reapply the style to the pasted cells. Alternatively, if there are table cells that contain the correct formatting, use the Format Painter to reformat the pasted cells as desired.

Tip

If you are inserting new cells into an existing table (as opposed to replacing existing material), insert blank rows so you have empty cells that you can select and into which you can paste the incoming cells. ■

Using Word Content in Excel

Going from Word into Excel isn't quite as tricky as going from Excel into Word, although there are some quirks worth being aware of.

Clipboard

When pasting content from Word into Excel — using the default Paste behavior — different kinds of content are handled differently. To see your options, make your selection in Word, and copy or cut it to the Clipboard. In Excel, click the Paste drop-down arrow for the options shown in Figure 41-8.

Note

When pasting a picture link, if the source text or tables material is updated, then it is automatically updated in Word. If you replace the picture, the picture will not be updated. If the source picture is updated (i.e., it is linked and the original picture changes, but it keeps the same name and location), then the picture will be updated. ■

When pasting text that includes one or no paragraph marks, it is inserted into the selected cell. If the selection contains multiple paragraphs, it is inserted into consecutive cells in the target column. For example, if the Clipboard contains three paragraphs and you paste into Row 1 Column 1, the three paragraphs are inserted into Row 1 Column 1, Row 2 Column 1, and Row 3 Column 1, respectively.

When pasting all or part of a table into Excel, the cells are inserted into separate cells matching the original selection in Word. Destination cells do not need to be selected. For example, to copy a 5 × 4 table from Word to Excel, select the table and copy or cut it to the Clipboard. Right-click in the upper-left cell of the 5 × 4 area where you want the table to appear, and choose Paste. Again, formatting and cell shading can be copied as well by clicking the Keep Source Formatting paste button.

FIGURE 41-8

When pasting text and/or table material from Word into Excel, the Paste Options buttons show a Live Preview of the result.

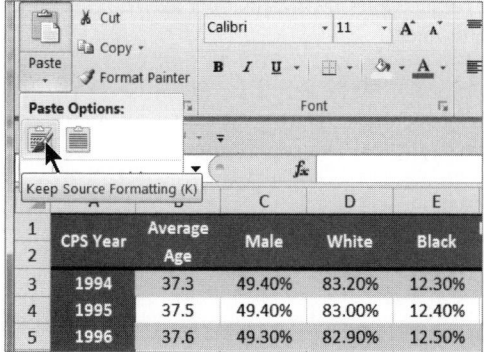

When you paste a picture from Word into Excel, it is inserted into Excel's drawing layer, rather than into cells. Note that Excel does not have an In Line with Text option for graphics.

Drag-and-Drop

Unlike when going from Excel to Word, when you go from Word to Excel, drag-and-drop *does* work, as long as drag-and-drop editing is enabled in Word (File ➪ Options ➪ Advanced ➪ Editing Options ➪ Allow Text to Be Dragged and Dropped).

Caution

When dragging from one program to another, the normal default is for text to be copied. When dragging from Word to Excel, the default action is to move the selection. If you really want to move the text, fine. If you instead merely want to copy, then the Ctrl key needs to be pressed when you drop the text. Ctrl doesn't need to be pressed when you begin the drag. However, it does need to be pressed when you drop. When you press the Ctrl key, notice that the drag icon suddenly gains a plus (+) sign, signifying that it will be copied. If you're not comfortable pressing the Ctrl key when dragging, you can right-drag, instead. When you right-drag, you will be provided a shortcut menu when you drop, allowing you to choose among copy, move, and other options. ■

Object

You can insert a new or existing Word document into an Excel file as an object. To insert part of an existing Word file as an object, select the portion you want and copy it to the Clipboard.

Click where you want it to reside, and choose the Paste button's drop-down arrow, and then Paste Special. In the Paste Special dialog box, shown in Figure 41-9, choose Microsoft Office Word Document Object. Select Display as Icon and Paste or Paste Link, as needed, and then click OK. Note that when using the Clipboard approach, you often can't get the entire document, even if you press Ctrl+A (Select All). That's because Ctrl+A excludes contents such as headers, footers, and footnotes. To insert the entire file as an object, therefore, you need to use a different approach.

FIGURE 41-9

Use Paste Special to paste the Clipboard's contents as a Word object.

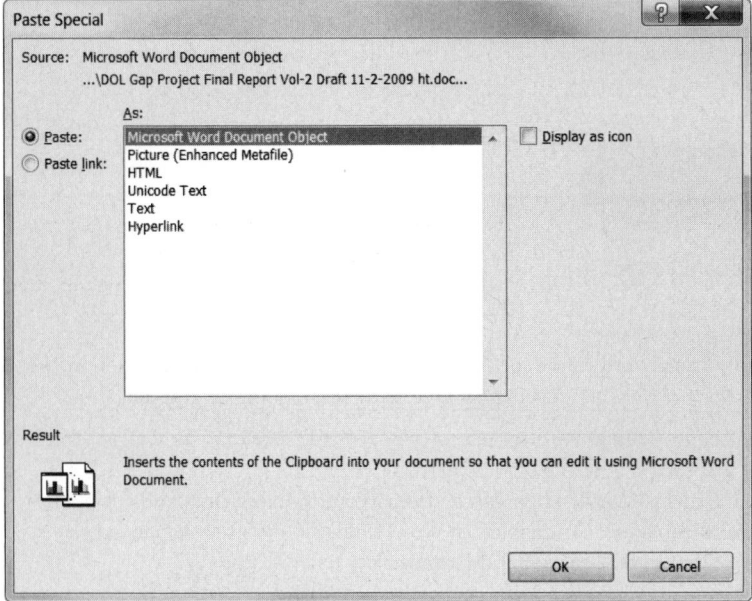

To insert the entire file as an object, in Excel, choose Insert ➪ Object. Using Create New or Create from File, proceed as shown earlier in this chapter.

PowerPoint

In some ways, Word and PowerPoint were meant to work together. That's because PowerPoint uses heading levels that are similar to Word's Heading styles. When creating a PowerPoint presentation, for example, it's a simple matter to convert a Word outline into a PowerPoint presentation (or at least the basis for one) or to use a PowerPoint presentation as an outline for a Word document.

Converting Word to PowerPoint Presentations

Converting a Word document outline into a PowerPoint presentation is simple — as long as you've used Word's Heading styles for your outline, and as long as the outline contains no other text. Unfortunately, PowerPoint is not able to extract just the outline from a Word document, so you're going to have to manage that trick yourself if the document has already been written.

Tip

A quick way to obtain an outline from a Word document that was formatted using Heading levels is to insert a table of contents. Copy the table of contents to another document, press Ctrl+Shift+F9 to convert it to static text, save it, and then proceed. ■

To convert a Word outline into a PowerPoint presentation, in PowerPoint, start a new PowerPoint presentation (Ctrl+N). In the Home Ribbon in PowerPoint, click the New Slide drop-down arrow, and choose Slides from Outline, as shown in Figure 41-10. In the Insert Outline dialog box, find the document containing your outline, select it, and click Insert.

Note

Once you've inserted an outline into a PowerPoint presentation, you'll often discover that stray or extra paragraph marks insinuate themselves prominently in the PowerPoint presentation, creating unsightly gaps. You can fix them in PowerPoint, or, if it's easier, press Ctrl+Z to undo the insert, clean up the outline in Word, and then try again. ■

Tip

In PowerPoint's Normal view, click the Outline tab. Working with a presentation in Outline view, you might find it as easy to clean up an imported outline there as it would be to go back to Word and start over. Note that some of Word's more useful outlining keystrokes, such as Alt+Shift+arrow keys, perform the same actions in PowerPoint as they do in Word — demoting, promoting, and moving selected outline headings. ■

Converting PowerPoint Presentations to Word Documents

You can also go in the other direction, using a PowerPoint presentation as a starting outline for a Word document. In PowerPoint, choose File ➪ Save As. Set the Save As Type to Outline/RTF (*.rtf) — near the bottom of the non-alphabetized list — and then click Save. Unlike Word, PowerPoint does not open or display the .rtf file, and it is immediately available for Word to open without your having to close anything in PowerPoint.

In Word, choose File ➪ Open, navigate to the .rtf file you just created, and open it. Then switch to Outline view. Look Ma! It's an outline! The top level for each slide was assigned Heading 1, the next level Heading 2, and so on.

You now have a Word outline of your document, and all you need to do now is fill in those petty details. You know — that stuff called content.

FIGURE 41-10

You can use a Word outline to create a PowerPoint presentation.

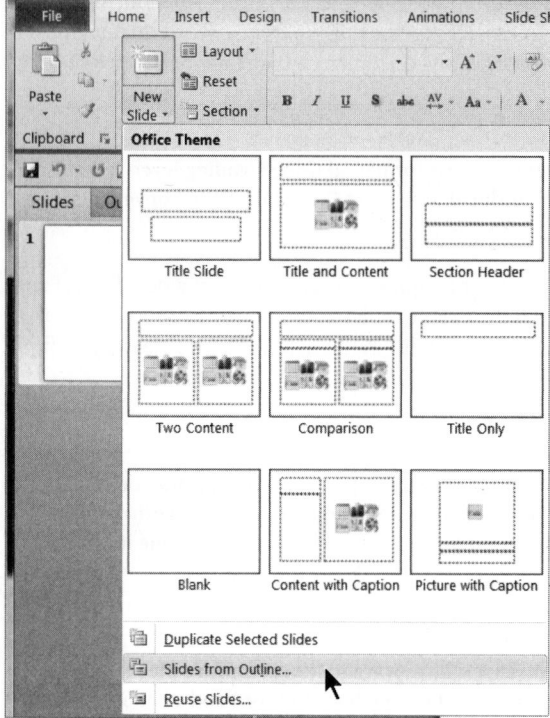

Outlook

In Office 2003 and earlier, Outlook and Word had a potentially much more intimate connection than they have in Office 2010. That's because you could use Word itself to view, edit, and compose your e-mail. Although Outlook's e-mail editor might look a whole lot like Word, it's not Word and is not connected to Word in any way. Instead, it's a small, mostly independent subset of Word, borrowed from the Word programming team. Even if you have only Outlook 2010 and do not have Word 2010, you still have the same Word-like editor in Outlook.

In fact, if your word processing needs are fairly simple, you might not even need Word. But, let's not be hasty. After all — we have a *Office 2010 Bible* we want to sell you!

You've already looked at how to use the Outlook Address Book to perform an e-mail merge. See Chapter 10 for the nitty-gritty details.

Using the Outlook Address Book in Word

One of the more conspicuous relationships between Word and Outlook is in the use of the Outlook Address Book for addresses in Word documents — especially letters and envelopes. For example, in the Mailings Ribbon, click Envelopes or Labels, and then click the Insert Address tool (see Figure 41-11).

You can access the Outlook Address Book using the Insert Address tool.

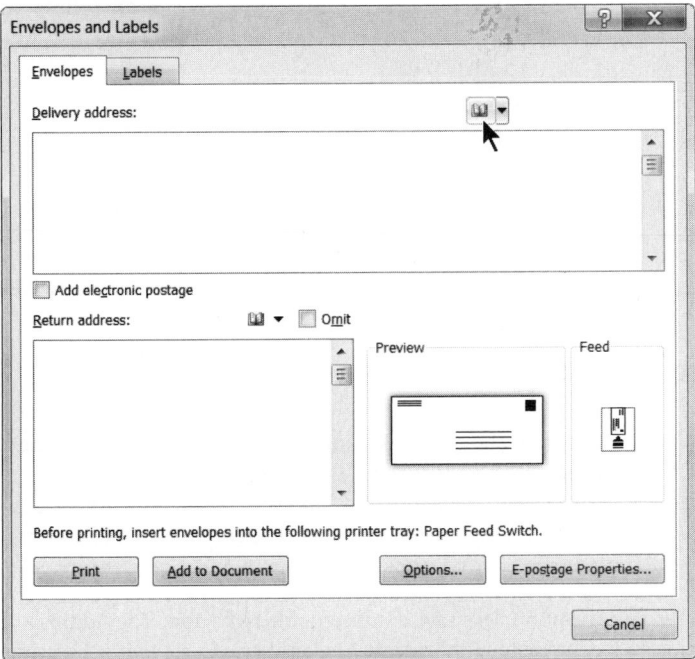

The Select Name dialog box appears, as shown in Figure 41-12. If you have multiple Contact folders set up as address books, click the Address Book drop-down arrow and choose the one you want. Note that the Search option enables you to search the Name Only or More Columns. When you use Name Only, the dialog box displays only names that start with what you type.

Alternatively, click More Columns, type what you're looking for, and click Go. This search feature searches for occurrences of the search text anywhere in any contact field. If that still gives you too many hits, click Advanced Find. Use the Find dialog box to search for names containing text you type. When you find the person or business whose address you want, select it and click OK.

FIGURE 41-12

Insert addresses in Outlook using the Address Book.

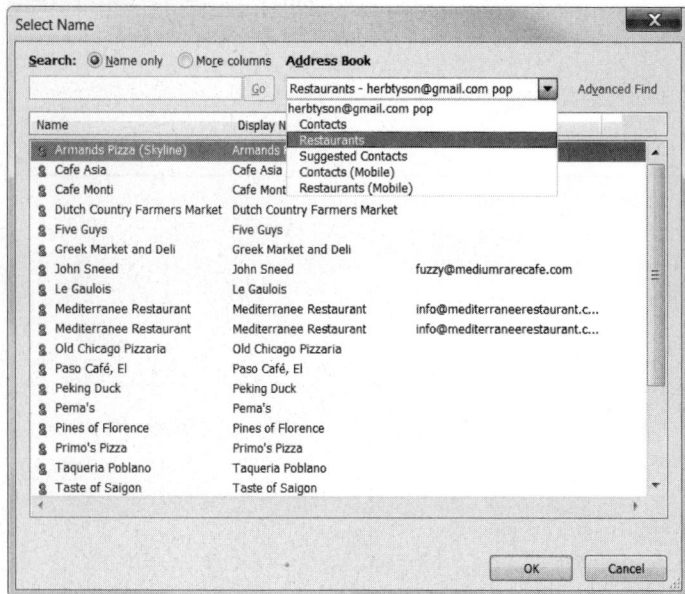

That's great for envelopes and labels, but what about for inserting the address in the body of the letter, or what if you want to type "**John's mailing address is . . .**"? You could simply use the envelope or label feature, select the address from the dialog box, and then dismiss the Envelopes and Labels dialog box (unless your Address Book is set up to display the contact's name, rather than name and e-mail address). Someone reading this does exactly that. Caught you, eh?

Rather than send you on a hunting expedition, let's save a little trouble right now. The Address Book or Insert Address tool does not exist in any Ribbon tab. The only way to get to it is by using the Envelopes and Labels dialog box.

However, there is a better way. If you were following along, dismiss the various dialog boxes, right-click on the Quick Access Toolbar, and choose Customize Quick Access Toolbar. You probably saw this coming, right? To drive home the point, set Choose Commands From to Commands Not in the Ribbon. About halfway down the first page of A commands, locate *Address Book*. Click on it and click Add. If you don't like where it is, you can use the up or down buttons to move it.

Note

The only difference between this Address Book tool and the one in the Envelopes and Labels dialog box is that the latter has a drop-down arrow from which you can select recently inserted addresses. ∎

Summary

In this chapter, you've learned how to share information between Word and OneNote as well as several ways to exchange data between Word and Excel. You've also seen how to convert Word outlines into PowerPoint presentations, and how to create a Word outline using a PowerPoint presentation. Additionally, you've looked at several ways that Outlook and Word stay in contact with, well, Contacts.

Index

D

E

G

O

Object Linking and Embedding (OLE), 1042
    controls, 1119–1120
ODBC files. *See* Open Database Connectivity files
ODF files. *See* Open Document Format files
Office 2003, menu keystrokes, 114
Office 2010. *See also* Excel 2010; PowerPoint 2010;
    Word 2010
    accessibility features, BC24–BC25
        Ease of Access, BC24
        Full Screen Reading, BC24
        speech recognition, BC25
        Zoom, BC24
    applications, 13–17
        closing, 16–17
        starting, 15–16
    Backstage, 42–43, 1031–1032
        sharing options, 43
        Word 2007, 42–43
    charts, 8, 10
    customization, BC1–BC13
        Access 2010 options, BC7–BC9
        common options, BC3–BC4
        dialog box, BC1–BC3
        Excel 2010 options, BC6–BC7
        options, BC1–BC10
        Outlook 2010 options, BC9–BC10
        PowerPoint 2010 options, BC7
        QAT, BC11–BC12
        Ribbon, BC12–BC13
        Word 2010 options, BC4–BC6
    database connections, 256
    dialog boxes, 48–50
        navigation, 48–49
        Options, 44
        Stay-on-Top, 48
        tabbed, 49–50
        typical, 48
    discoverability, 24–25
    file search, 17–19
        disk icons, 18
        folders, 18
        Open dialog box, 18
        Windows 7, 17

        Windows XP, 18–19
    functionality, 24
    galleries
        Picture gallery, 26
        Ribbon, 34–35
        Style gallery, 28
    graphics, 4, 6
    Help system, 19–21
        browsing, 19
        categories, 20
        Internet systems, 19–20
    installation, BC14–BC18
        activation, BC14–BC15
        adding/deleting features, BC16–BC17
        diagnostics, BC17
        repair, BC17–BC18
        setup disc, BC14
        updates, BC15
    language editing, BC20–BC22
    language translation, BC23
    legacy formats, 25
    list shortcuts, 256
    Live Preview, 25–26, 84–85
    menus, 24
    multiple windows, 69–71
        application switching, 69–71
        Ribbon, 69
        shortcut key combination, 70
        stacking, 70
        taskbar, 70
        Windows 7, 70
        Windows Vista, 70
Office.com, 19
    All Program Name choice, 19
OneNote 2010, 12–14
Open dialog box, 18–19
    finding files, 18
    Windows XP, 19
Options, 43–47, BC1–BC10
    Access 2010, BC7–BC9
    advanced, 45–47
    common, BC3–BC4
    dialog box, 44, BC1–BC3
    display, 45

P

S

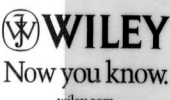